Großbritannien, Irland
Great Britain, Ireland
Grande Bretagne, Irlande
Groot-Brittanië, Ierland
Gran Bretagna, Irlanda
Gran Bretaña, Irlanda
Storbritannien, Irland

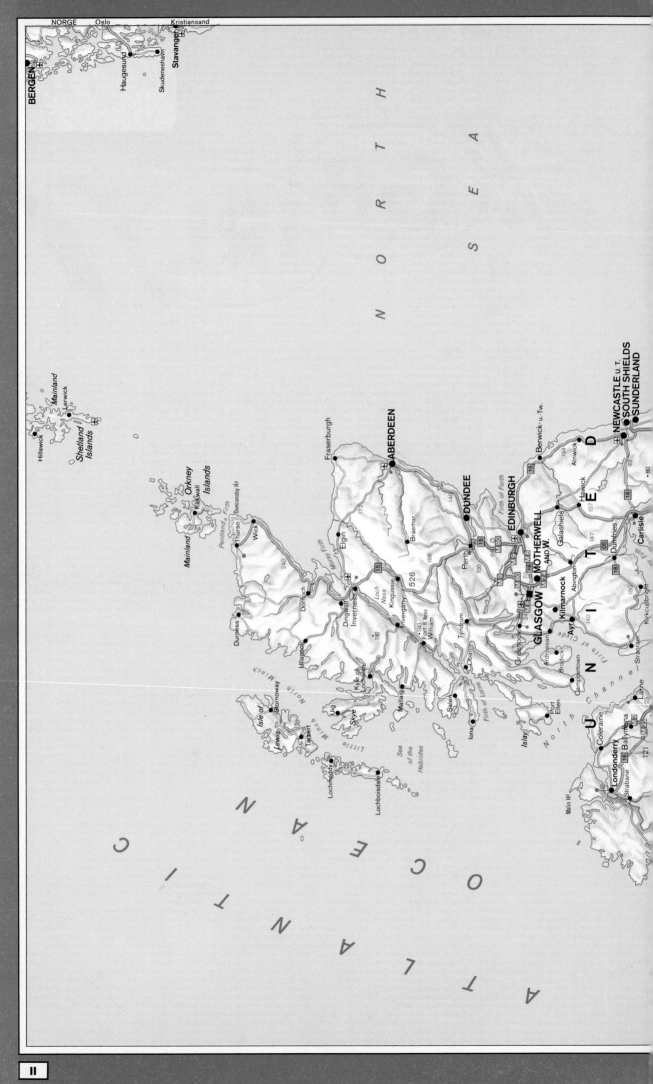

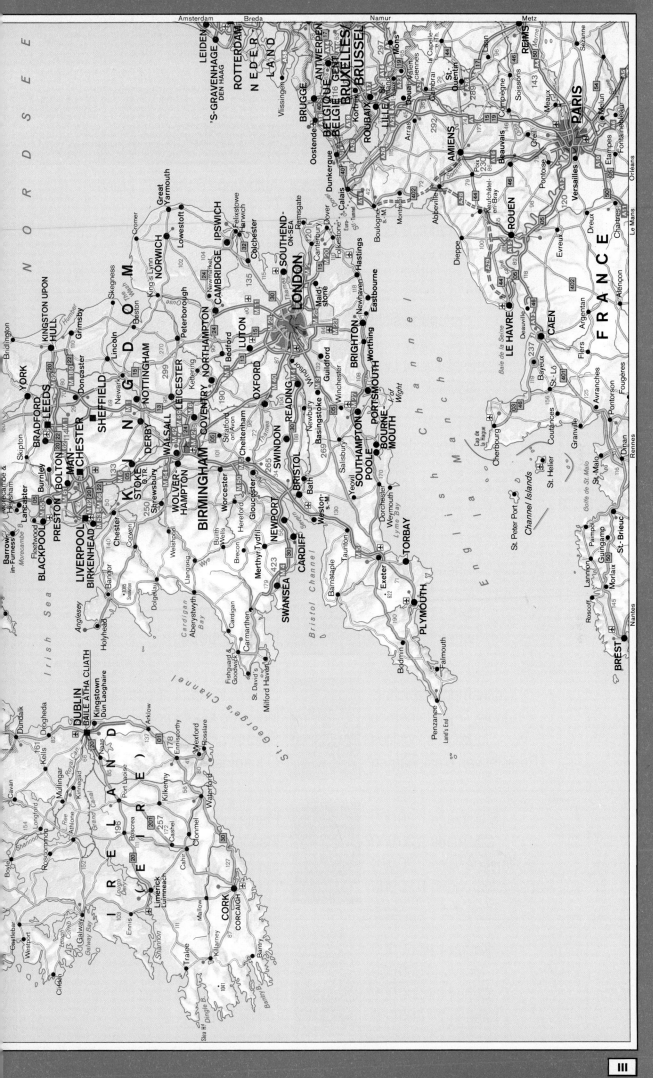

Inhaltsverzeichnis · Contents · Sommaire · Inhoud · Indice
Índice · Inholdsfortegnelse · Innehållsförteckning

Kartenübersicht · Key map · Carte d'assemblage · Overzichtskaart
Quadro d'unione · Mapa indice · Oversigtskort · Kartöversikt
1:300.000

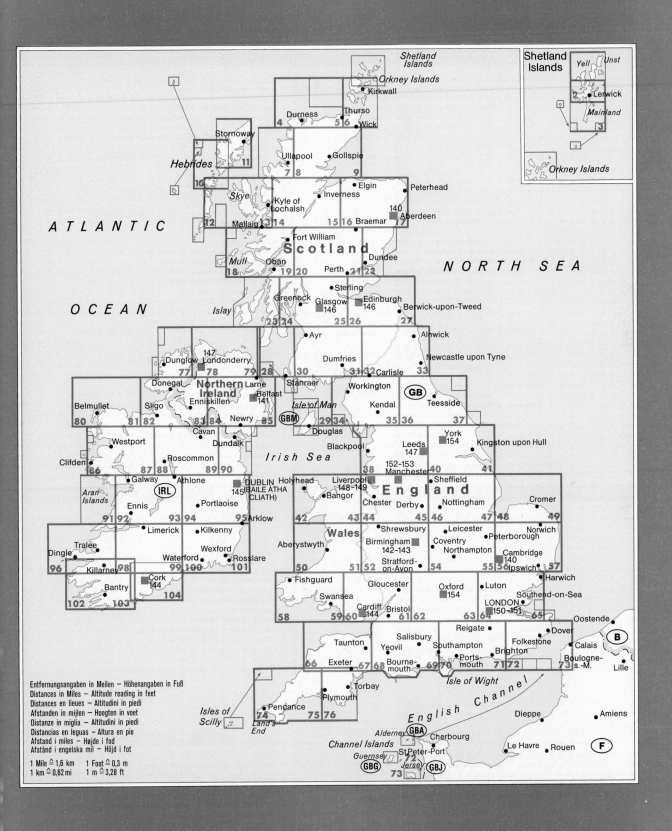

1:300.000

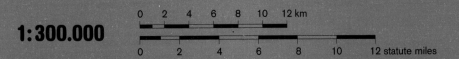

Zeichenerklärung · Legend
Légende · Legenda
1:300.000

VERKEHR - TRAFFIC | CIRCULATION - VERKEER

(D)
(GB)

Autobahn mit Anschlußstelle - Halbanschlußstelle - Tankstelle
- mit Kleinraststätte - Rasthaus - mit Motel
Motorway with junction - Half junction - Filling station
- with snackbar - Restaurant - with motel

Nur einbahnig - in Bau - geplant
Only single carriageway - under construction - projected

Vier- oder mehrspurige Autostraße, ein- oder zweibahnig - in Bau
Road with four or more lanes, single or dual carriageway - under construction

Bundes- bzw. Staats- oder Nationalstraße - Wichtige Hauptstraße - in Bau
National or federal road - Major main road - under construction

Hauptstraße - Nebenstraße
Main road - Secondary road

Fahrweg (nur bedingt befahrbar) - Fußweg
Practicable road (restricted passage) - Footpath

Straßenzustand: nicht staubfrei - sehr schlecht
Road condition: unsealed - very bad

Europastraßennummer
Number of main european route

Steigung - Paßstraße mit Wintersperre (von - bis)
Gradient - Mountain pass closed in winter (from - to)

Für Caravans nicht empfehlenswert - verboten
Not suitable - closed for caravans

Entfernungen an Autobahnen in Meilen
Distances on motorways in miles

Entfernungen an übrigen Straßen in Meilen
Distances on other roads in miles

Hauptbahn - Nebenbahn (mit Bahnhof bzw Haltepunkt)
Main railway - Other railway with station

Eisenbahn (nur Güterverkehr) - Zahnrad- oder Standseilbahn
Railway (freight haulage only) - Rackrailway or cabin lift

Seilschwebebahn - Sessellift - Skilift
Cable lift - Chair lift - T-bar

Autoverladung - Schiffahrtslinie
Railway ferry for cars - Shipping route

Schiffahrtslinie mit Autotransport - Autofähre an Flüssen
Car ferry route - Car ferry on river

Touristenstraße - Landschaftlich schöne Strecke
Tourist road - Scenic road

Mautstelle - Gebührenpflichtige Straße - für Kfz gesperrt
Toll - Toll road - Road closed for motor traffic

Flughafen - Flugplatz - Segelflugplatz - Hubschrauberlandeplatz
Airport - Airfield - Gliding field - Heliport

(F)
(NL)

Autoroute avec échangeur - Demi-échangeur - Poste d´essence -
avec snack - Restaurant - avec motel
Autosnelweg met op- en afritten - met of oprit of afrit - Benzinestation -
met snackbar - Restaurant - met motel

Seulement une chaussée - en construction - en projet
Slechts een rijbaan - in aanleg - gepland

Route à quatre ou plusieurs voies, à une ou deux chaussées - en construction
Weg met vier of meer rijstroken, een of twee rijbanen - in aanleg

Route nationale - Route principale importante - en construction
Rijksweg - Belangrijke hoofdweg - in aanbouw

Route principale - Route secondaire
Hoofdweg - Overige verharde wegen

Chemin carrossable (praticabilité non assurée) - Sentier
Weg (beperkt berijdbaar) - Voetpad

Etat des routes: route sans revêtement - route en très mauvais état
Toestand van het wegdek: onverhard - zeer slecht

Numéro des routes européennes
Europawegnummer

Côte - Col fermé en hiver (de - à)
Helling - Pas 's-winters gesloten (van - tot)

Non recommandé aux caravans - interdit
Voor caravans niet aanbevolen - verboden

Distances sur autoroutes en miles
Afstand in mijlen op autosnelwegen

Distances sur autres routes en miles
Afstand op overige wegen in mijlen

Chemin de fer principal - Chemin de fer secondaire (avec gare ou haltes)
Belangrijke Spoorweg - Spoorweg (met station)

Chemin de fer (trafic de marchandises) - Chemin de fer à crèmaillère ou funiculaire
Spoorweg (alleen goederenverkeer) - Tandradbaan of kabelspoorweg

Téléphérique - Télésiège - Téléski
Kabelbaan - Stoeltjeslift - Skilift

Navette par voie ferrée pour autos - Ligne maritime
Autoverlading - Scheepvaartlijn

Ligne maritime avec transport de voitures - Bac autos (rivière)
Scheepvaartlijn met autovervoer - Autoveer over rivier

Route touristique - Itinéraire pittoresque
Toeristische route - Landschappelijk mooie route

Péage - Route à péage - Route interdite
Tol - Tolweg - Verboden voor auto's

Aéroport - Aérodrome - Terrain pour vol à voile - Héliport
Luchthaven - Vliegveld - Zweefvliegveld - Heliport

SEHENSWÜRDIGKEITEN - PLACES OF INTEREST | CURIOSITÉS - BEZIENSWAARDIGHEDEN

Besonders sehenswerter Ort
Place of particular interest

Sehenswerter Ort
Place of interest

Besonders sehenswertes Bauwerk
Building of particular interest

Sehenswertes Bauwerk
Interesting building

Besondere Natursehenswürdigkeit
Natural object of particular interest

Sonstige Sehenswürdigkeit
Other object of interest

Botanischer Garten - Zoologischer Garten - Wildgehege
Botanical gardens - Zoological gardens - Game park

Nationalpark, Naturpark - Aussichtspunkt
Nature park - Viewpoint

Burg, Schloß - Kloster - Kirche, Kapelle - Ruinen
Castle - Monastery - Church, chapel - Ruins

Turm - Funk- oder Fernsehturm - Denkmal - Höhle
Tower - Radio- or TV tower - Monument - Cave

Leuchtturm - Feuerschiff - Windmühle
Lighthouse - Lightship - Windmill

CAMBRIDGE

BRIGHTON

Westminster Abbey

Bayham Abbey

The Needles

STONEHENGE

Sheffield Park

Localité pittoresque
Zeer bezienswaardige plaats

Localité remarquable
Bezienswaardige plaats

Bâtiment très intéressant
Zeer bezienswaardig gebouw

Bâtiment remarquable
Bezienswaardig gebouw

Curiosité naturelle intéressant
Zeer bezienswaardig natuurschoon

Autres curiosités
Overige bezienswaardigheden

Jardin botanique - Jardin zoologique - Parc à gibier
Botanische tuin - Dierentuin - Wildpark

Parc national, parc naturel - Point de vue
Nationaal park, Natuurpark - Uitzichtpunt

Château- fort, Château - Monastère - Église, chapelle - Ruines
Burcht, slot - Klooster - Kerk, kapel - Ruínes

Tour - Tour radio ou télévision - Monument - Grotte
Toren - Radio- of televisietoren - Monument - Grot

Phare - Bâteau- phare - Moulin à vent
Vuurtoren - Lichtschip - Windmolen

SONSTIGES - OTHER INFORMATION | AUTRES INDICATIONS - OVERIGE INFORMATIE

Jugendherberge - Motel - Alleinstehendes Hotel oder Gasthaus - Berghütte
Youth hostel - Motel - Isolated hotel or inn - Mountain hut

Campingplatz, ganzjährig - nur im Sommer - Wohnwagenplatz (Zelten nicht erlaubt)
Camping site, permanent - seasonal - Caravan site (not allowed for tents)

Guter Badestrand - Strandbad - Schwimmbad - Heilbad
Recommended beach - Bathing place - Swimming pool - Spa

Golfplatz - Boots- und Yachthafen - Unterwasserjagd verboten
Golf course - Harbour for boats and yachts - Underwater fishing prohibited

Einzelhof - Feriendorf - Römischer Limes mit Kastell
Isolated building - Holiday bungalows - Limes with castellum (roman)

Staatsgrenze - Grenzübergang - Verwaltungsgrenze
International boundary - Border crossing point - Administrative boundary

Wattenmeer - Sand und Dünen
Tidal flat - Sand and dunes

Wald - Heide
Forest - Heath

Gletscher - Sperrgebiet
Glacier - Restricted area

Auberge de jeunesse - Motel - Hôtel ou auberge isolé - Refuge de montagne
Jeugdherberg - Motel - Afgelegen hotel of restaurant - Berghut

Terrain de camping, permanent - saisonnier - Terrain pour caravans (interdite aux tents)
Camping, het gehele jaar - 's-zomers - Caravanplaats (niet voor tenten)

Plage recommandée - Baignade - Piscine - Station thermale
Strand met zwemgelegenheid - Strandbad - Openlucht- zwembad - Geneeskrachtige badplaats

Terrain de golf - Port de plaisance - Pêche sous-marine interdite
Golfterrein - Jachthaven - Jagen onder water verboden

Ferme - Village de vacances - Rempart romain (Limes) avec fortification
Vrijstaande boerderij - Vakantiedorp - Romeinse grensversterking met legerkamp

Frontière d´Etat - Passage frontalier - Limite des régions
Rijksgrens - Grensovergang - Regionale grens

Mer recouvrant les hauts-fonds - Sable et dunes
Bij eb droogvallende gronden - Zand en duinen

Bois - Lande
Bos - Heide

Glacier - Zone interdite
Gletsjer - Verboden gebied

Segni convenzionali · Signos convencionales
Tegnforklaring · Teckenförklaring
1:300.000

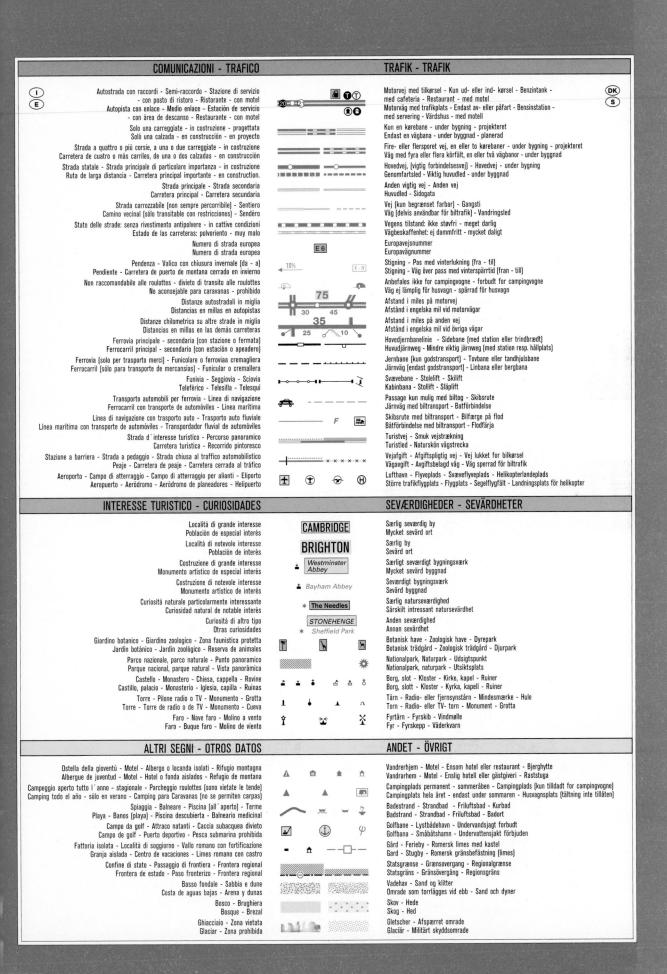

COMUNICAZIONI - TRAFICO / TRAFIK - TRAFIK

(I) (E) / **(DK) (S)**

Autostrada con raccordi - Semi-raccordo - Stazione di servizio - con posto di ristoro - Ristorante - con motel
Autopista con enlace - Medio enlace - Estación de servicio - con área de descanso - Restaurante - con motel

Motorvej med tilkørsel - Kun ud- eller ind- kørsel - Benzintank - med cafeteria - Restaurant - med motel
Motorväg med trafikplats - Endast av- eller påfart - Bensinstation - med servering - Värdshus - med motell

Solo una carreggiate - in costruzione - progettata
Solo una calzada - en construcción - en proyecto

Kun en kørebane - under bygning - projekteret
Endast en vägbana - under byggnad - planerad

Strada a quattro o più corsie, a una o due carreggiate - in costruzione
Carretera de cuatro o más carriles, de una o dos calzadas - en construcción

Fire- eller flersporet vej, en eller to kørebaner - under bygning - projekteret
Väg med fyra eller flera körfält, en eller två vägbanor - under byggnad

Strada statale - Strada principale di particolare importanza - in costruzione
Ruta de larga distancia - Carretera principal importante - en construction.

Hovedvej, (vigtig forbindelsesvej) - Hovedvej - under bygning
Genomfartsled - Viktig huvudled - under byggnad

Strada principale - Strada secondaria
Carretera principal - Carretera secundaria

Anden vigtig vej - Anden vej
Huvudled - Sidogata

Strada carrozzabile (non sempre percorribile) - Sentiero
Camino vecinal (sólo transitable con restricciones) - Sendero

Vej (kun begrænset farbar) - Gangsti
Väg (delvis användbar för biltrafik) - Vandringsled

Stato delle strade: senza rivestimento antipolvere - in cattive condizioni
Estado de las carreteras: polvoriento - muy malo

Vegens tilstand: ikke støvfri - meget darlig
Vägbeskaffenhet: ej dammfritt - mycket daligt

Numero di strada europea
Numero di strada europea

E 6

Europavejsnummer
Europavägnummer

Pendenza - Valico con chiusura invernale (da - a)
Pendiente - Carretera de puerto de montana cerrado en invierno

10% / X - IV

Stigning - Pas med vinterlukning (fra - til)
Stigning - Väg över pass med vinterspärrtid (fran - till)

Non raccomandabile alle roulottes - divieto di transito alle roulottes
No aconsejable para caravanas - prohibido

Anbefales ikke for campingvogne - forbudt for campingvogne
Väg ej lämplig för husvagn - spärrad för husvagn

Distanze autostradali in miglia
Distancias en millas en autopistas

75
30   45

Afstand i miles på motorvej
Afstånd i engelska mil vid motorvägar

Distanze chilometrica su altre strade in miglia
Distancias en millas en las demás carreteras

35
25   10

Afstand i miles på anden vej
Afstånd i engelska mil vid övriga vägar

Ferrovia principale - secondaria (con stazione o fermata)
Ferrocarril principal - secondario (con estación o apeadero)

Hovedjernbanelinie - Sidebane (med station eller trindbrædt)
Huvudjärnweg - Mindre viktig järnweg (med station resp. hållplats)

Ferrovia (solo per trasporto merci) - Funicolare o ferroviaa cremagliera
Ferrocarril (sólo para transporte de mercansias) - Funicular o cremallera

Jernbane (kun godstransport) - Tovbane eller tandhjulsbane
Järnväg (endast godstransport) - Linbana eller bergbana

Funivia - Seggiovia - Sciovia
Teleférico - Telesilla - Telesquí

Svævebane - Stolelift - Skilift
Kabinbana - Stollift - Släplift

Transporto automobili per ferrovia - Linea di navigazione
Ferrocarril con transporte de automóviles - Linea maritima

Passage kun mulig med biltog - Skibsrute
Järnväg med biltransport - Batförbindelse

Linea di navigazione con trasporto auto - Trasporto auto fluviale
Línea maritima con transporte de automóviles - Transportador fluvial de automóviles

F

Skibsrute med biltransport - Bilfærge på flod
Båtförbindelse med biltransport - Flodfärja

Strada d´interesse turistico - Percorso panoramico
Carretera turistica - Recorrido pintoresco

Turistvej - Smuk vejstrækning
Turistled - Naturskön vägstrecka

Stazione a barriera - Strada a pedaggio - Strada chiusa al traffico automobilistico
Peaje - Carretera de peaje - Carretera cerrada al tráfico

x x x x x x

Vejafgift - Afgiftspligtig vej - Vej lukket for bilkørsel
Vägavgift - Avgiftsbelagd väg - Väg sperrad för biltrafik

Aeroporto - Campo di atterraggio - Campo di atterraggio per alianti - Eliporto
Aeropuerto - Aeródromo - Aeródromo de planeadores - Helipuerto

Lufthavn - Flyveplads - Svæveflyveplads - Helikopterlandeplads
Större trafikflygplats - Flygplats - Segelflygfält - Landningsplats för helikopter

INTERESSE TURISTICO - CURIOSIDADES / SEVÆRDIGHEDER - SEVÄRDHETER

Località di grande interesse
Población de especial interés

CAMBRIDGE

Særlig seværdig by
Mycket sevärd ort

Località di notevole interesse
Población de interés

BRIGHTON

Særlig by
Sevärd ort

Costruzione di grande interesse
Monumento artistico de especial interés

Westminster Abbey

Særligt seværdigt bygningsværk
Mycket sevärd byggnad

Costruzione di notevole interesse
Monumento artistico de interés

Bayham Abbey

Seværdigt bygningsværk
Sevärd byggnad

Curiosità naturale particolarmente interessante
Curiosidad natural de notable interés

The Needles

Særlig naturseværdighed
Särskilt intressant naturevärdhet

Curiosità di altro tipo
Otras curiosidades

STONEHENGE
Sheffield Park

Anden seværdighed
Annan sevärdhet

Giardino botanico - Giardino zoologico - Zona faunistica protetta
Jardin botánico - Jardin zoológico - Reserva de animales

Botanisk have - Zoologisk have - Dyrepark
Botanisk trädgård - Zoologisk trädgård - Djurpark

Parco nazionale, parco naturale - Punto panoramico
Parque nacional, parque natural - Vista panorámica

Nationalpark, Naturpark - Udsigtspunkt
Nationalpark, naturpark - Utsiktsplats

Castello - Monastero - Chiesa, cappella - Rovine
Castillo, palacio - Monasterio - Iglesia, capilla - Ruinas

Borg, slot - Kloster - Kirke, kapel - Ruiner
Borg, slott - Kloster - Kyrka, kapell - Ruiner

Torre - Pilone radio o TV - Monumento - Grotta
Torre - Torre de radio o de TV - Monumento - Cueva

Tårn - Radio- eller fjernsynstårn - Mindesmærke - Hule
Torn - Radio- eller TV- torn - Monument - Grotta

Faro - Nave faro - Molino a vento
Faro - Buque faro - Molino de viento

Fyrtårn - Fyrskib - Vindmølle
Fyr - Fyrskepp - Väderkvarn

ALTRI SEGNI - OTROS DATOS / ANDET - ÖVRIGT

Ostella della gioventù - Motel - Albergo o locanda isolati - Rifugio montagna
Albergue de juventud - Motel - Hotel o fonda aislados - Refugio de montana

Vandrerhjem - Motel - Ensom hotel eller restaurant - Bjerghytte
Vandrarhem - Motel - Enslig hotell eller gästgiveri - Raststuga

Campeggio aperto tutto l´anno - stagionale - Parcheggio roulottes (sono vietate le tende)
Camping todo el año - sólo en verano - Camping para Caravanas (no se permiten carpas)

Campingplads permanent - sommeråben - Campingplads (kun tilldadt for campingvogne)
Campingplats hela året - endast under sommaren - Husvagnsplats (tältning inte tillåten)

Spiaggia - Balneare - Piscina (all´aperto) - Terme
Playa - Banos (playa) - Piscina descubierta - Balneario medicinal

Badestrand - Strandbad - Friluftsbad - Kurbad
Badstrand - Strandbad - Friluftsbad - Badort

Campo da golf - Attraco natanti - Caccia subacquea divieto
Campo de golf - Puerto deportivo - Pesca submarina prohibida

Golfbane - Lystbådehavn - Undervandsjagt forbudt
Golfbana - Småbåtshamn - Undervattensjakt förbjuden

Fattoria isolata - Località di soggiorno - Vallo romano con fortificazione
Granja aislada - Centro de vacaciones - Limes romano con castro

Gård - Ferieby - Romersk limes med kastel
Gård - Stugby - Romersk gränsbefästning (limes)

Confine di stato - Passaggio di frontiera - Frontera regional
Frontera de estado - Paso fronterizo - Frontera regional

Statsgrænse - Grænseovergang - Regionalgrænse
Statsgräns - Gränsövergång - Regionsgräns

Basso fondale - Sabbia e dune
Costa de aguas bajas - Arena y dunas

Vadehav - Sand og klitter
Omrade som torrlägges vid ebb - Sand och dyner

Bosco - Brughiera
Bosque - Brezal

Skov - Hede
Skog - Hed

Ghiacciaio - Zona vietata
Glaciar - Zona prohibida

Gletscher - Afspærret omrade
Glaciär - Militärt skyddsomrade

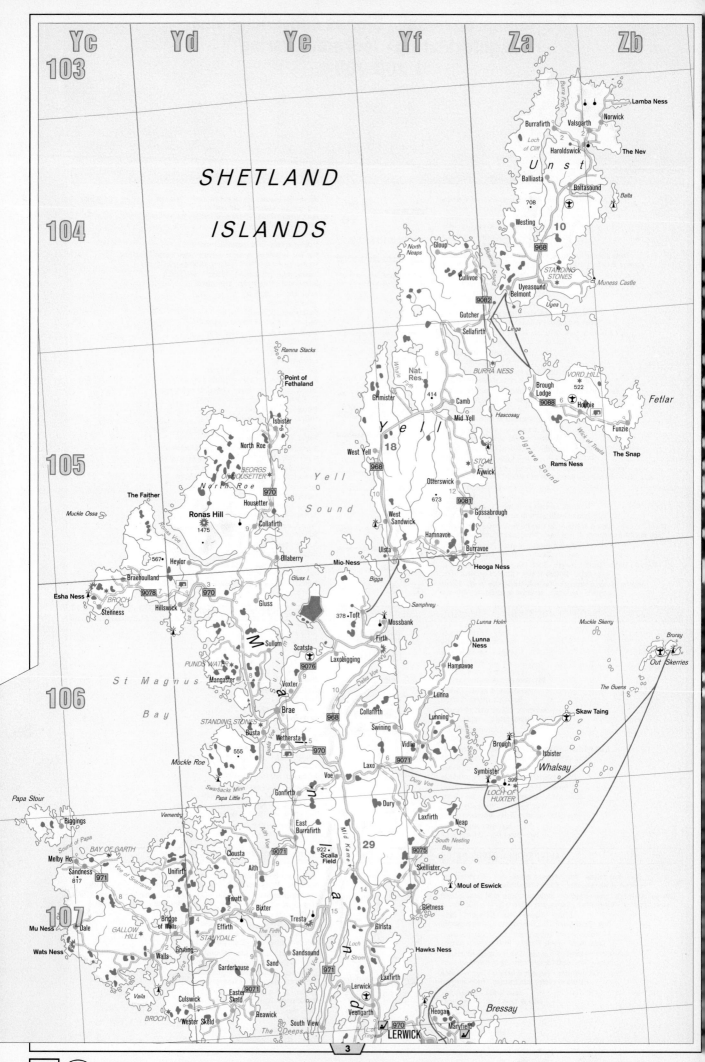

SHETLAND ISLANDS

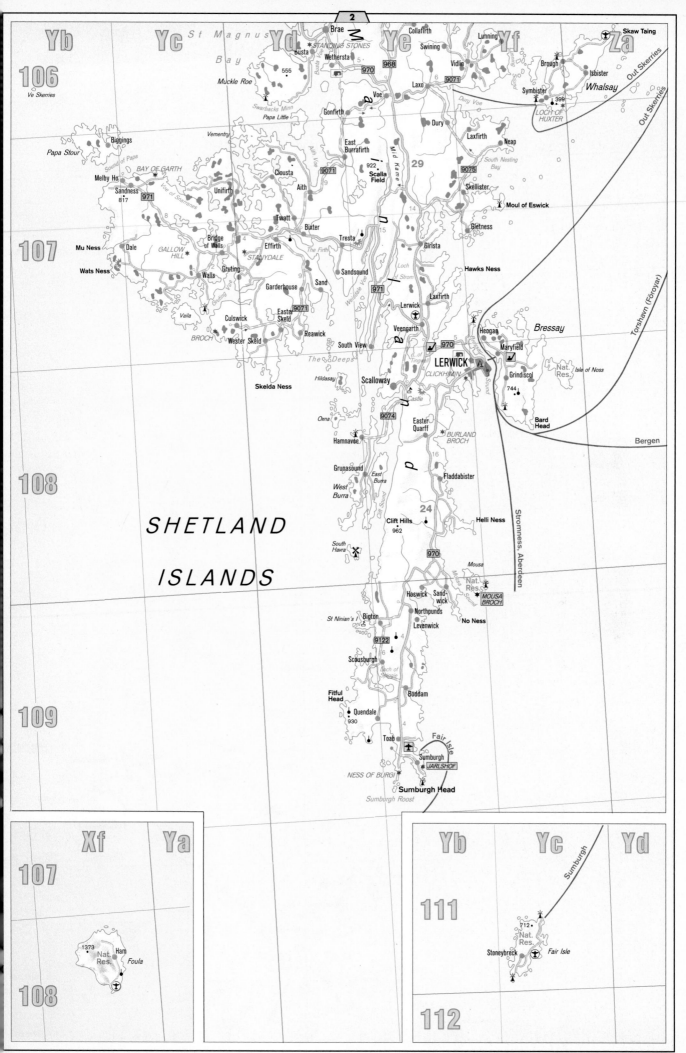

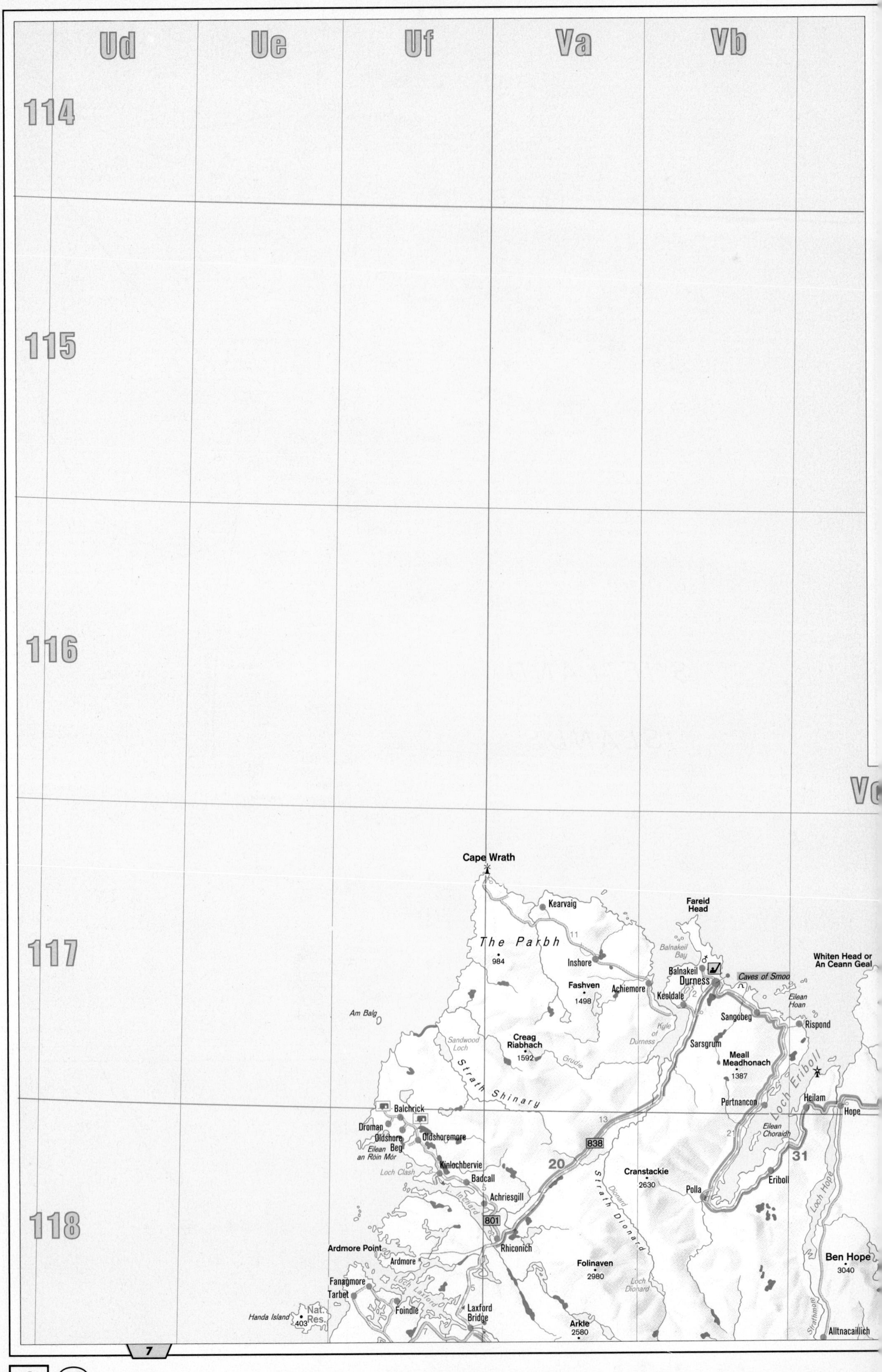

114

115

116

Vc

117

Cape Wrath

Kearvaig

Fareid
Head

The Parbh

11

Inshore

Whiten Head or
An Ceann Geal

984

*Balnakeil
Bay*

Fashven

Achiemore

Balnakeil
Durness

Caves of Smoo

*Eilean
Hoan*

Keoldale

1498

Am Balg

Sangobeg

Rispond

*Sandwood
Loch*

Creag
Riabhach

*Kyle
of
Durness*

Sarsgrum

Meall
Meadhonach

1592

Grudie

1387

Strath Shinary

Portnancon

Heilam

Hope

Balchrick

13

*Eilean
Choraidh*

Droman
Oldshore
Beg

Oldshoremore

838

20

31

*Eilean
an Ròin Mòr*

Cranstackie

Polla

Eriboll

Kinlochbervie

2630

Loch Clash

Badcall

Strath Dionard

Achriesgill

Loch Eriboll

Loch Hope

118

801

Ardmore Point

Rhiconich

Ardmore

Folinaven

Ben Hope

2980

3040

Fanagmore

Tarbet

*Loch
Dionard*

Foindle

Laxford
Bridge

Handa Island

Nat.
Res.

403

Arkle

2580

Strathmore

Alltnacaillich

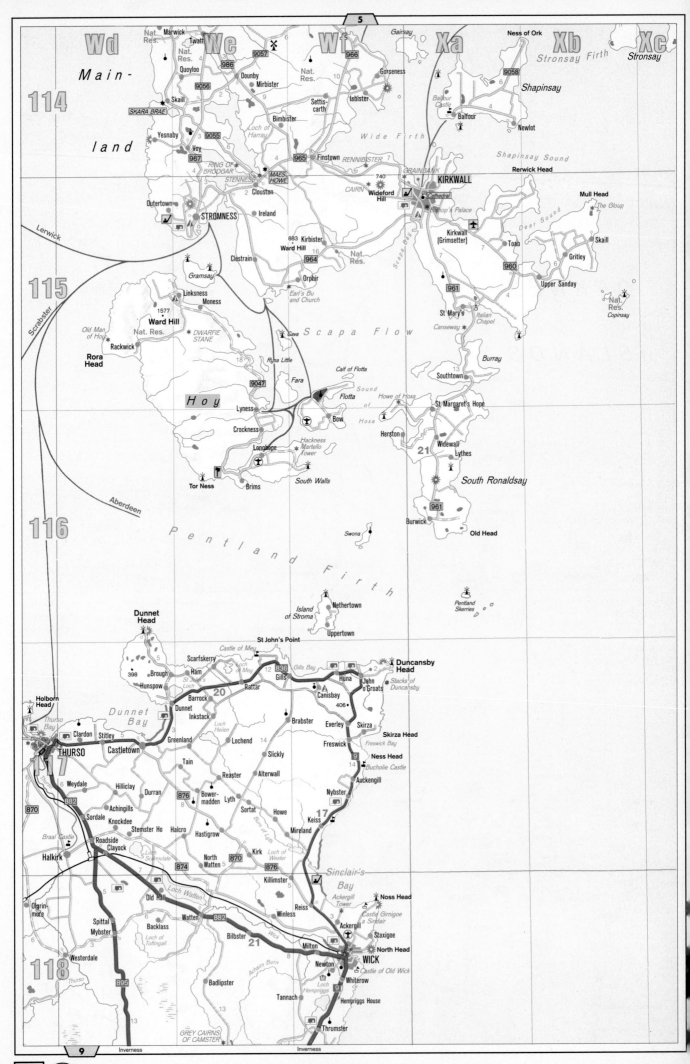

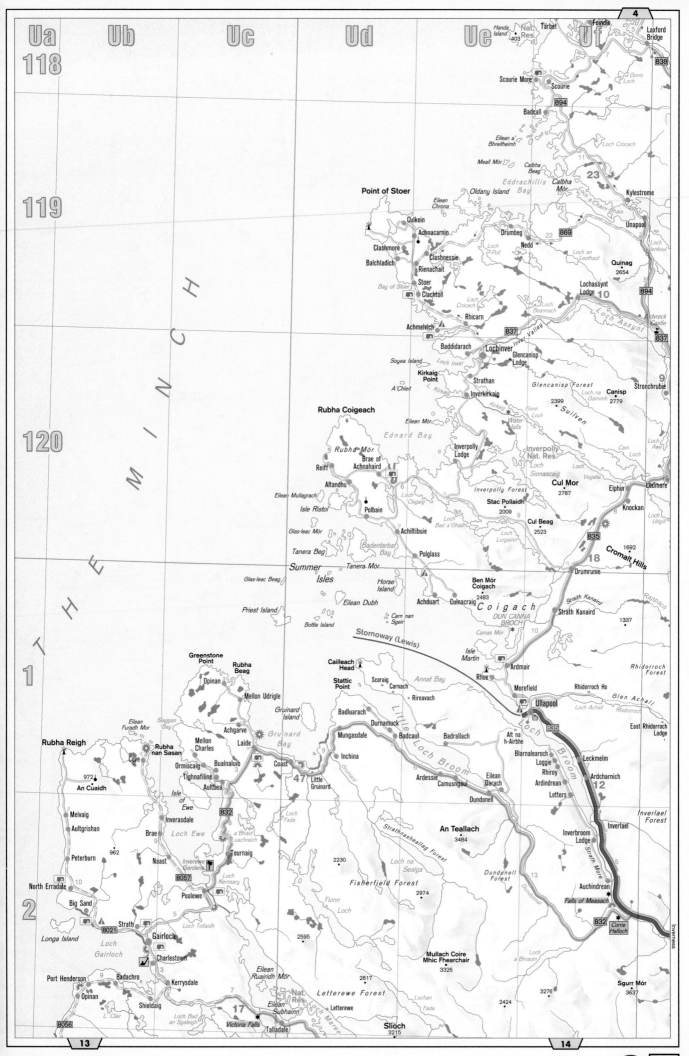

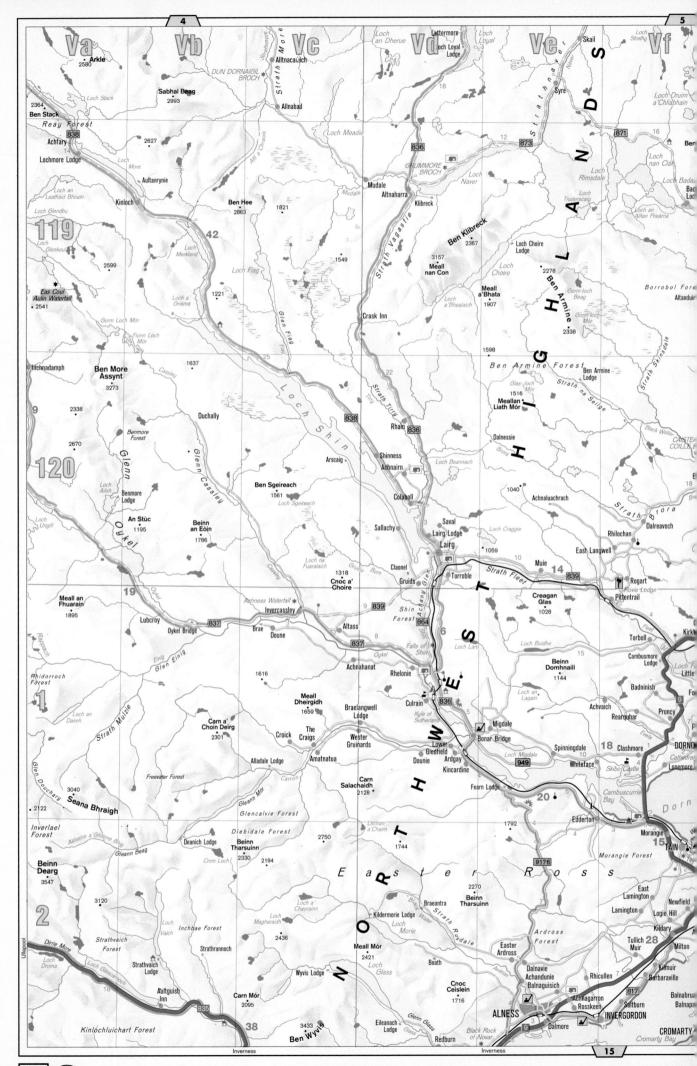

Va Vb Vc Vd Ve Vf

Arkle
2580

Loch an Dherue
Lettermore

Loch Loyal Lodge

Loch Strathy

Skail

Loch Druim a'Chliabhain

Ben

Dun Dornaigil Broch

Sabhal Beag
2993

Alltnacaillich

Strath More

Allnabad

Loch Meadie

Grummore Broch

Syre

Strathnaver

Loch Naver

Loch Rimsdale

Loch nan Clàr

Loch Badanloch

Loch Stack
2364
Ben Stack

Reay Forest

838

Achfary

Lochmore Lodge

2627

Loch More

Aultanrynie

Mudale

Mudale

Altnaharra

Klibreck

Ben Klibreck
2367

Loch Choire Lodge

2278

Ben Armine

Borrobol Forest

Altanduir

119

Loch Glenkoul

Eas Coul Aulin Waterfall
2541

2599

Kinloch

Ben Hee
2863

1821

42

1549

Meall nan Con
3157

Loch Choire

Meall a'Bhata
1907

Ben Armine Forest

Ben Armine Lodge

Loch an Leathaid Bhoain

Loch Glendhu

2338

Loch Merkland

Loch Fiag

Crask Inn

1598

Gorm-loch Beag

Gorm-loch Mòr

Strath Skinsdale

Loch Truderscaig

Black Water

CAISTEAL COILLE

Loch Glencoul

Gorm Loch Mòr

Fionn Loch Mòr

1221

1637

Meallan Liath Mòr
1516

Loch an Alltan Fheàrna

Inchnadamph

Ben More Assynt
3273

9

2338

Benmore Forest

Glenn Cassley

Glen Fiag

Loch Shin

Strath Tirry

Strath Terry

Rhain
836

Dalnessie

Loch Beannach

Strath Brora

2670

838

Shinness

Achnairn

1040

Achnaluachrach

Strath Brora

Rhilochan

Dalreavoch

120

Loch Ailsh

Benmore Lodge

Ben Sgeireach
1561

Arscaig

Coiaboll

Saval

East Langwell

Loch Urigill

An Stùc
1195

Loch Sgeireach

Sallachy

Lairg Lodge

Loch Craggie

1059

Muie

14

839

Rogart

Rowie Lodge

Beinn an Eòin
1786

Loch na Fuaralaich

Grudie Burn

Lairg

Claonel

Strath Fleet

Creagan Glas
1028

Pittentrail

Meall an Fhuarain
1895

Cnoc a' Choire
1318

Gruids

Torroble

10

839

Shin Forest

Kirk

Rhidorroch Forest

19

Lubcroy

Ashness Waterfall

Invercassley

9

864

6

Beinn Domhnaill
1144

Torboil

Cambusmore Lodge

Loch Fl

Little

Oykel Bridge

837

Brae

Doune

Altass

837

Altnas

Falls of Shin

Loch Laro

Loch Buidhe

Badninish

15

9

Fo

Rappach

Strath Mulzie

1

Loch an Daimh

Glen Einig

Glen Einig

1616

Achnahanat

Rhelonie

836

Loch an Laqain

Achvaich

Rearquhar

Proncy

DORNO

Meall Dheirgidh
1659

Braelangwell Lodge

Culrain

Migdale

Loch Migdale

Spinningdale

18

Clashmore

Rhidorroch

3040

Carn a' Choin Deirg
2301

Croick

The Craigs

Wester Gruinards

Kyle of Sutherland

Lower Gledfield

Bonar Bridge

Whiteface

Skibo Castle

Lonemore

Glen Douchary

2122

Seana Bhraigh

Alladale Lodge

Amatnatua

Dounie

Ardgay

Kincardine

949

Cambuscurrie Bay

Dorn

Inverlael Forest

Freevater Forest

Carron

Carn Salachaidh
2128

Fearn Lodge

20

Edderton

Beinn Dearg
3547

Glencalvie Forest

Gleann Mòr

Lochan a' Chairn

1792

Morangie

15

TAIN

3120

Diebidale Forest

Deanich Lodge

Beinn Tharsuinn
2330

2194

2750

1744

9176

Morangie Forest

East Lamington

2

Ullapool

Dirrie More

Strathvaich Forest

Crom Loch

Gleann Beag

Abhainn a'Ghlinne Bhig

NORTH

Braeantra

Beinn Tharsuinn
2270

Strath Rusdale

Ardross Forest

Dalnavie

Achandunie

Balnaguisich

Rhicullen

Lamington

Logie Hill

Kildary

Newfield

Kilmuir

Barbaraville

Loch Droma

Loch Glascarnoch

Strathvaich Lodge

Aultguish Inn

Carn Mòr
2095

Wyvis Lodge

2436

Inchbae Forest

Loch Vaich

Strathrannoch

Meall Mòr
2421

Loch Glass

Kildermorie Lodge

Loch Morie

Cnoc Ceislein
1716

Boath

Easter Ardross

Averon

EASTER ROSS

Dalmore

Tullich Muir

28

Milton

Balnabruaich

Kilmuir

Balnapaling

835

38

Kinlochluichart Forest

Ben Wyvis
3433

Eileanach Lodge

Glenn Glass

Redburn

Black Rock of Novar

ALNESS

Dalnavie

9

Rosskeen

Saltburn

INVERGORDON

CROMARTY

Cromarty Bay

Inverness

Inverness

Thurso

Wick

Wa   22

Forsinard

Loch More

Wb

Loch Ruard

Loch Sand

Wc

Lochan Thulachan

895

Loch Rangag

13 Achavanich

Wd

GREY CAIRNS OF CAMSTER

We

Thrumster

Wf

Sarclet

13

Camster

Loch of Yarrows

815 • Stemster Hill

9

Ulbster

Achentoul Forest

Dalganachar

1144 • Ben Alisky

741 •

44

RUMSTER FOREST

Houstry

CAIRN O'GET

STONES

Roster

Bruan

STONE ROWS

12

Halberry Head

37

Occumster

Lochside

1437

Knockfin Heights

953 •

Loch Dubh

Swiney

Latheren

Forse

Lybster

Achentoul

Kinbrace

1434

2313 • Morven

Braemore

Smerral

Berriedale Water

Janetstown

4

Dunbeath

897

1699 •

2055 Scaraben

Dunbeath Water

Borgue

16

Newport

Broch

Dunbeath Castle

Loch Ascaig

71

LEARABLE HILL CAIRNS

1819 •

Cnoe na Maoile

1305 •

Langwell W

9

Berriedale

eag Fiadh

Kildonan Lodge

Ousdale

BROCH

Craggie

18

Strath of Kildonan or Strath Ullie

Kilphedir

1134

1581

2060

Beinn Dhorain

1940 •

West Helmsdale

Gartymore Portgower

Helmsdale

Col-bheinn

1765 •

Glen Sletdale

Lothmore

12

Lothbeg

9

Gordonbush

21

Kintradwell

KINTRADWELL BROCH

West Clyne

NORTH

Loch Brora

Doll

Brora

Backies

5

CAIRN LIATH

SEA

5

Dunrobin Castle

olspie

Tarbat Ness

Innis Mhòr

Wilkhaven

2

Portmahomack

Innis Bheag

Inver Bay

Inver

10

Rockfield

Arboll

Tarrel

Lochslin

7

Eye

9165

Rhynie

Fearn

Loans of Tullich

Hilton of Cadboll Chapel

Hilton of Cadboll

Moray Firth

Balintore

Shandwick

Chapelhill

King's Cave

Halliman Skerries

BRANDERBURGH

LOSSIEMOUTH

Covesea Skerries

Lossiemouth

astlecraig

9040

h Sutor

Duffus

St Peter

Gordonstoun

9103

Cromarty Head

BURGHEAD

Burghead Well

Cummingstown

Roseisle

Hopeman

3

Duffus Castle

Loch Spynie

Spynie Palace

Lossie Forest

941

Spey Bay

Burghead Bay

9013

9012

6

9

Kingston

Spey Bay

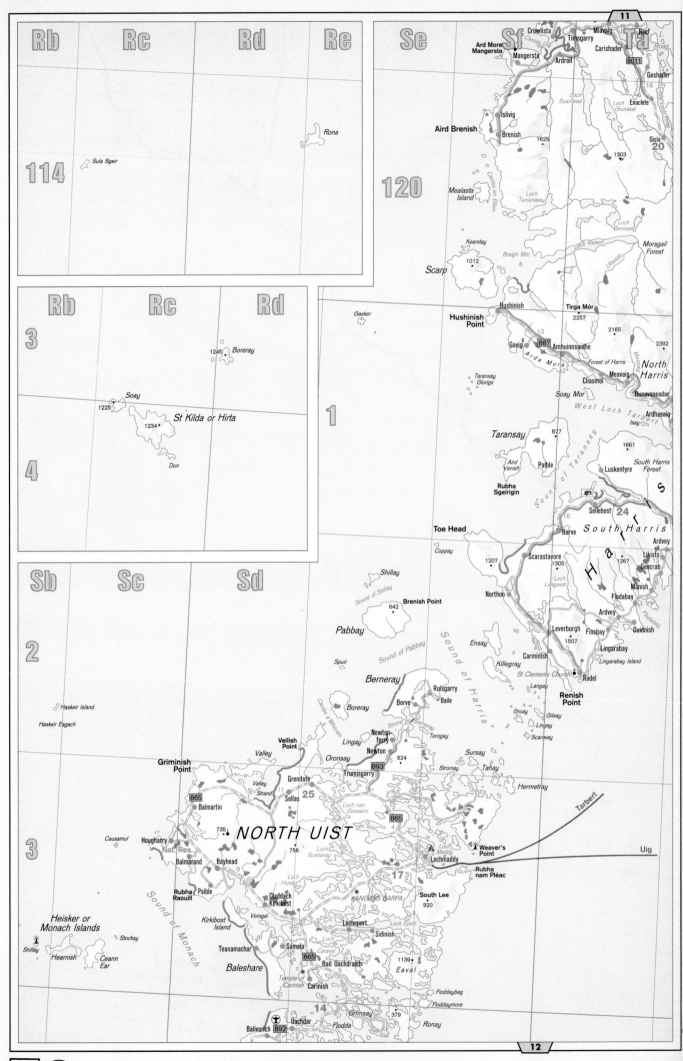

Rb **Rc** **Rd** **Re** **Se** **Sf** **Tا**

114 Sula Sgeir Rona

Crowlista
Miavaig
Ard More Timsgarry Reef
Mangersta Mangersta Carishader
Ardroil 8011
Geshader
16
Islivig Enaclete
Grunavat
Aird Brenish Brenish Gisla
1625 20
1303
Loch Suainaval
120
Mealasta
Island Loch
Tamanavay

Loch Resort Morsgail
Forest
Loch
Benisval

Kearstay Braigh Mór Ulladale
Scarp 1012

Gasker Hushinish Tirga Mór
Hushinish Hushinish 2257
Point 2165
13 2392
Govig 887 Amhuinnsuidhe North
Arda Mora Forest of Harris Harris
Taransay Cliasmol Meavaig
Glorigs Bunavoneadar
Soay Mor Ardhasaig
West Loch Tarbert Isay
877
Taransay 1661
Paible South Harris
Aird Luskentyre Forest
Vanish
Rubha Sellebost 24
Sgeirigin 16 South Harris
Borve Ardvey
Likisto
Toe Head 1207 Scarastavore 1267 Geocrab
1305 Manish
Coppay Loch Flodabay
Langavat Ardvey
Shillay Northton Quidnish
Brenish Point 642 1507 Finsbay
Sound of Shillay Leverburgh Lingarabay
Pabbay Carminish Lingarabay Island
Killegray St Clements Church
Spuir Ensay Langay Rodel
Sound of Pabbay Groay **Renish**
Berneray Gilsay **Point**
Ruisgarry Lingay
Borve Baile Scaravay
Haskeir Island Boreray Sound of Berneray Torogay Sursay
Haskeir Eagach Lingay Newton- Hermetray
Veilish ferry
Point Oronsay Newton 624
Griminish Valley 893 Stromay Tahay
Point Trumisgarry 5
Valley Grenitote Loch nan Tarbert
865 Strand 11 Sollas 25 Geireann 865
Balmartin 4
735 **NORTH UIST** Uig
Causamul Houghatry Nat. Res. 756 Loch Loch Weaver's
Scadavay Maddy **Point**
Balmarand Bayhead Lochmaddy
9 17 Rubha
nam Pléac
Rubha Paible KANGASS BARPA South Lee
Raouill Claddach 920
Kirkibost Vorogai 8
Kirkibost Locheport
Heisker or Island Sidinish
Monach Islands Teanamachar Samala 1139
Stockay 865 Caraval Eaval
Shillay Bail Uachdraich
Hearnish Ceann **Baleshare** Temple of
Ear Carinish Carinish Floddaybeg
14 Floddaymore
Uachdar Grimsay 379
Balivarich 892 Flodda Ronay

3 Rona

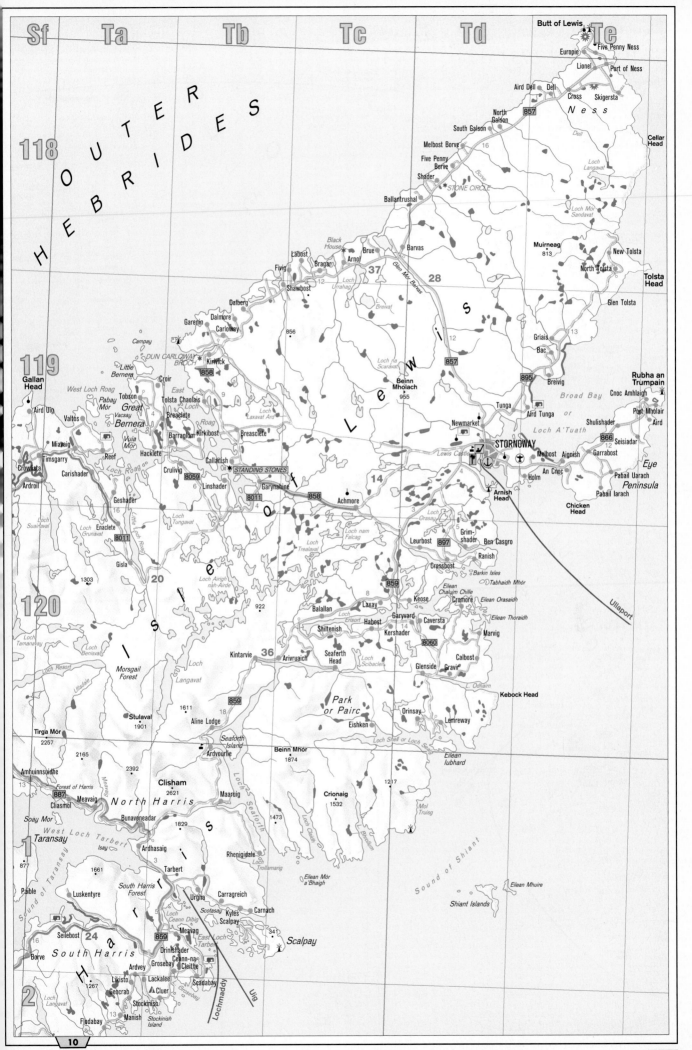

118

O U T E R   H E B R I D E S

119

120

Butt of Lewis
Five Penny Ness
Europie
Lionel
Port of Ness
Aird Dell Dell
Cross Skigersta
N e s s
857
North Galson
South Galson
Dell
Melbost Borve
16
Five Penny Borve
Shader
STONE CIRCLE
Ballantrushal
Black House
Brue Barvas
Labost
Bragar Arnol
Fivig
37 28
Shawbost
Loch Urrahag
Glen Mór Barvas
Dalberg
Garenin
Dalmore
Carloway
856
Muirneag
813
New Tolsta
North Tolsta
Glen Tolsta
Tolsta Head
Campay
DUN CARLOWAY BROCH
Kirivick
858
L e w i s
12
Loch na Scaraval
Beinn Mholach
955
857
895
Griais
Bac
Breivig
13
Rubha an Trumpain
Cnoc Amhlaigh
Port Mholair
Aird
866 Seisiadar
Garrabost
Eye Peninsula
Broad Bay
or
Loch A'Tuath
Gallan Head
Little Bernera
Croir
East Tolsta Chaolais
Pabay Mór Tobson
Vacsay
Great Bernera
Breaclete
Barraglom Kirkibost
Hacklete
Aird Uig
Valtos
Miavaig
Crowlista
Ardroil
Timsgarry
Carishader
Geshader
Reef
Vuia Mór
9
West Loch Roag
Loch Roag
Loch Laxavat Ard
Breasclete
Callanish
STANDING STONES
8059
Cruivig
Linshader
6
8011
Garynahine
858
Achmore
I s l e   o f   L e w i s
14
Newmarket
Lewis Castle
STORNOWAY
Melbost
Aignish
An Cnoc
Holm
Pabail Uarach
Pabail Iarach
Chicken Head
Tunga
Aird Tunga
Shulishader
Arnish Head
Ullaport
3
Loch Orasay
5
Grim-shader
Ben Casgro
Leurbost
897
Ranish
Crossbost
Barkin Isles
Tabhaidh Mhór
Eilean Chalum Chille
Eilean Orasaidh
Eilean Thoraidh
859
8
Keose
Cromore
Laxay
Garyvard
14
Caversta
Marvig
8060
Calbost
Glenside Gravir
L. Odhairn
Kebock Head
Balallan
Loch Erisort
Shiltenish
Habost
Kershader
Seaforth Head
Loch Scibacleit
Loch Suainaval
16
Enaclete
8011
Gisla
1303
20
Loch Airigh nah-Airde
922
Loch Trealaval
Loch nam Falcag
Loch Grunavat
Kintarvie
36
Arivruaich
Park or Pairc
Orinsay
Lemreway
Eishken
859
1611
18
Aline Lodge
Loch Langavat
Loch Tamanavay
Loch Benisval
Loch Resort
Ulladale
Morsgail Forest
Stulaval
1901
Tirga Mór
2257
2165
2392
Seaforth Island
Ardvourlie
Beinn Mhór
1874
Crionaig
1532
1217
Mol Truisg
Eilean Iubhard
Loch Shell or Loch Seaforth
Sound of Shiant
Amhuinnsuidhe
13
887
Forest of Harris
Meavaig
N o r t h   H a r r i s
Clisham
2621
Maartuig
Cliasmol
Bunaveneadar
1829
1473
Eilean Mór a'Bhaigh
Shiant Islands
Eilean Mhuire
Soay Mór
1
Taransay
877
West Loch Tarbert
Isay
Ardhasaig
3
Tarbert
Rhenigidale
Loch Trollamarig
Sound of Taransay
Paible
1661
Luskentyre
South Harris Forest
5
Urgha
Carragreich
Scotasay
Kyles Scalpay
Carnach
Scalpay
341
Loch Ceann Dibig
Loch Seaforth
1267
24
Seilebost
Borve
S o u t h   H a r r i s
859
Meavag
Drinishader
Ceann-na-Cleithe
Grosebay
Ardvey Lackalee
Likisto Geocrab
Cluer
Scadabay
Grosebay
Loch Langavat
2
Flodabay
13
Manish
Stockinish
Stockinish Island
Lochmaddy
Uig

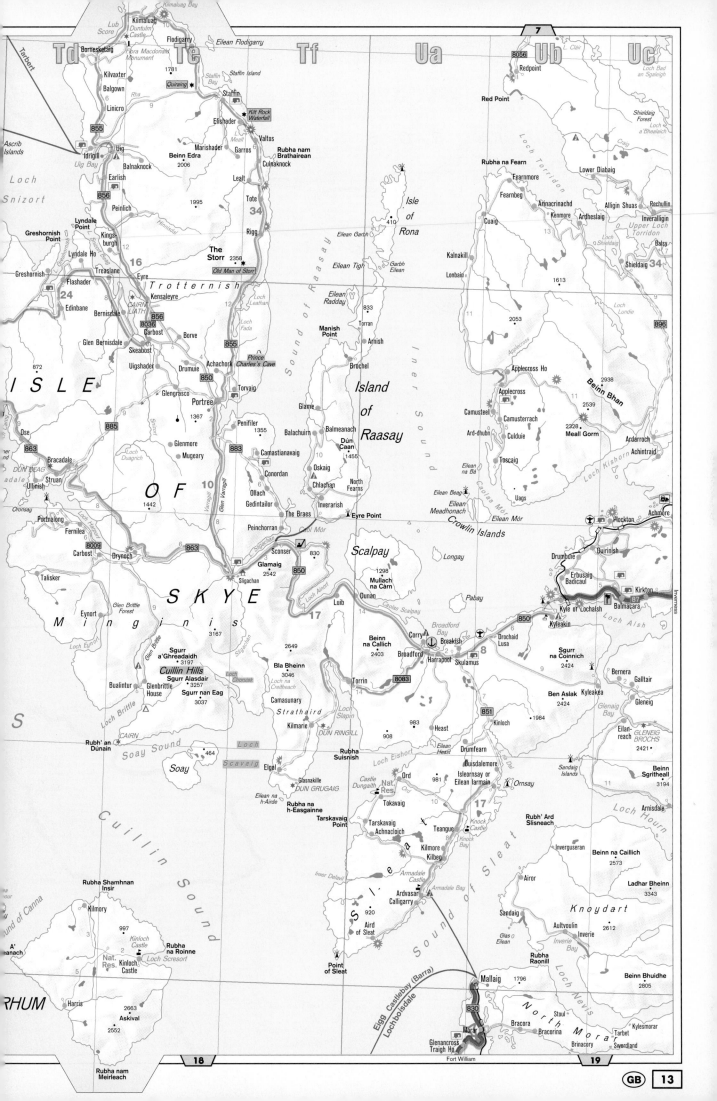

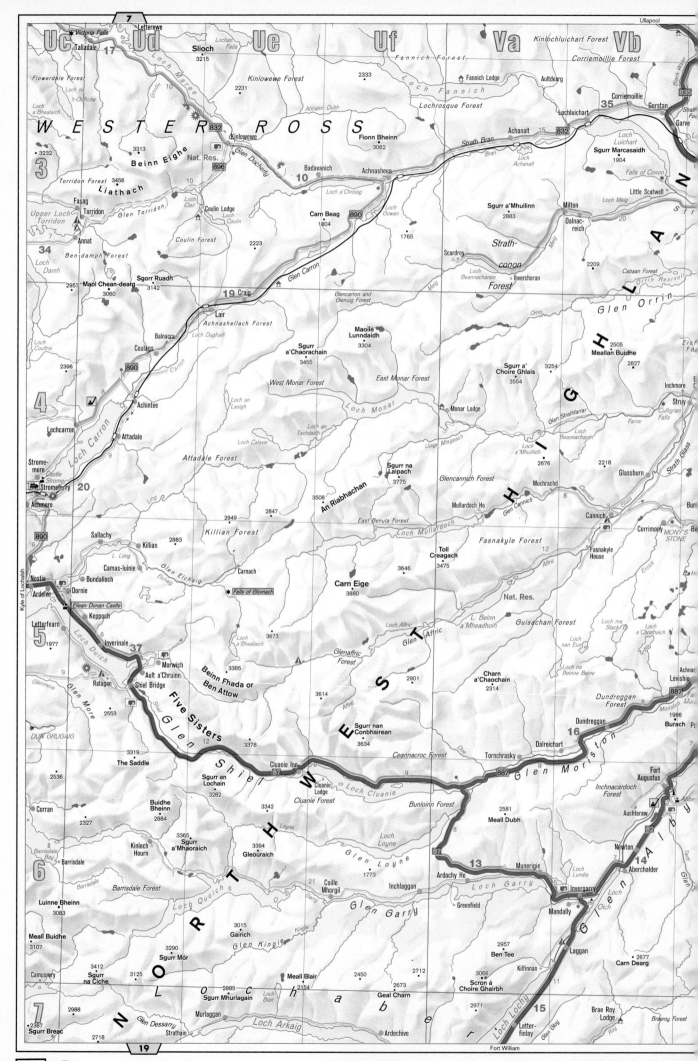

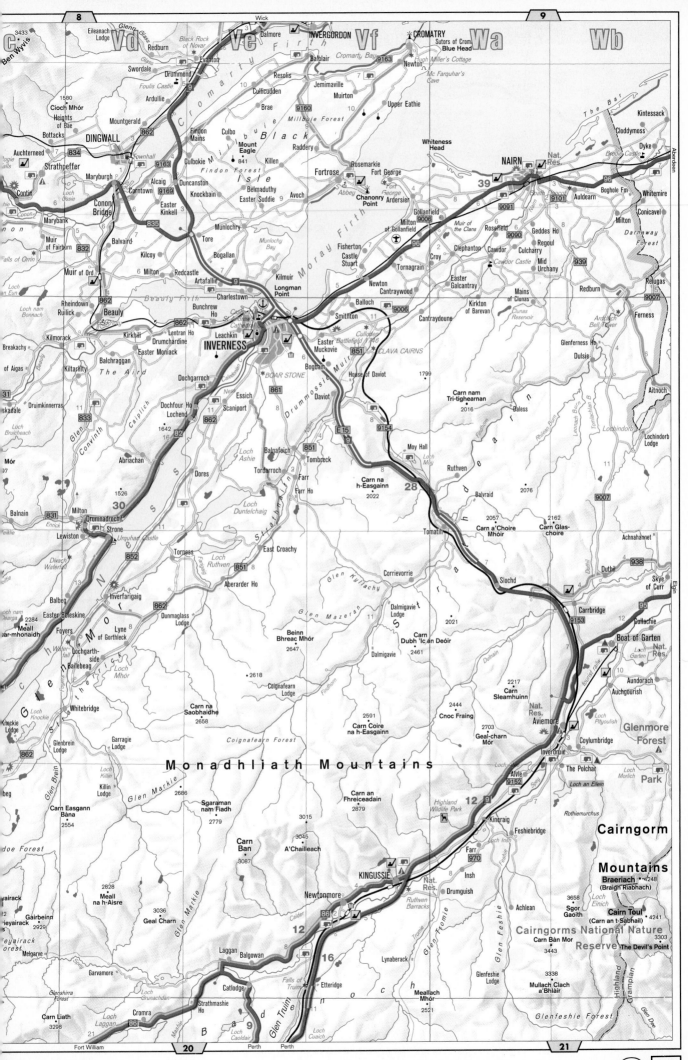

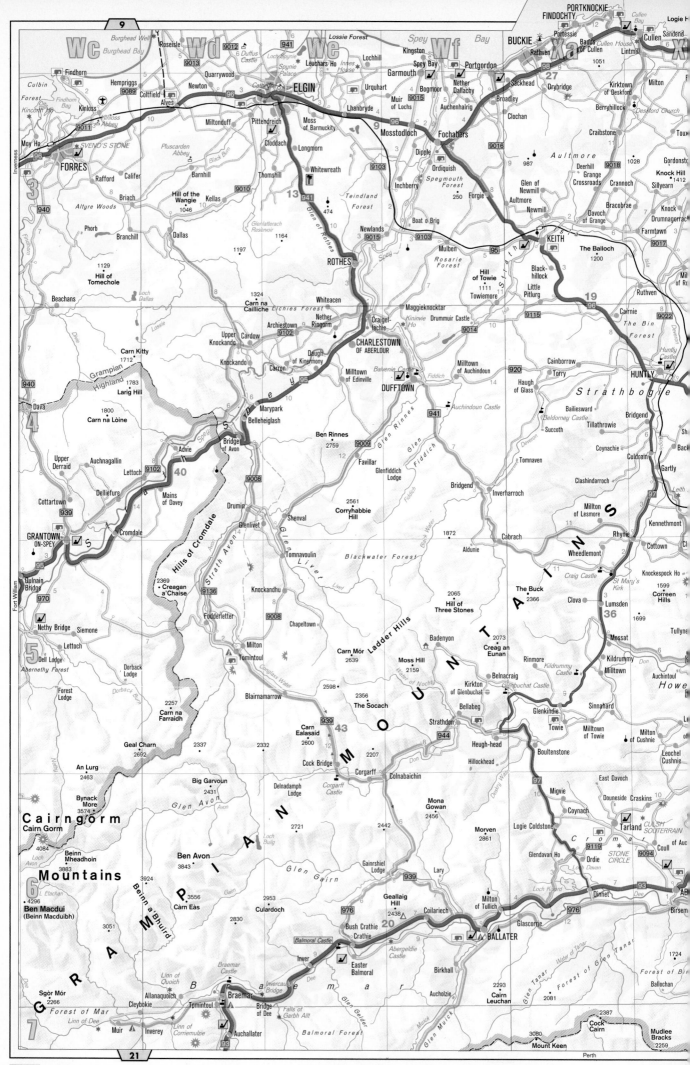

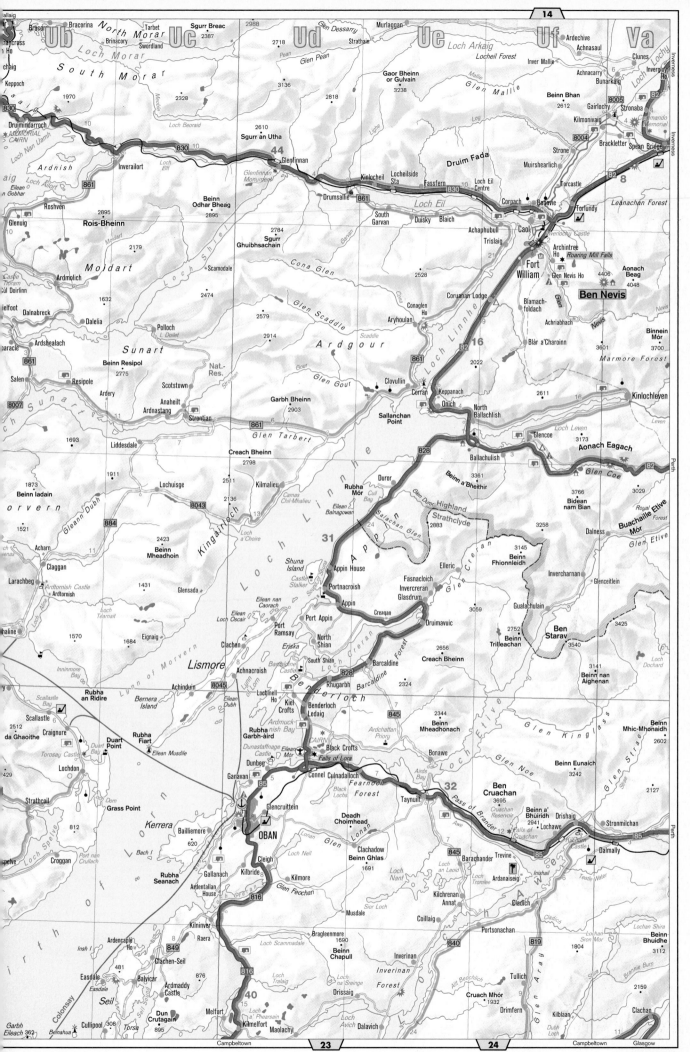

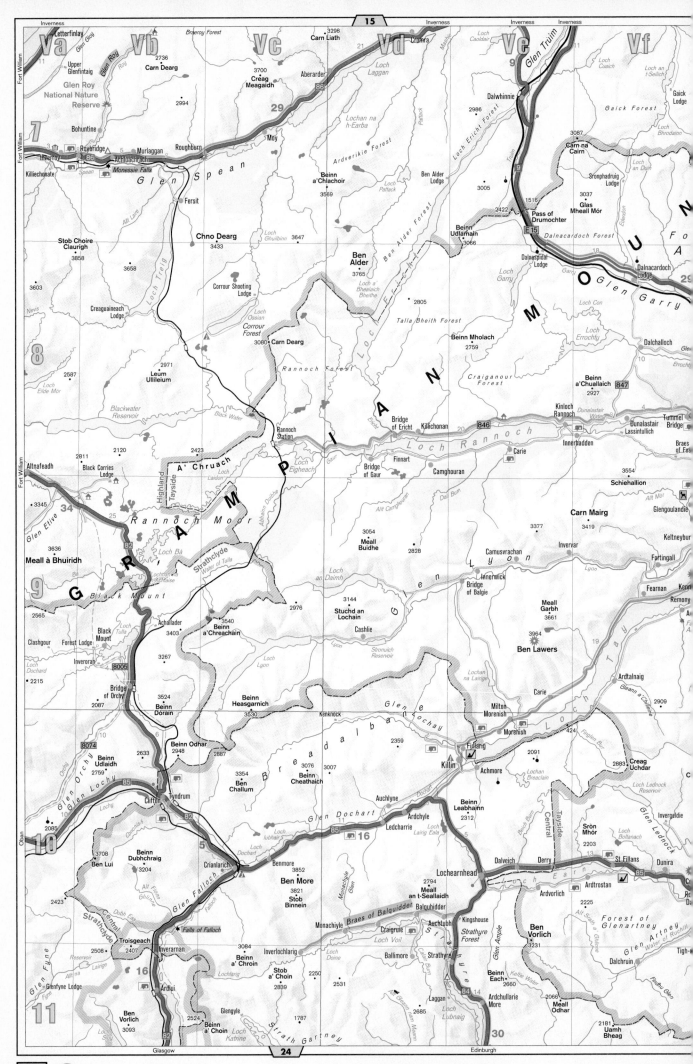

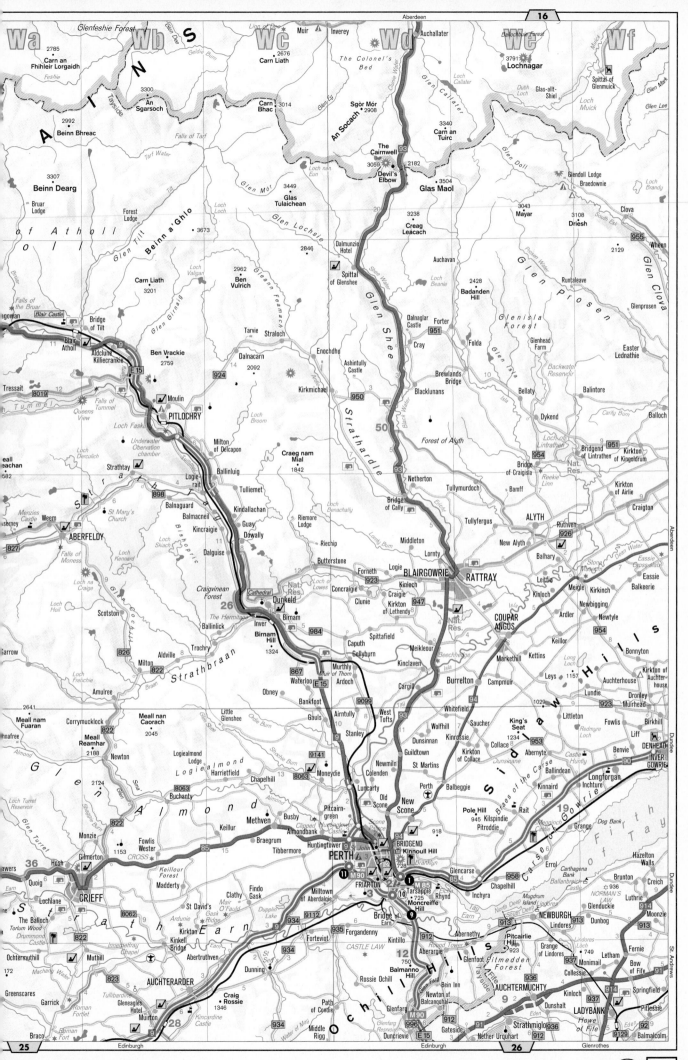

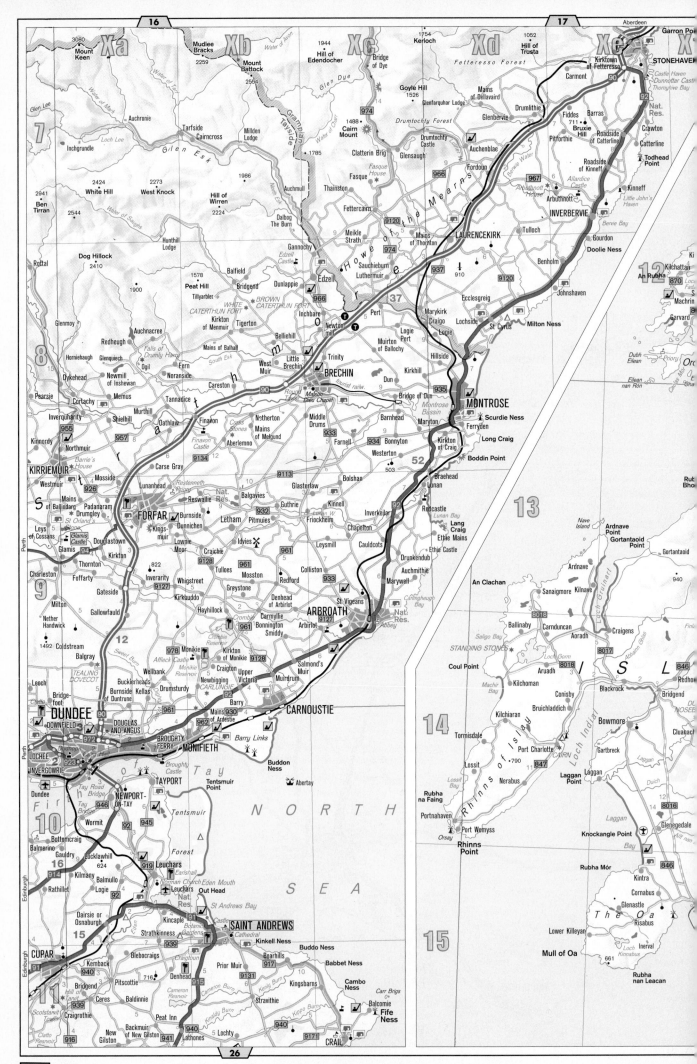

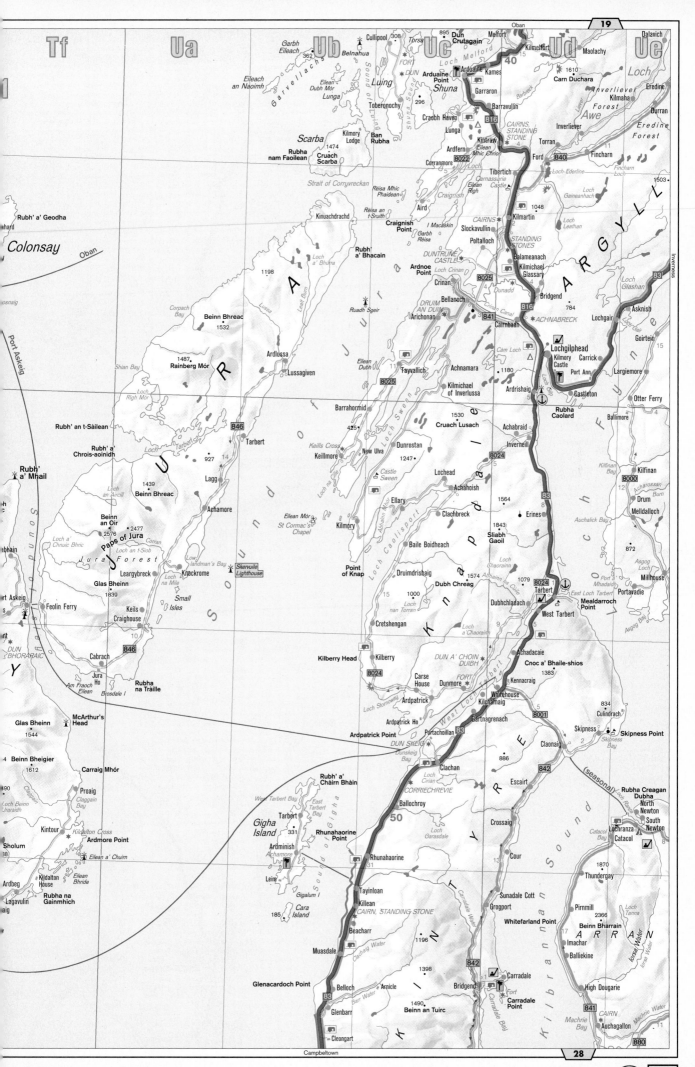

Tf   Ua   Ub   Uc   Ud   Ue

Garbh
Eileach   Belnahua   308
Culliepool   895   Dun
Crutagain   Oban
Eileach
an Naoimh   362   Eilean
Dubh Mór
Lunga   Torsa   Melfort
Kilmelfort   40   15   Maolachy   Dalavich
Loch Melford   Arduaine
Point   Arduaine   Kames   1610   Carn Duchara   Inverliever
Forest   Eredine
Loch
Awe
Luing   Shuna   Garraron
Toberonochy   296   Barravullin   Kilmaha
Forest   Durran   Eredine
Forest
Scarba   Kilmory
Lodge   Ban
Rubha   Craobh Haven   Lunga   816   Inverliever   Torran
Rubha
nam Faoilean   1474
Cruach
Scarba   Ardfern   Eilean
Mhic Chrion   Ford   840   Fincharn   1503
Kintraw   8022   Torran
Corranmore   Tibertich   Loch-Ederline   Loch
Fincharn
Strait of Corryvreckan   Réisa Mhic
Phaidean   Carnassarie
Castle   Loch
Gaineanhach
Aird   Réisa an
t-Sruith   Eilean
Righ
Colonsay   Oban   Kinuachdrachd   Craignish
Point   I Macaskin   CAIRNS   Kilmartin   1048
Garbh
Réisa   Slockavullin   1198   Rubh'
a' Bhacain   Poltalloch   STANDING
STONES   ARGYLL
Rubh' a' Geodha   Loch
a' Bhúrra   Ardnoe
Point   DUNTRUNE
CASTLE   Balmeanach
Kilmichael
Glassary   Loch
Glashan
Leal Burn   Crinan   Dunadd   Bridgend   784   Asknish
Corpach
Bay   Beinn Bhreac
1532   Ruadh Sgeir   Bellanoch   8025   816   Lochgair   Goirtein
Port Askaig   J   DRUIM
AN DUIM   ACHNABRECK   15
Arichonan   841   Cairnbaan
Cam Loch   Lochgilphead
Shian Bay   1487
Rainberg Mór   U   R   A   Ardlussa   Eilean
Dubh   1   Achnamara   1180   Kilmory
Castle   Carrick
Lussagiven   Tayvallich   8025   Port Ann   Largiemore
Loch
Righ Mór   Ardrishaig   Castleton
Loch Crinan
Otter Ferry
Rubh' an t-Sàilean   Barrahormid   1530   Cruach Lusach   Rubha
Caolard   Ballimore
846   425   Achabraid
Rubh' a'
Chrois-aoinidh   Tarbert   Keills Cross   New Ulva   Dunrostan   Inverneill   Loch
Tarbert   Kilfinan
Bay   Kilfinan
Rubh'
a' Mhail   927   14   Keillmore   1247   Lochead   8024   8000
Loch   83   12
Lagg   Castle
Sween   Achahoish   1564   Drum   Melldalloch
Beinn Bhreac
1439   Achamore   Ellary   1843
Sliabh
Gaoil   872
Beinn
an Oir   Kilmory   Clachbreck   Erines   Asgog
Loch
2576   2477   Eilean Mór
St Cormac's
Chapel   Baile Boidheach   Auchalick Bay   Millhouse
Jura Forest   Skervuile
Lighthouse   Point
of Knap   Druimdrishaig   1574   1079   8024   Portavadie
Leargybreck   Low
landman's Bay   Dubh Chreag   15   1000   Tarbert   Port à
Mhadaidh   East Loch Tarbert   Mealdarroch
Point
Glas Bheinn
1839   Knockrome   Loch
nan Torran   Dubhchladach   West Tarbert
Feolin Ferry   Keils   Small
Isles   Cretshengan   9   Loch
a' Chaorainn
Craighouse   Loch
na Mile   846   10   Kilberry Head   Kilberry   DUN A' CHOIN
DUIBH   Achadacaie   834
Culindrach
Cabrach   8024   Carse
House   FORT   1383   Cnoc a' Bhaile-shios   Skipness   Skipness Point
Am Fraoch
Eilean   Jura
Ho   Dunmore   Kennacraig   Skipness
Bay
Rubha
na Tràille   Brosdale I   Ardpatrick   Whitehouse   5   8001
McArthur's
Head   Ardpatrick Ho   Kilchamaig   Gartnagrenach   842
Glas Bheinn
1544   Loch Stornoway   886   Claonaig   Rubha Creagan
Dubha
Benn Bheigier
1612   Ardpatrick Point   Portachoillan   83   Escairt   North
Newton
DUN SKEIG   Rubh' a'
Chàirn Bhàin   (seasonal)   South
Newton
Carraig Mhór   Dunskeig
Bay   Clachan   Catacol
Bay   Lochranza
Proaig   West Tarbert Bay   East
Tarbert
Bay   CORRIECHREVIE   Ballochroy   Loch
Cirian   Catacol
Claggain
Bay   Tarbert   50   1870   Thundergay
Kintour   Gigha
Island   331   Rhunahaorine
Point   Loch
Garasdale   Crossaig   ARRAN
Ardminish   Rhunahaorine   Cour   130   Pirnmill   2366   Loch
Tanna
Sholum   Achamore   Sunadale Cott   Beinn Bharrain
Leim   Tayinloan   Grogport   Imachar
Ardbeg   Eilean a' Chuirn   Killean   Whitefarland Point   Iorsa Water
Kildalton
House   Gigalum I   CAIRN, STANDING STONE   Ballickine
Lagavulin   Rubha na
Gainmhich   Cara
Island   185   Beacharr   1196   High Dougarie
Muasdale   Clachaig Water   1398   Carradale   841   CAIRN   Auchagallon
Glenacardoch Point   Belloch   Arnicle   Beinn an Tuirc   842   Carradale
Point   Machrie
Bay   11
Glenbarr   Barr Water   1490   Bridgend   Fort   Machrie Water
Cleongart
Campbeltown   28

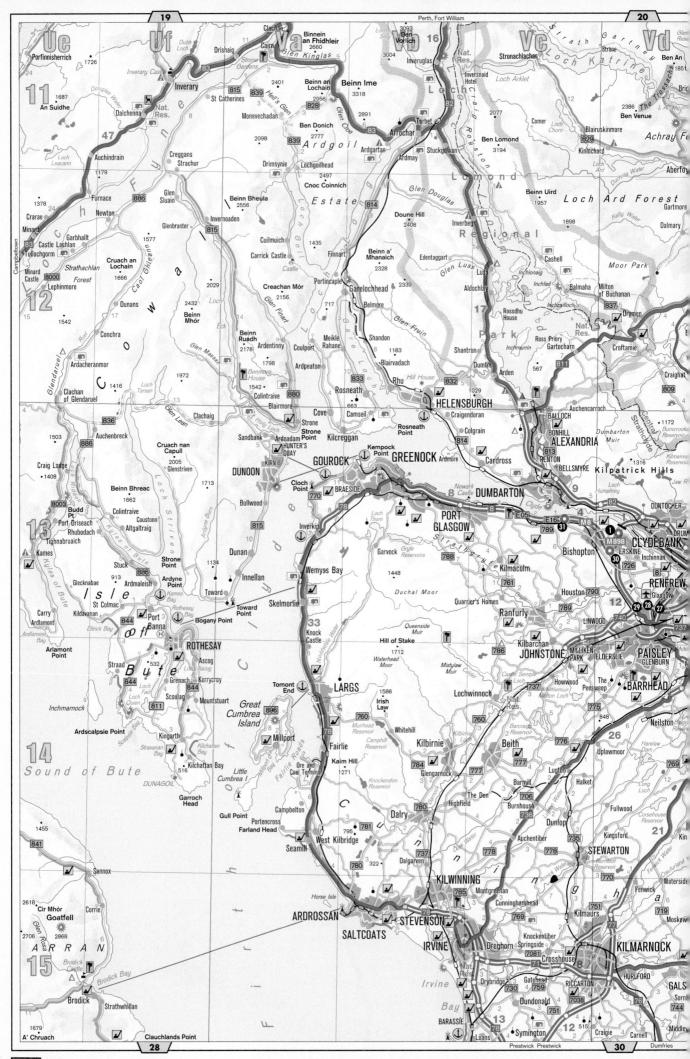

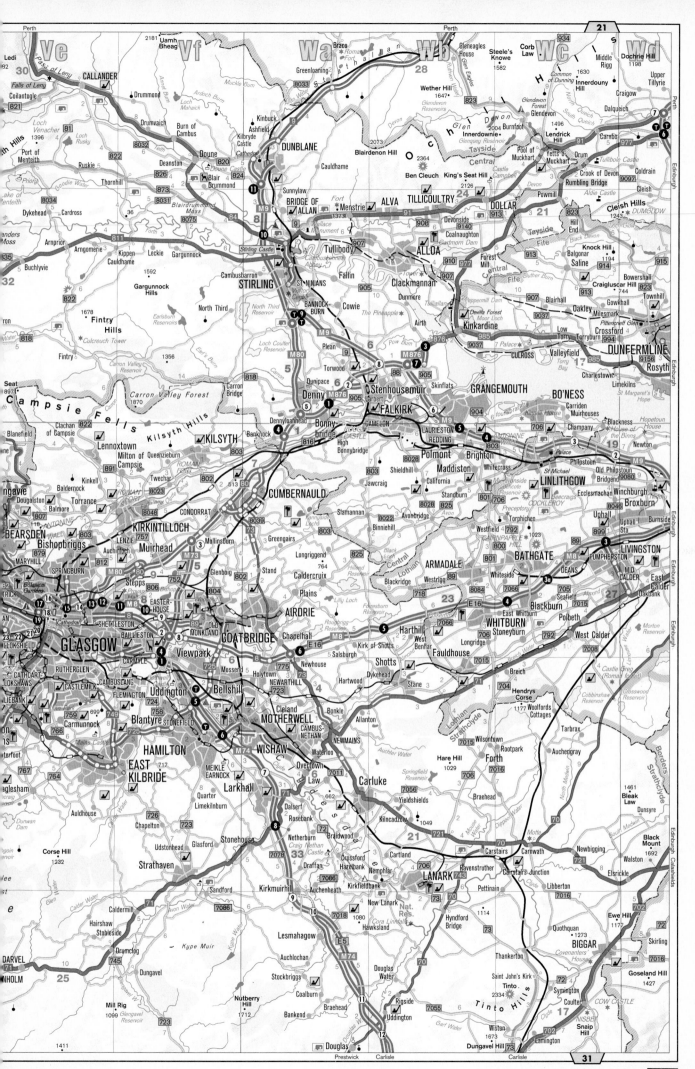

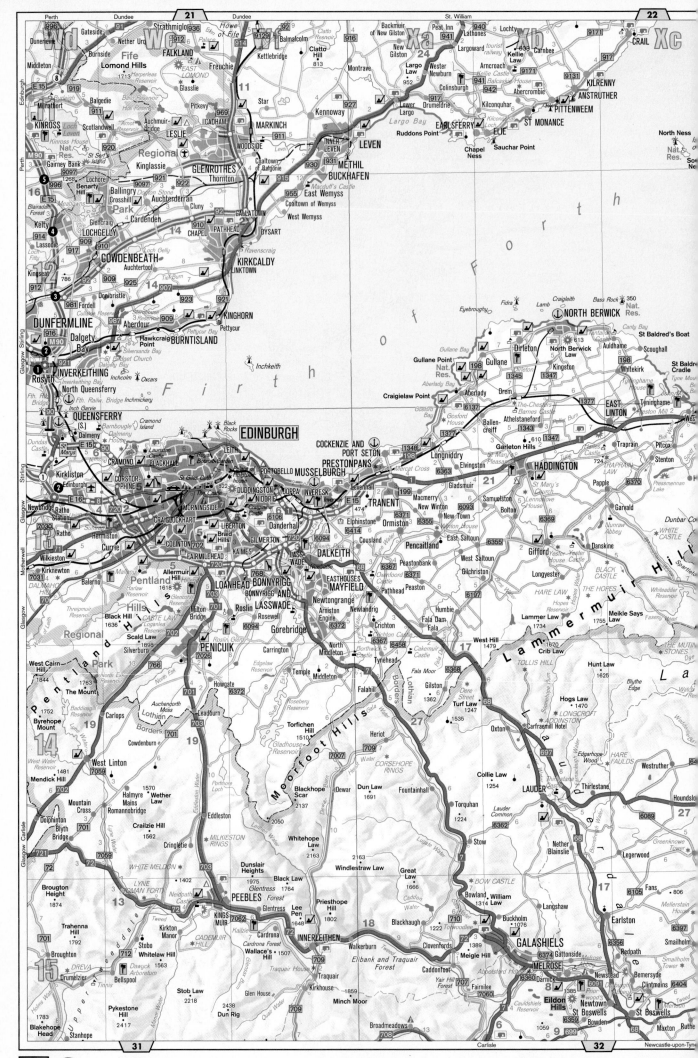

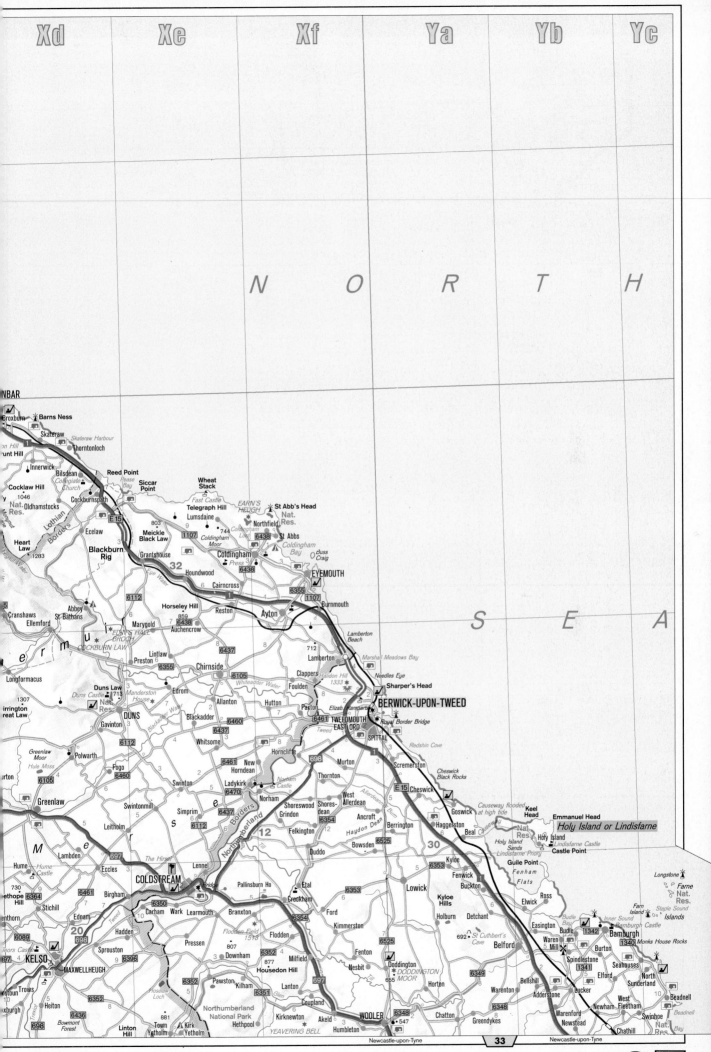

N   O   R   T   H

S   E   A

Broxburn   ⚓ Barns Ness
Skateraw   Skateraw Harbour
Thorntonloch
Innerwick   Bilsdean   Reed Point
Cocklaw Hill   Collegiate   Pease   Wheat
1046   Church   Bay   Siccar   Stack
Oldhamstocks   Cockburnspath   Point   Fast Castle
Nat.   E 15   EARN'S
Res.   803   HEUGH   St Abb's Head
Heart   Ecelaw   Telegraph Hill   Lumsdaine   Nat.
Law   Meickle   1107   744   Northfield   Res.
1283   Black Law   Coldingham   6438   St Abbs
Blackburn   Grantshouse   Moor   Coldingham   Buss
Rig   Press   Coldingham   Craig
32   Houndwood   Bay
Cranshaws   6112   Cairncross   EYEMOUTH
Ellemford   Horseley Hill   Reston   Ayton   6355
Abbey   859   1107
St Bathans   Marygold   6438   Burnmouth
EDIN'S HALL   Auchencrow   Lamberton
BROCH   Lintlaw   Beach
Longformacus   COCKBURN LAW   Preston   712   Marshall Meadows Bay
Chirnside   Lamberton   Needles Eye
6355   Clappers   Haldon Hill   Sharper's Head
Duns Law   6105   Foulden   1333
irrington   1713   Manderston   Whiteadder Water   Paxton   Elizab   Ramparts   BERWICK-UPON-TWEED
reat Law   Duns Castle   House   Edrom   6461   Royal Border Bridge
1307   Nat.   Allanton   Hutton   7   TWEEDMOUTH
Res.   DUNS   6460   EAST ORD
Gavinton   Blackadder   6437   Tweed   SPITTAL
Greenlaw   Polwarth   Whitsome   Horncliffe   698   Murton   Redshin Cove
Moor   6112   Ladykirk   6461   New   Thornton   Scremerston   Cheswick
Hule Moss   Fogo   Horndean   Norham   E 15   Cheswick   Black Rocks
6105   6460   Castle   Shoreswood   Shores-   West   Berrington   Goswick   Causeway flooded   Keel
Greenlaw   Swinton   Norham   dean   Allerdean   6354   Haggerston   at high tide   Head   Emmanuel Head
Leitholm   Simprim   6437   Grindon   Ancroft   Beal   Nat.   Holy Island or Lindisfarne
M   Lambden   697   6112   Felkington   Haydon Dean   Bowsden   6525   30   Holy Island   Holy Island
Hume   The Hirsel   12   Duddo   Kyloe   Sands   Lindisfarne Castle
Hume   Eccles   Lennel   Bowsden   6353   Buckton   Fenham   Guile Point   Castle Point
Castle   COLDSTREAM   Pallinsburn Ho   Etal   6353   Lowick   Fenwick   Flats   Longstone
730   6461   Birgham   Bridge   Crookham   Kyloe   Elwick   Ross   Farne
ethope   6364   6350   Wark   Learmouth   Branxton   Ford   Hills   Detchant   Nat.
Hill   Stichill   Carham   Kimmerston   Holburn   Buckton   Res.
nthorn   Ednam   6354   Flodden Field   Flodden   6525   692   St Cuthbert's   Easington   Budle   Farn   Islands
6089   20   698   1515   Fenton   Cave   Belford   Budle   1342   Island   Bamburgh Castle
997   KELSO   Hadden   Pressen   807   Nesbit   6349   Waren   Monks House Rocks
Trows   Sprouston   Downham   Milfield   Horton   Mill   1340
MAXWELLHEUGH   6396   6352   Doddington   Bellshill   Spindlestone
Heiton   6352   Housedon Hill   877   DODDINGTON   Burton   Seahouses
xburgh   6436   Pawston   Kilham   655   MOOR   Warenton   1341   Elford   North
698   Linton   881   Lanton   Coupland   Adderstone   Lucker   Sunderland
Hill   Town   Kirknewton   697   Chatton   6348   Warenford   West
Yetholm   Yetholm   Akeld   WOOLER   6348   Fleetham
Northumberland   Hethpool   Humbleton   Greendykes   Newstead   Swinhoe
National Park   YEAVERING BELL   547   Chathill   Beadnell
Newcastle-upon-Tyne   33   Newcastle-upon-Tyne   Nat.   Bay
Res.

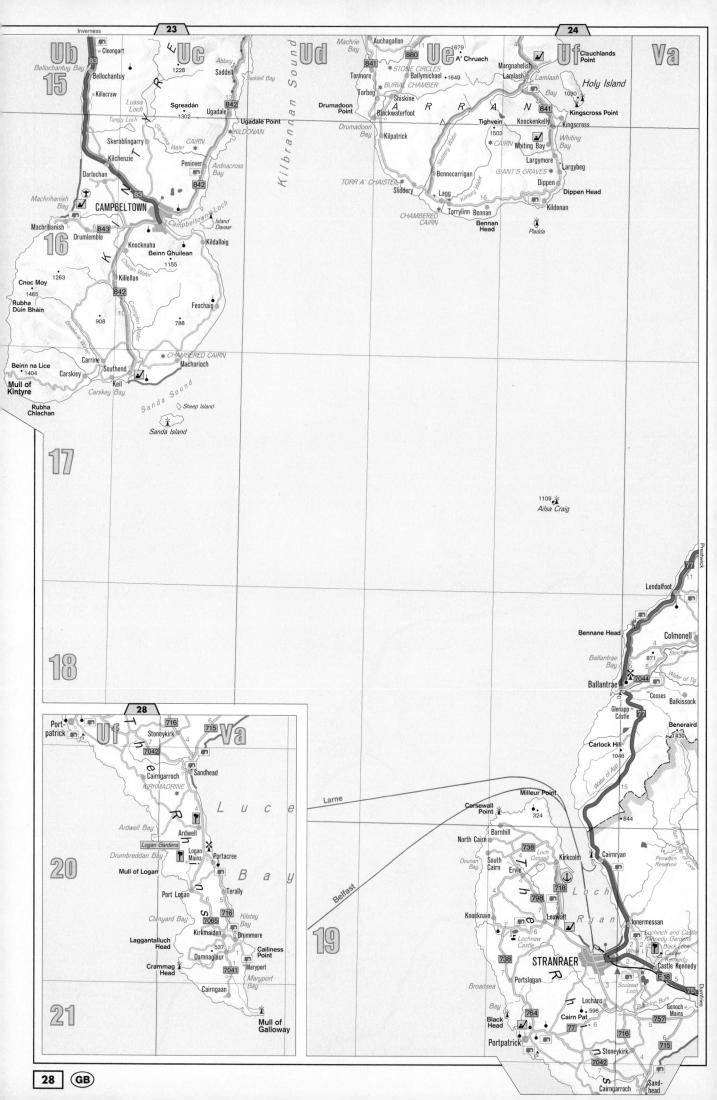

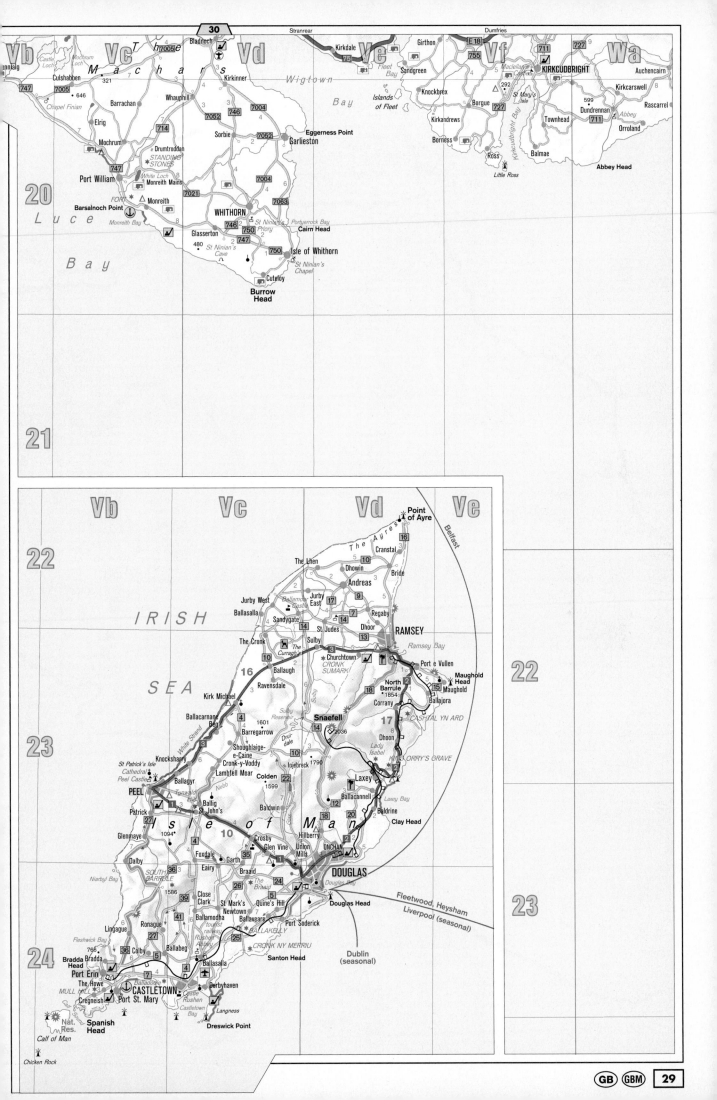

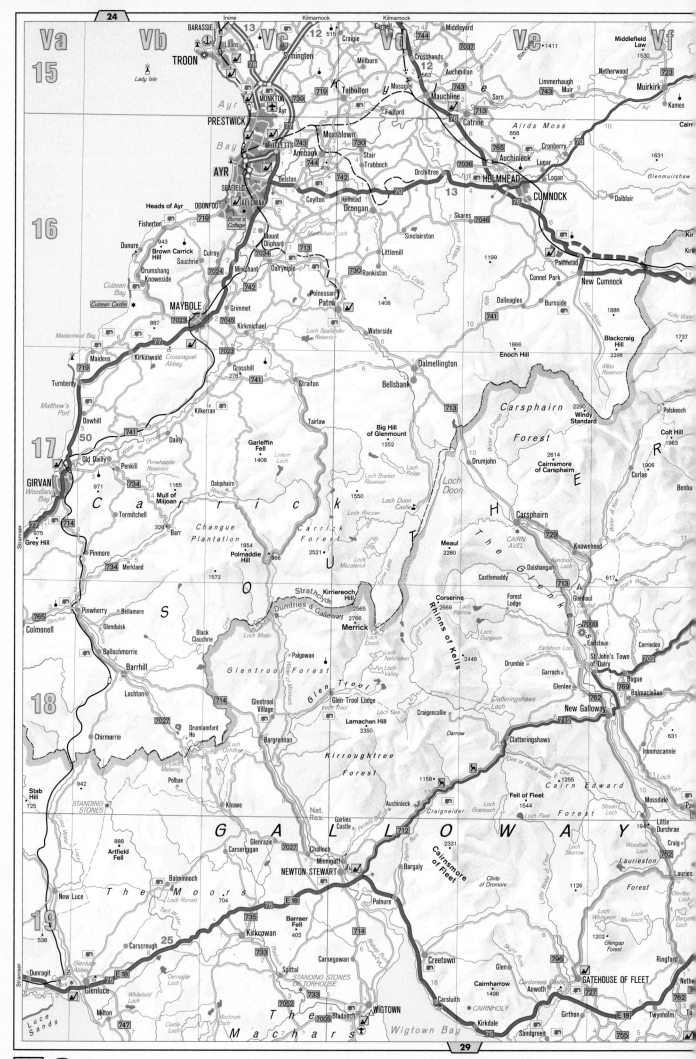

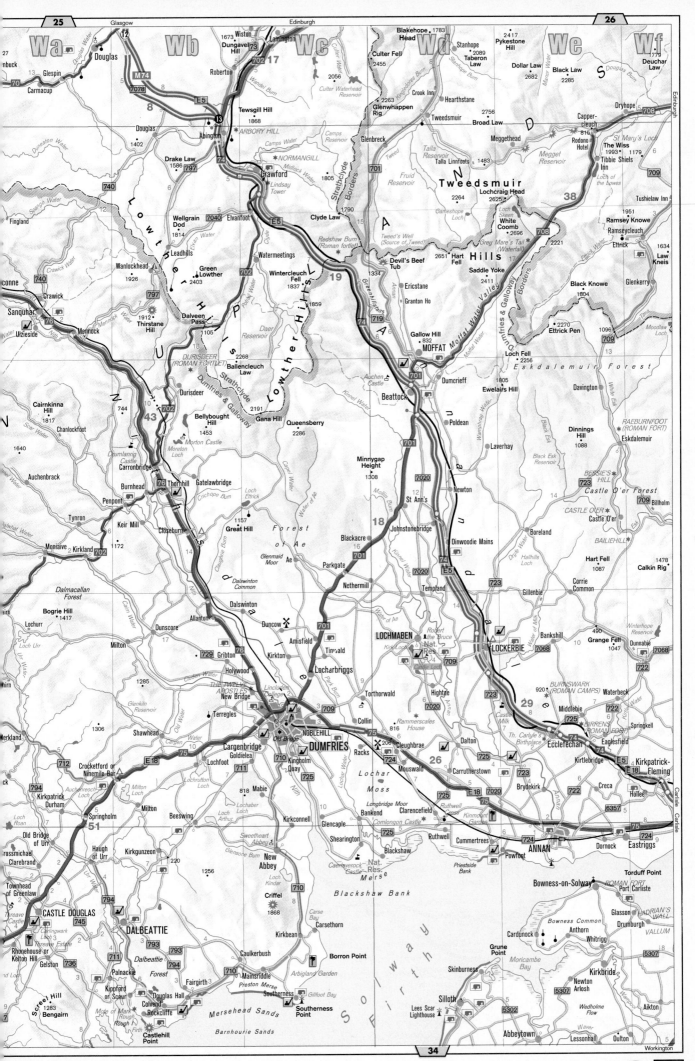

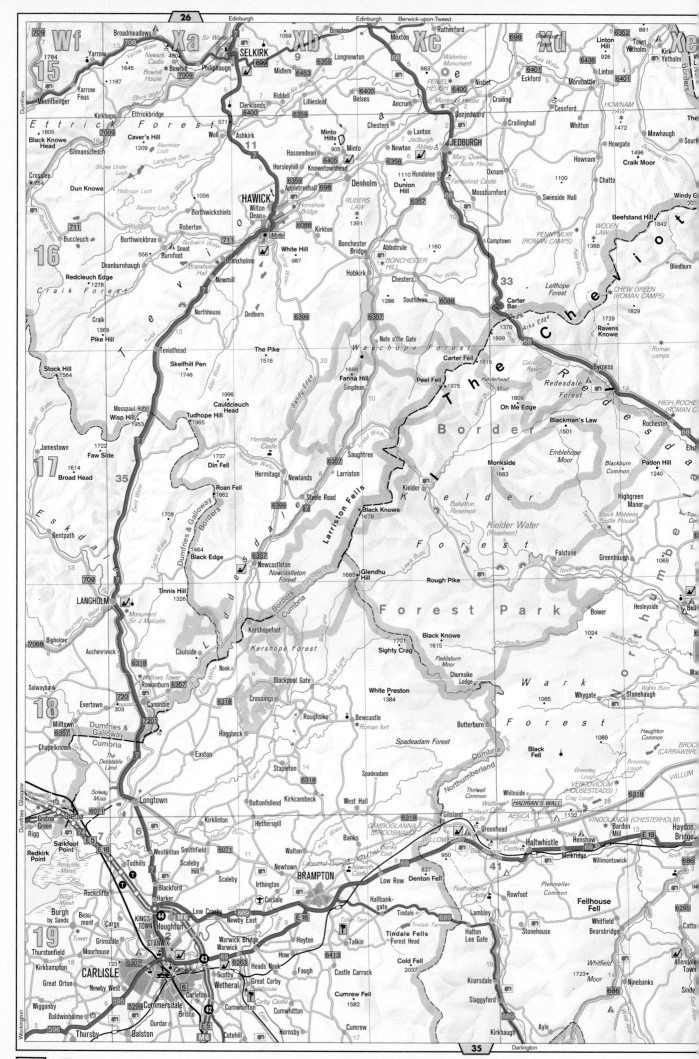

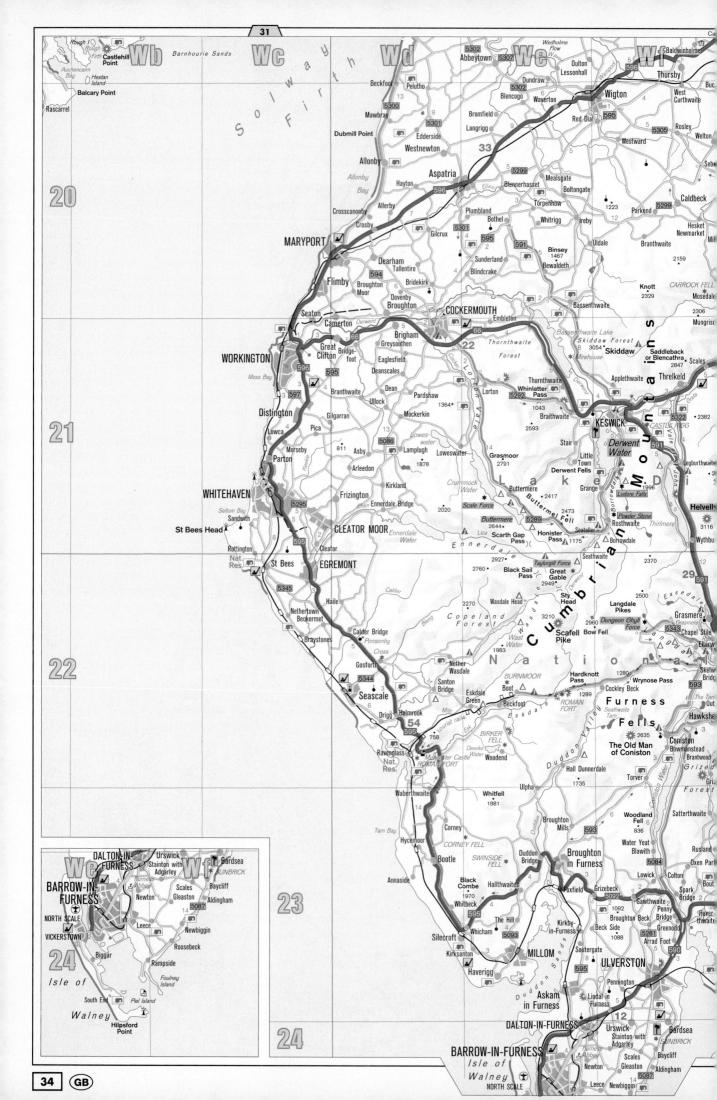

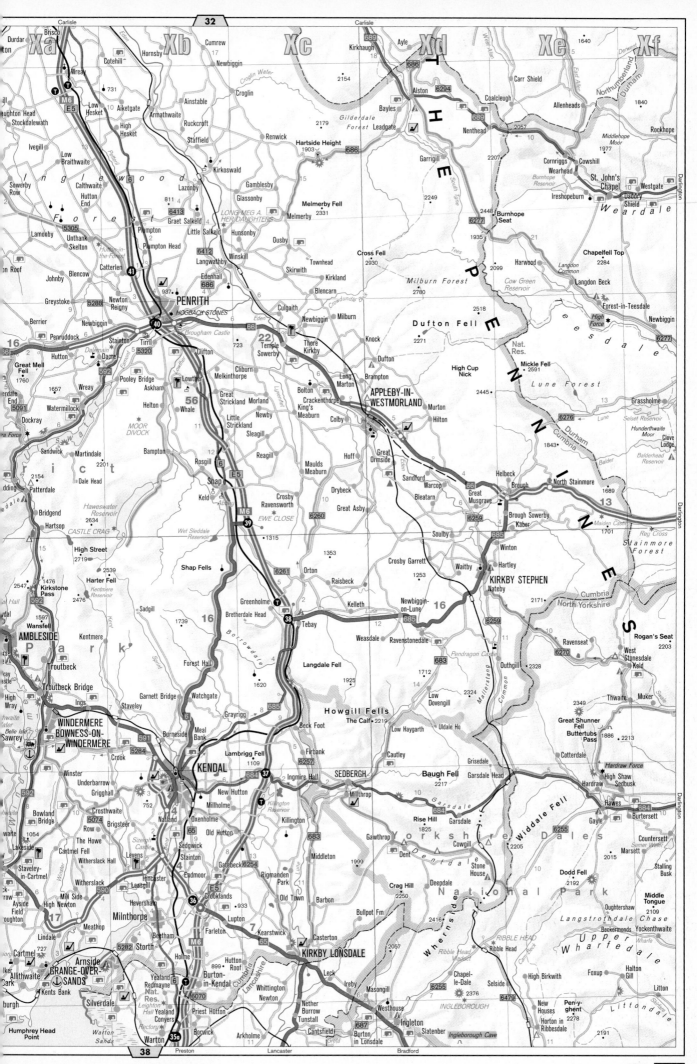

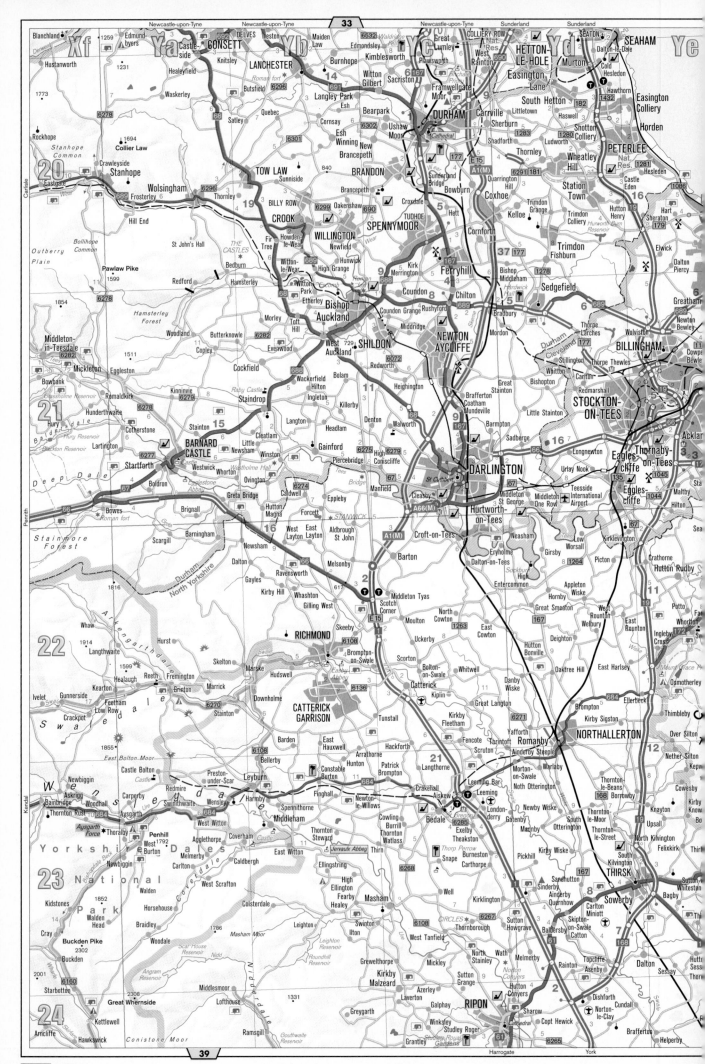

Scarborough
Cayton Bay
23
Lebberston
Gristhorpe   FILEY
Hertford
1039   Muston
Filey Bay
Hunmanby   18   165   Reighton
Speeton   Nat.
Res.
DANES'
Burton Fleming   DYKE
Bempton   Flamborough
WILLY   Grindale   1229   Head
HOWE   St Mary   Flamborough   1255   Sewerby Hall
24   Boynton   Sewerby
1253   BRIDLINGTON
Rudston   Bessingby   Bridlington
Carnaby   Bay
Haisthorpe   11   166   HILDER-
THORPE

Hartlepool Bay
HARTLEPOOL

Seaton Carew   Tees Bay

Coatham
REDCAR
Dormans-   MARSKE-BY-THE-SEA
town   1085   SALTBURN-BY-THE-SEA
174
South   Lazenby   New Marske
Bank   Grange-   Wilton   Upleatham   Skinningrove
ODDLES-   town   1269   173   Boulby   174   Staithes
OUGH   1380   Eston   793   SKELTON   BROTTON   700   Easington   8   Port Mulgrave
esby   ESTON NAB   Boosbeck   LOFTUS   Runswick
GUISBOROUGH   Priory   Lingdale   Liverton   Hinderwell   Bay   Runswick
171   Stanghow   1366   Roxby   Kettleness   Bay
172   Moorsholm   Ellerby   Goldsborough
Newton under   Scaling   Lythe   Sandsend
Great   Roseberry   Commondale   1266   645   6   WHITBY
Ayton   1078   Mickleby   174
esley   Captain Cook   North Yorkshire   Dunsley   Abbey
Monument   Newholm
173   Little   1064   Kildale   Danby   Houlskye   171   Aislaby   Stainsacre
Ayton   1099   Lealholm   8   Sleights   Hawsker
Easby   Battersby   Castleton   Egton   Ugglebarnby   Sneaton
Great   Ingleby   Street   Glaisdale   Grosmont   1416   Sneaton-   Raw
Busby   Greenhow   Westerdale   Esk   Egton   Littlebeck   thorpe   Robin Hood's Bay
Kirkby   Bridge   HIGH BRIDE   Fylingthorpe   Robin Hood's Bay
Great   846   Beck   STONES
Broughton   1427   No   r   t   h   Y   o   r   k   Hole   945   M   o   o   r   s
1422   Danby   Egton High Moor   Ravenscar
Urra   1490   Rigg   Mallyn Spout   Flask Inn   171   20
Seave   Westerdale   1407   Glaisdale   Goathland   Fylingdales
Green   1410   Moor   1418   959   Moor   Staindale
veland   1326   Moor   Hunt Ho   10
Cockayne Ridge   Church Houses   Wheeldale   18   Harwood   Silpho
The Grange   1257   Cockayne   1379   Moor   169   Langdale   Dale   Cloughton
Helmsley   Low Mill   Rosedale Abbey   Forest   Newlands
Fangdale Beck   Moor   Thorgill   Wheeldale   Cloughton
18   Spaunton   Bridestones   Langdale   Suffield   Burniston
National   Park   Moor   Cropton Forest   Stape   Levisham   End   Hackness   Scalby Ness
Hawnby   Keldy Castle   Everley   Scalby   Rocks
Helmsley   Lastingham   Newton-on-   Lockton   Dalby   Scalby   SCARBOROUGH
Moor   Gillamoor   Spaunton   Rawcliffe   Forest   Wykeham
Old Byland   Fadmoor   Hutton-   Appleton-   Keldholme   Wrelton   Forest   Hutton   Osgodby   Cayton Bay
Rievaulx   le-Hole   le-Moors   Nat.   Aislaby   Buscel   Ayton
Cold Kirby   Rievaulx   Carlton   Res.   Sinnington   Wilton   Irton   Seamer
Abbey   Puckley   Kirkbymoorside   Middleton   Thornton-   8   Sawdon   1261   Cayton
Scawton   Beadlam   Kirkby   170   le-Dale   Ebberston   Snainton   Wykeham   Lebberston
Nawton   Mills   13   Great   Marton   Allerston   Hall   5   Brompton   Gristhorpe
866   12   Wombleton   Edstone   Normanby   PICKERING   Ebberston   Hertford
Sproxton   Harome   Ryton   The   C   a   r   r   s   Folkton   1039
Oldstead   Salton   Little Barugh   169   Yedingham   Willerby   Flixton
Wass   1257   Nunnington   Ness   Kirby   Wykeham   1258   Sherburn   Ganton   Hunmanby
Ampleforth   Stonegrave   Ness Hall   Misperton   Great Barugh   Scampston   20   East   10
Coxwold   Oswaldkirk   Butterwick   Great Habton   Vale   of   Pickering   64   Hesterton   Fordon
Newburgh   Ampleforth   Gilling   Cawton   Brawby   Scagglethorpe   West   Staxton
Priory   College   East   Hovingham   Great   Ryton   Wykeham   Knapton   Hesterton   Wold
Thorpe Hall   Slingsby   Barton-   Old   1258   Wintringham   Newton   Burton
565   le-Street   Malton   Foxholes   Fleming
Husthwaite   1363   Howardian   Hills   Amotherby   Scampston   Thorpe   WILLY
Oulston   Coulton   Appleton-   13   Bassett   Place   Butterwick   HOWE
Brandsby   Scackleton   le-Street   Broughton   MALTON   Newton
Yearsley   Stearsby   Coneysthorpe   NORTON   Wintringham   Helperthorpe
dy Hall   Crayke   Settrington   Weaverthorpe
Marton   Terrington   Great Lake   Huttons Ambo   West Lutton   Thwing
Easingwold   Abbey   Whenby   Skewsby   Ganthorpe   Castle Howard   1249

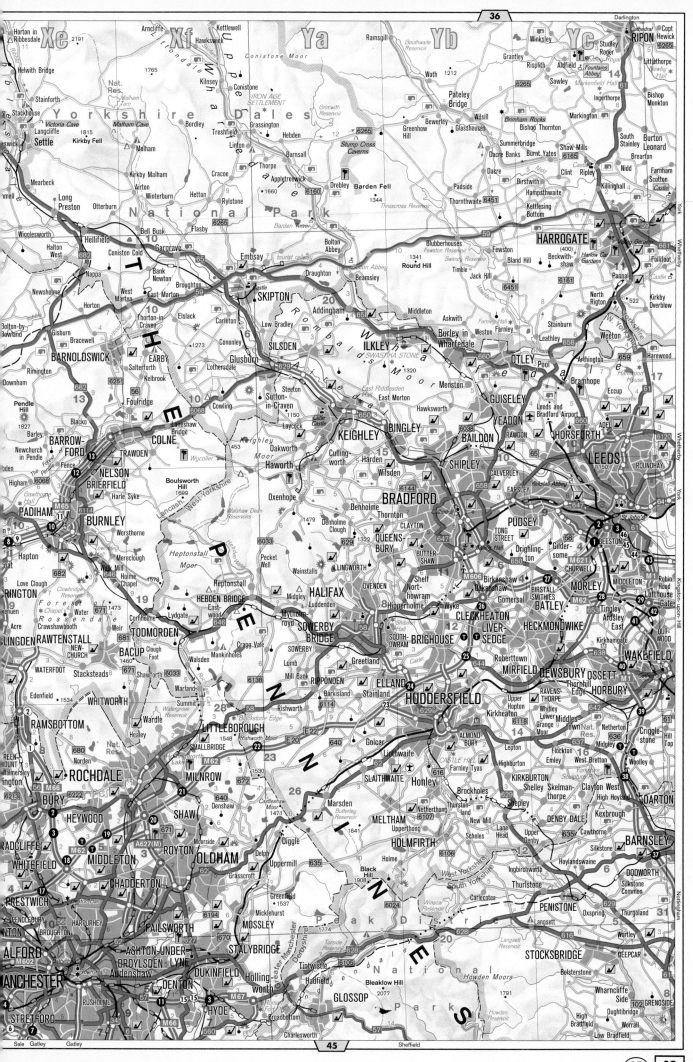

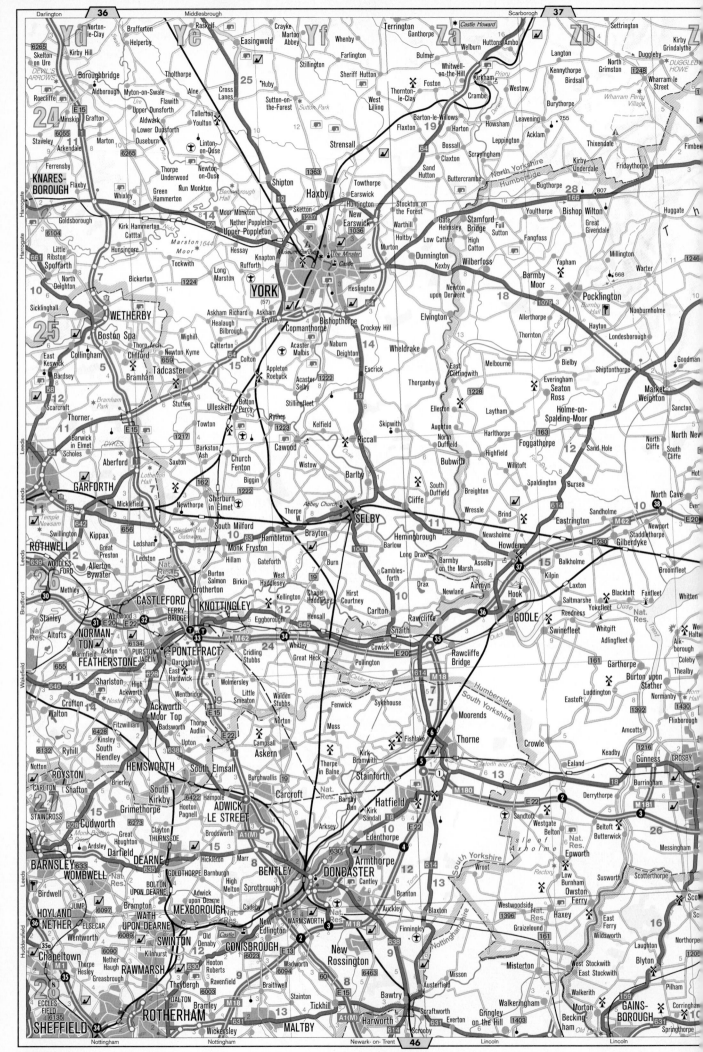

Dublin, Laoghaire

West Mouse
The Skerries
Cemaes Bay *Middle Mouse*
Llanbadrig Porthllechog
Bull Bay Amlwch Port
Cemlyn Bay
Carmel Head
Tregele ✕ Cemaes AMLWCH Point Lynas
Pengorffwysfa Llaneilian
Llanfairynghornwy Penysarn 580
Bodewryd Gadfa 5025 Dulas
Llanfechell Rhosgoch Dulas
City *Dulas Bay*
Llanrhyddlad Carreglefn Rhosybol Dulas Moelfre
Rhydwyn 15 Capel Parc Brynrefail DIN LLIGWY
Llanfflewyn Ceidio Llandyfrydog BURIAL CHAMBER
Llanfaethlu Elim Llanallgo
Llanfwrog Llanddeusant Llanerchymedd Maenaddwyn Marian-glas BURDD ARTHUR
North STANDING STONE Capel Coch Benllech
Stack Llantrisant Pen-llyn Carmel Bryngwran Llanbedrgoch Red Wharf Bay Lle
Holyhead 5025 369 Llechcynfarwy Brynteg *Red Wharf Bay* Llanddona
Mountain 722 Llanfachraeth BURIAL Llanbabo Bodffordd 5025
South Salt I CHAMBER Llanfigael 5112 Trefor 5111 Tregaian 5010 Pentraeth
Stack HOLYHEAD Llanynghenedl 5109 Llangwyllog Rhosmeirch 5109 Pen-y-Garnedd BEAUMAR
TY MAWR KINGSLAND CAERGYBI Penrhos Bodedern *A n g l e s e y* Rhoscefnhir 5025 Llansadwrn
STANDING STONES Dyffryn Caergeiliog Bryngwran Llynfaes Taiwrn Llandegfan 545
Penrhyn Mawr Four Mile E22 22 Heneglwys LLANGEFNI Penmynydd BAN
Trearddur 4545 Bridge Llanfihangel Gwalchmai Bodffordd Ceint 7 5420
Bodior yr Nhwyn Capel Gwyn Cerrigceinwen Pentre 5 Menai BRIDGE
Holy Island Rhoscolyn Llanfairyneubwll BURIAL Cefni Berw Llanfairpwllgwyngyll Cathedral
Cymyran Bay Valley CHAMBER Llangristiolus Gaerwen 5 Menai Suspension Bridge
Rhosneigr BURIAL Bethel 4422 Llanddaniel Fab 4080 E22
CHAMBER 4080 Trefdraeth 4419 CHAMBERED CAIRN Waen-wen Glasin
St Cwyfan Llangadwaladr Malltraeth Llangaffo Vaynol Tal-y-c: Tr
Aberffraw Hermon Brynsiencyn Hall Pentir 4366
Bodorgan 4421 PLAS NEWYDD Waen-wen Rhiwlas
Dwyran 4419 Y Felinheli 487 Dinas
*Malltraeth Niwbwrch CASTELL Llanddeiniolen 4366 Dinorwic M
Bay* BRYN GWYN Bethel Penisa'r Waun 4547
Newborough Pont-rug 5 Llanrug Clwyt-y
Nat. Res. Penr Caernarfon CAERNARFON
Llanddwyn I Warren Abermenai Castle Brpn Bras y-glo Cwm-
Point Roman Fort Caeathro Castle Llyn Padarn Llanberis
C a e r n a r f o n Llanfaglan Bontnewydd tourist
Forpd Bay Waunfawr Llanberis
Llanwnda Rhostryfan 4085 Moel Eilio Llan
499 3 2382
B a y Groeslon Rhosgadfan Betws Garmon
Llandwrog 487 Carmel Nantlle 2209 Llyn Cwellyn
DINAS DINLLE Penygroes Talysarn Nantlle 4418 Rhyd-Dd
Pontllyfni Llanllyfni *Llyn Nantlle Ffridd
Nebo Uchaf* Uchaf
S n o
Clynnog-fawr Capeluchaf Nasareth Garnedd- Beddgelert
10 Pant Glâs goch Pass of
Tai'n 6 2408 Aberglaslyn
Lôn CAERAU Moel
1712 Bwlch- 34 Hebog Pont Abe
Trefor Gyrn Ddu derwin Cennin Bryncir 1190 2566 Glasly
*TRE'R CEIRI Llanaelhaearn Garn Llanfihangel- 1811
1837 Pen-sarn Dolbenmaen y-pennant
Yr Eifl Cefn-caer-Ferch Dolbenmaen Golan
Llithfaen CARN PENTYRCH Rhoslan Tremadog
Pistyll Llwyndyrys Llangybi 4411 Penmorfa
Carreg Ddu 4417 Llanarmon Gell 497 PORTHMADOG
Morfa Nefyn Porth Nefyn Fron Chwilog Llanystumdwy Morfa
Dinllaen Y Ffôr Bychan Borth-
Edern GARN BODUAN Rhos- CRICCIETH y-Gest Portm
497 Boduan 4354 fawr Llannor 499 Abererch Llanfihan
Rhos-y-Llan 9 Llanbedrog Efailnewydd Pen-ychain y-traet
Tudweiliog Dinas CAER 2 Morfa
CARADOG Rhyd- PWLLHELI *Tremadog* Harlech
Garn 1218 y-clafdy Penrhos Harlech Castle
Penllech Llaniestyn Rhedyn *Bay*
4417 Sarn Nanhoron
Llangwnnadl Meyllteyrn Mynytho Llanbedrog
Tŷ-hen 4413 Botwnnog 499 Llanbedrog
Nethlern Bryncroes Llandegwning Inscribed stone Llanfihan
Rhydlios Llangian y-traet
Whistling 999 Llanengan St Tudwal's Morfa
Sands Rhoshirwaun Llawr Llanedd
Capel Carmel CASTELL Dref Abersoch Dyffryn
ODO Rhydolion Road Llandd
Llwchmynydd 4413 Rhiw Sarn Bach St Tudwal's Tal-y-l
Aberdaron Llanfaelrhys Bwlchtocyn Islands Dyffryn Ardudw
Braich Trwyn
y Pwll Uwchmynydd Cilan Trwyn yr Wylfa C A R D I G A N
Pen y Cil Uchaf Trwyn Cilan
Bardsey Sound Hell's Mouth Porth Neigwl
St Mary's Abbey B A Y
Bardsey Island 548
Ynys Ennlli

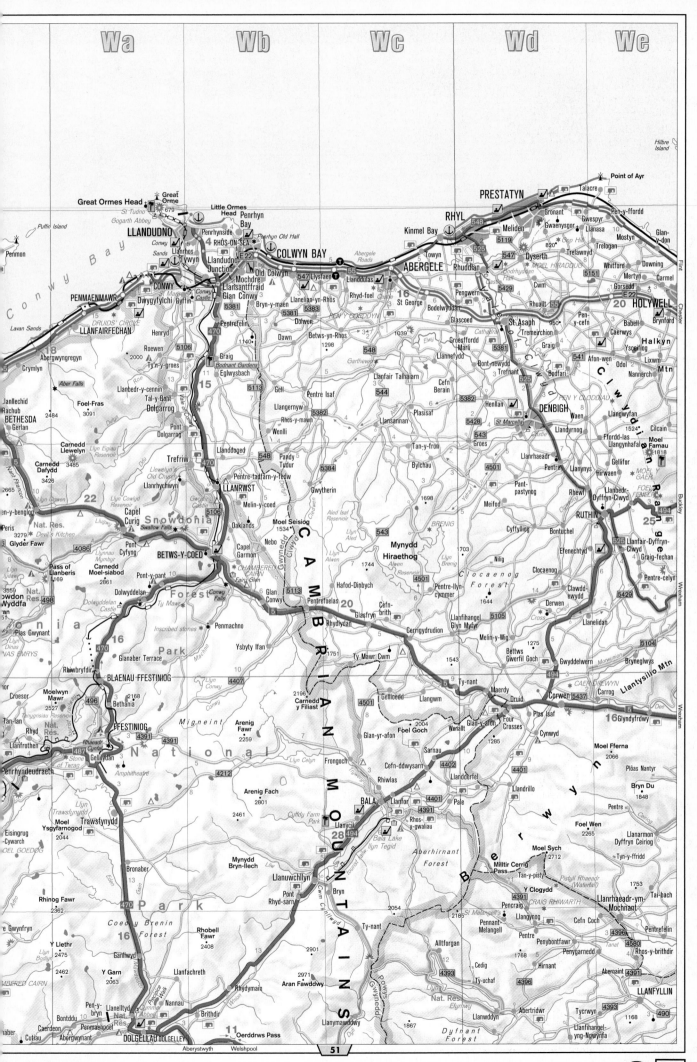

Hilbre
Island

Point of Ayr

Great Ormes Head
Great Orme
679
Little Ormes
Head
Penrhyn
Bay
St Tudno
Gogarth Abbey

PRESTATYN
Talacre
RHYL
548
Gronant
Gwespyr
Pen-y-ffordd
Meliden
Gwaenysgor
Llanasa
Mostyn
Glan-
y-don

LLANDUDNO
Conwy
Sands
Penrhynside
Llanrhos
Tywyn
RHOS-ON-SEA
Kinmel Bay
5119
Dyserth
Trelawnyd
Trelogan

COLWYN BAY
Abergele
Roads
547
Llysfaen
ABERGELE
Rhuddlan
525
547
Dyserth
820
Whitford
Downing
MOEL HIRADDUG

Old Colwyn
Llandudno
Junction
Mochdre
Llansantffraid
Glan Conwy
Llanelian-yn-Rhôs
5383
Rhyd-foel
St George
16
Pengwern
5429
Rhuallt
Cwm
Mertyn
Carmel
Gorsedd
E 22

CONWY
PENMAENMAWR
Dwygyfylchi
Byffin
Conwy
Castle
Bryn-y-maen
5381
Dolwen
PEN Y CORDDU
Bodelwyddan
Glascoed
St Asaph
Cathedral
Groesffordd
Marli
950
Pen-
y-cefn
Tremeirchion
5381
Babell
Caerwys
HOLYWELL
20

LLANFAIRFECHAN
Henryd
5106
Roewen
2000
Ty'n-y-groes
11
Bodnant Gardens
Eglwysbach
Gell
Pentre Isaf
544
Cefn
Berain
Llannefydd
Bont-newydd
Trefnant
525
Bodfari
541
Afon-wen
Odol
Graig
Lixwm
Nannerch
Halkyn
Ysceifiog
Mtn

18
Abergwyngregyn
Crymlyn
Aber Falls
Foel-Fras
3091
Tal-y-Bont
Dolgarrog
5113
Dawn
Betws-yn-Rhos
1298
548
Garthewin
1039
Elwy
Llanfair Talhaiarn
Plasisaf
5382
Henllan
5382
Llangwyfan
Cilcain
Moel
Famau
1818

BETHESDA
Gerlan
Rachub
2484
Carnedd
Llewelyn
Carnedd
Dafydd
3426
3485
Pont
Dolgarrog
Llewelyn's
Old Church
Llanbedr-y-cennin
Trefriw
470
Llanrhychwyn
5382
Rhos-y-mawn
Wenlli
548
Pandy
Tudur
Llansannan
Tan-y-fron
Bylchau
5384
543
Groes
Llanrhaeadr
St Marcella
5428
Waen
DENBIGH
Llandyrnog
Pentre
Hirwaen
Gellifor
Llanynys
Rhewl
Fford-las
Llangynhafal
MOEL
GAER
FOEL
FEMAU
Llanbedr-
Dyffryn-Clwyd
RANGE

22
Capel
Curig
Nat. Res.
Swallow Falls
Snowdonia
Melin-y-coed
Oaklands
Moel Seisiog
1534
Nebo
Capel
Garmon
Gwytherin
1698
Aled Isaf
Reservoir
Llyn
Aled
543
BRENIG
Meifod
Cyffylliog
Bontuchel
Clocaenog
Efenechtyd
RUTHIN
25
494
525
Llanfair-Dyffryn-
Clwyd
Graig-fechan

Glyder Fawr
3279
Devil's Kitchen
4086
Pont
Cyfyng
Carnedd
Moel-siabod
2861
BETWS-Y-COED
CHAMBERED
CAIRN
Fairy Glen
Glan
Conwy
5113
Pentrefoelas
20
Hafod-Dinbych
1744
Mynydd
Hiraethog
Alwen
Reservoir
Llyn
Brenig
1703
Nilig
Clocaenog
Forest
1644
14
Clawdd-
newydd
Derwen
Pentre-celyn
5429

Pass of
Llanberis
Carnedd
Moel-siabod
1169
Dolwyddelan
Dolwyddelan
Castle
Ty Mawr
Conwy
Falls
Glan
Conwy
Rhydlydan
Glasfryn
Cefn-
brith
Cerrigydrudion
Melin-y-Wig
1275
Bettws
Gwerfil Goch
Gwyddelwern
Bryneglwys
5104

498
Nat. Res.
Plas Gwynant
Inscribed stones
Penmachno
1751
Ty Mawr Cwm
1543
494
Llanfihangel
Glyn Myfyr
Cross
CAER DREWYN
Llantysilio Mtn

16
Rhiwbryfdir
470
Glanaber Terrace
Ysbyty Ifan
10
4407
4501
Gellioedd
Llangwm
Maerdy
Druid
Corwen
5437
Carrog
Llantysilio Mtn

BLAENAU FFESTINIOG
Moelwyn
Mawr
2527
496
Bethania
2168
Migneint
Arenig
Fawr
2259
2196
Carnedd
y Filiast
Foel Goch
2004
Glan-yr-afon
Sarnau
Wenallt
Plas Isaf
Four
Crosses
16
Glyndyfrdwy
Moel Fferna
2066
Plâas Nantyr

Croesor
Nat.
Res.
Rhaeadr
Cynfal
Ffestiniog
4391
4391
Llyn Celyn
Frongoch
Cefn-ddwysarn
4402
Llanderfel
Llandrillo
Bryn Du
1848
Pentre

Llanfrothen
487
Gellilydan
Amphitheatre
Arenig Fach
2801
Rhiwlas
4401
BALA
Llanfor
4401
Pale
Foel Wen
2265

Penrhyndeudraeth
Trawsfynydd
4212
Cuffty Farm
Park
2461
Llanycil
28
494
Rhos-y-
gwaliau
Bala Lake
Llyn Tegid
Aberhirnant
Forest
Moel Sych
2712
Llanarmon
Dyffryn Ceiriog
Tyn-y-ffridd

Eisingrug
Cywarch
Moel
Ysgyfarnogod
2044
OEL GOEDOG
Trawsfynydd
Mynydd
Bryn-llech
Llanuwchllyn
Bryn
Pont
Rhyd-sarn
2054
Ty-nant
2185
Milltir Cerrig
Pass
Tan-y-pisty
Pennant-
Melangell
Pistyll Rhaeadr
(Waterfall)
1753
Y Clogydd
CRAIG RHIWARTH
Llanrhaeadr-ym-
Mochnant
Tai-bach

Bronaber
13
Rhinog Fawr
2362
470
16
Coed y Brenin
Forest
Rhobell
Fawr
2408
Ganllwyd
13
Llanfachreth
2901
Rhydymain
2971
Aran Fawddwy
2971
Ty-nant
Alltforgan
Cedig
Ty-uchaf
1768
Hirnant
12
Pentre
Penygarnedd
4396
4393
4396
Abernaint
4391
LLANFYLLIN

Y Llethr
2475
Y Garn
2063
2462
AMBERED CAIRN
Pen-y-
bryn
Llanelltyd
Nant
Res.
Llanfihangel
Abbey
Nannau
Brithdir
1867
Llanymawddwy
Dyfnant
Forest
Llanwddyn
Nat. Res.
Abertridwr
Tycrwyn
4393
490
1168
Llanfihangel-
yng-Ngwynfa

Pennmaenpool
Abergwynant
Caerdeon
Bontddu
Penmaenpool
DOLGELLAU DOLGELLEY
Cymmer
Abbey
11
Oerddrws Pass

Aberystwyth Welshpool

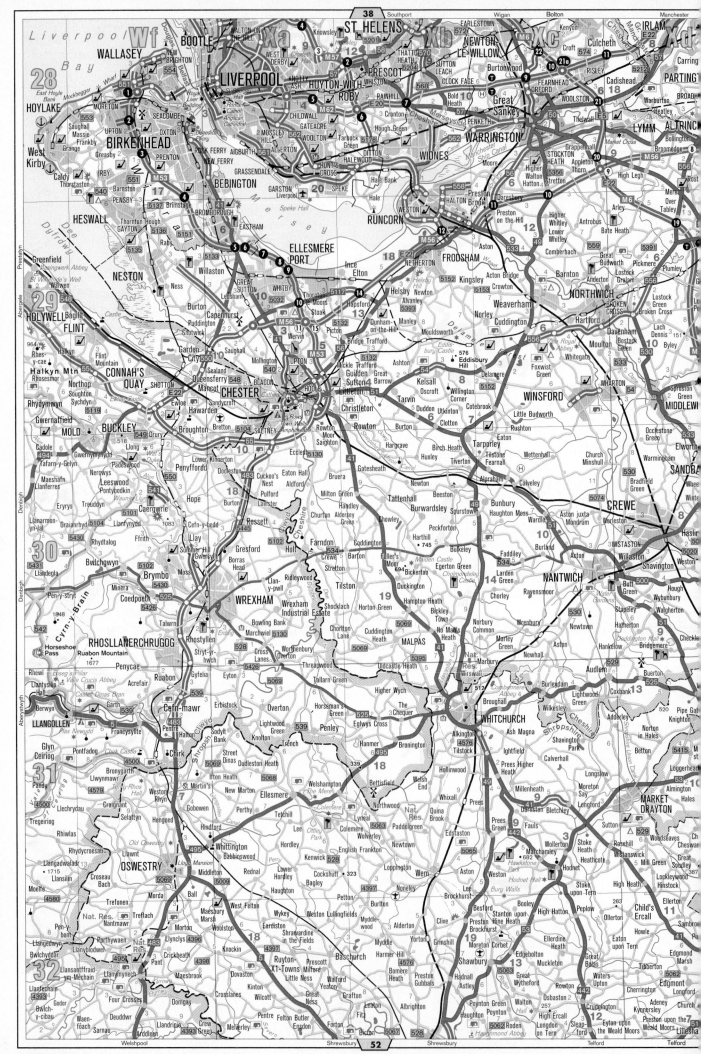

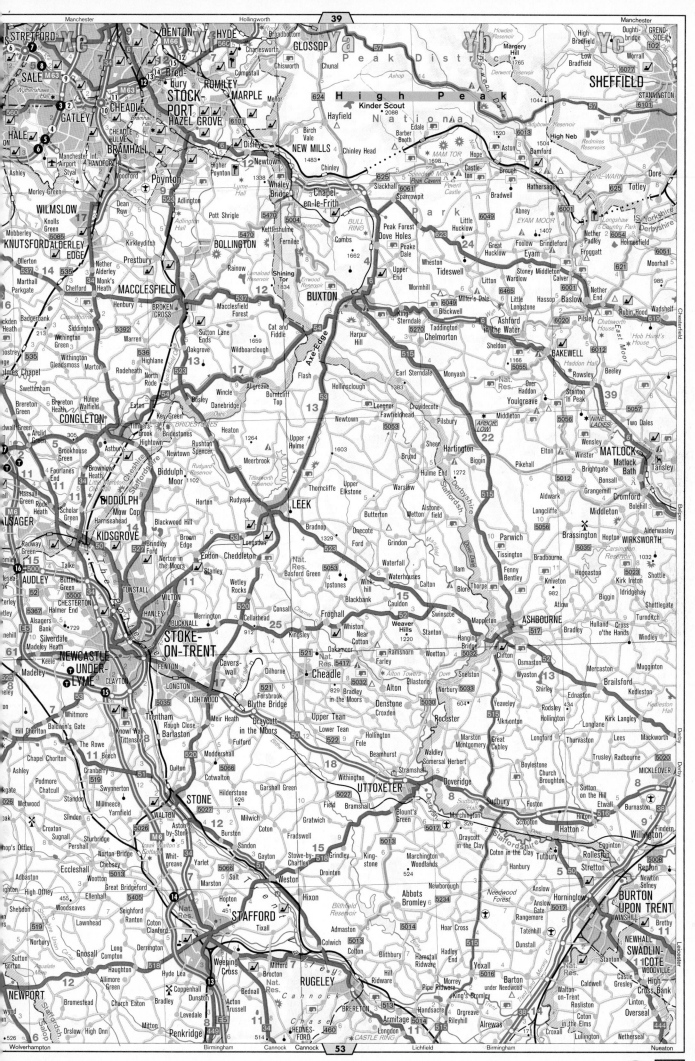

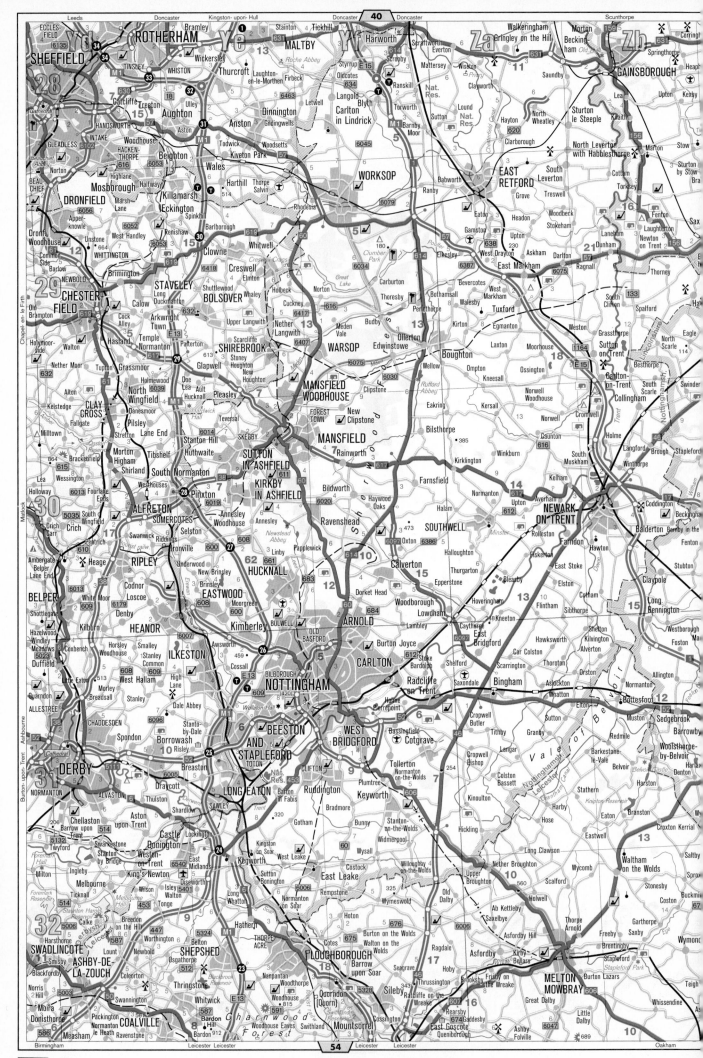

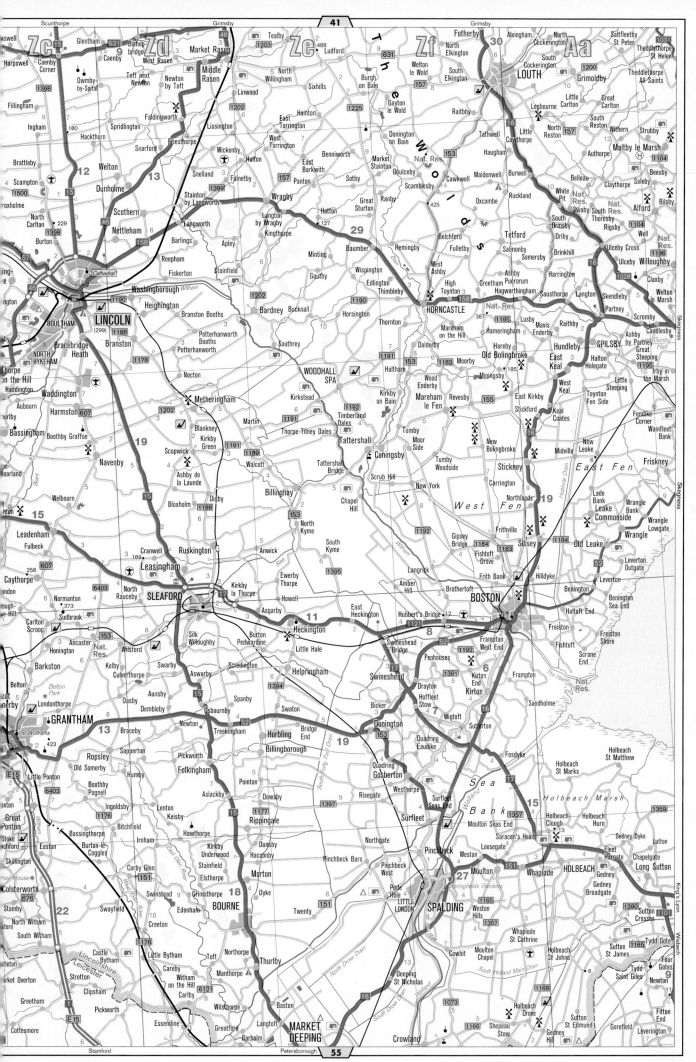

The Wash

Brancaster Roads

Holkham Bay

Brancaster Bay

28
MARBLETHORPE
1031
Theddlethorpe
St Helen
Thorpe
TRUSTHORPE
Sutton on Sea
Sutton le Marsh
1111
Hannah
52
Markby
6
Bilsby
29
Huttoft
Mumby
Authorpe
Row
Cumberworth
Hogsthorpe
Chapel Saint Leonards
Willoughby
Slothsby
10
Addlethorpe
Ingoldmells
Orby
Burgh
le Marsh
Winthorpe
Bratoft
158
11
52
SKEGNESS
Thorpe
St. Peter
Croft
1195
5
Sleeping River
Wainfleet
Bank
Wainfleet
All Saints
Nat.
Res.
Key's
Toft
Gibraltar
30
9

Lincoln
Boston

31

HUNSTANTON
Thornham
Nat.
Res.
Titchwell
9
Burnham
Deepdale
Burnham
Norton
Burnham
Overy Staithe
HOLKHAM
CAMP
Holkham
Hall
WELLS-NEXT-
THE-SEA
149
77
Warham
Stiffkey
Morston
Bla
Ringstead
Burnham Market
1155
Burnham
Thorpe
Holkham
Cockthorpe
Lan
Saxlingh
Binham
Heacham
Summerfield
Docking
289
North Creake
Stanhoe
1155
North Creake
10
South Creake
1355
Wighton
Egmere
Great
Walsingham
1388
Priory
Houghton
St Giles
Slipper
Chapel
Great
Snoring
Bale
Hindringham
Fie
Dal
22
Gun
Bri
Sedgeford
1454
Bircham
Newton
1155
1454
Fring
Syderstone
Stiffkey
East
Barsham
Sculthorpe
Little
Snoring
1105
Swan
Nov
149
Snettisham
Ingoldisthorpe
Great Bircham
Bagthorpe
1153
Tattersett
Dunton
Sbereford
7
117
Kettlestone
Stibbard
Shernborne
Dersingham
Anmer
New
Houghton
East
Rudham
Hempton
Tatterford
FAKENHAM
Southgate
Nat. Res.
Sandringham
West Newton
1440
West
Rudham
Helhoughton
Toftrees
Colkirk
Great
Ryburgh
Nat.
Res.
112
Twyfo
Gedney Drove End
Wolferton
Sandringham
House
Babingley
Flitcham
148
21
Harpley
272
South Raynham
East
Raynham
1065
Oxwick
Horningtoft
Gately
Bint
Guy's Head
Ongar Hill
14
North Wootton
Castle
Rising
Castle Rising
Hillington
Little Massingham
Great
Massingham
15
Weasenham
St Peter
Tittleshall
286
Brisley
East
Bilney
1146
Cathedral
North
Elmham
Billin
1145
KINGS'S
LYNN
162
SOUTH
WOOTTON
Roydon
Pott Row
Grimston
Massingham
Heath
311
Rougham
Weasenham
All Saints
Stainfield
1110
Wor
Mill S
Swar
Mo
Spalding
1359
Sutton Bridge
Terrington
St Clement
17
11
Little
London
Clenchwarton
West Lynn
2
1145
Gayton
1153
Ashwicken
1145
Mileham
Litcham
Beetley
Bittering
Hoe
227
Longham
Gressenhall
EAST
DEREHAM
Tydd Gote
Walpole
St Andrew
13
Tilney
All Saints
149
Saddle
Bow
West Winch
East Winch
East
Walton
West Acre
Castle Acre
Chapel
West
Lexham
Newton
Wendling
Four Gotes
9
St Peter
Terrington St John
Tilney High End
West Bilney
14
South
Acre
Great Dunham
Scarning
West
Walton
Walton
Highway
St John's
Highway
Wiggenhall
St Germans
Middleton
10
4
Blackborough
End
Setchey
Pentney
Narborough
269
Great
Palgrave
Great
Dunham
Little
Fransham
Great
Fransham
12
Daffy
Green
Yaxham
113
WISBECH
WALSOKEN
St John's
Fen End
Walpole
Highway
Wiggenhall
St Mary the Virgin
Wiggenhall
St Mary Magdalen
Wormegay
Watlington
134
7
Marham
Necton
East
Bradenham
Whinburgh
SWAFFHAM
62
47
Nar
310
Nene
Great Ouse
Ely
Thetford
Thetford

48 GB

Va Vb Vc Vd Ve

32

33

34

35

36

Bardsey Island
Ynys Ennlli
548

C A R D I G A N

B A Y

Barmouth
Bay

Llangelynnin
Rhoslefain
Llanfendigaid

Stradt

TYW

ABERYSTWY

PEN DINA

Blaenplw

487

Llandde

Llanrhystud

16 CAER
PENRHOS

Llansantffraed Llanon

Ma

RI
Ro

Nebo

Aberarth 4577 Cross
Inn Beth

Pennant

Monachty 4337

ABERAERON 761
Cilcennin

Foss-
y-ffin

Llwyn-
onn

NEW QUAY
CEINEWYDD

Llwyncelyn Ciliau-
Aeron Brynog Trefila

5342 Oakford 482 Tal-sarn

Gilfachreda Llanarth Aberm

Nanternis Dihewyd Ystrad Aeron
4342

Cross
Inn 486

Llwyndafydd Mydroilyn

Ynys-Lochtyn Temple Bar

Synod Inn

Caledrhydiau Pont
Creuddyn

Llangranog 21 487

Penbryn Cribyn

Pentregat 4338 Cribyn

Cardigan I. Tresaith 4334 Plwmp Gorsgoch
Parcllyn Sarnau 4337

Cemaes Talgarreg Aber
Head Aberporth Brynhoffnant 1062

Inscribed Bwlch-y- Cwrtnewydd Pentre-bac
stone Glynarthen fadfa

Gwbert Rhydlewis Castell 475
Howell Cwmsychbant Llanwnnen

Verwig Blaenannerch Tan-y- Capel 4459 Dre-fach Allybiaca
Groes Cynon Pont- 475

Tremain Blaenporth Ffostrasol Siân Rhydowen Llanwenog
4338 Pencarreg
CARDIGAN 4333 Betws Tre- Prengwyn Llanybydder
Ifan Maesllyn groes
St Dogmaels Penparc Pantgwyn Beulah Troedyraur Penrhiwpal Horeb Capel Dewi 4337

Moylcrove Abbey Brongest 486 Maesycrugiau Abergiar

Llangoedmor 4541 4334 Mynydd Myr
Ponthirwaun Aber- Llanbyther
Trwyn Monington 4570 Capel Llandygwydd banc Penrhiw-llan 1339
y Bwa 478 Tygwydd Cwm-Cou Llandyfriog 486 Llanllwni
Prembrokeshire 3 Llechryd
Dinas Coast National 645 Bridell Cilgerran Pentre-cagal
Head Tredrissi Park Llantood Abercych Inscribed NEWCASTLE Henllan Llandysul
Trewllyn 5 stone 484 EMLYN 4582

Milford Haven Tenby Carmarthen

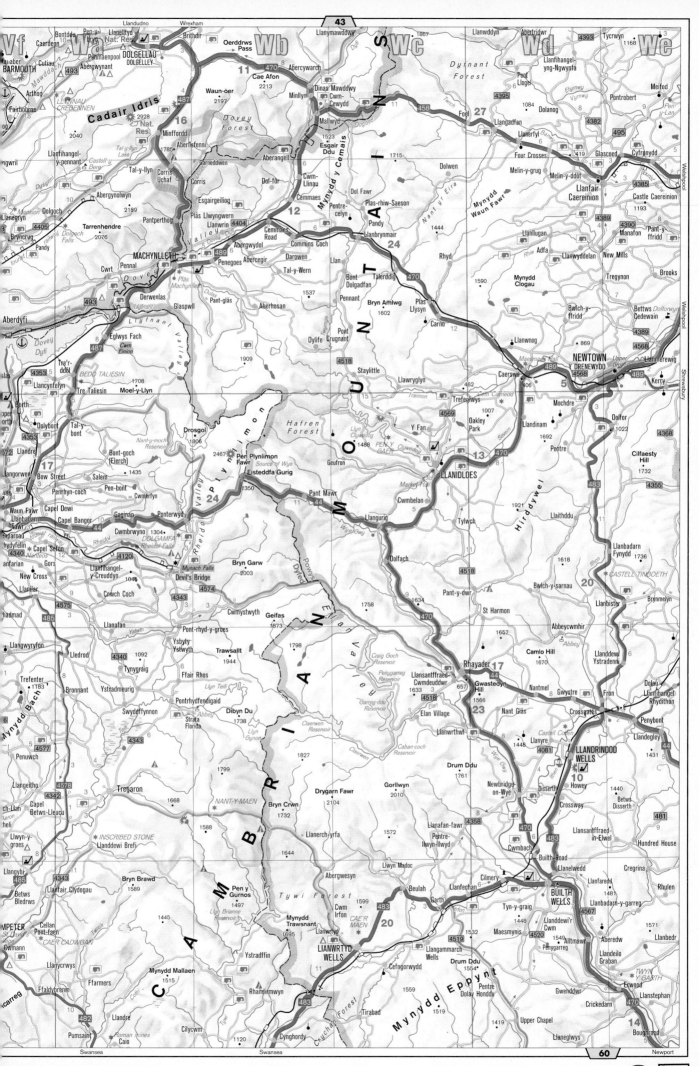

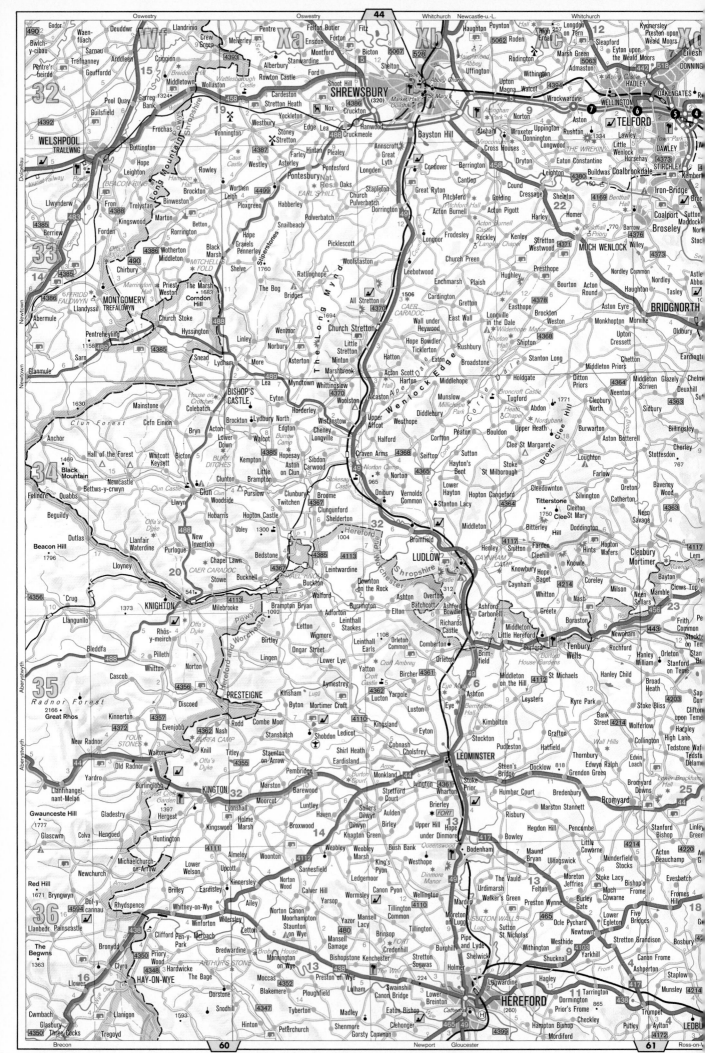

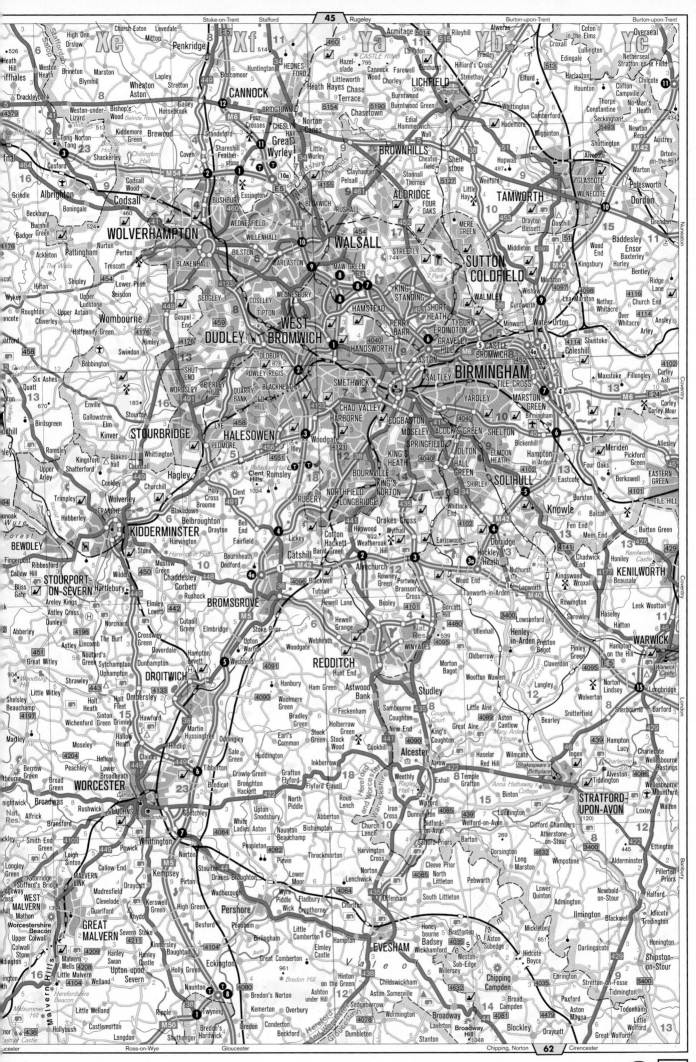

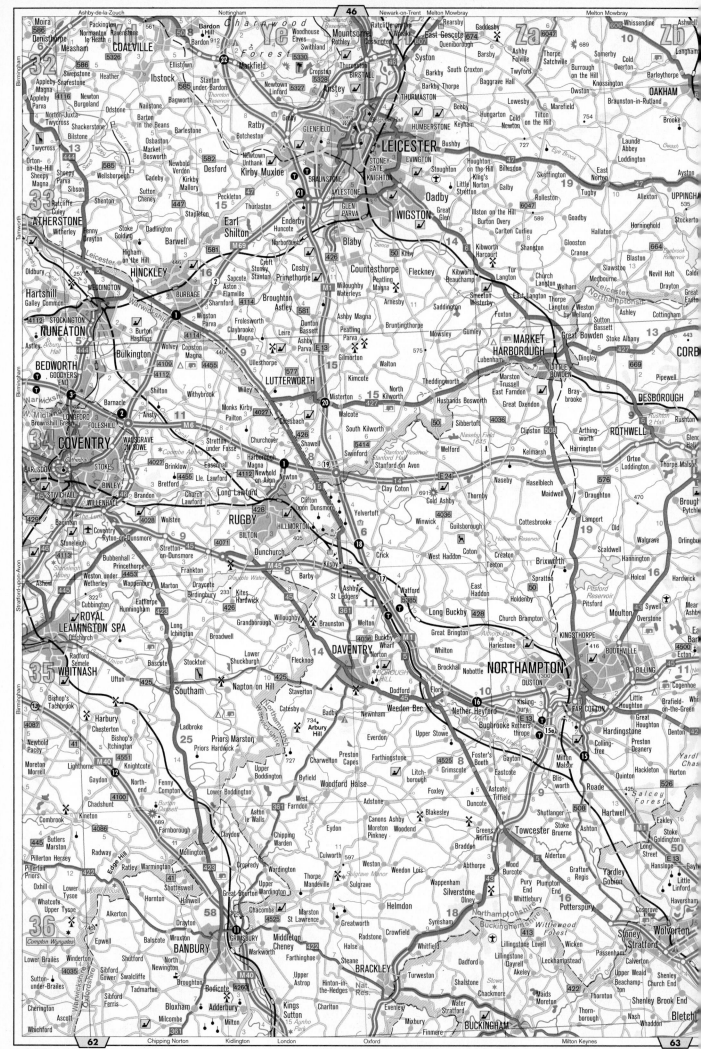

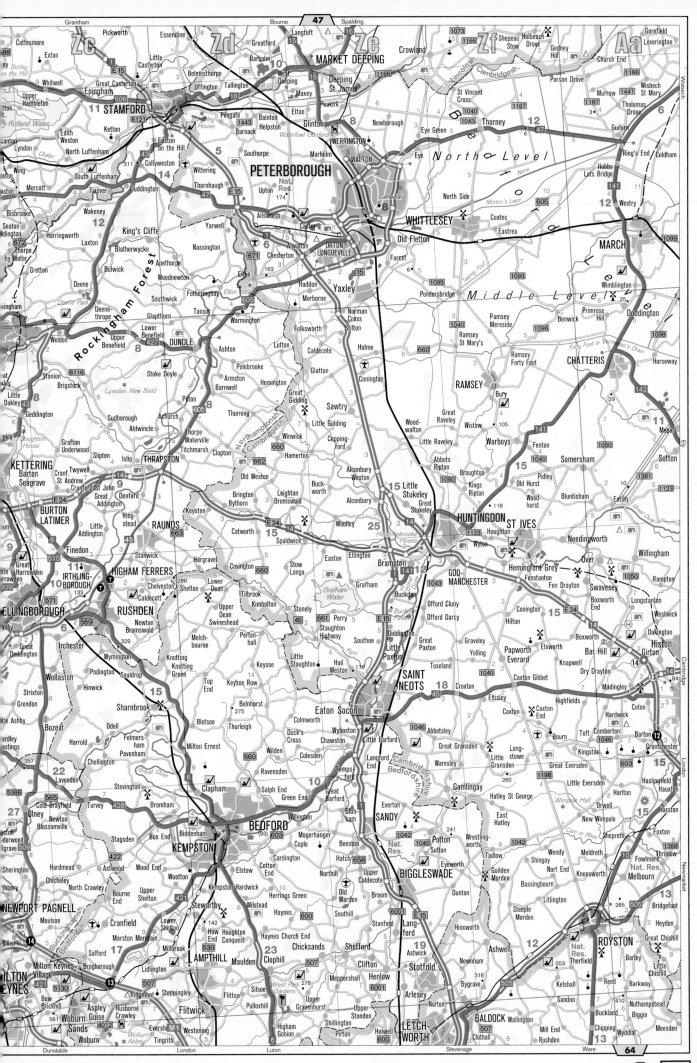

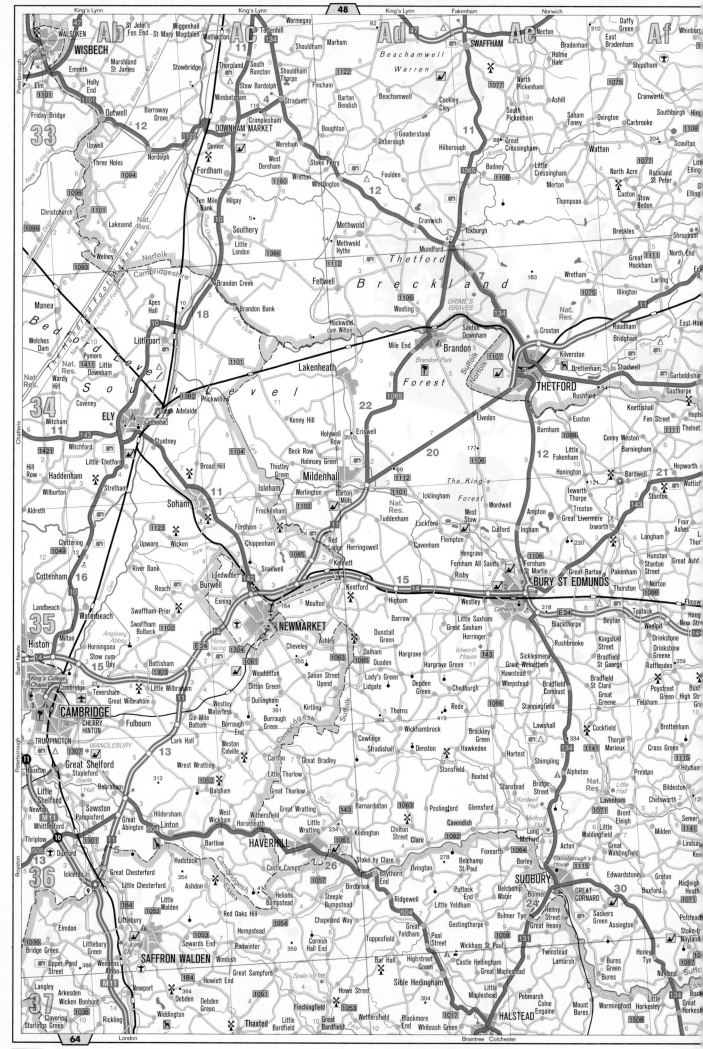

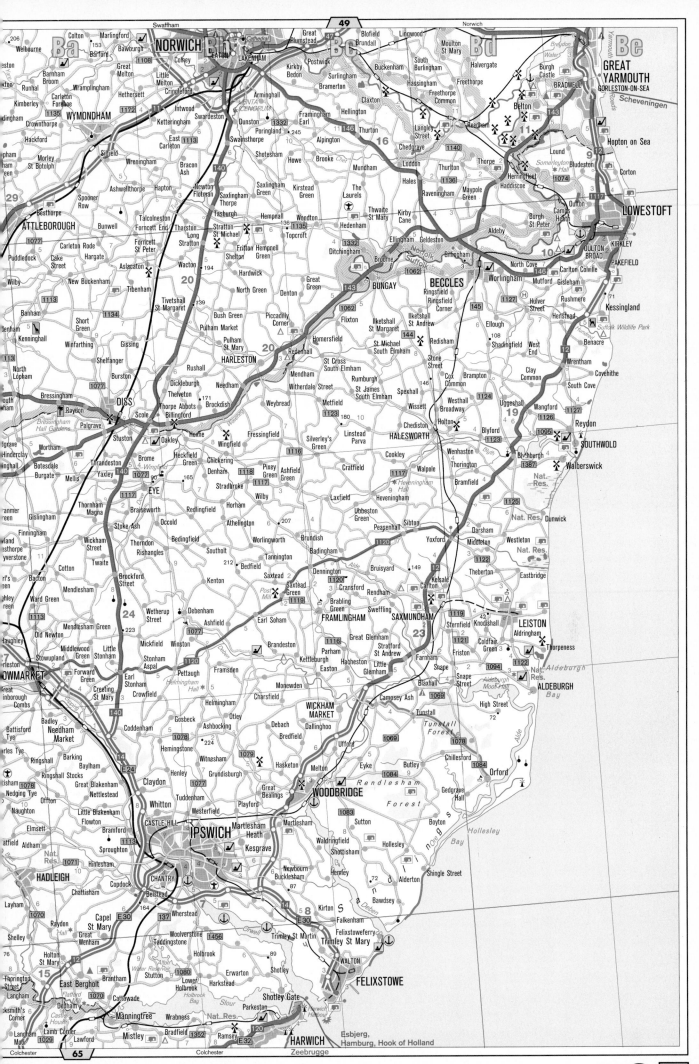

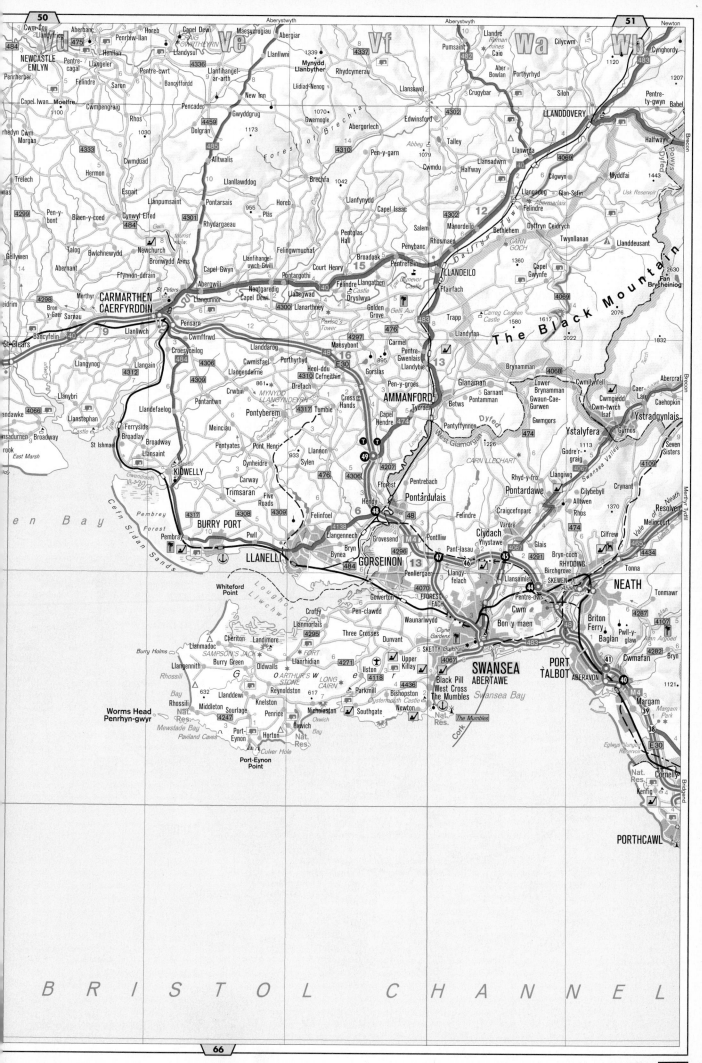

Aberystwyth Aberystwyth Newton

Cwm-Cou Llandyfriog Aberbanc Horeb Capel Dewi Maesycrugiau Abergiar Llandre nines Caio Cilycwm
484 475 Penrhiw-Ilan CRAIG GYRTHEYRN Pumsaint 482 1120 483
NEWCASTLE Henllan Llandysul Mynydd Llanbyther Rhydcymerau Llansawel Aber Porthyrhyd Pentre-ty-gwyn Cynghordy
EMLYN Pentre-cagal Llangeler 4336 4337 Bowlan 1207
Penrherber Pentre-cwrt New Inn Llidiad-Nenog Edwinsford Crugybar Siloh Babel
Felindre Saron Bancyffordd 9 Llanfihangel-ar-arth Abergorlech 4302 LLANDDOVERY Halfway
Capel Iwan Moelfre Cwmpengraig Pencader Gwernogle Abbey 4069 Myddfai 1443
1100 Rhos 4459 Forest of Brechfa Pen-y-garn Talley Llanwrda Glan-Sefin Halfway
Cwmduad Dolgran 1070 14 Cwmdu 40 Llangadog 12 1360 FAN
Trelech 1030 1173 485 4310 Brechfa 1042 Llanfynydd Capel Isaac Manordeilo Llansadwrn Bethlehem Dyffryn Ceidrych BRYCHEINIOG
Hermon Alltwalis Penybanc Salem Rhosmaen Twynllanan Llanddeusant 2630
Esgair Llanllawddog Pentlas Hall Capel Gwynfe
Pen-y- Blaen-y-coed Llanpumsaint Pontarsais Horeb Plâs Broadoak Pentrefelin LLANDEILO 1580 1617 2076 The Black Mountain
bont 484 4301 Rhydargaeau 955 Ffairfach CARN GOCH 2022
Talog Bwlchnewydd Newchurch Felingwmuchaf Court Henry 15 Pentre-Gwenlais Llandyfan Carreg Cennen 1832
Gellywen Bronwydd Arms Capel Gwyn Pontargothi Llangathen Golden Gelli Aur 7 Llandybie Castle
14 Ffynnon-ddrain Abergwili Nantgaredig Llanegwad Grove 476 Trapp 13
4299 Merthyr St Peters CARMARTHEN Llangunnor Capel Dewi 40 4300 Llanarthney Carmel Brynamman 4068
4298 CAERFYRDDIN Pensarn 4297 Maesybont Pen-y-groes Glanaman Cwmllynfell Abercraf
Bron Sarnau Llanllwch Cwmffrwd 48 E30 Gorslas AMMANFORD Garnant Lower Cwmgiedd Caer- Caehopkin
y-Gaer 40 9 Croesyceiliog Llanddarog Cwmisfael Heol-ddu Cefneithin Betws Pontamman Brynamman Cwm-twrch Lan Ystradgynlais
St-Clears Llangynog 484 4306 Porthyrhyd 4310 Tycroes Pantyffynnon Gwaun-Cae- Isaf
Llangain 4312 Crwbin Drefach Capel Gwmgors Godre'r- Ystalyfera Gurnos Seven
Llanybri 4309 MYNYDD Cross Hendre 474 1226 graig Sisters
4066 Llandefaelog LLANGYNDEYRN Hands 474 Gurnos 4109
Ferryside Pontantwn 4317 Tumble Fforest Rhyd-y-fro Llangiwg 1113 Swansea Valley
Llanstephan Broadlay Pontyberem Llannon 933 Pentrebach CARN LLECHART Pontardawe
Broadway Meinciau Sylen 4207 Pontàrdulais Cilybebyll Crynant
KIDWELLY St Ishmael Pontyates Pont Henri 476 4306 Hendy 48 Felindre Craigcefnparc Alltwen Resolven
Carway 49 Fforest Vardre Rhos 474
Trimsaran Cynheidre 48 Clydach Melincourt
Five Felinfoel 6 Pont-lliw Pant-lasau Bryn-coch 4067 4465 Cilfrew
Pembrey Roads 4308 4138 Grovesend M4 RHYDDING 4434
BURRY PORT 4317 4309 Llangennech 4296 47 46 45 4291 Birchgrove Tonna
Forest Pwll Bryn 4070 GORSEINON 13 Llansamlet SKEWEN NEATH
LLANELLI Bynea Penllergaer Llangy- 44 Tonmawr
Whiteford 484 6 Gowerton felach Pentre-dŵr Briton 4287
Point Croffy Pen-clawdd 3 Cwm Ferry 4107
Llanmorlais Waunarlwydd Bon y maen Baglan
Burry Holms Cheriton 4295 Three Crosses Dunvant FFOREST Clyne Pwll-y- Cwmafan
Llanmadoc SAMPSON'S JACK Ilston FACH Gardens 41 glaw Bryn
Llangennith Burry Green FORT Upper 4067 SWANSEA 40 4282
Oldwalls Llanrhidian Killay SKETTY ABERTAWE Margam
Rhossili ARTHUR'S Killay 4271 Black Pill PORT 39 Margam
G Reynoldston STONE Parkmill West Cross TÀLBOT ABERAVON Park
632 Llanddewi 617 4436 The Mumbles ABERAVON 38 1121
Middleton Knelston Nicholaston Oystermouth Castle Southgate Newton Swansea Bay
Worms Head 4247 Penrice Bishopston Nat. M4 E30
Penrhyn-gwyr Sourlage Oxwich Rès. The Mumbles
Mewslade Bay Port- Horton Culver Cork CORNELLY
Paviland Caves Eynon Hole Eglwys Nunydd Reservoir
Port-Eynon Nat. Kenfig
Point Rès.

PORTHCAWL

BRISTOL CHANNEL

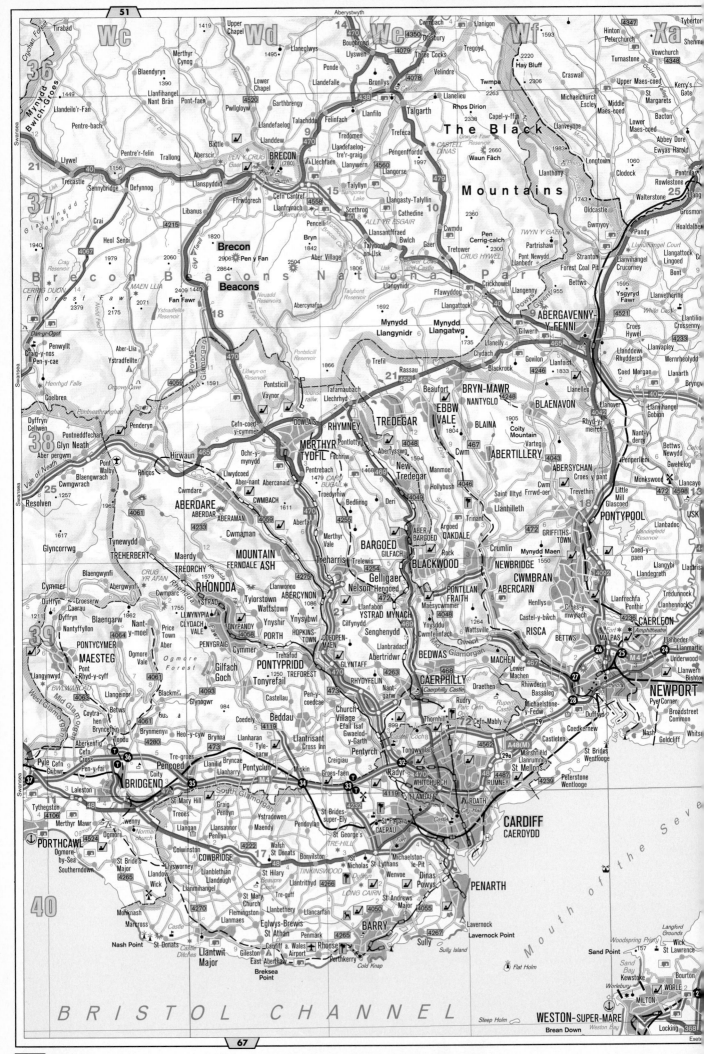

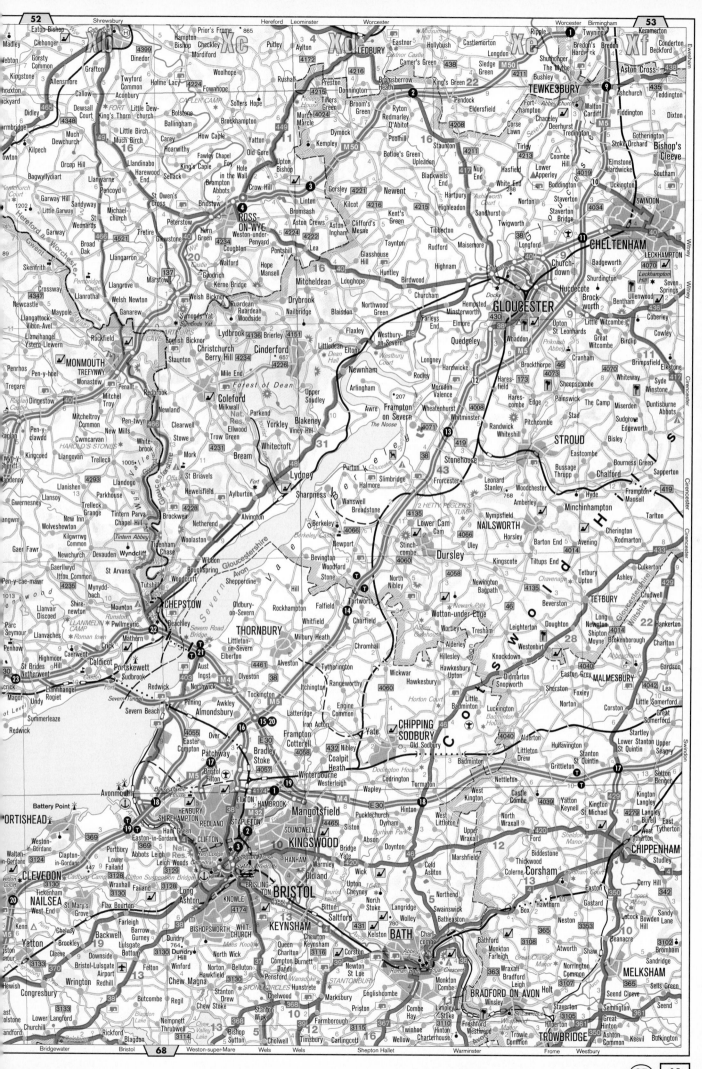

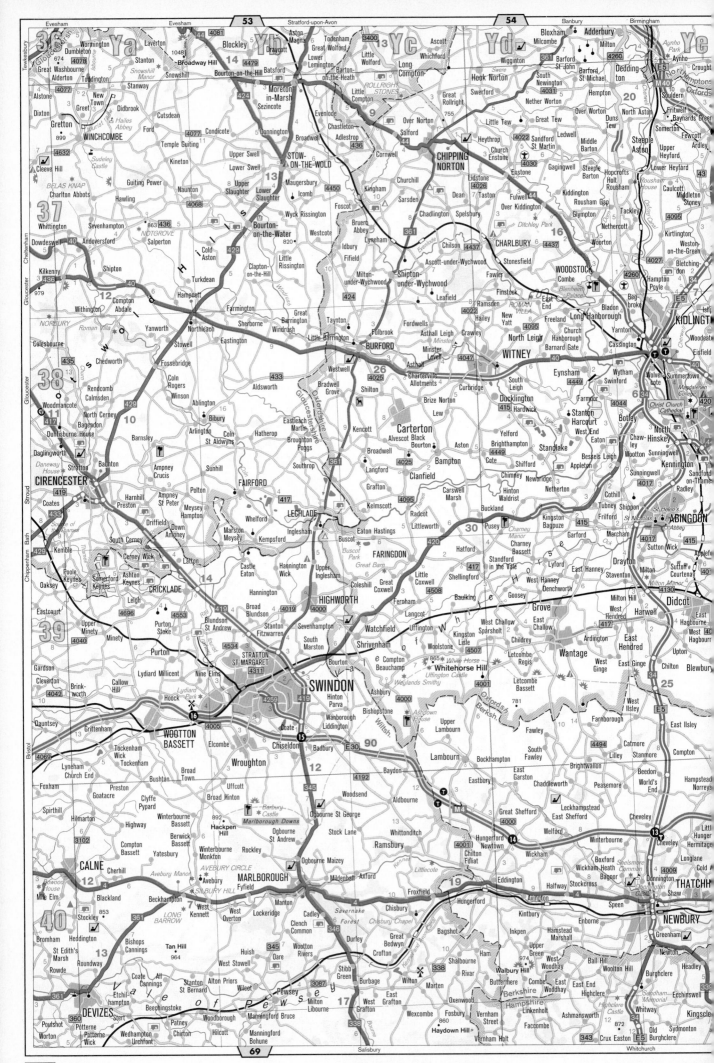

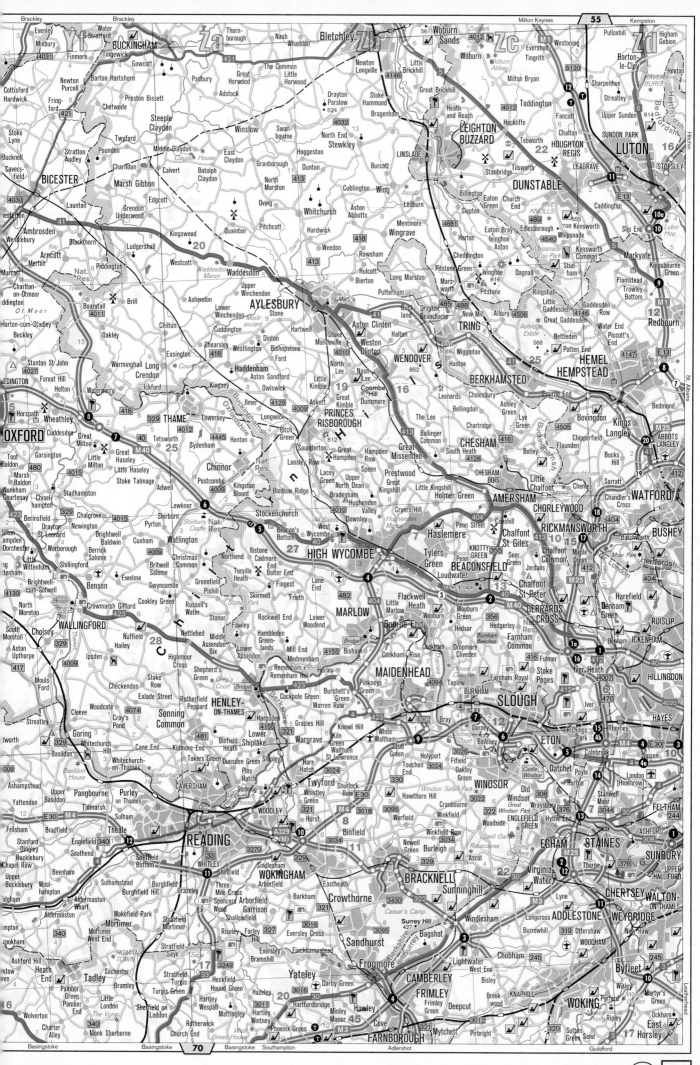

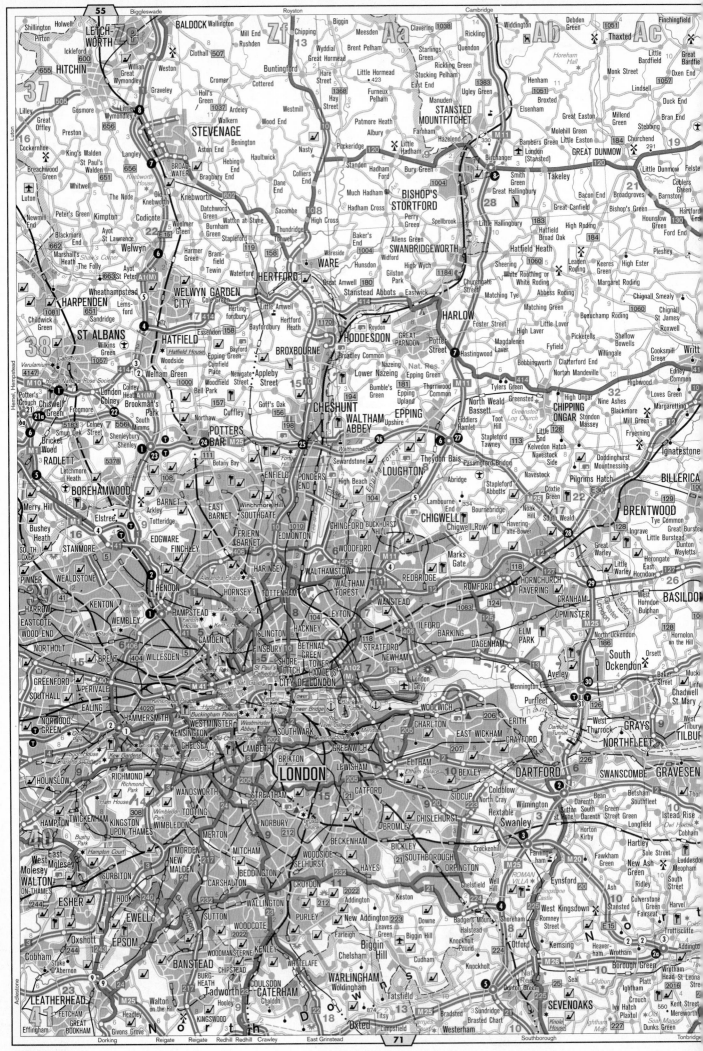

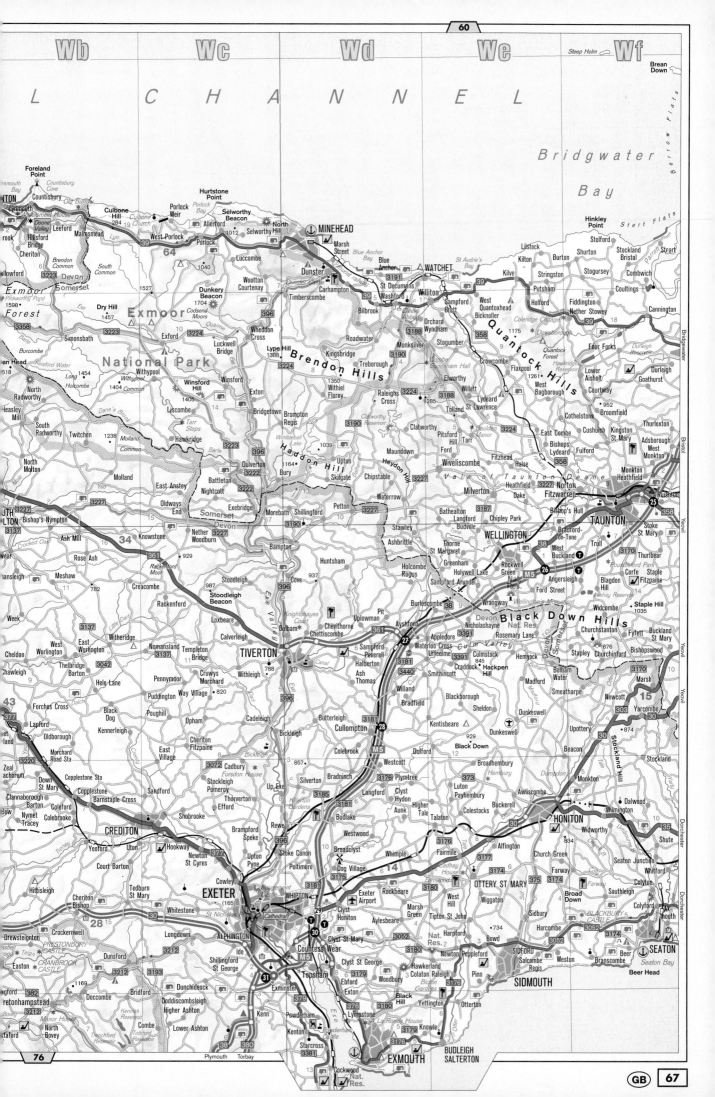

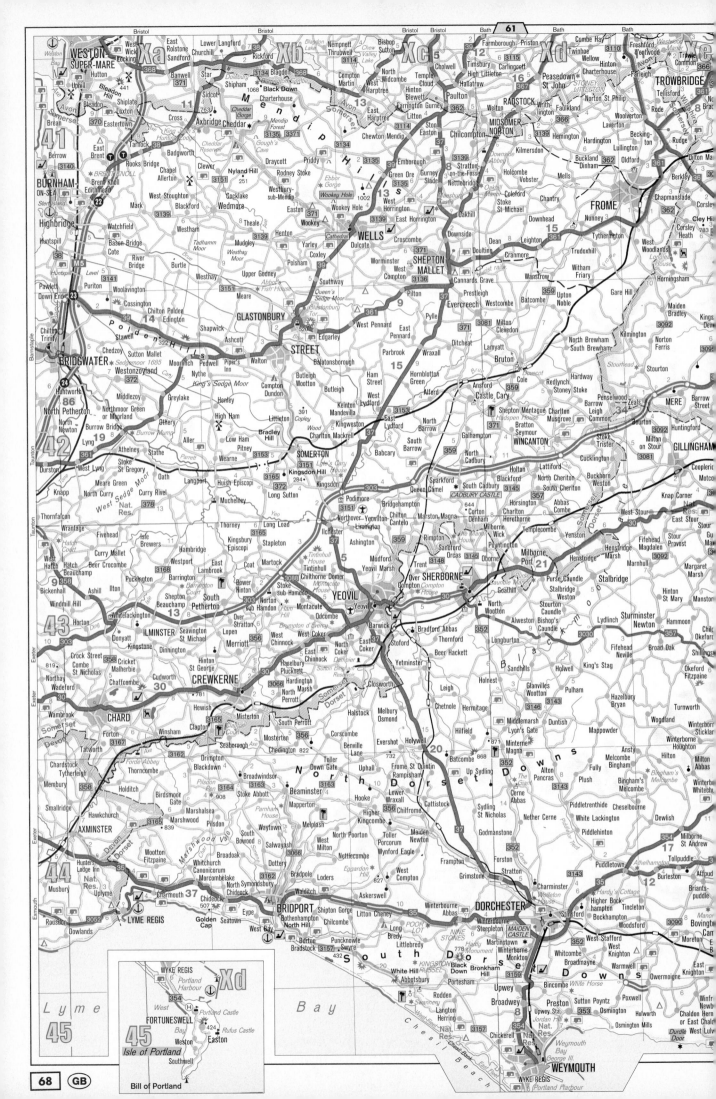

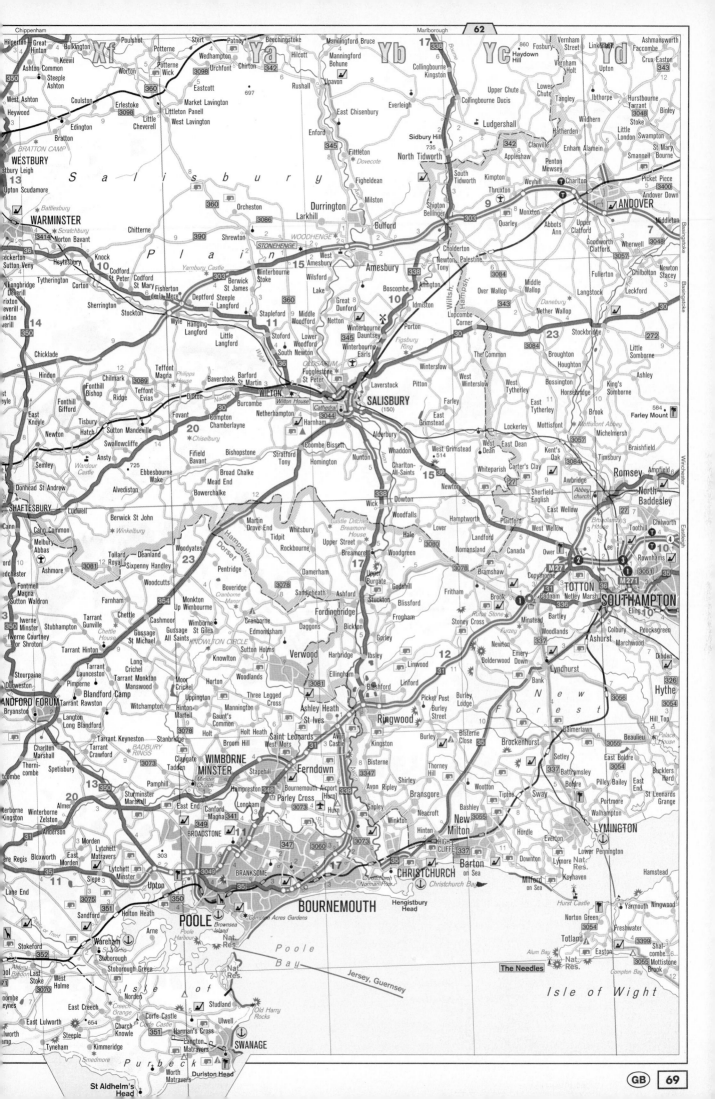

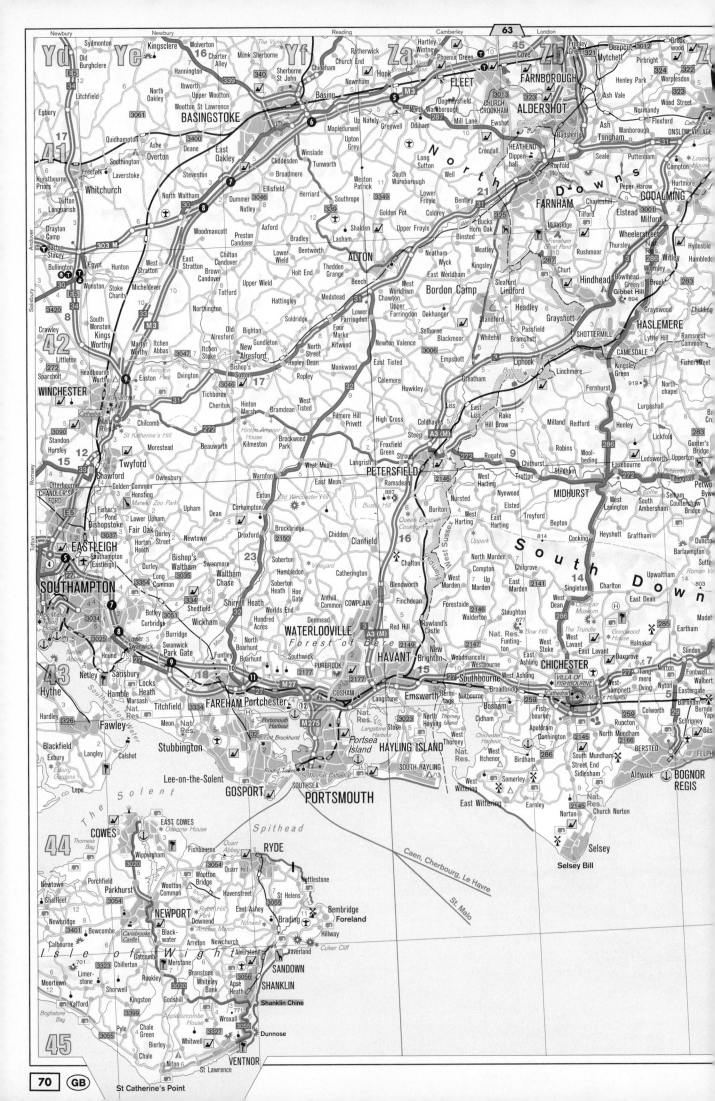

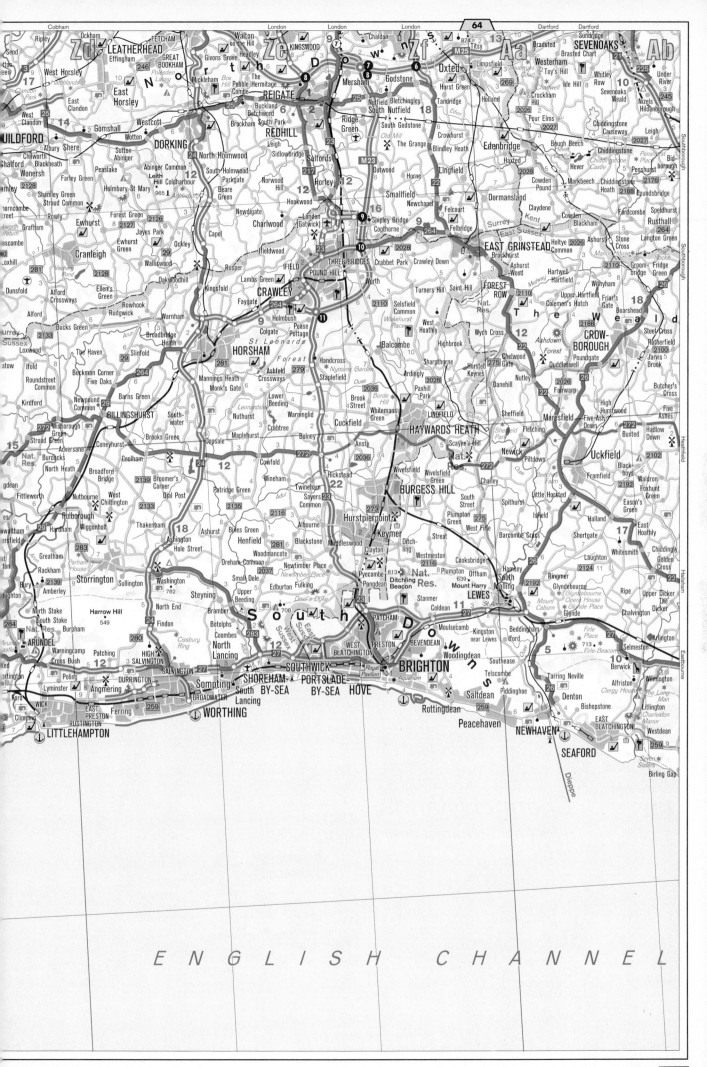

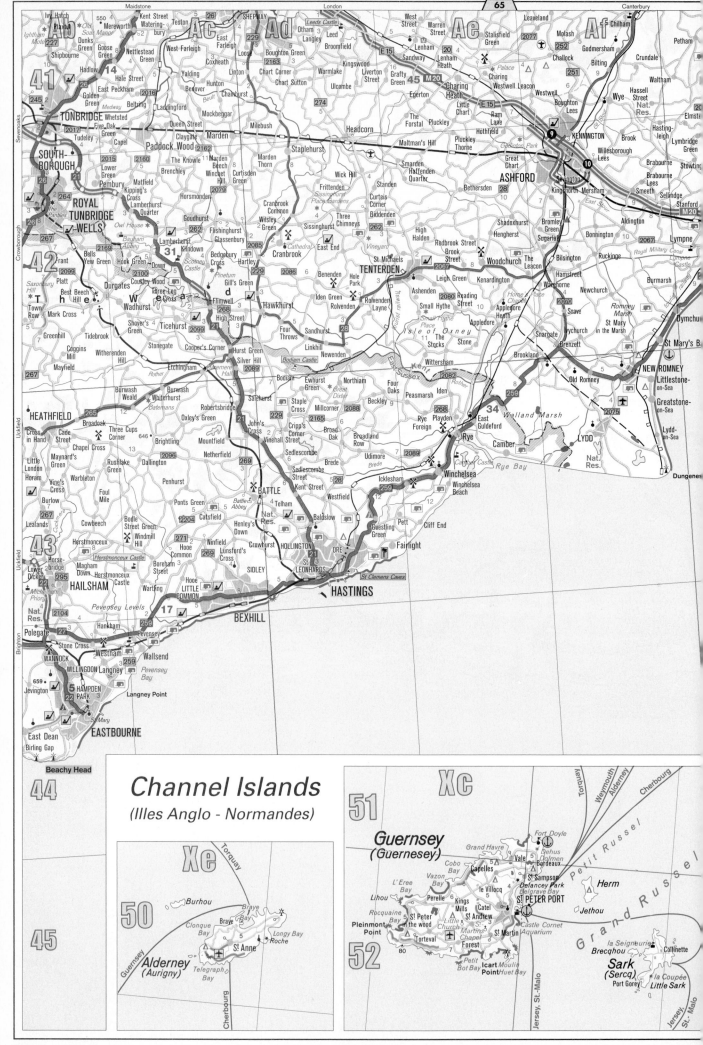

Channel Islands
(Illes Anglo - Normandes)

Guernsey
(Guernesey)

Alderney
(Aurigny)

Sark
(Sercq)

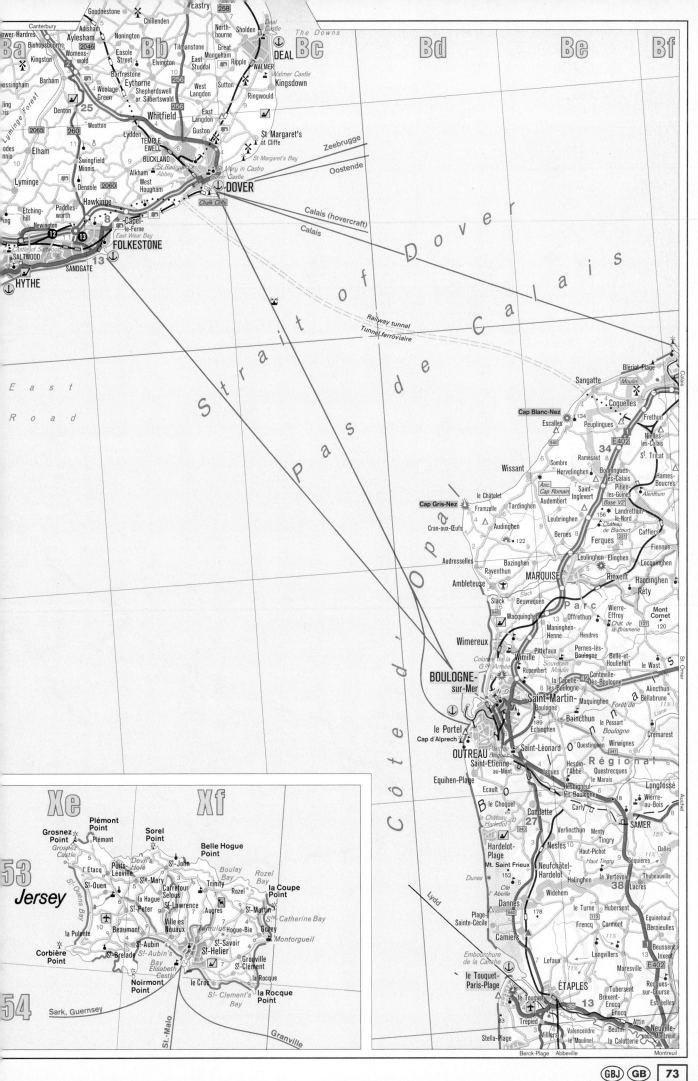

ATLANTIC

Seven Stones

OCEAN

Round Island
St Helen
129
White Island
St Martin's
Cromwell's Castle
Bryher
144
Tean
Higher Town
138
New Grimsby
Great Canilly
Tresco
Great Arthur
Eastern Isles
Abbey Gardens
Samson
BANT'S CARN
166 INNISIDGEN
3110
HUGH TOWN
St Mary's
Star Castle
PORTH HELLICK
Broad Sound
Scilly Isles-
St Mary
Annet
Gugh
Western Rocks
St Agnes

Penzance

Isles of Scilly

Whitesand Bay
MAEN CASTLE
30
Longships
Sennen Cove
Sennen
Land's End
3315
St Levan

Gwennap Head

Runnel S

Trevose Head

Uf

Treyarnon

Park Head
Bedruthan Steps
Bedruthan Steps
3276
Trenar
Mawgan Porth
Berryl's Point
Watergate Bay
Tregurrian
Trevelgue Head
Towan Head
Newq
St Mav
Fistral Bay
ST COLUMB MINOR
NEWQUAY
Quint
Dow
Kelsey Head
West Pentire
The Gannel
Holywell Bay
Crantock
Penhale Point
Holywell
3075
Trench Manor
St Newlyn East
Ligger or Perran Bay
Cubert
Penhale Sands
Rejerrah
St Piran's Oratory
Rose
Newlyn 490
Downs
Mitch
Perranporth
Goonhavern
Carland Cross
Bawden Rocks or Man and his man
3285
Perranzabuloe
Zelah
30
Rosemullion
St Agnes Head
Trevellas
Penhallow
St Allen
3076
St Agnes
Callestick
Trisp
The Beacon
629
Mithian
3284
St E
Mount Hawke
3277
Shortlanesend
Porthtowan
3284
Tregavethan
Blackwater
Menna
TRURO
Portreath
Cornwall Coast
Kenwyn
6
390
Illogan
3300
Scorrier
Mert
Navax Point
Crane Islands
3301
30
Chacewater
Malpas
Reskajeage Cliffs
3047
Twelveheads
Threemilestone
Godrevy Island
20
CARN BREA
REDRUTH
Baldhu
39
Gwithian
738
Carharrack
Bissoe
Playing Place
St Ives Bay
Roseworthy
3297
Lanner
Old Kea
The Island
30
Connor Downs
8
Carnon Downs
Michael Pen
Trendrine Hill
CARBIS BAY
3301
CAMBORNE
393
Devoran
Tretissi
Halsetown
3374
Angarrack
Troon
Penhalvean
Ponsanooth
Feock
Trelissick Gardens
ST IVES
3303
Four Lanes
Perranarworthal
812
Carnhell Green
3280
828
Mylor Bridge
St Ju
in Rosel
Towednack
Lelant
Gwinear
Wendron
Stithians
PENRYN
St Ma
Cripplesease
Trencrom Hill
Hayle
Barripper
Stithians Reservoir
4
Mylor
Gurnard's Head
MULFRA QUOIT CHYSAUSTER
3311
Canonstown
3302
Praze-an-Beeble
Rame
Longdowns
Pendeen Watch
3306
Carnell Green
Moors
Mabe Burnthouse
Porthmeor
MEN-AN-TOL
St Erth
728
Leedstown
Porkellis
Edgcumbe
FALMOUTH
Morvah
828
Crowan Beacon
3302
3303
Burncoose
Penjerrick
New Mill
Godolphin Cross
3297
Treverva
Pendennis Castle
Trewellard
CHUN CASTLE
Ludgvan
Crowlas
St Erth Praze
Nancegollan
Penryn
Falmouth Bay
Carnyorth
LANYON QUOIT
30
Townshend
Godolphin House
Wendron
Pennerick Gardens
Bojewyan
3318
Trewinnard Gardens
Relubbus
3280
Poldark Mining & Wendron Forge
10
Zoo
3071
Newbridge
Tremethick Cross
St Hilary
Crowntown
394
Mawnan Smith
Carnyorth
St Just
Longrock
St Michael's Mount
Trescowe
636
Tregonning Hill
Porth Navas
Rosemullion Head
CARN EUNY
Drift
Marazion
Ashton
24
Brill
Mawnan
The Brisons
3306
736
Drift Reservoir
Perranuthnoe
Breage
St Anthony-in-Meneage
BALLOWALL BARROW (CARN GLOOSE)
Sancreed
PENZANCE
Cudden Point
Praa Sands
3304
Mawgan
Helford
Kelynack
NEWLYN
Trewavas Head
Gweek
Land's End-
Catchall
Paul
HELSTON
Garras
Nare Point
St Just
3283
Crows-an-wra
Mousehole
Welloe
Culdrose
Porthallow
Whitesand Bay
30
St Clement's Isle
The Stone
Gwween
Lizard
MAEN CASTLE
St Buryan
3315
Berepper
Peninsula
Longships
Sennen Cove
MERRY MAIDENS
Boleigh
Cury
Newtown-in-St-Martin
Sennen
3315
TREGIFFAN
Mount's Bay
Porthleven
3083
Cury Cross
Manaccan
Land's End
Treen
Lamorna Cove
Goonhilly Downs
Traboe
St Keverne
St Levan
Poldhu Cove
Goonhilly Earth Station
Gwennap Head
Logan Rock
Poldhu Point
369
3293
Manacle Point
The Man
Runnel Stone
Mullion
Lowland Point
Porth Mellin
3296
Peninsula
Gwenter
Mullion Cove
Coverack
Mullion Island
Ruan Major
Black Head
Predannack Wollas
Ruan Minor
Cadgwith
Vellan Head
Kynance Cove
Hot Point
Lizard Town
Lizard Point

Hugh Town (Isles of Scilly)

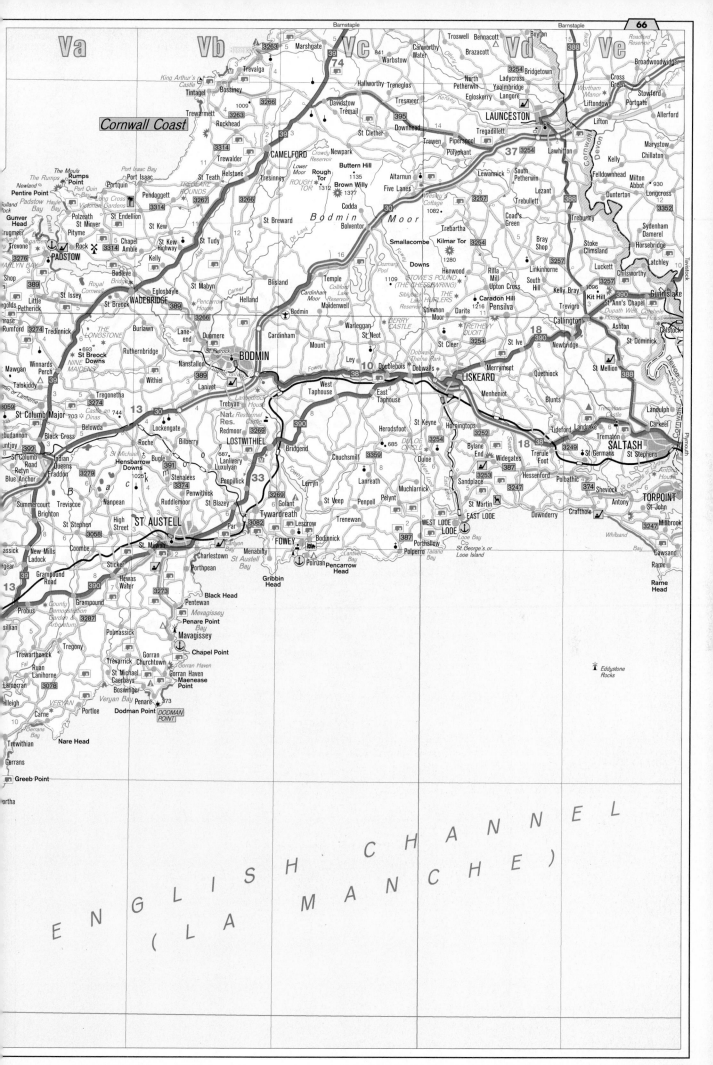

Va

Vb

Vc

Vd

Ve

Cornwall Coast

Barnstaple

Barnstaple

Broadwoodwidger

King Arthur's Castle

Tintagel
Bossiney
Trevalga

Trewarmett
Rockhead

1009
3266

3263

Marshgate

74
39

Hallworthy
Treneglos

Davidstow
Tremail

St Clether

395
Downhead

Troswell
Bennacott
Canworthy
Water
Warbstow

Boyton
Brazacott

North
Petherwin
Egloskerry

3254 Bridgetown
Ladycross
Yeolmbridge
Langore

Cross
Green

388

Roadford
Reservoir

15

Stowford
Portgate

Wortham
Manor

Liftondown

LAUNCESTON

Tregadillett
Piperspool

14

Trewen
Polyphant

37 3254

Lawhitton

Lifton

Marystow
Chillaton

Allerford

14

Camelford

Trewalder

Helstone
Tresinney

3314

3267

11

3266

St Teath

St Breward

Newpark

Crowdy
Reservoir

Buttern Hill
ROUGH
TOR

Rough
Tor
1312

1135
Brown Willy
1377

Codda

Altarnun
Five Lanes

Lewannick

South
Petherwin

Lezant
Trebullett

Trebartha

South
Hill

Wesley's
Cottage
1082

Kilmar Tor
1280

3257

Coad's
Green

Treburley

Bray
Shop

Stoke
Climsland

Linkinhorne

930

Longcross

3352

Dunterton

Milton
Abbot

Sydenham
Damerel

Horsebridge

Latchley

Chilsworthy

10

Pentire Point
The Rumps
Rumps
Point
Newland
Gunver
Head

The Mouls

Port Isaac Bay

Port Isaac

Port Quin

Portquin

TREGEARE
ROUNDS

Pendoggett

3314

3267

St Kew
Highway

St Kew

11

St Tudy

Blisland

Temple
Colliford
Lake

12

Bodmin Moor

Smallacombe

Downs

1109
STOWE'S POUND
(THE CHEESEWRING)

THE
HURLERS

Siblyback
Lake

Henwood

Rilla
Mill

Upton Cross

3257

Caradon Hill
Pensilva

1216
Darite

Common
Moor

Trevigro

Kelly Bray

1096
Kit Hill

St Ann's Chapel

Dupath Well

390

Gunnislake

3257

Ashton

Calstock

Cotehele
House

Polzeath
St Minver
Pityme
Rock

Chapel
Amble

Kelly

Marlyn Bay

Padstow
Hayle
Bay

Trevone

PADSTOW

St Issey

Bodieve

Royal
Cornwall

Egloshayle

WADEBRIDGE

389

St Mabyn

Helland

Cardinham

Bodmin

Warleggan
St Neot

BERRY
CASTLE

St Cleer

3254

St Ive

18
390

Newbridge

St Dominick

Landulph

Carkeel

Gunver
Head

Little
Petherick

Rumford

Tredinnick

3274

THE
LONGSTONE

St Breock

389

3266

Burlawn

Lane-
end

Dunmere

Mount

Ley

10
38

Doublebois

Dobwalls
Theme Park

Dobwalls

LISKEARD

Merrymeet

Quethiock

St Mellion

Trematon
Castle

SALTASH

St Stephens

Mawgan

Talskiddy

3059

Winnards
Perch

NINE
MAIDENS

693
St Breock
Downs

Ruthernbridge

Nanstallon

St Patrock

BODMIN

Lanivet

West
Taphouse

East
Taphouse

Herodsfoot

Horningtops

3252

Menheniot

Blunts

Tideford

Landrake

Plymouth

St Columb Major

703

744

13
30

Belowda

Tregonetha

3274

Lockengate

Roche

Bilberry

Trebyan

Nat.
Res.
Redmoor

Restormel
Castle

LOSTWITHIEL

390

Bridgend

Couchsmill

685

DULOE
CIRCLE

3254

Bylane
End

Duloe

Widegates

387

Trerule
Foot

18
39

3249

St Germans

3247

Antony
House

TORPOINT

St John

Black Cross

St Columb
Road
Retyn
Blue Anchor

Indian
Queens
Fraddon

3279

3392

Bugle

Stenalees

3374

Penwithick

391

1025

Ruddlemoor

Hensbarrow
Downs

Lanlivery
Luxulyan

Penpillick

Lerryn

Lanreath

Muchlarnick

Sandplace

3253

St Martin

Hessenford

Polbathic

374

Sheviock

Millbrook

Summercourt
Brighton
St Stephen

3058

Treviscoe

Nanpean

High
Street

ST AUSTELL

33

3269

Golant

St Veep

Penpoll

Pelynt

West Looe

Downderry

Crafthole

3247

Cawsand

Rame

assick
New Mills
Ladock

39

Grampound
Road

390

Coombe

St Mewan

3273

St Austell
Bay

Par

3082

Lescrow

Fowey

Bodinnick

Trenewan

387

Porthallow

Polperro

EAST LOOE
LOOE

Looe Bay

St George's or
Looe Island

Whitsand

Bay

Rame
Head

Probus

County
Demonstration
Garden &
Arboretum

3287

Hewas
Water

390

Charlestown
Porthpean

Black Head

Pentewan

Menabilly

Polruan

Gribbin
Head

Pencarrow
Head

Lantivet
Bay

13

sillian

Trewarthenick

Tregony

Polmassick

Trevarrick

Ruan
Lanihorne

3078

Lamorran

VERYAN

Carne

Portloe

Nare Head

Greeb Point

ortha

Penare Point
Bay

Mevagissey

MAVAGISSEY

Chapel Point

Gorran
Churchtown

Gorran Haven

Gorran Haven
Maenease
Point

St Michael
Caerhays
Boswinger

Penare

Veryan Bay

973

Dodman Point

DODMAN
POINT

Gerrans
Bay

Trewithian

Gerrans

Eddystone
Rocks

ENGLISH CHANNEL

(LA MANCHE)

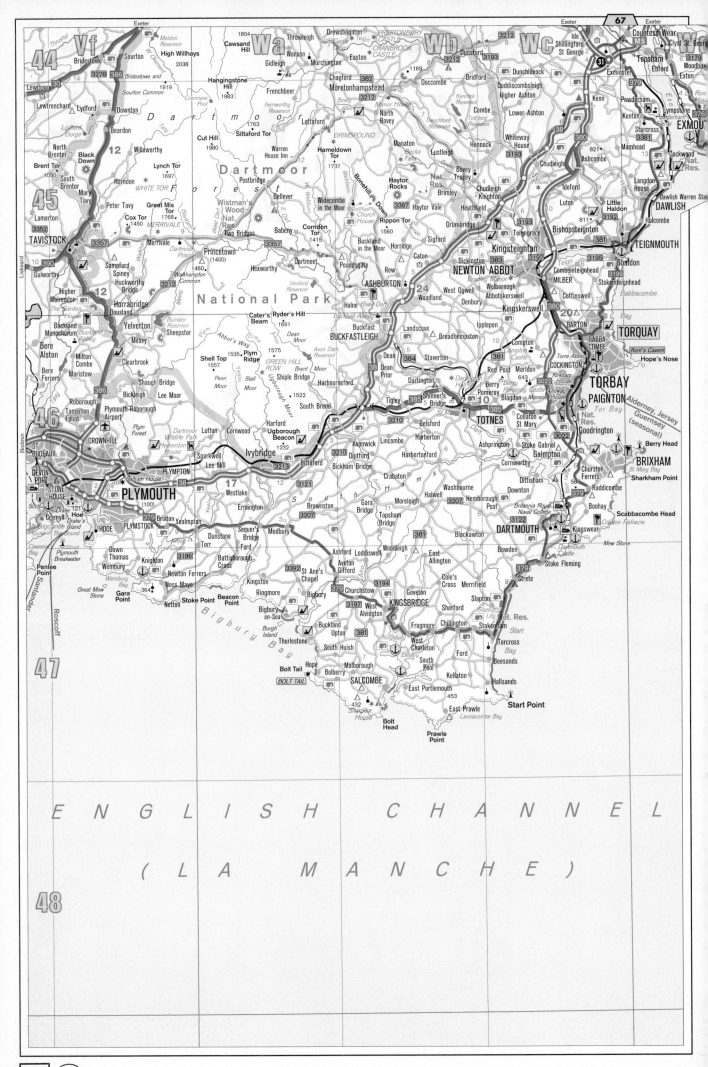

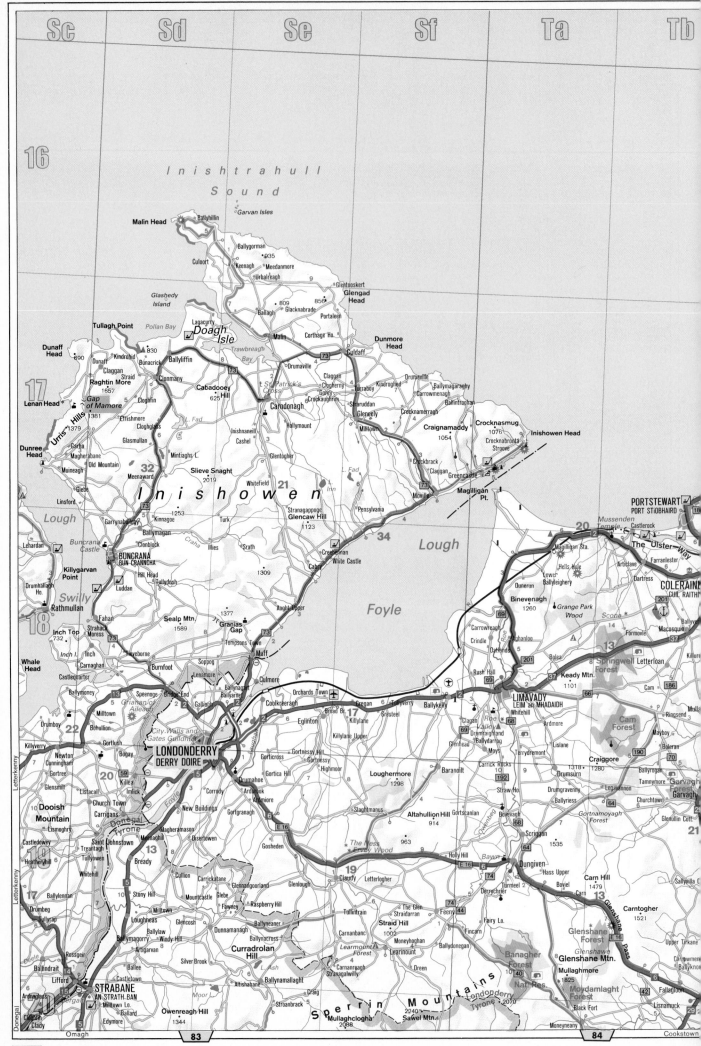

North Channel

Antrim Coast

Rathlin Sound

North Antrim

Bull Point
447
Crockantirrive
Ballyconagan
Robert the Bruce's Cave
Church Bay
Rathlin Island
196
Rue Point

Benbane Head
Rope Bridge
Sheep I.
Dunseverick
White Park Bay
Giant's Causeway
Tonduff
146
Ballintoy
672
Kinbane or
White Head
Benmore or
Fair Head
Views to Scotland
Murlough Bay

The Skerries
Ramore Head   Dunluce Castle
Bushmills   17
Lisnagunogue
Ballyallaght
Fallgarrive
Straid   17
Magheny Castle
Ballinlea
15
Clare Wood
Ballycastle Bay
Craigfad
Torr Head

RTRUSH
T RUS
4   2   2
62   7   66
17
Priestland
Magherintendry
Billy
Ballyloughbeg
Ballydivity
Liscolman
147
Moyarget
67
44
BALLYCASTLE
BAILE an CHAISTIL
Ballycastle Forest
Curragh
Carnanmore
1253
Runabay Head
880

29
17   Cloyfin   Ballywatt
Seneirl
Daneshill   Moyle Hill
Derrykeighan
67   Brook Hall   Benvardin Ho.
Ballyhoy   Africar Glinn
Dervock
Garry Reserve Wood   Ivy Ho.   Stranogum
Gracehill   147   15
Cape Castle
Knocklayd
1695
Armoy   Natur Reserve Breen Wood
Croghan
1368
Antrim
10
Ballypatrick Forest
18
Crockaneel
1321
Glenshesk
Agangarrive Hill
1225
2
92   Cushendun
Antrim Gorges

The Ulster Way

54
The Cuts
Ballindreen
Heagles
26
Cubbindall
Culramoney
147
147
BALLYMONEY
BAILE MONAIDH
16
Carnageeragh
2 Ballyboylands
Kilraghts
Pharis
High Tober
Aldorough
1670
Orra Lodge
Glendun
6
Oissan's Grave
14
Ballyrad
Red Arch
Cushendall
Red Bay

Fanneiry
englishtown Ho.
llyhotagh
Seacon
Cooldarragh
16
Knockaholet
Loughguile
Natur Reserve Slieveanorra Forest
Trostan
1817
Glenariff or Waterfoot
Milltown
Knockore
Garron Point
10
Garron Twr.

Banr
Ballynacree Ho.
26
16
Bendooragh
27
Barryduff
Checker Hall
Corkey
1325
Slievenanee
1782
14
Glenariff Forest Park Nat. Res.
Waterfalls
L. Fad

188   207   Curlycapple
Glasgort
Aghadowey
62
Finvoy
Caldanagh
Mullan Head
Dunloy
Clogh Mills
Irish Ombreae
43
Tuftarney Hill
Newtown-Crommelin
19
Dungonnell Dam
Collin Top
1426
Carnlough
Carnlough Bay

Mayoghill
64
Cahery
Vow
214
Craigs Wood
L. Naroon
16
Ballybogy
94
64
Martinstown
Gortnageeragh
Carncormick
Knockanully   1431
Soarns Hill
1326
Cranny Falls
Galdanagh
42
97
Glenarm
Glenarm Castle

22
54
Moneydig
Artnagross
Culmore Ho.
70
Rasharkin
93
Clogh
Doonbought
Mc Gregor's Corner
Berneyhill
Knockoochran
17
Killycarn
97
Doonan
Ballyvaddy
The Moat
Black Hill
1259
148   15
Milltown

64
Kilrea
75
Portna
64
64
Glarriford
94
Johnstonstown
Quarrytown
Ballyug
Skerry
The Sheddings
Carnalbanagh
Feystown
Ballygalley
Ballygalley Head
Ballygalley

Bovedy
Hervey Hill
96
Heath Park
26
Dromina
93
Dernaveagh
Tullaghgarley
Berneyhill
Buckna
Slievenamon
Aughaboy
Carncastle
1268

yletra Kill
Drumgarvagh
Timaconway
Moyaghney
Tamlaght
Lisnahunshin
12
Craigdunn   Craigs
93
Killyless
Milltown
Arthur House
Drumarkin
54
Broughshane
Tullog
Slemish Mountain
1446
Killybanway
Teenis
White Brae
Sallagh Braes
Drains Bay

10
9
Inishrush
Portglenore
Cullybackey
62
Ballyconelly
Glenhugh
Mount Davys
Ahoghill   Gracehill
Moravian Settlement
Crebilly
Ballygelly
Caherty
94
Ballygelly
Douglas
Capanagh
Knockintennons
148
E 1
E 18
LARNE

gha
10
Gulladuff
182
Culnady
Ballymacpeake
Ballynease
52
Cardearney
Hillhead
Cashelltown
Cromkill
Killybegs
93
Liminary
Deerfin
Mistyburn
Douglas Top
1325
Capanagh Wood
Agnews Hill
1563
Kilwaughter
E 1
E 18
Ballysnod

10
Cot of the Hill
Newferry
26
Moorfields
Shoptown
20
36
3

Stags of Broad Haven

Benwee Head　　Doonvinalla
Kid Island　　829　　Pig Island
761
Carrowteige　　The Arches
Erris Head　　Kilgalligan　　Cliff Boat Tunnel
Stonefield　　Porturlin
Curraunboy　　Sranataggl
Broad　　Ross Port
Eagle Island　　Haven　　9
Doonamo Point　　Aghadoon　　Duveel Point
Doonamo　　Clooneen　　Dooncarton
Fort　　Graghill　　Pullatomish
Corclogh　　434　　7　　Gortbrack North
Termoncarragh　　Tower Hill
Annagh Head　　Knocknalina
Termoncarragh L.　　Knocknalower　　Glename
Bingham Lo.　　Gortmellia
Seafield　　Belmullet　　Barnatra
Inishglora　　186　　58　　Carrowmore
Inishkeeragh　　Corraun　　An Geata Mòr　　Inishderry　　Derreens I.
Point　　Derrynameel
Cross L.　　Pollagarraun　　Muingingaun
Trawmore　　Bunnahowen
Bay　　Ederglen
Ardmore　　Srah　　Knocknascollop　　Carrowmore L.
Point　　788　　Glencullin Lowe
Fortress and
Carrickmoylenacurhogen　　8　　Ravine　　8
Elly Bay　　Barranagh　　7　　Glencullin Upp
Tiraun Point　　Island　　Doolough　　Attavally
Inishkea　　Point　　Srahmore　　58
North　　Clogher　　Bangor
Porteenbeg　　Aghleam
Knocknaskea　　59
Inishkea　　Termon　　Gweesalia　　Knocklettercuss
South　　345　　6　　Kanfinalta　　1208
Hill　　Blacksod　　Dooyork
Fallmore　　Point　　4　　Maumykel
Duvillaun More　　120
Duvillaun Beg　　Blacksod　　Tullaghan　　23
Bay　　Bay
143　　Deohooma
Kinrovar　　Tullaghanbaun
Srahnamanragh Bridge
Fahy L.　　Westport

ATLANTIC

Illanmaster
Glinsk
1002
Horse I.
Ballinapark
Belderg
Lougherglass
aralty
Benmore
1155
Maumakeogh
1247
10
Doonteeny
Ballyglas
Ballycastle
Downpatrick Head
Carrowcor
Gortmore
Lenabaun
606
Creevagh
Rathlackan
Benwee or Kilcummin Head
Kilcummin
214
Lenadoon Point
Walshestown
Easky
Killogeary
Faghill 5
Carrowmore
Rathlee
8
Killala
Bay
Ballymeeny
40
Donagh
Strahlagny
818
Mullaghnacross
Summerhill Ho.
Ross Point
Ross
Cabragh
Carranduff
40
Kilglass
Ballingen
eve Fyagh
Kincon
Ross Point
Bartragh I.
Sulphur
Baths
Drinaghan Cuffs Town
Oromore West
32
Cannaghanally
Templeboy
Sligo
Killala
125
Inishcrone
Owenbeg
Nacreeva
Farranmacfarrell
Ho.
Lugdoon
Strahnakilly
Belladooan
Moyne
Abbey
Ballynamona
Ballymona
Cullens
59
L. Loe
Cloonnakillore
119
Corbally
Finned
Formoyle
Strahnakilly
10
Rosserk Friary
40
Muingwore
Sligo
1685
Slieve
Oxe
Gamph
Mountains
L. Dahybaun
Stone Hall
Rathnamag
Carraun
7
Easky L.
1533
59
Eskeragh Br. Eskeragh
26
Rathmore
Knockanillaun
3
59
Crockets Town
Bunnyconnellan
Dooleeg More
11
Crossmolina
59
Tullysleva
BALLINA
BEAL AN ATNA
57
Kilgarvan
20
Tullyvellia
Loughs
Derry
Deel
Garrycloonagh
Rake Street
Annagh I.
Newtown Cloghans
87 Castlebar
L. Talt
Boyle
Sessuecommyn

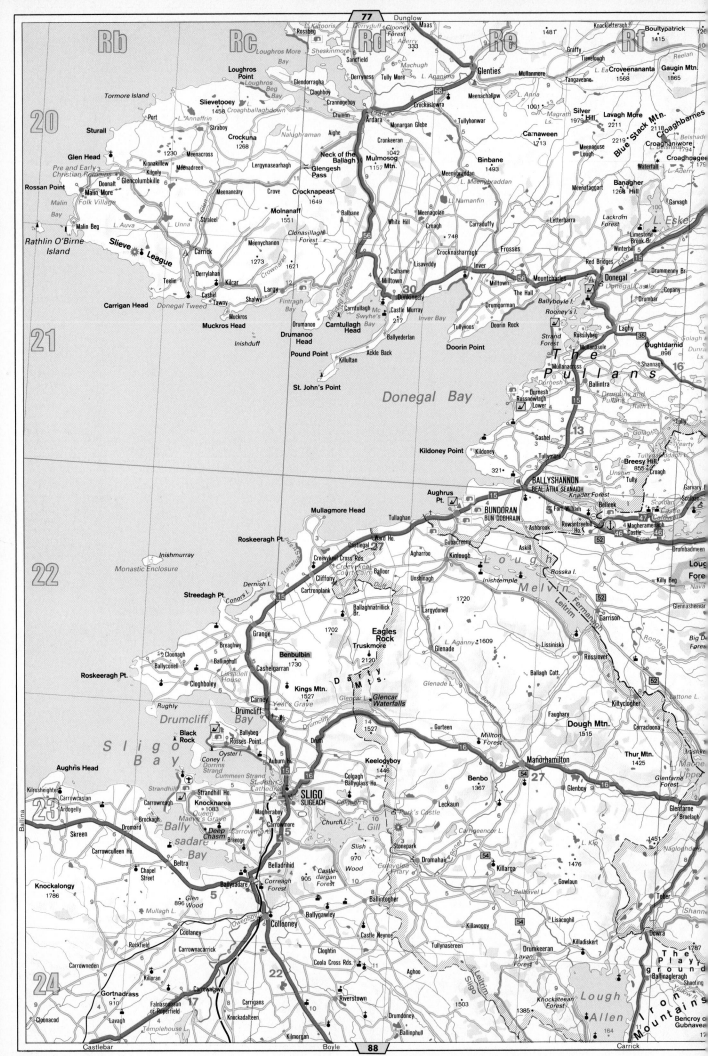

Rb
Rc
Rd
Re
Rf

20

Dunglow
Rossbeg
L. Kiltooris
L. Derryduff
Clooney Forest
Maas
Knockletteragh
Boultypatrick
1415
126

Loughros More Bay
Sheskinmore
L. Adery
333
1481
Graffy
Tievelough
Croveenananta
1568
Gaugin Mtn.
1865

Loughros Point
Loughros Beg Bay
Sandfield
Machugh
Glenties
Mullanmore
Tangaveane
L. Ea

Slievetooey
1458
Croaghballaghdown
Glendorragha
Cloghboy
Derryness
Tully More
L. Ananima
56
Meenachallow
L. Anna
1001
Magrath Ls.
Silver Hill
1979
2211
Lavagh More
Blue Stack Mtn.
2118
Croaghbarnes

Sturall
Crockuna
1268
Meenacross
Lergynasearhagh
Crumlin
Ardara
Crockaslowra
Tullyhonwar
Carnaween
1713
Meenaguse Lough
2219
Croaghaniwore
2118

Glen Head
1230
Meenadreen
Kilgoly
Aighe
Cronkeeran
1042
Mulmosog Mtn.
1157
Binbane
1493
Meenybraddan
Letterbarra
100
Croaghoge

Rossan Point
Doonalt
Glencolumbkille
Meenaneary
Crove
Balbane
L. Meenybraddan
Carraduffy
Lackrom Forest
L. Esker

Pre and Early Christian Remains
3
Malin More
Folk Village
Molnanaff
1551
White Hill
Croagh
L. Namanfin
Meenagolan
Limestone Brook Br.
Winterhill

Malin Bay
Straleel
Meenychanon
748
Crocknasharragh
Frosses
Red Bridges
Donegal

Malin Beg
L. Auva
L. Unna
Clonasillagh Forest
56
Calhame
Lisaveddy
Inver
Mountcharles
56
Donegal Castle

Rathlin O'Birne Island
Slieve   League
1273
1621
Crownarad
Milltown
Milltown
The Hall
Drumgorman
Ballyboyle I.
Rooney's I.
Laghy
35

Carrick
Derrylahan
Kilcar
Largy
12
Dunkineely
Castle Murray
Doorin Rock
Strand Forest
Rossilybeg
Oughtdarnid
898

Teelin
Cashel
Shalwy
Tawny
Fintragh Bay
Carntullagh
Mc Swyne's Bay
217
Ballyederlan
Tullyvoos
Doorin Point
Mullanasole
Shannagh
16

Carrigan Head
Donegal Tweed
Muckros
Drumanoo
Carntullagh Head
Ballintra
Drumbar
Company

Muckros Head
Drumanoo Head
Inishduff
Pound Point
Killultan
Ackle Back
Doorin Point
Durnesh
Rossnowlagh Lower
13

St. John's Point
Donegal Bay
Kildoney Point
Kildoney
321
Cashel
3
Tullymore
Breesy Hill
855
Croagh

Mullaghmore Head
Aughrus Pt.
Ballyshannon
Beal Atha Seanaidh
Knader Forest
Tully
Garvary

Roskeeragh Pt.
Tullaghan
15
Bundoran
Bun Dobhrain
Fort William
Belleek
Scolban

22

Inishmurray
Monastic Enclosure
Creevykeel Cross Rds.
Ward Ho.
Castlegal
Balloor
Agharroo
Gubacreeny
Ashbrook
Rowantreehill Ho.
52
46
46
Magheramenagh Castle
Drumbadmeen

Streedagh Pt.
Dernish I.
Cliffony
Cartronplank
Ballaghnatrillick Br.
Unshinagh
Kinlough
Askill
Inishtemple
Lough
Melvin
Rosska I.
Killy Beg
52
Loug
Fore

Roskeeragh Pt.
Conors I.
Travalley
15
1702
Eagles Rock
Truskmore
2120
Largydonell
1720
L. Aganny
1609
Glenade
Lissiniska
Garrison
Rossinver
Glennasheevar
Big De Fore

Breaghwy
Grange
Benbulbin
1730
Cashelgarran
Darty Mts.
Glenade L.
9
Ballagh Cott.
52

Roskeeragh Pt.
Cloonagh
Ballinphull
Lissadell House
Kings Mtn.
1527
Carney
Yeat's Grave
Glencar L.
Glencar Waterfalls
Boner
Kiltyclogher

Aughris Head
Rughly
Drumcliff
Drumcliff Bay
Ballybeg
Rosses Point
Drum
1527
Gurteen
Millton Forest
Manorhamilton
Dough Mtn.
1515
Carracloona

Kilrusheighter
Carrowcaslan
Ardogelly
Brockagh
Black Rock
Oyster I.
Coney I.
Dorrins Strand
Auburn Ho.
Keelogyboy
1446
Colgagh
96
Benbo
1367
54
27
Glenboy
9
16
Thur Mtn.
1425
Glenfarne Forest

Sligo Bay
Strandhill
Knocknarea
1083
Queen Maeve's Grave
Magheraboy
Colgagh L.
Carrowmore
Church I.
L. Gill
Park's Castle
Leckaun
Killarga
Gowlaun
Glenfarne
Broelagh

23

Dromard
Carrowreagh
Deep Chasm
15
16
St. John's Cathedral
Sligo
Sligeach
Slish Wood
970
Stonepark
Dromahair
Creevelea Friary
54
1476
Toher

Skreen
Carrowculleen Ho.
Bally sadare Bay
Breeoge
Belladrihid
Correagh Forest
Castle dargan Forest
905
Ballintogher
Ballygawley
Castle Neynoe
Carrigeencor L.
Belhavel L.
1451
Nagloghdara

Chapel Street
Beltra
Ballysadare
Killavoggy
54

Knockalongy
1786
Glen Wood
896
Mullagh L.
5
Colooney
Ballygawley
Cloghtin
Coola Cross Rds.
11
Aghoo
Tullynasereen
Drumkeeran
Lavan Forest
Killadiskert
The Playground
Ballinaleragh
1787

24
Rockfield
Carrownacarrick
22
Riverstown
1503
Knockateean Forest
1385
Lough
Allen
Iron
Mountains

Carrowneden
Kiloran
Carrowntawy
Carrigans
Knockadalteen
Drumdoney
Gortnadrass
910
Falnasoogaun or Roperfield
17
8
Lavagh
Templehouse L.
Kilmorgan
Ballinphull
164
Bencroy or Gubnavea

Cloonacod
Castlebar
Boyle
Carrick

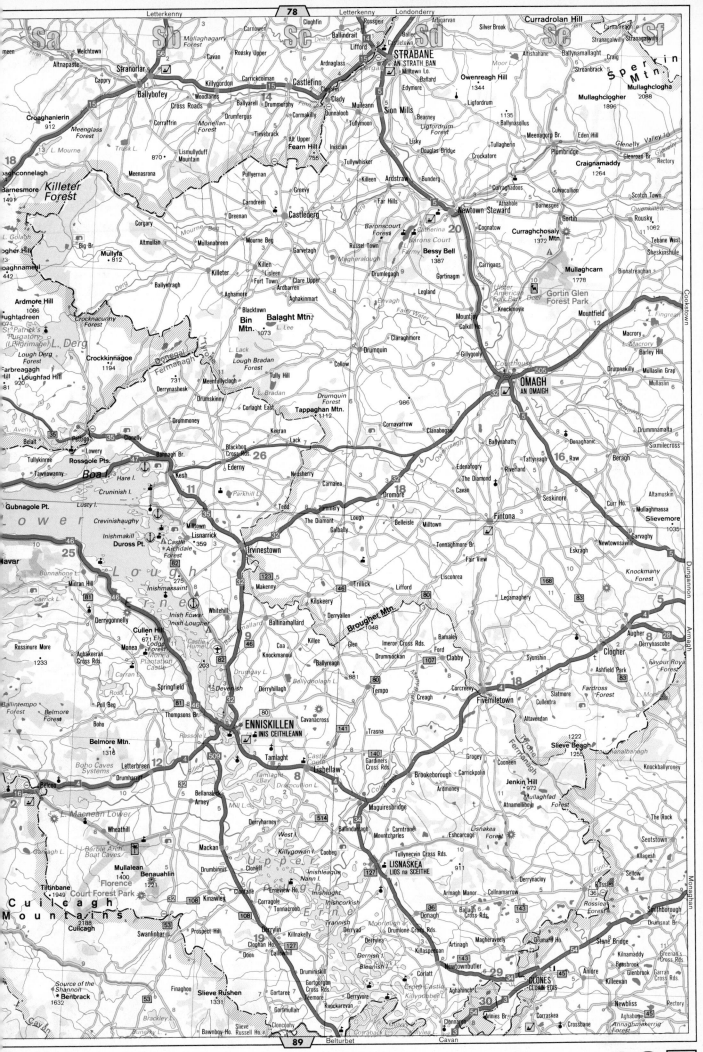

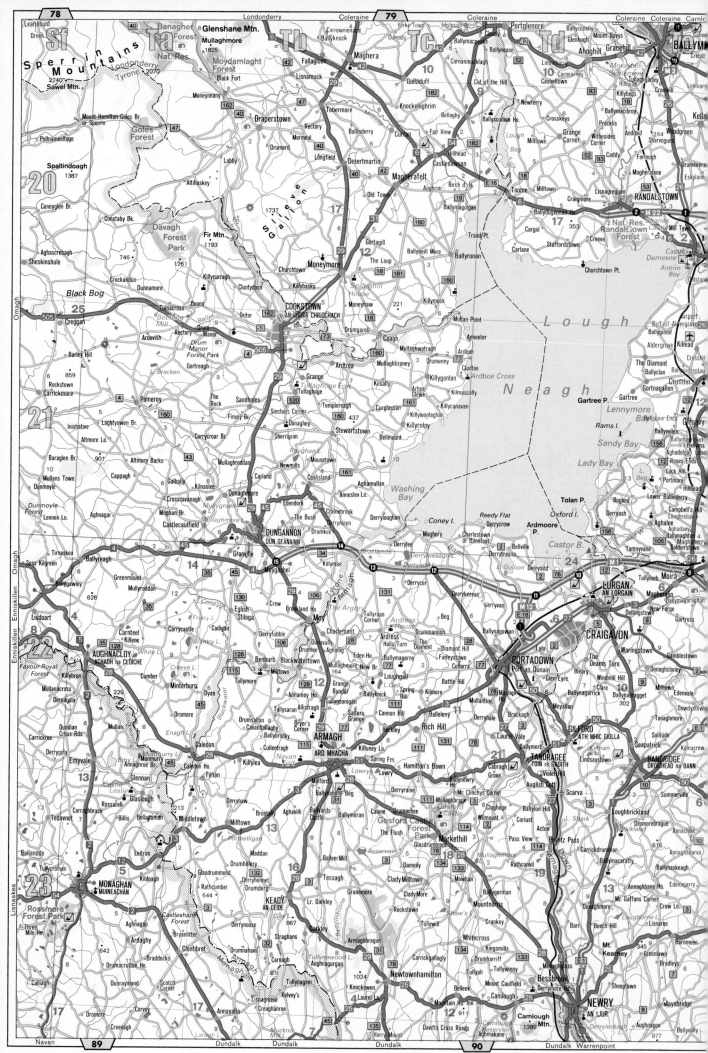

Carnlough

Stranraer

Tf
Ua
Ub
Uc
Ud

1446 Slemish Mountain
Tullog
Ballygelly
White Brae
Sallagh Braes
Drains Bay
Ballynahill
Douglas
Douglas Top
1325
Capanagh
Knockinennon
LARNE
Mistyburn
Capanagh Wood
Agnews Hill
148
Older Fleet
I. of Muck
90
Portmuck
Moorfields
Shoptown
1563
Kilwaughter
Four Corners
20
Glenwhirry
Ballysnod
Glynn
90
Browndod
Larne
Ballymoney
Island
Whappstown
1208
Ballyrickard
Gransha
90
Magee
Ballyboley
Ballylesson
Newlands
759
The Gobbins
Maxwells Walls
Big Collin
Forest
100
99
Ballykeel
1163
Tildarg
Ballystrudder
Carnlea
Dunamoy
Castletown
Ballynarry
Beltoy
Black Head
Five
Ballygowan
Carn Hill
WHITEHEAD
Tardree
Corners
Ballyeaston
58
99
1034
150
Forest 10
BALLYCLARE
Straid
Milebush
Woodburn and
Woodburn
North Carn Forest
War. Meml
Trooperslane
Town Walls, Castle
Douglas
CARRICKFERGUS
Carrickfergus Castle
Eden
GREENISLAND
Belfast
Light House Island
Mew Island
WHITEHOUSE
Grey P.
GROOMSPORT
Copeland Island
Lough
Helen's Bay
BANGOR
NEWTOWNABBEY
Craigavad
Ballyrobert
Kinnairds Corner
Foreland P.
BELFAST
HOLYWOOD
Newtownards

GB
85

Pe   Pf   Qa   Qb   Qc   Qd

25

Saddle Head

Ridge Point

Slievemore
2204

Doogort
Nambrack

Croaghaun
2192
*2000 Precipice

Achill
Head

Bellanasally

Keel Lough

Moyteoge
Head   Inishgalloon
Keel
Dooagh

1530   Cliff Scenery

Salia

Bunacurry

Achill Sound

Inishbiggle

Annagh I.

Fahy L.

Gortbrack South
Ballycroy

Owenduff

Srahill L.

Bellagarvaun

Srahduggaun

Bellaveeny

59

39

1509

Owenduff
6

Nephin Beg
2065

Bunaveela L.

Letterask

Keenagh
1274

Clendavoolagh Lo.

Boghadoor

Dumleen

2067
Glennamong

Corryloughaphuill L.

Bengorm
1912

Glenhes

Birreencorragh
2295

Beltra

Dooega Head

Knockmore
931
Sraheens

Dooega

Belfarsad

Mweewillin
Glassillaun

Atlantic Drive

Derreen

Cloghmore

Corraun

Corraun Hill
1715

Peninsula

Bolinglanna

Dooghbeg

Gubbaun Point

Moyrtish
More

Rosturk

Mallaranny

59

11

Furnace L.

Rockfleet Castle

Burrishoole Abb

Newport

L. Feeagh

1646

1935

Treanlaur Lo.

Cloondaff

Achillbeg Island

Newport
Bay

Inishbee

Island
More

Inishgort

Collan
More

Fahy

Clogher

Clogher L.

Islandady

11

Carrickfadda

Clew   Bay

59

27

Ballytoohy

Clare Island

1520

Harbour

Portnakilly

Westport Bay

Bartraw

Annagh
Islands

Westport
Quay

39

WESTPORT

CATHAIR
na MAIRT

Westport
House

60

11

26

Caher Island
620

Inishturk

Inishdalla

Roonah Quay

Emlagh Point

Old Head

Louisburgh
39
Askillaan
Carrowmore
5

Curraghmore
Point

Murrisk

Croagh Patrick
2510

Mullagh

Boleybrian

Prosped

Liscarney

6

Mountbrown Ho.

Aghagower

Corveagh

Cordarragh

Kiltarsaghaun

Bohaun
Bohaun
1294

Sraheen

Killeen

Roonah L.

7

Killadoon

Kinnadoohy

Corrymailley
941

Bunowen

1287

Tawnyslinnaun

Cregganhaun

12

Lugacolliwee L.

Owenmore
Br.

Owenmore

Carrowkennedy

Croaghrimbeg

Glennagashleeny

Partry Mountains

Tonakeera Point

Glencullin
L.

Doo L.

Sheeffry Hills
2504

2429

Srahlea Br.

59

L. Glenawough

1701

Toormakeady

27

Ardnagreevagh

Cashleen

Freaghhillaun South

1172
Letter More

Tully L.

Tully Cross

Gowlaun

Gubbadanbo

Mweelrea
Mountains

Mweelrea
2688

Salrock

Killary Harbour

Bundorragha

L. Muck

Garraun
1973

L. Fee

Ben Gorm
2303

6

Derrynaeleigh

Glenndgevlagh

Leenaun

Devilsmother

2131

Maumtrasna
2207

Errif

Tawnyard Lough

41

Nadirkmore

Owenbrin

Barnahowna

Cappanacreha

Trean

Fox Hill

Mask

Point
Aughrus

Emlagh

Aughrus More

Claddaghduff

Ballynakill L.

Cleggan

Bundouglas
5

Ballynakill
Harbour

Dawros

Letterfrack

Kylemore Abbey

Kylemore Ho.

Kylemore L.

Maumturk

2052

Skanafaraghaun

L. Nafooey
Bunnacunneen
1902

Maumtrasna

Finny

1539

Kilmore

Mayo

59

Streamstown
673

L. Anna

Connemara
National
Park

Benbrack
1922

Benbaun
2395

L. Nahillion

967

The Twelve Pins
or Benna Beola
2276

Letterbreckaun
2193

Mountains

Drishaghaun

Bohaun

Kilmeelickin

1628

Cloghbrack

Coolin L.

Clonbur

Omey
Isla

Inishturk

Eeshal
Island
Turbot Island

Kill
Belleek

Clifden
Bay

Clifden

Owenglin

Ballinaboy

Emlaghdaurbe
Loughanillaun

Benlettery

Bencorr

Ballynahinch

Derryclare L.

Benlettery

Connemara

Derryvoreada

L. Inagh

Maum

Maumcloghaloon

Crumlin

Cornamona

Errislannan Point

Curhownagh

Drinagh

Salt L.

Ballinaboy

Joyce   Country

2174

Corcogemore or
Leckavrea Mountain
2012

Castle Kirke

Claggan

Inishdoorus

Mannin
Bay

Emlaghbeg

Aughrus

Alcock and Brown
Transatlantic Landing
Site 1919

Anaserd

Ballyconneely

L. Bollard

L. Naweelaun

1024

Cashel

Recess

59

Glendollagh L.

11

L. Shindilla

Maam Cross

Loughanillaun

Dorid L.

1009

49

10

Inishkeeragh

Doonloughan

131

28

Bunowen Castle

Illaunurra

Callow

Maumeen L.

987
Errisbeg
12

Murvay

Roundstone

Inishnee

Inishlackan

Tawnaghbaun

Canower

Bertraghboy Bay

Loughanillaun

1178

Arderry Lough

Aphreaghaun

L. Bofin

L. Nahillon

Croaghnakeela
Island

St. Mc Dara's
Church

L. Bofa

L. Pilburn

Glnsk

Derryrush

1164

Pearse's Cottage

Kilbrickan

Illaunmore
Turloughbeg

Ls. Ahalia

Glentrasna

1138

Nagarrivhan

Letterfaffroe
908

Knocknalee Hil
960

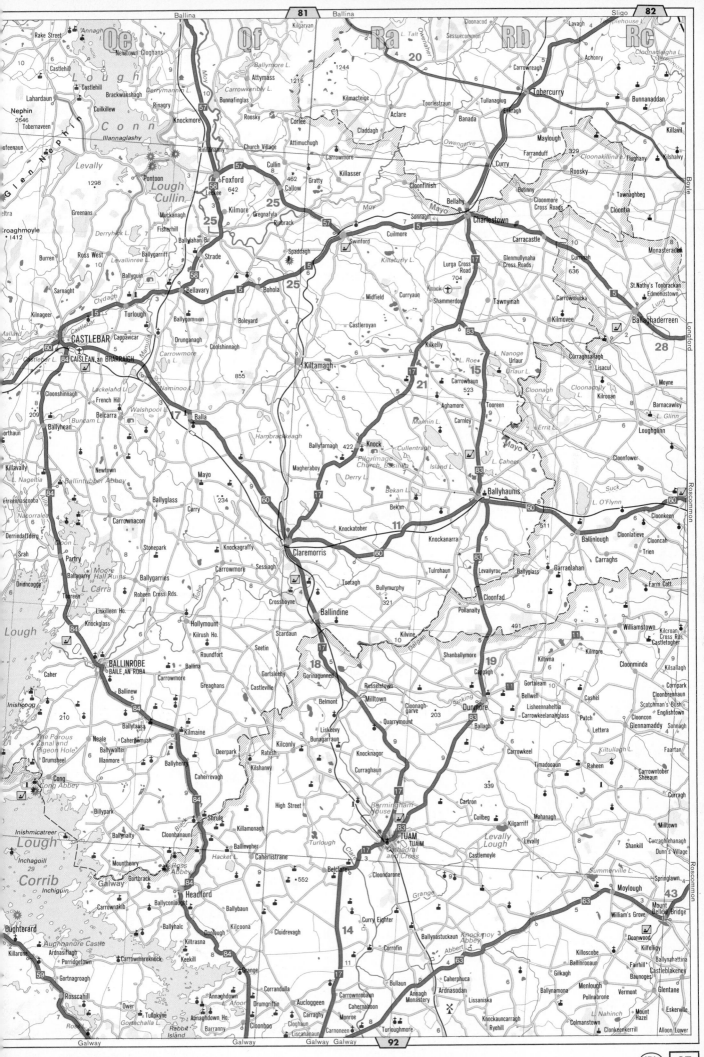

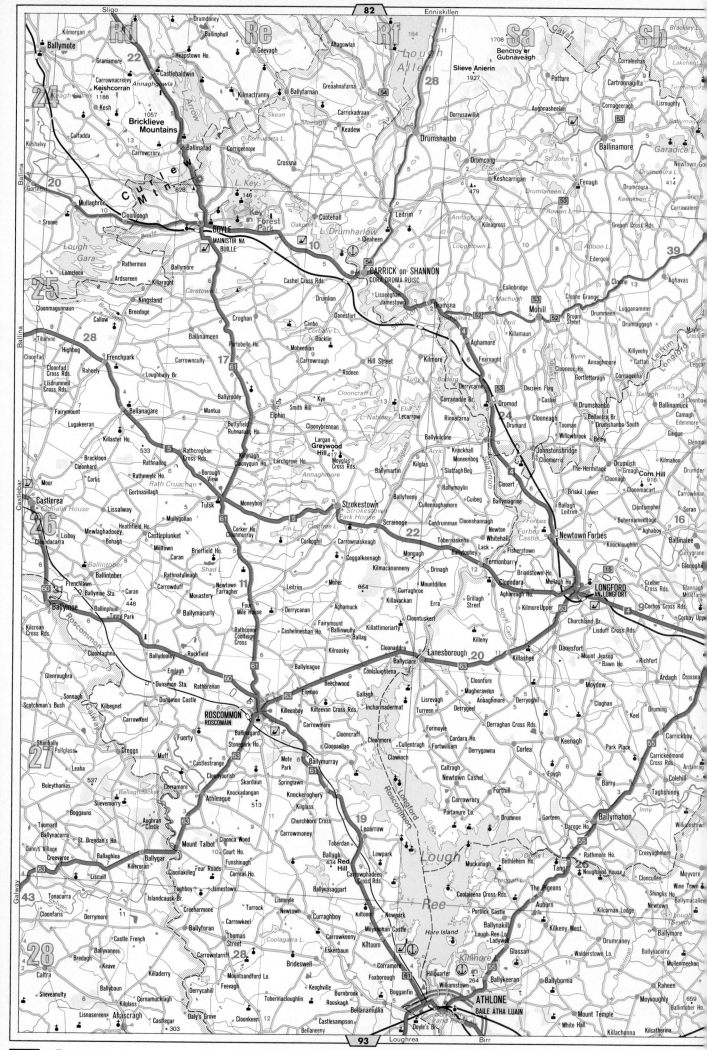

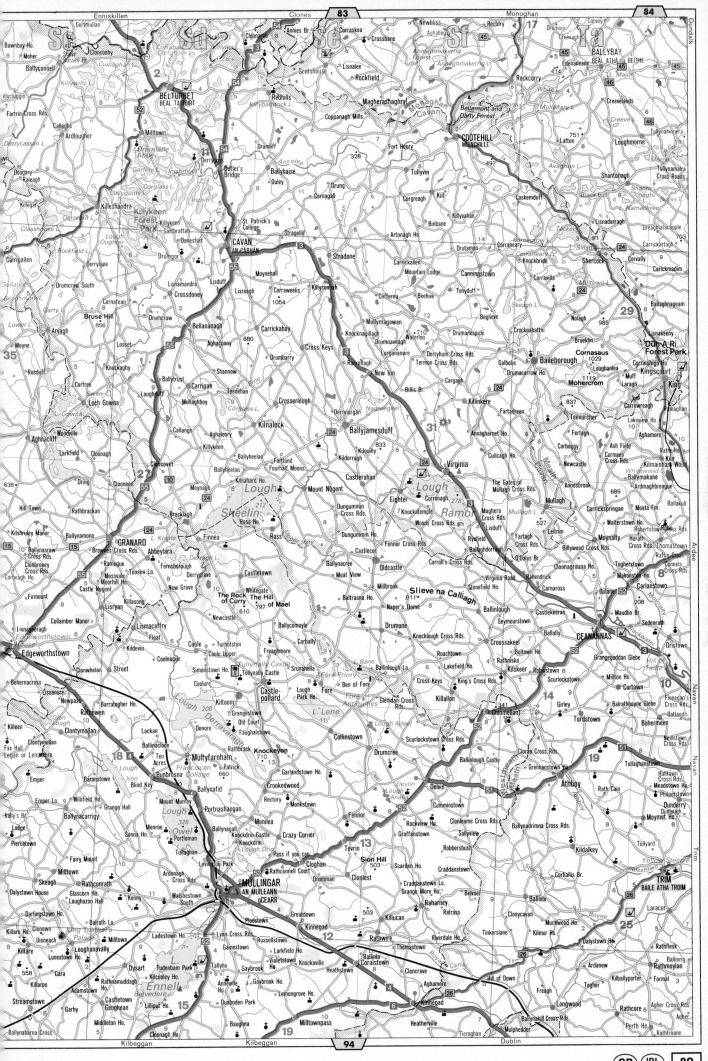

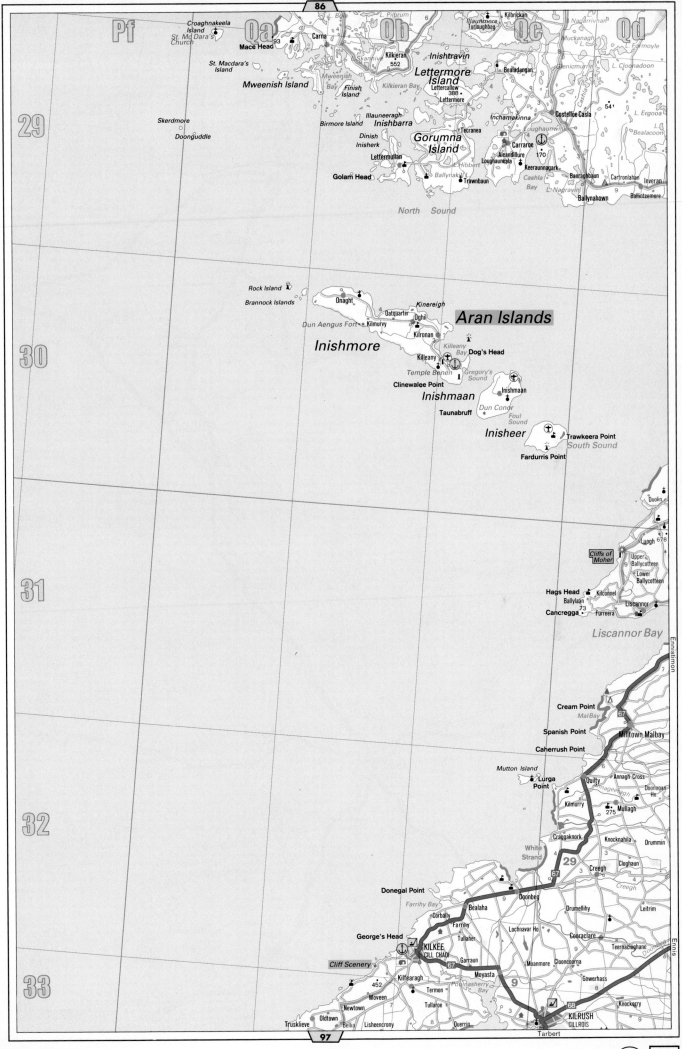

Pf

Qa

Qb

Qc

Qd

Croaghnakeela Island
St. Mc Dara's Church
St. Macdara's Island
Mace Head
93
Carna
L. Pilbrum
Béal
6
Illaunmore
Turloughbeg
Kilbrickan
Nagarrivhan
Formoyle
Mweenish
Bay
Kilkieran
552
Skannive
Inishtravin
Lettermore Island
Muckanagh
L.

Mweenish Island
Finish Island
Kilkieran Bay
Lettercallow
388
Lettermorn
Bealadangan
Glenicmurrin
L. Cloonadoon
L. Ergooa

29

Skerdmore
Doonguddle
Birmore Island
Illauneeragh
Inishbarra
Dinish
Inisherk
Lettermullan
Golam Head
Gorumna Island
Tecranea
L. Hibbert
Ballynakill L.
Trawnbaun
Inchamakinna
Loughaunwillin
Carraroe
Aleandillure
Loughauneala
170
Keeraunnagark
Costelloe Casla
54
Banraghbaun
Cartronlahan
Bealacoon
L. Nagravin
Cashla Bay
Inveran
Ballynahown
Ballinteemore

North   Sound

Rock Island
Brannock Islands
Onaght
Dun Aengus Fort
Kilmurvy
Oatquarter
Oghil
Kinereigh
Oghil

Aran Islands

30

Inishmore
Kilronan
Killeany
Temple Benen
Clinewalee Point
Killeany
Bay
Dog's Head
Gregory's
Sound
Killeany
Inishmaan
Inishmaan
Dun Conor
Taunabruff
Foul
Sound
Inisheer
Trawkeera Point
Fardurris Point
South Sound

Doolin

Lisdoon
Lackenareen
678
Cliffs of Moher
Upper Ballycotteen
Lower Ballycotteen

31

Hags Head
Ballylaan
Cancregga
73
Kilconnel
Furreera
Liscannor

Liscannor Bay

Ennistimon

Cream Point
Mal Bay
Spanish Point
Caherrush Point
Milltown Malbay
67

Annagh Cross
Doonogan Ho.
Mutton Island
Lurga Point
Quilty
Kilmurry
275
Mullagh

32

Craggaknork
Knocknahila
Drummin
White
Strand
29
67
Creegh
Cloghaun
Creegh

Donegal Point
Farrihy Bay
Bealaha
Corbally
Doonbeg
Drumellihy
Leitrim
Farrihy
Tullaher
Lochnavar Ho.
Cooraclare
Teernacleghane

George's Head
KILKEE
CILL CHADÍ
Garraun
Moanmore
Clooncoorna
Gowerhass
Cliff Scenery
Kilfearagh
Termon
Moyasta
9
452
Moveen
Tullaroe
Querrin
Poulnasherry Bay
68
Knockerry

33

Newtown
Bellia
Lisheencrony
9
Ennis
Trusklieve
Oldtown
KILRUSH
CILLROIS
Tarbert

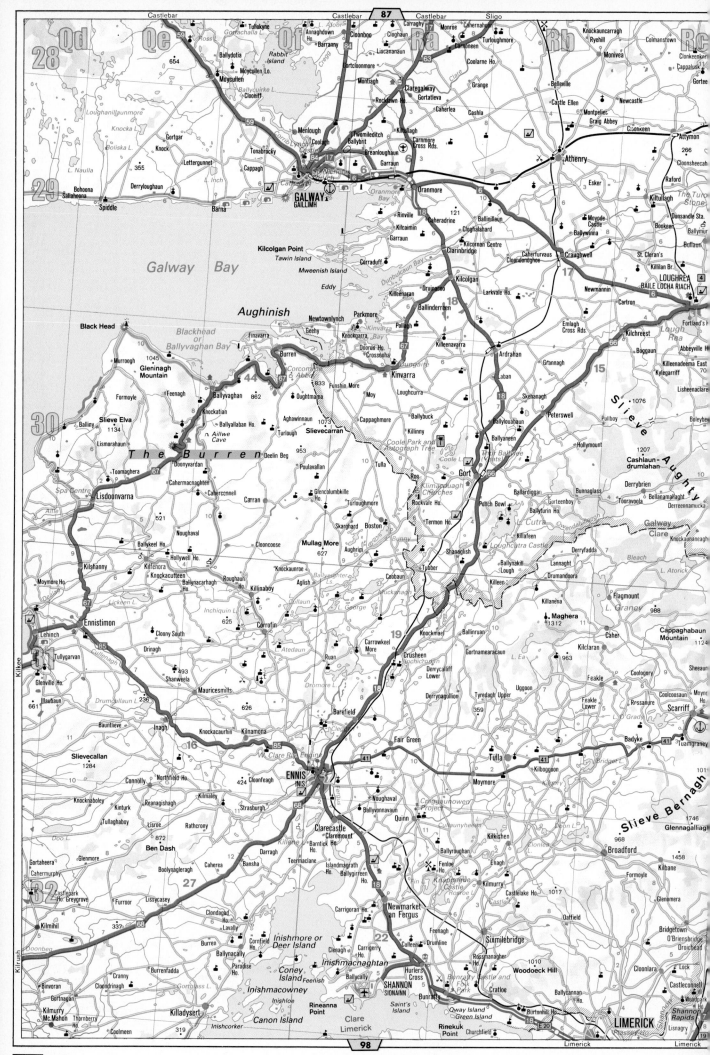

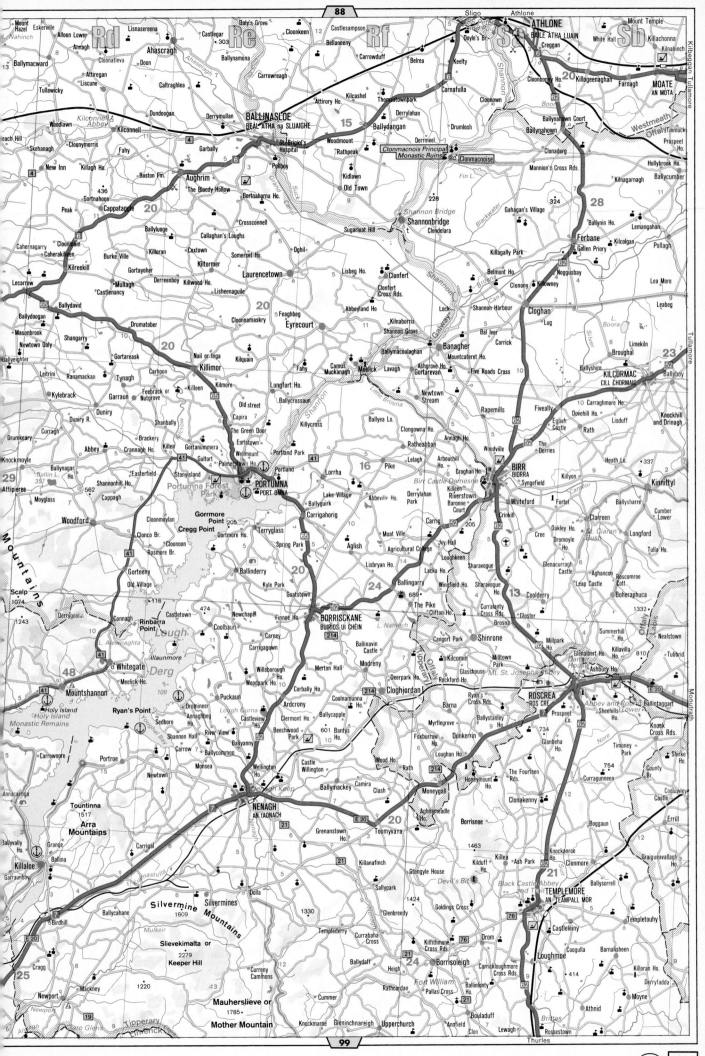

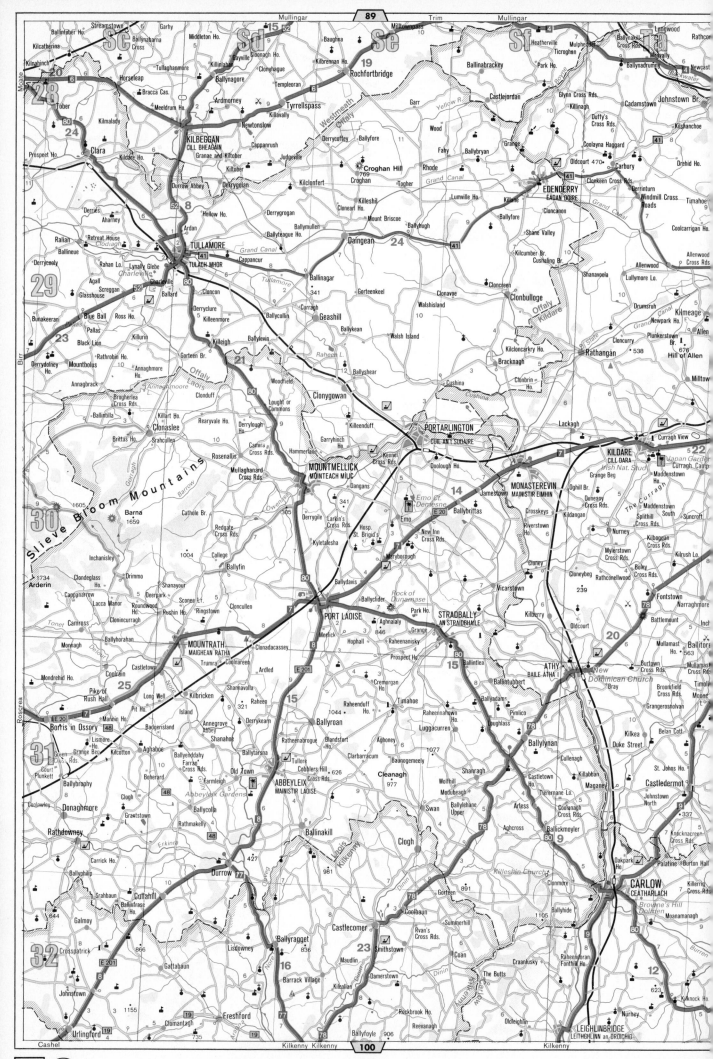

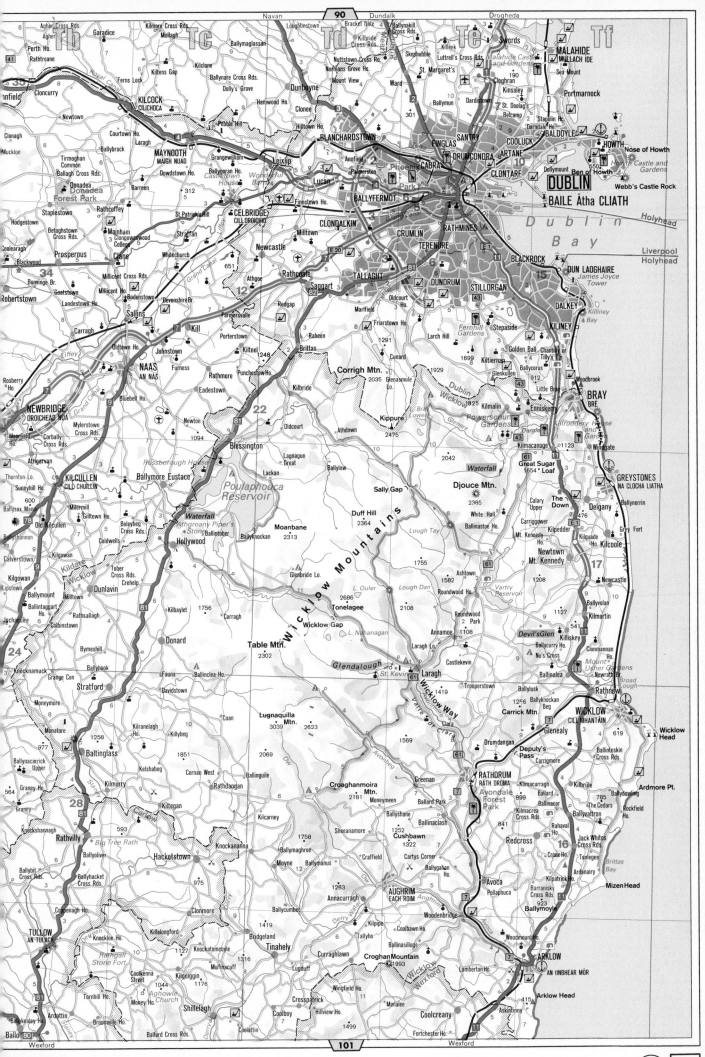

Brandon
Point
Br
Brandon
Head
1026
Masatiompan
2509
Brandon
Teer
Ballyquin
Brandon
Mauntain
3127
Cloonsharragh
8
Cappagh
Kilcummin
Faha
Ballydavid
Head
Ballyrue
5
Ballycurrane
Brando
Peak
2764
Cloghane
Ballyduff
Ballydavid
Feohanagh
Ballybrack
L. Cruttia
1945
Smerwick
Kilquane
Ballinloghig
Ardamore
D i n
Smerwick
Caherscullibeen
L. Gal
Balynagall
Murreagh
8
Ballysitteragh
2050
L. Adoon
L. Camclaun
Harbour
Ballyoughteragh
Gallerus Oratory
2026
Connor Pass
Ballinrolla
Ballineanig
5
Graigue
Ballyferriter
6
Emlagh
68 Ballybowter
Carhoo
Lateevebeg
Ballyeightragh
Knocknahoran
Lisdargan
Inishtooskert
Dunquin
11
Caherboshina
Milltown
DINGLE
AN DAINGEAN
68
11
Kildurrihg
Ventry
Tobernamoodane
Lispole
Mount Eagle
1696
Monaree
Lough
Ballynasare
Blasket
Sound
Beenacouma
Fahan
Burnham
Doonsheane
Doonmanagh
Minard Head
Slea Head
619
Ogham
Stones
Parkmore
Point
Bull's Head
Great Blasket Island

Inishnabro

Inishrickillane

Dingle Bay

Kerry

Roads

Knocknadobar
2267
70
Coomnahincht
Ring
9
Doulus Head
921 Killelan
Emlagh
Leacanabuaile
Fort
of
Beginish Island
Cahersiveen
888 Knight's Town
Reenard
11
Valencia Island
Chapeltown
Killoe
1235
Clynacarton
Portmagee
5
Folldogh
1639
Bray Head
7
70
102 Waterville

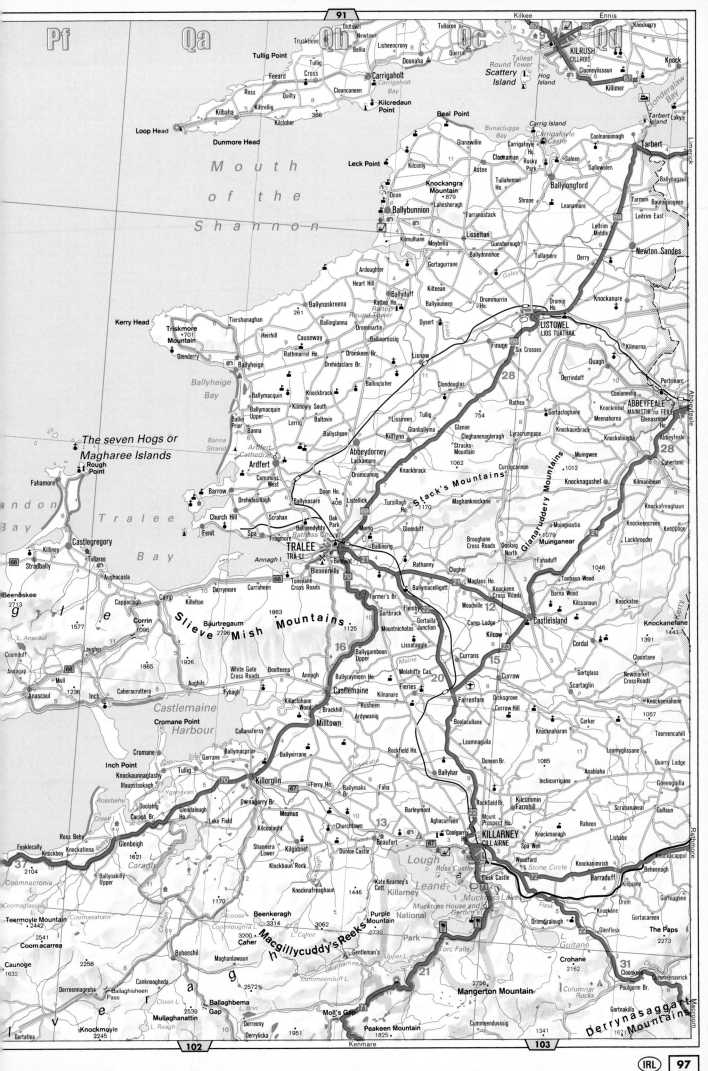

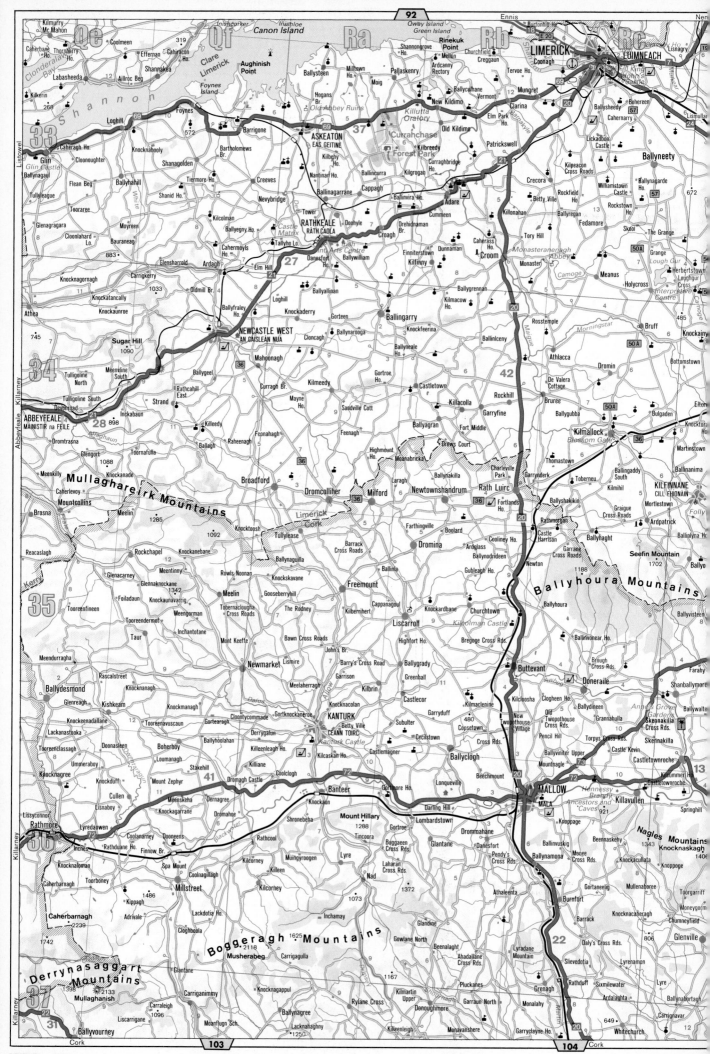

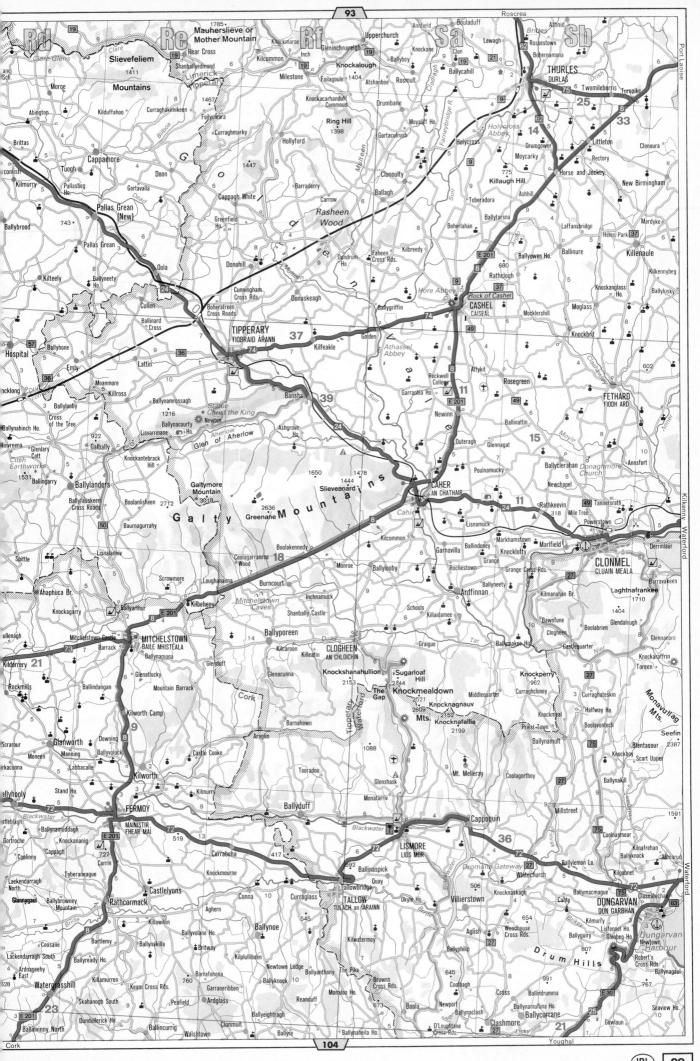

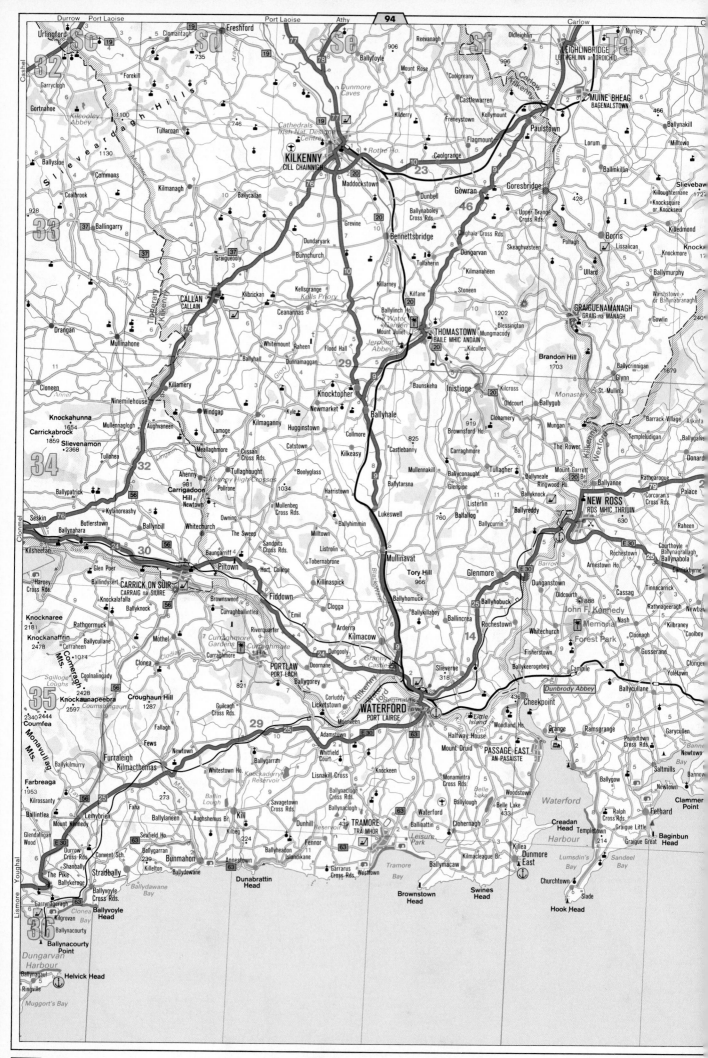

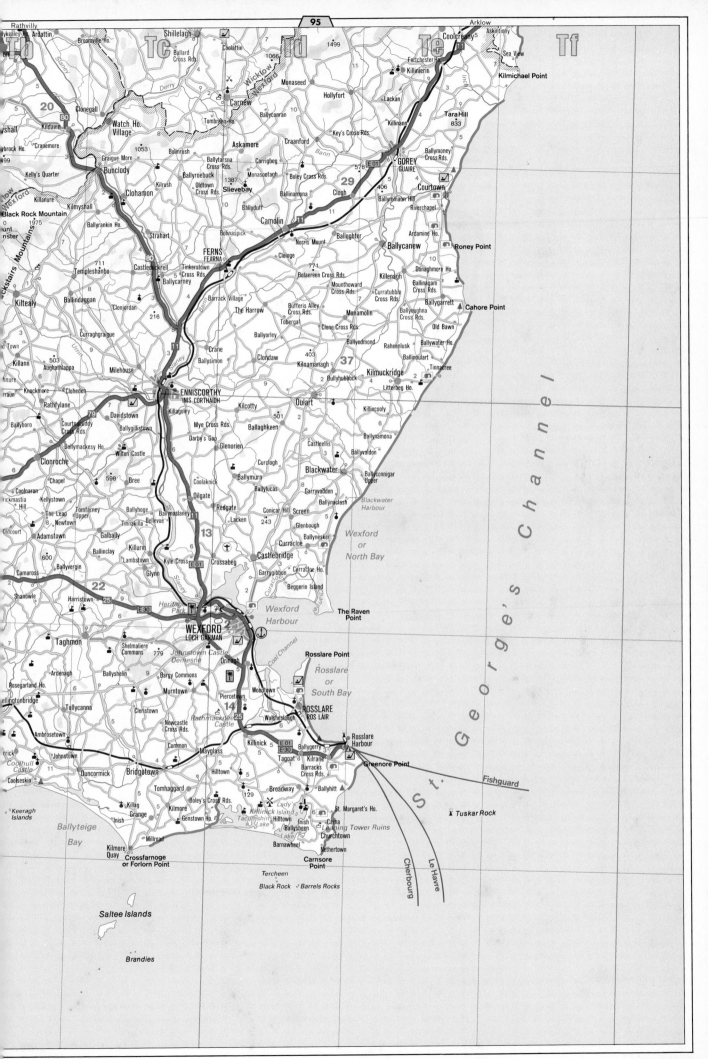

Rathvilly
Ardattin
kealey Ho.
Broomville Ho.
Shillelagh
Coolattin
Ballard
Cross Rds.
1066
1499
Arklow
Askintinny
Coolgreany
Sea View
Fortchester Ho.
Killinierin
Kilmichael Point

TC
Tc
Td
Te
Tf

20
80
Clonegall
Kildavin
Tombreen Ho.
Carnew
Monaseed
Hollyfort
Ballyconran
Lackan
Killinann
Tara Hill
833

brock Ho.
Cranemore
Kelly's Quarter
Watch Ho.
Village
1053
Bolinrush
Graigue More
Bunclody
Ballyroebuck
Askamore
Craanford
Carrigbeg
Boley Cross Rds.
Key's Cross Rds.
Bann
578
E 01
GOREY
GUAIRE
Ballymoney
Cross Rds.
Courtown
406

Killanure
Kilmyshall
Clohamon
Kilrush
Oldtown
Cross Rds.
711
Monasootagh
Ballinamona
29
Clogh
Ballymaun Hill
Riverchapel

Black Rock Mountain
1975
1387
Slievebay
Ballyduff
Camolin
11
11
Balloghter
Ardamine Ho.

unt
nster
Ballyrankin Ho.
Strahart
Bohnaspick
Norris Mount
Clologe
771
Ballycanew
Killenagh
Donaghmore Ho.
Roney Point

Kiltealy
Templeshanbo
80
Castledockrell
FERNS
FEARNA
Tinkerstown
Cross Rds.
Ballycarney
Barrack Village
Bolaereen Cross Rds.
Mounthoward
Cross Rds.
Curratubbin
Cross Rds.
Ballinagam
Cross Rds.
Ballygarrett
Cahore Point

Ballindaggan
Clonjordan
216
The Harrow
Bufferis Alley
Cross Rds.
Monamolin
Ballyoughna
Cross Rds.
Old Bawn

Curraghgraigue
Ballyorley
Tobergal
Clone Cross Rds.
Ballyedmond
Raheenlusk
Ballywater Ho.
Ballinoulart
Tinnacree

Killann
503
Aughathlappa
Milehouse
Crane
Ballysimon
403
Kilnamanagh
37
Bullyhubbock
Kilmuckridge
Litterbeg Ho.

hnure
rraun
Knockmore
Cloheden
Rathfylane
79
Davidstown
Killagoley
ENNISCORTHY
INIS CÓRTHAIDH
Kilcotty
Oulart
501
Killincooly

Ballyboro
Courtnacuddy
Cross Rds.
Ballymackesy Ho.
Ballygillistown
Mye Cross Rds.
Darby's Gap
Ballaghkeen
Castleellis
3
Ballynamona
Ballyvaldon

Clonroche
Chapel
598
Bree
Wilton Castle
Glenorien
Curclogh
Ballymurn
Ballylucas
Blackwater
8
Garryvadden
Ballyconnigar
Upper

Coolnaron
Kellystown
Hill
The Leap
Newtown
Oilgate
Coolaknick
Redgate
Garryvadden
Ballynaclash
Blackwater
Harbour

Oldcourt
Adamstown
Galbally
Ballyhoge
Tinnakilla
Bellevue
Ballynaslaney
Conicar Hill
243
Screen
Wexford
or
North Bay

600
Ballinclay
Killurin
11
Lacken
Glenbough
Ballynesker

Camaross
Ballyvergin
Lambstown
Glynn
Kyle Cross
E 01
Crossabeg
Curracloe
Curracloe Ho.

22
Harristown
25
Heritage
Park
E 30
13
Castlebridge
Garrygibbon
Beggerin Island
The Raven
Point

Shanowle
Taghmon
Shelmaliere
Commons
779
WEXFORD
LOCH GARMAN
Wexford
Harbour

Ardenagh
Rosegarland Ho.
Ballyshelin
Johnstown Castle
Demesne
Drinagh
Coal Channel
Rosslare Point

ellingtonbridge
Tullycanna
Bargy Commons
Murntown
Piercetown
Woodtown
Rosslare
or
South Bay

Cleristown
Newcastle
Cross Rds.
14
Rathmacknee
Castle
25
Walsheslough
ROSSLARE
ROS LÁIR

Ambrosetown
Johnstown
Common
Mayglass
Killinick
E 01
E 30
Ballygerry
Rosslare
Harbour

rrick
Coolhull
Castle
Coolseskin
11
Duncormick
Bridgetown
Hilltown
Kilrane
Tagoat
Barracks
Cross Rds.
Greenore Point
Fishguard

Keeragh
Islands
Tomhaggard
Killag
129
Broadway
Ballyhitt
Tuskar Rock

Ballyteige
Bay
Kilmore
Boley's Cross Rds.
Grange
Genstown Ho.
Lady's
Island
Killinick Island
Tacumshin
Lake
Hilltown
Inish
Ballysbeen
St. Margaret's Ho.
Carna
Leaning Tower Ruins
Churchtown

Millroad
Barnawheel
Nethertown

Kilmore
Quay
Crossfarnoge
or Forlorn Point
Carnsore
Point
Cherbourg
Le Havre
St. George's Channel

Tercheen
Black Rock
Barrels Rocks

Saltee Islands

Brandies

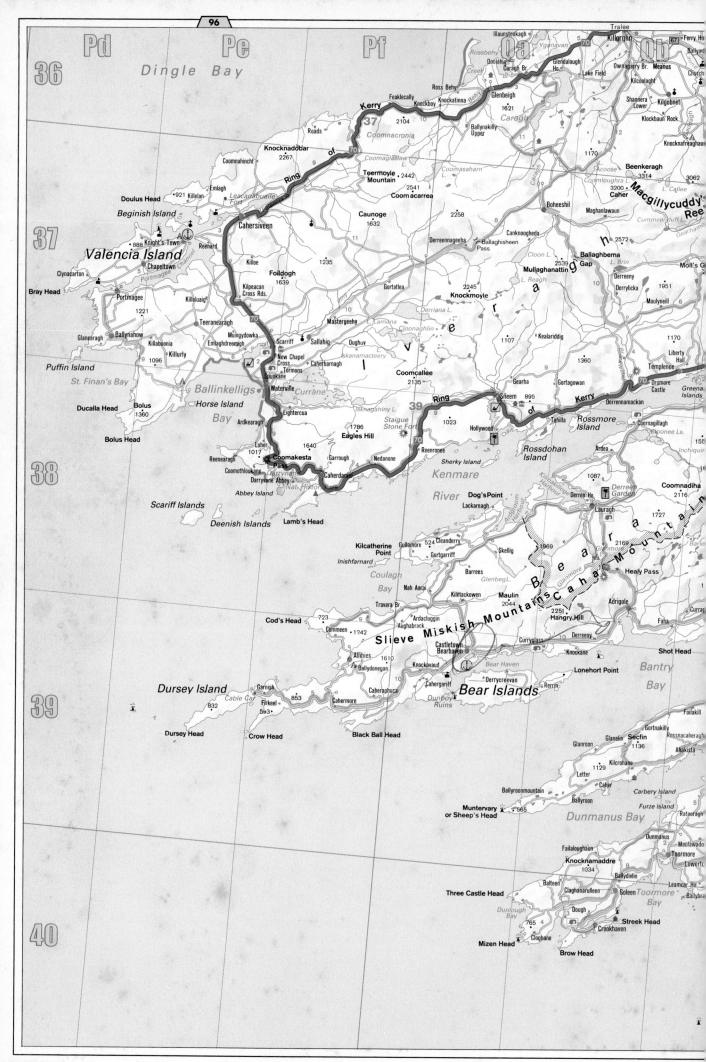

Dingle Bay

Pd **Pe** **Pf** **Oa** **Ob**

36

Tralee

Illaunstookagh

Killorglin 5 70 67 Ferry Br.
Rossbehy Yganavan Meanus
Doolahig Glandalough Ownagarry Br. Church
Ross Behy Caragh Br. Ho. Kilcoolaght
Feaklecally Knockboy Knockatinna Glenbeigh Lake Field Shannera Lower Kilgobnet
Knocknadobar Roads 2104 10 1621 Caragh Klockbaun Rock Knocknafreaghaun
Coomnacronia L.
Coomnahincht Coomaglaslaw Ballynakilly Upper 11 1170 Toacoose Beenkeragh
3314 3062
Kerry Teermoyle 2442 Coomasaharn L. Coomloughra L. 3200 Caher L. Callee
of Mountain 2541 Boheeshil Maghanlawaun Cummeenduff L. 3200 Macgillycuddy
Doulus Head 921 Killelan Coomacarrea 2258 Derreennageeha Canknoogheda Gearha Reeks
Emlagh Caunoge Ballaghisheen Cloon L. h 2572
Beginish Island Leacanabuaile 1632 Pass Ballaghbema
Fort Derreenageeha 2539 Gap Derreeny Moll's G
Cahersiveen Gortatlea Mullaghanattin g Derrylicka 1951
888 Knight's Town Reenard 1235 Knockmoyle 2245 L. Reagh a Maulyneill 6
Valencia Island Killoe Foildogh 1639 r 10
Chapeltown Kilpeacan 1107 Kealariddig 1360 1170
Clynacarton 5 Cross Rds. L. Lamona e Liberty
Portmagee Teeranearagh Mastergeehy Cloonaghlin L. 1360 Hall
Bray Head Killoluaig Muingydowka Oughuv v Templenoe
Glanearagh Ballynahow Emlaghdreenagh Scarriff Sallahig Caherbarnagh Coomcallee i Gearha Gortagowan 70 Dromore Greena
Killabuonia 7 New Chapel 2135 Srieem 895 of Castle Islands
Puffin Island Killurly 9 1096 6 2 Cross Tormons Hollywood Tahilla Kerry Derrennamackan
St. Finan's Bay Spunkane l Staigue Ring Rossmore 155
Ballinkelligs Waterville Currane Stone Fort 1023 Island Coornagillagh Inchiqui
Ducalla Head A Eightercua Isknagahiny L. 39 Ardea
Horse Island Bolus Ardkearagh 1786 1023 Rossdohan 1087
1360 Garrough Eagles Hill 870 Island Derreen Coomnadiha
Bolus Head Loher Coomakesta Nedanone Reenrooee 1727 Garden 2116
1017 Pass Caherdaniel Bleara 2169
Reeneragh Darrynane Sherky Island Kenmare 1969 Healy Pass
38 Coomothloukane Darrynane Abbey Dog's Point River Beara Mountains
Abbey Island Nat. History Park Lackareagh Derren Ho. Laragh Curra
Scariff Islands Kilcatherine Gullamore 524 Cleanderry b 2251 Hangry Hill Faha
Point Gortgarriff Skellig Glenmore Adrigole
Deenish Islands Lamb's Head Inishfarnard Barrees Slieve Miskish Mountains Cahac Mountain Shot Head
Coulagh Nah Aorai Glenbeg L. Maulin Derreeny Bantry
Bay Kilmackowen 2044 Bay
Cod's Head 723 Travara Br. Ardacluggin Castletown Curryglass 10 Knockane Lonehort Point
Cummeen 1242 Aughabrack Bearhaven Knockavaud Bear Haven Derrycreevan Rerrin
39 Allihies Knockavaud Cahergariff Derrycreevan Shot Head
1610 Caherphuca Dunpoy Bear Islands Caherphuca Ruins
Dursey Island Garnish Firkeel 853 5 Cahermore
Cable Car 832 593 Caheraphuca
Dursey Head Crow Head Black Ball Head Glanalin Secfin Rossnacaheragh
1136 Ahakista
40 Glanroon 1129 Kilcrohane
Letter Caher Carbery Island
Ballyroonmountain Ballyroon Furze Island
Muntervary 565 Knocknamaddre Dunmanus Maulawado
or Sheep's Head Failaloughaun 1034 Ballydivlin Toormore Lowerto
Goleen Toormore Leamcor Ho. Ballybra
Three Castle Head Balteen Claghanarulleen Bay
Dunlough Dough Streek Head
Bay 765 Crookhaven
Mizen Head Cloghane
Brow Head

Faha
Beaufort
Joe Castle
13
Barleymount
Aghacurreen
Mount Prospect Ho.
Rockfield Br.
Kilcummin Farmhill
Inchicorrigane
Anablaha
Gneeyguilla
Knocknagree
Knockduff
Mount Zephyr
11
Dromagh Castle
Coolclogh
Banteer
Knockaun
Mount Hillary
1288
Coolgarriv
67
KILLARNEY
CILL AIRNE
Knockmanagh
Scrahanaveal
Gullaun
Lissyconnor
Cullen
Lisnaboy
Meenskeha
Dernagree
Dromahoe
Drohane
72
41
Tincoora
Lyre
Woodford
Stone Circle
Spa Well
Lishabe
Rathmore
Lyredaowen
72
Coolanarney
Dooneens
Finnow Br.
Rathcool
Kilcorney
Killeen
Muingyroogen
Nad
Ross Castle
71
72
Barraduff
Knockanimrish
Beehenagh
Knockacappul
Inches
Rathduane Ho.
Spa Mount
Rathcool
Kilcorney
1073
Flesk Castle
Kiljuane
Drom
Gorthagane
Knocknaloman
Toorboney
Coolnagillagh
Lackdotia Ho.
Inchamay
Muckross Lake
Dromdiralough
Knockane
Gortacareen
Caherbarnagh
Kippagh
1486
Millstreet
Cloghboola
Adrivale
Inchamay
Purple Mountain
2739
Muckross House and Gardens
Glenflesk
The Paps
2273
Caherbarnagh
2239
1742
Boggeragh Mountains
Crohane
2162
Clydagh
Cloonkeen
Cummeenavrick
Glantane
2118
1625
Musherabeg
Carrigagulla
National Park
Mangerton Mountain
2756
Columnar Rocks
Poulgorm Br.
Cummeenduvasig
Gortnakilla
Mullaghanish
2133
Carriganimmy
Knocknagappul
Rylane Cross
Peakeen Mountain
East
1825
21
11
Milleeny
1671
Liscarrigane
Carraleigh
1096
Moanflugn Sch.
Ballynagree
Lacknahaghny
Gowlane
1278
Knockeens
1341
Coumaclovane
Bard Inch
Ballymakeery
Bawnatanaknoch
Cackanode
Garrane
1250
Bawnmore
Leadawillin
71
Kilfaddamore Ho.
Fuhiry
Coolea
869
Scronagare
Carrigaweigh
Garrane
Leades Ho.
Kilgarvan
Lackabaun
Derrytineen
Reananerree
Ballyvoge
Garrane
Bealnamoriye
Carrigacloodig Cross Rds.
Cleady
Letter
Glanlough
Carran
1986
Cahernacaha
Derrineanig
Aghacunna
Clonelud
MACROOM
MAIGH CHROMTHA
Kilmurry
Larchill Cross Rds.
Kilinardrish Ho.
Dromateuk
Curramore
Carran
2099
Carran
1776
Ballingeary
Turnaspidogy
Rossmore
Kilharry
Raleigh Ho.
64
Sleveen East
Ashton
Lehenagh
Shandangan Cross Rds.
1407
Letterdunane
Akinkeen
2280
1764
Gortafludig
L. Allua
64
Inchigeelagh
Derryvane
11
Moneyuesker
Annahatn
Toames
22
Kilmurry
Knockboy
2321
Coniger
1885
Gougane Barra Forest Park
The Pass of Keimaneigh
Doughill Mountain
1553
Bohanes Cross Rds.
Kilmiehael
Johnstown
Teerelton
Poulanargid
Lackareagh
947
Crookstown
Cork
25
1507
Ketra Cork
Sheny Mountains
Carrigarierk
1130
Knockaunnagorp
Slieveowen
Cappeen
Moneynacroha Cross Rds.
722
Quarry Cross Rds.
Glengarriff
1244
Illane
Maulavanig
Cahermuckee
1797
Tullugh
31
692
Slieveowen
Lissarourke
Newcetown
Farrannavane Ho.
Coomhola
64
Togher
Bandon
Behagh
Castletown
Scranahane Cross Rds.
65
Ardnagashel Ho.
Kealkill
Maughanaclea Hills
Breeny More
Ardrah
1424
Coomleagh
Derrynacaheragh
Toom
Clonamara
Enniskean
Murragh
Mt. Bernard
Reenadisert Court
Spave
Barnagowlane
1763
Dromdrasdil
Coolkellure
Behagh
Balteenbrack
Lissacroneen Cross Rds.
65
Ballineen
Cloonygorman
Mullaghmesha
1629
Glanbannoo Upper
Sillahertane
Dunmanway
35
65
Breaghna
Whiddy Island
Kilmore Lakes
5
Ardnamanagh Point
Barna Cross Rds.
1160
Moreagh
Ballynacarriga
Currabeg
711
Ballyvoige
13
Kilhessen Lo.
672
71
Beach Ho.
BANTRY
BEANNTRAÍ
Knocknaveagh
Trawiebane
Maunvough
Moyny
Shronacarton Cross Rds
987
Cloonkirgeen
Kilvurra
Ballingurteen
Kilmoyleane South
Curranvallihen Cross Rds.
Bantry House
71
Ardrah
Trawiebane
Drimoleague
65
Drinagh
Curraghalicky
Coolnaconarty
Knockmore
Rossmore
Gearagh
Ballinascarty
Clogagh
Kilmaloda Ho.
Gerahies
Coomkeen
734
Letterlicky Br.
65
Killeenleagh
Barna Cross Rds.
Derryclogh
Driminidy
Carrigbaun Cross Rds.
1031
Bealad Cross Rds.
Shannonvale
Durrus Court
Clashadoo
Ballycommane
978
Ballybane Ho.
Ballyourane
Bishops Village
457
CLONAKILTY
CLOICH na COILLTE
Nth. Ring
Aghafore
Durrus
Barnaghgeehy
990
Coosane
Rea Cross Rds.
Salvnure
311
Carrigeeny Cross Rds.
Mall Cross Rds.
Reanascreena
Sam's Cross Rds.
Woodfield
760
Inchydoney Island
Sth. Ring
Ballinglanna
Raheenroe
Rathruane
Fort View
Quakers Cross Rds.
Mount Gabriel
1339
Letter
Knockroe
Lissaclarig
Skeagli
Kilnaclasha
An Léim
71
Ross Carbery
412
Greenfield Ho.
Ardfield
Lehenagh
Clonakilty Bay
Tracking Station
Ballydehob
Kilcoe
Meen Br.
7
Hollybrook
Smórane
37
Glandore
565
Ballyviren Br.
Galley Head
Rossbrin
SKIBBEREEN
AN SCIOBAIRÍN
Kilnaclasha
Union Hall
Glandore Harbour
294
Donoure
Ballynoe
Skull
Seafort
Roaringwater
Cappaghglass
Kilkilleen
White Hall
Inishbeg
Creagh Gardens
Fookeen
Castletownshend
Myross
Rabbit Islands
Horse Island
Bay
Horse Island
Poulnacailee
652
534
Dooneen
Lickowen
Castle Island
Long Island
Lissamona
Ringarogy Island
Ardnagrena
Lough Hyne
Ballymacrown
Barloge
Horse Island
Hare Island
Calf Islands
Baltimore
435
Gokane Point
Teo Head
Kilmoon
Slievemore
Kedge Island
Sherkin Island
Ballyieragh
Cape Clear
Clear Island

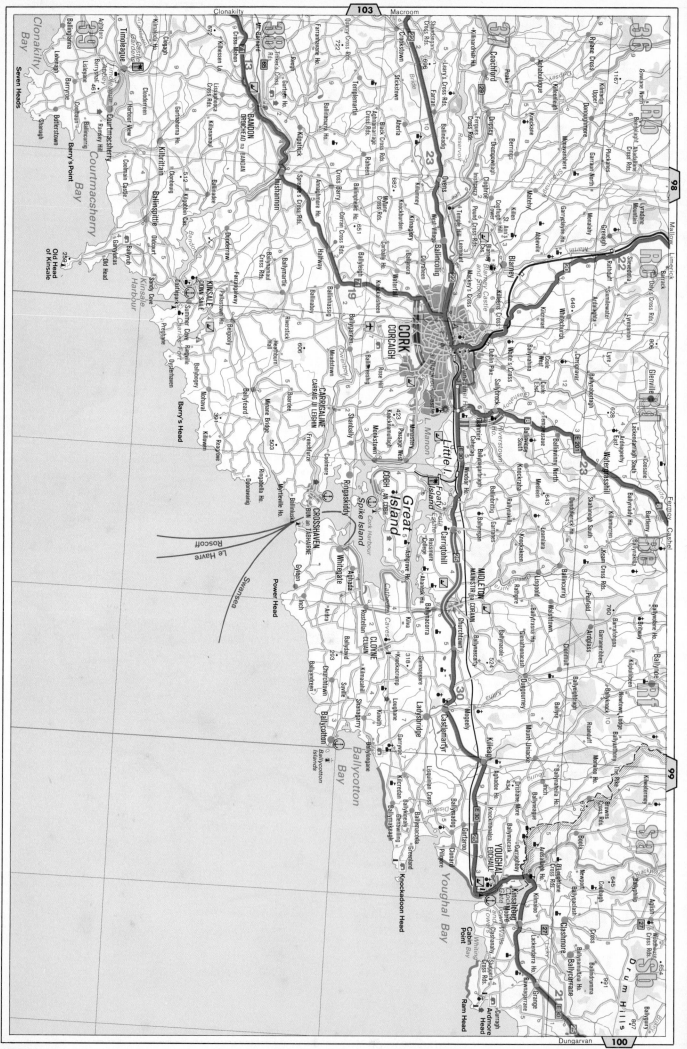

Ortsnamenverzeichnis · Index of place names · Index des localités
Register van plaatsnamen · Elenco dei nomi di località
Índice de topónimos · Stednavnsfortegnelse · Ortnamnsförteckning

Oxford	**GB**	(OXS)	62	Ye 38
Galway	**IRL**	(GAL)	92	Qf 29
①	②	③	④	⑤

	① Place name	② Country	③ County	④ Page number	⑤ Grid search reference
GB	Place name	Country	County	Page number	Grid search reference
D	Ortsname	Nationalität	Grafschaft	Seitenzahl	Suchfeldangabe
F	Localité	Nationalité	Comté	N° de page	Carreau
NL	Plaatsnaam	Nationaliteit	Graafschap	Nr. v. d. bladzijde	Zoekveld-gegevens
I	Località	Nazionalità	Contea	N° di pagina	Riquadro nel quale si trova il nome
E	Topónimo	Nacionalidad	Condado	Nro. de página	Datos casilla de localización
DK	Stednavn	Nationalitet	Grevskab	Sidetal	Kvadratangivelse
S	Ortnamn	Nationalitet	Grevskap	Sidnummer	Kartrutangivelse

② ③

GB	Großbritannien		
	und Nordirland		
	Great Britain		
	and Northern Ireland		
	Grande Bretagne		
	et Irelande du Nord		
	Groot-Brittanië		
	en Noord-Ierland		
	Gran Bretagna		
	e Irlanda Norte		
	Gran Bretaña		
	y Irlanda Norte		
	Storbritannien		
	og Nordirland		
	Storbritannien		
	och Nordirland		

			DEV	Devon		NRH	Northamptonshire
			DOS	Dorset		NTS	Nottinghamshire
			DOW	Down		ORK	Orkneys
			DSH	Derbyshire		OXS	Oxfordshire
			DUR	Durham		POW	Powys
			DYF	Dyfed		SFS	Staffordshire
			ESS	Essex		SGL	South Glamorgan
			ESX	East Sussex		SHL	Shetlands
			FER	Fermanagh		SHS	Shropshire
			FIF	Fife		SOM	Somerset
			GLS	Gloucestershire		SOY	South Yorkshire
			GRL	Greater London		STC	Strathdyde
			GRM	Greater Manchester		SUF	Suffolk
			GRP	Grampian		SUR	Surrey
			GWE	Gwent		TAW	Tyne and Wear
			GWY	Gwyn		TYR	Tyrone
			HAS	Hampshire		TYS	Tayside
			HGL	Highland		WGL	West Glamorgan
			HTS	Hertfordshire		WIL	Wiltshire
ANT	Antrim		HUS	Humberside		WMD	West Midlands
ARG	Armagh		HWC	Hereford and Worcester		WSX	West Sussex
AVN	Avon		IOW	Isle of Write		WWH	Warwickshire
BFS	Bedfordshire		KEN	Kent		WYO	West Yorkshire
BKS	Berkshire		LCS	Lancashire			
BOR	Borders		LDR	Londonderry			
BUS	Buckinghamshire		LEC	Leicester			
CBS	Cambridgeshire		LIN	Lincolnshire			
CEN	Central		LOT	Lothian			
CHS	Cheshire		MES	Merseyside		**GBA**	Alderney
CLE	Cleveland		MGL	Mid Glamorgan		**GBG**	Guernsey
CLW	Clywd		NHL	Northumberland		**GBJ**	Jersey
CNW	Cornwall		NOR	Norfolk		**GBM**	Isle of Man
CUB	Cumbria		NOY	North Yorkshire			
DAG	Dumfries and Galloway						

IRL	Irland
	Ireland
	Irlande
	Ierland
	Irlanda
CAV	Cavan
CLW	Carlow
COR	Cork
CRE	Clare
DON	Donegal
DUB	Dublin
GAL	Galway
KER	Kerry
KIL	Kildare
KLK	Kilkenny
LAO	Laois
LET	Leitrim
LGF	Longford
LIM	Limerick
LOT	Louth
MAY	Mayo
MOG	Monaghan
MT	Meath
OFF	Offaly
ROS	Roscommon
SLI	Sligo
TIP	Tipperary
WEX	Wexford
WKL	Wicklow
WMT	Westmeath
WTF	Waterford

A

Abbas Combe **GB** (SOM) 68 Xd 43
Abberley **GB** (HWC) 53 Xd 35
Abberton **GB** (ESS) 65 Af 38
Abberton **GB** (HWC) 53 Xf 35
Abbess Roding **GB** (ESS) 64 Ab 38
Abbeville **IRL** (COR) 104 Rc 37
Abbeville House **IRL** (TIP) 93 Rf 30
Abbey **IRL** (GAL) 93 Rd 30
Abbeycwmhir **GB** (POW) 51 Wd 35
Abbey Dore **GB** (HWC) 60 Xa 37
Abbeydorney **IRL** (KER) 97 Qb 34
Abbeyfeale **IRL** (LIM) 97 Qe 34
Abbeyland House **IRL** (GAL) 93 Rf 29
Abbeylara **IRL** (LGF) 89 Sd 26
Abbeyleix **IRL** (LAO) 94 Sd 31
Abbey Saint Bathans **GB** (BOR) 27 Xd 13
Abbeystead **GB** (LCS) 38 Xb 25
Abbeytown **GB** (CUB) 31 We 19
Abbey Village **GB** (LCS) 38 Xc 26
Abbeyville House **IRL** (GAL) 92 Rc 29
Abbotrule **GB** (BOR) 32 Xc 16
Abbots Ann **GB** (HAS) 69 Yc 41
Abbots Bromley **GB** (SFS) 45 Ya 32
Abbotsbury **GB** (DOS) 68 Xc 45
Abbotsham **GB** (DEV) 66 Ve 42
Abbotskerswell **GB** (DEV) 76 Wc 45
Abbots Langley **GB** (HTS) 63 Zd 38
Abbots Leigh **GB** (AVN) 61 Xc 40
Abbotsley **GB** (CBS) 55 Ze 35
Abbots Ripton **GB** (CBS) 55 Ze 34
Abdon **GB** (SHS) 52 Xc 34
Aber **GB** (DYF) 50 Ve 36
Aber **GB** (MGL) 60 Wc 39
Aberaeron **GB** (DYF) 50 Ve 35
Aberaman **GB** (MGL) 60 Wd 38
Aberangell **GB** (POW) 51 Wb 32
Aberarder **GB** (HGL) 20 Vd 7
Aberarder Ho **GB** (HGL) 15 Ve 5
Aberargie **GB** (TYS) 25 Wd 11
Aberarth **GB** (DYF) 50 Ve 35
Aberavon **GB** (WGL) 59 Wb 39
Aberbanc **GB** (DYF) 50 Vd 36
Aberbargoed **GB** (MGL) 60 We 38
Abercanaid **GB** (MGL) 60 Wd 38
Abercarn **GB** (GWE) 60 Wf 39
Abercastle **GB** (DYF) 58 Uf 37
Abercegir **GB** (POW) 51 Wb 33
Aberchalder **GB** (HGL) 14 Vb 6
Aberchirder **GB** (GRP) 17 Xc 3
Abercraf **GB** (POW) 59 Wb 38
Abercrombie **GB** (FIF) 26 Xb 11
Abercych **GB** (DYF) 50 Vc 36
Abercynon **GB** (MGL) 60 Wd 39
Abercywarch **GB** (GWY) 51 Wb 32
Aberdar = Aberdare **GB** (MGL) 60 Wd 38
Aberdare **GB** (MGL) 60 Wd 38
Aberdaron **GB** (GWY) 42 Vb 32
Aberdeen **GB** (GRP) 17 Xf 6
Aberdour **GB** (FIF) 26 We 12
Aberdyfi **GB** (GWY) 51 Vf 33
Aberedw **GB** (POW) 51 Wd 36
Abererch **GB** (GWY) 42 Vd 31
Aberfan **GB** (MGL) 60 Wd 38
Aberfeldy **GB** (TYS) 21 Wa 9
Aberffraw **GB** (GWY) 42 Vd 29
Aberford **GB** (WYO) 40 Yd 26
Aberfoyle **GB** (CEN) 24 Vd 11
Abergavenny **GB** (GWE) 60 Wf 38
Abergele **GB** (CLW) 43 Wc 29
Abergiar **GB** (DYF) 50 Ve 36
Abergorlech **GB** (DYF) 59 Vf 37
Abergwesyn **GB** (POW) 51 Wb 36
Abergwili **GB** (DYF) 59 Ve 37
Abergwydol **GB** (POW) 51 Wb 33
Abergwynant **GB** (GWY) 51 Wa 32
Abergwynfi **GB** (WGL) 60 Wc 39
Abergwyngregyn **GB** (GWY) 43 Vf 29
Abergynolwyn **GB** (GWY) 51 Wa 33
Aberhosan **GB** (POW) 51 Wb 33
Aberkenfig **GB** (MGL) 60 Wc 39
Aberlady **GB** (LOT) 26 Xa 12
Aberlemno **GB** (TYS) 22 Xb 8
Aberllefenni **GB** (GWY) 51 Wb 32
Abermeurig **GB** (DYF) 50 Vf 35
Abermule **GB** (POW) 52 We 33
Abernant **GB** (DYF) 59 Vd 37
Aber-nant **GB** (MGL) 60 Wd 38
Abernethy **GB** (TYS) 21 We 10
Abernyte **GB** (TYS) 21 We 10
Aber pergwm **GB** (WGL) 60 Wc 38
Aberporth **GB** (DYF) 50 Vc 36
Aberscir **GB** (POW) 60 Wd 37
Abersoch **GB** (GWY) 42 Vd 32
Abersychan **GB** (GWE) 60 Wf 38
Abertawe = Swansea **GB** (WGL) 59 Wa 39
Abertillery **GB** (GWE) 60 Wf 38
Abertridwr **GB** (MGL) 60 We 39
Abertridwr **GB** (POW) 43 Wd 32
Abertysswg **GB** (MGL) 60 We 38
Aberuthven **GB** (TYS) 21 Wc 11
Aber Village **GB** (POW) 60 We 37
Aberystwyth **GB** (DYF) 51 Vf 34
Abingdon **GB** (OXS) 62 Ye 38
Abinger Common **GB** (SUR) 71 Zd 41
Abington **GB** (STC) 31 Wb 16
Abington **IRL** (LIM) 99 Rd 33
Ab Kettleby **GB** (LEC) 46 Za 32
Ablington **GB** (GLS) 62 Ya 38
Abney **GB** (DSH) 45 Yb 29
Aboyne **GB** (GRP) 16 Xb 6
Abram **GB** (GRM) 38 Xc 27
Abriachan **GB** (HGL) 15 Vd 4
Abridge **GB** (ESS) 64 Aa 39
Abson **GB** (AVN) 61 Xd 40
Abthorpe **GB** (NRH) 54 Yf 36
Acaster Malbis **GB** (NOY) 40 Yf 25
Acaster Selby **GB** (NOY) 40 Yf 25
Accrington **GB** (LCS) 38 Xd 26
Acha **GB** (STC) 18 Tc 9
Achabraid **GB** (STC) 23 Ud 13
Achachork **GB** (HGL) 13 Te 4
Achadacaie **GB** (STC) 23 Ud 14
Achahoish **GB** (STC) 23 Uc 13
Achamore **GB** (STC) 23 Ua 13
Achanalt **GB** (HGL) 14 Va 3
Achandunie **GB** (HGL) 8 Ve 2
Achaphubuil **GB** (HGL) 19 Uf 7
Acharacle **GB** (HGL) 19 Ub 8
Achargary **GB** (HGL) 5 Ve 118
Acharn **GB** (TYS) 20 Vf 9
Achath **GB** (GRP) 17 Xd 5
Achavanich **GB** (HGL) 9 Wd 118
Achduart **GB** (HGL) 7 Ue 1
Achentoul **GB** (HGL) 9 Wa 119
Achfary **GB** (HGL) 8 Va 119
Achgarve **GB** (HGL) 7 Uc 1
Achiemore **GB** (HGL) 4 Vb 117
Achiemore **GB** (HGL) 5 Wa 118
A'Chill **GB** (HGL) 12 Tc 6
Achill Sound **IRL** (MAY) 86 Qa 25
Achiltibuie **GB** (HGL) 7 Ud 120
Achina **GB** (HGL) 5 Ve 117
Achinduin **GB** (STC) 19 Ub 10
Achingills **GB** (HGL) 6 Wd 117
Achintee **GB** (HGL) 14 Ud 4
Achintraid **GB** (HGL) 13 Uc 4
Achlean **GB** (HGL) 15 Wa 6
Achleck **GB** (STC) 18 Te 9
Achluachrach **GB** (HGL) 20 Vb 7
Achmelvich **GB** (HGL) 7 Ue 119
Achmore **GB** (CEN) 20 Ve 10
Achmore **GB** (HGL) 11 Tc 119
Achmore **GB** (HGL) 13 Uc 4
Achnacarnin **GB** (HGL) 7 Ue 119
Achnacloich **GB** (HGL) 13 Ua 6
Achnacroish **GB** (STC) 19 Ud 9
Achnadrish **GB** (STC) 18 Tf 9
Achnagarron **GB** (HGL) 8 Ve 2
Achnaha **GB** (HGL) 18 Tf 8
Achnahanat **GB** (HGL) 8 Vc 1
Achnairn **GB** (HGL) 8 Vd 120
Achnamara **GB** (STC) 23 Uc 12
Achnasaul **GB** (HGL) 19 Uf 7
Achnasheen **GB** (HGL) 14 Uf 3
Achonry **IRL** (MAY) 87 Rc 24
Achosnich **GB** (HGL) 18 Te 8
Achreamie **GB** (HGL) 5 Wb 117
Achriesgill **GB** (HGL) 4 Va 118
Achurch **GB** (NRH) 55 Zd 34
Achuvoldrach **GB** (HGL) 5 Vd 118
Achvaich **GB** (HGL) 8 Vf 1
Ackergill **GB** (HGL) 6 Wf 118
Acklam **GB** (CLE) 36 Ye 21
Acklam **GB** (NOY) 40 Zb 24
Ackle Back **IRL** (DON) 82 Rd 21
Ackleton **GB** (SHS) 53 Xd 34
Acklington **GB** (NHL) 33 Yc 17
Ackton **GB** (WYO) 40 Yd 26
Ackworth Moor Top **GB** (WYO) 40 Yd 27
Aclare **IRL** (SLI) 87 Ra 24
Aclare Lodge **IRL** (MT) 90 Tc 25
Acle **GB** (NOR) 49 Bd 33
Acock's Green **GB** (WMD) 53 Yb 34
Acol **GB** (KEN) 65 Bb 40
Acomb **GB** (NHL) 33 Xf 19
Aconbury **GB** (HWC) 61 Xb 37
Acre **GB** (LCS) 39 Xe 26
Acrefair **GB** (CLW) 44 Wf 31
Acton **GB** (CHS) 44 Xc 30
Acton **GB** (SHS) 52 Wf 34
Acton **GB** (SUF) 56 Ae 36
Acton Beauchamp **GB** (HWC) 52 Xd 36
Acton Bridge **GB** (CHS) 44 Xc 29
Acton Burnell **GB** (SHS) 52 Xb 33
Acton Green **GB** (HWC) 52 Xd 36
Acton Pigott **GB** (SHS) 52 Xb 33
Acton Round **GB** (SHS) 52 Xc 33
Acton Scott **GB** (SHS) 52 Xb 33
Acton Trussell **GB** (SFS) 45 Xf 32
Adamstown **IRL** (WEX) 101 Tb 34
Adamstown **IRL** (WMT) 89 Sc 28
Adamstown **IRL** (WTF) 100 Se 35
Adare **IRL** (LIM) 98 Rb 33
Adbaston **GB** (SFS) 45 Xd 31
Adderbury **GB** (OXS) 54 Ye 36
Adderley **GB** (SHS) 44 Xc 31
Adderstone **GB** (NHL) 27 Yb 15
Addingham **GB** (WYO) 39 Ya 25
Addington **GB** (GRL) 64 Zf 40
Addington **GB** (KEN) 64 Ac 41
Addlestone **GB** (SUR) 63 Zc 40
Addlethorpe **GB** (LIN) 48 Zf 29
Adel **GB** (WYO) 39 Yc 25
Adfa **GB** (POW) 51 Wd 33
Adforton **GB** (HWC) 52 Xa 35
Adisham **GB** (KEN) 65 Bb 41
Adlermaston **GB** (BKS) 63 Yf 40
Adlestrop **GB** (GLS) 62 Yc 37
Adlingfleet **GB** (HUS) 40 Zb 26
Adlington **GB** (CHS) 45 Xf 29
Adlington **GB** (LCS) 38 Xc 27
Admaston **GB** (SFS) 45 Ya 32
Admaston **GB** (SHS) 52 Xc 32
Admington **GB** (WWH) 53 Yb 36
Adrigole **IRL** (COR) 102 Qb 38
Adrivale **IRL** (COR) 98 Qf 36
Adsborough **GB** (SOM) 67 Wf 42
Adstock **GB** (BUS) 63 Za 37
Adstone **GB** (NRH) 54 Yf 36
Adversane **GB** (WSX) 71 Zd 43
Advie **GB** (HGL) 16 Wd 4
Adwell **GB** (OXS) 63 Za 38
Adwick le Street **GB** (SOY) 40 Ye 27
Adwick upon Dearne **GB** (SOY) 40 Ye 27
Ae **GB** (DAG) 31 Wc 17
Affleck **GB** (GRP) 17 Xe 5
Affpuddle **GB** (DOS) 68 Xe 44
Afon-wen **GB** (CLW) 43 We 29
Agall **IRL** (OFF) 94 Sc 29
Agglethorpe **GB** (NOY) 36 Ya 23
Aghaboe **IRL** (LAO) 94 Sc 31
Aghabog **IRL** (MOG) 83 Sf 24
Aghaboy **IRL** (LGF) 89 Sb 26
Aghabullogue **IRL** (COR) 104 Rb 37
Aghacony **IRL** (CAV) 89 Sd 25
Aghacunna **IRL** (COR) 103 Qf 37
Aghacurreen **IRL** (KER) 97 Qc 36
Aghadoe House **IRL** (COR) 104 Sa 37
Aghadoon **IRL** (MAY) 80 Pf 23
Aghadowey **GB** (LDR) 79 Tc 18
Aghafore **IRL** (COR) 103 Rb 39
Aghagower **IRL** (MAY) 87 Qd 26
Aghalee **GB** (ANT) 84 Te 21
Aghaloory **IRL** (CAV) 89 Sd 25
Aghamore **IRL** (LET) 88 Sa 25
Aghamore **IRL** (MAY) 87 Rb 26
Aghamore **IRL** (WMT) 89 Sf 28
Aghamuck **IRL** (ROS) 88 Rf 26
Aghancon **IRL** (OFF) 93 Sb 30
Aghareagh House **IRL** (LGF) 88 Sa 26
Agharroo **IRL** (LET) 82 Re 22
Aghavas **IRL** (LET) 89 Sb 25
'Aghawinnaun **IRL** (CRE) 92 Qf 30
Aghcross **IRL** (LAO) 94 Sf 31
Agher **IRL** (MT) 90 Tb 28
Agher Cross Roads **IRL** (MT) 90 Tb 28
Aghern **IRL** (COR) 99 Rf 36
Aghlattacru **IRL** (MOG) 90 Tb 25
Aghleam **IRL** (MAY) 80 Pf 24
Aghnacliff **IRL** (LGF) 89 Sc 25
Aghnafarcan **IRL** (MOG) 90 Tb 24
Aghnagap **IRL** (MOG) 84 Ta 23
Aghnalaly **IRL** (LAO) 94 Se 30
Aghnaleck **GB** (DOW) 85 Ua 22
Aghnamarrage Cross Roads **IRL** (COR) 104 Rb 38
Aghnameadle House **IRL** (OFF) 93 Sa 31
Aghnaskeagh **IRL** (LOT) 90 Td 24
Aghoney **IRL** (LAO) 94 Se 31
Aghoo **IRL** (SLI) 82 Re 24
Aglish **IRL** (CRE) 92 Ra 31
Aglish **IRL** (TIP) 93 Rf 30
Aglish **IRL** (WTF) 99 Sb 36
Agricultural College **IRL** (TIP) 93 Rf 30
Ahadallane Cross Roads **IRL** (COR) 98 Rb 36
Ahakista **IRL** (COR) 102 Qc 39
Ahanesk House **IRL** (COR) 104 Re 37
Ahaphuca Bridge **IRL** (COR) 99 Rd 35
Aharney **IRL** (OFF) 94 Sc 29
Ahascragh **IRL** (GAL) 88 Rd 28
Ahenny **IRL** (TIP) 100 Sd 34
Aherla **IRL** (COR) 104 Rb 37
Ahoghill **GB** (ANT) 79 Td 19
Aigburth **GB** (MES) 44 Xa 28
Aighe **IRL** (DON) 82 Rd 20
Aignish **GB** (HGL) 11 Te 119
Aike **GB** (HUS) 41 Zd 25
Aiketgate **GB** (CUB) 35 Xb 20
Aikton **GB** (CUB) 31 Wf 19
Ailey **GB** (HWC) 52 Xa 36
Aillroc Beg **IRL** (CRE) 98 Qe 33
Ailsworth **GB** (CBS) 55 Zd 33
Ainderby Quernhow **GB** (NOY) 36 Yd 23
Ainderby Steeple **GB** (NOY) 36 Yd 23
Aingers Green **GB** (ESS) 65 Ba 37
Ainsdale **GB** (MES) 38 Wf 27
Ainstable **GB** (CUB) 35 Xb 20
Ainsworth **GB** (GRM) 39 Xd 27
Aintree **GB** (MES) 38 Xa 28
Aird **GB** (HGL) 11 Tf 119
Aird **GB** (STC) 23 Uc 12
Aird Dell **GB** (HGL) 11 Te 118
Aird of Sleat **GB** (HGL) 13 Ua 6
Airdrie **GB** (STC) 25 Wa 13
Aird Tunga **GB** (HGL) 11 Te 119
Aird Uig **GB** (HGL) 11 Sf 119
Airmyn **GB** (HUS) 40 Za 26
Airntully **GB** (TYS) 21 Wd 9
Airor **GB** (HGL) 13 Ub 6
Airth **GB** (CEN) 25 Wb 12
Airton **GB** (NOY) 39 Xf 24
Aiskew **GB** (NOY) 36 Yc 23
Aislaby **GB** (NOY) 37 Zb 22
Aislaby **GB** (NOY) 37 Zb 23
Aith **GB** (ORK) 5 Xc 114
Aith **GB** (SHL) 2 Yd 107
Aitnoch **GB** (GRP) 15 Wb 4
Akeld **GB** (NHL) 27 Xf 15
Akeley **GB** (BUS) 54 Za 36
Alberbury **GB** (SHS) 52 Xa 32
Albourne **GB** (WSX) 71 Ze 43
Albrighton **GB** (SHS) 44 Xb 32
Albrighton **GB** (SHS) 53 Xe 34
Albury **GB** (HTS) 63 Zc 38
Albury **GB** (HTS) 64 Aa 37
Albury Shere **GB** (SUR) 71 Zd 41
Alby Hill **GB** (NOR) 49 Bb 31
Alcaig **GB** (HGL) 15 Vd 3
Alcaston **GB** (SHS) 52 Xb 34
Alcester **GB** (WWH) 53 Ya 35
Alconbury **GB** (CBS) 55 Ze 34
Alconbury Weston **GB** (CBS) 55 Ze 34
Aldborough **GB** (NOY) 40 Yd 24
Aldbourne **GB** (WIL) 62 Yc 40
Aldbrough **GB** (HUS) 41 Zf 26
Aldbrough Saint John **GB** (NOY) 36 Yb 22
Aldclune **GB** (TYS) 21 Wb 8
Aldeburgh **GB** (SUF) 57 Bd 36
Aldeby **GB** (NOR) 57 Bd 34
Alderbury **GB** (WIL) 69 Yb 42
Aldergrove **GB** (ANT) 84 Te 21
Alderley **GB** (GLS) 61 Xd 39
Alderley Edge **GB** (CHS) 45 Xe 29
Aldermaston Wharf **GB** (BKS) 63 Yf 40
Alderminster **GB** (WWH) 53 Yc 36
Aldershot **GB** (WIL) 70 Zb 41
Alderton **GB** (GLS) 62 Ya 36
Alderton **GB** (NRH) 54 Za 36
Alderton **GB** (SHS) 44 Xb 32
Alderton **GB** (SUF) 57 Bc 36
Alderton **GB** (WIL) 61 Xe 39
Alderwasley **GB** (DSH) 45 Yc 30
Aldfield **GB** (NOY) 39 Yc 24
Aldford **GB** (CHS) 44 Xa 30
Aldham **GB** (ESS) 65 Ae 37
Aldham **GB** (SUF) 57 Af 36
Aldingham **GB** (CUB) 38 Wf 24
Aldington **GB** (KEN) 72 Af 42
Aldochlay **GB** (STC) 24 Vc 12
Aldreth **GB** (CBS) 56 Aa 34
Aldridge **GB** (WMD) 53 Ya 33
Aldringham **GB** (SUF) 57 Bd 35
Aldsworth **GB** (GLS) 62 Yb 38
Aldville **GB** (TYS) 21 Wc 9
Aldwark **GB** (DSH) 45 Yc 30
Aldwark **GB** (NOY) 40 Ye 24
Aldwick **GB** (WSX) 70 Zb 44
Aldwincle **GB** (NRH) 55 Zc 34
Aldworth **GB** (BKS) 63 Ye 39
Aleandillure **IRL** (GAL) 91 Qc 29
Alexandria **GB** (STC) 24 Vc 13
Alfardisworthy **GB** (DEV) 66 Vd 43
Alfington **GB** (DEV) 67 We 44
Alford **GB** (GRP) 17 Xb 5
Alford **GB** (LIN) 47 Zf 29
Alford **GB** (SOM) 68 Xc 42
Alford **GB** (SUR) 71 Zc 42
Alford Crossways **GB** (SUR) 71 Zc 42
Alfreton **GB** (DSH) 46 Yc 30
Alfrick **GB** (HWC) 53 Xd 35
Alfriston **GB** (ESX) 71 Aa 44
Aline Lodge **GB** (HGL) 11 Tb 120
Alkborough **GB** (HUS) 40 Zc 26
Alkerton **GB** (OXS) 54 Yd 36
Alkham **GB** (KEN) 73 Ba 42
Alkington **GB** (SHS) 44 Xb 31
Alkmonton **GB** (DSH) 45 Yb 31
Allagesh **IRL** (MOG) 83 Sf 23
Allanaquoich **GB** (GRP) 16 Wd 6
Allanton **GB** (BOR) 27 Xe 14
Allanton **GB** (DAG) 31 Wb 18
Allanton **GB** (STC) 25 Wa 14
All Cannings **GB** (WIL) 62 Ya 40
Allen **IRL** (KIL) 94 Ta 29
Allendale Town **GB** (NHL) 32 Xe 19
Allenheads **GB** (NHL) 35 Xe 20
Allens Green **GB** (HTS) 64 Aa 38
Allensmore **GB** (HWC) 61 Xb 36
Allenwood **IRL** (KIL) 94 Ta 29
Allenwood Cross Roads **IRL** (KIL) 94 Ta 29
Aller **GB** (SOM) 68 Xa 42
Allerby **GB** (CUB) 34 Wd 20
Allerford **GB** (DEV) 66 Ve 45
Allerford **GB** (SOM) 67 Wc 41
Allerston **GB** (NOY) 37 Zc 23
Allerthorpe **GB** (HUS) 40 Zb 25
Allerton **GB** (MES) 44 Xa 28
Allerton Bywater **GB** (WYO) 40 Yd 26
Allesley **GB** (WMD) 53 Yc 34
Allestree **GB** (DSH) 46 Yd 31
Allexton **GB** (LEC) 54 Zb 33
Allgreave **GB** (CHS) 45 Xf 29
Allhallows **GB** (KEN) 65 Ad 40
Alligin Shuas **GB** (HGL) 13 Uc 3
Allihies **IRL** (COR) 102 Pf 39
Allimore Green **GB** (SFS) 45 Xe 32
Allington **GB** (LIN) 46 Zb 31
Allington **GB** (WIL) 69 Yb 42
Allithwaite **GB** (CUB) 35 Xa 23
Allnabad **GB** (HGL) 8 Vc 118
Alloa **GB** (CEN) 25 Wb 12
Allonby **GB** (CUB) 34 Wd 20
Alloon Lower **IRL** (GAL) 88 Rd 28
Alloway **GB** (STC) 30 Vc 16
Allscot **GB** (SHS) 53 Xd 34
All Stretton **GB** (SHS) 52 Xb 33
Alltforgan **GB** (POW) 43 Wc 32
Alltmawr **GB** (POW) 51 Wd 36
Alltnacaillich **GB** (HGL) 8 Vc 118
Alltwalis **GB** (DYF) 59 Ve 37
Alltwen **GB** (WGL) 59 Wb 38
Alltyblaca **GB** (DYF) 50 Vf 36
Almeley **GB** (HWC) 52 Xa 36
Almer **GB** (DOS) 69 Xf 44
Almington **GB** (SFS) 44 Xd 31
Almiston Cross **GB** (DEV) 66 Vd 43
Almondbank **GB** (TYS) 21 Wc 10
Almondbury **GB** (WYO) 39 Yb 27
Almondsbury **GB** (AVN) 61 Xc 39
Alne **GB** (NOY) 40 Ye 24
Alness **GB** (HGL) 8 Ve 2
Alnham **GB** (NHL) 33 Xf 16
Alnmouth **GB** (NHL) 33 Yc 16
Alnwick **GB** (NHL) 33 Yb 16
Alpheton **GB** (SUF) 56 Ae 36
Alphington **GB** (DEV) 67 Wc 44
Alpington **GB** (NOR) 57 Bc 33
Alpraham **GB** (CHS) 44 Xc 30
Alresford **GB** (ESS) 65 Ba 37
Alrewas **GB** (SFS) 45 Yb 32
Alsager **GB** (CHS) 45 Xe 30
Alsagers Bank **GB** (SFS) 45 Xe 30
Alston **GB** (CUB) 35 Xd 20
Alstone **GB** (GLS) 62 Xf 37
Alstonefield **GB** (SFS) 45 Yb 30
Alswear **GB** (DEV) 67 Wb 43
Altadush **IRL** (DON) 77 Sa 19
Altagowlan **IRL** (LET) 82 Rf 24
Altandhu **GB** (HGL) 7 Ud 120
Altarnun **GB** (CNW) 75 Vc 45
Altass **GB** (HGL) 8 Vc 1
Alterwall **GB** (HGL) 6 We 117
Altgaltraig **GB** (STC) 24 Uf 13
Altham **GB** (LCS) 38 Xd 26
Althorne **GB** (ESS) 65 Ae 39
Altnafeadh **GB** (HGL) 20 Va 8
Altnaharra **GB** (HGL) 8 Vd 119
Altnapaste **IRL** (DON) 77 Sa 20
Altofts **GB** (WYO) 40 Yd 26
Alton **GB** (DSH) 46 Yd 29
Alton **GB** (HAS) 70 Za 42
Alton **GB** (SFS) 45 Ya 31
Alton Pancras **GB** (DOS) 68 Xd 44
Alton Priors **GB** (WIL) 62 Ya 40
Altrincham **GB** (GRM) 45 Xd 28
Alt Upper **IRL** (DON) 83 Sc 20
Alva **GB** (CEN) 25 Wb 12
Alvanley **GB** (CHS) 44 Xb 29
Alvaston **GB** (DSH) 46 Yd 31
Alvechurch **GB** (HWC) 53 Ya 34
Alvecote **GB** (WWH) 53 Yc 33
Alvediston **GB** (WIL) 69 Xf 42
Alverdiscott **GB** (DEV) 66 Vf 42
Alverstone **GB** (IOW) 70 Ye 45
Alverton **GB** (NTS) 46 Zb 31
Alves **GB** (GRP) 16 Wd 3
Alvescot **GB** (OXS) 62 Yc 38
Alveston **GB** (AVN) 61 Xc 39
Alveston **GB** (WWH) 53 Yc 35
Alvie **GB** (HGL) 15 Wa 6
Alvingham **GB** (LIN) 41 Aa 28
Alvington **GB** (GLS) 61 Xc 38
Alwalton **GB** (CBS) 55 Ze 33
Alweston **GB** (DOS) 68 Xd 43
Alwinton **GB** (NHL) 33 Xf 16
Alyth **GB** (TYS) 21 We 9
Amatnatua **GB** (HGL) 8 Vc 1
Ambergate **GB** (DSH) 46 Yd 30
Amber Hill **GB** (LIN) 47 Zf 30
Amberley **GB** (GLS) 61 Xe 38
Amberley **GB** (WSX) 71 Zc 43
Amble-by-the-Sea **GB** (NHL) 33 Yc 17
Ambleside **GB** (CUB) 35 Xa 22
Ambleston **GB** (DYF) 58 Va 37
Ambrosden **GB** (OXS) 63 Yf 37
Ambrosetown **IRL** (WEX) 101 Tb 35
Amcotts **GB** (HUS) 40 Zb 27
Amersham **GB** (BUS) 63 Zc 38
Amesbury **GB** (WIL) 69 Yb 41
Amhuinnsuidhe **GB** (HGL) 11 Ta 1
Amisfield **GB** (DAG) 31 Wc 18
Amlwch **GB** (GWY) 42 Vd 28
Amlwch Port **GB** (GWY) 42 Vd 28
Ammanford **GB** (DYF) 59 Wa 38
Amotherby **GB** (NOY) 37 Za 24
Ampfield **GB** (HAS) 69 Yd 42
Ampleforth **GB** (NOY) 37 Yf 23
Ampleforth College **GB** (NOY) 37 Yf 23
Ampney Crucis **GB** (GLS) 62 Ya 38
Ampney Saint Peter **GB** (GLS) 62 Ya 38
Ampthill **GB** (BFS) 55 Zd 36
Ampton **GB** (SUF) 56 Ae 35
Amroth **GB** (DYF) 58 Vc 38
Amulree **GB** (TYS) 21 Wb 9
Anablaha **IRL** (KER) 97 Qd 36
Anaheilt **GB** (HGL) 19 Uc 8
Anascaul **IRL** (KER) 97 Pf 36
An Cabhán = Cavan **IRL** (CAV) 89 Sd 25
An Caisleán Nua = Newcastle West **IRL** (LIM) 98 Qf 34
Ancaster **GB** (LIN) 47 Zc 31
An Chathair = Caher **IRL** (TIP) 99 Sa 34
Anchor **GB** (SHS) 52 We 34
An Cnoc **GB** (HGL) 11 Te 119
Ancroft **GB** (NHL) 27 Xf 14
Ancrum **GB** (BOR) 32 Xc 15
Anderson **GB** (DOS) 69 Xf 44
Anderton **GB** (CHS) 44 Xc 29
Andover **GB** (HAS) 69 Yd 41
Andover Down **GB** (HAS) 69 Yd 41
Andoversford **GB** (GLS) 62 Ya 37
Andreas **GBM** 29 Vd 22
Angarrack **GB** (CNW) 74 Ud 47
An Geata Mór **IRL** (MAY) 80 Pf 23
Angersleigh **GB** (SOM) 67 Wf 43
Angle **GB** (DYF) 58 Uf 38
Angmering **GB** (WSX) 71 Zd 44
Angus, Douglas and **GB** (TYS) 22 Xa 10
Aninver **IRL** (DON) 77 Re 18
Anlaby **GB** (HUS) 41 Zd 26
An Leim **IRL** (COR) 103 Qf 39
An Longfort = Longford **IRL** (LGF) 88 Sb 26
Anlore **IRL** (MOG) 83 Se 23
Anmer **GB** (NOR) 48 Ad 32
Annacarriga **IRL** (CRE) 93 Rd 31
Annacloy **GB** (DOW) 85 Ub 22
Annacurragh **IRL** (WKL) 95 Td 31
Annagap **IRL** (KER) 97 Pf 36
Annagary **IRL** (DON) 77 Re 18
Annagassan **IRL** (LOT) 90 Td 25
Annagbrack **IRL** (OFF) 94 Sc 29
Annagh **IRL** (GAL) 93 Rd 28
Annagh **IRL** (KER) 97 Qb 35
Annagharnet House **IRL** (CAV) 89 Sf 25
Annaghbeg House **IRL** (TIP) 93 Re 31
Annagh Cross **IRL** (CRE) 91 Qd 32
Annaghdown **IRL** (GAL) 87 Qf 28
Annaghdown House **IRL** (GAL) 87 Qf 28
Annagh House **IRL** (TIP) 93 Sa 30
Annagh Monastery **IRL** (GAL) 87 Rb 28
Annaghmore **IRL** (LET) 88 Sb 25
Annaghmore **IRL** (LGF) 88 Sa 27
Annaghmore House **IRL** (COR) 104 Rc 38
Annaghmore House **IRL** (OFF) 94 Sc 29
Annaghroe Bridge **IRL** (MOG) 84 Ta 22
Annagleve **IRL** (MOG) 90 Tb 24
Annahatn **IRL** (COR) 103 Qf 37
Annahilt **GB** (DOW) 85 Ua 22
Annalittin **IRL** (MOG) 90 Tb 24
Annalong **GB** (DOW) 91 Ua 24
Annamoe **IRL** (WKL) 95 Te 30
Annan **GB** (DAG) 31 We 19
An Nás = Naas **IRL** (KIL) 95 Tb 29
Annaside **GB** (CUB) 34 Wd 23
Annat **GB** (HGL) 14 Uc 3
Annat **GB** (STC) 19 Ue 10
Annayalla **IRL** (MOG) 84 Tb 24
Annbank **GB** (STC) 30 Vc 16
Annegrove Abbey **IRL** (LAO) 94 Sd 31
Annesbrook **IRL** (MT) 89 Ta 26
Annesbrook or Loughanmore **IRL** (MT) 90 Td 27
Annesley **GB** (NTS) 46 Ye 30
Annesley Woodhouse **GB** (NTS) 46 Ye 30
Annestown **IRL** (WTF) 100 Se 36
Anneville House **IRL** (WMT) 89 Sd 28
Annfield **IRL** (DUB) 95 Td 28
Annfield **IRL** (TIP) 93 Sa 32
Annfield Plain **GB** (DUR) 33 Yb 19
Annochie **GB** (GRP) 17 Xf 4
Annscroft **GB** (SHS) 52 Xb 33
Annsfort **IRL** (TIP) 99 Sb 34
Ansford **GB** (SOM) 68 Xc 42
Ansley **GB** (WWH) 53 Yc 33
Anslow **GB** (SFS) 45 Yb 32
Anslow Gate **GB** (SFS) 45 Yb 32
Anstey **GB** (LEC) 54 Ye 32
Anston **GB** (SOY) 46 Ye 28
An Straidbhaile = Stradbally **IRL** (LAO) 94 Sf 30
Anstruther **GB** (FIF) 26 Xb 11
Ansty **GB** (DOS) 68 Xe 43
Ansty **GB** (WIL) 69 Xf 42
Ansty **GB** (WSX) 71 Zf 43
Ansty **GB** (WWH) 54 Yd 34
An tAonach = Nenach **IRL** (TIP) 93 Re 31
An Teampall Mór = Templemore **IRL** (TIP) 93 Sa 32
Anthill Common **GB** (HAS) 70 Yf 43
Anthorn **GB** (CUB) 31 We 19
An tInbhear Mór = Arklow **IRL** (WKL) 95 Tf 32
Antingham **GB** (NOR) 49 Bc 31
Antony **GB** (CNW) 75 Ve 46
Antrim **GB** (ANT) 84 Te 20
Antrobus **GB** (CHS) 44 Xc 29
An Tulach = Tullow **IRL** (CLW) 95 Tb 32
An Uaimh = Navan **IRL** (MT) 90 Tb 27
Anvil Corner **GB** (DEV) 66 Ve 44
Anwick **GB** (LIN) 47 Zd 30
Anwoth **GB** (DAG) 30 Ve 19
Aoradh **GB** (STC) 22 Td 14
Apes Hall **GB** (CBS) 56 Ab 40
Apethorpe **GB** (NRH) 55 Zd 33
Aphort **IRL** (DON) 77 Rc 19
Apley **GB** (LIN) 47 Zd 29
Apperknowle **GB** (DSH) 46 Yd 29
Appin **GB** (STC) 19 Ud 9
Appin House **GB** (STC) 19 Ud 9
Appleby **GB** (HUS) 41 Zc 27
Appleby-in-Westmorland **GB** (CUB) 35 Xd 21
Appleby Magna **GB** (LEC) 54 Yc 32
Appleby Parva **GB** (LEC) 54 Yc 32
Appleby Street **GB** (HTS) 64 Ab 38
Applecross **GB** (HGL) 13 Ub 4
Applecross House **GB** (HGL) 13 Ub 4
Appledore **GB** (DEV) 66 Ve 42
Appledore **GB** (DEV) 67 We 43
Appledore **GB** (KEN) 72 Ae 42
Appledore Heath **GB** (KEN) 72 Ae 42
Appleford **GB** (OXS) 62 Ye 39
Appleshaw **GB** (HAS) 69 Yc 41
Applethwaite **GB** (CUB) 34 Wf 21
Appleton **GB** (OXS) 62 Yd 38
Appleton-le-Moors **GB** (NOY) 37 Za 23
Appleton-le-Street **GB** (NOY) 37 Za 24
Appleton Roebuck **GB** (NOY) 40 Ye 25
Appleton Thorn **GB** (CHS) 44 Xc 28
Appleton Wiske **GB** (NOY) 36 Yd 22
Appletreehall **GB** (BOR) 32 Xb 16
Appletreewick **GB** (NOY) 39 Ya 24
Appley Bridge **GB** (LCS) 38 Xb 27
Apse Heath **GB** (IOW) 70 Ye 45
Apuldram **GB** (WSX) 70 Zb 44
Arabella **GB** (HGL) 8 Vf 2
Araglin **IRL** (COR) 99 Rf 35
Arbirlot **GB** (TYS) 22 Xc 9
Arboll **GB** (HGL) 9 Wa 2
Arborfield **GB** (BKS) 63 Za 40
Arborfield Garrison **GB** (BKS) 63 Za 40
Arbourhill House **IRL** (TIP) 93 Sa 30
Arbroath **GB** (TYS) 22 Xc 9
Arbuthnott **GB** (GRP) 22 Xe 7
Archiestown **GB** (GRP) 16 We 4
Archintree House **GB** (HGL) 19 Uf 8
Arclid Green **GB** (CHS) 45 Xe 30
Ardacheranmor **GB** (STC) 24 Ue 12
Ardacluggin **IRL** (COR) 102 Qa 38
Ardagh **IRL** (LGF) 89 Sb 26
Ardagh **IRL** (LIM) 98 Qf 34
Ardagh **IRL** (LOT) 90 Td 26
Ardagh **IRL** (MT) 90 Tb 25
Ardaghy **IRL** (LOT) 90 Te 24
Ardaghy **IRL** (MOG) 84 Ta 23
Ardalaghta **IRL** (COR) 98 Rc 36
Ardalanish **GB** (STC) 18 Te 11
Ardamine House **IRL** (WEX) 101 Te 33
Ardamore **IRL** (KER) 96 Pd 35
Ardan **IRL** (OFF) 94 Sd 29
Ardanairy **IRL** (WKL) 95 Tf 31
Ardanew **IRL** (MT) 89 Ta 28
Ardanragh **IRL** (LGF) 89 Sc 27
Ardara **IRL** (DON) 82 Rd 20
Ardarroch **GB** (HGL) 13 Uc 4
Ardattin **IRL** (CLW) 95 Tb 32
Ardbeg **GB** (STC) 23 Tf 15
Ardcanny Rectory **IRL** (LIM) 98 Rb 33
Ardcath **IRL** (MT) 90 Td 27
Ardcharnich **GB** (HGL) 7 Uf 1
Ardchiavaig **GB** (STC) 18 Te 11
Ardchullarie More **GB** (CEN) 20 Ve 11
Ardchyle **GB** (CEN) 20 Vd 10
Ardcrony **IRL** (TIP) 93 Rf 31
Ardderry Lough **IRL** (GAL) 86 Qd 28
Arddleen **GB** (POW) 52 Wf 32
Ardea **IRL** (KER) 102 Qb 38
Ardechive **GB** (HGL) 14 Uf 7
Ardee **IRL** (LOT) 90 Tc 25
Ardeley **GB** (HTS) 64 Zf 37
Ardelve **GB** (HGL) 14 Uc 5
Arden **GB** (STC) 24 Vc 12
Ardenagh **IRL** (WEX) 101 Tb 35
Ardentinny **GB** (STC) 24 Va 12
Arderra **IRL** (KLK) 100 Se 35
Ardersier **GB** (HGL) 15 Vf 3
Ardessie **GB** (HGL) 7 Ue 1
Ardfern **GB** (STC) 23 Uc 11
Ardfert **IRL** (KER) 97 Qb 35
Ardfield **IRL** (COR) 103 Ra 39
Ardfinnan **IRL** (TIP) 99 Sa 35
Ardgartan **GB** (STC) 24 Vb 11
Ardgay **GB** (HGL) 8 Vd 1
Ardglass **GB** (DOW) 85 Uc 23
Ardglass **IRL** (COR) 98 Rb 35
Ardglass **IRL** (COR) 99 Rf 36
Ardhasaig **GB** (HGL) 11 Ta 1
Ardheslaig **GB** (HGL) 13 Ub 3
Ardindrean **GB** (HGL) 7 Uf 1
Ardingly **GB** (WSX) 71 Zf 42
Ardington **GB** (OXS) 62 Yd 39
Ardivachar **GB** (HGL) 12 Sd 4
Ardkearagh **IRL** (KER) 102 Pe 38
Ardkeen **GB** (DOW) 85 Uc 22
Ardlair **GB** (GRP) 16 Xb 4
Ardled **IRL** (LAO) 94 Sd 31
Ardleigh **GB** (ESS) 65 Af 37
Ardler **GB** (TYS) 21 We 9
Ardley **GB** (OXS) 62 Ye 37
Ardlougher **IRL** (CAV) 89 Sc 24
Ardlui **GB** (STC) 20 Vb 11
Ardlussa **GB** (STC) 23 Ub 12
Ardmaddy Castle **GB** (STC) 19 Uc 11
Ardmaghbreague **IRL** (MT) 90 Ta 26
Ardmair **GB** (HGL) 7 Ue 1
Ardmaleish **GB** (STC) 24 Uf 13
Ardmay **GB** (STC) 24 Vb 11
Ardminish **GB** (STC) 23 Ub 14
Ardmolich **GB** (HGL) 19 Ub 8
Ardmorney **IRL** (WMT) 94 Sd 28
Ardnacross **GB** (HGL) 18 Ua 9
Ardnadam **GB** (STC) 24 Va 13
Ardnagashel House **IRL** (COR) 103 Qd 38
Ardnageehy East **IRL** (COR) 99 Rd 36
Ardnaglass **IRL** (DON) 77 Sc 20
Ardnagreevagh **IRL** (GAL) 86 Pf 27
Ardnagrena **IRL** (COR) 103 Qd 40
Ardnaree **IRL** (DON) 77 Sc 18
Ardnasillagh **IRL** (GAL) 87 Qe 28
Ardnasodan **IRL** (GAL) 87 Rb 28
Ardnastang **GB** (HGL) 19 Uc 8
Ardnave **GB** (STC) 22 Td 13
Ardoch **GB** (TYS) 21 Wd 9
Ardochy House **GB** (HGL) 14 Va 6
Ardogelly **IRL** (SLI) 82 Rb 23
Ardonagh Cross Roads **IRL** (WMT) 89 Sd 27
Ardoughter **IRL** (KER) 97 Qb 34
Ardpatrick **GB** (STC) 23 Uc 14
Ardpatrick **IRL** (LIM) 98 Rc 34
Ardpeaton **GB** (STC) 24 Va 12
Ardra **IRL** (COR) 104 Rf 38
Ardrah **IRL** (COR) 103 Qd 38
Ardrah **IRL** (COR) 103 Qd 39
Ardrahan **IRL** (GAL) 92 Rb 30
Ardress **GB** (ARG) 84 Tc 22
Ardrishaig **GB** (STC) 23 Ud 12
Ardroil **GB** (HGL) 11 Sf 119
Ardrossan **GB** (STC) 24 Vb 15
Ardsallagh House **IRL** (MT) 90 Tc 27
Ardsallagh House **IRL** (WTF) 104 Sa 37
Ardshealach **GB** (HGL) 19 Ub 8
Ardsley **GB** (SOY) 40 Yd 27
Ardsley East **GB** (WYO) 39 Yc 26
Ardslignish **GB** (HGL) 18 Ua 8
Ardsoreen **IRL** (SLI) 88 Rd 25
Ardstraw **GB** (TYR) 83 Sd 20
Ardtalnaig **GB** (TYS) 20 Vf 9
Ardtoe **GB** (HGL) 18 Ua 8
Ardtrea **GB** (TYR) 84 Tb 21
Ardtrostan **GB** (TYS) 20 Vf 10
Ardtully **IRL** (LOT) 90 Te 25
Arduaine **GB** (STC) 23 Uc 11
Ardullie **GB** (HGL) 15 Vd 3
Ardvasar **GB** (HGL) 13 Ua 6
Ardvey **GB** (HGL) 11 Ta 1
Ardvey **GB** (HGL) 11 Ta 2
Ardvorlich **GB** (TYS) 20 Ve 10
Ardvourlie **GB** (HGL) 11 Tb 1
Ardwell **GB** (DAG) 28 Va 20
Ardywanig **IRL** (KER) 97 Qb 36
Areley Kings **GB** (HWC) 53 Xe 34
Argoed **GB** (GWE) 60 We 38
Arichonan **GB** (STC) 23 Uc 12
Aridhglas **GB** (STC) 18 Td 11
Arileod **GB** (STC) 18 Tc 9
Arinacrinachd **GB** (HGL) 13 Ub 3
Arinagour **GB** (STC) 18 Tc 9
Arisaig **GB** (HGL) 19 Ua 7
Arivruaich **GB** (HGL) 11 Tc 120
Arkendale **GB** (NOY) 40 Yd 24
Arkesden **GB** (ESS) 56 Aa 37
Arkholme **GB** (LCS) 35 Xc 24
Arkley **GB** (GRL) 64 Ze 39
Arklow **IRL** (WKL) 95 Tf 32
Arksey **GB** (SOY) 40 Yf 27
Arkwright Town **GB** (DSH) 46 Yd 29
Arleedon **GB** (CUB) 34 Wc 21
Arlesey **GB** (BFS) 55 Ze 36
Arless **IRL** (LAO) 94 Sf 31
Arley **GB** (CHS) 44 Xd 29
Arley **GB** (WWH) 53 Yc 33
Arlingham **GB** (GLS) 61 Xd 38
Arlington **GB** (DEV) 66 Wa 42
Arlington **GB** (ESX) 71 Ab 43
Arlington **GB** (GLS) 62 Ya 38
Armadale **GB** (HGL) 5 Vf 117
Armadale **GB** (LOT) 25 Wb 13
Armagh **GB** (ARG) 84 Tc 22
Armathwaite **GB** (CUB) 35 Xb 20
Arminghall **GB** (NOR) 57 Bb 33
Armitage **GB** (SFS) 45 Ya 32
Armoy **GB** (ANT) 79 Te 18
Armston **GB** (NRH) 55 Zd 34

106 GB IRL Abbas Combe – Armston

Armthorpe **GB** (SOY) 40 Yf 27
Arnabost **GB** (STC) 18 Tc 9
Arncliffe **GB** (NOY) 36 Xf 24
Arncott **GB** (OXS) 63 Yf 37
Arncroach **GB** (FIF) 26 Xb 11
Arne **GB** (DOS) 69 Xf 44
Arnesby **GB** (LEC) 54 Yf 33
Arnestown House **IRL** (WEX) 100 Ta 34
Arney **GB** (FER) 83 Sb 23
Arngomerie **GB** (CEN) 25 Ve 12
Arnisdale **GB** (HGL) 13 Uc 6
Arnish **GB** (HGL) 13 Ua 4
Arniston Engine **GB** (LOT) 26 Wf 13
Arnol **GB** (HGL) 11 Tc 118
Arnold **GB** (NTS) 46 Yf 31
Arnprior **GB** (CEN) 25 Ve 12
Arnside **GB** (CUB) 35 Xb 23
Aros Mains **GB** (STC) 18 Ua 9
Arrad Foot **GB** (CUB) 34 Wf 23
Arram **GB** (HUS) 41 Zd 25
Arrathorne **GB** (NOY) 36 Yb 22
Arreton **GB** (IOW) 70 Ye 44
Arrochar **GB** (STC) 24 Vb 11
Arrow **GB** (WWH) 53 Ya 35
Arryheernabin **IRL** (DON) 77 Sc 17
Artafallie **GB** (HGL) 15 Ve 3
Artane **IRL** (DUB) 95 Te 28
Arthington **GB** (WYO) 39 Yc 25
Arthingworth **GB** (NRH) 54 Za 34
Arthog **GB** (GWY) 51 Vf 32
Arthrath **GB** (GRP) 17 Xf 4
Arthurstown House **IRL** (LOT) 90 Tc 25
Artonagh House **IRL** (CAV) 89 Sf 24
Artrochie **GB** (GRP) 17 Ya 4
Aruadh **GB** (STC) 22 Td 14
Arundel **GB** (WSX) 71 Zc 43
Arvagh **IRL** (CAV) 89 Sc 25
Aryhoulan **GB** (HGL) 19 Ue 8
Asby **GB** (CUB) 34 Wc 21
Ascog **GB** (STC) 24 Uf 14
Ascot **GB** (BKS) 63 Zb 40
Ascott **GB** (WWH) 54 Yc 36
Ascott-under-Wychwood **GB** (OXS) 62 Yc 37
Asenby **GB** (NOY) 36 Yd 23
Asfold Crossways **GB** (WSX) 71 Ze 42
Asfordby **GB** (LEC) 46 Za 32
Asfordby Hill **GB** (LEC) 46 Za 32
Asgarby **GB** (LIN) 47 Zd 31
Ash **GB** (DEV) 66 Vf 43
Ash **GB** (KEN) 64 Ab 40
Ash **GB** (KEN) 65 Bb 41
Ash **GB** (SUR) 70 Zb 41
Ashampstead **GB** (BKS) 63 Ye 40
Ashbocking **GB** (SUF) 57 Bb 36
Ashbourne **GB** (DSH) 45 Yb 30
Ashbourne **IRL** (MT) 90 Td 27
Ashbrittle **GB** (SOM) 67 Wd 43
Ashbrook **IRL** (DON) 82 Re 22
Ashburton **GB** (DEV) 76 Wb 45
Ashbury **GB** (OXS) 62 Yc 39
Ashbury House **IRL** (TIP) 93 Sb 31
Ashby **GB** (LIN) 47 Aa 29
Ashby cum Fenby **GB** (HUS) 41 Zf 28
Ashby de la Launde **GB** (LIN) 47 Zd 30
Ashby-de-la-Zouch **GB** (LEC) 46 Yd 32
Ashby Folville **GB** (LEC) 46 Za 32
Ashby Magna **GB** (LEC) 54 Ye 33
Ashby Parva **GB** (LEC) 54 Ye 34
Ashby Puerorum **GB** (LIN) 47 Zf 29
Ashby Saint Ledgers **GB** (NRH) 54 Yf 35
Ashchurch **GB** (GLS) 61 Xf 36
Ashcombe **GB** (DEV) 76 Wc 45
Ashcott **GB** (SOM) 68 Xb 42
Ashdon **GB** (ESS) 56 Ab 36
Ashe **GB** (HAS) 70 Ye 41
Asheldham **GB** (ESS) 65 Af 38
Ashenden **GB** (KEN) 72 Ae 42
Ashendon **GB** (BUS) 63 Za 38
Ashfield **GB** (CEN) 25 Wa 11
Ashfield **GB** (SUF) 57 Bb 35
Ash Field **IRL** (MT) 89 Ta 25
Ashfield Green **GB** (SUF) 57 Bb 35
Ashford **GB** (DEV) 66 Vf 42
Ashford **GB** (DEV) 76 Wa 47
Ashford **GB** (HAS) 69 Yb 43
Ashford **GB** (KEN) 72 Af 42
Ashford **GB** (SUR) 63 Zd 40
Ashford **IRL** (NIR) 84 Ta 23
Ashford Carbonell **GB** (SHS) 52 Xb 35
Ashford Hill **GB** (HAS) 63 Ye 40
Ashford in the Water **GB** (DSH) 45 Yb 29
Ashgrove House **IRL** (COR) 104 Re 37
Ashgrove House **IRL** (OFF) 93 Rf 29
Ashgrove House **IRL** (TIP) 99 Rf 34
Ashhill **IRL** (TIP) 99 Sb 33
Ashill **GB** (NOR) 56 Ae 33
Ashill **GB** (SOM) 68 Xa 43
Ashingdon **GB** (ESS) 65 Ae 39
Ashington **GB** (NHL) 33 Yc 17
Ashington **GB** (SOM) 68 Xc 43
Ashington **GB** (WSX) 71 Zd 43
Ashkirk **GB** (BOR) 32 Xa 16
Ashley **GB** (CBS) 56 Ac 35
Ashley **GB** (CHS) 45 Xd 28
Ashley **GB** (DEV) 66 Wa 43
Ashley **GB** (GLS) 61 Xf 39
Ashley **GB** (HAS) 69 Yd 42
Ashley **GB** (NRH) 54 Zb 33
Ashley **GB** (SFS) 45 Xd 31
Ashley Green **GB** (BUS) 63 Zc 38
Ashley Heath **GB** (DOS) 69 Yb 43
Ash Magna **GB** (SHS) 44 Xc 31
Ashmansworth **GB** (HAS) 62 Yd 41
Ashmansworthy **GB** (DEV) 66 Vd 43
Ash Mill **GB** (DEV) 67 Wb 43
Ashmore **GB** (DOS) 69 Xf 43
Ashow **GB** (WWH) 54 Yc 34
Ash Park **IRL** (TIP) 93 Sa 32
Ashperton **GB** (HWC) 52 Xc 36
Ashprington **GB** (DEV) 76 Wc 46
Ashreigney **GB** (DEV) 66 Wa 43
Ash Thomas **GB** (DEV) 67 Wd 43
Ashton **GB** (CHS) 44 Xb 29
Ashton **GB** (CNW) 74 Ud 48
Ashton **GB** (CNW) 75 Ve 46
Ashton **GB** (HWC) 52 Xb 34
Ashton **GB** (HWC) 52 Xb 35
Ashton **GB** (NRH) 54 Za 36
Ashton **GB** (NRH) 55 Zd 34
Ashton **IRL** (COR) 103 Ra 37
Ashton Common **GB** (WIL) 61 Xf 41
Ashton-in-Makerfield **GB** (GRM) 38 Xc 28
Ashton Keynes **GB** (WIL) 62 Ya 39
Ashton under Hill **GB** (HWC) 53 Xf 36
Ashton-under-Lyne **GB** (GRM) 39 Xf 28
Ashtown **IRL** (WKL) 95 Te 30
Ashurst **GB** (HAS) 69 Yc 43
Ashurst **GB** (KEN) 71 Aa 42
Ashurst **GB** (WSX) 71 Ze 43
Ashurst Wood **GB** (ESX) 71 Aa 42
Ash Vale **GB** (SUR) 70 Zb 41
Ashville **IRL** (LOT) 90 Tc 26
Ashwater **GB** (DEV) 66 Ve 44
Ashwell **GB** (HTS) 55 Zf 36
Ashwell **GB** (LEC) 46 Zb 32
Ashwellthorpe **GB** (NOR) 57 Ba 33
Ashwicken **GB** (NOR) 48 Ad 32
Askam in Furness **GB** (CUB) 34 We 23
Askeaton **IRL** (LIM) 98 Ra 33
Askern **GB** (SOY) 40 Yf 27
Askernish House **GB** (HGL) 12 Sd 5
Askerswell **GB** (DOS) 68 Xb 44
Askett **GB** (BUS) 63 Zb 38
Askham **GB** (CUB) 35 Xb 21
Askham **GB** (NTS) 46 Za 29
Askham Bryan **GB** (NOY) 40 Yf 25
Askham Richard **GB** (NOY) 40 Ye 25
Askill **IRL** (LET) 82 Re 22
Askillaan **IRL** (MAY) 86 Qa 26
Askintarney **IRL** (WEX) 100 Tb 34
Askintinny **IRL** (WKL) 95 Tf 32
Asknish **GB** (STC) 23 Ue 12
Askrigg **GB** (NOY) 36 Xf 23
Askwith **GB** (NOY) 39 Yb 25
Aslacaton **GB** (NOR) 57 Ba 34
Aslackby **GB** (LIN) 47 Zd 31
Aslockton **GB** (NTS) 46 Za 31
Aspatria **GB** (CUB) 34 Wd 20
Aspley Guise **GB** (BFS) 55 Zc 36
Aspull **GB** (GRM) 38 Xc 27
Asselby **GB** (HUS) 40 Za 26
Assington **GB** (SUF) 56 Ae 36
Astbury **GB** (CHS) 45 Xe 30
Astcote **GB** (NRH) 54 Yf 35
Astee **IRL** (KER) 97 Qc 33
Asterley **GB** (SHS) 52 Xa 33
Asterton **GB** (SHS) 52 Xa 33
Asthall **GB** (OXS) 62 Yc 38
Asthall Leigh **GB** (OXS) 62 Yc 38
Astley **GB** (HWC) 53 Xe 35
Astley **GB** (SHS) 44 Xb 32
Astley **GB** (WWH) 54 Yc 33
Astley Abbots **GB** (SHS) 52 Xd 33
Astley Cross **GB** (HWC) 53 Xe 35
Astley Green **GB** (GRM) 38 Xd 28
Aston **GB** (CHS) 44 Xc 29
Aston **GB** (CHS) 44 Xc 30
Aston **GB** (DSH) 45 Yb 28
Aston **GB** (OXS) 62 Yc 38
Aston **GB** (SFS) 45 Xd 31
Aston **GB** (SHS) 44 Xb 31
Aston **GB** (SHS) 52 Xc 32
Aston **GB** (SOY) 46 Ye 28
Aston **GB** (WMD) 53 Ya 34
Aston Abbotts **GB** (BUS) 63 Zb 37
Aston Botterell **GB** (SHS) 52 Xc 34
Aston-by-Stone **GB** (SFS) 45 Xf 31
Aston Cantlow **GB** (WWH) 53 Yb 35
Aston Clinton **GB** (BUS) 63 Zb 38
Aston Crews **GB** (HWC) 61 Xd 37
Aston Cross **GB** (GLS) 61 Xf 36
Aston End **GB** (HTS) 64 Zf 37
Aston Eyre **GB** (SHS) 52 Xc 33
Aston Flamville **GB** (LEC) 54 Ye 33
Aston Ingham **GB** (HWC) 61 Xd 37
Aston juxta Mondrum **GB** (CHS) 44 Xc 30
Aston le Walls **GB** (NRH) 54 Ye 36
Aston Magna **GB** (GLS) 53 Yb 36
Aston on Clun **GB** (SHS) 52 Xa 34
Aston-on-Trent **GB** (DSH) 46 Yd 31
Aston Sandford **GB** (BUS) 63 Za 38
Aston Somerville **GB** (HWC) 53 Ya 36
Aston Subedge **GB** (GLS) 53 Yb 36
Aston Upthorpe **GB** (OXS) 63 Ye 39
Astwick **GB** (BFS) 55 Ze 36
Astwood **GB** (BUS) 55 Zc 36
Astwood Bank **GB** (HWC) 53 Ya 35
Atcham **GB** (SHS) 52 Xb 32
Athaleenta **IRL** (COR) 98 Rc 36
Athboy **IRL** (MT) 89 Ta 27
Athdown **IRL** (WKL) 95 Td 29
Athea **IRL** (LIM) 98 Qe 34
Athelington **GB** (SUF) 57 Bb 35
Athelney **GB** (SOM) 68 Xa 42
Athelstaneford **GB** (LOT) 26 Xb 13
Athenry **IRL** (GAL) 92 Rb 29
Atherington **GB** (DEV) 66 Vf 43
Atherstone **GB** (WWH) 54 Yc 33
Atherstone on Stour **GB** (WWH) 53 Yb 36
Atherton **GB** (GRM) 38 Xd 27
Athgarvan **IRL** (KIL) 95 Tb 30
Athgoe **IRL** (DUB) 95 Tc 29
Athlacca **IRL** (LIM) 98 Rc 34
Athleague **IRL** (ROS) 88 Re 27
Athlone **IRL** (WMT) 88 Sa 28
Athnid **IRL** (TIP) 93 Sb 32
Athy **IRL** (KIL) 94 Ta 31
Atlow **GB** (DSH) 45 Yc 30
Atshanboe **IRL** (TIP) 99 Sa 32
Attadale **GB** (HGL) 14 Ud 4
Attavally **IRL** (MAY) 80 Qb 24
Attimuchugh **IRL** (MAY) 87 Qf 24
Attiregan **IRL** (GAL) 93 Rd 28
Attirory House **IRL** (ROS) 93 Rf 28
Attleborough **GB** (NOR) 57 Ba 33
Attlebridge **GB** (NOR) 49 Ba 32
Attykit **IRL** (TIP) 99 Sa 34
Attymass **IRL** (MAY) 87 Qf 24
Attymon **IRL** (GAL) 92 Rc 29
Atwick **GB** (HUS) 41 Ze 25
Atworth **GB** (WIL) 61 Xe 40
Aubourn **GB** (LIN) 47 Zc 30
Auburn **IRL** (WMT) 88 Sa 27
Auburn House **IRL** (SLI) 82 Rd 23
Auchagallon **GB** (STC) 23 Ud 15
Auchallater **GB** (GRP) 16 Wd 7
Aucharnie **GB** (GRP) 17 Xc 4
Auchattie **GB** (GRP) 17 Xc 6
Auchenblae **GB** (GRP) 22 Xd 7
Auchenbrack **GB** (DAG) 31 Wa 17
Auchenbreck **GB** (STC) 24 Uf 13
Auchencairn **GB** (DAG) 29 Wa 19
Auchencarroch **GB** (STC) 24 Vc 12
Auchencrow **GB** (BOR) 27 Xe 13
Auchengray **GB** (STC) 25 Wc 14
Auchenhalrig **GB** (GRP) 16 Wf 3
Auchenheath **GB** (STC) 25 Wa 14
Auchenmalg **GB** (DAG) 29 Vb 19
Auchenrivock **GB** (DAG) 32 Xa 18
Auchentiber **GB** (STC) 24 Vc 14
Auchgourish **GB** (HGL) 15 Wb 5
Auchindrain **GB** (STC) 24 Ue 11
Auchindrean **GB** (HGL) 7 Uf 2
Auchininna **GB** (GRP) 17 Xc 3
Auchinleck **GB** (STC) 30 Ve 16
Auchinloch **GB** (STC) 25 Vf 13
Auchlee **GB** (GRP) 17 Xe 6
Auchleven **GB** (GRP) 17 Xc 5
Auchlochan **GB** (STC) 25 Wa 15
Auchlunies **GB** (GRP) 17 Xe 6
Auchlyne **GB** (CEN) 20 Vd 10
Auchmacoy **GB** (GRP) 17 Xf 4
Auchmillan **GB** (STC) 30 Vd 15
Auchmithie **GB** (TYS) 22 Xc 9
Auchmuirbridge **GB** (FIF) 21 We 11
Auchnacree **GB** (TYS) 22 Xa 8
Auchnagallin **GB** (HGL) 16 Wc 4
Auchnagatt **GB** (GRP) 17 Xf 4
Auchterarder **GB** (TYS) 25 Wb 11
Auchterderran **GB** (FIF) 26 We 12
Auchterhouse **GB** (TYS) 21 Wf 9
Auchtermuchty **GB** (FIF) 21 We 11
Auchterneed **GB** (HGL) 15 Vc 3
Auchtertool **GB** (FIF) 26 We 12
Auchtubh **GB** (CEN) 20 Vd 10
Auckengill **GB** (HGL) 6 Wf 117
Auckley **GB** (SOY) 40 Yf 27
Aucloggeen **IRL** (GAL) 87 Ra 28
Audenshaw **GB** (GRM) 39 Xf 28
Audlem **GB** (CHS) 44 Xc 31
Audley **GB** (SFS) 45 Xe 30
Auds **GB** (GRP) 17 Xc 2
Aughabrack **IRL** (COR) 102 Qa 38
Aughacasla **IRL** (KER) 97 Qa 35
Aughagault **IRL** (DON) 77 Sb 19
Aughathlappa **IRL** (WEX) 101 Tb 33
Augher **GB** (TYR) 83 Se 22
Aughils **IRL** (KER) 97 Qa 36
Aughnacloy **GB** (TYR) 84 Ta 22
Aughnasheelan **IRL** (LET) 88 Sa 24
Aughran Castle **IRL** (GAL) 88 Re 27
Aughrim **IRL** (CRE) 92 Ra 30
Aughrim **IRL** (GAL) 93 Re 29
Aughrim **IRL** (WKL) 95 Te 31
Aughrus More **IRL** (GAL) 86 Pe 27
Aughshemus Bridge **IRL** (WTF) 100 Sd 35
Aughton **GB** (HUS) 40 Za 25
Aughton **GB** (LCS) 38 Xa 27
Aughton **GB** (LCS) 38 Xb 24
Aughton **GB** (SOY) 46 Ye 28
Aught Upper **IRL** (DON) 78 Se 18
Aughvaneen **IRL** (TIP) 100 Sd 34
Auldearn **GB** (HGL) 15 Wb 3
Aulden **GB** (HWC) 52 Xb 35
Auldhame **GB** (LOT) 26 Xc 12
Auldhouse **GB** (STC) 25 Ve 14
Ault a'Chruinn **GB** (HGL) 14 Ud 5
Aultbea **GB** (HGL) 7 Uc 1
Aultgrishan **GB** (HGL) 7 Ub 2
Aultguish Inn **GB** (HGL) 8 Vb 2
Ault Hucknall **GB** (DSH) 46 Ye 29
Aultmore **GB** (GRP) 16 Xa 3
Aulton **GB** (GRP) 17 Xc 4
Aultvoulin **GB** (HGL) 13 Ub 6
Aundorach **GB** (HGL) 15 Wb 5
Aunk **GB** (DEV) 67 Wd 44
Aunsby **GB** (LIN) 47 Zd 31
Auquhorthies **GB** (GRP) 17 Xe 4
Aust **GB** (AVN) 61 Xc 39
Austerfield **GB** (SOY) 40 Yf 28
Austrey **GB** (WWH) 53 Yc 33
Austwick **GB** (NOY) 38 Xd 24
Authorpe **GB** (LIN) 47 Aa 29
Authorpe Row **GB** (LIN) 48 Zf 29
Avebury **GB** (WIL) 62 Ya 40
Aveley **GB** (ESS) 64 Ab 40
Avening **GB** (GLS) 61 Xe 38
Averham **GB** (NTS) 46 Za 30
Aveton Gifford **GB** (DEV) 76 Wb 47
Aviemore **GB** (HGL) 15 Wb 5
Avington **GB** (BKS) 62 Yd 40
Avoca **IRL** (WKL) 95 Te 31
Avoch **GB** (HGL) 15 Ve 3
Avon **GB** (HAS) 69 Yb 44
Avonbridge **GB** (CEN) 25 Wb 13
Avon Castle **GB** (DOS) 69 Yb 44
Avonmouth **GB** (AVN) 61 Xb 40
Avonwick **GB** (DEV) 76 Wb 46
Awbridge **GB** (HAS) 69 Yc 42
Awkley **GB** (AVN) 61 Xc 39
Awliscombe **GB** (DEV) 67 We 44
Awre **GB** (GLS) 61 Xd 38
Awsworth **GB** (NTS) 46 Ye 31
Axbridge **GB** (SOM) 68 Xb 41
Axford **GB** (HAS) 70 Yf 41
Axford **GB** (WIL) 62 Yc 40
Axminster **GB** (DEV) 68 Xa 44
Axmouth **GB** (DEV) 67 Wf 44
Aylburton **GB** (GLS) 61 Xc 38
Ayle **GB** (NHL) 32 Xd 19
Aylesbeare **GB** (DEV) 67 Wd 44
Aylesbury **GB** (BUS) 63 Za 38
Aylesby **GB** (HUS) 41 Ze 27
Aylesford **GB** (KEN) 65 Ac 41
Aylesham **GB** (KEN) 65 Bb 41
Aylestone **GB** (LEC) 54 Yf 33
Aylmerton **GB** (NOR) 49 Bb 31
Aylsham **GB** (NOR) 49 Bb 32
Aylton **GB** (HWC) 52 Xd 36
Aymestrey **GB** (HWC) 52 Xa 35
Aynho **GB** (NRH) 62 Ye 37
Ayot Saint Lawrence **GB** (HTS) 64 Ac 38
Ayot Saint Peter **GB** (HTS) 64 Ze 38
Ayr **GB** (STC) 30 Vc 16
Aysgarth **GB** (NOY) 36 Ya 23
Ayshford **GB** (DEV) 67 Wd 43
Ayside **GB** (CUB) 35 Xa 23
Ayston **GB** (LEC) 54 Zb 33
Ayton **GB** (BOR) 27 Xf 13
Ayton **GB** (NOY) 37 Zd 23
Aywick **GB** (SHL) 2 Yf 105
Azerley **GB** (NOY) 36 Yc 24

B

Babbacombe **GB** (DEV) 76 Wc 46
Babbinswood **GB** (SHS) 44 Xa 31
Babcary **GB** (SOM) 68 Xc 42
Babel **GB** (DYF) 59 Wb 37
Babell **GB** (CLW) 43 We 29
Babeny **GB** (DEV) 76 Wa 45
Babraham **GB** (CBS) 56 Ab 36
Babworth **GB** (NTS) 46 Za 29
Bac **GB** (HGL) 11 Te 119
Backaland **GB** (ORK) 5 Xb 114
Backbarrow **GB** (CUB) 35 Xa 23
Backburn **GB** (GRP) 16 Xb 4
Backfolds **GB** (GRP) 17 Ya 3
Backhill **GB** (GRP) 17 Xd 4
Backhill **GB** (GRP) 17 Ya 4
Backhill of Clarckriach **GB** (GRP) 17 Xf 3
Backies **GB** (HGL) 9 Wa 1
Backlass **GB** (HGL) 6 Wd 118
Backmuir of New Gilston **GB** (FIF) 22 Xa 11
Back of Keppoch **GB** (HGL) 19 Ua 7
Backwell **GB** (AVN) 61 Xb 40
Bacon End **GB** (ESS) 64 Ab 37
Baconthorpe **GB** (NOR) 49 Ba 31
Bacton **GB** (HWC) 60 Xa 37
Bacton **GB** (SUF) 57 Ba 35
Bacup **GB** (LCS) 39 Xe 26
Badachro **GB** (HGL) 7 Ub 2
Badanloch Lodge **GB** (HGL) 8 Vf 119
Badavanich **GB** (HGL) 14 Ue 3
Badbury **GB** (WIL) 62 Yb 39
Badby **GB** (NRH) 54 Ye 35
Badcall **GB** (HGL) 4 Uf 118
Badcall **GB** (HGL) 7 Uf 119
Badcaul **GB** (HGL) 7 Ud 1
Baddesley Ensor **GB** (WWH) 53 Yc 33
Baddidarach **GB** (HGL) 7 Ue 120
Badenscoth **GB** (GRP) 17 Xd 4
Badenyon **GB** (GRP) 16 Wf 5
Badger **GB** (SHS) 53 Xd 34
Badgerbank **GB** (CHS) 45 Xe 29
Badgerisland **IRL** (LAO) 94 Sd 31
Badgers Mount **GB** (KEN) 64 Aa 40
Badgeworth **GB** (GLS) 61 Xf 37
Badgworth **GB** (SOM) 68 Xa 41
Badicaul **GB** (HGL) 13 Ub 5
Badingham **GB** (SUF) 57 Bc 35
Badley **GB** (SUF) 57 Ba 36
Badlipster **GB** (HGL) 9 We 118
Badluarach **GB** (HGL) 7 Ud 1
Badminton **GB** (AVN) 61 Xe 39
Badninish **GB** (HGL) 8 Vf 1
Badrallach **GB** (HGL) 7 Ue 1
Badsey **GB** (HWC) 53 Ya 36
Badshotlea **GB** (SUR) 70 Zb 41
Badsworth **GB** (WYO) 40 Ye 27
Badyke **IRL** (CRE) 92 Rc 31
Bagby **GB** (NOY) 36 Ye 23
Bage, The **GB** (HWC) 52 Wf 36
Bagenalstown = Muine Bheag **IRL** (CLW) 100 Ta 32
Bagendon **GB** (GLS) 62 Ya 38
Baggrave Hall **GB** (LEC) 54 Za 32
Bagillt **GB** (CLW) 44 Wf 29
Baginton **GB** (WWH) 54 Yd 34
Baglan **GB** (WGL) 59 Wb 39
Bagley **GB** (SHS) 44 Xa 31
Bagnor **GB** (BKS) 62 Yd 40
Bagshot **GB** (SUR) 63 Zb 40
Bagshot **GB** (WIL) 62 Yc 40
Bagthorpe **GB** (NOR) 48 Ad 31
Bagworth **GB** (LEC) 54 Ye 32
Bagwyllydiart **GB** (HWC) 61 Xb 37
Baildon **GB** (WYO) 39 Yb 25
Báile an Róba = Ballinrobe **IRL** (MAY) 87 Qe 27
Baile Átha Cliath = Dublin **IRL** (DUB) 95 Tf 28
Baile Atha Fhirdhia = Ardee **IRL** (LOT) 90 Tc 25
Baile Átha I = Athy **IRL** (KIL) 94 Ta 31
Baile Átha Troim = Trim **IRL** (MT) 90 Tb 27
Bailebeag **GB** (HGL) 15 Vd 5
Baile Boidheach **GB** (STC) 23 Uc 13
Baileborough **IRL** (CAV) 89 Ta 25
Baile Brigin = Balbriggan **IRL** (DUB) 90 Te 27
Baile Locha = Loughrea **IRL** (GAL) 92 Rc 29
Baile Mhic Andáin = Thomastown **IRL** (KLK) 100 Sf 33
Baile Mó **GB** (STC) 18 Td 10
Baileysmill **GB** (DOW) 85 Ua 22
Bailliemore **GB** (STC) 19 Uc 10
Baillieston **GB** (STC) 25 Vf 13
Bail Uachdraich **GB** (HGL) 10 Se 3
Bainbridge **GB** (NOY) 36 Xf 23
Bainton **GB** (CBS) 55 Zd 33
Bainton **GB** (HUS) 41 Zc 25
Baker's End **GB** (HTS) 64 Aa 38
Baker Street **GB** (ESS) 64 Ac 39
Bakewell **GB** (DSH) 45 Yb 29
Bala **GB** (GWY) 43 Wc 31
Balachuirn **GB** (HGL) 13 Tf 4
Balallan **GB** (HGL) 11 Tc 120
Balameanach **GB** (STC) 23 Ud 12
Balatonsborough **GB** (SOM) 68 Xc 42
Balbane **IRL** (DON) 82 Rd 20
Balbeg **GB** (HGL) 15 Vd 4
Balbeggie **GB** (TYS) 21 Wd 10
Balbithan **GB** (GRP) 17 Xe 5
Balbithan Ho **GB** (GRP) 17 Xe 5
Balblair **GB** (HGL) 15 Ve 2
Balbriggan **IRL** (DUB) 90 Te 27
Balbrobin House **IRL** (LOT) 90 Td 24
Balcherry **GB** (HGL) 9 Wa 2
Balchladich **GB** (HGL) 7 Ud 119
Balchraggan **GB** (HGL) 15 Vd 4
Balchrick **GB** (HGL) 4 Uf 118
Balcombe **GB** (WSX) 71 Zf 42
Balcomie **GB** (FIF) 22 Xc 11
Balcunnin **IRL** (MT) 90 Tf 27
Baldernock **GB** (STC) 25 Ve 13
Baldersby **GB** (NOY) 36 Yd 23
Balderton **GB** (NTS) 46 Zb 30
Baldhu **GB** (CNW) 74 Uf 47
Baldinnie **GB** (FIF) 22 Xa 11
Baldock **GB** (HTS) 55 Ze 37
Baldoyle **IRL** (DUB) 95 Tf 28
Baldrichard **IRL** (DUB) 90 Te 27
Baldrine **GBM** 29 Vd 23
Baldslow **GB** (ESX) 72 Ad 43
Baldwin **GBM** 29 Vc 23
Baldwinholme **GB** (CUB) 32 Wf 19
Baldwin's Gate **GB** (SFS) 45 Xe 31
Bale **GB** (NOR) 48 Af 31
Balemartine **GB** (STC) 18 Ta 10
Balephuil **GB** (STC) 18 Ta 10
Balerno **GB** (LOT) 26 Wd 13
Balevulin **GB** (STC) 18 Tf 10
Balevullin **GB** (STC) 18 Ta 9
Balfield **GB** (TYS) 22 Xb 8
Balfour **GB** (ORK) 6 Xa 114
Balfron **GB** (CEN) 25 Vd 12
Balgaveny **GB** (GRP) 17 Xc 4
Balgavies **GB** (TYS) 22 Xb 9
Balgedie **GB** (TYS) 26 Wd 11
Balgonar **GB** (FIF) 25 Wc 12
Balgove **GB** (GRP) 17 Xe 4
Balgowan **GB** (HGL) 15 Ve 6
Balgown **GB** (HGL) 13 Td 3
Balgray **GB** (TYS) 22 Xa 9
Balhalgardy **GB** (GRP) 17 Xd 5
Balhary **GB** (TYS) 21 We 9
Baligill **GB** (HGL) 5 Wa 117
Balintore **GB** (HGL) 9 Wa 2
Balintore **GB** (TYS) 21 Wf 8
Balivarich **GB** (HGL) 10 Sd 4
Bal Iver **IRL** (OFF) 93 Sa 29
Balkeerie **GB** (TYS) 21 Wf 9
Balkholme **GB** (HUS) 40 Zb 26
Balkissock **GB** (STC) 28 Va 18
Ball **GB** (SHS) 44 Wf 32
Balla **GB** (HGL) 12 Se 6
Balla **IRL** (MAY) 87 Qf 26
Ballabeg **GBM** 29 Vb 24
Ballacannell **GBM** 29 Vd 23
Ballacarnane Beg **GBM** 29 Vc 23
Ballachulish **GB** (HGL) 19 Uf 8
Balladangan **IRL** (ROS) 93 Rf 28
Ballag **IRL** (ROS) 88 Rf 26
Ballagan **IRL** (LOT) 90 Tf 24
Ballagh **IRL** (DON) 78 Se 17
Ballagh **IRL** (GAL) 87 Rb 27
Ballagh **IRL** (LGF) 88 Sa 26
Ballagh **IRL** (LIM) 98 Qf 34
Ballagh **IRL** (ROS) 88 Rf 27
Ballagh **IRL** (TIP) 99 Sa 33
Ballaghaderreen **IRL** (ROS) 88 Rc 25
Ballagh Cottage **IRL** (LET) 82 Rf 22
Ballagh Cross Roads **IRL** (KIL) 95 Tb 28
Ballaghdorragh **IRL** (CAV) 89 Sf 26
Ballaghkeen **IRL** (WEX) 101 Td 34
Ballaghlea **IRL** (GAL) 88 Rd 27
Ballaghnageam **IRL** (MOG) 90 Tb 25
Ballaghnatrillick Bridge **IRL** (SLI) 82 Rd 22
Ballagyr **GBM** 29 Vc 23
Ballajora **GBM** 29 Vd 23
Ballakull **IRL** (MT) 90 Tb 26
Ballally **IRL** (MT) 89 Ta 26
Ballamodha **GBM** 29 Vc 24
Ballantrae **GB** (STC) 28 Uf 18
Ballantrushal **GB** (HGL) 11 Td 118
Ballard **IRL** (OFF) 94 Sc 29
Ballard **IRL** (WKL) 95 Tf 31
Ballard Cross Roads **IRL** (WKL) 95 Tc 32
Ballardiggan **IRL** (GAL) 92 Rb 30
Ballard Park **IRL** (WKL) 95 Te 31
Ballasalla **GBM** 29 Vc 22
Ballasalla **GBM** 29 Vc 24
Ballater **GB** (GRP) 16 Wf 6
Ballaugh **GBM** 29 Vc 23
Ballaveare **GBM** 29 Vc 24
Ballcreiff **GB** (LOT) 26 Xb 13
Ball Hill **GB** (HAS) 62 Yd 40
Balliasta **GB** (SHL) 2 Za 104
Ballickmoyler **IRL** (LAO) 94 Sf 31
Balliekine **GB** (STC) 23 Ud 15
Ballig **GBM** 29 Vc 23
Balligan **GB** (DOW) 85 Ud 21
Ballimore **GB** (CEN) 20 Vd 11
Ballina **IRL** (MAY) 81 Qf 24
Ballina **IRL** (MAY) 87 Qf 27
Ballina **IRL** (TIP) 93 Rd 32
Ballinaboy **IRL** (COR) 104 Rc 38
Ballinaboy **IRL** (GAL) 86 Pf 28
Ballinabrackey **IRL** (MT) 94 Sf 28
Ballinaby **GB** (STC) 22 Td 14
Ballinaclash **IRL** (WKL) 95 Te 31
Ballinacloon **IRL** (WMT) 89 Sd 27
Ballinacor **IRL** (WKL) 95 Tf 31
Ballinacurra House **IRL** (COR) 104 Rb 38
Ballinadee **IRL** (COR) 104 Rc 38
Ballinafad **IRL** (SLI) 88 Re 24
Ballinagam Cross Roads **IRL** (WEX) 101 Te 33
Ballinagar **IRL** (OFF) 94 Sd 29
Ballinagard **IRL** (ROS) 88 Re 27
Ballinagarrane **IRL** (LIM) 98 Ra 33
Ballinagleragh **IRL** (LET) 82 Rf 24
Ballinakill **IRL** (LAO) 94 Se 31
Ballinalea **IRL** (WKL) 95 Tf 30
Ballinalee **IRL** (LGF) 89 Sc 26
Ballinamallard **GB** (FER) 83 Sc 22
Ballinameen **IRL** (ROS) 88 Re 25
Ballinamona **IRL** (WEX) 101 Td 33
Ballinamore **IRL** (LET) 88 Sb 24
Ballinamuck **IRL** (LGF) 89 Sb 25
Ballinanima **IRL** (LIM) 98 Rd 34
Ballinapark **IRL** (MAY) 81 Qc 23
Ballinard Cross **IRL** (TIP) 99 Re 34
Ballinascarty **IRL** (COR) 103 Ra 38
Ballinasilloge **IRL** (WKL) 95 Te 32
Ballinasloe **IRL** (GAL) 93 Re 29
Ballinaspick **IRL** (WTF) 99 Sa 36
Ballinastoe House **IRL** (WKL) 95 Te 30
Ballinattin **IRL** (TIP) 99 Sb 34
Ballinattin **IRL** (WTF) 100 Sf 35
Ballinavin Castle **IRL** (TIP) 93 Rf 31
Ballinbrittig **IRL** (COR) 104 Re 37
Ballinclay **IRL** (WEX) 101 Tc 34
Ballinclea House **IRL** (WKL) 95 Tc 31
Ballincloher **IRL** (KER) 97 Qb 34
Ballincollig **IRL** (COR) 104 Rc 37
Ballincrea **IRL** (KLK) 100 Sf 35
Ballincrick **IRL** (DON) 77 Rd 19
Ballincurra **IRL** (LIM) 98 Ra 33
Ballincurrig **IRL** (COR) 99 Re 37
Ballincurrig **IRL** (COR) 104 Rb 39
Ballindaggan **IRL** (WEX) 101 Tb 33
Ballindangan **IRL** (COR) 99 Re 35
Ballindean **GB** (TYS) 21 We 10
Ballinderreen **IRL** (GAL) 92 Ra 29
Ballinderry **IRL** (TIP) 93 Re 30
Ballindine **IRL** (MAY) 87 Ra 26
Ballindoney **IRL** (TIP) 99 Sa 34
Ballindrait **IRL** (DON) 78 Sc 19
Ballindrumma **IRL** (WTF) 99 Sb 36
Ballindysert **IRL** (WTF) 100 Sd 34
Ballineadig **IRL** (COR) 104 Rb 37
Ballineanig **IRL** (KER) 96 Pd 35
Ballineen **IRL** (COR) 103 Ra 38
Ballineue **IRL** (OFF) 94 Sc 29
Ballinew **IRL** (MAY) 87 Qe 27
Ballinfrase House **IRL** (LAO) 94 Sc 32
Ballingaddy South **IRL** (LIM) 98 Rc 34
Ballingarry **IRL** (LIM) 98 Ra 34
Ballingarry **IRL** (LIM) 99 Rd 34
Ballingarry **IRL** (TIP) 93 Rf 30
Ballingarry **IRL** (TIP) 100 Sc 33
Ballingeary **IRL** (COR) 103 Qe 37
Ballinger Common **GB** (BUS) 63 Zb 38
Ballingham **GB** (HWC) 61 Xc 37
Ballinglanna **IRL** (COR) 103 Rb 39
Ballinglanna **IRL** (KER) 97 Qb 34
Ballingry **GB** (FIF) 26 We 12
Ballinguile **IRL** (WKL) 95 Tc 31
Ballingurteen **IRL** (COR) 103 Qf 38
Ballinhassig **IRL** (COR) 104 Rc 38
Ballinillaun **IRL** (GAL) 92 Ra 29
Ballinkillin **IRL** (CLW) 100 Ta 33
Ballinla **IRL** (COR) 98 Ra 35
Ballinla **IRL** (WMT) 89 Se 28
Ballinlceny **IRL** (LIM) 98 Rb 34
Ballinlick **GB** (TYS) 21 Wc 9
Ballinloghig **IRL** (KER) 96 Pe 35
Ballinlonty House **IRL** (TIP) 93 Sa 32
Ballinlough **IRL** (MT) 89 Sf 26
Ballinlough **IRL** (ROS) 87 Rc 26
Ballinlough Castle **IRL** (WMT) 89 Sf 27
Ballinlough Lodge **IRL** (MT) 89 Se 26
Ballinluig **GB** (TYS) 21 Wc 9
Ballinluska **IRL** (COR) 104 Re 38
Ballinlyna House **IRL** (LIM) 98 Rd 34
Ballinorig **IRL** (KER) 97 Qc 35
Ballinorossig **IRL** (KER) 97 Qb 34
Ballinoulart **IRL** (WEX) 101 Te 33
Ballinphelic House **IRL** (COR) 104 Rc 38
Ballinphuill **IRL** (ROS) 88 Rd 26
Ballinphull **IRL** (SLI) 82 Rc 22
Ballinphull **IRL** (SLI) 82 Re 24
Ballin Prior **IRL** (KER) 97 Qa 34
Ballinreeshig **IRL** (COR) 104 Rd 37
Ballinrig **IRL** (MT) 90 Tb 28
Ballinrobe **IRL** (MAY) 87 Qe 27
Ballinrolla **IRL** (KER) 96 Pd 35
Ballinrooaun **IRL** (GAL) 87 Rc 28
Ballinruan **IRL** (CRE) 92 Rc 31
Ballinspittle **IRL** (COR) 104 Rc 38
Ballintaggart **IRL** (LAO) 93 Sb 31
Ballintaggart House **IRL** (KIL) 95 Tb 30
Ballinteemore **IRL** (GAL) 91 Qd 29
Ballinter House **IRL** (MT) 90 Tc 27
Ballinteskin Cross Roads **IRL** (WKL) 95 Tf 31
Ballintilla **IRL** (LAO) 94 Sc 30
Ballintlea **IRL** (LAO) 94 Sf 31
Ballintober **IRL** (ROS) 88 Rd 26
Ballintober **IRL** (WKL) 95 Tc 30
Ballintober House **IRL** (WMT) 89 Sc 28
Ballintogher **IRL** (SLI) 82 Rd 23
Ballintoy **GB** (ANT) 79 Td 17
Ballintra **IRL** (DON) 77 Rc 19
Ballintra **IRL** (DON) 82 Rf 21
Ballintroohan **IRL** (DON) 78 Sf 17
Ballintubbert **IRL** (LAO) 94 Sf 31
Ballinure **IRL** (TIP) 99 Sb 33
Ballinvinny North **IRL** (COR) 99 Rd 37
Ballinvinny South **IRL** (COR) 104 Rd 37
Ballinvira House **IRL** (LIM) 98 Ra 33
Ballinvoher **IRL** (GAL) 87 Qf 27
Ballinvonear House **IRL** (COR) 98 Rc 35
Ballinvreena **IRL** (LIM) 99 Rd 34
Ballinvuskig **IRL** (COR) 98 Rc 36
Ballinwully **IRL** (ROS) 88 Rf 26
Balliny **IRL** (CRE) 92 Qe 30
Ballitore **IRL** (KIL) 94 Tb 30
Ballivor **IRL** (MT) 89 Ta 27
Balloch **GB** (HGL) 15 Vf 4
Balloch **GB** (STC) 24 Vc 13
Balloch **GB** (TYS) 21 Wf 8
Balloch, The **GB** (TYS) 21 Wa 10
Ballochmorrie **GB** (STC) 30 Vb 18
Ballochroy **GB** (STC) 23 Uc 14
Balloghter **IRL** (WEX) 101 Td 33
Ballon **IRL** (CLW) 95 Tb 32
Balloo **GB** (DOW) 85 Ub 22
Balloor **IRL** (LET) 82 Rd 22
Ballough **IRL** (DUB) 90 Te 27
Balls Cross **GB** (WSX) 70 Zc 42
Ballyadams **IRL** (LAO) 94 Sf 31
Ballyagran **IRL** (LIM) 98 Rb 34
Ballyallaban House **IRL** (CRE) 92 Qf 30
Ballyallinan **IRL** (LIM) 98 Ra 34
Ballyandreen **IRL** (COR) 104 Rf 38
Ballyaneen **IRL** (GAL) 92 Rb 30
Ballyanne **IRL** (WEX) 100 Ta 34
Ballyanny **IRL** (TIP) 93 Re 31
Ballyanthony **IRL** (COR) 99 Rf 36
Ballyarell **IRL** (DON) 83 Sc 20
Ballyarthur **IRL** (COR) 99 Re 35
Ballybane House **IRL** (COR) 103 Qd 39
Ballybaun **IRL** (GAL) 87 Qf 28
Ballybaun **IRL** (GAL) 88 Rd 28
Ballybay **IRL** (MOG) 89 Ta 24
Ballybay House **IRL** (MOG) 90 Ta 24
Ballybeg **IRL** (SLI) 82 Rc 23
Ballybinaby **IRL** (LOT) 90 Tc 24
Ballybit Cross Roads **IRL** (CLW) 95 Tb 31
Ballyboe **IRL** (DON) 77 Sc 18
Ballybofey **IRL** (DON) 77 Sb 20
Ballybogey **IRL** (COR) 104 Rd 38
Ballyboghil **IRL** (DUB) 90 Te 27
Ballybogy **GB** (ANT) 79 Tc 18
Ballybornia **IRL** (WMT) 93 Sb 28
Ballyboro **IRL** (WEX) 101 Tb 34
Ballybowter **IRL** (KER) 96 Pe 36
Ballyboy **IRL** (OFF) 93 Sb 29
Ballyboy **IRL** (TIP) 99 Sa 32
Ballybrack **IRL** (COR) 102 Qc 39
Ballybrack **IRL** (KER) 96 Pe 35
Ballybrack **IRL** (KIL) 95 Tb 28
Ballybrit **IRL** (GAL) 92 Ra 29
Ballybrittas **IRL** (LAO) 94 Sf 30
Ballybrood **IRL** (LIM) 99 Rd 33
Ballybrophy **IRL** (LAO) 94 Sc 31
Ballybrowney Mountain **IRL** (COR) 99 Rd 36
Ballybryan **IRL** (OFF) 94 Sf 28
Ballybuck **IRL** (GAL) 92 Ra 30
Ballybunnion **IRL** (KER) 97 Qb 33
Ballycahane **IRL** (TIP) 93 Rd 32
Ballycahill **IRL** (TIP) 99 Sa 32
Ballycallan **IRL** (KLK) 100 Sd 33
Ballycally **IRL** (CRE) 92 Ra 32
Ballycanew **IRL** (WEX) 101 Te 33
Ballycannan House **IRL** (CRE) 92 Rc 32
Ballycapple **IRL** (TIP) 93 Rf 31
Ballycarney **IRL** (WEX) 101 Tc 33
Ballycarry **GB** (ANT) 85 Ub 20
Ballycastle **GB** (ANT) 79 Te 17
Ballycastle **IRL** (MAY) 81 Qd 23
Ballyclare **GB** (ANT) 85 Ua 20
Ballyclare **IRL** (ROS) 88 Rf 26
Ballyclerahan **IRL** (TIP) 99 Sb 34
Ballyclider **IRL** (LAO) 94 Se 30
Ballyclogh **IRL** (COR) 98 Rb 35
Ballycolla **IRL** (LAO) 94 Sd 31
Ballycollin **IRL** (OFF) 94 Sd 29
Ballycommane **IRL** (COR) 103 Qc 39
Ballycommon **IRL** (TIP) 93 Re 31
Ballycomoyle **IRL** (WMT) 89 Se 26
Ballyconaught **IRL** (KLK) 100 Sf 34
Ballyconell **IRL** (SLI) 82 Rc 22
Ballyconlought **IRL** (GAL) 87 Qf 28
Ballyconneely **IRL** (GAL) 86 Pf 28
Ballyconnell **IRL** (CAV) 89 Sc 24
Ballyconnigar Upper **IRL** (WEX) 101 Te 34
Ballyconran **IRL** (WEX) 101 Td 32
Ballycorus **IRL** (DUB) 95 Te 29
Ballycotton **IRL** (COR) 104 Rf 38
Ballycrinnigan **IRL** (CLW) 100 Ta 33
Ballycrossaun **IRL** (GAL) 93 Re 30
Ballycroy **IRL** (MAY) 86 Qb 24
Ballycullane **IRL** (LIM) 98 Rb 33
Ballycullane **IRL** (WEX) 100 Ta 35
Ballycullane **IRL** (WTF) 100 Sc 35
Ballycumber **IRL** (OFF) 93 Sb 29
Ballycumber **IRL** (WKL) 95 Td 31
Ballycunane **IRL** (KER) 96 Pe 35
Ballycurrane **IRL** (WTF) 99 Sb 36
Ballycurrin **IRL** (KLK) 100 Sf 34
Ballycurry House **IRL** (WKL) 95 Tf 30
Ballydaff **IRL** (TIP) 93 Rf 32
Ballydangan **IRL** (ROS) 93 Rf 28
Ballydavid **IRL** (COR) 104 Rf 38
Ballydavid **IRL** (GAL) 93 Rd 29
Ballydavid **IRL** (KER) 96 Pd 35
Ballydavis **IRL** (LAO) 94 Se 30
Ballydehob **IRL** (COR) 103 Qd 39

Armthorpe – Ballydehob (GB) (IRL) 107

Ballydesmond IRL (COR) 98 Qe 35
Ballydineen IRL (COR) 98 Rc 35
Ballydivlin IRL (COR) 102 Qb 39
Ballydonegan IRL (COR) 102 Pf 39
Ballydonohoe IRL (KER) 97 Qc 34
Ballydoogan IRL (GAL) 93 Rd 29
Ballydooley IRL (ROS) 88 Rd 27
Ballydotia IRL (GAL) 92 Qe 28
Ballydowane IRL (WTF) 100 Sd 36
Ballydowling IRL (WKL) 95 Tf 31
Ballyduff IRL (KER) 96 Pf 35
Ballyduff IRL (KER) 97 Qc 34
Ballyduff IRL (WEX) 101 Td 33
Ballyduff IRL (WTF) 99 Rf 36
Ballyea Lodge IRL (TIP) 93 Rf 30
Ballyeaston GB (ANT) 85 Ua 20
Ballyederlan IRL (DON) 82 Rd 21
Ballyedmond IRL (WEX) 101 Td 33
Ballyegny House IRL (LIM) 98 Qf 33
Ballyeighter IRL (GAL) 93 Rc 30
Ballyeightragh IRL (COR) 99 Rf 37
Ballyeightragh IRL (KER) 96 Pe 36
Ballyenddahy IRL (LAO) 94 Sd 31
Ballyendyhty IRL (KER) 97 Qb 35
Ballyfarnagh IRL (MAY) 87 Ra 26
Ballyfarnan IRL (ROS) 88 Re 24
Ballyfauskeen Cross Roads IRL (LIM) 99 Re 34
Ballyfeard IRL (COR) 104 Rd 38
Ballyfeeny IRL (ROS) 88 Rf 26
Ballyfermot IRL (DUB) 95 Td 28
Ballyferriter IRL (KER) 96 Pd 35
Ballyfin IRL (LAO) 94 Sd 30
Ballyforan IRL (ROS) 88 Re 28
Ballyfore IRL (OFF) 94 Se 28
Ballyfore IRL (OFF) 94 Sf 29
Ballyfoyle IRL (KLK) 100 Se 32
Ballyfraley House IRL (LIM) 98 Qf 34
Ballygahan IRL (WKL) 95 Te 31
Ballygalley GB (ANT) 79 Ua 19
Ballygalvert IRL (WEX) 100 Tb 34
Ballygamboon Upper IRL (KER) 97 Qb 35
Ballygar IRL (GAL) 88 Rd 27
Ballygarran IRL (WTF) 100 Sd 36
Ballygarran IRL (WTF) 100 Se 35
Ballygarrett IRL (WEX) 101 Te 33
Ballygarries IRL (MAY) 87 Qe 26
Ballygarriff IRL (MAY) 87 Qe 25
Ballygarry IRL (MAY) 87 Qe 26
Ballygarvan IRL (COR) 104 Rd 38
Ballygawley IRL (SLI) 82 Rd 23
Ballygeel IRL (LIM) 98 Qf 34
Ballygerry IRL (WEX) 101 Td 35
Ballygillistown IRL (WEX) 101 Tc 34
Ballygirreen House IRL (CRE) 92 Ra 32
Ballyglas IRL (MAY) 81 Qd 23
Ballyglass IRL (MAY) 87 Qe 26
Ballyglass IRL (MAY) 87 Rb 26
Ballyglass House IRL (SLI) 82 Rd 23
Ballygomartin GB (ANT) 85 Ua 21
Ballygommon IRL (MAY) 87 Qf 25
Ballygoran House IRL (KIL) 95 Tc 28
Ballygorey IRL (KLK) 100 Se 35
Ballygorman IRL (DON) 78 Se 16
Ballygow IRL (WEX) 100 Ta 35
Ballygowan GB (DOW) 85 Ub 21
Ballygown GB (STC) 18 Te 9
Ballygrady IRL (COR) 98 Rb 35
Ballygrant GB (STC) 23 Tf 14
Ballygrennan IRL (LIM) 98 Rb 34
Ballygriffin IRL (TIP) 99 Sa 33
Ballygub IRL (KLK) 100 Ta 34
Ballygubba IRL (LIM) 98 Rc 34
Ballyguin IRL (MAY) 87 Qe 25
Ballyguirk IRL (TIP) 93 Rf 30
Ballyguiry IRL (WTF) 99 Sb 36
Ballyhacket Cross Roads IRL (CLW) 95 Tb 31
Ballyhaght IRL (LIM) 98 Rc 34
Ballyhahill IRL (LIM) 98 Qe 33
Ballyhaise IRL (CAV) 89 Se 24
Ballyhalbert GB (DOW) 85 Ud 22
Ballyhalc IRL (GAL) 87 Qf 28
Ballyhale IRL (KLK) 100 Se 34
Ballyhall IRL (KLK) 100 Sd 33
Ballyhar IRL (KER) 97 Qc 36
Ballyhaugh GB (STC) 18 Tc 9
Ballyhaunis IRL (MAY) 87 Rb 26
Ballyheadon IRL (WTF) 100 Se 36
Ballyhean IRL (MAY) 87 Qe 26
Ballyheelan IRL (CAV) 89 Sd 25
Ballyheelan IRL (CAV) 89 Sd 26
Ballyheerin IRL (DON) 77 Sb 17
Ballyheige IRL (KER) 97 Qa 34
Ballyhenry IRL (MAY) 87 Qf 27
Ballyhide IRL (LAO) 94 Ta 32
Ballyhillin IRL (DON) 78 Sd 16
Ballyhimmin IRL (KLK) 100 Se 34
Ballyhitt IRL (WEX) 101 Td 35
Ballyhoge IRL (WEX) 101 Tc 34
Ballyhomuck IRL (KLK) 100 Sf 34
Ballyhone IRL (TIP) 99 Rd 34
Ballyhook IRL (WKL) 95 Tb 31
Ballyhoolahan IRL (COR) 98 Qf 35
Ballyhooly IRL (COR) 99 Rd 36
Ballyhorahan IRL (LAO) 94 Sc 31
Ballyhornan GB (DOW) 85 Uc 23
Ballyhoura IRL (COR) 98 Rc 35
Ballyhugh IRL (OFF) 94 Se 29
Ballyieragh IRL (COR) 103 Qc 40
Ballyjamesduff IRL (CAV) 89 Se 25
Ballykealey House IRL (CLW) 95 Tb 32
Ballykean IRL (OFF) 94 Se 29
Ballykeel GB (DOW) 85 Tf 22
Ballykeel House IRL (CRE) 92 Qe 30
Ballykeeran IRL (WMT) 88 Sa 28
Ballykeerogebeg IRL (WEX) 100 Ta 35
Ballykelly GB (LDR) 78 Sf 18
Ballykeroge IRL (WTF) 100 Sc 36
Ballykilcline IRL (ROS) 88 Sa 26
Ballykillaboy IRL (KLK) 100 Sf 35
Ballykilmurry IRL (WTF) 100 Sc 35
Ballykinealy IRL (COR) 104 Sa 37
Ballyknock IRL (COR) 99 Rf 36
Ballyknock IRL (KLK) 100 Sf 34
Ballyknock IRL (WTF) 99 Sc 36
Ballyknock IRL (WTF) 100 Sd 35
Ballyknockan IRL (WKL) 95 Tc 30
Ballyknockan Beg IRL (WKL) 95 Tf 31
Ballylaan IRL (CRE) 91 Qd 31
Ballylahan Bridge IRL (MAY) 87 Qf 25
Ballylanders IRL (LIM) 99 Rd 34
Ballylaneen IRL (WTF) 100 Sd 35
Ballylawn IRL (DON) 77 Sc 19
Ballyleague IRL (ROS) 88 Rf 27
Ballylehane Upper IRL (LAO) 94 Sf 31
Ballyleigh IRL (COR) 104 Rc 38
Ballylemon Lodge IRL (WTF) 99 Sb 36
Ballylennan IRL (DON) 78 Sc 19
Ballylesson GB (DOW) 85 Ua 21
Ballylevin IRL (OFF) 94 Sd 29
Ballylinch House IRL (KLK) 100 Se 33
Ballylongane IRL (COR) 104 Rf 37
Ballylongford IRL (KER) 97 Qd 33
Ballylooby IRL (LIM) 99 Rd 34
Ballylooby IRL (TIP) 99 Sa 35
Ballylouahaun IRL (GAL) 92 Rb 30
Ballylough IRL (WTF) 100 Sf 35
Ballylow IRL (WKL) 95 Td 30
Ballylucas IRL (WEX) 101 Td 34
Ballyluoge IRL (GAL) 93 Rd 29
Ballylusk IRL (WKL) 95 Tf 30
Ballylusky IRL (TIP) 99 Sc 33
Ballylynan IRL (LAO) 94 Sf 31
Ballymacallen IRL (WMT) 89 Sc 27
Ballymacask IRL (COR) 104 Sa 37
Ballymacaw IRL (WTF) 100 Sf 36
Ballymaceligott IRL (KER) 97 Qc 35
Ballymackesy House IRL (WEX) 101 Tb 34
Ballymackey IRL (TIP) 93 Rf 31
Ballymacmague IRL (WTF) 99 Sb 36
Ballymacoda IRL (COR) 104 Sa 37
Ballymacoolaghan House IRL (OFF) 93 Rf 29
Ballymacprior IRL (KER) 97 Qb 36
Ballymacquin IRL (KER) 97 Qb 34
Ballymacquin Upper IRL (KER) 97 Qb 34
Ballymacrown IRL (COR) 103 Qd 40
Ballymacurly IRL (ROS) 88 Re 26
Ballymacward IRL (GAL) 93 Rd 28
Ballymadog IRL (COR) 104 Sa 37
Ballymadun IRL (DUB) 90 Tc 26
Ballymagan IRL (DON) 78 Sd 18
Ballymagaraghy IRL (DON) 78 Sf 17
Ballymaghroe IRL (WKL) 95 Td 31
Ballymaglassan IRL (MT) 90 Tc 28
Ballymagorry GB (TYR) 78 Sd 19
Ballymagrine IRL (ROS) 88 Sa 26
Ballymahon IRL (LGF) 88 Sb 27
Ballymakane IRL (MT) 90 Ta 25
Ballymakeagh IRL (COR) 104 Sa 37
Ballymakee House IRL (WTF) 99 Sb 35
Ballymakeery IRL (COR) 103 Qf 37
Ballymakellett IRL (LOT) 90 Te 24
Ballymakenny IRL (LOT) 90 Td 26
Ballymalis Bridge IRL (KER) 97 Qb 36
Ballymanus IRL (WKL) 95 Td 31
Ballymartin GB (DOW) 91 Ua 24
Ballymartin IRL (ROS) 88 Rf 26
Ballymartle IRL (COR) 104 Rc 38
Ballymeeny IRL (SLI) 81 Ra 23
Ballymena GB (ANT) 79 Te 19
Ballymichael GB (STC) 28 Ue 15
Ballyminaun Hill IRL (WEX) 101 Te 33
Ballymoe IRL (GAL) 88 Rd 26
Ballymoe Station IRL (ROS) 88 Rd 26
Ballymoney GB (ANT) 79 Tc 18
Ballymoney IRL (DON) 78 Sc 18
Ballymoney Cross Roads IRL (WEX) 101 Te 32
Ballymore IRL (DON) 77 Sa 18
Ballymore IRL (WMT) 89 Sb 28
Ballymore Eustace IRL (KIL) 95 Tc 30
Ballymote IRL (SLI) 88 Rc 24
Ballymount IRL (KIL) 95 Tb 30
Ballymoylin IRL (ROS) 88 Sa 26
Ballymre IRL (ROS) 88 Re 25
Ballymun IRL (DUB) 95 Te 28
Ballymurn IRL (WEX) 101 Td 34
Ballymurphy IRL (CLW) 100 Ta 33
Ballymurray IRL (ROS) 88 Rf 27
Ballymurry IRL (GAL) 92 Rc 29
Ballynabarna Cross IRL (WMT) 89 Sc 28
Ballynabola IRL (WEX) 100 Ta 34
Ballynaboley Cross Roads IRL (KLK) 100 Sf 33
Ballynabortagh IRL (COR) 98 Rd 37
Ballynabucky IRL (GAL) 92 Ra 29
Ballynacally IRL (CRE) 92 Qf 32
Ballynacarhagh House IRL (CRE) 92 Qe 31
Ballynacarrick Upper IRL (KIL) 95 Tb 31
Ballynacarriga IRL (COR) 103 Qf 38
Ballynacarrigy IRL (WMT) 89 Sc 27
Ballynaclash IRL (WEX) 101 Td 34
Ballynaclash IRL (WTF) 99 Sb 36
Ballynaclogh IRL (WTF) 100 Se 35
Ballynaclogh Cross Roads IRL (WTF) 100 Se 35
Ballynacole IRL (COR) 104 Rf 37
Ballynacorra IRL (COR) 104 Re 37
Ballynacorra IRL (GAL) 88 Rd 27
Ballynacorra IRL (WMT) 89 Sb 28
Ballynacourty IRL (WTF) 100 Sc 36
Ballynacourty House IRL (TIP) 99 Re 34
Ballynacree IRL (MT) 89 Se 26
Ballynadrimna Cross Roads IRL (MT) 89 Ta 27
Ballynadrumny IRL (KIL) 94 Ta 28
Ballynafid IRL (WMT) 89 Sd 27
Ballynagall IRL (WMT) 89 Sd 27
Ballynagarbragh IRL (COR) 104 Rd 37
Ballynagarde House IRL (LIM) 98 Rc 33
Ballynagar House IRL (GAL) 93 Rd 30
Ballynagaul IRL (LIM) 97 Qe 33
Ballynagaul IRL (WTF) 100 Sc 36
Ballynagore IRL (WMT) 94 Sd 28
Ballynagrallagh IRL (WEX) 100 Tb 34
Ballynagree IRL (COR) 98 Ra 37
Ballynaguilla IRL (COR) 98 Ra 35
Ballynahara IRL (TIP) 100 Sc 34
Ballynahattina IRL (GAL) 88 Rc 28
Ballynaheila House IRL (COR) 99 Sa 37
Ballynahina IRL (COR) 104 Rd 37
Ballynahinch GB (DOW) 85 Ua 22
Ballynahinch House IRL (LIM) 99 Rd 34
Ballynahow IRL (KER) 102 Pd 37
Ballynahown IRL (GAL) 91 Qc 29
Ballynahown IRL (WMT) 93 Sa 28
Ballynakill IRL (CLW) 100 Ta 32
Ballynakill IRL (KIL) 89 Ta 28
Ballynakill IRL (WTF) 99 Sc 35
Ballynakilla IRL (COR) 98 Rb 34
Ballynakilla IRL (COR) 99 Re 36
Ballynakill Lough IRL (GAL) 92 Rb 30
Ballynakilly Upper IRL (KER) 97 Qa 36
Ballynalty IRL (MAY) 87 Qe 27
Ballynamallaght GB (TYR) 78 Se 19
Ballynamaul Cross Roads IRL (COR) 104 Rc 38
Ballynamona IRL (COR) 98 Rc 36
Ballynamona IRL (COR) 99 Re 35
Ballynamona IRL (GAL) 87 Rc 28
Ballynamona IRL (GAL) 93 Re 28
Ballynamona IRL (LGF) 89 Sc 26
Ballynamona IRL (SLI) 81 Qf 23
Ballynamona IRL (WEX) 101 Te 34
Ballynamrossagh IRL (TIP) 99 Re 34
Ballynamuddagh IRL (COR) 99 Rd 36
Ballynamult IRL (WTF) 99 Sb 35
Ballynamultina House IRL (WTF) 99 Sb 36
Ballynare Cross Roads IRL (MT) 95 Tc 28
Ballynarooga IRL (LIM) 98 Ra 34
Ballynasaggart IRL (ROS) 88 Rf 27
Ballynasare IRL (KER) 96 Pf 36
Ballynasare IRL (KER) 97 Qb 35
Ballynascarty IRL (COR) 104 Rf 37
Ballynaskreena IRL (KER) 97 Qb 34
Ballynaslaney IRL (WEX) 101 Tc 34
Ballynasraw Cross Roads IRL (LGF) 89 Sc 26
Ballynastuckaun IRL (GAL) 87 Rb 28
Ballyncill IRL (TIP) 100 Sd 34
Ballyneague IRL (COR) 104 Sa 37
Ballyneale IRL (KLK) 100 Sf 34
Ballyneale House IRL (LIM) 98 Ra 34
Ballynee IRL (MT) 90 Tb 26
Ballyneety IRL (TIP) 99 Sa 35
Ballyneety House IRL (LIM) 99 Re 33
Ballynerrin IRL (WKL) 95 Tf 30
Ballynes IRL (DON) 77 Rf 18
Ballynesker IRL (WEX) 101 Td 34
Ballynin House IRL (OFF) 93 Sb 29
Ballynodrideen IRL (COR) 98 Rb 35
Ballynoe IRL (COR) 99 Rf 36
Ballynoe IRL (COR) 103 Ra 39
Ballynora IRL (COR) 104 Rc 37
Ballynure GB (ANT) 85 Ua 20
Ballyoliver IRL (CLW) 95 Tb 31
Ballyorgan IRL (LIM) 98 Rd 35
Ballyorley IRL (WEX) 101 Td 33
Ballyoughna Cross Roads IRL (WEX) 101 Te 33
Ballyoughteragh IRL (KER) 96 Pd 35
Ballyouneen IRL (KER) 97 Qc 34
Ballyourane IRL (COR) 103 Qd 39
Ballyowen House IRL (TIP) 99 Sb 33
Ballypatrick IRL (TIP) 100 Sc 34
Ballyphilip IRL (LAO) 94 Sc 32
Ballyphilip IRL (WTF) 99 Sa 36
Ballyporeen IRL (TIP) 99 Rf 35
Ballyquin IRL (KER) 96 Pf 35
Ballyragget IRL (KLK) 94 Sd 32
Ballyrankin House IRL (WEX) 101 Tc 33
Ballyraymeen House IRL (KER) 97 Qb 35
Ballyre IRL (COR) 99 Rf 37
Ballyready House IRL (COR) 99 Re 36
Ballyreagh GB (TYR) 84 Ta 22
Ballyregan IRL (COR) 104 Re 37
Ballyregan IRL (LIM) 98 Rc 33
Ballyroan IRL (LAO) 94 Se 31
Ballyrobert GB (DOW) 85 Ub 21
Ballyrobert Cross Roads GB (ANT) 85 Ua 20
Ballyroddy IRL (ROS) 88 Re 25
Ballyroe IRL (KER) 96 Pd 35
Ballyroebuck IRL (WEX) 101 Tc 33
Ballyronan GB (LDR) 84 Tc 20
Ballyroney GB (DOW) 85 Tf 23
Ballyroon IRL (COR) 102 Qb 39
Ballyroonmountain IRL (COR) 102 Qb 39
Ballyroughan IRL (CRE) 92 Rb 32
Ballyrub IRL (COR) 104 Rc 39
Ballyrush IRL (MOG) 90 Tc 24
Ballysadare IRL (SLI) 82 Rc 23
Ballysax Manor IRL (KIL) 95 Tb 30
Ballyshakikin IRL (LIM) 98 Rc 34
Ballyshane IRL (WKL) 95 Te 31
Ballyshannon IRL (DON) 82 Re 21
Ballyshannon House IRL (KIL) 94 Tb 30
Ballysharre IRL (OFF) 93 Sb 30
Ballyshear IRL (OFF) 94 Se 29
Ballysheedy IRL (LIM) 98 Rc 33
Ballysheen IRL (KER) 97 Qb 34
Ballyshelin IRL (WEX) 101 Tc 35
Ballyshire IRL (OFF) 93 Sb 29
Ballysimon IRL (WEX) 101 Td 33
Ballysloe IRL (TIP) 100 Sc 33
Ballysorrell IRL (TIP) 93 Sb 32
Ballystanley House IRL (OFF) 93 Sa 31
Ballysteen IRL (LIM) 98 Ra 33
Ballytarsna IRL (KLK) 100 Se 34
Ballytarsna IRL (LAO) 94 Sd 31
Ballytarsna IRL (TIP) 99 Sa 33
Ballytarsna Cross Roads IRL (WEX) 101 Td 32
Ballytassa IRL (MAY) 87 Qf 27
Ballyteague House IRL (OFF) 94 Sd 29
Ballytoohey IRL (ROS) 88 Sa 26
Ballytoohy IRL (MAY) 86 Qa 26
Ballytrasna House IRL (COR) 104 Re 37
Ballytrust IRL (CAV) 89 Sd 25
Ballyturin House IRL (GAL) 92 Rb 30
Ballyvaghan IRL (CRE) 92 Qf 30
Ballyvaldon IRL (WEX) 101 Te 34
Ballyvally House IRL (CRE) 93 Rd 32
Ballyvaltron IRL (WKL) 95 Tf 31
Ballyvaneen IRL (GAL) 88 Rd 28
Ballyvergin IRL (WEX) 101 Tb 34
Ballyviniter Upper IRL (COR) 98 Rc 35
Ballyviren Bridge IRL (COR) 103 Qf 39
Ballyvirrane IRL (KER) 97 Qb 36
Ballyvisteen IRL (COR) 98 Rd 35
Ballyvoge IRL (COR) 103 Qf 37
Ballyvoige IRL (COR) 103 Ra 38
Ballyvolan IRL (WKL) 95 Tf 30
Ballyvolane House IRL (COR) 99 Re 36
Ballyvolock IRL (COR) 99 Re 35
Ballyvonnavaun IRL (CRE) 92 Ra 32
Ballyvourney IRL (COR) 103 Qe 37
Ballyvoyle Cross Roads IRL (WTF) 100 Sc 36
Ballywalter GB (DOW) 85 Ud 21
Ballywalter IRL (COR) 98 Rd 35
Ballywalter IRL (MAY) 87 Qe 27
Ballyward GB (DOW) 85 Tf 23
Ballywater House IRL (WEX) 101 Te 33
Ballywilliam IRL (LIM) 98 Ra 33
Ballywinna IRL (GAL) 92 Rb 29
Balmacara GB (HGL) 13 Uc 5
Balmaclellan GB (DAG) 30 Vf 18
Balmacneil GB (TYS) 21 Wc 9
Balmae GB (DAG) 29 Vf 20
Balmaha GB (CEN) 24 Vc 12
Balmalcolm GB (FIF) 21 Wf 11
Balmarand GB (HGL) 10 Sd 3
Balmartin GB (HGL) 10 Sd 3
Balmeanach GB (HGL) 13 Tf 4
Balmedie GB (GRP) 17 Xf 5
Balmerino GB (FIF) 21 Wf 10
Balmerlawn GB (HAS) 69 Yc 44
Balminnoch GB (DAG) 30 Vb 19
Balmore GB (STC) 25 Ve 13
Balmullo GB (FIF) 22 Xa 10
Balnabodach GB (HGL) 12 Sd 7
Balnabruaich GB (HGL) 8 Vf 2
Balnacoil GB (HGL) 8 Vf 120
Balnafoich GB (HGL) 15 Ve 4
Balnagall GB (HGL) 9 Wa 2
Balnaguard GB (TYS) 21 Wb 9
Balnaguisich GB (HGL) 8 Ve 2
Balnahard GB (STC) 18 Tf 10
Balnain GB (HGL) 15 Vc 4
Balnakeil GB (HGL) 4 Vb 117
Balnaknock GB (HGL) 13 Te 3
Balnapaling GB (HGL) 8 Vf 2
Balquhidder GB (CEN) 20 Vd 10
Balrathboyne Glebe IRL (MT) 89 Ta 26
Balrath House IRL (MT) 90 Tc 25
Balrath Lodge IRL (WMT) 89 Sc 27
Balreask Cross Roads IRL (MT) 90 Tb 27
Balrothery IRL (DUB) 90 Te 27
Balsall GB (WMD) 53 Yc 34
Balscaddan IRL (DUB) 90 Te 27
Balscote GB (OXS) 54 Yd 36
Balsham GB (CBS) 56 Ab 36
Baltasound GB (SHL) 2 Za 104
Balteen IRL (COR) 102 Qb 40
Balteenbrack IRL (COR) 103 Qf 38
Balterley GB (SFS) 45 Xd 30
Balthangie GB (GRP) 17 Xe 3
Baltimore IRL (COR) 103 Qd 40
Baltinglass IRL (WKL) 95 Tb 31
Baltovin IRL (KER) 97 Qb 34
Baltrasna IRL (MT) 90 Td 28
Baltrasna House IRL (MT) 89 Se 26
Baltray IRL (LOT) 90 Te 26
Balvaird GB (HGL) 15 Vd 3
Balvicar GB (STC) 19 Uc 11
Bamber Bridge GB (LCS) 38 Xc 26
Bambers Green GB (ESS) 64 Ab 37
Bamburgh GB (NHL) 27 Yb 15
Bamford GB (DSH) 45 Yb 28
Bampton GB (CUB) 35 Xb 21
Bampton GB (DEV) 67 Wd 43
Bampton GB (OXS) 62 Yc 38
Banada IRL (SLI) 87 Rb 24
Banagher IRL (OFF) 93 Sa 29
Banavie GB (HGL) 19 Uf 7
Banbridge GB (DOW) 84 Te 22
Banbury GB (OXS) 54 Yd 36
Banchory GB (GRP) 17 Xd 6
Banchory-Devenick GB (GRP) 17 Xf 6
Bancyfelin GB (DYF) 59 Vd 38
Bandon IRL (COR) 104 Rb 38
Banff GB (GRP) 17 Xc 2
Bangor GB (DOW) 85 Uc 21
Bangor GB (GWY) 42 Vf 29
Bangor IRL (MAY) 80 Qb 24
Banham GB (NOR) 57 Ba 34
Bank GB (HAS) 69 Yc 43
Bankend GB (DAG) 31 Wc 18
Bankend GB (STC) 25 Wa 15
Bankfoot GB (TYS) 21 Wc 9
Bankhead GB (GRP) 17 Xc 6
Bankhead GB (GRP) 17 Xe 5
Bank Newton GB (NOY) 39 Xf 25
Banknock GB (CEN) 25 Wa 13
Banks GB (CUB) 32 Xb 19
Banks GB (LCS) 38 Xa 26
Bankshill GB (DAG) 31 We 18
Bank Street GB (HWC) 52 Xc 35
Banna IRL (KER) 97 Qb 34
Banningham GB (NOR) 49 Bb 32
Bannockburn GB (CEN) 25 Wa 12
Bannow IRL (WEX) 100 Tb 35
Banraghbaun IRL (GAL) 91 Qc 29
Bansha IRL (CRE) 92 Qf 32
Bansha IRL (TIP) 99 Rf 34
Banstead GB (SUR) 64 Ze 41
Banteer IRL (COR) 98 Ra 36
Bantry IRL (COR) 103 Qd 38
Bantys House IRL (TIP) 93 Rf 31
Banwell GB (AVN) 68 Xa 41
Bapchild GB (KEN) 65 Ae 41
Barachander GB (STC) 19 Ue 10
Baralty IRL (MAY) 81 Qc 23
Baranoilt GB (LDR) 78 Sf 19
Barassie GB (STC) 24 Vc 15
Barbaraville GB (HGL) 8 Vf 2
Barbon GB (CUB) 35 Xc 23
Barbrook GB (DEV) 67 Wa 41
Barby GB (NRH) 54 Ye 35
Barcaldine GB (STC) 19 Ue 9
Barcombe Cross GB (ESX) 71 Aa 43
Barden GB (NOY) 36 Yb 22
Bard Inch IRL (COR) 103 Qe 37
Bardney GB (LIN) 47 Ze 29
Bardon GB (LEC) 46 Yd 32
Bardon Mill GB (NHL) 32 Xd 19
Bardsea GB (CUB) 34 Wf 24
Bardsey GB (WYO) 40 Yd 25
Bardwell GB (SUF) 56 Af 35
Barefield IRL (CRE) 92 Ra 31
Barewood GB (HWC) 52 Xa 35
Barford GB (NOR) 49 Ba 33
Barford GB (WWH) 53 Yc 35
Barford Saint John GB (OXS) 62 Yd 37
Barford Saint Martin GB (WIL) 69 Ya 42
Barford Saint Michael GB (OXS) 62 Yd 37
Barfrestone GB (KEN) 65 Bb 41
Bargaly GB (DAG) 30 Vd 19
Bargoed GB (MGL) 60 We 38
Bargrennan GB (DAG) 30 Vc 18
Bargy Commons IRL (WEX) 101 Tc 35
Bar Hall GB (ESS) 56 Ad 37
Barham GB (KEN) 73 Ba 41
Bar Hill GB (CBS) 55 Aa 35
Barholm GB (LIN) 47 Zd 32
Barkby GB (LEC) 54 Yf 32
Barkby Thorpe GB (LEC) 54 Yf 32
Barkestone-le-Vale GB (LEC) 46 Za 31
Barkham GB (BKS) 63 Za 40
Barking GB (GRL) 64 Aa 39
Barking GB (SUF) 57 Ba 36
Barkisland GB (WYO) 39 Ya 26
Barkston GB (LIN) 47 Zc 31
Barkston Ash GB (NOY) 40 Ye 26
Barkway GB (HTS) 55 Aa 36
Barlaston GB (SFS) 45 Xf 31
Barlavington GB (WSX) 70 Zc 43
Barlborough GB (DSH) 46 Ye 29
Barlby GB (NOY) 40 Yf 26
Barlestone GB (LEC) 54 Yd 33
Barley GB (HTS) 55 Aa 36
Barley GB (LCS) 39 Xe 25
Barleymont IRL (KER) 97 Qc 36
Barleythorpe GB (LEC) 54 Zb 32
Barling GB (ESS) 65 Ae 39
Barlings GB (LIN) 47 Zd 29
Barloge IRL (COR) 103 Qe 40
Barlow GB (DSH) 46 Yd 29
Barlow GB (NOY) 40 Yf 26
Barlow GB (TAW) 33 Yb 19
Barmby Moor GB (HUS) 40 Zb 25
Barmby on the Marsh GB (HUS) 40 Za 26
Barmeath IRL (LOT) 90 Td 26
Barmill GB (STC) 24 Vc 14
Barmouth GB (GWY) 51 Vf 32
Barmpton GB (DUR) 36 Yc 21
Barmston GB (HUS) 41 Ze 24
Barna IRL (GAL) 92 Qf 29
Barna IRL (OFF) 93 Sa 31
Barnacawley IRL (ROS) 88 Rc 25
Barnack GB (CBS) 55 Zd 33
Barnacle GB (WWH) 54 Yd 34
Barna Cross Roads IRL (COR) 103 Qd 39
Barnagowlane IRL (COR) 103 Qe 38
Barnahown IRL (TIP) 99 Rf 35
Barnahowna IRL (MAY) 86 Qd 27
Barnalisheen IRL (TIP) 93 Sb 32
Barnard Castle GB (DUR) 36 Ya 21
Barnard Gate GB (OXS) 62 Yd 38
Barnardiston GB (SUF) 56 Ad 36
Barnatra IRL (MAY) 80 Qa 23
Barnawheel IRL (WEX) 101 Td 35
Barna Wood IRL (KER) 97 Qd 35
Barnburgh GB (SOY) 40 Ye 27
Barnby Dun GB (SOY) 40 Yf 27
Barnby Moor GB (NTS) 46 Yf 28
Barnet GB (GRL) 64 Ze 39
Barnetby le Wold GB (HUS) 41 Zd 27
Barnham GB (SUF) 56 Ae 34
Barnham GB (WSX) 70 Zc 44
Barnham Broom GB (NOR) 57 Ba 33
Barnhead GB (TYS) 22 Xc 8
Barnhill GB (DAG) 28 Uf 19
Barnhill GB (GRP) 16 Wd 3
Barnhill Cross IRL (LOT) 90 Te 26
Barningham GB (DUR) 36 Ya 22
Barningham GB (SUF) 56 Af 34
Barnoldby le Beck GB (HUS) 41 Zf 27
Barnoldswick GB (LCS) 39 Xe 25
Barns Green GB (WSX) 71 Zd 42
Barnsley GB (GLS) 62 Ya 38
Barnsley GB (SOY) 40 Yd 27
Barnstaple GB (DEV) 66 Vf 42
Barnstaple Cross GB (DEV) 67 Wb 44
Barnston GB (CHS) 44 Wf 28
Barnston GB (ESS) 64 Ac 37
Barnt Green GB (HWC) 53 Ya 34
Barntick House IRL (CRE) 92 Ra 32
Barnton GB (CHS) 44 Xc 29
Barnwell GB (NRH) 55 Zd 34
Baronne Court IRL (TIP) 93 Sa 30
Baronstown IRL (WMT) 89 Sc 27
Barony, the GB (ORK) 5 We 114
Barr GB (STC) 23 Tf 14
Barr GB (STC) 30 Vb 17
Barrachan GB (DAG) 29 Vc 20
Barrack IRL (COR) 98 Rc 36
Barrack IRL (COR) 99 Re 35
Barrack Cross Roads IRL (COR) 98 Ra 35
Barracks Cross Roads IRL (WEX) 101 Td 35
Barrack Village IRL (KLK) 94 Se 32
Barrack Village IRL (WEX) 100 Ta 34
Barrack Village IRL (WEX) 101 Td 33
Barraderry IRL (TIP) 99 Rf 33
Barrafohona IRL (COR) 99 Rf 36
Barraglom GB (HGL) 11 Tb 119
Barrahormid GB (STC) 23 Ub 13
Barranisky Cross Roads IRL (WKL) 95 Tf 31
Barranny IRL (GAL) 87 Qf 28
Barrapol GB (STC) 18 Ta 10
Barras GB (GRP) 22 Xe 7
Barrasford GB (NHL) 33 Xf 18
Barratogher House IRL (WMT) 89 Sc 27
Barravakeen IRL (WTF) 99 Sc 35
Barravullin GB (STC) 23 Uc 11
Barreen IRL (KIL) 95 Tb 28
Barrees IRL (COR) 102 Qa 38
Barregarrow GBM 29 Vc 23
Barrhead GB (STC) 24 Vd 14
Barrhill GB (STC) 30 Vb 18
Barrigone IRL (LIM) 98 Qf 33
Barrington GB (SOM) 68 Xa 43
Barripper GB (CNW) 74 Ue 47
Barrock GB (HGL) 6 We 117
Barrow GB (LCS) 38 Xd 25
Barrow GB (SOM) 68 Xd 42
Barrow GB (SUF) 56 Ad 35
Barrow IRL (KER) 97 Qa 35
Barroway Drove GB (NOR) 56 Ab 33
Barrowby GB (LIN) 46 Zb 31
Barrowford GB (LCS) 39 Xe 25
Barrow Gurney GB (AVN) 61 Xb 40
Barrow-in-Furness GB (CUB) 38 We 24
Barrow Nook GB (LCS) 38 Xa 27
Barrow Street GB (WIL) 68 Xe 42
Barrow upon Humber GB (HUS) 41 Zd 26
Barrow upon Soar GB (LEC) 46 Yf 32
Barrow upon Trent GB (DSH) 46 Yd 31
Barry GB (SGL) 60 We 40
Barry GB (TYS) 22 Xb 9
Barry IRL (LGF) 88 Sb 27
Barry's Cross Road IRL (COR) 98 Ra 35
Barryroe IRL (COR) 104 Rb 39
Barryshall IRL (COR) 104 Rb 39
Barsby GB (LEC) 54 Za 32
Barston GB (WMD) 53 Yb 34
Barthol Chapel GB (GRP) 17 Xe 4
Bartholomews Bridge IRL (LIM) 98 Qf 33
Barthomley GB (CHS) 45 Xd 30
Bartlemy IRL (COR) 99 Re 36
Bartley GB (HAS) 69 Yc 43
Bartlow GB (CBS) 56 Ab 36
Barton GB (CBS) 55 Aa 35
Barton GB (CHS) 44 Xb 30
Barton GB (DEV) 76 Wc 46
Barton GB (LCS) 38 Xb 26
Barton GB (NOY) 36 Yc 22
Barton GB (WWH) 53 Ya 36
Barton Bendish GB (NOR) 56 Ad 33
Barton End GB (GLS) 61 Xe 38
Barton Hartshorn GB (BUS) 63 Yf 37
Barton in Fabis GB (NTS) 46 Ye 31
Barton in the Beans GB (LEC) 54 Yd 33
Barton-le-Cley GB (BFS) 63 Zd 37
Barton-le-Street GB (NOY) 37 Za 24
Barton-le-Willows GB (NOY) 40 Za 24
Barton Mills GB (SUF) 56 Ad 35
Barton on Sea GB (HAS) 69 Yc 44
Barton-on-the-Heath GB (WWH) 62 Yc 37
Barton Seagrave GB (NRH) 55 Zb 34
Barton Stacey GB (HAS) 69 Yd 42
Barton-under-Needwood GB (SFS) 45 Yb 32
Barton-upon-Humber GB (HUS) 41 Zd 26
Barvas GB (HGL) 11 Tc 118
Barwell GB (LEC) 54 Yd 33
Barwick GB (SOM) 68 Xc 43
Barwick in Elmet GB (WYO) 40 Yd 26
Baschurch GB (SHS) 44 Xa 32
Bascote GB (WWH) 54 Yd 35
Basford Green GB (SFS) 45 Xf 30
Bashall Eaves GB (LCS) 38 Xd 25
Bashley GB (HAS) 69 Yc 44
Basildon GB (BKS) 63 Yf 40
Basildon GB (ESS) 65 Ac 39
Basing GB (HAS) 70 Yf 41
Basingstoke GB (HAS) 70 Yf 41
Baslow GB (DSH) 45 Yc 29
Bason Bridge GB (SOM) 68 Xa 41
Bassaleg GB (GWE) 60 Wf 39
Bassenthwaite GB (CUB) 34 We 20
Basset's Cross GB (DEV) 66 Vf 44
Bassingbourn GB (CBS) 55 Zf 36
Bassingfield GB (NTS) 46 Yf 31
Bassingham GB (LIN) 47 Zc 30
Bassingthorpe GB (LIN) 47 Zc 31
Baston GB (LIN) 47 Zd 32
Bastwick GB (NOR) 49 Bd 32
Batchcott GB (SHS) 52 Xb 35
Batchworth GB (HTS) 63 Zd 39
Batcombe GB (DOS) 68 Xc 44
Batcombe GB (SOM) 68 Xd 42
Bate Heath GB (CHS) 44 Xd 29
Bath GB (AVN) 61 Xd 40
Batheaston GB (SOM) 67 We 42
Batheaston GB (AVN) 61 Xe 40
Bathford GB (AVN) 61 Xe 40
Bathgate GB (LOT) 25 Wc 13
Batley GB (WYO) 39 Yc 26
Batsford GB (GLS) 62 Yb 36
Battersby GB (NOY) 37 Yf 22
Batterstown IRL (MT) 90 Tc 28
Battisborough Cross GB (DEV) 76 Wa 47
Battisford Tye GB (SUF) 57 Af 36
Battle GB (ESX) 72 Ac 43
Battle GB (POW) 60 Wd 37
Battlemount IRL (KIL) 94 Ta 30
Battlesbridge GB (ESS) 65 Ad 39
Battleton GB (SOM) 67 Wc 42
Battramsley GB (HAS) 69 Yc 44
Bauds of Cullen GB (GRP) 16 Xa 2
Baughna IRL (WMT) 89 Se 28
Baughton GB (HWC) 53 Xe 36
Baulking GB (OXS) 62 Yc 39
Baumber GB (LIN) 47 Ze 29
Baungarrif IRL (KLK) 100 Sd 34
Baunogemeely IRL (LAO) 94 Se 31
Baunoges IRL (GAL) 88 Rc 28
Baunskeha IRL (KLK) 100 Sf 34
Bauntlieve IRL (CRE) 92 Qe 31
Baunton GB (GLS) 62 Ya 38
Bauragoogeen IRL (KER) 97 Qd 33
Bauraneag IRL (LIM) 98 Qe 33
Baurnagurrahy IRL (LIM) 99 Re 34
Baveney Wood GB (SHS) 52 Xd 34
Baverstock GB (WIL) 69 Ya 42
Bawburgh GB (NOR) 49 Bb 33
Bawdeswell GB (NOR) 49 Ba 32
Bawdsey GB (SUF) 57 Bc 36
Bawnagarrane IRL (WTF) 104 Sb 37
Bawnatanaknoch IRL (COR) 103 Qf 37
Bawnboy House IRL (CAV) 83 Sc 24
Bawn Cross Roads IRL (COR) 98 Ra 35
Bawnfune IRL (WTF) 99 Sb 35
Bawn House IRL (LGF) 88 Sb 26
Bawnmore IRL (COR) 103 Ra 37
Bawtry GB (SOY) 40 Yf 28
Baxenden GB (LCS) 39 Xd 26
Baxterley GB (WWH) 53 Yc 33
Baycliff GB (CUB) 34 Wf 24
Baydon GB (WIL) 62 Yc 39
Bayford GB (HTS) 64 Ab 38
Bayfordbury GB (HTS) 64 Ab 38
Bayhead GB (HGL) 10 Sd 3
Bayles GB (CUB) 35 Xd 20
Baylham GB (SUF) 57 Ba 36
Baynards Green GB (OXS) 62 Ye 37
Bayston Hill GB (SHS) 52 Xb 32
Baythorn End GB (ESS) 56 Ad 36
Bayton GB (HWC) 52 Xd 34
Beachampton GB (BUS) 54 Za 36
Beachamwell GB (NOR) 56 Ad 33
Beachans GB (GRP) 16 Wc 3
Beacharr GB (STC) 23 Ub 15
Beach Hill IRL (GAL) 93 Rc 29
Beach House IRL (COR) 103 Qd 38
Beachley GB (GLS) 61 Xc 39
Beacon GB (DEV) 67 We 43
Beacon End GB (ESS) 65 Ae 37
Beacon's Bottom GB (BUS) 63 Za 39
Beaconsfield GB (BUS) 63 Zc 39
Beadlam GB (NOY) 37 Za 23
Beadnell GB (NHL) 27 Yc 15
Beaford GB (DEV) 66 Vf 43
Beal GB (NHL) 27 Ya 14
Bealadangan IRL (GAL) 91 Qc 29
Bealad Cross Roads IRL (COR) 103 Ra 39
Bealaha IRL (CRE) 91 Qc 32
Beal Atha na Sluaighe = Ballinasloe IRL (GAL) 93 Re 29
Bealnablath IRL (COR) 103 Ra 38
Bealnamoriye IRL (COR) 103 Ra 37
Beamhurst GB (SFS) 45 Ya 31
Beaminster GB (DOS) 68 Xb 44
Beamish GB (DUR) 33 Yc 19
Beamsley GB (NOY) 39 Ya 25
Bean GB (KEN) 64 Ab 40
Beanacre GB (WIL) 61 Xf 40
Beanley GB (NHL) 33 Ya 16

108 GB IRL Ballydesmond – Beanley

Beardon **GB** (DEV) 66 Vf 45
Beare Green **GB** (SUR) 71 Ze 41
Bearley **GB** (WWH) 53 Yb 35
Bearpark **GB** (DUR) 36 Yc 20
Bearsbridge **GB** (NHL) 32 Xd 19
Bearsden **GB** (STC) 25 Vd 13
Bearsted **GB** (KEN) 65 Ad 41
Beattock **GB** (DAG) 31 Wd 17
Beauchamp Roding **GB** (ESS) 64 Ab 38
Beauchief **GB** (SOY) 46 Yd 29
Beaufort **GB** (GWE) 60 We 38
Beaufort **IRL** (KER) 97 Qc 36
Beaulieu **GB** (HAS) 69 Yd 44
Beauly **GB** (HGL) 15 Vd 4
Beaumaris **GB** (GWY) 42 Vf 29
Beaumont **GB** (CUB) 32 Wf 19
Beaumont **GB** (ESS) 65 Ba 37
Beaumont **GBJ** 73 Xf 53
Beaumont **IRL** (MT) 90 Td 27
Beausale **GB** (WWH) 53 Yc 34
Beauworth **GB** (HAS) 70 Ye 42
Beaworthy **GB** (DEV) 66 Ve 44
Beazley End **GB** (ESS) 65 Ad 37
Bebington **GB** (CHS) 44 Wf 28
Beccles **GB** (SUF) 57 Bd 34
Beckbury **GB** (SHS) 53 Xd 34
Beckenham **GB** (GRL) 64 Zf 40
Beckermet **GB** (CUB) 34 Wc 22
Beckfoot **GB** (CUB) 34 Wd 20
Beckfoot **GB** (CUB) 34 We 22
Beck Foot **GB** (CUB) 35 Xc 22
Beckford **GB** (HWC) 53 Xf 36
Beckhampton **GB** (WIL) 62 Ya 40
Beck Hole **GB** (NOY) 37 Zb 22
Beckingham **GB** (LIN) 46 Zb 30
Beckingham **GB** (NTS) 40 Za 28
Beckington **GB** (SOM) 68 Xe 41
Beckley **GB** (ESX) 72 Ad 43
Beckley **GB** (OXS) 63 Ye 38
Beck Row **GB** (SUF) 56 Ac 34
Beck Side **GB** (CUB) 34 We 23
Beckwithshaw **GB** (NOY) 39 Yc 25
Bective **IRL** (MT) 90 Tb 27
Bedale **GB** (NOY) 36 Yc 23
Bedburn **GB** (DUR) 36 Ya 20
Bedchester **GB** (DOS) 69 Xe 43
Beddau **GB** (MGL) 60 Wd 39
Beddgelert **GB** (GWY) 42 Vf 30
Beddingham **GB** (ESX) 71 Aa 43
Beddington **GB** (GRL) 64 Zf 40
Bedfield **GB** (SUF) 57 Bb 35
Bedford **GB** (BFS) 55 Zd 36
Bedgebury **GB** (KEN) 72 Ac 42
Bedingfield **GB** (SUF) 57 Bb 35
Bedlington **GB** (NHL) 33 Yc 18
Bedlinog **GB** (MGL) 60 We 38
Bedmond **GB** (HTS) 63 Zd 38
Bednall **GB** (SFS) 45 Xf 32
Bedruthan Steps **GB** (CNW) 74 Uf 46
Bedstone **GB** (SHS) 52 Xa 34
Bedwas **GB** (MGL) 60 We 39
Bedworth **GB** (WWH) 54 Yd 34
Beeby **GB** (LEC) 54 Yf 33
Beech **GB** (HAS) 70 Yf 42
Beech **GB** (SFS) 45 Xe 31
Beechingstoke **GB** (WIL) 62 Ya 40
Beechmount **IRL** (COR) 98 Rb 36
Beechwood **IRL** (ROS) 88 Rf 27
Beechwood Park **IRL** (TIP) 93 Rf 31
Beedon **GB** (BKS) 62 Ye 40
Beeford **GB** (HUS) 41 Ze 25
Beehive **IRL** (CAV) 89 Sf 25
Beeley **GB** (DSH) 45 Yc 29
Beelsby **GB** (HUS) 41 Ze 27
Beenacouma **IRL** (KER) 96 Pd 36
Beenalaght **IRL** (COR) 98 Rb 36
Beenham **GB** (BKS) 63 Yf 40
Beennaskehy **IRL** (COR) 98 Rc 36
Beer **GB** (DEV) 67 Wf 44
Beer Crocombe **GB** (SOM) 68 Xa 43
Beer Hackett **GB** (DOS) 68 Xc 43
Beesands **GB** (DEV) 76 Wc 47
Beesby **GB** (LIN) 47 Zf 29
Beeston **GB** (BFS) 55 Ze 36
Beeston **GB** (CHS) 44 Xb 30
Beeston **GB** (NOR) 48 Ae 32
Beeston **GB** (WYO) 39 Yc 26
Beeston and Stapleford **GB** (NTS) 46 Ye 31
Beeston Saint Lawrence **GB** (NOR) 49 Bc 32
Beeswing **GB** (DAG) 31 Wb 18
Beetham **GB** (CUB) 35 Xb 23
Beetley **GB** (NOR) 49 Af 32
Begbroke **GB** (OXS) 62 Ye 38
Begelly **GB** (DYF) 58 Vb 38
Beggerin Island **IRL** (WEX) 101 Td 34
Beglieve **IRL** (CAV) 89 Sf 25
Beguildy **GB** (POW) 52 We 34
Behagh **IRL** (COR) 103 Qf 38
Beheenagh **IRL** (KER) 97 Qe 36
Beighton **GB** (SOY) 46 Yd 28
Beihy **IRL** (LET) 88 Sb 25
Beith **GB** (STC) 24 Vc 14
Bekan **IRL** (MAY) 87 Ra 26
Bekesbourne **GB** (KEN) 65 Ba 41
Belalt **IRL** (DON) 83 Sa 21
Belan Cott. **IRL** (KIL) 94 Ta 31
Belbroughton **GB** (HWC) 53 Xf 34
Belcamp **IRL** (DUB) 95 Te 28
Belcarra **IRL** (MAY) 87 Qe 26
Belchamp Saint Paul **GB** (ESS) 56 Ad 36
Belchamp Water **GB** (ESS) 56 Ad 36
Belchford **GB** (LIN) 47 Zf 29
Belclare **IRL** (GAL) 87 Ra 28
Belcoo **GB** (FER) 83 Sa 23
Beldaragh **IRL** (DUB) 90 Te 27
Belderg **IRL** (MAY) 81 Qc 23
Belfarsad **IRL** (MAY) 86 Qa 25
Belfast **GB** (ANT) 85 Ua 21
Belford **GB** (NHL) 27 Yb 15
Belgooly House **IRL** (COR) 104 Rd 38
Belhelvie **GB** (GRP) 17 Xf 5
Bellabeg **GB** (GRP) 16 Wf 5
Belladooan **IRL** (MAY) 81 Qd 23
Belladrihid **IRL** (SLI) 82 Rd 23
Bellagarvaun **IRL** (MAY) 86 Qb 25
Bellahy **IRL** (SLI) 87 Rb 25
Bellanagare **IRL** (ROS) 88 Rd 25
Bellanamallaght **IRL** (GAL) 92 Rc 30
Bellanaman **IRL** (MOG) 84 Ta 23
Bellanamullia **IRL** (ROS) 88 Rf 28
Bellananagh **IRL** (CAV) 89 Sd 25
Bellanasally **IRL** (MAY) 86 Pf 25
Bellaneeny **IRL** (ROS) 88 Rf 28
Bellanoch **GB** (STC) 23 Uc 12
Bellanode **IRL** (MOG) 84 Sf 23
Bellantra Bridge **IRL** (LET) 88 Sb 25
Bellaty **GB** (TYS) 21 We 8
Bellavary **IRL** (MAY) 87 Qf 25
Bellaveeny **IRL** (MAY) 86 Qb 25
Bell Busk **GB** (NOY) 39 Xf 24
Belleau **GB** (LIN) 47 Aa 29
Belleek **IRL** (DON) 82 Rf 22
Belleek **IRL** (GAL) 86 Pf 28
Belleheiglash **GB** (GRP) 16 Wd 4
Belle Lake **IRL** (WTF) 100 Sf 35
Bell End **GB** (HWC) 53 Xf 34
Bellerby **GB** (NOY) 36 Yb 23
Bellever **GB** (DEV) 76 Wa 45
Belleville **IRL** (GAL) 92 Rb 28
Belle Vue **IRL** (MOG) 90 Tb 25
Bellevue **IRL** (WEX) 101 Tc 34
Bellewstown **IRL** (MT) 90 Td 27
Bellia **IRL** (CRE) 91 Qb 33
Belliehill **GB** (TYS) 22 Xb 8
Bellingdon **GB** (BUS) 63 Zc 38
Bellingham **GB** (NHL) 32 Xe 18
Belloch **GB** (STC) 23 Ub 15
Bellochantuy **GB** (STC) 28 Ub 15
Bell Park **GB** (HTS) 64 Ac 38
Bellsbank **GB** (STC) 30 Vd 17
Bellshill **GB** (NHL) 27 Yb 15
Bellshill **GB** (STC) 25 Vf 14
Bellsmyre **GB** (STC) 24 Vc 13
Bellspool **GB** (BOR) 26 We 14
Bells Yew Green **GB** (ESX) 72 Ab 42
Belluton **GB** (AVN) 61 Xc 40
Bellwell **IRL** (GAL) 87 Rb 27
Belmaduthy **GB** (HGL) 15 Ve 3
Belmesthorpe **GB** (LEC) 55 Zd 32
Belmont **GB** (ANT) 85 Ua 21
Belmont **GB** (LCS) 38 Xd 27
Belmont **GB** (SHL) 2 Za 104
Belmont **IRL** (GAL) 87 Ra 27
Belmont **IRL** (KER) 97 Qb 35
Belmont House **IRL** (OFF) 93 Sa 29
Belmore **GB** (STC) 24 Va 12
Belmullet **IRL** (MAY) 80 Qa 23
Belnacraig **GB** (GRP) 16 Wf 5
Belowda **GB** (CNW) 75 Va 46
Belper **GB** (DSH) 46 Yd 30
Belper Lane End **GB** (DSH) 46 Yc 30
Belrea **IRL** (ROS) 93 Rf 28
Belsay **GB** (NHL) 33 Ya 18
Belses **GB** (BOR) 32 Xb 15
Belsford **GB** (DEV) 76 Wb 46
Belstead **GB** (SUF) 57 Ba 36
Belston **GB** (STC) 30 Vc 16
Belstone **GB** (DEV) 66 Wa 44
Beltany **IRL** (DON) 77 Rf 18
Belthorn **GB** (LCS) 38 Xd 26
Beltoft **GB** (HUS) 40 Zb 27
Belton **GB** (HUS) 40 Zb 27
Belton **GB** (LEC) 46 Yd 32
Belton **GB** (LIN) 47 Zc 31
Belton **GB** (NOR) 57 Bd 33
Beltra **IRL** (MAY) 87 Qd 25
Beltra **IRL** (SLI) 82 Rc 23
Beltring **GB** (KEN) 72 Ac 41
Belturbet **IRL** (CAV) 89 Sd 24
Belvoir **GB** (LEC) 46 Zb 31
Belvue **IRL** (WMT) 89 Sf 27
Bembridge **GB** (IOW) 70 Yf 44
Bemersyde **GB** (BOR) 26 Xc 15
Bempton **GB** (HUS) 37 Ze 24
Benacre **GB** (SUF) 57 Be 34
Benbuie **GB** (DAG) 30 Vf 17
Benburb **GB** (TYR) 84 Tb 22
Ben Casgro **GB** (HGL) 11 Td 120
Benderloch **GB** (STC) 19 Ud 10
Bendooragh **GB** (ANT) 79 Tc 18
Benenden **GB** (KEN) 72 Ad 42
Benholm **GB** (GRP) 22 Xe 8
Benington **GB** (HTS) 64 Zf 37
Benington **GB** (LIN) 47 Aa 31
Benington Sea End **GB** (LIN) 47 Aa 31
Benllech **GB** (GWY) 42 Ve 29
Benmore **GB** (CEN) 20 Vc 10
Bennacott **GB** (CNW) 66 Vd 44
Bennan **GB** (STC) 28 Ue 16
Bennecarrigan **GB** (STC) 28 Ue 16
Bennettsbridge **IRL** (KLK) 100 Se 33
Benniworth **GB** (LIN) 47 Ze 29
Ben of Fore **IRL** (WMT) 89 Se 26
Benover **GB** (KEN) 72 Ac 41
Benson **GB** (OXS) 63 Yf 39
Benstonhall **GB** (ORK) 5 Xb 113
Bentham **GB** (GLS) 61 Xf 37
Bentley **GB** (HAS) 70 Za 41
Bentley **GB** (HUS) 41 Zd 26
Bentley **GB** (SOY) 40 Yf 27
Bentley **GB** (WWH) 53 Yc 33
Bentpath **GB** (DAG) 32 Wf 17
Bentworth **GB** (HAS) 70 Yf 42
Benvie **GB** (TYS) 21 Wf 10
Benville Lane **GB** (DOS) 68 Xc 44
Benwick **GB** (CBS) 55 Zf 34
Beoley **GB** (HWC) 53 Ya 35
Bepton **GB** (WSX) 70 Zb 43
Beragh **GB** (TYR) 83 Sf 21
Berea **GB** (DYF) 58 Ue 37
Bere Alston **GB** (DEV) 76 Ve 46
Bere Ferrers **GB** (DEV) 76 Ve 46
Berepper **GB** (CNW) 74 Ue 48
Bere Regis **GB** (DOS) 69 Xe 44
Berinsfield **GB** (OXS) 63 Ye 39
Berkeley **GB** (GLS) 61 Xd 38
Berkhamsted **GB** (HTS) 63 Zc 38
Berkley **GB** (SOM) 68 Xe 41
Berkswell **GB** (WMD) 53 Yc 34
Bernera **GB** (HGL) 13 Uc 5
Bernisdale **GB** (HGL) 13 Te 4
Berrick Salome **GB** (OXS) 63 Yf 39
Berriedale **GB** (HGL) 9 Wd 119
Berrier **GB** (CUB) 35 Xa 21
Berriew **GB** (POW) 52 We 33
Berrings **IRL** (COR) 104 Rb 37
Berrington **GB** (NHL) 27 Ya 14
Berrington **GB** (SHS) 52 Xb 33
Berrow **GB** (SOM) 68 Wf 41
Berrow Green **GB** (HWC) 53 Xd 35
Berry Hill **GB** (GLS) 61 Xc 38
Berryhillock **GB** (GRP) 16 Xb 3
Berrynarbor **GB** (DEV) 66 Vf 41
Berry Pomeroy **GB** (DEV) 76 Wc 46
Bersted **GB** (WSX) 70 Zb 44
Berwick **GB** (ESX) 71 Aa 44
Berwick Bassett **GB** (WIL) 62 Ya 40
Berwick Hill **GB** (NHL) 33 Yb 18
Berwick Saint James **GB** (WIL) 69 Ya 42
Berwick Saint John **GB** (WIL) 69 Xf 43
Berwick-upon-Tweed **GB** (NHL) 27 Xf 14
Berwyn **GB** (CLW) 44 We 31
Besboro House **IRL** (MT) 90 Td 27
Bescar **GB** (LCS) 38 Xa 27
Besford **GB** (HWC) 53 Xf 36
Besford **GB** (SHS) 44 Xb 32
Bessbrook **GB** (ARG) 84 Td 23
Bessbrook **IRL** (MOG) 83 Sf 23
Bessels Leigh **GB** (OXS) 62 Yd 38
Bessingby **GB** (HUS) 41 Ze 24
Bessingham **GB** (NOR) 49 Bb 31
Best Beech Hill **GB** (ESX) 72 Ab 42
Besthorpe **GB** (NOR) 57 Ba 33
Besthorpe **GB** (NTS) 46 Zb 29
Beswick **GB** (HUS) 41 Zd 25
Betaghstown Cross Roads **IRL** (KIL) 95 Tb 29
Betchword **GB** (SUR) 71 Ze 41
Bethania **GB** (DYF) 51 Vf 35
Bethania **GB** (GWY) 43 Wa 31
Bethel **GB** (GWY) 42 Vd 29
Bethel **GB** (GWY) 42 Ve 30
Bethersden **GB** (KEN) 72 Ae 42
Bethesda **GB** (DYF) 58 Vb 38
Bethesda **GB** (GWY) 43 Vf 29
Bethlehem **GB** (DYF) 59 Wa 37
Bethlehem House **IRL** (WMT) 88 Sa 27
Bethnal Green **GB** (GRL) 64 Zf 39
Betley **GB** (SFS) 45 Xd 30
Betsham **GB** (KEN) 64 Ab 40
Bettisfield **GB** (CLW) 44 Xb 31
Betton **GB** (SHS) 44 Xd 31
Bettws **GB** (GWE) 60 Wf 37
Bettws **GB** (GWE) 60 Wf 39
Bettws Cedewain **GB** (POW) 51 We 33
Bettws Gwerfil Goch **GB** (CLW) 43 Wd 30
Bettws Newydd **GB** (POW) 60 Xa 38
Bettws-y-crwyn **GB** (SHS) 52 We 34
Bettyfield **IRL** (ROS) 88 Re 25
Bettyhill **GB** (HGL) 5 Ve 117
Bettystown **IRL** (MT) 90 Te 26
Betty Ville **IRL** (COR) 98 Ra 35
Betty Ville **IRL** (LIM) 98 Rb 33
Betws **GB** (DYF) 59 Wa 38
Betws **GB** (MGL) 60 Wc 39
Betws Bledrws **GB** (DYF) 51 Vf 36
Betws Garmon **GB** (GWY) 42 Ve 30
Betws Ifan **GB** (DYF) 50 Vd 36
Betws-y-Coed **GB** (GWY) 43 Wb 30
Betws-yn-Rhos **GB** (CLW) 43 Wc 29
Beulah **GB** (DYF) 50 Vc 36
Beulah **GB** (POW) 51 Wc 36
Bevendean **GB** (ESX) 71 Zf 43
Bevercotes **GB** (NTS) 46 Za 29
Beverley **GB** (HUS) 41 Zd 25
Beverston **GB** (GLS) 61 Xe 39
Bevington **GB** (GLS) 61 Xd 38
Bewaldeth **GB** (CUB) 34 We 21
Bewcastle **GB** (CUB) 32 Xb 18
Bewdley **GB** (HWC) 53 Xe 34
Bewerley **GB** (NOY) 39 Yb 24
Bewholme **GB** (HUS) 41 Ze 25
Bexhill **GB** (ESX) 72 Ac 43
Bexley **GB** (GRL) 64 Aa 40
Beyton **GB** (SUF) 56 Ae 35
Bibury **GB** (GLS) 62 Yb 38
Bicester **GB** (OXS) 63 Yf 37
Bickenhall **GB** (SOM) 68 Wf 43
Bickenhill **GB** (WMD) 53 Yb 34
Bicker **GB** (LIN) 47 Ze 31
Bickerstaffe **GB** (LCS) 38 Xa 27
Bickerton **GB** (CHS) 44 Xb 30
Bickerton **GB** (NOY) 40 Ye 25
Bickham Bridge **GB** (DEV) 76 Wb 46
Bickington **GB** (DEV) 66 Vf 42
Bickington **GB** (DEV) 76 Wb 45
Bickleigh **GB** (DEV) 67 Wc 43
Bickleigh **GB** (DEV) 76 Vf 46
Bickley **GB** (GRL) 64 Aa 40
Bickley Town **GB** (CHS) 44 Xb 30
Bicknacre **GB** (ESS) 65 Ad 38
Bicknoller **GB** (SOM) 67 We 42
Bicknor **GB** (KEN) 65 Ae 41
Bickton **GB** (HAS) 69 Yb 43
Bicton **GB** (SHS) 44 Xb 32
Bicton **GB** (SHS) 52 Wf 34
Bidborough **GB** (KEN) 71 Ab 42
Biddenden **GB** (KEN) 72 Ad 42
Biddenham **GB** (BFS) 55 Zd 36
Biddestone **GB** (WIL) 61 Xe 40
Biddlestone **GB** (NHL) 33 Xf 16
Biddulph **GB** (SFS) 45 Xe 30
Biddulph Moor **GB** (SFS) 45 Xf 30
Bideford **GB** (DEV) 66 Ve 42
Bidford-on-Avon **GB** (WWH) 53 Ya 35
Bielby **GB** (HUS) 40 Zb 25
Bierley **GB** (IOW) 70 Ye 45
Bierton **GB** (BUS) 63 Zb 38
Bigbury **GB** (DEV) 76 Wa 47
Bigbury-on-Sea **GB** (DEV) 76 Wa 47
Bigby **GB** (LIN) 41 Zd 27
Biggar **GB** (CUB) 38 We 24
Biggar **GB** (STC) 25 Wc 15
Biggin **GB** (DSH) 45 Yb 30
Biggin **GB** (DSH) 45 Yc 30
Biggin **GB** (HTS) 55 Aa 37
Biggin **GB** (NOY) 40 Ye 26
Biggings **GB** (SHL) 3 Yb 107
Biggin Hill **GB** (GRL) 64 Aa 41
Biggleswade **GB** (BFS) 55 Ze 36
Bighouse **GB** (HGL) 5 Wa 117
Bighton **GB** (HAS) 70 Yf 42
Big Sand **GB** (HGL) 7 Ub 2
Bigton **GB** (SHL) 3 Ye 109
Bilberry **GB** (CNW) 75 Vb 46
Bilborough **GB** (NTS) 46 Ye 31
Bilbrook **GB** (SOM) 67 Wd 42
Bilbrough **GB** (NOY) 40 Ye 25
Bilbster **GB** (HGL) 9 We 118
Bildeston **GB** (SUF) 56 Af 36
Billericay **GB** (ESS) 64 Ac 39
Billesdon **GB** (LEC) 54 Za 33
Billing **GB** (NRH) 54 Zb 35
Billingborough **GB** (LIN) 47 Zd 31
Billinge **GB** (MES) 38 Xb 28
Billingford **GB** (NOR) 49 Af 32
Billingford **GB** (NOR) 57 Bb 34
Billingham **GB** (CLE) 36 Ye 21
Billinghay **GB** (LIN) 47 Ze 30
Billingshurst **GB** (WSX) 71 Zd 42
Billingsley **GB** (SHS) 53 Xd 34
Billington **GB** (BFS) 63 Zc 37
Billington **GB** (LCS) 38 Xd 26
Billis **IRL** (MOG) 84 Ta 23
Billis Bridge **IRL** (CAV) 89 Sf 25
Billockby **GB** (NOR) 49 Bd 33
Billypark **IRL** (MAY) 87 Qe 27
Billy Row **GB** (DUR) 36 Yb 20
Billywood Cross Roads **IRL** (MT) 89 Ta 26
Bilsborrow **GB** (LCS) 38 Xb 25
Bilsby **GB** (LIN) 47 Zf 29
Bilsdean **GB** (LOT) 27 Xd 13
Bilsham **GB** (WSX) 70 Zc 44
Bilsington **GB** (KEN) 72 Af 42
Bilsthorpe **GB** (NTS) 46 Yf 30
Bilston **GB** (WMD) 53 Xf 33
Bilstone **GB** (LEC) 54 Yd 33
Bilting **GB** (KEN) 72 Af 41
Bilton **GB** (HUS) 41 Ze 26
Bilton **GB** (NHL) 33 Yc 16
Bilton **GB** (WWH) 54 Ye 34
Bimbister **GB** (ORK) 6 Wf 114
Binbane **IRL** (CAV) 89 Sf 24
Binbrook **GB** (LIN) 41 Ze 28
Bincombe **GB** (DOS) 68 Xd 45
Bines Green **GB** (WSX) 71 Ze 43
Binfield **GB** (BKS) 63 Zb 40
Binfield Heath **GB** (OXS) 63 Za 40
Bingfield **GB** (NHL) 33 Xf 18
Bingham **GB** (DOS) 68 Xd 44
Bingham **GB** (NTS) 46 Za 31
Bingham Lodge **IRL** (MAY) 80 Pf 23
Bingham's Melcombe **GB** (DOS) 68 Xe 44
Bingley **GB** (WYO) 39 Yb 25
Binham **GB** (NOR) 48 Af 31
Binley **GB** (HAS) 69 Yd 41
Binley **GB** (WMD) 54 Yd 34
Binniehill **GB** (CEN) 25 Wb 13
Binroe Hill **IRL** (DON) 82 Rd 21
Binsted **GB** (HAS) 70 Za 42
Binsted **GB** (WSX) 70 Zc 43
Binton **GB** (WWH) 53 Yb 35
Bintree **GB** (NOR) 49 Af 32
Binvoran **IRL** (CRE) 92 Qe 32
Binweston **GB** (SHS) 52 Wf 33
Biorra = Birr **IRL** (OFF) 93 Sa 30
Birch **GB** (ESS) 65 Ae 37
Bircham Newton **GB** (NOR) 48 Ad 31
Birchanger **GB** (ESS) 64 Ab 37
Bircher **GB** (HWC) 52 Xb 35
Birchgrove **GB** (WGL) 59 Wa 38
Birch Heath **GB** (CHS) 44 Xb 30
Birchington **GB** (KEN) 65 Bb 40
Birch Vale **GB** (DSH) 45 Ya 28
Birdbrook **GB** (ESS) 56 Ac 36
Birdham **GB** (WSX) 70 Zb 44
Birdhill **IRL** (TIP) 93 Rd 32
Birdingbury **GB** (WWH) 54 Yd 35
Birdlip **GB** (GLS) 61 Xf 38
Birdsall **GB** (NOY) 40 Zb 24
Birdsgreen **GB** (SHS) 53 Xd 34
Birdsmoor Gate **GB** (DOS) 68 Xa 44
Birdwell **GB** (SOY) 40 Yd 27
Birdwood **GB** (GLS) 61 Xd 37
Birgham **GB** (BOR) 27 Xd 15
Birkenhead **GB** (CHS) 44 Wf 28
Birkenhills **GB** (GRP) 17 Xd 3
Birkenshaw **GB** (WYO) 39 Yb 26
Birkhall **GB** (GRP) 16 Wf 6
Birkhill **GB** (TYS) 21 Wf 10
Birkin **GB** (NOY) 40 Ye 26
Birley **GB** (HWC) 52 Xb 35
Birling **GB** (KEN) 65 Ac 41
Birling **GB** (NHL) 33 Yc 16
Birling Gap **GB** (ESX) 71 Ab 44
Birlingham **GB** (HWC) 53 Xf 36
Birmingham **GB** (WMD) 53 Yb 34
Birnam **GB** (TYS) 21 Wc 9
Birness **GB** (GRP) 17 Xf 4
Birr **IRL** (OFF) 93 Sa 30
Birsay **GB** (ORK) 5 We 114
Birse **GB** (GRP) 17 Xb 6
Birsemore **GB** (GRP) 16 Xb 6
Birstall **GB** (LEC) 54 Yf 32
Birstall Smithies **GB** (WYO) 39 Yc 26
Birstwith **GB** (NOY) 39 Yc 24
Birtley **GB** (HWC) 52 Xa 35
Birtley **GB** (NHL) 33 Xe 18
Birtley **GB** (TAW) 33 Yc 19
Bisbrooke **GB** (LEC) 55 Zb 33
Bisham **GB** (BKS) 63 Zb 39
Bishampton **GB** (HWC) 53 Xf 36
Bishop Auckland **GB** (DUR) 36 Yb 21
Bishopbridge **GB** (LIN) 41 Zd 28
Bishopbriggs **GB** (STC) 25 Ve 13
Bishop Burton **GB** (HUS) 41 Zd 25
Bishop Middleham **GB** (DUR) 36 Yd 20
Bishop Monkton **GB** (NOY) 39 Yd 24
Bishop Norton **GB** (LIN) 41 Zc 28
Bishopsbourne **GB** (KEN) 65 Ba 41
Bishops Cannings **GB** (WIL) 62 Ya 40
Bishop's Castle **GB** (SHS) 52 Wf 34
Bishop's Caundle **GB** (DOS) 68 Xd 43
Bishop's Cleeve **GB** 61 Xf 37
Bishop's Frome **GB** (HWC) 52 Xd 36
Bishop's Green **GB** (ESS) 64 Ac 38
Bishop's Hull **GB** (SOM) 67 Wf 42
Bishop's Itchington **GB** (WWH) 54 Yd 35
Bishops Lydeard **GB** (SOM) 67 We 42
Bishop's Nympton **GB** (DEV) 67 Wb 43
Bishop's Offley **GB** (SFS) 45 Xe 31
Bishop's Stortford **GB** (HTS) 64 Aa 37
Bishop's Sutton **GB** (HAS) 70 Yf 42
Bishop's Tachbrook **GB** (WWH) 54 Yc 35
Bishop's Tawton **GB** (DEV) 66 Vf 42
Bishopsteignton **GB** (DEV) 76 Wc 45
Bishopstoke **GB** (HAS) 70 Ye 43
Bishopston **GB** (WGL) 59 Vf 39
Bishopstone **GB** (BUS) 63 Za 38
Bishopstone **GB** (ESX) 71 Aa 44
Bishopstone **GB** (HWC) 52 Xa 36
Bishopstone **GB** (WIL) 62 Yc 39
Bishopstone **GB** (WIL) 69 Ya 42
Bishop Sutton **GB** (AVN) 61 Xc 41
Bishops Village **IRL** (COR) 103 Qe 39
Bishop's Waltham **GB** (HAS) 70 Ye 43
Bishop's Wood **GB** (SFS) 53 Xe 32
Bishopswood **GB** (SOM) 67 Wf 43
Bishopsworth **GB** (AVN) 61 Xc 40
Bishop Thornton **GB** (NOY) 39 Yc 24
Bishopthorpe **GB** (NOY) 40 Yf 25
Bishopton **GB** (DUR) 36 Yd 21
Bishopton **GB** (STC) 24 Vc 13
Bishop Wilton **GB** (HUS) 40 Zb 25
Bishton **GB** (GWE) 60 Wf 39
Bisley **GB** (GLS) 61 Xf 38
Bisley **GB** (SUR) 63 Zc 41
Bispham **GB** (LCS) 38 Wf 25
Bissoe **GB** (CNW) 74 Uf 47
Bisterne **GB** (HAS) 69 Yb 44
Bisterne Close **GB** (HAS) 69 Yb 44
Bitchfield **GB** (LIN) 47 Zc 31
Bittadon **GB** (DEV) 66 Vf 42
Bittaford **GB** (DEV) 76 Wa 46
Bittering **GB** (NOR) 48 Af 32
Bitterley **GB** (SHS) 52 Xc 34
Bitton **GB** (AVN) 61 Xd 40
Bix **GB** (OXS) 63 Za 39
Bixter **GB** (SHL) 2 Yd 107
Blaby **GB** (LEC) 54 Ye 33
Blackacre **GB** (DAG) 31 Wc 17
Blackadder **GB** (BOR) 27 Xe 14
Blackawton **GB** (DEV) 76 Wb 46
Blackbank **GB** (SFS) 45 Ya 30
Blackborough **GB** (DEV) 67 We 43
Blackborough End **GB** (NOR) 48 Ac 32
Black Bourton **GB** (OXS) 62 Yc 38
Blackboys **GB** (ESX) 71 Ab 43
Blackbrook **GB** (SFS) 45 Xd 31
Blackburn **GB** (GRP) 17 Xe 5
Blackburn **GB** (LCS) 38 Xd 26
Blackburn **GB** (LOT) 25 Wc 13
Black Callerton **GB** (TAW) 33 Yb 18
Blackcraig Hill **GB** (STC) 30 Vf 16
Black Crofts **GB** (STC) 19 Ud 10
Black Cross **GB** (CNW) 75 Va 46
Black Cross Roads **IRL** (COR) 104 Rb 37
Blackden Heath **GB** (CHS) 45 Xe 29
Black Dog **GB** (DEV) 67 Wb 43
Blackdog **GB** (GRP) 17 Xf 5
Blackdown **GB** (DOS) 68 Xa 44
Blackfield **GB** (HAS) 70 Yd 44
Blackford **GB** (CUB) 32 Xa 19
Blackford **GB** (SOM) 68 Xa 41
Blackford **GB** (SOM) 68 Xd 42
Blackford **GB** (TYS) 21 Wb 11
Blackfordby **GB** (LEC) 46 Yc 32
Blackhall **GB** (LOT) 26 We 13
Black Hall **IRL** (LOT) 90 Te 26
Blackham **GB** (ESX) 71 Aa 42
Blackhaugh **GB** (BOR) 26 Xa 15
Blackheath **GB** (ESS) 65 Af 37
Blackheath **GB** (SUR) 71 Zc 41
Blackheath **GB** (WMD) 53 Xf 34
Black Heddon **GB** (NHL) 33 Ya 18
Blackhill **GB** (DUR) 33 Ya 19
Blackhill **GB** (GRP) 17 Ya 3
Blackhill **GB** (GRP) 17 Ya 4
Blackhillock **GB** (GRP) 16 Xa 3
Black Hills **IRL** (MT) 90 Tf 27
Blackland **GB** (WIL) 62 Ya 40
Black Lion **IRL** (OFF) 94 Sc 29
Blacklunans **GB** (TYS) 21 Wd 8
Black Marsh **GB** (SHS) 52 Xa 33
Blackmill **GB** (MGL) 60 Wc 39
Blackmoor **GB** (HAS) 70 Za 42
Blackmoor Gate **GB** (DEV) 66 Wa 41
Blackmore **GB** (ESS) 64 Ab 38
Blackmore End **GB** (ESS) 56 Ad 37
Blackmore End **GB** (HTS) 64 Ac 38
Black Mount **GB** (STC) 20 Vb 9
Blackness **GB** (CEN) 25 Wc 13
Black Notley **GB** (ESS) 65 Ad 37
Blacko **GB** (LCS) 39 Xe 25
Black Pill **GB** (WGL) 59 Wa 39
Blackpool **GB** (LCS) 38 Wf 26
Blackpool Gate **GB** (CUB) 32 Xb 18
Blackridge **GB** (LOT) 25 Wb 13
Blackrock **GB** (GWE) 60 Wf 38
Blackrock **GB** (STC) 22 Te 14
Blackrock **IRL** (DUB) 95 Te 29
Blackrock **IRL** (LOT) 90 Td 25
Blackrod **GB** (GRM) 38 Xc 27
Blackshaw **GB** (DAG) 31 Wd 19
Blacksmith's Corner **GB** (ESS) 57 Af 37
Blackstone **GB** (WSX) 71 Ze 43
Blackthorn **GB** (OXS) 63 Yf 37
Blackthorpe **GB** (SUF) 56 Ae 35
Blacktoft **GB** (HUS) 40 Zb 26
Blacktop **GB** (GRP) 17 Xe 6
Black Torrington **GB** (DEV) 66 Ve 44
Blackwater **GB** (CNW) 74 Ue 47
Blackwater **GB** (IOW) 70 Ye 44
Blackwater **IRL** (WEX) 101 Td 34
Blackwaterfoot **GB** (STC) 28 Ue 15
Blackwatertown **GB** (ARG) 84 Tb 22
Blackwell **GB** (DSH) 45 Yb 29
Blackwell **GB** (HWC) 53 Xf 34
Blackwell **GB** (WWH) 53 Yc 36
Blackwells End **GB** (GLS) 61 Xe 37
Blackwood **GB** (GWE) 60 We 39
Blackwood **IRL** (KIL) 95 Tb 29
Blackwood Hill **GB** (SFS) 45 Xf 30
Blacon **GB** (CHS) 44 Xa 29
Bladnoch **GB** (DAG) 30 Vd 19
Bladon **GB** (OXS) 62 Yd 38
Blaenannerch **GB** (DYF) 50 Vc 36
Blaenau Ffestiniog **GB** (GWY) 43 Wa 31
Blaenavon **GB** (GWE) 60 Wf 38
Blaendyryn **GB** (POW) 60 Wc 36
Blaenffos **GB** (DYF) 58 Vc 36
Blaengarw **GB** (MGL) 60 Wc 39
Blaengwrach **GB** (WGL) 60 Wc 38
Blaengwynfi **GB** (WGL) 60 Wc 39
Blaenplwyf **GB** (DYF) 50 Vf 34
Blaenporth **GB** (DYF) 50 Vc 36
Blaenwaun **GB** (DYF) 58 Vc 37
Blaen-y-coed **GB** (DYF) 59 Vd 37
Blagdon **GB** (AVN) 61 Xb 41
Blagdon **GB** (DEV) 76 Wc 46
Blagdon Hill **GB** (SOM) 67 Wf 43
Blaich **GB** (HGL) 19 Ue 7
Blaina **GB** (GWE) 60 Wf 38
Blair Atholl **GB** (TYS) 21 Wa 8
Blairdaff **GB** (GRP) 17 Xc 5
Blair Drummond **GB** (CEN) 25 Vf 11
Blairgowrie **GB** (TYS) 21 Wd 9
Blairhall **GB** (FIF) 25 Wc 12
Blairmore **GB** (STC) 24 Va 13
Blairnamarrow **GB** (GRP) 16 We 5
Blairuskinmore **GB** (CEN) 24 Vc 11
Blairvadach **GB** (STC) 24 Vb 12
Blaisdon **GB** (GLS) 61 Xd 37
Blakedown **GB** (HWC) 53 Xe 34
Blakelaw **GB** (TAW) 33 Yc 19
Blakemere **GB** (HWC) 52 Xa 36
Blakeney **GB** (GLS) 61 Xd 38
Blakenhall **GB** (WMD) 53 Xf 33
Blakeshall **GB** (HWC) 53 Xe 34
Blakesley **GB** (NRH) 54 Yf 36
Blakestown Cross Roads **IRL** (LOT) 90 Tc 26
Blamachfoldach **GB** (HGL) 19 Uf 8
Blanchardstown **IRL** (DUB) 95 Td 28
Blanchland **GB** (NHL) 33 Xf 19
Blandford Camp **GB** (DOS) 69 Xf 43
Blandford Forum **GB** (DOS) 69 Xf 43
Bland Hill **GB** (NOY) 39 Yb 25
Blandsfort House **IRL** (LAO) 94 Se 31
Blanefield **GB** (CEN) 25 Ve 13
Blankney **GB** (LIN) 47 Zd 30
Blantyre **GB** (STC) 25 Vf 14
Blàr a'Chaoinn **GB** (HGL) 19 Uf 8
Blarnalearoch **GB** (HGL) 7 Uf 1
Blarney **IRL** (COR) 104 Rc 37
Blarney Castle **IRL** (COR) 104 Rc 37
Blashford **GB** (HAS) 69 Yb 43
Blaston **GB** (LEC) 54 Zb 33
Blatherwycke **GB** (NRH) 55 Zc 33
Blawith **GB** (CUB) 34 Wf 23
Blaxhall **GB** (SUF) 57 Bc 36
Blaxton **GB** (SOY) 40 Za 28
Blaydon **GB** (TAW) 33 Yb 19
Bleadon **GB** (AVN) 68 Xa 41
Bleasby **GB** (NTS) 46 Za 30
Bleatarn **GB** (CUB) 35 Xd 21
Blebocraigs **GB** (FIF) 22 Xa 11
Bleddfa **GB** (POW) 52 We 35
Bledlow Ridge **GB** (BUS) 63 Za 38
Blencarn **GB** (CUB) 35 Xc 20
Blencogo **GB** (CUB) 34 We 20
Blencow **GB** (CUB) 35 Xa 20
Blendworth **GB** (HAS) 70 Za 43
Blennerhasset **GB** (CUB) 34 We 20
Blennerville **IRL** (KER) 97 Qb 35
Blessington **IRL** (KLK) 100 Sf 33
Blessington **IRL** (WKL) 95 Tc 29
Bletchingdon **GB** (OXS) 62 Ye 37
Bletchingley **GB** (SUR) 71 Zf 41
Bletchley **GB** (BUS) 54 Zb 36
Bletchley **GB** (SHS) 44 Xc 31
Bletsoe **GB** (BFS) 55 Zd 35
Blewbury **GB** (OXS) 62 Ye 39
Blickling **GB** (NOR) 49 Bb 32
Blidworth **GB** (NTS) 46 Yf 30
Blindcrake **GB** (CUB) 34 We 20
Blind Key **IRL** (WMT) 89 Sd 27
Blindley Heath **GB** (SUR) 71 Zf 41
Blisland **GB** (CNW) 75 Vb 45
Blissford **GB** (HAS) 69 Yb 43
Bliss Gate **GB** (HWC) 53 Xd 34
Blisworth **GB** (NRH) 54 Za 35
Blithbury **GB** (SFS) 45 Ya 32
Blockley **GB** (GLS) 53 Yb 36
Blofield **GB** (NOR) 49 Bc 33
Bloody Hollow, The **IRL** (GAL) 93 Re 29
Blore **GB** (SFS) 45 Yb 30
Blount's Green **GB** (SFS) 45 Ya 31
Bloxham **GB** (OXS) 54 Yd 36
Bloxholm **GB** (LIN) 47 Zd 30
Bloxwich **GB** (WMD) 53 Ya 33
Bloxworth **GB** (DOS) 69 Xf 44
Blubberhouses **GB** (NOY) 39 Yb 25
Bludeston **GB** (SUF) 57 Be 33
Blue Anchor **GB** (CNW) 75 Va 46
Blue Anchor **GB** (SOM) 67 Wd 41
Blue Ball **IRL** (OFF) 94 Sc 29
Blue Bell Hill **GB** (KEN) 65 Ac 40
Bluebell House **IRL** (KIL) 95 Tb 29
Blundellsands **GB** (MES) 38 Wf 28
Blundson Saint Andrew **GB** (WIL) 62 Yb 39
Blunham **GB** (BFS) 55 Ze 36
Bluntisham **GB** (CBS) 55 Aa 34
Blunts **GB** (CNW) 75 Ve 46
Blyford **GB** (SUF) 57 Bd 34
Blymhill **GB** (SFS) 53 Xe 32
Blyth **GB** (NHL) 33 Yc 18
Blyth **GB** (NTS) 46 Yf 28
Blyth Bridge **GB** (BOR) 26 Wd 14
Blythburgh **GB** (SUF) 57 Bd 35
Blythe Bridge **GB** (SFS) 45 Xf 31
Blyton **GB** (LIN) 40 Zb 28
Boardee **IRL** (COR) 104 Rd 38
Boardsmills **GB** (DOW) 85 Ua 22
Boarhills **GB** (FIF) 22 Xb 11
Boarhunt **GB** (HAS) 70 Yf 43
Boarshead **GB** (ESX) 71 Ab 42
Boarstall **GB** (BUS) 63 Yf 38
Boasley Cross **GB** (DEV) 66 Vf 44
Boat of Garten **GB** (HGL) 15 Wb 5
Bobbing **GB** (KEN) 65 Ae 40
Bobbington **GB** (SFS) 53 Xe 33
Bobbingworth **GB** (ESS) 64 Ab 38
Bockhampton **GB** (BKS) 62 Yc 39
Bockhampton **GB** (DOS) 68 Xd 44
Bocking Churchstreet **GB** (ESS) 65 Ad 37
Boddam **GB** (GRP) 17 Yb 4
Boddam **GB** (SHL) 3 Ye 109
Boddington **GB** 61 Xf 37
Bodedern **GB** (GWY) 42 Vd 29
Bodelwyddan **GB** (CLW) 43 Wc 29
Bodenham **GB** (HWC) 52 Xb 36
Bodenstown **IRL** (KIL) 95 Tb 29
Bodewryd **GB** (GWY) 42 Vd 28
Bodfari **GB** (CLW) 43 Wd 29
Bodffordd **GB** (GWY) 42 Vd 29
Bodham Street **GB** (NOR) 49 Ba 31
Bodiam **GB** (ESX) 72 Ad 42
Bodicote **GB** (OXS) 54 Ye 36
Bodieve **GB** (CNW) 75 Vb 45
Bodinnick **GB** (CNW) 75 Vc 46
Bodior **GB** (GWY) 42 Vc 29
Bodle Street Green **GB** (ESX) 72 Ac 43
Bodmin **GB** (CNW) 75 Vb 46
Bodney **GB** (NOR) 56 Ae 33
Bodorgan **GB** (GWY) 42 Vd 29
Boduan **GB** (GWY) 42 Vd 31
Bofin **IRL** (GAL) 86 Pe 27
Bog, The **GB** (SHS) 52 Xa 33
Bogallan **GB** (HGL) 15 Ve 3
Bogay **IRL** (DON) 78 Sd 19
Bogbain **GB** (HGL) 15 Vf 4
Bogbrae **GB** (GRP) 17 Ya 4
Bogganfin **IRL** (ROS) 88 Sa 28
Bogganstown **IRL** (MT) 90 Tc 28
Boggaun **IRL** (GAL) 92 Rc 29
Boggaun **IRL** (TIP) 93 Sb 31
Boggauns **IRL** (GAL) 88 Rd 27
Boghadoon **IRL** (MAY) 87 Qd 24
Bogmoor **GB** (GRP) 16 Wf 3
Bogniebrae **GB** (GRP) 17 Xb 3
Bog of the Ring **IRL** (DUB) 90 Te 27
Bogton **GB** (GRP) 17 Xc 3
Bogue **GB** (DAG) 30 Vf 18
Bohagh **IRL** (ROS) 88 Rd 26
Boharboy **IRL** (LOT) 90 Tf 24
Bohaun **IRL** (GAL) 86 Qd 27
Bohaun **IRL** (MAY) 87 Qd 26
Boheeshil **IRL** (KER) 97 Qa 37
Boher **IRL** (LIM) 99 Rd 33
Boheraphuca **IRL** (OFF) 93 Sb 30
Boherard **IRL** (LAO) 94 Sc 31
Boheratreen Cross Roads **IRL** (TIP) 99 Re 33
Boherboy **IRL** (COR) 98 Qf 36
Bohereen **IRL** (LIM) 98 Rc 33
Boherlahan **IRL** (TIP) 99 Sa 33
Bohermeen **IRL** (MT) 90 Tb 27
Bohernacross **IRL** (LGF) 89 Sc 26
Bohernameeltoge **IRL** (LGF) 88 Sb 26
Bohernamona **IRL** (TIP) 99 Sb 32
Boherquill **IRL** (WMT) 89 Sd 26
Bohola **IRL** (MAY) 87 Qf 25
Bohoona **IRL** (GAL) 92 Qd 29
Bohortha **GB** (CNW) 75 Va 48
Bohullion **IRL** (DON) 78 Sd 18
Bohuntine **GB** (HGL) 20 Vb 7
Boisdale **GB** (HGL) 12 Sd 6
Bojewyan **GB** (CNW) 74 Uc 48
Bolaereen Cross Roads **IRL** (WEX) 101 Td 33
Bolam **GB** (DUR) 36 Yb 21
Bolberry **GB** (DEV) 76 Wa 47
Bolderwood **GB** (HAS) 69 Yc 43
Bold Heath **GB** (MES) 44 Xb 28
Boldon **GB** (TAW) 33 Yd 19
Boldre **GB** (HAS) 69 Yc 44
Boldron **GB** (DUR) 36 Ya 21
Bolehill **GB** (DSH) 45 Yc 30
Boleigh **GB** (CNW) 74 Uc 48
Boley's Cross Roads **IRL** (WEX) 101 Tc 35
Boleyard **IRL** (MAY) 87 Qf 25
Boleybeg **IRL** (GAL) 92 Rc 30

Beardon – Boleybeg (GB) (IRL) **109**

Boleybeg Cross Roads IRL (KIL) 95 Tc 30
Boleybrian IRL (MAY) 86 Qc 26
Boley Cross Roads IRL (KIL) 94 Ta 30
Boley Cross Roads IRL (WEX) 101 Td 33
Boleythomas IRL (GAL) 88 Rd 27
Bolham GB (DEV) 67 Wd 43
Bolham Water GB (DEV) 67 We 43
Bolinaspick IRL (WEX) 101 Td 33
Bolinglanna IRL (MAY) 86 Qa 25
Bolinrush IRL (WEX) 101 Tc 32
Bollington GB (CHS) 44 Xd 28
Bollington GB (CHS) 45 Xf 29
Bolney GB (WSX) 71 Ze 43
Bolnhurst GB (BFS) 55 Zd 35
Bolshan GB (TYS) 22 Xc 9
Bolsover GB (DSH) 46 Ye 29
Bolsterstone GB (SOY) 39 Yc 28
Bolstone GB (HWC) 61 Xc 37
Boltby GB (NOY) 36 Ye 23
Bolter End GB (BUS) 63 Za 39
Bolton GB (CUB) 35 Xc 21
Bolton GB (GRM) 38 Xd 27
Bolton GB (LOT) 26 Xb 13
Bolton GB (NHL) 33 Ya 16
Bolton Abbey GB (NOY) 39 Ya 25
Bolton-by-Bowland GB (LCS) 39 Xe 25
Boltonfellend GB (CUB) 32 Xb 18
Boltongate GB (CUB) 34 We 20
Bolton-le-Sands GB (LCS) 38 Xb 24
Bolton-on-Swale GB (NOY) 36 Yc 22
Bolton Percy GB (NOY) 40 Ye 25
Bolton upon Dearne GB (SOY) 40 Ye 27
Boltown House IRL (MT) 89 Ta 26
Bolventor GB (CNW) 75 Vc 45
Bomere Heath GB (SHS) 44 Xb 32
Bonar Bridge GB (HGL) 8 Vd 1
Bonawe GB (STC) 19 Ue 10
Bonby GB (HUS) 41 Zd 27
Boncath GB (DYF) 58 Vc 36
Bonchester Bridge GB (BOR) 32 Xc 16
Bondleigh GB (DEV) 66 Wa 44
Bo'ness GB (CEN) 25 Wc 12
Bonhill GB (STC) 24 Vc 13
Boningale GB (SHS) 53 Xe 33
Bonjedward GB (BOR) 32 Xc 15
Bonkle GB (STC) 25 Wa 14
Bonnington GB (KEN) 72 Af 42
Bonnington Smiddy GB (TYS) 22 Xb 9
Bonnybridge GB (CEN) 25 Wa 12
Bonnykelly GB (GRP) 17 Xe 3
Bonnyrigg GB (LOT) 26 Wf 13
Bonnyrigg and Lasswade GB (LOT) 26 Wf 13
Bonnyton GB (TYS) 21 Wf 9
Bonnyton GB (TYS) 22 Xc 8
Bonsall GB (DSH) 45 Yc 30
Bont GB (GWE) 60 Xa 37
Bontddu GB (GWY) 43 Wa 32
Bont Dolgadfan GB (POW) 51 Wc 33
Bont-goch (Elerch) GB (DYF) 51 Wa 34
Bont-newydd GB (CLW) 43 Wd 29
Bontnewydd GB (GWY) 42 Ve 30
Bontuchel GB (CLW) 43 Wd 30
Bonvilston GB (SGL) 60 Wd 40
Bonvinge Bridge IRL (KIL) 95 Tb 29
Bon y maen GB (WGL) 59 Wa 39
Boohay GB (DEV) 76 Wc 46
Bookeen IRL (GAL) 92 Rc 29
Boola IRL (WTF) 99 Sa 36
Boolabrien IRL (WTF) 99 Sb 35
Boolacullane IRL (KER) 97 Qc 36
Boolakennedy IRL (TIP) 99 Rf 34
Boolanlisheen IRL (LIM) 99 Re 34
Boolard IRL (COR) 98 Rb 35
Boolavontech IRL (WTF) 99 Sb 35
Booley GB (SHS) 44 Xc 32
Boolteens IRL (KER) 97 Qb 35
Boolyglass IRL (KLK) 100 Se 34
Boolynagleragh IRL (CRE) 92 Qf 32
Boosbeck GB (CLE) 37 Za 21
Boot GB (CUB) 34 We 22
Boothby Graffoe GB (LIN) 47 Zc 30
Boothby Pagnell GB (LIN) 47 Zc 31
Boothville GB (NRH) 54 Za 35
Bootle GB (CUB) 34 Wd 23
Bootle GB (MES) 38 Xa 28
Booton GB (NOR) 49 Ba 32
Boquhan GB (CEN) 24 Vd 12
Boraston GB (SHS) 52 Xc 35
Borden GB (KEN) 65 Ae 41
Bordley GB (NOY) 39 Xf 24
Bordon Camp GB (HAS) 70 Za 42
Boreham GB (ESS) 65 Ad 38
Boreham Street GB (ESX) 72 Ac 43
Borehamwood GB (HTS) 64 Ze 39
Boreland GB (DAG) 31 We 17
Borgie GB (HGL) 5 Ve 117
Borgue GB (DAG) 29 Vf 20
Borgue GB (HGL) 9 Wd 119
Borham GB (KEN) 65 Ac 41
Borley GB (ESS) 56 Ae 36
Borneskelaig GB (HGL) 13 Td 3
Borness GB (DAG) 29 Vf 20
Boroughbridge GB (NOY) 40 Yd 24
Borough Green GB (KEN) 64 Ab 41
Borough View IRL (ROS) 88 Re 26
Borras Head GB (CLW) 44 Xa 30
Borreraig GB (HGL) 12 Tb 4
Borris IRL (CLW) 100 Ta 33
Borris in Ossory IRL (LAO) 94 Sc 31
Borrisokane IRL (TIP) 93 Rf 31
Borrisoleigh IRL (TIP) 93 Sa 32
Borrowash GB (DSH) 46 Yd 31
Borrowby GB (NOY) 36 Yd 23
Borstal GB (KEN) 65 Ac 40
Borth GB (DYF) 51 Vf 34
Borthwickbrae GB (BOR) 32 Xa 16
Borthwickshiels GB (BOR) 32 Xa 16
Borth-y-Gest GB (GWY) 42 Vf 31
Borve GB (HGL) 10 Se 2
Borve GB (HGL) 11 Ta 1
Borve GB (HGL) 12 Sd 7
Borve GB (HGL) 13 Te 4
Borwick GB (LCS) 35 Xb 24
Bosbury GB (HWC) 52 Xd 36
Boscastle GB (CNW) 75 Vb 44
Boscombe GB (WIL) 69 Yb 42
Boscomoor GB (SFS) 53 Xf 32
Bosham GB (WSX) 70 Za 44
Bosherston GB (DYF) 58 Va 39
Bosley GB (CHS) 45 Xf 29
Bossall GB (NOY) 40 Za 24
Bossiney GB (CNW) 75 Vb 45
Bossingham GB (KEN) 72 Ba 41
Bossington GB (HAS) 69 Yc 42
Bostock Green GB (CHS) 44 Xd 29
Boston GB (LIN) 47 Zf 31
Boston IRL (CRE) 92 Ra 30
Boston Farm IRL (GAL) 93 Rd 29
Boston Spa GB (WYO) 40 Yd 25
Boswinger GB (CNW) 75 Vb 47
Botany Bay GB (GRL) 64 Ab 38
Botcheston GB (LEC) 54 Ye 33
Botesdale GB (SUF) 57 Ba 34
Bothal GB (NHL) 33 Yc 17
Bothamsall GB (NTS) 46 Za 29
Bothel GB (CUB) 34 We 20
Bothenhampton GB (DOS) 68 Xb 44
Botinny IRL (MAY) 87 Rb 25
Botley GB (BUS) 63 Zc 38
Botley GB (HAS) 70 Ye 43
Botley GB (OXS) 62 Ye 38
Botloe's Green GB (GLS) 61 Xd 37
Botolph Claydon GB (BUS) 63 Za 37
Botolphs GB (WSX) 71 Ze 43
Bottacks GB (HGL) 15 Vc 3
Bottesford GB (LEC) 46 Zb 31
Bottisham GB (CBS) 56 Ab 35
Bottomcraig GB (FIF) 22 Wf 10
Bottomstown IRL (LIM) 98 Rd 34
Botwnnog GB (GWY) 42 Vc 31
Bough Beech GB (KEN) 71 Aa 41
Boughrood GB (POW) 51 We 36
Boughspring GB (GLS) 61 Xc 39
Boughton GB (NOR) 56 Ad 33
Boughton GB (NTS) 46 Za 29
Boughton Green GB (KEN) 72 Ad 41
Boughton Lees GB (KEN) 72 Af 41
Boughton Street GB (KEN) 65 Af 41
Bouladuff IRL (TIP) 93 Sa 32
Boulby GB (NOY) 37 Zb 21
Bouldon GB (SHS) 52 Xb 34
Boulmer GB (NHL) 33 Yc 16
Boultenstone GB (GRP) 16 Xa 5
Boultham GB (LIN) 47 Zc 29
Bourn GB (CBS) 55 Zf 35
Bourne GB (LIN) 47 Zd 32
Bournebridge GB (ESS) 64 Ab 39
Bourne End GB (BFS) 55 Zc 36
Bourne End GB (BUS) 63 Zb 39
Bourne End GB (HTS) 63 Zc 38
Bournemouth GB (DOS) 69 Ya 44
Bourness Green GB (GLS) 61 Xf 38
Bournheath GB (HWC) 53 Xf 34
Bournmoor GB (DUR) 33 Yc 19
Bournville GB (WMD) 53 Ya 34
Bourton GB (AVN) 60 Xa 40
Bourton GB (DOR) 68 Xe 42
Bourton GB (OXS) 62 Yc 39
Bourton GB (SHS) 52 Xc 33
Bourton-on-the-Hill GB (GLS) 62 Yb 37
Bourton-on-the-Water GB (GLS) 62 Yb 37
Bousd GB (STC) 18 Td 8
Bouth GB (CUB) 34 Wf 23
Bovedy GB (LDR) 79 Tc 19
Boveney GB (BUS) 63 Zc 40
Boveridge GB (WIL) 69 Ya 43
Bovey Tracey GB (DEV) 76 Wb 45
Bovingdon GB (HTS) 63 Zc 38
Bovington Camp GB (DOS) 68 Xe 44
Bow GB (DEV) 67 Wb 44
Bow GB (ORK) 6 Wf 116
Bowbank GB (DUR) 36 Xf 21
Bow Brickhill GB (BUS) 55 Zb 36
Bowburn GB (DUR) 36 Yc 20
Bowcombe GB (IOW) 70 Ye 44
Bowd GB (DEV) 67 We 44
Bowden GB (BOR) 26 Xb 15
Bowden GB (DEV) 76 Wc 47
Bowden Hill GB (WIL) 61 Xf 40
Bowdon GB (GRM) 45 Xd 28
Bower GB (NHL) 32 Xd 18
Bowerchalke GB (WIL) 69 Ya 42
Bower Hinton GB (SOM) 68 Xb 43
Bowermadden GB (HGL) 6 We 117
Bowers Gifford GB (ESS) 65 Ad 39
Bowershall GB (FIF) 25 Wd 12
Bowes GB (DUR) 36 Xf 21
Bowgreave GB (LCS) 38 Xb 25
Bowhill GB (BOR) 32 Xa 15
Bowland GB (BOR) 26 Xa 15
Bowland Bridge GB (CUB) 35 Xa 23
Bowley GB (HWC) 52 Xb 35
Bowlhead Green GB (SUR) 70 Zb 42
Bowling Bank GB (CLW) 44 Xa 30
Bowmanstead GB (CUB) 34 Wf 22
Bowmore GB (STC) 22 Te 14
Bowness-on-Solway GB (CUB) 31 We 19
Bowness-on-Windermere GB (CUB) 35 Xa 22
Bow of Fife GB (FIF) 21 Wf 11
Bowsden GB (NHL) 27 Xf 14
Bow Street GB (DYF) 51 Vf 34
Box GB (WIL) 61 Xe 40
Box End GB (BFS) 55 Zc 36
Boxford GB (BKS) 62 Yd 40
Boxford GB (SUF) 56 Af 36
Boxgrove GB (WSX) 70 Zb 43
Boxley GB (KEN) 65 Ad 41
Boxted GB (SUF) 56 Ad 36
Boxted GB (ESS) 56 Af 37
Boxworth GB (CBS) 55 Zf 35
Boxworth End GB (CBS) 55 Zf 35
Boyerstown IRL (MT) 90 Tb 27
Boyle IRL (ROS) 88 Re 25
Boylestone GB (DSH) 45 Yb 31
Boyndie GB (GRP) 17 Xc 2
Boyndlie GB (GRP) 17 Xf 3
Boynton GB (HUS) 41 Ze 24
Boyton GB (CNW) 66 Vd 44
Boyton GB (SUF) 57 Bc 36
Bozeat GB (NRH) 55 Zb 35
Braaid GBM 29 Vc 24
Brabling Green GB (SUF) 57 Bc 35
Brabourne GB (KEN) 72 Af 42
Brabourne Lees GB (KEN) 72 Af 42
Brabster GB (HGL) 6 We 117
Bracadale GB (HGL) 13 Td 4
Bracca Castle IRL (WMT) 94 Sc 28
Bracebridge Heath GB (LIN) 47 Zc 29
Braceby GB (LIN) 47 Zd 31
Bracewell GB (LCS) 39 Xe 25
Brackenfield GB (DSH) 46 Yd 30
Brackery IRL (GAL) 93 Rd 30
Brackhill IRL (KER) 97 Qb 36
Bracklagh IRL (LGF) 89 Sd 26
Brackletter GB (HGL) 19 Va 7
Brackley GB (NRH) 54 Yf 36
Brackloon IRL (ROS) 88 Rd 26
Bracknagh IRL (OFF) 94 Sf 29
Bracknell GB (BKS) 63 Zb 40
Brackwanshagh IRL (MAY) 87 Qe 24
Braco GB (TYS) 21 Wa 11
Bracobrae GB (GRP) 16 Xb 3
Bracon Ash GB (NOR) 57 Bb 33
Bracora GB (HGL) 18 Ub 7
Bracorina GB (HGL) 13 Ub 7
Bradbourne GB (DSH) 45 Yb 30
Bradbury GB (DUR) 36 Yc 21
Bradda GBM 29 Vb 24
Bradden GB (NRH) 54 Yf 36
Braddocks IRL (MOG) 84 Ta 23
Bradenham GB (BUS) 63 Zb 38
Bradenham GB (NOR) 48 Af 33
Bradfield GB (BKS) 63 Yf 40
Bradfield GB (DEV) 67 Wd 43
Bradfield GB (ESS) 57 Ba 37
Bradfield GB (NOR) 49 Bc 31
Bradfield Combust GB (SUF) 56 Ae 35
Bradfield Green GB (CHS) 44 Xd 30
Bradfield Saint Clare GB (SUF) 56 Ae 35
Bradfield Saint George GB (SUF) 56 Ae 35
Bradford GB (WYO) 39 Yb 26
Bradford Abbas GB (DOS) 68 Xc 43
Bradford Leigh GB (WIL) 61 Xe 40
Bradford on Avon GB (WIL) 61 Xe 40
Bradford-on-Tone GB (SOM) 67 We 43
Brading GB (IOW) 70 Yf 44
Bradley GB (DSH) 45 Yc 30
Bradley GB (HAS) 70 Yf 41
Bradley GB (HUS) 41 Zf 27
Bradley Green GB (HWC) 53 Xf 35
Bradley in the Moors GB (SFS) 45 Ya 31
Bradley Stoke GB (AVN) 61 Xc 39
Bradmore GB (NTS) 46 Yf 31
Bradninch GB (DEV) 67 Wd 44
Bradnop GB (SFS) 45 Ya 30
Bradpole GB (DOS) 68 Xb 44
Bradsted GB (KEN) 64 Aa 41
Bradwall Green GB (CHS) 45 Xd 30
Bradwell GB (DSH) 45 Yb 29
Bradwell GB (ESS) 65 Ad 37
Bradwell GB (NOR) 57 Be 33
Bradwell GB (OXS) 62 Yc 38
Bradwell-on-Sea GB (ESS) 65 Af 38
Bradwell Waterside GB (ESS) 65 Af 38
Bradworthy GB (DEV) 66 Vd 43
Brae GB (HGL) 15 Ve 3
Brae GB (SHL) 2 Yd 106
Braefield GB (HGL) 14 Vc 4
Braegrum GB (TYS) 21 Wc 10
Braehead GB (STC) 25 Wa 15
Braehead GB (STC) 25 Wc 14
Braehead GB (TYS) 22 Xd 8
Braehoulland GB (SHL) 2 Yc 106
Braeklin IRL (CAV) 89 Ta 25
Braelangwell Lodge GB (HGL) 8 Vd 1
Braemar GB (GRP) 16 Wd 6
Braemore GB (HGL) 9 Wc 119
Brae of Achnahaird GB (HGL) 7 Ud 120
Brae Roy Lodge GB (HGL) 14 Vb 7
Braes, The GB (HGL) 13 Tf 4
Braeside GB (STC) 24 Vb 13
Braeswick GB (ORK) 5 Xb 113
Brafferton GB (DUR) 36 Yc 21
Brafferton GB (NOY) 36 Ye 24
Brafield-on-the-Green GB (NRH) 54 Zb 35
Bragar GB (HGL) 11 Tc 118
Bragbury End GB (HTS) 64 Zf 37
Bragenham GB (BUS) 63 Zb 37
Braides GB (LCS) 38 Xa 25
Braidley GB (NOY) 36 Ya 23
Braidwood GB (STC) 25 Wa 14
Brailsford GB (DSH) 45 Yc 31
Braintree GB (ESS) 65 Ad 37
Braiseworth GB (SUF) 57 Ba 35
Braishfield GB (HAS) 69 Yd 42
Braithwaite GB (CUB) 34 We 21
Braithwell GB (SOY) 40 Ye 28
Bramber GB (WSX) 71 Ze 43
Bramdean GB (HAS) 70 Yf 42
Bramerton GB (NOR) 57 Bc 33
Bramfield GB (HTS) 64 Ab 38
Bramfield GB (SUF) 57 Bd 35
Bramford GB (SUF) 57 Ba 36
Bramhall GB (GRM) 45 Xf 28
Bramham GB (WYO) 40 Yd 25
Bramhope GB (WYO) 39 Yc 25
Bramley GB (HAS) 63 Yf 41
Bramley GB (SOY) 40 Ye 28
Bramley GB (SUR) 71 Zc 41
Brampford Speke GB (DEV) 67 Wc 44
Brampton GB (CBS) 55 Ze 35
Brampton GB (CUB) 32 Xb 19
Brampton GB (CUB) 35 Xc 21
Brampton GB (SOY) 40 Yd 27
Brampton GB (SUF) 57 Bd 34
Brampton Abbots GB (HWC) 61 Xc 37
Brampton Bryan GB (HWC) 52 Xa 34
Bramshall GB (SFS) 45 Ya 31
Bramshaw GB (HAS) 69 Yc 43
Bramshill GB (HAS) 63 Za 40
Bramshott GB (HAS) 70 Zb 42
Branault GB (HGL) 18 Tf 8
Brancepeth GB (DUR) 36 Yc 20
Branchill GB (GRP) 16 Wc 3
Branderburgh GB (GRP) 9 We 2
Brandesburton GB (HUS) 41 Ze 25
Brandeston GB (SUF) 57 Bb 35
Brandis Corner GB (DEV) 66 Ve 44
Brandiston GB (NOR) 49 Ba 32
Brandon GB (DUR) 36 Yc 20
Brandon GB (LIN) 47 Zc 30
Brandon GB (NHL) 33 Ya 16
Brandon GB (SUF) 56 Ad 34
Brandon GB (WWH) 54 Yd 34
Brandon IRL (KER) 96 Pe 35
Brandon Bank GB (CBS) 56 Ac 34
Brandon Creek GB (CBS) 56 Ac 34
Brandsby GB (NOY) 37 Yf 24
Brandy Wharf GB (LIN) 41 Zd 28
Bran End GB (ESS) 64 Ac 37
Branksome GB (DOS) 69 Ya 44
Bransby GB (LIN) 46 Zb 29
Branscombe GB (DEV) 67 Wf 44
Bransford GB (HWC) 53 Xe 35
Bransgore GB (HAS) 69 Yb 44
Branson's Cross GB (HWC) 53 Ya 34
Branston GB (LEC) 46 Zb 31
Branston GB (LIN) 47 Zd 29
Branston Booths GB (LIN) 47 Zd 29
Branstone GB (IOW) 70 Ye 45
Brant Broughton GB (LIN) 47 Zc 30
Brantham GB (SUF) 57 Ba 37
Branthwaite GB (CUB) 34 Wc 21
Branthwaite GB (CUB) 34 Wf 20
Branton GB (NHL) 33 Ya 16
Branton GB (SOY) 40 Yf 27
Branxholme GB (BOR) 32 Xa 16
Branxton GB (NHL) 27 Xe 15
Brassington GB (DSH) 45 Yc 30
Brasted Chart GB (KEN) 64 Aa 41
Brathens GB (GRP) 17 Xc 6
Bratoft GB (LIN) 48 Ab 30
Brattleby GB (LIN) 47 Zc 29
Bratton GB (WIL) 69 Xf 41
Bratton Clovelly GB (DEV) 66 Ve 44
Bratton Fleming GB (DEV) 66 Wa 42
Bratton Seymour GB (SOM) 68 Xd 42
Braunston GB (NRH) 54 Ye 35
Braunstone GB (LEC) 54 Ye 33
Braunston-in-Rutland GB (LEC) 54 Zb 33
Braunton GB (DEV) 66 Ve 42
Brawby GB (NOY) 37 Za 23
Brawl GB (HGL) 5 Vf 117
Brawlbin GB (HGL) 5 We 118
Bray GB (BKS) 63 Zb 39
Bray IRL (KIL) 94 Ta 31
Bray IRL (WKL) 95 Tf 29
Braybrooke GB (NRH) 54 Za 34
Brayford GB (DEV) 66 Wa 42
Bray Shop GB (CNW) 75 Vd 45
Braystones GB (CUB) 34 Wc 22
Brayton GB (NOY) 40 Yf 26
Brazacott GB (CNW) 66 Vd 44
Bré = Bray IRL (WKL) 95 Tf 29
Brea GB (HGL) 7 Uc 2
Breachwood Green GB (HTS) 64 Ze 37
Breaclete GB (HGL) 11 Ta 119
Breadsall GB (DSH) 46 Yd 31
Breadstone GB (GLS) 61 Xd 38
Bready GB (TYR) 78 Sd 19
Breage GB (CNW) 74 Ud 48
Breaghna IRL (COR) 103 Ra 38
Breaghwy IRL (SLI) 82 Rc 22
Breakish GB (HGL) 13 Ua 5
Bream GB (GLS) 61 Xc 38
Breamore GB (HAS) 69 Yb 43
Brean GB (SOM) 68 Wf 41
Breanloughaun IRL (GAL) 92 Ra 29
Brearton GB (NOY) 39 Yd 24
Breasclete GB (HGL) 11 Tb 119
Breaston GB (DSH) 46 Ye 31
Brechfa GB (DYF) 59 Vf 37
Brechin GB (TYS) 22 Xc 8
Breckles GB (NOR) 56 Af 33
Brecon GB (POW) 60 Wd 37
Bredagh IRL (GAL) 88 Rd 28
Bredbury GB (GRM) 45 Xf 28
Brede GB (ESX) 72 Ad 43
Bredenbury GB (HWC) 52 Xc 35
Bredfield GB (SUF) 57 Bb 36
Bredgar GB (KEN) 65 Ae 41
Bredhurst GB (KEN) 65 Ad 41
Bredicot GB (HWC) 53 Xf 35
Bredon GB (HWC) 53 Xf 36
Bredon's Hardwick GB (HWC) 53 Xf 36
Bredon's Norton GB (HWC) 53 Xf 36
Bredwardine GB (HWC) 52 Xa 36
Bree IRL (WEX) 101 Tc 34
Breedoge IRL (ROS) 88 Rd 25
Breedon on the Hill GB (LEC) 46 Yd 32
Breeny More IRL (COR) 103 Qd 38
Breeoge IRL (SLI) 82 Rc 23
Bregoge Cross Roads IRL (COR) 98 Rb 35
Breich GB (LOT) 25 Wc 14
Breighton GB (HUS) 40 Za 26
Breivig GB (HGL) 11 Te 119
Brenchley GB (KEN) 72 Ac 42
Brendon GB (DEV) 66 Vd 43
Brenish GB (HGL) 10 Sf 120
Brent GB (GRL) 64 Ze 39
Brent Eleigh GB (SUF) 56 Ae 36
Brentingby GB (LEC) 46 Zb 32
Brent Knoll GB (SOM) 68 Xa 41
Brent Pelham GB (HTS) 64 Aa 37
Brentwood GB (ESS) 64 Ab 39
Brenzett GB (KEN) 72 Af 42
Brereton GB (SFS) 45 Ya 32
Brereton Green GB (CHS) 45 Xe 29
Brereton Heath GB (CHS) 45 Xe 29
Bressingham GB (NOR) 57 Ba 34
Bretby GB (DSH) 45 Yc 32
Bretford GB (WWH) 54 Yd 34
Bretforton GB (HWC) 53 Ya 36
Bretherton GB (LCS) 38 Xb 26
Brettenham GB (NOR) 56 Ae 34
Brettenham GB (SUF) 56 Af 36
Bretton GB (CLW) 44 Xa 30
Brewlands Bridge GB (TYS) 21 We 8
Brewood GB (SFS) 53 Xe 32
Briach GB (GRP) 16 Wc 3
Brianstown House IRL (LGF) 88 Sa 26
Briantspuddle GB (DOS) 68 Xe 44
Bricket Wood GB (HTS) 64 Zd 38
Bride GBM 29 Vd 22
Bridekirk GB (CUB) 34 Wd 20
Bridell GB (DYF) 50 Vc 36
Bridestones GB (SFS) 45 Xf 30
Bridestowe GB (DEV) 66 Vf 44
Brideswell GB (GRP) 17 Xb 4
Brideswell IRL (ROS) 88 Rf 28
Bridford GB (DEV) 67 Wb 45
Bridge GB (KEN) 65 Ba 41
Bridgeacrin IRL (LOT) 90 Td 24
Bridge End GB (LIN) 47 Ze 31
Bridge End IRL (DON) 78 Sd 18
Bridgefoot GB (CBS) 55 Aa 36
Bridgefoot GB (CUB) 34 Wc 21
Bridgefoot GB (TYS) 22 Wf 9
Bridge Green GB (ESS) 56 Aa 36
Bridgehampton GB (SOM) 68 Xc 42
Bridgeland IRL (WKL) 95 Td 32
Bridgemere GB (CHS) 44 Xd 30
Bridgend GB (CNW) 75 Vc 46
Bridgend GB (CUB) 35 Xa 21
Bridgend GB (FIF) 22 Xa 11
Bridgend GB (GRP) 16 Wf 4
Bridgend GB (GRP) 16 Xb 4
Bridgend GB (LOT) 25 Wc 13
Bridgend GB (MGL) 60 Wc 39
Bridgend GB (STC) 22 Te 14
Bridgend GB (STC) 23 Uc 15
Bridgend GB (STC) 23 Ud 12
Bridgend GB (TYS) 21 Wd 10
Bridgend GB (TYS) 22 Xb 8
Bridgend of Lintrathen GB (TYS) 21 Wf 8
Bridge of Alford GB (GRP) 16 Xb 5
Bridge of Allan GB (CEN) 25 Wa 12
Bridge of Avon GB (GRP) 16 Wd 4
Bridge of Balgie GB (TYS) 20 Ve 9
Bridge of Cally GB (TYS) 21 Wd 9
Bridge of Canny GB (GRP) 17 Xc 6
Bridge of Craigisla GB (TYS) 21 We 8
Bridge of Dee GB (DAG) 31 Wa 19
Bridge of Dee GB (GRP) 16 Wd 6
Bridge of Don GB (GRP) 17 Xf 5
Bridge of Dun GB (TYS) 22 Xc 8
Bridge of Dye GB (GRP) 17 Xc 7
Bridge of Earn GB (TYS) 21 Wd 10
Bridge of Ericht GB (TYS) 20 Vd 8
Bridge of Feugh GB (GRP) 17 Xd 6
Bridge of Forss GB (HGL) 5 Wc 117
Bridge of Gaur GB (TYS) 20 Vd 8
Bridge of Muchalls GB (GRP) 17 Xe 6
Bridge of Orchy GB (STC) 20 Vb 9
Bridge of Tilt GB (TYS) 21 Wb 8
Bridge of Walls GB (SHL) 2 Yc 107
Bridgerule GB (DEV) 66 Vd 44
Bridges GB (SHS) 52 Xa 33
Bridge Street GB (SUF) 56 Ae 36
Bridgetown GB (CNW) 66 Vd 44
Bridgetown GB (SOM) 67 Wc 42
Bridgetown IRL (CRE) 92 Rc 32
Bridgetown IRL (WEX) 101 Tc 35
Bridge Trafford GB (CHS) 44 Xb 29
Bridge Yate GB (AVN) 61 Xd 40
Bridgham GB (NOR) 56 Af 34
Bridgnorth GB (SHS) 52 Xd 33
Bridgtown GB (SFS) 53 Xf 32
Bridgwater GB (SOM) 68 Wf 42
Bridlington GB (HUS) 41 Ze 24
Bridport GB (DOS) 68 Xb 44
Bridstow GB (HWC) 61 Xc 37
Brierfield GB (LCS) 39 Xe 26
Brierfield House IRL (ROS) 88 Re 26
Brierley GB (GLS) 61 Xc 38
Brierley GB (HWC) 52 Xb 35
Brierley GB (SOY) 40 Yd 27
Brierley Hill GB (WMD) 53 Xf 34
Brigg GB (HUS) 41 Zd 27
Brigham GB (CUB) 34 Wc 21
Brighouse GB (WYO) 39 Yb 26
Brightgate GB (DSH) 45 Yc 30
Brighthampton GB (OXS) 62 Yd 38
Brightling GB (ESX) 72 Ac 43
Brightlingsea GB (ESS) 65 Ba 38
Brighton GB (CEN) 25 Wb 13
Brighton GB (CNW) 75 Va 46
Brighton GB (ESX) 71 Zf 44
Brightwallon GB (BKS) 62 Yd 39
Brightwell Baldwin GB (OXS) 63 Yf 39
Brightwell-cum-Sotwell GB (OXS) 63 Yf 39
Brignall GB (DUR) 36 Ya 21
Brig o' Turk GB (CEN) 24 Vd 11
Brigsley GB (HUS) 41 Zf 27
Brigsteer GB (CUB) 35 Xb 23
Brigstock GB (NRH) 55 Zc 34
Brill GB (BUS) 63 Yf 38
Brill GB (CNW) 74 Ue 48
Brilley GB (HWC) 52 Wf 36
Brimfield GB (HWC) 52 Xb 35
Brimington GB (DSH) 46 Yd 29
Brimley GB (DEV) 76 Wb 45
Brimpsfield GB (GLS) 61 Xf 38
Brimpton GB (BKS) 63 Ye 40
Brims GB (ORK) 6 We 116
Brimstage GB (CHS) 44 Wf 29
Brind GB (HUS) 40 Za 26
Brindle GB (LCS) 38 Xc 26
Brindley Ford GB (SFS) 45 Xe 30
Brineton GB (SFS) 53 Xe 32
Brington GB (CBS) 55 Zd 34
Brinian GB (ORK) 5 Xa 114
Brinkhill GB (LIN) 47 Aa 29
Brinklow GB (WWH) 54 Yd 34
Brinkworth GB (WIL) 62 Ya 39
Brinscall GB (LCS) 38 Xc 26
Brinsley GB (NTS) 46 Ye 30
Brinsop GB (HWC) 52 Xb 36
Brisco GB (CUB) 32 Xa 19
Briskil Lower IRL (LGF) 88 Sb 26
Brisley GB (NOR) 49 Af 32
Brislington GB (AVN) 61 Xc 40
Bristol GB (AVN) 61 Xc 40
Briston GB (NOR) 49 Ba 31
Brithdir GB (GWY) 43 Wb 32
Briton Ferry GB (WGL) 59 Wb 39
Brittas IRL (DUB) 95 Td 29
Brittas IRL (LIM) 99 Rd 33
Brittas House IRL (LAO) 94 Sc 30
Britway IRL (COR) 99 Re 36
Britwell Salome GB (OXS) 63 Yf 39
Brix GB (ESS) 65 Ad 38
Brixham GB (DEV) 76 Wc 46
Brixton GB (DEV) 76 Vf 46
Brixton GB (GRL) 64 Zf 40
Brixton Deverill GB (WIL) 69 Xe 42
Brixworth GB (NRH) 54 Za 35
Brize Norton GB (OXS) 62 Yc 38
Broad Blundson GB (WIL) 62 Yb 39
Broadbottom GB (GRM) 39 Xf 28
Broadbridge GB (WSX) 70 Za 43
Broadbridge Heath GB (WSX) 71 Zd 42
Broad Campden GB (GLS) 53 Yb 36
Broad Chalke GB (WIL) 69 Ya 42
Broadclyst GB (DEV) 67 Wd 44
Broadford GB (HGL) 13 Ua 5
Broadford IRL (CRE) 92 Rc 32
Broadford IRL (LIM) 98 Ra 34
Broadford Bridge GB (WSX) 71 Zd 43
Broad Green GB (ESS) 65 Ae 37
Broad Green GB (HWC) 53 Xd 35
Broadgroves GB (ESS) 64 Ac 37
Broad Haven GB (DYF) 58 Uf 38
Broadheath GB (GRM) 45 Xd 28
Broad Heath GB (HWC) 52 Xd 35
Broadhembury GB (DEV) 67 We 44
Broadhempston GB (DEV) 76 Wb 46
Broad Hill GB (CBS) 56 Ab 34
Broad Hinton GB (WIL) 62 Ya 40
Broadholme GB (NTS) 46 Zc 29
Broadland Row GB (ESX) 72 Ad 43
Broadlay GB (DYF) 59 Vd 38
Broadley GB (GRP) 16 Wf 3
Broadley Common GB (ESS) 64 Aa 38
Broadmayne GB (DOS) 68 Xd 44
Broadmeadows GB (BOR) 26 Xa 15
Broadmere GB (HAS) 70 Yf 41
Broadoak GB (DOS) 68 Xb 44
Broad Oak GB (DOS) 68 Xe 43
Broadoak GB (DYF) 59 Vf 37
Broadoak GB (ESX) 72 Ab 43
Broad Oak GB (ESX) 72 Ad 43
Broad Oak GB (HWC) 61 Xb 37
Broad Oak GB (KEN) 65 Ba 41
Broadstairs GB (KEN) 65 Bc 40
Broadstone GB (DOS) 69 Ya 44
Broadstone GB (SHS) 52 Xb 33
Broad Street GB (KEN) 65 Ad 41
Broadstreet Common GB (GWE) 60 Wf 39
Broad Street Green GB (ESS) 65 Ae 38
Broad Town GB (WIL) 62 Ya 39
Broadwas GB (HWC) 53 Xd 35
Broadwater GB (HTS) 64 Ze 37
Broadwater GB (WSX) 71 Zd 44
Broadway GB (DYF) 59 Vd 38
Broadway GB (HWC) 53 Ya 36
Broadway GB (SUF) 57 Bd 34
Broadway IRL (WEX) 101 Td 35
Broadwell GB (GLS) 62 Yb 37
Broadwell GB (OXS) 62 Yc 38
Broadwell GB (WWH) 54 Ye 35
Broadwey GB (DOS) 68 Xd 45
Broadwindsor GB (DOS) 68 Xb 44
Broadwoodkelly GB (DEV) 66 Wa 43
Broadwoodwidger GB (DEV) 66 Ve 44
Brochel GB (HGL) 13 Tf 4
Brockagh IRL (SLI) 82 Rc 23
Brockbridge GB (HAS) 70 Yf 43
Brockdish GB (NOR) 57 Bb 34
Brockenhurst GB (HAS) 69 Yc 44
Brockford Street GB (SUF) 57 Ba 35
Brockhall GB (NRH) 54 Yf 35
Brockham GB (SUR) 71 Ze 41
Brockhampton GB (HWC) 61 Xc 37
Brockholes GB (WYO) 39 Yb 27
Brockhurst GB (ESX) 71 Aa 42
Brocklesby GB (LIN) 41 Ze 27
Brockley GB (AVN) 61 Xb 40
Brockley Green GB (SUF) 56 Ae 36
Brockthorpe GB (GLS) 61 Xe 38
Brockton GB (SHS) 52 Wf 33
Brockton GB (SHS) 52 Xa 34
Brockton GB (SHS) 52 Xc 33
Brockton GB (SHS) 52 Xd 34
Brockweir GB (GLS) 61 Xc 38
Brockwood Park GB (HAS) 70 Yf 42
Brockworth GB (GLS) 61 Xf 37
Brocton GB (SFS) 45 Xf 32
Brodick GB (STC) 24 Uf 15
Brodsworth GB (SOY) 40 Ye 27
Broelagh IRL (LET) 82 Sa 23
Brogborough GB (BFS) 55 Zc 36
Brogherlea Cross Roads IRL (LAO) 94 Sc 29
Brokenborough GB (WIL) 61 Xf 39
Broken Cross GB (CHS) 44 Xd 29
Broken Cross GB (CHS) 45 Xf 29
Bromborough GB (CHS) 44 Xa 29
Brome GB (SUF) 57 Ba 34
Bromestead GB (SFS) 45 Xe 32
Bromfield GB (CUB) 34 We 20
Bromfield GB (SHS) 52 Xb 34
Bromham GB (BFS) 55 Zc 36
Bromham GB (WIL) 62 Xf 40
Bromley GB (GRL) 64 Aa 40
Bromley Green GB (KEN) 72 Af 42
Brompton GB (NOY) 36 Yd 22
Brompton GB (NOY) 37 Zc 23
Brompton-on-Swale GB (NOY) 36 Yb 22
Brompton Regis GB (SOM) 67 Wc 42
Bromsash GB (HWC) 61 Xc 37
Bromsberrow Heath GB (GLS) 61 Xd 37
Bromsgrove GB (HWC) 53 Xf 34
Bromyard GB (HWC) 52 Xc 35
Bromyard Downs GB (HWC) 52 Xd 35
Bronaber GB (GWY) 43 Wa 31
Brongest GB (DYF) 50 Vd 36
Bronington GB (CLW) 44 Xb 31
Bronllys GB (POW) 60 We 36
Bronnant GB (DYF) 51 Wa 35
Bronwydd Arms GB (DYF) 59 Ve 37
Bronydd GB (POW) 52 Wf 36
Bronygarth GB (SHS) 44 Wf 31
Brook GB (DYF) 59 Vc 38
Brook GB (HAS) 69 Yc 42
Brook GB (HAS) 69 Yc 43
Brook GB (IOW) 70 Yd 45
Brook GB (KEN) 72 Af 41
Brook GB (SUR) 70 Zb 42
Brook, Preston GB (CHS) 44 Xc 29
Brook Bridge IRL (DON) 82 Rf 20
Brooke GB (LEC) 54 Zb 33
Brooke GB (NOR) 57 Bc 33
Brookeborough GB (FER) 83 Sd 23
Brookfield Bridge GB (ANT) 85 Tf 20
Brookhouse GB (LCS) 38 Xb 24
Brookhouse Green GB (CHS) 45 Xe 30
Brookland GB (KEN) 72 Ae 42
Brookman's Park GB (HTS) 64 Ac 38
Brooks GB (POW) 51 We 33
Brooksby GB (LEC) 46 Yf 32
Brooks Green GB (WSX) 71 Zd 42
Brook Street GB (KEN) 72 Ae 42
Brook Street GB (WSX) 71 Zf 42
Brookwood GB (SUR) 63 Zc 41
Broom GB (BFS) 55 Ze 36
Broome GB (HWC) 53 Xf 34
Broome GB (NOR) 57 Bc 34
Broome GB (SHS) 52 Xa 34
Broomedge GB (CHS) 44 Xd 28
Broomer's Corner GB (WSX) 71 Zd 43
Broomfield GB (ESS) 65 Ac 38
Broomfield GB (GRP) 17 Xf 4
Broomfield GB (KEN) 65 Ad 41
Broomfield GB (SOM) 67 Wf 42
Broomfield IRL (MOG) 90 Tb 24
Broomfield Cross Roads IRL (KIL) 94 Ta 31
Broomfleet GB (HUS) 40 Zb 26
Broom Hill GB (DOS) 69 Ya 44
Broomhill GB (NHL) 33 Yc 17
Broom's Green GB (GLS) 61 Xd 37
Broom Street IRL (LET) 88 Sa 25
Broomville House IRL (CLW) 95 Tb 32
Brora GB (HGL) 9 Wa 120
Broseley GB (SHS) 52 Xd 33
Brosna IRL (KER) 98 Qe 35
Brosna IRL (OFF) 93 Sa 31
Brothertoft GB (LIN) 47 Zf 31
Brotherton GB (NOY) 40 Ye 26
Brotton GB (CLE) 37 Za 21
Broubster GB (HGL) 5 Wc 117
Brough GB (CUB) 35 Xe 21
Brough GB (DSH) 45 Yb 28
Brough GB (HGL) 6 Wd 117
Brough GB (HUS) 41 Zc 26
Brough GB (NTS) 46 Zb 30
Brough GB (SHL) 2 Za 106
Broughal IRL (OFF) 93 Sb 29
Broughall GB (SHS) 44 Xc 31
Broughane Cross Roads IRL (KER) 97 Qc 35
Brough Cross Roads IRL (COR) 98 Rc 35
Brough Lodge GB (SHL) 2 Za 105
Broughshane GB (ANT) 79 Te 19
Brough Sowerby GB (CUB) 35 Xe 21
Broughton GB (BOR) 26 Wd 15
Broughton GB (CBS) 55 Zf 34
Broughton GB (CLW) 44 Xa 30
Broughton GB (CUB) 34 Wd 20
Broughton GB (GRM) 39 Xe 27
Broughton GB (HAS) 69 Yc 42
Broughton GB (HUS) 41 Zc 27
Broughton GB (LCS) 38 Xb 26
Broughton GB (NOY) 37 Zb 24
Broughton GB (NOY) 39 Xf 25
Broughton GB (NRH) 54 Zb 34
Broughton GB (OXS) 54 Yd 36

110 GB IRL Boleybeg Cross Roads – Broughton

Broughton Astley **GB** (LEC) 54 Ye 33
Broughton Beck **GB** (CUB) 34 Wf 23
Broughton Hackett **GB** (HWC) 53 Xf 35
Broughton in Furness **GB** (CUB) 34 We 23
Broughton Mills **GB** (CUB) 34 We 23
Broughton Moor **GB** (CUB) 34 Wd 20
Broughton Poggs **GB** (OXS) 62 Yc 38
Broughtown **GB** (ORK) 5 Xc 113
Broughty Ferry **GB** (TYS) 22 Xa 10
Brown Candover **GB** (HAS) 70 Ye 42
Brown Edge **GB** (LCS) 38 Xa 27
Brown Edge **GB** (SFS) 45 Xf 30
Brownes Cross Roads **IRL** (LGF) 89 Sc 26
Brownhill **GB** (GRP) 17 Xe 4
Brownhills **GB** (WMD) 53 Ya 33
Brownieside **GB** (NHL) 33 Yb 15
Brownlow Heath **GB** (CHS) 45 Xe 30
Browns Cross Roads **IRL** (WTF) 99 Sa 36
Brownsford House **IRL** (KLK) 100 Sf 34
Brownshill Green **GB** (WMD) 54 Yc 34
Brownston **GB** (DEV) 76 Wa 46
Brownswood **IRL** (WTF) 100 Sd 35
Broxbourne **GB** (HTS) 64 Ab 38
Broxburn **GB** (LOT) 25 Wd 13
Broxburn **GB** (LOT) 27 Xd 13
Broxholme **GB** (LIN) 47 Zc 29
Broxted **GB** (ESS) 64 Ab 37
Broxwood **GB** (HWC) 52 Xa 35
Bruan **GB** (HGL) 9 We 118
Brue **GB** (HGL) 11 Tc 118
Bruera **GB** (CHS) 44 Xa 30
Bruern Abbey **GB** (OXS) 62 Yc 37
Bruernish **GB** (HGL) 12 Sd 7
Bruff **IRL** (LIM) 98 Rc 34
Bruichladdich **GB** (STC) 22 Td 14
Bruisyard **GB** (SUF) 57 Bc 35
Brund **GB** (SFS) 45 Ya 30
Brundall **GB** (NOR) 49 Bc 33
Brundish **GB** (SUF) 57 Bb 35
Bruntingthorpe **GB** (LEC) 54 Yf 33
Brunton **GB** (FIF) 21 Wf 10
Brunton **GB** (NHL) 33 Yb 15
Bruree **IRL** (LIM) 98 Rc 34
Bruton **GB** (SOM) 68 Xd 42
Bryanlitter **IRL** (MOG) 84 Ta 23
Bryansford **GB** (DOW) 85 Ua 23
Bryanston **GB** (DOS) 69 Xe 43
Brydekirk **GB** (DAG) 31 We 18
Brymbo **GB** (CLW) 44 Wf 30
Bryn **GB** (DYF) 59 Vf 38
Bryn **GB** (GRM) 38 Xc 27
Bryn **GB** (GWY) 43 Wc 31
Bryn **GB** (SHS) 52 Wf 34
Bryn **GB** (WGL) 59 Wb 39
Brynamman **GB** (WGL) 59 Wa 38
Brynberian **GB** (DYF) 58 Vb 37
Bryncae **GB** (MGL) 60 Wd 39
Bryncethin **GB** (MGL) 60 Wc 39
Bryncir **GB** (GWY) 42 Ve 31
Bryn-côch **GB** (WGL) 59 Wb 38
Bryncroes **GB** (GWY) 42 Vc 31
Bryncrug **GB** (GWY) 51 Vf 33
Bryneglwys **GB** (CLW) 43 We 30
Brynford **GB** (CLW) 43 We 29
Bryn Gates **GB** (GRM) 38 Xc 27
Bryngwran **GB** (GWY) 42 Vd 29
Bryngwyn **GB** (POW) 52 We 36
Bryngwyn **GB** (POW) 60 Xa 38
Brynhenllan **GB** (DYF) 58 Va 36
Brynhoffnant **GB** (DYF) 50 Vd 36
Bryn-Mawr **GB** (GWE) 60 We 38
Brynmenyn **GB** (MGL) 60 Wc 39
Brynna **GB** (MGL) 60 Wd 39
Brynrefail **GB** (GWY) 42 Ve 28
Brynsiencyn **GB** (GWY) 42 Ve 29
Brynteg **GB** (GWY) 42 Ve 29
Bryn-y-maen **GB** (CLW) 43 Wb 29
Bualintur **GB** (HGL) 13 Te 5
Bualnaluib **GB** (HGL) 7 Uc 1
Buarthfa **GB** (MGL) 60 Wc 39
Bubbenhall **GB** (WWH) 54 Yd 34
Bubwith **GB** (HUS) 40 Za 26
Buccleuch **GB** (BOR) 32 Wf 16
Buchanty **GB** (TYS) 21 Wb 10
Buchlyvie **GB** (CEN) 25 Ve 12
Buckabank **GB** (CUB) 34 Xa 20
Buckby Wharf **GB** (NRH) 54 Yf 35
Buckden **GB** (CBS) 55 Ze 35
Buckden **GB** (NOY) 36 Xf 23
Buckenham **GB** (NOR) 57 Bc 33
Buckerell **GB** (DEV) 67 We 44
Buckfast **GB** (DEV) 76 Wb 46
Buckfastleigh **GB** (DEV) 76 Wb 46
Buckhafen **GB** (FIF) 26 Wf 11
Buckholm **GB** (BOR) 26 Xb 15
Buckhorn Weston **GB** (DOS) 68 Xd 42
Buckhurst Hill **GB** (ESS) 64 Aa 39
Buckie **GB** (GRP) 16 Xa 2
Buckingham **GB** (BUS) 54 Za 36
Buckland **GB** (BUS) 63 Zb 38
Buckland **GB** (DEV) 76 Wa 47
Buckland **GB** (HTS) 55 Zf 37
Buckland **GB** (KEN) 73 Ba 42
Buckland **GB** (OXS) 62 Yc 38
Buckland **GB** (SUR) 71 Ze 41
Buckland Brewer **GB** (DEV) 66 Ve 43
Buckland Dinham **GB** (SOM) 68 Xd 41
Buckland Filleigh **GB** (DEV) 66 Ve 43
Buckland in the Moor **GB** (DEV) 76 Wb 45
Buckland Monochorum **GB** (DEV) 76 Vf 46
Buckland Saint Mary **GB** (SOM) 67 Wf 43
Bucklerheads **GB** (TYS) 22 Xa 9
Bucklers Hard **GB** (HAS) 69 Yd 44
Bucklesham **GB** (SUF) 57 Bb 36
Buckley **GB** (CLW) 44 Wf 30
Buckman Corner **GB** (WSX) 71 Zd 42
Buckminster **GB** (LEC) 46 Zb 32
Bucknall **GB** (LIN) 47 Ze 29
Bucknall **GB** (SFS) 45 Xf 30
Bucknell **GB** (OXS) 63 Ye 37
Bucknell **GB** (SHS) 52 Xa 34
Bucksburn **GB** (GRP) 17 Xe 5
Buck's Cross **GB** (DEV) 66 Vd 43
Bucks Green **GB** (WSX) 71 Zd 42
Bucks Hill **GB** (HTS) 63 Zd 38
Bucks Horn Oak **GB** (HAS) 70 Za 41
Buck's Mills **GB** (DEV) 66 Vd 43
Buckton **GB** (HWC) 52 Xa 34
Buckton **GB** (NHL) 27 Ya 15
Buckworth **GB** (CBS) 55 Ze 34
Budby **GB** (NTS) 46 Yf 29
Bude **GB** (CNW) 66 Vc 44
Budlake **GB** (DEV) 67 Wd 44
Budle **GB** (NHL) 27 Yb 15
Budleigh Salterton **GB** (DEV) 67 We 45
Buerton **GB** (CHS) 44 Xd 31
Bufferis Alley Cross Roads **IRL** (WEX) 101 Td 33
Bugbrooke **GB** (NRH) 54 Yf 35
Buggaeen Cross Roads **IRL** (COR) 98 Rb 36
Bugle **GB** (CNW) 75 Vb 46
Bugthorpe **GB** (HUS) 40 Va 24
Buildwas **GB** (SHS) 52 Xc 33
Builth Road **GB** (POW) 51 Wd 35
Builth Wells **GB** (POW) 51 Wd 36
Buiríos uí Chéin = Borrisokane **IRL** (TIP) 93 Rf 31
Buldoo **GB** (HGL) 5 Wb 117
Bulford **GB** (WIL) 69 Yb 41
Bulgaden **IRL** (LIM) 98 Rc 34
Bulkeley **GB** (CHS) 44 Xb 30
Bulkington **GB** (WIL) 61 Xf 41
Bulkington **GB** (WWH) 54 Yd 34
Bulkworthy **GB** (DEV) 66 Ve 43
Bullaun **IRL** (GAL) 87 Ra 28
Bullaun **IRL** (GAL) 92 Rc 29
Bullington **GB** (HAS) 70 Yd 42
Bullpot Fm **GB** (CUB) 35 Xc 23
Bullwood **GB** (STC) 24 Va 13
Bullyhubbock **IRL** (WEX) 101 Te 33
Bullymurphy **IRL** (MAY) 87 Ra 26
Bulmer **GB** (ESS) 56 Ae 36
Bulmer **GB** (NOY) 40 Za 24
Bulmer Tye **GB** (ESS) 56 Ae 36
Bulphan **GB** (ESS) 64 Ac 39
Bulwell **GB** (NTS) 46 Ye 30
Bulwick **GB** (NRH) 55 Zc 33
Bumble's Green **GB** (ESS) 64 Aa 38
Bunacrick **IRL** (DON) 78 Sd 17
Bunacurry **IRL** (MAY) 86 Qa 25
Bunagarraun **IRL** (GAL) 87 Ra 27
Bunakeeran **IRL** (OFF) 94 Sb 29
Bunarkaig **GB** (HGL) 19 Va 7
Bunavoneadar **GB** (HGL) 11 Ta 1
Bunbeg **IRL** (DON) 77 Re 18
Bunbrosna **IRL** (WMT) 89 Sd 27
Bunbury **GB** (CHS) 44 Xc 30
Bunchrew Ho **GB** (HGL) 15 Ve 4
Bunclody **IRL** (WEX) 101 Tc 33
Buncrana **IRL** (DON) 78 Sd 18
Bundalloch **GB** (HGL) 14 Ud 5
Bundoran **IRL** (DON) 82 Re 22
Bundorragha **IRL** (MAY) 86 Qb 27
Bundouglas **IRL** (GAL) 86 Pf 27
Bunessan **GB** (STC) 18 Te 11
Bungay **GB** (SUF) 57 Bc 34
Bunmahon **IRL** (WTF) 100 Sd 36
Bunnafinglas **IRL** (MAY) 87 Qf 24
Bunnaglass **IRL** (GAL) 92 Rb 30
Bunnahabhain **GB** (STC) 23 Tf 13
Bunnahowen **IRL** (MAY) 80 Qa 23
Bunnanaddan **IRL** (SLI) 88 Rc 24
Bunny **GB** (NTS) 46 Yf 31
Bunnyconnellan **IRL** (MAY) 81 Qf 24
Bunowen Castle **IRL** (GAL) 86 Pf 28
Bunratty **IRL** (CRE) 92 Rb 32
Buntait **GB** (HGL) 14 Vc 4
Buntingford **GB** (HTS) 64 Zf 37
Bunwell **GB** (NOR) 57 Ba 33
Burbage **GB** (LEC) 54 Yd 33
Burbage **GB** (WIL) 62 Yc 40
Burchett's Green **GB** (BKS) 63 Zb 39
Burcombe **GB** (WIL) 69 Ya 42
Burcott **GB** (BUS) 63 Zb 37
Burdocks **GB** (WSX) 71 Zc 43
Bures **GB** (SUF) 56 Ae 37
Bures Green **GB** (SUF) 56 Ae 37
Burford **GB** (OXS) 62 Yc 38
Burford **GB** (SHS) 52 Xc 35
Burg **GB** (STC) 18 Te 9
Burgate **GB** (SUF) 57 Ba 35
Burgess Hill **GB** (ESX) 71 Zf 43
Burgh **GB** (LIN) 48 Ab 30
Burgh by Sands **GB** (CUB) 32 Wf 19
Burgh Castle **GB** (NOR) 57 Bd 33
Burghclere **GB** (HAS) 62 Ye 40
Burghead **GB** (GRP) 9 Wd 2
Burgheath **GB** (SUR) 64 Ze 41
Burghfield **GB** (BKS) 63 Yf 40
Burghfield Hill **GB** (BKS) 63 Yf 40
Burghill **GB** (HWC) 52 Xb 36
Burgh next Aylsham **GB** (NOR) 49 Bb 32
Burgh on Bain **GB** (LIN) 47 Ze 28
Burgh Saint Margaret **GB** (NOR) 49 Bd 32
Burgh Saint Peter **GB** (NOR) 57 Bd 34
Burghwallis **GB** (SOY) 40 Ye 27
Buriton **GB** (HAS) 70 Za 43
Burke Ville **IRL** (GAL) 93 Rd 29
Burland **GB** (CHS) 44 Xc 30
Burlawn **GB** (CNW) 75 Vb 46
Burleigh **GB** (BKS) 63 Zb 40
Burlescombe **GB** (DEV) 67 We 43
Burleston **GB** (DOS) 68 Xe 44
Burley **GB** (HAS) 69 Yb 44
Burley **GB** (LEC) 55 Zb 32
Burleydam **GB** (CHS) 44 Xc 31
Burley Gate **GB** (HWC) 52 Xc 36
Burley in Wharfedale **GB** (WYO) 39 Yb 25
Burley Lodge **GB** (HAS) 69 Yc 43
Burley Street **GB** (HAS) 69 Yb 43
Burlingiobb **GB** (POW) 52 Wf 35
Burlow **GB** (ESX) 72 Ab 43
Burlton **GB** (SHS) 44 Xb 32
Burmarsh **GB** (KEN) 72 Af 42
Burn **GB** (NOY) 40 Yf 26
Burnaston **GB** (DSH) 45 Yc 31
Burnbrook **IRL** (ROS) 88 Rf 28
Burnchurch **IRL** (KLK) 100 Se 33
Burncourt **IRL** (TIP) 99 Rf 35
Burndell **GB** (WSX) 70 Zc 44
Burneside **GB** (CUB) 35 Xb 22
Burness **GB** (ORK) 5 Xc 113
Burneston **GB** (NOY) 36 Yc 23
Burnett **GB** (AVN) 61 Xd 40
Burnfoot **GB** (BOR) 32 Xa 16
Burnfoot **GB** (TYS) 25 Wc 11
Burnfoot **IRL** (DON) 78 Sd 18
Burnfort **IRL** (COR) 98 Rc 36
Burnham **GB** (BUS) 63 Zc 39
Burnham **GB** (HUS) 41 Zd 27
Burnham **IRL** (KER) 96 Pe 36
Burnham Deepdale **GB** (NOR) 48 Ae 31
Burnham Green **GB** (HTS) 64 Ab 38
Burnham Market **GB** (NOR) 48 Ae 31
Burnham Norton **GB** (NOR) 48 Ae 31
Burnham-on-Crouch **GB** (ESS) 65 Ae 39
Burnham-On-Sea **GB** (SOM) 68 Wf 41
Burnham Overy Staithe **GB** (NOR) 48 Ae 31
Burnham Thorpe **GB** (NOR) 48 Ae 31
Burnhaven **GB** (GRP) 17 Yb 4
Burnhead **GB** (DAG) 31 Wb 17
Burnhervie **GB** (GRP) 17 Xd 5
Burnhill Green **GB** (SFS) 53 Xe 33
Burnhope **GB** (DUR) 33 Yb 20
Burnhouse **GB** (STC) 24 Vc 14
Burniston **GB** (NOY) 37 Zd 23
Burnley **GB** (LCS) 39 Xe 26
Burnmouth **GB** (BOR) 27 Xf 13
Burn of Cambus **GB** (CEN) 25 Vf 11
Burnopfield **GB** (DUR) 33 Yb 19
Burnsall **GB** (NOY) 39 Ya 24
Burnside **GB** (LOT) 25 Wd 13
Burnside **GB** (STC) 30 Ve 16
Burnside **GB** (TYS) 22 Xb 9
Burnside **GB** (TYS) 26 Wd 11
Burnside of Duntrune **GB** (TYS) 22 Xa 9
Burntcliff Top **GB** (CHS) 45 Xf 29
Burntisland **GB** (FIF) 26 We 12
Burntwood **GB** (SFS) 53 Ya 32
Burntwood Green **GB** (SFS) 53 Ya 32
Burnt Yates **GB** (NOY) 39 Yc 24
Burpham **GB** (WSX) 71 Zc 43
Burradon **GB** (NHL) 33 Xf 16
Burrafirth **GB** (SHL) 2 Za 104
Burravoe **GB** (SHL) 2 Yf 105
Burrelton **GB** (TYS) 21 We 9
Burren **GB** (DOW) 90 Te 24
Burren **IRL** (CRE) 92 Qf 30
Burren **IRL** (CRE) 92 Qf 32
Burren **IRL** (MAY) 87 Qe 25
Burrenfadda **IRL** (CRE) 92 Qe 32
Burridge **GB** (HAS) 70 Ye 43
Burrill **GB** (NOY) 36 Yc 23
Burringham **GB** (HUS) 40 Zb 27
Burrington **GB** (DEV) 66 Wa 43
Burrington **GB** (HWC) 52 Xb 34
Burrough End **GB** (CBS) 56 Ac 35
Burrough Green **GB** (CBS) 56 Ac 35
Burrough on the Hill **GB** (LEC) 54 Za 32
Burrow Bridge **GB** (SOM) 68 Xa 42
Burrowhill **GB** (SUR) 63 Zc 40
Burry Green **GB** (WGL) 59 Ve 39
Burry Port **GB** (DYF) 59 Ve 38
Burscough Bridge **GB** (LCS) 38 Xa 27
Bursea **GB** (HUS) 40 Zb 26
Burshill **GB** (HUS) 41 Zd 25
Burston **GB** (NOR) 57 Ba 34
Burston **GB** (SFS) 45 Xf 31
Burstwick **GB** (HUS) 41 Zf 26
Burtersett **GB** (NOY) 35 Xe 23
Burtle **GB** (SOM) 68 Xa 41
Burton **GB** (CHS) 44 Wf 29
Burton **GB** (CHS) 44 Xb 30
Burton **GB** (CLW) 44 Xa 30
Burton **GB** (DYF) 58 Va 38
Burton **GB** (LIN) 47 Zc 29
Burton **GB** (NHL) 27 Yb 15
Burton **GB** (SOM) 67 Wf 41
Burton Agnes **GB** (HUS) 41 Ze 24
Burton Bradstock **GB** (DOS) 68 Xb 44
Burton Constable **GB** (HUS) 41 Ze 26
Burton Green **GB** (WWH) 53 Yc 34
Burton Hall **IRL** (CLW) 94 Ta 31
Burton Hastings **GB** (WWH) 54 Yd 33
Burtonhill House **IRL** (CRE) 92 Rb 32
Burton-in-Kendal **GB** (CUB) 35 Xb 23
Burton in Lonsdale **GB** (NOY) 35 Xc 24
Burton Joyce **GB** (NTS) 46 Yf 31
Burton Latimer **GB** (NRH) 55 Zb 34
Burton Lazars **GB** (LEC) 46 Za 32
Burton-le-Coggles **GB** (LIN) 47 Zc 32
Burton Leonard **GB** (NOY) 39 Yd 24
Burton on the Wolds **GB** (LEC) 46 Yf 32
Burton Overy **GB** (LEC) 54 Za 33
Burton Pedwardine **GB** (LIN) 47 Ze 31
Burton Pidsea **GB** (HUS) 41 Zf 26
Burtonport **IRL** (DON) 77 Rd 19
Burton Salmon **GB** (NOY) 40 Ye 26
Burton upon Stather **GB** (HUS) 40 Zb 27
Burton upon Trent **GB** (SFS) 45 Yc 32
Burtonwood **GB** (CHS) 44 Xc 28
Burtown Cross Roads **IRL** (KIL) 94 Ta 31
Burwardsley **GB** (CHS) 44 Xb 30
Burwarton **GB** (SHS) 52 Xc 34
Burwash **GB** (ESX) 72 Ac 42
Burwash Weald **GB** (ESX) 72 Ac 43
Burwell **GB** (CBS) 56 Ab 35
Burwell **GB** (LIN) 47 Aa 29
Burwick **GB** (ORK) 6 Xa 116
Bury **GB** (CBS) 55 Zf 34
Bury **GB** (GRM) 39 Xe 27
Bury **GB** (SOM) 67 Wc 42
Bury **GB** (WSX) 71 Zc 43
Bury Green **GB** (HTS) 64 Aa 37
Bury Saint Edmunds **GB** (SUF) 56 Ae 35
Burythorpe **GB** (NOY) 40 Zb 24
Busby **GB** (TYS) 21 Wc 10
Buscot **GB** (OXS) 62 Yc 38
Bush, The **IRL** (LOT) 90 Te 25
Bush Bank **GB** (HWC) 52 Xb 36
Bushbury **GB** (WMD) 53 Xf 33
Bushby **GB** (LEC) 54 Yf 33
Bush Crathie **GB** (GRP) 16 We 6
Bushey **GB** (HTS) 63 Zd 39
Bushey Heath **GB** (HTS) 64 Zd 39
Bush Green **GB** (NOR) 57 Bb 34
Bushley **GB** (HWC) 53 Xe 36
Bushmills **GB** (ANT) 79 Tc 17
Bushton **GB** (WIL) 62 Ya 40
Bussage **GB** (GLS) 61 Xf 38
Busta **GB** (SHL) 2 Yd 106
Butcher's Cross **GB** (ESX) 71 Ab 42
Butcombe **GB** (AVN) 61 Xb 40
Butleigh **GB** (SOM) 68 Xb 42
Butleigh Wootton **GB** (SOM) 68 Xb 42
Butler's Bridge **IRL** (CAV) 89 Sd 24
Butlers Marston **GB** (WWH) 54 Yc 36
Butlerstown **IRL** (COR) 104 Rb 39
Butlerstown **IRL** (TIP) 100 Sc 34
Butley **GB** (SUF) 57 Bc 36
Butsfield **GB** (DUR) 36 Yb 20
Butterburn **GB** (CUB) 32 Xc 18
Butterknowle **GB** (DUR) 36 Ya 21
Butterleigh **GB** (DEV) 67 Wd 43
Buttermere **GB** (CUB) 34 We 21
Buttermere **GB** (WIL) 62 Yc 40
Butters Green **GB** (SFS) 45 Xe 30
Buttershaw **GB** (WYO) 39 Yb 26
Butterstone **GB** (TYS) 21 Wc 9
Butterton **GB** (SFS) 45 Ya 30
Butterwick **GB** (HUS) 40 Zb 27
Butterwick **GB** (NOY) 37 Za 23
Buttevant **IRL** (COR) 98 Rb 35
Butt Green **GB** (CHS) 44 Xd 30
Buttington **GB** (POW) 52 Wf 32
Buttonoak **GB** (SHS) 53 Xd 34
Butts, The **IRL** (CLW) 94 Tb 33
Buxhall **GB** (SUF) 56 Af 35
Buxted **GB** (ESX) 71 Aa 43
Buxton **GB** (DSH) 45 Ya 29
Buxton **GB** (NOR) 49 Bb 32
Bwlch **GB** (POW) 60 We 37
Bwlch-derwin **GB** (GWY) 42 Ve 31
Bwlchgwyn **GB** (CLW) 44 Wf 30
Bwlch-Llan **GB** (DYF) 51 Vf 35
Bwlchnewydd **GB** (DYF) 59 Vd 37
Bwlchtocyn **GB** (GWY) 42 Vc 32
Bwlch-y-cibau **GB** (POW) 44 We 32
Bwlchyddar **GB** (CLW) 44 We 32
Bwlch-y-fadfa **GB** (DYF) 50 Ve 36
Bwlch-y-ffridd **GB** (POW) 51 Wd 33
Bwlchygroes **GB** (DYF) 58 Vc 37
Bwlch-y-sarnau **GB** (POW) 51 Wd 34
Byfield **GB** (NRH) 54 Ye 35
Byfleet **GB** (SUR) 63 Zd 41
Bygrave **GB** (HTS) 55 Zf 36
Byker **GB** (TAW) 33 Yc 19
Bylane End **GB** (CNW) 75 Vd 46
Bylchau **GB** (CLW) 43 Wc 30
Byley **GB** (CHS) 44 Xd 29
Bymeshill **IRL** (WKL) 95 Tb 30
Bynea **GB** (DYF) 59 Vf 38
Byrness **GB** (NHL) 32 Xd 17
Bythorn **GB** (CBS) 55 Zd 34
Byton **GB** (HWC) 52 Xa 35
Bywater, Allerton **GB** (WYO) 40 Yd 26
Bywell **GB** (NHL) 33 Ya 19
Byworth **GB** (WSX) 70 Zc 43

C

Cabourne **GB** (LIN) 41 Ze 27
Cabra **IRL** (DUB) 95 Te 28
Cabrach **GB** (GRP) 16 Wf 5
Cabrach **GB** (STC) 23 Tf 14
Cabragh **IRL** (SLI) 81 Qf 23
Cabry **IRL** (DON) 78 Se 18
Cackanode **IRL** (COR) 103 Ra 37
Cadamstown **IRL** (KIL) 94 Ta 28
Cadbury **GB** (DEV) 67 Wc 44
Cadbury Barton **GB** (DEV) 66 Wa 43
Caddington **GB** (BFS) 63 Zd 37
Caddonfoot **GB** (BOR) 26 Xa 15
Cadeby **GB** (LEC) 54 Yd 33
Cadeby **GB** (SOY) 40 Ye 27
Cadeleigh **GB** (DEV) 67 Wc 43
Cade Street **GB** (ESX) 72 Ab 43
Cadgwith **GB** (CNW) 74 Ue 49
Cadham **GB** (FIF) 26 Wf 11
Cadishead **GB** (GRM) 44 Xd 28
Cadley **GB** (WIL) 62 Yb 40
Cadmore End **GB** (BUS) 63 Za 39
Cadnam **GB** (HAS) 69 Yc 43
Cadney **GB** (HUS) 41 Zd 27
Cadole **GB** (CLW) 44 We 30
Caeathro **GB** (GWY) 42 Ve 30
Caehopkin **GB** (POW) 59 Wb 38
Caenby **GB** (LIN) 41 Zd 28
Caenby Corner **GB** (LIN) 41 Zc 28
Caerau **GB** (MGL) 60 Wc 39
Caerau **GB** (SGL) 60 We 40
Caerdeon **GB** (GWY) 43 Wa 32
Caerdydd = Cardiff **GB** (SGL) 60 Wf 40
Caerfyrddin = Carmarthen **GB** (DYF) 59 Vd 37
Caergeiliog **GB** (GWY) 42 Vc 29
Caergwrle **GB** (CLW) 44 Wf 30
Caer-Lan **GB** (POW) 59 Wb 38
Caerleon **GB** (GWE) 60 Xa 39
Caernarfon **GB** (GWY) 42 Ve 30
Caerphilly **GB** (MGL) 60 We 39
Caersws **GB** (POW) 51 Wd 33
Caerwent **GB** (GWE) 61 Xb 39
Caerwys **GB** (CLW) 43 We 29
Caheny **GB** (LDR) 79 Tc 19
Caher **IRL** (COR) 102 Qb 39
Caher **IRL** (CRE) 92 Rc 31
Caher **IRL** (MAY) 87 Qe 27
Caher **IRL** (TIP) 99 Sa 34
Caheracruttera **IRL** (KER) 97 Qa 36
Caheradrine **IRL** (GAL) 92 Ra 29
Caheragh House **IRL** (LIM) 98 Qe 33
Caherakilleen **IRL** (GAL) 93 Rd 29
Caheraphuca **IRL** (COR) 102 Pf 39
Caherass House **IRL** (LIM) 98 Rb 33
Caherbane House **IRL** (CRE) 98 Qe 33
Caherbarnagh **IRL** (KER) 98 Qe 36
Caherbarnagh **IRL** (KER) 102 Pf 37
Caherboshina **IRL** (KER) 96 Pd 36
Caherconlish **IRL** (LIM) 99 Rd 33
Caherconnell **IRL** (CRE) 92 Qf 30
Caherdaniel **IRL** (KER) 102 Pf 38
Caherea **IRL** (CRE) 92 Qf 32
Caherfurvaus **IRL** (GAL) 92 Rb 29
Cahergariff **IRL** (COR) 102 Qa 39
Caherhemush **IRL** (MAY) 87 Qe 27
Caherlag **IRL** (COR) 104 Rd 37
Caherlane **IRL** (LIM) 97 Qe 34
Caherlea **IRL** (GAL) 92 Ra 29
Caherlevoy **IRL** (LIM) 98 Qe 34
Caherlistrane **IRL** (GAL) 87 Qf 28
Cahermacnaghten **IRL** (CRE) 92 Qe 30
Cahermore **IRL** (COR) 102 Pf 39
Cahermoyls House **IRL** (LIM) 98 Qf 33
Cahermuckee **IRL** (COR) 103 Qe 38
Cahermurphy **IRL** (CRE) 92 Qe 32
Cahernacaha **IRL** (COR) 103 Qe 37
Cahernagarry **IRL** (GAL) 93 Rc 29
Cahernahoon **IRL** (GAL) 87 Ra 28
Cahernarry **IRL** (LIM) 98 Rc 33
Caherpeak **IRL** (GAL) 92 Ra 29
Caherphuca **IRL** (GAL) 87 Rb 28
Caherrevagh **IRL** (MAY) 87 Qf 27
Cahersculllibeen **IRL** (KER) 96 Pd 35
Cahersiveen **IRL** (KER) 96 Pe 37
Cahiracon House **IRL** (CRE) 98 Qf 33
Cainborrow **GB** (GRP) 16 Xa 4
Caio **GB** (DYF) 51 Wa 36
Cairn **GB** (STC) 24 Va 11
Cairnbaan **GB** (STC) 23 Ud 12
Cairnbrogie **GB** (GRP) 17 Xe 5
Cairncross **GB** (BOR) 27 Xe 13
Cairncross **GB** (TYS) 22 Xb 7
Cairngaan **GB** (DAG) 34 Va 21
Cairngarroch **GB** (DAG) 28 Uf 20
Cairnhill **GB** (GRP) 17 Xc 4
Cairnie **GB** (GRP) 16 Xa 4
Cairnryan **GB** (DAG) 28 Uf 19
Cairstairs Junction **GB** (STC) 25 Wc 14
Caiseal = Cashel **IRL** (TIP) 99 Sa 33
Caisleán an Bharraigh = Castlebar **IRL** (MAY) 87 Qe 25
Caister-on-Sea **GB** (NOR) 49 Be 33
Caistor **GB** (LIN) 41 Ze 27
Caistron **GB** (NHL) 33 Xf 17
Cake Street **GB** (NOR) 57 Ba 34
Calary Upper **IRL** (WKL) 95 Tf 30
Calbost **GB** (HGL) 11 Td 120
Calbourne **GB** (IOW) 70 Yd 44
Caldbeck **GB** (CUB) 34 Wf 20
Caldbergh **GB** (NOY) 36 Ya 23
Caldecote **GB** (CBS) 55 Ze 34
Caldecott **GB** (LEC) 54 Zb 33
Caldecott **GB** (NRH) 55 Zc 35
Calder Bridge **GB** (CUB) 34 Wd 22
Caldercruix **GB** (STC) 25 Wa 13
Calder Mains **GB** (HGL) 6 Wc 117
Caldermill **GB** (STC) 25 Vf 15
Caldicot **GB** (GWE) 61 Xb 39
Caldwell **GB** (DSH) 45 Yc 32
Caldwell **GB** (NOY) 36 Yb 21
Caldy **GB** (CHS) 44 Wf 28
Caledon **GB** (TYR) 84 Ta 22
Caledrhydiau **GB** (DYF) 50 Ve 36
Calfsound **GB** (ORK) 5 Xb 113
Calgary **GB** (STC) 18 Te 9
Calhame **IRL** (DON) 82 Rd 21
Califer **GB** (GRP) 16 Wc 3
California **GB** (CEN) 25 Wb 13
California **GB** (NOR) 49 Be 32
Calke **GB** (DSH) 46 Yd 32
Callaghan's Loughs **IRL** (GAL) 93 Re 29
Callaghs **IRL** (CAV) 89 Sc 24
Callain = Callan **IRL** (KLK) 100 Sd 33
Callaly **GB** (NHL) 33 Ya 16
Callan **IRL** (KLK) 100 Sd 33
Callanafersy **IRL** (KER) 97 Qb 36
Callander **GB** (CEN) 25 Ve 11
Callangh **IRL** (CAV) 89 Sd 25
Callanish **GB** (HGL) 11 Tb 119
Callenberg House **IRL** (MOG) 90 Tc 25
Callestick **GB** (CNW) 74 Uf 47
Calliagh **IRL** (MOG) 84 Sf 23
Calligarry **GB** (HGL) 13 Ua 6
Callington **GB** (CNW) 75 Ve 45
Callow **GB** (HWC) 61 Xb 36
Callow **IRL** (GAL) 86 Pf 28
Callow **IRL** (MAY) 87 Qf 25
Callow **IRL** (ROS) 88 Rd 25
Callow End **GB** (HWC) 53 Xe 36
Callow Hill **GB** (HWC) 53 Xd 34
Callow Hill **GB** (WIL) 62 Ya 39
Calmsden **GB** (GLS) 62 Ya 38
Calne **GB** (WIL) 62 Xf 40
Calow **GB** (DSH) 46 Yd 29
Calshot **GB** (HAS) 70 Ye 44
Calstock **GB** (CNW) 75 Ve 46
Calthorpe **GB** (NOR) 49 Bb 31
Calthwaite **GB** (CUB) 35 Xb 20
Calton **GB** (SFS) 45 Ya 30
Caltra **IRL** (GAL) 88 Rd 28
Caltragh **IRL** (LGF) 88 Sa 27
Caltraghlea **IRL** (GAL) 93 Re 28
Calveley **GB** (CHS) 44 Xc 30
Calver **GB** (DSH) 45 Yc 29
Calverhall **GB** (SHS) 44 Xc 31
Calver Hill **GB** (HWC) 52 Xa 36
Calverleigh **GB** (DEV) 67 Wc 43
Calverley **GB** (WYO) 39 Yb 26
Calverstown **IRL** (KIL) 95 Tb 30
Calvert **GB** (BUS) 63 Za 37
Calverton **GB** (BUS) 54 Za 36
Calverton **GB** (NTS) 46 Yf 30
Calvine **GB** (TYS) 21 Wa 8
Cam **GB** (GLS) 61 Xd 38
Camagh **IRL** (LGF) 89 Sc 25
Camaross **IRL** (WEX) 101 Tb 34
Camas-luinie **GB** (HGL) 14 Ud 5
Camastianavaig **GB** (HGL) 13 Tf 4
Camasunary **GB** (HGL) 13 Tf 5
Camb **GB** (SHL) 2 Yf 105
Camber **GB** (ESX) 72 Ae 43
Camberley **GB** (SUR) 63 Zb 41
Camblesforth **GB** (NOY) 40 Yf 26
Cambo **GB** (NHL) 33 Ya 18
Camborne **GB** (CNW) 74 Ue 47
Cambridge **GB** (CBS) 56 Aa 35
Cambusbarron **GB** (CEN) 25 Wa 12
Cambuslang **GB** (STC) 25 Ve 14
Cambusnethan **GB** (STC) 25 Wa 14
Camden **GB** (GRL) 64 Zf 39
Camelford **GB** (CNW) 75 Vb 45
Camelon **GB** (CEN) 25 Wb 12
Camer's Green **GB** (HWC) 61 Xe 36
Camerton **GB** (CUB) 34 Wd 20
Camesdale **GB** (SUR) 70 Zb 42
Camfield Place **GB** (HTS) 64 Ab 38
Camghouran **GB** (TYS) 20 Vd 8
Camira **IRL** (TIP) 93 Rf 31
Camira Cross Roads **IRL** (LAO) 94 Sd 30
Camlough **GB** (ARG) 84 Td 23
Cammachmore **GB** (GRP) 17 Xf 6
Camolin **IRL** (WEX) 101 Td 33
Camp **IRL** (KER) 97 Qa 35
Camp, The **GB** (GLS) 61 Xf 38
Campbelton **GB** (STC) 24 Va 14
Campbeltown **GB** (STC) 28 Uc 16
Campile **IRL** (WEX) 100 Ta 35
Camp Lodge **IRL** (KER) 97 Qc 35
Campmuir **GB** (TYS) 21 We 9
Campsall **GB** (SOY) 40 Ye 27
Campsey Ash **GB** (SUF) 57 Bc 36
Camps Heath **GB** (SUF) 57 Be 34
Camrose **GB** (DYF) 58 Uf 37
Camross **IRL** (LAO) 94 Sc 30
Camseil **GB** (STC) 24 Vb 13
Camster **GB** (HGL) 9 We 118
Camus **IRL** (GAL) 93 Rf 29
Camusmore Bay **IRL** (DON) 77 Re 17
Camusngaul **GB** (HGL) 7 Ue 1
Camusteel **GB** (HGL) 13 Ub 4
Camusterrach **GB** (HGL) 13 Ub 4
Camusvrachan **GB** (TYS) 20 Ve 9
Canada **GB** (HAS) 69 Yc 43
Canbo **IRL** (ROS) 88 Rf 25
Candlesby **GB** (LIN) 47 Zf 29
Cane End **GB** (OXS) 63 Yf 39
Canewdon **GB** (ESS) 65 Ae 39
Canford Magna **GB** (DOS) 69 Ya 44
Cangort Park **IRL** (OFF) 93 Sa 31
Canisbay **GB** (HGL) 6 Wf 117
Canknoogheda **IRL** (KER) 97 Qa 37
Cann **GB** (DOS) 69 Xe 43
Cannaghanally **IRL** (SLI) 81 Ra 23
Cannards Grave **GB** (SOM) 68 Xc 41
Cann Common **GB** (DOS) 69 Xf 43
Cannich **GB** (HGL) 14 Vb 4
Canningstown **IRL** (CAV) 89 Sf 25
Cannington **GB** (SOM) 67 Wf 42
Cannock **GB** (SFS) 53 Xf 32
Cannock Wood **GB** (SFS) 53 Ya 32
Canonbie **GB** (DAG) 32 Xa 18
Canon Bridge **GB** (HWC) 52 Xb 36
Canon Frome **GB** (HWC) 52 Xc 36
Canon Pyon **GB** (HWC) 52 Xb 36
Canons Ashby **GB** (NRH) 54 Yf 36
Canonstown **GB** (CNW) 74 Ud 48
Canower **IRL** (GAL) 86 Qa 28
Canterbury **GB** (KEN) 65 Ba 41
Cantley **GB** (SOY) 40 Yf 27
Cantlop **GB** (SHS) 52 Xb 33
Cantraydoune **GB** (HGL) 15 Vf 4
Cantraywood **GB** (HGL) 15 Vf 3
Cantsfield **GB** (LCS) 35 Xc 24
Canty **IRL** (WTF) 99 Sb 36
Canvey Island **GB** (ESS) 65 Ad 39
Canworthy Water **GB** (CNW) 66 Vc 44
Caol **GB** (HGL) 19 Uf 7
Caolas **GB** (STC) 18 Tb 9
Caolis **GB** (HGL) 12 Sc 7
Capel **GB** (KEN) 72 Ac 41
Capel **GB** (SUR) 71 Ze 42
Capel Bangor **GB** (DYF) 51 Wa 34
Capel Betws-Lleucu **GB** (DYF) 51 Vf 35
Capel Carmel **GB** (GWY) 42 Vb 32
Capel Coch **GB** (GWY) 42 Ve 29
Capel Curig **GB** (GWY) 43 Wa 30
Capel Cynon **GB** (DYF) 50 Vd 36
Capel Dewi **GB** (DYF) 50 Ve 36
Capel Dewi **GB** (DYF) 51 Vf 34
Capel Dewi **GB** (DYF) 59 Ve 37
Capel Garmon **GB** (GWY) 43 Wb 30
Capel Gwyn **GB** (DYF) 59 Ve 37
Capel Gwyn **GB** (GWY) 42 Vd 29
Capel Gwynfe **GB** (DYF) 59 Wa 37
Capel Hendre **GB** (DYF) 59 Vf 38
Capel Isaac **GB** (DYF) 59 Vf 37
Capel Iwan **GB** (DYF) 59 Vd 36
Capel-le-Ferne **GB** (KEN) 73 Ba 42
Capelles **GBG** 100 Xc 52
Capel Parc **GB** (GWY) 42 Ve 28
Capel Saint Mary **GB** (SUF) 57 Ba 36
Capel Sefon **GB** (DYF) 51 Vf 34
Capel Tygwydd **GB** (DYF) 50 Vc 36
Capeluchaf **GB** (GWY) 42 Vd 30
Capenhurst **GB** (CHS) 44 Xa 29
Capernwray **GB** (LCS) 35 Xb 24
Capheaton **GB** (NHL) 33 Ya 18
Capira **IRL** (GAL) 93 Re 30
Cappaclogh **IRL** (KER) 97 Qa 35
Cappagh **IRL** (COR) 99 Rd 36
Cappagh **IRL** (GAL) 87 Rb 27
Cappagh **IRL** (GAL) 92 Qf 29
Cappagh **IRL** (GAL) 93 Rd 30
Cappagh **IRL** (KER) 96 Pe 35
Cappagh **IRL** (LIM) 98 Ra 33
Cappaghglass **IRL** (COR) 103 Qd 39
Cappaghmore **IRL** (GAL) 92 Ra 30
Cappagh White **IRL** (TIP) 99 Re 33
Cappalusk **IRL** (GAL) 92 Rc 28
Cappamore **IRL** (LIM) 99 Rd 33
Cappanacreha **IRL** (MAY) 86 Qd 27
Cappanagoul **IRL** (COR) 98 Rb 35
Cappanarrow **IRL** (LAO) 94 Sc 30
Cappancur **IRL** (OFF) 94 Sd 29
Cappanrush **IRL** (WMT) 94 Sd 28
Cappataggle **IRL** (GAL) 93 Rd 29
Cappavicar **IRL** (MAY) 87 Qe 25
Cappeen **IRL** (COR) 103 Ra 38
Cappercleuch **GB** (BOR) 31 We 16
Cappoquin **IRL** (WTF) 99 Sa 36
Cappry **IRL** (DON) 77 Sb 20
Capstone **GB** (KEN) 65 Ad 40
Caputh **GB** (TYS) 21 Wd 9
Cara **IRL** (WMT) 89 Sc 28
Caragh Bridge **IRL** (KER) 97 Qa 36
Caran **IRL** (ROS) 88 Rd 26
Caran **IRL** (ROS) 88 Re 26
Carbis Bay **GB** (CNW) 74 Ud 47
Carbost **GB**, (HGL) 13 Td 5
Carbost **GB** (HGL) 13 Te 4
Carbrooke **GB** (NOR) 56 Af 33
Carburton **GB** (NTS) 46 Yf 29
Carbury **IRL** (KIL) 94 Ta 28
Car Colston **GB** (NTS) 46 Za 31
Carcroft **GB** (SOY) 40 Ye 27
Cardenden **GB** (FIF) 26 We 12
Cardeston **GB** (SHS) 52 Xa 32
Cardiff **GB** (SGL) 60 Wf 40
Cardigan **GB** (DYF) 50 Vc 36
Cardington **GB** (BFS) 55 Zd 36
Cardington **GB** (SHS) 52 Xb 33
Cardinham **GB** (CNW) 75 Vc 46
Cardow **GB** (GRP) 16 Wd 4
Cardrona **GB** (BOR) 26 Wf 15
Cardross **GB** (STC) 24 Vc 13
Cardunock **GB** (CUB) 31 We 19
Careby **GB** (LIN) 47 Zd 32
Careston **GB** (TYS) 22 Xb 8
Carew **GB** (DYF) 58 Vb 38
Carey **GB** (HWC) 61 Xc 37
Cargagh **IRL** (CAV) 89 Sf 25
Cargenbridge **GB** (DAG) 31 Wc 18
Cargill **GB** (TYS) 21 Wd 9
Cargo **GB** (CUB) 32 Xa 19
Carha **IRL** (DON) 78 Sc 17
Carham **GB** (NHL) 27 Xe 15
Carhampton **GB** (SOM) 67 Wd 41
Carharrack **GB** (CNW) 74 Ue 47
Carhoo **IRL** (KER) 96 Pd 36
Carhoon **IRL** (GAL) 93 Rd 30
Carickmadim **IRL** (MOG) 90 Tb 25
Carie **GB** (TYS) 20 Ve 8
Carie **GB** (TYS) 20 Ve 9
Carinish **GB** (HGL) 10 Se 3
Carishader **GB** (HGL) 11 Ta 119
Cark **GB** (CUB) 35 Xa 23
Cark **IRL** (DON) 77 Sa 19
Carkeel **GB** (CNW) 75 Ve 46
Carker **IRL** (KER) 97 Qd 36
Carland Cross **GB** (CNW) 74 Uf 46
Carlanstown **IRL** (MT) 90 Ta 26
Carlby **GB** (LIN) 47 Zd 32
Carlecotes **GB** (SOY) 39 Yb 27
Carleton **GB** (CUB) 32 Xa 19
Carleton **GB** (LCS) 38 Wf 25
Carleton **GB** (NOY) 39 Xf 25
Carleton Forehoe **GB** (NOR) 57 Ba 33
Carleton Rode **GB** (NOR) 57 Ba 34
Carlingcott **GB** (AVN) 61 Xd 41
Carlingford **IRL** (LOT) 90 Te 24
Carlisle **GB** (CUB) 32 Xa 19
Carlops **GB** (BOR) 26 Wd 14
Carlow **IRL** (CLW) 94 Ta 31
Carloway **GB** (HGL) 11 Tb 119
Carlton **GB** (CBS) 56 Ac 36
Carlton **GB** (CLE) 36 Yd 21

Broughton Astley – Carlton (GB) (IRL) 111

Carlton **GB** (NOY) 36 Ya 23
Carlton **GB** (NOY) 37 Yf 23
Carlton **GB** (NOY) 40 Yf 26
Carlton **GB** (NTS) 46 Yf 31
Carlton **GB** (SOY) 40 Yd 27
Carlton **GB** (SUF) 57 Bc 35
Carlton Colville **GB** (SUF) 57 Be 34
Carlton Curlieu **GB** (LEC) 54 Za 33
Carlton Husthwaite **GB** (NOY) 37 Ye 23
Carlton in Cleveland **GB** (NOY) 37 Ye 22
Carlton in Lindrick **GB** (NTS) 46 Yf 28
Carlton-le-Moorland **GB** (LIN) 47 Zc 30
Carlton Miniott **GB** (NOY) 36 Yd 23
Carlton on Trent **GB** (NTS) 46 Zb 29
Carlton Scroop **GB** (LIN) 47 Zc 31
Carluke **GB** (STC) 25 Wa 14
Carmacup **GB** (STC) 31 Wa 15
Carmarthen **GB** (DYF) 59 Vd 37
Carmel **GB** (CLW) 43 We 29
Carmel **GB** (DYF) 59 Vf 38
Carmel **GB** (GWY) 42 Vd 29
Carmel **GB** (GWY) 42 Ve 30
Carminish **GB** (HGL) 10 Ta 2
Carmont **GB** (GRP) 22 Xe 7
Carmunnock **GB** (STC) 25 Ve 14
Carmyle **GB** (STC) 25 Vf 14
Carmyllie **GB** (TYS) 22 Xb 9
Carna **IRL** (GAL) 91 Qa 29
Carna **IRL** (WEX) 101 Td 35
Carnaby **GB** (HUS) 41 Ze 24
Carnach **GB** (HGL) 11 Tb 1
Carnaghan **IRL** (DON) 78 Sd 18
Carnalbanagh **GB** (ANT) 79 Tf 19
Carnaross **IRL** (MT) 89 Ta 26
Carnbee **GB** (FIF) 26 Xb 11
Carnbo **GB** (TYS) 25 Wc 11
Carndonagh **IRL** (DON) 78 Se 17
Carnduncan **GB** (STC) 22 Td 14
Carne **GB** (CNW) 75 Va 47
Carnell **GB** (STC) 24 Vd 15
Carnes **IRL** (MT) 90 Td 27
Carnew **IRL** (WKL) 101 Tc 32
Carney **IRL** (SLI) 82 Rc 22
Carney **IRL** (TIP) 93 Re 31
Carnforth **GB** (LCS) 38 Xb 24
Carnhedryn **GB** (DYF) 58 Ue 37
Carnhell Green **GB** (CNW) 74 Ud 47
Carnie **GB** (GRP) 17 Xe 6
Carnley **IRL** (MAY) 87 Rb 26
Carnlough **GB** (ANT) 79 Ua 19
Carnmoney **GB** (ANT) 85 Ua 20
Carnmore Cross Roads **IRL** (GAL) 92 Ra 29
Carno **GB** (POW) 51 Wc 33
Carnon Downs **GB** (CNW) 74 Uf 47
Carnoneen **IRL** (GAL) 87 Ra 28
Carnoustie **GB** (TYS) 22 Xb 9
Carnowen **IRL** (DON) 77 Sc 19
Carnteel **GB** (TYR) 84 Ta 22
Carntullagh **IRL** (DON) 82 Rd 21
Carnwath **GB** (STC) 25 Wc 14
Carnyorth **GB** (CNW) 74 Ub 48
Carowcanon **IRL** (DON) 77 Rf 18
Carperby **GB** (NOY) 36 Ya 23
Carracastle **IRL** (MAY) 87 Rb 25
Carradale **GB** (STC) 23 Ud 15
Carraduffy **IRL** (DON) 82 Re 20
Carragh **IRL** (KIL) 95 Tb 29
Carraghmore **IRL** (KLK) 100 Sf 34
Carraghmore House **IRL** (OFF) 93 Sb 30
Carraghs **IRL** (ROS) 87 Rc 26
Carraghy **IRL** (GAL) 87 Ra 28
Carragreich **GB** (HGL) 11 Tb 1
Carraig Mhachaire = Carrickmacross **IRL** (MOG) 90 Tb 25
Carraig na Siúire = Carrick on Suir **IRL** (TIP) 100 Sd 34
Carraleigh **IRL** (COR) 98 Qf 37
Carran **IRL** (COR) 103 Qd 38
Carran **IRL** (CRE) 92 Qf 30
Carranadoe Bridge **IRL** (ROS) 88 Sa 25
Carranduff **IRL** (SLI) 81 Qf 23
Carraroe **IRL** (GAL) 91 Qc 29
Carraun **IRL** (SLI) 81 Qf 24
Carrbridge **GB** (HGL) 15 Wb 5
Carrefour Selous **GBJ** 73 Xf 53
Carreglefn **GB** (GWY) 42 Vd 28
Carrick **GB** (STC) 23 Ud 12
Carrick **IRL** (DON) 82 Rc 21
Carrick **IRL** (OFF) 93 Sa 29
Carrick **IRL** (WEX) 101 Tb 35
Carrickaboy **IRL** (CAV) 89 Se 25
Carrickadraan **IRL** (ROS) 88 Rf 24
Carrickallen **IRL** (CAV) 89 Sf 25
Carrickart **IRL** (DON) 77 Sb 17
Carrickartagh **IRL** (MOG) 90 Tb 24
Carrickashedoge **IRL** (MOG) 90 Tb 25
Carrickboy **IRL** (LGF) 89 Sb 27
Carrickbyrne **IRL** (WEX) 100 Tb 34
Carrick Castle **GB** (STC) 24 Va 12
Carrickcolman **IRL** (DON) 77 Sc 20
Carrickedmond Cross Roads **IRL** (LGF) 89 Sb 27
Carrickfergus **GB** (ANT) 85 Ub 20
Carrick House **IRL** (LAO) 94 Sc 31
Carrickloughmore Cross Roads **IRL** (TIP) 93 Sa 32
Carrickmacross **IRL** (MOG) 90 Tb 25
Carrickmastia Hill **IRL** (WEX) 101 Tb 34
Carrickmore **GB** (TYR) 84 Sf 21
Carrick on Shannon **IRL** (LET) 89 Rf 25
Carrick on Suir **IRL** (TIP) 100 Sd 34
Carrickroe **IRL** (MOG) 84 Sf 22
Carrickspringan **IRL** (MT) 89 Ta 26
Carriden **GB** (CEN) 25 Wc 12
Carrig **IRL** (TIP) 93 Sa 30
Carrigaclodig Cross Roads **IRL** (COR) 103 Ra 37
Carrigafoyle House **IRL** (KER) 97 Qd 33
Carrigagown **IRL** (TIP) 93 Re 31
Carrigagulla **IRL** (COR) 98 Ra 36
Carrigaholt **IRL** (CRE) 97 Qb 33
Carrigahorig **IRL** (TIP) 93 Rf 30
Carrigal **IRL** (TIP) 93 Re 32
Carrigaline **IRL** (COR) 104 Rd 38
Carrigallen **IRL** (LET) 89 Sc 25
Carrigan **IRL** (CAV) 89 Sd 25
Carriganimmy **IRL** (COR) 98 Qf 37
Carrigans **IRL** (DON) 78 Sd 19
Carrigans **IRL** (SLI) 82 Rc 24
Carrigaweigh **IRL** (COR) 103 Qf 37
Carrigbaun Cross Roads **IRL** (COR) 103 Qf 39
Carrigbeg **IRL** (WEX) 101 Td 32
Carrig East **IRL** (KER) 103 Qc 37
Carrigeeny Cross Roads **IRL** (COR) 103 Qe 39
Carrigerry House **IRL** (CRE) 92 Ra 32
Carriggower **IRL** (WKL) 95 Tf 30
Carrigkerry **IRL** (LIM) 98 Qf 34
Carrigmore **IRL** (WKL) 95 Tf 31
Carrignavar **IRL** (COR) 98 Rd 37
Carrigoran House **IRL** (CRE) 92 Ra 32
Carrigtohill **IRL** (COR) 104 Re 37
Carrine **GB** (STC) 28 Ub 17
Carrington **GB** (GRM) 38 Xd 28
Carrington **GB** (LIN) 47 Zf 30
Carrington **GB** (LOT) 26 Wf 14
Carrog **GB** (CLW) 43 We 31
Carroll's Cross Roads **IRL** (MT) 89 Sf 26
Carron **GB** (GRP) 16 We 4
Carron Bridge **GB** (CEN) 25 Vf 12
Carronbridge **GB** (DAG) 31 Wb 17
Carrow **IRL** (TIP) 93 Re 31
Carrow **IRL** (TIP) 99 Rf 33
Carrowbaun **IRL** (MAY) 87 Rb 25
Carrowcaslan **IRL** (SLI) 82 Rb 23
Carrowcor **IRL** (MAY) 81 Qe 23
Carrowcrory **IRL** (SLI) 88 Rd 24
Carrowculleen House **IRL** (SLI) 82 Rb 23
Carrowdore **GB** (DOW) 85 Uc 21
Carrowduff **IRL** (ROS) 88 Re 26
Carrowduff **IRL** (ROS) 93 Rf 28
Carrowkeel **IRL** (DON) 77 Sc 18
Carrowkeel **IRL** (GAL) 87 Rb 27
Carrowkeel **IRL** (ROS) 88 Rd 27
Carrowkeel **IRL** (ROS) 88 Re 28
Carrowkeelanahglass **IRL** (GAL) 87 Rb 27
Carrowkeel More **IRL** (CRE) 92 Ra 31
Carrowkeeny **IRL** (ROS) 88 Rf 28
Carrowkennedy **IRL** (MAY) 86 Qc 26
Carrowlinan **IRL** (LGF) 89 Sb 26
Carrowmenagh **IRL** (DON) 78 Sf 17
Carrowmore **IRL** (MAY) 80 Qb 23
Carrowmore **IRL** (MAY) 81 Qe 23
Carrowmore **IRL** (MAY) 86 Qb 26
Carrowmore **IRL** (MAY) 87 Qf 26
Carrowmore **IRL** (MAY) 87 Qf 27
Carrowmore **IRL** (MAY) 87 Ra 24
Carrowmore **IRL** (ROS) 88 Rf 27
Carrowmore **IRL** (SLI) 82 Rd 23
Carrowmoreknock **IRL** (GAL) 87 Qe 28
Carrownacarrick **IRL** (SLI) 82 Rc 24
Carrownacon **IRL** (MAY) 87 Qe 26
Carrownacreevy **IRL** (SLI) 88 Rd 24
Carrownakib **IRL** (GAL) 87 Qe 28
Carrownaskeagh **IRL** (ROS) 88 Rf 26
Carrowncully **IRL** (ROS) 88 Re 25
Carrowneden **IRL** (SLI) 82 Rb 24
Carrownlucka **IRL** (MAY) 87 Rb 25
Carrownrooaun **IRL** (GAL) 87 Ra 28
Carrowntarriff **IRL** (ROS) 88 Re 28
Carrowntawy **IRL** (SLI) 82 Rc 24
Carrowntober Sheeaun **IRL** (GAL) 88 Rc 27
Carrowoore **IRL** (CRE) 93 Rd 31
Carrowphadeen Cross Roads **IRL** (ROS) 88 Rf 27
Carrowreagh **GB** (ANT) 79 Td 18
Carrowreagh **IRL** (CAV) 90 Ta 25
Carrowreagh **IRL** (ROS) 88 Re 25
Carrowreagh **IRL** (ROS) 93 Re 28
Carrowreagh **IRL** (SLI) 82 Rc 23
Carrowreagh **IRL** (SLI) 87 Rb 24
Carrowrory **IRL** (LGF) 88 Sa 27
Carrowteige **IRL** (MAY) 80 Qb 23
Carr Shield **GB** (NHL) 35 Xe 20
Carrutherstown **GB** (DAG) 31 Wd 18
Carrville **GB** (DUR) 36 Yc 20
Carry **GB** (STC) 24 Ue 13
Carryduff **GB** (DOW) 85 Ua 21
Carsaig **GB** (STC) 18 Ua 11
Carscreugh **GB** (DAG) 30 Vb 19
Carsegowan **GB** (DAG) 30 Vd 19
Carse Gray **GB** (TYS) 22 Xa 8
Carse House **GB** (STC) 23 Uc 14
Carseriggan **GB** (DAG) 30 Vc 19
Carsethorn **GB** (DAG) 31 Wc 19
Carshalton **GB** (GRL) 64 Ze 40
Carskiey **GB** (STC) 28 Ub 17
Carsluith **GB** (DAG) 30 Vd 19
Carsphairn **GB** (DAG) 30 Ve 17
Carstairs **GB** (STC) 25 Wb 14
Carswell Marsh **GB** (OXS) 62 Yc 38
Carter's Clay **GB** (HAS) 69 Yc 42
Carterton **GB** (OXS) 62 Yc 38
Carthorpe **GB** (NOY) 36 Yc 23
Cartington **GB** (NHL) 33 Ya 17
Cartland **GB** (STC) 25 Wb 14
Cartmel **GB** (CUB) 35 Xa 23
Cartmel Fell **GB** (CUB) 35 Xa 23
Cartron **IRL** (GAL) 87 Rb 27
Cartron **IRL** (GAL) 92 Rc 29
Cartronlahan **IRL** (GAL) 91 Qd 29
Cartronnagilta **IRL** (LET) 88 Sb 24
Cartronplank **IRL** (SLI) 82 Rd 22
Cartys Corner **IRL** (WKL) 95 Te 31
Carway **GB** (DYF) 59 Ve 38
Cascob **GB** (POW) 52 Wf 35
Cashel **IRL** (DON) 77 Sa 18
Cashel **IRL** (DON) 78 Se 17
Cashel **IRL** (DON) 82 Rc 21
Cashel **IRL** (DON) 82 Re 21
Cashel **IRL** (GAL) 86 Qb 28
Cashel **IRL** (GAL) 87 Rc 27
Cashel **IRL** (LET) 88 Sa 25
Cashel **IRL** (TIP) 99 Sa 33
Cashel Cross Roads **IRL** (ROS) 88 Rf 25
Cashelgarran **IRL** (SLI) 82 Rc 22
Cashel Glebe **IRL** (DON) 77 Sb 17
Cashelmechan House **IRL** (ROS) 88 Re 26
Cashelmore **IRL** (DON) 77 Sa 18
Cashelnagor **IRL** (DON) 77 Rf 18
Cashla **IRL** (GAL) 92 Ra 29
Cashleen **IRL** (GAL) 86 Pf 27
Cashlie **GB** (TYS) 20 Vd 9
Cashmoor **GB** (DOS) 69 Xf 43
Cassag **IRL** (WEX) 100 Ta 34
Cassington **GB** (OXS) 62 Yd 38
Castellau **GB** (MGL) 60 Wd 39
Castell Howell **GB** (DYF) 50 Ve 36
Castel-y-bwch **GB** (GWE) 60 Wf 39
Casterton **GB** (CUB) 35 Xc 23
Castle Acre **GB** (NOR) 48 Ae 32
Castle Ashby **GB** (NRH) 54 Zb 35
Castlebaldwin **IRL** (SLI) 88 Rd 24
Castlebanny **IRL** (KLK) 100 Se 34
Castlebar **IRL** (MAY) 87 Qe 25
Castlebay **GB** (HGL) 12 Sd 7
Castlebellingham **IRL** (LOT) 90 Td 25
Castleblagh **IRL** (COR) 99 Rd 36
Castleblakeney **IRL** (GAL) 88 Rd 28
Castleblayney **IRL** (MOG) 90 Tb 24
Castle Bolton **GB** (NOY) 36 Ya 23
Castlebridge **IRL** (WEX) 101 Td 34
Castle Bromwich **GB** (WMD) 53 Yb 33
Castle Bytham **GB** (LIN) 47 Zc 32
Castle Caereinion **GB** (POW) 52 We 33
Castle Camps **GB** (CBS) 56 Ac 36
Castle Carrock **GB** (CUB) 32 Xb 19
Castle Cary **GB** (SOM) 68 Xc 42
Castlecaulfield **GB** (TYR) 84 Tb 21
Castle Combe **GB** (WIL) 61 Xe 40
Castlecomer **IRL** (KLK) 94 Se 32
Castleconnell **IRL** (LIM) 92 Rc 32
Castle Cooke **IRL** (COR) 99 Re 35
Castlecor **IRL** (COR) 98 Rb 35
Castlecor **IRL** (MT) 89 Se 26
Castlecraig **GB** (HGL) 9 Wa 2
Castledawson **GB** (LDR) 84 Tc 20
Castlederg **GB** (TYR) 83 Sc 20
Castledermot **IRL** (KIL) 94 Ta 31
Castledockrell **IRL** (WEX) 101 Tc 33
Castle Donington **GB** (LEC) 46 Yd 31
Castle Douglas **GB** (DAG) 31 Wa 19
Castledowey **IRL** (DON) 77 Sc 19
Castle Eaton **GB** (WIL) 62 Yb 39
Castle Eden **GB** (DUR) 36 Ye 20
Castle Ellen **IRL** (GAL) 92 Rb 28
Castleellis **IRL** (WEX) 101 Td 34
Castlefinn **IRL** (DON) 77 Sc 20
Castleford **GB** (WYO) 40 Yd 26
Castle French **IRL** (GAL) 88 Rd 28
Castlegal **IRL** (SLI) 82 Rd 22
Castlegar **IRL** (GAL) 88 Re 28
Castlegregory **IRL** (KER) 97 Pf 35
Castle Gresley **GB** (DSH) 45 Yc 32
Castle Harrison **IRL** (COR) 98 Rc 35
Castle Hedingham **GB** (ESS) 56 Ad 37
Castle Hill **GB** (SUF) 57 Ba 36
Castlehill **IRL** (MAY) 87 Qd 24
Castleisland **IRL** (KER) 97 Qd 35
Castlejordan **IRL** (MT) 94 Sf 28
Castlekeeran **IRL** (MT) 89 Ta 26
Castle Kennedy **GB** (DAG) 28 Va 18
Castle Kevin **IRL** (COR) 98 Rc 35
Castlekevin **IRL** (WKL) 95 Te 30
Castle Lachlan **GB** (STC) 24 Ue 12
Castlelake House **IRL** (CRE) 92 Rb 32
Castleleiny **IRL** (TIP) 93 Sb 32
Castlelyons **IRL** (COR) 99 Re 36
Castlemagner **IRL** (COR) 98 Rb 35
Castlemaine **IRL** (KER) 97 Qb 35
Castlemartin **GB** (DYF) 58 Uf 39
Castlemartyr **IRL** (COR) 104 Rf 37
Castlemilk **GB** (STC) 25 Ve 14
Castlemorris **GB** (DYF) 58 Uf 37
Castlemorton **GB** (HWC) 53 Xe 36
Castlemoyle **IRL** (GAL) 87 Rb 27
Castle Murray **IRL** (DON) 82 Rd 21
Castlenancy **IRL** (GAL) 93 Rd 29
Castlenavan **GB** (DOW) 85 Ub 22
Castle Neynoe **IRL** (SLI) 82 Rd 23
Castle Nugent **IRL** (LGF) 89 Sc 26
Castle O'er **GB** (DAG) 31 We 17
Castlepark **IRL** (COR) 104 Rc 38
Castlepark House **IRL** (CRE) 92 Qe 32
Castleplunket **IRL** (ROS) 88 Rd 26
Castlepollard **IRL** (WMT) 89 Se 26
Castlequarter **IRL** (DON) 78 Sd 18
Castlequarter **IRL** (WTF) 99 Sb 35
Castlerahan **IRL** (CAV) 89 Se 26
Castlerea **IRL** (ROS) 88 Rd 26
Castlerock **IRL** (LDR) 78 Tb 17
Castleroyan **IRL** (MAY) 87 Ra 25
Castlesampson **IRL** (ROS) 88 Rf 28
Castle Shanaghan **IRL** (DON) 77 Sc 19
Castleside **GB** (DUR) 33 Ya 20
Castlestrange **IRL** (ROS) 88 Re 27
Castle Stuart **GB** (HGL) 15 Vf 3
Castletogher **IRL** (ROS) 88 Rc 26
Castleton **GB** (DSH) 45 Yb 28
Castleton **GB** (GWE) 60 Wf 39
Castleton **GB** (NOY) 37 Za 22
Castleton **GB** (STC) 23 Ud 12
Castletow **GB** (TAW) 33 Yd 19
Castletown **GB** (HGL) 6 Wd 117
Castletown **GBM** 29 Vc 24
Castletown **IRL** (COR) 103 Ra 38
Castletown **IRL** (LAO) 94 Sd 31
Castletown **IRL** (LIM) 98 Rb 34
Castletown **IRL** (MT) 90 Tb 26
Castletown **IRL** (TIP) 93 Re 31
Castletown **IRL** (WMT) 89 Sd 26
Castletown Bearhaven **IRL** (COR) 102 Qa 39
Castletown Geoghean **IRL** (WMT) 89 Sd 28
Castletown House **IRL** (LAO) 94 Sf 31
Castletownroche **IRL** (COR) 98 Rc 36
Castletownroche **IRL** (COR) 98 Rd 35
Castletownshend **IRL** (COR) 103 Qe 39
Castletown Tara **IRL** (MT) 90 Tc 27
Castleview House **IRL** (TIP) 93 Re 31
Castleville **IRL** (MAY) 87 Qf 27
Castlewarren **IRL** (KLK) 100 Sf 32
Castlewellan **GB** (DOW) 85 Ua 23
Castle Willington **IRL** (TIP) 93 Rf 31
Castle Wray **IRL** (DON) 77 Sb 19
Caston **GB** (NOR) 56 Af 33
Castor **GB** (CBS) 55 Ze 33
Catacol **GB** (STC) 23 Ue 14
Cat and Fiddle **GB** (CHS) 45 Ya 29
Catchall **GB** (CNW) 74 Uc 48
Catcliffe **GB** (SOY) 46 Yd 28
Caterham **GB** (SUR) 64 Zf 41
Caterway Heads **GB** (NHL) 33 Ya 19
Catesby **GB** (NRH) 54 Ye 35
Catford **GB** (GRL) 64 Zf 40
Cathair na Mairt = Westport **IRL** (MAY) 86 Qc 26
Catham **GB** (KEN) 65 Zd 40
Cathcart **GB** (STC) 25 Ve 14
Cathedine **GB** (POW) 60 We 37
Catherington **GB** (HAS) 70 Yf 43
Catherton **GB** (SHS) 52 Xc 34
Cathole Bridge **IRL** (LAO) 94 Sd 30
Catlodge **GB** (HGL) 15 Ve 6
Catmore **GB** (BKS) 62 Yd 39
Caton **GB** (DEV) 76 Wb 45
Caton **GB** (LCS) 38 Xb 24
Catrine **GB** (STC) 30 Ve 15
Catsfield **GB** (ESX) 72 Ac 43
Catshill **GB** (HWC) 53 Xf 34
Catstown **IRL** (KLK) 100 Se 34
Cattal **GB** (NOY) 40 Ye 25
Cattan **IRL** (LET) 88 Sb 25
Cattawade **GB** (SUF) 57 Ba 37
Catteral **GB** (LCS) 38 Xb 25
Catterick **GB** (NOY) 36 Yc 22
Catterick Garrison **GB** (NOY) 36 Yb 22
Catterlen **GB** (CUB) 35 Xb 20
Catterline **GB** (GRP) 22 Xe 7
Catterton **GB** (NOY) 40 Ye 25
Cattistock **GB** (DOS) 68 Xc 44
Catton **GB** (NHL) 32 Xe 19
Catton **GB** (NOY) 36 Yd 23
Catwick **GB** (HUS) 41 Ze 25
Catworth **GB** (CBS) 55 Zd 34
Caulcott **GB** (OXS) 62 Ye 37
Cauldcots **GB** (TYS) 22 Xc 9
Cauldhame **GB** (CEN) 25 Ve 12
Cauldhame **GB** (CEN) 25 Wa 11
Cauldon **GB** (SFS) 45 Ya 30
Caulkerbush **GB** (DAG) 31 Wb 19
Caulside **GB** (DAG) 32 Xa 18
Caunsall **GB** (HWC) 53 Xe 34
Caunton **GB** (NTS) 46 Za 30
Causeway **IRL** (KER) 97 Qb 34
Causeyend **GB** (GRP) 17 Xf 5
Causey Park **GB** (NHL) 33 Yb 17
Causey Park Bridge **GB** (NHL) 33 Yb 17
Cautley **GB** (CUB) 35 Xd 22
Cavan **IRL** (CAV) 89 Sd 25
Cavan **IRL** (DON) 77 Sb 20
Cavendish **GB** (SUF) 56 Ad 36
Cavenham **GB** (SUF) 56 Ad 35
Caversfield **GB** (OXS) 63 Yf 37
Caversham **GB** (BKS) 63 Za 40
Caversta **GB** (HGL) 11 Td 120
Caverswall **GB** (SFS) 45 Xf 31
Cavetown **IRL** (ROS) 88 Re 25
Cawdor **GB** (HGL) 15 Wa 3
Cawkwell **GB** (LIN) 47 Zf 29
Cawood **GB** (NOY) 40 Yf 25
Cawsand **GB** (CNW) 75 Ve 46
Cawston **GB** (NOR) 49 Ba 32
Cawthorne **GB** (SOY) 39 Yc 27
Cawton **GB** (NOY) 37 Yf 23
Caxton **GB** (CBS) 55 Zf 35
Caxton End **GB** (CBS) 55 Zf 35
Caxton Gibbet **GB** (CBS) 55 Zf 35
Caynham **GB** (SHS) 52 Xc 34
Caythorpe **GB** (LIN) 47 Zc 30
Caythorpe **GB** (NTS) 46 Za 30
Cayton **GB** (NOY) 37 Zd 23
Ceanannas **IRL** (KLK) 100 Se 33
Ceanannas **IRL** (MT) 89 Ta 26
Ceann-na-Cleithe **GB** (HGL) 11 Tb 1
Ceann Toirc = Kanturk **IRL** (COR) 98 Ra 35
Ceatharlach = Carlow **IRL** (CLW) 94 Ta 31
Cecilstown **IRL** (COR) 98 Rb 35
Cedars, The **IRL** (WKL) 95 Tf 31
Cefn Berain **GB** (CLW) 43 Wc 29
Cefn-brith **GB** (CLW) 43 Wc 30
Cefn Cantref **GB** (POW) 60 Wd 37
Cefn Coch **GB** (POW) 43 We 32
Cefn-coed-y-cymmer **GB** (MGL) 60 Wd 38
Cefn Cribwr **GB** (MGL) 60 Wc 39
Cefn Cross **GB** (MGL) 60 Wc 39
Cefn-ddwysarn **GB** (GWY) 43 Wc 31
Cefn Einion **GB** (SHS) 52 Wf 34
Cefneithin **GB** (DYF) 59 Vf 38
Cefngorwydd **GB** (POW) 51 Wc 36
Cefn Mably **GB** (MGL) 60 Wf 39
Cefn-mawr **GB** (CLW) 44 Wf 31
Cefn-y-bedd **GB** (CLW) 44 Wf 30
Cefn-y-pant **GB** (DYF) 58 Vc 37
Ceinewydd = New Quay **GB** (DYF) 50 Vd 35
Ceint **GB** (GWY) 42 Ve 29
Celbridge **IRL** (KIL) 95 Tc 29
Cellan **GB** (DYF) 51 Vf 36
Cellarhead **GB** (SFS) 45 Xf 30
Cemaes **GB** (GWY) 42 Vd 28
Cemmaes **GB** (POW) 51 Wb 33
Cemmaes Road **GB** (POW) 51 Wb 33
Cennin **GB** (GWY) 42 Ve 31
Ceres **GB** (FIF) 22 Xa 11
Cerne Abbas **GB** (DOS) 68 Xd 44
Cerney Wick **GB** (GLS) 62 Ya 39
Cerrigceinwen **GB** (GWY) 42 Vd 29
Cerrigydrudion **GB** (CLW) 43 Wc 30
Cessford **GB** (BOR) 32 Xd 15
Chaceley **GB** (GLS) 61 Xe 37
Chacewater **GB** (CNW) 74 Uf 47
Chackmore **GB** (BUS) 54 Za 36
Chacombe **GB** (NRH) 54 Ye 36
Chadderton **GB** (GRM) 39 Xf 27
Chaddesden **GB** (DSH) 46 Yd 31
Chaddesley Corbett **GB** (HWC) 53 Xf 34
Chaddleworth **GB** (BKS) 62 Yd 40
Chadlington **GB** (OXS) 62 Yc 37
Chadshunt **GB** (WWH) 54 Yd 35
Chad Valley **GB** (WMD) 53 Ya 34
Chadwell Saint Mary **GB** (ESS) 64 Ac 40
Chadwick End **GB** (WMD) 53 Yb 34
Chaffcombe **GB** (SOM) 68 Xa 43
Chagford **GB** (DEV) 67 Wa 44
Chailey **GB** (ESX) 71 Zf 43
Chainhurst **GB** (KEN) 72 Ac 41
Chaldon **GB** (SUR) 64 Zf 41
Chaldon Herring or East Chaldon **GB** (DOS) 68 Xe 45
Chale **GB** (IOW) 70 Ye 45
Chale Green **GB** (IOW) 70 Ye 45
Chalfont Common **GB** (BUS) 63 Zc 39
Chalfont Saint Giles **GB** (BUS) 63 Zc 39
Chalfont Saint Peter **GB** (BUS) 63 Zc 39
Chalford **GB** (GLS) 61 Xf 38
Chalgrove **GB** (OXS) 63 Yf 38
Challacombe **GB** (DEV) 66 Wa 42
Challoch **GB** (DAG) 30 Vc 19
Challock **GB** (KEN) 72 Af 41
Chalton **GB** (BFS) 63 Zd 37
Chalton **GB** (HAS) 70 Za 43
Chalvington **GB** (ESX) 71 Aa 43
Champany **GB** (CEN) 25 Wc 13
Chandler's Cross **GB** (HTS) 63 Zd 38
Chandler's Ford **GB** (HAS) 70 Yd 43
Chanonrock **IRL** (LOT) 90 Tc 25
Chantilly or Tilly's T.n **IRL** (DUB) 95 Tf 29
Chantry **GB** (SOM) 68 Xd 41
Chantry **GB** (SUF) 57 Ba 36
Chapel **GB** (FIF) 26 We 12
Chapel Allerton **GB** (SOM) 68 Xa 41
Chapel Amble **GB** (CNW) 75 Vb 45
Chapeland Way **GB** (ESS) 56 Ac 36
Chapel Chorlton **GB** (SFS) 45 Xe 31
Chapel Cross **GB** (ESX) 72 Ab 43
Chapel-en-le-Frith **GB** (DSH) 45 Ya 29
Chapelgate **GB** (LIN) 47 Aa 32
Chapel Haddlesey **GB** (NOY) 40 Yf 26
Chapelhall **GB** (STC) 25 Wa 13
Chapel Hill **GB** (GRP) 17 Xa 4
Chapel Hill **GB** (GWE) 61 Xb 38
Chapelhill **GB** (HGL) 9 Wa 2
Chapel Hill **GB** (LIN) 47 Ze 30
Chapelhill **GB** (TYS) 21 Wc 10
Chapelhill **GB** (TYS) 21 We 10
Chapelknowe **GB** (DAG) 32 Wf 18
Chapel Lawn **GB** (SHS) 52 Wf 34
Chapel-le-Dale **GB** (NOY) 35 Xd 23
Chapel Row **GB** (BKS) 63 Ye 40
Chapel Stile **GB** (CUB) 34 Wf 22
Chapel St Leonards **GB** (LIN) 48 Zf 29
Chapel Street **IRL** (SLI) 82 Rc 23
Chapelton **GB** (STC) 25 Vf 14
Chapelton **GB** (TYS) 22 Xc 9
Chapeltown **GB** (DOW) 85 Uc 23
Chapeltown **GB** (SOY) 40 Yd 28
Chapeltown **IRL** (KER) 96 Pd 37
Chapet **IRL** (WEX) 101 Tb 34
Chapmanslade **GB** (WIL) 68 Xe 41
Chappel **GB** (ESS) 65 Ae 37
Chard **GB** (SOM) 68 Xa 43
Chardstock **GB** (DEV) 68 Xa 44
Charfield **GB** (AVN) 61 Xd 39
Charing **GB** (KEN) 72 Zc 41
Charing Heath **GB** (KEN) 72 Ae 41
Charlbury **GB** (OXS) 62 Yd 37
Charlcombe **GB** (AVN) 61 Xd 40
Charlecote **GB** (WWH) 53 Yc 35
Charlemont **GB** (ARG) 84 Tb 22
Charles **GB** (DEV) 66 Wa 42
Charleshill **GB** (SUR) 70 Zb 41
Charleston **GB** (TYS) 22 Wf 9
Charlestown **GB** (CNW) 75 Vb 47
Charlestown **GB** (FIF) 25 Wc 12
Charlestown **GB** (GRP) 17 Xf 6
Charlestown **GB** (HGL) 7 Ub 2
Charlestown **GB** (HGL) 15 Ve 3
Charlestown **IRL** (LOT) 90 Tc 25
Charlestown **IRL** (MAY) 87 Rb 25
Charlestown of Aberlour **GB** (GRP) 16 We 4
Charles Tye **GB** (SUF) 57 Af 36
Charlesworth **GB** (SOY) 39 Yc 28
Charleville **IRL** (OFF) 94 Sc 29
Charleville Park **IRL** (COR) 98 Rb 34
Charlton **GB** (GRL) 64 Aa 40
Charlton **GB** (HAS) 69 Yd 41
Charlton **GB** (HWC) 53 Ya 36
Charlton **GB** (NRH) 54 Ye 36
Charlton **GB** (WIL) 61 Xf 39
Charlton **GB** (WSX) 70 Zb 43
Charlton Abbots **GB** (GLS) 62 Ya 37
Charlton-All-Saints **GB** (WIL) 69 Yb 42
Charlton Horethorne **GB** (SOM) 68 Xd 42
Charlton Mackrell **GB** (SOM) 68 Xb 42
Charlton Marshall **GB** (DOS) 69 Xf 44
Charlton Musgrove **GB** (SOM) 68 Xd 42
Charlton-on-Otmoor **GB** (OXS) 63 Ye 37
Charlwood **GB** (SUR) 71 Ze 42
Charminster **GB** (DOS) 68 Xd 44
Charmouth **GB** (DOS) 68 Xa 44
Charndon **GB** (BUS) 63 Yf 37
Charney Bassett **GB** (OXS) 62 Yd 39
Charnock Richard **GB** (LCS) 38 Xc 27
Charsfield **GB** (SUF) 57 Bb 36
Chart Corner **GB** (KEN) 72 Ad 41
Charter Alley **GB** (HAS) 63 Yf 41
Charterhouse **GB** (SOM) 68 Xb 41
Charterville Allotments **GB** (OXS) 62 Yc 38
Chartham **GB** (KEN) 65 Ba 41
Chartham Hatch **GB** (KEN) 65 Af 41
Chartridge **GB** (BUS) 63 Zc 38
Chart Sutton **GB** (KEN) 72 Ad 41
Charwelton **GB** (NRH) 54 Ye 35
Chase Terrace **GB** (SFS) 53 Ya 32
Chasetown **GB** (SFS) 53 Ya 32
Chastleton **GB** (OXS) 62 Yc 37
Chasty **GB** (DEV) 66 Vd 44
Chatburn **GB** (LCS) 38 Xd 25
Chatcull **GB** (SFS) 45 Xe 31
Chatham **GB** (KEN) 65 Ad 40
Chathill **GB** (NHL) 27 Yb 15
Chattenden **GB** (KEN) 65 Ad 40
Chatteris **GB** (CBS) 55 Aa 34
Chattisham **GB** (SUF) 57 Ba 36
Chatto **GB** (BOR) 32 Xd 16
Chatton **GB** (NHL) 27 Ya 15
Chawleigh **GB** (DEV) 67 Wa 43
Chawley **GB** (OXS) 63 Ye 38
Chawston **GB** (BFS) 55 Ze 35
Chawton **GB** (HAS) 70 Za 42
Cheadle **GB** (GRM) 45 Xe 28
Cheadle **GB** (SFS) 45 Ya 31
Cheadle Hulme **GB** (GRM) 45 Xe 28
Chearsley **GB** (BUS) 63 Za 38
Chebsey **GB** (SFS) 45 Xe 31
Checkendon **GB** (OXS) 63 Yf 39
Checkley **GB** (CHS) 44 Xd 30
Checkley **GB** (HWC) 52 Xc 36
Chedburgh **GB** (SUF) 56 Ad 35
Cheddar **GB** (SOM) 68 Xb 41
Cheddington **GB** (BUS) 63 Zb 37
Cheddleton **GB** (SFS) 45 Xf 30
Chedgrave **GB** (NOR) 57 Bc 33
Chedington **GB** (DOS) 68 Xb 43
Chediston **GB** (SUF) 57 Bc 34
Chedworth **GB** (GLS) 62 Ya 38
Chedzoy **GB** (SOM) 68 Xa 42
Cheekpoint **IRL** (WTF) 100 Ta 35
Cheldon **GB** (DEV) 67 Wb 43
Chelford **GB** (CHS) 45 Xe 29
Chellaston **GB** (DSH) 46 Yd 31
Chellington **GB** (BFS) 55 Zc 35
Chelmarsh **GB** (SHS) 52 Xd 34
Chelmorton **GB** (DSH) 45 Yb 29
Chelmsford **GB** (ESS) 65 Ac 38
Chelsea **GB** (GRL) 64 Ze 40
Chelsfield **GB** (GRL) 64 Aa 40
Chelsham **GB** (SUR) 64 Zf 41
Chelsworth **GB** (SUF) 56 Af 36
Cheltenham **GB** (GLS) 61 Xf 37
Chelveston **GB** (NRH) 55 Zc 35
Chelvey **GB** (AVN) 61 Xb 40
Chelwood **GB** (AVN) 61 Xc 40
Chelwood Gate **GB** (ESX) 71 Aa 42
Cheney Longville **GB** (SHS) 52 Xa 34
Chenies **GB** (BUS) 63 Zc 38
Chepstow **GB** (GLS) 61 Xc 39
Chequer, The **GB** (CLW) 44 Xb 31
Cherhill **GB** (WIL) 62 Ya 40
Cherington **GB** (GLS) 61 Xf 38
Cherington **GB** (WWH) 54 Yc 36
Cheriton **GB** (DEV) 67 Wb 41
Cheriton **GB** (DYF) 58 Va 39
Cheriton **GB** (HAS) 70 Yf 42
Cheriton **GB** (WGL) 59 Ve 39
Cheriton Bishop **GB** (DEV) 67 Wb 44
Cheriton Fitzpaine **GB** (DEV) 67 Wc 43
Cherrington **GB** (SHS) 44 Xc 32
Cherry Burton **GB** (HUS) 41 Zd 25
Cherry Hinton **GB** (CBS) 56 Ab 35
Chertsey **GB** (SUR) 63 Zc 40
Cheselbourne **GB** (DOS) 68 Xe 44
Chesham **GB** (BUS) 63 Zc 38
Chesham Bois **GB** (BUS) 63 Zc 38
Cheshunt **GB** (HTS) 64 Ab 38
Cheslyn Hay **GB** (SFS) 53 Xf 33
Chester **GB** (CHS) 44 Xa 29
Chesterfield **GB** (DSH) 46 Yd 29
Chesterfield **GB** (KEN) 65 Ba 40
Chesterfield **GB** (SFS) 53 Ya 33
Chester-Le Street **GB** (DUR) 33 Yc 19
Chesters **GB** (BOR) 32 Xc 16
Chesterton **GB** (CBS) 55 Zd 33
Chesterton **GB** (OXS) 63 Ye 37
Chesterton **GB** (SFS) 45 Xe 30
Chesterton **GB** (WWH) 54 Yd 35
Cheswardine **GB** (SHS) 45 Xd 31
Cheswick **GB** (NHL) 27 Ya 14
Chetnole **GB** (DOS) 68 Xc 43
Chettiscombe **GB** (DEV) 67 Wd 43
Chettle **GB** (DOS) 69 Xf 43
Chetton **GB** (SHS) 52 Xd 33
Chetwode **GB** (BUS) 63 Yf 37
Chetwynd Aston **GB** (SHS) 45 Xd 32
Cheveley **GB** (BKS) 62 Ye 40
Cheveley **GB** (CBS) 56 Ac 35
Chevithorne **GB** (DEV) 67 Wd 43
Chew Magna **GB** (AVN) 61 Xc 40
Chew Stoke **GB** (AVN) 61 Xc 40
Chewton Keynsham **GB** (AVN) 61 Xc 40
Chewton Mendip **GB** (SOM) 68 Xc 41
Chicheley **GB** (BUS) 55 Zb 36
Chichester **GB** (WSX) 70 Zb 43
Chickerell **GB** (DOS) 68 Xc 45
Chickering **GB** (SUF) 57 Bb 34
Chicklade **GB** (WIL) 69 Xf 42
Chicksands **GB** (BFS) 55 Zd 36
Chidden **GB** (HAS) 70 Yf 43
Chiddingfold **GB** (SUR) 70 Zc 42
Chiddingly **GB** (ESX) 71 Ab 43
Chiddingstone **GB** (KEN) 71 Aa 41
Chiddingstone Causeway **GB** (KEN) 71 Ab 41
Chiddingstone Hoath **GB** (KEN) 71 Aa 42
Chideock **GB** (DOS) 68 Xb 44
Chignall Saint James **GB** (ESS) 64 Ac 38
Chignall Smealy **GB** (ESS) 64 Ac 38
Chigwell **GB** (ESS) 64 Aa 39
Chigwell Row **GB** (ESS) 64 Aa 39
Chilbolton **GB** (HAS) 69 Yd 42
Chilcomb **GB** (HAS) 70 Ye 42
Chilcombe **GB** (DOS) 68 Xb 44
Chilcompton **GB** (SOM) 68 Xc 41
Chilcote **GB** (LEC) 53 Yc 32
Child Okeford **GB** (DOS) 68 Xe 43
Childrey **GB** (OXS) 62 Yd 39
Child's Ercall **GB** (SHS) 44 Xd 32
Childswickham **GB** (HWC) 53 Ya 36
Childwall **GB** (MES) 44 Xa 28
Childwick Green **GB** (HTS) 64 Zd 38
Chilfrome **GB** (DOS) 68 Xc 44
Chilgrove **GB** (WSX) 70 Zb 43
Chilham **GB** (KEN) 65 Af 41
Chillaton **GB** (DEV) 75 Ve 45
Chillenden **GB** (KEN) 65 Bb 41
Chillerton **GB** (IOW) 70 Ye 45
Chillesford **GB** (SUF) 57 Bc 36
Chillingham **GB** (NHL) 33 Ya 15
Chillington **GB** (DEV) 76 Wb 47
Chilmark **GB** (WIL) 69 Xf 42
Chilson **GB** (OXS) 62 Yc 37
Chilsworthy **GB** (CNW) 75 Ve 45
Chilsworthy **GB** (DEV) 66 Vd 43
Chilthorne Domer **GB** (SOM) 68 Xb 43
Chilton **GB** (BUS) 63 Yf 38
Chilton **GB** (DUR) 36 Yc 21
Chilton **GB** (OXS) 62 Ye 39
Chilton Candover **GB** (HAS) 70 Yf 42
Chilton Cantelo **GB** (SOM) 68 Xc 43
Chilton Foliat **GB** (WIL) 62 Yc 40
Chilton Polden **GB** (SOM) 68 Xa 42
Chilton Street **GB** (SUF) 56 Ad 36
Chilton Trinity **GB** (SOM) 68 Wf 42
Chilworth **GB** (HAS) 69 Yd 43
Chilworth **GB** (SUR) 71 Zc 41
Chimney **GB** (OXS) 62 Yd 38
Chineham **GB** (HAS) 70 Yf 41
Chingford **GB** (GRL) 64 Zf 39
Chinley **GB** (DSH) 45 Ya 28
Chinley Head **GB** (DSH) 45 Ya 28
Chinnor **GB** (OXS) 63 Za 38
Chipchase Castle **GB** (NHL) 33 Xe 18
Chipley Park **GB** (SOM) 67 We 42
Chipnall **GB** (SHS) 45 Xd 31
Chippenham **GB** (CBS) 56 Ac 35
Chippenham **GB** (WIL) 61 Xf 40
Chipperfield **GB** (HTS) 63 Ad 38
Chipping **GB** (HTS) 55 Zf 37
Chipping **GB** (LCS) 38 Xc 25
Chipping Campden **GB** (GLS) 53 Yb 36
Chipping Norton **GB** (OXS) 62 Yc 37
Chipping Ongar **GB** (ESS) 64 Ab 38
Chipping Sodbury **GB** (AVN) 61 Xd 39
Chipping Warden **GB** (NRH) 54 Ye 36
Chipstable **GB** (SOM) 67 Wd 42
Chirbury **GB** (SHS) 52 Wf 33
Chirk **GB** (CLW) 44 Wf 31
Chirmorrie **GB** (STC) 30 Vb 18
Chirnside **GB** (BOR) 27 Xe 14
Chirton **GB** (WIL) 62 Ya 41
Chisbury **GB** (WIL) 62 Yc 40
Chiseldon **GB** (WIL) 62 Yb 39
Chiselhampton **GB** (OXS) 63 Yf 38
Chislehurst **GB** (GRL) 64 Aa 40
Chiswell Green **GB** (HTS) 64 Zd 38
Chisworth **GB** (DSH) 45 Xf 28
Chithurst **GB** (WSX) 70 Zb 42
Chittering **GB** (CBS) 56 Ab 35
Chitterne **GB** (WIL) 69 Xf 41
Chittlehamholt **GB** (DEV) 66 Wa 43
Chittlehampton **GB** (DEV) 66 Wa 42
Chivenor **GB** (DEV) 66 Vf 42
Chlachan **GB** (HGL) 13 Tf 4

112 GB IRL **Carlton – Chlachan**

Chobham **GB** (SUR) 63 Zc 40
Cholderton **GB** (WIL) 69 Yb 41
Cholesbury **GB** (BUS) 63 Zc 38
Cholsey **GB** (OXS) 63 Yf 39
Cholsfrey **GB** (HWC) 52 Xb 35
Cholwell **GB** (AVN) 61 Xc 41
Chopwell **GB** (TAW) 33 Yb 19
Chorley **GB** (CHS) 44 Xc 30
Chorley **GB** (LCS) 38 Xc 27
Chorley **GB** (SFS) 53 Ya 32
Chorley **GB** (SHS) 52 Xd 34
Chorleywood **GB** (HTS) 63 Zc 39
Chorlton Lane **GB** (CHS) 44 Xb 30
Chowley **GB** (CHS) 44 Xb 30
Christchurch **GB** (CBS) 56 Ab 33
Christchurch **GB** (DOS) 69 Yb 44
Christchurch **GB** (GLS) 61 Xc 38
Christleton **GB** (CHS) 44 Xa 29
Christmas Common **GB** (OXS) 63 Za 39
Christon Bank **GB** (NHL) 33 Yb 16
Chromer **GB** (NOR) 49 Bb 31
Chromhall **GB** (AVN) 61 Xd 39
Chudleigh **GB** (DEV) 76 Wc 45
Chudleigh Knighton **GB** (DEV) 76 Wc 45
Chulmleigh **GB** (DEV) 66 Wa 43
Chumneyfield **IRL** (COR) 98 Rd 36
Chunal **GB** (DSH) 45 Ya 28
Church **GB** (LCS) 38 Xd 26
Churcham **GB** (GLS) 61 Xd 37
Church Ballee **GB** (DOW) 85 Uc 23
Churchboro Cross **IRL** (ROS) 88 Rf 27
Church Brampton **GB** (NRH) 54 Za 35
Church Broughton **GB** (DSH) 45 Yb 31
Church Crookham **GB** (HAS) 70 Za 41
Churchdown **GB** (GLS) 61 Xf 37
Church Eaton **GB** (SFS) 45 Xe 32
Church End **GB** (BFS) 63 Zc 37
Church End **GB** (CBS) 55 Aa 33
Churchend **GB** (ESS) 64 Ac 37
Church End **GB** (ESS) 65 Ad 37
Churchend **GB** (ESS) 65 Af 39
Church End **GB** (HAS) 63 Yf 41
Church End **GB** (WIL) 62 Ya 39
Church End **GB** (WWH) 53 Yc 33
Church Enstone **GB** (OXS) 62 Yd 37
Church Fenton **GB** (NOY) 40 Ye 26
Churchfield **IRL** (CRE) 92 Rb 32
Churchfield **IRL** (MAY) 87 Qd 27
Churchgate Street **GB** (ESS) 64 Aa 38
Church Green **GB** (DEV) 67 We 44
Church Hanborough **GB** (OXS) 62 Yd 38
Church Hill **IRL** (DON) 77 Sa 19
Church Hill **IRL** (KER) 97 Qb 35
Church Houses **GB** (NOY) 37 Za 22
Churchill **GB** (AVN) 61 Xb 41
Churchill **GB** (HWC) 53 Xe 34
Churchill **GB** (OXS) 62 Yc 37
Churchinford **GB** (SOM) 67 Wf 43
Church Knowle **GB** (DOS) 69 Xf 45
Churchland Bridge **IRL** (LGF) 88 Sb 26
Church Langton **GB** (LEC) 54 Za 33
Church Lawford **GB** (WWH) 54 Yd 34
Church Lench **GB** (HWC) 53 Ya 36
Church Minshull **GB** (CHS) 44 Xc 30
Church Norton **GB** (WSX) 70 Zb 44
Churchover **GB** (WWH) 54 Ye 34
Church Preen **GB** (SHS) 52 Xb 33
Church Pulverbatch **GB** (SHS) 52 Xa 33
Churchstanton **GB** (SOM) 67 Wf 43
Church Stoke **GB** (POW) 52 Wf 33
Churchstow **GB** (DEV) 76 Wb 47
Church Stretton **GB** (SHS) 52 Xb 33
Churchtown **GB** (DEV) 66 Wa 41
Churchtown **GB** (LCS) 38 Xb 25
Churchtown **GBM** 29 Vd 23
Churchtown **IRL** (COR) 98 Rb 35
Churchtown **IRL** (COR) 104 Rf 37
Churchtown **IRL** (COR) 104 Rf 38
Church Town **IRL** (DON) 78 Sd 19
Churchtown **IRL** (KER) 97 Qb 36
Churchtown **IRL** (WEX) 100 Ta 36
Churchtown **IRL** (WEX) 101 Td 35
Church Village **GB** (MGL) 60 We 39
Church Village **IRL** (MAY) 87 Qf 24
Churston Ferrers **GB** (DEV) 76 Wc 46
Churt **GB** (SUR) 70 Zb 42
Churton **GB** (CHS) 44 Xa 30
Churwell **GB** (WYO) 39 Yc 26
Chwilog **GB** (GWY) 42 Ve 31
Cidham **GB** (WSX) 70 Za 44
Cilan Uchaf **GB** (GWY) 42 Vc 32
Cilcain **GB** (CLW) 43 We 29
Cilcennin **GB** (DYF) 50 Vf 35
Cilfrew **GB** (WGL) 59 Wb 38
Cilfynydd **GB** (MGL) 60 We 39
Cilgerran **GB** (DYF) 50 Vc 36
Cilgwyn **GB** (DYF) 58 Vb 37
Ciliau-Aeron **GB** (DYF) 50 Ve 35
Cilichoca = Kilcock **IRL** (KIL) 95 Tb 28
Cill Chainnigh = Kilkenny **IRL** (KLK) 100 Se 33
Cill Chaoi = Kilkee **IRL** (CRE) 91 Qc 32
Cill Chormaic = Kilcormac **IRL** (OFF) 93 Sb 29
Cill Chuillin = Kilcullen **IRL** (KIL) 95 Tb 30
Cill Dara = Kildare **IRL** (KIL) 94 Ta 30
Cill Droichid = Celbridge **IRL** (KIL) 95 Tc 29
Cill Fhíonáin = Kilfinnane **IRL** (LIM) 98 Rd 34
Cill Mhantáin = Wicklow **IRL** (WKL) 95 Tf 31
Cillrois = Killrush **IRL** (CRE) 91 Qd 33
Cilmery **GB** (POW) 51 Wd 36
Cilrhedyn **GB** (DYF) 59 Vc 37
Cilybebyll **GB** (WGL) 59 Wb 38
Cilycwm **GB** (DYF) 51 Wb 36
Cinderford **GB** (GLS) 61 Xc 38
Cirencester **GB** (GLS) 62 Ya 38
City Dulas **GB** (GWY) 42 Ve 28
City of London **GB** (GRL) 64 Zf 39
Civil Hollow **IRL** (LOT) 90 Te 25
Clabby **GB** (FER) 83 Sd 22
Clachadow **GB** (STC) 19 Ue 10
Clachaig **GB** (STC) 24 Uf 13
Clachan **GB** (STC) 19 Ud 9
Clachan **GB** (STC) 19 Va 11
Clachan **GB** (STC) 23 Uc 14
Clachan Mór **GB** (STC) 18 Ta 9
Clachan of Campsie **GB** (STC) 25 Ve 13
Clachan of Glendaruel **GB** (STC) 24 Ue 12
Clachbreck **GB** (STC) 23 Uc 13
Clachen-Seil **GB** (STC) 19 Uc 11
Clachtoll **GB** (HGL) 7 Ue 119
Clackmannan **GB** (CEN) 25 Wb 12
Clacton-on-Sea **GB** (ESS) 65 Ba 38
Claddach Kirkibost **GB** (HGL) 10 Sd 3
Claddagh **IRL** (SLI) 87 Ra 24
Claddaghduff **IRL** (GAL) 86 Pf 27
Cladich **GB** (STC) 19 Uf 10
Clady **GB** (TYR) 83 Sc 20
Clady Milltown **GB** (ARG) 84 Tc 23
Claggan **GB** (HGL) 19 Ub 9
Claggan **IRL** (DON) 77 Sa 17
Claggan **IRL** (DON) 78 Sd 17
Claggan **IRL** (DON) 78 Se 17
Claggan **IRL** (DON) 78 Sf 17
Claggan **IRL** (MAY) 86 Qd 28
Claghanarulleen **IRL** (COR) 102 Qb 40
Claigan **GB** (HGL) 12 Tc 4
Claines **GB** (HWC) 53 Xe 35
Clane **IRL** (KIL) 95 Tb 29
Clanfield **GB** (HAS) 70 Yf 43
Clanfield **GB** (OXS) 62 Yc 38
Clannaborough Barton **GB** (DEV) 67 Wb 44
Clanville **GB** (HAS) 69 Yc 41
Claonaig **GB** (STC) 23 Ud 14
Clapgate **GB** (DOS) 69 Ya 44
Clapham **GB** (BFS) 55 Zd 36
Clapham **GB** (NOY) 38 Xd 24
Clappers **GB** (BOR) 27 Xf 14
Clappersgate **GB** (CUB) 35 Xa 22
Clapton **GB** (SOM) 68 Xb 43
Clapton-in-Gordano **GB** (AVN) 61 Xb 40
Clapton-on-the-Hill **GB** (GLS) 62 Yb 37
Clapworthy **GB** (DEV) 66 Wa 43
Clara **IRL** (OFF) 94 Sc 28
Clara **IRL** (WKL) 95 Te 31
Clarbarracum **IRL** (LAO) 94 Se 31
Clarbeston **GB** (DYF) 58 Va 37
Clarbeston Road **GB** (DYF) 58 Va 37
Clarborough **GB** (NTS) 46 Za 28
Clardon **GB** (HGL) 6 Wd 117
Clare **GB** (SUF) 56 Ad 36
Clarebrand **GB** (DAG) 31 Wa 19
Clarecastle **IRL** (CRE) 92 Ra 32
Claregalway **IRL** (GAL) 92 Ra 28
Claremorris **IRL** (MAY) 87 Ra 26
Clare Mount **IRL** (MT) 90 Te 27
Clarencefield **GB** (DAG) 31 Wd 18
Clarina **IRL** (LIM) 98 Rb 33
Clarinbridge **IRL** (GAL) 92 Ra 29
Clarreen **IRL** (OFF) 93 Sb 30
Clash **IRL** (TIP) 93 Rf 31
Clashadoo **IRL** (COR) 103 Qc 39
Clashanahy **IRL** (WTF) 104 Sb 37
Clashmore **GB** (HGL) 7 Ud 119
Clashmore **GB** (HGL) 8 Vf 1
Clashmore **IRL** (WTF) 99 Sb 36
Clashnessie **GB** (HGL) 7 Ue 119
Clasnalochan **IRL** (WTF) 99 Sc 36
Clathy **GB** (TYS) 21 Wc 10
Clatt **GB** (GRP) 16 Xb 5
Clatterford End **GB** (ESS) 64 Ab 38
Clatterin Brig **GB** (GRP) 22 Xc 7
Clatteringshaws **GB** (DAG) 30 Ve 18
Clatworthy **GB** (SOM) 67 Wd 42
Claudy **GB** (LDR) 78 Sf 19
Claughton **GB** (LCS) 38 Xb 24
Claughton **GB** (LCS) 38 Xb 25
Claverdon **GB** (WWH) 53 Yb 35
Clavering **GB** (ESS) 56 Aa 37
Claverley **GB** (SHS) 53 Xe 33
Clawdd-newydd **GB** (CLW) 43 Wd 30
Clawinch **IRL** (LGF) 88 Rf 27
Clawton **GB** (DEV) 66 Vd 44
Claxby **GB** (LIN) 41 Ze 28
Claxby **GB** (LIN) 47 Aa 29
Claxton **GB** (NOR) 57 Bc 33
Claxton **GB** (NOY) 40 Za 24
Claybrooke Magna **GB** (LEC) 54 Ye 34
Clay Common **GB** (SUF) 57 Bd 34
Clay Coton **GB** (NRH) 54 Yf 34
Clay Cross **GB** (DSH) 46 Yc 30
Claydene **GB** (KEN) 71 Aa 42
Claydon **GB** (OXS) 54 Ye 36
Claydon **GB** (SUF) 57 Ba 36
Claygate **GB** (KEN) 72 Ac 41
Clayhanger **GB** (WMD) 53 Ya 33
Claylock **GB** (HGL) 6 Wd 117
Claypole **GB** (LIN) 46 Zb 30
Claythorpe **GB** (LIN) 47 Aa 29
Clayton **GB** (SFS) 45 Xe 31
Clayton **GB** (SOY) 40 Ye 27
Clayton **GB** (WSX) 71 Zf 43
Clayton **GB** (WYO) 39 Yb 26
Clayton-le-Moors **GB** (LCS) 38 Xd 26
Clayton West **GB** (WYO) 39 Yc 27
Clayworth **GB** (NTS) 46 Za 28
Cleadale **GB** (HGL) 18 Tf 7
Cleady **IRL** (KER) 103 Qc 37
Cleaheen **IRL** (ROS) 88 Rf 25
Cleanderry **IRL** (COR) 102 Qa 38
Clearbrook **GB** (DEV) 76 Vf 46
Clearwell **GB** (GLS) 61 Xc 38
Cleasby **GB** (NOY) 36 Yc 21
Cleat **GB** (HGL) 12 Sd 6
Cleatlam **GB** (DUR) 36 Yb 21
Cleator **GB** (CUB) 34 Wc 21
Cleator Moor **GB** (CUB) 34 Wc 21
Cleckheaton **GB** (WYO) 39 Yb 26
Cleedownton **GB** (SHS) 52 Xc 34
Cleehill **GB** (SHS) 52 Xc 34
Clee Saint Margaret **GB** (SHS) 52 Xc 34
Cleethorpes **GB** (HUS) 41 Zf 27
Cleeton Saint Mary **GB** (SHS) 52 Xc 34
Cleeve **GB** (AVN) 61 Xb 40
Cleeve **GB** (OXS) 63 Yf 39
Cleeve Hill **GB** (GLS) 62 Xf 37
Cleeve Prior **GB** (HWC) 53 Ya 36
Cleggan **IRL** (GAL) 86 Pf 27
Clehonger **GB** (HWC) 52 Xb 36
Cleigh **GB** (STC) 19 Ud 10
Cleland **GB** (STC) 25 Wa 14
Clenagh **IRL** (CRE) 92 Ra 32
Clench Common **GB** (WIL) 62 Yb 40
Clenchwarton **GB** (NOR) 48 Ac 32
Clendavoolagh Lodge **IRL** (MAY) 86 Qc 24
Clent **GB** (HWC) 53 Xf 34
Cleobury Mortimer **GB** (SHS) 52 Xd 34
Cleobury North **GB** (SHS) 52 Xc 34
Clephanton **GB** (HGL) 15 Wa 3
Cleristown **IRL** (WEX) 101 Tc 35
Clerklands **GB** (BOR) 32 Xb 15
Clermont House **IRL** (TIP) 93 Rf 31
Clermont Park **IRL** (LOT) 90 Td 25
Clestrain **GB** (ORK) 6 We 115
Cleughbrae **GB** (DAG) 31 Wd 18
Clevedon **GB** (AVN) 61 Xa 40
Cleveleys **GB** (LCS) 38 Wf 25
Clevelode **GB** (HWC) 53 Xe 36
Cleverton **GB** (AVN) 62 Xf 39
Clewer **GB** (SOM) 68 Xb 41
Cleybokie **GB** (GRP) 16 Wc 7
Cley next the Sea **GB** (NOR) 49 Ba 31
Cliasmol **GB** (HGL) 11 Ta 1
Cliburn **GB** (CUB) 35 Xc 21
Cliddesden **GB** (HAS) 70 Yf 41
Clifden **IRL** (GAL) 86 Pf 28
Cliffe **GB** (KEN) 65 Ac 40
Cliffe **GB** (NOY) 40 Za 26
Cliff End **GB** (ESX) 72 Ae 43
Cliffena **IRL** (CAV) 89 Se 25
Cliffe Woods **GB** (KEN) 65 Ac 40
Cliffony **IRL** (SLI) 82 Rd 22
Clifford **GB** (HWC) 52 Wf 36
Clifford **GB** (WYO) 40 Yd 25
Clifford Chambers **GB** (WWH) 53 Yb 35
Clifford's Mesne **GB** (GLS) 61 Xd 37
Cliffs End **GB** (KEN) 65 Bc 40
Clifton **GB** (AVN) 61 Xc 40
Clifton **GB** (BFS) 55 Ze 36
Clifton **GB** (CEN) 20 Vb 10
Clifton **GB** (CUB) 35 Xb 21
Clifton **GB** (DSH) 45 Yb 31
Clifton **GB** (LCS) 38 Xb 26
Clifton **GB** (NTS) 46 Ye 31
Clifton **IRL** (TIP) 93 Sa 30
Clifton Campville **GB** (SFS) 53 Yc 32
Clifton Hampden **GB** (OXS) 63 Ye 39
Clifton House **IRL** (TIP) 93 Sa 30
Clifton upon Dunsmore **GB** (WWH) 54 Ye 34
Clifton upon Teme **GB** (HWC) 52 Xd 35
Climping **GB** (WSX) 71 Zc 44
Clint **GB** (NOY) 39 Yc 24
Clinterty **GB** (GRP) 17 Xe 5
Clint Green **GB** (NOR) 56 Af 33
Clintmains **GB** (BOR) 26 Xc 15
Clipsham **GB** (LEC) 47 Zc 32
Clipston **GB** (NRH) 54 Za 34
Clipstone **GB** (NTS) 46 Yf 29
Clitheroe **GB** (LCS) 38 Xd 25
Clive **GB** (SHS) 44 Xb 32
Cliveden **GB** (BUS) 63 Zb 39
Clocaenog **GB** (CLW) 43 Wd 30
Clochan **GB** (GRP) 16 Xa 3
Clock Face **GB** (MES) 44 Xb 28
Cloddach **GB** (GRP) 16 We 3
Cloddymoss **GB** (GRP) 15 Wb 3
Clodock **GB** (HWC) 60 Xa 37
Clogagh **IRL** (COR) 103 Rb 38
Clogga **IRL** (KLK) 100 Se 35
Clogh **GB** (ANT) 79 Te 19
Clogh **IRL** (KLK) 94 Se 31
Clogh **IRL** (LAO) 94 Sc 31
Clogh **IRL** (WEX) 101 Td 33
Cloghala Cross Roads **IRL** (KLK) 100 Sf 33
Cloghalahard **IRL** (GAL) 92 Ra 29
Cloghan **IRL** (DON) 77 Sa 19
Cloghan **IRL** (LGF) 88 Sb 27
Cloghan **IRL** (MT) 90 Td 27
Cloghan **IRL** (OFF) 93 Sa 29
Cloghan **IRL** (WMT) 89 Se 27
Cloghane **IRL** (COR) 102 Qb 40
Cloghane **IRL** (KER) 96 Pe 35
Cloghanenagleragh **IRL** (KER) 97 Qc 34
Cloghaun **IRL** (CRE) 91 Qd 32
Cloghaun **IRL** (GAL) 87 Ra 28
Cloghboley **IRL** (SLI) 82 Rc 22
Cloghboola **IRL** (COR) 98 Qf 36
Cloghboy **IRL** (DON) 77 Rd 20
Cloghbrack **IRL** (GAL) 86 Qd 27
Clogheen **IRL** (TIP) 99 Sa 35
Clogheen **IRL** (WTF) 99 Sb 35
Clogheen House **IRL** (COR) 98 Rc 35
Clogher **GB** (TYR) 83 Se 22
Clogher **IRL** (KER) 97 Qc 35
Clogher **IRL** (MAY) 80 Pf 24
Clogher **IRL** (MAY) 87 Qd 25
Clogherhead **IRL** (LOT) 90 Te 26
Clogherny **IRL** (DON) 78 Se 17
Cloghfin **IRL** (DON) 77 Sc 19
Cloghfin **IRL** (DON) 78 Sc 20
Cloghfin **IRL** (DON) 78 Sd 17
Cloghglass **IRL** (DON) 78 Sd 17
Cloghjordan **IRL** (TIP) 93 Rf 31
Cloghmacoo Cross Roads **IRL** (MT) 90 Tb 25
Cloghmore **IRL** (MAY) 86 Qa 25
Cloghran **IRL** (DUB) 95 Te 28
Cloghroe **IRL** (COR) 104 Rc 37
Cloghroe **IRL** (DON) 77 Sb 19
Cloghtin **IRL** (SLI) 82 Rd 24
Cloghy **GB** (DOW) 85 Ud 22
Clohamon **IRL** (WEX) 101 Tc 33
Cloheden **IRL** (WEX) 101 Tb 33
Clohernagh **IRL** (WTF) 100 Sf 35
Clola **GB** (GRP) 17 Ya 4
Cloloige **IRL** (WEX) 101 Td 33
Clomantagh **IRL** (KLK) 94 Sd 32
Clon **IRL** (TIP) 99 Sa 32
Clonadacassey **IRL** (LAO) 94 Sd 30
Clonaderg **IRL** (OFF) 93 Sa 28
Clonagh **IRL** (KIL) 95 Tb 28
Clonakenny **IRL** (TIP) 93 Sa 31
Clonakilty **IRL** (COR) 103 Ra 39
Clonalvy **IRL** (MT) 90 Td 27
Clonamara **IRL** (COR) 103 Ra 38
Clonamery **IRL** (KLK) 100 Sf 34
Clonard **IRL** (COR) 104 Sa 37
Clonaslee **IRL** (LAO) 94 Sc 30
Clonavoe **IRL** (OFF) 94 Sf 29
Clonblock **IRL** (DON) 78 Sd 18
Clonbouig **IRL** (COR) 104 Rc 38
Clonbrin House **IRL** (OFF) 94 Sf 29
Clonbroney Cross Roads **IRL** (LGF) 89 Sc 26
Clonbullogue **IRL** (OFF) 94 Sf 29
Clonbur **IRL** (GAL) 87 Qd 27
Cloncagh **IRL** (LIM) 98 Ra 34
Cloncanon **IRL** (OFF) 94 Sf 29
Clonco Bridge **IRL** (GAL) 93 Rd 30
Cloncon **IRL** (OFF) 94 Sd 29
Cloncovet **IRL** (CAV) 89 Sd 26
Cloncrave **IRL** (WMT) 89 Sf 28
Cloncreen **IRL** (OFF) 94 Sf 29
Cloncullen **IRL** (LAO) 94 Sd 30
Cloncullen **IRL** (WMT) 88 Sb 27
Cloncurry **IRL** (KIL) 94 Ta 29
Cloncurry **IRL** (KIL) 95 Tb 28
Clondagad House **IRL** (CRE) 92 Qf 32
Clondalkin **IRL** (DUB) 95 Td 29
Clondaw **IRL** (WEX) 101 Td 33
Clondeglass House **IRL** (LAO) 94 Sc 30
Clondelara **IRL** (OFF) 93 Sa 29
Clondouglas **IRL** (KER) 97 Qc 34
Clonduff **IRL** (LAO) 94 Sd 29
Clonea **IRL** (WTF) 100 Sd 35
Clonearl House **IRL** (OFF) 94 Se 29
Clone Cross Roads **IRL** (WEX) 101 Td 33
Clonee **IRL** (MT) 95 Td 28
Cloneen **IRL** (TIP) 100 Sc 34
Clonegall **IRL** (CLW) 101 Tc 32
Clonelud **IRL** (COR) 103 Qf 37
Clones **IRL** (MOG) 83 Se 23
Cloney **IRL** (KIL) 94 Sf 30
Cloneybeg **IRL** (KIL) 94 Ta 30
Clonfert **IRL** (GAL) 93 Rf 29
Clonfert Cross Roads **IRL** (GAL) 93 Rf 29
Clongeen **IRL** (WEX) 100 Tb 35
Clongill **IRL** (MT) 90 Tb 26
Clongoweswood College **IRL** (KIL) 95 Tb 29
Clongowna House **IRL** (TIP) 93 Rf 30
Clonincurragh **IRL** (LAO) 94 Sc 30
Clonjordan **IRL** (WEX) 101 Tc 33
Clonkeen Cross Roads **IRL** (KIL) 94 Ta 28
Clonkeenkerrill **IRL** (GAL) 87 Rc 28
Clonleame Cross Roads **IRL** (WMT) 89 Sf 27
Clonlost **IRL** (WMT) 89 Se 27
Clonmacnoise **IRL** (OFF) 93 Sa 29
Clonmannan House **IRL** (WKL) 95 Tf 30
Clonmany **IRL** (DON) 78 Sd 17
Clonmel **IRL** (TIP) 99 Sb 34
Clonmellon **IRL** (WMT) 89 Sf 27
Clonmore **IRL** (CLW) 95 Tc 32
Clonmore **IRL** (LAO) 94 Ta 31
Clonmore **IRL** (LOT) 90 Te 25
Clonmore **IRL** (TIP) 93 Sb 32
Clonmult **IRL** (COR) 99 Rf 37
Clonony **IRL** (OFF) 93 Sa 29
Clonoulty **IRL** (TIP) 99 Sa 33
Clonoura **IRL** (TIP) 99 Sc 33
Clonroche **IRL** (WEX) 101 Tb 34
Clontarf **IRL** (DUB) 95 Te 28
Clontibret **IRL** (MOG) 84 Ta 23
Clontrain **IRL** (MOG) 90 Tb 25
Clontumpher **IRL** (LGF) 89 Sb 26
Clontymullan **IRL** (WMT) 89 Sc 27
Clonwhelan **IRL** (LGF) 89 Sc 26
Clonycavan **IRL** (MT) 89 Ta 27
Clonygowan **IRL** (OFF) 94 Se 29
Clonyhague **IRL** (WMT) 94 Sd 28
Clooart **IRL** (LGF) 88 Sa 26
Clooderreen **IRL** (COR) 104 Rb 39
Cloomorris **IRL** (LGF) 88 Sa 26
Cloonacool **IRL** (SLI) 82 Rb 24
Cloonaddra **IRL** (ROS) 88 Rf 26
Cloonagh **IRL** (LGF) 88 Sb 26
Cloonagh **IRL** (LGF) 89 Sc 25
Cloonagh **IRL** (SLI) 82 Rc 22
Cloonagh **IRL** (WEX) 100 Ta 35
Cloonaghgarve **IRL** (GAL) 87 Ra 27
Cloonagh House **IRL** (WMT) 89 Sd 28
Cloonagrouna House **IRL** (MT) 89 Ta 26
Cloonakilleg **IRL** (ROS) 88 Re 27
Cloonatleva **IRL** (GAL) 93 Rd 28
Cloonback **IRL** (LGF) 89 Sc 25
Cloonbanaun **IRL** (MAY) 87 Qf 27
Cloonboo **IRL** (GAL) 87 Qf 28
Cloonbrennaun **IRL** (GAL) 88 Rc 27
Clooncah **IRL** (ROS) 88 Rc 26
Cloonca Wood **IRL** (ROS) 88 Re 27
Clooncon **IRL** (GAL) 88 Rc 27
Clooncoeen **IRL** (CRE) 97 Qb 33
Clooncoorna **IRL** (CRE) 91 Qd 32
Clooncoose **IRL** (CRE) 92 Qf 30
Clooncraff **IRL** (ROS) 88 Rf 27
Cloondacarra **IRL** (ROS) 88 Rd 26
Cloondaff **IRL** (MAY) 87 Qd 25
Cloondara **IRL** (LGF) 88 Sa 26
Cloondarone **IRL** (GAL) 87 Ra 28
Cloondonoghoe **IRL** (GAL) 92 Rb 29
Cloondrinagh **IRL** (CRE) 92 Qe 32
Clooneagh **IRL** (LET) 88 Sb 25
Clooneagh **IRL** (LET) 88 Sa 25
Clooneen **IRL** (LGF) 89 Sd 26
Clooneen **IRL** (MAY) 80 Pf 23
Cloone Grange **IRL** (LET) 88 Sb 25
Clooneoc House **IRL** (LET) 88 Sa 25
Clooney **IRL** (DON) 77 Rd 19
Clooney **IRL** (DON) 77 Sc 18
Clooneylissaun **IRL** (CRE) 97 Qd 33
Cloonfad **IRL** (ROS) 87 Rb 26
Cloonfad **IRL** (ROS) 88 Rc 25
Cloonfad Cross Roads **IRL** (ROS) 88 Rd 25
Cloonfaghna **IRL** (GAL) 88 Rd 27
Cloonfaris **IRL** (GAL) 88 Rd 28
Cloonfeagh **IRL** (CRE) 92 Qf 31
Cloonfinish **IRL** (MAY) 87 Ra 25
Cloonfore **IRL** (LGF) 88 Sa 27
Cloonfower **IRL** (ROS) 87 Rc 26
Cloonhard **IRL** (ROS) 88 Rd 26
Clooniff **IRL** (GAL) 92 Qf 29
Cloonkeen **IRL** (GAL) 92 Rc 29
Cloonkeen **IRL** (KER) 96 Qe 37
Cloonkeen **IRL** (ROS) 88 Rc 26
Cloonkeen **IRL** (ROS) 88 Re 28
Cloonkirgeen **IRL** (COR) 103 Qf 38
Cloonlahard Lodge **IRL** (LIM) 98 Qe 33
Cloonlara **IRL** (CRE) 92 Rc 32
Cloonlatieve **IRL** (ROS) 88 Rc 26
Cloonlough **IRL** (SLI) 88 Rd 25
Cloonmacart **IRL** (LGF) 88 Sb 26
Cloonmagunnaun **IRL** (ROS) 88 Rd 25
Cloonmain **IRL** (GAL) 93 Rd 29
Cloonminda **IRL** (GAL) 88 Rc 27
Cloonmore **IRL** (ROS) 88 Rf 27
Cloonmore Cross Roads **IRL** (MAY) 87 Rb 25
Cloonmoylan **IRL** (GAL) 93 Re 30
Cloonmurray **IRL** (ROS) 88 Re 26
Cloonnamaskry **IRL** (GAL) 93 Re 29
Cloonoon **IRL** (GAL) 93 Re 30
Cloonoughter **IRL** (LIM) 98 Qe 33
Cloonsellan **IRL** (ROS) 88 Rf 27
Cloonshannagh **IRL** (ROS) 88 Sa 26
Cloonsharragh **IRL** (KER) 96 Pe 35
Cloonsheecahill **IRL** (GAL) 92 Rc 29
Cloonshinnagh **IRL** (MAY) 87 Qe 26
Cloontia **IRL** (MAY) 88 Rc 25
Cloontuskert **IRL** (ROS) 88 Rf 26
Cloontycarthy **IRL** (COR) 103 Qf 37
Cloontycommade **IRL** (COR) 98 Ra 35
Cloonybrennan **IRL** (ROS) 88 Rf 26
Cloonygorman **IRL** (COR) 103 Qd 38
Cloonymorris **IRL** (GAL) 93 Rd 29
Cloonyourish **IRL** (ROS) 88 Re 27
Cloonyquin House **IRL** (ROS) 88 Re 26
Cloony South **IRL** (CRE) 92 Qe 31
Clophill **GB** (BFS) 55 Zd 36
Clopton **GB** (NRH) 55 Zd 34
Cloran Cross Roads **IRL** (WMT) 89 Ta 27
Closeburn **GB** (DAG) 31 Wb 17
Close Clark **GBM** 29 Vc 24
Closworth **GB** (SOM) 68 Xc 43
Clothall **GB** (HTS) 55 Zf 37
Clotton **GB** (CHS) 44 Xb 29
Clough **GB** (DOW) 85 Ua 23
Cloughmore **IRL** (LOT) 90 Te 24
Cloughton **GB** (NOY) 37 Zd 23
Cloughton Newlands **GB** (NOY) 37 Zd 22
Clountane **IRL** (KER) 97 Qd 35
Clountane **IRL** (KER) 97 Qe 35
Clousta **GB** (SHL) 2 Yd 107
Clouston **GB** (ORK) 6 We 115
Clova **GB** (GRP) 16 Xa 5
Clova **GB** (TYS) 21 Wf 7
Clovelly **GB** (DEV) 66 Vd 42
Clovelly Cross **GB** (DEV) 66 Vd 43
Clovenfords **GB** (BOR) 26 Xa 15
Clovullin **GB** (HGL) 19 Ue 8
Clowanstown **IRL** (MT) 90 Tc 27
Clowne **GB** (DSH) 46 Ye 29
Clows Top **GB** (HWC) 52 Xd 34
Cloyne **IRL** (COR) 104 Rf 37
Cluain Meala = Clonmel **IRL** (TIP) 99 Sb 34
Cluanach **GB** (STC) 22 Te 14
Cluanie Inn **GB** (HGL) 14 Uf 6
Cluer **GB** (HGL) 11 Tb 2
Cluidrevagh **IRL** (GAL) 87 Ra 28
Clun **GB** (SHS) 52 Wf 34
Clunbury **GB** (SHS) 52 Xa 34
Clunderwen **GB** (DYF) 58 Vb 37
Clunes **GB** (HGL) 19 Va 7
Clungunford **GB** (SHS) 52 Xa 34
Clunie **GB** (TYS) 21 Wd 9
Clunton **GB** (SHS) 52 Xa 34
Cluny **GB** (FIF) 26 We 12
Clwyt-y-bont **GB** (GWY) 42 Vf 30
Clydach **GB** (GWE) 60 Wf 38
Clydach **GB** (WGL) 59 Wa 38
Clydach Vale **GB** (MGL) 60 Wd 39
Clydebank **GB** (STC) 24 Vd 13
Clydey **GB** (DYF) 58 Vc 37
Clyffe Pypard **GB** (WIL) 62 Ya 40
Clynacarton **IRL** (KER) 96 Pd 37
Clynnog-fawr **GB** (GWY) 42 Vd 30
Clyro **GB** (POW) 52 Wf 36
Clyst Honiton **GB** (DEV) 67 Wd 44
Clyst Hydon **GB** (DEV) 67 Wd 44
Clyst Saint George **GB** (DEV) 67 Wd 44
Clyst Saint Mary **GB** (DEV) 67 Wd 44
Cnoc Amhlaigh **GB** (HGL) 11 Te 119
Cnwch Coch **GB** (DYF) 51 Wa 34
Coachford **IRL** (COR) 104 Rb 37
Coad's Green **GB** (CNW) 75 Vd 45
Coagh **GB** (TYR) 84 Tc 21
Coalbrook **IRL** (TIP) 100 Sc 33
Coalbrookdale **GB** (SHS) 52 Xd 33
Coalburn **GB** (STC) 25 Wa 15
Coalcleugh **GB** (NHL) 35 Xe 20
Coalnaughton **GB** (CEN) 25 Wb 12
Coalpit Heath **GB** (AVN) 61 Xd 39
Coalport **GB** (SHS) 52 Xd 33
Coaltown of Balgonie **GB** (FIF) 26 Wf 11
Coaltown of Wemyss **GB** (FIF) 26 Wf 12
Coalville **GB** (LEC) 46 Yd 32
Coan **IRL** (KLK) 94 Sf 32
Coan **IRL** (WKL) 95 Tc 31
Coast **GB** (HGL) 7 Ud 1
Coat **GB** (SOM) 68 Xb 43
Coatbridge **GB** (STC) 25 Vf 13
Coate **GB** (WIL) 62 Ya 40
Coate **GB** (WIL) 62 Yb 39
Coates **GB** (CBS) 55 Zf 33
Coates **GB** (GLS) 62 Xf 38
Coates **GB** (WSX) 71 Zc 43
Coatham **GB** (CLE) 37 Yf 21
Coatham Mundeville **GB** (DUR) 36 Yc 21
Cobbaton **GB** (DEV) 66 Wa 42
Cobblers Hill Cross Roads **IRL** (LAO) 94 Se 31
Coberley **GB** (GLS) 61 Xf 37
Cobh **IRL** (COR) 104 Re 37
Cobham **GB** (KEN) 64 Ac 40
Cobham **GB** (SUR) 64 Zd 41
Coblers Green **GB** (ESS) 64 Ac 37
Cobnash **GB** (HWC) 52 Xb 35
Cock Alley **GB** (DSH) 46 Yd 29
Cockayne **GB** (NOY) 37 Yf 22
Cock Bridge **GB** (GRP) 16 We 5
Cockburnspath **GB** (BOR) 27 Xd 13
Cock Clarks **GB** (ESS) 65 Ad 38
Cockenzie and Port Seton **GB** (LOT) 26 Xa 13
Cockerham **GB** (LCS) 38 Xb 25
Cockermouth **GB** (CUB) 34 Wd 21
Cockernhoe **GB** (HTS) 64 Zd 37
Cockfield **GB** (DUR) 36 Yb 21
Cockfield **GB** (SUF) 56 Ae 36
Cocking **GB** (WSX) 70 Zb 43
Cockington **GB** (DEV) 76 Wc 46
Cocklake **GB** (SOM) 68 Xb 41
Cockley Beck **GB** (CUB) 34 Wf 22
Cockley Cley **GB** (NOR) 56 Ad 33
Cockney **GB** (GRP) 17 Xe 6
Cockpole Green **GB** (BKS) 63 Za 39
Cockshutt **GB** (SHS) 44 Xa 31
Cockthorpe **GB** (NOR) 48 Af 31
Cockwood **GB** (DEV) 76 Wd 45
Cockyard **GB** (HWC) 61 Xa 36
Codda **GB** (CNW) 75 Vc 45
Coddenham **GB** (SUF) 57 Ba 36
Coddington **GB** (CHS) 44 Xb 30
Coddington **GB** (HWC) 53 Xd 36
Coddington **GB** (NTS) 46 Zb 30
Codford Saint Mary **GB** (WIL) 69 Xf 42
Codford Saint Peter **GB** (WIL) 69 Xf 42
Codicote **GB** (HTS) 64 Ze 37
Codnor **GB** (DSH) 46 Yd 30
Codrington **GB** (AVN) 61 Xd 39
Codsall **GB** (SFS) 53 Xe 34
Codsall Wood **GB** (SFS) 53 Xe 33
Coedely **GB** (MGL) 60 Wd 39
Coedkernew **GB** (GWE) 60 Wf 39
Coed Morgan **GB** (POW) 60 Xa 38
Coedpenmaen **GB** (MGL) 60 Wd 39
Coedpoeth **GB** (CLW) 44 Wf 30
Coed-y-paen **GB** (GWE) 60 Xa 38
Coelbren **GB** (POW) 60 Wc 38
Coeshill **GB** (BUS) 63 Zc 39
Coffcott Green **GB** (DEV) 66 Vd 44
Coffinswell **GB** (DEV) 76 Wc 45
Cofton Hackett **GB** (HWC) 53 Ya 34
Cogenhoe **GB** (NRH) 54 Zb 35
Coggalkeenagh **IRL** (ROS) 88 Rf 26
Coggeshall **GB** (ESS) 65 Ae 37
Coggins Mill **GB** (ESX) 72 Ab 42
Coilantogle **GB** (CEN) 25 Ve 11
Coillariech **GB** (GRP) 16 Wf 6
Coillaig **GB** (STC) 19 Ue 10
Coille Mhorgil **GB** (HGL) 14 Uf 6
Coity **GB** (MGL) 60 Wc 39
Colaboll **GB** (HGL) 8 Vd 120
Colaton Raleigh **GB** (DEV) 67 We 44
Colbinstown **IRL** (KIL) 95 Tb 30
Colbost **GB** (HGL) 12 Tc 4
Colbury **GB** (HAS) 69 Yd 43
Colby **GB** (CUB) 35 Xc 21
Colby **GB** (NOR) 49 Bb 31
Colby **GBM** 29 Vb 24
Colchester **GB** (ESS) 65 Af 37
Cold Ash **GB** (BKS) 62 Ye 40
Cold Ashby **GB** (NRH) 54 Yf 34
Cold Ashton **GB** (AVN) 61 Xd 40
Cold Aston **GB** (GLS) 62 Yb 37
Coldbackie **GB** (HGL) 5 Vd 117
Cold Blow **GB** (DYF) 58 Vb 38
Coldblow **GB** (GRL) 64 Aa 40
Cold Brayfield **GB** (BUS) 55 Zc 36
Coldean **GB** (ESX) 71 Zf 43
Colden Common **GB** (HAS) 70 Ye 43
Coldfair Green **GB** (SUF) 57 Bd 35
Coldham **GB** (CBS) 55 Aa 33
Coldharbour **GB** (SUR) 71 Zd 41
Coldhayes **GB** (HAS) 70 Za 42
Cold Hesledon **GB** (DUR) 33 Yd 20
Coldingham **GB** (BOR) 27 Xf 13
Cold Kirby **GB** (NOY) 37 Ye 23
Cold Newton **GB** (LEC) 54 Za 33
Cold Norton **GB** (ESS) 65 Ae 38
Cold Overton **GB** (LEC) 54 Zb 32
Coldrain **GB** (TYS) 25 Wd 11
Coldrey **GB** (HAS) 70 Za 41
Coldridge **GB** (DEV) 66 Wa 43
Coldstream **GB** (BOR) 27 Xe 15
Coldstream **GB** (TYS) 22 Xa 9
Coldwaltham **GB** (WSX) 71 Zc 43
Coldwells **GB** (GRP) 17 Yb 4
Coldwells **IRL** (KIL) 95 Tc 30
Coldwells, Milton **GB** (GRP) 17 Xf 4
Cole **GB** (SOM) 68 Xd 42
Colebatch **GB** (SHS) 52 Wf 34
Colebrook **GB** (DEV) 67 Wd 43
Colebrooke **GB** (DEV) 67 Wb 44
Coleby **GB** (HUS) 40 Zc 27
Coleford **GB** (DEV) 67 Wb 44
Coleford **GB** (GLS) 61 Xc 38
Coleford **GB** (SOM) 68 Xd 41
Cole Green **GB** (HTS) 64 Zf 38
Colehill **IRL** (LGF) 89 Sb 27
Coleman's Hatch **GB** (ESX) 71 Aa 42
Colemere **GB** (SHS) 44 Xa 31
Colemore **GB** (HAS) 70 Za 42
Colenden **GB** (TYS) 21 Wd 10
Coleorton **GB** (LEC) 46 Yd 32
Coleraine **GB** (LDR) 78 Tb 18
Colerne **GB** (WIL) 61 Xe 40
Colesbourne **GB** (GLS) 62 Xf 38
Cole's Cross **GB** (DEV) 76 Wb 47
Colesden **GB** (BFS) 55 Zd 35
Coleshill **GB** (OXS) 62 Yc 39
Coleshill **GB** (WWH) 53 Yb 33
Colestocks **GB** (DEV) 67 We 44
Colgagh **IRL** (SLI) 82 Rd 23
Colgate **GB** (WSX) 71 Ze 42
Colgrain **GB** (STC) 24 Vb 13
Colinsburgh **GB** (FIF) 26 Xa 11
Colinton **GB** (LOT) 26 We 13
Colintraive **GB** (STC) 24 Uf 13
Colintraive **GB** (STC) 24 Va 12
Colkirk **GB** (NOR) 49 Af 32
Collace **GB** (TYS) 21 We 10
Collafirth **GB** (SHL) 2 Yd 105
Collafirth **GB** (SHL) 2 Ye 106
Collamber Manor **IRL** (LGF) 89 Sc 26
Collamoor Head **GB** (CNW) 66 Vc 44
Collaton Saint Mary **GB** (DEV) 76 Wc 46
College **IRL** (LAO) 94 Sd 30
College Cross Roads **IRL** (MT) 90 Tb 25
Collegeland **IRL** (MT) 90 Tb 28
Collessie **GB** (FIF) 21 Wf 11
Colliers End **GB** (HTS) 64 Zf 37
Colliery Row **GB** (TAW) 33 Yd 19
Collieston **GB** (GRP) 17 Ya 4
Collin **GB** (DAG) 31 Wc 18
Collingbourne Ducis **GB** (WIL) 69 Yc 41
Collingbourne Kingston **GB** (WIL) 62 Yc 41
Collingham **GB** (NTS) 46 Zb 30
Collingham **GB** (WYO) 40 Yd 25
Collington **GB** (HWC) 52 Xc 35
Collingtree **GB** (NRH) 54 Za 35
Collinstown **IRL** (WMT) 89 Se 27
Colliston **GB** (TYS) 22 Xc 9
Collmore **IRL** (KLK) 100 Se 34
Collon **IRL** (LOT) 90 Td 26
Collooney **IRL** (SLI) 82 Rd 23
Collyweston **GB** (NRH) 55 Zc 33
Colmanstown **IRL** (GAL) 87 Rc 28
Colmonell **GB** (STC) 28 Va 18
Colmworth **GB** (BFS) 55 Zd 35
Colnabaichin **GB** (GRP) 16 Wf 6
Colnbrook **GB** (GRL) 63 Zc 40
Colne **GB** (LCS) 39 Xf 25
Colne Engaine **GB** (ESS) 56 Ae 37
Colney **GB** (NOR) 49 Bb 33
Colney Heath **GB** (HTS) 64 Ac 38
Colney Street **GB** (HTS) 64 Ac 38
Coln Rogers **GB** (GLS) 62 Ya 38
Coln Saint Aldwyns **GB** (GLS) 62 Yb 38
Colonsay **GB** (STC) 22 Te 12
Colp **GB** (GRP) 17 Xd 3
Colpy **GB** (GRP) 17 Xc 4
Colsterdale **GB** (NOY) 36 Yb 23
Colsterworth **GB** (LIN) 47 Zc 32
Colston Bassett **GB** (NTS) 46 Za 31
Coltfield **GB** (GRP) 16 Wd 3
Coltishall **GB** (NOR) 49 Bc 32
Colton **GB** (CUB) 34 Wf 23
Colton **GB** (NOR) 49 Ba 33
Colton **GB** (NOY) 40 Ye 25
Colton **GB** (SFS) 45 Ya 32
Colvend **GB** (DAG) 31 Wb 19
Colwall Stone **GB** (HWC) 53 Xd 36
Colwell **GB** (NHL) 33 Xf 18
Colwich **GB** (SFS) 45 Ya 32
Colwinston **GB** (SGL) 60 Wc 40
Colworth **GB** (WSX) 70 Zb 44
Colwyn Bay **GB** (CLW) 43 Wb 29
Colyford **GB** (DEV) 67 Wf 44
Colyton **GB** (DEV) 67 Wf 44
Combe **GB** (BKS) 62 Yd 40
Combe **GB** (DEV) 67 Wc 45

Chobham – Combe GB IRL 113

Combe **GB** (OXS) 62 Yd 37
Combe Hay **GB** (AVN) 61 Xd 40
Combeinteignhead **GB** (DEV) 76 Wc 45
Combe Martin **GB** (DEV) 66 Vf 41
Combe Moor **GB** (HWC) 52 Xa 35
Comber **GB** (DOW) 85 Ub 21
Comberbach **GB** (CHS) 44 Xc 29
Comberford **GB** (SFS) 53 Yb 32
Comberton **GB** (CBS) 55 Aa 35
Comberton **GB** (HWC) 52 Xb 35
Combe Saint Nicholas **GB** (SOM) 68 Xa 43
Combrook **GB** (WWH) 54 Yc 36
Combs **GB** (DSH) 45 Ya 29
Combs **GB** (SUF) 57 Af 35
Combwich **GB** (SOM) 67 Wf 41
Comers **GB** (GRP) 17 Xc 6
Commeen **IRL** (DON) 77 Rf 19
Commeen **IRL** (DON) 77 Sa 20
Commins Coch **GB** (POW) 51 Wb 33
Common **IRL** (WEX) 101 Tc 35
Common, The **GB** (WIL) 69 Yc 42
Commondale **GB** (NOY) 37 Za 22
Common Edge **GB** (LCS) 38 Wf 26
Common Moor **GB** (CNW) 75 Vd 45
Commons **IRL** (TIP) 100 Sc 33
Common Side **GB** (DSH) 46 Yd 29
Commons Lower **IRL** (DUB) 90 Td 27
Commons West **IRL** (KER) 97 Qb 35
Compass, Square and **GB** (DYF) 58 Uf 37
Compstall **GB** (GRM) 45 Xf 28
Compton **GB** (BKS) 62 Ye 39
Compton **GB** (DEV) 76 Wc 46
Compton **GB** (SUR) 70 Zc 41
Compton **GB** (WSX) 70 Za 43
Compton Abdale **GB** (GLS) 62 Ya 37
Compton Bassett **GB** (WIL) 62 Ya 40
Compton Beauchamp **GB** (OXS) 62 Yc 39
Compton Chamberlayne **GB** (WIL) 69 Ya 42
Compton Dando **GB** (AVN) 61 Xc 40
Compton Dundon **GB** (SOM) 68 Xb 42
Compton Martin **GB** (AVN) 68 Xc 41
Comrie **GB** (TYS) 20 Wa 10
Conchra **GB** (STC) 24 Uf 12
Concraigie **GB** (TYS) 21 Wd 9
Conder Green **GB** (LCS) 38 Xb 25
Conderton **GB** (HWC) 53 Xf 36
Condicote **GB** (GLS) 62 Yb 37
Condorrat **GB** (STC) 25 Vf 13
Condover **GB** (SHS) 52 Xb 33
Coneyhurst **GB** (WSX) 71 Zd 42
Coneysthorpe **GB** (NOY) 37 Za 24
Coney Weston **GB** (SUF) 56 Af 34
Cong **IRL** (MAY) 87 Qe 27
Congleton **GB** (CHS) 45 Xe 30
Congresbury **GB** (AVN) 61 Xb 40
Conicar Hill **IRL** (WEX) 101 Td 34
Conicavel **GB** (GRP) 15 Wb 3
Coningsby **GB** (LIN) 47 Ze 30
Conington **GB** (CBS) 55 Ze 34
Conington **GB** (CBS) 55 Zf 35
Conisbrough **GB** (SOY) 40 Ye 28
Conisby **GB** (STC) 22 Td 14
Conisholme **GB** (LIN) 41 Aa 28
Coniston **GB** (CUB) 34 Wf 22
Coniston **GB** (HUS) 41 Ze 26
Coniston Cold **GB** (NOY) 39 Xf 25
Conistone **GB** (NOY) 39 Xf 24
Conna **IRL** (COR) 99 Rf 36
Connagh **IRL** (GAL) 93 Rd 31
Connah's Quay **GB** (CLW) 44 Wf 29
Connel **GB** (STC) 19 Ud 10
Connel Park **GB** (STC) 30 Ve 16
Connels Cross Roads **IRL** (MT) 90 Tb 26
Connolly **IRL** (CRE) 92 Qe 32
Connor **GB** (ANT) 84 Te 20
Connor Downs **GB** (CNW) 74 Ud 47
Conon Bridge **GB** (HGL) 15 Vd 3
Cononley **GB** (NOY) 39 Xf 25
Conordan **GB** (HGL) 13 Tf 4
Consall **GB** (SFS) 45 Xf 30
Consett **GB** (DUR) 33 Yb 19
Constable Burton **GB** (NOY) 36 Yb 23
Contin **GB** (HGL) 15 Vc 3
Contlaw **GB** (GRP) 17 Xe 6
Convent School **IRL** (WTF) 100 Sd 36
Convoy **IRL** (DON) 77 Sb 19
Conwy **GB** (GWY) 43 Wa 29
Conyer **GB** (KEN) 65 Ae 40
Coobaun **IRL** (CRE) 92 Ra 31
Cooflugh Tower **IRL** (COR) 104 Rc 37
Coogulla **IRL** (TIP) 93 Sb 32
Cookbury **GB** (DEV) 66 Ve 44
Cookham **GB** (BKS) 63 Zb 39
Cookham Rise **GB** (BKS) 63 Zb 39
Cookhill **GB** (HWC) 53 Ya 35
Cookley **GB** (HWC) 53 Xe 34
Cookley **GB** (SUF) 57 Bc 35
Cookley Green **GB** (OXS) 63 Yf 39
Cooksbridge **GB** (ESX) 71 Zf 43
Cooksmill Green **GB** (ESS) 64 Ac 38
Cookstown **GB** (TYR) 84 Tb 21
Coola Cross Roads **IRL** (SLI) 82 Rd 24
Coolagarranroe Wood **IRL** (TIP) 99 Rf 35
Coolagh **IRL** (GAL) 92 Qf 29
Coolagortboy **IRL** (WTF) 99 Sb 35
Coolaknick **IRL** (WEX) 101 Tc 34
Coolaleena Cross Roads **IRL** (WMT) 88 Sa 27
Coolanagh Cross Roads **IRL** (LAO) 94 Ta 31
Coolanarney **IRL** (COR) 98 Qf 36
Coolaneelig **IRL** (KER) 97 Qd 34
Coolaney **IRL** (SLI) 82 Rc 23
Coolarne House **IRL** (GAL) 92 Ra 28
Coolattin **IRL** (WKL) 95 Tc 32
Coolayna Haggard **IRL** (KIL) 94 Sf 28
Coolbagh **IRL** (WTF) 99 Sa 36
Coolbaun **IRL** (COR) 104 Rb 39
Coolbaun **IRL** (KLK) 94 Se 32
Coolbaun **IRL** (TIP) 93 Re 31
Coolbawn House **IRL** (WKL) 95 Te 32
Coolboy **IRL** (WEX) 100 Tb 35
Coolboy **IRL** (WKL) 95 Td 32
Coolcarrigan House **IRL** (KIL) 94 Ta 29
Coolclogh **IRL** (COR) 98 Ra 36
Coolcoosaun **IRL** (CRE) 92 Rc 31
Coolcreany **IRL** (WEX) 95 Te 32
Coolderry **IRL** (OFF) 93 Sa 30
Coole **IRL** (WMT) 89 Sd 26
Coolea **IRL** (COR) 103 Qe 37
Coolearagh **IRL** (KIL) 95 Tb 29
Coole East **IRL** (COR) 104 Rd 37
Coole Upper **IRL** (WMT) 89 Sd 26
Coole West **IRL** (COR) 104 Rd 37
Coolgarriv House **IRL** (KER) 97 Qc 36
Coolgrange **IRL** (KLK) 100 Sf 33
Coolgreany **IRL** (KLK) 100 Sf 32
Coolham **GB** (WSX) 71 Zd 43
Coolieragh **IRL** (COR) 103 Qc 38
Cooliney House **IRL** (COR) 98 Rb 35
Cooling **GB** (KEN) 65 Ad 40
Coolinny **IRL** (COR) 99 Rd 36
Coolkellure **IRL** (COR) 103 Qe 38
Coolkenna Street **IRL** (WKL) 95 Tc 32
Coolkreeragh **GB** (LDR) 78 Se 18
Coolmain Castle **IRL** (COR) 104 Rc 39
Coolmeen **IRL** (CRE) 92 Qe 33
Coolmore **IRL** (COR) 104 Rd 38
Coolnaconarty **IRL** (COR) 103 Qf 39
Coolnagillagh **IRL** (COR) 98 Qf 36
Coolnagun **IRL** (WMT) 89 Sd 26
Coolnalingady **IRL** (WTF) 100 Sc 36
Coolnamunna House **IRL** (TIP) 93 Rf 31
Coolnanoonagh **IRL** (KER) 97 Qd 33
Coolnareen **IRL** (LAO) 94 Sd 31
Coolnaron **IRL** (WEX) 101 Tb 34
Coolnasmear **IRL** (WTF) 99 Sc 36
Coolology **IRL** (CRE) 92 Rc 31
Coolowley **IRL** (LAO) 94 Sc 31
Coolrain **IRL** (LAO) 94 Sc 31
Coolseskin **IRL** (WEX) 101 Tb 35
Coolshinnagh **IRL** (MAY) 87 Qf 25
Coolsluightena **IRL** (ROS) 88 Rf 27
Cooluck **IRL** (DUB) 95 Te 28
Coolure **IRL** (WMT) 89 Sd 26
Coomarkane **IRL** (COR) 103 Qc 38
Coombe **GB** (CNW) 75 Va 47
Coombe Bissett **GB** (WIL) 69 Ya 42
Coombe Hill **GB** 61 Xf 37
Coombe Keynes **GB** (DOS) 69 Xe 45
Coombes **GB** (WSX) 71 Ze 43
Coomkeen **IRL** (COR) 103 Qc 39
Coomleagh **IRL** (COR) 103 Qe 38
Coomnahincht **IRL** (KER) 96 Pe 37
Coomothloukane **IRL** (KER) 102 Pe 38
Coonagh **IRL** (CRE) 98 Rb 32
Cooper's Corner **GB** (ESX) 72 Ac 42
Coopleridge **GB** (DOR) 68 Xe 42
Cooraclare **IRL** (CRE) 91 Qd 32
Coornagillagh **IRL** (KER) 102 Qb 38
Coosane **IRL** (COR) 99 Rd 36
Coosane **IRL** (COR) 103 Qd 39
Cootehall **IRL** (ROS) 88 Rf 25
Cootehill **IRL** (CAV) 89 Sf 24
Copany **IRL** (DON) 82 Rf 21
Copdock **GB** (SUF) 57 Ba 36
Cople **GB** (BFS) 55 Zd 36
Copley **GB** (DUR) 36 Ya 21
Copmanthorpe **GB** (NOY) 40 Yf 25
Coppanagh Mills **IRL** (CAV) 89 Se 24
Coppathorne **GB** (CNW) 66 Vc 44
Coppenagh House **IRL** (CLW) 95 Tb 32
Coppenhall **GB** (SFS) 45 Xf 32
Coppingford **GB** (CBS) 55 Ze 34
Copplestone **GB** (DEV) 67 Wb 44
Coppull **GB** (LCS) 38 Xc 27
Copsale **GB** (WSX) 71 Ze 43
Copsetown Cross Roads **IRL** (COR) 98 Rb 35
Copster Green **GB** (LCS) 38 Xd 26
Copston Magna **GB** (WWH) 54 Ye 34
Copt Hewick **GB** (NOY) 36 Yd 24
Copthorne **GB** (SUR) 71 Zf 42
Copy Lake **GB** (DEV) 66 Wa 43
Copythorne **GB** (HAS) 69 Yc 43
Cora Droma Rúisc = Carrick on Shannon **IRL** (LET) 89 Rf 25
Coralstown **IRL** (WMT) 89 Se 28
Corballis Bridge **IRL** (MT) 89 Ta 27
Corbally **IRL** (CRE) 91 Qc 32
Corbally **IRL** (SLI) 81 Qf 23
Corbally **IRL** (WMT) 89 Se 26
Corbally Cross Roads **IRL** (KIL) 95 Tb 30
Corbally House **IRL** (COR) 104 Rc 37
Corbally House **IRL** (TIP) 93 Rf 31
Corbay Upper **IRL** (LGF) 89 Sb 26
Corbeagh House **IRL** (LGF) 89 Sc 26
Corboggy **IRL** (MT) 89 Ta 25
Corboghil **IRL** (ROS) 88 Rf 26
Corboy Cross Roads **IRL** (LGF) 89 Sb 26
Corbridge **GB** (NHL) 33 Xf 19
Corby **GB** (NRH) 55 Zb 34
Corby Glen **GB** (LIN) 47 Zc 32
Corclogh **IRL** (MAY) 80 Pf 23
Corcoran's Cross Roads **IRL** (WEX) 100 Ta 34
Corcreeghagh **IRL** (LOT) 90 Tc 25
Corcreggan **IRL** (DON) 77 Rf 18
Cordal **IRL** (KER) 97 Qd 35
Cordara House **IRL** (LGF) 88 Sa 27
Cordarragh **IRL** (MAY) 86 Qc 26
Cordrumman **IRL** (ROS) 88 Sa 26
Corduff **IRL** (DUB) 90 Te 27
Coreley **GB** (SHS) 52 Xc 34
Corfe **GB** (SOM) 67 Wf 43
Corfe Castle **GB** (DOS) 69 Xf 45
Corfree **IRL** (CAV) 89 Sc 25
Corfton **GB** (SHS) 52 Xb 34
Corgarff **GB** (GRP) 16 We 6
Corgreagh **IRL** (CAV) 89 Sf 24
Corhampton **GB** (HAS) 70 Yf 43
Cork **IRL** (COR) 104 Rd 37
Corker House **IRL** (ROS) 88 Re 26
Corlae **GB** (DAG) 30 Vf 17
Corlea **IRL** (LGF) 88 Sa 27
Corlee **IRL** (MAY) 87 Qf 24
Corley **GB** (WWH) 53 Yc 34
Corley Ash **GB** (WWH) 53 Yc 34
Corlis **IRL** (ROS) 88 Rd 26
Corluddy **IRL** (KLK) 100 Se 35
Cormakilly **IRL** (DON) 83 Sc 20
Cormeen Cross Roads **IRL** (MT) 89 Ta 25
Cornabus **GB** (STC) 22 Te 15
Cornafean **IRL** (CAV) 89 Sd 25
Cornafulla **IRL** (ROS) 93 Rf 28
Cornagall **IRL** (CAV) 89 Se 24
Cornageeha **IRL** (LET) 88 Sb 25
Cornageeragh **IRL** (LET) 88 Sb 24
Cornamona **IRL** (GAL) 86 Qd 27
Cornamucklagh **IRL** (GAL) 88 Re 28
Cornan West **IRL** (WKL) 95 Tc 31
Cornaquillagh **IRL** (DON) 77 Sb 19
Cornelly **GB** (WGL) 59 Wb 39
Corney **GB** (CUB) 34 Wd 23
Cornfield House **IRL** (CRE) 92 Qf 32
Cornforth **GB** (DUR) 36 Yc 20
Cornhill **GB** (GRP) 17 Xb 3
Cornholme **GB** (WYO) 39 Xf 26
Cornish Hall End **GB** (ESS) 56 Ac 36
Cornpark **IRL** (GAL) 88 Rc 27
Cornriggs **GB** (DUR) 35 Xe 20
Cornsay **GB** (DUR) 36 Yb 20
Corntown **GB** (HGL) 15 Vd 3
Cornwell **GB** (OXS) 62 Yc 37
Cornwood **GB** (DEV) 76 Wa 46
Cornworthy **GB** (DEV) 76 Wc 46
Corpach **GB** (HGL) 19 Uf 7
Corpusty **GB** (NOR) 49 Ba 32
Corraduff **IRL** (GAL) 92 Ra 29
Corraffrin **IRL** (DON) 83 Sb 20
Corragh **IRL** (WKL) 95 Tc 30
Corraghbrack **IRL** (MOG) 84 Ta 23
Corraleehan **IRL** (LET) 88 Sb 24
Corramore **IRL** (ROS) 88 Re 27
Corramore **IRL** (ROS) 88 Rf 28
Corran **GB** (HGL) 14 Uc 6
Corran **GB** (HGL) 19 Ue 8
Corranagh **IRL** (DON) 77 Sb 19
Corran Cross Roads **IRL** (COR) 104 Rc 38
Corrandulla **IRL** (GAL) 87 Ra 28
Corraneary **IRL** (CAV) 89 Sf 25
Corrany **GBM** 29 Vd 23
Corraskea **IRL** (MOG) 83 Se 24
Corraun **IRL** (MAY) 86 Qa 25
Corravilla **IRL** (CAV) 89 Ta 25
Corrawaleen **IRL** (LET) 89 Sb 24
Corraweelis **IRL** (CAV) 89 Se 25
Correal House **IRL** (ROS) 88 Re 27
Corrie **GB** (STC) 24 Uf 15
Corrie Common **GB** (DAG) 31 We 18
Corriemoillie **GB** (HGL) 14 Vb 3
Corrievorrie **GB** (HGL) 15 Vf 5
Corrigeenroe **IRL** (ROS) 88 Re 24
Corrimony **GB** (HGL) 14 Vb 4
Corrin **IRL** (COR) 99 Re 36
Corringham **GB** (ESS) 65 Ac 39
Corringham **GB** (LIN) 40 Zb 28
Corrinshigo House **IRL** (CAV) 90 Ta 25
Corrinshigo House **IRL** (CAV) 90 Tb 25
Corris **GB** (GWY) 51 Wa 33
Corris Uchaf **GB** (GWY) 51 Wa 33
Corrofin **IRL** (CRE) 92 Qf 31
Corrofin **IRL** (GAL) 87 Ra 28
Corronagh **IRL** (CAV) 89 Sf 26
Corry **GB** (HGL) 13 Ua 5
Corrymailley **IRL** (MAY) 86 Qa 26
Corrymucklock **GB** (TYS) 21 Wb 10
Corscombe **GB** (DOS) 68 Xb 43
Corse **GB** (GRP) 17 Xc 4
Corse Lawn **GB** (HWC) 61 Xe 37
Corsham **GB** (WIL) 61 Xe 40
Corsindae **GB** (GRP) 17 Xc 5
Corsley **GB** (WIL) 68 Xe 41
Corsley Heath **GB** (WIL) 68 Xe 41
Corsock **GB** (DAG) 31 Wa 18
Corston **GB** (AVN) 61 Xd 40
Corston **GB** (WIL) 61 Xf 39
Corstorphine **GB** (LOT) 26 We 13
Corstown Cross **IRL** (LOT) 90 Te 25
Cortachy **GB** (TYS) 22 Xa 8
Corthage House **IRL** (DON) 78 Se 17
Corton **GB** (SUF) 57 Be 33
Corton **GB** (WIL) 69 Xf 42
Corton Denham **GB** (SOM) 68 Xc 43
Cortown **IRL** (MT) 89 Ta 26
Coruanan Lodge **GB** (HGL) 19 Uf 8
Corvally **IRL** (MOG) 90 Ta 25
Corveagh **IRL** (MAY) 86 Qd 26
Corveen **IRL** (DON) 77 Re 18
Corvoy **IRL** (MOG) 84 Ta 24
Corwen **GB** (CLW) 43 Wd 31
Cosby **GB** (LEC) 54 Ye 33
Coseley **GB** (WMD) 53 Xf 33
Cosford **GB** (SHS) 53 Xe 32
Cosgrove **GB** (BUS) 54 Za 36
Cosham **GB** (HAS) 70 Yf 43
Cosheston **GB** (DYF) 58 Va 38
Coskemduff **IRL** (CAV) 89 Ta 24
Cossall **GB** (NTS) 46 Ye 31
Cossington **GB** (LEC) 46 Yf 32
Cossington **GB** (SOM) 68 Xa 42
Costelloe Casla **IRL** (GAL) 91 Qc 29
Costessey **GB** (NOR) 49 Ba 33
Costock **GB** (NTS) 46 Yf 32
Coston **GB** (LEC) 46 Zb 32
Cote **GB** (OXS) 62 Yd 38
Cote **GB** (SOM) 68 Xa 41
Cotebrook **GB** (CHS) 44 Xc 29
Cotehill **GB** (CUB) 32 Xb 19
Cotehill Muinchille **IRL** (CAV) 89 Sf 24
Cotes **GB** (LEC) 54 Ye 32
Cotesbach **GB** (LEC) 54 Ye 34
Cotgrave **GB** (NTS) 46 Yf 31
Cothall **GB** (GRP) 17 Xe 5
Cotham **GB** (NTS) 46 Zb 30
Cothelstone **GB** (SOM) 67 We 42
Cotherstone **GB** (DUR) 36 Ya 21
Cothill **GB** (OXS) 63 Ye 38
Coton **GB** (CBS) 55 Aa 35
Coton **GB** (NRH) 54 Yf 34
Coton **GB** (SFS) 45 Xf 31
Coton in the Clay **GB** (SFS) 45 Yb 31
Coton in the Elms **GB** (DSH) 45 Yc 32
Cottam **GB** (LCS) 38 Xb 26
Cottam **GB** (NTS) 46 Zb 29
Cottartown **GB** (HGL) 16 Wc 4
Cottehill **IRL** (CAV) 89 Sf 24
Cottenham **GB** (CBS) 56 Aa 35
Cotterdale **GB** (NOY) 35 Xe 22
Cottered **GB** (HTS) 64 Zf 37
Cottesbrooke **GB** (NRH) 54 Za 34
Cottesmore **GB** (LEC) 47 Zc 32
Cottian **IRL** (DON) 77 Sb 18
Cottingham **GB** (HUS) 41 Zd 26
Cottingham **GB** (NRH) 54 Zb 33
Cottisford **GB** (OXS) 63 Yf 37
Cotton **GB** (SUF) 57 Ba 35
Cotton End **GB** (BFS) 55 Zd 36
Cottown **GB** (GRP) 16 Xb 5
Cottown **GB** (GRP) 17 Xd 5
Cottown **GB** (GRP) 17 Xe 4
Cotwalton **GB** (SFS) 45 Xf 31
Couchsmill **GB** (CNW) 75 Vc 46
Coughton **GB** (HWC) 61 Xc 37
Coughton **GB** (WWH) 53 Ya 35
Coulags **GB** (HGL) 14 Ud 4
Coulin Lodge **GB** (HGL) 14 Ud 3
Coull **GB** (GRP) 16 Xb 6
Coulport **GB** (STC) 24 Va 12
Coulsdon **GB** (GRL) 64 Zf 41
Coulston **GB** (WIL) 69 Xf 41
Coulter **GB** (STC) 25 Wc 15
Coultershaw Bridge **GB** (WSX) 70 Zc 43
Coultings **GB** (SOM) 67 Wf 42
Coulton **GB** (NOY) 40 Yf 25
Coumaclovane **IRL** (COR) 103 Qe 37
Coumduff **IRL** (KER) 97 Pf 35
Cound **GB** (SHS) 52 Xc 33
Coundon **GB** (DUR) 36 Yc 21
Coundon Grange **GB** (DUR) 36 Yc 21
Countersett **GB** (NOY) 35 Xf 23
Countess Wear **GB** (DEV) 67 Wd 44
Countesthorpe **GB** (LEC) 54 Yf 33
Countisbury **GB** (DEV) 67 Wb 41
County Bridge **IRL** (LAO) 93 Sb 31
Coupar Angus **GB** (TYS) 21 We 9
Coupland **GB** (NHL) 27 Xf 15
Cour **GB** (STC) 23 Ud 14
Court Barton **GB** (DEV) 67 Wb 44
Court Henry **GB** (DYF) 59 Vf 37
Court House **IRL** (ROS) 88 Re 27
Courthoyle **IRL** (WEX) 100 Tb 34
Courtlough House **IRL** (DUB) 90 Te 27
Courtmacsherry **IRL** (COR) 104 Rb 39
Courtnacuddy Cross Roads **IRL** (WEX) 101 Tb 34
Courtown **IRL** (WEX) 101 Te 33
Courtown House **IRL** (KIL) 95 Tb 28
Court Plunkett **IRL** (LAO) 94 Sc 31
Courtsend **GB** (ESS) 65 Af 39
Courtway **GB** (SOM) 67 Wf 42
Cousland **GB** (LOT) 26 Xa 13
Cousley Wood **GB** (ESX) 72 Ac 42
Cove **GB** (DEV) 67 Wd 43
Cove **GB** (HAS) 63 Zb 41
Cove **GB** (HGL) 7 Ub 1
Cove **GB** (STC) 24 Va 12
Cove Bay **GB** (GRP) 17 Xf 6
Covehithe **GB** (SUF) 57 Be 34
Coven **GB** (SFS) 53 Xf 33
Coveney **GB** (CBS) 56 Ab 34
Covenham Saint Mary **GB** (LIN) 41 Aa 28
Coventry **GB** (WMD) 54 Yc 34
Coverack **GB** (CNW) 74 Uf 48
Coverham **GB** (NOY) 36 Ya 23
Covington **GB** (CBS) 55 Zd 35
Cowbeech **GB** (ESX) 72 Ab 43
Cowbit **GB** (LIN) 47 Zf 32
Cowbridge **GB** (SGL) 60 Wd 40
Cowden **GB** (KEN) 71 Aa 42
Cowdenbeath **GB** (FIF) 26 Wd 12
Cowden Pound **GB** (KEN) 71 Aa 42
Cowes **GB** (IOW) 70 Ye 44
Cowesby **GB** (NOY) 36 Ye 23
Cowfold **GB** (WSX) 71 Ze 43
Cowgill **GB** (CUB) 35 Xd 23
Cowick **GB** (HUS) 40 Yf 26
Cowie **GB** (CEN) 25 Wa 12
Cowlam Manor **GB** (HUS) 41 Zc 24
Cowley **GB** (DEV) 67 Wc 44
Cowley **GB** (GLS) 61 Xf 38
Cowling **GB** (NOY) 36 Yc 23
Cowling **GB** (NOY) 39 Xf 25
Cowlinge **GB** (SUF) 56 Ad 36
Cowpen **GB** (NHL) 33 Yc 18
Cowpen Bewley **GB** (CLE) 36 Ye 21
Cowplain **GB** (HAS) 70 Yf 43
Cowshill **GB** (DUR) 35 Xe 20
Coxbank **GB** (CHS) 44 Xc 31
Coxbench **GB** (DSH) 46 Yd 31
Cox Common **GB** (SUF) 57 Bd 34
Coxheath **GB** (KEN) 72 Ac 41
Coxhoe **GB** (DUR) 36 Yc 20
Coxley **GB** (SOM) 68 Xb 41
Coxtie Green **GB** (ESS) 64 Ab 39
Coxtown **IRL** (GAL) 93 Re 29
Coxwold **GB** (NOY) 37 Ye 23
Coylton **GB** (STC) 30 Vc 16
Coylumbridge **GB** (HGL) 15 Wb 5
Coynach **GB** (GRP) 16 Xa 6
Coytrahen **GB** (MGL) 60 Wc 39
Cozey Lodge **IRL** (MT) 90 Td 27
Craanford **IRL** (WEX) 101 Td 32
Craanlusky **IRL** (CLW) 94 Tb 33
Crabaton **GB** (DEV) 76 Wb 46
Crabbet Park **GB** (WSX) 71 Zf 42
Crabtree **GB** (WSX) 71 Ze 42
Crackenthorpe **GB** (CUB) 35 Xc 21
Crackington **GB** (CNW) 66 Vc 44
Crackington Haven **GB** (CNW) 66 Vc 44
Crackleybank **GB** (SHS) 53 Xd 32
Crackpot **GB** (NOY) 36 Xf 22
Cracoe **GB** (NOY) 39 Xf 24
Craddanstown **IRL** (WMT) 89 Sf 27
Craddanstown Lodge **IRL** (WMT) 89 Sf 27
Craddock **GB** (DEV) 67 We 43
Craffield **IRL** (WKL) 95 Td 31
Crafthole **GB** (CNW) 75 Ve 46
Cragg **IRL** (TIP) 93 Rd 32
Craggaknork **IRL** (CRE) 91 Qd 32
Cragg Vale **GB** (WYO) 39 Ya 26
Craghead **GB** (DUR) 33 Yb 19
Crai **GB** (POW) 60 Wc 37
Craibstone **GB** (GRP) 16 Xa 3
Craibstone **GB** (GRP) 17 Xe 5
Craichie **GB** (TYS) 22 Xb 9
Craig **GB** (HGL) 14 Ue 4
Craigavad **GB** (DOW) 85 Ub 21
Craigavon **GB** (ARG) 84 Td 22
Craigcefnparc **GB** (WGL) 59 Wa 38
Craigdam **GB** (GRP) 17 Xe 4
Craigearn **GB** (GRP) 17 Xd 5
Craigellachie **GB** (GRP) 16 We 4
Craigendoran **GB** (STC) 24 Vb 13
Craigens **GB** (STC) 22 Te 14
Craighat **GB** (CEN) 24 Vd 12
Craighouse **GB** (STC) 23 Ua 13
Craigie **GB** (GRP) 17 Xf 5
Craigie **GB** (STC) 24 Vd 15
Craigie **GB** (TYS) 21 Wd 9
Craiglockhart **GB** (LOT) 26 We 13
Craig Lodge **GB** (STC) 24 Ue 13
Craignant **GB** (SHS) 44 Wf 31
Craignure **GB** (STC) 19 Ub 10
Craigo **GB** (TYS) 22 Xd 8
Craigow **GB** (TYS) 25 Wd 11
Craigrothie **GB** (FIF) 22 Wf 11
Craigruie **GB** (CEN) 20 Vd 10
Craigs, the **GB** (HGL) 8 Vc 1
Craigton **GB** (TYS) 21 Wf 9
Craigton **GB** (TYS) 22 Xb 9
Craig-y-nos **GB** (POW) 60 Wb 38
Crail **GB** (FIF) 22 Xc 11
Crailing **GB** (BOR) 32 Xd 15
Crailinghall **GB** (BOR) 32 Xd 16
Crakehall **GB** (NOY) 36 Yc 23
Crambe **GB** (NOY) 40 Za 24
Cramlington **GB** (NHL) 33 Yc 18
Cramond **GB** (LOT) 26 We 13
Cranage **GB** (CHS) 45 Xd 29
Cranberry **GB** (SFS) 45 Xe 31
Cranborne **GB** (DOS) 69 Ya 43
Cranbourne **GB** (BKS) 63 Zb 40
Cranbrook **GB** (KEN) 72 Ad 42
Cranbrook Common **GB** (KEN) 72 Ad 42
Crane **IRL** (WEX) 101 Tc 33
Cranemore **IRL** (CLW) 101 Tb 32
Cranfield **GB** (BFS) 55 Zc 36
Cranford **GB** (DEV) 66 Vd 43
Cranford Saint Andrew **GB** (NRH) 55 Zc 34
Cranford Saint John **GB** (NRH) 55 Zc 34
Cranham **GB** (GLS) 61 Xf 38
Cranham **GB** (GRL) 64 Ab 39
Crank **GB** (MES) 38 Xb 28
Cranleigh **GB** (SUR) 71 Zd 42
Cranmer Green **GB** (SUF) 57 Af 35
Cranmore **GB** (SOM) 68 Xd 41
Cranna **GB** (GRP) 17 Xc 3
Crannagh House **IRL** (GAL) 93 Rd 30
Crannoch **GB** (GRP) 16 Xa 3
Crannogeboy **IRL** (DON) 77 Rd 20
Cranny **IRL** (CRE) 92 Qe 32
Cranoe **GB** (LEC) 54 Za 33
Cransford **GB** (SUF) 57 Bc 35
Cranshaws **GB** (BOR) 27 Xd 13
Cranstal **GBM** 29 Vd 22
Cranswick, Hutton **GB** (HUS) 41 Zd 25
Crantock **GB** (CNW) 74 Uf 46
Cranwell **GB** (LIN) 47 Zd 30
Cranwich **GB** (NOR) 56 Ad 33
Cranworth **GB** (NOR) 56 Af 33
Craobh Haven **GB** (STC) 23 Uc 11
Crarae **GB** (STC) 24 Ue 12
Crask Inn **GB** (HGL) 8 Vd 119
Craskins **GB** (GRP) 16 Xb 6
Craster **GB** (NHL) 33 Yc 16
Craswall **GB** (HWC) 60 Wf 36
Cratfield **GB** (SUF) 57 Bc 35
Crathes **GB** (GRP) 17 Xd 6
Crathie **GB** (GRP) 16 We 6
Crathorne **GB** (NOY) 36 Ye 22
Cratloe **IRL** (CRE) 92 Rb 32
Craughwell **IRL** (GAL) 92 Rb 29
Craven Arms **GB** (SHS) 52 Xa 34
Crawcrook **GB** (TAW) 33 Yb 19
Crawford **GB** (STC) 31 Wc 16
Crawick **GB** (DAG) 31 Wa 16
Crawley **GB** (HAS) 70 Yd 42
Crawley **GB** (OXS) 62 Yc 38
Crawley **GB** (WSX) 71 Ze 42
Crawley Down **GB** (WSX) 71 Zf 42
Crawleyside **GB** (DUR) 36 Xf 20
Crawshawbooth **GB** (LCS) 39 Xe 26
Crawton **GB** (GRP) 22 Xe 7
Cray **GB** (NOY) 36 Xf 23
Cray **GB** (TYS) 21 Wd 8
Crayford **GB** (GRL) 64 Ab 40
Crayke **GB** (NOY) 37 Yf 24
Crays Hill **GB** (ESS) 65 Ac 39
Cray's Pond **GB** (OXS) 63 Yf 39
Crazy Corner **IRL** (WMT) 89 Se 27
Creacombe **GB** (DEV) 67 Wb 43
Creaghanroe **IRL** (MOG) 84 Tb 23
Creagorry **GB** (HGL) 12 Se 4
Creaton **GB** (NRH) 54 Za 34
Creca **GB** (DAG) 31 We 18
Crecora **IRL** (LIM) 98 Rb 33
Credenhill **GB** (HWC) 52 Xb 36
Crediton **GB** (DEV) 67 Wc 44
Cree **IRL** (OFF) 93 Sa 30
Cree's Cross **GB** (DOW) 85 Ub 21
Creegh **IRL** (CRE) 91 Qd 32
Creeharmore **IRL** (ROS) 88 Re 28
Creehennan **IRL** (DON) 78 Se 18
Creeslough **IRL** (DON) 77 Sa 18
Creeting Saint Mary **GB** (SUF) 57 Ba 35
Creeton **GB** (LIN) 47 Zd 32
Creetown **GB** (DAG) 30 Vd 19
Creevagh **IRL** (MAY) 81 Qe 23
Creevagh **IRL** (MOG) 84 Ta 24
Creeve Cross Roads **IRL** (LGF) 89 Sb 26
Creevelands **IRL** (MOG) 89 Ta 24
Creeveroe **IRL** (GAL) 88 Rd 27
Creeves **IRL** (LIM) 98 Qf 33
Creevykeel Cross Roads **IRL** (SLI) 82 Rd 22
Creeyaghmore **IRL** (LGF) 88 Sb 27
Creggan **GB** (TYR) 84 Sf 21
Cregganhaun **IRL** (MAY) 86 Qb 26
Creggans **GB** (STC) 24 Uf 11
Creggaun **IRL** (CRE) 98 Rb 32
Creggs **IRL** (GAL) 88 Rd 27
Cregnafyla **IRL** (MAY) 87 Qf 25
Cregneish **GBM** 29 Vb 24
Cregrina **GB** (POW) 51 We 36
Crehelp **IRL** (WKL) 95 Tc 30
Creich **GB** (FIF) 21 Wf 10
Creigiau **GB** (MGL) 60 We 39
Cremorgan House **IRL** (LAO) 94 Se 31
Cremyll **GB** (CNW) 76 Ve 46
Cressage **GB** (SHS) 52 Xc 33
Cresselly **GB** (DYF) 58 Vb 38
Cressing **GB** (ESS) 65 Ad 37
Cresswell **GB** (NHL) 33 Yc 17
Cresswell Quay **GB** (DYF) 58 Vb 38
Creswell **GB** (DSH) 46 Ye 29
Cretshengan **GB** (STC) 23 Uc 13
Crewe **GB** (CHS) 44 Xa 30
Crewe **GB** (CHS) 44 Xd 30
Crew Green **GB** (POW) 44 Wf 32
Crewkerne **GB** (SOM) 68 Xb 43
Crianlarich **GB** (CEN) 20 Vc 10
Cribyn **GB** (DYF) 50 Vf 36
Criccieth **GB** (GWY) 42 Ve 31
Crich **GB** (DSH) 46 Yd 30
Crich Carr **GB** (DSH) 46 Yd 30
Crichie **GB** (GRP) 17 Xf 4
Crichton **GB** (LOT) 26 Xa 13
Crick **GB** (GWE) 61 Xb 39
Crick **GB** (NRH) 54 Yf 34
Crickedarn **GB** (POW) 51 We 36
Cricket Malherbie **GB** (SOM) 68 Xa 43
Crickheath **GB** (SHS) 44 Wf 32
Crickhowell **GB** (POW) 60 Wf 37
Cricklade **GB** (WIL) 62 Ya 39
Cridling Stubbs **GB** (NOY) 40 Ye 26
Crieff **GB** (TYS) 21 Wa 10
Criggion **GB** (POW) 52 Wf 32
Crigglestone **GB** (WYO) 39 Yc 27
Crimonmogate **GB** (GRP) 17 Ya 3
Crimplesham **GB** (NOR) 56 Ac 33
Crinan **GB** (STC) 23 Uc 12
Cringleford **GB** (NOR) 57 Bb 33
Cringletie **GB** (BOR) 26 We 14
Crinkill **IRL** (OFF) 93 Sa 30
Crinow **GB** (DYF) 58 Vb 38
Cripplesease **GB** (CNW) 74 Uc 47
Cripp's Corner **GB** (ESX) 72 Ad 43
Croagh **IRL** (DON) 82 Rd 20
Croagh **IRL** (DON) 82 Rf 21
Croagh **IRL** (LIM) 98 Ra 33
Croaghlosky **IRL** (DON) 77 Rf 18
Croaghrimbeg **IRL** (MAY) 86 Qd 26
Crockaslowra **IRL** (DON) 77 Rd 20
Crockaughrim **IRL** (DON) 78 Se 17
Crockbrack **IRL** (DON) 78 Sf 17
Crockenhill **GB** (KEN) 64 Aa 40
Crockernwell **GB** (DEV) 67 Wb 44
Crockerton **GB** (WIL) 69 Xe 41
Crocketford or Ninemile Bar **GB** (DAG) 31 Wb 18
Crockets Town **IRL** (MAY) 81 Qf 24
Crockey Hill **GB** (NOY) 40 Yf 25
Crockglass **IRL** (DON) 77 Sa 18
Crockham Hill **GB** (KEN) 71 Aa 41
Crockhasharragh **IRL** (DON) 82 Re 21
Crockleford Heath **GB** (ESS) 65 Af 37
Crocknabronta **IRL** (DON) 78 Ta 17
Crocknahattni **IRL** (CAV) 89 Sf 25
Crocknamerragh **IRL** (DON) 78 Sf 17
Crocknasharragh **IRL** (DON) 82 Rd 20
Crockness **GB** (ORK) 6 We 116
Crock Street **GB** (SOM) 68 Xa 43
Croeserw **GB** (WGL) 60 Wc 39
Croes-goch **GB** (DYF) 58 Uf 37
Croes Hywel **GB** (POW) 60 Xa 38
Croesor **GB** (GWY) 43 Vf 31
Croesyceilog **GB** (DYF) 59 Ve 38
Croes-y-mwylach **GB** (GWE) 60 Wf 39
Croes y pant **GB** (GWE) 60 Wf 38
Croft **GB** (CHS) 38 Xc 28
Croft **GB** (LEC) 54 Ye 33
Croft **GB** (LIN) 48 Ab 30
Croftamie **GB** (CEN) 24 Vd 12
Crofton **GB** (WIL) 62 Yc 40
Crofton **GB** (WYO) 40 Yd 27
Croft-on-Tees **GB** (NOY) 36 Yc 22
Crofts of Haddo **GB** (GRP) 17 Xe 4
Crofts of Inverthernie **GB** (GRP) 17 Xd 4
Crofty **GB** (WGL) 59 Vf 39
Croggan **GB** (STC) 19 Ub 10
Croghan **IRL** (OFF) 94 Se 28
Croghan **IRL** (ROS) 88 Re 25
Croghan House **IRL** (TIP) 93 Sa 30
Croglin **GB** (CUB) 35 Xc 20
Croick **GB** (HGL) 8 Vc 1
Croir **GB** (HGL) 11 Ta 119
Crolla **IRL** (DON) 77 Re 18
Cromane **IRL** (KER) 97 Qa 36
Cromarty **GB** (HGL) 8 Vf 2
Crombie Mill **GB** (TYS) 22 Xb 9
Cromdale **GB** (HGL) 16 Wc 4
Cromer **GB** (HTS) 64 Zf 37
Cromford **GB** (DSH) 45 Yc 30
Cromore **GB** (HGL) 11 Td 120
Cromra **GB** (HGL) 15 Vd 7
Cromwell **GB** (NTS) 46 Zb 30
Cronberry **GB** (STC) 30 Ve 16
Crondall **GB** (HAS) 70 Za 41
Crone House **IRL** (WKL) 95 Tf 31
Cronk, The **GBM** 29 Vc 23
Cronkeeran **IRL** (DON) 82 Rd 20
Cronk-y-Voddy **GBM** 29 Vc 23
Cronton **GB** (MES) 44 Xb 28
Crook **GB** (CUB) 35 Xb 22
Crook **GB** (DUR) 36 Yb 20
Crookedwood **IRL** (WMT) 89 Se 27
Crookham **GB** (BKS) 63 Ye 40
Crookham **GB** (NHL) 27 Xf 15
Crookhaven **IRL** (COR) 102 Qb 40
Crooklands **GB** (CUB) 35 Xb 23
Crook of Devon **GB** (TYS) 25 Wc 11
Crookstown **IRL** (COR) 103 Ra 37
Croom **IRL** (LIM) 98 Rb 33
Cropredy **GB** (OXS) 54 Ye 36
Cropston **GB** (LEC) 54 Ye 32
Cropthorne **GB** (HWC) 53 Xf 36
Cropton **GB** (NOY) 37 Zb 23
Cropwell Bishop **GB** (NTS) 46 Za 31
Cropwell Butler **GB** (NTS) 46 Za 31
Crosby **GB** (CUB) 34 Wd 20
Crosby **GB** (HUS) 40 Zb 27
Crosby **GB** (MES) 44 Wf 28
Crosby **GBM** 29 Vc 23
Crosby Garrett **GB** (CUB) 35 Xd 22
Crosby Ravensworth **GB** (CUB) 35 Xc 21
Croscombe **GB** (SOM) 68 Xc 41
Croseau Bach **GB** (SHS) 44 Wf 31
Cross **GB** (HGL) 11 Te 118
Cross **GB** (SOM) 68 Xa 41
Cross **IRL** (CRE) 97 Qb 33
Cross **IRL** (WTF) 99 Sb 36
Crossabeg **IRL** (WEX) 101 Tc 34
Crossaig **GB** (STC) 23 Ud 14
Crossakeel **IRL** (MT) 89 Sf 26
Crossapol **GB** (STC) 18 Ta 10
Cross Ash **GB** (GWE) 60 Xa 37
Cross-at-Hand **GB** (KEN) 72 Ad 41
Crossbane **IRL** (MOG) 83 Se 24
Cross Barry **IRL** (COR) 104 Rc 38
Crossbost **GB** (HGL) 11 Td 120
Crossboyne **IRL** (MAY) 87 Qf 26
Cross Bush **GB** (WSX) 71 Zc 43
Crosscanonby **GB** (CUB) 34 Wd 20
Crossconnell **IRL** (GAL) 93 Re 29
Crossdale Street **GB** (NOR) 49 Bb 31
Crossdoney **IRL** (CAV) 89 Sd 25
Crossdougal **GB** (HGL) 12 Sd 6
Crossea **IRL** (LGF) 88 Sc 26
Crosserlough **IRL** (CAV) 89 Se 25
Crossford **GB** (FIF) 25 Wd 12
Crossford **GB** (STC) 25 Wa 14
Crossgar **GB** (DOW) 85 Ub 22
Crossgates **GB** (POW) 51 Wd 35
Crossgill **GB** (LCS) 38 Xb 24
Cross Green **GB** (DEV) 66 Ve 44
Cross Green **GB** (SUF) 56 Af 36
Crosshands **GB** (DYF) 58 Vc 37
Cross Hands **GB** (DYF) 59 Vf 38
Crosshands **GB** (STC) 30 Ve 15
Crosshaven **IRL** (COR) 104 Re 38
Crosshill **GB** (FIF) 26 We 12
Crosshill **GB** (STC) 30 Vc 17
Crosshouse **GB** (STC) 24 Vc 15
Cross Houses **GB** (SHS) 52 Xb 33
Crossings **GB** (CUB) 32 Xb 18
Cross in Hand **GB** (ESX) 71 Ab 43
Cross Inn **GB** (DYF) 50 Vd 35
Cross Inn **GB** (DYF) 50 Vf 35
Cross Inn **GB** (MGL) 60 Wd 39
Cross Keys **IRL** (CAV) 89 Se 25
Crosskeys **IRL** (KIL) 94 Sf 30
Cross Keys **IRL** (MT) 89 Sf 26
Cross Keys **IRL** (MT) 90 Tc 27
Crosskirk **GB** (HGL) 5 Wc 117
Cross Lanes **GB** (CLW) 44 Xa 30
Cross Lanes **GB** (NOY) 40 Ye 24
Crosslanes **GB** (SHS) 44 Wf 32
Crosslee **GB** (BOR) 32 Wf 16
Crossmacool **IRL** (MT) 90 Td 27
Crossmaglen **GB** (ARG) 90 Tc 24
Cross Mahon **IRL** (COR) 104 Rb 38
Crossmichael **GB** (DAG) 31 Wa 19
Crossmolina **IRL** (MAY) 81 Qe 24

114 GB IRL **Combe – Crossmolina**

Dooncarton **IRL** (MAY) 80 Qa 23
Dooneen **IRL** (COR) 103 Qe 39
Dooneens **IRL** (COR) 98 Qf 36
Doonfoot **GB** (STC) 30 Vc 16
Doon House **IRL** (KER) 97 Qb 35
Doonloughan **IRL** (GAL) 86 Pf 28
Doonmanagh **IRL** (KER) 96 Pf 36
Doonogan House **IRL** (CRE) 91 Qd 32
Doonsheane **IRL** (KER) 96 Pe 36
Doonteeny **IRL** (MAY) 81 Qd 23
Doonwood **IRL** (GAL) 88 Rc 28
Doonyvardan **IRL** (CRE) 92 Qe 30
Doorin Rock **IRL** (DON) 82 Re 21
Doornane **IRL** (KLK) 100 Se 35
Doorus House **IRL** (GAL) 92 Ra 30
Dooyork **IRL** (MAY) 80 Qa 24
Dorchester **GB** (DOS) 68 Xd 44
Dorchester **GB** (OXS) 63 Yf 39
Dordon **GB** (WWH) 53 Yc 33
Dore **GB** (DSH) 45 Yc 29
Dore **IRL** (DON) 77 Re 18
Dores **GB** (HGL) 15 Ve 4
Dorket Head **GB** (NTS) 46 Yf 30
Dorking **GB** (SUR) 71 Ze 41
Dormansland **GB** (SUR) 71 Aa 42
Dormanstown **GB** (CLE) 37 Yf 21
Dormington **GB** (HWC) 52 Xc 36
Dorney **GB** (BUS) 63 Zc 39
Dornie **GB** (HGL) 14 Uc 5
Dornoch **GB** (HGL) 8 Vf 1
Dornock **GB** (DAG) 31 We 19
Dorridge **GB** (WMD) 53 Yb 34
Dorrington **GB** (SHS) 52 Xb 33
Dorrusawillin **IRL** (LET) 88 Rf 24
Dorsington **GB** (WWH) 53 Yb 36
Dorstone **GB** (HWC) 52 Wf 36
Dosthill **GB** (SFS) 53 Yb 33
Dottery **GB** (DOS) 68 Xb 44
Doublebois **GB** (CNW) 75 Vc 46
Dougalston **GB** (STC) 25 Ve 13
Dough **IRL** (COR) 102 Qb 40
Doughton **GB** (GLS) 61 Xe 39
Douglas **GB** (STC) 25 Wa 15
Douglas **GB** (STC) 31 Wb 16
Douglas **GBM** 29 Vd 24
Douglas and Angus **GB** (TYS) 22 Xa 10
Douglas Hall **GB** (DAG) 31 Wb 19
Douglastown **GB** (TYS) 22 Xa 9
Douglas Water **GB** (STC) 25 Wb 15
Doulting **GB** (SOM) 68 Xc 41
Dounby **GB** (ORK) 6 We 114
Doune **GB** (CEN) 25 Vf 11
Doune **GB** (HGL) 8 Vc 1
Dounie **GB** (HGL) 8 Vd 1
Dounreay **GB** (HGL) 5 Wb 117
Dousland **GB** (DEV) 76 Vf 45
Dovaston **GB** (SHS) 44 Xa 32
Dovehill House **IRL** (OFF) 93 Sb 30
Dove Holes **GB** (DSH) 45 Ya 29
Dovenby **GB** (CUB) 34 Wd 20
Dover **GB** (KEN) 73 Ba 42
Doverdale **GB** (HWC) 53 Xe 35
Doveridge **GB** (DSH) 45 Yb 31
Dowally **GB** (TYS) 21 Wc 9
Dowdeswell **GB** (GLS) 62 Ya 37
Dowdstown House **IRL** (KIL) 95 Tc 28
Dowhill **GB** (STC) 30 Vb 17
Dowlais **GB** (MGL) 60 Wd 38
Dowland **GB** (DEV) 66 Vf 43
Dowlands **GB** (DEV) 68 Wf 44
Down **GB** (KEN) 72 Ac 42
Down Ampney **GB** (GLS) 62 Ya 38
Downderry **GB** (CNW) 75 Vd 46
Downe **GB** (GRL) 64 Aa 41
Downend **GB** (IOW) 70 Ye 44
Down End **GB** (SOM) 68 Xa 42
Downfield **GB** (TYS) 22 Xa 10
Downham **GB** (ESS) 65 Ac 39
Downham **GB** (LCS) 39 Xe 25
Downham **GB** (NHL) 27 Xe 15
Downham Market **GB** (NOR) 56 Ac 33
Downhead **GB** (CNW) 66 Vc 45
Downhead **GB** (SOM) 68 Xd 41
Downholme **GB** (NOY) 36 Yb 22
Downies **GB** (GRP) 17 Xf 6
Downing **GB** (CLW) 43 We 29
Downing **IRL** (COR) 99 Re 35
Downley **GB** (BUS) 63 Zb 39
Downpatrick **GB** (DOW) 85 Ub 22
Down Saint Mary **GB** (DEV) 67 Wb 44
Downside **GB** (AVN) 61 Xb 40
Downside **GB** (SOM) 68 Xc 41
Down Thomas **GB** (DEV) 76 Vf 47
Downton **GB** (DEV) 66 Vf 45
Downton **GB** (DEV) 76 Wc 46
Downton **GB** (HAS) 69 Yc 44
Downton on the Rock **GB** (HWC) 52 Xa 34
Dowra **IRL** (CAV) 82 Rf 23
Dowsby **GB** (LIN) 47 Zd 31
Dowth **IRL** (MT) 90 Td 26
Dowton **GB** (WIL) 69 Yb 43
Doyle's Bridge **IRL** (ROS) 88 Sa 28
Doynton **GB** (AVN) 61 Xd 40
Draethen **GB** (MGL) 60 Wf 39
Draffan **GB** (STC) 25 Wa 14
Drakes Broughton **GB** (HWC) 53 Xf 36
Drakes Cross **GB** (HWC) 53 Ya 34
Drangan **IRL** (TIP) 100 Sc 33
Draperstown **GB** (LDR) 84 Tb 20
Draughton **GB** (NOY) 39 Ya 25
Draughton **GB** (NRH) 54 Za 34
Drax **GB** (NOY) 40 Za 26
Draycote **GB** (WWH) 54 Yd 35
Draycott **GB** (DSH) 46 Yd 31
Draycott **GB** (GLS) 53 Yb 36
Draycott **GB** (HWC) 53 Xe 36
Draycott **GB** (SOM) 68 Xb 41
Draycott in the Clay **GB** (SFS) 45 Yb 31
Draycott in the Moors **GB** (SFS) 45 Xf 31
Drayton **GB** (HWC) 53 Xf 34
Drayton **GB** (LEC) 54 Zb 33
Drayton **GB** (LIN) 47 Zf 31
Drayton **GB** (NOR) 49 Bb 32
Drayton **GB** (OXS) 54 Yd 36
Drayton **GB** (OXS) 62 Ye 39
Drayton Bassett **GB** (SFS) 53 Yb 33
Drayton Beauchamp **GB** (BUS) 63 Zb 38
Drayton Camp **GB** (HAS) 70 Yd 41
Drayton Parslow **GB** (BUS) 63 Zb 37
Drayton Saint Leonard **GB** (OXS) 63 Yf 39
Drebley **GB** (NOY) 39 Ya 24
Dreenhill **GB** (DYF) 58 Uf 38
Dre-fach **GB** (DYF) 50 Ve 36
Drefach **GB** (DYF) 59 Vf 38
Dreghorn **GB** (STC) 24 Vc 15
Drehidaclare Bridge **IRL** (KER) 97 Qb 34
Drehidasillagh **IRL** (KER) 97 Qb 35
Drehid House **IRL** (KIL) 94 Ta 28
Drehidnaman Bridge **IRL** (LIM) 98 Ra 33
Drem **GB** (LOT) 26 Xb 12
Drews Court **IRL** (LIM) 98 Rb 34
Drewsteignton **GB** (DEV) 67 Wb 44
Driby **GB** (LIN) 47 Aa 29
Driffield **GB** (GLS) 62 Ya 38
Driffield **GB** (HUS) 41 Zd 24
Drigg **GB** (CUB) 34 Wd 22
Drighlington **GB** (WYO) 39 Yc 26
Drimfern **GB** (STC) 19 Uf 11
Driminidy **IRL** (COR) 103 Qe 39
Drimmo **IRL** (LAO) 94 Sc 30
Drimnin **GB** (HGL) 18 Ua 9
Drimoleague **IRL** (COR) 103 Qe 39
Drimpton **GB** (DOS) 68 Xb 43
Drimsynie **GB** (STC) 24 Va 11
Drinagh **IRL** (COR) 103 Qf 39
Drinagh **IRL** (CRE) 92 Qe 31
Drinagh **IRL** (GAL) 86 Pf 28
Drinagh **IRL** (ROS) 88 Sa 26
Drinagh **IRL** (WEX) 101 Td 35
Drinaghan **IRL** (SLI) 81 Qf 23
Dring **IRL** (LGF) 89 Sc 26
Drinishader **GB** (HGL) 11 Tb 1
Drinkstone **GB** (SUF) 56 Af 35
Drinkstone Greene **GB** (SUF) 56 Af 35
Drioncoggy **IRL** (MAY) 87 Qd 26
Dripsey **IRL** (COR) 104 Rb 37
Drishaghaun **IRL** (GAL) 86 Qc 27
Drishaig **GB** (STC) 19 Uf 10
Drishaig **GB** (STC) 24 Va 11
Drishane More **IRL** (COR) 104 Sa 37
Drissaig **GB** (STC) 19 Ue 11
Drogheda **IRL** (LOT) 90 Td 26
Droichead Átha =Drogheda **IRL** (LOT) 90 Td 26
Droichead Nua = Newbridge **IRL** (KIL) 95 Tb 29
Drointon **GB** (SFS) 45 Ya 31
Droitwich **GB** (HWC) 53 Xf 35
Drom **IRL** (KER) 97 Qd 36
Drom **IRL** (TIP) 93 Sa 32
Dromagh Castle **IRL** (COR) 98 Ra 36
Dromahair **IRL** (LET) 82 Re 23
Dromahoe **IRL** (COR) 98 Ra 36
Droman **GB** (HGL) 4 Uf 118
Dromara **GB** (DOW) 85 Tf 22
Dromatouk **IRL** (KER) 103 Qc 37
Dromcolliher **IRL** (LIM) 98 Ra 34
Dromcunnig **IRL** (KER) 97 Qb 35
Dromdiralough **IRL** (KER) 97 Qd 36
Dromdrasdil **IRL** (COR) 103 Qe 38
Dromgownagh **IRL** (COR) 104 Rb 37
Dromin **IRL** (LIM) 98 Rc 34
Dromina **IRL** (COR) 98 Rb 35
Dromineer **IRL** (TIP) 93 Re 31
Dromin House **IRL** (KER) 97 Qd 34
Dromiskin **IRL** (LOT) 90 Td 25
Dromkeen Bridge **IRL** (KER) 97 Qb 34
Drommahane **IRL** (COR) 98 Rb 36
Drommartin **IRL** (KER) 97 Qb 34
Drommurrin House **IRL** (KER) 97 Qc 34
Dromod **IRL** (LET) 88 Sa 25
Dromore **GB** (DOW) 85 Tf 22
Dromore **GB** (TYR) 83 Sd 21
Dromore **IRL** (MOG) 84 Ta 24
Dromore Castle **IRL** (KER) 102 Qb 37
Dromore West **IRL** (SLI) 81 Ra 23
Dromoyle House **IRL** (OFF) 93 Sb 30
Dromtrasna **IRL** (LIM) 98 Qe 34
Dronfield **GB** (DSH) 46 Yd 29
Dronfield Woodhouse **GB** (DSH) 45 Yc 29
Drongan **GB** (STC) 30 Vd 16
Dronley **GB** (TYS) 21 Wf 9
Dropmore **GB** (BUS) 63 Zb 39
Droxford **GB** (HAS) 70 Yf 43
Droylsden **GB** (GRM) 39 Xf 28
Druid **GB** (CLW) 43 Wd 31
Druidston **GB** (DYF) 58 Uf 38
Druimavuic **GB** (STC) 19 Ue 9
Druimdrishaig **GB** (STC) 23 Uc 13
Druimindarroch **GB** (HGL) 19 Ub 7
Druinacoo **IRL** (GAL) 92 Ra 29
Drum **GB** (STC) 23 Ue 13
Drum **GB** (TYS) 25 Wc 11
Drum **IRL** (SLI) 82 Rd 23
Drumacarrow House **IRL** (CAV) 89 Sf 25
Drumacruttan House **IRL** (MOG) 84 Ta 23
Drumahoe **GB** (LDR) 78 Se 19
Drumakill **IRL** (MOG) 90 Tb 24
Drumandoora **IRL** (CRE) 92 Rb 30
Drumanespick **IRL** (CAV) 89 Sf 25
Drumanoo **IRL** (DON) 82 Rd 21
Drumanoss **GB** (DOW) 85 Ua 22
Drumard **IRL** (LET) 88 Sa 25
Drumard House **IRL** (MOG) 83 Se 23
Drumatober **IRL** (GAL) 93 Rd 29
Drumaville **IRL** (DON) 78 Se 17
Drumaville **IRL** (DON) 78 Sf 17
Drumbane **IRL** (TIP) 99 Sa 33
Drumbar **IRL** (DON) 82 Rf 21
Drumbarry **IRL** (CAV) 89 Se 25
Drumbeg **GB** (DOW) 85 Ua 21
Drumbeg **GB** (HGL) 7 Ue 119
Drumbeg **IRL** (DON) 77 Sc 19
Drumblade **GB** (GRP) 17 Xb 4
Drumblair **GB** (GRP) 17 Xc 4
Drumbo **GB** (DOW) 85 Ua 21
Drumbo **IRL** (MOG) 90 Tb 25
Drumbologe **IRL** (DON) 77 Sa 19
Drumboy **IRL** (DON) 78 Sc 18
Drumbrick **IRL** (LET) 89 Sc 24
Drumbride House **IRL** (MT) 90 Tb 25
Drumbridge **GB** (DEV) 76 Wb 45
Drumbroagh **IRL** (MOG) 90 Tb 24
Drumbuie **GB** (HGL) 13 Ub 5
Drumburgh **GB** (CUB) 31 Wf 19
Drumcar **IRL** (LOT) 90 Td 25
Drumcattan **IRL** (MOG) 90 Tc 24
Drumchapel **GB** (STC) 24 Vd 13
Drumchardine **GB** (HGL) 15 Vd 4
Drumcliff **IRL** (SLI) 82 Rd 23
Drumclog **GB** (STC) 25 Ve 15
Drumcondra **IRL** (DUB) 95 Te 28
Drumcondra **IRL** (MT) 90 Tc 25
Drumcong **IRL** (LET) 88 Sa 24
Drumcoura **IRL** (LET) 88 Sb 24
Drumcree **IRL** (WMT) 89 Sf 27
Drumcrow **IRL** (CAV) 89 Sd 25
Drumcrow South **IRL** (CAV) 89 Sc 25
Drumdangan **IRL** (WKL) 95 Te 31
Drumderg **IRL** (LGF) 89 Sc 26
Drumdoney **IRL** (SLI) 82 Re 24
Drumdoo **IRL** (DON) 77 Rf 18
Drumeldrie **GB** (FIF) 26 Xa 11
Drumellihy **IRL** (CRE) 91 Qd 32
Drumelzier **GB** (BOR) 26 Wd 15
Drumfearn **GB** (HGL) 13 Ua 5
Drumganny **IRL** (MOG) 90 Tc 24
Drumgeeny **IRL** (MOG) 90 Tc 25
Drumgley **GB** (TYS) 22 Xa 9
Drumgor **IRL** (CAV) 89 Sd 25
Drumgorman **IRL** (DON) 82 Re 21
Drumgower **IRL** (TIP) 99 Sb 33
Drumgowna **IRL** (LOT) 90 Tc 25
Drumgriftin **IRL** (GAL) 87 Ra 28
Drumguish **GB** (HGL) 15 Wa 6
Drumgumberland **IRL** (DON) 77 Sb 19
Drumhallagh House **IRL** (DON) 78 Sc 18
Drumin **GB** (GRP) 16 Wd 4
Drumin **IRL** (LOT) 90 Td 25
Druming **IRL** (LGF) 89 Sb 27
Drumjohn **GB** (DAG) 30 Ve 17
Drumkeary **IRL** (GAL) 93 Rd 30
Drumkeeran **IRL** (LET) 82 Rf 23
Drumlaggagh **IRL** (LET) 88 Sb 25
Drumlassie **GB** (GRP) 17 Xc 6
Drumlemble **GB** (STC) 28 Ub 16
Drumliff **IRL** (CAV) 89 Se 24
Drumligair **GB** (GRP) 17 Xf 5
Drumline **IRL** (CRE) 92 Ra 32
Drumlion **IRL** (ROS) 88 Rf 25
Drumlish **IRL** (LGF) 88 Sb 26
Drumlithie **GB** (GRP) 22 Xd 7
Drumman **IRL** (WMT) 89 Se 27
Drummanreagh **IRL** (MOG) 90 Tb 24
Drummeen **IRL** (LET) 88 Sb 25
Drummenny Bridge **IRL** (DON) 82 Rf 21
Drummin **IRL** (CRE) 91 Qd 32
Drummond **GB** (CEN) 25 Vf 11
Drummond **GB** (HGL) 15 Ve 3
Drummore **GB** (DAG) 28 Va 20
Drummurphy **IRL** (DON) 83 Sc 20
Drumnadowan **IRL** (DON) 77 Sc 19
Drumnadrochit **GB** (HGL) 15 Vd 4
Drumnagorrach **GB** (GRP) 16 Xb 3
Drumnagrella **IRL** (MOG) 90 Tc 25
Drumnaha **IRL** (DON) 77 Rf 19
Drumnaveagh **IRL** (CAV) 89 Se 25
Drumnee **IRL** (LGF) 88 Sa 27
Drumoak **GB** (GRP) 17 Xd 6
Drumoghill **IRL** (DON) 77 Sc 19
Drumone **IRL** (MT) 89 Sf 26
Drumquin **GB** (TYR) 83 Sd 21
Drumraney **IRL** (WMT) 93 Sb 28
Drumree **IRL** (MT) 90 Tc 27
Drumrunie **GB** (HGL) 7 Ue 120
Drums **GB** (GRP) 17 Xf 5
Drumsallie **GB** (HGL) 19 Ud 7
Drumshanbo **IRL** (LET) 88 Rf 24
Drumshanbo **IRL** (LET) 88 Sb 25
Drumshanbo South **IRL** (LET) 88 Sb 25
Drumshang **GB** (STC) 30 Vb 16
Drumsheel **IRL** (MAY) 87 Qe 27
Drumsna **IRL** (LET) 88 Rf 25
Drumsnat Bridge **IRL** (MOG) 83 Sf 23
Drumsruh **IRL** (KIL) 94 Ta 29
Drumsturdy **GB** (TYS) 22 Xb 9
Drumsurn **GB** (LDR) 78 Tb 19
Drumuie **GB** (HGL) 13 Te 4
Drumvaich **GB** (CEN) 25 Vf 11
Drumwhindle **GB** (GRP) 17 Xf 4
Drung **IRL** (CAV) 89 Se 24
Drunganagh **IRL** (MAY) 87 Qf 25
Drunkendub **GB** (TYS) 22 Xc 9
Drury **GB** (CLW) 44 Wf 29
Drutamon **IRL** (CAV) 89 Sf 25
Drybeck **GB** (CUB) 35 Xc 21
Drybridge **GB** (GRP) 16 Xa 3
Drybridge **GB** (STC) 24 Vc 15
Drybrook **GB** (GLS) 61 Xc 37
Dry Drayton **GB** (CBS) 55 Aa 35
Dryhope **GB** (BOR) 31 Wf 15
Drymen **GB** (CEN) 24 Vd 12
Drymuir **GB** (GRP) 17 Xf 3
Drynoch **GB** (HGL) 13 Te 5
Dryslwyn **GB** (DYF) 59 Vf 37
Dry Street **GB** (ESS) 65 Ac 39
Dryton **GB** (SHS) 52 Xc 33
Duagh **IRL** (KER) 97 Qd 34
Dubford **GB** (GRP) 17 Xe 3
Dubhchladach **GB** (STC) 23 Ud 13
Dublin **IRL** (DUB) 95 Te 28
Dublin Pike **IRL** (COR) 104 Rd 37
Duchally **GB** (HGL) 8 Vb 120
Duck End **GB** (ESS) 64 Ac 37
Duckington **GB** (CHS) 44 Xb 30
Ducklington **GB** (OXS) 62 Yd 38
Duck's Cross **GB** (BFS) 55 Zd 35
Duddingston **GB** (LOT) 26 Wf 13
Duddington **GB** (NRH) 55 Zc 33
Duddleswell **GB** (ESX) 71 Aa 42
Duddo **GB** (NHL) 27 Xf 14
Duddon **GB** (CHS) 44 Xb 29
Duddon Bridge **GB** (CUB) 34 We 23
Dudleston Heath **GB** (SHS) 44 Xa 31
Dudley **GB** (TAW) 33 Yc 18
Dudley **GB** (WMD) 53 Xf 33
Duffield **GB** (DSH) 46 Yd 31
Duffryn **GB** (GWE) 60 Wf 39
Duffryn **GB** (WGL) 60 Wb 39
Dufftown **GB** (GRP) 16 Wf 4
Duffus **GB** (GRP) 9 Wd 2
Duffy's Cross Roads **IRL** (KIL) 94 Sf 28
Duffy's Cross Roads **IRL** (LOT) 90 Td 25
Dufton **GB** (CUB) 35 Xd 21
Duggleby **GB** (NOY) 40 Zc 24
Duirinish **GB** (HGL) 13 Ub 5
Duisdalemore **GB** (HGL) 13 Ub 6
Duisky **GB** (HGL) 19 Ue 7
Duke Street **IRL** (KIL) 94 Ta 31
Dukinfield **GB** (GRM) 39 Xf 28
Dulane **IRL** (MT) 89 Ta 26
Dulas **GB** (GWY) 42 Ve 28
Dulcote **GB** (SOM) 68 Xc 41
Duleek **IRL** (MT) 90 Td 27
Dulford **GB** (DEV) 67 We 43
Dull **GB** (TYS) 21 Wa 9
Dullingham **GB** (CBS) 56 Ac 35
Dulnain Bridge **GB** (HGL) 16 Wc 5
Duloe **GB** (CNW) 75 Vd 46
Dulsie **GB** (HGL) 15 Wb 4
Dulverton **GB** (SOM) 67 Wc 42
Dumbarton **GB** (STC) 24 Vc 13
Dumbleton **GB** (GLS) 53 Ya 36
Dumcrieff **GB** (DAG) 31 Wd 17
Dumfin **GB** (STC) 24 Vc 12
Dumfries **GB** (DAG) 31 Wc 18
Dummer **GB** (HAS) 70 Yf 41
Dumnacross **IRL** (DON) 77 Sb 19
Dun **GB** (TYS) 22 Xc 8
Dunaff **IRL** (DON) 78 Sd 17
Dunalastair **GB** (TYS) 20 Vf 8
Dunamon Castle **IRL** (ROS) 88 Re 27
Dunamon Station **IRL** (ROS) 88 Re 27
Dunan **GB** (HGL) 13 Ua 5
Dunan **GB** (STC) 24 Va 13
Dunans **GB** (STC) 24 Uf 12
Dunany House **IRL** (LOT) 90 Te 25
Dunbar **GB** (LOT) 27 Xc 13
Dunbeath **GB** (HGL) 9 Wd 119
Dunbeg **GB** (STC) 19 Ud 10
Dunbell **IRL** (KLK) 100 Sf 33
Dunblane **GB** (CEN) 25 Wa 11
Dunboden Park **IRL** (WMT) 89 Sd 28
Dunbog **GB** (FIF) 21 Wf 10
Dunboyne **IRL** (MT) 95 Td 28
Duncanston **GB** (HGL) 15 Vd 3
Duncanstone **GB** (GRP) 17 Xb 5
Dunchideock **GB** (DEV) 67 Wc 44
Dunchurch **GB** (WWH) 54 Ye 34
Duncormick **IRL** (WEX) 101 Tc 35
Duncote **GB** (NRH) 54 Yf 36
Duncow **GB** (DAG) 31 Wc 18
Duncrievie **GB** (TYS) 21 Wd 11
Duncton **GB** (WSX) 70 Zc 43
Dundalk **IRL** (LOT) 90 Td 24
Dundaryark **IRL** (KLK) 100 Se 33
Dundee **GB** (TYS) 22 Xa 10
Dunderrow **IRL** (COR) 104 Rc 38
Dunderry **IRL** (MT) 90 Tb 27
Dundian Cross Roads **IRL** (MOG) 84 Ta 22
Dundonald **GB** (DOW) 85 Ub 21
Dundonald **GB** (STC) 24 Vc 15
Dundonell **GB** (HGL) 7 Ue 1
Dundoogan **IRL** (GAL) 93 Rd 28
Dundraw **GB** (CUB) 34 We 19
Dundreggan **GB** (HGL) 14 Vb 5
Dundrennan **GB** (DAG) 29 Wa 20
Dundrum **GB** (DOW) 85 Ua 23
Dundrum **IRL** (DUB) 95 Te 29
Dundrum House **IRL** (TIP) 99 Rf 33
Dundry **GB** (AVN) 61 Xc 40
Dundullerick House **IRL** (COR) 99 Re 37
Duneany Cross Roads **IRL** (KIL) 94 Ta 30
Dunecht **GB** (GRP) 17 Xd 5
Dunfanaghy **IRL** (DON) 77 Sa 17
Dunfermline **GB** (FIF) 25 Wd 12
Dungannon **GB** (TYR) 84 Tb 21
Dunganstown **IRL** (WEX) 100 Ta 34
Dungarvan **IRL** (KLK) 100 Sf 33
Dungarvan **IRL** (WTF) 99 Sc 36
Dungavel **GB** (STC) 25 Vf 15
Dungiven **GB** (LDR) 78 Ta 19
Dunglow **IRL** (DON) 77 Rd 19
Dungolman **IRL** (WMT) 93 Sb 28
Dungooly **IRL** (KLK) 100 Se 35
Dungooly Cross Roads **IRL** (LOT) 90 Td 24
Dungourney **IRL** (COR) 104 Rf 37
Dungummin Cross Roads **IRL** (CAV) 89 Se 26
Dungummin House **IRL** (CAV) 89 Se 26
Dunham **GB** (NTS) 46 Zb 29
Dunham-on-the-Hill **GB** (CHS) 44 Xb 29
Dunhampton **GB** (HWC) 53 Xe 35
Dunhill **IRL** (WTF) 100 Se 35
Dunholme **GB** (LIN) 47 Zd 29
Dunipace **GB** (CEN) 25 Wa 12
Dunira **GB** (TYS) 20 Vf 10
Duniry **IRL** (GAL) 93 Rd 30
Duniry River **IRL** (GAL) 93 Rd 30
Dunkeld **GB** (TYS) 21 Wc 9
Dunkerrin **IRL** (OFF) 93 Sa 31
Dunkeswell **GB** (DEV) 67 We 43
Dunkineely **IRL** (DON) 82 Rd 21
Dunkirk **GB** (KEN) 65 Af 41
Dunks Green **GB** (KEN) 72 Ab 41
Dun Laoghaire **IRL** (DUB) 95 Tf 29
Dunlappie **GB** (TYS) 22 Xb 8
Dunlavin **IRL** (WKL) 95 Tb 30
Dunleer **IRL** (LOT) 90 Td 26
Dunlewy **IRL** (DON) 77 Rf 18
Dunley **GB** (HWC) 53 Xe 35
Dunloe Castle **IRL** (KER) 97 Qc 36
Dunlop **GB** (STC) 24 Vc 14
Dunlough **IRL** (MT) 90 Tb 27
Dunloy **GB** (ANT) 79 Td 18
Dunmanus **IRL** (COR) 102 Qb 39
Dunmanway **IRL** (COR) 103 Qf 38
Dunmaurice **IRL** (MOG) 90 Ta 24
Dunmere **GB** (CNW) 75 Vb 46
Dunmore **GB** (CEN) 25 Wb 12
Dunmore **GB** (STC) 23 Uc 14
Dunmore **IRL** (DON) 77 Sc 18
Dunmore **IRL** (GAL) 87 Rb 27
Dunmore East **IRL** (WTF) 100 Ta 36
Dunmurry **GB** (ANT) 85 Tf 21
Dunn's Village **IRL** (GAL) 88 Rd 27
Dunnaloob **IRL** (DON) 83 Sc 20
Dunnamaggan **IRL** (KLK) 100 Se 33
Dunnaman **IRL** (LIM) 98 Rb 33
Dunnamanagh **GB** (TYR) 78 Se 19
Dunnet **GB** (HGL) 6 Wd 117
Dunnichen **GB** (TYS) 22 Xb 9
Dunning **GB** (TYS) 21 Wc 11
Dunnington **GB** (HUS) 41 Ze 25
Dunnington **GB** (NOY) 40 Za 25
Dunnington **GB** (WWH) 53 Ya 35
Dunoon **GB** (STC) 24 Va 13
Dunquin **IRL** (KER) 96 Pd 36
Dunragit **GB** (DAG) 30 Va 18
Dunraymond **IRL** (MOG) 84 Ta 23
Dunrostan **GB** (STC) 23 Uc 13
Duns **GB** (BOR) 27 Xd 14
Dunsandle Station **IRL** (GAL) 92 Rc 29
Dunsany Castle **IRL** (MT) 90 Tc 27
Dunsany Cross Roads **IRL** (MT) 90 Tc 27
Dunsby **GB** (LIN) 47 Zd 32
Dunscore **GB** (DAG) 31 Wb 18
Dunsden Green **GB** (OXS) 63 Za 40
Dunsfold **GB** (SUR) 71 Zc 42
Dunsford **GB** (DEV) 67 Wb 44
Dunshalt **GB** (FIF) 21 We 11
Dunshaughlin **IRL** (MT) 90 Tc 27
Dunsinnan **GB** (TYS) 21 Wd 10
Dunsland Cross **GB** (DEV) 66 Ve 44
Dunsley **GB** (NOY) 37 Zb 22
Dunsmore **GB** (BUS) 63 Zb 38
Dunsop Bridge **GB** (LCS) 38 Xc 25
Dunstable **GB** (BFS) 63 Zc 37
Dunstall **GB** (SFS) 45 Yb 32
Dunstall Green **GB** (SUF) 56 Ad 35
Dunstan **GB** (NHL) 33 Yc 16
Dunster **GB** (SOM) 67 Wd 41
Duns Tew **GB** (OXS) 62 Yd 37
Dunston **GB** (NOR) 57 Bb 33
Dunston **GB** (SFS) 45 Xf 32
Dunston **GB** (TAW) 33 Yc 19
Dunstone **GB** (DEV) 76 We 46
Dunswell **GB** (HUS) 41 Zd 26
Dunsyre **GB** (STC) 25 Wd 14
Dunterton **GB** (DEV) 75 Ve 45
Duntisbourne Abbots **GB** (GLS) 61 Xf 38
Duntisbourne House **GB** (GLS) 62 Xf 38
Duntish **GB** (DOS) 68 Xd 43
Duntocher **GB** (STC) 24 Vd 13
Dunton **GB** (BFS) 55 Ze 36
Dunton **GB** (BUS) 63 Zb 37
Dunton **GB** (NOR) 48 Ae 32
Dunton Bassett **GB** (LEC) 54 Ye 33
Dunton Green **GB** (KEN) 64 Ab 41
Dunton Wayletts **GB** (ESS) 64 Ac 39
Dunure **GB** (STC) 30 Vb 16
Dunvant **GB** (WGL) 59 Vf 39
Dunvegan **GB** (HGL) 12 Tc 4
Dunwick **GB** (SUF) 57 Bd 35
Durdar **GB** (CUB) 32 Xa 19
Durgates **GB** (ESX) 72 Ac 42
Durham **GB** (DUR) 36 Yc 20
Durisdeer **GB** (DAG) 31 Wb 17
Durlas = Thurles **IRL** (TIP) 99 Sb 32
Durleigh **GB** (SOM) 67 Wf 42
Durley **GB** (HAS) 70 Ye 43
Durley **GB** (WIL) 62 Yc 40
Durley Street **GB** (HAS) 70 Ye 43
Durnamuck **GB** (HGL) 7 Ud 1
Durnesh **IRL** (DON) 82 Re 21
Durness **GB** (HGL) 4 Vb 117
Durno **GB** (GRP) 17 Xd 4
Duror **GB** (HGL) 19 Ue 9
Durran **GB** (HGL) 6 Wd 117
Durran **GB** (STC) 23 Ue 11
Durrington **GB** (WIL) 69 Yb 41
Durrington **GB** (WSX) 71 Zd 44
Durrow **IRL** (LAO) 94 Sd 31
Durrow Abbey **IRL** (OFF) 94 Sc 29
Durrow Cross Roads **IRL** (WTF) 100 Sc 36
Durrus **IRL** (COR) 103 Qc 39
Durrus Court **IRL** (COR) 103 Qc 39
Dursley **GB** (GLS) 61 Xd 38
Durston **GB** (SOM) 68 Wf 42
Durweston **GB** (DOS) 69 Xe 43
Dury **GB** (SHL) 2 Ye 107
Duston **GB** (NRH) 54 Za 35
Duthil **GB** (HGL) 15 Wb 5
Dutlas **GB** (POW) 52 We 34
Duxford **GB** (CBS) 56 Aa 36
Dwygyfylchi **GB** (GWY) 43 Wa 29
Dwyran **GB** (GWY) 42 Ve 29
Dyce **GB** (GRP) 17 Xe 5
Dyffryn **GB** (GWY) 42 Vc 29
Dyffryn **GB** (MGL) 60 Wc 39
Dyffryn Ardudwy **GB** (GWY) 42 Vf 32
Dyffryn Ceidrych **GB** (DYF) 59 Wa 37
Dyffryn Cellwen **GB** (POW) 60 Wb 38
Dyke **GB** (GRP) 15 Wb 3
Dyke **GB** (LIN) 47 Zd 32
Dykehead **GB** (CEN) 25 Ve 12
Dykehead **GB** (STC) 25 Wb 14
Dykehead **GB** (TYS) 22 Xa 8
Dykend **GB** (TYS) 21 We 8
Dylife **GB** (POW) 51 Wb 33
Dymchurch **GB** (KEN) 72 Af 42
Dymock **GB** (GLS) 61 Xd 37
Dyrham **GB** (AVN) 61 Xd 40
Dysart **GB** (FIF) 26 Wf 12
Dysart **IRL** (WMT) 89 Sd 28
Dysert **IRL** (KER) 97 Qc 34
Dyserth **GB** (CLW) 43 Wd 29

E

Each Roim = Aughrim **IRL** (WKL) 95 Te 31
Éadan Doire = Edenderry **IRL** (OFF) 94 Sf 28
Eadestown **IRL** (KIL) 95 Tc 29
Eagland Hall **GB** (LCS) 38 Xa 25
Eagle **GB** (LIN) 46 Zb 29
Eaglescliffe **GB** (CLE) 36 Yd 21
Eaglesfield **GB** (CUB) 34 Wc 21
Eaglesfield **GB** (DAG) 31 We 18
Eaglesham **GB** (STC) 25 Ve 14
Eairy **GBM** 29 Vc 24
Eakley **GB** (BUS) 54 Zb 36
Eakring **GB** (NTS) 46 Za 30
Ealand **GB** (HUS) 40 Zb 27
Ealing **GB** (GRL) 64 Ze 40
Earby **GB** (LCS) 39 Xf 25
Eardington **GB** (SHS) 52 Xd 34
Eardisland **GB** (HWC) 52 Xa 35
Eardisley **GB** (HWC) 52 Wf 36
Eardiston **GB** (SHS) 44 Xa 32
Earith **GB** (CBS) 55 Aa 34
Earle **GB** (NHL) 33 Xf 15
Earlestown **GB** (MES) 38 Xc 28
Earlish **GB** (HGL) 13 Td 3
Earls Barton **GB** (NRH) 54 Zb 35
Earls Colne **GB** (ESS) 56 Ae 37
Earl's Common **GB** (HWC) 53 Xf 35
Earlsdon **GB** (WMD) 54 Yc 34
Earlsferry **GB** (FIF) 26 Xa 11
Earlsford **GB** (GRP) 17 Xe 4
Earl's Green **GB** (SUF) 57 Af 35
Earl Shilton **GB** (LEC) 54 Ye 33
Earl Soham **GB** (SUF) 57 Bb 35
Earl Sterndale **GB** (DSH) 45 Ya 29
Earlston **GB** (BOR) 26 Xb 15
Earl Stonham **GB** (SUF) 57 Ba 35
Earlstown **IRL** (GAL) 93 Re 30
Earlswood **GB** (WWH) 53 Yb 34
Earnley **GB** (WSX) 70 Za 44
Earsary **GB** (HGL) 12 Sd 7
Earswick **GB** (NOY) 40 Yf 24
Eartham **GB** (WSX) 70 Zc 43
Easby **GB** (NOY) 37 Yf 22
Easdale **GB** (STC) 19 Uc 11
Easebourne **GB** (WSX) 70 Zb 43
Easenhall **GB** (WWH) 54 Ye 34
Eas Geitine = Askeaton **IRL** (LIM) 98 Ra 33
Easington **GB** (BUS) 63 Yf 38
Easington **GB** (CLE) 37 Za 21
Easington **GB** (HUS) 41 Aa 27
Easington **GB** (NHL) 27 Yb 15
Easington **GB** (TAW) 36 Yd 20
Easington Colliery **GB** (DUR) 36 Ye 20
Easingwold **GB** (NOY) 37 Ye 24
Easky **IRL** (SLI) 81 Ra 23
Easole Street **GB** (KEN) 65 Bb 41
Eason's Green **GB** (ESX) 71 Aa 43
Eassie **GB** (TYS) 21 Wf 9
East Aberthaw **GB** (SGL) 60 Wd 40
East Allington **GB** (DEV) 76 Wb 47
East Anstey **GB** (DEV) 67 Wc 42
East Ashey **GB** (IOW) 70 Ye 44
East Ashling **GB** (WSX) 70 Za 43
East Barkwith **GB** (LIN) 47 Ze 29
East Barnet **GB** (GRL) 64 Zf 39
East Barsham **GB** (NOR) 48 Af 31
East Beckham **GB** (NOR) 49 Bb 31
East Bergholt **GB** (SUF) 57 Ba 37
East Bilney **GB** (NOR) 49 Af 32
East Blatchington **GB** (ESX) 71 Aa 44
East Boldre **GB** (HAS) 69 Yd 44
Eastbourne **GB** (ESX) 72 Ab 44
East Bradenham **GB** (NOR) 48 Af 33
East Brent **GB** (SOM) 68 Xa 41
Eastbridge **GB** (SUF) 57 Bd 35
East Bridgford **GB** (NTS) 46 Za 31
East Buckland **GB** (DEV) 66 Wa 42
East Burrafirth **GB** (SHL) 2 Yd 107
East Burton **GB** (DOS) 68 Xe 44
Eastbury **GB** (BKS) 62 Yc 40
East Calder **GB** (LOT) 25 Wd 13
East Carleton **GB** (NOR) 57 Bb 33
East Chaldon, Chaldon Herning or **GB** (DOS) 68 Xe 45
East Challow **GB** (OXS) 62 Yd 39
East Chinnock **GB** (SOM) 68 Xb 43
East Chisenbury **GB** (WIL) 69 Yb 41
Eastchurch **GB** (KEN) 65 Af 40
East Clandon **GB** (SUR) 71 Zd 41
East Claydon **GB** (BUS) 63 Za 37
East Coker **GB** (SOM) 68 Xc 43
Eastcombe **GB** (GLS) 61 Xf 38
East Combe **GB** (SOM) 67 We 42
Eastcote **GB** (GRL) 64 Zd 39
Eastcote **GB** (NRH) 54 Yf 35
Eastcote **GB** (WMD) 53 Yb 34
Eastcott **GB** (DEV) 66 Vd 43
Eastcott **GB** (WIL) 69 Ya 41
East Cottingwith **GB** (HUS) 40 Za 25
Eastcourt **GB** (WIL) 62 Xf 39
East Cowes **GB** (IOW) 70 Ye 44
East Cowton **GB** (NOY) 36 Yc 22
East Creech **GB** (DOS) 69 Xf 45
East Croachy **GB** (HGL) 15 Ve 5
East Dean **GB** (ESX) 72 Ab 44
East Dean **GB** (HAS) 69 Yc 42
East Dean **GB** (WSX) 70 Zb 43
East Dereham **GB** (NOR) 49 Af 32
East Down **GB** (DEV) 66 Vf 42
East End **GB** (DOS) 69 Ya 44
East End **GB** (HAS) 62 Yd 40
East End **GB** (HAS) 69 Yd 44
East End **GB** (HTS) 64 Aa 37
East End **GB** (KEN) 72 Ad 42
East End **GB** (OXS) 62 Yd 38
Easter Ardross **GB** (HGL) 8 Ve 2
Easter Balmoral **GB** (GRP) 16 We 6
Easter Boleskine **GB** (HGL) 15 Vd 5
Easter Compton **GB** (AVN) 61 Xc 39
Easterfield **IRL** (GAL) 93 Rd 30
Easter Galcantray **GB** (HGL) 15 Wa 3
Eastergate **GB** (WSX) 70 Zc 43
Easterhouse **GB** (STC) 25 Vf 13
Easter Kinkell **GB** (HGL) 15 Vd 3
Easter Lednathie **GB** (TYS) 21 Wf 8
Easter Moniack **GB** (HGL) 15 Vd 4
Easter Muckovie **GB** (HGL) 15 Vf 4
Eastern Green **GB** (WMD) 53 Yc 34
Easter Ord **GB** (GRP) 17 Xe 6
Easter Quarff **GB** (SHL) 3 Ye 108
Easter Skeld **GB** (SHL) 2 Yd 107
Easter Suddie **GB** (HGL) 15 Ve 3
Eastertown **GB** (SOM) 68 Xa 41
Easter Whyntie **GB** (GRP) 17 Xc 2
East Farleigh **GB** (KEN) 65 Ac 41
East Farndon **GB** (NRH) 54 Za 34
East Ferry **GB** (LIN) 40 Zb 28
Eastfield **GB** (NOY) 37 Zd 23
Eastfield Hall **GB** (NHL) 33 Yc 16
East Garston **GB** (BKS) 62 Yd 40
Eastgate **GB** (DUR) 36 Xf 20
Eastgate **GB** (NOR) 49 Bb 32
East Ginge **GB** (OXS) 62 Yd 39
East Goscote **GB** (LEC) 46 Yf 32
East Grafton **GB** (WIL) 62 Yc 40
East Grimstead **GB** (WIL) 69 Yb 42
East Grinstead **GB** (WSX) 71 Zf 42
East Guldeford **GB** (ESX) 72 Ae 43
East Haddon **GB** (NRH) 54 Yf 35
East Hagbourne **GB** (OXS) 62 Ye 39
East Halton **GB** (HUS) 41 Ze 27
Eastham **GB** (CHS) 44 Xa 29
East Hanney **GB** (OXS) 62 Yd 39
East Hanningfield **GB** (ESS) 65 Ad 38
East Hardwick **GB** (WYO) 40 Ye 27
East Harling **GB** (NOR) 56 Af 34
East Harlsey **GB** (NOY) 36 Yd 22
East Harptree **GB** (AVN) 68 Xc 41
East Harting **GB** (WSX) 70 Za 43
East Hatley **GB** (CBS) 55 Zf 36
East Hauxwell **GB** (NOY) 36 Yb 22
Eastheath **GB** (BKS) 63 Za 40
East Heckington **GB** (LIN) 47 Ze 31
East Hendred **GB** (OXS) 62 Yd 39
East Heslerton **GB** (NOY) 37 Zc 23
East Hoathly **GB** (ESX) 71 Ab 43
Easthope **GB** (SHS) 52 Xc 33
East Horndon **GB** (ESS) 64 Ac 39
Easthorpe **GB** (ESS) 65 Ae 37
East Horrington **GB** (SOM) 68 Xc 41
East Horsley **GB** (SUR) 71 Zd 41
Easthouses **GB** (LOT) 26 Wf 13
East Ilsley **GB** (BKS) 62 Ye 39
Eastington **GB** (GLS) 62 Yb 38
East Keal **GB** (LIN) 47 Aa 30
East Keswick **GB** (WYO) 40 Yd 25
East Kilbride **GB** (STC) 25 Ve 14
East Kirkby **GB** (LIN) 47 Zf 30
East Knighton **GB** (DOS) 68 Xe 44
East Knoyle **GB** (WIL) 69 Xf 42
East Lambrook **GB** (SOM) 68 Xb 43
East Lamington **GB** (HGL) 8 Vf 2
East Langdon **GB** (KEN) 73 Bb 41
East Langton **GB** (LEC) 54 Za 33
East Langwell **GB** (HGL) 8 Vf 120
East Lavant **GB** (WSX) 70 Zb 43
East Layton **GB** (NOY) 36 Yb 22
Eastleach Martin **GB** (GLS) 62 Yb 38
East Leake **GB** (NTS) 46 Ye 32
East Leigh **GB** (DEV) 67 Wa 44
Eastleigh **GB** (HAS) 70 Yd 43
East Lexham **GB** (NOR) 48 Ae 32
East Lilburn **GB** (NHL) 33 Ya 15
Eastling **GB** (KEN) 65 Ae 41
East Linton **GB** (LOT) 26 Xc 13
East Liss **GB** (HAS) 70 Za 42
East Looe **GB** (CNW) 75 Vd 46
East Lulworth **GB** (DOS) 69 Xe 45
East Lydford **GB** (SOM) 68 Xc 42
East Mains **GB** (GRP) 17 Xc 6
East Malling **GB** (KEN) 65 Ac 41
East Marden **GB** (WSX) 70 Za 43
East Markham **GB** (NTS) 46 Za 29
East Marton **GB** (NOY) 39 Xf 25
East Meon **GB** (HAS) 70 Yf 43
East Mersea **GB** (ESS) 65 Af 38
East Molesey **GB** (SUR) 64 Zd 40
East Morden **GB** (DOS) 69 Xf 44
East Morton **GB** (WYO) 39 Ya 25
Eastnor **GB** (HWC) 53 Xd 36
East Norton **GB** (LEC) 54 Zb 33
East Oakley **GB** (HAS) 70 Ye 41
Eastoft **GB** (HUS) 40 Zb 27
Easton **GB** (CBS) 55 Ze 35
Easton **GB** (CUB) 32 Xa 18
Easton **GB** (DEV) 67 Wb 44
Easton **GB** (DOS) 68 Xd 45
Easton **GB** (HAS) 69 Yc 44
Easton **GB** (HAS) 70 Ye 42

116 GB IRL Dooncarton – Easton

Easton **GB** (LIN) 47 Zc 32
Easton **GB** (NOR) 49 Ba 33
Easton **GB** (SOM) 68 Xb 41
Easton **GB** (SUF) 57 Bc 35
Easton **GB** (WIL) 61 Xf 40
Easton Grey **GB** (WIL) 61 Xe 39
Easton-in-Gordano **GB** (AVN) 61 Xb 40
Easton on the Hill **GB** (NRH) 55 Zc 33
East Ord **GB** (NHL) 27 Xf 14
East Peckham **GB** (KEN) 72 Ac 41
East Pennard **GB** (SOM) 68 Xc 42
East Portlemouth **GB** (DEV) 76 Wb 47
East Prawle **GB** (DEV) 76 Wb 47
East Preston **GB** (WSX) 71 Zd 44
East Putford **GB** (DEV) 66 Ve 43
East Ravendale **GB** (HUS) 41 Zf 28
East Raynham **GB** (NOR) 48 Ae 32
Eastrea **GB** (CBS) 55 Zf 33
East Retford **GB** (NTS) 46 Za 29
Eastriggs **GB** (DAG) 31 We 19
Eastrington **GB** (HUS) 40 Zb 26
East Rolstone **GB** (AVN) 61 Xa 40
East Rounton **GB** (NOY) 36 Yd 22
East Rudham **GB** (NOR) 48 Ae 32
East Ruston **GB** (NOR) 49 Bc 32
Eastry **GB** (KEN) 65 Bb 41
East Saltoun **GB** (LOT) 26 Xa 13
East Shefford **GB** (BKS) 62 Yd 40
East Somerton **GB** (NOR) 49 Be 32
East Stockwith **GB** (LIN) 40 Zb 28
East Stoke **GB** (NTS) 46 Za 30
East Stour **GB** (DOR) 68 Xe 42
East Stourmouth **GB** (KEN) 65 Bb 41
East Stratton **GB** (HAS) 70 Ye 42
East Studdal **GB** (KEN) 73 Bb 41
East Taphouse **GB** (CNW) 75 Vc 46
East-The-Water **GB** (DEV) 66 Ve 42
East Tilbury **GB** (ESS) 65 Ac 40
East Tisted **GB** (HAS) 70 Za 42
East Torrington **GB** (LIN) 47 Ze 28
East Town **IRL** (DON) 77 Re 17
East Tuddenham **GB** (NOR) 49 Ba 33
East Tytherley **GB** (HAS) 69 Yc 42
East Tytherton **GB** (WIL) 61 Xf 40
East Village **GB** (DEV) 67 Wc 44
East Wall **GB** (SHS) 52 Xb 33
East Walton **GB** (NOR) 48 Ad 32
Eastwell **GB** (LEC) 46 Za 31
East Wellow **GB** (HAS) 69 Yc 43
East Wemyss **GB** (FIF) 26 Wf 12
East Whitburn **GB** (LOT) 25 Wc 13
Eastwick **GB** (HTS) 64 Aa 38
East Wickham **GB** (GRL) 64 Aa 40
East Williamston **GB** (DYF) 58 Vb 38
East Winch **GB** (NOR) 48 Ad 32
East Wittering **GB** (WSX) 70 Za 44
East Witton **GB** (NOY) 36 Yb 23
Eastwood **GB** (NTS) 46 Ye 30
Eastwood **GB** (WYO) 39 Xf 26
East Woodhay **GB** (HAS) 62 Yd 40
East Worldham **GB** (HAS) 70 Za 42
East Worlington **GB** (DEV) 67 Wb 43
Eathorpe **GB** (WWH) 54 Yd 35
Eaton **GB** (CHS) 44 Xc 30
Eaton **GB** (CHS) 45 Xe 29
Eaton **GB** (LEC) 46 Zb 31
Eaton **GB** (NOR) 57 Bb 33
Eaton **GB** (NTS) 46 Za 29
Eaton **GB** (OXS) 62 Yd 38
Eaton Bishop **GB** (HWC) 52 Xb 36
Eaton Bray **GB** (BUS) 63 Zc 37
Eaton Constantine **GB** (SHS) 52 Xc 33
Eaton Green **GB** (BFS) 63 Zc 37
Eaton Hall **GB** (CHS) 44 Xa 30
Eaton Hastings **GB** (OXS) 62 Yc 38
Eaton Socon **GB** (CBS) 55 Ze 35
Eaton upon Tern **GB** (SHS) 44 Xc 32
Ebberston **GB** (NOY) 37 Zc 23
Ebbesbourne Wake **GB** (WIL) 69 Xf 42
Ebbw Vale **GB** (GWE) 60 We 38
Ebchester **GB** (DUR) 33 Ya 19
Ebford **GB** (DEV) 67 Wd 44
Ebrington **GB** (GLS) 53 Yb 36
Ecchinswell **GB** (HAS) 62 Ye 41
Ecclefechan **GB** (DAG) 31 We 18
Eccles **GB** (BOR) 27 Xd 15
Eccles **GB** (GRM) 39 Xd 28
Eccles **GB** (KEN) 65 Ac 41
Ecclesfield **GB** (SOY) 40 Yd 28
Ecclesgreig **GB** (GRP) 22 Xd 8
Eccleshall **GB** (SFS) 45 Xe 31
Ecclesmachan **GB** (LOT) 25 Wc 13
Eccles Road **GB** (NOR) 56 Af 34
Eccleston **GB** (CHS) 44 Xa 30
Eccleston **GB** (LCS) 38 Xb 27
Eccleston **GB** (MES) 38 Xb 28
Eccup **GB** (WYO) 39 Yc 25
Ecelaw **GB** (BOR) 27 Xd 13
Echt **GB** (GRP) 17 Xd 6
Eckford **GB** (BOR) 32 Xd 15
Eckington **GB** (DSH) 46 Yd 29
Eckington **GB** (HWC) 53 Xf 36
Ecton **GB** (NRH) 54 Zb 35
Edale **GB** (DSH) 45 Yb 28
Edburton **GB** (WSX) 71 Ze 43
Edderside **GB** (CUB) 34 Wd 20
Edderton **GB** (HGL) 8 Vf 1
Eddington **GB** (BKS) 62 Yd 40
Eddleston **GB** (BOR) 26 We 14
Edenaneane **IRL** (MOG) 89 Ta 24
Edenbridge **GB** (KEN) 71 Aa 41
Edenderry **IRL** (OFF) 94 Sf 28
Edenfield **GB** (LCS) 39 Xe 26
Edenhall **GB** (CUB) 35 Xb 20
Edenham **GB** (LIN) 47 Zd 32
Edenmore **IRL** (LGF) 89 Sc 25
Edenthorpe **GB** (SOY) 40 Yf 27
Ederglen **IRL** (MAY) 80 Qb 23
Edergole **IRL** (LET) 88 Sb 25
Edern **GB** (GWY) 42 Vc 31
Ederny **GB** (FER) 83 Sc 21
Edgarley **GB** (SOM) 68 Xb 42
Edgbaston **GB** (WMD) 53 Ya 34
Edgcott **GB** (BUS) 63 Yf 37
Edgcumbe **GB** (CNW) 74 Ue 48
Edge **GB** (GLS) 61 Xe 38
Edge **GB** (SHS) 52 Xa 32
Edgebolton **GB** (SHS) 44 Xc 32
Edgefield **GB** (NOR) 49 Ba 31
Edgeworth **GB** (GLS) 61 Xf 38
Edgeworthstown **IRL** (LGF) 89 Sc 26
Edgmont **GB** (SHS) 44 Xd 32
Edgton **GB** (SHS) 52 Xa 34
Edgware **GB** (GRL) 64 Ze 39
Edgworth **GB** (LCS) 38 Xd 27
Edial **GB** (SFS) 53 Ya 32
Edinbane **GB** (HGL) 13 Td 4
Edinburgh **GB** (LOT) 26 We 13
Edingale **GB** (SFS) 53 Yb 32
Edington **GB** (SOM) 68 Xa 42
Edington **GB** (WIL) 69 Xf 41
Edithmead **GB** (SOM) 68 Xa 41
Edith Weston **GB** (LEC) 55 Zc 33
Edlesborough **GB** (BFS) 63 Zc 37
Edlingham **GB** (NHL) 33 Yb 16
Edlington **GB** (LIN) 47 Zf 29
Edmondsham **GB** (DOS) 69 Ya 43
Edmondsley **GB** (DUR) 33 Yc 19
Edmondstown **IRL** (LOT) 90 Tc 25
Edmondstown **IRL** (ROS) 88 Rc 25
Edmonton **GB** (GRL) 64 Zf 39
Edmundbyers **GB** (DUR) 33 Ya 19
Ednam **GB** (BOR) 27 Xd 15
Ednaston **GB** (DSH) 45 Yc 31
Edney Common **GB** (ESS) 64 Ac 38
Edrom **GB** (BOR) 27 Xe 14
Edstaston **GB** (SHS) 44 Xb 31
Edwardstone **GB** (SUF) 56 Af 36
Edwinsford **GB** (DYF) 59 Wa 37
Edwinstone **GB** (NTS) 46 Za 29
Edwyn Ralph **GB** (HWC) 52 Xc 35
Edzell **GB** (TYS) 22 Xc 8
Efail Isaf **GB** (MGL) 60 We 39
Efailnewydd **GB** (GWY) 42 Vd 31
Efailwen **GB** (DYF) 58 Vb 37
Efenechtyd **GB** (CLW) 43 Wd 30
Effernan **IRL** (CRE) 98 Qe 33
Effingham **GB** (SUR) 71 Zd 41
Effirth **GB** (SHL) 2 Yd 107
Effishmore **IRL** (DON) 78 Sd 17
Efford **GB** (DEV) 67 Wc 44
Egbury **GB** (HAS) 70 Yd 41
Egdean **GB** (WSX) 71 Zc 43
Egerton **GB** (GRM) 38 Xd 27
Egerton **GB** (KEN) 72 Ac 41
Egerton Green **GB** (CHS) 44 Xb 30
Eggborough **GB** (NOY) 40 Yf 26
Egginton **GB** (DSH) 45 Yc 31
Egglescliffe **GB** (CLE) 36 Yd 21
Eggleston **GB** (DUR) 36 Ya 21
Egleton **GB** (LEC) 55 Zb 33
Eglingham **GB** (NHL) 33 Yb 16
Eglinton **GB** (LDR) 78 Se 18
Eglish Castle **IRL** (OFF) 93 Sa 30
Eglish Stiloga **GB** (TYR) 84 Tb 22
Egloshayle **GB** (CNW) 75 Vb 45
Egloskerry **GB** (CNW) 66 Vd 45
Eglwysbach **GB** (GWY) 43 Wb 29
Eglwys-Brewis **GB** (SGL) 60 Wd 40
Eglwys Cross **GB** (CLW) 44 Xb 31
Eglwys Fach **GB** (DYF) 51 Wa 33
Eglwyswrw **GB** (DYF) 58 Vb 36
Egmanton **GB** (NTS) 46 Za 29
Egmere **GB** (NOR) 48 Ae 31
Egremont **GB** (CUB) 34 Wc 22
Egton **GB** (NOY) 37 Zb 22
Egton Bridge **GB** (NOY) 37 Zb 22
Egypt **GB** (HAS) 70 Ye 42
Eight Ash Green **GB** (ESS) 65 Ae 37
Eighter **IRL** (CAV) 89 Sf 26
Eighter **IRL** (MAY) 87 Qd 24
Eightercua **IRL** (KER) 102 Pf 38
Eilanreach **GB** (HGL) 13 Uc 5
Eilean Darach **GB** (HGL) 7 Ue 1
Eilean Iarmain, Isleornsay or **GB** (HGL) 13 Ub 6
Eisfield **GB** (OXS) 62 Ye 38
Eishken **GB** (HGL) 11 Tc 120
Eisingrug **GB** (GWY) 43 Vf 31
Elan Village **GB** (POW) 51 Wc 35
Elberton **GB** (AVN) 61 Xc 39
Elcombe **GB** (WIL) 62 Yb 39
Eldersfield **GB** (HWC) 61 Xe 37
Elderslie **GB** (STC) 24 Vd 14
Eldroth **GB** (NOY) 38 Xd 24
Elford **GB** (NHL) 27 Yb 15
Elford **GB** (SFS) 53 Yb 32
Elgin **GB** (GRP) 16 We 3
Elgol **GB** (HGL) 13 Tf 6
Elham **GB** (KEN) 73 Ba 42
Elie **GB** (FIF) 26 Xb 11
Elim **GB** (GWY) 42 Vd 29
Eling **GB** (HAS) 69 Yd 43
Elishader **GB** (HGL) 13 Te 3
Elishaw **GB** (NHL) 32 Xe 17
Elkesley **GB** (NTS) 46 Za 29
Elkstone **GB** (GLS) 61 Xf 38
Elland **GB** (WYO) 39 Ya 26
Ellary **GB** (STC) 23 Uc 13
Ellastone **GB** (SFS) 45 Yb 31
Ellemford **GB** (BOR) 27 Xd 13
Ellenhall **GB** (SFS) 45 Xe 32
Ellen's Green **GB** (SUR) 71 Zd 42
Ellerbeck **GB** (NOY) 36 Ye 22
Ellerby **GB** (NOY) 37 Zb 21
Ellerdine Heath **GB** (SHS) 44 Xc 32
Elleric **GB** (STC) 19 Ue 9
Ellerker **GB** (HUS) 41 Zc 26
Ellerton **GB** (HUS) 40 Za 25
Ellesmere **GB** (SHS) 44 Xa 31
Ellesmere Port **GB** (CHS) 44 Xa 29
Ellingham **GB** (HAS) 69 Yb 43
Ellingham **GB** (NHL) 33 Yb 15
Ellingham **GB** (NOR) 57 Bc 34
Ellingstring **GB** (NOY) 36 Yb 23
Ellington **GB** (CBS) 55 Ze 35
Ellington **GB** (NHL) 33 Yc 17
Ellisfield **GB** (HAS) 70 Yf 41
Ellistown **GB** (LEC) 54 Yd 32
Ellistrin **IRL** (DON) 77 Sb 19
Ellon **GB** (GRP) 17 Xf 4
Ellough **GB** (SUF) 57 Bd 34
Elloughton **GB** (HUS) 41 Zc 26
Ellwood **GB** (GLS) 61 Xc 38
Elm **GB** (CBS) 56 Ab 33
Elmbridge **GB** (HWC) 53 Xf 35
Elmdon **GB** (ESS) 56 Aa 36
Elmdon Heath **GB** (WMD) 53 Yb 34
Elm Hill **IRL** (LIM) 98 Qf 33
Elmhurst **GB** (SFS) 53 Yb 32
Elmley Castle **GB** (HWC) 53 Xf 36
Elmley Lovett **GB** (HWC) 53 Xe 35
Elmore **GB** (GLS) 61 Xe 38
Elm Park **GB** (GRL) 64 Ab 39
Elm Park House **IRL** (LIM) 98 Rb 33
Elmscott **GB** (DEV) 66 Vc 43
Elmsett **GB** (SUF) 57 Af 36
Elmsted **GB** (KEN) 72 Ba 41
Elmstone **GB** (KEN) 65 Bb 41
Elmstone Hardwicke **GB** 61 Xf 37
Elmswell **GB** (SUF) 56 Af 35
Elmton **GB** (DSH) 46 Ye 29
Elphin **GB** (HGL) 7 Ue 120
Elphin **IRL** (ROS) 88 Re 25
Elphinstone **GB** (LOT) 26 Xa 13
Elrick **GB** (GRP) 17 Xe 6
Elrig **GB** (DAG) 29 Vc 20
Elsdon **GB** (NHL) 33 Xf 17
Elsecar **GB** (SOY) 40 Yd 28
Elsenham **GB** (ESS) 64 Ab 37
Elsham **GB** (HUS) 41 Zd 27
Elsing **GB** (NOR) 49 Ba 32
Elslack **GB** (NOY) 39 Xf 25
Elsrickle **GB** (STC) 25 Wd 14
Elstead **GB** (SUR) 70 Zb 41
Elsted **GB** (WSX) 70 Za 43
Elsthorpe **GB** (LIN) 47 Zd 32
Elston **GB** (NTS) 46 Za 30
Elstone **GB** (DEV) 66 Wa 43
Elstow **GB** (BFS) 55 Zd 36
Elstree **GB** (GRL) 64 Ze 39
Elstronwick **GB** (HUS) 41 Zf 26
Elswick **GB** (LCS) 38 Xa 25
Elsworth **GB** (CBS) 55 Zf 35
Elterwater **GB** (CUB) 34 Wf 22
Eltham **GB** (GRL) 64 Aa 40
Eltisley **GB** (CBS) 55 Zf 35
Elton **GB** (CBS) 55 Zd 33
Elton **GB** (CHS) 44 Xb 29
Elton **GB** (DSH) 45 Yc 30
Elton **GB** (GLS) 61 Xd 38
Elton **GB** (HWC) 52 Xb 35
Elton **GB** (NTS) 46 Za 31
Elton **IRL** (LIM) 98 Rd 34
Elvanfoot **GB** (STC) 31 Wc 16
Elveden **GB** (SUF) 56 Ae 34
Elvingston **GB** (LOT) 26 Xa 13
Elvington **GB** (KEN) 65 Bb 41
Elvington **GB** (NOY) 40 Za 25
Elwick **GB** (CLE) 36 Ye 20
Elwick **GB** (NHL) 27 Yb 15
Elworth **GB** (CHS) 44 Xd 30
Elworthy **GB** (SOM) 67 We 42
Ely **GB** (CBS) 56 Ab 34
Embleton **GB** (CUB) 34 We 21
Embleton **GB** (NHL) 33 Yc 16
Embo **GB** (HGL) 9 Wa 1
Emborough **GB** (SOM) 68 Xc 41
Embsay **GB** (NOY) 39 Ya 25
Emery Down **GB** (HAS) 69 Yc 43
Emil **IRL** (KLK) 100 Se 35
Emlagh **IRL** (GAL) 86 Pf 27
Emlagh **IRL** (KER) 96 Pd 35
Emlagh **IRL** (KER) 96 Pe 37
Emlagh **IRL** (ROS) 88 Re 27
Emlagh Cross Roads **IRL** (GAL) 92 Rb 29
Emlaghdauroe **IRL** (GAL) 86 Qa 28
Emlaghdreenagh **IRL** (KER) 102 Pe 37
Emley **GB** (WYO) 39 Yc 27
Emly **IRL** (TIP) 99 Rd 34
Emmoo **IRL** (ROS) 88 Rf 27
Emneth **GB** (NOR) 56 Ab 33
Emo **IRL** (LAO) 94 Se 30
Emper **IRL** (WMT) 89 Sc 27
Emper Lodge **IRL** (WMT) 89 Sc 27
Empshott **GB** (HAS) 70 Za 42
Emsworth **GB** (HAS) 70 Za 43
Emyvale **IRL** (MOG) 84 Ta 22
Enaclete **GB** (HGL) 11 Ta 120
Enagh **IRL** (CRE) 92 Rb 32
Enborne **GB** (BKS) 62 Yd 40
Enchmarsh **GB** (SHS) 52 Xb 33
Enderby **GB** (LEC) 54 Ye 33
Endmoor **GB** (CUB) 35 Xb 23
Endon **GB** (SFS) 45 Xf 30
Enfield **GB** (GRL) 64 Zf 39
Enford **GB** (WIL) 69 Yb 41
Engine Common **GB** (AVN) 61 Xd 39
Englefield **GB** (BKS) 63 Yf 40
Englefield Green **GB** (SUR) 63 Zc 40
Engleseabrook **GB** (CHS) 45 Xd 30
English Bicknor **GB** (GLS) 61 Xc 38
Englishcombe **GB** (AVN) 61 Xd 40
English Frankton **GB** (SHS) 44 Xb 31
Englishtown **IRL** (GAL) 88 Rc 27
Enham Alamein **GB** (HAS) 69 Yd 41
Ennerdale Bridge **GB** (CUB) 34 Wc 21
Ennis **IRL** (CRE) 92 Ra 31
Enniscorthy **IRL** (WEX) 101 Tc 33
Enniskean **IRL** (COR) 103 Ra 38
Enniskillen **GB** (FER) 83 Sc 22
Ennistimon **IRL** (CRE) 92 Qe 31
Enochdhu **GB** (TYS) 21 Wc 8
Ensay **GB** (STC) 18 Te 9
Ensdon **GB** (SHS) 44 Xa 32
Ensis **GB** (DEV) 66 Vf 42
Enstone **GB** (OXS) 62 Yd 37
Enville **GB** (SFS) 53 Xe 34
Eochar **GB** (HGL) 12 Sd 4
Eoligary **GB** (HGL) 12 Sd 6
Epingham **GB** (LEC) 55 Zc 33
Epperstone **GB** (NTS) 46 Yf 30
Epping **GB** (ESS) 64 Aa 38
Epping Green **GB** (ESS) 64 Aa 38
Epping Green **GB** (HTS) 64 Zf 38
Epping Upland **GB** (ESS) 64 Aa 38
Eppleby **GB** (NOY) 36 Yb 21
Epsom **GB** (SUR) 64 Ze 40
Epwell **GB** (OXS) 54 Yd 36
Epworth **GB** (HUS) 40 Zb 27
Erbistock **GB** (CLW) 44 Xa 31
Erbusaig **GB** (HGL) 13 Ub 5
Erdington **GB** (WMD) 53 Yb 33
Eredine **GB** (STC) 23 Ue 11
Eriboll **GB** (HGL) 4 Vb 118
Ericstane **GB** (DAG) 31 Wd 16
Erines **GB** (STC) 23 Ud 13
Eriswell **GB** (SUF) 56 Ad 34
Erith **GB** (GRL) 64 Ab 40
Erlestoke **GB** (WIL) 69 Xf 41
Ermington **GB** (DEV) 76 Wa 46
Erpingham **GB** (NOR) 49 Bb 31
Erra **IRL** (ROS) 88 Sa 26
Errill **IRL** (LAO) 93 Sb 31
Errol **GB** (TYS) 21 We 10
Erskine **GB** (STC) 24 Vd 13
Ervie **GB** (DAG) 28 Uf 18
Erwarton **GB** (SUF) 57 Bb 37
Erwood **GB** (POW) 51 We 36
Eryholme **GB** (NOY) 36 Yc 22
Eryrys **GB** (CLW) 44 We 30
Escart **GB** (STC) 23 Ud 14
Escrick **GB** (NOY) 40 Yf 25
Esgairgeiliog **GB** (POW) 51 Wb 33
Esgair **GB** (DYF) 59 Vd 37
Esh **GB** (DUR) 36 Yb 20
Esher **GB** (SUR) 64 Zd 40
Eshott **GB** (NHL) 33 Yb 17
Esh Winning **GB** (DUR) 36 Yb 20
Eskadale **GB** (HGL) 15 Vc 4
Eskdale Green **GB** (CUB) 34 We 22
Eskdalemuir **GB** (DAG) 31 We 17
Esker **IRL** (GAL) 92 Rb 29
Eskeragh Bridge **IRL** (MAY) 81 Qd 24
Eskerbaun **IRL** (ROS) 88 Rf 28
Eskerville **IRL** (GAL) 88 Rd 28
Eskham **GB** (LIN) 41 Aa 28
Esknish **GB** (STC) 22 Te 14
Eskragh **IRL** (SLI) 87 Rb 24
Eslinbridge **IRL** (LET) 88 Sa 25
Espley Hall **GB** (NHL) 33 Yb 17
Esprick **GB** (LCS) 38 Xa 26
Essendine **GB** (LEC) 47 Zd 32
Essendon **GB** (HTS) 64 Zf 38
Essexford **IRL** (LOT) 90 Tc 25
Essich **GB** (HGL) 15 Ve 4
Essington **GB** (SFS) 53 Xf 33
Esslemont **GB** (GRP) 17 Xf 4
Eston **GB** (CLE) 37 Yf 21
Etal **GB** (NHL) 27 Xf 15
Etchilhampton **GB** (WIL) 62 Ya 40
Etchingham **GB** (ESX) 72 Ac 42
Etchinghill **GB** (KEN) 73 Ba 42
Etherley **GB** (DUR) 36 Yb 21
Ethie Mains **GB** (TYS) 22 Xd 9
Eton **GB** (BKS) 63 Zc 40
Ettington **GB** (WWH) 53 Yc 36
Etton **GB** (CBS) 55 Ze 33
Etton **GB** (HUS) 41 Zc 25
Ettrickbridge **GB** (BOR) 32 Xa 15
Etwall **GB** (DSH) 45 Yc 31
Europie **GB** (HGL) 11 Te 117
Euston **GB** (SUF) 56 Ae 34
Euxton **GB** (LCS) 38 Xb 26
Evanton **GB** (HGL) 15 Ve 2
Evenjobb **GB** (POW) 52 Wf 35
Evenley **GB** (NRH) 54 Yf 36
Evenlode **GB** (GLS) 62 Yb 37
Evenwood **GB** (DUR) 36 Yb 21
Everbay **GB** (ORK) 5 Xc 114
Evercreech **GB** (SOM) 68 Xc 42
Everdon **GB** (NRH) 54 Yf 35
Everingham **GB** (HUS) 40 Zb 25
Everleigh **GB** (WIL) 69 Yb 41
Everley **GB** (HGL) 6 Wf 117
Everley **GB** (NOY) 37 Zd 23
Eversholt **GB** (BFS) 55 Zc 37
Evershot **GB** (DOS) 68 Xc 43
Eversley **GB** (HAS) 63 Za 40
Eversley Cross **GB** (HAS) 63 Za 40
Everton **GB** (BFS) 55 Ze 36
Everton **GB** (HAS) 69 Yc 44
Everton **GB** (NTS) 40 Za 28
Evertown **GB** (DAG) 32 Wf 18
Evesbatch **GB** (HWC) 52 Xd 36
Evesham **GB** (HWC) 53 Ya 36
Evington **GB** (LEC) 54 Yf 33
Ewell **GB** (SUR) 64 Ze 40
Ewelme **GB** (OXS) 63 Yf 39
Ewenny **GB** (MGL) 60 Wc 40
Ewerby Thorpe **GB** (LIN) 47 Ze 30
Ewhurst **GB** (SUR) 71 Zd 42
Ewhurst Green **GB** (ESX) 72 Ad 43
Ewhurst Green **GB** (SUR) 71 Zd 42
Ewloe **GB** (CLW) 44 Wf 29
Eworthy **GB** (DEV) 66 Ve 44
Ewshot **GB** (WIL) 70 Zb 41
Ewyas Harold **GB** (HWC) 60 Xa 37
Exbourne **GB** (DEV) 66 Wa 44
Exbury **GB** (HAS) 70 Yd 44
Exebridge **GB** (SOM) 67 Wc 42
Exelby **GB** (NOY) 36 Yc 23
Exeter **GB** (DEV) 67 Wc 44
Exford **GB** (SOM) 67 Wc 42
Exhall **GB** (WWH) 53 Ya 35
Exlade Street **GB** (OXS) 63 Yf 39
Exminster **GB** (DEV) 67 Wd 44
Exmouth **GB** (DEV) 67 Wd 45
Exning **GB** (SUF) 56 Ac 35
Exton **GB** (DEV) 67 Wd 44
Exton **GB** (HAS) 70 Yf 43
Exton **GB** (LEC) 55 Zc 32
Exton **GB** (SOM) 67 Wc 42
Eyam **GB** (DSH) 45 Yb 29
Eydon **GB** (NRH) 54 Ye 36
Eye **GB** (CBS) 55 Ze 33
Eye **GB** (HWC) 52 Xb 35
Eye **GB** (SUF) 57 Ba 35
Eye Green **GB** (CBS) 55 Ze 33
Eyemouth **GB** (BOR) 27 Xf 13
Eyeworth **GB** (BFS) 55 Ze 36
Eyhorne Street **GB** (KEN) 65 Ad 41
Eyke **GB** (SUF) 57 Bc 36
Eynort **GB** (HGL) 13 Td 5
Eynsford **GB** (KEN) 64 Ab 40
Eynsham **GB** (OXS) 62 Yd 38
Eype **GB** (DOS) 68 Xb 44
Eyre **GB** (HGL) 13 Te 4
Eyrecourt **IRL** (GAL) 93 Rf 29
Eythorne **GB** (KEN) 73 Bb 41
Eyton **GB** (CLW) 44 Xa 31
Eyton **GB** (HWC) 52 Xb 35
Eyton **GB** (SHS) 52 Xa 34
Eyton upon the Weald Moors **GB** (SHS) 44 Xc 32

F

Faartan **IRL** (GAL) 88 Rd 27
Faccombe **GB** (HAS) 62 Yd 41
Faceby **GB** (NOY) 36 Ye 22
Faddiley **GB** (CHS) 44 Xc 30
Fadmoor **GB** (NOY) 37 Za 23
Faghill **IRL** (MAY) 81 Qe 23
Faha **IRL** (COR) 102 Qb 38
Faha **IRL** (KER) 96 Pe 35
Faha **IRL** (KER) 97 Qc 36
Faha **IRL** (WTF) 100 Sd 35
Fahaduff **IRL** (KER) 97 Qd 35
Fahamore **IRL** (KER) 97 Pf 35
Fahan **IRL** (DON) 78 Sd 18
Fahan **IRL** (KER) 96 Pd 36
Faheen Cross Roads **IRL** (TIP) 99 Sa 33
Fahy **IRL** (GAL) 93 Rd 29
Fahy **IRL** (GAL) 93 Re 29
Fahy **IRL** (MAY) 86 Qd 25
Fahy **IRL** (OFF) 94 Se 28
Failaloughaun **IRL** (COR) 102 Qb 39
Failand **GB** (AVN) 61 Xb 40
Failford **GB** (STC) 30 Vd 15
Failsworth **GB** (GRM) 39 Xf 27
Fairbourne **GB** (GWY) 51 Vf 32
Fairfield **GB** (HWC) 53 Xf 34
Fairford **GB** (GLS) 62 Yb 38
Fairgirth **GB** (DAG) 31 Wb 19
Fair Green **IRL** (CRE) 92 Ra 31
Fairhill **IRL** (GAL) 88 Rc 28
Fairlie **GB** (STC) 24 Va 14
Fairlight **GB** (ESX) 72 Ad 43
Fairmile **GB** (DEV) 67 We 44
Fairmilehead **GB** (LOT) 26 We 13
Fair Oak **GB** (HAS) 70 Ye 43
Fairoak **GB** (SFS) 45 Xd 31
Fairseat **GB** (KEN) 64 Ab 41
Fairstead **GB** (ESS) 65 Ad 38
Fairstead **GB** (NOR) 49 Bc 32
Fairwarp **GB** (ESX) 71 Aa 42
Fairy Cross **GB** (DEV) 66 Ve 43
Fairyhouse Race Course **IRL** (MT) 90 Td 28
Fairymount **IRL** (ROS) 88 Rd 26
Fairymount **IRL** (ROS) 88 Rf 26
Fairy Mount **IRL** (WMT) 89 Sc 27
Fakenham **GB** (NOR) 49 Af 32
Fala **GB** (LOT) 26 Xa 13
Fala Dam **GB** (LOT) 26 Xa 13
Falahill **GB** (BOR) 26 Xa 14
Falcarragh **IRL** (DON) 77 Rf 18
Faldingworth **GB** (LIN) 47 Zd 28
Falfield **GB** (AVN) 61 Xd 39
Falkenham **GB** (SUF) 57 Bb 36
Falkirk **GB** (CEN) 25 Wb 12
Falkland **GB** (FIF) 26 We 11
Fallagh **IRL** (WTF) 100 Sd 35
Fallagloon **GB** (LDR) 78 Tb 19
Fallgate **GB** (DSH) 46 Yd 30
Fallin **GB** (CEN) 25 Wa 12
Fallmore **IRL** (MAY) 80 Pf 24
Falls **GB** (ANT) 85 Ua 21
Falmouth **GB** (CNW) 74 Uf 48
Falnasoogaun or Roperfield **IRL** (SLI) 82 Rc 24
Falstone **GB** (NHL) 32 Xd 17
Fanagmore **GB** (HGL) 4 Uf 118
Fancott **GB** (BFS) 63 Zc 37
Fangdale Beck **GB** (NOY) 37 Yf 22
Fangfoss **GB** (HUS) 40 Za 25
Fanmore **GB** (STC) 18 Te 9
Fans **GB** (BOR) 26 Xc 15
Farahy **IRL** (COR) 98 Rd 35
Farcet **GB** (CBS) 55 Ze 33
Far Cotton **GB** (NRH) 54 Za 35
Farden **GB** (SHS) 52 Xc 34
Fareham **GB** (HAS) 70 Ye 43
Farewell **GB** (SFS) 53 Ya 32
Faringdon **GB** (OXS) 62 Yc 39
Farington **GB** (LCS) 38 Xb 26
Farleigh **GB** (AVN) 61 Xb 40
Farleigh **GB** (SOM) 68 Xe 41
Farleigh **GB** (SUR) 64 Zf 41
Farleton **GB** (CUB) 35 Xb 23
Farley **GB** (SFS) 45 Ya 31
Farley **GB** (SHS) 52 Xa 33
Farley **GB** (WIL) 69 Yb 42
Farley Green **GB** (SUR) 71 Zd 41
Farley Hill **GB** (BKS) 63 Za 40
Farleys End **GB** (GLS) 61 Xe 38
Farlington **GB** (NOY) 40 Yf 24
Farlow **GB** (SHS) 52 Xc 34
Farmborough **GB** (AVN) 61 Xd 40
Farm Cott. **IRL** (GAL) 88 Rc 26
Farmer's Bridge **IRL** (KER) 97 Qc 35
Farmersvale **IRL** (KIL) 95 Tc 29
Farmington **GB** (GLS) 62 Yb 37
Farmleigh **IRL** (LAO) 94 Sd 31
Farmoor **GB** (OXS) 62 Yd 38
Farmtown **GB** (GRP) 16 Xb 3
Farnagh **IRL** (WMT) 93 Sb 28
Farnborough **GB** (BKS) 62 Yd 39
Farnborough **GB** (HAS) 63 Zb 41
Farnborough **GB** (WWH) 54 Yd 36
Farndon **GB** (CHS) 44 Xa 30
Farndon **GB** (NTS) 46 Za 30
Farnell **GB** (TYS) 22 Xc 8
Farnham **GB** (DOS) 69 Xf 43
Farnham **GB** (ESS) 64 Aa 37
Farnham **GB** (NOY) 39 Yd 24
Farnham **GB** (SUF) 57 Bc 35
Farnham **GB** (SUR) 70 Zb 41
Farnham Common **GB** (BUS) 63 Zc 39
Farnham Royal **GB** (BUS) 63 Zc 39
Farningham **GB** (KEN) 64 Ab 40
Farnley **GB** (NOY) 39 Yb 25
Farnley Tyas **GB** (WYO) 39 Yb 27
Farnsfield **GB** (NTS) 46 Yf 30
Farnworth **GB** (GRM) 38 Xd 27
Farr **GB** (HGL) 5 Ve 117
Farr **GB** (HGL) 15 Ve 4
Farr **GB** (HGL) 15 Wa 6
Farran **IRL** (COR) 104 Rb 37
Farranastack **IRL** (KER) 97 Qc 33
Farran Cross Roads **IRL** (LAO) 94 Sd 31
Farranduff **IRL** (SLI) 87 Rb 24
Farrangalway **IRL** (COR) 104 Rc 38
Farranhavane House **IRL** (COR) 103 Rb 38
Farranmacfarrell House **IRL** (SLI) 81 Ra 23
Farrenfore **IRL** (KER) 97 Qc 35
Farrihy **IRL** (CRE) 91 Qc 32
Farrington Gurney **GB** (AVN) 68 Xc 41
Farsley **GB** (WYO) 39 Yb 26
Fartadreen **IRL** (CAV) 89 Sf 25
Fartagh Cross Roads **IRL** (CAV) 89 Ta 26
Farthinghoe **GB** (NRH) 54 Ye 36
Farthingstone **GB** (NRH) 54 Yf 35
Farthingville **IRL** (COR) 98 Rb 35
Fartrin Cross Roads **IRL** (CAV) 89 Sc 24
Farway **GB** (DEV) 67 Wf 44
Fasag **GB** (HGL) 14 Uc 3
Fascadale **GB** (HGL) 18 Tf 8
Fasnacloich **GB** (STC) 19 Ue 9
Fasque **GB** (GRP) 22 Xc 7
Fassfern **GB** (HGL) 19 Ue 7
Fattahead **GB** (GRP) 17 Xc 3
Faugh **GB** (CUB) 32 Xb 19
Faughalstown **IRL** (WMT) 89 Se 27
Faughary **IRL** (LET) 82 Rf 22
Faugher **IRL** (DON) 77 Sa 17
Fauldhouse **GB** (LOT) 25 Wb 14
Faulkbourne **GB** (ESS) 65 Ad 38
Faulkland **GB** (SOM) 68 Xd 41
Fauls **GB** (SHS) 44 Xc 31
Fauna **IRL** (WKL) 95 Tc 31
Faversham **GB** (KEN) 65 Af 41
Favillar **GB** (GRP) 16 We 4
Fawdon **GB** (TAW) 33 Yc 18
Fawfieldhead **GB** (SFS) 45 Ya 29
Fawkham Green **GB** (KEN) 64 Ab 40
Fawler **GB** (OXS) 62 Yd 37
Fawley **GB** (BKS) 62 Yd 39
Fawley **GB** (BUS) 63 Za 39
Fawley **GB** (HAS) 70 Yd 44
Faxfleet **GB** (HUS) 40 Zb 26
Fax Hall **IRL** (LGF) 89 Sc 27
Faygate **GB** (WSX) 71 Ze 42
Feaghbeg **IRL** (GAL) 93 Re 29
Feakle **IRL** (CRE) 92 Rc 31
Feaklecally **IRL** (KER) 97 Pf 36
Feakle Lower **IRL** (CRE) 92 Rc 31
Fearby **GB** (NOY) 36 Yb 23
Fearna = Ferns **IRL** (WEX) 101 Td 33
Fearnagh **IRL** (LET) 88 Sa 25
Fearnan **GB** (TYS) 20 Vf 9
Fearnbeg **GB** (HGL) 13 Ub 3
Fearnhead **GB** (CHS) 44 Xc 28
Fearnmore **GB** (HGL) 13 Ub 3
Featherstone **GB** (SFS) 53 Xf 33
Featherstone **GB** (WYO) 40 Yd 26
Feckenham **GB** (HWC) 53 Ya 35
Fedamore **IRL** (LIM) 98 Rc 33
Fedderate **GB** (GRP) 17 Xe 3
Feeard **IRL** (CRE) 97 Qb 33
Feebrack or Nutgrove **IRL** (GAL) 93 Rd 30
Feegavla **IRL** (MOG) 90 Tc 24
Feenagh **IRL** (CRE) 92 Qe 30
Feenagh **IRL** (CRE) 92 Rb 32
Feenagh **IRL** (LIM) 98 Ra 34
Feeny **GB** (LDR) 78 Sf 19
Feering **GB** (ESS) 65 Ae 37
Feetham **GB** (NOY) 36 Xf 22
Feevagh **IRL** (ROS) 88 Re 28
Felbridge **GB** (SUR) 71 Zf 42
Felcourt **GB** (SUR) 71 Zf 42
Felindre **GB** (DYF) 59 Vd 36
Felindre **GB** (DYF) 59 Vf 37
Felindre **GB** (DYF) 59 Wa 37
Felindre **GB** (POW) 52 We 34
Felindre **GB** (WGL) 59 Wa 38
Felindre Farchog **GB** (DYF) 58 Vb 36
Felinfach **GB** (POW) 60 We 37
Felinfoel **GB** (DYF) 59 Vf 38
Felingwmuchaf **GB** (DYF) 59 Ve 37
Felixkirk **GB** (NOY) 36 Ye 23
Felixstowe **GB** (SUF) 57 Bc 37
Felixstoweferry **GB** (SUF) 57 Bc 37
Felkington **GB** (NHL) 27 Xf 14
Felldownhead **GB** (DEV) 75 Ve 45
Felling **GB** (TAW) 33 Yc 19
Felmersham **GB** (BFS) 55 Zc 35
Felmingham **GB** (NOR) 49 Bc 32
Felpham **GB** (WSX) 70 Zc 44
Felsham **GB** (SUF) 56 Af 35
Felsted **GB** (ESS) 64 Ac 37
Feltham **GB** (GRL) 63 Zd 40
Felton **GB** (AVN) 61 Xb 40
Felton **GB** (HWC) 52 Xc 36
Felton **GB** (NHL) 33 Yb 17
Felton Butler **GB** (SHS) 44 Xa 32
Feltwell **GB** (NOR) 56 Ad 34
Fenagh **IRL** (LET) 88 Sa 24
Fence **GB** (LCS) 39 Xe 25
Fencote **GB** (NOY) 36 Yc 22
Fendike Corner **GB** (LIN) 47 Aa 30
Fen Drayton **GB** (CBS) 55 Zf 35
Fen End **GB** (WMD) 53 Yb 34
Fenhouses **GB** (LIN) 47 Zf 31
Feniscowles **GB** (LCS) 38 Xc 26
Fenit **IRL** (KER) 97 Qa 35
Fenloe House **IRL** (CRE) 92 Rb 32
Fennor **IRL** (WMT) 89 Se 27
Fennor **IRL** (WTF) 100 Se 36
Fennor Cross Roads **IRL** (MT) 89 Sf 26
Fenny Bentley **GB** (DSH) 45 Yb 30
Fenny Compton **GB** (WWH) 54 Yd 35
Fenny Drayton **GB** (LEC) 54 Yd 33
Fenrother **GB** (NHL) 33 Yb 17
Fenstanton **GB** (CBS) 55 Zf 35
Fen Street **GB** (SUF) 56 Af 34
Fenton **GB** (CBS) 55 Zf 34
Fenton **GB** (LIN) 46 Zb 29
Fenton **GB** (LIN) 46 Zb 30
Fenton **GB** (NHL) 27 Xf 15
Fenton **GB** (SFS) 45 Xf 31
Fenwick **GB** (NHL) 27 Ya 15
Fenwick **GB** (NHL) 33 Ya 18
Fenwick **GB** (SOY) 40 Yf 27
Fenwick **GB** (STC) 24 Vd 15
Feochaig **GB** (STC) 28 Uc 16
Feock **GB** (CNW) 74 Uf 47
Feohanagh **IRL** (KER) 96 Pd 35
Feolin Ferry **GB** (STC) 23 Tf 13
Feonahagh **IRL** (LIM) 98 Ra 34
Ferbane **IRL** (OFF) 93 Sb 29
Fergues Cross Roads **IRL** (COR) 104 Rb 37
Ferniquarrie **GB** (HGL) 12 Tb 4
Fermoy **IRL** (COR) 99 Re 36
Fern **GB** (TYS) 22 Xa 8
Ferndale **GB** (MGL) 60 Wd 39
Ferndown **GB** (DOS) 69 Ya 44
Ferness **GB** (HGL) 15 Wb 4
Fernham **GB** (OXS) 62 Yc 39
Fernhill **GB** (HWC) 53 Xd 36
Fernhurst **GB** (WSX) 70 Zb 42
Fernie **GB** (FIF) 21 Wf 11
Fernilea **GB** (HGL) 13 Td 5
Fernilee **GB** (DSH) 45 Ya 29
Ferns **IRL** (WEX) 101 Td 33
Fernsborough **IRL** (LGF) 89 Sd 26
Ferns Lock **IRL** (MT) 95 Tb 28
Ferrensby **GB** (NOY) 40 Yd 24
Ferring **GB** (WSX) 71 Zd 44
Ferrybridge **GB** (WYO) 40 Ye 26
Ferryden **GB** (TYS) 22 Xd 8
Ferryhill **GB** (DUR) 36 Yc 20
Ferry House **IRL** (KER) 97 Qb 36
Ferryside **GB** (DYF) 59 Vd 38
Fersit **GB** (HGL) 20 Vb 7
Fertagh **IRL** (MT) 89 Ta 25
Feshiebridge **GB** (HGL) 15 Wa 6
Fetcham **GB** (SUR) 64 Zd 41
Fethard **IRL** (TIP) 99 Sb 34
Fethard **IRL** (WEX) 100 Ta 35
Fetterangus **GB** (GRP) 17 Xf 3
Fettercairn **GB** (GRP) 22 Xc 7
Fewcott **GB** (OXS) 62 Ye 37
Fewston **GB** (NOY) 39 Yb 25
Ffairfach **GB** (DYF) 59 Wa 37
Ffair Rhos **GB** (DYF) 51 Wa 35
Ffaldybrenin **GB** (DYF) 51 Wa 36
Ffarmers **GB** (DYF) 51 Wa 36
Ffawyddog **GB** (POW) 60 Wf 37
Ffestiniog **GB** (GWY) 43 Wa 31
Ffordd-las **GB** (CLW) 43 We 29
Fforest **GB** (DYF) 59 Vf 38
Fforestfach **GB** (WGL) 59 Wa 39
Ffostrasol **GB** (DYF) 50 Vd 36
Ffridd Uchaf **GB** (GWY) 42 Vf 30
Ffrith **GB** (CLW) 44 Wf 30
Ffrwdgrech **GB** (POW) 60 Wd 37
Ffynnon-ddrain **GB** (DYF) 59 Ve 37
Fiddes **GB** (GRP) 22 Xe 7
Fiddington **GB** (GLS) 61 Xf 37
Fiddington **GB** (SOM) 67 Wf 42
Fiddlers Hamlet **GB** (ESS) 64 Aa 38
Fiddown **IRL** (KLK) 100 Se 34
Field **GB** (SFS) 45 Ya 31
Field Broughton **GB** (CUB) 35 Xa 23
Field Dalling **GB** (NOR) 48 Af 31
Fieries **IRL** (KER) 97 Qc 35
Fifehead Magdalen **GB** (DOS) 68 Xe 43
Fifehead Neville **GB** (DOS) 68 Xe 43
Fifield **GB** (BKS) 63 Zb 40
Fifield **GB** (OXS) 62 Yc 37
Fifield Bavant **GB** (WIL) 69 Ya 42
Figart **IRL** (DON) 77 Sc 19
Figheldean **GB** (WIL) 69 Yb 41
Filby **GB** (NOR) 49 Bd 33
Filey **GB** (NOY) 37 Ze 23
Filgrave **GB** (BUS) 55 Zb 36
Filleigh **GB** (DEV) 66 Wa 42
Fillingham **GB** (LIN) 47 Zc 28
Fillongley **GB** (WWH) 53 Yc 34
Filmore Hill **GB** (HAS) 70 Yf 42
Filton **GB** (AVN) 61 Xc 40
Fimber **GB** (HUS) 40 Zc 24
Finaghoo **IRL** (CAV) 83 Sb 24
Finaghy **GB** (ANT) 85 Ua 21
Finavarra **IRL** (CRE) 92 Qf 30
Finavon **GB** (TYS) 22 Xb 8
Fincham **GB** (NOR) 56 Ac 33
Fincharn **GB** (STC) 23 Ud 11
Finchdean **GB** (HAS) 70 Za 43
Finchhampstead **GB** (BKS) 63 Za 40
Finchingfield **GB** (ESS) 56 Ac 37
Finchley **GB** (GRL) 64 Ze 39
Findern **GB** (DSH) 45 Yc 31
Findhorn **GB** (GRP) 16 Wc 3
Findochty **GB** (GRP) 16 Xa 2
Findo Gask **GB** (TYS) 21 Wc 10
Findon **GB** (GRP) 17 Xf 6
Findon **GB** (WSX) 71 Zd 43
Findon Mains **GB** (HGL) 15 Vd 3
Finedon **GB** (NRH) 55 Zc 34
Fingask **GB** (GRP) 17 Xd 4
Fingerpost **GB** (HWC) 53 Xd 34
Fingest **GB** (BUS) 63 Za 39
Finghall **GB** (NOY) 36 Yb 23
Finglas **IRL** (DUB) 95 Te 28
Fingringhoe **GB** (ESS) 65 Af 37
Finlarig **GB** (CEN) 20 Ve 10
Finmere **GB** (OXS) 63 Yf 37
Finnart **GB** (STC) 24 Vb 12

Easton – Finnart (GB) (IRL) 117

Finnea IRL (WMT) 89 Sd 26
Finnegan's Cross Roads IRL (MT) 90 Tb 26
Finningham GB (SUF) 57 Ba 35
Finningley GB (SOY) 40 Za 28
Finnis GB (DOW) 85 Tf 22
Finniterstown IRL (LIM) 98 Rb 33
Finnoe House IRL (TIP) 93 Re 31
Finnow Bridge IRL (COR) 98 Qf 36
Finnstown House IRL (DUB) 95 Td 28
Finny IRL (MAY) 86 Qd 27
Finnygaud GB (GRP) 17 Xc 3
Finsbay GB (HGL) 10 Ta 2
Finsbury GB (GRL) 64 Zf 39
Finsthwaite GB (CUB) 35 Xa 23
Finstock GB (OXS) 62 Yd 37
Finstown GB (ORK) 6 Wf 114
Fintona GB (TYR) 83 Se 21
Fintry GB (CEN) 25 Ve 12
Fintry GB (GRP) 17 Xd 3
Finuge IRL (KER) 97 Qc 34
Finvoy GB (ANT) 79 Tc 18
Finzean GB (GRP) 17 Xc 6
Fiodh Ard = Fethard IRL (TIP) 99 Sb 34
Fionnachaidh IRL (DON) 77 Sa 17
Fionnphort GB (STC) 18 Td 11
Firbank GB (CUB) 35 Xc 22
Firbeck GB (SOY) 46 Yf 28
Firkeel IRL (COR) 102 Pf 39
Firmount IRL (LGF) 89 Sc 26
Firth GB (SHL) 2 Ye 106
Fir Tree GB (DUR) 36 Yb 20
Fishbourne GB (IOW) 70 Ye 44
Fishbourne GB (WSX) 70 Zb 44
Fishburn GB (DUR) 36 Yd 20
Fisherford GB (GRP) 17 Xc 4
Fisherhill IRL (MAY) 87 Qe 25
Fisher's Pond GB (HAS) 70 Ye 43
Fisherstown IRL (LGF) 88 Sa 26
Fisherstown IRL (WEX) 100 Ta 35
Fisherstreet GB (WSX) 70 Zc 42
Fisherton GB (HGL) 15 Vf 3
Fisherton GB (STC) 30 Vb 16
Fisherton de la Mere GB (WIL) 69 Ya 42
Fishguard GB (DYF) 58 Va 37
Fishlake GB (SOY) 40 Yf 27
Fishley Barton GB (DEV) 66 Vf 42
Fishtoft GB (LIN) 47 Aa 31
Fishtoft Drove GB (LIN) 47 Zf 30
Fiskerton GB (LIN) 47 Zd 29
Fiskerton GB (NTS) 46 Za 30
Fittleton GB (WIL) 69 Yb 41
Fittleworth GB (WSX) 71 Zc 43
Fitton End GB (CBS) 47 Aa 32
Fitz GB (SHS) 44 Xb 32
Fitzhead GB (SOM) 67 We 42
Fitzwilliam GB (WYO) 40 Yd 27
Fiunary GB (HGL) 18 Ua 9
Fiveally IRL (OFF) 93 Sa 30
Five Ash Down GB (ESX) 71 Aa 43
Five Ashes GB (ESX) 71 Ab 42
Five Bridges GB (HWC) 52 Xc 36
Fivehead GB (SOM) 68 Xa 43
Five Lanes GB (CNW) 75 Vc 45
Fivemiletown GB (TYR) 83 Se 22
Five Oak Green GB (KEN) 72 Ac 41
Five Oaks GB (WSX) 71 Zd 42
Five Penny Borve GB (HGL) 11 Td 118
Five Penny Ness GB (HGL) 11 Te 117
Five Roads GB (DYF) 59 Ve 38
Five Roads Cross IRL (OFF) 93 Sa 29
Flackwell Heath GB (BUS) 63 Zb 39
Fladbury GB (HWC) 53 Xf 36
Fladdabister GB (SHL) 3 Ye 108
Flagmount IRL (CRE) 92 Rc 31
Flagmount IRL (KLK) 100 Sf 33
Flamborough GB (HUS) 37 Zf 24
Flamstead GB (HTS) 63 Zd 38
Flasby GB (NOY) 39 Xf 24
Flash GB (SFS) 45 Ya 29
Flashader GB (HGL) 13 Td 4
Flaunden GB (HTS) 63 Zc 38
Flawith GB (NOY) 40 Ye 24
Flax Bourton GB (AVN) 61 Xb 40
Flaxby GB (NOY) 40 Yd 24
Flaxley GB (GLS) 61 Xd 38
Flaxpool GB (SOM) 67 We 42
Flaxton GB (NOY) 40 Za 24
Flean Beg IRL (LIM) 98 Qe 33
Fleckney GB (LEC) 54 Yf 33
Flecknoe GB (WWH) 54 Ye 35
Fleet GB (HAS) 70 Za 41
Fleet Hargate GB (LIN) 47 Aa 32
Fleetwood GB (LCS) 38 Wf 25
Flemby IRL (KER) 97 Qc 35
Flemingston GB (SGL) 60 Wd 40
Flemington GB (STC) 25 Vf 14
Flempton GB (SUF) 56 Ad 35
Flesk Castle IRL (KER) 97 Qd 36
Fletching GB (ESX) 71 Aa 43
Flexbury GB (CNW) 66 Vc 43
Flexford GB (SUR) 70 Zc 41
Flimby GB (CUB) 34 Wc 20
Flimwell GB (ESX) 72 Ac 42
Flint GB (CLW) 44 Wf 29
Flintham GB (NTS) 46 Za 30
Flint Mountain GB (CLW) 44 Wf 29
Flinton GB (HUS) 41 Zf 26
Flishinghurst GB (KEN) 72 Ac 42
Flitcham GB (NOR) 48 Ad 32
Flitton GB (BFS) 55 Zd 36
Flitwick GB (BFS) 55 Zd 36
Flixborough GB (HUS) 40 Zb 27
Flixton GB (NOY) 37 Zd 23
Flixton GB (SUF) 57 Bc 34
Float IRL (WMT) 89 Sd 26
Flockton GB (WYO) 39 Yc 27
Flodabay GB (HGL) 11 Ta 2
Flodden GB (NHL) 27 Xf 15
Flodigarry GB (HGL) 13 Te 2
Flood Hall IRL (KLK) 100 Se 33
Flookburgh GB (CUB) 35 Xa 23
Flore GB (NRH) 54 Yf 35
Flotterton GB (NHL) 33 Ya 17
Flowton GB (SUF) 57 Ba 36
Flughany IRL (MAY) 88 Rc 24
Flushing GB (GRP) 17 Ya 3
Flyford Flavell GB (HWC) 53 Xf 35
Fochabers GB (GRP) 16 Wf 3
Fochriw GB (MGL) 60 We 38
Fodderletter GB (GRP) 16 Wd 5
Foel GB (POW) 51 Wd 32
Foffarty GB (TYS) 22 Xa 9
Foggathorpe GB (HUS) 40 Za 26
Fogo GB (BOR) 27 Xd 14
Foiladuan IRL (COR) 98 Qf 35
Foilagoule IRL (TIP) 99 Rf 32
Foilakill IRL (COR) 102 Qc 39
Foilycleara IRL (LIM) 99 Re 33
Foindle GB (HGL) 4 Uf 118
Folda GB (TYS) 21 We 8
Fole GB (SFS) 45 Ya 31
Foleshill GB (WMD) 54 Yd 34
Folkestone GB (KEN) 73 Ba 42
Folkingham GB (LIN) 47 Zd 31
Folksworth GB (CBS) 55 Ze 34
Folkton GB (NOY) 37 Zd 23
Folla Rule GB (GRP) 17 Xd 4
Follifoot GB (NOY) 39 Yd 25
Folly GB (DYF) 58 Uf 37
Folly, The GB (HTS) 64 Ze 38
Folly Gate GB (DEV) 66 Vf 44
Fonthill Bishop GB (WIL) 69 Xf 42
Fonthill Gifford GB (WIL) 69 Xf 42
Fontmell Magna GB (DOS) 69 Xe 43
Fontstown IRL (KIL) 94 Ta 30
Fontwell GB (WSX) 70 Zc 43
Fookeen IRL (COR) 103 Qe 39
Foolow GB (DSH) 45 Yb 29
Forcett GB (NOY) 36 Yb 21
Forches Cross GB (DEV) 67 Wb 43
Ford GB (BUS) 63 Za 38
Ford GB (DEV) 66 Ve 42
Ford GB (DEV) 76 Wa 46
Ford GB (DEV) 76 Wb 47
Ford GB (GLS) 62 Ya 37
Ford GB (NHL) 27 Xf 15
Ford GB (SFS) 45 Ya 30
Ford GB (SHS) 52 Xa 32
Ford GB (SOM) 67 We 42
Ford GB (STC) 23 Ud 11
Ford GB (WIL) 61 Xe 40
Ford GB (WSX) 71 Zc 44
Fordcombe GB (KEN) 71 Ab 42
Fordell GB (FIF) 26 Wd 12
Forden GB (POW) 52 Wf 33
Ford End GB (ESS) 64 Ac 38
Fordham GB (CBS) 56 Ac 35
Fordham GB (ESS) 65 Ae 37
Fordham GB (NOR) 56 Ac 33
Fordingbridge GB (HAS) 69 Yb 43
Fordoun GB (GRP) 22 Xd 7
Ford Street GB (SOM) 67 We 43
Fordwells GB (OXS) 62 Yc 38
Fordwich GB (KEN) 65 Ba 41
Fordyce GB (GRP) 16 Xb 3
Fore IRL (WMT) 89 Se 26
Forekill IRL (KLK) 99 Sc 32
Forest GBG 100 Xc 52
Forestburn Gate GB (NHL) 33 Ya 17
Forest Coal Pit GB (GWE) 60 Wf 37
Forest Green GB (SUR) 71 Zd 42
Forest Hall GB (CUB) 35 Xb 22
Forest Hill GB (OXS) 63 Yf 38
Forest-in-Teesdale GB (DUR) 35 Xe 21
Forest Mill GB (CEN) 25 Wb 12
Forest Row GB (ESX) 71 Aa 42
Forestside GB (WSX) 70 Za 43
Forest Town GB (NTS) 46 Yf 30
Forfar GB (TYS) 22 Xa 9
Forgandenny GB (TYS) 21 Wd 10
Forgie GB (GRP) 16 Wf 3
Forkill GB (ARG) 90 Td 24
Formal IRL (MT) 90 Tb 28
Formby GB (MES) 38 Wf 27
Formoyle IRL (CRE) 92 Qe 30
Formoyle IRL (CRE) 92 Rc 32
Formoyle IRL (LGF) 88 Sa 27
Formoyle IRL (MAY) 81 Qd 24
Forncett End GB (NOR) 57 Ba 33
Forncett Saint Peter GB (NOR) 57 Bb 34
Forneth GB (TYS) 21 Wd 9
Fornham All Saints GB (SUF) 56 Ae 35
Fornham Saint Martin GB (SUF) 56 Ae 35
Forres GB (GRP) 16 Wc 3
Forsbrook GB (SFS) 45 Xf 31
Forse GB (HGL) 9 We 119
Forsinard GB (HGL) 9 Wa 118
Forstal, the GB (KEN) 72 Ae 41
Forston GB (DOS) 68 Xd 44
Fort Augustus GB (HGL) 14 Vb 6
Fortchester House IRL (WEX) 95 Te 32
Fortel IRL (OFF) 93 Sa 30
Forter GB (TYS) 21 Wd 8
Forteviot GB (TYS) 21 Wc 10
Fort George GB (HGL) 15 Vf 3
Forth GB (STC) 25 Wb 14
Forthampton GB (GLS) 61 Xe 37
Fort Henry IRL (CAV) 89 Se 24
Forthill IRL (LGF) 88 Sa 27
Fortingall GB (TYS) 20 Vf 9
Fortland IRL (CAV) 89 Se 25
Fortlands House IRL (COR) 98 Rb 34
Fortland's House IRL (GAL) 92 Rc 29
Fort Middle IRL (LIM) 98 Rb 34
Forton GB (HAS) 69 Yd 41
Forton GB (LCS) 38 Xb 25
Forton GB (SFS) 45 Xd 32
Forton GB (SHS) 44 Xa 32
Forton GB (SOM) 68 Xa 43
Fortrie GB (GRP) 17 Xc 4
Fortrie GB (GRP) 17 Xf 4
Fortrose GB (HGL) 15 Vf 3
Fort Stewart IRL (DON) 77 Sc 18
Fortuneswell GB (DOS) 68 Xd 45
Fort View IRL (COR) 103 Qd 39
Fort William GB (HGL) 19 Uf 8
Fort William IRL (LET) 82 Rf 22
Fortwilliam IRL (LGF) 88 Sa 27
Fort William IRL (TIP) 93 Sa 32
Forward Green GB (SUF) 57 Ba 35
Fosbury GB (WIL) 62 Yc 41
Foscot GB (GLS) 62 Yc 37
Fosdyke GB (LIN) 47 Zf 31
Foss GB (TYS) 21 Wa 8
Fossebridge GB (GLS) 62 Ya 38
Foss-y-ffin GB (DYF) 50 Ve 35
Foster's Booth GB (NRH) 54 Yf 35
Foster Street GB (ESS) 64 Aa 38
Foston GB (DSH) 45 Yb 31
Foston GB (LIN) 46 Zb 31
Foston GB (NOY) 40 Za 24
Foston on the Wolds GB (HUS) 41 Ze 25
Fotherby GB (LIN) 41 Zf 28
Fotheringhay GB (NRH) 55 Zd 33
Foulden GB (BOR) 27 Xf 13
Foulden GB (NOR) 56 Ad 33
Foul Mile GB (ESX) 72 Ab 43
Foulridge GB (LCS) 39 Xf 25
Foulsham GB (NOR) 49 Ba 32
Fountainhall GB (BOR) 26 Xa 14
Four Ashes GB (SUF) 56 Af 35
Four Crosses GB (CLW) 43 Wd 31
Four Crosses GB (POW) 44 Wf 32
Four Crosses GB (POW) 51 Wd 32
Four Crosses GB (SFS) 53 Xf 32
Four Elms GB (KEN) 71 Aa 41
Four Forks GB (SOM) 67 Wf 42
Four Gotes GB (CBS) 48 Aa 32
Fourhalf Moons IRL (CAV) 89 Se 25
Fourhalf Moons IRL (CAV) 89 Se 26
Fourlane Ends GB (DSH) 46 Yd 30
Four Lanes GB (CNW) 74 Ue 47
Fourlanes End GB (CHS) 45 Xe 30
Four Marks GB (HAS) 70 Yf 42
Four Mile Bridge GB (GWY) 42 Vc 29
Four Mile House IRL (ROS) 88 Re 26
Four Oaks GB (ESX) 72 Ad 43
Four Oaks GB (WMD) 53 Ya 33
Four Oaks GB (WMD) 53 Yc 34
Fourpenny GB (HGL) 8 Vf 1
Four Roads IRL (ROS) 88 Re 27
Fourstones GB (NHL) 33 Xe 18
Fourteen Roads, The IRL (TIP) 93 Sa 31
Four Throws GB (KEN) 72 Ad 42
Fovant GB (WIL) 69 Ya 42
Fowey GB (CNW) 75 Vc 46
Fowlis GB (TYS) 21 Wf 10
Fowlis Wester GB (TYS) 21 Wb 10
Fowlmere GB (CBS) 55 Aa 36
Fownhope GB (HWC) 61 Xc 36
Foxborough IRL (ROS) 88 Rf 28
Foxburrow House IRL (OFF) 93 Sa 31
Foxdale GBM 29 Vc 23
Foxearth GB (ESS) 56 Ae 36
Foxfield GB (CUB) 34 We 23
Foxford IRL (MAY) 87 Qf 25
Foxhall IRL (LOT) 90 Td 26
Foxham GB (WIL) 62 Xf 40
Fox Hill IRL (MAY) 87 Qd 27
Foxhunt Green GB (ESX) 71 Ab 43
Foxley GB (NOR) 49 Ba 32
Foxley GB (NRH) 54 Yf 36
Foxley GB (WIL) 61 Xf 39
Foxton GB (CBS) 55 Aa 36
Foxton GB (LEC) 54 Za 33
Foxup GB (NOY) 35 Xe 23
Foxwist Green GB (CHS) 44 Xc 29
Foy GB (HWC) 61 Xc 37
Foyers GB (HGL) 15 Vd 5
Foygh IRL (LGF) 88 Sb 27
Foynes IRL (LIM) 98 Qf 33
Fraddon GB (CNW) 75 Va 46
Fradswell GB (SFS) 45 Xf 31
Fraigh House GB (HGL) 19 Ua 7
Fraisthorpe GB (HUS) 41 Ze 24
Framfield GB (ESX) 71 Aa 43
Framingham Earl GB (NOR) 57 Bc 33
Framlingham GB (SUF) 57 Bc 35
Frampton GB (DOS) 68 Xc 44
Frampton GB (LIN) 47 Zf 31
Frampton Cotterell GB (AVN) 61 Xd 39
Frampton Mansell GB (GLS) 61 Xf 38
Frampton on Severn GB (GLS) 61 Xd 38
Frampton West End GB (LIN) 47 Zf 31
Framsden GB (SUF) 57 Bb 35
Framwellgate Moor GB (DUR) 36 Yc 20
Franche GB (HWC) 53 Xe 34
Frankby GB (CHS) 44 Wf 28
Frankton GB (WWH) 54 Yd 34
Frant GB (ESX) 72 Ab 42
Fraserburgh GB (GRP) 17 Xf 2
Frating Green GB (ESS) 65 Ba 37
Freagh IRL (MT) 89 Ta 28
Freaghmore IRL (WMT) 89 Se 26
Freckenham GB (SUF) 56 Ac 35
Freckleton GB (LCS) 38 Xa 26
Freeby GB (LEC) 46 Zb 32
Freefolk GB (HAS) 70 Ye 41
Freeland GB (OXS) 62 Yd 38
Freemount IRL (COR) 98 Ra 35
Freethorpe GB (NOR) 57 Bd 33
Freethorpe Common GB (NOR) 57 Bd 33
Freiston GB (LIN) 47 Aa 31
Freiston Shore GB (LIN) 47 Aa 31
Fremington GB (DEV) 66 Vf 42
Fremington GB (NOY) 36 Ya 22
Frenchbeer GB (DEV) 66 Wa 45
Frenchfurze IRL (COR) 104 Rd 38
French Hill IRL (MAY) 87 Qe 26
Frenchlawn IRL (ROS) 88 Rd 26
Frenchpark IRL (ROS) 88 Rd 25
Freneystown IRL (KLK) 100 Sf 32
Fresgoe GB (HGL) 5 Wb 117
Freshford GB (AVN) 61 Xe 40
Freshford IRL (KLK) 94 Sd 32
Freshwater GB (IOW) 69 Yd 44
Freshwater East GB (DYF) 58 Va 39
Fressingfield GB (SUF) 57 Bb 34
Freswick GB (HGL) 6 Wf 117
Frettenham GB (NOR) 49 Bb 32
Freuchie GB (FIF) 26 Wf 11
Freystrop GB (DYF) 58 Va 38
Friar's Gate GB (ESX) 71 Aa 42
Friarstown House IRL (DUB) 95 Td 29
Friarton GB (TYS) 21 Wd 10
Friday Bridge GB (CBS) 48 Aa 33
Fridaythorpe GB (HUS) 40 Va 24
Fridge Green GB (ESX) 71 Ab 42
Friern Barnet GB (GRL) 64 Zf 39
Friesthorpe GB (LIN) 47 Zd 28
Frieth GB (BUS) 63 Za 39
Frilford GB (OXS) 62 Yd 38
Frilsham GB (BKS) 63 Ye 40
Frimley GB (SUR) 63 Zb 41
Frimley Green GB (SUR) 63 Zb 41
Fring GB (NOR) 48 Ad 31
Fringford GB (OXS) 63 Yf 37
Frinsted GB (KEN) 65 Ae 41
Frinton-on-Sea GB (ESS) 65 Bb 38
Friockheim GB (TYS) 22 Xc 9
Friog GB (GWY) 51 Vf 32
Frisby on the Wreake GB (LEC) 46 Za 32
Friskney GB (LIN) 47 Ab 30
Friston GB (SUF) 57 Bd 35
Fritham GB (HAS) 69 Yc 43
Frith Bank GB (LIN) 47 Zf 30
Frith Common GB (HWC) 52 Xd 35
Frithelstock Stone GB (DEV) 66 Ve 43
Frithville GB (LIN) 47 Zf 30
Frittenden GB (KEN) 72 Ad 42
Fritton GB (NOR) 57 Bb 34
Fritwell GB (OXS) 62 Ye 37
Frizington GB (CUB) 34 Wc 21
Frochas GB (POW) 52 Wf 32
Frodesley GB (SHS) 52 Xb 33
Frodsham GB (CHS) 44 Xb 29
Froggatt GB (DSH) 45 Yc 29
Froghall GB (SFS) 45 Ya 30
Frogham GB (HAS) 69 Yb 43
Frogmore GB (BKS) 63 Zb 40
Frogmore GB (DEV) 76 Wb 47
Frogmore GB (HTS) 64 Ze 38
Frogmore IRL (KER) 97 Qb 35
Frolesworth GB (LEC) 54 Ye 33
Frome GB (SOM) 68 Xe 41
Frome Saint Quintin GB (DOS) 68 Xc 44
Fromes Hill GB (HWC) 52 Xd 36
Fron GB (GWY) 42 Vd 31
Fron GB (POW) 51 Wd 35
Fron GB (POW) 52 Wf 33
Froncysyllte GB (CLW) 44 Wf 31
Frongoch GB (GWY) 43 Wc 31
Frorcester GB (GLS) 61 Xe 38
Frosses IRL (DON) 82 Re 21
Frosterley GB (DUR) 36 Ya 20
Froxfield GB (WIL) 62 Yc 40
Froxfield Green GB (HAS) 70 Za 42
Fryerning GB (ESS) 64 Ac 38
Fuerty IRL (ROS) 88 Re 27
Fugglestone Saint Peter GB (WIL) 69 Ya 42
Fuhiry IRL (COR) 103 Qe 37
Fulbeck GB (LIN) 47 Zc 30
Fulbourn GB (CBS) 56 Ab 35
Fulbrook GB (OXS) 62 Yc 38
Fulford GB (SFS) 45 Xf 31
Fulford GB (SOM) 67 Wf 42
Fulking GB (WSX) 71 Ze 43
Fuller's Moor GB (CHS) 44 Xb 30
Fuller Street GB (ESS) 65 Ad 38
Fullerton GB (HAS) 69 Yd 42
Fulletby GB (LIN) 47 Zf 29
Full Sutton GB (HUS) 40 Za 25
Fullwood GB (STC) 24 Vd 14
Fully GB (DOS) 68 Xd 44
Fulmer GB (BUS) 63 Zc 39
Fulnetby GB (LIN) 47 Zd 29
Fulstow GB (LIN) 41 Zf 28
Fulwell GB (OXS) 62 Yd 37
Fulwood GB (LCS) 38 Xb 26
Funshinagh IRL (ROS) 88 Re 27
Funshin More IRL (GAL) 92 Ra 30
Funtington GB (WSX) 70 Za 43
Funtley GB (HAS) 70 Ye 43
Funzie GB (SHL) 2 Zb 105
Furnace GB (STC) 24 Ue 12
Furness IRL (KIL) 95 Tc 29
Furneux Pelham GB (HTS) 64 Aa 37
Furraleigh IRL (WTF) 100 Sc 35
Furreera IRL (CRE) 91 Qd 31
Furroor IRL (CRE) 92 Qe 32
Fybagh IRL (KER) 97 Qb 36
Fyfett GB (SOM) 67 Wf 43
Fyfield GB (ESS) 64 Ab 38
Fyfield GB (WIL) 62 Yb 40
Fylingthorpe GB (NOY) 37 Zc 22
Fyvie GB (GRP) 17 Xd 4

G

Gaddesden Row GB (HTS) 63 Ad 38
Gadfa GB (GWY) 42 Ve 28
Gaer GB (POW) 60 We 37
Gaer Fawr GB (GWE) 61 Xb 38
Gaerllwyd GB (GWE) 61 Xb 39
Gaerwen GB (GWY) 42 Ve 29
Gagingwell GB (OXS) 62 Yd 37
Gahagan's Village IRL (OFF) 93 Sa 29
Gaigue IRL (LGF) 89 Sb 25
Gailey GB (SFS) 53 Xf 32
Gainestown IRL (WMT) 89 Se 28
Gainford GB (DUR) 36 Yb 21
Gainsborough GB (LIN) 40 Zb 28
Gainstown IRL (MT) 90 Tb 27
Gairloch GB (HGL) 7 Ub 2
Gairlochy GB (HGL) 19 Va 7
Gairney Bank GB (TYS) 26 Wd 11
Gaitsgill GB (CUB) 35 Xa 20
Galashiels GB (BOR) 26 Xb 15
Galbally IRL (LIM) 99 Re 34
Galbally IRL (WEX) 101 Tc 34
Galbolie IRL (CAV) 89 Ta 25
Galby GB (LEC) 54 Za 33
Galgate GB (LCS) 38 Xb 25
Galhampton GB (SOM) 68 Xc 42
Gallagh IRL (ROS) 88 Rf 27
Gallanach GB (STC) 18 Tc 9
Gallanach GB (STC) 19 Uc 10
Gallatown GB (FIF) 26 Wf 12
Gallen Priory IRL (OFF) 93 Sb 29
Galley Common GB (WWH) 54 Yc 33
Galleyend GB (ESS) 65 Ac 38
Galleywood GB (ESS) 65 Ac 38
Gallowfauld GB (TYS) 22 Xa 9
Gallowstree Elm GB (SFS) 53 Xe 34
Galltair GB (HGL) 13 Uc 5
Galmisdale GB (HGL) 18 Tf 7
Galmoy IRL (KLK) 94 Sc 32
Galmpton GB (DEV) 76 Wc 46
Galphay GB (NOY) 36 Yc 24
Galston GB (STC) 24 Vd 15
Galtrigill GB (HGL) 12 Tb 4
Galtrim House IRL (MT) 90 Tb 27
Galway IRL (GAL) 92 Qf 29
Gamblesby GB (CUB) 35 Xc 20
Gamlingay GB (CBS) 55 Ze 36
Gammaton Moor GB (DEV) 66 Vf 43
Gamston GB (NTS) 46 Za 29
Ganarew GB (HWC) 61 Xb 37
Ganavan GB (STC) 19 Ud 10
Ganllwyd GB (GWY) 43 Wa 32
Gannochy GB (TYS) 22 Xc 8
Ganthorpe GB (NOY) 37 Za 24
Ganton GB (NOY) 37 Zd 23
Gara Bridge GB (DEV) 76 Wb 46
Garadice IRL (MT) 90 Tb 28
Garbally IRL (GAL) 93 Re 29
Garbhallt GB (STC) 24 Ue 12
Garboldisham GB (NOR) 56 Af 34
Garden City GB (CLW) 44 Wf 29
Gardenstown GB (GRP) 17 Xd 2
Garderhouse GB (SHL) 2 Yd 107
Gardson GB (WIL) 61 Xf 39
Gare Hill GB (SOM) 68 Xe 42
Garelochhead GB (STC) 24 Va 12
Garenin GB (HGL) 11 Tb 119
Garford GB (OXS) 62 Yd 39
Gargrave GB (NOY) 39 Xf 25
Gargunnock GB (CEN) 25 Vf 12
Garhy IRL (WMT) 89 Sc 28
Garlandstown House IRL (WMT) 89 Se 27
Garlieston GB (DAG) 29 Vd 20
Garlogie GB (GRP) 17 Xd 6
Garlow Cross IRL (MT) 90 Tc 27
Garmond GB (GRP) 17 Xe 3
Garmony GB (STC) 19 Ub 9
Garmouth GB (GRP) 16 Wf 3
Garn GB (GWY) 42 Vc 31
Garnant GB (DYF) 59 Wa 38
Garnavilla IRL (TIP) 99 Sa 34
Garn Dolbenmaen GB (GWY) 42 Ve 31
Garnett Bridge GB (CUB) 35 Xb 22
Garnish IRL (COR) 102 Pf 39
Garr IRL (OFF) 94 Se 28
Garrabost GB (HGL) 11 Te 119
Garran Cross Roads IRL (MOG) 83 Sf 23
Garrane IRL (COR) 103 Qf 37
Garrane IRL (KER) 97 Qa 36
Garrane Cross Roads IRL (COR) 98 Rc 35
Garranerribben IRL (COR) 99 Rf 36
Garranes IRL (COR) 104 Re 37
Garranlahan IRL (ROS) 87 Rc 26
Garranlea House IRL (TIP) 99 Sa 34
Garraron GB (STC) 23 Uc 11
Garrarus Cross Roads IRL (WTF) 100 Se 36
Garras GB (CNW) 74 Ue 48
Garraun IRL (CRE) 91 Qc 32
Garraun IRL (GAL) 92 Ra 29
Garraun IRL (GAL) 93 Rd 30
Garraun IRL (WEX) 101 Tb 34
Garraunboy IRL (CRE) 93 Rd 32
Garraun North IRL (COR) 98 Rb 37
Garreg GB (GWY) 43 Vf 31
Garreg Bank GB (POW) 52 Wf 32
Garrick GB (TYS) 21 Wa 11
Garrigill GB (CUB) 35 Xd 20
Garrison GB (FER) 82 Rf 22
Garrison IRL (COR) 98 Ra 35
Garristown IRL (DUB) 90 Td 27
Garros GB (HGL) 13 Te 3
Garrough IRL (KER) 102 Pf 38
Garrow GB (TYS) 21 Wa 9
Garryblagh IRL (DON) 77 Sc 17
Garryclayne House IRL (COR) 98 Rc 37
Garryclogh IRL (TIP) 99 Sc 32
Garrycloonagh IRL (MAY) 81 Qe 24
Garryduff IRL (COR) 98 Rb 35
Garryfine IRL (LIM) 98 Rb 34
Garrygibbon IRL (WEX) 101 Td 34
Garryhinch House IRL (OFF) 94 Se 30
Garrylucas IRL (COR) 104 Rc 39
Garrynabullogy IRL (DON) 78 Sd 18
Garrynageragh IRL (WTF) 100 Sc 36
Garrynamonie GB (HGL) 12 Sd 6
Garrynderk IRL (LIM) 98 Rb 34
Garryvadden IRL (WEX) 101 Td 34
Garryvoe IRL (COR) 104 Rf 37
Garsdale GB (CUB) 35 Xd 23
Garsdale Head GB (CUB) 35 Xe 23
Garshall Green GB (SFS) 45 Xf 31
Garsington GB (OXS) 63 Yf 38
Garstang GB (LCS) 38 Xb 25
Garston GB (MES) 44 Xa 28
Garswood GB (MES) 38 Xb 28
Gartbrattan IRL (CAV) 89 Sd 24
Garth GB (CLW) 44 Wf 31
Garth GB (POW) 51 Wc 36
Garth GBM 29 Vc 23
Garthbrengy GB (POW) 60 Wd 37
Gartheli GB (DYF) 51 Vf 35
Garthorpe GB (HUS) 40 Zb 27
Garthorpe GB (LEC) 46 Zb 32
Gartly GB (GRP) 16 Xb 4
Gartmore GB (CEN) 24 Vd 12
Gartnagrenach GB (STC) 23 Uc 14
Gartocharn GB (STC) 24 Vc 12
Garton GB (HUS) 41 Zf 26
Garton-on-the-Wolds GB (HUS) 41 Zc 24
Gartree GB (ANT) 84 Te 21
Gartymore GB (HGL) 9 Wb 120
Garvagh GB (LDR) 79 Tb 19
Garvagh IRL (DON) 82 Rf 20
Garvald GB (LOT) 26 Xc 13
Garvard GB (STC) 22 Te 12
Garve GB (HGL) 14 Vb 3
Garveston GB (NOR) 57 Af 33
Garvock GB (STC) 24 Vb 13
Garway GB (HWC) 61 Xb 37
Garway Hill GB (HWC) 61 Xb 37
Garycullen IRL (WEX) 100 Tb 35
Garynahine GB (HGL) 11 Tb 119
Garyvard GB (HGL) 11 Td 120
Gastard GB (WIL) 61 Xe 40
Gasthorpe GB (NOR) 56 Af 34
Gatcombe GB (IOW) 70 Ye 44
Gateacre GB (MES) 44 Xa 28
Gatebeck GB (CUB) 35 Xb 23
Gateforth GB (NOY) 40 Yf 26
Gatehead GB (STC) 24 Vc 15
Gate Helmsley GB (NOY) 40 Za 25
Gatehouse of Fleet GB (DAG) 30 Ve 19
Gatelawbridge GB (DAG) 31 Wb 17
Gately GB (NOR) 49 Af 32
Gatenby GB (NOY) 36 Yc 23
Gateshead GB (TAW) 33 Yc 19
Gatesheath GB (CHS) 44 Xb 30
Gateside GB (FIF) 21 We 11
Gateside GB (TYS) 22 Xa 9
Gates of Mullagh Cross Roads, The IRL (CAV) 89 Ta 26
Gathurst GB (GRM) 38 Xb 27
Gatley GB (GRM) 45 Xe 28
Gattabaun IRL (KLK) 94 Sd 32
Gattonside GB (BOR) 26 Xb 15
Gauldry GB (FIF) 22 Wf 10
Gauls GB (TYS) 21 Wc 10
Gaulstown IRL (MT) 90 Tc 27
Gaulstown IRL (MT) 90 Tc 28
Gaunt's Common GB (DOS) 69 Ya 43
Gautby GB (LIN) 47 Ze 29
Gavinton GB (BOR) 27 Xd 14
Gawcott GB (BUS) 63 Yf 37
Gawthrop GB (CUB) 35 Xd 23
Gawthwaite GB (CUB) 34 Wf 23
Gaybrook IRL (WMT) 89 Se 28
Gaybrook House IRL (WMT) 89 Se 28
Gaydon GB (WWH) 54 Yd 35
Gayhurst GB (BUS) 54 Zb 36
Gayle GB (NOY) 35 Xe 23
Gayles GB (NOY) 36 Yb 22
Gayton GB (CHS) 44 Wf 29
Gayton GB (NOR) 48 Ad 32
Gayton GB (NRH) 54 Za 35
Gayton GB (SFS) 45 Xf 31
Gayton le Wold GB (LIN) 47 Zf 28
Gayville IRL (WMT) 94 Sd 28
Geaagh IRL (COR) 103 Ra 39
Gearha IRL (KER) 102 Qa 37
Geary GB (HGL) 12 Tc 3
Geashill IRL (OFF) 94 Se 29
Geddes Ho GB (HGL) 15 Wa 3
Geddington GB (NRH) 55 Zb 34
Gedgrave Hall GB (SUF) 57 Bd 36
Gedintailor GB (HGL) 13 Tf 4
Gedney GB (LIN) 47 Aa 32
Gedney Broadgate GB (LIN) 47 Aa 32
Gedney Drove End GB (LIN) 48 Ab 31
Gedney Dyke GB (LIN) 47 Aa 32
Gedney Hill GB (LIN) 47 Zf 32
Geehy IRL (GAL) 92 Qf 29
Geevagh IRL (SLI) 88 Re 24
Geldeston GB (NOR) 57 Bd 34
Gell GB (CLW) 43 Wb 29
Gell GB (GWY) 42 Ve 31
Gelli GB (DYF) 58 Vb 37
Gellifor GB (CLW) 43 We 30
Gelligaer GB (MGL) 60 We 39
Gellilydan GB (GWY) 43 Wa 31
Gellioedd GB (CLW) 43 Wc 31
Gellyburn GB (TYS) 21 Wd 9
Gellywen GB (DYF) 59 Vc 37
Gelston GB (DAG) 31 Wa 19
Genstown House IRL (WEX) 101 Td 35
Gentleman's IRL (KER) 97 Qc 37
Geocrab GB (HGL) 11 Ta 2
Georgeham GB (DEV) 66 Ve 42
George Nympton GB (DEV) 66 Wa 43
Georth GB (ORK) 5 Wf 114
Gerahies IRL (COR) 103 Qc 39
Gerlan GB (GWY) 43 Vf 29
Gerrardstown House IRL (DUB) 90 Te 27
Gerrans GB (CNW) 75 Va 47
Gerrards Cross GB (BUS) 63 Zc 39
Geshader GB (HGL) 11 Ta 119
Gestingthorpe GB (ESS) 56 Ad 36
Geuffordd GB (POW) 52 We 32
Gibraltar GB (LIN) 48 Ab 30
Gidleigh GB (DEV) 66 We 44
Gifford GB (LOT) 26 Xb 13
Giggleswick GB (NOY) 39 Xe 24
Gilberdyke GB (HUS) 40 Zb 26
Gilchriston GB (LOT) 26 Xb 13
Gilcrux GB (CUB) 34 Wd 20
Gildersome GB (WYO) 39 Yc 26
Gildingwells GB (SOY) 46 Yf 28
Gileston GB (SGL) 60 Wd 40
Gilfach GB (MGL) 60 We 38
Gilfach Goch GB (MGL) 60 Wd 39
Gilfachreda GB (DYF) 50 Ve 35
Gilford GB (DOW) 84 Td 22
Gilgarran GB (CUB) 34 Wc 21
Gilkagh IRL (GAL) 87 Rc 28
Gillamoor GB (NOY) 37 Za 23
Gillen GB (HGL) 12 Tc 3
Gillenbie GB (DAG) 31 We 18
Gilling East GB (NOY) 37 Yf 23
Gillingham GB (DOR) 68 Xe 42
Gillingham GB (KEN) 65 Ad 40
Gillingham GB (NOR) 57 Bd 34
Gilling West GB (NOY) 36 Yb 22
Gills GB (HGL) 6 We 117
Gill's Green GB (KEN) 72 Ad 42
Gilltown House IRL (KIL) 95 Tb 30
Gilmanscleuch GB (BOR) 32 Wf 16
Gilmerton GB (LOT) 26 Wf 13
Gilmerton GB (TYS) 21 Wb 10
Gilmorton GB (LEC) 54 Yf 34
Gilsland GB (NHL) 32 Xc 19
Gilston GB (LOT) 26 Xa 14
Gilston Park GB (HTS) 64 Aa 38
Gilwern GB (GWE) 60 Wf 38
Gipsey Bridge GB (LIN) 47 Zf 30
Girley IRL (MT) 89 Ta 27
Girlsta GB (SHL) 2 Ye 107
Girmingham GB (NOR) 49 Bc 31
Girsby GB (NOY) 36 Yd 22
Girthon GB (DAG) 30 Ve 19
Girton GB (CBS) 55 Aa 35
Girvan GB (STC) 30 Va 17
Gisburn GB (LCS) 39 Xe 25
Gisla GB (HGL) 11 Ta 120
Gisleham GB (SUF) 57 Be 34
Gislingham GB (SUF) 57 Ba 35
Gissing GB (NOR) 57 Ba 34
Givons Grove GB (SUR) 64 Ze 41
Glacknabrade IRL (DON) 78 Se 17
Gladestry GB (POW) 52 Wf 35
Gladsmuir GB (LOT) 26 Xa 13
Glais GB (WGL) 59 Wa 38
Glaisdale GB (NOY) 37 Zb 22
Glame GB (HGL) 13 Tf 4
Glamis GB (TYS) 22 Xa 9
Glan IRL (COR) 103 Qc 39
Glanaber Terrace GB (GWY) 43 Wa 30
Glanalin IRL (COR) 102 Qb 39
Glanaman GB (DYF) 59 Wa 38
Glanawillin IRL (KER) 97 Qc 34
Glanballyma IRL (KER) 97 Qc 34
Glanbannoo Upper IRL (COR) 103 Qd 38
Glanbeha House IRL (TIP) 93 Sb 31
Glan Conwy GB (GWY) 43 Wb 30
Glandford GB (NOR) 49 Ba 31
Glandine IRL (COR) 98 Rb 36
Glandore IRL (COR) 103 Qf 39
Glandwr GB (DYF) 58 Vc 37
Glanearagh IRL (KER) 102 Pd 37
Glanlough IRL (COR) 103 Qc 39
Glanlough IRL (KER) 103 Qd 37
Glanmire IRL (COR) 104 Rd 37
Glanmule GB (POW) 52 We 33
Glannagaul IRL (COR) 99 Rd 36
Glannagh IRL (LGF) 89 Sc 26
Glanoe IRL (KER) 97 Qc 34
Glanroon IRL (COR) 102 Qb 39
Glantane IRL (COR) 98 Qf 37
Glantane IRL (COR) 98 Rb 36
Glanton GB (NHL) 33 Ya 16
Glanvilles Wootton GB (DOS) 68 Xd 43
Glanworth IRL (COR) 99 Rd 35
Glan-y-don GB (CLW) 43 We 29
Glan-yr-afon GB (GWY) 43 Wc 31
Glan-yr-afon GB (GWY) 43 Wd 31
Glapthorn GB (NRH) 55 Zd 34
Glapwell GB (DSH) 46 Ye 29
Glasbury GB (POW) 52 We 36
Glascoed GB (CLW) 43 Wc 29
Glascoed GB (GWE) 60 Xa 38
Glascoed GB (POW) 51 We 32
Glascorn House IRL (WMT) 89 Sc 27
Glascorrie GB (GRP) 16 Xa 6
Glascote GB (SFS) 53 Yc 33
Glascwm GB (POW) 52 We 35
Glasdrum GB (STC) 19 Ue 9
Glasford GB (STC) 25 Vf 14
Glasfryn GB (CLW) 43 Wc 30
Glasgow GB (STC) 25 Ve 13
Glashagh IRL (DON) 77 Rf 19
Glasinfryn GB (GWY) 42 Vf 29
Glaslough IRL (MOG) 84 Ta 23
Glasmullan IRL (DON) 78 Sd 17
Glaspwll GB (POW) 51 Wa 33
Glassburn GB (HGL) 14 Vb 4
Glassenbury GB (KEN) 72 Ac 42
Glasserton GB (DAG) 29 Vd 20
Glasshouse IRL (OFF) 93 Sa 31
Glasshouse IRL (OFF) 94 Se 29
Glasshouse Hill GB (GLS) 61 Xd 37
Glasshouses GB (NOY) 39 Yb 24
Glassillaun IRL (MAY) 86 Qa 25
Glasslaw GB (GRP) 17 Xe 3
Glasslie GB (FIF) 26 We 11
Glasson GB (CUB) 31 Wf 19
Glasson GB (LCS) 38 Xa 25
Glassonby GB (CUB) 35 Xc 20
Glasterlaw GB (TYS) 22 Xc 9
Glaston GB (LEC) 55 Zb 33
Glastonbury GB (SOM) 68 Xb 42
Glastry GB (DOW) 85 Ud 22
Glatton GB (CBS) 55 Ze 34
Glazely GB (SHS) 52 Xd 34
Gleadless GB (SOY) 46 Yd 28
Gleadsmoss GB (CHS) 45 Xe 29
Gleaston GB (CUB) 38 Wf 24
Glebe IRL (DON) 78 Sc 17
Glemduff IRL (KER) 97 Qc 35
Glemsford GB (SUF) 56 Ad 36
Glen GB (DAG) 30 Ve 19

Glen **IRL** (DON) 77 Sb 18
Glenacarney **IRL** (COR) 98 Qe 35
Glenacunna **IRL** (TIP) 99 Rf 35
Glenacurragh Castle **IRL** (OFF) 93 Sb 30
Glenade **IRL** (LET) 82 Re 22
Glenagragara **IRL** (LIM) 98 Qe 33
Glenalbert House **IRL** (TIP) 93 Sb 31
Glenamoy **IRL** (MAY) 80 Qb 23
Glenancross **GB** (HGL) 13 Ua 7
Glenariffor Waterfoot **GB** (ANT) 79 Tf 18
Glenarm **GB** (ANT) 79 Ua 19
Glenasmole Lodge **IRL** (DUB) 95 Td 29
Glenasrone House **IRL** (LIM) 97 Qe 34
Glenastle **GB** (STC) 22 Te 15
Glenathonacash **IRL** (COR) 104 Rf 37
Glenatlucky **IRL** (COR) 99 Re 35
Glenavy **GB** (ANT) 84 Te 21
Glenawilling **IRL** (COR) 104 Sa 37
Glenbarr **GB** (STC) 23 Ub 15
Glenbeg **GB** (HGL) 18 Ua 8
Glenbeg House **IRL** (WTF) 99 Sb 36
Glenbeigh **IRL** (KER) 97 Qa 36
Glen Bernisdale **GB** (HGL) 13 Te 4
Glenbervie **GB** (GRP) 22 Xd 7
Glenboig **GB** (STC) 25 Vf 13
Glenborrodale **GB** (HGL) 18 Ua 8
Glenbough **IRL** (WEX) 101 Td 34
Glenboy **IRL** (LET) 82 Rf 23
Glenbreck **GB** (BOR) 31 Wd 16
Glenbreedy **IRL** (TIP) 93 Rf 32
Glenbride Lodge **IRL** (WKL) 95 Td 30
Glenbrien **IRL** (WEX) 101 Td 34
Glenbrittle House **GB** (HGL) 13 Te 5
Glenbrook **IRL** (MOG) 83 Sf 23
Glenbuck **GB** (STC) 31 Wa 15
Glenburn **GB** (STC) 24 Vd 14
Glencanisp Lodge **GB** (HGL) 7 Ue 120
Glencaple **GB** (DAG) 31 Wc 18
Glencarse **GB** (TYS) 21 We 10
Glencoe **GB** (HGL) 19 Uf 8
Glencolumbkille **IRL** (DON) 82 Rb 20
Glencolumbkille House **IRL** (CRE) 92 Qf 30
Glencraig **GB** (FIF) 26 We 12
Glencruittein **GB** (STC) 19 Ud 10
Glencullin Lower **IRL** (MAY) 80 Qb 23
Glencullin Upper **IRL** (MAY) 80 Qb 23
Glendalligan Wood **IRL** (WTF) 100 Sc 36
Glendalough **IRL** (WTF) 99 Sc 35
Glendalough House **IRL** (KER) 97 Qa 36
Glenderry **IRL** (KER) 97 Qa 34
Glendevon **GB** (TYS) 25 Wc 11
Glendoebeg **GB** (HGL) 14 Vc 6
Glendon Hall **GB** (NRH) 54 Zb 34
Glendoon Hill **IRL** (DON) 77 Sb 19
Glendorragha **IRL** (DON) 77 Rc 20
Glendowan **IRL** (DON) 77 Sa 19
Glenduckie **GB** (FIF) 21 Wf 10
Glenduff **IRL** (COR) 99 Re 35
Gleneagles House **GB** (TYS) 25 Wb 11
Glenealy **IRL** (WKL) 95 Tf 31
Gleneely **IRL** (DON) 78 Sf 17
Glenegedale **GB** (STC) 22 Te 14
Gleneig **GB** (HGL) 13 Uc 5
Glenfarg **GB** (TYS) 21 Wd 11
Glenfarne **IRL** (LET) 82 Sa 23
Glenfield **GB** (LEC) 54 Ye 33
Glenfinnan **GB** (HGL) 19 Ud 7
Glenflesk **IRL** (KER) 97 Qd 36
Glenfoot **GB** (TYS) 21 We 11
Glengarnock **GB** (STC) 24 Vb 14
Glengarriff **IRL** (COR) 103 Qc 38
Glengormley **GB** (ANT) 85 Ua 20
Glengort **IRL** (LIM) 98 Qe 34
Glengoulandie **GB** (TYS) 20 Vf 9
Glengrasco **GB** (HGL) 13 Te 4
Glen House **GB** (BOR) 26 Wf 15
Glenidan Cross Roads **IRL** (MT) 89 Sf 26
Glenkerry **GB** (BOR) 31 Wf 16
Glenkindie **GB** (GRP) 16 Xa 5
Glenkullen **IRL** (DUB) 95 Te 29
Glenlary Cott **IRL** (LIM) 99 Rd 34
Glenlee **GB** (DAG) 30 Ve 18
Glenlivet **GB** (GRP) 16 Wd 4
Glenluce **GB** (DAG) 30 Va 19
Glenmaquin **IRL** (DON) 77 Sb 19
Glenmaye **GBM** 29 Vb 23
Glenmore **GB** (HGL) 13 Te 4
Glenmore **IRL** (CRE) 92 Qe 32
Glenmore **IRL** (KLK) 100 Sf 34
Glenmore **IRL** (LGF) 89 Sc 25
Glenmullynaha Cross Roads **IRL** (MAY) 87 Rb 25
Glennagashleeny **IRL** (MAY) 87 Qd 26
Glennagat **IRL** (TIP) 99 Sa 34
Glennageare **IRL** (COR) 104 Rf 37
Glennaknockane **IRL** (COR) 98 Qf 35
Glennamaddy **IRL** (GAL) 88 Rc 27
Glennan **IRL** (MOG) 84 Ta 23
Glennanore **IRL** (WTF) 99 Sc 35
Glenndgevlagh **IRL** (GAL) 86 Qb 27
Glen of Newmill **GB** (GRP) 16 Xa 3
Glenoghil **IRL** (LGF) 89 Sb 26
Glenoghil **IRL** (LGF) 89 Sc 26
Glenomera **IRL** (CRE) 92 Rc 32
Glen Parva **GB** (LEC) 54 Yf 33
Glenpipe **IRL** (KLK) 100 Sf 34
Glen Poer **IRL** (WTF) 100 Sc 34
Glenrazie **GB** (DAG) 30 Vc 19
Glenreagh **IRL** (COR) 98 Qe 35
Glenree **IRL** (DON) 77 Sb 18
Glenridding **GB** (CUB) 35 Xa 21
Glenrothes **GB** (FIF) 26 Wf 11
Glenroughra **IRL** (GAL) 88 Rd 27
Glensaugh **GB** (GRP) 22 Xc 7
Glensharrold **IRL** (LIM) 98 Qf 33
Glenshask **IRL** (WTF) 99 Sa 35
Glenside **GB** (HGL) 11 Td 120
Glen Sluain **GB** (STC) 24 Uf 12
Glensmill **IRL** (DON) 78 Sc 19
Glentane **IRL** (GAL) 88 Rc 28
Glentham **GB** (LIN) 41 Zd 28
Glenties **IRL** (DON) 77 Re 20
Glentogher **IRL** (DON) 78 Se 17
Glen Tolsta **GB** (HGL) 11 Te 119
Glenton **GB** (GRP) 17 Xc 5
Glentooskert **IRL** (DON) 78 Se 16
Glentrasna **IRL** (GAL) 86 Qc 28
Glentress **GB** (BOR) 26 Wf 15
Glen Trool Lodge **GB** (DAG) 30 Vd 18
Glentrool Village **GB** (DAG) 30 Vc 18
Glenuig **GB** (HGL) 19 Ub 8
Glenvar **IRL** (DON) 77 Sc 18
Glenville **IRL** (COR) 98 Rd 36
Glenville House **IRL** (CRE) 92 Qd 31
Glen Vine **GBM** 29 Vc 23
Glespin **GB** (STC) 31 Wa 15
Gletness **GB** (SHL) 2 Yf 107
Glewstone **GB** (HWC) 61 Xc 37
Glin **IRL** (LIM) 98 Qe 33
Glinsk **IRL** (DON) 77 Sb 17
Glinsk **IRL** (GAL) 86 Qb 28
Glinton **GB** (CBS) 55 Ze 33
Glooston **GB** (LEC) 54 Za 33
Glossop **GB** (DSH) 39 Ya 28
Gloster **IRL** (OFF) 93 Sa 30
Gloucester **GB** (GLS) 61 Xe 37
Gloup **GB** (SHL) 2 Yf 104
Glusburn **GB** (NOY) 39 Ya 25
Gluss **GB** (SHL) 2 Yd 106
Glympton **GB** (OXS) 62 Yd 37
Glynarthen **GB** (DYF) 50 Uc 36
Glyn Ceiriog **GB** (CLW) 44 We 31
Glyncorrwg **GB** (WGL) 60 Wc 38
Glynde **GB** (ESX) 71 Aa 43
Glyndebourne **GB** (ESX) 71 Aa 43
Glyndyfrdwy **GB** (CLW) 43 We 31
Glynn **GB** (ANT) 85 Ub 20
Glynn **IRL** (CLW) 100 Ta 33
Glynn **IRL** (WEX) 101 Tc 34
Glynn Cross Roads **IRL** (KIL) 94 Sf 28
Glyn Neath **GB** (WGL) 60 Wc 38
Glynogwr **GB** (MGL) 60 Wd 39
Glyntaff **GB** (MGL) 60 We 39
Gneevguilla **IRL** (KER) 97 Qe 36
Gnosall **GB** (SFS) 45 Xe 32
Goadby **GB** (LEC) 54 Za 33
Goatacre **GB** (WIL) 62 Ya 40
Goathill **GB** (DOS) 68 Xd 43
Goathland **GB** (NOY) 37 Zb 22
Goathurst **GB** (SOM) 67 Wf 42
Goatstown **IRL** (KIL) 95 Tb 29
Goatstown **IRL** (TIP) 93 Rf 30
Gobowen **GB** (SHS) 44 Wf 31
Godalming **GB** (SUR) 70 Zc 41
Godmanchester **GB** (CBS) 55 Zf 35
Godmanstone **GB** (DOS) 68 Xd 44
Godmersham **GB** (KEN) 65 Af 41
Godolphin Cross **GB** (CNW) 74 Ud 48
Godre'r-graig **GB** (WGL) 59 Wb 38
Godshill **GB** (IOW) 70 Ye 45
Godstone **GB** (SUR) 71 Zf 41
Goff's Oak **GB** (HTS) 64 Zf 38
Goginan **GB** (DYF) 51 Wa 34
Goirtein **GB** (STC) 23 Ue 12
Golan **GB** (GWY) 42 Ve 31
Golant **GB** (CNW) 75 Vc 46
Golborne **GB** (GRM) 38 Xc 28
Golcar **GB** (WYO) 39 Ya 27
Goldcliff **GB** (GWE) 60 Xa 39
Golden **IRL** (TIP) 99 Sa 34
Golden Ball **IRL** (DUB) 95 Te 29
Golden Cross **GB** (ESX) 71 Ab 43
Golden Green **GB** (KEN) 72 Ac 41
Golden Grove **GB** (DYF) 59 Vf 37
Golden Pot **GB** (HAS) 70 Za 41
Goldhanger **GB** (ESS) 65 Ae 38
Goldielea **GB** (DAG) 31 Wc 18
Golding **GB** (SHS) 52 Xb 33
Goldings Cross **IRL** (TIP) 93 Sa 32
Goldsborough **GB** (NOY) 37 Zb 21
Goldsborough **GB** (NOY) 40 Yd 25
Goldthorpe **GB** (SOY) 40 Ye 27
Goleen **IRL** (COR) 102 Qb 40
Gollanfield **GB** (HGL) 15 Wa 3
Golspie **GB** (HGL) 9 Wa 1
Golval **GB** (HGL) 5 Wa 117
Gomersal **GB** (WYO) 39 Yb 26
Gomshall **GB** (SUR) 71 Zd 41
Gonfirth **GB** (SHL) 2 Ye 106
Gooderstone **GB** (NOR) 56 Ad 33
Goodmanham **GB** (HUS) 40 Zc 25
Goodnestone **GB** (KEN) 65 Af 41
Goodnestone **GB** (KEN) 65 Bb 41
Goodrich **GB** (HWC) 61 Xc 37
Goodrington **GB** (DEV) 76 Wc 46
Goodwick **GB** (DYF) 58 Uf 36
Goodworth Clatford **GB** (HAS) 69 Yd 41
Goodyers End **GB** (WWH) 54 Yc 34
Goole **GB** (HUS) 40 Za 26
Goonhavern **GB** (CNW) 74 Uf 46
Gooseberryhill **IRL** (COR) 98 Ra 35
Goose Green **GB** (KEN) 72 Ac 41
Goosey **GB** (OXS) 62 Yd 39
Goosnargh **GB** (LCS) 38 Xc 26
Goostrey **GB** (CHS) 45 Xd 29
Gorcott Hill **GB** (WWH) 53 Ya 35
Gordon **GB** (BOR) 26 Xc 14
Gordonbush **GB** (HGL) 9 Wa 120
Gordonstown **GB** (GRP) 16 Xb 3
Gordonstown **GB** (GRP) 17 Xd 4
Gorebridge **GB** (LOT) 26 Wf 13
Gorefield **GB** (CBS) 47 Aa 32
Goresbridge **IRL** (KLK) 100 Ta 33
Gorey **GBJ** 73 Xf 53
Gorey **IRL** (DON) 78 Se 17
Gorey **IRL** (WEX) 101 Te 32
Goringagunned **IRL** (GAL) 87 Ra 27
Goring **GB** (OXS) 63 Yf 39
Gorleston-on-Sea **GB** (NOR) 57 Be 33
Gorley **GB** (HAS) 69 Yb 43
Gormanlough Cross Roads **IRL** (MT) 90 Tc 26
Gormanstown **IRL** (MT) 90 Te 27
Gorrachie **GB** (GRP) 17 Xd 3
Gorran Churchtown **GB** (CNW) 75 Vb 47
Gorran Haven **GB** (CNW) 75 Vb 47
Gors **GB** (DYF) 51 Vf 34
Gorsedd **GB** (CLW) 43 We 29
Gorseinon **GB** (WGL) 59 Vf 38
Gorseness **GB** (ORK) 6 Wf 114
Gorsgoch **GB** (DYF) 50 Ve 36
Gorslas **GB** (DYF) 59 Vf 38
Gorsley **GB** (GLS) 61 Xd 37
Gorstan **GB** (HGL) 14 Vb 3
Gorsty Common **GB** (HWC) 52 Xb 36
Gort **IRL** (GAL) 92 Rb 30
Gortacareen **IRL** (KER) 97 Qe 36
Gortacloghane **IRL** (KER) 97 Qd 34
Gortaculrush **IRL** (TIP) 99 Sa 33
Gortafludig **IRL** (COR) 103 Qe 37
Gortagowan **IRL** (KER) 102 Qa 37
Gortagurrane **IRL** (KER) 97 Qc 34
Gortaheera **IRL** (CRE) 92 Qe 32
Gortahork **IRL** (DON) 77 Rf 18
Gortalla Junction **IRL** (KER) 97 Qc 35
Gortaleam **IRL** (GAL) 87 Rb 27
Gortaneelig **IRL** (COR) 98 Rc 36
Gortanummera **IRL** (GAL) 93 Re 30
Gortareask **IRL** (GAL) 93 Rd 29
Gortarevan **IRL** (OFF) 93 Rf 29
Gortaroo **IRL** (COR) 104 Sa 37
Gortatlea **IRL** (KER) 97 Pf 37
Gortatleva **IRL** (GAL) 92 Ra 28
Gortavalla **IRL** (LIM) 99 Re 33
Gortaway **IRL** (DON) 77 Sc 18
Gortayoher **IRL** (GAL) 93 Rd 29
Gortbrack **IRL** (KER) 97 Qc 35
Gortbrack **IRL** (MAY) 87 Qe 28
Gortbrack North **IRL** (MAY) 80 Qa 23
Gortbrack South **IRL** (MAY) 86 Qb 24
Gortcloonmore **IRL** (GAL) 92 Ra 28
Gortearagh **IRL** (COR) 98 Qf 35
Gorteen **IRL** (GAL) 92 Rc 28
Gorteen **IRL** (KLK) 94 Sf 32
Gorteen **IRL** (LGF) 88 Sb 27
Gorteen **IRL** (LIM) 98 Ra 34
Gorteen **IRL** (SLI) 88 Rc 25
Gorteenboy **IRL** (GAL) 92 Rb 30
Gorteen Bridge **IRL** (OFF) 94 Sd 29
Gorteenkeel **IRL** (OFF) 94 Se 29
Gorteeny **IRL** (GAL) 93 Rd 30
Gortgar **IRL** (GAL) 92 Qe 29
Gortgarriff **IRL** (COR) 102 Qa 38
Gortglass **IRL** (KER) 97 Qd 35
Gorthaun **IRL** (MAY) 87 Qd 26
Gortin **GB** (TYR) 83 Se 20
Gortknockaneroe **IRL** (COR) 98 Ra 35
Gortletteragh **IRL** (LET) 88 Sb 25
Gortlush **IRL** (DON) 78 Sd 19
Gortmellia **IRL** (MAY) 80 Qa 23
Gortmore **IRL** (MAY) 81 Qd 23
Gortmore House **IRL** (COR) 98 Rb 36
Gortmore House **IRL** (TIP) 93 Re 30
Gortnabrade **IRL** (DON) 77 Sb 18
Gortnagallon **GB** (ANT) 84 Te 21
Gortnagan **IRL** (CRE) 92 Qe 32
Gortnagane **IRL** (KER) 97 Qe 36
Gortnagroagh **IRL** (GAL) 87 Qe 28
Gortnahoe **IRL** (TIP) 99 Sc 32
Gortnahoon **IRL** (GAL) 93 Rd 29
Gortnahorna House **IRL** (COR) 104 Rb 38
Gortnahorna House **IRL** (GAL) 93 Re 29
Gortnahoughtee **IRL** (COR) 103 Qf 38
Gortnakilla **IRL** (KER) 96 Qe 37
Gortnakilly **IRL** (COR) 102 Qb 39
Gortnamearacaun **IRL** (CRE) 92 Rc 31
Gortnasillagh **IRL** (ROS) 88 Rd 26
Gortree **IRL** (DON) 78 Sc 19
Gortroche **IRL** (COR) 99 Rd 36
Gortroe **IRL** (COR) 98 Rb 36
Gortroe House **IRL** (LIM) 98 Ra 34
Gortsleehy **IRL** (MAY) 87 Qf 27
Gosbeck **GB** (SUF) 57 Ba 36
Gosberton **GB** (LIN) 47 Zf 31
Gosfield **GB** (ESS) 65 Ad 37
Gosforth **GB** (CUB) 34 Wd 22
Gosforth **GB** (TAW) 33 Yc 18
Gosmore **GB** (HTS) 64 Ze 37
Gospel End **GB** (SFS) 53 Xf 33
Gosport **GB** (HAS) 70 Yf 44
Gossabrough **GB** (SHL) 2 Yf 105
Goswick **GB** (NHL) 27 Ya 14
Gotham **GB** (NTS) 46 Ye 31
Gotherington **GB** 61 Xf 37
Goudhurst **GB** (KEN) 72 Ac 42
Goulceby **GB** (LIN) 47 Zf 29
Gourdas **GB** (GRP) 17 Xd 4
Gourdon **GB** (GRP) 22 Xe 8
Gourock **GB** (STC) 24 Vb 13
Govan **GB** (STC) 25 Ve 13
Goveton **GB** (DEV) 76 Wb 47
Govig **GB** (HGL) 11 Sf 1
Govilon **GB** (GWE) 60 Wf 38
Gowanhill **GB** (GRP) 17 Ya 3
Gowerhass **IRL** (CRE) 91 Qd 32
Gowerton **GB** (WGL) 59 Vf 39
Gowkhall **GB** (FIF) 25 Wc 12
Gowlane **IRL** (KER) 103 Qc 37
Gowlane North **IRL** (COR) 98 Rb 36
Gowlaun **IRL** (GAL) 86 Qa 27
Gowlaun **IRL** (LET) 82 Rf 23
Gowlaun **IRL** (WTF) 99 Sc 36
Gowlin **IRL** (CLW) 100 Ta 33
Gowran **IRL** (KLK) 100 Sf 33
Goxhill **GB** (HUS) 41 Ze 26
Gracehill **GB** (ANT) 79 Te 19
Graet Salkeld **GB** (CUB) 35 Xb 20
Graffanstown **IRL** (WMT) 89 Sf 27
Graffham **GB** (WSX) 70 Zb 43
Graffy **IRL** (DON) 77 Rf 20
Grafham **GB** (CBS) 55 Ze 35
Grafham **GB** (SUR) 71 Zc 42
Grafton **GB** (HWC) 52 Xc 35
Grafton **GB** (HWC) 61 Xb 36
Grafton **GB** (NOY) 40 Yd 24
Grafton **GB** (OXS) 62 Yc 38
Grafton **GB** (SHS) 44 Xa 32
Grafton Flyford **GB** (HWC) 53 Xf 35
Grafton Regis **GB** (NRH) 54 Za 36
Grafton Underwood **GB** (NRH) 55 Zc 34
Grafty Green **GB** (KEN) 72 Zc 41
Graghill **IRL** (MAY) 80 Qa 23
Graianrhyd **GB** (CLW) 44 We 30
Graig **GB** (CLW) 43 Wd 29
Graig **GB** (GWY) 43 Wb 29
Graig Abbey **IRL** (GAL) 92 Rb 29
Graig-fechan **GB** (CLW) 43 We 30
Graig na Managh = Graiguenamanagh **IRL** (KLK) 100 Ta 33
Graigneavallagh **IRL** (LAO) 93 Sc 31
Graig Penllyn **GB** (SGL) 60 Wd 40
Graigue **IRL** (KER) 96 Pd 36
Graigue **IRL** (TIP) 99 Sa 35
Graigue Cross Roads **IRL** (LIM) 98 Rc 34
Graigue Great **IRL** (WEX) 100 Ta 35
Graigue Little **IRL** (WEX) 100 Ta 35
Graigue More **IRL** (WEX) 101 Tc 33
Graiguenamanagh **IRL** (KLK) 100 Ta 33
Graigueooly **IRL** (KLK) 100 Sd 33
Grain **GB** (KEN) 65 Ae 40
Grainsby **GB** (LIN) 41 Zf 28
Grainthorpe **GB** (LIN) 41 Aa 28
Graizelound **GB** (HUS) 40 Za 28
Grampound **GB** (CNW) 75 Va 47
Grampound Road **GB** (CNW) 75 Va 47
Granae and Kiltober **IRL** (WMT) 94 Sd 28
Granard **IRL** (LGF) 89 Sd 26
Granborough **GB** (BUS) 63 Za 37
Granby **GB** (NTS) 46 Za 31
Grandborough **GB** (WWH) 54 Ye 35
Grande **IRL** (LIM) 98 Rc 33
Graney **IRL** (KIL) 95 Tb 31
Graney House **IRL** (KIL) 95 Tb 31
Granford **IRL** (DON) 77 Sb 18
Grange **GB** (CHS) 44 We 28
Grange **GB** (CUB) 34 Wf 21
Grange **GB** (KEN) 65 Ad 40
Grange **GB** (TYR) 84 Tb 21
Grange **GB** (TYS) 21 We 10
Grange **IRL** (GAL) 87 Qf 28
Grange **IRL** (GAL) 92 Ra 28
Grange **IRL** (LAO) 94 Se 30
Grange **IRL** (LOT) 90 Te 24
Grange **IRL** (OFF) 94 Sf 28
Grange **IRL** (SLI) 82 Rc 22
Grange **IRL** (TIP) 93 Rd 32
Grange **IRL** (TIP) 99 Sb 34
Grange **IRL** (WEX) 101 Tc 35
Grange **IRL** (WTF) 104 Sb 37
Grange Beg **IRL** (KIL) 94 Ta 30
Grange Beg **IRL** (LAO) 94 Sc 31
Grangebellew **IRL** (LOT) 90 Te 26
Grange Con **IRL** (WKL) 95 Tb 31
Grange Corner **GB** (ANT) 84 Td 20
Grange Crossroads **GB** (GRP) 16 Xa 3
Grange Cross Roads **IRL** (TIP) 99 Sb 35
Grangegeeth **IRL** (MT) 90 Tc 26
Grangegeeth Cross Roads **IRL** (MT) 90 Tc 26
Grangegoddan Glebe **IRL** (MT) 89 Ta 26
Grange Hall **IRL** (WMT) 89 Sd 27
Grangemill **GB** (DSH) 45 Yc 30
Grange Moor **GB** (WYO) 39 Yc 27
Grange More House **IRL** (WMT) 89 Sf 27
Grangemouth **GB** (CEN) 25 Wb 12
Grange of Lindores **GB** (FIF) 21 We 10
Grange-over-Sands **GB** (CUB) 35 Xa 23
Grangerosnolvan **IRL** (KIL) 94 Ta 31
Grangestown **IRL** (WMT) 89 Sd 27
Grangetown **GB** (CLE) 37 Yf 21
Grange Villa **GB** (DUR) 33 Yc 19
Grangewilliam **IRL** (KIL) 95 Tc 28
Graniamore **IRL** (SLI) 88 Rd 24
Grannagh **IRL** (GAL) 92 Rb 30
Grannahulla **IRL** (COR) 98 Rc 35
Gransmoor **GB** (HUS) 41 Ze 24
Granston **GB** (DYF) 58 Uf 37
Grantchester **GB** (CBS) 55 Aa 35
Grantham **GB** (LIN) 47 Zc 31
Grantley **GB** (NOY) 36 Yc 24
Grantlodge **GB** (GRP) 17 Xd 5
Granton House **GB** (DAG) 31 Wd 16
Grantown-on-Spey **GB** (HGL) 16 Wc 4
Grantshouse **GB** (BOR) 27 Xe 13
Grantstown Lough **IRL** (LAO) 94 Sc 31
Granville **GB** (TYR) 84 Tb 22
Grappenhall **GB** (CHS) 44 Xc 28
Grasby **GB** (LIN) 41 Zd 27
Grasmere **GB** (CUB) 34 Wf 22
Grasscroft **GB** (GRM) 39 Xf 27
Grassendale **GB** (MES) 44 Xa 28
Grassholme **GB** (DUR) 35 Xf 21
Grassington **GB** (NOY) 39 Ya 24
Grassmoor **GB** (DSH) 46 Yd 29
Grassthorpe **GB** (NTS) 46 Zb 29
Gratty **IRL** (MAY) 87 Qf 25
Gratwich **GB** (SFS) 45 Ya 31
Graveley **GB** (CBS) 55 Zf 35
Graveley **GB** (HTS) 64 Ze 37
Gravelly Hill **GB** (WMD) 53 Ya 33
Gravels **GB** (SHS) 52 Xa 33
Graveney **GB** (KEN) 65 Af 41
Gravesend **GB** (KEN) 64 Ac 40
Gravir **GB** (HGL) 11 Td 120
Grawfordsburn **GB** (DOW) 85 Ub 21
Grayingham **GB** (LIN) 41 Zc 28
Grayrigg **GB** (CUB) 35 Xc 22
Grays **GB** (ESS) 64 Ab 40
Grayshott **GB** (HAS) 70 Zb 42
Grayswood **GB** (SUR) 70 Zb 42
Grazeley **GB** (BKS) 63 Za 40
Grazies Hill **GB** (BKS) 63 Za 39
Greaahnafarna **IRL** (ROS) 88 Rf 24
Greagh **IRL** (LGF) 88 Sb 26
Greaghans **IRL** (MAY) 87 Qf 27
Greagh Cross Roads **IRL** (LET) 88 Sb 25
Greaghlatacapple **IRL** (MOG) 90 Tb 24
Greasbrough **GB** (SOY) 40 Yd 28
Greasby **GB** (CHS) 44 Wf 28
Great Abington **GB** (CBS) 56 Ab 36
Great Addington **GB** (NRH) 55 Zc 34
Great Alne **GB** (WWH) 53 Yb 35
Great Altcar **GB** (LCS) 38 Wf 27
Great Amwell **GB** (HTS) 64 Zf 38
Great Asby **GB** (CUB) 35 Xd 21
Great Ashfield **GB** (SUF) 56 Af 35
Great Ayton **GB** (NOY) 37 Yf 22
Great Baddow **GB** (ESS) 65 Ac 38
Great Bardfield **GB** (ESS) 56 Ac 37
Great Barford **GB** (BFS) 55 Zd 36
Great Barrington **GB** (GLS) 62 Yb 38
Great Barrow **GB** (CHS) 44 Xb 29
Great Barton **GB** (SUF) 56 Ae 35
Great Barugh **GB** (NOY) 37 Za 23
Great Bealings **GB** (SUF) 57 Bb 36
Great Bedwyn **GB** (WIL) 62 Yc 40
Great Bentley **GB** (ESS) 65 Ba 37
Great Bircham **GB** (NOR) 48 Ad 31
Great Blakenham **GB** (SUF) 57 Ba 36
Great Bolas **GB** (SHS) 44 Xc 32
Great Bookham **GB** (SUR) 64 Zd 41
Great Bourton **GB** (OXS) 54 Yd 36
Great Bowden **GB** (LEC) 54 Za 34
Great Bradley **GB** (SUF) 56 Ac 36
Great Braxted **GB** (ESS) 65 Ae 38
Great Brickhill **GB** (BUS) 63 Zb 37
Great Bridgeford **GB** (SFS) 45 Xe 31
Great Brington **GB** (NRH) 54 Yf 35
Great Bromley **GB** (ESS) 65 Ba 37
Great Broughton **GB** (NOY) 37 Yf 22
Great Budworth **GB** (CHS) 44 Xc 29
Great Burstead **GB** (ESS) 64 Ac 39
Great Busby **GB** (NOY) 37 Ye 22
Great Canfield **GB** (ESS) 64 Ab 38
Great Carlton **GB** (LIN) 47 Aa 28
Great Casterton **GB** (LEC) 55 Zc 32
Great Chart **GB** (KEN) 72 Ae 42
Great Chesterford **GB** (ESS) 56 Ab 36
Great Chishill **GB** (CBS) 55 Aa 36
Great Clacton **GB** (ESS) 65 Ba 38
Great Clifton **GB** (CUB) 34 Wc 21
Great Coates **GB** (HUS) 41 Zf 27
Great Comberton **GB** (HWC) 53 Xf 36
Great Corby **GB** (CUB) 32 Xb 19
Great Cornard **GB** (SUF) 56 Ae 36
Great Cowden **GB** (HUS) 41 Zf 25
Great Coxwell **GB** (OXS) 62 Yc 39
Great Cressingham **GB** (NOR) 56 Ae 33
Great Crosby **GB** (MES) 38 Wf 28
Great Cubley **GB** (DSH) 45 Yb 31
Great Dalby **GB** (LEC) 46 Za 32
Great Doddington **GB** (NRH) 55 Zb 35
Greatdown **IRL** (WMT) 89 Se 27
Great Dunford **GB** (WIL) 69 Yb 42
Great Dunham **GB** (NOR) 48 Ae 32
Great Dunmow **GB** (ESS) 64 Ac 37
Great Easton **GB** (ESS) 64 Ab 37
Great Easton **GB** (LEC) 54 Zb 33
Great Eccleston **GB** (LCS) 38 Xa 25
Great Edstone **GB** (NOY) 37 Za 23
Great Ellingham **GB** (NOR) 56 Af 33
Great Eversden **GB** (CBS) 55 Zf 36
Great Finborough **GB** (SUF) 57 Af 35
Greatford **GB** (LIN) 47 Zd 32
Great Fransham **GB** (NOR) 48 Ae 32
Great Gaddesden **GB** (HTS) 63 Zc 38
Great Gidding **GB** (CBS) 55 Zd 34
Great Givendale **GB** (HUS) 40 Zb 25
Great Glemham **GB** (SUF) 57 Bc 35
Great Glen **GB** (LEC) 54 Yf 33
Great Gonerby **GB** (LIN) 47 Zc 31
Great Gransden **GB** (CBS) 55 Zf 35
Great Green **GB** (NOR) 57 Bc 34
Great Greene **GB** (BFS) 55 Zc 36
Great Habton **GB** (NOY) 37 Za 23
Great Hallingbury **GB** (ESS) 64 Ab 37
Greatham **GB** (CLE) 36 Ye 21
Greatham **GB** (HAS) 70 Za 42
Greatham **GB** (WSX) 71 Zc 43
Great Hampden **GB** (BUS) 63 Zb 38
Great Harrowden **GB** (NRH) 55 Zb 35
Great Harwood **GB** (LCS) 38 Xd 26
Great Haseley **GB** (OXS) 63 Yf 38
Great Hatfield **GB** (HUS) 41 Ze 25
Great Heck **GB** (NOY) 40 Yf 26
Great Henny **GB** (ESS) 56 Ae 36
Great Hinton **GB** (WIL) 61 Xf 41
Great Hockham **GB** (NOR) 56 Af 34
Great Holland **GB** (ESS) 65 Bb 38
Great Horkesley **GB** (ESS) 56 Af 37
Great Hormead **GB** (HTS) 64 Aa 37
Great Horwood **GB** (BUS) 63 Za 37
Great Houghton **GB** (NRH) 54 Za 35
Great Houghton **GB** (SOY) 40 Yd 27
Great Hucklow **GB** (DSH) 45 Yb 29
Great Kelk **GB** (HUS) 41 Ze 24
Great Kimble **GB** (BUS) 63 Zb 38
Great Kingshill **GB** (BUS) 63 Zb 38
Great Langton **GB** (NOY) 36 Yc 22
Great Leighs **GB** (ESS) 65 Ad 38
Great Limber **GB** (LIN) 41 Ze 27
Great Livermere **GB** (SUF) 56 Ae 35
Great Lumley **GB** (DUR) 33 Yc 19
Great Lyth **GB** (SHS) 52 Xb 33
Great Malvern **GB** (HWC) 53 Xe 36
Great Maplestead **GB** (ESS) 56 Ad 37
Great Marton **GB** (LCS) 38 Wf 26
Great Massingham **GB** (NOR) 48 Ae 32
Great Melton **GB** (NOR) 57 Ba 33
Great Milton **GB** (OXS) 63 Yf 38
Great Missenden **GB** (BUS) 63 Zb 38
Great Mitton **GB** (LCS) 38 Xd 25
Great Mongeham **GB** (KEN) 65 Bc 41
Great Musgrave **GB** (CUB) 35 Xd 21
Great Ness **GB** (SHS) 44 Xa 32
Great Oakley **GB** (ESS) 65 Bb 37
Great Oakley **GB** (NRH) 55 Zb 34
Great Offley **GB** (HTS) 64 Ze 37
Great Ormside **GB** (CUB) 35 Xd 21
Great Orton **GB** (CUB) 32 Wf 19
Great Oxendon **GB** (NRH) 54 Za 34
Great Palgrave **GB** (NOR) 48 Ae 32
Great Parndon **GB** (ESS) 64 Aa 38
Great Paxton **GB** (CBS) 55 Ze 35
Great Plumstead **GB** (NOR) 49 Bc 33
Great Ponton **GB** (LIN) 47 Zc 31
Great Preston **GB** (WYO) 40 Yd 26
Great Raveley **GB** (CBS) 55 Zf 34
Great Rollright **GB** (OXS) 62 Yc 37
Great Ryburgh **GB** (NOR) 49 Af 32
Great Ryle **GB** (NHL) 33 Ya 16
Great Ryton **GB** (SHS) 52 Xb 33
Great Saling **GB** (ESS) 65 Ac 37
Great Sampford **GB** (ESS) 56 Ac 37
Great Sankey **GB** (CHS) 44 Xc 28
Great Saxham **GB** (SUF) 56 Ad 35
Great Shefford **GB** (BKS) 62 Yd 40
Great Shelford **GB** (CBS) 56 Aa 36
Great Smeaton **GB** (NOY) 36 Yd 22
Great Snoring **GB** (NOR) 48 Af 31
Great Somerford **GB** (WIL) 61 Xf 39
Great Soudley **GB** (SHS) 45 Xd 31
Great Stainton **GB** (DUR) 36 Yd 21
Great Stambridge **GB** (ESS) 65 Ae 39
Great Steeping **GB** (LIN) 47 Aa 30
Great Stonar **GB** (KEN) 65 Bb 41
Greatstone-on-Sea **GB** (KEN) 72 Af 43
Great Strickland **GB** (CUB) 35 Xb 21
Great Stukeley **GB** (CBS) 55 Ze 34
Great Sturton **GB** (LIN) 47 Ze 29
Great Sutton **GB** (CHS) 44 Xa 29
Great Swinburne **GB** (NHL) 33 Xf 18
Great Tew **GB** (OXS) 62 Yd 37
Great Tey **GB** (ESS) 65 Ae 37
Great Thurlow **GB** (SUF) 56 Ac 36
Great Torrington **GB** (DEV) 66 Vf 43
Great Tosson **GB** (NHL) 33 Ya 17
Great Totham **GB** (ESS) 65 Ae 38
Great Wakering **GB** (ESS) 65 Ae 39
Great Waldingfield **GB** (SUF) 56 Ae 36
Great Walsingham **GB** (NOR) 48 Af 31
Great Waltham **GB** (ESS) 65 Ac 38
Great Warley **GB** (ESS) 64 Ab 39
Great Washbourne **GB** (GLS) 62 Xf 36
Great Welnetham **GB** (SUF) 56 Ae 35
Great Wenham **GB** (SUF) 57 Ba 36
Great Whittington **GB** (NHL) 33 Ya 18
Great Wigborough **GB** (ESS) 65 Af 38
Great Wilbraham **GB** (CBS) 56 Ab 35
Great Witcombe **GB** (GLS) 61 Xf 38
Great Witley **GB** (HWC) 53 Xd 35
Great Wolford **GB** (WWH) 53 Yc 36
Greatworth **GB** (NRH) 54 Ye 36
Great Wratting **GB** (SUF) 56 Ac 36
Great Wymondley **GB** (HTS) 64 Ze 37
Great Wyrley **GB** (SFS) 53 Xf 33
Great Wytheford **GB** (SHS) 44 Xc 32
Great Yarmouth **GB** (NOR) 57 Be 33
Great Yeldham **GB** (ESS) 56 Ad 36
Greenan **IRL** (WKL) 95 Te 31
Greenan's Cross Roads **IRL** (MOG) 83 Sf 23
Greenans **IRL** (MAY) 87 Qe 25
Greenanstown **IRL** (MT) 90 Te 27
Greencastle **GB** (ANT) 85 Ua 21
Greencastle **IRL** (DON) 78 Ta 17
Green Cross Roads **IRL** (LAO) 94 Sc 31
Green Door, The **IRL** (GAL) 93 Re 30
Greendykes **GB** (NHL) 27 Ya 15
Green End **GB** (BFS) 55 Zd 36
Greenfield **GB** (CLW) 44 We 29
Greenfield **GB** (GRM) 39 Ya 27
Greenfield **GB** (OXS) 63 Za 39
Greenfield House **IRL** (COR) 103 Ra 39
Greenfield House **IRL** (TIP) 99 Re 33
Greenford **GB** (GRL) 64 Zd 39
Greengairs **GB** (STC) 25 Wa 13
Greenhall **IRL** (COR) 98 Rb 35
Greenham **GB** (BKS) 62 Ye 40
Greenham **GB** (SOM) 67 We 43
Green Hammerton **GB** (NOY) 40 Ye 24
Greenhaugh **GB** (NHL) 32 Xe 17
Greenhead **GB** (NHL) 32 Xc 19
Greenhill **GB** (ESX) 72 Ab 42
Greenholm **GB** (STC) 25 Ve 15
Greenholme **GB** (CUB) 35 Xc 22
Greenhow Hill **GB** (NOY) 39 Yb 24
Greenisland **GB** (ANT) 85 Ua 20
Greenland **GB** (HGL) 6 We 117
Greenland **IRL** (COR) 104 Sa 37
Greenlands **GB** (BUS) 63 Za 39
Greenlaw **GB** (BOR) 27 Xd 14
Greenloaning **GB** (TYS) 25 Wa 11
Greenmount **GB** (GRM) 39 Xe 27
Greenmount **IRL** (LOT) 90 Td 25
Greenock **GB** (STC) 24 Vb 13
Greenodd **GB** (CUB) 34 Wf 23
Green Ore **GB** (SOM) 68 Xc 41
Greenore **IRL** (LOT) 90 Tf 24
Greenscares **GB** (TYS) 21 Wa 11
Greenside **GB** (TAW) 33 Yb 19
Greenskares **GB** (GRP) 17 Xd 3
Greens Norton **GB** (NRH) 54 Yf 36
Greenstead Green **GB** (ESS) 65 Ad 37
Greensted **GB** (ESS) 64 Ab 38
Green Street Green **GB** (KEN) 64 Ab 40
Greenwich **GB** (GRL) 64 Zf 40
Greet **GB** (GLS) 62 Ya 37
Greete **GB** (SHS) 52 Xc 35
Greetham **GB** (LEC) 47 Zc 32
Greetham **GB** (LIN) 47 Zf 29
Greetland **GB** (WYO) 39 Ya 26
Greevagh **IRL** (DON) 77 Sa 18
Grenach **GB** (STC) 24 Uf 14
Grenagh **IRL** (COR) 98 Rc 36
Grenanstown House **IRL** (TIP) 93 Rf 31
Grendon **GB** (NRH) 55 Zb 35
Grendon **GB** (WWH) 53 Yc 33
Grendon Green **GB** (HWC) 52 Xc 35
Grendon Underwood **GB** (BUS) 63 Yf 37
Grenitote **GB** (HGL) 10 Se 3
Grennanstown House **IRL** (MT) 89 Ta 27
Grenoside **GB** (SOY) 39 Yc 28
Gresford **GB** (CLW) 44 Xa 30
Gresham **GB** (NOR) 49 Bb 31
Greshornish **GB** (HGL) 13 Td 3
Gressenhall **GB** (NOR) 48 Af 32
Gressingham **GB** (LCS) 38 Xc 24
Greta Bridge **GB** (DUR) 36 Ya 21
Gretna **GB** (DAG) 32 Wf 19
Gretna Green **GB** (DAG) 32 Wf 18
Gretton **GB** (GLS) 62 Ya 37
Gretton **GB** (NRH) 55 Zc 33
Gretton **GB** (SHS) 52 Xb 33
Grevine **IRL** (KLK) 100 Se 33
Grewelthorpe **GB** (NOY) 36 Yc 23
Greyabbey **GB** (DOW) 85 Uc 21
Grey Fort **IRL** (WKL) 95 Tf 30
Greygarth **GB** (NOY) 36 Yb 24
Greygrove **IRL** (CRE) 92 Qe 32
Greylake **GB** (SOM) 68 Xa 42
Greysouthen **GB** (CUB) 34 Wc 21
Greystoke **GB** (CUB) 35 Xa 20
Greystone **GB** (TYS) 22 Xb 9
Greystones **IRL** (WKL) 95 Tf 30
Greywell **GB** (HAS) 70 Za 41
Griais **GB** (HGL) 11 Te 119
Gribton **GB** (DAG) 31 Wb 18
Griffithstown **GB** (GWE) 60 Wf 38
Grigghall **GB** (CUB) 35 Xb 23
Grillagh Street **IRL** (LGF) 88 Sa 26
Grimethorpe **GB** (SOY) 40 Yd 27
Griminish **GB** (HGL) 12 Sd 4
Grimister **GB** (SHL) 2 Yf 105
Grimley **GB** (HWC) 53 Xe 35
Grimmet **GB** (STC) 30 Vc 16
Grimoldby **GB** (LIN) 47 Aa 28
Grimsargh **GB** (LCS) 38 Xc 26
Grimsbury **GB** (OXS) 54 Yd 36
Grimsby **GB** (HUS) 41 Zf 27
Grimscote **GB** (NRH) 54 Yf 35
Grimscott **GB** (CNW) 66 Vd 43
Grimshader **GB** (HGL) 11 Td 120
Grimsthorpe **GB** (LIN) 47 Zd 32
Grimston **GB** (NOR) 48 Ad 32
Grimstone **GB** (DOS) 68 Xc 44
Grindale **GB** (HUS) 37 Ze 24
Grindiscol **GB** (SHL) 3 Yf 108
Grindle **GB** (SHS) 53 Xd 34
Grindleford **GB** (DSH) 45 Yc 29
Grindleton **GB** (LCS) 38 Xd 25
Grindley **GB** (SFS) 45 Ya 31
Grindon **GB** (NHL) 27 Xf 14
Grindon **GB** (SFS) 45 Ya 30
Gringley on the Hill **GB** (NTS) 40 Za 28
Grinsdale **GB** (CUB) 32 Xa 19
Grinshill **GB** (SHS) 44 Xb 32
Grinton **GB** (NOY) 36 Ya 22
Grishipoll **GB** (STC) 18 Tc 9
Gristhorpe **GB** (NOY) 37 Ze 23
Gritley **GB** (ORK) 6 Xb 115
Grittenham **GB** (WIL) 62 Ya 39
Grittleton **GB** (WIL) 61 Xe 39
Grizebeck **GB** (CUB) 34 We 23
Grizedale **GB** (CUB) 34 Wf 22
Grobister **GB** (ORK) 5 Xc 114
Groby **GB** (LEC) 54 Ye 33
Groes **GB** (CLW) 43 Wd 29

Glen – Groes (GB) (IRL) 119

Groes-faen **GB** (MGL) 60 Wd 39
Groesffordd Marli **GB** (CLW) 43 Wd 29
Groeslon **GB** (GWY) 42 Ve 30
Grogport **GB** (STC) 23 Ud 15
Gronant **GB** (CLW) 43 Wd 29
Groombridge **GB** (ESX) 71 Ab 42
Groomsport **GB** (ANT) 85 Uc 20
Grosebay **GB** (HGL) 11 Tb 1
Grosmont **GB** (GWE) 60 Xa 37
Grosmont **GB** (NOY) 37 Zb 22
Groton **GB** (SUF) 56 Af 36
Grouville Saint-Clément **GBJ** 73 Xf 53
Grove **GB** (KEN) 65 Bb 41
Grove **GB** (NTS) 46 Za 29
Grove **GB** (OXS) 62 Yd 39
Grovesend **GB** (WGL) 59 Vf 38
Gruids **GB** (HGL) 8 Vd 120
Gruline **GB** (STC) 18 Ua 10
Gruline House **GB** (STC) 18 Ua 10
Grunasound **GB** (SHL) 3 Yd 108
Grundisburgh **GB** (SUF) 57 Bb 36
Gruting **GB** (SHL) 2 Yd 107
Gtengyle House **IRL** (TIP) 93 Sa 32
Guaire = Gorey **IRL** (WEX) 101 Te 32
Gualachulain **GB** (HGL) 19 Uf 9
Guarlford **GB** (HWC) 53 Xe 36
Guay **GB** (TYS) 21 Wc 9
Gubacreeny **IRL** (LET) 82 Re 22
Gubbadanbo **IRL** (GAL) 86 Qa 27
Gubleagh House **IRL** (COR) 98 Rb 35
Guestling Green **GB** (ESX) 72 Ad 43
Guestwick **GB** (NOR) 49 Ba 32
Guide Post **GB** (NHL) 33 Yc 18
Guihirn **GB** (CBS) 55 Aa 33
Guilcagh Cross Roads **IRL** (WTF) 100 Sd 35
Guilden Morden **GB** (CBS) 55 Zf 36
Guilden Sutton **GB** (CHS) 44 Xb 29
Guildtown **GB** (TYS) 21 Wd 10
Guilsborough **GB** (NRH) 54 Yf 34
Guilsfield **GB** (POW) 52 Wf 32
Guisborough **GB** (CLE) 37 Yf 21
Guiseley **GB** (WYO) 39 Yb 25
Guiting Power **GB** (GLS) 62 Ya 37
Gulladuff **GB** (LDR) 79 Tc 20
Gullamore **IRL** (COR) 102 Qa 38
Gullane **GB** (LOT) 26 Xb 12
Gullaun **IRL** (KER) 97 Qe 36
Gultort **IRL** (GAL) 93 Re 30
Gulworthy **GB** (DEV) 76 Ve 45
Gumfrestor **GB** (DYF) 58 Vb 38
Gumley **GB** (LEC) 54 Za 33
Gundleton **GB** (HAS) 70 Yf 42
Gunn **GB** (DEV) 66 Wa 42
Gunnerside **GB** (NOY) 36 Xf 22
Gunnerton **GB** (NHL) 33 Xf 18
Gunness **GB** (HUS) 40 Zb 27
Gunnislake **GB** (CNW) 75 Ve 45
Gunsborough **IRL** (KER) 97 Qc 34
Gunter's Bridge **GB** (WSX) 70 Zc 42
Gunthorpe **GB** (NOR) 48 Af 31
Gurney Slade **GB** (SOM) 68 Xc 41
Gurnos **GB** (POW) 59 Wb 38
Gurteen **IRL** (LET) 82 Re 23
Gurteen House **IRL** (COR) 104 Rb 38
Gussage All Saints **GB** (DOS) 69 Ya 43
Gussage Saint Michael **GB** (DOS) 69 Xf 43
Gusserane **IRL** (WEX) 100 Ta 35
Guston **GB** (KEN) 73 Ba 42
Gutcher **GB** (SHL) 2 Yf 104
Guthrie **GB** (TYS) 22 Xb 9
Guy's Head **GB** (LIN) 48 Ab 32
Guy's Marsh **GB** (DOS) 69 Xe 43
Guyzance **GB** (NHL) 33 Yb 17
Gwaelod-y-Garth **GB** (MGL) 60 We 39
Gwaenysgor **GB** (CLW) 43 Wd 29
Gwalchmai **GB** (GWY) 42 Vd 29
Gwaun-Cae-Gurwen **GB** (WGL) 59 Wa 38
Gwbert **GB** (DYF) 50 Vb 36
Gweedore **IRL** (DON) 77 Re 18
Gweek **GB** (CNW) 74 Ue 48
Gweesalia **IRL** (MAY) 80 Qa 24
Gwehelog **GB** (GWE) 60 Xa 38
Gwenddwr **GB** (POW) 51 Wd 36
Gwenter **GB** (CNW) 74 Uf 48
Gwernaffield **GB** (CLW) 44 We 29
Gwernesney **GB** (GWE) 61 Xa 38
Gwernymynydd **GB** (CLW) 44 We 30
Gwersyllt **GB** (CLW) 44 Wf 30
Gwespyr **GB** (CLW) 43 Wd 29
Gwinear **GB** (CNW) 74 Ud 47
Gwithian **GB** (CNW) 74 Ud 47
Gwmgors **GB** (WGL) 59 Wa 38
Gwyddelwern **GB** (CLW) 43 Wd 30
Gwyddgrug **GB** (DYF) 59 Ve 37
Gwystre **GB** (POW) 51 Wd 35
Gwytherin **GB** (CLW) 43 Wb 30
Gyfelia **GB** (CLW) 44 Wf 31
Gyffin **GB** (GWY) 43 Wa 29
Gyleen **IRL** (COR) 104 Re 38

H

Habberley **GB** (HWC) 53 Xe 34
Habberley **GB** (SHS) 52 Xa 33
Habost **GB** (HGL) 11 Tc 120
Habrough **GB** (HUS) 41 Ze 27
Hacconby **GB** (LIN) 47 Zd 32
Hacheston **GB** (SUF) 57 Bc 35
Hackballs Cross **IRL** (LOT) 90 Tc 24
Hackenthorpe **GB** (SOY) 46 Yd 28
Hacketstown **IRL** (CLW) 95 Tc 31
Hacketts Cross **IRL** (LOT) 90 Te 26
Hackford **GB** (NOR) 57 Ba 33
Hackforth **GB** (NOY) 36 Yc 22
Hacklete **GB** (HGL) 11 Ta 119
Hackleton **GB** (NRH) 54 Zb 35
Hackness **GB** (NOY) 37 Zc 23
Hackney **GB** (GRL) 64 Zf 39
Hadden **GB** (BOR) 27 Xd 15
Haddenham **GB** (BUS) 63 Za 38
Haddenham **GB** (CBS) 56 Aa 34
Haddington **GB** (LIN) 47 Zc 30
Haddiscoe **GB** (NOR) 57 Bd 33
Haddon **GB** (CBS) 55 Ze 33
Hademore **GB** (SFS) 53 Yb 32
Hadfield **GB** (DSH) 39 Ya 28
Hadham Cross **GB** (HTS) 64 Aa 37
Hadham Ford **GB** (HTS) 64 Aa 37
Hadleigh **GB** (ESS) 65 Ad 39
Hadleigh **GB** (SUF) 57 Af 36
Hadleigh Heath **GB** (SUF) 56 Af 36
Hadley **GB** (SHS) 52 Xd 32
Hadley End **GB** (SFS) 45 Yb 32
Hadlow **GB** (KEN) 72 Ab 41
Hadlow Down **GB** (ESX) 71 Ab 43
Hadnall **GB** (SHS) 44 Xb 32
Hadstock **GB** (ESS) 56 Ab 36
Haedington **GB** (OXS) 62 Ye 38
Haffenden Quarter **GB** (KEN) 72 Ae 42
Hafod-Dinbych **GB** (CLW) 43 Wc 30
Haggbeck **GB** (CUB) 32 Xb 18
Haggerston **GB** (NHL) 27 Ya 14
Hagley **GB** (HWC) 52 Xc 36
Hagley **GB** (HWC) 53 Xf 34
Hagworthingham **GB** (LIN) 47 Aa 29
Haigh **GB** (GRM) 38 Xc 27
Haighton Green **GB** (LCS) 38 Xc 26
Haile **GB** (CUB) 34 Wd 22
Hailey **GB** (OXS) 62 Yd 38
Hailey **GB** (OXS) 63 Yf 39
Hailsham **GB** (ESX) 72 Ab 43
Hail Weston **GB** (CBS) 55 Ze 35
Hainton **GB** (LIN) 47 Ze 28
Hairshaw **GB** (STC) 25 Ve 15
Haisthorpe **GB** (HUS) 41 Ze 24
Halam **GB** (NTS) 46 Za 30
Halberton **GB** (DEV) 67 Wd 43
Halcro **GB** (HGL) 6 We 117
Hale **GB** (CHS) 44 Xb 29
Hale **GB** (GRM) 45 Xd 28
Hale Bank **GB** (MES) 44 Xb 28
Hales **GB** (NOR) 57 Bd 33
Hales **GB** (SFS) 44 Xd 31
Halesowen **GB** (WMD) 53 Xf 34
Hale Street **GB** (KEN) 72 Ac 41
Halesworth **GB** (SUF) 57 Bc 34
Halewood **GB** (MES) 44 Xb 28
Halford **GB** (SHS) 52 Xb 34
Halford **GB** (WWH) 53 Yc 36
Halfpenny Green **GB** (SFS) 53 Xe 33
Halfway **GB** (BKS) 62 Yd 40
Halfway **GB** (DYF) 59 Wa 37
Halfway **GB** (DYF) 59 Wb 37
Halfway **GB** (SOY) 46 Yd 29
Halfway **IRL** (COR) 104 Rc 38
Halfway House **IRL** (WTF) 99 Sb 35
Halfway House **IRL** (WTF) 100 Sf 35
Halfway Houses **GB** (KEN) 65 Ae 40
Halifax **GB** (WYO) 39 Ya 26
Halistra **GB** (HGL) 12 Tc 3
Halket **GB** (STC) 24 Vc 14
Halkirk **GB** (HGL) 6 Wd 117
Halkyn **GB** (CLW) 44 We 29
Hall, The **IRL** (DON) 82 Re 21
Halland **GB** (ESX) 71 Aa 43
Hallaton **GB** (LEC) 54 Zb 33
Hallatrow **GB** (AVN) 68 Xc 41
Hallbankgate **GB** (CUB) 32 Xc 19
Hall Dunnerdale **GB** (CUB) 34 We 22
Hall Green **GB** (WMD) 53 Ya 34
Halliburton **GB** (BOR) 27 Xc 14
Hallin **GB** (HGL) 12 Tc 3
Halling **GB** (KEN) 65 Ac 40
Hallington **GB** (NHL) 33 Xf 18
Hall of the Forest **GB** (SHS) 52 We 34
Halloughton **GB** (NTS) 46 Za 30
Hallow **GB** (HWC) 53 Xe 35
Hallow Heath **GB** (HWC) 53 Xe 35
Halls **GB** (LOT) 26 Xc 13
Hallsands **GB** (DEV) 76 Wc 47
Hallthwaites **GB** (CUB) 34 We 23
Halltown Cross Roads **IRL** (MT) 90 Tb 27
Hallworthy **GB** (CNW) 66 Vc 45
Halmer End **GB** (SFS) 45 Xe 30
Halmore **GB** (GLS) 61 Xd 38
Halmyre Mains **GB** (BOR) 26 We 14
Halnaker **GB** (WSX) 70 Zb 43
Halsall **GB** (LCS) 38 Xa 27
Halse **GB** (NRH) 54 Ye 36
Halse **GB** (SOM) 67 We 42
Halsetown **GB** (CNW) 74 Ud 47
Halsinger **GB** (DEV) 66 Vf 42
Halstead **GB** (ESS) 56 Ad 37
Halstead **GB** (KEN) 64 Aa 41
Halstock **GB** (DOS) 68 Xc 43
Haltham **GB** (LIN) 47 Zf 30
Haltoft End **GB** (LIN) 47 Aa 31
Halton **GB** (BUS) 63 Zb 38
Halton **GB** (CHS) 44 Xb 29
Halton **GB** (CLW) 44 Wf 31
Halton **GB** (LCS) 38 Xb 24
Halton Gill **GB** (NOY) 35 Xe 23
Halton Holegate **GB** (LIN) 47 Aa 30
Halton Lea Gate **GB** (NHL) 32 Xc 19
Halton West **GB** (NOY) 39 Xe 25
Haltwhistle **GB** (NHL) 32 Xd 19
Halvergate **GB** (NOR) 57 Bd 33
Halwell **GB** (DEV) 76 Wb 46
Halwill **GB** (DEV) 66 We 44
Halwill Junction **GB** (DEV) 66 Ve 44
Ham **GB** (HGL) 6 We 117
Ham **GB** (SHL) 3 Xf 108
Ham **GB** (WIL) 62 Yc 40
Hamble **GB** (HAS) 70 Ye 43
Hambleden **GB** (BUS) 63 Za 39
Hambledon **GB** (HAS) 70 Yf 43
Hambledon **GB** (SUR) 70 Zc 42
Hambleton **GB** (LCS) 38 Xa 25
Hambleton **GB** (NOY) 40 Yf 26
Hambridge **GB** (SOM) 68 Xa 43
Hambrook **GB** (AVN) 61 Xc 40
Hameringham **GB** (LIN) 47 Zf 29
Hamerton **GB** (CBS) 55 Ze 34
Ham Green **GB** (AVN) 61 Xb 40
Ham Green **GB** (HWC) 53 Ya 35
Hamilton **GB** (STC) 25 Vf 14
Hamilton's Bawn **GB** (ARG) 84 Tc 22
Hammerlane **IRL** (OFF) 94 Se 30
Hammersmith **GB** (GRL) 64 Ze 40
Hammerwich **GB** (SFS) 53 Ya 32
Hammoon **GB** (DOS) 68 Xe 43
Hamnavoe **GB** (SHL) 2 Yf 105
Hamnavoe **GB** (SHL) 2 Yf 106
Hamnavoe **GB** (SHL) 3 Yd 108
Hampden Park **GB** (ESX) 72 Ab 44
Hampden Row **GB** (BUS) 63 Zb 38
Hampnett **GB** (GLS) 62 Ya 37
Hampole **GB** (SOY) 40 Ye 27
Hampreston **GB** (DOS) 69 Ya 44
Hampshire **GB** (HAS) 69 Ya 43
Hampstead **GB** (GRL) 64 Ze 39
Hampstead Norreys **GB** (BKS) 62 Ye 40
Hampsthwaite **GB** (NOY) 39 Yc 24
Hampton **GB** (GRL) 64 Zd 40
Hampton **GB** (HWC) 53 Ya 36
Hampton **GB** (SHS) 52 Xd 34
Hampton Bishop **GB** (HWC) 52 Xc 36
Hampton Heath **GB** (CHS) 44 Xb 30
Hampton in Arden **GB** (WMD) 53 Yb 34
Hampton Lovett **GB** (HWC) 53 Xf 35
Hampton Lucy **GB** (WWH) 53 Yc 35
Hampton on the Hill **GB** (WWH) 53 Yc 35
Hampton Poyle **GB** (OXS) 62 Ye 37
Hamptworth **GB** (WIL) 69 Yc 43
Hamsey **GB** (ESX) 71 Aa 43
Hamstall Ridware **GB** (SFS) 45 Ya 32
Hamstead **GB** (IOW) 69 Yd 44
Hamstead **GB** (WMD) 53 Ya 33
Hamstead Marshall **GB** (BKS) 62 Yd 40
Hamsterley **GB** (DUR) 33 Yb 19
Hamsterley **GB** (DUR) 36 Yb 20
Hamstreet **GB** (KEN) 72 Af 42
Ham Street **GB** (SOM) 68 Xc 42
Hamwood House **IRL** (MT) 95 Tc 28
Hanbury **GB** (HWC) 53 Xf 35
Hanbury **GB** (SFS) 45 Yb 31
Handcross **GB** (WSX) 71 Ze 42
Handforth **GB** (CHS) 45 Xe 28
Handley **GB** (CHS) 44 Xb 30
Handsacre **GB** (SFS) 45 Ya 32
Handsworth **GB** (SOY) 46 Yd 28
Handsworth **GB** (WMD) 53 Ya 33
Hanging Bridge **GB** (SFS) 45 Yb 30
Hanging Langford **GB** (WIL) 69 Ya 42
Hanham **GB** (AVN) 61 Xc 40
Hankelow **GB** (CHS) 44 Xd 30
Hankerton **GB** (WIL) 62 Xf 39
Hankham **GB** (ESX) 72 Ab 44
Hanley **GB** (SFS) 45 Xe 30
Hanley Castle **GB** (HWC) 53 Xe 36
Hanley Child **GB** (HWC) 52 Xc 35
Hanley Swan **GB** (HWC) 53 Xe 36
Hanley William **GB** (HWC) 52 Xd 35
Hanmer **GB** (CLW) 44 Xb 31
Hannah **GB** (LIN) 48 Zf 29
Hannington **GB** (HAS) 70 Ye 41
Hannington **GB** (NRH) 54 Zb 35
Hannington **GB** (WIL) 62 Yb 39
Hannington Wick **GB** (WIL) 62 Yb 39
Hanslope **GB** (BUS) 54 Zb 36
Hanwell **GB** (OXS) 54 Yd 36
Hanwood **GB** (SHS) 52 Xb 32
Hanworth **GB** (NOR) 49 Bb 31
Happisburgh **GB** (NOR) 49 Bd 32
Happisburgh Common **GB** (NOR) 49 Bd 32
Hapsford **GB** (CHS) 44 Xb 29
Hapton **GB** (LCS) 39 Xe 26
Hapton **GB** (NOR) 57 Bb 33
Harberton **GB** (DEV) 76 Wb 46
Harbertonford **GB** (DEV) 76 Wb 46
Harborne **GB** (WMD) 53 Ya 34
Harborough Magna **GB** (WWH) 54 Ye 34
Harbottle **GB** (NHL) 33 Xf 17
Harbour **IRL** (MAY) 86 Qa 26
Harbour **IRL** (MT) 90 Tb 26
Harbourneford **GB** (DEV) 76 Wb 46
Harbour View **IRL** (COR) 104 Rb 39
Harbridge **GB** (HAS) 69 Yb 43
Harbury **GB** (WWH) 54 Yd 35
Harby **GB** (LEC) 46 Za 31
Harby **GB** (NTS) 46 Zb 29
Harcombe **GB** (DEV) 67 We 44
Harden **GB** (WYO) 39 Ya 25
Hardgate **GB** (GRP) 17 Xd 6
Hardham **GB** (WSX) 71 Zc 43
Hardingham **GB** (NOR) 57 Ba 33
Hardingstone **GB** (NRH) 54 Za 35
Hardington **GB** (SOM) 68 Xd 41
Hardington Marsh **GB** (SOM) 68 Xb 43
Hardley **GB** (HAS) 70 Yd 43
Hardmead **GB** (BUS) 55 Zc 36
Hardraw **GB** (NOY) 35 Xe 23
Hardway **GB** (SOM) 68 Xd 42
Hardwick **GB** (BUS) 63 Zb 37
Hardwick **GB** (CBS) 55 Aa 35
Hardwick **GB** (NOR) 57 Bb 34
Hardwick **GB** (NRH) 54 Zb 35
Hardwick **GB** (OXS) 62 Yd 38
Hardwick **GB** (OXS) 63 Ye 37
Hardwicke **GB** (GLS) 61 Xe 38
Hardwicke **GB** (HWC) 52 Wf 36
Hardy's Green **GB** (HTS) 65 Ae 37
Hareby **GB** (LIN) 47 Zf 29
Harefield **GB** (GRL) 63 Zd 39
Hare Hatch **GB** (BKS) 63 Za 40
Harescombe **GB** (GLS) 61 Xe 38
Haresfield **GB** (GLS) 61 Xe 38
Hare Street **GB** (HTS) 64 Aa 37
Harewood **GB** (WYO) 39 Yc 25
Harewood End **GB** (HWC) 61 Xb 37
Harford **GB** (DEV) 76 Wa 46
Hargate **GB** (NOR) 57 Ba 34
Hargrave **GB** (CHS) 44 Xb 30
Hargrave **GB** (NRH) 55 Zd 35
Hargrave **GB** (SUF) 56 Ad 35
Hargrave Green **GB** (SUF) 56 Ad 35
Haringey **GB** (GRL) 64 Zf 39
Harker **GB** (CUB) 32 Xa 19
Harkstead **GB** (SUF) 57 Bb 37
Harlaston **GB** (SFS) 53 Yb 32
Harlaxton **GB** (LIN) 46 Zb 31
Harlech **GB** (GWY) 42 Vf 31
Harleston **GB** (NOR) 57 Bb 34
Harleston **GB** (SUF) 57 Af 35
Harlestone **GB** (NRH) 54 Za 35
Harle Syke **GB** (LCS) 39 Xe 26
Harley **GB** (SHS) 52 Xc 33
Harlosh **GB** (HGL) 13 Tc 4
Harlow **GB** (ESS) 64 Aa 38
Harlow Hill **GB** (NHL) 33 Ya 18
Harlthorpe **GB** (HUS) 40 Za 26
Harlton **GB** (CBS) 55 Aa 36
Harmby **GB** (NOY) 36 Yb 23
Harmer Green **GB** (HTS) 64 Zf 38
Harmer Hill **GB** (SHS) 44 Xb 32
Harmston **GB** (LIN) 47 Zc 30
Harney Cross Roads **IRL** (WTF) 100 Sc 34
Harnham **GB** (WIL) 69 Yb 42
Harnhill **GB** (GLS) 62 Ya 38
Haroldston West **GB** (DYF) 58 Uf 38
Haroldswick **GB** (SHL) 2 Za 104
Harome **GB** (NOY) 37 Yf 23
Harpenden **GB** (HTS) 64 Zd 38
Harpford **GB** (DEV) 67 We 44
Harpham **GB** (HUS) 41 Ze 24
Harpley **GB** (HWC) 52 Xd 35
Harpley **GB** (NOR) 48 Ad 32
Harpsden **GB** (OXS) 63 Za 39
Harpswell **GB** (LIN) 41 Zc 28
Harpurhey **GB** (GRM) 39 Xe 27
Harpur Hill **GB** (DSH) 45 Ya 29
Harrapool **GB** (HGL) 13 Ua 5
Harrietfield **GB** (TYS) 21 Wc 10
Harrington **GB** (LIN) 47 Aa 29
Harrington **GB** (NRH) 54 Za 34
Harringworth **GB** (NRH) 55 Zc 33
Harris **GB** (HGL) 13 Td 7
Harriseahead **GB** (SFS) 45 Xe 30
Harristown **IRL** (KLK) 100 Se 34
Harristown **IRL** (WEX) 101 Tc 34
Harrogate **GB** (NOY) 39 Yc 25
Harrold **GB** (BFS) 55 Zc 35
Harrow **GB** (GRL) 64 Zd 39
Harrow, The **IRL** (WEX) 101 Td 33
Harsthorne **GB** (DSH) 46 Yc 32
Harston **GB** (CBS) 55 Aa 36
Harston **GB** (LEC) 46 Zb 31
Hart **GB** (CLE) 36 Ye 20
Hartburn **GB** (NHL) 33 Ya 17
Hartest **GB** (SUF) 56 Ae 36
Hartfield **GB** (ESX) 71 Aa 42
Hartford **GB** (CHS) 44 Xc 29
Hartfordbridge **GB** (HAS) 63 Za 41
Hartford End **GB** (ESS) 64 Ac 38
Harthill **GB** (CHS) 44 Xb 30
Harthill **GB** (LOT) 25 Wb 13
Harthill **GB** (SOY) 46 Ye 29
Hartington **GB** (DSH) 45 Yb 30
Hartland **GB** (DEV) 66 Vd 43
Hartlebury **GB** (HWC) 53 Xe 34
Hartlepool **GB** (CLE) 36 Ye 20
Hartley **GB** (CUB) 35 Xd 22
Hartley **GB** (KEN) 64 Ab 40
Hartley **GB** (KEN) 72 Ad 42
Hartley **GB** (NHL) 33 Yd 18
Hartley Wespall **GB** (HAS) 63 Za 41
Hartley Wintney **GB** (HAS) 63 Za 41
Hartlip **GB** (KEN) 65 Ad 40
Harton **GB** (NOY) 40 Za 24
Harton **GB** (SHS) 52 Xb 34
Harton **GB** (TAW) 33 Yd 19
Hartpury **GB** (GLS) 61 Xe 37
Hartshill **GB** (WWH) 54 Yc 33
Hartsop **GB** (CUB) 35 Xa 21
Hartwell **GB** (BUS) 63 Za 38
Hartwell **GB** (ESX) 71 Aa 42
Hartwell **GB** (NRH) 54 Za 36
Hartwood **GB** (STC) 25 Wa 14
Harvel **GB** (KEN) 64 Ac 40
Harvington **GB** (HWC) 53 Xe 34
Harvington Cross **GB** (HWC) 53 Ya 36
Harwell **GB** (OXS) 62 Ye 39
Harwich **GB** (ESS) 57 Bb 37
Harwood **GB** (DUR) 35 Xe 20
Harwood Dale **GB** (NOY) 37 Zc 22
Harworth **GB** (NTS) 40 Yf 28
Hascombe **GB** (SUR) 71 Zc 42
Haselbech **GB** (NRH) 54 Za 34
Haselbury Plucknett **GB** (SOM) 68 Xb 43
Haseley **GB** (WWH) 53 Yc 35
Haselor **GB** (WWH) 53 Yb 35
Hasfield **GB** (GLS) 61 Xe 37
Hasguard **GB** (DYF) 58 Uf 38
Haskayne **GB** (LCS) 38 Xa 27
Hasketon **GB** (SUF) 57 Bb 36
Hasland **GB** (DSH) 46 Yd 29
Haslemere **GB** (BUS) 63 Zb 39
Haslemere **GB** (SUR) 70 Zb 42
Haslingden **GB** (LCS) 39 Xe 26
Haslingden Grane **GB** (LCS) 38 Xd 26
Haslingfield **GB** (CBS) 55 Aa 36
Haslington **GB** (CHS) 44 Xd 30
Hassall **GB** (CHS) 45 Xd 30
Hassall Green **GB** (CHS) 45 Xe 30
Hassell Street **GB** (KEN) 72 Af 41
Hassendean **GB** (BOR) 32 Xb 16
Hassingham **GB** (NOR) 57 Bc 33
Hassop **GB** (DSH) 45 Yc 29
Hastigrow **GB** (HGL) 6 We 117
Hastingleigh **GB** (KEN) 72 Af 41
Hastings **GB** (ESX) 72 Ad 43
Hastingwood **GB** (ESS) 64 Aa 38
Hastoe **GB** (HTS) 63 Zb 38
Haswell **GB** (DUR) 36 Yd 20
Hatch **GB** (BFS) 55 Ze 36
Hatch **GB** (WIL) 69 Xf 42
Hatch Beauchamp **GB** (SOM) 68 Wf 43
Hatfield **GB** (HTS) 64 Ze 38
Hatfield **GB** (HWC) 52 Xc 35
Hatfield **GB** (SOY) 40 Yf 27
Hatfield Broad Oak **GB** (ESS) 64 Ab 38
Hatfield Heath **GB** (ESS) 64 Ab 38
Hatfield Peverel **GB** (ESS) 65 Ad 38
Hatford **GB** (OXS) 62 Yc 39
Hatherden **GB** (HAS) 69 Yc 41
Hatherleigh **GB** (DEV) 66 Vf 44
Hathern **GB** (LEC) 46 Ye 32
Hatherop **GB** (GLS) 62 Yb 38
Hathersage **GB** (DSH) 45 Yc 31
Hatherton **GB** (CHS) 44 Xd 30
Hatley Saint George **GB** (CBS) 55 Zf 36
Hattingley **GB** (HAS) 70 Yf 42
Hatton **GB** (CHS) 44 Xc 28
Hatton **GB** (DSH) 45 Yb 31
Hatton **GB** (GRP) 17 Ya 4
Hatton **GB** (LIN) 47 Ze 29
Hatton **GB** (SHS) 52 Xb 33
Hatton **GB** (WWH) 53 Yc 35
Hattoncrook **GB** (GRP) 17 Xe 5
Hatton of Fintray **GB** (GRP) 17 Xe 5
Haugham **GB** (LIN) 47 Aa 29
Haugh Head **GB** (NHL) 33 Ya 15
Haughley **GB** (SUF) 57 Af 35
Haughley Green **GB** (SUF) 57 Af 35
Haugh of Glass **GB** (GRP) 16 Xa 4
Haugh of Urr **GB** (DAG) 31 Wa 19
Haughton **GB** (SFS) 45 Xe 32
Haughton **GB** (SHS) 44 Xa 31
Haughton **GB** (SHS) 44 Xb 32
Haughton **GB** (SHS) 52 Xd 33
Haughton Moss **GB** (CHS) 44 Xc 30
Haugley New Street **GB** (SUF) 56 Af 35
Haultwick **GB** (HTS) 64 Zf 37
Haunton **GB** (SFS) 53 Yc 32
Hauxley **GB** (NHL) 33 Yc 17
Hauxton **GB** (CBS) 55 Aa 36
Havant **GB** (HAS) 70 Za 43
Haven **GB** (HWC) 52 Xa 35
Haven, The **GB** (WSX) 71 Zd 42
Havenstreet **GB** (IOW) 70 Ye 44
Haverfordwest **GB** (DYF) 58 Va 38
Haverhill **GB** (SUF) 56 Ac 36
Haverigg **GB** (CUB) 34 We 23
Havering **GB** (GRL) 64 Ab 39
Havering-atte-Bower **GB** (GRL) 64 Ab 39
Haversham **GB** (BUS) 54 Zb 36
Haverthwaite **GB** (CUB) 34 Wf 23
Hawarden **GB** (CLW) 44 Wf 29
Hawes **GB** (NOY) 35 Xe 23
Hawford **GB** (HWC) 53 Xe 35
Hawick **GB** (BOR) 32 Xb 16
Hawkchurch **GB** (DEV) 68 Xa 44
Hawkedon **GB** (SUF) 56 Ad 36
Hawkerland **GB** (DEV) 67 We 44
Hawkesbury **GB** (AVN) 61 Xd 39
Hawkesbury Upton **GB** (AVN) 61 Xe 39
Hawkhurst **GB** (KEN) 72 Ad 42
Hawkinge **GB** (KEN) 73 Ba 42
Hawkley **GB** (HAS) 70 Za 42
Hawkridge **GB** (SOM) 67 Wc 42
Hawkshead **GB** (CUB) 34 Xa 22
Hawksland **GB** (STC) 25 Wa 15
Hawkswick **GB** (NOY) 36 Xf 24
Hawksworth **GB** (NTS) 46 Za 31
Hawkwell **GB** (ESS) 65 Ad 39
Hawley **GB** (HAS) 63 Zb 41
Hawling **GB** (GLS) 62 Ya 37
Hawnby **GB** (NOY) 37 Yf 23
Haworth **GB** (WYO) 39 Ya 25
Hawsker **GB** (NOY) 37 Zc 22
Hawstead **GB** (SUF) 56 Ae 35
Hawthorn **GB** (DUR) 36 Yd 20
Hawthorn **GB** (WIL) 61 Xe 40
Hawthorn Hill **GB** (BKS) 63 Zb 40
Hawthorpe **GB** (LIN) 47 Zd 31
Hawton **GB** (NTS) 46 Zb 30
Haxby **GB** (NOY) 40 Yf 24
Haxey **GB** (HUS) 40 Za 28
Haxted **GB** (SUR) 71 Aa 41
Haydock **GB** (MES) 38 Xc 28
Haydon Bridge **GB** (NHL) 32 Xe 19
Hayes **GB** (GRL) 63 Zd 39
Hayes **GB** (GRL) 64 Zf 40
Hayfield **GB** (DSH) 45 Ya 28
Hayhillock **GB** (TYS) 22 Xb 9
Hayle **GB** (CNW) 74 Ud 47
Hayling Island **GB** (HAS) 70 Za 44
Haynes **GB** (BFS) 55 Zd 36
Haynes Church End **GB** (BFS) 55 Zd 36
Hay-on-Wye **GB** (POW) 52 Wf 36
Hayscastle **GB** (DYF) 58 Uf 37
Hayscastle Cross **GB** (DYF) 58 Uf 37
Hay Street **GB** (HTS) 64 Aa 37
Hayton **GB** (CUB) 32 Xb 19
Hayton **GB** (CUB) 34 Wd 20
Hayton **GB** (HUS) 40 Zb 25
Hayton **GB** (NTS) 46 Za 28
Hayton's Bent **GB** (SHS) 52 Xb 34
Haytor Vale **GB** (DEV) 76 Wb 45
Haywards Heath **GB** (WSX) 71 Zf 42
Haywood Oaks **GB** (NTS) 46 Yf 30
Hazelbank **GB** (STC) 25 Wa 14
Hazelbury Bryan **GB** (DOS) 68 Xd 43
Hazeleigh **GB** (ESS) 65 Ad 38
Hazelend **GB** (ESS) 62 Yb 37
Hazeley **GB** (HAS) 63 Za 41
Hazel Grove **GB** (GRM) 45 Xf 28
Hazelslade **GB** (SFS) 53 Ya 32
Hazelton Walls **GB** (FIF) 21 Wf 10
Hazelwood **GB** (DSH) 46 Yc 30
Heacham **GB** (NOR) 48 Ac 31
Headbourne Worthy **GB** (HAS) 70 Ye 42
Head Bridge **GB** (DEV) 66 Wa 43
Headcorn **GB** (KEN) 72 Ad 41
Headfort **IRL** (GAL) 87 Qf 28
Headlam **GB** (DUR) 36 Yb 21
Headley **GB** (HAS) 62 Ye 40
Headley **GB** (HAS) 70 Zb 42
Headley **GB** (SUR) 64 Ze 41
Headon **GB** (NTS) 46 Za 29
Heads Nook **GB** (CUB) 32 Xb 19
Heage **GB** (DSH) 46 Yd 30
Healaugh **GB** (NOY) 36 Ya 22
Healaugh **GB** (NOY) 40 Ye 25
Heale **GB** (DEV) 66 Wa 41
Healey **GB** (LCS) 39 Xe 27
Healey **GB** (NHL) 33 Ya 19
Healey **GB** (NOY) 36 Yb 23
Healeyfield **GB** (DUR) 36 Yb 20
Healing **GB** (HUS) 41 Zf 27
Heanish **GB** (STC) 18 Tb 10
Heanor **GB** (DSH) 46 Yd 30
Heapham **GB** (LIN) 46 Zb 28
Heapstown House **IRL** (SLI) 88 Rd 24
Heart Hill **IRL** (KER) 97 Qb 34
Hearthstane **GB** (BOR) 31 Wd 15
Heasley Mill **GB** (DEV) 67 Wb 42
Heast **GB** (HGL) 13 Ua 5
Heath and Reach **GB** (BFS) 63 Zc 37
Heathburn Hall **IRL** (COR) 104 Rd 38
Heathcote **GB** (SHS) 44 Xc 31
Heath End **GB** (HAS) 63 Yf 40
Heathend **GB** (SUR) 70 Zb 41
Heather **GB** (LEC) 54 Yd 32
Heatherville **IRL** (MT) 89 Sf 28
Heatheryhill **IRL** (DON) 77 Sc 19
Heathfield **GB** (DEV) 76 Wc 45
Heathfield **GB** (ESX) 72 Ab 43
Heathfield **GB** (SOM) 67 We 42
Heathfield House **IRL** (ROS) 88 Rd 26
Heath Hayes **GB** (SFS) 53 Ya 32
Heath Hill **GB** (SHS) 53 Xd 32
Heath Lodge **IRL** (OFF) 93 Sb 30
Heathstown **IRL** (WMT) 89 Se 28
Heatley **GB** (CHS) 44 Xd 28
Heaton **GB** (LCS) 38 Xa 24
Heaton **GB** (SFS) 45 Xf 30
Heaton **GB** (TAW) 33 Yc 19
Heaverham **GB** (KEN) 64 Ab 41
Hebburn **GB** (TAW) 33 Yc 19
Hebden **GB** (NOY) 39 Ya 24
Hebden Bridge **GB** (WYO) 39 Xf 26
Hebing End **GB** (HTS) 64 Zf 37
Hebron **GB** (NHL) 33 Yb 17
Heckfield **GB** (HAS) 63 Za 40
Heckfield Green **GB** (SUF) 57 Bb 34
Heckfordbridge **GB** (ESS) 65 Ae 37
Heckington **GB** (LIN) 47 Ze 31
Heckmondwike **GB** (WYO) 39 Yc 26
Heddington **GB** (WIL) 62 Xf 40
Hedenham **GB** (NOR) 57 Bc 34
Hedgerley **GB** (BUS) 63 Zc 39
Hedley on the Hill **GB** (NHL) 33 Ya 19
Hednesford **GB** (SFS) 53 Xf 32
Hedon **GB** (HUS) 41 Ze 26
Hedsor **GB** (BUS) 63 Zb 39
Hegdon Hill **GB** (HWC) 52 Xc 35
Heigh **IRL** (TIP) 93 Sa 32
Heighington **GB** (DUR) 36 Yc 21
Heighington **GB** (LIN) 47 Zd 29
Heights of Bae **GB** (HGL) 15 Vd 3
Heilam **GB** (HGL) 4 Vc 117
Heirhill **IRL** (KER) 97 Qb 34
Heiton **GB** (BOR) 27 Xd 15
Helbeck **GB** (CUB) 35 Xe 21
Hele **GB** (DEV) 66 Vf 41
Hele Bridge **GB** (DEV) 66 Vf 43
Hele Lane **GB** (DEV) 67 Wb 43
Helen's Bay **GB** (ANT) 85 Ub 20
Helen Park **IRL** (TIP) 99 Sb 33
Helensburgh **GB** (STC) 24 Vb 12
Helford **GB** (CNW) 74 Uf 48
Helhoughton **GB** (NOR) 48 Ae 32
Helions Bumpstead **GB** (ESS) 56 Ac 36
Helland **GB** (CNW) 75 Vb 45
Hellifield **GB** (NOY) 39 Xe 24
Hellington **GB** (NOR) 57 Bc 33
Helmdon **GB** (NRH) 54 Yf 36
Helmingham **GB** (SUF) 57 Bb 36
Helmsdale **GB** (HGL) 9 Wc 120
Helmsley **GB** (NOY) 37 Yf 23
Helperby **GB** (NOY) 36 Ye 24
Helperthorpe **GB** (NOY) 37 Zc 24
Helpringham **GB** (LIN) 47 Ze 31
Helpston **GB** (CBS) 55 Zd 33
Helsby **GB** (CHS) 44 Xb 29
Helston **GB** (CNW) 74 Ue 48
Helstone **GB** (CNW) 75 Vb 45
Helton **GB** (CUB) 35 Xb 21
Helwith Bridge **GB** (NOY) 39 Xe 24
Hemblington **GB** (NOR) 49 Bc 33
Hemborough Post **GB** (DEV) 76 Wc 46
Hemel Hempstead **GB** (HTS) 63 Zd 38
Hemingbrough **GB** (NOY) 40 Za 26
Hemingby **GB** (LIN) 47 Zf 29
Hemingford Grey **GB** (CBS) 55 Zf 35
Hemingstone **GB** (SUF) 57 Ba 36
Hemington **GB** (NRH) 55 Zd 34
Hemington **GB** (SOM) 68 Xd 41
Hemley **GB** (SUF) 57 Bb 36
Hempholme **GB** (HUS) 41 Zd 25
Hempnall **GB** (NOR) 57 Bb 33
Hempnell Green **GB** (NOR) 57 Bb 34
Hempriggs **GB** (GRP) 16 Wc 3
Hempstead **GB** (ESS) 56 Ac 36
Hempstead **GB** (NOR) 49 Ba 31
Hempstead **GB** (NOR) 49 Bd 32
Hempsted **GB** (GLS) 61 Xe 37
Hempton **GB** (NOR) 48 Ae 32
Hempton **GB** (OXS) 62 Yd 37
Hemsby **GB** (NOR) 49 Be 32
Hemswell **GB** (LIN) 41 Zc 28
Hemsworth **GB** (WYO) 40 Yd 27
Hemyock **GB** (DEV) 67 We 43
Henbury **GB** (AVN) 61 Xc 40
Henbury **GB** (CHS) 45 Xe 29
Hendon **GB** (GRL) 64 Ze 39
Hendon **GB** (TAW) 33 Yd 19
Hendy **GB** (DYF) 59 Vf 38
Heneglwys **GB** (GWY) 42 Vd 29
Henford **GB** (DEV) 66 Ve 44
Henghurst **GB** (KEN) 72 Ae 42
Hengoed **GB** (MGL) 60 We 39
Hengoed **GB** (POW) 52 Wf 35
Hengoed **GB** (SHS) 44 Wf 31
Hengrave **GB** (SUF) 56 Ae 35
Henham **GB** (ESS) 64 Ab 37
Henley **GB** (SHS) 52 Xb 34
Henley **GB** (SOM) 68 Xb 42
Henley **GB** (SUF) 57 Ba 36
Henley **GB** (WSX) 70 Zb 42
Henley-in-Arden **GB** (WWH) 53 Yb 35
Henley-on-Thames **GB** (OXS) 63 Za 39
Henley Park **GB** (SUR) 70 Zc 41
Henley's Down **GB** (ESX) 72 Ac 43
Henllan **GB** (CLW) 43 Wd 29
Henllan **GB** (DYF) 50 Vd 36
Henllan Amgoes **GB** (DYF) 58 Vc 37
Henllys **GB** (GWE) 60 Wf 39
Henlow **GB** (BFS) 55 Ze 36
Hennock **GB** (DEV) 76 Wc 45
Henny Street **GB** (ESS) 56 Ae 36
Henryd **GB** (GWY) 43 Wa 29
Hensall **GB** (NOY) 40 Yf 26
Henshaw **GB** (NHL) 32 Xd 19
Henstead **GB** (SUF) 57 Bd 34
Hensting **GB** (HAS) 70 Ye 43
Henstridge **GB** (SOM) 68 Xd 43
Henstridge Marsh **GB** (SOM) 68 Xd 43
Henton **GB** (OXS) 63 Za 38
Henton **GB** (SOM) 68 Xb 41
Henwood **GB** (CNW) 75 Vd 45
Heogan **GB** (SHL) 2 Yf 107
Heol-ddu **GB** (DYF) 59 Vf 38
Heol Senni **GB** (POW) 60 Wc 37
Heol-y-Cyw **GB** (MGL) 60 Wc 39
Hepburn **GB** (NHL) 33 Ya 15
Hepple **GB** (NHL) 33 Xf 17
Hepscott **GB** (NHL) 33 Yc 18
Heptonstall **GB** (WYO) 39 Xf 26
Hepworth **GB** (SUF) 56 Af 35
Herbertstown **IRL** (LIM) 98 Rd 33
Herbrandston **GB** (DYF) 58 Uf 38
Hergest **GB** (HWC) 52 Wf 35
Heriot **GB** (BOR) 26 Xa 14
Hermiston **GB** (LOT) 26 We 13
Hermitage **GB** (BKS) 62 Ye 40
Hermitage **GB** (BOR) 32 Xb 17
Hermitage **GB** (DOS) 68 Xc 43
Hermitage **GB** (WSX) 70 Za 43
Hermitage, The **GB** (SUR) 71 Ze 41
Hermitage, The **IRL** (LGF) 88 Sb 26
Hermon **GB** (DYF) 58 Vc 37
Hermon **GB** (DYF) 59 Vd 37
Hermon **GB** (GWY) 42 Vd 29
Herne Bay **GB** (KEN) 65 Ba 40
Herner **GB** (DEV) 66 Vf 42
Hernhill **GB** (KEN) 65 Af 41
Herodsfoot **GB** (CNW) 75 Vc 46
Herongate **GB** (ESS) 64 Ac 39
Herriard **GB** (HAS) 70 Yf 41
Herringfleet **GB** (SUF) 57 Bd 33
Herrings Green **GB** (BFS) 55 Zd 36
Herringswell **GB** (SUF) 56 Ad 35
Herrington **GB** (TAW) 33 Yd 19
Hersden **GB** (KEN) 65 Ba 41
Herstmonceux **GB** (ESX) 72 Ab 43
Herstmonceux Castle **GB** (ESX) 72 Ab 43
Herston **GB** (ORK) 6 Wf 116
Hertford **GB** (HTS) 64 Zf 38
Hertford Heath **GB** (HTS) 64 Zf 38
Hertingfordbury **GB** (HTS) 64 Zf 38
Hesketh Bank **GB** (LCS) 38 Xa 26
Hesketh Lane **GB** (LCS) 38 Xc 25
Hesket Newmarket **GB** (CUB) 34 Wf 20
Heskin Green **GB** (LCS) 38 Xb 27
Hesleden **GB** (DUR) 36 Ye 20
Heslington **GB** (NOY) 40 Yf 25
Hessay **GB** (NOY) 40 Ye 25
Hessenford **GB** (CNW) 75 Vd 46
Hessle **GB** (HUS) 41 Zd 26
Hest Bank **GB** (LCS) 38 Xb 24
Heswall **GB** (CHS) 44 Wf 29
Hethersett **GB** (NOR) 57 Bb 33
Hethersgill **GB** (CUB) 32 Xb 19
Hethpool **GB** (NHL) 27 Xe 15
Hett **GB** (DUR) 36 Yc 20
Hetton **GB** (NOY) 39 Xf 24
Hetton **GB** (TAW) 33 Yd 20
Heugh **GB** (NHL) 33 Ya 18
Heugh-head **GB** (GRP) 16 Wf 5
Heveningham **GB** (SUF) 57 Bc 35
Hever **GB** (KEN) 71 Aa 41
Heversham **GB** (CUB) 35 Xb 23
Hevingham **GB** (NOR) 49 Bb 32
Hewas Water **GB** (CNW) 75 Va 47
Hewell Grange **GB** (HWC) 53 Ya 35
Hewell Lane **GB** (HWC) 53 Ya 35
Hewelsfield **GB** (GLS) 61 Xc 38
Hewish **GB** (AVN) 61 Xa 40
Hewish **GB** (SOM) 68 Xb 43
Hewton **GB** (DEV) 66 Vf 44
Hexham **GB** (NHL) 33 Xf 19
Hextable **GB** (KEN) 64 Ab 40

120 GB IRL Groes-faen – Hextable

Hexton GB (HTS) 63 Zd 37
Hexworthy GB (DEV) 76 Wa 45
Heybridge GB (ESS) 65 Ae 38
Heydon GB (CBS) 55 Aa 36
Heylipol GB (STC) 18 Ta 10
Heylor GB (SHL) 2 Yd 105
Heysham GB (LCS) 38 Xa 24
Heyshott GB (WSX) 70 Zb 43
Heytesbury GB (WIL) 69 Xf 41
Heythrop GB (OXS) 62 Yd 37
Heywood GB (GRM) 39 Xe 27
Heywood GB (WIL) 69 Xe 41
Hibaldstow GB (HUS) 41 Zc 27
Hickleton GB (SOY) 40 Ye 27
Hickling GB (NOR) 49 Bd 32
Hickling GB (NTS) 46 Za 31
Hickling Heath GB (NOR) 49 Bd 32
Hickstead GB (WSX) 71 Ze 43
Hidcote Boyce GB (GLS) 53 Yb 36
Hiendley GB (WYO) 40 Yd 27
High Ackworth GB (WYO) 40 Yd 27
Higham GB (DSH) 46 Yd 30
Higham GB (KEN) 65 Ac 40
Higham GB (LCS) 39 Xe 26
Higham GB (SUF) 56 Ad 35
Higham Ferrers GB (NRH) 55 Zc 35
Higham Gobion GB (BFS) 55 Zd 37
Higham on the Hill GB (LEC) 54 Yd 33
Highampton GB (DEV) 66 Vf 44
High Beach GB (ESS) 64 Aa 39
High Bentham GB (NOY) 38 Xc 24
High Bickington GB (DEV) 66 Wa 43
High Birkwith GB (NOY) 35 Xe 23
Highbog IRL (ROS) 88 Rd 25
High Bonnybridge GB (CEN) 25 Wa 13
High Bradfield GB (SOY) 39 Yc 28
Highbridge GB (SOM) 68 Xa 41
Highbrook GB (WSX) 71 Zf 42
High Bullen GB (DEV) 66 Vf 43
Highburton GB (WYO) 39 Yb 27
High Buston GB (NHL) 33 Yc 16
High Catton GB (HUS) 40 Za 25
Highclere GB (HAS) 62 Yd 40
Highcliffe GB (DOS) 69 Yb 44
High Coniscliffe GB (DUR) 36 Yc 21
High Cross GB (HAS) 70 Za 42
High Cross GB (HTS) 64 Zf 37
High Cross Bank GB (DSH) 45 Yc 32
High Dougarie GB (STC) 23 Ud 15
High Ellington GB (NOY) 36 Yb 23
High Entercommon GB (NOY) 36 Yd 22
Higher Ashton GB (DEV) 67 Wc 45
Higher Ballam GB (LCS) 38 Xa 26
Higher Bockhampton GB (DOS) 68 Xd 44
High Ercall GB (SHS) 44 Xc 32
Higher Kingcombe GB (DOS) 68 Xc 44
Higher Penwortham GB (LCS) 38 Xb 26
Higher Poynton GB (CHS) 45 Xf 28
Higher Tale GB (DEV) 67 We 44
Higher Town GB 74 Te 49
Higher Walreddon GB (DEV) 76 Vf 45
Higher Walton GB (CHS) 44 Xc 28
Higher Walton GB (LCS) 38 Xc 26
Higher Whitley GB (CHS) 44 Xc 29
Higher Wych GB (CHS) 44 Xb 31
High Ester GB (ESS) 64 Ac 38
Highfield GB (HUS) 40 Za 26
Highfield GB (STC) 24 Vb 14
Highfields GB (CBS) 55 Zf 35
Highfort House IRL (COR) 98 Rb 35
High Garrett GB (ESS) 65 Ad 37
High Grange GB (DUR) 36 Yb 20
High Green GB (HWC) 53 Xe 36
Highgreen Manor GB (NHL) 32 Xe 17
High Halden GB (KEN) 72 Ae 42
High Halstow GB (KEN) 65 Ad 40
High Ham GB (SOM) 68 Xb 42
High Hatton GB (SHS) 44 Xc 32
High Heath GB (SHS) 44 Xd 31
High Hesket GB (CUB) 35 Xb 20
High Hoyland GB (SOY) 39 Yc 27
High Hunsley GB (HUS) 41 Zc 26
High Hurstwood GB (ESX) 71 Aa 42
Highlane GB (CHS) 45 Xe 29
Highlane GB (DSH) 46 Yd 28
High Lane GB (DSH) 46 Yd 31
High Lane GB (HWC) 52 Xd 35
Highleadon GB (GLS) 61 Xe 37
High Legh GB (CHS) 44 Xd 28
Highley GB (SHS) 53 Xd 34
High Littleton GB (AVN) 68 Xc 41
High Lover GB (ESS) 64 Ab 38
High Melton GB (SOY) 40 Ye 27
Highmoor Cross GB (OXS) 63 Za 39
Highmoor Hill GB (GWE) 61 Xb 39
Highmount House IRL (LIM) 98 Ra 34
Highnam GB (GLS) 61 Xe 37
High Newton GB (CUB) 35 Xa 23
High Newton-by-the-Sea GB (NHL) 33 Yc 15
High Offley GB (SFS) 45 Xe 32
High Ongar GB (ESS) 64 Ab 38
High Onn GB (SFS) 45 Xe 32
High Roding GB (ESS) 64 Ab 38
High Salvington GB (WSX) 71 Zd 43
High Shaw GB (NOY) 35 Xe 23
High Speen GB (TAW) 33 Yb 19
Highsted GB (KEN) 65 Ae 41
High Street GB (CNW) 75 Va 46
High Street GB (KEN) 72 Ac 42
High Street GB (SUF) 57 Bd 36
High Street IRL (GAL) 87 Ra 27
Highstreet Green GB (ESS) 56 Ad 37
High Street Green GB (SUF) 56 Af 36
Hightae GB (DAG) 31 Wd 18
Hightown GB (CHS) 45 Xe 30
Hightown GB (MES) 38 Wf 27
High Toynton GB (LIN) 47 Zf 29
High Trewhill GB (NHL) 33 Ya 16
Highway GB (WIL) 62 Ya 40
Highwood GB (ESS) 64 Ac 38
Highworth GB (WIL) 62 Yb 39
High Wray GB (CUB) 35 Xa 22
High Wych GB (HTS) 64 Aa 38
High Wycombe GB (BUS) 63 Zb 39
Hilborough GB (NOR) 56 Ae 33
Hilcott GB (WIL) 62 Yb 41
Hildenborough GB (KEN) 71 Ab 41
Hildersham GB (CBS) 56 Ab 36
Hilderstone GB (SFS) 45 Xf 31
Hilderthorpe GB (HUS) 41 Ze 24
Hilfield GB (DOS) 68 Xc 43
Hilgay GB (NOR) 56 Ac 33
Hill GB (AVN) 61 Xc 39
Hillam GB (NOY) 40 Ye 26
Hillberry GBM 29 Vd 23
Hillbrae GB (GRP) 17 Xc 3
Hillbrae GB (GRP) 17 Xd 5
Hill Brow GB (WSX) 70 Za 42
Hill Chorlton GB (SFS) 45 Xe 31
Hilldyke GB (LIN) 47 Aa 30
Hill End GB (DUR) 36 Ya 20
Hill End GB (FIF) 25 Wc 12
Hillesley GB (AVN) 61 Xd 39
Hillhead GB (STC) 30 Vd 16
Hill Head IRL (DON) 78 Sd 18
Hillhead of Auchentumb GB (GRP) 17 Xf 3
Hillhead of Cocklaw GB (GRP) 17 Ya 4
Hilliard's Cross GB (SFS) 53 Yb 32
Hilliclay GB (HGL) 6 Wd 117
Hillingdon GB (GRL) 63 Zd 39
Hillington GB (NOR) 48 Ad 32
Hillmorton GB (WWH) 54 Ye 34
Hill Mountain GB (DYF) 58 Va 38
Hill of Down IRL (MT) 89 Sf 28
Hill of Fearn GB (HGL) 9 Wa 2
Hillquarter IRL (WMT) 88 Sa 28
Hill Ridware GB (SFS) 45 Ya 32
Hill Row GB (CBS) 56 Aa 34
Hillsborough GB (DOW) 85 Tf 22
Hillsford Bridge GB (DEV) 67 Wb 41
Hillside GB (GRP) 17 Xf 6
Hillside GB (TYS) 22 Xd 8
Hill Street IRL (ROS) 88 Rf 25
Hillswick GB (SHL) 2 Yd 106
Hill Top GB (HAS) 69 Yd 44
Hill Top GB (WYO) 39 Yd 27
Hilltown GB (DOW) 85 Tf 23
Hill Town IRL (LGF) 89 Sc 26
Hilltown IRL (MT) 90 Td 27
Hilltown IRL (WEX) 101 Td 35
Hilltown House IRL (MT) 95 Td 28
Hillview House IRL (WEX) 95 Td 32
Hillway GB (IOW) 70 Yf 44
Hilmarton GB (WIL) 62 Ya 40
Hilperton GB (WIL) 61 Xe 41
Hilton GB (CBS) 55 Zf 35
Hilton GB (CLE) 36 Ye 22
Hilton GB (CUB) 35 Xd 21
Hilton GB (DOS) 68 Xe 44
Hilton GB (DSH) 45 Yc 31
Hilton GB (DUR) 36 Yb 21
Hilton GB (GRP) 17 Xf 4
Hilton GB (SHS) 53 Xe 33
Hilton of Cadboll GB (HGL) 9 Wa 2
Himley GB (SFS) 53 Xe 33
Hincaster GB (CUB) 35 Xb 23
Hinckley GB (LEC) 54 Yd 33
Hinderclay GB (SUF) 57 Af 34
Hinderwell GB (NOY) 37 Zb 21
Hindford GB (SHS) 44 Xa 31
Hindhead GB (SUR) 70 Zb 42
Hindley GB (GRM) 38 Xc 27
Hindlip GB (HWC) 53 Xe 35
Hindolveston GB (NOR) 49 Ba 32
Hindon GB (WIL) 69 Xf 42
Hindringham GB (NOR) 48 Af 31
Hingham GB (NOR) 56 Af 33
Hinlesham GB (SUF) 57 Ba 36
Hinstock GB (SHS) 44 Xd 31
Hinton GB (AVN) 61 Xd 40
Hinton GB (HAS) 69 Yb 44
Hinton GB (HWC) 52 Xa 36
Hinton GB (SHS) 52 Xa 33
Hinton Blewett GB (AVN) 68 Xc 41
Hinton Charterhouse GB (AVN) 61 Xe 41
Hinton-in-the-Hedges GB (NRH) 54 Ye 36
Hinton Marsh GB (HAS) 70 Yf 42
Hinton Martell GB (DOS) 69 Ya 43
Hinton on the Green GB (HWC) 53 Ya 36
Hinton Parva GB (WIL) 62 Yb 39
Hinton Saint George GB (SOM) 68 Xb 43
Hinton Saint Mary GB (DOS) 68 Xe 43
Hinton Waldrist GB (OXS) 62 Yd 38
Hints GB (SHS) 52 Xc 34
Hinwick GB (BFS) 55 Zc 35
Hinxworth GB (HTS) 55 Ze 36
Hipperholme GB (WYO) 39 Yb 26
Hirnant GB (POW) 43 Wd 32
Hirnfield GB (GRP) 17 Xd 6
Hirst GB (NHL) 33 Yc 17
Hirst Courtney GB (NOY) 40 Yf 26
Hirwaen GB (CLW) 43 We 30
Hirwaun GB (MGL) 60 Wc 38
Histon GB (CBS) 56 Aa 35
Hitcham GB (SUF) 56 Af 36
Hitchin GB (HTS) 64 Ze 37
Hittisleigh GB (DEV) 67 Wb 44
Hixon GB (SFS) 45 Ya 32
Hoaden GB (KEN) 65 Bb 41
Hoaldalbert GB (GWE) 60 Xa 37
Hoar Cross GB (SFS) 45 Yb 32
Hoarwithy GB (HWC) 61 Xc 37
Hoath GB (KEN) 65 Ba 41
Hobarris GB (SHS) 52 Wf 34
Hobbs Lots Bridge GB (CBS) 55 Aa 33
Hobkirk GB (BOR) 32 Xc 16
Hoby GB (LEC) 46 Yf 32
Hockering GB (NOR) 49 Ba 32
Hockley GB (ESS) 65 Ad 39
Hockley Heath GB (WMD) 53 Yb 34
Hockliffe GB (BFS) 63 Zc 37
Hockwold cum Wilton GB (NOR) 56 Ad 34
Hoddesdon GB (HTS) 64 Zf 38
Hoddlesden GB (LCS) 38 Xd 26
Hodgeston GB (DYF) 58 Va 39
Hodgestown IRL (KIL) 95 Tb 29
Hodnet GB (SHS) 44 Xc 31
Hoe GB (NOR) 48 Af 32
Hoe Gate GB (HAS) 70 Yf 43
Hoe Saint Werburgh GB (KEN) 65 Ad 40
Hoff GB (CUB) 35 Xc 21
Hoffleet Stow GB (LIN) 47 Zf 31
Hogans Bridge IRL (LIM) 98 Ra 33
Hoggeston GB (BUS) 63 Zb 37
Hoghton GB (LCS) 38 Xc 26
Hognaston GB (DSH) 45 Yc 30
Hogsthorpe GB (LIN) 48 Zf 29
Holbeach GB (LIN) 47 Aa 32
Holbeach Clough GB (LIN) 47 Aa 32
Holbeach Drove GB (LIN) 47 Zf 32
Holbeach Hurn GB (LIN) 47 Aa 32
Holbeach Saint Johns GB (LIN) 47 Aa 32
Holbeach Saint Marks GB (LIN) 47 Aa 31
Holbeach Saint Matthew GB (LIN) 47 Aa 31
Holbeck GB (NTS) 46 Ye 29
Holberrow Green GB (HWC) 53 Ya 35
Holbrook GB (SUF) 57 Ba 37
Holburn GB (NHL) 27 Ya 15
Holcol GB (NRH) 54 Zb 35
Holcombe GB (DEV) 76 Wd 45
Holcombe GB (SOM) 68 Xd 41
Holcombe Rogus GB (DEV) 67 Wd 43
Holden GB (LCS) 38 Xd 25
Holdenby GB (NRH) 54 Za 35
Holdgate GB (SHS) 52 Xc 34
Holditch GB (DOS) 68 Xa 44
Hole in the Wall GB (HWC) 61 Xc 37
Hole Street GB (WSX) 71 Zd 43
Holford GB (SOM) 67 We 42
Holker GB (CUB) 35 Xa 23
Holkham GB (NOR) 48 Ae 31
Hollacombe GB (DEV) 66 Ve 44
Holland GB (ORK) 5 Xa 112
Holland GB (SUR) 71 Aa 41
Holland-on-Sea GB (ESS) 65 Bb 38
Hollandstrom GB (ORK) 5 Xd 112
Hollee GB (DAG) 31 Wf 18
Hollesley GB (SUF) 57 Bc 36
Hollingbourne GB (KEN) 65 Ad 41
Hollington GB (DSH) 45 Yc 31
Hollington GB (ESX) 72 Ad 43
Hollington GB (SFS) 45 Ya 31
Hollingworth GB (GRM) 39 Ya 28
Hollinsclough GB (SFS) 45 Ya 29
Hollinwood GB (SHS) 44 Xb 31
Holloway GB (DSH) 46 Yc 30
Hollow House IRL (OFF) 94 Sd 29
Holl's Green GB (HTS) 64 Zf 37
Hollybrock House IRL (CLW) 101 Tb 32
Hollybrook IRL (COR) 103 Qe 39
Hollybrook House IRL (OFF) 93 Sb 29
Hollybush GB (GWE) 60 We 38
Hollybush GB (HWC) 53 Xd 36
Holly End GB (NOR) 56 Ab 33
Hollyford IRL (TIP) 99 Rf 33
Hollyfort IRL (WEX) 101 Td 32
Holly Green GB (HWC) 53 Xe 36
Hollym GB (HUS) 41 Aa 26
Hollymount IRL (DON) 78 Se 17
Hollymount IRL (GAL) 92 Rb 30
Hollymount IRL (MAY) 87 Qf 27
Hollywell House IRL (GRE) 92 Qe 31
Hollywood IRL (KER) 102 Qa 38
Hollywood IRL (WKL) 95 Tc 30
Holm GB (HGL) 11 Te 119
Holmbury Saint Mary GB (SUR) 71 Zd 41
Holmbush GB (WSX) 71 Ze 42
Holme GB (CBS) 55 Ze 34
Holme GB (CUB) 35 Xb 23
Holme GB (NTS) 46 Zb 30
Holme GB (WYO) 39 Ya 27
Holme Chapel GB (LCS) 39 Xe 26
Holme Hale GB (NOR) 56 Ae 33
Holme Lacy GB (HWC) 61 Xc 36
Holme Marsh GB (HWC) 52 Xa 35
Holme-on-Spalding-Moor GB (HUS) 40 Zb 25
Holme on the Wolds GB (HUS) 41 Zc 25
Holme Pierrepoint GB (NTS) 46 Yf 31
Holmer GB (HWC) 52 Xb 36
Holmer Green GB (BUS) 63 Zb 38
Holmes Chapel GB (CHS) 44 Xd 29
Holmesfield GB (DSH) 45 Yc 29
Holmeswood GB (LCS) 38 Xa 27
Holmewood GB (DSH) 46 Yd 29
Holmfirth GB (WYO) 39 Yb 27
Holmhead GB (STC) 30 Ve 16
Holmpton GB (HUS) 41 Aa 26
Holmrook GB (CUB) 34 Wd 22
Holmsey Green GB (SUF) 56 Ac 34
Holne GB (DEV) 76 Wb 45
Holnest GB (DOS) 68 Xd 43
Holsworthy GB (DEV) 66 Vd 44
Holsworthy Beacon GB (DEV) 66 Ve 43
Holt GB (CLW) 44 Xa 30
Holt GB (DOS) 69 Ya 43
Holt GB (NOR) 49 Ba 31
Holt GB (WIL) 61 Xe 40
Holtby GB (NOY) 40 Za 25
Holt End GB (HAS) 70 Yf 42
Holt Fleet GB (HWC) 53 Xe 35
Holt Heath GB (DOS) 69 Ya 43
Holt Heath GB (HWC) 53 Xe 35
Holton GB (LIN) 47 Ze 29
Holton GB (OXS) 63 Yf 38
Holton GB (SOM) 68 Xd 42
Holton GB (SUF) 57 Bd 34
Holton Heath GB (DOS) 69 Xf 44
Holton le Clay GB (LIN) 41 Zf 27
Holton le Moor GB (LIN) 41 Zd 28
Holton St Mary GB (ESS) 65 Ba 37
Holtye Common GB (ESX) 71 Aa 42
Holwell GB (DOS) 68 Xd 43
Holwell GB (HTS) 55 Ze 37
Holwell GB (LEC) 46 Za 32
Holy Cross GB (HWC) 53 Xf 34
Holycross IRL (LIM) 98 Rc 33
Holycross IRL (TIP) 99 Sa 33
Holyhead GB (GWY) 42 Vc 29
Holy Island GB (NHL) 27 Yb 14
Holymoorside GB (DSH) 46 Yd 29
Holyport GB (BKS) 63 Zb 40
Holystone GB (NHL) 33 Xf 17
Holytown GB (STC) 25 Wa 14
Holywell GB (CLW) 44 We 29
Holywell GB (CNW) 74 Uf 46
Holywell GB (DOS) 68 Xc 43
Holywell Lake GB (SOM) 67 We 43
Holywell Row GB (SUF) 56 Ad 34
Holywood GB (ANT) 85 Ua 21
Holywood GB (DAG) 31 Wc 18
Homer GB (SHS) 52 Xc 33
Homersfield GB (SUF) 57 Bc 34
Homington GB (WIL) 69 Yb 42
Honeybourne GB (HWC) 53 Ya 36
Honey Hill GB (KEN) 65 Ba 41
Honeymount House IRL (TIP) 93 Sa 31
Honey Tye GB (SUF) 56 Af 37
Honiley GB (WWH) 53 Yc 34
Honing GB (NOR) 49 Bc 32
Honington GB (LIN) 47 Zc 31
Honington GB (SUF) 56 Ae 35
Honington GB (WWH) 53 Yc 36
Honiton GB (DEV) 67 We 44
Honley GB (WYO) 39 Yb 27
Hoock GB (WIL) 62 Ya 39
Hooe GB (DEV) 76 Vf 46
Hooe GB (ESX) 72 Ac 43
Hooe Common GB (ESX) 72 Ac 43
Hook GB (DYF) 58 Va 38
Hook GB (GRL) 64 Ze 40
Hook GB (HAS) 70 Za 41
Hook GB (HUS) 40 Za 26
Hooke GB (DOS) 68 Xc 44
Hookgate GB (SFS) 45 Xd 31
Hook Green GB (KEN) 72 Ac 42
Hook Norton GB (OXS) 62 Yd 37
Hookway GB (DEV) 67 Wc 44
Hookwood GB (SUR) 71 Ze 42
Hoole GB (CHS) 44 Xa 29
Hooley GB (SUR) 64 Ze 41
Hooton Pagnell GB (SOY) 40 Ye 27
Hooton Roberts GB (SOY) 40 Ye 28
Hopcrofts Holt GB (OXS) 62 Ye 37
Hope GB (CLW) 44 Wf 30
Hope GB (DEV) 76 Wa 47
Hope GB (DSH) 45 Yb 28
Hope GB (HGL) 4 Vc 117
Hope GB (POW) 52 Wf 33
Hope GB (SHS) 52 Xa 33
Hope Bagot GB (SHS) 52 Xc 34
Hope Bowdler GB (SHS) 52 Xb 33
Hopeman GB (GRP) 9 Wd 2
Hope Mansell GB (HWC) 61 Xc 37
Hopesay GB (SHS) 52 Xa 34
Hope under Dinmore GB (HWC) 52 Xb 35
Hophall IRL (LAO) 94 Se 30
Hopkinstown GB (MGL) 60 Wd 39
Hopton GB (DSH) 45 Yc 30
Hopton GB (SFS) 45 Xf 32
Hopton GB (SUF) 56 Af 34
Hopton Cangeford GB (SHS) 52 Xb 34
Hopton Castle GB (SHS) 52 Xa 34
Hopton on Sea GB (NOR) 57 Be 33
Hopton Wafers GB (SHS) 52 Xc 34
Hopwas GB (SFS) 53 Yb 33
Hopwood GB (HWC) 53 Ya 34
Horam GB (ESX) 72 Ab 43
Horath Cross Roads IRL (MT) 90 Ta 26
Horath Cross Roads IRL (MT) 90 Tb 26
Horbling GB (LIN) 47 Zd 31
Horbury GB (WYO) 39 Yc 27
Horden GB (DUR) 36 Ye 20
Horderley GB (SHS) 52 Xa 34
Hordle GB (HAS) 69 Yc 44
Hordley GB (SHS) 44 Xa 31
Horeb GB (DYF) 50 Vd 36
Horeb GB (DYF) 59 Vf 37
Horham GB (SUF) 57 Bb 35
Horkesley Heath GB (ESS) 65 Af 37
Horkstow GB (HUS) 41 Zc 27
Horley GB (SUR) 71 Ze 41
Hornblotton Green GB (SOM) 68 Xc 42
Hornby GB (LCS) 38 Xc 24
Hornby GB (NOY) 36 Yd 22
Horncastle GB (LIN) 47 Zf 29
Hornchurch GB (GRL) 64 Ab 39
Horncliffe GB (NHL) 27 Xf 14
Horndon GB (DEV) 76 Vf 45
Horndon on the Hill GB (ESS) 64 Ac 39
Horne GB (SUR) 71 Zf 41
Horn Green GB (HWC) 61 Xc 37
Horninghold GB (LEC) 54 Zb 33
Horninglow GB (SFS) 45 Yc 32
Horningsea GB (CBS) 56 Ab 35
Horningsham GB (WIL) 68 Xe 41
Horningtoft GB (NOR) 49 Af 32
Horningtops GB (CNW) 75 Vd 46
Hornsby GB (CUB) 32 Xb 19
Horns Cross GB (DEV) 66 Ve 43
Hornsea GB (HUS) 41 Zf 25
Hornsey GB (GRL) 64 Zf 39
Hornton GB (OXS) 54 Yd 36
Horrabridge GB (DEV) 76 Vf 45
Horridge GB (DEV) 76 Wb 45
Horringer GB (SUF) 56 Ae 35
Horse and Jockey IRL (TIP) 99 Sb 33
Horsebridge GB (DEV) 75 Ve 45
Horsebridge GB (ESX) 72 Ab 43
Horsebridge GB (HAS) 69 Yc 42
Horsebrook GB (SFS) 53 Xe 32
Horseford GB (NOR) 49 Bb 32
Horsehay GB (SHS) 52 Xd 33
Horseheath GB (CBS) 56 Ac 36
Horsehouse GB (NOY) 36 Ya 23
Horseleap IRL (WMT) 94 Sc 28
Horseman's Green GB (CLW) 44 Xb 31
Horseway GB (CBS) 55 Aa 34
Horsforth GB (WYO) 39 Yc 25
Horsham GB (WSX) 71 Ze 42
Horsham Saint Faith GB (NOR) 49 Bb 32
Horsington GB (LIN) 47 Ze 29
Horsington GB (SOM) 68 Xd 42
Horsley GB (GLS) 61 Xe 38
Horsley GB (NHL) 33 Ya 19
Horsley Cross GB (ESS) 65 Ba 37
Horsleycross Street GB (ESS) 65 Ba 37
Horsleyhill GB (BOR) 32 Xb 16
Horsley Woodhouse GB (DSH) 46 Yd 31
Horsmonden GB (KEN) 72 Ac 42
Horspath GB (OXS) 63 Ye 38
Horstead GB (NOR) 49 Bc 32
Horsted Keynes GB (WSX) 71 Zf 42
Hort. College IRL (KLK) 100 Se 34
Horton GB (BKS) 63 Zc 40
Horton GB (BUS) 63 Zc 37
Horton GB (DOS) 69 Ya 43
Horton GB (LCS) 39 Xe 25
Horton GB (NHL) 27 Ya 15
Horton GB (NRH) 54 Zb 35
Horton GB (SFS) 45 Xf 30
Horton GB (SOM) 68 Xa 43
Horton GB (WGL) 59 Ve 39
Horton-cum-Studley GB (OXS) 63 Yf 38
Horton Grange GB (TAW) 33 Yb 18
Horton Green GB (CHS) 44 Xb 30
Horton Heath GB (HAS) 70 Ye 43
Horton in Ribblesdale GB (NOY) 35 Xe 24
Horton Kirby GB (KEN) 64 Ab 40
Horwich GB (GRM) 38 Xc 27
Horwood GB (DEV) 66 Vf 42
Hose GB (LEC) 46 Za 31
Hosh GB (TYS) 21 Wa 10
Hospital IRL (LIM) 99 Rd 34
Hospital Saint Brigid's IRL (LAO) 94 Se 30
Hoswick GB (SHL) 3 Ye 109
Hotham GB (HUS) 40 Zc 26
Hothfield GB (KEN) 72 Ae 42
Hoton GB (LEC) 46 Yf 32
Houbie GB (SHL) 2 Za 105
Hough GB (CHS) 44 Xd 30
Hougharry GB (HGL) 10 Sc 3
Hough Green GB (CHS) 44 Xb 28
Hough-on-the-Hill GB (LIN) 47 Zc 30
Houghton GB (CBS) 55 Zf 35
Houghton GB (CUB) 32 Xa 19
Houghton GB (DYF) 58 Va 38
Houghton GB (HAS) 69 Yc 42
Houghton GB (WSX) 71 Zc 43
Houghton Conquest GB (BFS) 55 Zd 36
Houghton-le-Spring GB (TAW) 33 Yd 19
Houghton on the Hill GB (LEC) 54 Za 33
Houghton Regis GB (BFS) 63 Zc 37
Houghton Saint Giles GB (NOR) 48 Af 31
Houlskye GB (NOY) 37 Za 22
Hound GB (HAS) 70 Ye 43
Hound Green GB (HAS) 63 Za 41
Houndslow GB (BOR) 26 Xc 14
Houndwood GB (BOR) 27 Xe 13
Hounslow GB (GRL) 64 Zd 40
Hounslow Green GB (ESS) 64 Ac 38
Housetter GB (SHL) 2 Yd 105
Houston GB (STC) 24 Vc 13
Houstry GB (HGL) 9 Wd 119
Hove GB (ESX) 71 Ze 44
Hoveringham GB (NTS) 46 Za 30
Hoveton GB (NOR) 49 Bc 32
Hovingham GB (NOY) 37 Za 23
How GB (CUB) 32 Xb 19
How Caple GB (HWC) 61 Xc 37
Howden GB (DUR) 36 Yb 20
Howden GB (HUS) 40 Za 26
Howe GB (HGL) 6 We 117
Howe GB (NOR) 57 Bc 33
Howe Green GB (ESS) 65 Ad 38
Howell GB (LIN) 47 Ze 30
How End GB (BFS) 55 Zd 36
Howe of Teuchar GB (GRP) 17 Xd 3
Howe Street GB (ESS) 56 Ac 37
Howe Street GB (ESS) 65 Ac 38
Howey GB (POW) 51 Wd 35
Howgate GB (BOR) 32 Xd 16
Howgate GB (LOT) 26 We 14
Howick GB (NHL) 33 Yc 16
Howle GB (SHS) 44 Xd 32
Howlett End GB (ESS) 56 Ab 37
Howmore GB (HGL) 12 Sd 5
Hownam GB (BOR) 32 Xd 16
Howsham GB (HUS) 41 Zd 27
Howsham GB (NOY) 40 Za 24
Howth IRL (DUB) 95 Tf 28
Howton GB (HWC) 60 Xa 37
Howwood GB (STC) 24 Vc 14
Hoxne GB (SUF) 57 Bb 34
Hoylake GB (CHS) 44 We 28
Hoyland Nether GB (SOY) 40 Yd 27
Hoylandswaine GB (SOY) 39 Yc 27
Hubbert's Bridge GB (LIN) 47 Zf 31
Huby GB (NOY) 40 Yf 24
Hucclecote GB (GLS) 61 Xe 37
Hucking GB (KEN) 65 Ad 41
Hucknall GB (NTS) 46 Ye 30
Huckworthy Bridge GB (DEV) 76 Vf 45
Huddersfield GB (WYO) 39 Yb 27
Huddington GB (HWC) 53 Xf 35
Hudswell GB (NOY) 36 Yb 22
Huggate GB (HUS) 40 Zc 25
Hugginstown IRL (KLK) 100 Se 34
Hughenden Valley GB (BUS) 63 Zb 39
Hughley GB (SHS) 52 Xc 33
Hugh Town GB 74 Te 49
Huish GB (WIL) 62 Yb 40
Huish Episcopi GB (SOM) 68 Xb 42
Hulcott GB (BUS) 63 Zb 37
Hull, Kingston upon GB (HUS) 41 Zd 26
Hulland GB (DSH) 45 Yc 30
Hullavington GB (WIL) 61 Xf 39
Hullbridge GB (ESS) 65 Ad 39
Hulme End GB (SFS) 45 Ya 30
Hulme Walfield GB (CHS) 45 Xe 29
Hulver Street GB (SUF) 57 Bd 34
Humber Court GB (HWC) 52 Xb 35
Humberston GB (HUS) 41 Zf 27
Humberstone GB (LEC) 54 Yf 33
Humbie GB (LOT) 26 Xa 13
Humbleton GB (HUS) 41 Zf 26
Humbleton GB (NHL) 27 Xf 15
Humby GB (LIN) 47 Zc 31
Hume GB (BOR) 27 Xd 15
Humshaugh GB (NHL) 33 Xf 18
Huna GB (HGL) 6 Wf 117
Huncoat GB (LCS) 39 Xe 26
Huncote GB (LEC) 54 Ye 33
Hundalee GB (BOR) 32 Xc 16
Hunderthwaite GB (DUR) 36 Xf 21
Hundleby GB (LIN) 47 Aa 29
Hundred Acres GB (HAS) 70 Yf 43
Hundred End GB (LCS) 38 Xa 26
Hundred House GB (POW) 51 We 35
Hungarton GB (LEC) 54 Za 33
Hungerford GB (BKS) 62 Yc 40
Hungerford Newtown GB (BKS) 62 Yd 40
Hungleton GB (DYF) 58 Va 39
Hunmanby GB (NOY) 37 Ze 23
Hunningham GB (WWH) 54 Yd 35
Hunsdon GB (HTS) 64 Aa 38
Hunsingore GB (NOY) 40 Yd 25
Hunsonby GB (CUB) 35 Xc 20
Hunspow GB (HGL) 6 Wd 117
Hunstanton GB (NOR) 48 Ac 31
Hunston GB (SUF) 56 Af 35
Hunstrete GB (AVN) 61 Xc 40
Hunt End GB (HWC) 53 Ya 35
Hunter's Quay GB (STC) 24 Va 13
Huntingdon GB (CBS) 55 Ze 34
Huntingford GB (DOR) 68 Xe 42
Huntington GB (HWC) 52 Wf 35
Huntington GB (NOY) 40 Yf 25
Huntington GB (SFS) 53 Xf 32
Huntingtower GB (TYS) 21 Wc 10
Huntley GB (GLS) 61 Xd 37
Huntly GB (GRP) 16 Xb 4
Hunton GB (HAS) 70 Ye 42
Hunton GB (KEN) 72 Ac 41
Hunton GB (NOY) 36 Yb 23
Hunt's Cross GB (MES) 44 Xa 28
Huntsham GB (DEV) 67 Wd 43
Huntshaw Cross GB (DEV) 66 Vf 43
Huntspill GB (SOM) 68 Xa 41
Huntworth GB (SOM) 68 Xa 42
Hunwick GB (DUR) 36 Yb 20
Hunworth GB (NOR) 49 Ba 31
Hurcle IRL (MT) 90 Td 26
Hurlers Cross IRL (CRE) 92 Ra 32
Hurley GB (BKS) 63 Zb 39
Hurley GB (WWH) 53 Yc 33
Hurlford GB (STC) 24 Vd 15
Hurn GB (DOS) 69 Yb 44
Hursley GB (HAS) 70 Yd 42
Hurst GB (BKS) 63 Za 40
Hurst GB (NOY) 36 Ya 22
Hurstbourne Priors GB (HAS) 70 Yd 41
Hurstbourne Tarrant GB (HAS) 69 Yd 41
Hurst Green GB (ESX) 72 Ac 42
Hurst Green GB (LCS) 38 Xd 25
Hurst Green GB (SUR) 71 Zf 41
Hurstpierpoint GB (WSX) 71 Ze 43
Hurtmore GB (SUR) 70 Zc 41
Hurtworth-on-Tees GB (DUR) 36 Yc 22
Hury GB (DUR) 36 Xf 21
Husbands Bosworth GB (LEC) 54 Yf 34
Husborne Crawley GB (BFS) 55 Zc 36
Hushinish GB (HGL) 10 Sf 1
Hustanworth GB (DUR) 36 Xf 20
Husthwaite GB (NOY) 37 Ye 23
Huthwaite GB (NTS) 46 Ye 30
Huttoft GB (LIN) 48 Zf 29
Hutton GB (AVN) 68 Xa 41
Hutton GB (BOR) 27 Xf 14
Hutton GB (CUB) 35 Xa 21
Hutton GB (LCS) 38 Xb 26
Hutton Bonville GB (NOY) 36 Yd 22
Hutton Buscel GB (NOY) 37 Zc 23
Hutton Conyers GB (NOY) 36 Yc 24
Hutton Cranswick GB (HUS) 41 Zd 25
Hutton End GB (CUB) 35 Xa 20
Hutton Henry GB (DUR) 36 Yd 20
Hutton Magna GB (DUR) 36 Yb 21
Hutton Roof GB (CUB) 35 Xa 20
Hutton Roof GB (CUB) 35 Xc 23
Hutton Rudby GB (NOY) 36 Ye 22
Huttons Ambo GB (NOY) 37 Za 24
Hutton Sessay GB (NOY) 36 Ye 23
Huxley GB (CHS) 44 Xb 30
Huyton-with-Roby GB (MES) 44 Xb 28
Hycemoor GB (CUB) 34 Wd 23
Hyde GB (GLS) 61 Xf 38
Hyde GB (GRM) 39 Xf 28
Hyde Lea GB (SFS) 45 Xf 32
Hydestile GB (SUR) 70 Zc 42
Hyndford Bridge GB (STC) 25 Wb 15
Hynestown IRL (DUB) 90 Te 27
Hynish GB (STC) 18 Ta 10
Hyssington GB (POW) 52 Wf 33
Hythe GB (HAS) 70 Yd 43
Hythe GB (KEN) 73 Ba 42
Hythe End GB (BKS) 63 Zc 40

I

Ibsley GB (HAS) 69 Yb 43
Ibstock GB (LEC) 54 Yd 32
Ibstone GB (BUS) 63 Za 39
Ibthorpe GB (HAS) 69 Yd 41
Ibworth GB (HAS) 70 Ye 41
Ickburgh GB (NOR) 56 Ae 33
Ickenham GB (GRL) 63 Zd 39
Ickford GB (BUS) 63 Yf 38
Ickleford GB (HTS) 64 Ze 37
Icklesham GB (ESX) 72 Ae 43
Ickleton GB (CBS) 56 Ab 36
Icklingham GB (SUF) 56 Ad 35
Icomb GB (GLS) 62 Yb 37
Idbury GB (OXS) 62 Yc 37
Iddesleigh GB (DEV) 66 Vf 43
Ide GB (DEV) 67 Wc 44
Ideford GB (DEV) 76 Wc 45
Ide Hill GB (KEN) 71 Aa 41
Iden GB (ESX) 72 Ae 43
Iden Green GB (KEN) 72 Ad 42
Idlicote GB (WWH) 53 Yc 36
Idmiston GB (WIL) 69 Yb 42
Idridgehay GB (DSH) 45 Yc 30
Idrigill GB (HGL) 13 Td 3
Idvies GB (TYS) 22 Xb 9
Ifield GB (WSX) 71 Ze 42
Ifieldwood GB (WSX) 71 Ze 42
Ifold GB (WSX) 71 Zc 42
Iford GB (ESX) 71 Aa 43
Ifton Heath GB (SHS) 44 Wf 31
Ightfield GB (SHS) 44 Xc 31
Ightham GB (KEN) 64 Ab 41
Ignatestone GB (ESS) 64 Ac 38
Ilam GB (SFS) 45 Yb 30
Ilchester GB (SOM) 68 Xb 43
Ilderton GB (NHL) 33 Ya 16
Ilford GB (GRL) 64 Aa 39
Ilfracombe GB (DEV) 66 Vf 41
Ilkeston GB (DSH) 46 Ye 31
Ilketshall Saint Andrew GB (SUF) 57 Bc 34
Ilketshall Saint Margaret GB (SUF) 57 Bc 34
Ilkley GB (WYO) 39 Yb 25
Illane IRL (COR) 103 Qd 38
Illanmore IRL (MAY) 87 Qe 27
Illaubaun IRL (CRE) 92 Qe 31
Illaunstookagh IRL (KER) 97 Qa 36
Illey GB (WMD) 53 Xf 34
Illies IRL (DON) 78 Sd 18
Illington GB (NOR) 56 Af 34
Illingworth GB (WYO) 39 Ya 26
Illogan GB (CNW) 74 Ue 47
Illston on the Hill GB (LEC) 54 Za 33
Ilmer GB (BUS) 63 Za 38
Ilmington GB (WWH) 53 Yb 36
Ilminster GB (SOM) 68 Xa 43
Ilston GB (WGL) 59 Vf 39
Ilton GB (NOY) 36 Yb 23
Ilton GB (SOM) 68 Xa 43
Imachar GB (STC) 23 Ud 15
Imlick IRL (DON) 78 Sd 19
Immingham GB (HUS) 41 Ze 27
Inagh IRL (CRE) 92 Qe 31
Ince GB (CHS) 44 Xb 29
Ince Blundell GB (MES) 38 Wf 27
Inch IRL (COR) 104 Re 38
Inch IRL (COR) 104 Sa 37
Inch IRL (DON) 78 Sd 18
Inch IRL (KER) 97 Qa 36
Inch IRL (TIP) 99 Rf 32
Inchamay IRL (COR) 98 Ra 36
Inchanisley IRL (LAO) 94 Sc 30
Inchantotane IRL (COR) 98 Qf 35
Inchaquire IRL (KIL) 95 Tb 30
Incharmadermat IRL (ROS) 88 Rf 27
Inchbare GB (TYS) 22 Xc 8
Inchberry GB (GRP) 16 Wf 3
Inches IRL (KER) 98 Qe 36
Inchicorrigane IRL (KER) 97 Qd 36
Inchigeelagh IRL (COR) 103 Qf 37
Inchina GB (HGL) 7 Ud 1
Inchinnan GB (STC) 24 Vd 13
Inchisine IRL (COR) 103 Qf 37
Inchlaggan GB (HGL) 14 Uf 6
Inchnadamph GB (HGL) 8 Va 120
Inchnamuck IRL (TIP) 99 Rf 35
Inchture GB (TYS) 21 We 10
Inchyra GB (TYS) 21 We 10
Inckabaun IRL (LIM) 98 Qe 34
Indian Queens GB (CNW) 75 Va 46
Ingbirchworth GB (SOY) 39 Yc 27
Ingham GB (LIN) 47 Zc 28
Ingham GB (NOR) 49 Bd 32
Ingham GB (SUF) 56 Ae 35
Ingleby GB (DSH) 46 Yd 31
Ingleby Cross GB (NOY) 36 Ye 22
Ingleby Greenhow GB (NOY) 37 Yf 22
Inglesham GB (GLS) 62 Yb 38
Ingleton GB (DUR) 36 Yb 21
Ingleton GB (NOY) 35 Xd 24

Hexton – Ingleton GB IRL 121

Inglewhite **GB** (LCS) 38 Xb 25
Ingmire Hall **GB** (CUB) 35 Xc 23
Ingoe **GB** (NHL) 33 Ya 18
Ingoldisthorpe **GB** (NOR) 48 Ad 31
Ingoldmells **GB** (LIN) 48 Zf 29
Ingoldsby **GB** (LIN) 47 Zd 31
Ingon **GB** (WWH) 53 Yb 35
Ingram **GB** (NHL) 33 Ya 16
Ingrave **GB** (ESS) 64 Ac 39
Ings **GB** (CUB) 35 Xa 22
Ingst **GB** (AVN) 61 Xc 39
Inis = Ennis **IRL** (CRE) 92 Ra 31
Inis Córthaidh = Enniscorthy **IRL** (WEX) 101 Tc 33
Inish **IRL** (WEX) 101 Tc 35
Inishannon **IRL** (COR) 104 Rc 38
Inish Ballysheen **IRL** (WEX) 101 Td 35
Inishcarra **IRL** (COR) 104 Rc 37
Inishcrone **IRL** (SLI) 81 Qf 23
Inishmaan **IRL** (CRE) 91 Qc 30
Inishnaneill **IRL** (DON) 78 Se 17
Inistioge **IRL** (KLK) 100 Sf 34
Inkberrow **GB** (HWC) 53 Ya 35
Inkpen **GB** (BKS) 62 Yd 40
Inkstack **GB** (HGL) 6 We 117
Innellan **GB** (STC) 24 Va 13
Innerhadden **GB** (TYS) 20 Vf 8
Innerleithen **GB** (BOR) 26 Wf 15
Innerleven **GB** (FIF) 26 We 11
Innermessan **GB** (DAG) 28 Va 18
Innerwick **GB** (LOT) 27 Xd 13
Innerwick **GB** (TYS) 20 Ve 9
Innfield **IRL** (MT) 95 Tb 28
Inniskeen **IRL** (MOG) 90 Tc 24
Insch **GB** (GRP) 17 Xc 4
Insh **GB** (HGL) 15 Wa 6
Inshore **GB** (HGL) 4 Va 117
Inskip **GB** (LCS) 38 Xb 26
Instow **GB** (DEV) 66 Ve 42
Intake **GB** (SOY) 46 Yd 28
Intwood **GB** (NOR) 57 Bb 33
Inver **GB** (GRP) 16 We 6
Inver **GB** (HGL) 9 Wa 2
Inver **GB** (TYS) 21 Wc 9
Inver **IRL** (DON) 82 Re 21
Inverailort **GB** (HGL) 19 Uc 7
Inveralligin **GB** (HGL) 13 Uc 3
Inverallochy **GB** (GRP) 17 Ya 2
Inveran **IRL** (GAL) 91 Qd 29
Inverarish **GB** (HGL) 13 Tf 4
Inverarity **GB** (TYS) 22 Xa 9
Inverarnan **GB** (STC) 20 Vb 11
Inverary **GB** (STC) 24 Uf 11
Inverasdale **GB** (HGL) 7 Uc 2
Inverbeg **GB** (STC) 24 Vc 12
Inverbervie **GB** (GRP) 22 Xe 7
Inverbroom Lodge **GB** (HGL) 7 Uf 2
Invercassley **GB** (HGL) 8 Vc 1
Invercharnan **GB** (HGL) 19 Uf 9
Invercreran **GB** (STC) 19 Ue 9
Inverdruie **GB** (HGL) 15 Wb 5
Inverebrie **GB** (GRP) 17 Xf 4
Inveresk **GB** (LOT) 26 Wf 13
Inverey **GB** (GRP) 16 Wc 7
Inverfarigaig **GB** (HGL) 15 Vd 5
Invergarry **GB** (HGL) 14 Vb 6
Invergloy House **GB** (HGL) 19 Va 7
Invergordon **GB** (HGL) 8 Vf 2
Invergowrie **GB** (TYS) 21 Wf 10
Inverharroch **GB** (GRP) 16 Wf 4
Inverie **GB** (HGL) 13 Ub 6
Inverinate **GB** (HGL) 14 Ud 5
Inverinan **GB** (STC) 19 Ue 11
Inverkeilor **GB** (TYS) 22 Xc 9
Inverkeithing **GB** (FIF) 26 Wd 12
Inverkeithny **GB** (GRP) 17 Xc 3
Inverkip **GB** (STC) 24 Va 13
Inverkirkaig **GB** (HGL) 7 Ue 120
Inverlael **GB** (HGL) 7 Uf 2
Inverliever **GB** (STC) 23 Ud 11
Inverlochlarig **GB** (CEN) 24 Vc 11
Invermoriston **GB** (HGL) 15 Vc 5
Inverneill **GB** (STC) 23 Ud 13
Inverness **GB** (HGL) 15 Ve 4
Invernoaden **GB** (STC) 24 Uf 12
Inverpolly Lodge **GB** (HGL) 7 Ue 120
Inverquharity **GB** (TYS) 22 Xa 8
Inverroy **GB** (HGL) 20 Va 7
Inverugie **GB** (GRP) 17 Yb 3
Inveruglas **GB** (STC) 24 Vb 11
Inverurie **GB** (GRP) 17 Xd 5
Invervar **GB** (TYS) 20 Ve 9
Inwardleigh **GB** (DEV) 66 Vf 44
Inworth **GB** (ESS) 65 Ae 38
Ipplepen **GB** (DEV) 76 Wc 46
Ipsden **GB** (OXS) 63 Yf 39
Ipstones **GB** (SFS) 45 Ya 30
Ipswich **GB** (SUF) 57 Bb 36
Irby **GB** (CHS) 44 Wf 28
Irby **GB** (LIN) 47 Ab 30
Irby upon Humber **GB** (HUS) 41 Ze 27
Irchester **GB** (NRH) 55 Zc 35
Ireby **GB** (CUB) 34 We 20
Ireby **GB** (LCS) 35 Xc 23
Ireland **GB** (ORK) 6 We 115
Ireshopeburn **GB** (DUR) 35 Xe 20
Irishford **IRL** (MT) 90 Tb 26
Irlam **GB** (GRM) 38 Xd 28
Irnham **GB** (LIN) 47 Zd 32
Iron Acton **GB** (AVN) 61 Xd 39
Iron-Bridge **GB** (SHS) 52 Xd 33
Iron Cross **GB** (WWH) 53 Ya 35
Ironmacannie **GB** (DAG) 30 Vf 18
Ironside **GB** (GRP) 17 Xe 3
Ironville **GB** (DSH) 46 Yd 30
Irstead **GB** (NOR) 49 Bd 32
Irthington **GB** (CUB) 32 Xb 19
Irthlingborough **GB** (NRH) 55 Zc 35
Irton **GB** (NOY) 37 Zd 23
Irvine **GB** (STC) 24 Vc 15
Irvinestown **GB** (FER) 83 Sc 22
Isauld **GB** (HGL) 5 Wb 117
Isbister **GB** (ORK) 6 Wf 114
Isbister **GB** (SHL) 2 Ye 105
Isbister **GB** (SHL) 2 Za 106
Isfield **GB** (ESX) 71 Aa 43
Isham **GB** (NRH) 55 Zb 34
Island **IRL** (LAO) 94 Sd 31
Islandcausk Bridge **IRL** (GAL) 88 Re 28
Islandikane **IRL** (WTF) 100 Se 36
Islandmagrath House **IRL** (CRE) 92 Ra 32
Isle Brewers **GB** (SOM) 68 Xa 43
Isleham **GB** (CBS) 56 Ac 35
Isle of Whithorn **GB** (DAG) 29 Vd 20
Isleornsay or Eilean Iarmain **GB** (HGL) 13 Ub 6
Isley Walton **GB** (LEC) 46 Yd 32
Islington **GB** (GRL) 64 Zf 39
Islip **GB** (NRH) 55 Zc 34
Islip **GB** (OXS) 62 Ye 38
Islivig **GB** (HGL) 10 Sf 120
Istead Rise **GB** (KEN) 64 Ac 40
Itchen Abbas **GB** (HAS) 70 Ye 42
Itchen Stoke **GB** (HAS) 70 Ye 42
Itchington **GB** (AVN) 61 Xd 39
Itteringham **GB** (NOR) 49 Bb 32
Itton **GB** (DEV) 66 Wa 44
Itton Common **GB** (GWE) 61 Xb 39
Ivegill **GB** (CUB) 35 Xa 20
Ivelet **GB** (NOY) 36 Xf 22
Iver **GB** (BUS) 63 Zc 39
Iver Heath **GB** (BUS) 63 Zc 39
Iveston **GB** (DUR) 33 Yb 19
Ivinghoe **GB** (BUS) 63 Zc 38
Ivinghoe Aston **GB** (BUS) 63 Zc 37
Ivington **GB** (HWC) 52 Xb 35
Ivybridge **GB** (DEV) 76 Wa 46
Ivychurch **GB** (KEN) 72 Af 42
Ivy Hatch **GB** (KEN) 64 Ab 41
Iwade **GB** (KEN) 65 Ae 40
Iwerne Courtney or Shroton **GB** (DOS) 69 Xe 43
Iwerne Minster **GB** (DOS) 69 Xe 43
Ixworth **GB** (SUF) 56 Ae 35
Ixworth Thorpe **GB** (SUF) 56 Ae 35

J

Jack Hill **GB** (NOY) 39 Yb 25
Jackstown **GB** (GRP) 17 Xd 4
Jack Whites Cross Roads **IRL** (WKL) 95 Tf 31
Jacobstowe **GB** (DEV) 66 Vf 44
Jameston **GB** (DYF) 58 Vb 39
Jamestown **GB** (DAG) 32 Wf 17
Jamestown **IRL** (LAO) 94 Sf 30
Jamestown **IRL** (LET) 88 Rf 25
Jamestown **IRL** (ROS) 88 Re 27
Janetstown **GB** (HGL) 9 Wd 119
Jarrow **GB** (TAW) 33 Yd 19
Jarvis Brook **GB** (ESX) 71 Ab 42
Jawcraig **GB** (CEN) 25 Wa 13
Jayes Park **GB** (SUR) 71 Zd 42
Jaywick **GB** (ESS) 65 Ba 38
Jedburgh **GB** (BOR) 32 Xc 16
Jeffreyston **GB** (DYF) 58 Vb 38
Jemimaville **GB** (HGL) 15 Vf 3
Jenkinstown Cross **IRL** (LOT) 90 Te 24
Jesmond **GB** (TAW) 33 Yc 19
Jessop, Mount **IRL** (LGF) 88 Sb 26
Jevington **GB** (ESX) 72 Ab 44
John's Bridge **IRL** (COR) 98 Ra 35
Johnby **GB** (CUB) 35 Xa 20
John o'Groats **GB** (HGL) 6 Wf 117
John's Cross **GB** (ESX) 72 Ac 43
Johnshaven **GB** (GRP) 22 Xe 8
Johnston **GB** (DYF) 58 Va 38
Johnstone **GB** (STC) 24 Vc 14
Johnstonebridge **GB** (DAG) 31 Wd 17
Johnstonsbridge **IRL** (LET) 88 Sa 26
Johnstown **IRL** (COR) 103 Qf 38
Johnstown **IRL** (KIL) 95 Tc 29
Johnstown **IRL** (KLK) 94 Sc 32
Johnstown **IRL** (MT) 90 Tc 27
Johnstown **IRL** (WEX) 101 Tb 35
Johnstown Bridge **IRL** (KIL) 94 Ta 28
Johnstown North **IRL** (KIL) 94 Ta 31
Jonesborough **GB** (ARG) 90 Td 24
Joppa **GB** (LOT) 26 Wf 13
Jordans **GB** (BUS) 63 Ae 39
Judgeville **IRL** (WMT) 94 Sd 28
Julianstown **IRL** (MT) 90 Te 26
Jump **GB** (SOY) 40 Yd 27
Jurby East **GBM** 29 Vd 22
Jurby West **GBM** 29 Vc 22
Jvy Hall **IRL** (TIP) 93 Sa 30

K

Kaber **GB** (CUB) 35 Xe 21
Kaimes **GB** (LOT) 26 Wf 13
Kalnakill **GB** (HGL) 13 Ua 3
Kames **GB** (STC) 23 Uc 11
Kames **GB** (STC) 24 Ue 13
Kames **GB** (STC) 30 Vf 15
Kanturk **IRL** (COR) 98 Ra 35
Kate Kearney's Cottage **IRL** (KER) 97 Qc 36
Keadby **GB** (HUS) 40 Zb 27
Keadew **IRL** (ROS) 88 Rf 24
Keady **GB** (ARG) 84 Tb 23
Kealariddig **IRL** (KER) 102 Qa 37
Keal Coates **GB** (LIN) 47 Aa 30
Kealkill **IRL** (COR) 103 Qd 38
Kealvaugh **IRL** (COR) 103 Qe 38
Keam Cross Roads **IRL** (COR) 99 Re 36
Kearstwick **GB** (CUB) 35 Xc 23
Kearton **GB** (NOY) 36 Xf 22
Kearvaig **GB** (HGL) 4 Va 117
Keasden **GB** (NOY) 38 Xd 24
Keave **IRL** (GAL) 88 Rd 28
Kedington **GB** (SUF) 56 Ac 36
Kedleston **GB** (DSH) 45 Yc 31
Keekill **IRL** (GAL) 87 Qf 28
Keel **IRL** (LGF) 88 Sb 27
Keel **IRL** (MAY) 86 Pf 25
Keelby **GB** (LIN) 41 Ze 27
Keele **GB** (SFS) 45 Xe 30
Keenagh **IRL** (DON) 78 Se 16
Keenagh **IRL** (LGF) 88 Sb 27
Keenagh **IRL** (MAY) 87 Qd 24
Keeran House **IRL** (MT) 90 Tc 26
Keeraunnagark **IRL** (GAL) 91 Qc 29
Keeres Green **GB** (ESS) 64 Ab 38
Keeston **GB** (DYF) 58 Uf 38
Keevil **GB** (WIL) 61 Xf 41
Kegworth **GB** (LEC) 46 Ye 31
Kehelland **GB** (CNW) 74 Ue 47
Keig **GB** (GRP) 17 Xc 5
Keighley **GB** (WYO) 39 Ya 25
Keil **GB** (STC) 28 Ub 17
Keilhill **GB** (GRP) 17 Xd 3
Keillmore **GB** (STC) 23 Ub 13
Keillor **GB** (TYS) 21 We 9
Keills **GB** (STC) 23 Tf 13
Keillur **GB** (TYS) 21 Wc 10
Keils **GB** (STC) 23 Ua 13
Keinton Mandeville **GB** (SOM) 68 Xc 42
Keir Mill **GB** (DAG) 31 Wb 17
Keisby **GB** (LIN) 47 Zd 31
Keiss **GB** (HGL) 6 Wf 117
Keith **GB** (GRP) 16 Xa 3
Kelbrook **GB** (LCS) 39 Xf 25
Kelby **GB** (LIN) 47 Zc 31
Keld **GB** (CUB) 35 Xb 21
Keld **GB** (NOY) 35 Xf 22
Keldholme **GB** (NOY) 37 Za 23
Keldy Castle **GB** (NOY) 37 Zb 23
Kelfield **GB** (NOY) 40 Yf 25
Kelham **GB** (NTS) 46 Za 30
Kellan **GB** (STC) 18 Tf 10
Kellas **GB** (GRP) 16 Wd 3
Kellas **GB** (TYS) 22 Xa 9
Kellaton **GB** (DEV) 76 Wb 47
Kelleth **GB** (CUB) 35 Xc 22
Kelleythorpe **GB** (HUS) 41 Zd 25
Kelling **GB** (NOR) 49 Ba 31
Kellington **GB** (NOY) 40 Yf 26
Kelloe **GB** (DUR) 36 Yd 20
Kells **GB** (ANT) 84 Te 20
Kellsgrange **IRL** (KLK) 100 Se 33
Kelly **GB** (CNW) 75 Vb 45
Kelly **GB** (DEV) 75 Ve 45
Kelly's Bridge **IRL** (WMT) 89 Sc 27
Kelly's Quarter **IRL** (CLW) 101 Tb 33
Kelly Bray **GB** (CNW) 75 Ve 45
Kellymount **IRL** (KLK) 100 Sf 32
Kellystown **IRL** (WEX) 101 Tb 34
Kelmarsh **GB** (NRH) 55 Za 34
Kelmscott **GB** (OXS) 62 Yc 38
Kelsale **GB** (SUF) 57 Bc 35
Kelsall **GB** (CHS) 44 Xb 29
Kelshabeg **IRL** (WKL) 95 Tc 31
Kelshall **GB** (HTS) 55 Zf 36
Kelso **GB** (BOR) 27 Xd 15
Kelstedge **GB** (DSH) 46 Yd 29
Kelston **GB** (AVN) 61 Xd 40
Keltneyburn **GB** (TYS) 20 Vf 9
Kelton Hill, Rhonehouse or **GB** (DAG) 31 Wa 19
Kelty **GB** (FIF) 26 Wd 12
Kelvedon **GB** (ESS) 65 Ae 38
Kelvedon Hatch **GB** (ESS) 64 Ab 38
Kelynack **GB** (CNW) 74 Ub 48
Kemback **GB** (FIF) 22 Xa 11
Kemberton **GB** (SHS) 52 Xd 34
Kemble **GB** (GLS) 62 Xf 38
Kemerton **GB** (HWC) 53 Xf 36
Kemnay **GB** (GRP) 17 Xd 5
Kempley **GB** (GLS) 61 Xd 37
Kempsey **GB** (HWC) 53 Xe 36
Kempsford **GB** (GLS) 62 Yb 38
Kempston **GB** (BFS) 55 Zd 36
Kempston Hardwick **GB** (BFS) 55 Zd 36
Kempton **GB** (SHS) 52 Xa 34
Kemsing **GB** (KEN) 64 Ab 41
Kenardington **GB** (KEN) 72 Ae 42
Kenchester **GB** (HWC) 52 Xb 36
Kencott **GB** (OXS) 62 Yc 38
Kendal **GB** (CUB) 35 Xb 23
Kenilworth **GB** (WWH) 53 Yc 34
Kenley **GB** (GRL) 64 Zf 41
Kenley **GB** (SHS) 52 Xc 33
Kenmare **IRL** (KER) 103 Qc 37
Kenmore **GB** (TYS) 20 Wa 9
Kenn **GB** (AVN) 61 Xa 40
Kenn **GB** (DEV) 67 Wc 45
Kennel Cross Roads **IRL** (LAO) 94 Se 30
Kennerleigh **GB** (DEV) 67 Wb 43
Kennethmont **GB** (GRP) 16 Xb 4
Kennett **GB** (CBS) 56 Ac 35
Kenninghall **GB** (NOR) 57 Af 34
Kennington **GB** (KEN) 72 Af 41
Kennington **GB** (OXS) 62 Ye 38
Kennoway **GB** (FIF) 26 Wf 11
Kenny **IRL** (WMT) 89 Sd 27
Kenny Hill **GB** (SUF) 56 Ac 34
Kennythorpe **GB** (NOY) 40 Zb 24
Kenovay **GB** (STC) 18 Ta 9
Kensaleyre **GB** (HGL) 13 Te 4
Kensington **GB** (GRL) 64 Ze 40
Kensworth **GB** (BFS) 63 Zd 37
Kensworth Common **GB** (BFS) 63 Zd 37
Kentford **GB** (SUF) 56 Ad 35
Kentig **GB** (WGL) 59 Wb 39
Kentisbeare **GB** (DEV) 67 We 43
Kentisbury Ford **GB** (DEV) 66 Wa 42
Kentmere **GB** (CUB) 35 Xa 22
Kenton **GB** (DEV) 67 Wd 45
Kenton **GB** (GRL) 64 Ze 39
Kenton **GB** (SUF) 57 Bb 35
Kenton **GB** (TAW) 33 Yc 18
Kentra **GB** (HGL) 19 Ua 8
Kents Bank **GB** (CUB) 35 Xa 23
Kent's Green **GB** (GLS) 61 Xd 37
Kent's Oak **GB** (HAS) 69 Yc 42
Kentstown **IRL** (MT) 90 Tc 27
Kent Street **GB** (ESX) 72 Ad 43
Kent Street **GB** (KEN) 64 Ac 41
Kenwick **GB** (SHS) 44 Xa 31
Kenyon **GB** (GRM) 38 Xc 28
Keoghville **IRL** (ROS) 88 Rf 28
Keoldale **GB** (HGL) 4 Vb 117
Keose **GB** (HGL) 11 Td 120
Keppoch **GB** (HGL) 14 Ud 5
Kepwick **GB** (NOY) 36 Ye 23
Kerne Bridge **GB** (HWC) 61 Xc 37
Kerry **GB** (POW) 51 We 33
Kerrycroy **GB** (STC) 24 Uf 14
Kerrysdale **GB** (HGL) 7 Uc 2
Kerry's Gate **GB** (HWC) 60 Xa 37
Kersall **GB** (NTS) 46 Za 30
Kersey **GB** (SUF) 56 Af 36
Kershader **GB** (HGL) 11 Tc 120
Kershopefoot **GB** (CUB) 32 Xb 18
Kerswell Green **GB** (HWC) 53 Xe 36
Kesgrave **GB** (SUF) 57 Bb 36
Kesh **GB** (FER) 83 Sb 21
Kesh **IRL** (SLI) 88 Rd 24
Keshcarrigan **IRL** (LET) 88 Sa 24
Kessingland **GB** (SUF) 57 Be 34
Kestle Mill **GB** (CNW) 74 Uf 46
Keston **GB** (GRL) 64 Aa 40
Keswick **GB** (CUB) 34 Wf 21
Keswick **GB** (NOR) 49 Bc 31
Kettering **GB** (NRH) 55 Zb 34
Ketteringham **GB** (NOR) 57 Bb 33
Kettins **GB** (TYS) 21 We 9
Kettlebridge **GB** (FIF) 26 Wf 11
Kettleburgh **GB** (SUF) 57 Bb 35
Kettleness **GB** (NOY) 37 Zb 21
Kettleshulme **GB** (CHS) 45 Xf 29
Kettlesing Bottom **GB** (NOY) 39 Yc 24
Kettlestone **GB** (NOR) 48 Af 31
Kettletoft **GB** (ORK) 5 Xc 113
Kettlewell **GB** (NOY) 36 Xf 24
Ketton **GB** (LEC) 55 Zc 33
Kewstoke **GB** (AVN) 60 Xa 40
Kexbrough **GB** (SOY) 39 Yc 27
Kexby **GB** (LIN) 46 Zb 28
Kexby **GB** (NOY) 40 Za 25
Key's Cross Roads **IRL** (WEX) 101 Td 32
Key Green **GB** (CHS) 45 Xf 29
Keyham **GB** (LEC) 54 Za 33
Keyhaven **GB** (HAS) 69 Yc 44
Keyingham **GB** (HUS) 41 Zf 26
Keymer **GB** (WSX) 71 Zf 43
Keynsham **GB** (AVN) 61 Xc 40
Keysoe **GB** (BFS) 55 Zd 35
Keysoe Row **GB** (BFS) 55 Zd 35
Key's Toft **GB** (LIN) 48 Ab 30
Keyston **GB** (CBS) 55 Zd 34
Keyworth **GB** (NTS) 46 Yf 31
Kibblesworth **GB** (TAW) 33 Yc 19
Kibworth Beauchamp **GB** (LEC) 54 Za 33
Kibworth Harcourt **GB** (LEC) 54 Za 33
Kiddemore Green **GB** (SFS) 53 Xe 32
Kidderminster **GB** (HWC) 53 Xe 34
Kiddington **GB** (OXS) 62 Yd 37
Kidlawn **IRL** (ROS) 93 Rf 29
Kidlington **GB** (OXS) 62 Ye 38
Kidmore End **GB** (OXS) 63 Za 39
Kidsgrove **GB** (SFS) 45 Xe 30
Kidstones **GB** (NOY) 36 Xf 23
Kidwelly **GB** (DYF) 59 Ve 38
Kiel Crofts **GB** (STC) 19 Ud 10
Kielder **GB** (NHL) 32 Xc 17
Kilbaha **IRL** (CRE) 97 Qa 33
Kilballyporter **IRL** (MT) 90 Tb 28
Kilbane **IRL** (CRE) 92 Rc 32
Kilbarchan **GB** (STC) 24 Vc 13
Kilbarry **IRL** (COR) 103 Qf 37
Kilbaylet **IRL** (WKL) 95 Tc 30
Kilbeg **GB** (HGL) 13 Ua 6
Kilbeg **IRL** (WTF) 100 Se 36
Kilbeggan **IRL** (WMT) 94 Sd 28
Kilbegnet **IRL** (ROS) 88 Rd 27
Kilbeheny **IRL** (LIM) 99 Re 35
Kilbehy House **IRL** (LIM) 98 Ra 33
Kilberrihert **IRL** (COR) 98 Ra 35
Kilberry **GB** (STC) 23 Uc 14
Kilberry **IRL** (KIL) 94 Sf 30
Kilberry **IRL** (MT) 90 Tb 26
Kilbirnie **GB** (STC) 24 Vb 14
Kilboggan Cross Roads **IRL** (KIL) 94 Ta 30
Kilboggoon **IRL** (CRE) 92 Rb 31
Kilbraney **IRL** (WEX) 100 Tb 35
Kilbreedy **IRL** (TIP) 99 Sa 33
Kilbrennan House **IRL** (WMT) 94 Sd 28
Kilbrickan **IRL** (GAL) 86 Qc 28
Kilbrickan **IRL** (KLK) 100 Sd 33
Kilbricken **IRL** (LAO) 94 Sd 31
Kilbride **GB** (HGL) 12 Sd 6
Kilbride **GB** (STC) 19 Ud 10
Kilbride **IRL** (WKL) 95 Td 29
Kilbrin **IRL** (COR) 98 Ra 35
Kilbrittain **IRL** (COR) 104 Rb 38
Kilbrüle **IRL** (WKL) 95 Tf 31
Kilburn **GB** (DSH) 46 Yd 30
Kilburn **GB** (NOY) 37 Ye 23
Kilby **GB** (LEC) 54 Yf 33
Kilcaimin **IRL** (GAL) 92 Ra 29
Kilcar **IRL** (DON) 82 Rc 21
Kilcarney **IRL** (WKL) 95 Td 31
Kilcaroon **IRL** (TIP) 99 Rf 35
Kilcashel **IRL** (ROS) 93 Rf 28
Kilcaskan House **IRL** (COR) 98 Ra 36
Kilcatherina **IRL** (WMT) 89 Sb 28
Kilchamaig **GB** (STC) 23 Uc 14
Kilchattan **GB** (STC) 22 Te 12
Kilchattan Bay **GB** (STC) 24 Uf 14
Kilchenzie **GB** (STC) 28 Ub 16
Kilchiaran **GB** (STC) 22 Td 14
Kilchoan **GB** (HGL) 18 Tf 8
Kilchoman **GB** (STC) 22 Td 14
Kilchreest **IRL** (GAL) 92 Rc 29
Kilchrenan **GB** (STC) 19 Ue 10
Kilclaran **IRL** (CRE) 92 Rc 31
Kilclief **GB** (DOW) 85 Uc 22
Kilcloher **IRL** (CRE) 97 Qb 33
Kilcloncarkry House **IRL** (OFF) 94 Sf 29
Kilclone **IRL** (MT) 95 Tc 28
Kilclonfert **IRL** (WMT) 94 Sd 29
Kilcloosha **IRL** (COR) 98 Rb 35
Kilcock **IRL** (KIL) 95 Tb 28
Kilcoe **IRL** (COR) 103 Qd 39
Kilcolgan **IRL** (GAL) 92 Ra 29
Kilcolgan **IRL** (OFF) 93 Sb 29
Kilcollan **IRL** (KLK) 94 Se 32
Kilcolman **IRL** (LIM) 98 Qf 33
Kilcomin **IRL** (OFF) 93 Sa 31
Kilcommon **IRL** (TIP) 99 Rf 32
Kilcommon **IRL** (TIP) 99 Sa 34
Kilconly **IRL** (KER) 97 Qc 33
Kilconnel **IRL** (CRE) 91 Qd 31
Kilconnell **IRL** (GAL) 93 Rd 28
Kilconquhar **GB** (FIF) 26 Xb 11
Kilcoo **GB** (DOW) 85 Tf 23
Kilcoolaght **IRL** (KER) 97 Qb 36
Kilcoole **IRL** (WKL) 95 Tf 30
Kilcooley House **IRL** (WMT) 89 Sd 28
Kilcoona **IRL** (GAL) 87 Qf 28
Kilcormac **IRL** (OFF) 93 Sb 29
Kilcornan Centre **IRL** (GAL) 92 Ra 29
Kilcornan Lodge **IRL** (WMT) 88 Sb 27
Kilcorney **IRL** (COR) 98 Ra 36
Kilcot **GB** (GLS) 61 Xd 37
Kilcotton **IRL** (LAO) 94 Sc 31
Kilcotty **IRL** (WEX) 101 Td 34
Kilcoy **GB** (HGL) 15 Vd 3
Kilcredan **IRL** (COR) 104 Sa 37
Kilcreggan **GB** (STC) 24 Vb 13
Kilcroan Cross Roads **IRL** (GAL) 88 Rd 26
Kilcrohane **IRL** (COR) 102 Qb 39
Kilcronan **IRL** (COR) 104 Rc 37
Kilcross **IRL** (KLK) 100 Sf 34
Kilcullen **IRL** (KIL) 95 Tb 30
Kilcullen **IRL** (KLK) 100 Sf 33
Kilcumber Bridge **IRL** (OFF) 94 Sf 29
Kilcummer House **IRL** (COR) 98 Rd 36
Kilcummin **IRL** (KER) 97 Pf 35
Kilcummin **IRL** (MAY) 81 Qe 23
Kilcummin Farmhill **IRL** (KER) 97 Qd 36
Kilcurly **IRL** (LOT) 90 Td 24
Kilcusnaun **IRL** (KER) 97 Qd 35
Kildale **GB** (NOY) 37 Yf 22
Kildalkey **IRL** (MT) 89 Ta 27
Kildalloig **GB** (STC) 28 Uc 16
Kildangan **IRL** (KIL) 94 Sf 30
Kildare **IRL** (KIL) 94 Ta 30
Kildare House **IRL** (OFF) 94 Sc 28
Kildary **GB** (HGL) 8 Vf 2
Kildavin **IRL** (CLW) 101 Tb 32
Kildemock House **IRL** (LOT) 90 Tc 25
Kilderry **IRL** (KLK) 100 Se 32
Kildevin **IRL** (WMT) 89 Sd 26
Kildoagh **IRL** (MOG) 84 Ta 23
Kildonan **GB** (STC) 28 Uf 16
Kildonan Lodge **GB** (HGL) 9 Wa 119
Kildoney **IRL** (DON) 82 Re 21
Kildonnan **GB** (HGL) 18 Tf 7
Kildorragh **IRL** (CAV) 89 Se 25
Kildorrery **IRL** (COR) 99 Rd 35
Kildrummy **GB** (GRP) 16 Xa 5
Kilduffahoo **IRL** (LIM) 99 Re 33
Kilduff House **IRL** (TIP) 93 Sa 32
Kildurrihy **IRL** (KER) 96 Pd 36
Kilfaddamore House **IRL** (KER) 103 Qd 37
Kilfane **IRL** (KLK) 100 Sf 33
Kilfeakle **IRL** (TIP) 99 Rf 34
Kilfearagh **IRL** (CRE) 91 Qc 33
Kilfelligy **IRL** (GAL) 88 Rc 28
Kilfenora **IRL** (CRE) 92 Qe 31
Kilfinan **GB** (STC) 23 Ue 13
Kilfinnane **IRL** (LIM) 98 Rd 34
Kilfinny **IRL** (LIM) 98 Rb 33
Kilfithmone Cross Roads **IRL** (TIP) 93 Sa 32
Kilflynn **IRL** (KER) 97 Qc 34
Kilgalligan **IRL** (MAY) 80 Qa 23
Kilgarriff **IRL** (GAL) 87 Rb 27
Kilgarvan **IRL** (KER) 103 Qd 37
Kilgarvan **IRL** (MAY) 81 Qf 24
Kilgetty **GB** (DYF) 58 Vb 38
Kilglas **IRL** (ROS) 88 Rf 26
Kilglass **IRL** (GAL) 88 Rd 28
Kilglass **IRL** (ROS) 88 Rf 27
Kilglass **IRL** (SLI) 81 Qf 23
Kilgobbin Castle **IRL** (COR) 104 Rc 38
Kilgobnet **IRL** (KER) 97 Qb 36
Kilgobnet **IRL** (WTF) 99 Sc 36
Kilgoly **IRL** (DON) 82 Rb 20
Kilgowan **IRL** (KIL) 95 Tb 30
Kilgrogan **IRL** (LIM) 98 Ra 33
Kilgrovan **IRL** (WTF) 100 Sc 36
Kilham **GB** (HUS) 41 Zd 24
Kilham **GB** (NHL) 27 Xe 15
Kilhessen Lodge **IRL** (COR) 103 Rb 38
Kiliney **IRL** (DUB) 95 Tf 29
Kilkea **IRL** (KIL) 94 Ta 31
Kilkeasy **IRL** (KLK) 100 Se 34
Kilkee **IRL** (CRE) 91 Qc 32
Kilkeel **GB** (DOW) 90 Tf 24
Kilkelly **IRL** (MAY) 87 Ra 25
Kilkenneth **GB** (STC) 18 Ta 10
Kilkenny **GB** (GLS) 62 Ya 37
Kilkenny **IRL** (KLK) 100 Se 33
Kilkennybeg **IRL** (TIP) 99 Sa 33
Kilkeny West **IRL** (WMT) 93 Sb 28
Kilkerin **IRL** (CRE) 92 Qf 32
Kilkhampton **GB** (CNW) 66 Vd 43
Kilkieran **IRL** (GAL) 91 Qb 29
Kilkilleen **IRL** (COR) 103 Qd 39
Kilkishen **IRL** (CRE) 92 Rb 32
Kilknock House **IRL** (CLW) 94 Tb 32
Kill **IRL** (CAV) 89 Sf 24
Kill **IRL** (GAL) 86 Pf 27
Kill **IRL** (KIL) 95 Tc 29
Kill **IRL** (WTF) 100 Sd 35
Killabban **IRL** (LAO) 94 Ta 31
Killabney **IRL** (KER) 97 Qc 36
Killabuonia **IRL** (KER) 102 Pe 37
Killachonna **IRL** (WMT) 93 Sb 28
Killaclohane Wood **IRL** (KER) 97 Qb 36
Killacolla **IRL** (LIM) 98 Rb 34
Killaderry **IRL** (GAL) 88 Re 28
Killadiskert **IRL** (LET) 82 Rf 23
Killadooley House **IRL** (LAO) 94 Sc 31
Killadoon **IRL** (MAY) 86 Qa 26
Killadysert **IRL** (CRE) 92 Qf 32
Killafeen **IRL** (GAL) 92 Rb 30
Killag **IRL** (WEX) 101 Tc 35
Killagally Park **IRL** (OFF) 93 Sa 29
Killagh House **IRL** (GAL) 93 Rd 29
Killagoley **IRL** (WEX) 101 Tc 34
Killaidamee **IRL** (TIP) 99 Sa 35
Killala **IRL** (MAY) 81 Qe 23
Killallon **IRL** (MT) 89 Sf 26
Killaloe **IRL** (CRE) 93 Rd 32
Killalongford **IRL** (CLW) 95 Tc 32
Killamarsh **GB** (DSH) 46 Ye 29
Killamaun **IRL** (LET) 88 Sa 25
Killamery **IRL** (KLK) 100 Sd 34
Killamonagh **IRL** (GAL) 87 Qf 27
Killamurren **IRL** (COR) 99 Re 36
Killanafinch **IRL** (TIP) 93 Rf 32
Killanamaul **IRL** (COR) 104 Rb 38
Killane **IRL** (OFF) 94 Sf 29
Killanena **IRL** (CRE) 92 Rb 31
Killann **IRL** (WEX) 101 Tb 33
Killanure **IRL** (WEX) 101 Tb 33
Killaraght **IRL** (SLI) 88 Rd 25
Killare **IRL** (WMT) 89 Sc 28
Killare House **IRL** (WMT) 89 Sc 28
Killarga **IRL** (LET) 82 Re 23
Killarney **IRL** (KER) 97 Qc 36
Killarney **IRL** (KLK) 100 Se 33
Killarone **IRL** (GAL) 87 Qe 28
Killaroo **IRL** (WMT) 89 Sd 28
Killart House **IRL** (LAO) 94 Sc 30
Killashee **IRL** (LGF) 88 Sa 26
Killasong **IRL** (LGF) 89 Sd 26
Killasser **IRL** (MAY) 87 Ra 25
Killaster House **IRL** (ROS) 88 Rd 26
Killattimoriarty **IRL** (ROS) 88 Rf 26
Killavackan **IRL** (ROS) 88 Rf 26
Killavally **IRL** (MAY) 87 Qd 26
Killavally **IRL** (WMT) 94 Sd 28
Killavil **IRL** (SLI) 88 Rc 24
Killavilla House **IRL** (OFF) 93 Sb 31
Killavoggy **IRL** (LET) 82 Re 23
Killavullen **IRL** (COR) 98 Rc 36
Killawillin **IRL** (COR) 99 Re 36
Killea **IRL** (DON) 78 Sd 19
Killea **IRL** (TIP) 93 Sa 32
Killea **IRL** (WTF) 100 Sf 35
Killead **GB** (ANT) 84 Te 21
Killeagh **IRL** (COR) 104 Sa 37
Killean **GB** (STC) 23 Uc 15
Killeany **IRL** (CRE) 91 Qc 30
Killearn **GB** (CEN) 24 Vd 12
Killeatin **IRL** (TIP) 99 Rf 35
Killedmond **IRL** (CLW) 100 Ta 33
Killeedy **IRL** (LIM) 98 Qf 34
Killeek **IRL** (DUB) 90 Te 28
Killeen **IRL** (COR) 98 Ra 36
Killeen **IRL** (GAL) 92 Rb 31
Killeen **IRL** (GAL) 93 Re 30
Killeen **IRL** (LGF) 89 Sc 27
Killeen **IRL** (MAY) 86 Qa 26
Killeen **IRL** (TIP) 93 Sa 30
Killeenadeema East **IRL** (GAL) 92 Rc 30
Killeenaran **IRL** (GAL) 92 Ra 29
Killeenavarra **IRL** (GAL) 92 Ra 30
Killeenboy **IRL** (ROS) 88 Rf 27
Killeen Castle **IRL** (MT) 90 Tc 27
Killeenduff **IRL** (OFF) 94 Se 30
Killeenleagh House **IRL** (COR) 98 Ra 36
Killeenleigh **IRL** (COR) 98 Rb 37
Killeenmore **IRL** (OFF) 94 Sd 29
Killeens Cross **IRL** (COR) 104 Rc 37
Killeevan **IRL** (MOG) 83 Sf 23
Killegar **IRL** (LET) 89 Sc 24
Killeigh **IRL** (OFF) 94 Sd 29
Killelan **IRL** (KER) 96 Pe 37
Killellan **GB** (STC) 28 Uc 16
Killelton **IRL** (KER) 97 Qa 35
Killelton **IRL** (WTF) 100 Sd 36
Killen **GB** (HGL) 15 Ve 3
Killen **GB** (TYR) 83 Sb 21
Killen **IRL** (COR) 104 Rc 37
Killen **IRL** (GAL) 93 Re 30
Killenagh **IRL** (WEX) 101 Te 33
Killenaule **IRL** (TIP) 99 Sb 33
Killeny **IRL** (LGF) 88 Sa 26
Killerby **GB** (DUR) 36 Yb 21
Killeroran **IRL** (GAL) 88 Rd 27
Killerrig Cross Roads **IRL** (CLW) 94 Tb 31
Killeshandra **IRL** (CAV) 89 Sc 24
Killeshil **IRL** (OFF) 94 Se 29
Killeter **GB** (TYR) 83 Sb 20
Killian **GB** (HGL) 14 Ud 5
Killiane **IRL** (COR) 98 Ra 36
Killichonan **GB** (TYS) 20 Vd 8
Killiechronan **GB** (STC) 18 Ua 9
Killiecrankie **GB** (TYS) 21 Wb 8
Killiemor **GB** (STC) 18 Tf 10
Killilan Bridge **IRL** (GAL) 92 Rc 29
Killimer **IRL** (CRE) 97 Qd 33
Killimor **IRL** (GAL) 93 Re 29
Killimster **GB** (HGL) 9 We 118
Killin **GB** (CEN) 20 Ve 10
Killinaboy **IRL** (CRE) 92 Qf 31
Killinagh **IRL** (KIL) 94 Sf 28
Killinann **IRL** (WEX) 101 Te 32
Killinardrish House **IRL** (COR) 103 Ra 37
Killinaspick **IRL** (KLK) 100 Se 34
Killinchy **GB** (DOW) 85 Ub 22
Killincooly **IRL** (WEX) 101 Te 34
Killiney **IRL** (KER) 97 Pf 35
Killinghall **GB** (NOY) 39 Yc 24
Killington **GB** (CUB) 35 Xc 23
Killinick **IRL** (WEX) 101 Td 35
Killinierin **IRL** (WEX) 101 Te 32
Killinkere **IRL** (CAV) 89 Sf 25
Killinlahan **IRL** (WMT) 94 Sd 28
Killinny **IRL** (GAL) 92 Ra 30
Killiskey **IRL** (WKL) 95 Tf 30
Killoe **IRL** (KER) 96 Pe 37
Killogeary **IRL** (MAY) 81 Qe 23
Killogeenaghan **IRL** (WMT) 93 Sb 28
Killoluaig **IRL** (KER) 102 Pe 37
Killonahan **IRL** (LIM) 98 Rb 33
Killoran **IRL** (GAL) 93 Rd 29
Killoran **IRL** (SLI) 82 Rc 24
Killoran House **IRL** (TIP) 93 Sb 32
Killorglin **IRL** (KER) 97 Qb 36
Killoscobe **IRL** (GAL) 87 Rc 28
Killough **GB** (DOW) 85 Uc 23
Killoughternane **IRL** (CLW) 100 Ta 33
Killowen **IRL** (COR) 104 Rd 38
Killowen **IRL** (KER) 103 Qc 37
Killowney **IRL** (OFF) 93 Sa 29
Killross **IRL** (TIP) 99 Re 34
Killsallaghan **IRL** (DUB) 90 Te 28
Killucan **IRL** (WMT) 89 Sf 27
Killultan **IRL** (DON) 82 Rd 21
Killumney **IRL** (COR) 104 Rc 37
Killundine **GB** (HGL) 18 Ua 9
Killurin **IRL** (OFF) 94 Sc 29
Killurin **IRL** (WEX) 101 Tc 34
Killwood House **IRL** (GAL) 93 Re 29
Killybeg **IRL** (WKL) 95 Tc 31
Killybron **IRL** (MOG) 84 Sf 22
Killyclug **IRL** (DON) 77 Sb 19
Killycluggin **IRL** (CAV) 89 Sc 24
Killycolpy **GB** (TYR) 84 Tc 21
Killyconnan **IRL** (CAV) 89 Se 25
Killycross **IRL** (TIP) 93 Rf 30
Killygonlan **GB** (TYR) 84 Tc 21
Killygordon **IRL** (DON) 77 Sb 20
Killykeen **IRL** (CAV) 89 Sd 24
Killykeen **IRL** (CAV) 89 Sd 25
Killykergan **GB** (LDR) 79 Tb 18
Killylea **GB** (ARG) 84 Tb 22
Killyleagh **GB** (DOW) 85 Uc 22
Killynagh **IRL** (ROS) 88 Re 26
Killyon **IRL** (OFF) 93 Sb 30
Killyvahan **IRL** (CAV) 89 Sf 24
Killyverry **IRL** (DON) 76 Sc 19
Kilmacahill **IRL** (COR) 104 Rf 37
Kilmacananneny **IRL** (ROS) 88 Rf 26
Kilmacanoge **IRL** (WKL) 95 Tf 29
Kilmackowen **IRL** (COR) 102 Qa 38
Kilmacleague Bridge **IRL** (WTF) 100 Sf 36
Kilmaclenine **IRL** (COR) 98 Rb 35
Kilmacolm **GB** (STC) 24 Vc 13
Kilmacow **IRL** (KLK) 100 Se 35
Kilmacow House **IRL** (LIM) 98 Rb 34
Kilmacrea Ballinacor Cross Roads **IRL** (WKL) 95 Te 31
Kilmacrenan **IRL** (DON) 77 Sb 18
Kilmacteige **IRL** (SLI) 87 Ra 24
Kilmacthomas **IRL** (WTF) 100 Sd 35
Kilmactranny **IRL** (SLI) 88 Re 24
Kilmaganny **IRL** (KLK) 100 Se 34
Kilmaha **GB** (STC) 23 Ue 11
Kilmahon **IRL** (LGF) 89 Sb 26
Kilmainham Wood **IRL** (MT) 90 Tb 25
Kilmalady **IRL** (OFF) 94 Sc 28
Kilmaley **IRL** (CRE) 92 Qf 32
Kilmalieu **GB** (HGL) 19 Ud 9
Kilmalin **IRL** (WKL) 95 Te 29
Kilmallock **IRL** (LIM) 98 Rc 34
Kilmaloda House **IRL** (COR) 103 Rb 39
Kilmaloo **IRL** (WTF) 104 Sb 37
Kilmaluag **GB** (HGL) 13 Te 2
Kilmanagh **IRL** (KLK) 100 Sd 33
Kilmanahan Bridge **IRL** (WTF) 99 Sb 35
Kilmanaheen **IRL** (KLK) 100 Sf 33
Kilmanihen **IRL** (KER) 97 Qd 35
Kilmany **GB** (FIF) 22 Xa 10
Kilmarie **GB** (HGL) 13 Tf 5
Kilmarnock **GB** (STC) 24 Vd 15
Kilmartin **GB** (STC) 23 Ud 12
Kilmartin **IRL** (WKL) 95 Tf 30
Kilmartin Upper **IRL** (COR) 98 Rb 37
Kilmaurs **GB** (STC) 24 Vc 15
Kilmeage **IRL** (KIL) 94 Ta 29
Kilmeedy **IRL** (LIM) 98 Ra 34
Kilmeelickin **IRL** (GAL) 86 Qc 27
Kilmelfort **GB** (STC) 19 Ud 11
Kilmersdon **GB** (SOM) 68 Xd 41
Kilmessan **IRL** (MT) 90 Tc 27
Kilmeston **GB** (HAS) 70 Yf 42
Kilmichael Glassary **GB** (STC) 23 Ud 12
Kilmichael of Inverlussa **GB** (STC) 23 Uc 12
Kilmichael **IRL** (COR) 103 Qf 37
Kilmihil **IRL** (CRE) 92 Qe 32
Kilmihil **IRL** (LIM) 98 Rc 34
Kilmington **GB** (WIL) 68 Xe 42
Kilmonivaig **GB** (HGL) 19 Uf 7
Kilmoon **IRL** (COR) 103 Qd 40
Kilmoon **IRL** (MT) 90 Td 27
Kilmorack **GB** (HGL) 15 Vc 4
Kilmore **GB** (DOW) 85 Ub 22
Kilmore **GB** (HGL) 13 Ua 6
Kilmore **GB** (STC) 19 Ud 10
Kilmore **IRL** (GAL) 87 Rc 27
Kilmore **IRL** (GAL) 93 Re 30
Kilmore **IRL** (MAY) 86 Qd 27
Kilmore **IRL** (MAY) 87 Qf 25
Kilmore **IRL** (MT) 90 Tc 28
Kilmore **IRL** (ROS) 88 Rf 25
Kilmore **IRL** (WEX) 101 Tc 35
Kilmore Cross Roads **IRL** (MT) 90 Tc 28

122 GB IRL Inglewhite – Kilmore Cross Roads

Kilmore Lakes **IRL** (COR) 103 Qc 38
Kilmore Quay **IRL** (WEX) 101 Tc 35
Kilmore Upper **IRL** (LGF) 88 Sa 26
Kilmorgan **IRL** (SLI) 82 Rd 24
Kilmorna **IRL** (KER) 97 Qd 34
Kilmory **GB** (HGL) 13 Td 6
Kilmory **GB** (HGL) 18 Tf 8
Kilmory **GB** (STC) 23 Ub 13
Kilmovee **IRL** (MAY) 87 Rb 25
Kilmoyleane South **IRL** (COR) 103 Ra 38
Kilmoyly South **IRL** (KER) 97 Qb 34
Kilmuckridge **IRL** (WEX) 101 Te 33
Kilmuir **GB** (HGL) 8 Vf 2
Kilmuir **GB** (HGL) 12 Tc 4
Kilmuir **GB** (HGL) 15 Ve 3
Kilmulhane **IRL** (KER) 97 Qc 34
Kilmur House **IRL** (MT) 89 Ta 27
Kilmurry **IRL** (COR) 99 Re 36
Kilmurry **IRL** (COR) 103 Ra 37
Kilmurry **IRL** (CRE) 91 Qd 32
Kilmurry **IRL** (CRE) 92 Rb 32
Kilmurry **IRL** (LIM) 99 Rd 33
Kilmurry **IRL** (WKL) 95 Tb 31
Kilmurry **IRL** (WTF) 99 Sb 36
Kilmurry Mc.Mahon **IRL** (CRE) 92 Qe 33
Kilmurvy **IRL** (CRE) 91 Qb 30
Kilmyshall **IRL** (WEX) 101 Tc 33
Kilnaborris **IRL** (GAL) 93 Rf 29
Kilnaclasha **IRL** (COR) 103 Qe 39
Kilnafrehan **IRL** (WTF) 99 Sc 36
Kilnagarnagh **IRL** (OFF) 93 Sb 29
Kilnageer **IRL** (MAY) 87 Qd 25
Kilnagross **IRL** (LET) 88 Sa 25
Kilnahard House **IRL** (CAV) 89 Sd 26
Kilnahinch **IRL** (WMT) 93 Sb 28
Kilnaleck **IRL** (CAV) 89 Se 25
Kilnamaddy **IRL** (MOG) 83 Sf 23
Kilnamanagh **IRL** (WEX) 101 Td 33
Kilnamona **IRL** (CRE) 92 Qf 31
Kilnanare **IRL** (KER) 97 Qc 35
Kilnave **GB** (STC) 22 Td 13
Kilncadzow **GB** (STC) 25 Wb 14
Kiln Green **GB** (BKS) 63 Zb 40
Kilnhurst **GB** (SOY) 40 Ye 28
Kilninian **GB** (STC) 18 Te 9
Kilninver **GB** (STC) 19 Uc 10
Kiln Pit Hill **GB** (NHL) 33 Ya 19
Kilnsea **GB** (HUS) 41 Aa 27
Kilnsey **GB** (NOY) 39 Xf 24
Kiloran **GB** (STC) 22 Te 12
Kilpatrick **GB** (STC) 28 Ue 16
Kilpatrick **IRL** (COR) 104 Rb 38
Kilpatrick House **IRL** (WKL) 95 Tf 31
Kilpeacon Cross Roads **IRL** (KER) 102 Pe 37
Kilpeacon Cross Roads **IRL** (LIM) 98 Rc 33
Kilpech **GB** (HWC) 61 Xb 37
Kilpedder **IRL** (WKL) 95 Tf 30
Kilpheder **GB** (HGL) 12 Sd 6
Kilphedir **GB** (HGL) 9 Wb 120
Kilpin **GB** (HUS) 40 Zb 26
Kilpipe **IRL** (WKL) 95 Td 32
Kilplullibeen **IRL** (COR) 99 Rf 36
Kilquade House **IRL** (WKL) 95 Tf 30
Kilquain **IRL** (GAL) 93 Re 29
Kilquane **IRL** (KER) 96 Pe 35
Kilquane **IRL** (KER) 97 Qe 36
Kilquiggin **IRL** (WKL) 95 Tc 32
Kilquilly **IRL** (CAV) 89 Se 25
Kilrane **IRL** (WEX) 101 Td 35
Kilranelagh House **IRL** (WKL) 95 Tc 31
Kilrea **GB** (LDR) 79 Tc 19
Kilreekill **IRL** (GAL) 93 Rd 29
Kilrenny **GB** (FIF) 26 Xb 11
Kilronan **IRL** (CRE) 91 Qb 30
Kilrooan **IRL** (ROS) 87 Rc 25
Kilroosky **IRL** (ROS) 88 Rf 26
Kilrossanty **IRL** (WTF) 100 Sc 35
Kilrush **IRL** (CRE) 91 Qd 33
Kilrush **IRL** (WEX) 101 Tc 33
Kilrusheighter **IRL** (SLI) 82 Rb 23
Kilrush House **IRL** (MAY) 87 Qf 27
Kilrush Lodge **IRL** (KIL) 94 Ta 30
Kilsallagh **IRL** (GAL) 88 Rc 27
Kilsaran **IRL** (LOT) 90 Td 25
Kilsby **GB** (NRH) 54 Ye 34
Kilshalvy **IRL** (SLI) 88 Rc 24
Kilshanchoe **IRL** (KIL) 94 Ta 28
Kilshanny **IRL** (CRE) 92 Qe 31
Kilshanvy **IRL** (GAL) 87 Qf 27
Kilsheelan **IRL** (TIP) 100 Sc 34
Kilshruley Manor **IRL** (LGF) 89 Sc 26
Kilskeer **IRL** (MT) 89 Ta 26
Kilskeery **GB** (TYR) 83 Sc 22
Kilspindie **GB** (TYS) 21 We 10
Kilsyth **GB** (STC) 25 Vf 13
Kiltale **IRL** (MT) 90 Tc 27
Kiltallaght House **IRL** (LOT) 90 Te 26
Kiltamagh **IRL** (MAY) 87 Ra 25
Kiltarlity **GB** (HGL) 15 Vd 4
Kiltarsaghaun **IRL** (MAY) 87 Qd 26
Kiltealy **IRL** (WEX) 101 Tb 33
Kilteean **IRL** (KER) 97 Qc 34
Kilteel **IRL** (KIL) 95 Tc 29
Kilteely **IRL** (LIM) 99 Rd 33
Kilteevan Cross Roads **IRL** (ROS) 88 Rf 27
Kiltegan **IRL** (WKL) 95 Tc 31
Kiltens Gap **IRL** (MT) 95 Tc 28
Kiltiernan **IRL** (DUB) 95 Te 29
Kiltivna **IRL** (GAL) 87 Rb 27
Kiltober **IRL** (WMT) 94 Sd 28
Kilton **GB** (SOM) 67 We 41
Kiltoom **IRL** (ROS) 88 Rf 28
Kiltoom **IRL** (WMT) 89 Sd 26
Kiltormer **IRL** (GAL) 93 Re 29
Kiltrasna **IRL** (GAL) 87 Qf 28
Kiltrellig **IRL** (CRE) 97 Qa 33
Kiltrough **IRL** (MT) 90 Te 26
Kiltubbrid **IRL** (NIR) 84 Ta 23
Kiltullagh **IRL** (GAL) 92 Ra 29
Kiltullagh **IRL** (GAL) 92 Rc 29
Kiltybegs **IRL** (MOG) 90 Tc 25
Kiltyclogher **IRL** (LET) 82 Rf 22
Kilva **IRL** (COR) 104 Rf 37
Kilvaxter **GB** (HGL) 13 Td 3
Kilve **GB** (SOM) 67 We 41
Kilverston **GB** (NOR) 56 Ae 34
Kilvine **IRL** (MAY) 87 Ra 27
Kilvington **GB** (NTS) 46 Zb 31
Kilvirra **IRL** (COR) 103 Ra 38
Kilwatermoy **IRL** (WTF) 99 Sa 36
Kilwaughter **GB** (ANT) 79 Ua 20
Kilwinning **GB** (STC) 24 Vb 15
Kilworth **IRL** (COR) 99 Re 35
Kilworth Camp **IRL** (COR) 99 Re 35
Kimberley **GB** (NOR) 57 Ba 33
Kimberley **GB** (NTS) 46 Ye 31
Kimblesworth **GB** (DUR) 33 Yc 20
Kimbolton **GB** (CBS) 55 Zd 35
Kimbolton **GB** (HWC) 52 Xb 35
Kimcote **GB** (LEC) 54 Yf 34
Kimmeridge **GB** (DOS) 69 Xf 45
Kimmerston **GB** (NHL) 27 Xf 15
Kimpton **GB** (HAS) 69 Yc 41
Kimpton **GB** (HTS) 64 Ze 37
Kinawley **GB** (FER) 83 Sc 23
Kinbrace **GB** (HGL) 9 Wa 119
Kinbuck **GB** (CEN) 25 Wa 11
Kincaple **GB** (FIF) 22 Xa 10
Kincardine **GB** (HGL) 8 Vd 1
Kincardine O'Neil **GB** (GRP) 17 Xb 6
Kincaslough **IRL** (DON) 77 Rd 18
Kinclaven **GB** (TYS) 21 Wd 9
Kincon **IRL** (MAY) 81 Qe 23
Kincraig **GB** (HGL) 15 Wa 6
Kincraigie **GB** (TYS) 21 Wc 9
Kindallachan **GB** (TYS) 21 Wc 9
Kindroghed **IRL** (DON) 78 Sf 17
Kindrohid **IRL** (DON) 78 Sd 17
Kineton **GB** (GLS) 62 Ya 37
Kineton **GB** (WWH) 54 Yc 36
King's Cross Roads **IRL** (MT) 89 Sf 26
Kingarth **GB** (STC) 24 Uf 14
Kingcoed **GB** (GWE) 61 Xb 38
Kingham **GB** (OXS) 62 Yc 37
Kingholm Quay **GB** (DAG) 31 Wc 18
Kinghorn **GB** (FIF) 26 We 12
Kinglassie **GB** (FIF) 26 We 11
Kingsbarns **GB** (FIF) 22 Xc 11
Kingsbourne Green **GB** (HTS) 63 Zd 38
Kingsbridge **GB** (DEV) 76 Wb 47
Kingsbridge **GB** (SOM) 67 Wd 42
King's Bromley **GB** (SFS) 45 Yb 32
Kingsburgh **GB** (HGL) 13 Td 3
Kingsbury **GB** (WWH) 53 Yb 33
Kingsbury Episcopi **GB** (SOM) 68 Xb 43
King's Caple **GB** (HWC) 61 Xc 37
Kingsclere **GB** (HAS) 62 Ye 41
King's Cliffe **GB** (NRH) 55 Zc 33
Kingscote **GB** (GLS) 61 Xe 39
Kingscott **GB** (DEV) 66 Vf 43
King's Coughton **GB** (WWH) 53 Ya 35
Kingscourt **IRL** (CAV) 90 Tb 25
Kingscross **GB** (STC) 28 Uf 15
Kingsdon **GB** (SOM) 68 Xb 42
Kingsdown **GB** (KEN) 73 Bc 41
Kingseat **GB** (FIF) 26 Wd 12
Kingsey **GB** (BUS) 63 Za 38
Kingsfold **GB** (WSX) 71 Ze 42
Kingsford **GB** (HWC) 53 Xe 34
Kingsford **GB** (STC) 24 Vd 14
King's Green **GB** (GLS) 61 Xe 36
Kingshall Street **GB** (SUF) 56 Ae 35
King's Heath **GB** (WMD) 53 Ya 34
Kingskerswell **GB** (DEV) 76 Wc 46
Kingsland **GB** (GWY) 42 Vc 29
Kingsland **GB** (HWC) 52 Xb 35
Kingsland **IRL** (ROS) 88 Rd 25
Kings Langley **GB** (HTS) 63 Zd 38
Kingsley **GB** (CHS) 44 Xb 29
Kingsley **GB** (HAS) 70 Za 42
Kingsley **GB** (SFS) 45 Ya 30
Kingsley Green **GB** (WSX) 70 Zb 42
King's Lynn **GB** (NOR) 48 Ac 32
King's Meaburn **GB** (CUB) 35 Xc 21
Kings Muir **GB** (BOR) 26 Wd 15
Kingsmuir **GB** (TYS) 22 Xa 9
King's Newton **GB** (DSH) 46 Yd 32
Kingsnorth **GB** (KEN) 65 Ad 40
Kingsnorth **GB** (KEN) 72 Af 42
King's Norton **GB** (LEC) 54 Za 33
King's Norton **GB** (WMD) 53 Ya 34
King's Pyon **GB** (HWC) 52 Xb 36
Kings Ripton **GB** (CBS) 55 Zf 34
King's Somborne **GB** (HAS) 69 Yd 42
King's Stag **GB** (DOS) 68 Xd 43
Kings Sutton **GB** (NRH) 54 Ye 36
Kingstanding **GB** (WMD) 53 Ya 33
Kingsteignton **GB** (DEV) 76 Wc 45
King Sterndale **GB** (DSH) 45 Ya 29
King's Thorn **GB** (HWC) 61 Xb 37
Kingsthorpe **GB** (NRH) 54 Za 35
Kingston **GB** (CBS) 55 Zf 35
Kingston **GB** (DEV) 76 Wa 47
Kingston **GB** (GRP) 9 Wf 2
Kingston **GB** (HAS) 69 Yb 44
Kingston **GB** (IOW) 70 Ye 45
Kingston **GB** (KEN) 65 Ba 41
Kingston **GB** (LOT) 26 Xb 12
Kingston Bagpuze **GB** (OXS) 62 Yd 38
Kingston Blount **GB** (OXS) 63 Za 38
Kingston Deverill **GB** (WIL) 69 Xe 42
Kingstone **GB** (HWC) 61 Xa 36
Kingstone **GB** (SFS) 45 Ya 31
Kingstone **GB** (SOM) 68 Xa 43
Kingston Lisle **GB** (OXS) 62 Yc 39
Kingston near Lewes **GB** (ESX) 71 Zf 43
Kingston on Soar **GB** (NTS) 46 Ye 31
Kingston Saint Mary **GB** (SOM) 67 Wf 42
Kingston Seymour **GB** (AVN) 61 Xa 40
Kingston upon Hull **GB** (HUS) 41 Zd 26
Kingston upon Thames **GB** (GRL) 64 Ze 40
Kingstown **GB** (CUB) 32 Xa 19
King's Walden **GB** (HTS) 64 Ze 37
Kingswear **GB** (DEV) 76 Wc 46
Kingswells **GB** (STC) 24 Vd 14
Kingswood **GB** (AVN) 61 Xc 40
Kingswood **GB** (BUS) 63 Za 37
Kingswood **GB** (HWC) 52 Wf 35
Kingswood **GB** (KEN) 72 Ad 41
Kingswood **GB** (POW) 52 Wf 33
Kingswood **GB** (SUR) 64 Ze 41
Kingswood **GB** (WWH) 53 Yb 34
Kings Worthy **GB** (HAS) 70 Ye 42
Kingthorpe **GB** (LIN) 47 Ze 29
Kington **GB** (HWC) 52 Wf 35
Kington Langley **GB** (WIL) 61 Xf 40
Kington Saint Michael **GB** (WIL) 61 Xf 40
Kingussie **GB** (HGL) 15 Vf 6
Kingweston **GB** (SOM) 68 Xb 42
Kinharrachie **GB** (GRP) 17 Xf 4
Kinkardine **GB** (FIF) 25 Wb 12
Kinkell **GB** (STC) 25 Ve 13
Kinkell Bridge **GB** (TYS) 21 Wb 11
Kinknockie **GB** (GRP) 17 Ya 4
Kinloch **GB** (FIF) 21 Wf 11
Kinloch **GB** (HGL) 8 Vb 119
Kinloch **GB** (TYS) 21 Wd 9
Kinloch **GB** (TYS) 21 We 9
Kinlochard **GB** (CEN) 24 Vd 11
Kinlochbervie **GB** (HGL) 4 Uf 118
Kinloch Castle **GB** (HGL) 13 Te 6
Kinlocheil **GB** (HGL) 19 Ue 7
Kinloch Hourn **GB** (HGL) 14 Ud 6
Kinlochleven **GB** (HGL) 19 Va 8
Kinloch Rannoch **GB** (TYS) 20 Ve 8
Kinlochspelve **GB** (STC) 19 Ub 10
Kinloss **GB** (GRP) 16 Wc 3
Kinlough **IRL** (LET) 82 Re 22
Kinlowewe **GB** (HGL) 14 Ue 3
Kinmel Bay **GB** (CLW) 43 Wc 29
Kinmuck **GB** (GRP) 17 Xe 5
Kinmundy **GB** (GRP) 17 Xe 5
Kinnadie **GB** (GRP) 17 Xf 4
Kinnadoohy **IRL** (MAY) 86 Qa 26
Kinnagoe **IRL** (DON) 78 Sd 18
Kinnaird **GB** (TYS) 21 We 10
Kinnakillew **IRL** (DON) 82 Rb 20
Kinneff **GB** (GRP) 22 Xe 7
Kinnegad **IRL** (WMT) 89 Se 27
Kinnegad **IRL** (WMT) 89 Sf 28
Kinnell **GB** (TYS) 22 Xc 9
Kinnersley **GB** (HWC) 52 Xa 36
Kinnersley **GB** (HWC) 53 Xe 36
Kinnerton **GB** (POW) 52 Wf 35
Kinninvie **GB** (DUR) 36 Ya 21
Kinnitty **IRL** (OFF) 93 Sb 30
Kinnordy **GB** (TYS) 22 Wf 8
Kinoith **IRL** (COR) 104 Rf 37
Kinoulton **GB** (NTS) 46 Za 31
Kinross **GB** (TYS) 26 Wd 11
Kinrossie **GB** (TYS) 21 We 10
Kinsale **IRL** (COR) 104 Rc 38
Kinsalebeg **IRL** (WTF) 104 Sb 37
Kinsaley **IRL** (DUB) 95 Te 28
Kinsham **GB** (HWC) 52 Xa 35
Kinsley South **GB** (WYO) 40 Yd 27
Kintarvie **GB** (HGL) 11 Tb 120
Kintbury **GB** (BKS) 62 Yd 40
Kintessack **GB** (GRP) 15 Wb 3
Kintillo **GB** (TYS) 21 Wd 10
Kinton **GB** (SHS) 44 Xa 32
Kintore **GB** (GRP) 17 Xd 5
Kintour **GB** (STC) 23 Tf 14
Kintra **GB** (STC) 22 Te 15
Kintradwell **GB** (HGL) 9 Wb 120
Kintraw **GB** (STC) 23 Ud 11
Kinturk **IRL** (CRE) 92 Qe 32
Kinvarra **IRL** (GAL) 92 Ra 30
Kinver **GB** (SFS) 53 Xe 34
Kiplin **GB** (NOY) 36 Yc 22
Kippagh **IRL** (COR) 98 Qf 36
Kippax **GB** (WYO) 40 Yd 26
Kippen **GB** (CEN) 25 Ve 12
Kippford or Scaur **GB** (DAG) 31 Wb 19
Kipping's Cross **GB** (KEN) 72 Ac 42
Kirbister **GB** (ORK) 6 Wf 115
Kirby Bellars **GB** (LEC) 46 Za 32
Kirby Cane **GB** (NOR) 57 Bc 34
Kirby Cross **GB** (ESS) 65 Bb 37
Kirby Grindalythe **GB** (NOY) 40 Zc 24
Kirby Hill **GB** (NOY) 36 Yb 22
Kirby Hill **GB** (NOY) 40 Yd 24
Kirby Knowle **GB** (NOY) 36 Ye 23
Kirby-le-Soken **GB** (ESS) 65 Bb 37
Kirby Misperton **GB** (NOY) 37 Zb 23
Kirby Muxloe **GB** (LEC) 54 Ye 33
Kirby Sigston **GB** (NOY) 36 Yd 22
Kirby Underdale **GB** (HUS) 40 Va 24
Kirby Wiske **GB** (NOY) 36 Yd 23
Kircubbin **GB** (DOW) 85 Uc 22
Kirdford **GB** (WSX) 71 Zc 42
Kirivick **GB** (HGL) 11 Tb 119
Kirk **GB** (HGL) 6 We 117
Kirkbampton **GB** (CUB) 32 Wf 19
Kirkbean **GB** (DAG) 31 Wc 19
Kirk Bramwith **GB** (SOY) 40 Yf 27
Kirkbride **GB** (CUB) 31 We 19
Kirkbuddo **GB** (TYS) 22 Xb 9
Kirkburn **GB** (HUS) 41 Zc 25
Kirkburton **GB** (WYO) 39 Yb 27
Kirkby **GB** (LIN) 41 Zd 28
Kirkby **GB** (MES) 38 Xa 28
Kirkby **GB** (NOY) 37 Ye 22
Kirkby Bedon **GB** (NOR) 57 Bc 33
Kirkby Fleetham **GB** (NOY) 36 Yc 22
Kirkby Green **GB** (LIN) 47 Zd 30
Kirkby in Ashfield **GB** (NTS) 46 Ye 30
Kirkby-in-Furness **GB** (CUB) 34 We 23
Kirkby la Thorpe **GB** (LIN) 47 Zd 30
Kirkby Lonsdale **GB** (CUB) 35 Xc 23
Kirkby Malham **GB** (NOY) 39 Xe 24
Kirkby Mallory **GB** (LEC) 54 Ye 33
Kirkby Malzeard **GB** (NOY) 36 Yc 24
Kirkby Mills **GB** (NOY) 37 Za 23
Kirkbymoorside **GB** (NOY) 37 Za 23
Kirkby on Bain **GB** (LIN) 47 Zf 30
Kirkby Overblow **GB** (NOY) 39 Yc 25
Kirkby Stephen **GB** (CUB) 35 Xd 22
Kirkby Underwood **GB** (LIN) 47 Zd 32
Kirkcaldy **GB** (FIF) 26 Wf 12
Kirkcambeck **GB** (CUB) 32 Xb 18
Kirkcarswell **GB** (DAG) 29 Wa 20
Kirkcolm **GB** (DAG) 28 Uf 19
Kirkconne **GB** (STC) 25 Wa 15
Kirkconnell **GB** (DAG) 31 Wc 18
Kirkcowan **GB** (DAG) 29 Vc 19
Kirkcudbright **GB** (DAG) 29 Vf 19
Kirkdale **GB** (DAG) 30 Ve 19
Kirk Ella **GB** (HUS) 41 Zd 26
Kirkfieldbank **GB** (STC) 25 Wb 14
Kirkgunzeon **GB** (DAG) 31 Wb 19
Kirkham **GB** (LCS) 38 Xa 26
Kirkham **GB** (NOY) 40 Za 24
Kirkhamgate **GB** (WYO) 39 Yc 26
Kirk Hammerton **GB** (NOY) 40 Ye 25
Kirkharle **GB** (NHL) 33 Ya 18
Kirkhaugh **GB** (NHL) 32 Xd 19
Kirkheaton **GB** (NHL) 33 Ya 18
Kirkheaton **GB** (WYO) 39 Yb 27
Kirkhill **GB** (HGL) 15 Vd 4
Kirkhill **GB** (TYS) 22 Xc 8
Kirkhope **GB** (BOR) 32 Xa 15
Kirkhouse **GB** (BOR) 26 Wf 15
Kirkibost **GB** (HGL) 11 Tb 119
Kirkinch **GB** (TYS) 21 Wf 9
Kirkinner **GB** (DAG) 29 Vd 20
Kirkintilloch **GB** (STC) 25 Vf 13
Kirk Ireton **GB** (DSH) 45 Yc 30
Kirkistown **GB** (DOW) 85 Ud 22
Kirkland **GB** (CUB) 34 Wc 21
Kirkland **GB** (CUB) 35 Xc 20
Kirkland **GB** (DAG) 31 Wa 17
Kirk Langley **GB** (DSH) 45 Yc 31
Kirklevington **GB** (CLE) 36 Yd 22
Kirkley **GB** (SUF) 57 Be 34
Kirkleyditch **GB** (CHS) 45 Xe 29
Kirklington **GB** (NOY) 36 Yc 23
Kirklington **GB** (NTS) 46 Za 30
Kirklinton **GB** (CUB) 32 Xa 19
Kirkliston **GB** (LOT) 26 Wd 13
Kirkmaiden **GB** (DAG) 28 Va 20
Kirk Merrington **GB** (DUR) 36 Yc 20
Kirkmichael **GB** (STC) 30 Vc 16
Kirkmichael **GB** (TYS) 21 Wd 8
Kirk Michael **GBM** 29 Vc 23
Kirkmond le Mire **GB** (LIN) 41 Ze 28
Kirkmuirhill **GB** (STC) 25 Wa 14
Kirknewton **GB** (LOT) 26 Wd 13
Kirknewton **GB** (NHL) 27 Xf 15
Kirk of Shotts **GB** (STC) 25 Wa 13
Kirkoswald **GB** (CUB) 35 Xb 20
Kirkoswald **GB** (STC) 30 Vb 17
Kirkpatrick Durham **GB** (DAG) 31 Wa 18
Kirkpatrick-Fleming **GB** (DAG) 31 Wf 18
Kirk Sandall **GB** (SOY) 40 Yf 27
Kirksanton **GB** (CUB) 34 We 23
Kirkstead **GB** (LIN) 47 Ze 30
Kirkton **GB** (BOR) 32 Xb 16
Kirkton **GB** (DAG) 31 Wc 18
Kirkton **GB** (GRP) 17 Xc 3
Kirkton **GB** (GRP) 17 Xc 5
Kirkton **GB** (HGL) 8 Vf 1
Kirkton **GB** (HGL) 13 Uc 5
Kirkton **GB** (TYS) 21 Wb 10
Kirkton **GB** (TYS) 22 Xa 9
Kirkton Manor **GB** (BOR) 26 Wd 15
Kirkton of Airlie **GB** (TYS) 21 Wf 9
Kirkton of Auchterhouse **GB** (TYS) 21 Wf 9
Kirkton of Auchterless **GB** (GRP) 17 Xd 4
Kirkton of Barevan **GB** (HGL) 15 Wa 3
Kirkton of Bourtie **GB** (GRP) 17 Xe 5
Kirkton of Collace **GB** (TYS) 21 We 10
Kirkton of Craig **GB** (TYS) 22 Xd 8
Kirkton of Culsalmond **GB** (GRP) 17 Xc 4
Kirkton of Durris **GB** (GRP) 17 Xd 6
Kirkton of Glenbuchat **GB** (GRP) 16 Wf 5
Kirkton of Kingoldrum **GB** (TYS) 21 Wf 8
Kirkton of Lethendy **GB** (TYS) 21 Wd 9
Kirkton of Logie Buchan **GB** (GRP) 17 Xf 4
Kirkton of Maryculter **GB** (GRP) 17 Xe 6
Kirkton of Menmuir **GB** (TYS) 22 Xb 8
Kirkton of Monikie **GB** (TYS) 22 Xb 9
Kirkton of Rayne **GB** (GRP) 17 Xc 4
Kirkton of Skene **GB** (GRP) 17 Xe 6
Kirkton of Tough **GB** (GRP) 17 Xc 5
Kirktown **GB** (GRP) 17 Ya 3
Kirktown of Alveh **GB** (GRP) 17 Xc 3
Kirktown of Deskford **GB** (GRP) 16 Xb 3
Kirktown of Fetteresso **GB** (GRP) 17 Xe 7
Kirkwall **GB** (ORK) 6 Xa 115
Kirkwhelpington **GB** (NHL) 33 Xf 18
Kirk Yetholm **GB** (BOR) 27 Xe 15
Kirmington **GB** (HUS) 41 Ze 27
Kirn **GB** (STC) 24 Va 13
Kirriemuir **GB** (TYS) 22 Wf 8
Kirstead Green **GB** (NOR) 57 Bc 33
Kirtlebridge **GB** (DAG) 31 We 18
Kirtling **GB** (CBS) 56 Ac 35
Kirtlington **GB** (OXS) 62 Ye 37
Kirtomy **GB** (HGL) 5 Vf 117
Kirton **GB** (LIN) 47 Zf 31
Kirton **GB** (NTS) 46 Za 29
Kirton **GB** (SUF) 57 Bb 36
Kirton End **GB** (LIN) 47 Zf 31
Kirton in Lindsey **GB** (HUS) 41 Zc 28
Kishkeam **IRL** (COR) 98 Qf 35
Kislingbury **GB** (NRH) 54 Za 35
Kismeolon Bridge **GB** (DEV) 66 Vd 43
Kitchenstown **IRL** (DUB) 90 Te 27
Kites Hardwick **GB** (WWH) 54 Ye 35
Kitwood **GB** (HAS) 70 Yf 42
Kiveton Park **GB** (SOY) 46 Ye 28
Klimacurragh **IRL** (WKL) 95 Te 31
Klindown **GB** (KEN) 72 Ac 42
Klockbaun Rock **IRL** (KER) 97 Qb 36
Knackbrack **IRL** (KER) 97 Qc 34
Knaith **GB** (LIN) 46 Zb 28
Knap Corner **GB** (DOR) 68 Xe 42
Knaphill **GB** (SUR) 63 Zc 41
Knapp **GB** (SOM) 68 Wf 42
Knapton **GB** (NOR) 49 Bc 31
Knapton **GB** (NOY) 37 Zc 23
Knapton **GB** (NOY) 40 Yf 25
Knapton Green **GB** (HWC) 52 Xb 35
Knapwell **GB** (CBS) 55 Zf 35
Knaresborough **GB** (NOY) 40 Yd 24
Knarsdale **GB** (NHL) 32 Xc 19
Knaven **GB** (GRP) 17 Xf 4
Knayton **GB** (NOY) 36 Ye 23
Knebworth **GB** (HTS) 64 Ze 37
Kneesall **GB** (NTS) 46 Za 29
Kneesworth **GB** (CBS) 55 Zf 36
Kneeton **GB** (NTS) 46 Za 30
Knelston **GB** (WGL) 59 Ve 39
Knettishall **GB** (SUF) 56 Af 34
Knight's Town **IRL** (KER) 96 Pe 37
Knightacott **GB** (DEV) 66 Wa 42
Knightcote **GB** (WWH) 54 Yd 35
Knighton **GB** (DEV) 76 Vf 47
Knighton **GB** (LEC) 54 Yf 33
Knighton **GB** (POW) 52 Wf 34
Knighton **GB** (SFS) 45 Xd 31
Knightwick **GB** (HWC) 53 Xd 35
Knill **GB** (HWC) 52 Wf 35
Knitsley **GB** (DUR) 33 Yb 20
Kniveton **GB** (DSH) 45 Yb 30
Knock **GB** (CUB) 35 Xc 21
Knock **GB** (GRP) 16 Xb 3
Knock **GB** (STC) 18 Ua 10
Knock **GB** (WIL) 69 Xf 41
Knock **IRL** (GAL) 92 Qe 29
Knock **IRL** (MAY) 87 Ra 26
Knockacappul **IRL** (KER) 97 Qe 36
Knockacarharduff Commous **IRL** (TIP) 99 Rf 33
Knockacaurhin **IRL** (CRE) 92 Qf 31
Knockacrump **IRL** (COR) 104 Rf 37
Knockaculiata **IRL** (COR) 98 Rc 36
Knockacutteen **IRL** (CRE) 92 Qe 31
Knockadalteen **IRL** (SLI) 82 Rc 24
Knockadangan **IRL** (ROS) 88 Re 27
Knockaderry **IRL** (LIM) 98 Ra 34
Knockafreaghaun **IRL** (KER) 97 Qe 35
Knockagarrane **IRL** (COR) 98 Qf 36
Knockagarry **IRL** (COR) 99 Rd 35
Knockaghy **IRL** (CAV) 89 Sc 25
Knockagraffy **IRL** (MAY) 87 Qf 26
Knockaholet **GB** (ANT) 79 Td 18
Knockakeen **IRL** (COR) 104 Re 37
Knockalafalla **IRL** (WTF) 100 Sc 35
Knockalisheen **IRL** (COR) 104 Rc 37
Knockalougha **IRL** (KER) 97 Qd 34
Knockan **GB** (HGL) 7 Ue 120
Knockanade **IRL** (LIM) 98 Qe 34
Knockanaffrin **IRL** (WTF) 99 Sc 35
Knockananig **IRL** (COR) 99 Rd 36
Knockananna **IRL** (WKL) 95 Td 31
Knockanarra **IRL** (MAY) 87 Rb 26
Knockandhu **GB** (GRP) 16 We 5
Knockando **GB** (GRP) 16 Wd 4
Knockane **IRL** (COR) 102 Qb 39
Knockane **IRL** (COR) 104 Rb 37
Knockane **IRL** (KER) 97 Qd 36
Knockane **IRL** (TIP) 99 Sa 32
Knockanebane **IRL** (COR) 98 Qf 35
Knockanglass House **IRL** (TIP) 99 Sb 33
Knockanillaun **IRL** (MAY) 81 Qe 24
Knockanimrish **IRL** (KER) 97 Qd 36
Knockanroe House **IRL** (TIP) 93 Sb 31
Knockantebrack Hill **IRL** (LIM) 99 Re 34
Knockanure **IRL** (KER) 97 Qd 34
Knockardbane **IRL** (COR) 98 Rb 35
Knockatancally **IRL** (LIM) 98 Qe 34
Knockatee **IRL** (KER) 97 Qd 35
Knockatemple **IRL** (CAV) 89 Sf 26
Knockatian **IRL** (CRE) 92 Qf 30
Knockatinna **IRL** (KER) 97 Qa 36
Knockatober **IRL** (MAY) 87 Ra 26
Knockatomcoyle **IRL** (WKL) 95 Tc 32
Knockaun **IRL** (COR) 98 Ra 36
Knockaunaneagh **IRL** (GAL) 92 Rc 30
Knockaunavarrig **IRL** (COR) 98 Qf 35
Knockaunbrack **IRL** (KER) 97 Qd 34
Knockauncarragh **IRL** (GAL) 87 Rb 28
Knockaunnaglashy **IRL** (KER) 97 Qa 36
Knockaunnagorp **IRL** (COR) 103 Qf 38
Knockaunroe **IRL** (CRE) 92 Qf 31
Knockaunroe **IRL** (LIM) 98 Qe 34
Knockavaud **IRL** (COR) 102 Qa 39
Knockaville **IRL** (WMT) 89 Se 28
Knockbain **GB** (HGL) 15 Ve 3
Knockballyroney **IRL** (MOG) 83 Sf 23
Knockbidge **IRL** (LOT) 90 Td 25
Knockboy **IRL** (KER) 97 Pf 36
Knockboy **IRL** (WTF) 99 Sb 35
Knockbrack **IRL** (DON) 77 Sb 19
Knockbrack **IRL** (KER) 97 Qb 34
Knockbreckan **GB** (DOW) 85 Ua 21
Knockbrex **GB** (DAG) 29 Ve 20
Knockbride **IRL** (CAV) 89 Ta 25
Knockbrit **IRL** (TIP) 99 Sb 33
Knockburden **IRL** (COR) 104 Rc 37
Knock Castle **GB** (STC) 24 Va 14
Knock Cross Roads **IRL** (TIP) 93 Sb 31
Knockdee **GB** (HGL) 6 Wd 117
Knockdown **GB** (GLS) 61 Xe 39
Knockdrin **IRL** (WMT) 89 Se 27
Knockdrin Castle **IRL** (WMT) 89 Sd 27
Knockduff **IRL** (COR) 98 Qf 36
Knockduff **IRL** (KER) 103 Qc 38
Knockeen **IRL** (WTF) 100 Se 35
Knockeenadallane **IRL** (COR) 98 Qe 35
Knockeenahone **IRL** (KER) 97 Qe 35
Knockeencreen **IRL** (KER) 97 Qd 35
Knockeen Cross Roads **IRL** (KER) 97 Qc 35
Knockeens **IRL** (KER) 103 Qd 37
Knockeloghrim **GB** (LDR) 84 Tc 20
Knockenkelly **GB** (STC) 28 Uf 16
Knockentiber **GB** (STC) 24 Vc 15
Knockeroghery **IRL** (ROS) 88 Rf 27
Knockerry **IRL** (CRE) 91 Qd 33
Knockfeerina **IRL** (LIM) 98 Rb 34
Knockfola **IRL** (DON) 77 Re 18
Knockgarra **IRL** (GAL) 92 Ra 30
Knockglass **IRL** (MAY) 87 Qe 27
Knockhall **IRL** (ROS) 88 Sa 26
Knockholt **GB** (KEN) 64 Aa 41
Knockholt Pound **GB** (KEN) 64 Aa 41
Knockin **GB** (SHS) 44 Xa 32
Knockletteragh **IRL** (DON) 77 Rf 20
Knockloe House **IRL** (WKL) 95 Tb 32
Knocklofty **IRL** (TIP) 99 Sb 34
Knocklong **IRL** (LIM) 99 Rd 34
Knocklough Cross Roads **IRL** (MT) 89 Sf 26
Knockloughlin **IRL** (LGF) 88 Sb 26
Knockmael **IRL** (CRE) 92 Ra 31
Knockmanagh **IRL** (COR) 98 Qf 35
Knockmanagh **IRL** (KER) 97 Qf 36
Knockmaroe **IRL** (TIP) 93 Rf 32
Knockmeal **IRL** (KER) 97 Qd 34
Knockmeal **IRL** (WTF) 99 Sb 35
Knockmonalea **IRL** (COR) 104 Sa 37
Knockmore **IRL** (CLW) 100 Ta 33
Knockmore **IRL** (COR) 103 Qf 39
Knockmore **IRL** (MAY) 86 Pf 25
Knockmore **IRL** (MAY) 87 Qe 24
Knockmore **IRL** (WEX) 101 Tb 33
Knockmourne **IRL** (COR) 99 Rf 36
Knockmoyle **IRL** (GAL) 93 Rd 30
Knocknaboley **IRL** (CRE) 92 Qe 32
Knocknabooly **IRL** (LIM) 98 Qf 33
Knocknacaheragh **IRL** (COR) 98 Rd 36
Knocknacolan **IRL** (COR) 98 Ra 35
Knocknacree Cross Roads **IRL** (KIL) 94 Tb 31
Knocknafreaghaun **IRL** (KER) 97 Qb 36
Knocknagappul **IRL** (COR) 98 Ra 37
Knocknagashel **IRL** (KER) 97 Qd 35
Knocknagillagh **IRL** (CAV) 89 Se 25
Knocknagor **IRL** (GAL) 87 Ra 27
Knocknagornagh **IRL** (LIM) 98 Qe 34
Knocknagree **IRL** (COR) 98 Qe 36
Knocknaha **GB** (STC) 28 Uc 16
Knocknaharan **IRL** (KER) 97 Qd 36
Knocknahila **IRL** (CRE) 91 Qd 32
Knocknahoran **IRL** (KER) 96 Pe 36
Knocknain **GB** (DAG) 28 Uf 19
Knocknalina **IRL** (MAY) 80 Qa 23
Knocknaloman **IRL** (KER) 98 Qe 36
Knocknalower **IRL** (MAY) 80 Qb 23
Knocknamuck **IRL** (WKL) 95 Tb 31
Knocknamullagh **IRL** (COR) 104 Rd 37
Knocknanagh **IRL** (COR) 98 Qf 35
Knocknaskagh **IRL** (WTF) 99 Sb 36
Knocknaskea **IRL** (MAY) 80 Pe 24
Knocknaveagh **IRL** (COR) 103 Qd 38
Knockraha **IRL** (COR) 104 Rd 37
Knockroe **IRL** (COR) 103 Qd 39
Knockrome **GB** (STC) 23 Ua 13
Knockshannagh **IRL** (KIL) 95 Tb 31
Knocksharry **GBM** 29 Vc 23
Knockskavane **IRL** (COR) 98 Ra 35
Knocksquire or Knockseur **IRL** (CLW) 100 Ta 33
Knocktoosh **IRL** (LIM) 98 Ra 35
Knocktopher **IRL** (KLK) 100 Se 34
Knocktoran House **IRL** (LIM) 98 Rd 34
Knodishall **GB** (SUF) 57 Bd 35
Knolls Green **GB** (CHS) 45 Xe 29
Knolton **GB** (CLW) 44 Xa 31
Knoppage **IRL** (COR) 98 Rc 36
Knoppoge **IRL** (COR) 98 Rd 36
Knoppoge **IRL** (KER) 97 Qe 35
Knossington **GB** (LEC) 54 Zb 32
Knott End-on-Sea **GB** (LCS) 38 Xa 25
Knotting **GB** (BFS) 55 Zc 35
Knotting Green **GB** (BFS) 55 Zc 35
Knottingley **GB** (WYO) 40 Ye 26
Knotty Ash **GB** (MES) 44 Xa 28
Knotty Green **GB** (BUS) 63 Zc 39
Knowbury **GB** (SHS) 52 Xc 34
Knowe **GB** (DAG) 30 Vc 18
Knowehead **GB** (DAG) 30 Ve 17
Knowesgate **GB** (NHL) 33 Xf 18
Knoweside **GB** (STC) 30 Vb 16
Knowes of Elrick **GB** (GRP) 17 Xc 3
Knowetownhead **GB** (BOR) 32 Xb 16
Knowle **GB** (AVN) 61 Xc 40
Knowle **GB** (DEV) 66 Vf 42
Knowle **GB** (DEV) 67 Wd 45
Knowle **GB** (SHS) 52 Xc 34
Knowle **GB** (WMD) 53 Yb 34
Knowle, The **GB** (KEN) 72 Ac 42
Knowle Green **GB** (LCS) 38 Xc 25
Knowl Hill **GB** (BKS) 63 Zb 39
Knowlton **GB** (DOS) 69 Ya 43
Knowl Wall **GB** (SFS) 45 Xe 31
Knowsley **GB** (MES) 38 Xa 28
Knowstone **GB** (DEV) 67 Wb 43
Knowth House **IRL** (MT) 90 Td 26
Knutsford **GB** (CHS) 45 Xd 29
Kye **IRL** (ROS) 88 Rf 25
Kylanoreashy **IRL** (TIP) 100 Sc 34
Kyle **IRL** (KLK) 100 Se 34
Kyleakin **GB** (HGL) 13 Ub 5
Kylebrack **IRL** (GAL) 93 Rd 30
Kyle Cross **IRL** (WEX) 101 Tc 34
Kylegarriff **IRL** (GAL) 92 Rc 30
Kylemore House **IRL** (GAL) 86 Qb 27
Kyle of Lochalsh **GB** (HGL) 13 Ub 5
Kyle Park **IRL** (TIP) 93 Re 30
Kylerhea **GB** (HGL) 13 Uc 4
Kyles Scalpay **GB** (HGL) 11 Tb 1
Kylestrome **GB** (HGL) 7 Uf 119
Kyletalesha **IRL** (LAO) 94 Se 30
Kyloe **GB** (NHL) 27 Ya 15
Kynnersley **GB** (SHS) 44 Xd 32
Kyre Park **GB** (HWC) 52 Xc 35

L

Laban **IRL** (GAL) 92 Rb 30
Labasheeda **IRL** (CRE) 98 Qe 33
Labbacalle **IRL** (COR) 99 Rd 35
Labost **GB** (HGL) 11 Tc 118
Lacca Manor **IRL** (LAO) 94 Sc 30
Laceby **GB** (HUS) 41 Zf 27
Lacey Green **GB** (BUS) 63 Zb 38
Lach Dennis **GB** (CHS) 44 Xd 29
Lack **IRL** (ROS) 88 Sa 26
Lackabaun **IRL** (KER) 103 Qe 37
Lackagh **IRL** (KIL) 94 Sf 30
Lacka House **IRL** (TIP) 93 Sa 30
Lackalee **GB** (HGL) 11 Tb 2
Lackamore **IRL** (KER) 97 Qc 34
Lackan **IRL** (WEX) 101 Te 32
Lackan **IRL** (WKL) 95 Td 30
Lackan **IRL** (WMT) 89 Sd 27
Lackanastooka **IRL** (KER) 98 Qe 36
Lackanatleeve **IRL** (SLI) 81 Qf 23
Lackareagh **IRL** (COR) 102 Qa 38
Lackareagh **IRL** (COR) 103 Ra 38
Lackbrooder **IRL** (KER) 97 Qd 35
Lackdotia House **IRL** (COR) 98 Qf 36
Lacken **IRL** (WEX) 101 Td 34
Lackendarragh North **IRL** (COR) 99 Rd 36
Lackendarragh South **IRL** (COR) 99 Rd 36
Lackendarra House **IRL** (WTF) 104 Sb 37
Lackford **GB** (SUF) 56 Ad 35
Lacknahaghny **IRL** (COR) 98 Ra 37
Lacock **GB** (WIL) 61 Xf 40
Ladbroke **GB** (WWH) 54 Yd 35
Laddingford **GB** (KEN) 72 Ac 41
Lade Bank **GB** (LIN) 47 Aa 30
Ladestown House **IRL** (WMT) 89 Sd 28
Ladock **GB** (CNW) 75 Va 47
Ladybank **GB** (FIF) 21 Wf 11
Ladybrook (Belfast) **GB** (ANT) 85 Tf 21
Ladycross **GB** (CNW) 66 Vd 44
Ladykirk **GB** (BOR) 27 Xe 14
Ladysbridge **IRL** (COR) 104 Rf 37
Ladysford **GB** (GRP) 17 Xf 3
Lady's Green **GB** (SUF) 56 Ad 35
Laffansbridge **IRL** (TIP) 99 Sb 33
Lagacurry **IRL** (DON) 78 Sd 17
Lagavulin **GB** (STC) 23 Tf 15
Lagg **GB** (STC) 23 Ua 13
Lagg **GB** (STC) 28 Ue 16
Laggan **GB** (HGL) 14 Vb 6
Laggan **GB** (HGL) 15 Ve 6
Laggan **GB** (STC) 22 Te 14
Lagganulva **GB** (STC) 18 Tf 10
Laghtane Sch. **IRL** (LIM) 92 Rd 32
Laghy **IRL** (DON) 82 Rf 21
Lagnagun Great **IRL** (WKL) 95 Td 30
Laharan Cross Roads **IRL** (COR) 98 Rb 36
Lahardaun **IRL** (MAY) 87 Qe 24
Laheseragh **IRL** (KER) 97 Qc 33
Laide **GB** (HGL) 7 Uc 1
Lair **GB** (HGL) 14 Ue 4
Lairg **GB** (HGL) 8 Vd 120
Lairg Lodge **GB** (HGL) 8 Vd 120
Lake **GB** (WIL) 69 Yb 42
Lake Field **IRL** (KER) 97 Qa 36
Lakefield House **IRL** (MT) 89 Sf 26
Lakenham **GB** (NOR) 49 Bb 33
Lakenheath **GB** (SUF) 56 Ad 34
Lakesend **GB** (NOR) 56 Ab 33

Kilmore Lakes – Lakesend GB IRL **123**

Little Staughton GB (BFS) 55 Zd 35
Little Steeping GB (LIN) 47 Aa 30
Littlestone-on-Sea GB (KEN) 72 Af 43
Little Stonham GB (SUF) 57 Ba 35
Little Stretton GB (LEC) 54 Yf 33
Little Stretton GB (SHS) 52 Xb 33
Little Strickland GB (CUB) 35 Xb 21
Little Stukeley GB (CBS) 55 Ze 34
Little Tew GB (OXS) 62 Yd 37
Little Tey GB (ESS) 65 Ae 37
Little Thetford GB (CBS) 56 Ab 34
Littlethorpe GB (NOY) 39 Yc 24
Little Thurlow GB (SUF) 56 Ac 36
Littleton GB (CHS) 44 Xa 29
Littleton GB (HAS) 70 Yd 42
Littleton GB (SOM) 68 Xb 42
Littleton GB (TYS) 21 We 10
Littleton IRL (TIP) 99 Sb 33
Littleton Drew GB (WIL) 61 Xe 39
Littleton-on-Severn GB (AVN) 61 Xc 39
Littleton Panell GB (WIL) 69 Ya 41
Little Torrington GB (DEV) 66 Vf 43
Little Totham GB (ESS) 65 Ae 38
Little Town GB (CUB) 34 We 21
Littletown GB (DUR) 36 Yd 20
Little Wakering GB (ESS) 65 Ae 39
Little Walden GB (ESS) 56 Ab 36
Little Waldingfield GB (SUF) 56 Ae 36
Little Waltham GB (ESS) 65 Ac 38
Little Warley GB (ESS) 64 Ab 39
Little Weighton GB (HUS) 41 Zd 26
Little Welland GB (HWC) 53 Xe 36
Little Wenlock GB (SHS) 52 Xc 33
Little Wilbraham GB (CBS) 56 Ab 35
Little Witcombe GB (GLS) 61 Xf 37
Little Witley GB (HWC) 53 Xe 35
Little Wittenham GB (OXS) 63 Ye 39
Little Wolford GB (WWH) 53 Yc 36
Littleworth GB (OXS) 62 Yc 38
Littleworth GB (SFS) 53 Ya 32
Little Wratting GB (SUF) 56 Ac 36
Little Wurley GB (SFS) 53 Ya 33
Little Wymondley GB (HTS) 64 Ze 37
Little Yeldham GB (ESS) 56 Ad 36
Litton GB (DSH) 45 Yb 29
Litton GB (NOY) 35 Xf 24
Litton GB (SOM) 68 Xc 41
Litton Cheney GB (DOS) 68 Xc 44
Liverpool GB (MES) 44 Xa 28
Liversedge GB (WYO) 39 Yb 26
Liverton GB (CLE) 37 Za 21
Liverton Street GB (KEN) 72 Ae 41
Livingston GB (LOT) 25 Wc 13
Lixnaw IRL (KER) 97 Qc 34
Lixwm GB (CLW) 43 We 29
Lizard Town GB (CNW) 74 Ue 49
Llaingoch GB (GWY) 42 Vc 29
Llaithddu GB (POW) 51 Wd 34
Llan GB (POW) 51 Wc 33
Llanaber GB (GWY) 43 Vf 32
Llanaelhaearn GB (GWY) 42 Vd 31
Llanafan GB (DYF) 51 Wa 35
Llanafan-Fawr GB (POW) 51 Wc 35
Llanallgo GB (GWY) 42 Ve 28
Llanarmon GB (GWY) 42 Vd 31
Llanarmon Dyffryn Ceiriog GB (CLW) 43 We 31
Llanarmon-yn-lal GB (CLW) 44 We 30
Llanarth GB (DYF) 50 Ve 35
Llanarth GB (POW) 60 Xa 38
Llanarthney GB (DYF) 59 Vf 37
Llanasa GB (CLW) 43 Wd 29
Llanbabo GB (GWY) 42 Vd 28
Llanbadarn Fawr GB (DYF) 51 Vf 34
Llanbadarn Fynydd GB (POW) 51 We 34
Llanbadarn-y-garreg GB (POW) 51 We 36
Llanbadoc GB (GWE) 60 Xa 38
Llanbadrig GB (GWY) 42 Vd 28
Llanbeder GB (GWE) 60 Wf 39
Llanbedr GB (GWY) 42 Vf 32
Llanbedr GB (POW) 51 We 36
Llanbedr GB (POW) 60 Wf 37
Llanbedr-Dyffryn-Clwyd GB (CLW) 43 We 30
Llanbedrgoch GB (GWY) 42 Ve 29
Llanbedrog GB (GWY) 42 Vd 31
Llanbedr-y-cennin GB (GWY) 43 Wa 29
Llanberis GB (GWY) 42 Vf 30
Llanbethery GB (SGL) 60 Wd 40
Llanbister GB (POW) 51 We 34
Llanblethian GB (SGL) 60 Wd 40
Llanboidy GB (DYF) 58 Vc 37
Llanbradach GB (MGL) 60 We 39
Llanbrynmair GB (POW) 51 Wc 33
Llancarfan GB (SGL) 60 Wd 40
Llancayo GB (GWE) 60 Xa 38
Llancynfelyn GB (DYF) 51 Vf 33
Llandaff GB (SGL) 60 We 40
Llandawke GB (DYF) 59 Vd 38
Llanddaniel Fab GB (GWY) 42 Ve 29
Llanddarog GB (DYF) 59 Ve 38
Llanddeiniol GB (DYF) 50 Vf 35
Llanddeiniolen GB (GWY) 42 Ve 29
Llandderfel GB (GWY) 43 Wc 31
Llanddeusant GB (DYF) 59 Wb 37
Llanddeusant GB (GWY) 42 Vd 28
Llanddew GB (POW) 60 Wd 37
Llanddewi GB (WGL) 59 Ve 39
Llanddewi Brefi GB (DYF) 51 Wa 35
Llanddewi'r Cwm GB (POW) 51 Wd 36
Llanddewi Rhydderch GB (POW) 60 Xa 38
Llanddewi Velfrey GB (DYF) 58 Vb 38
Llanddewi Ystradenni GB (POW) 51 We 35
Llanddoged GB (GWY) 43 Wb 30
Llanddona GB (GWY) 42 Vf 29
Llanddovery GB (DYF) 59 Wb 37
Llanddowror GB (DYF) 58 Vc 38
Llanddulas GB (CLW) 43 Wc 29
Llanddywe GB (GWY) 42 Vf 32
Llanddyfnan GB (GWY) 42 Ve 29
Llandefaelog GB (DYF) 59 Ve 38
Llandefaelog GB (POW) 60 Wd 37
Llandefaelog-tre'r-graig GB (POW) 60 We 37
Llandefalle GB (POW) 60 We 36
Llandegfan GB (GWY) 42 Vf 29
Llandegla GB (CLW) 44 We 30
Llandegley GB (POW) 51 We 35
Llandegreth GB (GWE) 60 Wf 39
Llandegwning GB (GWY) 42 Vc 31
Llandeilo Graban GB (POW) 51 We 36
Llandeilo'r-Fan GB (POW) 60 Wc 37
Llandeloy GB (DYF) 58 Uf 37
Llandenny GB (GWE) 61 Xa 38
Llandinabo GB (HWC) 61 Xb 37
Llandinam GB (POW) 51 Wd 34
Llandissilio GB (DYF) 58 Vb 37
Llandogo GB (GWE) 61 Xb 38
Llandough GB (SGL) 60 Wd 40
Llandow GB (SGL) 60 Wc 40
Llandre GB (DYF) 51 Vf 34
Llandre GB (DYF) 51 Wa 36
Llandrillo GB (CLW) 43 Wd 31
Llandrindod Wells GB (POW) 51 Wd 35
Llandrinio GB (POW) 44 Wf 32
Llandsadurnen GB (DYF) 59 Vd 38
Llandudno GB (GWY) 43 Wa 29
Llandudno Junction GB (GWY) 43 Wb 29
Llandwrog GB (GWY) 42 Ve 30
Llandybie GB (DYF) 59 Vf 38
Llandyfan GB (DYF) 59 Wa 37
Llandyfriog GB (DYF) 50 Vd 36
Llandyfrydog GB (GWY) 42 Vd 28
Llandygwydd GB (DYF) 50 Vc 36
Llandyrnog GB (CLW) 43 Wd 29
Llandyssil GB (POW) 52 We 33
Llandysul GB (DYF) 50 Ve 36
Llaneglwys GB (POW) 51 Wd 36
Llanegryn GB (GWY) 51 Vf 33
Llanegwad GB (DYF) 59 Vf 37
Llanelian-yn-Rhôs GB (CLW) 43 Wb 29
Llanelidan GB (CLW) 43 Wd 30
Llanelieu GB (POW) 60 We 37
Llanellen GB (GWE) 60 Wf 38
Llanelli GB (DYF) 59 Vf 38
Llanelltyd GB (GWY) 43 Wa 32
Llanelly GB (GWE) 60 Wf 38
Llanelwedd GB (POW) 51 Wd 36
Llanenddwyn GB (GWY) 42 Vf 32
Llanengan GB (GWY) 42 Vc 32
Llanerchymedd GB (GWY) 42 Vd 29
Llanerch-yrfa GB (DYF) 51 Wb 35
Llanerfyl GB (POW) 51 Wd 32
Llanfabon GB (MGL) 60 We 39
Llanfachraeth GB (GWY) 42 Vc 29
Llanfachreth GB (GWY) 43 Wa 32
Llanfaelrhys GB (GWY) 42 Vc 32
Llanfaes GB (GWY) 42 Vf 29
Llanfaethlu GB (GWY) 42 Vc 28
Llanfaglan GB (GWY) 42 Ve 30
Llanfair GB (GWY) 42 Vf 31
Llanfair Caereinion GB (POW) 51 Wd 33
Llanfair Clydogau GB (DYF) 51 Vf 36
Llanfair-Dyffryn-Clwyd GB (CLW) 43 We 30
Llanfairfechan GB (GWY) 43 Wa 29
Llanfair-Nant-Gwyn GB (DYF) 58 Vb 36
Llanfairpwllgwyngyll GB (GWY) 42 Ve 29
Llanfair Talhaiarn GB (CLW) 43 Wc 29
Llanfair Waterdine GB (SHS) 52 Wf 34
Llanfairyneubwll GB (GWY) 42 Vc 29
Llanfairynghornwy GB (GWY) 42 Vc 28
Llanfallteg GB (DYF) 58 Vb 37
Llanfarian GB (DYF) 51 Vf 34
Llanfechain GB (POW) 44 We 32
Llanfechan GB (POW) 51 Wc 36
Llanfechell GB (GWY) 42 Vd 28
Llanfendigaid GB (GWY) 50 Vf 33
Llanferres GB (CLW) 44 We 30
Llanfflewyn GB (GWY) 42 Vd 28
Llanfigael GB (GWY) 42 Vc 29
Llanfihangel-ar-arth GB (DYF) 59 Ve 36
Llanfihangel Glyn Myfyr GB (CLW) 43 Wc 30
Llanfihangel Nant Brân GB (POW) 60 Wc 37
Llanfihangel-nant-Melan GB (POW) 52 We 35
Llanfihangel Rhydithon GB (POW) 52 We 35
Llanfihangel Rogiet GB (GWE) 61 Xb 39
Llanfihangel-y-Creuddyn GB (DYF) 51 Wa 34
Llanfihangel-yng-Ngwynfa GB (POW) 43 Wd 32
Llanfihangel yn Nhowyn GB (GWY) 42 Vc 29
Llanfihangel-y-pennant GB (GWY) 42 Ve 31
Llanfihangel-y-pennant GB (GWY) 51 Wa 33
Llanfihangel-y-traethau GB (GWY) 42 Vf 31
Llanfilo GB (POW) 60 We 37
Llanfoist GB (GWE) 60 Wf 38
Llanfor GB (GWY) 43 Wc 31
Llanfrechfa GB (GWE) 60 Wf 39
Llanfrothen GB (GWY) 43 Vf 31
Llanfrynach GB (POW) 60 Wd 37
Llanfwrog GB (GWY) 42 Vc 29
Llanfyllin GB (POW) 43 We 32
Llanfynydd GB (CLW) 44 Wf 30
Llanfynydd GB (DYF) 59 Vf 37
Llanfyrnach GB (DYF) 58 Vc 37
Llangadfan GB (POW) 51 Wd 32
Llangadog GB (DYF) 59 Wa 37
Llangadwaladr GB (CLW) 44 We 31
Llangadwaladr GB (GWY) 42 Vd 29
Llangaffo GB (GWY) 42 Ve 29
Llangain GB (DYF) 59 Vd 38
Llangammarch Wells GB (POW) 51 Wc 36
Llangan GB (SGL) 60 Wc 40
Llangarron GB (HWC) 61 Xb 37
Llangasty-Talyllin GB (POW) 60 We 37
Llangathen GB (DYF) 59 Vf 37
Llangattock GB (POW) 60 Wf 37
Llangattock Lingoed GB (GWE) 60 Xa 37
Llangattock-Vibon-Avel GB (GWE) 61 Xb 37
Llangedwyn GB (CLW) 44 We 32
Llangefni GB (GWY) 42 Ve 29
Llangeinor GB (MGL) 60 Wc 39
Llangeitho GB (DYF) 51 Vf 35
Llangeler GB (DYF) 59 Vd 36
Llangelynnin GB (GWY) 50 Vf 33
Llangendeirne GB (DYF) 59 Ve 38
Llangennech GB (DYF) 59 Vf 38
Llangennith GB (WGL) 59 Ve 39
Llangenny GB (POW) 60 Wf 37
Llangernyw GB (CLW) 43 Wb 29
Llangian GB (GWY) 42 Vc 32
Llangiwg GB (WGL) 59 Wa 38
Llanglydwen GB (DYF) 58 Vc 37
Llangoed GB (GWY) 42 Vf 29
Llangoedmor GB (DYF) 50 Vc 36
Llangollen GB (CLW) 44 We 31
Llangolman GB (DYF) 58 Vb 37
Llangorse GB (POW) 60 We 37
Llangorwen GB (DYF) 51 Vf 34
Llangovan GB (GWE) 61 Xb 38
Llangranog GB (DYF) 50 Vd 36
Llangristiolus GB (GWY) 42 Vd 29
Llangrove GB (HWC) 61 Xb 37
Llangua GB (GWE) 60 Xa 37
Llangunllo GB (POW) 52 Wf 35
Llangunnor GB (DYF) 59 Ve 37
Llangurig GB (POW) 51 Wc 34
Llangwm GB (CLW) 43 Wc 31
Llangwm GB (DYF) 58 Va 38
Llangwm GB (GWE) 61 Xa 38
Llangwnnadl GB (GWY) 42 Vb 31
Llangwyfan GB (CLW) 43 We 29
Llangwyllog GB (GWY) 42 Vd 29
Llangwyryfon GB (DYF) 51 Vf 35
Llangybi GB (DYF) 51 Vf 36
Llangybi GB (GWE) 60 Wf 39
Llangybi GB (GWY) 42 Vd 31
Llangy-felach GB (WGL) 59 Wa 38
Llangynhafal GB (CLW) 43 We 30
Llangynidr GB (POW) 60 We 37
Llangynin GB (DYF) 58 Vc 37
Llangynog GB (DYF) 59 Vd 38
Llangynog GB (POW) 43 Wd 32
Llangynwyd GB (MGL) 60 Wc 39
Llanharan GB (MGL) 60 Wd 39
Llanharry GB (MGL) 60 Wd 39
Llanhennock GB (GWE) 60 Wf 39
Llanhilleth GB (GWE) 60 Wf 38
Llanidloes GB (POW) 51 Wc 34
Llaniestyn GB (GWY) 42 Vc 31
Llanigon GB (POW) 52 Wf 36
Llanilar GB (DYF) 51 Vf 34
Llanilid GB (MGL) 60 Wd 39
Llanishen GB (GWE) 61 Xb 38
Llanllawddog GB (DYF) 59 Ve 37
Llanllechid GB (GWY) 43 Vf 29
Llanllugan GB (POW) 51 Wd 33
Llanllwch GB (DYF) 59 Vd 37
Llanllwni GB (DYF) 50 Ve 36
Llanllyfni GB (GWY) 42 Ve 30
Llanmadoc GB (WGL) 59 Ve 39
Llanmaes GB (SGL) 60 Wd 40
Llanmartin GB (GWE) 60 Wf 39
Llanmerewig GB (POW) 52 We 33
Llanmihangel GB (SGL) 60 Wd 40
Llanmorlais GB (WGL) 59 Vf 39
Llannefydd GB (CLW) 43 Wc 29
Llannon GB (DYF) 59 Vf 38
Llannor GB (GWY) 42 Vd 31
Llanon GB (DYF) 50 Ve 35
Llanover GB (GWE) 60 Xa 38
Llanpumsaint GB (DYF) 59 Ve 37
Llanrhaeadr GB (CLW) 43 Wd 30
Llanrhaeadr-ym-Mochnant GB (CLW) 43 We 32
Llanrhian GB (DYF) 58 Ue 37
Llanrhidian GB (WGL) 59 Vf 39
Llanrhos GB (GWY) 43 Wb 29
Llanrhychwyn GB (GWY) 43 Wa 30
Llanrhyddlad GB (GWY) 42 Vc 28
Llanrhystud GB (DYF) 50 Vf 35
Llanrothal GB (HWC) 61 Xb 37
Llanrug GB (GWY) 42 Ve 30
Llanrumney GB (SGL) 60 Wf 39
Llanrwst GB (GWY) 43 Wb 30
Llansadwrn GB (DYF) 59 Wa 37
Llansadwrn GB (GWY) 42 Vf 29
Llansaint GB (DYF) 59 Vd 38
Llansamlet GB (WGL) 59 Wa 39
Llansannan GB (CLW) 43 Wc 29
Llansannor GB (SGL) 60 Wd 40
Llansantffraed GB (DYF) 50 Ve 35
Llansantffraed GB (POW) 60 We 37
Llansantffraed-Cwmdeuddwr GB (POW) 51 Wc 35
Llansantffraed-in-Elwel GB (POW) 51 We 35
Llansantffraid Glan Conwy GB (GWY) 43 Wb 29
Llansantffraid-ym-Mechain GB (POW) 44 Wf 32
Llansawel GB (DYF) 59 Vf 36
Llansilin GB (CLW) 44 We 31
Llansoy GB (GWE) 61 Xb 38
Llanspyddid GB (POW) 60 Wd 37
Llanstadwell GB (DYF) 58 Va 38
Llanstephan GB (DYF) 59 Vd 38
Llanstephan GB (POW) 51 We 36
Llanteg GB (DYF) 58 Vc 38
Llanthony GB (GWE) 60 Wf 37
Llantilio Crossenny GB (POW) 60 Xa 38
Llantood GB (DYF) 50 Vb 36
Llantrisant GB (GWE) 60 Wf 39
Llantrisant GB (GWY) 42 Vd 29
Llantrisant GB (MGL) 60 Wd 39
Llantrithyd GB (SGL) 60 Wd 40
Llantwit Major GB (SGL) 60 Wd 40
Llantysilio Hall GB (CLW) 44 We 31
Llanuwchllyn GB (GWY) 43 Wb 31
Llanvaches GB (GWE) 61 Xb 39
Llanvair Discoed GB (GWE) 61 Xb 39
Llanvapley GB (POW) 60 Xa 38
Llanvetherine GB (GWE) 60 Xa 37
Llanveynoe GB (HWC) 60 Wf 37
Llanvihangel Crucorney GB (GWE) 60 Xa 37
Llanvihangel Gobion GB (POW) 60 Xa 38
Llanvihangel Ystern-Llewern GB (GWE) 61 Xb 38
Llanwarne GB (HWC) 61 Xb 37
Llanwddyn GB (POW) 43 Wd 32
Llanwenog GB (DYF) 50 Ve 36
Llanwern GB (GWE) 60 Wf 39
Llanwinio GB (DYF) 59 Vc 37
Llanwnda GB (DYF) 58 Uf 36
Llanwnda GB (GWY) 42 Ve 30
Llanwnnen GB (DYF) 50 Vf 36
Llanwnog GB (POW) 51 Wd 33
Llanwonno GB (MGL) 60 Wd 39
Llanwrda GB (DYF) 59 Wa 37
Llanwrin GB (POW) 51 Wb 33
Llanwrthwl GB (POW) 51 Wc 35
Llanwrtyd GB (POW) 51 Wc 36
Llanwyddelan GB (POW) 51 Wd 33
Llanyblodwel GB (SHS) 44 Wf 32
Llanybri GB (DYF) 59 Vd 38
Llanybydder GB (DYF) 50 Vf 36
Llanycefn GB (DYF) 58 Vb 37
Llanychaer GB (DYF) 58 Va 37
Llanycil GB (GWY) 43 Wc 31
Llanycrwys GB (DYF) 51 Wa 36
Llanymawddwy GB (GWY) 43 Wc 32
Llanymynech GB (POW) 44 Wf 32
Llanynghenedl GB (GWY) 42 Vc 29
Llanynys GB (CLW) 43 Wd 30
Llan-y-pwll GB (CLW) 44 Xa 30
Llanyre GB (POW) 51 Wd 35
Llanystumdwy GB (GWY) 42 Ve 31
Llanywern GB (POW) 60 We 37
Llawhaden GB (DYF) 58 Vb 38
Llawnt GB (SHS) 44 Wf 31
Llawr Dref GB (GWY) 42 Vc 32
Llawryglyn GB (POW) 51 Wc 33
Llay GB (CLW) 44 Wf 30
Llechcynfarwy GB (GWY) 42 Vd 29
Llechfaen GB (POW) 60 Wd 37
Llechrhyd GB (MGL) 60 We 38
Llechryd GB (DYF) 50 Vc 36
Llechrydau GB (CLW) 44 Wf 31
Lledrod GB (DYF) 51 Wa 35
Llithfaen GB (GWY) 42 Vd 31
Llong GB (CLW) 44 Wf 30
Llowes GB (POW) 52 We 36
Lloyney GB (POW) 52 Wf 34
Llwchmynydd GB (GWY) 42 Vb 32
Llwydcoed GB (MGL) 60 Wd 38
Llwyn GB (SHS) 52 Wf 34
Llwyncelyn GB (DYF) 50 Ve 35
Llwyndafydd GB (DYF) 50 Vd 35
Llwynderw GB (POW) 52 We 33
Llwyndyrys GB (GWY) 42 Vd 31
Llwyngwril GB (GWY) 51 Vf 33
Llwynmawr GB (CLW) 44 Wf 31
Llwyn-onn GB (DYF) 50 Ve 35
Llwyn-y-groes GB (DYF) 51 Vf 35
Llwynypia GB (MGL) 60 Wd 39
Llynclys GB (SHS) 44 Wf 32
Llynfaes GB (GWY) 42 Vd 29
Llysfaen GB (CLW) 43 Wc 29
Llyswen GB (POW) 60 We 36
Llysworney GB (SGL) 60 Wd 40
Llywel GB (POW) 60 Wc 37
Loanends GB (ANT) 85 Tf 21
Loanhead GB (LOT) 26 Wf 13
Loans GB (STC) 30 Vc 15
Loans of Tullich GB (HGL) 9 Wa 2
Lobinstown IRL (MT) 90 Tc 26
Lochaline GB (HGL) 19 Ub 9
Lochans GB (DAG) 28 Uf 18
Locharbriggs GB (DAG) 31 Wc 18
Lochassynt Lodge GB (HGL) 7 Uf 119
Lochawe GB (STC) 19 Uf 10
Lochboisdale GB (HGL) 12 Se 6
Lochbui GB (STC) 18 Ua 10
Lochcarnan GB (HGL) 12 Se 4
Lochcarron GB (HGL) 14 Uc 4
Lochdon GB (STC) 19 Ub 10
Lochead GB (STC) 23 Uc 13
Lochearnhead GB (CEN) 20 Ve 10
Lochee GB (TYS) 21 Wf 10
Locheilside Station GB (HGL) 19 Ue 7
Lochend GB (HGL) 6 We 117
Lochend GB (HGL) 15 Ve 4
Locheport GB (HGL) 10 Se 3
Lochfoot GB (DAG) 31 Wb 18
Lochgair GB (STC) 23 Ud 12
Loch Garman = Wexford IRL (WEX) 101 Td 34
Lochgarthside GB (HGL) 15 Vd 5
Lochgelly GB (FIF) 26 We 12
Lochgilphead GB (STC) 23 Ud 12
Lochgoilhead GB (STC) 24 Va 11
Loch Gowna IRL (CAV) 89 Sc 25
Lochhill GB (GRP) 16 We 2
Lochinver GB (HGL) 7 Ue 120
Lochlane GB (TYS) 21 Wa 10
Lochluichart GB (HGL) 14 Vb 3
Lochmaben GB (DAG) 31 Wd 18
Lochmaddy GB (HGL) 10 Sf 3
Lochmore Lodge GB (HGL) 8 Va 119
Lochnavar House IRL (CRE) 91 Qd 32
Lochore GB (FIF) 26 We 12
Lochranza GB (STC) 23 Ue 14
Lochside GB (GRP) 22 Xd 8
Lochside GB (HGL) 9 Wa 119
Lochskipport GB (HGL) 12 Se 5
Lochslin GB (HGL) 9 Wa 2
Lochton GB (GRP) 17 Xd 6
Lochton GB (STC) 30 Vb 18
Lochty GB (FIF) 22 Xb 11
Lochuisge GB (HGL) 19 Uc 9
Lochwinnoch GB (STC) 24 Vc 14
Lock IRL (CRE) 92 Rc 32
Lock IRL (OFF) 93 Sa 29
Lockengate GB (CNW) 75 Vb 46
Lockerbie GB (DAG) 31 Wd 18
Lockeridge GB (WIL) 62 Yb 40
Lockerley GB (HAS) 69 Yc 42
Locking GB (AVN) 60 Xa 41
Lockington GB (HUS) 41 Zd 25
Lockington GB (LEC) 46 Ye 31
Lockleywood GB (SHS) 44 Xd 31
Locks Heath GB (HAS) 70 Ye 43
Lockton GB (NOY) 37 Zb 23
Loddington GB (LEC) 54 Zb 33
Loddington GB (NRH) 54 Zb 34
Loddiswell GB (DEV) 76 Wb 47
Loddon GB (NOR) 57 Bc 33
Loders GB (DOS) 68 Xb 44
Lodsworth GB (WSX) 70 Zb 43
Lofthouse GB (NOY) 36 Ya 24
Lofthouse Gate GB (WYO) 39 Yd 26
Loftus GB (CLE) 37 Za 21
Logan GB (STC) 30 Ve 16
Loggerheads GB (SFS) 44 Xd 31
Loggie GB (HGL) 7 Uf 1
Loghill IRL (LIM) 98 Qe 33
Loghill IRL (LIM) 98 Ra 34
Logie GB (FIF) 22 Xa 10
Logie GB (TYS) 21 Wd 9
Logie GB (TYS) 22 Xd 8
Logie Coldstone GB (GRP) 16 Xa 6
Logie Hill GB (HGL) 8 Vf 2
Logie Newton GB (GRP) 17 Xc 4
Logie Pert GB (TYS) 22 Xc 8
Logierait GB (TYS) 21 Wb 9
Loher IRL (KER) 102 Pe 38
Lombardstown IRL (COR) 98 Rb 36
Lomcloon IRL (SLI) 88 Rd 25
Londesborough GB (HUS) 40 Zb 25
London GB (GRL) 64 Zf 40
London Colney GB (HTS) 64 Ze 38
Londonderry GB (LDR) 78 Sd 19
Londonderry GB (NOY) 36 Yc 23
Londonthorpe GB (LIN) 47 Zc 31
Lonemore GB (HGL) 8 Vf 1
Long Ashton GB (AVN) 61 Xc 40
Long Bennington GB (LIN) 46 Zb 31
Longbenton GB (TAW) 33 Yc 18
Long Bredy GB (DOS) 68 Xc 44
Longbridge GB (WMD) 53 Ya 34
Longbridge GB (WWH) 53 Yc 35
Longbridge Deverill GB (WIL) 69 Xe 42
Long Buckby GB (NRH) 54 Yf 35
Longburton GB (DOS) 68 Xc 43
Long Clawson GB (LEC) 46 Za 31
Longcliffe GB (DSH) 45 Yc 30
Long Common GB (HAS) 70 Ye 43
Long Compton GB (SFS) 45 Xe 32
Long Compton GB (WWH) 62 Yc 37
Long Crendon GB (BUS) 63 Yf 38
Long Crichel GB (DOS) 69 Xf 43
Longcross GB (DEV) 75 Ve 45
Longcross GB (SUR) 63 Zc 40
Longden GB (SHS) 52 Xb 33
Longdon GB (HWC) 53 Xe 36
Longdon GB (SFS) 45 Ya 32
Longdon on Tern GB (SHS) 44 Xc 32
Longdown GB (DEV) 67 Wc 44
Longdowns GB (CNW) 74 Uf 48
Long Drax GB (NOY) 40 Za 26
Long Duckmanton GB (DSH) 46 Yd 29
Long Eaton GB (DSH) 46 Ye 31
Longfield GB (KEN) 64 Ab 40
Longford GB (DSH) 45 Yb 31
Longford GB (GLS) 61 Xe 37
Longford GB (SHS) 44 Xc 31
Longford GB (WMD) 54 Yd 34
Longford IRL (LGF) 88 Sb 26
Longford IRL (OFF) 93 Sb 30
Longforgan GB (TYS) 21 Wf 10
Longformacus GB (BOR) 27 Xd 14
Longfort House IRL (GAL) 93 Re 30
Longframlington GB (NHL) 33 Yb 17
Long Gill GB (NOY) 39 Xe 24
Longham GB (DOS) 69 Ya 44
Longham GB (NOR) 48 Af 32
Long Hanborough GB (OXS) 62 Yd 38
Longhirst GB (NHL) 33 Yc 17
Longhope GB (GLS) 61 Xd 37
Longhope GB (ORK) 6 We 116
Longhorsley GB (NHL) 33 Yb 17
Longhoughton GB (NHL) 33 Yc 16
Long Itchington GB (WWH) 54 Yd 35
Longlane GB (BKS) 62 Ye 40
Longlane GB (DSH) 45 Yc 31
Long Lawford GB (WWH) 54 Ye 34
Longley Green GB (HWC) 53 Xd 36
Long Load GB (SOM) 68 Xb 42
Longmanhill GB (GRP) 17 Xd 3
Long Marston GB (HTS) 63 Zb 38
Long Marston GB (NOY) 40 Ye 25
Long Marston GB (WWH) 53 Yb 36
Long Marton GB (CUB) 35 Xc 21
Long Melford GB (BFS) 55 Zc 36
Longmorn GB (GRP) 16 We 3
Long Newnton GB (GLS) 61 Xf 39
Longnewton GB (BOR) 32 Xc 15
Longnewton GB (CLE) 36 Yd 21
Longney GB (GLS) 61 Xd 38
Longniddry GB (LOT) 26 Xa 13
Longnor GB (SFS) 45 Ya 29
Longnor GB (SHS) 52 Xb 33
Longparish GB (HAS) 70 Yd 41
Long Preston GB (NOY) 39 Xe 24
Longridge GB (LCS) 38 Xc 25
Longridge GB (LOT) 25 Wb 13
Longriggend GB (STC) 25 Wa 13
Long Riston GB (HUS) 41 Ze 25
Longrock GB (CNW) 74 Ud 48
Longsdon GB (SFS) 45 Xf 30
Longside GB (GRP) 17 Ya 3
Longslow GB (SHS) 44 Xc 31
Longstanton GB (CBS) 55 Aa 35
Longstowe GB (CBS) 55 Zf 35
Long Stratton GB (NOR) 57 Bb 34
Long Street GB (BUS) 54 Zb 36
Long Sutton GB (HAS) 70 Za 41
Long Sutton GB (LIN) 47 Aa 32
Long Sutton GB (SOM) 68 Xb 42
Long Thurlow GB (SUF) 56 Af 35
Longton GB (LCS) 38 Xb 26
Longton GB (SFS) 45 Xf 31
Longtown GB (CUB) 32 Xa 18
Longtown GB (HWC) 60 Xa 37
Longville in the Dale GB (SHS) 52 Xb 33
Long Well IRL (LAO) 94 Sd 31
Long Whatton GB (LEC) 54 Ye 32
Longwick GB (BUS) 63 Za 38
Long Wittenham GB (OXS) 63 Ye 39
Longwitton GB (NHL) 33 Ya 17
Longwood GB (SHS) 52 Xc 33
Longwood IRL (MT) 89 Ta 28
Longyester GB (LOT) 26 Xb 13
Lonqueville IRL (COR) 98 Rb 36
Looe GB (CNW) 75 Vd 46
Loose GB (KEN) 72 Ad 41
Loosegate GB (LIN) 47 Zf 32
Loosley Row GB (BUS) 63 Zb 38
Lopcombe Corner GB (WIL) 69 Yc 42
Lopen GB (SOM) 68 Xb 43
Loppington GB (SHS) 44 Xb 31
Lorbottle GB (NHL) 33 Ya 16
Lornty GB (TYS) 21 Wd 9
Lorrha IRL (TIP) 93 Rf 30
Lorton GB (CUB) 34 We 21
Lorum IRL (CLW) 100 Ta 33
Loscoe GB (DSH) 46 Yd 30
Losset IRL (CAV) 89 Sd 25
Lossiemouth GB (GRP) 9 We 2
Lossit GB (STC) 22 Td 14
Lostock Gralam GB (CHS) 44 Xd 29
Lostock Green GB (CHS) 44 Xd 29
Lostock Junction GB (GRM) 38 Xd 27
Lostwithiel GB (CNW) 75 Vb 46
Lothbeg GB (HGL) 9 Wb 120
Lothersdale GB (NOY) 39 Xf 25
Lothmore GB (HGL) 9 Wb 120
Loudwater GB (BUS) 63 Zb 39
Lough IRL (KER) 96 Pe 36
Loughananna IRL (LIM) 99 Re 35
Loughanavally IRL (WMT) 89 Sc 28
Loughane IRL (COR) 104 Rf 37
Loughan House IRL (OFF) 93 Sa 31
Loughanillann IRL (GAL) 86 Qa 28
Loughanlea IRL (CAV) 89 Ta 25
Loughanure IRL (DON) 77 Re 19
Loughaunealа IRL (GAL) 91 Qc 29
Loughazon Hall IRL (WMT) 89 Sc 27
Loughbally Bridge IRL (ROS) 88 Rd 25
Loughborough GB (LEC) 46 Ye 32
Loughbrickland GB (DOW) 84 Te 23
Loughcurra IRL (GAL) 92 Ra 30
Loughduff IRL (CAV) 89 Sd 25
Lougher IRL (MT) 90 Td 26
Loughgall GB (ARG) 84 Tc 22
Loughglinn IRL (ROS) 88 Rc 26
Loughguile GB (ANT) 79 Te 18
Loughgur Cross IRL (LIM) 98 Rc 33
Loughkeen IRL (TIP) 93 Sa 30
Loughlass IRL (LAO) 94 Sf 31
Loughmoe IRL (TIP) 93 Sa 32
Loughmorne IRL (MOG) 90 Ta 24
Loughneas GB (TYR) 78 Sd 19
Lough Park House IRL (WMT) 89 Se 26
Loughrea IRL (GAL) 92 Rc 29
Loughshinny IRL (MT) 90 Tf 27
Loughton GB (ESS) 64 Aa 39
Loughton GB (SHS) 52 Xc 34
Lought or Commons IRL (LAO) 94 Sd 29
Louisburgh IRL (MAY) 86 Qb 26
Loumanagh IRL (COR) 98 Qf 36
Lound GB (NTS) 46 Za 28
Lound GB (SUF) 57 Be 33
Lount GB (LEC) 46 Yd 32
Louth GB (LIN) 47 Zf 28
Louth IRL (LOT) 90 Tc 25
Love Clough GB (LCS) 39 Xe 26
Lover GB (WIL) 69 Yb 43
Lover Higham GB (KEN) 65 Ac 40
Loves Green GB (ESS) 64 Ac 38
Loveston GB (DYF) 58 Vb 38
Low Bentham GB (NOY) 38 Xc 24
Low Bradfield GB (SOY) 39 Yc 28
Low Bradley GB (NOY) 39 Ya 25
Low Braithwaite GB (CUB) 35 Xa 20
Low Brunton GB (NHL) 33 Xf 18
Low Burnham GB (HUS) 40 Zb 27
Lowca GB (CUB) 34 Wc 21
Low Catton GB (HUS) 40 Za 25
Low Crosby GB (CUB) 32 Xa 19
Lowdham GB (NTS) 46 Yf 30
Low Dovengill GB (CUB) 35 Xd 22
Lower Aisholt GB (SOM) 67 Wf 42
Lower Apperley GB (GLS) 61 Xe 37
Lower Ashton GB (DEV) 67 Wc 45
Lower Assendon GB (OXS) 63 Za 39
Lower Ballycotteen IRL (CRE) 91 Qd 31
Lower Beeding GB (WSX) 71 Ze 42
Lower Benefield GB (NRH) 55 Zc 34
Lower Boddington GB (NRH) 54 Ye 35
Lower Brailes GB (WWH) 54 Yc 36
Lower Breinton GB (HWC) 52 Xb 36
Lower Broadheath GB (HWC) 53 Xe 35
Lower Brynamman GB (WGL) 59 Wa 38
Lower Cam GB (GLS) 61 Xd 38
Lower Chapel GB (POW) 60 Wd 36
Lower Chute GB (WIL) 69 Yc 41
Lower Dean GB (BFS) 55 Zd 35
Lower Diabaig GB (HGL) 13 Ub 3
Lower Dicker GB (ESX) 72 Ab 43
Lower Down GB (SHS) 52 Xa 34
Lower Dunsforth GB (NOY) 40 Ye 24
Lower Egleton GB (HWC) 52 Xc 36
Lower Failand GB (AVN) 61 Xb 40
Lower Farringdon GB (HAS) 70 Za 42
Lower Froyle GB (HAS) 70 Za 41
Lower Gledfield GB (HGL) 8 Vd 1
Lower Green GB (KEN) 72 Ab 42
Lower Halstow GB (KEN) 65 Ae 40
Lower Hardres GB (KEN) 65 Ba 41
Lower Hayton GB (SHS) 52 Xb 34
Lower Heyford GB (OXS) 62 Ye 37
Lower Holbrook GB (SUF) 57 Ba 37
Lower Hordley GB (SHS) 44 Xa 31
Lower Killeyan GB (STC) 22 Te 15
Lower Kinnerton GB (CHS) 44 Xa 30
Lower Langford GB (AVN) 61 Xb 40
Lower Largo GB (FIF) 26 Xa 11
Lower Lemington GB (GLS) 62 Yb 36
Lower Lye GB (HWC) 52 Xa 35
Lower Machen GB (GWE) 60 Wf 39
Lower Maes-coed GB (HWC) 60 Xa 37
Lower Moor GB (HWC) 53 Xf 36
Lower Nazeing GB (ESS) 64 Aa 38
Lower Penn GB (SFS) 53 Xe 33
Lower Pennington GB (HAS) 69 Yc 44
Lower Peover GB (CHS) 44 Xd 29
Lower Quinton GB (WWH) 53 Yb 36
Lower Shelton GB (BFS) 55 Zc 36
Lower Shiplake GB (OXS) 63 Za 39
Lower Shuckburgh GB (WWH) 54 Ye 35
Lower Slaughter GB (GLS) 62 Yb 37
Lower Stanton Saint Quintin GB (WIL) 61 Xf 39
Lower Stoke GB (KEN) 65 Ad 40
Lower Swanwick GB (HAS) 70 Ye 43
Lower Swell GB (GLS) 62 Yb 37
Lower Tean GB (SFS) 45 Ya 31
Lowertown IRL (COR) 102 Qc 39
Lower Tysoe GB (WWH) 54 Yc 36
Lower Upham GB (HAS) 70 Ye 43
Lower Welson GB (HWC) 52 Wf 36
Lower Whitley GB (CHS) 44 Xc 29
Lower Wield GB (HAS) 70 Yf 42
Lower Winchendon GB (BUS) 63 Za 38
Lower Woodend GB (BUS) 63 Zb 39
Lower Woodford GB (WIL) 69 Yb 42
Lower Wraxall GB (DOS) 68 Xc 44
Lowesby GB (LEC) 54 Za 33
Lowestoft GB (SUF) 57 Be 34
Loweswater GB (CUB) 34 Wc 21
Low Gate GB (NHL) 33 Xf 19
Lowgill GB (LCS) 38 Xc 24
Low Ham GB (SOM) 68 Xb 42
Low Haygarth GB (CUB) 35 Xd 22
Low Hesket GB (CUB) 35 Xb 20
Low Hesleyhurst GB (NHL) 33 Ya 17
Lowick GB (CUB) 34 Wf 23
Lowick GB (NHL) 27 Ya 15
Low Mill GB (NOY) 37 Za 22
Low Moor GB (LCS) 38 Xd 25
Lownie Moor GB (TYS) 22 Xa 9
Lowpark IRL (ROS) 88 Rf 27
Low Row GB (CUB) 32 Xc 19
Low Row GB (NOY) 36 Xf 22
Lowsonford GB (WWH) 53 Yb 35
Low Street GB (NOR) 49 Bc 32
Lowther GB (CUB) 35 Xb 21
Lowtherstone IRL (DUB) 90 Te 27
Lowthorpe GB (HUS) 41 Zd 24
Lowton Common GB (GRM) 38 Xc 28
Low Torry GB (FIF) 25 Wc 12
Lowtown GB (DOW) 85 Tf 23
Low Worsall GB (NOY) 36 Yd 22
Loxbeare GB (DEV) 67 Wc 43
Loxhill GB (SUR) 71 Zc 42
Loxhore GB (DEV) 66 Wa 42
Loxley GB (WWH) 53 Yc 35
Loxton GB (AVN) 68 Xa 41
Loxwood GB (WSX) 71 Zc 42
Lubber IRL (DON) 77 Sb 19
Lubcroy GB (HGL) 8 Vb 1
Lubenham GB (LEC) 54 Za 34
Lucan IRL (DUB) 95 Td 28
Luccombe GB (SOM) 67 Wc 41
Lucker GB (NHL) 27 Yb 15
Luckett GB (CNW) 75 Ve 45
Luckington GB (WIL) 61 Xe 39
Lucklawhill GB (FIF) 22 Xa 10
Luckwell Bridge GB (SOM) 67 Wc 42
Lucton GB (HWC) 52 Xb 35
Ludag GB (HGL) 12 Se 6

Little Staughton – Ludag (GB) (IRL) 125

Middleton One Row **GB** (DUR) 36 Yd 21
Middleton on the Hill **GB** (HWC) 52 Xb 35
Middleton-on-the-Wolds **GB** (HUS) 41 Zc 25
Middleton Priors **GB** (SHS) 52 Xc 33
Middleton Saint George **GB** (DUR) 36 Yd 21
Middleton Scriven **GB** (SHS) 52 Xd 34
Middleton Stoney **GB** (OXS) 62 Ye 37
Middleton Tyas **GB** (NOY) 36 Yc 22
Middletown **GB** (POW) 52 Wf 32
Middletown **IRL** (NIR) 84 Ta 23
Middle Wallop **GB** (HAS) 69 Yc 42
Middlewich **GB** (CHS) 44 Xd 29
Middle Woodford **GB** (WIL) 69 Yb 42
Middlewood Green **GB** (SUF) 57 Ba 35
Middleyard **GB** (STC) 24 Vd 15
Middlezoy **GB** (SOM) 68 Xa 42
Midridge **GB** (DUR) 36 Yc 21
Midfield **GB** (HGL) 5 Vd 117
Midfield **IRL** (MAY) 87 Ra 25
Midgham **GB** (BKS) 63 Ye 40
Midgley **GB** (WYO) 39 Ya 26
Midgley **GB** (WYO) 39 Yc 27
Midhurst **GB** (WSX) 70 Zb 43
Midlem **GB** (BOR) 32 Xb 15
Midleton **IRL** (COR) 104 Re 37
Midsomer Norton **GB** (AVN) 68 Xd 41
Mid Town **IRL** (DON) 77 Sb 18
Mid Urchany **GB** (HGL) 15 Wa 3
Midville **GB** (LIN) 47 Aa 30
Mid Yell **GB** (SHL) 2 Yf 105
Migdale **GB** (HGL) 8 Ve 1
Migvie **GB** (GRP) 16 Xa 6
Milber **GB** (DEV) 76 Wc 45
Milborne Port **GB** (SOM) 68 Xd 43
Milborne Saint Andrew **GB** (DOS) 68 Xe 44
Milborne Wick **GB** (SOM) 68 Xd 43
Milbourne **GB** (NHL) 33 Yb 18
Milburn **GB** (CUB) 35 Xc 21
Milbury Heath **GB** (AVN) 61 Xd 39
Milcombe **GB** (OXS) 54 Yd 36
Milden **GB** (SUF) 56 Af 36
Mildenhall **GB** (SUF) 56 Ad 34
Mildenhall **GB** (WIL) 62 Yb 40
Milebrooke **GB** (POW) 52 Wf 34
Milebush **GB** (KEN) 72 Ad 41
Mile Elm **GB** (WIL) 62 Xf 40
Mile End **GB** (ESS) 65 Af 37
Mile End **GB** (GLS) 61 Xc 38
Mile End **GB** (SUF) 56 Ad 34
Mileham **GB** (NOR) 49 Af 32
Milehouse **IRL** (WEX) 101 Tc 33
Milermill **IRL** (KIL) 95 Tb 30
Milesmark **GB** (FIF) 25 Wd 12
Milestone **IRL** (TIP) 99 Rf 32
Mile Tree **IRL** (TIP) 99 Sb 34
Milfield **GB** (NHL) 27 Xf 15
Milford **GB** (DEV) 66 Vc 43
Milford **GB** (SFS) 45 Xf 32
Milford **GB** (SHS) 44 Xa 32
Milford **GB** (SUR) 70 Zc 41
Milford **IRL** (COR) 98 Ra 34
Milford Haven **GB** (DYF) 58 Uf 38
Milford on Sea **GB** (HAS) 69 Yc 44
Milkwall **GB** (GLS) 61 Xc 38
Milland **GB** (WSX) 70 Zb 42
Mill Bank **GB** (WYO) 39 Ya 26
Millbreck **GB** (GRP) 17 Ya 4
Millbrex **GB** (GRP) 17 Xe 4
Millbridge **GB** (SUR) 70 Zb 41
Millbrook **GB** (BFS) 55 Zc 36
Millbrook **IRL** (MT) 89 Sf 26
Millbrook **GB** (STC) 30 Vd 15
Millcorner **GB** (ESX) 72 Ad 43
Milleen **IRL** (COR) 98 Qf 35
Milleeny **IRL** (COR) 103 Qe 37
Mill End **GB** (BUS) 63 Za 39
Mill End **GB** (HTS) 55 Zf 37
Millend Green **GB** (ESS) 64 Ac 37
Millenheath **GB** (SHS) 44 Xc 31
Miller's Dale **GB** (DSH) 45 Yb 29
Millford **IRL** (DON) 77 Sb 18
Mill Green **GB** (ESS) 64 Ac 38
Mill Green **GB** (SHS) 44 Xd 31
Millholme **GB** (CUB) 35 Xb 23
Millhouse **GB** (CUB) 34 Xa 20
Millhouse **GB** (STC) 23 Ue 13
Millicent Cross Roads **IRL** (KIL) 95 Tb 29
Millicent House **IRL** (KIL) 95 Tb 29
Millikenpark **GB** (STC) 24 Vc 14
Millington **GB** (HUS) 40 Zb 25
Millisle **GB** (DOW) 85 Uc 21
Mill Lane **GB** (HAS) 70 Za 41
Millmeece **GB** (SFS) 45 Xe 31
Millmount **IRL** (DON) 77 Rf 18
Mill of Fortune **GB** (TYS) 21 Wa 10
Millom **GB** (CUB) 34 We 23
Millpark House **IRL** (OFF) 93 Sb 31
Millport **GB** (STC) 24 Va 14
Millroad **IRL** (WEX) 101 Tc 35
Mill Side **GB** (CUB) 35 Xa 23
Mill Street **GB** (NOR) 48 Af 32
Millstreet **IRL** (COR) 98 Qf 36
Millstreet **IRL** (WTF) 99 Sb 36
Millthrop **GB** (CUB) 35 Xc 23
Millton House **IRL** (MT) 89 Ta 26
Millton of Lesmore **GB** (GRP) 16 Xa 4
Milltown **GB** (ANT) 79 Tf 18
Milltown **GB** (ARG) 84 Tb 23
Milltown **GB** (DAG) 32 Wf 18
Milltown **GB** (DEV) 66 Vf 42
Milltown **GB** (DOW) 90 Te 24
Milltown **GB** (DSH) 46 Yd 30
Milltown **GB** (GRP) 16 Xa 5
Milltown **IRL** (CAV) 89 Sd 24
Milltown **IRL** (CLW) 100 Ta 32
Milltown **IRL** (DON) 78 Sd 18
Milltown **IRL** (DON) 78 Sf 17
Milltown **IRL** (DON) 82 Rd 21
Milltown **IRL** (DON) 82 Re 21
Milltown **IRL** (DUB) 95 Td 29
Milltown **IRL** (GAL) 88 Rc 27
Milltown **IRL** (KER) 96 Pe 36
Milltown **IRL** (KER) 97 Qb 36
Milltown **IRL** (KIL) 94 Ta 29
Milltown **IRL** (KLK) 100 Se 34
Milltown **IRL** (LOT) 90 Te 26
Mill Town **IRL** (MOG) 90 Tb 24
Milltown **IRL** (ROS) 88 Rd 26
Milltown **IRL** (WKL) 95 Tb 30
Milltown **IRL** (WMT) 89 Sc 27
Milltown **IRL** (WMT) 89 Sd 28
Milltown House **IRL** (LIM) 98 Ra 33
Milltown Malbay **IRL** (CRE) 91 Qd 31
Milltown of Aberdalgie **GB** (TYS) 21 Wd 10
Milltown of Auchindoun **GB** (GRP) 16 Wf 4
Milltown of Craigston **GB** (GRP) 17 Xd 3
Milltown of Edinville **GB** (GRP) 16 We 4
Milltown of Rothiemay **GB** (GRP) 16 Xb 3
Milltown of Towie **GB** (GRP) 16 Xa 5
Milltown Park **IRL** (OFF) 93 Sa 31
Milltownpass **IRL** (WMT) 89 Se 28
Milnathort **GB** (TYS) 26 Wd 11
Milngavie **GB** (STC) 25 Ve 13
Milnrow **GB** (GRM) 39 Xf 27
Milnthorpe **GB** (CUB) 35 Xb 23
Milovaig **GB** (HGL) 12 Tb 4
Milson **GB** (SHS) 52 Xc 34
Milsted **GB** (KEN) 65 Ae 41
Milston **GB** (WIL) 69 Yb 41
Milton **GB** (AVN) 60 Xa 40
Milton **GB** (CBS) 56 Aa 35
Milton **GB** (DAG) 30 Vb 19
Milton **GB** (DAG) 31 Wb 18
Milton **GB** (DSH) 46 Yc 31
Milton **GB** (GRP) 16 Wd 5
Milton **GB** (GRP) 16 Xb 3
Milton **GB** (HGL) 6 Wf 118
Milton **GB** (HGL) 8 Vf 2
Milton **GB** (HGL) 14 Va 3
Milton **GB** (HGL) 15 Vd 3
Milton **GB** (HGL) 15 Vd 4
Milton **GB** (HGL) 15 Wb 3
Milton **GB** (OXS) 54 Yd 36
Milton **GB** (OXS) 62 Ye 39
Milton **GB** (SFS) 45 Xf 30
Milton **GB** (TYS) 21 Wb 9
Milton **GB** (TYS) 22 Wf 9
Milton Abbas **GB** (DOS) 68 Xe 44
Milton Abbot **GB** (DEV) 75 Ve 45
Milton Bridge **GB** (LOT) 26 We 13
Milton Bryan **GB** (BFS) 63 Zc 37
Milton Clevedon **GB** (SOM) 68 Xd 42
Milton Coldwells **GB** (GRP) 17 Xf 4
Milton Combe **GB** (DEV) 76 Vf 46
Milton Damerel **GB** (DEV) 66 Ve 43
Miltonduff **GB** (GRP) 16 Wd 3
Milton Ernest **GB** (BFS) 55 Zc 35
Milton Green **GB** (CHS) 44 Xb 30
Milton Hill **GB** (OXS) 62 Ye 39
Milton Keynes **GB** (BUS) 54 Zb 36
Milton Keynes Village **GB** (BUS) 55 Zb 36
Milton Libourne **GB** (WIL) 62 Yb 40
Milton Malsor **GB** (NRH) 54 Za 35
Milton Morenish **GB** (TYS) 20 Ve 10
Milton of Auchinhove **GB** (GRP) 16 Xb 6
Milton of Buchanan **GB** (CEN) 24 Vc 12
Milton of Campfield **GB** (GRP) 17 Xc 6
Milton of Campsie **GB** (STC) 25 Vf 13
Milton of Cushnie **GB** (GRP) 16 Xb 5
Milton of Delcapon **GB** (TYS) 21 Wc 8
Milton of Gollanfield **GB** (HGL) 15 Vf 3
Milton of Tullich **GB** (GRP) 16 Wf 6
Milton on Stour **GB** (DOR) 68 Xe 42
Milton-under-Wychwood **GB** (OXS) 62 Yc 37
Milverton **GB** (SOM) 67 We 42
Milwich **GB** (SFS) 45 Xf 31
Minane Bridge **IRL** (COR) 104 Rd 38
Minard **GB** (STC) 24 Ue 12
Minchinhampton **GB** (GLS) 61 Xe 38
Minehead **GB** (SOM) 67 Wd 41
Minera **GB** (CLW) 44 Wf 30
Minety **GB** (WIL) 62 Ya 39
Minffordd **GB** (GWY) 42 Vf 31
Minffordd **GB** (GWY) 51 Wa 32
Mingary **GB** (HGL) 12 Sd 5
Miningsby **GB** (LIN) 47 Zf 30
Minishant **GB** (STC) 30 Vc 16
Minley Manor **GB** (HAS) 63 Zb 41
Minllyn **GB** (GWY) 51 Wb 32
Minnes **GB** (GRP) 17 Xf 5
Minnigaff **GB** (DAG) 30 Vd 19
Minnonie **GB** (GRP) 17 Xd 3
Minskip **GB** (NOY) 40 Yd 24
Minstead **GB** (HAS) 69 Yc 43
Minster **GB** (KEN) 65 Ae 40
Minster **GB** (KEN) 65 Bb 40
Minsteracres **GB** (NHL) 33 Ya 19
Minster Lovell **GB** (OXS) 62 Yc 38
Minsterworth **GB** (GLS) 61 Xe 37
Minterburn **GB** (TYR) 84 Ta 22
Minterne Magna **GB** (DOS) 68 Xd 44
Mintiaghs Lough **IRL** (DON) 78 Sd 17
Minting **GB** (LIN) 47 Ze 29
Mintlaw **GB** (GRP) 17 Ya 3
Minto **GB** (BOR) 32 Xb 16
Minton **GB** (SHS) 52 Xa 33
Minworth **GB** (WMD) 53 Yb 33
Mirbister **GB** (ORK) 6 We 114
Mireland **GB** (HGL) 6 We 117
Mirfield **GB** (WYO) 39 Yb 26
Miserden **GB** (GLS) 61 Xf 38
Miskin **GB** (MGL) 60 Wd 39
Misson **GB** (NTS) 40 Za 28
Misterton **GB** (LEC) 54 Ye 34
Misterton **GB** (NTS) 40 Za 28
Misterton **GB** (SOM) 68 Xb 43
Mistley **GB** (ESS) 57 Ba 37
Mitcham **GB** (GRL) 64 Zf 40
Mitcheldean **GB** (GLS) 61 Xd 37
Mitchell **GB** (CNW) 74 Uf 46
Mitchelstown **IRL** (COR) 99 Re 35
Mitchelstown Castle **IRL** (COR) 99 Re 35
Mitchel Troy **GB** (GWE) 61 Xb 38
Mitcheltroy Common **GB** (GWE) 61 Xb 38
Mitford **GB** (NHL) 33 Yb 17
Mithian **GB** (CNW) 74 Uf 47
Mitton **GB** (SFS) 45 Xe 32
Mixbury **GB** (OXS) 54 Yf 36
Moanabricka **IRL** (COR) 98 Rb 34
Moanamanagh **IRL** (CLW) 94 Tb 32
Moanflugn Sch. **IRL** (COR) 98 Ra 37
Moanmore **IRL** (CRE) 91 Qc 32
Moanmore **IRL** (TIP) 99 Re 34
Moata Farm **IRL** (MT) 90 Ta 26
Moate **IRL** (WMT) 93 Sb 28
Moatfarrell **IRL** (LGF) 89 Sc 26
Moat View **IRL** (MT) 89 Se 26
Moat Ville **IRL** (TIP) 93 Rf 30
Mobberley **GB** (CHS) 45 Xe 29
Moccas **GB** (HWC) 52 Xa 36
Mochdre **GB** (CLW) 43 Wb 29
Mochdre **GB** (POW) 51 Wd 34
Mochrum **GB** (DAG) 29 Vc 20
Mockbeggar **GB** (KEN) 72 Ac 41
Mockerkin **GB** (CUB) 34 Wc 21
Mocklershill **IRL** (TIP) 99 Sb 33
Modbury **GB** (DEV) 76 Wa 46
Moddershall **GB** (SFS) 45 Xf 31
Modreny **IRL** (TIP) 93 Rf 31
Modubeagh **IRL** (LAO) 94 Sf 31
Moelfe **GB** (CLW) 44 We 31
Moelfre **GB** (GWY) 42 Ve 28
Moffat **GB** (DAG) 31 Wd 16
Mogeely **IRL** (COR) 104 Rf 37
Mogerhanger **GB** (BFS) 55 Ze 36
Moglass **IRL** (TIP) 99 Sb 33
Moheedian **IRL** (ROS) 88 Re 25
Moher **IRL** (CAV) 89 Sc 24
Moher **IRL** (ROS) 88 Rf 26
Mohill **IRL** (LET) 88 Sa 25
Moig **IRL** (LIM) 98 Ra 33
Moine Ho **GB** (HGL) 4 Vc 117
Moira **GB** (DOW) 84 Te 22
Moira **GB** (LEC) 46 Yc 32
Molahiffe Castle **IRL** (KER) 97 Qc 35
Molash **GB** (KEN) 65 Af 41
Mold **GB** (CLW) 44 Wf 30
Molehill Green **GB** (ESS) 64 Ab 37
Molland **GB** (DEV) 67 Wb 42
Mollington **GB** (CHS) 44 Xa 29
Mollington **GB** (OXS) 54 Yd 36
Mollinsburn **GB** (STC) 25 Vf 13
Monachyle **GB** (CEN) 20 Vd 10
Monaghan **IRL** (MOG) 84 Ta 23
Monalahy **IRL** (COR) 98 Rc 37
Monalee **IRL** (WEX) 95 Te 32
Monalia **IRL** (MOG) 90 Tb 24
Monaloo House **IRL** (COR) 99 Sa 36
Monamintra Cross Roads **IRL** (WTF) 100 Sf 35
Monamolin **IRL** (WEX) 101 Td 33
Monaree **IRL** (KER) 96 Pe 36
Monargan Glebe **IRL** (DON) 82 Rd 20
Monarud **IRL** (WTF) 99 Sc 36
Monaseed **IRL** (WEX) 101 Td 32
Monasootagh **IRL** (WEX) 101 Td 33
Monaster **IRL** (LIM) 98 Rb 33
Monasteraden **IRL** (SLI) 88 Rc 25
Monasterevin **IRL** (KIL) 94 Sf 30
Monastery **IRL** (COR) 104 Rd 37
Monastery **IRL** (ROS) 88 Re 26
Monatarriv **IRL** (WTF) 99 Sa 35
Monatore **IRL** (WKL) 95 Tb 31
Monavanshere **IRL** (COR) 98 Rb 37
Mondrehid House **IRL** (LAO) 94 Sc 31
Monea **GB** (FER) 83 Sb 22
Monee Cross Roads **IRL** (COR) 98 Rc 36
Moneen **IRL** (COR) 99 Rd 35
Moneenbog **IRL** (ROS) 88 Sa 26
Moness **GB** (ORK) 6 We 115
Monevechadan **GB** (STC) 24 Va 11
Monewden **GB** (SUF) 57 Bb 35
Moneyboy **IRL** (ROS) 88 Re 26
Moneydie **GB** (TYS) 21 Wc 10
Moneydig **GB** (LDR) 79 Tc 19
Moneyeusker **IRL** (COR) 103 Qf 37
Moneygall **IRL** (OFF) 93 Sa 31
Moneygorm **IRL** (COR) 98 Rd 36
Moneyhaughly **IRL** (DON) 77 Sc 19
Money House **IRL** (WKL) 95 Tc 32
Moneymeen **IRL** (WKL) 95 Td 31
Moneymore **GB** (LDR) 84 Tc 20
Moneymore **IRL** (WKL) 95 Tb 31
Moneynacroha Cross Roads **IRL** (COR) 103 Ra 38
Moneyreagh **GB** (DOW) 85 Ub 21
Monganagh **IRL** (ROS) 88 Rf 26
Moniaive **GB** (DAG) 31 Wa 17
Monifieth **GB** (TYS) 22 Xb 10
Monikie **GB** (TYS) 22 Xb 9
Monilea **IRL** (WMT) 89 Se 27
Monimail **GB** (FIF) 21 Wf 11
Monington **GB** (DYF) 50 Vb 36
Monivea **IRL** (GAL) 92 Rb 28
Monk Fryston **GB** (NOY) 40 Ye 26
Monkhopton **GB** (SHS) 52 Xc 33
Monkland **GB** (HWC) 52 Xb 35
Monkleigh **GB** (DEV) 66 Ve 43
Monknash **GB** (SGL) 60 Wc 40
Monknetown **IRL** (MT) 90 Td 26
Monkokehampton **GB** (DEV) 66 Vf 44
Monkseaton **GB** (TAW) 33 Yd 18
Monk's Gate **GB** (WSX) 71 Ze 42
Monk's Heath **GB** (CHS) 45 Xe 29
Monk Sherborne **GB** (HAS) 63 Yf 41
Monkshill **GB** (GRP) 17 Xd 4
Monksilver **GB** (SOM) 67 We 42
Monks Kirby **GB** (WWH) 54 Ye 34
Monkstown **IRL** (COR) 104 Rd 37
Monkstown **IRL** (WMT) 89 Se 27
Monk Street **GB** (ESS) 64 Ac 37
Monkswood **GB** (GWE) 60 Xa 38
Monkton **GB** (DEV) 67 Wf 44
Monkton **GB** (KEN) 65 Bb 40
Monkton **GB** (STC) 30 Vc 15
Monkton **GB** (TAW) 33 Yd 19
Monkton Combe **GB** (AVN) 61 Xe 40
Monkton Deverill **GB** (WIL) 69 Xe 42
Monkton Farleigh **GB** (WIL) 61 Xe 40
Monkton Heathfield **GB** (SOM) 67 Wf 42
Monkton Up Wimborne **GB** (WIL) 69 Ya 43
Monkwearmouth **GB** (TAW) 33 Yd 19
Monkwood **GB** (HAS) 70 Yf 42
Monmouth **GB** (GWE) 61 Xb 38
Monmurry **IRL** (MOG) 84 Ta 22
Monnagh **IRL** (LAO) 94 Sc 31
Monnington on Wye **GB** (HWC) 52 Xa 36
Monreith **GB** (DAG) 29 Vc 20
Monroe **IRL** (GAL) 87 Ra 28
Monroe **IRL** (TIP) 99 Rf 35
Monroe **IRL** (WMT) 89 Sd 27
Monsea **IRL** (TIP) 93 Re 31
Montacute **GB** (SOM) 68 Xb 43
Montford **GB** (SHS) 52 Xa 32
Montgarrie **GB** (GRP) 17 Xb 5
Montgomery **GB** (POW) 52 Wf 33
Montgreenan **GB** (STC) 24 Vc 15
Montiagh **IRL** (GAL) 92 Ra 28
Mont Keeffe **IRL** (COR) 98 Ra 35
Montpelier **IRL** (GAL) 92 Rb 28
Montrave **GB** (FIF) 26 Xa 11
Montrose **GB** (TYS) 22 Xd 8
Monxton **GB** (HAS) 69 Yc 41
Monyash **GB** (DSH) 45 Yb 29
Monymusk **GB** (GRP) 17 Xc 5
Monzie **GB** (TYS) 21 Wb 10
Moone **IRL** (KIL) 94 Tb 31
Moonveen **IRL** (KLK) 100 Se 35
Moonzie **GB** (FIF) 21 Wf 10
Moor **IRL** (ROS) 88 Rd 26
Moorby **GB** (LIN) 47 Zf 30
Moor Cock **GB** (LCS) 38 Xc 24
Moorcot **GB** (HWC) 52 Xa 35
Moor Crichel **GB** (DOS) 69 Ya 43
Moord **IRL** (WTF) 104 Sb 37
Moore **GB** (CHS) 44 Xc 28
Moorends **GB** (SOY) 40 Za 27
Mooretown House **IRL** (MT) 90 Tc 26
Moorfield House **IRL** (KIL) 95 Tb 29
Moorfields **GB** (ANT) 79 Tf 20
Moorgreen **GB** (NTS) 46 Ye 30
Moorhall **GB** (DSH) 45 Yc 29
Moorhampton **GB** (HWC) 52 Xa 36
Moorhill House **IRL** (LGF) 89 Sc 26
Moorhouse **GB** (CUB) 32 Wf 19
Moorhouse **GB** (NTS) 46 Za 29
Moorlinch **GB** (SOM) 68 Xa 42
Moor Monkton **GB** (NOY) 40 Ye 24
Moorsholm **GB** (CLE) 37 Za 21
Moorside **GB** (GRM) 39 Xf 25
Moor Side **GB** (LIN) 47 Zf 30
Moortown **GB** (IOW) 70 Yd 45
Moortown **GB** (LIN) 41 Zd 28
Morangie **GB** (HGL) 8 Vf 2
Morar **GB** (HGL) 13 Ub 7
Morborne **GB** (CBS) 55 Ze 33
Morcombelake **GB** (DOS) 68 Xa 44
Morcott **GB** (LEC) 55 Zc 33
Morda **GB** (SHS) 44 Wf 31
Morden **GB** (DOS) 69 Xf 44
Morden **GB** (GRL) 64 Ze 40
Mordiford **GB** (HWC) 52 Xc 36
Mordon **GB** (DUR) 36 Yd 21
More **GB** (SHS) 52 Xa 33
Moreagh **IRL** (COR) 103 Qf 38
Morebath **GB** (DEV) 67 Wd 42
Morebattle **GB** (BOR) 32 Xd 15
Morecambe **GB** (LCS) 38 Xa 24
Moredon Valence **GB** (GLS) 61 Xe 38
Morefield **GB** (HGL) 7 Ue 1
Moreleigh **GB** (DEV) 76 Wb 46
Morenish **GB** (TYS) 20 Ve 10
Morestead **GB** (HAS) 70 Ye 42
Moreton **GB** (CHS) 44 Wf 28
Moreton **GB** (DOS) 68 Xe 44
Moreton Corbet **GB** (SHS) 44 Xc 32
Moretonhampstead **GB** (DEV) 67 Wb 45
Moreton-in-Marsh **GB** (GLS) 62 Yb 37
Moreton Jeffries **GB** (HWC) 52 Xc 36
Moreton Morrell **GB** (WWH) 54 Yc 35
Moreton on Lugg **GB** (HWC) 52 Xb 36
Moreton Pinkney **GB** (NRH) 54 Yf 36
Moreton Say **GB** (SHS) 44 Xc 31
Morfa Bychan **GB** (GWY) 42 Vf 31
Morfa Nefyn **GB** (GWY) 42 Vc 31
Morganstown House **IRL** (LOT) 90 Td 26
Mork **GB** (GLS) 61 Xc 38
Morland **GB** (CUB) 35 Xc 21
Morley **GB** (DSH) 46 Yd 31
Morley **GB** (DUR) 36 Yb 21
Morley **GB** (WYO) 39 Yc 26
Morley Green **GB** (CHS) 45 Xe 29
Morley Saint Botolph **GB** (NOR) 57 Ba 33
Morningside **GB** (LOT) 26 We 13
Mornington **IRL** (MT) 90 Te 26
Mornington House **IRL** (MT) 90 Te 26
Moroe **IRL** (LIM) 99 Rd 33
Morpeth **GB** (NHL) 33 Yb 18
Morrey **GB** (SFS) 45 Yb 32
Morseby **GB** (CUB) 34 Wc 21
Morston **GB** (NOR) 48 Af 31
Mortehoe **GB** (DEV) 66 Ve 41
Mortimer **GB** (BKS) 63 Yf 40
Mortimer Croft **GB** (HWC) 52 Xa 35
Mortimer West End **GB** (HAS) 63 Yf 40
Mortlestown **IRL** (LIM) 98 Rc 34
Morton **GB** (DSH) 46 Yd 30
Morton **GB** (LIN) 40 Zb 28
Morton **GB** (LIN) 47 Zd 32
Morton **GB** (NOR) 49 Ba 32
Morton **GB** (SHS) 44 Wf 32
Morton Bagot **GB** (WWH) 53 Yb 35
Morton-on-Swale **GB** (NOY) 36 Yd 23
Morvah **GB** (CNW) 74 Uc 48
Morville **GB** (SHS) 52 Xd 33
Morwenstow **GB** (CNW) 66 Vc 43
Morwich **GB** (HGL) 14 Ud 5
Mosborough **GB** (SOY) 46 Yd 29
Mosedale **GB** (CUB) 34 Wf 20
Moseley **GB** (HWC) 53 Xe 35
Moseley **GB** (WMD) 53 Ya 34
Moskow **GB** (STC) 24 Vd 15
Mosney **IRL** (MT) 90 Te 27
Moss **GB** (CLW) 44 Wf 30
Moss **GB** (SOY) 40 Yf 27
Moss **GB** (STC) 18 Ta 10
Mossat **GB** (GRP) 16 Xa 5
Moss Bank **GB** (MES) 38 Xb 28
Mossbank **GB** (SHL) 2 Ye 106
Mossblown **GB** (STC) 30 Vc 16
Mossburnford **GB** (BOR) 32 Xc 16
Mossdale **GB** (DAG) 30 Vf 18
Mossend **GB** (STC) 25 Vf 14
Mossgiel **GB** (STC) 30 Vd 15
Mosside **GB** (TYS) 22 Xa 9
Mossley **GB** (GRM) 39 Xf 27
Mossley Hill **GB** (MES) 44 Xa 28
Moss of Barmuckity **GB** (GRP) 16 We 3
Moss Side **GB** (LCS) 38 Xa 26
Mosstodloch **GB** (GRP) 16 Wf 3
Mosston **GB** (TYS) 22 Xb 9
Mossvale **IRL** (LGF) 89 Sc 26
Mosterton **GB** (DOS) 68 Xb 43
Mostyn **GB** (CLW) 43 We 29
Motcombe **GB** (DOR) 69 Xe 42
Mote Park **IRL** (ROS) 88 Rf 27
Mothel **IRL** (WTF) 100 Sd 35
Motherwell **GB** (STC) 25 Wa 14
Mottisfont **GB** (HAS) 69 Yc 42
Mottistone **GB** (IOW) 70 Yd 45
Mouldsworth **GB** (CHS) 44 Xb 29
Moulin **GB** (TYS) 21 Wb 8
Moulsecomb **GB** (ESX) 71 Zf 43
Mouls Ford **GB** (OXS) 63 Yf 39
Moulsoe **GB** (BUS) 55 Zb 36
Moulton **GB** (CHS) 44 Xc 29
Moulton **GB** (LIN) 47 Zf 32
Moulton **GB** (NOY) 36 Yc 22
Moulton **GB** (NRH) 54 Za 35
Moulton **GB** (SUF) 56 Ac 35
Moulton Chapel **GB** (LIN) 47 Zf 32
Moulton Saint Mary **GB** (NOR) 49 Bd 33
Moulton Seas End **GB** (LIN) 47 Zf 32
Mount **GB** (CNW) 75 Vc 46
Mountain Ash **GB** (MGL) 60 Wd 38
Mountain Barrack **IRL** (COR) 99 Re 35
Mountain Cross **GB** (BOR) 26 Wd 14
Mountain Lodge **IRL** (CAV) 89 Sf 25
Mount Bellew Bridge **IRL** (GAL) 88 Rc 28
Mountbenger **GB** (BOR) 32 Wf 15
Mount Bernard **IRL** (COR) 103 Rb 38
Mountbolus **IRL** (OFF) 94 Sc 29
Mount Briscoe **IRL** (OFF) 94 Se 29
Mountbrown House **IRL** (MAY) 86 Qd 26
Mount Bures **GB** (ESS) 56 Ae 37
Mountcateret House **IRL** (OFF) 93 Sa 29
Mountcharles **IRL** (DON) 82 Re 21
Mountcollins **IRL** (LIM) 98 Qe 35
Mountdillon **IRL** (ROS) 88 Rf 26
Mount Druid **IRL** (WTF) 100 Sf 35
Mountfield **GB** (ESX) 72 Ac 43
Mountfield **GB** (TYR) 83 Sf 21
Mount Garrett Bridge **IRL** (KLK) 100 Ta 34
Mountgerald **GB** (HGL) 15 Vd 3
Mount Hawke **GB** (CNW) 74 Ue 47
Mount Hazel **IRL** (GAL) 88 Rc 28
Mounthenry **IRL** (MAY) 87 Qe 28
Mounthoward Cross Roads **IRL** (WEX) 101 Td 33
Mountjoy **GB** (CNW) 75 Va 46
Mountjoy **GB** (TYR) 83 Sd 21
Mount Juliet **IRL** (KLK) 100 Se 33
Mount Kennedy **IRL** (WTF) 100 Sc 35
Mount Kennedy House **IRL** (WKL) 95 Tf 30
Mount Melleray **IRL** (WTF) 99 Sa 35
Mount Murray **IRL** (WMT) 89 Sd 27
Mountnagle **IRL** (COR) 98 Rc 36
Mountnessing **GB** (ESS) 64 Ac 39
Mountnicholas **IRL** (KER) 97 Qc 35
Mountnorris **GB** (ARG) 84 Td 23
Mount Nugent **IRL** (CAV) 89 Se 26
Mount Oliphant **GB** (STC) 30 Vc 16
Mounton **GB** (GWE) 61 Xb 39
Mount Prospect House **IRL** (KER) 97 Qd 36
Mountrath **IRL** (LAO) 94 Sd 30
Mount Rose **IRL** (KLK) 100 Se 32
Mountsandford Lodge **IRL** (ROS) 88 Re 28
Mountshannon **IRL** (CRE) 93 Rd 31
Mountsorrel **GB** (LEC) 46 Yf 32
Mountstuart **GB** (STC) 24 Uf 14
Mount Talbot **IRL** (ROS) 88 Re 27
Mount Temple **IRL** (WMT) 93 Sb 28
Mount Uniacke **IRL** (COR) 104 Rf 37
Mount View **IRL** (MT) 95 Td 28
Mount Zephyr **IRL** (COR) 98 Qf 36
Mousehole **GB** (CNW) 74 Uc 48
Mouswald **GB** (DAG) 31 Wd 18
Moveen **IRL** (CRE) 91 Qb 33
Moville **IRL** (DON) 78 Sf 17
Mow Cop **GB** (CHS) 45 Xe 30
Mowhaugh **GB** (BOR) 32 Xe 16
Mowsley **GB** (LEC) 54 Yf 34
Mowtie **GB** (GRP) 17 Xe 7
Moy **GB** (HGL) 20 Vc 7
Moy **GB** (TYR) 84 Tb 22
Moy **IRL** (GAL) 92 Ra 30
Moyad **GB** (DOW) 90 Tf 24
Moyagh **IRL** (DON) 77 Sb 18
Moyaliff House **IRL** (TIP) 99 Sa 33
Moyasta **IRL** (CRE) 91 Qc 32
Moybella **IRL** (KER) 97 Qc 34
Moycarky **IRL** (TIP) 99 Sb 33
Moycullen **IRL** (GAL) 92 Qe 28
Moycullen Lodge **IRL** (GAL) 92 Qf 28
Moydow **IRL** (LGF) 88 Sb 27
Moygashel **GB** (TYR) 84 Tb 22
Moyglas Cross Roads **IRL** (ROS) 88 Rf 26
Moyglass **IRL** (GAL) 93 Rd 30
Moy Ho **GB** (GRP) 16 Wc 3
Moylcrove **GB** (DYF) 50 Vb 36
Moyles Mill **IRL** (MOG) 90 Tc 24
Moylough **IRL** (GAL) 88 Rc 28
Moymet House **IRL** (MT) 90 Tb 27
Moymore **IRL** (CRE) 92 Rb 31
Moymore House **IRL** (CRE) 92 Qd 31
Moynagh **IRL** (CAV) 89 Sd 26
Moynalty **IRL** (MT) 89 Ta 26
Moynalvy **IRL** (MT) 90 Tb 28
Moyne **IRL** (LGF) 89 Sc 25
Moyne **IRL** (ROS) 88 Rc 25
Moyne **IRL** (TIP) 93 Sb 32
Moyne **IRL** (WKL) 95 Td 31
Moyne Cross Roads **IRL** (LGF) 89 Sc 25
Moynehall **IRL** (CAV) 89 Se 25
Moynoe House **IRL** (CRE) 92 Rc 31
Moyny **IRL** (COR) 103 Qe 38
Moyode Castle **IRL** (GAL) 92 Rb 29
Moyra **IRL** (DON) 77 Rf 18
Moyreen **IRL** (LIM) 98 Qe 33
Moyvally **IRL** (KIL) 94 Ta 28
Moyvannan Castle **IRL** (ROS) 88 Rf 28
Moyvore **IRL** (WMT) 89 Sc 27
Moyvoughly **IRL** (WMT) 89 Sb 28
Muasdale **GB** (STC) 23 Ub 15
Muchalls **GB** (GRP) 17 Xf 6
Much Birch **GB** (HWC) 61 Xb 37
Much Cowarne **GB** (HWC) 52 Xc 36
Much Dewchurch **GB** (HWC) 61 Xb 37
Muchelney **GB** (SOM) 68 Xb 42
Much Hadham **GB** (HTS) 64 Aa 37
Much Hoole **GB** (LCS) 38 Xb 26
Muchlarnick **GB** (CNW) 75 Vc 46
Much Wenlock **GB** (SHS) 52 Xc 33
Muchwood House **IRL** (MT) 89 Ta 27
Muckanagh **IRL** (GAL) 93 Rf 29
Muckanagh **IRL** (MAY) 87 Qe 25
Muckanagh **IRL** (WMT) 88 Sa 27
Mucking **GB** (ESS) 64 Ac 39
Mucklestone **GB** (SFS) 44 Xd 31
Muckleton **GB** (SHS) 44 Xc 32
Mucklon **IRL** (KIL) 95 Tb 28
Muckros **IRL** (DON) 82 Rc 21
Mudale **GB** (HGL) 8 Vd 119
Muddiford **GB** (DEV) 66 Vf 42
Muddleswood **GB** (WSX) 71 Ze 43
Mudford **GB** (SOM) 68 Xc 43
Mudgley **GB** (SOM) 68 Xb 41
Muff **IRL** (CAV) 90 Ta 25
Muff **IRL** (DON) 78 Se 18
Muff **IRL** (ROS) 88 Re 27
Mugeary **GB** (HGL) 13 Te 4
Mugginton **GB** (DSH) 45 Yc 31
Muie **GB** (HGL) 8 Ve 120
Muileann **GB** (TYR) 83 Sc 20
Muineagh **IRL** (DON) 78 Sc 17
Muine Bheag **IRL** (CLW) 100 Ta 32
Muing **IRL** (KER) 97 Qb 35
Muingingaun **IRL** (MAY) 80 Qb 23
Muingvautia **IRL** (KER) 97 Qd 35
Muingwee **IRL** (KER) 97 Qd 34
Muingwore **IRL** (SLI) 81 Qf 23
Muingydowka **IRL** (KER) 102 Pe 37
Muingyroogen **IRL** (COR) 98 Ra 36
Muir **GB** (GRP) 16 Wc 7
Muirden **GB** (GRP) 17 Xd 3
Muirdrum **GB** (TYS) 22 Xb 9
Muirhead **GB** (STC) 25 Vf 13
Muirhead **GB** (TYS) 21 Wf 10
Muirhouses **GB** (CEN) 25 Wc 12
Muirkirk **GB** (STC) 30 Vf 15
Muir of Fairburn **GB** (HGL) 15 Vc 3
Muir of Fowlis **GB** (GRP) 16 Xb 5
Muir of Lochs **GB** (GRP) 16 Wf 3
Muir of Ord **GB** (HGL) 15 Vd 3
Muirshearlich **GB** (HGL) 19 Uf 7
Muirskie **GB** (GRP) 17 Xe 6
Muirtack **GB** (GRP) 17 Xf 4
Muirton **GB** (HGL) 15 Vf 3
Muirton **GB** (TYS) 21 Wb 11
Muirton of Ballochy **GB** (TYS) 22 Xc 8
Muiryfold **GB** (GRP) 17 Xd 3
Muker **GB** (NOY) 35 Xf 22
Mulben **GB** (GRP) 16 Wf 3
Mull **IRL** (KER) 97 Pf 36
Mullabohy Cross Roads **IRL** (LOT) 90 Td 25
Mullach Ide = Malahide **IRL** (DUB) 95 Tf 28
Mullagh **IRL** (CAV) 89 Ta 26
Mullagh **IRL** (CRE) 91 Qd 32
Mullagh **IRL** (GAL) 93 Rd 29
Mullagh **IRL** (MAY) 86 Qb 26
Mullagh **IRL** (MT) 90 Tc 28
Mullaghard **IRL** (MT) 90 Tb 26
Mullaghattin **IRL** (LOT) 90 Te 24
Mullaghboy **IRL** (CAV) 89 Sd 25
Mullagh House **IRL** (LGF) 88 Sb 26
Mullaghnacross **IRL** (MAY) 81 Qe 23
Mullaghroe **IRL** (SLI) 88 Rd 25
Mullamast **IRL** (KIL) 94 Ta 30
Mullamast Cross Roads **IRL** (KIL) 94 Ta 31
Mullan **GB** (LDR) 79 Tb 18
Mullan **IRL** (MOG) 84 Ta 22
Mullanacross **IRL** (DON) 82 Rf 21
Mullanacross **IRL** (MOG) 84 Ta 22
Mullanasole **IRL** (DON) 82 Rf 21
Mullanmore **IRL** (DON) 77 Re 20
Mullenaboree **IRL** (COR) 98 Rd 36
Mullenbeg Cross Roads **IRL** (KLK) 100 Se 34
Mullenmeehan **IRL** (WMT) 89 Sb 28
Mullennaglogh **IRL** (TIP) 100 Sd 34
Mullennakill **IRL** (KLK) 100 Sf 34
Mullinacuff **IRL** (WKL) 95 Tc 32
Mullinahone **IRL** (TIP) 100 Sc 33
Mullinavat **IRL** (KLK) 100 Se 34
Mullingar **IRL** (WMT) 89 Sd 27
Mullion **GB** (CNW) 74 Ue 48
Mullygollan **IRL** (ROS) 88 Re 26
Mullymagowan **IRL** (CAV) 89 Se 25
Mulphedder **IRL** (KIL) 89 Ta 28
Mulroy House **IRL** (DON) 77 Sb 17
Multyfarnham **IRL** (WMT) 89 Sd 27
Mumbles, The **GB** (WGL) 59 Wa 39
Mumby **GB** (LIN) 48 Zf 29
Munderfield Stocks **GB** (HWC) 52 Xc 36
Mundesley **GB** (NOR) 49 Bc 31
Mundford **GB** (NOR) 56 Ad 33
Mundham **GB** (NOR) 57 Bc 33
Mundon Hill **GB** (ESS) 65 Ae 38
Munerigie **GB** (HGL) 14 Va 6
Mungan **IRL** (KLK) 100 Ta 34
Mungasdale **GB** (HGL) 7 Ud 1
Mungmacody **IRL** (KLK) 100 Sf 33
Mungret **IRL** (LIM) 98 Rb 33
Mungrisdale **GB** (CUB) 34 Xa 21
Munlochry **GB** (HGL) 15 Ve 3
Munsley **GB** (HWC) 52 Xd 36
Munslow **GB** (SHS) 52 Xb 34
Murchington **GB** (DEV) 66 Wa 44
Murch Marcle **GB** (HWC) 61 Xd 37
Murcott **GB** (OXS) 63 Ye 37
Murlaggan **GB** (HGL) 14 Ue 7
Murlaggan **GB** (HGL) 20 Vb 7
Murnaghbeg **IRL** (COR) 103 Qe 37
Murntown **IRL** (WEX) 101 Tc 35
Murragh **IRL** (COR) 103 Ra 38
Murreagh **IRL** (KER) 96 Pd 35
Murrisk **IRL** (MAY) 86 Qc 26
Murroogh **IRL** (CRE) 92 Qe 30
Murrow **GB** (CBS) 55 Aa 33
Murston **GB** (KEN) 65 Ae 40
Murthill **GB** (TYS) 22 Xa 8
Murthly **GB** (TYS) 21 Wd 9
Murton **GB** (CUB) 35 Xd 21
Murton **GB** (DUR) 36 Yd 20
Murton **GB** (NHL) 27 Xf 14
Murton **GB** (NOY) 40 Yf 25
Murvay **IRL** (GAL) 86 Pf 28
Musbury **GB** (DEV) 68 Wf 44
Musselburgh **GB** (LOT) 26 Wf 13
Muston **GB** (LEC) 46 Zb 31
Muston **GB** (NOY) 37 Ze 23
Mustow Green **GB** (HWC) 53 Xe 34
Mutford **GB** (SUF) 57 Bd 34
Muthill **GB** (TYS) 21 Wb 11
Mweewillin **IRL** (MAY) 86 Qa 25
Mybster **GB** (HGL) 6 Wd 118
Myddfai **GB** (DYF) 59 Wb 37
Myddle **GB** (SHS) 44 Xb 32
Mydroilyn **GB** (DYF) 50 Ve 35
Mye Cross Roads **IRL** (WEX) 101 Tc 34
Mylane Cross Roads **IRL** (COR) 104 Rc 37
Mylerstown Cross Roads **IRL** (KIL) 94 Ta 30
Mylerstown Cross Roads **IRL** (KIL) 95 Tb 29
Mylor **GB** (CNW) 74 Uf 47
Mylor Bridge **GB** (CNW) 74 Uf 47
Mynachlog-ddu **GB** (DYF) 58 Vb 37
Myndtown **GB** (SHS) 52 Xa 33
Mynydd-bach **GB** (GWE) 61 Xb 39
Mynydd Llandegai **GB** (GWY) 42 Vf 29
Mynytho **GB** (GWY) 42 Vc 31
Myross **IRL** (COR) 103 Qf 39
Myrtlegrove **IRL** (OFF) 93 Sa 31
Myrtleville House **IRL** (COR) 104 Re 38
Myshall **IRL** (CLW) 101 Tb 32
Mytchett **GB** (SUR) 63 Zb 41
Mytholmroyd **GB** (WYO) 39 Ya 26
Myton-on-Swale **GB** (NOY) 40 Ye 24

N

Naas **IRL** (KIL) 95 Tb 29
Naast **GB** (HGL) 7 Uc 2
Naburn **GB** (NOY) 40 Yf 25
Na Clocha Liatha = Greystones **IRL** (WKL) 95 Tf 30

Middleton One Row – Na Clocha Liatha = Greystones GB IRL 127

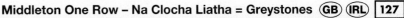

Nacreeva IRL (SLI) 81 Ra 23
Nad IRL (COR) 98 Ra 36
Nafferton GB (HUS) 41 Zd 24
Naglack IRL (MOG) 90 Tb 25
Nah Aoraí IRL (COR) 102 Qa 38
Nailbridge GB (GLS) 61 Xc 37
Nail or Inga IRL (GAL) 93 Re 29
Nailsea GB (AVN) 61 Xb 40
Nailstone GB (LEC) 54 Yd 33
Nailsworth GB (GLS) 61 Xe 38
Nairn GB (HGL) 15 Wa 3
Nambrack IRL (MAY) 86 Qa 24
Nancegollan GB (CNW) 74 Ue 48
Nanhoron GB (GWY) 42 Vc 31
Nannau GB (GWY) 43 Wa 32
Nannerch GB (CLW) 43 We 29
Nanpantan GB (LEC) 54 Ye 32
Nanpean GB (CNW) 75 Va 46
Nanstallon GB (CNW) 75 Vb 46
Nanternis GB (DYF) 50 Vd 35
Nantgaredig GB (DYF) 59 Ve 37
Nantgarw GB (MGL) 60 We 39
Nant Glâs GB (POW) 51 Wd 35
Nantinan House IRL (LIM)
98 Ra 33
Nantlle GB (GWY) 42 Ve 30
Nantmawr GB (SHS) 44 Wf 32
Nantmel GB (POW) 51 Wd 35
Nantmor GB (GWY) 43 Vf 31
Nant Peris GB (GWY) 43 Vf 30
Nantwich GB (CHS) 44 Xc 30
Nant-y-derry GB (POW) 60 Xa 38
Nantyffyllon GB (MGL) 60 Wc 39
Nantyglo GB (GWE) 60 Wf 38
Nant-y-moel GB (MGL) 60 Wc 39
Naper's Dome IRL (MT) 89 Sf 26
Nappa GB (NOY) 39 Xe 25
Napton on the Hill GB (WWH)
54 Ye 35
Naran IRL (DON) 77 Rd 19
Narberth GB (DYF) 58 Vb 38
Narborough GB (LEC) 54 Ye 33
Narborough GB (NOR) 48 Ad 32
Narraghmore IRL (KIL) 94 Ta 30
Nasareth GB (GWY) 42 Ve 30
Na Sceirí = Skerries IRL (MT)
90 Tf 27
Naseby GB (NRH) 54 Za 34
Nash GB (BUS) 54 Za 36
Nash GB (GWE) 60 Xa 39
Nash GB (HWC) 52 Wf 35
Nash GB (SHS) 52 Xc 34
Nash IRL (WEX) 100 Ta 35
Nash Lee GB (BUS) 63 Zb 38
Nassington GB (NRH) 55 Zd 33
Nasty GB (HTS) 64 Zf 37
Nateby GB (CUB) 35 Xd 22
Nateby GB (LCS) 38 Xb 25
Natland GB (CUB) 35 Xb 23
Naughton GB (SUF) 56 Af 36
Naul IRL (DUB) 90 Te 27
Naunton GB (GLS) 62 Yb 37
Naunton GB (HWC) 53 Xe 36
Naunton Beauchamp GB (HWC)
53 Xf 35
Navan IRL (MT) 90 Tb 27
Navenby GB (LIN) 47 Zc 30
Navestock GB (ESS) 64 Ab 39
Navestock Side GB (ESS) 64 Ab 39
Nawton GB (NOY) 37 Za 23
Nayland GB (SUF) 56 Af 37
Nazeing GB (ESS) 64 Aa 38
Neacroft GB (HAS) 69 Yb 44
Neale IRL (MAY) 87 Qe 27
Nealstown IRL (LAO) 93 Sb 31
Neap GB (SHL) 2 Yf 107
Near Cotton GB (SFS) 45 Ya 30
Neasham GB (DUR) 36 Yd 22
Neath GB (WGL) 59 Wb 39
Neatham GB (HAS) 70 Za 42
Neatishead GB (NOR) 49 Bc 32
Nebo GB (DYF) 50 Vf 35
Nebo GB (GWY) 42 Ve 30
Nebo GB (GWY) 43 Wb 30
Necton GB (NOR) 48 Ae 33
Nedanone IRL (KER) 102 Pf 38
Nedd GB (HGL) 7 Ue 119
Nedging Tye GB (SUF) 57 Af 36
Needham GB (NOR) 57 Bb 34
Needham Market GB (SUF)
57 Ba 36
Needingworth GB (CBS) 55 Zf 35
Neen Savage GB (SHS) 52 Xd 34
Neen Sollars GB (SHS) 52 Xc 34
Neenton GB (SHS) 52 Xc 34
Nefyn GB (GWY) 42 Vc 31
Neillstown Cross Roads IRL (MT)
90 Tb 27
Neilston GB (STC) 24 Vd 14
Nelson GB (LCS) 39 Xe 26
Nelson GB (MGL) 60 We 39
Nemphlar GB (STC) 25 Wb 14
Nempnett Thrubwell GB (AVN)
61 Xb 40
Nenagh IRL (TIP) 93 Re 31
Nenthead GB (CUB) 35 Xd 20
Nenthorn GB (BOR) 27 Xc 15
Nerabus GB (STC) 22 Td 14
Nercwys GB (CLW) 44 Wf 30
Nesbit GB (NHL) 27 Xf 15
Ness GB (CHS) 44 Wf 29
Ness GB (NOY) 37 Za 23
Neston GB (CHS) 44 Wf 29
Neston GB (WIL) 61 Xe 40
Nether Alderley GB (CHS) 45 Xe 29
Nether Blainslie GB (BOR)
26 Xb 14
Netherbrae GB (GRP) 17 Xd 3
Nether Broughton GB (LEC)
46 Za 32
Netherburn GB (STC) 25 Wa 14
Nether Burrow GB (LCS) 35 Xc 23
Nether Cerne GB (DOS) 68 Xd 44
Nethercott GB (OXS) 62 Ye 37
Nether Crimond GB (GRP) 17 Xe 5
Nether Dallachy GB (GRP) 16 Wf 3
Nether End GB (DSH) 45 Yc 29
Netherend GB (GLS) 61 Xc 38
Netherfield GB (ESX) 72 Ac 43
Netherhampton GB (WIL) 69 Ya 42
Nether Haugh GB (SOY) 40 Yd 28
Nether Heyford GB (NRH) 54 Yf 35
Nether Kellet GB (LCS) 38 Xb 24
Nether Kinmundy GB (GRP)
17 Ya 4
Nether Langwith GB (DSH)
46 Ye 29
Netherley GB (GRP) 17 Xe 6
Nethermill GB (DAG) 31 Wc 17
Nether Moor GB (DSH) 46 Yd 29
Nethermuir GB (GRP) 17 Xf 4
Nether Padley GB (DSH) 45 Yc 29
Nether Poppleton GB (NOY)
40 Yf 25
Nether Ringorm GB (GRP) 16 We 4
Netherseal GB (DSH) 45 Yc 32
Nether Silton GB (NOY) 36 Ye 23
Nether Stowey GB (SOM) 67 Wf 42
Netherthird GB (DAG) 30 Vf 19
Netherthong GB (WYO) 39 Yb 27
Netherton GB (CHS) 44 Xb 29
Netherton GB (MES) 38 Xa 28
Netherton GB (NHL) 33 Xf 16
Netherton GB (OXS) 62 Yd 38
Netherton GB (TYS) 21 Wd 9
Netherton GB (TYS) 22 Xb 8
Netherton GB (WYO) 39 Yc 27
Nethertown GB (CUB) 34 Wc 22
Nethertown GB (HGL) 6 Wf 116
Nethertown IRL (WEX) 101 Td 35
Nether Urquhart GB (FIF) 21 We 11
Nether Wallop GB (HAS) 69 Yc 42
Nether Wasdale GB (CUB)
34 Wd 22
Nether Whitacre GB (WWH)
53 Yc 33
Netherwitton GB (NHL) 33 Ya 17
Netherwood GB (STC) 30 Vf 15
Nether Woodburn GB (DEV)
67 Wc 43
Nether Worton GB (OXS) 62 Yd 37
Nethlern GB (GWY) 42 Vb 31
Nethy Bridge GB (HGL) 16 Wc 5
Netley GB (HAS) 70 Yd 43
Netley Marsh GB (HAS) 69 Yc 43
Nettlebed GB (OXS) 63 Za 39
Nettlebridge GB (SOM) 68 Xc 41
Nettlecombe GB (DOS) 68 Xb 44
Nettleden GB (HTS) 63 Zc 38
Nettleham GB (LIN) 47 Zd 29
Nettlestead GB (SUF) 57 Ba 36
Nettlestead Green GB (KEN)
72 Ac 41
Nettlestone GB (IOW) 70 Yf 44
Nettleton GB (LIN) 41 Zd 28
Nettleton GB (WIL) 61 Xe 39
Netton GB (DEV) 76 Vf 47
Netton GB (WIL) 69 Yb 42
Neuk, the GB (GRP) 17 Xd 6
Nevendon GB (ESS) 65 Ad 39
Nevern GB (DYF) 58 Vb 36
Nevill Holt GB (LEC) 54 Zb 33
Nevybridge IRL (LIM) 98 Ra 33
New Abbey GB (DAG) 31 Wc 19
New Aberdour GB (GRP) 17 Xe 3
New Addington GB (GRL) 64 Zf 40
New Alresford GB (HAS) 70 Yf 42
New Alyth GB (TYS) 21 We 9
Newark on Trent GB (NTS)
46 Zb 30
Newarthill GB (STC) 25 Wa 14
New Ash Green GB (KEN)
64 Ab 40
Newbawn IRL (WEX) 100 Tb 34
New Bewick GB (NHL) 33 Ya 16
Newbiggin GB (CUB) 35 Xb 19
Newbiggin GB (CUB) 35 Xb 21
Newbiggin GB (CUB) 35 Xc 21
Newbiggin GB (CUB) 38 Wf 24
Newbiggin GB (DUR) 35 Xf 21
Newbiggin GB (NOY) 36 Xf 23
Newbiggin GB (NOY) 36 Ya 23
Newbiggin-by-the-Sea GB (NHL)
33 Yc 17
Newbigging GB (STC) 25 Wc 14
Newbigging GB (TYS) 21 Wf 9
Newbigging GB (TYS) 22 Xb 9
Newbiggin-on-Lune GB (CUB)
35 Xd 22
New Birmingham IRL (TIP)
99 Sc 33
Newbliss IRL (MOG) 83 Sf 24
Newbold GB (DSH) 46 Yd 29
Newbold GB (LEC) 46 Yd 32
Newbold on Avon GB (WWH)
54 Ye 34
Newbold on Stour GB (WWH)
53 Yc 36
Newbold Pacey GB (WWH)
54 Yc 35
Newbold Verdon GB (LEC)
54 Yd 33
New Bolingbroke GB (LIN) 47 Zf 30
Newborough GB (CBS) 55 Ze 33
Newborough GB (SFS) 45 Yb 32
Newbourn GB (SUF) 57 Bb 36
New Brancepeth GB (DUR)
36 Yc 20
Newbridge GB (CNW) 74 Uc 48
Newbridge GB (CNW) 75 Ve 46
New Bridge GB (DAG) 31 Wc 18
Newbridge GB (GWE) 60 Wf 39
Newbridge GB (IOW) 70 Yd 44
Newbridge GB (LOT) 26 Wd 13
Newbridge IRL (KIL) 95 Tb 29
Newbridge-on-Wye GB (POW)
51 Wd 35
New Brighton GB (CHS) 44 Wf 28
New Brighton GB (HAS) 70 Za 44
New Brinsley GB (NTS) 46 Ye 30
Newbrough GB (NHL) 33 Xe 18
New Buckenham GB (NOR)
57 Ba 34
New Buildings GB (LDR) 78 Sd 19
Newburgh GB (FIF) 21 We 10
Newburgh GB (GRP) 17 Xf 5
Newburgh GB (LCS) 38 Xb 27
Newburgh Priory GB (NOY)
37 Ye 23
Newburn GB (TAW) 33 Yb 19
Newby GB (CUB) 35 Xc 21
Newby GB (NOY) 37 Ye 21
Newby GB (NOY) 38 Xd 24
Newby Bridge GB (CUB) 35 Xa 23
Newby East GB (CUB) 32 Xb 19
New Byth GB (GRP) 17 Xe 3
Newby West GB (CUB) 32 Xa 19
Newby Wiske GB (NOY) 36 Yd 23
Newcastle GB (DOW) 85 Ua 23
Newcastle GB (GWE) 61 Xb 37
Newcastle GB (SHS) 52 Wf 34
Newcastle IRL (DUB) 95 Tc 29
Newcastle IRL (GAL) 92 Rb 28
Newcastle IRL (MT) 89 Ta 25
Newcastle IRL (MT) 94 Ta 28
Newcastle IRL (WKL) 95 Tf 30
Newcastle IRL (WMT) 89 Sd 26
Newcastle Cross Roads IRL (WEX)
101 Tc 35
Newcastle Emlyn GB (DYF)
50 Vd 36
Newcastleton GB (BOR) 32 Xb 17
Newcastle-under-Lyme GB (SFS)
45 Xe 30
Newcastle upon Tyne GB (TAW)
33 Yc 19
Newcastle West IRL (LIM) 98 Qf 34
Newcetown IRL (COR) 103 Ra 38
Newchapel GB (DYF) 58 Vc 36
Newchapel GB (SUR) 71 Zf 42
Newchapel IRL (TIP) 93 Re 31
Newchapel IRL (TIP) 99 Sb 34
New Chapel Cross IRL (KER)
102 Pe 37
Newchurch GB (DYF) 59 Vd 37
Newchurch GB (GWE) 61 Xb 38
Newchurch GB (IOW) 70 Ye 44
Newchurch GB (KEN) 72 Af 42
Newchurch GB (LCS) 39 Xe 26
Newchurch GB (POW) 52 Wf 36
Newchurch in Pendle GB (LCS)
39 Xe 25
New Clipstone GB (NTS) 46 Yf 30
New Costessey GB (NOR)
49 Bb 33
Newcott GB (DEV) 67 Wf 43
New Cross GB (DYF) 51 Vf 34
New Cumnock GB (STC) 30 Ve 16
New Deer GB (GRP) 17 Xe 3
Newdigate GB (SUR) 71 Ze 42
New Earswick GB (NOY) 40 Yf 25
New Edlington GB (SOY) 40 Ye 28
New Ellerby GB (HUS) 41 Ze 25
Newell Green GB (BKS) 63 Zb 40
New End GB (HWC) 53 Ya 35
Newenden GB (KEN) 72 Ad 42
Newent GB (GLS) 61 Xd 37
New Ferry GB (CHS) 44 Xa 28
Newfield GB (DUR) 36 Yb 20
Newfield GB (HGL) 8 Vf 2
Newgale GB (DYF) 58 Uf 37
New Galloway GB (DAG) 30 Vf 18
Newgate Street GB (HTS) 64 Zf 38
New Gilston GB (FIF) 22 Xa 11
New Grimsby GB 74 Te 49
New Grove IRL (LGF) 89 Sd 26
Newhall GB (CHS) 44 Xc 30
Newhall GB (DSH) 45 Yc 32
Newham GB (GRL) 64 Aa 39
Newham GB (NHL) 27 Yb 15
New Hartley GB (NHL) 33 Yc 18
Newhaven GB (ESX) 71 Aa 44
New Haw GB (SUR) 63 Zd 40
New Hedges GB (DYF) 58 Vb 38
New Holland GB (HUS) 41 Zd 26
Newholm GB (NOY) 37 Zc 22
New Horndean GB (BOR) 27 Xf 14
New Houghton GB (DSH) 46 Ye 29
New Houghton GB (NOR)
48 Ad 32
Newhouse GB (STC) 25 Wa 14
Newhouse IRL (LOT) 90 Te 26
New Houses GB (NOY) 35 Xe 24
New Hutton GB (CUB) 35 Xb 23
New Hythe GB (KEN) 65 Ac 41
Newick GB (ESX) 71 Aa 43
Newington GB (KEN) 65 Ad 40
Newington GB (OXS) 63 Yf 39
Newington Bagpath GB (GLS)
61 Xe 39
New Inn GB (DYF) 59 Ve 36
New Inn GB (GWE) 61 Xb 38
New Inn IRL (CAV) 89 Se 25
New Inn IRL (GAL) 93 Rd 29
Newinn IRL (TIP) 99 Sa 34
New Inn Cross Roads IRL (LAO)
94 Se 30
New Invention GB (SHS) 52 Wf 34
New Kildimo IRL (LIM) 98 Rb 33
New Lanark GB (STC) 25 Wb 15
Newland GB (GLS) 61 Xc 38
Newland GB (HUS) 40 Za 26
Newlandrig GB (LOT) 26 Wf 13
Newlands GB (BOR) 32 Xb 17
Newlands GB (GRP) 16 Wf 3
Newlands GB (NHL) 33 Ya 19
Newlands of Geise GB (HGL)
5 Wc 117
New Lane GB (LCS) 38 Xa 27
New Leake GB (LIN) 47 Aa 30
New Leeds GB (GRP) 17 Xf 3
New Line Cross IRL (LOT)
90 Td 26
New Longton GB (LCS) 38 Xb 26
Newlot GB (ORK) 6 Xb 114
New Luce GB (DAG) 30 Va 18
Newlyn GB (CNW) 74 Uc 48
Newmacher GB (GRP) 17 Xe 5
Newmains GB (STC) 25 Wa 14
New Malden GB (GRL) 64 Ze 40
Newmannin IRL (GAL) 92 Rb 29
Newmarket GB (HGL) 11 Td 119
Newmarket GB (SUF) 56 Ac 35
Newmarket IRL (COR) 98 Qf 35
Newmarket IRL (KLK) 100 Se 34
Newmarket an Fergus IRL (CRE)
92 Ra 32
Newmarket Cross Roads IRL (KER)
97 Qe 35
New Marske GB (CLE) 37 Yf 21
New Marton GB (SHS) 44 Xa 31
Newmill GB (BOR) 32 Xa 16
New Mill GB (CNW) 74 Uc 48
Newmill GB (GRP) 16 Xa 3
New Mill GB (HTS) 63 Zc 38
New Mill GB (WYO) 39 Yb 27
Newmill End GB (BFS) 64 Zd 37
Newmill of Inshewan GB (TYS)
22 Xa 8
New Mills GB (CNW) 75 Va 47
New Mills GB (DSH) 45 Xf 28
New Mills GB (GWE) 61 Xb 38
New Mills GB (POW) 51 Wd 33
Newmiln GB (TYS) 21 Wd 10
Newmilns GB (STC) 25 Vd 15
New Milton GB (HAS) 69 Yc 44
New Moat GB (DYF) 58 Vb 37
Newnham GB (GLS) 61 Xd 38
Newnham GB (HAS) 70 Za 41
Newnham GB (HTS) 55 Ze 36
Newnham GB (HWC) 52 Xc 35
Newnham GB (KEN) 65 Ae 41
Newnham GB (NRH) 54 Yf 35
Neworidge GB (OXS) 62 Yd 38
Newpark GB (CNW) 75 Vc 45
Newpark IRL (ROS) 88 Rf 28
Newpark House IRL (KIL) 94 Ta 29
Newpass IRL (WMT) 89 Sc 27
New Pitsligo GB (GRP) 17 Xe 3
Newport GB (DEV) 66 Vf 42
Newport GB (DYF) 58 Va 36
Newport GB (ESS) 56 Ab 37
Newport GB (GLS) 61 Xd 38
Newport GB (GWE) 60 Xa 39
Newport GB (HGL) 9 Wd 119
Newport GB (HUS) 40 Zb 26
Newport GB (IOW) 70 Ye 44
Newport GB (NOR) 49 Be 32
Newport GB (SHS) 45 Xd 32
Newport IRL (MAY) 86 Qc 25
Newport IRL (TIP) 93 Rd 32
Newport IRL (WTF) 99 Sa 36
Newport-on-Tay GB (FIF) 22 Xa 10
Newport Pagnell GB (BUS)
55 Zb 36
Newpound Common GB (WSX)
71 Zd 42
Newquay GB (CNW) 74 Uf 46
New Quay GB (DYF) 50 Vd 35
New Rackheath GB (NOR)
49 Bc 33
New Radnor GB (POW) 52 Wf 35
Newrath Bridge IRL (WKL) 95 Tf 30
New Romney GB (KEN) 72 Af 43
New Ross IRL (WEX) 100 Ta 34
New Rossington GB (SOY)
40 Yf 28
New Row GB (LCS) 38 Xc 25
Newry GB (DOW) 84 Td 23
New Salhouse GB (NOR) 49 Bc 32
New Scone GB (TYS) 21 Wd 10
Newsham GB (LCS) 38 Xb 26
Newsham GB (NHL) 33 Yc 18
Newsham GB (NOY) 36 Yb 22
Newsholme GB (HUS) 40 Za 26
Newsholme GB (LCS) 39 Xe 25
New Silksworth GB (TAW)
33 Yd 19
Newstead GB (BOR) 26 Xb 15
Newstead GB (NHL) 27 Yb 15
Newthorpe GB (NOY) 40 Ye 26
Newtimber Place GB (WSX)
71 Ze 43
New Tolsta GB (HGL) 11 Te 118
Newton GB (BOR) 32 Xc 16
Newton GB (CBS) 47 Aa 32
Newton GB (CBS) 56 Aa 36
Newton GB (CHS) 44 Xb 29
Newton GB (CHS) 44 Xb 30
Newton GB (CUB) 38 We 24
Newton GB (DAG) 31 Wd 17
Newton GB (GRP) 16 Wd 3
Newton GB (GRP) 17 Ya 4
Newton GB (HAS) 62 Ye 40
Newton GB (HAS) 69 Yc 43
Newton GB (HGL) 6 Wf 118
Newton GB (HGL) 10 Se 2
Newton GB (HGL) 14 Vb 6
Newton GB (HGL) 15 Vf 2
Newton GB (HGL) 15 Vf 3
Newton GB (LCS) 35 Xc 23
Newton GB (LCS) 38 Xd 25
Newton GB (LIN) 47 Zd 31
Newton GB (LOT) 25 Wd 13
Newton GB (NHL) 33 Ya 19
Newton GB (NOR) 48 Ae 32
Newton GB (STC) 24 Uf 12
Newton GB (TYS) 21 Wb 10
Newton GB (WGL) 59 Vf 39
Newton GB (WIL) 69 Xf 42
Newton GB (WIL) 69 Yc 42
Newton GB (WWH) 54 Ye 34
Newton IRL (COR) 98 Rb 35
Newton IRL (DON) 78 Sc 19
Newton IRL (KIL) 95 Tb 28
Newton IRL (KIL) 95 Tc 29
Newton IRL (ROS) 88 Sa 26
Newton IRL (TIP) 99 Re 34
Newton Abbot GB (DEV) 76 Wc 45
Newton Arlosh GB (CUB) 31 We 19
Newton Aycliffe GB (DUR) 36 Yc 21
Newton Bewley GB (CLE) 36 Ye 21
Newton Blossomville GB (BUS)
55 Zc 36
Newton Bromswold GB (NRH)
55 Zc 35
Newton Burgoland GB (LEC)
54 Yd 32
Newton by Toft GB (LIN) 47 Zd 28
Newton Ferrers GB (DEV) 76 Vf 47
Newtonferry GB (HGL) 10 Se 2
Newton Flotman GB (NOR)
57 Bb 33
Newtongrange GB (LOT) 26 Wf 13
Newtonhill GB (GRP) 17 Xf 6
Newton Kyme GB (NOY) 40 Ye 25
Newton-le-Willows GB (MES)
38 Xc 28
Newton-le-Willows GB (NOY)
36 Yb 23
Newton Longville GB (BUS)
63 Zb 37
Newton Mearns GB (STC)
25 Ve 14
Newtonmill GB (TYS) 22 Xc 8
Newtonmore GB (HGL) 15 Vf 6
Newton of Balcanquhal GB (TYS)
21 Wd 11
Newton-on-Ouse GB (NOY)
40 Ye 24
Newton-on-Rawcliffe GB (NOY)
37 Zb 23
Newton on the Moor GB (NHL)
33 Yb 16
Newton on Trent GB (LIN)
46 Zb 29
Newton Platin IRL (MT) 90 Td 26
Newton Poppleford GB (DEV)
67 We 44
Newton Purcell GB (OXS) 63 Yf 37
Newton Regis GB (WWH) 53 Yc 33
Newton Reigny GB (CUB) 35 Xb 20
Newton Saint Cyres GB (DEV)
67 Wc 44
Newton Saint Faith GB (NOR)
49 Bb 32
Newton Saint Loe GB (AVN)
61 Xd 40
Newton Saint Petrock GB (DEV)
66 Ve 43
Newton Sandes IRL (KER)
97 Qd 33
Newtonslow IRL (WMT) 94 Sd 28
Newton Solney GB (DSH) 45 Yc 32
Newton Stacey GB (HAS) 69 Yd 42
Newton Stewart GB (DAG)
30 Vd 19
Newton Tony GB (WIL) 69 Yb 42
Newton Tracey GB (DEV) 66 Vf 42
Newton under Roseberry GB (CLE)
37 Yf 21
Newton upon Derwent GB (HUS)
40 Za 25
Newton Valence GB (HAS)
70 Za 42
Newtown GB (CHS) 44 Xc 30
Newtown GB (CUB) 32 Xb 19
Newtown GB (DSH) 45 Xf 28
New Town GB (GLS) 62 Ya 37
Newtown GB (HAS) 70 Ye 43
Newtown GB (HWC) 52 Xc 36
Newtown GB (IOW) 70 Yd 44
New Town GB (LOT) 26 Xb 13
Newtown GB (NHL) 33 Ya 15
Newtown GB (NHL) 33 Ya 17
Newtown GB (POW) 51 We 33
Newtown GB (SFS) 45 Xf 30
Newtown GB (SFS) 45 Ya 30
Newtown GB (SHS) 44 Xb 31
Newtown GBM 29 Vc 24
Newtown IRL (CRE) 91 Qb 33
Newtown IRL (LOT) 90 Td 26
Newtown IRL (MAY) 87 Qe 26
Newtown IRL (MT) 90 Tc 26
Newtown IRL (ROS) 88 Rf 28
Newtown IRL (TIP) 93 Re 31
Newtown IRL (TIP) 100 Sd 34
Newtown IRL (WEX) 100 Tb 35
Newtown IRL (WEX) 101 Tb 34
Newtown IRL (WMT) 89 Sb 27
Newtown IRL (WTF) 99 Sc 36
Newtown IRL (WTF) 100 Sd 35
Newtownabbey GB (ANT)
85 Ua 20
Newtownards GB (DOW) 85 Ub 21
Newtownbutler GB (FER) 83 Sd 23
Newtown Cashel IRL (LGF)
88 Sa 27
Newtown Cloghans IRL (MAY)
81 Qe 24
Newtown-Crommelin GB (ANT)
79 Te 19
Newtown Daly IRL (GAL) 93 Rd 29
Newtown Farragher IRL (ROS)
88 Re 26
Newtown Forbes IRL (LGF)
88 Sa 26
Newtown Gore IRL (LET) 89 Sb 24
Newtownhamilton GB (ARG)
84 Tc 23
Newtown-in-Saint-Martin GB (CNW)
74 Uf 48
Newtown Linford GB (LEC)
54 Ye 32
Newtown Lodge IRL (COR)
99 Rf 36
Newtownlynch IRL (GAL) 92 Qf 29
Newtown Mount Kennedy IRL
(WKL) 95 Tf 30
Newtown Saint Boswells GB (BOR)
26 Xb 15
Newtownshandrum IRL (COR)
98 Rb 34
Newtown Steward GB (TYR)
83 Sd 20
Newtown Stream IRL (OFF)
93 Rf 30
Newtown Unthank GB (LEC)
54 Ye 33
New Tredegar GB (MGL) 60 We 38
New Twopothouse Village IRL
(COR) 98 Rb 35
Newtyle GB (TYS) 21 Wf 9
New Waltham GB (HUS) 41 Zf 27
New Wimpole GB (CBS) 55 Zf 36
New Winton GB (LOT) 26 Xa 13
New Yatt GB (OXS) 62 Yd 38
New York GB (LIN) 47 Zf 30
Neyland GB (DYF) 58 Va 38
Nibley GB (AVN) 61 Xd 39
Nicholashayne GB (DEV) 67 We 43
Nicholaston GB (WGL) 59 Vf 39
Nicholastown House IRL (LOT)
90 Tc 25
Nidd GB (NOY) 39 Yc 24
Niddrie GB (LOT) 26 Wf 13
Nigg GB (HGL) 9 Wa 2
Nightcott GB (SOM) 67 Wc 42
Nine Ashes GB (ESS) 64 Ab 38
Ninebanks GB (NHL) 32 Xd 19
Nine Elms GB (WIL) 62 Ya 39
Ninemile Bar, Crocketford or GB
(DAG) 31 Wb 18
Ninemilehouse IRL (TIP) 100 Sd 34
Ninfield GB (ESX) 72 Ac 43
Ningwood GB (IOW) 69 Yd 44
Nisbet GB (BOR) 32 Xc 15
Niton GB (IOW) 70 Ye 45
Nitshill GB (STC) 24 Vd 14
Niwbwrch GB (GWY) 42 Vd 30
Nizels GB (KEN) 71 Ab 41
Noak Hill GB (GRL) 64 Ab 39
Nobber IRL (MT) 90 Tb 26
Noblehill GB (DAG) 31 Wc 18
Nobottle GB (NRH) 54 Yf 35
Nocton GB (LIN) 47 Zd 30
Noggusbay IRL (OFF) 93 Sa 29
Nohaval IRL (COR) 104 Rd 38
Nolagh IRL (CAV) 89 Ta 25
Nolton GB (DYF) 58 Uf 38
No Man's Heath GB (CHS)
44 Xb 30
No Man's Heath GB (WWH)
53 Yc 32
Nomansland GB (DEV) 67 Wc 43
Nomansland GB (HAS) 69 Yc 43
Noneley GB (SHS) 44 Xb 31
Nonington GB (KEN) 65 Bb 41
Noose The GB (GLS) 61 Xd 38
Noranside GB (TYS) 22 Xa 8
Norbury GB (DSH) 45 Yb 31
Norbury GB (GRL) 64 Zf 40
Norbury GB (SFS) 45 Xe 32
Norbury GB (SHS) 52 Xa 33
Norbury Common GB (CHS)
44 Xc 30
Norchard GB (HWC) 53 Xe 35
Nordelph GB (NOR) 56 Ab 33
Norden GB (DOS) 69 Xf 45
Norden GB (GRM) 39 Xe 27
Nordley GB (SHS) 52 Xd 33
Norham GB (NHL) 27 Xf 14
Norley GB (CHS) 44 Xc 29
Normanby GB (HUS) 40 Zb 27
Normanby GB (NOY) 37 Za 23
Norman Cross GB (CBS) 55 Ze 34
Normandy GB (SUR) 70 Zb 41
Normans Grove House IRL (MT)
95 Td 28
Normanton GB (DSH) 46 Yd 31
Normanton GB (LEC) 46 Zb 31
Normanton GB (LIN) 47 Zc 30
Normanton GB (NTS) 46 Za 30
Normanton on Soar GB (NTS)
54 Ye 32
Normoss GB (LCS) 38 Xa 26
Norrington Common GB (WIL)
61 Xe 40
Norris Hill GB (LEC) 46 Yc 32
Norris Mount IRL (WEX) 101 Td 33
Nort End GB (CBS) 55 Zf 36
North Acre GB (NOR) 56 Af 33
Northallerton GB (NOY) 36 Yd 22
Northall Green GB (NOR) 48 Af 32
Northam GB (DEV) 66 Ve 42
Northampton GB (NRH) 54 Za 35
North Aston GB (OXS) 62 Ye 37
Northaw GB (HTS) 64 Ze 38
Northay GB (SOM) 68 Wf 43
North Baddesley GB (HAS)
69 Yd 43
North Ballachlish GB (HGL)
19 Ue 8
North Barrow GB (SOM) 68 Xc 42
North Benfleet GB (ESS) 65 Ad 39
North Berwick GB (LOT) 26 Xb 12
North Boarhunt GB (HAS) 70 Yf 43
Northbourne GB (KEN) 65 Bb 41
North Bovey GB (DEV) 67 Wb 45
North Bradley GB (WIL) 69 Xe 41
North Brentor GB (DEV) 76 Vf 45
North Brewham GB (SOM)
68 Xd 42
North Cadbury GB (SOM) 68 Xc 42
North Cairn GB (DAG) 28 Uf 19
North Carlton GB (LIN) 47 Zc 29
North Cave GB (HUS) 40 Zc 26
North Cerney GB (GLS) 62 Ya 38
Northchapel GB (WSX) 70 Zc 42
North Charlton GB (NHL) 33 Yb 16
North Cheriton GB (SOM) 68 Xd 42
North Chideock GB (DOS)
68 Xb 44
North Cliffe GB (HUS) 40 Zb 26
North Cockerington GB (LIN)
41 Aa 28
North Coker GB (SOM) 68 Xc 43
North Cotes GB (LIN) 41 Aa 28
Northcott GB (DEV) 66 Vd 44
North Cove GB (SUF) 57 Bd 34
North Cowton GB (NOY) 36 Yc 22
North Crawley GB (BUS) 55 Zc 36
North Cray GB (GRL) 64 Aa 40
North Creake GB (NOR) 48 Ae 31
North Curry GB (SOM) 68 Xa 42
North Dalton GB (HUS) 41 Zc 25
North Deighton GB (NOY) 40 Yd 25
North Duffield GB (NOY) 40 Za 26
North Elkington GB (LIN) 41 Zf 28
North Elmham GB (NOR) 49 Af 32
Northend GB (AVN) 61 Xe 40
Northend GB (BUS) 63 Za 39
North End GB (BUS) 63 Zb 37
North End GB (NOR) 56 Af 34
North End GB (WSX) 71 Zd 43
Northend GB (WWH) 54 Yd 35
North Erradale GB (HGL) 7 Ub 2
North Ferriby GB (HUS) 41 Zc 26
Northfield GB (BOR) 27 Xf 13
Northfield GB (WMD) 53 Ya 34
Northfield House IRL (CRE)
92 Qe 31
Northfleet GB (KEN) 64 Ac 40
North Frodingham GB (HUS)
41 Ze 25
North Galson GB (HGL) 11 Td 118
Northgate GB (LIN) 47 Ze 32
North Green GB (NOR) 57 Bb 34
North Grimston GB (NOY)
40 Zb 24
North Hayling GB (HAS) 70 Za 44
North Heath GB (WSX) 71 Zd 43
North Hinksey GB (OXS) 62 Ye 38
North Holmwood GB (SUR)
71 Ze 41
North Hykeham GB (LIN) 47 Zc 29
Northiam GB (ESX) 72 Ad 43
Northill GB (BFS) 55 Ze 36
Northington GB (HAS) 70 Ye 42
North Kelsey GB (LIN) 41 Zd 27
North Killingholme GB (HUS)
41 Ze 27
North Kilvington GB (NOY)
36 Yd 23
North Kilworth GB (LEC) 54 Yf 34
North Kyme GB (LIN) 47 Ze 30
North Lancing GB (WSX) 71 Ze 43
Northlands GB (LIN) 47 Aa 30
Northleach GB (GLS) 62 Ya 38
North Lee GB (BUS) 63 Zb 38
Northleigh GB (DEV) 66 Wa 42
North Leigh GB (OXS) 62 Yd 38
North Leverton with Habblesthorpe
GB (NTS) 46 Za 28
Northlew GB (DEV) 66 Vf 44
North Littleton GB (HWC) 53 Ya 36
North Lopham GB (NOR) 57 Af 34
North Luffenham GB (LEC)
55 Zc 33
North Marden GB (WSX) 70 Za 43
North Marston GB (BUS) 63 Za 37
North Middleton GB (LOT)
26 Wf 14
North Molton GB (DEV) 67 Wb 42
Northmoor GB (DEV) 66 Vd 43
Northmoor Green or Moorland GB
(SOM) 68 Xa 42
North Moreton GB (OXS) 63 Ye 39
Northmuir GB (TYS) 22 Xa 8
North Mundham GB (WSX)
70 Zb 44
North Newbald GB (HUS) 40 Zc 26
North Newington GB (OXS)
54 Yd 36
North Newton GB (SOM) 68 Wf 42
North Newton GB (STC) 23 Ue 14
North Nibley GB (GLS) 61 Xd 39
North Oakley GB (HAS) 70 Ye 41
North Ockendon GB (GRL)
64 Ab 39
Northolt GB (GRL) 64 Zd 39
Northon GB (HGL) 11 Sf 2
Northop GB (CLW) 44 Wf 29
Northorpe GB (LIN) 40 Zc 28
Northorpe GB (LIN) 47 Zd 32
North Otterington GB (NOY)
36 Yd 23
Northover GB (SOM) 68 Xb 42
North Owersby GB (LIN) 41 Zd 28
Northowram GB (WYO) 39 Yb 26
North Perrott GB (SOM) 68 Xb 43
North Petherton GB (SOM)
68 Wf 42
North Petherwin GB (CNW)
66 Vd 44
North Pickenham GB (NOR)
56 Ae 33
North Piddle GB (HWC) 53 Xf 35
North Poorton GB (DOS) 68 Xb 44
Northpunds GB (SHL) 3 Ye 109
North Queensferry GB (FIF)
26 Wd 12
North Radworthy GB (DEV)
67 Wb 42
North Rauceby GB (LIN) 47 Zd 30
North Reston GB (LIN) 47 Aa 29
North Rigton GB (NOY) 39 Yc 25
North Ring IRL (COR) 103 Ra 39
North Rode GB (CHS) 45 Xf 29
North Roe GB (SHL) 2 Yd 105
North Scale GB (CUB) 38 We 24
North Scarle GB (LIN) 46 Zb 29
North Shian GB (STC) 19 Ud 9
North Shields GB (TAW) 33 Yd 18
North Side GB (CBS) 55 Zf 33
North Somercotes GB (LIN)
41 Aa 28
North Stainley GB (NOY) 36 Yc 23
North Stainmore GB (CUB)
35 Xe 21
North Stoke GB (AVN) 61 Xd 40
North Stoke GB (WSX) 71 Zc 43
North Street GB (HAS) 70 Yf 42
North Sunderland GB (NHL)
27 Yc 15
North Tamerton GB (CNW)
66 Vd 44
North Tawton GB (DEV) 66 Wa 44
North Third GB (CEN) 25 Wa 12
North Thoresby GB (LIN) 41 Zf 28
North Tidworth GB (WIL) 69 Yc 41
North Tolsta GB (HGL) 11 Te 118
North Town GB (DEV) 66 Vf 43
North Tuddenham GB (NOR)
49 Ba 32
North Walsham GB (NOR)
49 Bc 32
North Waltham GB (HAS) 70 Ye 41
North Warnborough GB (HAS)
70 Za 41
North Watten GB (HGL) 6 We 117
North Weald Bassett GB (ESS)
64 Aa 38
Northwell GB (ORK) 5 Xd 113
North Wheatley GB (NTS) 46 Za 28
Northwich GB (CHS) 44 Xc 29
Northwick GB (AVN) 61 Xc 39
North Wick GB (AVN) 61 Xc 40
North Widcombe GB (AVN)
61 Xc 41
North Willingham GB (LIN)
47 Ze 28
North Wingfield GB (DSH) 46 Yd 29
North Witham GB (LIN) 47 Zc 32
Northwood GB (SHS) 44 Xb 31
Northwood Green GB (GLS)
61 Xd 37
North Wootton GB (DOS) 68 Xd 43
North Wootton GB (NOR) 48 Ac 32
North Wraxall GB (WIL) 61 Xe 40
Norton GB (GLS) 61 Xe 37
Norton GB (HTS) 55 Ze 37
Norton GB (HWC) 53 Xe 36
Norton GB (HWC) 53 Ya 36
Norton GB (NOY) 37 Zb 24
Norton GB (NRH) 54 Yf 35
Norton GB (NTS) 46 Yf 29
Norton GB (POW) 52 Wf 35

128 GB IRL Nacreeva – Norton

Norton **GB** (SHS) 52 Xb 34
Norton **GB** (SHS) 52 Xc 32
Norton **GB** (SHS) 52 Xd 34
Norton **GB** (SOY) 40 Ye 27
Norton **GB** (SOY) 46 Yd 29
Norton **GB** (SUF) 56 Af 35
Norton **GB** (WIL) 61 Xf 39
Norton **GB** (WSX) 70 Zb 43
Norton **GB** (WSX) 70 Zb 44
Norton Bavant **GB** (WIL) 69 Xf 41
Norton Bridge **GB** (SFS) 45 Xe 31
Norton Canes **GB** (SFS) 53 Ya 32
Norton Canon **GB** (HWC) 52 Xa 36
Norton Ferris **GB** (WIL) 68 Xe 42
Norton Fitzwarren **GB** (SOM) 67 Wf 42
Norton Green **GB** (HAS) 69 Yc 44
Norton Hawkfield **GB** (AVN) 61 Xc 40
Norton in Hales **GB** (SHS) 45 Xd 31
Norton in the Moors **GB** (SFS) 45 Xf 30
Norton-Juxta-Twycross **GB** (LEC) 54 Yc 33
Norton-le-Clay **GB** (NOY) 36 Yd 24
Norton Lindsey **GB** (WWH) 53 Yc 35
Norton Mandeville **GB** (ESS) 64 Ab 38
Norton Saint Philip **GB** (SOM) 68 Xe 41
Norton sub Hamdon **GB** (SOM) 68 Xb 43
Norwell **GB** (NTS) 46 Za 30
Norwell Woodhouse **GB** (NTS) 46 Za 30
Norwich **GB** (NOR) 49 Ba 33
Norwick **GB** (SHL) 2 Zb 104
Norwood Green **GB** (GRL) 64 Zd 40
Norwood Hill **GB** (SUR) 71 Ze 41
Noss Mayo **GB** (DEV) 76 Vf 47
Nostie **GB** (HGL) 14 Uc 5
Nottingham **GB** (NTS) 46 Yf 31
Notton **GB** (WYO) 40 Yd 27
Noughaval **IRL** (CRE) 92 Qe 30
Noughaval **IRL** (CRE) 92 Ra 31
Noughaval House **IRL** (WMT) 88 Sb 27
Noutard's Green **GB** (HWC) 53 Xe 35
Nox **GB** (SHS) 52 Xa 32
Noyadd Trefawr **GB** (DYF) 50 Vc 36
Nu's Cross **IRL** (WKL) 95 Tf 30
Nuffield **GB** (OXS) 63 Yf 39
Nunburnholme **GB** (HUS) 40 Zb 25
Nuneaton **GB** (WWH) 54 Yd 33
Nuneham Courtenay **GB** (OXS) 63 Ye 38
Nun Monkton **GB** (NOY) 40 Ye 24
Nunney **GB** (SOM) 68 Xd 41
Nunnington **GB** (NOY) 37 Za 23
Nunnykirk **GB** (NHL) 33 Ya 17
Nunton **GB** (HGL) 12 Sd 4
Nunton **GB** (WIL) 69 Yb 42
Nunwick **GB** (NHL) 33 Xe 18
Nup End **GB** (GLS) 61 Xe 37
Nurney **IRL** (CLW) 94 Ta 32
Nurney **IRL** (KIL) 94 Ta 30
Nursted **GB** (WSX) 70 Za 43
Nurton **GB** (SFS) 53 Xe 33
Nutbourne **GB** (WSX) 70 Za 43
Nutbourne **GB** (WSX) 71 Zd 43
Nutfield **GB** (SUR) 71 Zf 41
Nuthampstead **GB** (HTS) 55 Aa 37
Nuthurst **GB** (WSX) 71 Ze 42
Nuthurst **GB** (WWH) 53 Yb 34
Nutley **GB** (ESX) 71 Aa 42
Nutley **GB** (HAS) 70 Yf 41
Nuttstown Cross Roads **IRL** (MT) 95 Td 28
Nybster **GB** (HGL) 6 Wf 117
Nyewood **GB** (WSX) 70 Za 43
Nymet Rowland **GB** (DEV) 67 Wb 43
Nymet Tracey **GB** (DEV) 67 Wb 44
Nympsfield **GB** (GLS) 61 Xe 38
Nythe **GB** (SOM) 68 Xb 42
Nyton **GB** (WSX) 70 Zc 43

O

O'Briensbridge Droichead **IRL** (LIM) 92 Rd 32
O'Dalys Bridge **IRL** (MT) 89 Ta 26
Oadby **GB** (LEC) 54 Yf 33
Oad Street **GB** (KEN) 65 Ae 41
Oak **GB** (DEV) 66 Vf 44
Oakamoor **GB** (SFS) 45 Ya 31
Oakbank **GB** (LOT) 25 Wd 13
Oakdale **GB** (GWE) 60 We 38
Oake **GB** (SOM) 67 We 42
Oakenclough **GB** (LCS) 38 Xb 25
Oakengates **GB** (SHS) 52 Xd 32
Oakenshaw **GB** (DUR) 36 Yb 20
Oakenshaw **GB** (WYO) 39 Yb 26
Oakford **GB** (DYF) 50 Ve 35
Oakgrove **GB** (CHS) 45 Xe 29
Oakham **GB** (LEC) 54 Zb 32
Oakhanger **GB** (HAS) 70 Za 42
Oakhill **GB** (SOM) 68 Xc 41
Oakington **GB** (CBS) 55 Aa 35
Oaklands **GB** (GWY) 43 Wb 30
Oakley **GB** (BUS) 63 Yf 38
Oakley **GB** (FIF) 25 Wc 12
Oakley **GB** (SUF) 57 Bb 34
Oakley Green **GB** (BKS) 63 Zb 40
Oakley House **IRL** (OFF) 93 Sb 30
Oakley Park **GB** (POW) 51 Wd 34
Oak Park **IRL** (KER) 97 Qb 35
Oakpark House **IRL** (CLW) 94 Ta 31
Oaks **GB** (SHS) 52 Xa 33
Oaksey **GB** (WIL) 62 Xf 39
Oaktree Hill **GB** (NOY) 36 Yd 22
Oakwoodhill **GB** (SUR) 71 Zd 42
Oakworth **GB** (WYO) 39 Ya 25
Oare **GB** (KEN) 65 Af 41
Oare **GB** (WIL) 62 Yb 40
Oasby **GB** (LIN) 47 Zc 31
Oatfield **IRL** (CRE) 92 Rb 32
Oath **GB** (SOM) 68 Xa 42
Oathlaw **GB** (TYS) 22 Xa 8
Oatlands **IRL** (MT) 90 Tb 27
Oatquarter **IRL** (CRE) 91 Qb 30
Oban **GB** (STC) 19 Ud 10
Obertstown Cross Roads **IRL** (MT) 90 Tc 27
Obney **GB** (TYS) 21 Wc 9
Oborne **GB** (DOS) 68 Xd 43
Occlestone Green **GB** (CHS) 44 Xd 30
Occold **GB** (SUF) 57 Ba 35
Occumster **GB** (HGL) 9 We 119
Ochr-y-mynydd **GB** (MGL) 60 Wd 38
Ochtermuthill **GB** (TYS) 21 Wa 11
Ockham **GB** (SUR) 63 Zd 41
Ockle **GB** (HGL) 18 Ua 8
Ockley **GB** (SUR) 71 Zd 42
Ocle Pychard **GB** (HWC) 52 Xc 36
Odcombe **GB** (SOM) 68 Xb 43
Odder Castle **IRL** (MT) 90 Tc 27
Oddingley **GB** (HWC) 53 Xf 35
Oddington **GB** (OXS) 63 Ye 38
Odell **GB** (BFS) 55 Zc 35
Odie **GB** (ORK) 5 Xc 114
Odiham **GB** (HAS) 70 Za 41
Odol **GB** (CLW) 43 We 29
Odstone **GB** (LEC) 54 Yd 32
Offchurch **GB** (WWH) 54 Yd 35
Offenham **GB** (HWC) 53 Ya 36
Offham **GB** (ESX) 71 Zf 43
Offord Cluny **GB** (CBS) 55 Ze 35
Offord Darcy **GB** (CBS) 55 Ze 35
Offton **GB** (SUF) 57 Ba 36
Ogbourne Maizey **GB** (WIL) 62 Yb 40
Ogbourne Saint Andrew **GB** (WIL) 62 Yb 40
Ogbourne Saint George **GB** (WIL) 62 Yb 40
Oghil **IRL** (CRE) 91 Qb 30
Oghil **IRL** (GAL) 93 Re 29
Oghill Bridge **IRL** (KIL) 94 Sf 30
Ogle **GB** (NHL) 33 Yb 18
Ogmore **GB** (MGL) 60 Wc 40
Ogmore-by-Sea **GB** (MGL) 60 Wc 40
Ogmore Vale **GB** (MGL) 60 Wc 39
Oilgate **IRL** (WEX) 101 Tc 34
Okeford Fitzpaine **GB** (DOS) 68 Xe 43
Okehampton **GB** (DEV) 66 Vf 44
Okyle House **IRL** (WTF) 99 Sa 36
Old **GB** (NRH) 54 Za 34
Old Alresford **GB** (HAS) 70 Yf 42
Old Basford **GB** (NTS) 46 Ye 31
Old Bawn **IRL** (WEX) 101 Te 33
Oldberrow **GB** (WWH) 53 Yb 35
Old Bewick **GB** (NHL) 33 Ya 16
Old Bolingbroke **GB** (LIN) 47 Aa 30
Oldborough **GB** (DEV) 67 Wb 43
Old Brampton **GB** (DSH) 46 Yd 29
Old Bridge of Urr **GB** (DAG) 31 Wa 19
Old Burghclere **GB** (HAS) 62 Ye 41
Oldbury **GB** (SHS) 52 Xd 34
Oldbury **GB** (WMD) 53 Xf 33
Oldbury **GB** (WWH) 54 Yc 33
Oldbury-on-Severn **GB** (AVN) 61 Xc 39
Old Byland **GB** (NOY) 37 Yf 23
Oldcastle **GB** (GWE) 60 Xa 37
Oldcastle **IRL** (MT) 89 Sf 26
Oldcastle Heath **GB** (CHS) 44 Xb 30
Old Colwyn **GB** (CLW) 43 Wb 29
Old Copper Mine **IRL** (MT) 90 Tf 27
Oldcotes **GB** (NTS) 46 Yf 28
Oldcourt **IRL** (COR) 104 Rc 38
Oldcourt **IRL** (KIL) 94 Sf 28
Oldcourt **IRL** (KIL) 94 Ta 30
Oldcourt **IRL** (KLK) 100 Sf 34
Oldcourt **IRL** (WEX) 101 Tb 34
Oldcourt **IRL** (WKL) 95 Td 29
Old Court **IRL** (WMT) 89 Sd 27
Oldcourt **IRL** (WEX) 100 Ta 34
Oldcourt House **IRL** (DUB) 95 Td 29
Old Dailly **GB** (STC) 30 Vb 17
Old Dalby **GB** (LEC) 46 Yf 32
Old Deer **GB** (GRP) 17 Xf 3
Old Denaby **GB** (SOY) 40 Ye 28
Old Ellerby **GB** (HUS) 41 Ze 26
Old Fletton **GB** (CBS) 55 Ze 33
Oldford **GB** (SOM) 68 Xe 41
Old Gore **GB** (HWC) 61 Xc 37
Old Hall **GB** (HGL) 6 Wd 118
Oldham **GB** (GRM) 39 Xf 27
Oldhamstocks **GB** (LOT) 27 Xd 13
Old Head **IRL** (COR) 104 Rc 39
Old Heath **GB** (ESS) 65 Af 37
Old Hill **GB** (WMD) 53 Xf 34
Old Hurst **GB** (CBS) 55 Zf 34
Old Hutton **GB** (CUB) 35 Xb 23
Old Kea **GB** (CNW) 74 Uf 47
Old Kilcullen **IRL** (KIL) 95 Tb 30
Old Kildimo **IRL** (LIM) 98 Rb 33
Old Kinnemie **GB** (GRP) 17 Xd 5
Old Knebworth **GB** (HTS) 64 Ze 37
Oldland **GB** (AVN) 61 Xd 40
Old Leake **GB** (LIN) 47 Aa 30
Oldleighlin **IRL** (CLW) 94 Tb 33
Old Malton **GB** (NOY) 37 Zb 24
Oldmeldrum **GB** (GRP) 17 Xe 4
Oldmill Bridge **IRL** (LIM) 98 Qf 34
Old Monkland **GB** (STC) 25 Vf 13
Old Mountain **IRL** (DON) 78 Sd 17
Old Newton **GB** (SUF) 57 Af 35
Oldpark **GB** (ANT) 85 Ua 21
Old Philpstoun **GB** (LOT) 25 Wd 13
Old Radnor **GB** (POW) 52 Wf 35
Old Rayne **GB** (GRP) 17 Xc 4
Old Romney **GB** (KEN) 72 Af 43
Old Scone **GB** (TYS) 21 Wd 10
Oldshore Beg **GB** (HGL) 4 Uf 118
Oldshoremore **GB** (HGL) 4 Uf 118
Old Sodbury **GB** (AVN) 61 Xd 39
Old Somerby **GB** (LIN) 47 Zc 31
Oldstead **GB** (NOY) 37 Ye 23
Oldstreet **IRL** (GAL) 93 Re 30
Old Swarland **GB** (NHL) 33 Yb 17
Old Town **GB** (CUB) 35 Xc 23
Oldtown **IRL** (CRE) 91 Qb 33
Old Town **IRL** (DON) 77 Sc 18
Oldtown **IRL** (DUB) 90 Te 27
Old Town **IRL** (LAO) 94 Sd 31
Old Town **IRL** (ROS) 93 Rf 29
Old Town **IRL** (WEX) 101 Tb 33
Oldtown Cross Roads **IRL** (WEX) 101 Tc 33
Old Town Farm **GB** (NHL) 33 Xe 17
Oldtown House **IRL** (KIL) 95 Tb 29
Oldtown of Ord **GB** (GRP) 17 Xc 3
Old Twopothouse Cross Roads **IRL** (COR) 98 Rc 35
Old Village **IRL** (GAL) 93 Re 30
Oldwalls **GB** (WGL) 59 Ve 39
Old Warden **GB** (BFS) 55 Ze 36
Oldways End **GB** (DEV) 67 Wc 42
Old Weston **GB** (CBS) 55 Zd 34
Old Windsor **GB** (BKS) 63 Zc 40
Old Wives Lees **GB** (KEN) 65 Af 41
Olgrinmore **GB** (HGL) 6 Wc 118
Ollaberry **GB** (SHL) 2 Yd 105
Ollach **GB** (HGL) 13 Tf 4
Ollerton **GB** (CHS) 45 Xe 29
Ollerton **GB** (NTS) 46 Za 29
Ollerton **GB** (SHS) 44 Xc 32
Olney **GB** (BUS) 55 Zb 36
Olney **GB** (NRH) 54 Yf 36
Olton **GB** (WMD) 53 Yb 34
Olveston **GB** (AVN) 61 Xc 39
Omagh **GB** (TYR) 83 Se 21
Ombersley **GB** (HWC) 53 Xe 35
Omeath **IRL** (LOT) 90 Te 24
Omeath Park **IRL** (LOT) 90 Te 24
Ompton **GB** (NTS) 46 Za 29
Onaght **IRL** (CRE) 91 Qb 30
Onchan **GBM** 29 Vd 23
Onecote **GB** (SFS) 45 Ya 30
Ongar Hill **GB** (NOR) 48 Ac 32
Ongar Street **GB** (HWC) 52 Xa 35
Onibury **GB** (SHS) 52 Xb 34
Onich **GB** (HGL) 19 Ue 8
Onneley **GB** (SHS) 45 Xd 31
Onslow Village **GB** (SUR) 70 Zc 41
Oola **IRL** (LIM) 99 Re 33
Opinan **GB** (HGL) 7 Ub 2
Opinan **GB** (HGL) 7 Uc 1
Oranmore **IRL** (GAL) 92 Ra 29
Orby **GB** (LIN) 48 Zf 29
Orchard Wyndham **GB** (SOM) 67 Wd 42
Orcheston **GB** (WIL) 69 Ya 41
Orchiltree **GB** (STC) 30 Vd 16
Orcop Hill **GB** (HWC) 61 Xb 37
Ord **GB** (HGL) 13 Ua 6
Ordhead **GB** (GRP) 17 Xc 5
Ordie **GB** (GRP) 16 Xa 6
Ordiquish **GB** (GRP) 16 Wf 3
Ore **GB** (ESX) 72 Ad 43
Oreham Common **GB** (WSX) 71 Ze 43
Oreton **GB** (SHS) 52 Xc 34
Orford **GB** (CHS) 44 Xc 28
Orford **GB** (SUF) 57 Bd 36
Orgreave **GB** (SFS) 45 Yb 32
Orinsay **GB** (HGL) 11 Td 120
Oristown **IRL** (MT) 90 Tb 26
Orleton **GB** (HWC) 52 Xb 35
Orleton **GB** (HWC) 52 Xd 35
Orlingbury **GB** (NRH) 54 Zb 34
Ormesby **GB** (CLE) 37 Ye 21
Ormesby **GB** (NOR) 49 Bd 32
Ormesby Saint Margaret **GB** (NOR) 49 Be 32
Ormiclate Castle **GB** (HGL) 12 Sd 5
Ormiscaig **GB** (HGL) 7 Uc 1
Ormiston **GB** (LOT) 26 Xa 13
Ormsaigmore **GB** (HGL) 18 Tf 8
Ormskirk **GB** (LCS) 38 Xa 27
Orphir **GB** (ORK) 6 Wf 115
Orpington **GB** (GRL) 64 Aa 40
Orrell **GB** (GRM) 38 Xb 27
Orroland **GB** (DAG) 29 Wa 20
Orsett **GB** (ESS) 64 Ac 39
Orslow **GB** (SFS) 45 Xe 32
Orston **GB** (NTS) 46 Za 31
Orton **GB** (CUB) 35 Xc 22
Orton **GB** (NRH) 54 Zb 34
Orton Longueville **GB** (CBS) 55 Ze 33
Orton-on-the-Hill **GB** (LEC) 54 Yc 33
Orwell **GB** (CBS) 55 Zf 36
Osbaldeston **GB** (LCS) 38 Xc 26
Osbaston **GB** (LEC) 54 Yd 33
Osbaston **GB** (SHS) 44 Xc 32
Osbournby **GB** (LIN) 47 Zd 31
Oscroft **GB** (CHS) 44 Xb 29
Ose **GB** (HGL) 13 Td 4
Osgathorpe **GB** (LEC) 46 Yd 32
Osgodby **GB** (NOY) 37 Zd 23
Oskaig **GB** (HGL) 13 Tf 4
Osmaston **GB** (DSH) 45 Yb 31
Osmington **GB** (DOS) 68 Xd 45
Osmotherley **GB** (NOY) 36 Ye 22
Osnaburgh, Dairsie or **GB** (FIF) 22 Xa 10
Ossett **GB** (WYO) 39 Yc 26
Ossington **GB** (NTS) 46 Za 29
Ostend **GB** (ESS) 65 Ae 39
Oswaldkirk **GB** (NOY) 37 Yf 23
Oswaldtwistle **GB** (LCS) 38 Xd 26
Oswestry **GB** (SHS) 44 Wf 31
Otford **GB** (KEN) 64 Ab 41
Otham **GB** (KEN) 65 Ad 41
Othery **GB** (SOM) 68 Xa 42
Otley **GB** (SUF) 57 Bb 36
Otley **GB** (WYO) 39 Yb 25
Otterbourne **GB** (HAS) 70 Yd 42
Otterburn **GB** (NHL) 33 Xe 17
Otterburn **GB** (NOY) 39 Xe 24
Otterburn Camp **GB** (NHL) 33 Xe 17
Otterden Place **GB** (KEN) 65 Ae 41
Otter Ferry **GB** (STC) 23 Ue 12
Ottershaw **GB** (SUR) 63 Zc 40
Otterswick **GB** (SHL) 2 Yf 105
Otterton **GB** (DEV) 67 We 45
Ottery Saint Mary **GB** (DEV) 67 We 44
Ottringham **GB** (HUS) 41 Zf 26
Oughterard **IRL** (GAL) 87 Qe 28
Oughtibridge **GB** (SOY) 39 Yc 28
Oughtiv **IRL** (KER) 102 Pf 37
Oughtmama **IRL** (CRE) 92 Qf 30
Ouldnish **GB** (HGL) 10 Ta 2
Oulart **IRL** (WEX) 101 Td 33
Oulley **IRL** (CAV) 89 Se 24
Oulston **GB** (NOY) 37 Yf 23
Oulton **GB** (CUB) 31 We 19
Oulton **GB** (SFS) 45 Xf 31
Oulton **GB** (SUF) 57 Be 34
Oulton Broad **GB** (SUF) 57 Be 34
Oulton Street **GB** (NOR) 49 Bb 32
Oundle **GB** (NRH) 55 Zd 34
Ousby **GB** (CUB) 35 Xc 20
Ousdale **GB** (HGL) 9 Wc 120
Ousden **GB** (SUF) 56 Ad 35
Ouseburn **GB** (NOY) 40 Ye 24
Ouston **GB** (DUR) 33 Yc 19
Outeragh **IRL** (TIP) 99 Sa 34
Outertown **GB** (ORK) 6 We 115
Outgate **GB** (CUB) 34 Xa 22
Outhgill **GB** (CUB) 35 Xd 22
Out Rawcliffe **GB** (LCS) 38 Xa 25
Outwell **GB** (NOR) 56 Ab 33
Outwood **GB** (WYO) 39 Yd 26
Ovenden **GB** (WYO) 39 Ya 26
Over **GB** (AVN) 61 Xc 39
Over **GB** (CBS) 55 Aa 35
Overbury **GB** (HWC) 53 Xf 36
Over Compton **GB** (DOS) 68 Xc 43
Over Haddon **GB** (DSH) 45 Yb 29
Over Kellet **GB** (LCS) 38 Xb 24
Over Kiddington **GB** (OXS) 62 Yd 37
Over Norton **GB** (OXS) 62 Yc 37
Overseal **GB** (DSH) 45 Yc 32
Over Silton **GB** (NOY) 36 Ye 22
Overstone **GB** (NRH) 54 Zb 35
Overstrand **GB** (NOR) 49 Bc 31
Over Stratton **GB** (SOM) 68 Xb 43
Over Tabley **GB** (CHS) 44 Xd 29
Overton **GB** (CLW) 44 Xa 30
Overton **GB** (CLW) 44 Xa 31
Overton **GB** (GRP) 17 Xe 5
Overton **GB** (HAS) 70 Ye 41
Overton **GB** (LCS) 38 Xa 24
Overton **GB** (SHS) 52 Xb 34
Overtown **GB** (STC) 25 Wa 14
Over Wallop **GB** (HAS) 69 Yc 41
Over Whitacre **GB** (WWH) 53 Yc 33
Over Worton **GB** (OXS) 62 Yd 37
Oving **GB** (BUS) 63 Za 37
Oving **GB** (WSX) 70 Zb 43
Ovingham **GB** (NHL) 33 Ya 19
Ovington **GB** (DUR) 36 Yb 21
Ovington **GB** (ESS) 56 Ad 36
Ovington **GB** (HAS) 70 Ye 42
Ovington **GB** (NHL) 33 Ya 19
Ovington **GB** (NOR) 56 Af 33
Owenbeg **IRL** (SLI) 81 Ra 23
Owenduff **IRL** (MAY) 86 Qa 25
Owenmore Bridge **IRL** (MAY) 86 Qc 26
Ower **IRL** (GAL) 87 Qe 28
Owermoigne **GB** (DOS) 68 Xe 44
Owlesbury **GB** (HAS) 70 Ye 42
Owlswick **GB** (BUS) 63 Za 38
Owmby-by-Spital **GB** (LIN) 47 Zd 28
Owning **IRL** (KLK) 100 Sd 34
Owston **GB** (LEC) 54 Za 33
Owston Ferry **GB** (HUS) 40 Zb 28
Owstwick **GB** (HUS) 41 Zf 26
Oxborough **GB** (NOR) 56 Ad 33
Oxcombe **GB** (LIN) 47 Zf 29
Oxen End **GB** (ESS) 64 Ac 37
Oxenholme **GB** (CUB) 35 Xb 23
Oxenhope **GB** (WYO) 39 Ya 26
Oxen Park **GB** (CUB) 34 Wf 23
Oxenwood **GB** (WIL) 62 Yc 40
Oxford **GB** (OXS) 62 Ye 38
Oxhill **GB** (WWH) 54 Yc 36
Oxley's Green **GB** (ESX) 72 Ac 43
Oxnam **GB** (BOR) 32 Xd 16
Oxshott **GB** (SUR) 64 Zd 41
Oxspring **GB** (SOY) 39 Yc 27
Oxted **GB** (SUR) 71 Zf 41
Oxton **GB** (BOR) 26 Xb 14
Oxton **GB** (CHS) 44 Wf 28
Oxton **GB** (NTS) 46 Yf 30
Oxwich **GB** (WGL) 59 Vf 39
Oxwick **GB** (NOR) 48 Ae 32
Oykel Bridge **GB** (HGL) 8 Vb 1
Oyne **GB** (GRP) 17 Xc 5
Oysterhaven **IRL** (COR) 104 Rd 38

P

Pabail Iarach **GB** (HGL) 11 Te 119
Pabail Uarach **GB** (HGL) 11 Te 119
Packington **GB** (LEC) 46 Yd 32
Padanaram **GB** (TYS) 22 Xa 9
Padbury **GB** (BUS) 63 Za 37
Paddlesworth **GB** (KEN) 73 Ba 42
Paddock Wood **GB** (KEN) 72 Ac 41
Paddolgreen **GB** (SHS) 44 Xb 31
Padeswood **GB** (CLW) 44 Wf 30
Padiham **GB** (LCS) 39 Xe 26
Padside **GB** (NOY) 39 Yb 24
Padstow **GB** (CNW) 75 Va 45
Paglesham Churchend **GB** (ESS) 65 Ae 39
Paglesham Eastend **GB** (ESS) 65 Ae 39
Pagnell, Hooton **GB** (SOY) 40 Ye 27
Paible **GB** (HGL) 10 Sd 3
Paible **GB** (HGL) 11 Sf 1
Paignton **GB** (DEV) 76 Wc 46
Pailton **GB** (WWH) 54 Ye 34
Painestown **IRL** (MT) 90 Td 27
Painscastle **GB** (POW) 52 We 36
Painshawfield **GB** (NHL) 33 Ya 19
Painswick **GB** (GLS) 61 Xe 38
Paisley **GB** (STC) 24 Vd 13
Pakefield **GB** (SUF) 57 Be 34
Pakenham **GB** (SUF) 56 Ae 35
Palace **IRL** (WEX) 100 Tb 34
Palace House **GB** (HAS) 69 Yd 44
Palatine **IRL** (CLW) 94 Ta 31
Pale **GB** (GWY) 43 Wc 31
Palestine **GB** (HAS) 69 Yc 41
Palgrave **GB** (SUF) 57 Ba 34
Pallas **IRL** (OFF) 94 Sc 29
Pallasbeg House **IRL** (LIM) 99 Rd 33
Pallas Cross **IRL** (TIP) 93 Sa 32
Pallas Grean **IRL** (LIM) 99 Rd 33
Pallas Grean (New) **IRL** (LIM) 99 Rd 33
Pallaskenry **IRL** (LIM) 98 Ra 33
Pallastown House **IRL** (COR) 104 Rc 38
Pallatomish **IRL** (MAY) 80 Qb 23
Palmerston **IRL** (DUB) 95 Td 28
Palmerstown House **IRL** (GAL) 93 Re 30
Palnackie **GB** (DAG) 31 Wa 19
Palnure **GB** (DAG) 30 Vd 19
Palterton **GB** (DSH) 46 Ye 29
Pamber End **GB** (HAS) 63 Yf 41
Pamber Green **GB** (HAS) 63 Yf 41
Pamphill **GB** (DOS) 69 Xf 44
Pampisford **GB** (CBS) 56 Ab 36
Pancrasweek **GB** (DEV) 66 Vd 44
Pandy **GB** (CLW) 44 We 31
Pandy **GB** (GWE) 60 Xa 37
Pandy **GB** (POW) 51 Wc 33
Pandy Tudur **GB** (CLW) 43 Wb 30
Panfield **GB** (ESS) 65 Ad 37
Pangbourne **GB** (BKS) 63 Yf 40
Pangdean **GB** (WSX) 71 Zf 43
Pannal **GB** (NOY) 39 Yc 25
Pant **GB** (SHS) 44 Wf 32
Panteg **GB** (DYF) 58 Uf 37
Pant Glâs **GB** (GWY) 42 Ve 30
Pantgwyn **GB** (DYF) 50 Vc 36
Pant-lasau **GB** (WGL) 59 Wa 38
Pant Mawr **GB** (POW) 51 Wb 34
Panton **GB** (LIN) 47 Ze 29
Pant-pastynog **GB** (CLW) 43 Wd 30
Pantperthog **GB** (GWY) 51 Wa 33
Pant-y-dwr **GB** (POW) 51 Wd 34
Pant-y-ffridd **GB** (POW) 51 We 33
Pantyffynnon **GB** (WGL) 60 Wa 38
Panxworth **GB** (NOR) 49 Bc 33
Papple **GB** (LOT) 26 Xc 13
Papplewick **GB** (NTS) 46 Ye 30
Papworth Everard **GB** (CBS) 55 Zf 35
Par **GB** (CNW) 75 Vb 46
Paradise House **IRL** (CRE) 92 Qf 32
Parbold **GB** (LCS) 38 Xb 27
Parbrook **GB** (SOM) 68 Xc 42
Parcllyn **GB** (DYF) 50 Vc 36
Parc Seymour **GB** (GWE) 61 Xa 39
Pardshaw **GB** (CUB) 34 Wc 21
Parham **GB** (SUF) 57 Bc 35
Parkacunna **IRL** (COR) 99 Rd 35
Parkend **GB** (CUB) 34 Wf 20
Parkend **GB** (GLS) 61 Xc 38
Park End **GB** (NHL) 33 Xe 18
Parkeston **GB** (ESS) 57 Bb 37
Parkgate **GB** (CHS) 45 Xe 29
Parkgate **GB** (DAG) 31 Wc 17
Park Gate **GB** (HAS) 70 Ye 43
Parkgate **GB** (SUR) 71 Ze 41
Parkham **GB** (DEV) 66 Ve 43
Parkhouse **GB** (GWE) 61 Xb 38
Park House **IRL** (LAO) 94 Se 30
Park House **IRL** (MT) 94 Sf 28
Parkhurst **GB** (IOW) 70 Ye 44
Parkmill **GB** (WGL) 59 Vf 39
Parkmore **IRL** (GAL) 92 Ra 29
Parknatomogard **IRL** (DON) 77 Rd 19
Park Place **IRL** (LGF) 88 Sb 27
Parley Cross **GB** (DOS) 69 Ya 44
Parracombe **GB** (DEV) 66 Wa 41
Parrog **GB** (DYF) 58 Va 36
Parson Drove **GB** (CBS) 55 Aa 33
Partanure Lodge **IRL** (LGF) 88 Sa 27
Partington **GB** (GRM) 44 Xd 28
Partney **GB** (LIN) 47 Aa 29
Parton **GB** (CUB) 34 Wc 21
Parton **GB** (DAG) 30 Vf 18
Partrishaw **GB** (POW) 60 Wf 37
Partry **IRL** (MAY) 87 Qe 26
Parwich **GB** (DSH) 45 Yb 30
Passage East **IRL** (WTF) 100 Ta 35
Passage West **IRL** (COR) 104 Rd 37
Passenham **GB** (NRH) 54 Za 36
Passfield **GB** (HAS) 70 Zb 42
Pass if you can **IRL** (WMT) 89 Se 27
Passingford Bridge **GB** (ESS) 64 Ab 39
Paston **GB** (NOR) 49 Bc 31
Patch **IRL** (GAL) 87 Rc 27
Patcham **GB** (ESX) 71 Zf 43
Patching **GB** (WSX) 71 Zd 43
Patchole **GB** (DEV) 66 Wa 42
Patchway **GB** (AVN) 61 Xc 39
Pateley Bridge **GB** (NOY) 39 Yb 24
Path **GB** (TYS) 21 Wc 11
Pathhead **GB** (FIF) 26 Wf 12
Pathhead **GB** (LOT) 26 Xa 13
Pathhead **GB** (STC) 30 Ve 16
Patmore Heath **GB** (HTS) 64 Aa 37
Patna **GB** (STC) 30 Vd 16
Patney **GB** (WIL) 62 Ya 41
Patrick **GB** (STC) 25 Ve 13
Patrick **GBM** 29 Vb 23
Patrick **IRL** (WMT) 89 Sd 27
Patrick Brompton **GB** (NOY) 36 Yc 23
Patrickswell **IRL** (LIM) 98 Rb 33
Patridge Green **GB** (WSX) 71 Ze 43
Patrington **GB** (HUS) 41 Zf 26
Patterdale **GB** (CUB) 35 Xa 21
Pattingham **GB** (SFS) 53 Xe 34
Pattiswick **GB** (ESS) 65 Ad 37
Paul **GB** (CNW) 74 Uc 48
Paull **GB** (HUS) 41 Ze 26
Paulstown **IRL** (KLK) 100 Sf 32
Paulton **GB** (AVN) 68 Xc 41
Pauperhaugh **GB** (NHL) 33 Ya 17
Pavenham **GB** (BFS) 55 Zc 35
Pawlett **GB** (SOM) 68 Wf 41
Pawston **GB** (NHL) 27 Xe 15
Paxford **GB** (GLS) 53 Yb 36
Paxhill Park **GB** (WSX) 71 Zf 42
Paxton **GB** (BOR) 27 Xf 14
Payhembury **GB** (DEV) 67 We 44
Peacehaven **GB** (ESX) 71 Zf 44
Peachley **GB** (HWC) 53 Xe 35
Peafield **IRL** (COR) 99 Re 36
Peak **IRL** (GAL) 93 Rd 29
Peake **IRL** (COR) 104 Rb 37
Peake Dale **GB** (DSH) 45 Ya 29
Peak Forest **GB** (DSH) 45 Yb 29
Peakirk **GB** (CBS) 55 Ze 33
Pearsie **GB** (TYS) 22 Wf 8
Peasedown Saint John **GB** (AVN) 68 Xd 41
Peasemore **GB** (BKS) 62 Yd 40
Peasenhall **GB** (SUF) 57 Bc 35
Pease Pottage **GB** (WSX) 71 Ze 42
Peaslake **GB** (SUR) 71 Zd 41
Peasmarsh **GB** (ESX) 72 Ae 43
Peaston **GB** (LOT) 26 Xa 13
Peastonbank **GB** (LOT) 26 Xa 13
Peathill **GB** (GRP) 17 Xf 2
Peat Inn **GB** (FIF) 22 Xa 11
Peatling Magna **GB** (LEC) 54 Yf 33
Peatling Parva **GB** (LEC) 54 Yf 33
Peaton **GB** (SHS) 52 Xb 34
Pebble Combe **GB** (SUR) 71 Ze 41
Pebble Hill **IRL** (KIL) 95 Tc 28
Pebmarsh **GB** (ESS) 56 Ae 37
Pebworth **GB** (HWC) 53 Yb 36
Pecket Well **GB** (WYO) 39 Xf 26
Peckforton **GB** (CHS) 44 Xb 30
Peckleton **GB** (LEC) 54 Ye 33
Pedmore **GB** (WMD) 53 Xf 34
Pedwell **GB** (SOM) 68 Xb 42
Peebles **GB** (BOR) 26 Wd 15
Peel **GBM** 29 Vb 23
Peesweep, The **GB** (STC) 24 Vd 14
Pegswood **GB** (NHL) 33 Yc 17
Peinchorran **GB** (HGL) 13 Tf 5
Peinlich **GB** (HGL) 13 Te 3
Pelcomb Cross **GB** (DYF) 58 Uf 38
Peldon **GB** (ESS) 65 Af 38
Pelletstown Cross Roads **IRL** (MT) 90 Tc 28
Pelsall **GB** (WMD) 53 Ya 33
Pelutho **GB** (CUB) 34 Wd 20
Pelynt **GB** (CNW) 75 Vc 46
Pembray **GB** (DYF) 59 Ve 38
Pembridge **GB** (HWC) 52 Xa 35
Pembroke **GB** (DYF) 58 Va 39
Pembroke Dock **GB** (DYF) 58 Va 38
Pembury **GB** (KEN) 72 Ab 42
Penally **GB** (DYF) 58 Vb 39
Penare **GB** (CNW) 75 Vb 47
Penarth **GB** (SGL) 60 Wf 40
Pen-bont **GB** (DYF) 51 Wa 34
Penbryn **GB** (DYF) 50 Vd 36
Pencader **GB** (DYF) 59 Ve 36
Pencaitland **GB** (LOT) 26 Xa 13
Pencarreg **GB** (DYF) 50 Vf 36
Pencelli **GB** (POW) 60 We 37
Pencil Hill **IRL** (COR) 98 Rc 35
Pen-clawdd **GB** (WGL) 59 Vf 39
Pencoed **GB** (MGL) 60 Wd 39
Pencombe **GB** (HWC) 52 Xc 35
Pencoyd **GB** (HWC) 61 Xb 37
Pencraig **GB** (POW) 43 Wd 32
Penderyn **GB** (MGL) 60 Wc 38
Pendine **GB** (DYF) 58 Vc 38
Pendlebury **GB** (GRM) 39 Xe 27
Pendleton **GB** (LCS) 38 Xd 25
Pendock **GB** (HWC) 61 Xe 37
Pendoggett **GB** (CNW) 75 Vb 45
Pendoylan **GB** (SGL) 60 Wd 40
Pendy's Cross Roads **IRL** (COR) 98 Rb 36
Penegoes **GB** (POW) 51 Wb 33
Penffordd **GB** (DYF) 58 Vb 37
Penfro = Pembroke **GB** (DYF) 58 Va 39
Pengenffordd **GB** (POW) 60 We 37
Pengorffwysfa **GB** (GWY) 42 Ve 28
Pengwern **GB** (CLW) 43 Wd 29
Penhallow **GB** (CNW) 74 Uf 47
Penhalvean **GB** (CNW) 74 Ue 47
Penhow **GB** (GWE) 61 Xa 39
Penhurst **GB** (ESX) 72 Ac 43
Penicuik **GB** (LOT) 26 We 14
Penifiler **GB** (HGL) 13 Te 4
Pen-llyn **GB** (GWY) 42 Vd 29
Peninver **GB** (STC) 28 Uc 16
Penisa'r Waun **GB** (GWY) 42 We 30
Penistone **GB** (SOY) 39 Yc 27
Penjerrick **GB** (CNW) 74 Uf 48
Penketh **GB** (CHS) 44 Xc 28
Penkill **GB** (STC) 30 Vb 17
Penkridge **GB** (SFS) 45 Xf 32
Penley **GB** (CLW) 44 Xa 31
Penllergaer **GB** (WGL) 59 Vf 39
Penllyn **GB** (SGL) 60 Wd 40
Penmachno **GB** (GWY) 43 Wb 30
Penmaenmawr **GB** (GWY) 43 Wa 29
Penmaenpool **GB** (GWY) 43 Wa 32
Penmark **GB** (SGL) 60 Wd 40
Penmon **GB** (GWY) 43 Vf 29
Penmorfa **GB** (GWY) 42 Vf 31
Penmynydd **GB** (GWY) 42 Ve 29
Penn **GB** (BUS) 63 Zb 39
Pennal **GB** (GWY) 51 Wa 33
Pennan **GB** (GRP) 17 Xe 2
Pennant **GB** (DYF) 50 Ve 35
Pennant **GB** (POW) 51 Wc 33
Pennant-Melangell **GB** (POW) 43 Wd 32
Pennerley **GB** (SHS) 52 Xa 33
Pennington **GB** (CUB) 34 Wf 23
Penn Street **GB** (BUS) 63 Zc 39
Penny Bridge **GB** (CUB) 34 Wf 23
Pennycross **GB** (STC) 18 Tf 10
Pennygown **GB** (STC) 18 Ua 9
Pennymoor **GB** (DEV) 67 Wc 43
Penparc **GB** (DYF) 50 Vc 36
Penparcau **GB** (DYF) 51 Vf 34
Penperlleni **GB** (POW) 60 Xa 38
Penpillick **GB** (CNW) 75 Vb 46
Penpoll **GB** (CNW) 75 Vc 46
Penpont **GB** (DAG) 31 Wb 17
Penrherber **GB** (DYF) 59 Vd 36
Penrhiw-llan **GB** (DYF) 50 Vd 36
Penrhiwpal **GB** (DYF) 50 Vd 36
Penrhos **GB** (GWE) 61 Xa 38
Penrhos **GB** (GWY) 42 Vc 29
Penrhyn Bay **GB** (GWY) 43 Wb 29
Penrhyn-coch **GB** (DYF) 51 Wa 34
Penrhyndeudraeth **GB** (GWY) 43 Vf 31
Penrhynside **GB** (GWY) 43 Wb 29
Penrice **GB** (WGL) 59 Ve 39
Penrith **GB** (CUB) 35 Xb 21
Penrose **GB** (CNW) 75 Va 46
Penruddock **GB** (CUB) 35 Xa 21
Penryn **GB** (CNW) 74 Uf 47
Pensarn **GB** (DYF) 59 Ve 37
Pen-sarn **GB** (GWY) 42 Ve 31
Pen-sarn **GB** (GWY) 42 Vf 32
Pensax **GB** (HWC) 52 Xd 35
Pensby **GB** (CHS) 44 Wf 28
Penselwood **GB** (SOM) 68 Xd 42
Pensford **GB** (AVN) 61 Xc 40
Pensham **GB** (HWC) 53 Xf 36
Penshurst **GB** (KEN) 71 Ab 41
Pensilva **GB** (CNW) 75 Vd 46
Pensylvania **IRL** (DON) 78 Sf 17
Pentewan **GB** (CNW) 75 Vb 47
Pentglas Hall **GB** (DYF) 59 Vd 36
Pentir **GB** (GWY) 42 Vf 29
Pentlepoir **GB** (DYF) 58 Vb 38
Pentney **GB** (NOR) 48 Ad 32
Penton Mewsey **GB** (HAS) 69 Yc 41
Pentraeth **GB** (GWY) 42 Ve 29
Pentre **GB** (CLW) 43 Wd 30
Pentre **GB** (CLW) 44 Wf 31
Pentre **GB** (POW) 43 Wd 32
Pentre **GB** (POW) 51 Wd 34
Pentre **GB** (SHS) 44 Xa 32
Pentre-bâch **GB** (DYF) 50 Vf 36
Pentrebach **GB** (MGL) 60 Wd 38
Pentre-bach **GB** (POW) 60 Wc 37
Pentrebach **GB** (WGL) 59 Vf 38
Pentre Berw **GB** (GWY) 42 Ve 29
Pentrecagal **GB** (DYF) 59 Vd 36
Pentre-celyn **GB** (CLW) 43 We 30
Pentre-celyn **GB** (POW) 51 Wc 33
Pentre-cwrt **GB** (DYF) 59 Vd 36
Pentre Dolav Honddu **GB** (POW) 51 Wd 36
Pentre-dwr **GB** (WGL) 59 Wa 39
Pentrefelin **GB** (CLW) 43 We 32
Pentrefelin **GB** (DYF) 59 Vf 37
Pentrefelin **GB** (GWY) 43 Wb 29
Pentrefoelas **GB** (CLW) 43 Wb 30
Pentre-galar **GB** (DYF) 58 Vc 37
Pentregat **GB** (DYF) 50 Vd 36
Pentre-Gwenlais **GB** (DYF) 59 Vf 38
Pentre Gwynfryn **GB** (GWY) 43 Vf 32
Pentreheyling **GB** (SHS) 52 Wf 33
Pentre-llwyn-llwyd **GB** (POW) 51 Wc 35
Pentre Isaf **GB** (CLW) 43 Wb 29
Pentre-llyn-cymmer **GB** (CLW) 43 Wc 30
Pentre'r beirdd **GB** (POW) 52 We 32
Pentre'r-felin **GB** (POW) 60 Wc 37
Pentre-tafarn-y-fedw **GB** (GWY) 43 Wb 30
Pentre-ty-gwyn **GB** (DYF) 59 Wb 36
Pentrich **GB** (DSH) 46 Yd 30
Pentridge **GB** (WIL) 69 Ya 43
Pen-twyn **GB** (GWE) 61 Xb 38
Pentyrch **GB** (MGL) 60 We 39
Penuwch **GB** (DYF) 51 Vf 35
Penwithick **GB** (CNW) 75 Vb 46
Penwyllt **GB** (POW) 60 Wc 38
Penybanc **GB** (DYF) 59 Vf 37
Pen-y-benglog **GB** (GWY) 43 Vf 30
Pen-y-bont **GB** (CLW) 44 We 32
Pen-y-bont **GB** (DYF) 59 Vd 37
Penybont **GB** (POW) 51 We 35
Penybontfawr **GB** (POW) 43 Wd 32
Pen-y-bryn **GB** (GWY) 43 Wa 32
Penycae **GB** (CLW) 44 Wf 31
Pen-y-cae **GB** (POW) 60 Wb 38
Pen-y-cae-mawr **GB** (GWE) 61 Xa 39
Pen-y-cefn **GB** (CLW) 43 We 29
Pen-y-clawdd **GB** (GWE) 61 Xb 38
Pen-y-coedcae **GB** (MGL) 60 Wd 39
Penycwm **GB** (DYF) 58 Uf 37
Pen-y-fai **GB** (MGL) 60 Wc 39
Pen-y-ffordd **GB** (CLW) 43 We 29
Penyffordd **GB** (CLW) 44 Wf 30
Pen-y-garn **GB** (DYF) 59 Vf 37
Pen-y-garnedd **GB** (GWY) 42 Ve 29
Penygarnedd **GB** (POW) 43 We 32
Penygraig **GB** (MGL) 60 Wd 39
Pen-y-groes **GB** (DYF) 59 Vf 38
Penygroes **GB** (GWY) 42 Ve 30
Pen-y-Park **GB** (HWC) 52 Wf 36
Pen-yr-heol **GB** (GWE) 61 Xb 38
Penysarn **GB** (GWY) 42 Ve 28
Pen-y-stryt **GB** (CLW) 44 We 30
Penzance **GB** (CNW) 74 Uc 48
Peopleton **GB** (HWC) 53 Xf 36
Peper Harow **GB** (SUR) 70 Zc 41
Peplow **GB** (SHS) 44 Xc 32
Pepperstown Cross Roads **IRL** (LOT) 90 Tc 25
Perivale **GB** (GRL) 64 Ze 39
Perlethorpe **GB** (NTS) 46 Yf 29

Norton – Perlethorpe (GB) (IRL) **129**

Perranarworthal GB (CNW) 74 Uf 47
Perranporth GB (CNW) 74 Uf 46
Perranuthnoe GB (CNW) 74 Ud 48
Perranzabuloe GB (CNW) 74 Uf 47
Perry GB (CBS) 55 Ze 35
Perry Barr GB (WMD) 53 Ya 33
Perry Green GB (HTS) 64 Aa 37
Pershall GB (SFS) 45 Xe 31
Pershore GB (HWC) 53 Xf 36
Pert GB (TYS) 22 Xc 8
Pertenhall GB (BFS) 55 Zd 35
Perth GB (TYS) 21 Wd 10
Perth House IRL (MT) 90 Tb 28
Perthy GB (SHS) 44 Xa 31
Perton GB (SFS) 53 Xe 33
Peterborough GB (CBS) 55 Ze 33
Peterburn GB (HGL) 7 Ub 2
Peterchurch GB (HWC) 52 Xa 36
Peterculter GB (GRP) 17 Xe 6
Peterhead GB (GRP) 17 Yb 3
Peterlee GB (DUR) 36 Ye 20
Petersfield GB (HAS) 70 Za 42
Peter's Green GB (HTS) 64 Ze 37
Peters Marland GB (DEV) 66 Vf 43
Peterstone Wentlooge GB (GWE) 60 Wf 39
Peterstow GB (HWC) 61 Xc 37
Peterswell IRL (GAL) 92 Rb 30
Peter Tavy GB (DEV) 76 Vf 45
Petham GB (KEN) 65 Ba 41
Pett GB (ESX) 72 Ae 43
Pettaugh GB (SUF) 57 Ba 35
Pettigo IRL (DON) 83 Sb 21
Pettinain GB (STC) 25 Wc 14
Petton GB (DEV) 67 Wd 42
Petton GB (SHS) 44 Xa 32
Petty GB (GRP) 17 Xd 4
Pettycur GB (FIF) 26 We 12
Pettymuick GB (GRP) 17 Xf 5
Petworth GB (WSX) 70 Zc 43
Pevensey GB (ESX) 72 Ac 44
Pewsey GB (WIL) 62 Yb 40
Philham GB (DEV) 66 Vd 43
Philiphaugen GB (BOR) 32 Xa 15
Philipstown IRL (LOT) 90 Td 26
Philleigh GB (CNW) 75 Va 47
Philpotstown IRL (MT) 90 Tb 27
Philpstoun GB (LOT) 25 Wc 13
Phoenix Green GB (HAS) 63 Za 41
Pica GB (CUB) 34 Wc 21
Piccadilly Corner GB (NOR) 57 Bc 34
Piccott's End GB (HTS) 63 Zd 38
Pickerells GB (ESS) 64 Ab 38
Pickering GB (NOY) 37 Zb 23
Picket Piece GB (HAS) 69 Yd 41
Pickford Green GB (WMD) 53 Yc 34
Pickhill GB (NOY) 36 Yd 23
Picklescott GB (SHS) 52 Xa 33
Pickmere GB (CHS) 44 Xd 29
Pickwell GB (DEV) 66 Ve 42
Pickworth GB (LEC) 47 Zc 32
Pickworth GB (LIN) 47 Zd 31
Picton GB (CHS) 44 Xa 29
Picton GB (NOY) 36 Yd 22
Piddinghoe GB (ESX) 71 Aa 44
Piddington GB (OXS) 63 Yf 37
Piddlehinton GB (DOS) 68 Xd 44
Piddletrenthide GB (DOS) 68 Xd 44
Pidley GB (CBS) 55 Zf 34
Piercebridge GB (DUR) 36 Yb 21
Piercetown IRL (WEX) 101 Td 35
Piercetown IRL (WMT) 89 Sc 27
Piercetown House IRL (MT) 90 Td 27
Pierowall GB (ORK) 5 Xa 113
Pigdon GB (NHL) 33 Yb 17
Pigeons, The IRL (WMT) 88 Sb 27
Pike IRL (TIP) 93 Rf 30
Pike, The IRL (WTF) 99 Sa 36
Pike, The IRL (WTF) 100 Sc 36
Pikehall GB (DSH) 45 Yb 30
Pike of Rush Hall IRL (LAO) 94 Sc 31
Pilgrims Hatch GB (ESS) 64 Ab 39
Pilham GB (LIN) 40 Zb 28
Pillerton Hersey GB (WWH) 54 Yc 36
Pillerton Priors GB (WWH) 54 Yc 36
Pilleth GB (POW) 52 Wf 35
Pilley Bailey GB (HAS) 69 Yc 44
Pilling GB (LCS) 38 Xa 25
Pilling Lane GB (LCS) 38 Xa 25
Pillmore IRL (COR) 104 Sa 37
Pilning GB (AVN) 61 Xc 39
Pilsbury GB (DSH) 45 Yb 30
Pilsdon GB (DOS) 68 Xb 44
Pilsgate GB (CBS) 55 Zd 33
Pilsley GB (DSH) 45 Yc 29
Pilsley GB (DSH) 46 Yd 30
Piltdown GB (ESX) 71 Aa 43
Pilton GB (DEV) 66 Vf 42
Pilton GB (NRH) 55 Zd 34
Pilton GB (SOM) 68 Xc 41
Piltown IRL (KLK) 100 Sd 34
Pimlico IRL (LAO) 94 Sf 31
Pimperne GB (DOS) 69 Xf 43
Pinchbeck GB (LIN) 47 Zf 32
Pinchbeck Bars GB (LIN) 47 Ze 32
Pinchbeck West GB (LIN) 47 Ze 32
Pinchmore IRL (WMT) 88 Sa 27
Pinfold GB (LCS) 38 Xa 27
Pinkneys Green GB (BKS) 63 Zb 39
Pinley Green GB (WWH) 53 Yb 35
Pinmore GB (STC) 30 Vb 17
Pinn GB (DEV) 67 We 44
Pinner GB (GRL) 64 Zd 39
Pinvin GB (HWC) 53 Xf 36
Pinwherry GB (STC) 30 Vb 18
Pinxton GB (DSH) 46 Ye 30
Pipe and Lyde GB (HWC) 52 Xb 36
Pipe Gate GB (SHS) 45 Xd 31
Pipe Ridware GB (SFS) 45 Ya 32
Piper's Inn GB (SOM) 68 Xb 42
Piperspool GB (CNW) 66 Vd 45
Pipewell GB (NRH) 54 Zb 34
Pirbright GB (SUR) 63 Zc 41
Pirnmill GB (STC) 23 Ud 15
Pirton GB (HTS) 55 Ze 37
Pirton GB (HWC) 53 Xe 36
Pishill GB (OXS) 63 Za 39
Pistyll GB (GWY) 42 Vd 31
Pit GB (DEV) 67 Wd 43
Pitagowan GB (TYS) 21 Wa 8
Pitcairngreen GB (TYS) 21 Wc 10
Pitchcombe GB (GLS) 61 Xe 38
Pitchcott GB (BUS) 63 Za 37
Pitchford GB (SHS) 52 Xb 33
Pitch Green GB (BUS) 63 Za 38
Pitcox GB (LOT) 26 Xc 13
Pitfichie GB (GRP) 17 Xc 5
Pitforthie GB (GRP) 22 Xe 7
Pitgrudy GB (HGL) 8 Vf 1
Pit House IRL (LAO) 94 Sc 31
Pitkevy GB (FIF) 26 We 11
Pitlessie GB (FIF) 21 Wf 11
Pitlochry GB (TYS) 21 Wb 8
Pitmedden GB (GRP) 17 Xe 4
Pitmuies GB (TYS) 22 Xb 9
Pitmunie GB (GRP) 17 Xc 5
Pitney GB (SOM) 68 Xb 42
Pitroddie GB (TYS) 21 We 10
Pitscottie GB (FIF) 22 Xa 11
Pitsford GB (NRH) 54 Za 35
Pitsford Hill GB (SOM) 67 We 42
Pitstone GB (BUS) 63 Zc 38
Pitstone Green GB (BUS) 63 Zc 38
Pittendreich GB (GRP) 16 Wd 3
Pittentrail GB (HGL) 8 Vf 1
Pittenweem GB (FIF) 26 Xb 11
Pitton GB (WIL) 69 Yb 42
Pityme GB (CNW) 75 Va 45
Pixey Green GB (SUF) 57 Bb 35
Place Newton GB (NOY) 37 Zc 24
Plains GB (STC) 25 Wa 13
Plaish GB (SHS) 52 Xb 33
Plaistow GB (WSX) 71 Zc 42
Plaitford GB (WIL) 69 Yc 43
Plas Gwynant GB (GWY) 43 Vf 30
Plasisaf GB (CLW) 43 We 29
Plas Isaf GB (CLW) 43 Wd 31
Plâs Llwyngwern GB (POW) 51 Wa 33
Plas Llysyn GB (POW) 51 Wc 33
Plas-rhiw-Saeson GB (POW) 51 Wc 33
Plastow Green GB (HAS) 63 Ye 40
Platt GB (ESX) 72 Ab 42
Platt GB (KEN) 64 Ab 41
Plawsworth GB (DUR) 33 Yc 20
Plaxtol GB (KEN) 64 Ab 41
Playden GB (ESX) 72 Ae 43
Playford GB (SUF) 57 Bb 36
Play Hatch GB (OXS) 63 Za 40
Playing Place GB (CNW) 74 Uf 47
Plealey GB (SHS) 52 Xa 33
Plean GB (CEN) 25 Wa 12
Pleasington GB (LCS) 38 Xc 26
Pleasley GB (DSH) 46 Ye 29
Plémont GBJ 73 Xe 53
Pleshey GB (ESS) 64 Ac 38
Plockton GB (HGL) 13 Uc 4
Plodstown IRL (WMT) 89 Se 27
Ploughfield GB (HWC) 52 Xa 36
Ploxgreen GB (SHS) 52 Xa 33
Pluck IRL (DON) 77 Sc 19
Pluckanes IRL (COR) 98 Rb 37
Pluckley GB (KEN) 72 Zc 41
Pluckley Thorne GB (KEN) 72 Ae 42
Plumbland GB (CUB) 34 We 20
Plumbridge GB (TYR) 83 Se 20
Plumley GB (CHS) 44 Xd 29
Plumpton GB (CUB) 35 Xb 20
Plumpton GB (ESX) 71 Zf 43
Plumpton GB (LCS) 38 Xa 26
Plumpton End GB (NRH) 54 Za 36
Plumpton Green GB (ESX) 71 Zf 43
Plumpton Head GB (CUB) 35 Xb 20
Plumstead GB (NOR) 49 Ba 31
Plumtree GB (NTS) 46 Yf 31
Plunkerstown Bridge IRL (KIL) 94 Ta 29
Plush GB (DOS) 68 Xd 44
Plwmp GB (DYF) 50 Vd 36
Plymouth GB (DEV) 76 Vf 46
Plympton GB (DEV) 76 Vf 46
Plymstock GB (DEV) 76 Vf 46
Plymtree GB (DEV) 67 Wd 44
Pockley GB (NOY) 37 Yf 23
Pocklington GB (HUS) 40 Zb 25
Pode Hole GB (LIN) 47 Ze 32
Podimore GB (SOM) 68 Xc 42
Podington GB (BFS) 55 Zc 35
Podmore GB (SFS) 45 Xe 31
Point IRL (LOT) 90 Td 24
Pointon GB (LIN) 47 Zd 31
Polbain GB (HGL) 7 Ud 120
Polbathic GB (CNW) 75 Ve 46
Polbeth GB (LOT) 25 Wc 13
Polchar, the GB (HGL) 15 Wb 6
Poldean GB (DAG) 31 Wd 17
Polebrooke GB (NRH) 55 Zd 34
Polegate GB (ESX) 72 Ab 44
Pole of Itlaw, the GB (GRP) 17 Xc 3
Polesworth GB (WWH) 53 Yc 33
Polglass GB (HGL) 7 Ue 120
Poling GB (WSX) 71 Zc 44
Polla GB (HGL) 4 Vb 118
Pollachar GB (HGL) 12 Sd 6
Pollagarraun IRL (MAY) 80 Qa 23
Pollagh IRL (GAL) 92 Ra 29
Pollagh IRL (KLK) 100 Ta 33
Pollagh IRL (OFF) 93 Sb 29
Pollanalty IRL (ROS) 87 Rb 26
Pollaphuca Cross Roads IRL (WKL) 95 Te 31
Pollboy IRL (CRE) 92 Rb 30
Pollboy IRL (GAL) 93 Re 29
Pollglass IRL (GAL) 88 Rd 27
Pollington GB (HUS) 40 Yf 26
Pollnabrone IRL (GAL) 92 Rc 28
Polloch GB (HGL) 19 Uc 8
Pollokshaws GB (STC) 25 Ve 14
Pollokshields GB (STC) 25 Ve 13
Pollrone IRL (KLK) 100 Sd 34
Polmassick GB (CNW) 75 Va 47
Polmont GB (CEN) 25 Wb 13
Polnessan GB (STC) 30 Vd 16
Polperro GB (CNW) 75 Vc 47
Polruan GB (CNW) 75 Vc 47
Polsham GB (SOM) 68 Xb 41
Polstead GB (SUF) 56 Af 36
Poltalloch GB (STC) 23 Uc 12
Poltimore GB (DEV) 67 Wd 44
Polton GB (GLS) 62 Ya 38
Polwarth GB (BOR) 27 Xd 14
Polyphant GB (CNW) 75 Vd 45
Polzeath GB (CNW) 75 Va 45
Pomeroy GB (TYR) 84 Ta 21
Ponde GB (POW) 60 We 36
Pondersbridge GB (CBS) 55 Zf 33
Ponders End GB (GRL) 64 Zf 39
Ponsanooth GB (CNW) 74 Uf 47
Pont Aber Glaslyn GB (GWY) 42 Vf 31
Pontamman GB (DYF) 59 Wa 38
Pontantwn GB (DYF) 59 Ve 38
Pontardawe GB (WGL) 59 Wa 38
Pontardulais GB (WGL) 59 Wa 38
Pontargothi GB (DYF) 59 Ve 37
Pontarsais GB (DYF) 59 Ve 37
Pont Creuddyn GB (DYF) 50 Vf 36
Pont Crugnant GB (POW) 51 Wc 33
Pont Cyfyng GB (GWY) 43 Wa 30
Pont Dolgarrog GB (GWY) 43 Wa 29
Pontefract GB (WYO) 40 Ye 26
Ponteland GB (NHL) 33 Yb 18
Ponterwyd GB (DYF) 51 Wa 34
Pontesbury GB (SHS) 52 Xa 33
Pontesford GB (SHS) 52 Xa 33
Pontfadog GB (CLW) 44 Wf 31
Pont-faen GB (DYF) 51 Vf 36
Pontfaen GB (DYF) 58 Va 37
Pont-faen GB (POW) 60 Wd 37
Pont Henri GB (DYF) 59 Ve 38
Ponthir GB (GWE) 60 Wf 39
Ponthirwaun GB (DYF) 50 Vc 36
Pontllanfraith GB (GWE) 60 We 39
Pontlliw GB (WGL) 59 Vf 38
Pont Llogel GB (POW) 51 Wd 32
Pontllyfni GB (GWY) 42 Vd 30
Pontlottyn GB (MGL) 60 We 38
Pontneddfechan GB (POW) 60 Wc 38
Pontoon IRL (MAY) 87 Qe 25
Pontrhydfendigaid GB (DYF) 51 Wa 35
Pont Rhyd-sarn GB (GWY) 43 Wb 31
Pont Rhyd-y-cyff GB (MGL) 60 Wc 39
Pont-rhyd-y-groes GB (DYF) 51 Wa 35
Pontrilas GB (HWC) 60 Xa 37
Pontrobert GB (POW) 51 We 32
Pont-rug GB (GWY) 42 Ve 30
Ponts Green GB (ESX) 72 Ac 43
Pontshill GB (HWC) 61 Xc 37
Pont-Siân GB (DYF) 50 Ve 36
Pontsticill GB (MGL) 60 Wd 38
Pont Walby GB (WGL) 60 Wc 38
Pontyates GB (DYF) 59 Ve 38
Pontyberem GB (DYF) 59 Ve 38
Pontybodkin GB (CLW) 44 Wf 30
Pontyclun GB (MGL) 60 Wd 39
Pontycymer GB (MGL) 60 Wc 39
Pont-y-pant GB (GWY) 43 Wa 30
Pontypool GB (GWE) 60 Wf 38
Pontypridd GB (MGL) 60 Wd 39
Poocksgreen GB (HAS) 69 Yd 43
Pool GB (WYO) 39 Yc 25
Poole GB (DOS) 69 Ya 44
Poole Keynes GB (GLS) 62 Ya 39
Poolewe GB (HGL) 7 Uc 2
Pooley Bridge GB (CUB) 35 Xb 21
Poolhill GB (GLS) 61 Xd 37
Pool of Muckhart GB (CEN) 25 Wc 11
Pool Quay GB (POW) 52 Wf 32
Pool Street GB (ESS) 56 Ad 36
Porchfield GB (IOW) 70 Yd 44
Poringland GB (NOR) 57 Bc 33
Porkellis GB (CNW) 74 Ue 48
Porlock GB (SOM) 67 Wc 41
Porlock Weir GB (SOM) 67 Wc 41
Porridgetown IRL (GAL) 87 Qe 28
Port IRL (DON) 82 Rb 20
Port IRL (LOT) 90 Te 25
Portacree GB (DAG) 28 Va 20
Portadown GB (ARG) 84 Td 22
Portaleen IRL (DON) 78 Se 17
Port Appin GB (STC) 19 Ud 9
Port Askaig GB (STC) 23 Tf 13
Portaterry GB (DOW) 85 Uc 22
Portavadie GB (STC) 23 Ue 13
Portavogie GB (DOW) 85 Ud 22
Port Banna GB (STC) 24 Uf 13
Portbury GB (AVN) 61 Xb 40
Port Carliste GB (CUB) 31 We 19
Port Charlotte GB (STC) 22 Td 14
Portchester GB (HAS) 70 Yf 43
Portclair GB (HGL) 14 Vc 5
Port Driseach GB (STC) 24 Ue 13
Porteenbeg IRL (MAY) 80 Pe 24
Port Ellen GB (STC) 22 Te 15
Port Elphinstone GB (GRP) 17 Xd 5
Portencross GB (STC) 24 Va 14
Port Erin GBM 29 Vb 24
Porterstown IRL (KIL) 95 Tc 29
Portesham GB (DOS) 68 Xc 44
Portessie GB (GRP) 16 Xa 2
Port e Vullen GBM 29 Vd 23
Port-Eynon GB (WGL) 59 Ve 39
Portfield Gate GB (DYF) 58 Uf 38
Portgate GB (DEV) 66 Ve 45
Port Glasgow GB (STC) 24 Vb 13
Portglenore GB (ANT) 79 Td 19
Portgordon GB (GRP) 16 Wf 2
Portgower GB (HGL) 9 Wb 120
Porth GB (MGL) 60 Wd 39
Porthallow GB (CNW) 74 Uf 48
Porthallow GB (CNW) 75 Vc 46
Porthcawl GB (MGL) 59 Wb 40
Port Henderson GB (HGL) 7 Ub 2
Porthgain GB (DYF) 58 Ue 37
Porthkerry GB (SGL) 60 We 40
Porthleven GB (CNW) 74 Ue 48
Porthllechog GB (GWY) 42 Vd 28
Porthmadog GB (GWY) 42 Vf 31
Porth Mellin GB (CNW) 74 Ue 48
Porthmeor GB (CNW) 74 Uc 47
Porth Navas GB (CNW) 74 Uf 48
Porthpean GB (CNW) 75 Vb 47
Porthtowan GB (CNW) 74 Ue 47
Porthyrhyd GB (DYF) 59 Vf 38
Porthyrhyd GB (DYF) 59 Wa 36
Porth y waen GB (SHS) 44 Wf 32
Portincaple GB (STC) 24 Va 12
Portinnisherrich GB (STC) 24 Ue 11
Port Isaac GB (CNW) 75 Vb 45
Portishead GB (AVN) 61 Xb 40
Portknockie GB (GRP) 16 Xa 2
Portland IRL (TIP) 93 Re 30
Portland Park IRL (GAL) 93 Re 30
Port Laoise IRL (LAO) 94 Se 30
Portlaw IRL (WTF) 100 Se 35
Portlethen GB (GRP) 17 Xf 6
Portlethen Village GB (GRP) 17 Xf 6
Portloe GB (CNW) 75 Va 47
Port Logan GB (DAG) 28 Va 20
Portloman IRL (WMT) 89 Sd 27
Portmagee IRL (KER) 96 Pd 37
Portmahomack GB (HGL) 9 Wb 1
Portmarnock IRL (DUB) 95 Tf 28
Port Mholair GB (HGL) 11 Tf 119
Port Mòr GB (HGL) 18 Te 7
Portmore GB (HAS) 69 Yc 44
Port Mulgrave GB (NOY) 37 Zb 21
Portnacroish GB (STC) 19 Ud 9
Portnahaven GB (STC) 22 Tc 14
Portnakilly IRL (MAY) 86 Qa 26
Portnalong GB (HGL) 13 Td 5
Portnaluchaig GB (HGL) 18 Ua 7
Portnancon GB (HGL) 4 Vb 117
Portnashangan IRL (WMT) 89 Sd 27
Portnoo IRL (DON) 77 Rd 19
Portobello GB (LOT) 26 Wf 13
Portobello House IRL (ROS) 88 Re 25
Port of Menteith GB (CEN) 25 Ve 11
Port of Ness GB (HGL) 11 Te 118
Port Omna = Portumna IRL (GAL) 93 Re 30
Porton GB (WIL) 69 Yb 42
Portpatrick GB (DAG) 28 Uf 19
Portquin GB (CNW) 75 Va 45
Portraine IRL (DUB) 95 Tf 28
Port Ramsay GB (STC) 19 Ud 9
Portreath GB (CNW) 74 Ue 47
Portree GB (HGL) 13 Te 4
Portrinarc IRL (LIM) 97 Qe 34
Portroe IRL (TIP) 93 Rd 31
Portrush GB (ANT) 79 Tc 17
Port Saint Mary GBM 29 Vb 24
Portsalon IRL (DON) 77 Sc 17
Port Seton, Cockenzie and GB (LOT) 26 Xa 13
Portskerra GB (HGL) 5 Wa 117
Portskewett GB (GWE) 61 Xb 39
Portslade-by-Sea GB (ESX) 71 Ze 44
Portslogan GB (DAG) 28 Uf 18
Portsmouth GB (HAS) 70 Yf 44
Port Soderick GBM 29 Vc 24
Portsonachan GB (STC) 19 Uf 10
Portsoy GB (GRP) 17 Xb 2
Portstewart GB (LDR) 78 Tb 17
Port Talbot GB (WGL) 59 Wb 39
Portuairk GB (HGL) 18 Te 8
Portumna IRL (GAL) 93 Re 30
Porturlin IRL (MAY) 80 Qb 23
Port Wemyss GB (STC) 22 Tc 14
Port William GB (DAG) 29 Vc 20
Poslingford GB (SUF) 56 Ad 36
Postbridge GB (DEV) 76 Wa 45
Postcombe GB (OXS) 63 Za 38
Postling GB (KEN) 72 Ba 42
Postwick GB (NOR) 49 Bc 33
Potarch GB (GRP) 17 Xc 6
Potten End GB (HTS) 63 Zc 38
Potterhanworth GB (LIN) 47 Zd 29
Potterhanworth Booths GB (LIN) 47 Zd 29
Potter Higham GB (NOR) 49 Bd 32
Potterne GB (WIL) 62 Xf 41
Potterne Wick GB (WIL) 62 Ya 41
Potters Bar GB (HTS) 64 Ze 38
Potter's Crouch GB (HTS) 64 Zd 38
Potterspury GB (NRH) 54 Za 36
Potter Street GB (ESS) 64 Aa 38
Potterton GB (GRP) 17 Xf 5
Potto GB (NOY) 36 Ye 22
Potton GB (BFS) 55 Ze 36
Pottore IRL (LET) 88 Sa 24
Pott Row GB (NOR) 48 Ad 32
Pott Shrigley GB (CHS) 45 Xe 29
Poughill GB (CNW) 66 Vc 43
Poughill GB (DEV) 67 Wc 43
Poulanargid IRL (COR) 103 Ra 37
Poulavallan IRL (CRE) 92 Qf 30
Poulgorm Bridge IRL (KER) 96 Qe 37
Poulnacallee IRL (COR) 103 Qd 39
Poulnamucky IRL (TIP) 99 Sb 34
Poulshot GB (WIL) 62 Xf 40
Poulton-le-Fylde GB (LCS) 38 Xa 25
Pound Cross Roads IRL (COR) 104 Rc 37
Poundgate GB (ESX) 71 Aa 42
Pound Hill GB (WSX) 71 Ze 42
Poundon GB (BUS) 63 Yf 37
Poundsbridge GB (KEN) 71 Ab 42
Poundsgate GB (DEV) 76 Wb 45
Poundstock GB (CNW) 66 Vc 44
Poundtown Cross Roads IRL (WEX) 100 Ta 35
Powburn GB (NHL) 33 Ya 16
Powderham GB (DEV) 67 Wd 45
Powerstown IRL (TIP) 99 Sb 34
Powfoot GB (DAG) 31 We 19
Pow Green GB (HWC) 52 Xd 36
Powick GB (HWC) 53 Xe 35
Powler's Piece GB (DEV) 66 Ve 43
Powmill GB (TYS) 25 Wc 12
Poxwell GB (DOS) 68 Xd 45
Poyle GB (SUR) 63 Zc 40
Poyntington GB (DOS) 68 Xc 43
Poynton GB (CHS) 45 Xf 28
Poynton GB (SHS) 44 Xc 32
Poynton Green GB (SHS) 44 Xc 32
Poyntz Pass GB (ARG) 84 Td 23
Poystreet Green GB (SUF) 56 Af 35
Praa Sands GB (CNW) 74 Ud 48
Praze-an-Beeble GB (CNW) 74 Ue 47
Predannack Wollas GB (CNW) 74 Ue 49
Prees GB (SHS) 44 Xb 31
Preesall GB (LCS) 38 Xa 25
Prees Green GB (SHS) 44 Xc 31
Prees Higher Heath GB (SHS) 44 Xc 31
Preghane IRL (COR) 104 Rd 38
Prendwick GB (NHL) 33 Ya 16
Prengwyn GB (DYF) 50 Ve 36
Prenteg GB (GWY) 42 Vf 31
Prenton GB (CHS) 44 Wf 28
Prescot GB (MES) 44 Xb 28
Prescott GB (SHS) 44 Xa 32
Pressen GB (NHL) 27 Xe 15
Prestatyn GB (CLW) 43 Wd 28
Prestbury GB (CHS) 45 Xf 29
Presteigne GB (HWC) 52 Wf 35
Presthope GB (SHS) 52 Xc 33
Prestleigh GB (SOM) 68 Xc 42
Preston GB (BOR) 27 Xe 14
Preston GB (DOS) 68 Xd 45
Preston GB (ESX) 71 Zf 43
Preston GB (GLS) 62 Ya 38
Preston GB (HTS) 64 Ze 37
Preston GB (HUS) 41 Ze 26
Preston GB (HWC) 61 Xd 36
Preston GB (KEN) 65 Bb 41
Preston GB (LCS) 38 Xb 26
Preston GB (LEC) 55 Zb 33
Preston GB (NHL) 33 Yb 15
Preston GB (SUF) 56 Ae 36
Preston GB (WIL) 62 Ya 40
Preston Bagot GB (WWH) 53 Yb 35
Preston Bissett GB (BUS) 63 Yf 37
Preston Brockhurst GB (SHS) 44 Xb 32
Preston Brook GB (CHS) 44 Xc 29
Preston Candover GB (HAS) 70 Yf 42
Preston Capes GB (NRH) 54 Yf 35
Preston Deanery GB (NRH) 54 Za 35
Preston Gubbals GB (SHS) 44 Xb 32
Preston on the Hill GB (CHS) 44 Xc 29
Preston on Wye GB (HWC) 52 Xa 36
Prestonpans GB (LOT) 26 Xa 13
Preston-under-Scar GB (NOY) 36 Ya 23
Preston upon the Weald Moors GB (SHS) 44 Xd 32
Preston Wynne GB (HWC) 52 Xc 36
Prestwich GB (GRM) 39 Xe 27
Prestwick GB (NHL) 33 Yb 18
Prestwick GB (STC) 30 Vc 16
Prestwood GB (BUS) 63 Zb 38
Price Town GB (MGL) 60 Wc 39
Prickwillow GB (CBS) 56 Ac 34
Priddy GB (SOM) 68 Xb 41
Priest Hutton GB (LCS) 35 Xb 24
Priest Town IRL (TIP) 99 Sb 35
Priest Weston GB (SHS) 52 Wf 33
Primatepark IRL (LOT) 90 Te 26
Primatestown IRL (MT) 90 Td 27
Primethorpe GB (LEC) 54 Ye 33
Primrose Green GB (NOR) 49 Ba 32
Primrose Hill GB (CBS) 55 Aa 34
Princes Gate GB (DYF) 58 Vb 38
Princes Risborough GB (BUS) 63 Za 38
Princethorpe GB (WWH) 54 Yd 34
Princetown GB (DEV) 76 Wa 45
Prior Muir GB (FIF) 22 Xb 11
Prior's Frome GB (HWC) 52 Xc 36
Priors Hardwick GB (WWH) 54 Ye 35
Priors Marston GB (WWH) 54 Ye 35
Priory Wood GB (HWC) 52 Wf 36
Priston GB (AVN) 61 Xd 40
Privett GB (HAS) 70 Yf 42
Prixford GB (DEV) 66 Vf 42
Proaig GB (STC) 23 Tf 14
Probus GB (CNW) 75 Va 47
Proncy GB (HGL) 8 Vf 1
Prospect Hill IRL (NIR) 83 Sb 23
Prospect House IRL (LAO) 94 Se 30
Prosped IRL (MAY) 86 Qc 26
Prospeet House IRL (OFF) 93 Sb 28
Prospect Lodge IRL (TIP) 93 Sb 31
Prosperous IRL (KIL) 95 Tb 29
Proudstown IRL (MT) 90 Tc 27
Prudhoe GB (NHL) 33 Ya 19
Puckaun IRL (TIP) 93 Re 31
Puckeridge GB (HTS) 64 Aa 37
Puckington GB (SOM) 68 Xa 43
Pucklechurch GB (AVN) 61 Xd 40
Puddington GB (CHS) 44 Wf 29
Puddington GB (DEV) 67 Wc 43
Puddledock GB (NOR) 57 Ba 34
Puddletown GB (DOS) 68 Xd 44
Pudleston GB (HWC) 52 Xc 35
Pudsey GB (WYO) 39 Yc 26
Puits-Léoville GBJ 73 Xe 53
Pulborough GB (WSX) 71 Zc 43
Pulford GB (CHS) 44 Xa 30
Pulham GB (DOS) 68 Xd 43
Pulham Market GB (NOR) 57 Bb 34
Pulham Saint Mary GB (NOR) 57 Bb 34
Pulloxhill GB (BFS) 55 Zd 36
Pulverbatch GB (SHS) 52 Xa 33
Pumpherston GB (LOT) 25 Wc 13
Pumsaint GB (DYF) 51 Wa 36
Punch Bowl IRL (GAL) 92 Rb 30
Puncheston GB (DYF) 58 Va 37
Punchestown House IRL (KIL) 95 Tc 29
Puncknowle GB (DOS) 68 Xc 44
Purbrook GB (HAS) 70 Yf 43
Purfleet GB (ESS) 64 Ab 40
Puriton GB (SOM) 68 Xa 41
Purleigh GB (ESS) 65 Ad 38
Purley GB (GRL) 64 Zf 40
Purley on Thames GB (BKS) 63 Yf 40
Purlogue GB (SHS) 52 Wf 34
Purse Caundle GB (DOS) 68 Xd 43
Purslow GB (SHS) 52 Xa 34
Purston Jaglin GB (WYO) 40 Yd 26
Purton GB (GLS) 61 Xd 38
Purton GB (WIL) 62 Ya 39
Purton Stoke GB (WIL) 62 Ya 39
Pury End GB (NRH) 54 Za 36
Pusey GB (OXS) 62 Yd 39
Putley GB (HWC) 52 Xc 36
Putsham GB (SOM) 67 We 41
Puttenham GB (SUR) 70 Zb 41
Putterham GB (HTS) 63 Zb 38
Puttock End GB (ESS) 56 Ad 36
Pwll GB (DYF) 59 Ve 38
Pwllcrochan GB (DYF) 58 Uf 38
Pwllgloyw GB (POW) 60 Wd 37
Pwllheli GB (GWY) 42 Vd 31
Pwllmeyric GB (GWE) 61 Xb 39
Pwll-y-glaw GB (WGL) 59 Wb 39
Pyecombe GB (WSX) 71 Zf 43
Pye Corner GB (GWE) 60 Wf 39
Pyle GB (IOW) 70 Ye 45
Pyle GB (WGL) 60 Wb 39
Pylle GB (SOM) 68 Xc 42
Pymore GB (CBS) 56 Ab 34
Pyrford GB (SUR) 63 Zc 41
Pyrton GB (OXS) 63 Yf 39
Pytchley GB (NRH) 54 Zb 34
Pyworthy GB (DEV) 66 Vd 44

Q

Quabbs GB (SHS) 52 We 34
Quadring GB (LIN) 47 Ze 31
Quadring Eaudike GB (LIN) 47 Zf 31
Quainton GB (BUS) 63 Za 37
Quakers Cross Roads IRL (COR) 103 Qf 39
Quarley GB (HAS) 69 Yc 41
Quarndon GB (DSH) 46 Yc 31
Quarr Hill GB (IOW) 70 Ye 44
Quarrier's Homes GB (STC) 24 Vc 13
Quarrington Hill GB (DUR) 36 Yd 20
Quarry Bank GB (WMD) 53 Xf 34
Quarry Cross Roads IRL (COR) 103 Rb 38
Quarry Lodge IRL (KER) 97 Qe 36
Quarrymount IRL (GAL) 87 Ra 27
Quarrywood GB (GRP) 16 Wd 3
Quarter GB (STC) 25 Vf 14
Quatford GB (SHS) 53 Xd 34
Quatt GB (SHS) 53 Xd 34
Quay IRL (WTF) 99 Sa 36
Quebec GB (DUR) 36 Yb 20
Quedgeley GB (GLS) 61 Xe 38
Queen Adelaide GB (CBS) 56 Ab 34
Queenborough GB (KEN) 65 Ae 40
Queen Camel GB (SOM) 68 Xc 42
Queen Charlton GB (AVN) 61 Xc 40
Queensbury GB (WYO) 39 Ya 26
Queensferry GB (CLW) 44 Wf 29
Queensferry GB (LOT) 26 Wd 13
Queen Street GB (KEN) 72 Ac 41
Queenzieburn GB (STC) 25 Vf 13
Quendale GB (SHL) 3 Yd 109
Quendon GB (ESS) 64 Ab 37
Queniborough GB (LEC) 46 Yf 32
Quenmore GB (LCS) 38 Xb 24
Querrin IRL (CRE) 91 Qc 33
Quethiock GB (CNW) 75 Vd 46
Quidenham GB (NOR) 57 Af 34
Quidhampton GB (HAS) 70 Ye 41
Quilquox GB (GRP) 17 Xf 4
Quilty IRL (CRE) 91 Qd 32
Quilty IRL (CRE) 97 Qb 33
Quina Brook GB (SHS) 44 Xb 31
Quine's Hill GBM 29 Vc 24
Quinn IRL (CRE) 92 Ra 32
Quinton GB (NRH) 54 Za 35
Quintrell Downs GB (CNW) 74 Uf 46
Quoditch GB (DEV) 66 Ve 44
Quoig GB (TYS) 21 Wa 10
Quorn, Quorndon GB (LEC) 46 Yf 32
Quorndon (Quorn) GB (LEC) 46 Yf 32
Quothquan GB (STC) 25 Wc 15
Quoyloo GB (ORK) 6 We 114
Qutwood GB (SUR) 71 Zf 41

R

Raby GB (CHS) 44 Wf 29
Race End IRL (DON) 77 Sb 18
Rachub GB (GWY) 43 Vf 29
Rackenford GB (DEV) 67 Wc 43
Rackham GB (WSX) 71 Zc 43
Rackheath GB (NOR) 49 Bc 32
Racks GB (DAG) 31 Wc 18
Rackwick GB (ORK) 6 Wd 115
Radbourne GB (DSH) 45 Yc 31
Radcliff GB (NHL) 33 Yc 17
Radcliffe GB (GRM) 39 Xe 27
Radcliffe on Trent GB (NTS) 46 Yf 31
Radcot GB (OXS) 62 Yc 38
Raddery GB (HGL) 15 Vf 3
Raddicombe GB (DEV) 76 Wc 46
Radford Semele GB (WWH) 54 Yd 35
Radlett GB (HTS) 64 Ze 38
Radley GB (OXS) 63 Ye 38
Radstock GB (AVN) 68 Xd 41
Radstone GB (NRH) 54 Yf 36
Radway GB (WWH) 54 Yd 36
Radway Green GB (CHS) 45 Xe 30
Radwinter GB (ESS) 56 Ac 36
Radyr GB (SGL) 60 We 39
Raffin Cross IRL (MT) 90 Tb 26
Rafford GB (GRP) 16 Wc 3
Raford IRL (GAL) 92 Rc 29
Ragdale GB (LEC) 46 Yf 32
Raglan GB (GWE) 61 Xa 38
Ragnall GB (NTS) 46 Zb 29
Rahan Lodge IRL (OFF) 94 Sc 29
Raharney IRL (WMT) 89 Sf 27
Rahaval House IRL (WKL) 95 Tf 31
Raheely IRL (ROS) 88 Rd 25
Raheen IRL (COR) 104 Rb 38
Raheen IRL (DUB) 95 Td 29
Raheen IRL (GAL) 92 Rc 27
Raheen IRL (KER) 97 Qd 36
Raheen IRL (KLK) 100 Se 33
Raheen IRL (LAO) 94 Sd 31
Raheen IRL (WEX) 100 Tb 34
Raheen IRL (WMT) 89 Sb 28
Raheenagh IRL (LIM) 98 Qf 34
Raheenanisky IRL (LAO) 94 Se 30
Raheendoran Fonthill House IRL (CLW) 94 Ta 32
Raheenlusk IRL (WEX) 101 Te 33
Raheennahown House IRL (LAO) 94 Sf 31
Raheenroe IRL (COR) 103 Qc 39
Rahendrick IRL (MT) 89 Ta 26
Rahheenduff House IRL (LAO) 94 Se 31
Rainford GB (MES) 38 Xb 28
Rainhill GB (MES) 44 Xb 28
Rainow GB (CHS) 45 Xe 29
Rainton GB (NOY) 36 Yd 23
Rainworth GB (NTS) 46 Yf 30
Raisbeck GB (CUB) 35 Xc 22
Rait GB (TYS) 21 We 10
Raithby GB (LIN) 47 Zf 28
Raithby GB (LIN) 47 Aa 29
Rake GB (WSX) 70 Za 42
Rake Street IRL (MAY) 81 Qd 24
Raleagh IRL (CAV) 89 Sc 24
Raleigh House IRL (COR) 103 Qf 37
Raleighs Cross GB (SOM) 67 Wd 42
Ralian IRL (OFF) 94 Sc 29
Rallynakilla IRL (COR) 104 Re 37
Raloaghan IRL (MT) 90 Tb 25
Ralph Cross Roads IRL (WEX) 100 Ta 35
Ramasaig GB (HGL) 12 Tb 4
Rame GB (CNW) 74 Ue 48
Rame GB (CNW) 75 Ve 47
Ram Lane GB (KEN) 72 Zc 41
Ramogue IRL (LGF) 89 Sc 26
Rampark IRL (LOT) 90 Te 25
Rampisham GB (DOS) 68 Xc 44
Rampside GB (CUB) 38 We 24
Rampton GB (CBS) 55 Aa 35
Ramsbottom GB (GRM) 39 Xe 27
Ramsbury GB (WIL) 62 Yc 40
Ramsdean GB (HAS) 70 Za 43
Ramsden GB (OXS) 62 Yd 37
Ramsden Bellhouse GB (ESS) 65 Ac 39
Ramsden Heath GB (ESS) 65 Ac 39
Ramsey GB (CBS) 55 Zf 34
Ramsey GB (ESS) 57 Bb 37
Ramsey GBM 29 Vd 23
Ramseycleuch GB (BOR) 31 Wf 16
Ramsey Forty Foot GB (CBS) 55 Zf 34
Ramsey Hill IRL (COR) 104 Rb 39
Ramsey Mereside GB (CBS) 55 Zf 34
Ramsey Saint Mary's GB (CBS) 55 Zf 34
Ramsgate GB (KEN) 65 Bc 41
Ramsgill GB (NOY) 36 Yb 24
Ramsgrange IRL (WEX) 100 Ta 35
Ramshorn GB (SFS) 45 Ya 30
Ramsnest Common GB (SUR) 70 Zc 42
Ranamackan IRL (GAL) 93 Rd 30
Ranby GB (LIN) 47 Zf 29
Ranby GB (NTS) 46 Za 29
Randalstown GB (ANT) 84 Te 20
Randwick GB (GLS) 61 Xe 38
Ranfurly GB (STC) 24 Vc 13
Rangemore GB (SFS) 45 Yb 32
Rangeworthy GB (AVN) 61 Xd 39
Ranish GB (HGL) 11 Td 120
Rankiston GB (STC) 30 Vd 16
Ranks Green GB (ESS) 65 Ad 38
Ranrenagh IRL (CAV) 89 Se 25
Ranskill GB (NTS) 46 Yf 28
Ranton GB (SFS) 45 Xe 32
Ranworth GB (NOR) 49 Bc 32
Rapemills IRL (OFF) 93 Sa 30
Raphoe IRL (DON) 77 Sc 19
Rapness GB (ORK) 5 Xa 113
Rascalstreet IRL (COR) 98 Qe 35
Rascarrel GB (DAG) 29 Wa 20
Rasharkin GB (ANT) 79 Td 19
Rashedoge IRL (DON) 77 Sa 19
Raskelf GB (NOY) 37 Ye 24
Rassau GB (GWE) 60 We 38
Ratby GB (LEC) 54 Ye 33
Ratcliffe Culey GB (LEC) 54 Yc 33
Ratcliffe on the Wreake GB (LEC) 46 Yf 32
Ratesh IRL (GAL) 87 Qf 27
Rath IRL (OFF) 93 Rf 31

130 GB IRL Perranarworthal – Rath

Rath **IRL** (OFF) 93 Sb 30
Rathangán **IRL** (KIL) 94 Ta 29
Rathanny **IRL** (KER) 97 Qc 35
Rathbrack **IRL** (WMT) 89 Sd 27
Rathbrackan **IRL** (LGF) 89 Sc 26
Rathbran More **IRL** (MT) 90 Tc 26
Rathbrenan **IRL** (ROS) 88 Re 27
Rathbrist House **IRL** (LOT) 90 Tc 25
Rathcahill East **IRL** (LIM) 98 Qf 34
Rath Cain **IRL** (MT) 89 Ta 27
Ráth Caola = Rathkeale **IRL** (LIM) 98 Ra 33
Rathcardan **IRL** (TIP) 93 Sa 32
Rathclogh **IRL** (TIP) 99 Sb 33
Rathcoffey **IRL** (KIL) 95 Tb 28
Rathconellwood **IRL** (KIL) 94 Ta 30
Rathconnell Court **IRL** (WMT) 89 Se 27
Rathconor Coolteige Cross **IRL** (ROS) 88 Re 26
Rathconrath **IRL** (WMT) 89 Sc 27
Rathcool **IRL** (COR) 98 Ra 36
Rathcoole **GB** (ANT) 85 Ua 21
Rathcoole **IRL** (DUB) 95 Td 29
Rathcor **IRL** (LOT) 90 Te 25
Rathcore **IRL** (MT) 89 Ta 28
Rathcormack **IRL** (COR) 99 Re 36
Rathcroghan Cross Roads **IRL** (ROS) 88 Re 26
Rathcrony **IRL** (CRE) 92 Qf 32
Rathdangan **IRL** (WKL) 95 Tc 31
Rathdonnel House **IRL** (DON) 77 Sb 19
Rathdowney **IRL** (LAO) 94 Sc 31
Rathdrinagh Cross Roads **IRL** (MT) 90 Tc 27
Ráth Droma = Rathdrum **IRL** (WKL) 95 Te 31
Rathdrum **IRL** (WKL) 95 Te 31
Rathduane House **IRL** (COR) 98 Qf 36
Rathduff **IRL** (COR) 98 Rc 36
Rathea **IRL** (KER) 97 Qd 34
Ratheabban **IRL** (TIP) 93 Rf 30
Ratheenabrogue **IRL** (LAO) 94 Sd 31
Rathe House **IRL** (MT) 90 Tb 25
Rathen **GB** (GRP) 17 Ya 3
Rathermon **IRL** (SLI) 88 Rd 25
Rathescar Cross **IRL** (LOT) 90 Td 26
Rathfeigh **IRL** (MT) 90 Td 27
Rathflesk **IRL** (MT) 90 Tb 27
Rathfriland **GB** (DOW) 85 Tf 23
Rathfylane **IRL** (WEX) 101 Tb 34
Rathgarogue **IRL** (WEX) 100 Ta 34
Rathgire **IRL** (COR) 104 Re 37
Rathgormuck **IRL** (WTF) 100 Sd 35
Rathillet **GB** (FIF) 22 Wf 10
Rathkeale **IRL** (LIM) 98 Ra 33
Rathkeevin **IRL** (TIP) 99 Sb 34
Rathkenny **IRL** (MT) 90 Tc 26
Rathkenny House **IRL** (MT) 90 Tb 26
Rathlackan **IRL** (MAY) 81 Qe 23
Rathlee **IRL** (SLI) 81 Qf 23
Rath Luirc **IRL** (COR) 98 Rb 34
Rathmakelly **IRL** (LAO) 94 Sd 31
Rathmell **GB** (NOY) 39 Xe 24
Rathmelton **IRL** (DON) 77 Sc 18
Rathmines **IRL** (DUB) 95 Te 29
Rathmore **IRL** (KER) 98 Qe 36
Rathmore **IRL** (KIL) 95 Tc 29
Rathmore **IRL** (MAY) 81 Qd 24
Rathmore House **IRL** (LGF) 88 Sb 27
Rathmorgan **IRL** (COR) 98 Rc 34
Rathmorrel House **IRL** (KER) 97 Qb 34
Rathmoylan **IRL** (MT) 90 Tb 28
Rathmoyle House **IRL** (ROS) 88 Rd 26
Rathmullan **IRL** (DON) 78 Sc 18
Rathnageeragh **IRL** (WEX) 100 Ta 34
Rathnallog **IRL** (ROS) 88 Rd 26
Rathnamag **IRL** (MAY) 81 Qe 24
Rathnamuddagh House **IRL** (WMT) 89 Sd 28
Rathnatulleagh **IRL** (ROS) 88 Re 26
Rathneestin House **IRL** (LOT) 90 Tc 25
Rathnew **IRL** (WKL) 95 Tf 31
Rathniska **IRL** (MT) 89 Sf 26
Rathnure **IRL** (WEX) 101 Tb 33
Ratho **GB** (LOT) 26 Wd 13
Ratho Station **GB** (LOT) 26 Wd 13
Rathowen **IRL** (WMT) 89 Sc 27
Rathpeak **IRL** (ROS) 93 Rf 29
Rathrobin House **IRL** (OFF) 94 Sc 29
Rathruane **IRL** (COR) 103 Qc 39
Rathsallagh **IRL** (WKL) 95 Tb 30
Rathtroane **IRL** (MT) 95 Tb 28
Rathven **GB** (GRP) 16 Xa 2
Rathvilly **IRL** (CLW) 95 Tb 31
Rathwire **IRL** (WMT) 89 Sf 27
Ratley **GB** (WWH) 54 Yd 36
Ratlinghope **GB** (SHS) 52 Xa 33
Ratoath **IRL** (MT) 90 Td 27
Ratooragh **IRL** (COR) 102 Qc 39
Ratrass **IRL** (WMT) 89 Sf 27
Rattav **GB** (HGL) 6 We 117
Rattlesden **GB** (SUF) 56 Af 35
Rattoo House **IRL** (KER) 97 Qc 34
Rattray **GB** (TYS) 21 We 9
Raughton Head **GB** (CUB) 35 Xa 20
Raunds **GB** (NRH) 55 Zc 34
Ravenfield **GB** (SOY) 40 Ye 28
Ravenglass **GB** (CUB) 34 Wd 22
Raveningham **GB** (NOR) 57 Bd 33
Ravenscar **GB** (NOY) 37 Zd 22
Ravensdale **GBM** 29 Vc 23
Ravensdale **IRL** (LOT) 90 Td 24
Ravensden **GB** (BFS) 55 Zd 35
Ravenseat **GB** (NOY) 35 Xe 22
Ravenshead **GB** (NTS) 46 Yf 30
Ravensmoor **GB** (CHS) 44 Xc 30
Ravensthorpe **GB** (WYO) 39 Yc 26
Ravenstone **GB** (LEC) 46 Yd 32
Ravenstonedale **GB** (CUB) 35 Xd 22
Ravenstruther **GB** (STC) 25 Wb 14
Ravensworth **GB** (NOY) 36 Yb 22
Raw **GB** (NOY) 37 Zc 22
Rawcliffe **GB** (HUS) 40 Za 26
Rawcliffe Bridge **GB** (HUS) 40 Za 26
Rawdon **GB** (WYO) 39 Yb 25
Rawmarsh **GB** (SOY) 40 Yd 28
Rawreth **GB** (ESS) 65 Ad 39
Rawtenstall **GB** (LCS) 39 Xe 26
Ray **IRL** (DON) 77 Rf 18
Ray **IRL** (DON) 77 Sc 18
Raydon **GB** (SUF) 57 Af 36
Raylees **GB** (NHL) 33 Xf 17
Rayleigh **GB** (ESS) 65 Ad 39
Rayne **GB** (ESS) 65 Ad 37
Rea, Lough **IRL** (GAL) 92 Rc 29
Reacaslagh **IRL** (KER) 98 Qe 35
Reach **GB** (CBS) 56 Ab 35
Rea Cross Roads **IRL** (COR) 103 Qe 39
Read **GB** (LCS) 38 Xd 26
Reading **GB** (BKS) 63 Za 40
Reading Street **GB** (KEN) 72 Ae 42
Reaghstown **IRL** (LOT) 90 Tc 25
Reagill **GB** (CUB) 35 Xc 21
Reagrove **IRL** (COR) 104 Rd 38
Realtoge **IRL** (MT) 90 Tc 27
Reanagishagh **IRL** (CRE) 92 Qe 32
Reananerree **IRL** (COR) 103 Qf 37
Reanascreena **IRL** (COR) 103 Qf 39
Reanduff **IRL** (COR) 99 Rf 36
Rear Cross **IRL** (TIP) 99 Re 32
Rearquhar **GB** (HGL) 8 Vf 1
Rearsby **GB** (LEC) 46 Yf 32
Rearyvale House **IRL** (LAO) 94 Sd 30
Reaster **GB** (HGL) 6 We 117
Reawick **GB** (SHL) 2 Yd 107
Reay **GB** (HGL) 5 Wb 117
Recess **IRL** (GAL) 86 Qb 28
Rectory **IRL** (MOG) 83 Sf 24
Rectory **IRL** (TIP) 99 Sb 33
Rectory **IRL** (WMT) 89 Se 27
Redberth **GB** (DYF) 58 Vb 38
Redbourn **GB** (HTS) 63 Zd 38
Redbourne **GB** (HUS) 41 Zc 28
Redbridge **GB** (GRL) 64 Aa 39
Red Bridges **IRL** (DON) 82 Rf 21
Redbrook **GB** (GLS) 61 Xb 38
Redbrook Street **GB** (KEN) 72 Ae 42
Redburn **GB** (HGL) 15 Vd 2
Redburn **GB** (HGL) 15 Wb 3
Redcar **GB** (CLE) 37 Yf 21
Redcastle **GB** (HGL) 15 Vd 3
Redcastle **GB** (TYS) 22 Xc 9
Redcross **IRL** (WKL) 95 Tf 31
Red Dial **GB** (CUB) 34 Wf 20
Redding **GB** (CEN) 25 Wb 13
Redditch **GB** (HWC) 53 Ya 35
Rede **GB** (SUF) 56 Ad 35
Redenhall **GB** (NOR) 57 Bb 34
Redford **GB** (DUR) 36 Ya 20
Redford **GB** (TYS) 22 Xb 9
Redford **GB** (WSX) 70 Zb 42
Redgap **IRL** (DUB) 95 Td 29
Redgate **IRL** (WEX) 101 Td 34
Redgate Cross Roads **IRL** (LAO) 94 Sd 30
Redgrave **GB** (SUF) 57 Af 34
Redheugh **GB** (TYS) 22 Xa 8
Redhill **GB** (AVN) 61 Xb 40
Redhill **GB** (GRP) 17 Xd 6
Red Hill **GB** (HAS) 70 Za 43
Redhill **GB** (SHS) 52 Xd 32
Redhill **GB** (SUR) 71 Zf 41
Red Hill **GB** (WWH) 53 Yb 35
Redhills **IRL** (CAV) 89 Se 24
Redhouses **GB** (STC) 22 Te 14
Redisham **GB** (SUF) 57 Bd 34
Redland **GB** (AVN) 61 Xc 40
Redland **GB** (ORK) 5 Wf 114
Redlingfield **GB** (SUF) 57 Bb 35
Red Lodge **GB** (SUF) 56 Ac 35
Redlynch **GB** (SOM) 68 Xd 42
Redmarley D'Abitot **GB** (GLS) 61 Xd 37
Redmarshall **GB** (CLE) 36 Yd 21
Redmile **GB** (LEC) 46 Zb 31
Redmire **GB** (NOY) 36 Ya 23
Redmoor **GB** (CNW) 75 Vb 46
Rednal **GB** (SHS) 44 Xa 31
Red Oaks Hill **GB** (ESS) 56 Ab 36
Redpath **GB** (BOR) 26 Xc 15
Redpoint **GB** (HGL) 13 Ub 3
Red Post **GB** (CNW) 66 Vd 44
Red Post **GB** (DEV) 76 Wc 46
Red Roses **GB** (DYF) 58 Vc 38
Red Row **GB** (NHL) 33 Yc 17
Redruth **GB** (CNW) 74 Ue 47
Red Wharf Bay **GB** (GWY) 42 Ve 29
Redwick **GB** (AVN) 61 Xc 39
Redwick **GB** (GWE) 61 Xa 39
Redworth **GB** (DUR) 36 Yc 21
Reed **GB** (HTS) 55 Zf 36
Reedham **GB** (NOR) 57 Bd 33
Reedness **GB** (HUS) 40 Zb 26
Reef **GB** (HGL) 11 Ta 119
Reen **IRL** (KER) 103 Qc 37
Reenadisert Court **IRL** (COR) 103 Qd 38
Reenard **IRL** (KER) 96 Pe 37
Reenearagh **IRL** (KER) 102 Pe 38
Reenronee **IRL** (KER) 102 Qa 38
Reepham **GB** (LIN) 47 Zd 29
Reepham **GB** (NOR) 49 Ba 32
Reeth **GB** (NOY) 36 Ya 22
Reevanagh **IRL** (KLK) 94 Sf 32
Regaby **GBM** 29 Vd 22
Regil **GB** (AVN) 61 Xb 40
Regional Tech.College **IRL** (LOT) 90 Td 25
Regoul **GB** (HGL) 15 Wa 3
Reiff **GB** (HGL) 7 Ud 120
Reigate **GB** (SUR) 71 Ze 41
Reighton **GB** (NOY) 37 Ze 24
Reiss **GB** (HGL) 6 Wf 118
Rejerrah **GB** (CNW) 74 Uf 46
Relubbus **GB** (CNW) 74 Ud 48
Relugas **GB** (GRP) 15 Wb 3
Remenham **GB** (BKS) 63 Za 39
Remenham Hill **GB** (BKS) 63 Za 39
Remony **GB** (TYS) 20 Vf 9
Rempstone **GB** (NTS) 46 Yf 32
Rendcomb **GB** (GLS) 62 Ya 38
Rendham **GB** (SUF) 57 Bc 35
Renfrew **GB** (STC) 24 Vd 13
Renishaw **GB** (DSH) 46 Ye 29
Rennington **GB** (NHL) 33 Yb 16
Renton **GB** (STC) 24 Vc 13
Renwick **GB** (CUB) 35 Xc 20
Repton **GB** (DSH) 45 Yc 31
Rerrin **IRL** (COR) 102 Qb 39
Reservoir **IRL** (WTF) 100 Se 35
Resfon **GB** (BOR) 27 Xe 13
Resipole **GB** (HGL) 19 Ub 8
Resolven **GB** (POW) 60 Wb 38
Reswallie **GB** (TYS) 22 Xb 9
Retreat House **IRL** (OFF) 94 Sc 29
Rettendon **GB** (ESS) 65 Ad 39
Rettendon Place **GB** (ESS) 65 Ad 39
Retyn **GB** (CNW) 75 Va 46
Revesby **GB** (LIN) 47 Zf 30
Rew **GB** (DEV) 76 Wb 45
Rewe **GB** (DEV) 67 Wd 44
Reydon **GB** (SUF) 57 Bd 34
Reynalton **GB** (DYF) 58 Vb 38
Reynold's Town **IRL** (LOT) 90 Te 26
Reynoldston **GB** (WGL) 59 Ve 39
Rhadmad **GB** (DYF) 51 Vf 34
Rhain **GB** (HGL) 8 Vd 120
Rhandirmwyn **GB** (DYF) 51 Wb 36
Rhayader **GB** (POW) 51 Wc 35
Rhedyn **GB** (GWY) 42 Vc 31
Rheindown **GB** (HGL) 15 Vd 4
Rhelonie **GB** (HGL) 8 Vd 1
Rhemore **GB** (HGL) 18 Ua 9
Rhenigidale **GB** (HGL) 11 Tb 1
Rhes-y-cae **GB** (CLW) 44 We 29
Rhewl **GB** (CLW) 43 Wd 30
Rhewl **GB** (CLW) 44 We 31
Rhicarn **GB** (HGL) 7 Ue 119
Rhiconich **GB** (HGL) 4 Va 118
Rhicullen **GB** (HGL) 8 Ve 2
Rhigos **GB** (MGL) 60 Wc 38
Rhilochan **GB** (HGL) 8 Vf 120
Rhiroy **GB** (HGL) 7 Uf 1
Rhiw **GB** (GWY) 42 Vc 32
Rhiwbryfdir **GB** (GWY) 43 Wa 30
Rhiwderin **GB** (GWE) 60 Wf 39
Rhiwlas **GB** (CLW) 44 We 31
Rhiwlas **GB** (GWY) 42 Vf 29
Rhiwlas **GB** (GWY) 43 Wc 31
Rhode **IRL** (OFF) 94 Se 28
Rhodesia **GB** (NTS) 46 Za 29
Rhodes Minnis **GB** (KEN) 73 Ba 42
Rhondda **GB** (MGL) 60 Wd 39
Rhonehouse or Kelton Hill **GB** (DAG) 31 Wa 19
Rhoose **GB** (SGL) 60 Wd 40
Rhos **GB** (DYF) 59 Vd 37
Rhos **GB** (WGL) 59 Wb 38
Rhoscefnhir **GB** (GWY) 42 Ve 29
Rhoscolyn **GB** (GWY) 42 Vc 29
Rhoscrowther **GB** (DYF) 58 Uf 38
Rhosesmor **GB** (CLW) 44 We 29
Rhos-fawr **GB** (GWY) 42 Vd 31
Rhosgadfan **GB** (GWY) 42 Ve 30
Rhosgoch **GB** (GWY) 42 Vd 28
Rhos Hill **GB** (DYF) 58 Vc 36
Rhoshirwaun **GB** (GWY) 42 Vb 32
Rhoslan **GB** (GWY) 42 Ve 31
Rhoslefain **GB** (GWY) 50 Vf 33
Rhosllanerchrugog **GB** (CLW) 44 Wf 30
Rhosmaen **GB** (DYF) 59 Wa 37
Rhosmeirch **GB** (GWY) 42 Ve 29
Rhosneigr **GB** (GWY) 42 Vc 29
Rhôs-on-Sea **GB** (CLW) 43 Wb 29
Rhossili **GB** (WGL) 59 Ve 39
Rhosson **GB** (DYF) 58 Ue 37
Rhostryfan **GB** (GWY) 42 Ve 30
Rhostyllen **GB** (CLW) 44 Wf 30
Rhosybol **GB** (GWY) 42 Vd 28
Rhos-y-brithdir **GB** (POW) 43 We 32
Rhos-y-llan **GB** (GWY) 42 Vc 31
Rhôs-y-meirch **GB** (POW) 52 Wf 35
Rhu **GB** (STC) 24 Vb 12
Rhuallt **GB** (CLW) 43 Wd 29
Rhubodach **GB** (STC) 24 Uf 13
Rhuddlan **GB** (CLW) 43 Wd 29
Rhude Cross **GB** (CNW) 66 Vd 43
Rhue **GB** (HGL) 7 Ue 1
Rhugarbh **GB** (STC) 19 Ud 9
Rhulen **GB** (POW) 51 We 36
Rhunahaorine **GB** (STC) 23 Uc 14
Rhyd **GB** (GWY) 43 Vf 31
Rhyd **GB** (POW) 51 Wc 33
Rhydargaeau **GB** (DYF) 59 Ve 37
Rhydcymerau **GB** (DYF) 50 Vf 36
Rhydd **GB** (HWC) 53 Xe 36
Rhyd-Ddu **GB** (GWY) 42 Vf 30
Rhydding **GB** (WGL) 59 Wb 38
Rhŷd-foel **GB** (CLW) 43 Wc 29
Rhydlewis **GB** (DYF) 50 Vd 36
Rhydlios **GB** (GWY) 42 Vb 31
Rhydlydan **GB** (CLW) 43 Wc 30
Rhydolion **GB** (GWY) 42 Vc 32
Rhydowen **GB** (DYF) 50 Ve 36
Rhyd-Rosser **GB** (DYF) 50 Vf 35
Rhydspence **GB** (HWC) 52 Wf 36
Rhydtalog **GB** (CLW) 44 Wf 30
Rhydwyn **GB** (GWY) 42 Vc 28
Rhyd-y-clafdy **GB** (GWY) 42 Vd 31
Rhydycroesau **GB** (SHS) 44 Wf 31
Rhydyfelin **GB** (DYF) 51 Vf 34
Rhydyfelin **GB** (MGL) 60 We 39
Rhyd-y-fro **GB** (WGL) 59 Wa 38
Rhydymain **GB** (GWY) 43 Wb 32
Rhyd-y-meirch **GB** (GWE) 60 Wf 38
Rhydymwyn **GB** (CLW) 44 We 29
Rhyl **GB** (CLW) 43 Wd 29
Rhymney **GB** (MGL) 60 We 38
Rhynd **GB** (TYS) 21 Wd 10
Rhynie **GB** (GRP) 16 Xb 5
Rhynie **GB** (HGL) 9 Wa 2
Ribbesford **GB** (HWC) 53 Xe 34
Ribbleton **GB** (LCS) 38 Xc 26
Ribchester **GB** (LCS) 38 Xc 26
Riby **GB** (LIN) 41 Ze 27
Riccall **GB** (NOY) 40 Yf 25
Riccarton **GB** (STC) 24 Vc 15
Richards Castle **GB** (HWC) 52 Xb 35
Richfort **IRL** (LGF) 88 Sb 26
Rich Hill **GB** (ARG) 84 Tc 22
Richings Park **GB** (GRL) 63 Zc 40
Richmond **GB** (GRL) 64 Ze 40
Richmond **GB** (NOY) 36 Yb 22
Rickarton **GB** (GRP) 17 Xe 7
Rickford **GB** (AVN) 61 Xb 41
Rickinghall **GB** (SUF) 57 Af 34
Rickling **GB** (ESS) 56 Ab 37
Rickling Green **GB** (ESS) 64 Ab 37
Rickmansworth **GB** (HTS) 63 Zc 39
Riddell **GB** (BOR) 32 Xb 15
Riddings **GB** (DSH) 46 Yd 30
Riddlecombe **GB** (DEV) 66 Wa 43
Ridge **GB** (WIL) 69 Xf 42
Ridge Green **GB** (SUR) 71 Zf 41
Ridge Lane **GB** (WWH) 53 Yc 33
Ridgeway Cross **GB** (HWC) 53 Xd 36
Ridgewell **GB** (ESS) 56 Ad 36
Ridgmont **GB** (BFS) 55 Zc 36
Riding Mill **GB** (NHL) 33 Ya 19
Ridley **GB** (KEN) 64 Ab 40
Ridleywood **GB** (CLW) 44 Xa 30
Ridsdale **GB** (NHL) 33 Xf 18
Rienachait **GB** (HGL) 7 Ue 119
Rievaulx **GB** (NOY) 37 Yf 23
Rigg **GB** (DAG) 32 Wf 19
Rigg **GB** (HGL) 13 Tf 3
Rigmanden Park **GB** (CUB) 35 Xc 23
Rigsby **GB** (LIN) 47 Aa 29
Rigside **GB** (STC) 25 Wb 15
Rileyhill **GB** (SFS) 45 Yb 32
Rilla Mill **GB** (CNW) 75 Vd 45
Rimington **GB** (LCS) 39 Xe 25
Rimpton **GB** (SOM) 68 Xc 43
Rimswell **GB** (HUS) 41 Zf 26
Rinagry **IRL** (MAY) 87 Qe 24
Rinaston **GB** (DYF) 58 Va 37
Rinbrack **IRL** (MAY) 87 Qf 25
Ringabella House **IRL** (COR) 104 Re 38
Ringaskiddy **IRL** (COR) 104 Re 38
Ringford **GB** (DAG) 30 Vf 19
Ringmer **GB** (ESX) 71 Aa 43
Ringmore **GB** (DEV) 76 Wa 47
Ring's End **GB** (CBS) 55 Aa 33
Ringsfield **GB** (SUF) 57 Bd 34
Ringsfield Corner **GB** (SUF) 57 Bd 34
Ringshall **GB** (HTS) 63 Zc 38
Ringshall **GB** (SUF) 57 Af 36
Ringshall Stocks **GB** (SUF) 57 Af 36
Ringstead **GB** (NOR) 48 Ad 31
Ringstead **GB** (NRH) 55 Zc 34
Ringstown **IRL** (LAO) 94 Sd 30
Ringville **IRL** (COR) 104 Rd 38
Ringville **IRL** (WTF) 100 Sc 36
Ringwood **GB** (HAS) 69 Yb 43
Ringwood House **IRL** (KLK) 100 Ta 34
Ringwould **GB** (KEN) 73 Bc 41
Rinmore **GB** (GRP) 16 Xa 5
Rinnafarna **IRL** (ROS) 88 Sa 25
Rinnananny **IRL** (MAY) 87 Qf 24
Rinville **IRL** (GAL) 92 Ra 29
Ripe **GB** (ESX) 71 Aa 43
Ripley **GB** (DSH) 46 Yc 30
Ripley **GB** (HAS) 69 Yb 44
Ripley **GB** (NOY) 39 Yc 24
Ripley **GB** (SUR) 63 Zd 41
Riplingham **GB** (HUS) 41 Zc 26
Ripon **GB** (NOY) 36 Yc 24
Rippingale **GB** (LIN) 47 Zd 31
Ripple **GB** (HWC) 53 Xe 36
Ripple **GB** (KEN) 65 Bc 41
Ripponden **GB** (WYO) 39 Ya 26
Risabus **GB** (STC) 22 Te 15
Risbury **GB** (HWC) 52 Xc 35
Risby **GB** (HUS) 41 Zc 27
Risby **GB** (SUF) 56 Ad 35
Risca **GB** (GWE) 60 Wf 39
Rise **GB** (HUS) 41 Ze 25
Risegate **GB** (LIN) 47 Ze 31
Riseley **GB** (BKS) 63 Za 40
Rishangles **GB** (SUF) 57 Ba 35
Rishton **GB** (LCS) 38 Xd 26
Rishworth **GB** (WYO) 39 Ya 27
Risley **GB** (CHS) 44 Xc 28
Risley **GB** (DSH) 46 Ye 31
Risplith **GB** (NOY) 39 Yc 24
Rispond **GB** (HGL) 4 Vc 117
Rivar **GB** (WIL) 62 Yc 40
Rivenhall **GB** (ESS) 65 Ad 38
River Bank **GB** (CBS) 56 Ab 35
River Bridge **GB** (SOM) 68 Xa 41
Riverchapel **IRL** (WEX) 101 Te 33
Riverdale House **IRL** (WMT) 89 Sf 27
Riverquarter **IRL** (KLK) 100 Se 35
Riverstick **IRL** (COR) 104 Rd 38
Riverstown **IRL** (SLI) 82 Rd 24
Riverstown **IRL** (TIP) 93 Sa 30
Riverstown House **IRL** (KIL) 94 Sf 30
River View **IRL** (TIP) 93 Re 31
Rivington **GB** (LCS) 38 Xc 27
Roachtown **IRL** (MT) 89 Sf 26
Roade **GB** (NRH) 54 Za 36
Roads **IRL** (KER) 96 Pf 36
Roadside **GB** (HGL) 6 Wd 117
Roadside of Catterline **GB** (GRP) 22 Xe 7
Roadside of Kinneff **GB** (GRP) 22 Xe 7
Roadstown **IRL** (LOT) 90 Te 25
Roadwater **GB** (SOM) 67 Wd 42
Roag **GB** (HGL) 12 Tc 4
Roath **GB** (SGL) 60 Wf 40
Robbersbush **IRL** (WMT) 89 Sf 27
Robeen Cross Roads **IRL** (MAY) 87 Qe 26
Robert's Cross Roads **IRL** (WTF) 99 Sc 36
Roberton **GB** (BOR) 32 Xa 16
Roberton **GB** (STC) 31 Wb 15
Robertsbridge **GB** (ESX) 72 Ac 43
Robertstown **IRL** (KIL) 95 Tb 29
Robertstown Cross Roads **IRL** (MT) 90 Tb 26
Roberttown **GB** (WYO) 39 Yb 26
Robeston Cross **GB** (DYF) 58 Uf 38
Robeston Wathen **GB** (DYF) 58 Vb 38
Robin Hood **GB** (DSH) 45 Yc 29
Robin Hood **GB** (WYO) 39 Yc 26
Robin Hood's Bay **GB** (NOY) 37 Zc 22
Robins **GB** (WSX) 70 Zb 42
Robinson's Cross Roads **IRL** (MT) 90 Td 27
Robinstown **IRL** (MT) 89 Ta 26
Robinstown **IRL** (MT) 90 Tb 27
Roborough **GB** (DEV) 66 Vf 43
Roborough **GB** (DEV) 76 Vf 46
Roby Mill **GB** (LCS) 38 Xb 27
Rocester **GB** (SFS) 45 Yb 31
Roch **GB** (DYF) 58 Uf 37
Rochdale **GB** (GRM) 39 Xf 27
Roche **GB** (CNW) 75 Vb 46
Rochester **GB** (KEN) 65 Ac 40
Rochester **GB** (NHL) 32 Xe 17
Rochestown **IRL** (KLK) 100 Sf 35
Rochestown **IRL** (TIP) 99 Sa 34
Rochestown **IRL** (WEX) 100 Ta 34
Rochford **GB** (ESS) 65 Ae 39
Rochford **GB** (HWC) 52 Xc 35
Rochfortbridge **IRL** (WMT) 94 Se 28
Rock **GB** (CNW) 75 Va 45
Rock **GB** (GWE) 60 We 38
Rock **GB** (HWC) 53 Xd 34
Rock **GB** (NHL) 33 Yb 16
Rock, The **GB** (TYR) 84 Tb 21
Rock, The **IRL** (MOG) 83 Sf 23
Rockbeare **GB** (DEV) 67 Wd 44
Rockbourne **GB** (HAS) 69 Ya 43
Rockbrook House **IRL** (KLK) 94 Se 32
Rockchapel **IRL** (COR) 98 Qf 35
Rockcliffe **GB** (CUB) 32 Wf 19
Rockcliffe **GB** (DAG) 31 Wb 19
Rockcorry **IRL** (MOG) 89 Sf 24
Rock Ferry **GB** (CHS) 44 Wf 28
Rockfield **GB** (GWE) 61 Xb 38
Rockfield **GB** (HGL) 9 Wb 2
Rockfield **IRL** (ROS) 88 Re 27
Rockfield **IRL** (SLI) 82 Rc 24
Rockfield Bridge **IRL** (KER) 97 Qc 36
Rockfield House **IRL** (KER) 97 Qc 36
Rockfield House **IRL** (LIM) 98 Rc 33
Rockfield House **IRL** (WKL) 95 Tf 31
Rockford House **IRL** (OFF) 93 Sa 31
Rockhampton **GB** (AVN) 61 Xc 39
Rockhead **GB** (CNW) 75 Vb 45
Rockhill **IRL** (LIM) 98 Rb 34
Rockingham **GB** (NRH) 54 Zb 33
Rocking Stone **IRL** (DON) 77 Re 18
Rockland Saint Peter **GB** (NOR) 56 Af 33
Rocklawn House **IRL** (GAL) 92 Ra 29
Rockley **GB** (WIL) 62 Yb 40
Rockmills **IRL** (COR) 99 Rd 35
Rockstown House **IRL** (LIM) 98 Rc 33
Rockvale House **IRL** (CRE) 92 Ra 30
Rockview House **IRL** (WMT) 89 Sf 27
Rockwell College **IRL** (TIP) 99 Sa 34
Rockwell End **GB** (BUS) 63 Za 39
Rockwell Green **GB** (SOM) 67 We 43
Rodd **GB** (HWC) 52 Wf 35
Roddam **GB** (NHL) 33 Ya 16
Rodden **GB** (DOS) 68 Xc 45
Rode **GB** (SOM) 68 Xe 41
Rodeen **IRL** (ROS) 88 Rf 25
Rodeheath **GB** (CHS) 45 Xe 29
Rode Heath **GB** (CHS) 45 Xe 30
Rodel **GB** (HGL) 10 Ta 2
Roden **GB** (SHS) 44 Xc 32
Rodington **GB** (SHS) 52 Xc 32
Rodley **GB** (GLS) 61 Xd 38
Rodmarton **GB** (GLS) 61 Xf 38
Rodmersham **GB** (KEN) 65 Ae 41
Rodney Stoke **GB** (SOM) 68 Xb 41
Rodsley **GB** (DSH) 45 Yb 31
Roebuck, Appleton **GB** (NOY) 40 Ye 25
Roecliffe **GB** (NOY) 40 Yd 24
Roevehagh **IRL** (GAL) 92 Ra 29
Roewen **GB** (GWY) 43 Wa 29
Rogart **GB** (HGL) 8 Vf 120
Rogate **GB** (WSX) 70 Za 42
Rokeby Hall **IRL** (LOT) 90 Td 26
Roker **GB** (TAW) 33 Yd 19
Rollesby **GB** (NOR) 49 Bd 32
Rolleston **GB** (LEC) 54 Za 33
Rolleston **GB** (NTS) 46 Za 30
Rolleston **GB** (SFS) 45 Yc 31
Rolston **GB** (HUS) 41 Zf 25
Rolvenden **GB** (KEN) 72 Ad 42
Rolvenden Layne **GB** (KEN) 72 Ad 42
Romaldkirk **GB** (DUR) 36 Xf 21
Romanby **GB** (NOY) 36 Yd 22
Romannobridge **GB** (BOR) 26 Wd 14
Romansleigh **GB** (DEV) 67 Wb 43
Romford **GB** (GRL) 64 Aa 39
Romiley **GB** (GRM) 45 Xf 28
Romney Street **GB** (KEN) 64 Ab 41
Romsey **GB** (HAS) 69 Yd 42
Romsley **GB** (HWC) 53 Xf 34
Romsley **GB** (SHS) 53 Xe 34
Ronague **GBM** 29 Vb 24
Roo **IRL** (GAL) 92 Ra 30
Rookhope **GB** (DUR) 35 Xf 20
Rookley **GB** (IOW) 70 Ye 45
Rooks Bridge **GB** (SOM) 68 Xa 41
Roos **GB** (HUS) 41 Zf 26
Roosebeck **GB** (CUB) 38 Wf 24
Rooskagh **IRL** (ROS) 88 Rf 28
Roosky **IRL** (MAY) 87 Qf 24
Roosky **IRL** (MAY) 87 Rb 24
Roosky Upper **IRL** (DON) 77 Sc 20
Rootpark **GB** (STC) 25 Wc 14
Ropley **GB** (HAS) 70 Yf 42
Ropley Dean **GB** (HAS) 70 Yf 42
Ropsley **GB** (LIN) 47 Zc 31
Rora **GB** (GRP) 17 Ya 3
Rorrington **GB** (SHS) 52 Wf 33
Ros, The **GB** (DYF) 58 Va 38
Rosberry House **IRL** (KIL) 95 Tb 29
Roscomáin = Roscommon **IRL** (ROS) 88 Re 27
Roscommon **IRL** (ROS) 88 Re 27
Roscomroe Cott **IRL** (OFF) 93 Sb 30
Ros Cre = Roscrea **IRL** (TIP) 93 Sb 31
Roscrea **IRL** (TIP) 93 Sb 31
Rosduff **IRL** (LGF) 89 Sc 25
Rose **GB** (CNW) 74 Uf 46
Rose Ash **GB** (DEV) 67 Wb 43
Rosebank **GB** (STC) 25 Wa 14
Rosebush **GB** (DYF) 58 Vb 37
Rosedale Abbey **GB** (NOY) 37 Za 22
Roseden **GB** (NHL) 33 Ya 16
Rosefield **GB** (HGL) 15 Wa 3
Rosegarland House **IRL** (WEX) 101 Tb 35
Rose Greene **GB** (ESS) 65 Ae 37
Rosehearty **GB** (GRP) 17 Xf 2
Rosehill **GB** (SHS) 44 Xc 31
Rose Hill **IRL** (COR) 104 Rd 37
Roseisle **GB** (GRP) 9 Wd 2
Rosemarket **GB** (DYF) 58 Va 38
Rosemarkie **GB** (HGL) 15 Vf 3
Rosemary Lane **GB** (DEV) 67 We 43
Rosenallis **IRL** (LAO) 94 Sd 30
Rosepool **GB** (DYF) 58 Uf 38
Rosetta **GB** (ANT) 85 Ua 21
Rosewell **GB** (LOT) 26 Wf 13
Roseworthy **GB** (CNW) 74 Ud 47
Rosgill **GB** (CUB) 35 Xb 21
Roshven **GB** (HGL) 19 Ub 7
Roskhill **GB** (HGL) 12 Tc 4
Rosley **GB** (CUB) 34 Wf 20
Roslin **GB** (LOT) 26 Wf 13
Rosliston **GB** (DSH) 45 Yc 32
Ros Mhic Thriúin = New Ross **IRL** (WEX) 100 Ta 34
Rosmore Bridge **IRL** (GAL) 93 Re 30
Rosmult **IRL** (TIP) 99 Sa 32
Rosnakill **IRL** (DON) 77 Sb 17
Rosneath **GB** (STC) 24 Vb 12
Ross **GB** (DAG) 29 Vf 20
Ross **GB** (NHL) 27 Yb 15
Ross **GB** (TYS) 20 Wa 10
Ross **IRL** (CRE) 97 Qa 33
Ross **IRL** (LOT) 90 Tc 25
Ross **IRL** (MAY) 81 Qe 23
Ross **IRL** (MT) 89 Se 26
Rossanure **IRL** (CRE) 92 Rc 31
Rossarell **IRL** (MOG) 84 Ta 23
Rossbeg **IRL** (DON) 77 Rc 20
Ross Behy **IRL** (KER) 97 Qa 36
Rossbrin **IRL** (COR) 103 Qd 39
Rosscahill **IRL** (GAL) 87 Qe 28
Ross Carbery **IRL** (COR) 103 Qf 39
Rosses Point **IRL** (SLI) 82 Rc 23
Rossestown **IRL** (TIP) 93 Sb 32
Rossett **GB** (CLW) 44 Xa 30
Rossgeir **IRL** (DON) 78 Sd 19
Ross House **IRL** (MT) 89 Se 26
Ross House **IRL** (OFF) 94 Sc 29
Rossie Ochill **GB** (TYS) 21 Wd 11
Rossilybeg **IRL** (DON) 82 Rf 21
Rossinver **IRL** (LET) 82 Rf 22
Rosskeen **GB** (HGL) 8 Ve 2
Rosslare **IRL** (WEX) 101 Td 35
Rosslea **GB** (FER) 83 Se 23
Rossmanagher House **IRL** (CRE) 92 Rb 32
Rossmore **IRL** (COR) 103 Qf 37
Rossmore **IRL** (COR) 103 Ra 38
Rossmore College **IRL** (COR) 104 Re 37
Rossnacaheragh **IRL** (COR) 102 Qc 39
Rossnegrena **IRL** (COR) 103 Qc 38
Rossnowlagh Lower **IRL** (DON) 82 Re 21
Ross-on-Wye **GB** (HWC) 61 Xc 37
Ross Port **IRL** (MAY) 80 Qb 23
Rosstemple **IRL** (LIM) 98 Rb 34
Ross West **IRL** (MAY) 87 Qe 25
Rostellan **IRL** (COR) 104 Re 37
Roster **GB** (HGL) 9 We 118
Rostherne **GB** (CHS) 44 Xd 28
Rosthwaite **GB** (CUB) 34 Wf 21
Rostrevor **GB** (DOW) 90 Te 24
Rosturk **IRL** (MAY) 86 Qb 25
Rosyth **GB** (FIF) 26 Wd 12
Rothbury **GB** (NHL) 33 Ya 17
Rotherfield **GB** (ESX) 71 Ab 42
Rotherfield Peppard **GB** (OXS) 63 Za 39
Rotherham **GB** (SOY) 40 Yd 28
Rothersthorpe **GB** (NRH) 54 Za 35
Rotherwick **GB** (HAS) 63 Za 41
Rothes **GB** (GRP) 16 We 3
Rothesay **GB** (STC) 24 Uf 14
Rothiebrisbane **GB** (GRP) 17 Xd 4
Rothienorman **GB** (GRP) 17 Xd 4
Rothiesholm **GB** (ORK) 6 Xc 114
Rothwell **GB** (LIN) 41 Ze 28
Rothwell **GB** (NRH) 54 Zb 34
Rottal **GB** (TYS) 22 Wf 8
Rottingdean **GB** (ESX) 71 Zf 44
Rottington **GB** (CUB) 34 Wc 22
Roudham **GB** (NOR) 56 Af 34
Rough **IRL** (COR) 104 Rb 38
Rougham **GB** (NOR) 48 Ae 32
Roughaun House **IRL** (CRE) 92 Qf 31
Roughburn **GB** (HGL) 20 Vb 7
Rough Close **GB** (SFS) 45 Xf 31
Rough Common **GB** (KEN) 65 Ba 41
Roughsike **GB** (CUB) 32 Xb 18
Roughton **GB** (NOR) 49 Bb 31
Roughton **GB** (SHS) 53 Xd 34
Roundfort **IRL** (MAY) 87 Qf 27
Roundhay **GB** (WYO) 39 Yc 26
Roundstreet Common **GB** (WSX) 71 Zc 42
Roundway **GB** (WIL) 62 Ya 40
Roundwood House **IRL** (LAO) 94 Sc 30
Roundwood House **IRL** (WKL) 95 Te 30
Roundwood Park **IRL** (WKL) 95 Te 30
Rounstone **IRL** (GAL) 86 Qa 28
Rourkes Town **IRL** (LOT) 90 Te 24
Rousdon **GB** (DEV) 68 Wf 44
Rousham **GB** (OXS) 62 Ye 37
Rousham Gap **GB** (OXS) 62 Ye 37
Rousky **GB** (TYR) 83 Sf 20
Rous Lench **GB** (HWC) 53 Ya 35
Routh **GB** (HUS) 41 Zd 25
Row **GB** (CUB) 35 Xa 23
Rowanburn **GB** (DAG) 32 Xa 18
Rowantreehill House **IRL** (LET) 82 Rf 22
Rowde **GB** (WIL) 62 Xf 40
Rower, The **IRL** (KLK) 100 Ta 34
Rowfoot **GB** (NHL) 32 Xd 19
Row Heath **GB** (ESS) 65 Ba 38
Rowhedge **GB** (BUS) 63 Zb 37
Rowhook **GB** (WSX) 71 Zd 42
Rowington **GB** (WWH) 53 Yb 35
Rowland's Castle **GB** (HAS) 70 Za 43
Rowlands Gill **GB** (TAW) 33 Yb 19
Rowlestone **GB** (HWC) 60 Xa 37
Rowley **GB** (SHS) 52 Wf 33
Rowley Regis **GB** (WMD) 53 Xf 34
Rowls Noonan **IRL** (COR) 98 Qf 35
Rowly **GB** (SUR) 71 Zc 42
Rowney Green **GB** (HWC) 53 Ya 34
Rownhams **GB** (HAS) 69 Yd 43
Rowsham **GB** (BUS) 63 Zb 37
Rowsley **GB** (DSH) 45 Yc 29
Rowton **GB** (CHS) 44 Xb 29
Rowton **GB** (SHS) 44 Xc 32
Rowton Castle **GB** (SHS) 52 Xa 32
Rowton Moor **GB** (CHS) 44 Xa 29
Roxburgh **GB** (BOR) 27 Xd 15
Roxby **GB** (HUS) 41 Zc 27
Roxby **GB** (NOY) 37 Zb 21
Roxwell **GB** (ESS) 64 Ac 38
Royal British Legion Village **GB** (KEN) 65 Ac 41
Royal Tunbrigde Wells **GB** (KEN) 72 Ab 42
Roybridge **GB** (HGL) 20 Va 7
Roydon **GB** (ESS) 64 Aa 38
Roydon **GB** (NOR) 48 Ad 32
Roydon **GB** (NOR) 57 Ba 34
Royston **GB** (HTS) 55 Zf 36
Royston **GB** (SOY) 40 Yd 27
Royton **GB** (GRM) 39 Xf 27
Ruabon **GB** (CLW) 44 Wf 31
Ruaig **GB** (STC) 18 Tb 9
Ruan **IRL** (CRE) 92 Ra 31
Ruan Lanihorne **GB** (CNW) 75 Va 47
Ruan Major **GB** (CNW) 74 Ue 48
Ruan Minor **GB** (CNW) 74 Ue 49
Ruardean **GB** (GLS) 61 Xc 37
Ruardean Woodside **GB** (GLS) 61 Xc 37
Rubane **GB** (DOW) 85 Uc 22
Rubery **GB** (WMD) 53 Xf 34
Ruckcroft **GB** (CUB) 35 Xb 20
Ruckinge **GB** (KEN) 72 Af 42
Ruckland **GB** (LIN) 47 Zf 29
Ruckley **GB** (SHS) 52 Xb 33
Ruddington **GB** (NTS) 46 Yf 31
Ruddlemoor **GB** (CNW) 75 Vb 46
Rudford **GB** (GLS) 61 Xe 37
Rudge **GB** (SOM) 68 Xe 41
Rudgwick **GB** (WSX) 71 Zd 42
Rudley Green **GB** (ESS) 65 Ad 38
Rudry **GB** (MGL) 60 Wf 39
Rudston **GB** (HUS) 41 Ze 24
Rudyard **GB** (SFS) 45 Xf 30
Rufford **GB** (LCS) 38 Xb 27
Rufforth **GB** (NOY) 40 Ye 25
Rugby **GB** (WWH) 54 Ye 34
Rugeley **GB** (SFS) 45 Ya 32
Ruilick **GB** (HGL) 15 Vd 4
Ruisgarry **GB** (HGL) 10 Sf 2
Ruishton **GB** (SOM) 67 Wf 42
Ruislip **GB** (GRL) 63 Zd 39
Rumbling Bridge **GB** (TYS) 25 Wc 11
Rumburgh **GB** (SUF) 57 Bc 34
Rumford **GB** (CNW) 75 Va 46
Rumney **GB** (SGL) 60 Wf 39
Runcorn **GB** (CHS) 44 Xb 29
Runcton **GB** (WSX) 70 Zb 44
Runfold **GB** (SUR) 70 Zb 41
Runhal **GB** (NOR) 57 Ba 33
Runham **GB** (NOR) 49 Bd 33
Runnaruag House **IRL** (ROS) 88 Re 26
Runswick Bay **GB** (NOY) 37 Zb 21
Runwell **GB** (ESS) 65 Ad 39
Rush **IRL** (MT) 90 Tf 27
Rushall **GB** (HWC) 61 Xc 36
Rushall **GB** (NOR) 57 Bb 34
Rushall **GB** (WIL) 69 Yb 41
Rushall **GB** (WMD) 53 Ya 33
Rushbrooke **GB** (SUF) 56 Ae 35
Rushbury **GB** (SHS) 52 Xb 33

Rath – Rushbury (GB) (IRL) 131

Rushden **GB** (HTS) 55 Zf 37
Rushden **GB** (NRH) 55 Zc 35
Rusheen **IRL** (KER) 97 Qc 36
Rushford **GB** (NOR) 56 Ae 34
Rushin House **IRL** (LAO) 94 Sd 30
Rushlake Green **GB** (ESX) 72 Ab 43
Rushmere **GB** (SUF) 57 Be 34
Rushmoor **GB** (SUR) 70 Zb 42
Rushock **GB** (HWC) 53 Xe 34
Rusholme **GB** (GRM) 39 Xe 28
Rushton **GB** (CHS) 44 Xc 29
Rushton **GB** (NRH) 54 Zb 34
Rushton **GB** (SHS) 52 Xc 32
Rushton Spencer **GB** (SFS) 45 Xf 30
Rushwee **IRL** (MT) 90 Tc 26
Rushwick **GB** (HWC) 53 Xe 35
Rushyford **GB** (DUR) 36 Yc 21
Ruskie **GB** (CEN) 25 Ve 11
Ruskington **GB** (LIN) 47 Zd 30
Rusky Park **IRL** (KER) 97 Qd 33
Rusland **GB** (CUB) 34 Wf 23
Rusper **GB** (WSX) 71 Ze 42
Russelstown **IRL** (WMT) 89 Se 28
Russell's Water **GB** (OXS) 63 Za 39
Russelstown **IRL** (GAL) 87 Ra 27
Rusthall **GB** (KEN) 71 Ab 42
Rustington **GB** (WSX) 71 Zc 44
Ruston Parva **GB** (HUS) 41 Zd 24
Rutherford **GB** (BOR) 26 Xc 15
Rutherglen **GB** (STC) 25 Ve 14
Ruthernbridge **GB** (CNW) 75 Vb 46
Ruthin **GB** (CLW) 43 We 30
Ruthven **GB** (GRP) 16 Xb 3
Ruthven **GB** (HGL) 15 Wa 4
Ruthven **GB** (TYS) 21 Wf 9
Ruthwell **GB** (DAG) 31 Wd 19
Ruyton-XI-Towns **GB** (SHS) 44 Xa 32
Ryan's Cross Roads **IRL** (KLK) 94 Sf 32
Ryal **GB** (NHL) 33 Ya 18
Ryal Fold **GB** (LCS) 38 Xc 26
Ryan's Cross Roads **IRL** (OFF) 93 Sa 31
Rydal **GB** (CUB) 35 Xa 22
Ryde **GB** (IOW) 70 Yf 44
Rydon **GB** (DEV) 66 Vd 44
Rye **GB** (ESX) 72 Ae 43
Ryefield **IRL** (CAV) 89 Sf 26
Rye Foreign **GB** (ESX) 72 Ae 43
Ryehill **IRL** (GAL) 87 Rb 28
Ryhill **GB** (WYO) 40 Yd 27
Ryhope **GB** (TAW) 33 Yd 19
Rylane Cross **IRL** (COR) 98 Ra 37
Rylstone **GB** (NOY) 39 Xf 24
Ryther **GB** (NOY) 40 Yf 25
Ryton **GB** (GLS) 61 Xd 37
Ryton **GB** (NOY) 37 Zb 23
Ryton **GB** (TAW) 33 Yb 19
Ryton-on-Dunsmore **GB** (WWH) 54 Yd 34

S

Sabden **GB** (LCS) 39 Xe 25
Sackers Green **GB** (SUF) 56 Ae 36
Sackhead **GB** (GRP) 16 Xa 3
Sacombe **GB** (HTS) 64 Zf 37
Sacriston **GB** (DUR) 36 Yc 20
Sadberge **GB** (DUR) 36 Yd 21
Saddell **GB** (STC) 28 Uc 15
Saddington **GB** (LEC) 54 Yf 33
Saddle Bow **GB** (NOR) 48 Ac 32
Saffron Walden **GB** (ESS) 56 Ab 36
Sageston **GB** (DYF) 58 Vb 38
Saggart **IRL** (DUB) 95 Td 29
Saham Toney **GB** (NOR) 56 Ae 33
Saighton **GB** (CHS) 44 Xa 30
Saint Abbs **GB** (BOR) 27 Xf 13
Saint Agnes **GB** (CNW) 74 Ue 47
Saint Albans **GB** (HTS) 64 Zd 38
Saint Allen **GB** (CNW) 74 Uf 47
Saint Andrew **GBG** 72 Xc 52
Saint Andrew **GBG** 100 Xc 52
Saint Andrews **GB** (FIF) 22 Xb 10
Saint Andrews Major **GB** (SGL) 60 We 40
Saint Ann's Hill **IRL** (COR) 104 Rc 37
Saint Anne **GBA** 72 Xe 50
Saint Anne's **GB** (LCS) 38 Wf 26
Saint Anne's, Lytham **GB** (LCS) 38 Wf 26
Saint Ann's **GB** (DAG) 31 Wd 17
Saint Ann's Chapel **GB** (CNW) 75 Ve 45
Saint Ann's Chapel **GB** (DEV) 76 Wa 47
Saint Anthony-in-Meneage **GB** (CNW) 74 Uf 48
Saint Arvans **GB** (GWE) 61 Xb 39
Saint Asaph **GB** (CLW) 43 Wd 29
Saint Athan **GB** (SGL) 60 Wd 40
Saint-Aubin **GBJ** 73 Xf 53
Saint Austell **GB** (CNW) 75 Vb 46
Saint Bees **GB** (CUB) 34 Wc 22
Saint Blazey **GB** (CNW) 75 Vb 46
Saint Boswells **GB** (BOR) 26 Xc 15
Saint-Brelade **GBJ** 73 Xe 53
Saint Brendan's House **IRL** (GAL) 88 Rd 27
Saint Breock **GB** (CNW) 75 Va 45
Saint Breward **GB** (CNW) 75 Vb 45
Saint Briavels **GB** (GLS) 61 Xc 38
Saint Brides **GB** (DYF) 58 Ue 38
Saint Bride's Major **GB** (MGL) 60 Wc 40
Saint Brides Netherwent **GB** (GWE) 61 Xb 39
Saint Brides-super-Ely **GB** (SGL) 60 We 40
Saint Brides Wentlooge **GB** (GWE) 60 Wf 39
Saint Brigiol's Hospital **IRL** (GAL) 93 Re 29
Saint Budeaux **GB** (DEV) 76 Ve 46
Saint Buryan **GB** (CNW) 74 Uc 48
Saint Catherines **GB** (STC) 24 Uf 11
Saint Clears **GB** (DYF) 59 Vd 38
Saint Cleer **GB** (CNW) 75 Vd 46
Saint Cleran's **IRL** (GAL) 92 Rc 29
Saint Clether **GB** (CNW) 66 Vc 45
Saint Colmac **GB** (STC) 24 Uf 13
Saint Columb Major **GB** (CNW) 75 Va 46
Saint Columb Minor **GB** (CNW) 74 Uf 46
Saint Columb Road **GB** (CNW) 75 Va 46
Saint Combs **GB** (GRP) 17 Ya 3
Saint Cross South Elmham **GB** (SUF) 57 Bc 34
Saint Cyrus **GB** (GRP) 22 Xd 8
Saint David's **GB** (DYF) 58 Ue 37
Saint David's **GB** (TYS) 21 Wb 10
Saint Decumans **GB** (SOM) 67 Wd 41
Saint Dogmaels **GB** (DYF) 50 Vb 36
Saint Dominick **GB** (CNW) 75 Ve 46
Saint Donats **GB** (SGL) 60 Wc 40
Saint Doolag's **IRL** (DUB) 95 Te 28
Saint Edith's Marsh **GB** (WIL) 62 Xf 40
Sainte-Mary **GBJ** 73 Xf 53
Saint Endellion **GB** (CNW) 75 Vb 45
Saint Erme **GB** (CNW) 74 Uf 47
Saint Erth **GB** (CNW) 74 Ud 48
Saint Erth Praze **GB** (CNW) 74 Ud 48
Saint Fagans **GB** (SGL) 60 We 40
Saint Fergus **GB** (GRP) 17 Yb 3
Saintfield **GB** (DOW) 85 Ub 22
Saint Fillans **GB** (TYS) 20 Vf 10
Saint Florence **GB** (DYF) 58 Vb 38
Saint George **GB** (CLW) 43 Wc 29
Saint George's **GB** (SGL) 60 We 40
Saint Germans **GB** (CNW) 75 Ve 46
Saint Giles in the Wood **GB** (DEV) 66 Vf 43
Saint Harmon **GB** (POW) 51 Wd 34
Saint Helena **GB** (NOR) 49 Bb 32
Saint Helens **GB** (IOW) 70 Yf 44
Saint Helens **GB** (MES) 38 Xb 28
Saint-Helier **GBJ** 73 Xf 53
Saint Hilary **GB** (CNW) 74 Ud 48
Saint Hilary **GB** (SGL) 60 Wd 40
Saint Hill **GB** (WSX) 71 Zf 42
Saint Illtyd **GB** (GWE) 60 Wf 38
Saint Ishmael's **GB** (DYF) 58 Uf 38
Saint Issey **GB** (CNW) 75 Va 45
Saint Ita's Hospital **IRL** (DUB) 90 Tf 28
Saint Ive **GB** (CNW) 75 Vd 46
Saint Ives **GB** (CBS) 55 Zf 35
Saint Ives **GB** (CNW) 74 Ud 47
Saint Ives **GB** (DOS) 69 Yb 43
Saint James South Elmham **GB** (SUF) 57 Bc 34
Saint John **GB** (CNW) 75 Ve 46
Saint-John **GBJ** 73 Xf 53
Saint Johns **GB** (HWC) 53 Xe 35
Saint John's **GBM** 29 Vc 23
Saint John's Chapel **GB** (DEV) 66 Vf 42
Saint John's Chapel **GB** (DUR) 35 Xe 20
Saint John's Highway **GB** (NOR) 48 Ab 32
Saint Johns House **IRL** (KIL) 94 Ta 31
Saint Johnstown **IRL** (DON) 78 Sd 19
Saint John's Town of Dalry **GB** (DAG) 30 Vf 18
Saint John's Fen End **GB** (NOR) 48 Ab 32
Saint Judes **GBM** 29 Vd 22
Saint Just **GB** (CNW) 74 Ub 48
Saint Just in Roseland **GB** (CNW) 74 Uf 47
Saint Katharines **GB** (GRP) 17 Xd 4
Saint Keverne **GB** (CNW) 74 Uf 48
Saint Kew **GB** (CNW) 75 Vb 45
Saint Kew Highway **GB** (CNW) 75 Vb 45
Saint Keyne **GB** (CNW) 75 Vd 46
Saint Lawrence **GB** (ESS) 65 Af 38
Saint Lawrence **GB** (IOW) 70 Ye 45
Saint-Lawrence **GBJ** 73 Xf 53
Saint Leonards **GB** (BUS) 63 Zb 38
Saint Leonards **GB** (DOS) 69 Ya 43
Saint Leonards **GB** (ESX) 72 Ad 43
Saint Leonards Grange **GB** (HAS) 69 Yd 44
Saint Leonards Street **GB** (KEN) 64 Ac 41
Saint Levan **GB** (CNW) 74 Uc 48
Saint Lythans **GB** (SGL) 60 We 40
Saint Mabyn **GB** (CNW) 75 Vb 45
Saint Margaret's **IRL** (DUB) 95 Te 28
Saint Margaret's House **IRL** (WEX) 101 Td 35
Saint Margarets **GB** (HWC) 60 Xa 37
Saint Margaret's at Cliffe **GB** (KEN) 73 Bc 42
Saint Margaret's Hope **GB** (ORK) 6 Xa 116
Saint Mark's **GBM** 29 Vc 24
Saint Martin **GB** (CNW) 75 Vd 46
Saint Martin **GBG** 100 Xc 52
Saint-Martin **GBJ** 73 Xf 53
Saint Martins **GB** (TYS) 21 Wd 10
Saint Martin's **GB** (SHS) 44 Wf 31
Saint Mary **GB** (KEN) 72 Af 42
Saint Mary Bourne **GB** (HAS) 70 Yd 41
Saint Mary Church **GB** (SGL) 60 Wd 40
Saint Mary Hill **GB** (SGL) 60 Wd 40
Saint Mary's **GB** (ORK) 6 Xa 115
Saint Mary's Bay **GB** (KEN) 72 Af 42
Saint Mary's Grove **GB** (AVN) 61 Xb 40
Saint Mawes **GB** (CNW) 74 Uf 48
Saint Mawgan **GB** (CNW) 75 Va 46
Saint Mellion **GB** (CNW) 75 Ve 46
Saint Mellons **GB** (SGL) 60 Wf 39
Saint Michael Caerhays **GB** (CNW) 75 Va 47
Saint Michael Penkevil **GB** (CNW) 74 Uf 47
Saint Michaels **GB** (HWC) 52 Xc 35
Saint Michaels **GB** (KEN) 72 Ae 42
Saint Michael's on Wyre **GB** (LCS) 38 Xb 25
Saint Michael South Elmham **GB** (SUF) 57 Bc 34
Saint Minver **GB** (CNW) 75 Va 45
Saint Monance **GB** (FIF) 26 Xb 11
Saint Mullin's **IRL** (CLW) 100 Ta 34
Saint Nathy's Toobrackan **IRL** (ROS) 88 Rc 25
Saint Neot **GB** (CNW) 75 Vc 46
Saint Neots **GB** (CBS) 55 Ze 35
Saint Newlyn East **GB** (CNW) 74 Uf 46
Saint Nicholas **GB** (DYF) 58 Uf 37
Saint Nicholas **GB** (SGL) 60 We 40
Saint Nicholas at Wade **GB** (KEN) 65 Bb 40
Saint Ninians **GB** (CEN) 25 Wa 12
Saint Osyth **GB** (ESS) 65 Ba 38
Saint-Ouen **GBJ** 73 Xe 53
Saint Owen's Cross **GB** (HWC) 61 Xb 37
Saint Patrick's College **IRL** (CAV) 89 Sd 24
Saint Patrick's Hill **IRL** (KIL) 95 Tc 29
Saint Paul's Walden **GB** (HTS) 64 Ze 37
Saint-Peter **GBJ** 73 Xf 53
Saint Peter in the wood **GBG** 100 Xc 52
Saint Peter Port **GBG** 100 Xc 52
Saint Petrox **GB** (DYF) 58 Va 39
Saint Sampson **GBG** 72 Xd 51
Saint Samson **GBG** 100 Xc 52
Saint-Savoir **GBJ** 73 Xf 53
Saint Stephen **GB** (CNW) 75 Va 46
Saint Stephens **GB** (CNW) 75 Ve 46
Saint Teath **GB** (CNW) 75 Vb 45
Saint Tudy **GB** (CNW) 75 Vb 45
Saint Twynnells **GB** (DYF) 58 Va 39
Saint Veep **GB** (CNW) 75 Vc 46
Saint Vigeans **GB** (TYS) 22 Xc 9
Saint Vincent Cross **GB** (CBS) 55 Zf 33
Saint Weonards **GB** (HWC) 61 Xb 37
Salcombe **GB** (DEV) 76 Wb 47
Salcombe Regis **GB** (DEV) 67 We 44
Salcott **GB** (ESS) 65 Ae 38
Sale **GB** (GRM) 45 Xe 28
Saleby **GB** (LIN) 47 Zf 29
Saleen **IRL** (KER) 97 Qd 33
Sale Green **GB** (HWC) 53 Xf 35
Salehurst **GB** (ESX) 72 Ac 43
Salem **GB** (DYF) 51 Wa 34
Salem **GB** (DYF) 59 Vf 37
Salen **GB** (HGL) 19 Ub 8
Salen **GB** (STC) 18 Ua 9
Salesbury **GB** (LCS) 38 Xd 26
Salfords **GB** (SUR) 71 Ze 41
Salford **GB** (BFS) 55 Zc 36
Salford **GB** (GRM) 39 Xe 28
Salford **GB** (OXS) 62 Yc 37
Salford Priors **GB** (WWH) 53 Ya 36
Salia **IRL** (MAY) 86 Qa 25
Saliahoona **IRL** (GAL) 92 Qd 29
Saline **GB** (FIF) 25 Wc 12
Salisbury **GB** (WIL) 69 Yb 42
Sallachie **GB** (HGL) 14 Ud 5
Sallachy **GB** (HGL) 8 Vd 120
Sallahig **IRL** (KER) 102 Pf 37
Sallins **IRL** (KIL) 95 Tb 29
Sallowolen **IRL** (KER) 97 Qd 33
Sallybrock **IRL** (COR) 104 Rd 37
Sallypark **IRL** (TIP) 93 Rf 32
Sallyview **IRL** (WMT) 89 Sf 27
Salmonby **GB** (LIN) 47 Zf 29
Salmond's Muir **GB** (TYS) 22 Xb 9
Salperton **GB** (GLS) 62 Ya 37
Salph End **GB** (BFS) 55 Zd 36
Salrock **IRL** (GAL) 86 Qa 27
Salsburgh **GB** (STC) 25 Wa 13
Salt **GB** (SFS) 45 Xf 31
Saltash **GB** (CNW) 75 Ve 46
Saltburn **GB** (HGL) 8 Vf 2
Saltburn-by-the-Sea **GB** (CLE) 37 Za 21
Saltby **GB** (LEC) 46 Zb 32
Saltcoats **GB** (STC) 24 Vb 15
Saltdean **GB** (ESX) 71 Zf 44
Salter **GB** (LCS) 38 Xc 24
Salterforth **GB** (LCS) 39 Xf 25
Salterstown **IRL** (LOT) 90 Te 25
Saltfleet **GB** (LIN) 41 Ab 28
Saltfleetby Saint Peter **GB** (LIN) 41 Aa 28
Saltfleet Saint Clement **GB** (LIN) 41 Ab 28
Saltford **GB** (AVN) 61 Xd 40
Salthouse **GB** (NOR) 49 Ba 31
Saltley **GB** (WMD) 53 Ya 34
Saltmarshe **GB** (HUS) 40 Zb 26
Saltmills **IRL** (WEX) 100 Tb 35
Saltney **GB** (CHS) 44 Xa 29
Salton **GB** (NOY) 37 Za 24
Saltwick **GB** (NHL) 33 Yb 18
Saltwood **GB** (KEN) 73 Ba 42
Salvington **GB** (WSX) 71 Zd 44
Salwayash **GB** (DOS) 68 Xb 44
Sam's Cross Roads **IRL** (COR) 103 Ra 39
Samala **GB** (HGL) 10 Sd 3
Sambourne **GB** (WWH) 53 Ya 35
Samlesbury **GB** (LCS) 38 Xc 26
Samlesbury Bottoms **GB** (LCS) 38 Xc 26
Sampford Arundel **GB** (SOM) 67 We 43
Sampford Brett **GB** (SOM) 67 We 42
Sampford Courtenay **GB** (DEV) 66 Wa 44
Sampford Peverell **GB** (DEV) 67 Wd 43
Sampford Spiney **GB** (DEV) 76 Vf 45
Samuelston **GB** (LOT) 26 Xb 13
Sanaigmore **GB** (STC) 22 Td 13
Sancreed **GB** (CNW) 74 Uc 48
Sancton **GB** (HUS) 40 Zc 25
Sand **GB** (SHL) 2 Yd 107
Sandaig **GB** (HGL) 13 Ub 6
Sandbach **GB** (CHS) 44 Xd 30
Sandbank **GB** (STC) 24 Va 13
Sandend **GB** (GRP) 16 Xb 2
Sandfield **IRL** (DON) 77 Rd 20
Sandford **GB** (AVN) 61 Xa 41
Sandford **GB** (CUB) 35 Xd 21
Sandford **GB** (DEV) 67 Wc 44
Sandford **GB** (DOS) 69 Xf 44
Sandford **GB** (STC) 25 Vf 15
Sandfordhill **GB** (GRP) 17 Yb 4
Sandford-on-Thames **GB** (OXS) 62 Ye 38
Sandford Orcas **GB** (DOS) 68 Xc 43
Sandford Saint Martin **GB** (OXS) 62 Yd 37
Sandgate **GB** (KEN) 73 Ba 42
Sandgreen **GB** (DAG) 30 Ve 19
Sandhaven **GB** (GRP) 17 Xf 2
Sandhead **GB** (DAG) 28 Va 20
Sandhills **GB** (DOS) 68 Xd 43
Sandhoe **GB** (NHL) 33 Xf 19
Sand Hole **GB** (HUS) 40 Zb 26
Sandholes **GB** (TYR) 84 Tb 21
Sandholme **GB** (HUS) 40 Zb 26
Sandholme **GB** (LIN) 47 Zf 31
Sandhurst **GB** (BKS) 63 Zb 40
Sandhurst **GB** (GLS) 61 Xe 37
Sandhurst **GB** (KEN) 72 Ad 42
Sandhutton **GB** (NOY) 36 Yd 23
Sand Hutton **GB** (NOY) 40 Za 24
Sandleheath **GB** (HAS) 69 Yb 43
Sandling **GB** (KEN) 65 Ad 41
Sandness **GB** (SHL) 2 Yc 107
Sandon **GB** (ESS) 65 Ad 38
Sandon **GB** (HTS) 55 Zf 37
Sandon **GB** (SFS) 45 Xf 31
Sandown **GB** (IOW) 70 Yf 45
Sandpits Cross Roads **IRL** (KLK) 100 Se 34
Sandplace **GB** (CNW) 75 Vd 46
Sandridge **GB** (HTS) 64 Ze 38
Sandridge **GB** (WIL) 61 Xf 40
Sandringham **GB** (NOR) 48 Ad 32
Sandsend **GB** (NOY) 37 Zb 21
Sandsound **GB** (SHL) 2 Yd 107
Sandtoft **GB** (HUS) 40 Za 27
Sandville Cott **IRL** (LIM) 98 Ra 34
Sandway **GB** (KEN) 72 Ac 41
Sandwich **GB** (KEN) 65 Bb 41
Sandwick **GB** (HGL) 12 Se 4
Sandwick **GB** (SHL) 3 Ye 109
Sandwith **GB** (CUB) 34 Wc 21
Sandy **GB** (BFS) 55 Ze 36
Sandy Cove **IRL** (COR) 104 Rc 38
Sandycroft **GB** (CLW) 44 Xa 29
Sandygate **GBM** 29 Vc 22
Sandy Lane **GB** (WIL) 61 Xf 40
Sandymount **IRL** (LOT) 90 Td 25
Sandyway **GB** (HWC) 61 Xb 37
Sangobeg **GB** (HGL) 4 Vb 117
Sanna **GB** (HGL) 18 Te 8
Sannox **GB** (STC) 24 Uf 15
Sanquhar **GB** (DAG) 31 Wa 16
Santon **GB** (HUS) 41 Zc 27
Santon Bridge **GB** (CUB) 34 Wd 22
Santon Downham **GB** (SUF) 56 Ad 34
Santry **IRL** (DUB) 95 Te 28
Sapcote **GB** (LEC) 54 Ye 33
Sapey Common **GB** (HWC) 52 Xd 35
Sapperton **GB** (GLS) 61 Xf 38
Sapperton **GB** (LIN) 47 Zd 31
Saracen's Head **GB** (LIN) 47 Zf 32
Sarclet **GB** (HGL) 9 Wf 118
Sarisbury **GB** (HAS) 70 Ye 43
Sarn **GB** (POW) 52 We 33
Sarnaght **IRL** (MAY) 87 Qe 25
Sarnau **GB** (DYF) 50 Vd 36
Sarnau **GB** (DYF) 59 Vd 37
Sarnau **GB** (GWY) 43 Wc 31
Sarnau **GB** (POW) 44 Wf 32
Sarn Bach **GB** (GWY) 42 Vc 32
Sarnesfield **GB** (HWC) 52 Xa 36
Sarn Meyllteyrn **GB** (GWY) 42 Vc 31
Saron **GB** (DYF) 59 Vd 36
Sarratt **GB** (HTS) 63 Zd 38
Sarre **GB** (KEN) 65 Bb 40
Sarsden **GB** (OXS) 62 Yc 37
Sarsgrum **GB** (HGL) 4 Vb 117
Satley **GB** (DUR) 36 Yb 20
Satterleigh **GB** (DEV) 66 Wa 43
Satterthwaite **GB** (CUB) 34 Wf 23
Sauchen **GB** (GRP) 17 Xd 5
Saucher **GB** (TYS) 21 We 10
Sauchieburn **GB** (GRP) 22 Xc 8
Sauchrie **GB** (STC) 30 Vb 16
Saughall **GB** (CHS) 44 Xa 29
Saughall Massie **GB** (CHS) 44 Wf 28
Saughtree **GB** (BOR) 32 Xb 17
Saundersfoot **GB** (DYF) 58 Vb 38
Saunderton **GB** (BUS) 63 Za 38
Saunton **GB** (DEV) 66 Ve 42
Sausthorpe **GB** (LIN) 47 Aa 29
Savagetown Cross Roads **IRL** (WTF) 100 Se 35
Saval **GB** (HGL) 8 Vd 120
Savary **GB** (HGL) 18 Ua 9
Sawbridge Worth **GB** (HTS) 64 Aa 38
Sawdon **GB** (NOY) 37 Zc 23
Sawley **GB** (LCS) 39 Xd 25
Sawley **GB** (NOY) 39 Yc 24
Sawley **GB** (NTS) 46 Ye 31
Sawrey **GB** (CUB) 35 Xa 23
Sawston **GB** (CBS) 56 Aa 36
Sawtry **GB** (CBS) 55 Ze 34
Saxby **GB** (LEC) 46 Zb 32
Saxelbye **GB** (LEC) 46 Za 32
Saxilby **GB** (LIN) 46 Zc 29
Saxlingham **GB** (NOR) 48 Ba 31
Saxlingham Green **GB** (NOR) 57 Bb 33
Saxlingham Thorpe **GB** (NOR) 57 Bb 33
Saxmundham **GB** (SUF) 57 Bc 35
Saxondale **GB** (NTS) 46 Za 31
Saxon Street **GB** (CBS) 56 Ac 35
Saxtead **GB** (SUF) 57 Bb 35
Saxtead Green **GB** (SUF) 57 Bb 35
Saxthorpe **GB** (NOR) 49 Ba 32
Saxton **GB** (NOY) 40 Ye 26
Sayers Common **GB** (WSX) 71 Ze 43
Scackleton **GB** (NOY) 40 Yf 25
Scadabay **GB** (HGL) 11 Tb 1
Scagglethorpe **GB** (NOY) 37 Zb 24
Scalasaig **GB** (STC) 22 Te 12
Scalby **GB** (NOY) 37 Zd 23
Scaldwell **GB** (NRH) 54 Za 34
Scaleby **GB** (CUB) 32 Xa 19
Scaleby Hill **GB** (CUB) 32 Xa 19
Scales **GB** (CUB) 34 Wf 21
Scales **GB** (CUB) 34 Wf 24
Scalford **GB** (LEC) 46 Za 32
Scaling **GB** (CLE) 37 Za 21
Scallastle **GB** (STC) 19 Tf 10
Scalloway **GB** (SHL) 3 Ye 108
Scamblesby **GB** (LIN) 47 Zf 29
Scampston **GB** (NOY) 37 Zb 23
Scampton **GB** (LIN) 47 Zc 29
Scaniport **GB** (HGL) 15 Ve 4
Scarastavore **GB** (HGL) 11 Sf 2
Scarborough **GB** (NOY) 37 Zd 23
Scarcliffe **GB** (DSH) 46 Ye 29
Scarcroft **GB** (WYO) 40 Yd 25
Scardaun **IRL** (MAY) 87 Qf 27
Scarden House **IRL** (WMT) 89 Sf 27
Scarfskerry **GB** (HGL) 6 We 117
Scargill **GB** (DUR) 36 Ya 22
Scarinish **GB** (STC) 18 Tb 9
Scarisbrick **GB** (LCS) 38 Xa 27
Scarning **GB** (NOR) 48 Af 32
Scarriff **IRL** (CRE) 92 Rc 31
Scarriff **IRL** (KER) 102 Pe 37
Scarrington **GB** (NTS) 46 Za 31
Scartaglin **IRL** (KER) 97 Qd 35
Scarth Hill **GB** (LCS) 38 Xa 27
Scartho **GB** (HUS) 41 Zf 27
Scart Upper **IRL** (WTF) 99 Sc 35
Scarva **GB** (DOW) 84 Td 23
Scaur, Kippford or **GB** (DAG) 31 Wb 19
Scawby **GB** (HUS) 41 Zc 27
Scawton **GB** (NOY) 37 Yf 23
Scayne's Hill **GB** (WSX) 71 Zf 43
Scethrog **GB** (POW) 60 We 37
Scholar Green **GB** (CHS) 45 Xe 30
Scholes **GB** (WYO) 39 Yb 27
Scholes **GB** (WYO) 40 Yd 26
Schoolhill **GB** (GRP) 17 Xd 6
Schools **IRL** (TIP) 99 Sa 35
Schripney **GB** (WSX) 70 Zb 44
Scleddau **GB** (DYF) 58 Va 37
Scole **GB** (NOR) 57 Ba 34
Scolton **GB** (DYF) 58 Va 37
Sconee L.r **IRL** (LAO) 94 Sd 30
Sconser **GB** (HGL) 13 Tf 5
Scopwick **GB** (LIN) 47 Zd 30
Scorborough **GB** (HUS) 41 Zd 25
Scorrier **GB** (CNW) 74 Ue 47
Scorton **GB** (LCS) 38 Xb 25
Scorton **GB** (NOY) 36 Yc 22
Sco Ruston **GB** (NOR) 49 Bc 32
Scotby **GB** (CUB) 32 Xa 19
Scotch Corner **GB** (NOY) 36 Yc 22
Scotch Corner **IRL** (MOG) 84 Ta 23
Scotchman's Bush **IRL** (GAL) 88 Rd 27
Scotforth **GB** (LCS) 38 Xb 24
Scothern **GB** (LIN) 47 Zd 29
Scotlandwell **GB** (TYS) 26 We 11
Scotshouse **IRL** (MOG) 89 Se 24
Scotston **GB** (TYS) 21 Wb 9
Scotstown **GB** (HGL) 19 Uc 8
Scotter **GB** (LIN) 40 Zb 28
Scotterthorpe **GB** (LIN) 40 Zb 27
Scotton **GB** (LIN) 40 Zb 28
Scotton **GB** (NOY) 39 Yd 24
Scoughall **GB** (LOT) 26 Xc 12
Scoulag **GB** (STC) 24 Uf 14
Scoulton **GB** (NOR) 56 Af 33
Scourie **GB** (HGL) 7 Uf 118
Scourie More **GB** (HGL) 7 Uf 118
Scousburgh **GB** (SHL) 3 Ye 109
Scrabster **GB** (HGL) 6 Wc 117
Scraftworth **GB** (NTS) 40 Za 28
Scrahan **IRL** (KER) 97 Qb 35
Scrahanaveal **IRL** (KER) 97 Qe 36
Scrainoge **IRL** (ROS) 88 Rf 26
Scrainwood **GB** (NHL) 33 Xf 16
Scrane End **GB** (LIN) 47 Aa 31
Scranhane Cross Roads **IRL** (COR) 103 Ra 38
Scrarour **IRL** (COR) 99 Rd 35
Scrayingham **GB** (NOY) 40 Za 24
Scredington **GB** (LIN) 47 Zd 31
Screen **IRL** (WEX) 101 Td 34
Screggan **IRL** (OFF) 94 Sc 29
Scremby **GB** (LIN) 47 Aa 29
Scremerston **GB** (NHL) 27 Ya 14
Scriggan **GB** (LDR) 78 Ta 19
Scronagare **IRL** (COR) 103 Qf 37
Scrooby **GB** (NTS) 40 Yf 28
Scropton **GB** (DSH) 45 Yb 31
Scrowmore **IRL** (LIM) 99 Re 35
Scrub Hill **GB** (LIN) 47 Zf 30
Scruton **GB** (NOY) 36 Yc 23
Sculthorpe **GB** (NOR) 48 Ae 31
Scunthorpe **GB** (HUS) 40 Zc 27
Scurlockstown **IRL** (MT) 89 Ta 26
Scurlockstown Cross Roads **IRL** (WMT) 89 Sf 27
Seaborough **GB** (DOS) 68 Xb 43
Seacombe **GB** (CHS) 44 Wf 28
Seafield **GB** (LOT) 25 Wc 13
Seafield **GB** (STC) 30 Vc 16
Seafield **IRL** (MAY) 80 Pf 23
Seafield House **IRL** (WTF) 100 Sd 36
Seaford **GB** (ESX) 71 Aa 44
Seaforde **GB** (DOW) 85 Ua 23
Seafort **IRL** (COR) 103 Qc 39
Seaforth Head **GB** (HGL) 11 Tc 120
Seaham **GB** (DUR) 33 Yd 19
Seahouses **GB** (NHL) 27 Yb 15
Seal **GB** (KEN) 64 Ab 41
Sealand **GB** (CLW) 44 Xa 29
Seale **GB** (SUR) 70 Zb 41
Seamer **GB** (NOY) 36 Ye 22
Seamer **GB** (NOY) 37 Zd 23
Seamill **GB** (STC) 24 Va 14
Sea Mount **IRL** (DUB) 95 Tf 28
Sea Palling **GB** (NOR) 49 Bd 32
Seapatrick **GB** (DOW) 84 Te 22
Searby **GB** (LIN) 41 Zd 27
Seascale **GB** (CUB) 34 Wd 22
Seaton **GB** (CUB) 34 Wc 21
Seaton **GB** (DEV) 67 Wf 44
Seaton **GB** (DUR) 33 Yd 19
Seaton **GB** (HUS) 41 Ze 25
Seaton **GB** (LEC) 55 Zc 33
Seaton **GB** (NHL) 33 Yd 18
Seaton Burn **GB** (TAW) 33 Yc 18
Seaton Carew **GB** (CLE) 37 Ye 21
Seaton Delaval **GB** (NHL) 33 Yc 18
Seaton Junction **GB** (DEV) 67 Wf 44
Seaton Ross **GB** (HUS) 40 Zb 25
Seatown **GB** (DOS) 68 Xb 44
Seave Green **GB** (NOY) 37 Yf 22
Sea View **IRL** (WKL) 101 Tf 32
Seaview House **IRL** (WTF) 99 Sc 36
Seavington Saint Michael **GB** (SOM) 68 Xa 43
Sebergham **GB** (CUB) 34 Xa 20
Seckington **GB** (WWH) 53 Yc 33
Sedbergh **GB** (CUB) 35 Xc 23
Sedboro **IRL** (TIP) 93 Re 31
Sedbusk **GB** (NOY) 35 Xe 23
Sedenrath **IRL** (MT) 90 Tb 26
Sedgeberrow **GB** (HWC) 53 Ya 36
Sedgebrook **GB** (LIN) 46 Zb 31
Sedgefield **GB** (DUR) 36 Yd 21
Sedgeford **GB** (NOR) 48 Ad 31
Sedgley **GB** (WMD) 53 Xf 33
Sedgwick **GB** (CUB) 35 Xb 23
Sedlescombe **GB** (ESX) 72 Ad 43
Sedlescombe Street **GB** (ESX) 72 Ad 43
Seend **GB** (WIL) 61 Xf 40
Seend Cleeve **GB** (WIL) 61 Xf 40
Seer Green **GB** (BUS) 63 Zc 39
Seetin **IRL** (MAY) 87 Qf 27
Sefton **GB** (MES) 38 Xa 27
Seifton **GB** (SHS) 52 Xb 34
Seighford **GB** (SFS) 45 Xe 32
Seilebost **GB** (HGL) 11 Ta 1
Seisdon **GB** (SFS) 53 Xe 33
Seisiadar **GB** (HGL) 11 Te 119
Selattyn **GB** (SHS) 44 Wf 31
Selborne **GB** (HAS) 70 Za 42
Selby **GB** (NOY) 40 Yf 26
Selham **GB** (WSX) 70 Zc 43
Selhurst **GB** (GRL) 64 Zf 40
Selkirk **GB** (BOR) 26 Xb 15
Sellack **GB** (HWC) 61 Xc 37
Sellafirth **GB** (SHL) 2 Yf 105
Sellindge **GB** (KEN) 72 Af 42
Selling **GB** (KEN) 65 Af 41
Sellow **IRL** (MOG) 83 Sf 23
Sells Green **GB** (WIL) 61 Xf 40
Selmeston **GB** (ESX) 71 Aa 43
Selsey **GB** (WSX) 70 Zb 44
Selsfield Common **GB** (WSX) 71 Zf 42
Selside **GB** (NOY) 35 Xe 23
Selston **GB** (NTS) 46 Ye 30
Selworthy **GB** (SOM) 67 Wc 41
Semer **GB** (SUF) 56 Af 36
Semington **GB** (WIL) 61 Xf 40
Semley **GB** (WIL) 69 Xf 42
Send **GB** (SUR) 63 Zc 41
Senghenydd **GB** (MGL) 60 We 39
Sennen **GB** (CNW) 74 Ub 48
Sennen Cove **GB** (CNW) 74 Ub 48
Sennybridge **GB** (POW) 60 Wc 37
Seotstown **IRL** (MOG) 83 Sf 23
Sequer's Bridge **GB** (DEV) 76 Wa 46
Seskin **IRL** (TIP) 100 Sc 34
Seskinore **GB** (TYR) 83 Se 21
Sessay **GB** (NOY) 36 Ye 23
Sessiagh **IRL** (MAY) 87 Qf 26
Sessuecommon **IRL** (SLI) 81 Rb 24
Setchey **GB** (NOR) 48 Ac 32
Setley **GB** (HAS) 69 Yc 44
Settiscarth **GB** (ORK) 6 Wf 114
Settle **GB** (NOY) 39 Xe 24
Settrington **GB** (NOY) 37 Zb 24
Sevenhampton **GB** (GLS) 62 Ya 37
Sevenhampton **GB** (WIL) 62 Yb 39
Sevenoaks **GB** (KEN) 64 Ab 41
Sevenoaks Weald **GB** (KEN) 71 Ab 41
Seven Sisters **GB** (WGL) 59 Wb 38
Seven Springs **GB** (GLS) 61 Xf 37
Severn Beach **GB** (GLS) 61 Xb 39
Severn Stoke **GB** (HWC) 53 Xe 36
Sevington **GB** (KEN) 72 Af 42
Sewards End **GB** (ESS) 56 Ab 36
Sewardstone **GB** (ESS) 64 Zf 39
Sewerby **GB** (HUS) 41 Zf 24
Seymourstown **IRL** (MT) 89 Sf 26
Sezincote **GB** (GLS) 62 Yb 37
Shackerley **GB** (SHS) 53 Xe 34
Shackerstone **GB** (LEC) 54 Yd 33
Shader **GB** (HGL) 11 Td 118
Shadforth **GB** (DUR) 36 Yd 20
Shadingfield **GB** (SUF) 57 Bd 34
Shadoxhurst **GB** (KEN) 72 Ae 42
Shadwell **GB** (NOR) 56 Af 34
Shaftesbury **GB** (DOR) 69 Xe 42
Shafton **GB** (SOY) 40 Yd 27
Shalbourne **GB** (WIL) 62 Yc 40
Shalcombe **GB** (IOW) 69 Yd 44
Shalden **GB** (HAS) 70 Yf 41
Shaldon **GB** (DEV) 76 Wc 45
Shalfleet **GB** (IOW) 70 Yd 44
Shalford **GB** (SUR) 71 Zc 41
Shalford Green **GB** (ESS) 65 Ac 37
Shallogan **IRL** (DON) 77 Re 20
Shallowfield **GB** (BKS) 63 Za 40
Shallowford **GB** (DEV) 67 Wa 41
Shalmsford Street **GB** (KEN) 65 Ba 41
Shalstone **GB** (BUS) 54 Yf 36
Shalwy **IRL** (DON) 82 Rc 21
Shamley Green **GB** (SUR) 71 Zc 41
Shammerdoo **IRL** (MAY) 87 Ra 25
Shanagarry **IRL** (COR) 104 Rf 37
Shanagh **IRL** (COR) 104 Rb 39
Shanaglish **IRL** (GAL) 92 Ra 30
Shanagolden **IRL** (LIM) 98 Qf 33
Shanahoe **IRL** (LAO) 94 Sd 31
Shanavoola **IRL** (KIL) 94 Ta 29
Shanayour **IRL** (LAO) 94 Sd 30
Shanbally **IRL** (COR) 104 Rd 38
Shanbally **IRL** (DON) 77 Sa 18
Shanbally **IRL** (GAL) 88 Rd 27
Shanbally **IRL** (GAL) 93 Rd 30
Shanbally **IRL** (WTF) 100 Sc 36
Shanbally Castle **IRL** (TIP) 99 Rf 35
Shanballyedmond **IRL** (TIP) 99 Re 32
Shanballymore **IRL** (COR) 98 Rd 35
Shanballymore **IRL** (GAL) 87 Rb 27
Shanbo **IRL** (WMT) 90 Tb 27
Shandangan Cross Roads **IRL** (COR) 103 Ra 37
Shandon **GB** (ANT) 85 Ua 21
Shandon **GB** (STC) 24 Vb 12
Shandwick **GB** (HGL) 9 Wa 2
Shane Valley **IRL** (OFF) 94 Sf 29
Shangarry **IRL** (GAL) 93 Rd 29
Shangton **GB** (LEC) 54 Za 33
Shanid House **IRL** (LIM) 98 Qf 33
Shankill **IRL** (GAL) 88 Rc 27
Shanklin **GB** (IOW) 70 Ye 45
Shanlis Cross Roads **IRL** (LOT) 90 Tc 25
Shannagh **IRL** (DON) 82 Rf 21
Shannakea **IRL** (CRE) 98 Qf 33
Shannavolla **IRL** (LAO) 94 Sd 31
Shannera Lower **IRL** (KER) 97 Qb 36
Shannon **IRL** (CRE) 92 Ra 32
Shannonbridge **IRL** (OFF) 93 Rf 29
Shannon Grove **IRL** (GAL) 93 Rf 29
Shannongrove House **IRL** (LIM) 98 Ra 33
Shannon Hall **IRL** (TIP) 93 Re 31
Shannon Harbour **IRL** (OFF) 93 Sa 29
Shannonhill House **IRL** (GAL) 93 Rd 30
Shannonvale **IRL** (COR) 103 Ra 39
Shannow **IRL** (CAV) 89 Sd 25
Shanowle **IRL** (WEX) 101 Tb 34
Shanragh **IRL** (LAO) 94 Sf 31
Shantonagh **IRL** (MOG) 89 Ta 24
Shantron **GB** (STC) 24 Vc 12
Shanweela **IRL** (CRE) 92 Qe 31
Shap **GB** (CUB) 35 Xb 21
Shapwick **GB** (SOM) 68 Xa 42
Sharavogue **IRL** (OFF) 93 Sa 30
Sharavogue House **IRL** (OFF) 93 Sa 30
Shardlow **GB** (DSH) 46 Yd 31
Shareshill **GB** (SFS) 53 Xf 33
Sharlston **GB** (WYO) 40 Yd 27
Sharnbrook **GB** (BFS) 55 Zc 35
Sharnford **GB** (LEC) 54 Ye 33
Sharoe Green **GB** (LCS) 38 Xb 26
Sharow **GB** (NOY) 36 Yd 24
Sharpenhoe **GB** (BFS) 63 Zd 37
Sharperton **GB** (NHL) 33 Xf 17
Sharpness **GB** (GLS) 61 Xd 38
Sharpthorne **GB** (ESX) 71 Zf 42
Sharrington **GB** (NOR) 49 Ba 31
Shatterford **GB** (HWC) 53 Xe 34
Shaugh Bridge **GB** (DEV) 76 Vf 46
Shavington **GB** (CHS) 44 Xd 30
Shavington Park **GB** (SHS) 44 Xc 31
Shaw **GB** (BKS) 62 Ye 40
Shaw **GB** (GRM) 39 Xf 27
Shaw **GB** (WIL) 61 Xf 40
Shawbost **GB** (HGL) 11 Tb 119
Shawbury **GB** (SHS) 44 Xc 32
Shawell **GB** (LEC) 54 Ye 34
Shawford **GB** (HAS) 70 Ye 42
Shawforth **GB** (LCS) 39 Xf 26
Shawhead **GB** (DAG) 31 Wb 18
Shaw Mills **GB** (NOY) 39 Yc 24
Shearington **GB** (DAG) 31 Wc 19
Shebbear **GB** (DEV) 66 Ve 43
Shebdon **GB** (SFS) 45 Xd 32
Shebster **GB** (HGL) 5 Wb 117
Sheddings, The **GB** (ANT) 79 Tf 19
Shedfield **GB** (HAS) 70 Ye 43
Sheeanamore **IRL** (WKL) 95 Td 31
Sheeaun **IRL** (CRE) 92 Rc 31
Sheehills House **IRL** (TIP) 93 Sb 31
Sheen **GB** (SFS) 45 Yb 30
Sheephouse **IRL** (MT) 90 Td 26
Sheepscombe **GB** (GLS) 61 Xf 38
Sheepstor **GB** (DEV) 76 Vf 46
Sheepwash **GB** (DEV) 66 Vf 43
Sheepy Magna **GB** (LEC) 54 Yc 33
Sheepy Parva **GB** (LEC) 54 Yc 33
Sheering **GB** (ESS) 64 Ab 38
Sheerness **GB** (KEN) 65 Ae 40
Sheffield **GB** (ESX) 71 Aa 42
Sheffield **GB** (SOY) 46 Yd 28
Sheffield Bottom **GB** (BKS) 63 Yf 40
Shefford **GB** (BFS) 55 Ze 36
Sheinton **GB** (SHS) 52 Xc 33
Shelderton **GB** (SHS) 52 Xa 34
Sheldon **GB** (DEV) 67 We 43
Sheldon **GB** (DSH) 45 Yb 29

132 GB IRL Rushden – Sheldon

Sheldon **GB** (WMD) 53 Yb 34
Sheldwich **GB** (KEN) 65 Af 41
Shelf **GB** (WYO) 39 Yb 26
Shelfanger **GB** (NOR) 57 Ba 34
Shelford **GB** (NTS) 46 Yf 31
Shellbrook **IRL** (DON) 77 Sc 18
Shelley **GB** (SUF) 57 Af 36
Shelley **GB** (WYO) 39 Yb 27
Shellingford **GB** (OXS) 62 Yc 39
Shellow Bowells **GB** (ESS) 64 Ab 38
Shelmaliere Commons **IRL** (WEX) 101 Tc 35
Shelsley Beauchamp **GB** (HWC) 53 Xd 35
Shelton **GB** (BFS) 55 Zd 35
Shelton **GB** (NOR) 57 Bb 34
Shelton **GB** (NTS) 46 Za 31
Shelton **GB** (SHS) 52 Xb 32
Shelve **GB** (SHS) 52 Xa 33
Shelwick **GB** (HWC) 52 Xb 36
Shenley **GB** (HTS) 64 Ze 38
Shenley Brook End **GB** (BUS) 54 Zb 36
Shenleybury **GB** (HTS) 64 Ze 38
Shenley Church End **GB** (BUS) 54 Zb 36
Shenmore **GB** (HWC) 52 Xa 36
Shenstone **GB** (SFS) 53 Ya 33
Shenton **GB** (LEC) 54 Yd 33
Shenval **GB** (GRP) 16 We 4
Shepeau Stow **GB** (LIN) 47 Zf 32
Shepherd's Green **GB** (OXS) 63 Za 39
Shepherdswell or Silbertswold **GB** (KEN) 73 Bb 41
Shepley **GB** (WYO) 39 Yb 27
Shepperdine **GB** (AVN) 61 Xc 39
Shepreth **GB** (CBS) 55 Aa 36
Shepshed **GB** (LEC) 46 Ye 32
Shepton Beauchamp **GB** (SOM) 68 Xa 43
Shepton Mallet **GB** (SOM) 68 Xc 41
Shepton Montague **GB** (SOM) 68 Xd 42
Shepway **GB** (KEN) 65 Ad 41
Sheraton **GB** (DUR) 36 Ye 20
Sherborne **GB** (DOS) 68 Xc 43
Sherborne **GB** (GLS) 62 Yb 38
Sherborne Saint John **GB** (HAS) 70 Yf 41
Sherbourne **GB** (WWH) 53 Yc 35
Sherburn **GB** (DUR) 36 Yc 20
Sherburn **GB** (NOY) 37 Zc 23
Sherburn in Elmet **GB** (NOY) 40 Ye 26
Shercock **IRL** (CAV) 89 Ta 25
Shereford **GB** (NOR) 48 Ae 32
Sherfield English **GB** (HAS) 69 Yc 42
Sherfield on Loddon **GB** (HAS) 63 Yf 41
Sherford **GB** (DEV) 76 Wb 47
Sheriffhales **GB** (SHS) 53 Xd 32
Sheriff Hutton **GB** (NOY) 40 Yf 24
Sheringham **GB** (NOR) 49 Bb 31
Sherington **GB** (BUS) 55 Zb 36
Shernborne **GB** (NOR) 48 Ad 31
Sherrington **GB** (WIL) 69 Xf 42
Sherston **GB** (WIL) 61 Xe 39
Sheskinapoll **IRL** (DON) 77 Sc 19
Sheskinshule **GB** (TYR) 83 Sf 20
Shettleston **GB** (STC) 25 Vf 13
Shevington **GB** (GRM) 38 Xb 27
Sheviock **GB** (CNW) 75 Ve 46
Shiel Bridge **GB** (HGL) 14 Ud 5
Shieldaig **GB** (HGL) 7 Ub 2
Shieldaig **GB** (HGL) 13 Uc 3
Shieldhill **GB** (CEN) 25 Wb 13
Shielfoot **GB** (HGL) 19 Ub 8
Shielhill **GB** (TYS) 22 Xa 8
Shifford **GB** (OXS) 62 Yd 38
Shifnal **GB** (SHS) 53 Xd 33
Shilbottle **GB** (NHL) 33 Yb 16
Shildon **GB** (DUR) 36 Yc 21
Shillelagh **IRL** (WKL) 95 Tc 32
Shillingford **GB** (DEV) 67 Wd 42
Shillingford **GB** (OXS) 63 Yf 39
Shillingford Saint George **GB** (DEV) 67 Wc 44
Shillingstone **GB** (DOS) 68 Xe 43
Shillington **GB** (BFS) 55 Zd 37
Shillmoor **GB** (NHL) 33 Xe 16
Shiltenish **GB** (HGL) 11 Tc 120
Shilton **GB** (OXS) 62 Yc 38
Shilton **GB** (WWH) 54 Yd 34
Shimpling **GB** (SUF) 56 Ae 36
Shiney Row **GB** (TAW) 33 Yd 19
Shinfield **GB** (BKS) 63 Za 40
Shingay **GB** (CBS) 55 Zf 36
Shingle Street **GB** (SUF) 57 Bc 36
Shinglis House **IRL** (WMT) 89 Sb 27
Shinner's Bridge **GB** (DEV) 76 Wb 46
Shinness **GB** (HGL) 8 Vd 120
Shinrone **IRL** (OFF) 93 Sa 31
Shipbourne **GB** (KEN) 72 Ab 41
Shipdham **GB** (NOR) 56 Af 33
Shipham **GB** (SOM) 68 Xb 41
Shiplate **GB** (AVN) 68 Xa 41
Shiple Bridge **GB** (DEV) 76 Wa 46
Shipley **GB** (OXS) 63 Za 40
Shipley **GB** (SHS) 53 Xe 33
Shipley **GB** (WYO) 39 Yb 25
Shipley Bridge **GB** (SUR) 71 Zf 42
Shippon **GB** (OXS) 63 Ye 38
Shipston-on-Stour **GB** (WWH) 53 Yc 36
Shipton **GB** (GLS) 62 Ya 37
Shipton **GB** (NOY) 40 Yf 24
Shipton **GB** (SHS) 52 Xc 33
Shipton Bellinger **GB** (HAS) 69 Yc 41
Shipton Gorge **GB** (DOS) 68 Xb 44
Shipton Moyne **GB** (GLS) 61 Xf 39
Shiptonthorpe **GB** (HUS) 40 Zb 25
Shipton-under-Wychwood **GB** (OXS) 62 Yc 37
Shirburn **GB** (OXS) 63 Yf 39
Shirdley Hill **GB** (LCS) 38 Xa 27
Shirebrook **GB** (DSH) 46 Ye 29
Shirehampton **GB** (AVN) 61 Xb 40
Shiremoor **GB** (TAW) 33 Yc 18
Shirenewton **GB** (GWE) 61 Xb 39
Shirke House **IRL** (LAO) 93 Sc 31
Shirland **GB** (DSH) 46 Yd 30
Shirley **GB** (DSH) 45 Yb 31
Shirley **GB** (HAS) 69 Yb 44
Shirley **GB** (WMD) 53 Yb 34
Shirl Heath **GB** (HWC) 52 Xa 35
Shirrell Heath **GB** (HAS) 70 Ye 43
Shirwell **GB** (DEV) 66 Vf 42
Shirwell Cross **GB** (DEV) 66 Vf 42
Shiskine **GB** (STC) 28 Ue 15
Shobdon **GB** (HWC) 52 Xa 35
Shobrooke **GB** (DEV) 67 Wc 44
Shocklach **GB** (CHS) 44 Xa 30
Shoeburyness **GB** (ESS) 65 Ae 39
Sholden **GB** (KEN) 65 Bc 41
Shoot Hill **GB** (SHS) 52 Xa 32
Shooting Lodge **IRL** (LET) 82 Sa 24
Shop **GB** (CNW) 66 Vc 43
Shop **GB** (CNW) 75 Va 45
Shoptown **GB** (ANT) 79 Tf 20
Shoreditch **GB** (GRL) 64 Zf 39
Shoreham **GB** (KEN) 64 Ab 41
Shoreham-by-Sea **GB** (WSX) 71 Ze 44
Shoresdean **GB** (NHL) 27 Xf 14
Shoreswood **GB** (NHL) 27 Xf 14
Shorne **GB** (KEN) 65 Ac 40
Shortgate **GB** (ESX) 71 Aa 43
Short Green **GB** (NOR) 57 Ba 34
Short Heath **GB** (WMD) 53 Ya 33
Shortlanesend **GB** (CNW) 74 Uf 47
Shorwell **GB** (IOW) 70 Yd 45
Shotesham **GB** (NOR) 57 Bb 33
Shotley **GB** (SUF) 57 Bb 37
Shotley Bridge **GB** (DUR) 33 Ya 19
Shotley Gate **GB** (SUF) 57 Bb 37
Shottenden **GB** (KEN) 65 Af 41
Shottermill **GB** (SUR) 70 Zb 42
Shotteswell **GB** (WWH) 54 Yd 36
Shottisham **GB** (SUF) 57 Bc 36
Shottle **GB** (DSH) 45 Yc 30
Shottlegate **GB** (DSH) 46 Yc 30
Shotton **GB** (CLW) 44 Wf 29
Shotton Colliery **GB** (DUR) 36 Yd 20
Shotts **GB** (STC) 25 Wb 14
Shotwick **GB** (CHS) 44 Xa 29
Shoughlaige-e-Caine **GBM** 29 Vc 23
Shouldham **GB** (NOR) 56 Ac 33
Shouldham Thorpe **GB** (NOR) 56 Ac 33
Shover's Green **GB** (ESX) 72 Ac 42
Shrawardine **GB** (SHS) 52 Xa 32
Shrawley **GB** (HWC) 53 Xe 35
Shrewley **GB** (WWH) 53 Yb 35
Shrewsbury **GB** (SHS) 52 Xb 32
Shrewton **GB** (WIL) 69 Ya 41
Shrine **IRL** (LOT) 90 Td 24
Shrivenham **GB** (OXS) 62 Yc 39
Shronacarton Cross Roads **IRL** (COR) 103 Qe 38
Shrone **IRL** (KER) 97 Qd 33
Shronebeha **IRL** (COR) 98 Ra 36
Shropham **GB** (NOR) 56 Af 34
Shroton, Iwerne Courtney or **GB** (DOS) 69 Xe 43
Shrule **IRL** (MAY) 87 Qf 27
Shucknall **GB** (HWC) 52 Xc 36
Shulishader **GB** (HGL) 11 Te 119
Shurdington **GB** (GLS) 61 Xf 37
Shurlock Row **GB** (BKS) 63 Aa 40
Shurrery **GB** (HGL) 5 Wc 117
Shurton **GB** (SOM) 67 Wf 41
Shustoke **GB** (WWH) 53 Yc 33
Shute **GB** (DEV) 67 Wf 44
Shut End **GB** (WMD) 53 Xf 33
Shutford **GB** (OXS) 54 Yd 36
Shuthonger **GB** (GLS) 61 Xf 36
Shutlanger **GB** (NRH) 54 Za 36
Shuttington **GB** (WWH) 53 Yc 33
Shuttlewood **GB** (DSH) 46 Ye 29
Sibbertoft **GB** (NRH) 54 Yf 34
Sibdon Carwood **GB** (SHS) 52 Xa 34
Sibford Ferris **GB** (OXS) 54 Yd 36
Sibford Gower **GB** (OXS) 54 Yd 36
Sible Hedingham **GB** (ESS) 56 Ad 37
Sibsey **GB** (LIN) 47 Aa 30
Sibson **GB** (LEC) 54 Yd 33
Sibthorpe **GB** (NTS) 46 Za 31
Sibton **GB** (SUF) 57 Bc 35
Sicklesmere **GB** (SUF) 56 Ae 35
Sicklinghall **GB** (NOY) 40 Yd 25
Sidbury **GB** (DEV) 67 We 44
Sidbury **GB** (SHS) 52 Xd 34
Sidcot **GB** (AVN) 68 Xb 41
Sidcup **GB** (GRL) 64 Aa 40
Siddan **IRL** (MT) 90 Tc 26
Siddington **GB** (CHS) 45 Xe 29
Sidestrand **GB** (NOR) 49 Bc 31
Sidford **GB** (DEV) 67 We 44
Sidinish **GB** (HGL) 10 Se 3
Sidlesham **GB** (WSX) 70 Zb 44
Sidley **GB** (ESX) 72 Ac 43
Sidlowbridge **GB** (SUR) 71 Ze 41
Sidmouth **GB** (DEV) 67 We 44
Sigford **GB** (DEV) 76 Wb 45
Sigglesthorne **GB** (HUS) 41 Ze 25
Silbertswold, Shepherdswell or **GB** (KEN) 73 Bb 41
Silchester **GB** (HAS) 63 Yf 40
Sileby **GB** (LEC) 46 Yf 32
Silecroft **GB** (CUB) 34 Wd 23
Silfield **GB** (NOR) 57 Ba 33
Silian **GB** (DYF) 50 Vf 36
Silkstone **GB** (SOY) 39 Yc 27
Silkstone Common **GB** (SOY) 39 Yc 27
Silk Willoughby **GB** (LIN) 47 Zd 31
Silahertane **IRL** (COR) 103 Qe 38
Silloth **GB** (CUB) 31 Wd 19
Sillyearn **GB** (GRP) 16 Xb 3
Siloh **GB** (DYF) 59 Wb 36
Silpho **GB** (NOY) 37 Zc 23
Silsden **GB** (WYO) 39 Ya 25
Silsoe **GB** (BFS) 55 Zd 36
Silverburn **GB** (LOT) 26 We 14
Silverdale **GB** (LCS) 35 Xb 24
Silverdale **GB** (SFS) 45 Xe 30
Silver End **GB** (ESS) 65 Ad 37
Silverford **GB** (GRP) 17 Xd 2
Silver Hill **GB** (ESX) 72 Ac 42
Silverley's Green **GB** (SUF) 57 Bc 34
Silvermines **IRL** (TIP) 93 Re 32
Silverstone **GB** (NRH) 54 Yf 36
Silverton **GB** (DEV) 67 Wd 44
Silvington **GB** (SHS) 52 Xc 34
Simonburn **GB** (NHL) 33 Xe 18
Simonsbath **GB** (SOM) 67 Wb 42
Simonstown House **IRL** (WMT) 89 Sd 26
Simprim **GB** (BOR) 27 Xe 14
Sinclairston **GB** (STC) 30 Vd 16
Sinderby **GB** (NOY) 36 Yd 23
Sinderhope **GB** (NHL) 32 Xe 19
Sindlesham **GB** (BKS) 63 Za 40
Singleton **GB** (LCS) 38 Xa 25
Singleton **GB** (WSX) 70 Zb 43
Sinnahard **GB** (GRP) 16 Xa 5
Sinnington **GB** (NOY) 37 Za 23
Sinton Green **GB** (HWC) 53 Xe 35
Sionainn = Shannon **IRL** (CRE) 92 Ra 32
Sion Mills **GB** (TYR) 83 Sd 20
Sipson **GB** (GRL) 63 Zd 40
Sissinghurst **GB** (KEN) 72 Ad 42
Siston **GB** (AVN) 61 Xd 40
Sittingbourne **GB** (KEN) 65 Ae 40
Six Ashes **GB** (SHS) 53 Xe 34
Six Crosses **IRL** (KER) 97 Qc 34
Sixhills **GB** (LIN) 47 Ze 28
Six Mile **IRL** (MOG) 84 Ta 23
Six Mile Bottom **GB** (CBS) 56 Ab 35
Sixmilebridge **IRL** (CRE) 92 Rb 32
Sixmilecross **GB** (TYR) 83 Sf 21
Sixmilewater **IRL** (COR) 98 Rc 36
Sixpenny Handley **GB** (WIL) 69 Ya 43
Six Road Ends **GB** (DOW) 85 Uc 21
Skahanogh South **IRL** (COR) 99 Re 36
Skail **GB** (HGL) 5 Ve 118
Skaill **GB** (ORK) 6 Wa 114
Skaill **GB** (ORK) 6 Xb 115
Skanafaraghaun **IRL** (GAL) 86 Qc 27
Skardaun **IRL** (ROS) 88 Re 27
Skares **GB** (STC) 30 Ve 16
Skarghard **IRL** (CRE) 92 Ra 30
Skateraw **GB** (LOT) 27 Xd 13
Skeabost **GB** (HGL) 13 Te 4
Skeagh **IRL** (WMT) 89 Sc 27
Skeaghvasteen **IRL** (KLK) 100 Ta 33
Skeeby **GB** (NOY) 36 Yb 22
Skeffington **GB** (LEC) 54 Za 33
Skeffling **GB** (HUS) 41 Aa 27
Skegby **GB** (NTS) 46 Ye 30
Skegness **GB** (LIN) 48 Ac 30
Skehanagh **IRL** (GAL) 92 Rb 30
Skehanagh **IRL** (GAL) 93 Rc 29
Skellig **IRL** (COR) 102 Qa 38
Skellingthorpe **GB** (LIN) 47 Zc 29
Skellister **GB** (SHL) 2 Yf 107
Skelmanthorpe **GB** (WYO) 39 Yc 27
Skelmersdale **GB** (LCS) 38 Xb 27
Skelmonae **GB** (GRP) 17 Xe 4
Skelmorlie **GB** (STC) 24 Va 13
Skelpick **GB** (HGL) 5 Ve 118
Skelton **GB** (CLE) 37 Za 21
Skelton **GB** (CUB) 35 Xa 20
Skelton **GB** (NOY) 36 Ya 22
Skelton **GB** (NOY) 40 Yf 25
Skelton on Ure **GB** (NOY) 40 Yd 24
Skelwick **GB** (ORK) 5 Xa 113
Skelwith Bridge **GB** (CUB) 34 Wf 22
Skendleby **GB** (LIN) 47 Aa 29
Skenfrith **GB** (GWE) 61 Xb 37
Skephubble **IRL** (DUB) 90 Te 28
Skerne **GB** (HUS) 41 Zd 25
Skeroblingarry **GB** (STC) 28 Uc 16
Skerray **GB** (HGL) 5 Ve 117
Skerries **IRL** (MT) 90 Tf 27
Sketty **GB** (WGL) 59 Wa 39
Skewen **GB** (WGL) 59 Wa 39
Skewsby **GB** (NOY) 37 Yf 24
Skibbereen **IRL** (COR) 103 Qe 39
Skidby **GB** (HUS) 41 Zd 26
Skigersta **GB** (HGL) 11 Te 118
Skilgate **GB** (SOM) 67 Wd 42
Skillington **GB** (LIN) 47 Zc 32
Skinburness **GB** (CUB) 31 Wd 19
Skinflats **GB** (CEN) 25 Wb 12
Skinidin **GB** (HGL) 12 Tc 4
Skinningrove **GB** (CLE) 37 Za 21
Skipness **GB** (STC) 23 Ud 14
Skipsea **GB** (HUS) 41 Ze 25
Skipton **GB** (NOY) 39 Xf 25
Skipton-on-Swale **GB** (NOY) 36 Yd 23
Skipwith **GB** (NOY) 40 Yf 25
Skirling **GB** (BOR) 25 Wd 15
Skirmett **GB** (BUS) 63 Za 39
Skirwith **GB** (CUB) 35 Xc 20
Skirza **GB** (HGL) 6 Wf 117
Skool **IRL** (LIM) 98 Rc 33
Skreen **IRL** (MT) 90 Tc 27
Skreen **IRL** (SLI) 82 Rb 23
Skulamus **GB** (HGL) 13 Ua 5
Skull **IRL** (COR) 103 Qc 39
Skullomie **GB** (HGL) 5 Vd 117
Skye of Curr **GB** (HGL) 15 Wb 5
Slackhall **GB** (DSH) 45 Ya 28
Slade **IRL** (WEX) 100 Ta 36
Slaggyford **GB** (NHL) 32 Xc 19
Slaidburn **GB** (LCS) 38 Xd 25
Slaithwaite **GB** (WYO) 39 Ya 27
Slaley **GB** (NHL) 33 Xf 19
Slamannan **GB** (CEN) 25 Wa 13
Slane **IRL** (MT) 90 Tc 26
Slapton **GB** (BUS) 63 Zc 37
Slapton **GB** (DEV) 76 Wc 47
Slatenber **GB** (NOY) 35 Xd 24
Slattagh Beg **IRL** (ROS) 88 Sa 26
Slawston **GB** (LEC) 54 Za 33
Sleaford **GB** (HAS) 70 Za 42
Sleaford **GB** (LIN) 47 Zd 31
Sleagill **GB** (CUB) 35 Xc 21
Sleapford **GB** (SHS) 44 Xc 32
Sledge Green **GB** (HWC) 61 Xe 36
Sledmere **GB** (HUS) 41 Zc 24
Sleights **GB** (NOY) 37 Zc 22
Slepe **GB** (DOS) 69 Xf 44
Sleveen East **IRL** (COR) 103 Ra 37
Slickly **GB** (HGL) 6 We 117
Sliddery **GB** (STC) 28 Ue 16
Slieve **IRL** (LOT) 90 Td 24
Slieveanulty **IRL** (GAL) 88 Rd 28
Slievedotia **IRL** (COR) 98 Rc 36
Slievemore **IRL** (COR) 103 Qd 40
Slievemurry **IRL** (GAL) 88 Rd 27
Slieveowen **IRL** (COR) 103 Qf 38
Slieveroe **IRL** (KLK) 100 Sf 35
Slieve Russell House **IRL** (CAV) 83 Sc 24
Sligo **IRL** (SLI) 82 Rd 23
Slimbridge **GB** (GLS) 61 Xd 38
Slindon **GB** (SFS) 45 Xe 31
Slindon **GB** (WSX) 70 Zc 43
Slinfold **GB** (WSX) 71 Zd 42
Slingsby **GB** (NOY) 37 Za 23
Slioch **GB** (GRP) 16 Xb 4
Slip End **GB** (BFS) 63 Zd 37
Slipton **GB** (NRH) 55 Zc 34
Slochd **GB** (HGL) 15 Wa 5
Slockavullin **GB** (STC) 23 Uc 12
Sloley **GB** (NOR) 49 Bc 32
Slothsby **GB** (LIN) 48 Zf 29
Slough **GB** (BKS) 63 Zc 39
Sluggera Cross Roads **IRL** (WTF) 104 Sb 37
Smailholm **GB** (BOR) 26 Xc 15
Smallbridge **GB** (GRM) 39 Xf 27
Small Dole **GB** (WSX) 71 Ze 43
Smalley **GB** (DSH) 46 Yd 31
Smallfield **GB** (SUR) 71 Zf 42
Small Hythe **GB** (KEN) 72 Ae 42
Smallridge **GB** (DEV) 68 Wf 44
Smannell **GB** (HAS) 69 Yd 41
Smarden **GB** (KEN) 72 Ae 42
Smarmore **IRL** (LOT) 90 Tc 26
Smeatharpe **GB** (DEV) 67 Wf 43
Smeeth **GB** (KEN) 72 Af 42
Smeeton Westerby **GB** (LEC) 54 Za 33
Smerral **GB** (HGL) 9 Wd 119
Smerwick **IRL** (KER) 96 Pd 35
Smethwick **GB** (WMD) 53 Ya 34
Smisby **GB** (DSH) 46 Yd 32
Smithborough **IRL** (MOG) 83 Sf 23
Smith End Green **GB** (HWC) 53 Xe 35
Smithfield **GB** (CUB) 32 Xa 19
Smith Green **GB** (ESS) 64 Ab 37
Smith Hill **IRL** (ROS) 88 Re 25
Smithincott **GB** (DEV) 67 Wd 43
Smithstown **IRL** (KLK) 94 Se 32
Smithton **GB** (HGL) 15 Vf 4
Smithy Green **GB** (CHS) 44 Xd 29
Smorane **IRL** (COR) 103 Qe 39
Smug Oak **GB** (HTS) 63 Zd 38
Smyths Green **GB** (ESS) 65 Ae 38
Snailbeach **GB** (SHS) 52 Xa 33
Snailwell **GB** (CBS) 56 Ac 35
Snainton **GB** (NOY) 37 Zc 23
Snaith **GB** (HUS) 40 Yf 26
Snape **GB** (NOY) 36 Yc 23
Snape **GB** (SUF) 57 Bc 35
Snape Street **GB** (SUF) 57 Bc 36
Snarestone **GB** (LEC) 54 Yd 32
Snarford **GB** (LIN) 47 Zd 29
Snargate **GB** (KEN) 72 Af 42
Snave **GB** (KEN) 72 Af 42
Snead **GB** (POW) 52 Wf 33
Sneaton **GB** (NOY) 37 Zc 22
Sneatonthorpe **GB** (NOY) 37 Zc 22
Sneem **IRL** (KER) 102 Qa 37
Snelland **GB** (LIN) 47 Zd 29
Snelston **GB** (DSH) 45 Yb 31
Snettisham **GB** (NOR) 48 Ad 31
Snitter **GB** (NHL) 33 Ya 17
Snitterby **GB** (LIN) 41 Zc 28
Snitterfield **GB** (WWH) 53 Yb 35
Snitton **GB** (SHS) 52 Xc 34
Snodhill **GB** (HWC) 52 Xa 36
Snodland **GB** (KEN) 65 Ac 41
Snopworth **GB** (WIL) 61 Xe 39
Snowshill **GB** (GLS) 62 Ya 36
Soberton **GB** (HAS) 70 Yf 43
Soberton Heath **GB** (HAS) 70 Yf 43
Sodylt Bank **GB** (SHS) 44 Xa 31
Soham **GB** (CBS) 56 Ab 35
Soldon Cross **GB** (DEV) 66 Vd 43
Soldridge **GB** (HAS) 70 Yf 42
Sole Street **GB** (KEN) 64 Ac 40
Solihull **GB** (WMD) 53 Yb 34
Sollas **GB** (HGL) 10 Sd 3
Sollers Dilwyn **GB** (HWC) 52 Xa 35
Sollers Hope **GB** (HWC) 61 Xc 37
Sollom **GB** (LCS) 38 Xb 27
Solva **GB** (DYF) 58 Ue 37
Somerby **GB** (LEC) 54 Za 32
Somercotes **GB** (DSH) 46 Yd 30
Somerford Keynes **GB** (GLS) 62 Ya 39
Somerley **GB** (WSX) 70 Za 44
Somersal Herbert **GB** (DSH) 45 Yb 31
Somersby **GB** (LIN) 47 Aa 29
Somerset House **IRL** (GAL) 93 Re 29
Somersham **GB** (CBS) 55 Zf 34
Somerton **GB** (OXS) 62 Ye 37
Somerton **GB** (SOM) 68 Xb 42
Sompson Cross **GB** (DYF) 58 Uf 38
Sompting **GB** (WSX) 71 Ze 44
Sonnagh **IRL** (GAL) 88 Rd 27
Sonnagh **IRL** (MAY) 87 Ra 25
Sonna House **IRL** (WMT) 89 Sd 27
Sonning **GB** (BKS) 63 Za 40
Sonning Common **GB** (OXS) 63 Za 39
Sopley **GB** (HAS) 69 Yb 44
Soppog **IRL** (DON) 78 Se 18
Soran **IRL** (LGF) 89 Sb 26
Sorbie **GB** (DAG) 29 Vd 20
Sordale **GB** (HGL) 6 Wd 117
Sorisdale **GB** (STC) 18 Td 8
Sorn **GB** (STC) 30 Ve 15
Sornhill **GB** (STC) 24 Vd 15
Sortat **GB** (HGL) 6 We 117
Sotby **GB** (LIN) 47 Ze 29
Soughton **GB** (CLW) 44 Wf 29
Soulby **GB** (CUB) 35 Xd 22
Souldern **GB** (OXS) 62 Ye 37
Souldrop **GB** (BFS) 55 Zc 35
Soundwell **GB** (AVN) 61 Xc 40
Sourhope **GB** (BOR) 32 Xe 16
Sourlage **GB** (WGL) 59 Ve 39
Sourton **GB** (DEV) 66 Vf 44
Soutergate **GB** (CUB) 34 We 23
South Acre **GB** (NOR) 48 Ad 32
Southall **GB** (GRL) 64 Zd 39
Southam **GB** 61 Xf 37
Southam **GB** (WWH) 54 Yd 35
South Ambersham **GB** (WSX) 70 Zb 43
Southampton **GB** (HAS) 70 Yd 43
South Bank **GB** (CLE) 37 Ye 21
South Barrow **GB** (SOM) 68 Xc 42
South Benfleet **GB** (ESS) 65 Ad 39
Southborough **GB** (GRL) 64 Aa 40
Southborough **GB** (KEN) 72 Ab 42
Southbourne **GB** (WSX) 70 Za 43
South Bowood **GB** (DOS) 68 Xb 44
South Brend **GB** (DEV) 76 Wa 46
South Brentor **GB** (DEV) 76 Vf 45
South Brewham **GB** (SOM) 68 Xd 42
Southburgh **GB** (NOR) 56 Af 33
South Burlingham **GB** (NOR) 49 Bd 33
South Cadbury **GB** (SOM) 68 Xc 42
South Cairn **GB** (DAG) 28 Ue 19
South Cave **GB** (HUS) 41 Zc 26
South Cerney **GB** (GLS) 62 Ya 38
South Charlton **GB** (NHL) 33 Yb 16
South Cheriton **GB** (SOM) 68 Xd 42
South Cliffe **GB** (HUS) 40 Zb 26
South Clifton **GB** (NTS) 46 Zb 29
South Cockerington **GB** (LIN) 41 Aa 28
South Cove **GB** (SUF) 57 Bd 34
South Creake **GB** (NOR) 48 Ae 31
South Croxton **GB** (LEC) 54 Za 32
South Dalton **GB** (HUS) 41 Zc 25
South Darenth **GB** (KEN) 64 Ab 40
South Duffield **GB** (NOY) 40 Za 26
Southease **GB** (ESX) 71 Aa 44
South Elkington **GB** (LIN) 47 Zf 28
South Elmsall **GB** (WYO) 40 Ye 27
Southend **GB** (BKS) 63 Yf 40
Southend **GB** (STC) 28 Uc 17
Southend-on-Sea **GB** (ESS) 65 Ae 39
Southerndown **GB** (MGL) 60 Wc 40
Southerness **GB** (DAG) 31 Wc 19
Southery **GB** (NOR) 56 Ac 33
South Fambridge **GB** (ESS) 65 Ae 39
South Fawley **GB** (BKS) 62 Yd 39
South Ferriby **GB** (HUS) 41 Zc 26
Southfleet **GB** (KEN) 64 Ab 40
South Galson **GB** (HGL) 11 Td 118
South Garvan **GB** (HGL) 19 Ue 7
Southgate **GB** (GRL) 64 Zf 39
Southgate **GB** (NOR) 48 Ac 31
Southgate **GB** (WGL) 59 Vf 39
South Godstone **GB** (SUR) 71 Zf 41
South Hanningfield **GB** (ESS) 65 Ad 39
South Hayling **GB** (HAS) 70 Za 44
South Heath **GB** (BUS) 63 Zb 38
South Hetton **GB** (DUR) 36 Yd 20
South Hill **GB** (CNW) 75 Vd 45
South Holmwood **GB** (SUR) 71 Ze 41
South Huish **GB** (DEV) 76 Wa 47
South Hylton **GB** (TAW) 33 Yd 19
Southill **GB** (BFS) 55 Ze 36
Southington **GB** (HAS) 70 Ye 41
South Kelsey **GB** (LIN) 41 Zd 28
South Killingholme **GB** (HUS) 41 Ze 27
South Kilvington **GB** (NOY) 36 Yd 23
South Kilworth **GB** (LEC) 54 Yf 34
South Kirkby **GB** (WYO) 40 Ye 27
South Kirkton **GB** (GRP) 17 Xd 6
South Kyme **GB** (LIN) 47 Ze 30
South Lancing **GB** (WSX) 71 Ze 44
Southleigh **GB** (DEV) 67 Wf 44
South Leigh **GB** (OXS) 62 Yd 38
South Leverton **GB** (NTS) 41 Zb 29
South Littleton **GB** (HWC) 53 Ya 36
South Lochboisdale **GB** (HGL) 12 Se 6
South Lopham **GB** (NOR) 57 Af 34
South Luffenham **GB** (LEC) 55 Zc 33
South Malling **GB** (ESX) 71 Aa 43
South Marston **GB** (WIL) 62 Yb 39
South Milford **GB** (NOY) 40 Ye 26
South Mimms **GB** (HTS) 64 Ze 38
Southminster **GB** (ESS) 65 Ae 39
South Molton **GB** (DEV) 67 Wa 42
South Moor **GB** (DUR) 33 Yb 19
South Moreton **GB** (OXS) 63 Ye 39
South Mundham **GB** (WSX) 70 Zb 44
South Muskham **GB** (NTS) 46 Zb 30
South Newington **GB** (OXS) 62 Yd 37
South Newton **GB** (STC) 23 Ue 14
South Newton **GB** (WIL) 69 Ya 42
South Normanton **GB** (DSH) 46 Yd 30
South Nutfield **GB** (SUR) 71 Zf 41
South Ockendon **GB** (ESS) 64 Ab 39
Southoe **GB** (CBS) 55 Ze 35
Southolt **GB** (SUF) 57 Bb 35
South Ormsby **GB** (LIN) 47 Aa 29
Southorpe **GB** (CBS) 55 Zd 33
South Otterington **GB** (NOY) 36 Yd 23
Southowram **GB** (WYO) 39 Ya 26
South Oxey **GB** (HTS) 63 Zd 39
South Park **GB** (SUR) 71 Ze 41
South Perrott **GB** (DOS) 68 Xb 43
South Petherton **GB** (SOM) 68 Xb 43
South Petherwin **GB** (CNW) 75 Vd 45
South Pickenham **GB** (NOR) 56 Ae 33
South Pool **GB** (DEV) 76 Wb 47
Southport **GB** (MES) 38 Wf 27
South Radworthy **GB** (DEV) 67 Wb 42
Southrepps **GB** (NOR) 49 Bc 31
South Reston **GB** (LIN) 47 Aa 29
Southrey **GB** (LIN) 47 Ze 29
South Ring **IRL** (COR) 103 Ra 39
Southrop **GB** (GLS) 62 Yb 38
Southrope **GB** (HAS) 70 Yf 41
South Runcton **GB** (NOR) 56 Ac 33
South Scarle **GB** (NTS) 46 Zb 29
South Shields **GB** (TAW) 33 Yd 18
South Skirlaugh **GB** (HUS) 41 Ze 25
South Somercotes **GB** (LIN) 41 Aa 28
South Stainley **GB** (NOY) 39 Yc 24
South Stoke **GB** (WSX) 71 Zc 43
South Street **GB** (ESX) 71 Zf 43
South Street **GB** (KEN) 64 Ac 40
South Thoresby **GB** (LIN) 47 Aa 29
South Tidworth **GB** (HAS) 69 Yc 41
Southtown **GB** (ORK) 6 Xa 115
South View **GB** (SHL) 2 Ye 107
South Walsham **GB** (NOR) 49 Bc 33
Southwark **GB** (GRL) 64 Zf 40
South Warnborough **GB** (HAS) 70 Za 41
Southwater **GB** (WSX) 71 Zd 42
Southway **GB** (SOM) 68 Xb 41
South Weald **GB** (ESS) 64 Ab 39
Southwell **GB** (DOS) 68 Xd 45
Southwell **GB** (NTS) 46 Za 30
South Wheatley **GB** (CNW) 66 Vd 44
Southwick **GB** (HAS) 70 Yf 43
Southwick **GB** (NRH) 55 Zd 33
Southwick **GB** (TAW) 33 Yd 19
Southwick **GB** (WSX) 71 Ze 44
South Wingfield **GB** (DSH) 46 Yd 30
South Witham **GB** (LIN) 47 Zc 32
Southwold **GB** (SUF) 57 Bd 35
South Wonston **GB** (HAS) 70 Ye 42
South Woodham Ferrers **GB** (ESS) 65 Ad 39
South Wootton **GB** (NOR) 48 Ac 32
South Zeal **GB** (DEV) 66 Wa 44
Sowerby **GB** (NOY) 36 Yd 23
Sowerby **GB** (WYO) 39 Ya 26
Sowerby Bridge **GB** (WYO) 39 Ya 26
Sowerby Row **GB** (CUB) 35 Xa 20
Spa **IRL** (KER) 97 Qb 35
Spa Common **GB** (NOR) 49 Bc 32
Spaddagh **IRL** (MAY) 87 Qf 25
Spalding **GB** (LIN) 47 Zf 32
Spaldington **GB** (HUS) 40 Za 26
Spaldwick **GB** (CBS) 55 Zd 34
Spalford **GB** (NTS) 46 Zb 29
Spa Mount **IRL** (COR) 98 Qf 36
Spanby **GB** (LIN) 47 Zd 31
Sparham **GB** (NOR) 49 Ba 32
Spark Bridge **GB** (CUB) 34 Wf 23
Sparkford **GB** (SOM) 68 Xc 42
Sparkwell **GB** (DEV) 76 Wa 46
Sparrowpit **GB** (DSH) 45 Ya 29
Sparsholt **GB** (HAS) 70 Yd 42
Sparsholt **GB** (OXS) 62 Yd 39
Spaunton **GB** (NOY) 37 Za 23
Spave **IRL** (COR) 103 Qd 38
Spa Well **IRL** (KER) 97 Qd 36
Spean Bridge **GB** (HGL) 19 Va 7
Speen **GB** (BKS) 62 Yd 40
Speen **GB** (BUS) 63 Zb 38
Speenoge **IRL** (DON) 78 Sd 18
Speeton **GB** (NOY) 37 Ze 24
Speke **GB** (MES) 44 Xa 28
Speldhurst **GB** (KEN) 71 Ab 42
Spellbrook **GB** (HTS) 64 Aa 38
Spelsbury **GB** (OXS) 62 Yd 37
Spencers Wood **GB** (BKS) 63 Za 40
Spennithorne **GB** (NOY) 36 Yb 23
Spennymoor **GB** (DUR) 36 Yc 20
Spetchley **GB** (HWC) 53 Xf 35
Spetisbury **GB** (DOS) 69 Xf 44
Spexhall **GB** (SUF) 57 Bc 34
Spey Bay **GB** (GRP) 9 Wf 2
Spiddle **IRL** (GAL) 92 Qe 29
Spilsby **GB** (LIN) 47 Aa 29
Spindlestone **GB** (NHL) 27 Yb 15
Spinkhill **GB** (DSH) 46 Ye 29
Spinningdale **GB** (HGL) 8 Ve 1
Spirthill **GB** (WIL) 62 Xf 40
Spithurst **GB** (ESX) 71 Aa 43
Spittafield **GB** (TYS) 21 Wd 9
Spittal **GB** (DAG) 30 Vc 19
Spittal **GB** (DYF) 58 Va 37
Spittal **GB** (HGL) 6 Wd 118
Spittal **GB** (NHL) 27 Ya 14
Spittal of Glenshee **GB** (TYS) 21 Wd 8
Spittle **IRL** (LIM) 99 Rd 35
Splithill Cross Roads **IRL** (KIL) 94 Ta 30
Spofforth **GB** (NOY) 40 Yd 25
Spondon **GB** (DSH) 46 Yd 31
Spooner Row **GB** (NOR) 57 Ba 33
Spott **GB** (LOT) 26 Xc 13
Spratton **GB** (NRH) 54 Za 35
Spreade's Cross Roads **IRL** (COR) 104 Rc 38
Spreyton **GB** (DEV) 67 Wa 44
Spridlington **GB** (LIN) 47 Zd 28
Springburn **GB** (STC) 25 Ve 13
Springfield **GB** (FER) 83 Sb 22
Springfield **GB** (FIF) 21 Wf 11
Springfield **GB** (WMD) 53 Ya 34
Springhill **IRL** (COR) 98 Rd 36
Springholm **GB** (DAG) 31 Wa 18
Springlawn **IRL** (GAL) 88 Rc 27
Springlawn **IRL** (ROS) 88 Rf 27
Spring Park **IRL** (TIP) 93 Rf 30
Springside **GB** (STC) 24 Vc 15
Springthorpe **GB** (LIN) 40 Zb 28
Spring Vale **IRL** (DON) 77 Sb 19
Sproatley **GB** (HUS) 41 Ze 26
Sproston Green **GB** (CHS) 44 Xd 29
Sprotbrough **GB** (SOY) 40 Ye 27
Sproughton **GB** (SUF) 57 Ba 36
Sprouston **GB** (BOR) 27 Xd 15
Sprowston **GB** (NOR) 49 Bb 33
Sproxton **GB** (LEC) 46 Zb 32
Sproxton **GB** (NOY) 37 Yf 23
Spunkane **IRL** (KER) 102 Pe 37
Spurstow **GB** (CHS) 44 Xb 30
Square and Compass **GB** (DYF) 58 Uf 37
Srah **IRL** (MAY) 80 Qa 23
Srah **IRL** (MAY) 87 Qd 26
Srahbaun **IRL** (KLK) 94 Sc 32
Srahcullen **IRL** (LAO) 94 Sc 30
Srahduggaun **IRL** (MAY) 86 Qb 24
Sraheen **IRL** (MAY) 87 Qd 26
Sraheens **IRL** (MAY) 86 Qa 25
Srahlea Bridge **IRL** (MAY) 86 Qc 26
Srahmore **IRL** (MAY) 80 Qb 24
Srahnakilly **IRL** (MAY) 81 Qc 24
Srahnamanragh Bridge **IRL** (MAY) 80 Qa 24
Sranataggle **IRL** (MAY) 80 Qb 23
Srath **IRL** (DON) 78 Se 18
Sroove **IRL** (SLI) 88 Rc 25
Srunahella **IRL** (WMT) 89 Se 26
Stabannan **IRL** (LOT) 90 Td 25
Stackallan **IRL** (MT) 90 Tc 26
Stackhouse **GB** (NOY) 39 Xe 24
Stackpole **GB** (DYF) 58 Va 39
Stacksteads **GB** (LCS) 39 Xe 26
Stad **GB** (GLS) 61 Xe 38
Staddlethorpe **GB** (HUS) 40 Zb 26
Stadhampton **GB** (OXS) 63 Yf 38
Staffield **GB** (CUB) 35 Xb 20
Staffin **GB** (HGL) 13 Te 3
Stafford **GB** (SFS) 45 Xf 32
Stagsden **GB** (BFS) 55 Zc 36
Stainburn **GB** (NOY) 39 Yc 25
Stainby **GB** (LIN) 47 Zc 32
Staincross **GB** (SOY) 40 Yd 27
Staindrop **GB** (DUR) 36 Yb 21
Staines **GB** (SUR) 63 Zc 40
Stainfield **GB** (LIN) 47 Zd 29
Stainfield **GB** (LIN) 47 Zd 32
Stainfield **GB** (NOR) 49 Af 32
Stainforth **GB** (NOY) 39 Xe 24
Stainforth **GB** (SOY) 40 Yf 27
Staining **GB** (LCS) 38 Xa 26
Stainland **GB** (WYO) 39 Ya 26
Stainsacre **GB** (NOY) 37 Zc 22
Stainton **GB** (CLE) 36 Ye 21
Stainton **GB** (CUB) 35 Xb 21
Stainton **GB** (CUB) 35 Xb 23
Stainton **GB** (DUR) 36 Ya 21
Stainton **GB** (NOY) 36 Ya 22
Stainton **GB** (SOY) 40 Ye 28
Stainton by Langworth **GB** (LIN) 47 Zd 29
Staintondale **GB** (NOY) 37 Zd 22
Stainton le Vale **GB** (LIN) 41 Ze 28
Stainton with Adgarley **GB** (CUB) 34 Wf 24
Stair **GB** (CUB) 34 We 21
Stair **GB** (STC) 30 Vd 16
Staithes **GB** (NOY) 37 Zb 21
Stakeford **GB** (NHL) 33 Yc 18
Stakehill **IRL** (COR) 98 Qf 36
Stake Pool **GB** (LCS) 38 Xa 25
Stalbridge **GB** (DOS) 68 Xd 43
Stalbridge Weston **GB** (DOS) 68 Xd 43
Stalham **GB** (NOR) 49 Bd 32
Stalham Green **GB** (NOR) 49 Bd 32
Stalisfield Green **GB** (KEN) 65 Ae 41
Stallingborough **GB** (HUS) 41 Ze 27
Stalmine **GB** (LCS) 38 Xa 25
Stalybridge **GB** (GRM) 39 Xf 28
Stamford **GB** (LIN) 55 Zd 33
Stamford Bridge **GB** (HUS) 40 Za 25
Stamfordham **GB** (NHL) 33 Ya 18
Stamullin **IRL** (MT) 90 Te 27
Stanbridge **GB** (BFS) 63 Zc 37
Stanbridge **GB** (DOS) 69 Xf 44
Stand **GB** (STC) 25 Wa 13
Standburn **GB** (CEN) 25 Wb 13
Standeford **GB** (SFS) 53 Xf 33
Standen **GB** (KEN) 72 Ad 42
Standford **GB** (HAS) 70 Za 42
Standford in the Vale **GB** (OXS) 62 Yd 39
Standford -le -Hope **GB** (ESS) 65 Ac 39
Stand House **IRL** (COR) 99 Re 36
Standish **GB** (GRM) 38 Xc 27
Standlake **GB** (OXS) 62 Yd 38
Standon **GB** (HAS) 70 Yd 42
Standon **GB** (HTS) 64 Aa 37
Standon **GB** (SFS) 45 Xe 31
Stane **GB** (STC) 25 Wb 14
Stanford **GB** (BFS) 55 Ze 36
Stanford **GB** (KEN) 72 Ba 42
Stanford Bishop **GB** (HWC) 52 Xd 35
Stanford Bridge **GB** (HWC) 52 Xd 35
Stanford Dingley **GB** (BKS) 63 Ye 40

Sheldon – Stanford Dingley GB IRL 133

Stanford on Avon **GB** (NRH) 54 Yf 34
Stanford on Teme **GB** (HWC) 52 Xd 35
Stanghow **GB** (CLE) 37 Za 21
Stanhoe **GB** (NOR) 48 Ae 31
Stanhope **GB** (BOR) 26 Wd 15
Stanhope **GB** (DUR) 36 Xf 20
Stanion **GB** (NRH) 55 Zc 34
Stanley **GB** (DSH) 46 Yd 31
Stanley **GB** (DUR) 33 Yb 19
Stanley **GB** (SFS) 45 Xf 30
Stanley **GB** (TYS) 21 Wd 10
Stanley **GB** (WYO) 40 Yd 26
Stanley Common **GB** (DSH) 46 Yd 31
Stanmer **GB** (ESX) 71 Zf 43
Stanmore **GB** (BKS) 62 Ye 40
Stanmore **GB** (GRL) 64 Ze 39
Stanningfield **GB** (SUF) 56 Ae 35
Stannington **GB** (NHL) 33 Yb 18
Stannington **GB** (SOY) 45 Yc 28
Stansbatch **GB** (HWC) 52 Xa 35
Stansfield **GB** (SUF) 56 Ad 36
Stanstead **GB** (SUF) 56 Ae 36
Stanstead Abbots **GB** (HTS) 64 Aa 38
Stansted **GB** (KEN) 64 Ab 40
Stansted Mountfitchet **GB** (ESS) 64 Ab 37
Stanton **GB** (DSH) 45 Yc 32
Stanton **GB** (GLS) 62 Ya 36
Stanton **GB** (GWE) 60 Wf 37
Stanton **GB** (NHL) 33 Yb 17
Stanton **GB** (SFS) 45 Yb 30
Stanton **GB** (SUF) 56 Af 35
Stanton by Bridge **GB** (DSH) 46 Yd 31
Stanton-by-Dale **GB** (DSH) 46 Ye 31
Stanton Drew **GB** (AVN) 61 Xc 40
Stanton Fitzwarren **GB** (WIL) 62 Yb 39
Stanton Harcourt **GB** (OXS) 62 Yd 38
Stanton Hill **GB** (NTS) 46 Ye 30
Stanton in Peak **GB** (DSH) 45 Yc 29
Stanton Lacy **GB** (SHS) 52 Xb 34
Stanton Long **GB** (SHS) 52 Xc 33
Stanton-on-the-Wolds **GB** (NTS) 46 Yf 31
Stanton Saint Bernard **GB** (WIL) 62 Ya 40
Stanton Saint John **GB** (OXS) 63 Yf 38
Stanton Saint Quintin **GB** (WIL) 61 Xf 39
Stanton Street **GB** (SUF) 56 Af 35
Stanton under Bardon **GB** (LEC) 54 Ye 32
Stanton upon Hine Heath **GB** (SHS) 44 Xc 32
Stanton Wick **GB** (AVN) 61 Xc 40
Stanwardine in the Fields **GB** (SHS) 44 Xa 32
Stanway **GB** (ESS) 65 Ae 37
Stanwell Moor **GB** (SUR) 63 Zc 40
Stanwick **GB** (NRH) 55 Zc 35
Stanwix **GB** (CUB) 32 Xa 19
Stape **GB** (NOY) 37 Zb 23
Stapehill **GB** (DOS) 69 Ya 44
Stapeley **GB** (CHS) 44 Xd 30
Staple **GB** (KEN) 65 Bb 41
Staple Cross **GB** (ESX) 72 Ad 43
Staplefield **GB** (WSX) 71 Ze 42
Staple Fitzpaine **GB** (SOM) 67 Wf 43
Stapleford **GB** (CBS) 56 Aa 36
Stapleford **GB** (HTS) 64 Zf 38
Stapleford **GB** (LEC) 46 Zb 32
Stapleford **GB** (LIN) 46 Zb 30
Stapleford **GB** (WIL) 69 Ya 42
Stapleford, Beeston and **GB** (NTS) 46 Ye 31
Stapleford Abbotts **GB** (ESS) 64 Ab 39
Stapleford Tawney **GB** (ESS) 64 Ab 38
Staplehurst **GB** (KEN) 72 Ad 42
Staplestown **IRL** (KIL) 95 Tb 29
Stapleton **GB** (AVN) 61 Xc 40
Stapleton **GB** (CUB) 32 Xb 18
Stapleton **GB** (LEC) 54 Yd 33
Stapleton **GB** (SHS) 52 Xb 33
Stapleton **GB** (SOM) 68 Xb 43
Stapley **GB** (SOM) 67 Wf 43
Staplow **GB** (HWC) 52 Xd 36
Stapolin House **IRL** (DUB) 95 Te 28
Star **GB** (DYF) 58 Vc 37
Star **GB** (FIF) 26 Wf 11
Star **GB** (SOM) 68 Xb 41
Starbotton **GB** (NOY) 36 Xf 23
Starcross **GB** (DEV) 67 Wd 45
Starinagh **IRL** (MT) 90 Td 26
Starlings Green **GB** (ESS) 56 Aa 37
Startforth **GB** (DUR) 36 Ya 21
Startley **GB** (WIL) 61 Xf 39
Stathe **GB** (SOM) 68 Xa 42
Stathern **GB** (LEC) 46 Za 31
Station Town **GB** (DUR) 36 Yd 20
Staughton Highway **GB** (CBS) 55 Zd 35
Staunton **GB** (GLS) 61 Xc 38
Staunton **GB** (GLS) 61 Xe 37
Staunton on Arrow **GB** (HWC) 52 Xa 35
Staunton on Wye **GB** (HWC) 52 Xa 36
Staveley **GB** (CUB) 35 Xb 22
Staveley **GB** (DSH) 46 Yd 29
Staveley **GB** (NOY) 40 Yd 24
Staveley-in-Cartmel **GB** (CUB) 35 Xa 23
Staventon **GB** (OXS) 62 Yd 39
Staverton **GB** (DEV) 76 Wb 46
Staverton **GB** (GLS) 61 Xf 37
Staverton **GB** (NRH) 54 Ye 35
Staverton **GB** (WIL) 61 Xe 40
Staverton Bridge **GB** (GLS) 61 Xf 37
Stawley **GB** (SOM) 67 Wd 43
Staxigoe **GB** (HGL) 6 Wf 118
Staxton **GB** (NOY) 37 Zd 23
Staylittle **GB** (POW) 51 Wc 33
Steane **GB** (NRH) 54 Ye 36
Stearsby **GB** (NOY) 37 Yf 24
Steart **GB** (SOM) 67 Wf 41
Stebbing **GB** (ESS) 64 Ac 37
Stedham **GB** (WSX) 70 Zb 43
Steel Cross **GB** (ESX) 71 Ab 42
Steele Road **GB** (BOR) 32 Xb 17
Steen's Bridge **GB** (HWC) 52 Xb 35
Steep **GB** (HAS) 70 Za 42
Steeple **GB** (DOS) 69 Xf 45
Steeple **GB** (ESS) 65 Ae 38
Steeple Ashton **GB** (WIL) 69 Xf 41
Steeple Aston **GB** (OXS) 62 Ye 37
Steeple Barton **GB** (OXS) 62 Yd 37
Steeple Bumpstead **GB** (ESS) 56 Ac 36
Steeple Claydon **GB** (BUS) 63 Za 37
Steeple Langford **GB** (WIL) 69 Ya 42
Steeple Morden **GB** (CBS) 55 Zf 36
Steeton **GB** (WYO) 39 Ya 25
Steinmanhill **GB** (GRP) 17 Xd 4
Stelling Minnis **GB** (KEN) 72 Ba 41
Stemster Ho **GB** (HGL) 6 Wd 117
Stenalees **GB** (CNW) 75 Vb 46
Stenhousemuir **GB** (CEN) 25 Wb 12
Stenness **GB** (SHL) 2 Yc 106
Stenton **GB** (LOT) 26 Xc 13
Stepaside **GB** (DYF) 58 Vb 38
Stepaside **IRL** (DUB) 95 Te 29
Stephenstown House **IRL** (MT) 90 Tb 26
Steppingley **GB** (BFS) 55 Zc 36
Stepps **GB** (STC) 25 Vf 13
Sternfield **GB** (SUF) 57 Bc 35
Sterridge **GB** (DEV) 66 Vf 41
Stert **GB** (WIL) 62 Ya 41
Stevenage **GB** (HTS) 64 Ze 37
Stevenson **GB** (STC) 24 Vb 15
Steventon **GB** (HAS) 70 Ye 41
Stevington **GB** (BFS) 55 Zc 35
Stewartby **GB** (BFS) 55 Zd 36
Stewarton **GB** (STC) 24 Vc 14
Stewartstown **GB** (TYR) 84 Tb 21
Stewkley **GB** (BUS) 63 Zb 37
Stewton **GB** (LIN) 47 Aa 28
Steyning **GB** (WSX) 71 Ze 43
Steynton **GB** (DYF) 58 Uf 38
Stibb **GB** (CNW) 66 Vc 43
Stibbard **GB** (NOR) 49 Af 32
Stibb Cross **GB** (DEV) 66 Ve 43
Stibb Green **GB** (WIL) 62 Yb 40
Stichill **GB** (BOR) 27 Xd 15
Sticker **GB** (CNW) 75 Va 47
Stickford **GB** (LIN) 47 Aa 30
Sticklepath **GB** (DEV) 66 Wa 44
Stickney **GB** (LIN) 47 Aa 30
Stickstown **IRL** (COR) 104 Rb 37
Stiffkey **GB** (NOR) 48 Af 31
Stifford's Bridge **GB** (HWC) 53 Xd 36
Stilligary **GB** (HGL) 12 Sd 5
Stillingfleet **GB** (NOY) 40 Yf 25
Stillington **GB** (CLE) 36 Yd 21
Stillington **GB** (NOY) 40 Yf 24
Stillorgan **IRL** (DUB) 95 Te 29
Stilton **GB** (CBS) 55 Ze 34
Stinchcombe **GB** (GLS) 61 Xd 38
Stinsford **GB** (DOS) 68 Xd 44
Stirchley **GB** (SHS) 52 Xd 33
Stirling **GB** (CEN) 25 Wa 12
Stisted **GB** (ESS) 65 Ad 37
Stithians **GB** (CNW) 74 Ue 47
Stitley **GB** (HGL) 6 Wd 117
Stivichall **GB** (WMD) 54 Yc 34
St Levan **GB** (CNW) 74 Uc 48
Stoak **GB** (CHS) 44 Xa 29
Stobieside **GB** (STC) 25 Ve 15
Stobo **GB** (BOR) 26 Wd 15
Stoborough **GB** (DOS) 69 Xf 44
Stoborough Green **GB** (DOS) 69 Xf 44
Stock **GB** (ESS) 65 Ac 39
Stockbridge **GB** (HAS) 69 Yd 42
Stockbriggs **GB** (STC) 25 Wa 15
Stockbury **GB** (KEN) 65 Ad 41
Stockcross **GB** (BKS) 62 Yd 40
Stockdalewath **GB** (CUB) 35 Xa 20
Stockenchurch **GB** (BUS) 63 Za 39
Stockerton **GB** (LEC) 54 Zb 33
Stock Green **GB** (HWC) 53 Xf 35
Stockingford **GB** (WWH) 54 Yd 33
Stocking Pelham **GB** (HTS) 64 Aa 37
Stockinish **GB** (HGL) 11 Tb 2
Stockland **GB** (DEV) 67 Wf 43
Stockland Bristol **GB** (SOM) 67 Wf 41
Stock Lane **GB** (WIL) 62 Yc 40
Stockleigh Pomeroy **GB** (DEV) 67 Wc 44
Stockley **GB** (WIL) 62 Xf 40
Stockport **GB** (GRM) 45 Xf 28
Stocks, The **GB** (KEN) 72 Ae 42
Stocksbridge **GB** (SOY) 39 Yc 28
Stockton **GB** (HWC) 52 Xb 35
Stockton **GB** (SHS) 52 Xd 34
Stockton **GB** (WIL) 69 Xf 42
Stockton **GB** (WWH) 54 Yd 35
Stockton Heath **GB** (CHS) 44 Xc 28
Stockton-on-Tees **GB** (CLE) 36 Ye 21
Stockton on Teme **GB** (HWC) 52 Xd 35
Stockton on the Forest **GB** (NOY) 40 Za 25
Stock Wood **GB** (HWC) 53 Ya 35
Stodday **GB** (LCS) 38 Xb 24
Stoer **GB** (HGL) 7 Ue 119
Stoford **GB** (SOM) 68 Xc 43
Stoford **GB** (WIL) 69 Ya 42
Stogumber **GB** (SOM) 67 We 42
Stogursey **GB** (SOM) 67 Wf 41
Stoke **GB** (HAS) 69 Yd 41
Stoke **GB** (HAS) 70 Za 43
Stoke **GB** (KEN) 65 Ad 40
Stoke **GB** (WMD) 54 Yd 34
Stoke Abbott **GB** (DOS) 68 Xb 44
Stoke Albany **GB** (NRH) 54 Zb 34
Stoke Ash **GB** (SUF) 57 Ba 35
Stoke Bardolph **GB** (NTS) 46 Yf 31
Stoke Bliss **GB** (HWC) 52 Xc 35
Stoke Bruerne **GB** (NRH) 54 Za 36
Stoke by Clare **GB** (SUF) 56 Ad 36
Stoke-by-Nayland **GB** (SUF) 56 Af 37
Stoke Canon **GB** (DEV) 67 Wc 44
Stoke Charity **GB** (HAS) 70 Ye 42
Stoke Climsland **GB** (CNW) 75 Ve 45
Stoke D'Abernon **GB** (SUR) 64 Zd 41
Stoke Doyle **GB** (NRH) 55 Zd 34
Stoke Ferry **GB** (NOR) 56 Ad 33
Stoke Fleming **GB** (DEV) 76 Wc 47
Stokeford **GB** (DOS) 69 Xe 44
Stoke Gabriel **GB** (DEV) 76 Wc 46
Stoke Golding **GB** (LEC) 54 Yd 33
Stoke Goldington **GB** (BUS) 54 Zb 36
Stokeham **GB** (NTS) 46 Zb 29
Stoke Hammond **GB** (BUS) 63 Zb 37
Stoke Heath **GB** (SHS) 44 Xc 31
Stokeinteignhead **GB** (DEV) 76 Wc 45
Stoke Lacy **GB** (HWC) 52 Xc 36
Stoke Lyne **GB** (OXS) 63 Ye 37
Stoke Mandeville **GB** (BUS) 63 Zb 38
Stokenham **GB** (DEV) 76 Wb 47
Stoke on Tern **GB** (SHS) 44 Xc 31
Stoke-on-Trent **GB** (SFS) 45 Xe 30
Stoke Orchard **GB** 61 Xf 37
Stoke Poges **GB** (BUS) 63 Zc 39
Stoke Prior **GB** (HWC) 52 Xb 35
Stoke Prior **GB** (HWC) 53 Xf 35
Stoke Rivers **GB** (DEV) 66 Wa 42
Stoke Rochford **GB** (LIN) 47 Zc 32
Stoke Row **GB** (OXS) 63 Yf 39
Stoke Saint Gregory **GB** (SOM) 68 Xa 42
Stoke Saint Mary **GB** (SOM) 67 Wf 43
Stoke Saint Michael **GB** (SOM) 68 Xd 41
Stoke Saint Milborough **GB** (SHS) 52 Xc 34
Stokesby **GB** (NOR) 49 Bd 33
Stokesley **GB** (NOY) 37 Ye 22
Stoke sub Hamdon **GB** (SOM) 68 Xb 43
Stoke Talmage **GB** (OXS) 63 Yf 38
Stoke Trister **GB** (SOM) 68 Xd 42
Stolford **GB** (SOM) 67 Wf 41
Stondon Massey **GB** (ESS) 64 Ab 38
Stone **GB** (BUS) 63 Za 38
Stone **GB** (GLS) 61 Xd 39
Stone **GB** (HWC) 53 Xe 34
Stone **GB** (KEN) 72 Ae 42
Stone **GB** (SFS) 45 Xf 31
Ston Easton **GB** (SOM) 68 Xc 41
Stone Bridge **IRL** (MOG) 83 Sf 23
Stone Cross **GB** (ESX) 72 Ab 44
Stone Cross **GB** (KEN) 71 Ab 42
Stoneen **IRL** (KLK) 100 Sf 33
Stonefield **GB** (STC) 25 Vf 14
Stonefield **IRL** (MAY) 80 Qb 23
Stonefield House **IRL** (MT) 89 Sf 26
Stonegate **GB** (ESX) 72 Ac 42
Stonegrave **GB** (NOY) 37 Za 23
Stone Hall **IRL** (MAY) 81 Qd 24
Stonehaugh **GB** (NHL) 32 Xd 18
Stonehaven **GB** (GRP) 17 Xe 7
Stone House **GB** (CUB) 35 Xd 23
Stonehouse **GB** (DEV) 76 Vf 46
Stonehouse **GB** (GLS) 61 Xe 38
Stonehouse **GB** (NHL) 32 Xd 19
Stonehouse **GB** (STC) 25 Wa 14
Stoneleigh **GB** (WWH) 54 Yc 34
Stonely **GB** (CBS) 55 Zd 35
Stonepark **IRL** (LET) 82 Re 23
Stonepark **IRL** (MAY) 87 Qe 26
Stonepark House **IRL** (ROS) 88 Re 27
Stonesby **GB** (LEC) 46 Zb 32
Stonesfield **GB** (OXS) 62 Yd 37
Stones Green **GB** (ESS) 65 Ba 37
Stone Street **GB** (SUF) 57 Bc 34
Stoneybreck **GB** (SHL) 3 Yc 111
Stoneybridge **GB** (HGL) 12 Sd 5
Stoneyburn **GB** (LOT) 25 Wc 13
Stoney Cross **GB** (HAS) 69 Yc 43
Stoneygate **GB** (GRP) 17 Ya 4
Stoneygate **GB** (LEC) 54 Yf 33
Stoneyhills **GB** (ESS) 65 Ae 39
Stoney Houghton **GB** (DSH) 46 Ye 29
Stoneykirk **GB** (DAG) 28 Va 18
Stoney Middleton **GB** (DSH) 45 Yc 29
Stoney Stanton **GB** (LEC) 54 Ye 33
Stoney Stoke **GB** (SOM) 68 Xd 42
Stoney Stratford **GB** (BUS) 54 Zb 36
Stoney Stretton **GB** (SHS) 52 Xa 32
Stonham Aspal **GB** (SUF) 57 Ba 35
Stonnall **GB** (SFS) 53 Ya 33
Stonor **GB** (OXS) 63 Za 39
Stonyisland **IRL** (GAL) 93 Re 30
Stoodleigh **GB** (DEV) 67 Wc 43
Stopsley **GB** (BFS) 63 Zd 37
Stornoway **GB** (HGL) 11 Td 119
Storridge **GB** (HWC) 53 Xd 36
Storrington **GB** (WSX) 71 Zd 43
Storth **GB** (CUB) 35 Xb 23
Stotfold **GB** (BFS) 55 Ze 36
Stottesdon **GB** (SHS) 52 Xd 34
Stoughton **GB** (LEC) 54 Yf 33
Stoughton **GB** (WSX) 70 Za 43
Stoulton **GB** (HWC) 53 Xf 36
Stourbridge **GB** (WMD) 53 Xf 34
Stourpaine **GB** (DOS) 69 Xe 43
Stourport-on-Severn **GB** (HWC) 53 Xe 34
Stour Provost **GB** (DOS) 68 Xe 43
Stour Row **GB** (DOS) 68 Xe 43
Stourton **GB** (SFS) 53 Xe 34
Stourton **GB** (WIL) 68 Xe 42
Stourton Caundle **GB** (DOS) 68 Xd 43
Stow **GB** (BOR) 26 Xa 14
Stow **GB** (LIN) 46 Zb 29
Stow Bardolph **GB** (NOR) 56 Ac 33
Stow Bedon **GB** (NOR) 56 Af 33
Stowbridge **GB** (NOR) 56 Ac 33
Stow cum Quy **GB** (CBS) 56 Ab 35
Stowe **GB** (GLS) 61 Xc 38
Stowe **GB** (SHS) 52 Wf 34
Stowe-by-Chartley **GB** (SFS) 45 Ya 31
Stowell **GB** (GLS) 62 Ya 38
Stowford **GB** (DEV) 66 Ve 45
Stow Longa **GB** (CBS) 55 Zd 35
Stow Maries **GB** (ESS) 65 Ad 39
Stowmarket **GB** (SUF) 57 Af 35
Stow-on-the-Wold **GB** (GLS) 62 Yb 37
Stowting **GB** (KEN) 72 Ba 42
Stowupland **GB** (SUF) 57 Ba 35
Straad **GB** (STC) 24 Uf 14
Strabally **IRL** (GAL) 92 Ra 29
Strabane **GB** (TYR) 78 Sd 20
Straboy **IRL** (DON) 82 Rc 20
Strachur **GB** (STC) 24 Uf 11
Stracks-Mountain **IRL** (KER) 97 Qc 34
Stradbally **IRL** (KER) 97 Pf 35
Stradbally **IRL** (LAO) 94 Sf 30
Stradbally **IRL** (WTF) 100 Sd 36
Stradbroke **GB** (SUF) 57 Bb 35
Strade **IRL** (MAY) 87 Qf 25
Stradishall **GB** (SUF) 56 Ad 36
Stradone **IRL** (CAV) 89 Se 25
Stradsett **GB** (NOR) 56 Ac 33
Straffan **IRL** (KIL) 95 Tc 29
Stragellif **IRL** (CAV) 89 Se 24
Strahack Moress **IRL** (DON) 78 Sd 18
Strahart **IRL** (WEX) 101 Tc 33
Strahlaghy **IRL** (MAY) 81 Qc 23
Straid **GB** (ANT) 85 Ua 20
Straid **IRL** (DON) 78 Sd 17
Straiton **GB** (STC) 30 Vc 17
Straleel **IRL** (DON) 82 Rc 20
Straloch **GB** (TYS) 21 Wc 8
Stralongfort **IRL** (DON) 77 Sb 19
Stramshall **GB** (SFS) 45 Ya 31
Stranabrooey **IRL** (DON) 77 Re 18
Stranagappoge **IRL** (DON) 78 Se 17
Strand **IRL** (LIM) 98 Qf 34
Strandhill House **IRL** (SLI) 82 Rc 23
Strangford **GB** (DOW) 85 Uc 22
Stranmillis **GB** (ANT) 85 Ua 21
Stranorlar **IRL** (DON) 77 Sb 20
Stranraer **GB** (DAG) 28 Uf 19
Straruddan **IRL** (DON) 78 Sf 17
Strasburgh **IRL** (CRE) 92 Qf 32
Stratfield Mortimer **GB** (BKS) 63 Yf 40
Stratfield Saye **GB** (HAS) 63 Yf 40
Stratfield Turgis **GB** (HAS) 63 Yf 41
Stratford **GB** (GRL) 64 Aa 39
Stratford **IRL** (WKL) 95 Tb 31
Stratford Saint Andrew **GB** (SUF) 57 Bc 35
Stratford Tony **GB** (WIL) 69 Ya 42
Stratford-upon-Avon **GB** (WWH) 53 Yb 35
Strath **GB** (HGL) 7 Ub 2
Strathan **GB** (HGL) 7 Ue 120
Strathaven **GB** (STC) 25 Vf 14
Strathblane **GB** (CEN) 25 Ve 13
Strathcoil **GB** (STC) 19 Ub 10
Strathdon **GB** (GRP) 16 Wf 5
Strath Kanaird **GB** (HGL) 7 Uf 1
Strathkinness **GB** (FIF) 22 Xa 10
Strathmiglo **GB** (FIF) 21 We 11
Strathpeffer **GB** (HGL) 15 Vc 3
Strathtay **GB** (TYS) 21 Wb 8
Strathwhillan **GB** (STC) 24 Uf 15
Strathy **GB** (HGL) 5 Wa 117
Strathyre **GB** (CEN) 20 Ve 11
Stratton **GB** (CNW) 66 Vc 44
Stratton **GB** (DOS) 68 Xd 44
Stratton **GB** (GLS) 62 Ya 38
Stratton **GB** (NOR) 49 Bb 32
Stratton Audley **GB** (OXS) 63 Yf 37
Stratton-on-the-Fosse **GB** (SOM) 68 Xd 41
Stratton Saint Margaret **GB** (WIL) 62 Yb 39
Stratton Saint Michael **GB** (NOR) 57 Bb 34
Stravithie **GB** (FIF) 22 Xb 11
Streamstown **IRL** (GAL) 86 Pf 27
Streamstown **IRL** (WMT) 89 Sc 28
Streat **GB** (ESX) 71 Zf 43
Streatham **GB** (GRL) 64 Zf 40
Streatley **GB** (BFS) 63 Zd 37
Streatley **GB** (BKS) 63 Yf 39
Street **GB** (LCS) 38 Xb 25
Street **GB** (NOY) 37 Za 22
Street **GB** (SOM) 68 Xb 42
Street **IRL** (WMT) 89 Sd 26
Street Dinas **GB** (SHS) 44 Xa 31
Street End **GB** (WSX) 70 Zb 44
Streethay **GB** (SFS) 53 Yb 32
Streetly **GB** (WMD) 53 Ya 33
Strensall **GB** (NOY) 40 Yf 24
Strete **GB** (DEV) 76 Wc 47
Stretford **GB** (GRM) 39 Xe 28
Stretford Court **GB** (HWC) 52 Xb 35
Stretham **GB** (CBS) 56 Ab 34
Stretton **GB** (CHS) 44 Xb 30
Stretton **GB** (CHS) 44 Xc 28
Stretton **GB** (DSH) 46 Yd 30
Stretton **GB** (LEC) 47 Zc 32
Stretton **GB** (SFS) 45 Yc 31
Stretton **GB** (SFS) 53 Xe 32
Stretton en le Field **GB** (LEC) 53 Yc 32
Stretton Grandison **GB** (HWC) 52 Xc 36
Stretton Heath **GB** (SHS) 52 Xa 32
Stretton-on-Dunsmore **GB** (WWH) 54 Yd 34
Stretton-on-Fosse **GB** (WWH) 53 Yb 36
Stretton Sugwas **GB** (HWC) 52 Xb 36
Stretton under Fosse **GB** (WWH) 54 Yd 34
Stretton Westwood **GB** (SHS) 52 Xc 33
Strichen **GB** (GRP) 17 Xf 3
Stringston **GB** (SOM) 67 We 41
Strixton **GB** (NRH) 55 Zb 35
Strokestown **IRL** (ROS) 88 Rf 26
Stromeferry **GB** (HGL) 14 Uc 4
Stromemore **GB** (HGL) 14 Uc 4
Stromness **GB** (ORK) 6 We 115
Stronaba **GB** (HGL) 19 Va 7
Stronachlachar **GB** (CEN) 24 Vc 11
Stronchrubie **GB** (HGL) 7 Va 120
Strone **GB** (HGL) 15 Vd 5
Strone **GB** (HGL) 19 Uf 7
Strone **GB** (STC) 24 Va 13
Stronmilchan **GB** (STC) 19 Va 10
Strontian **GB** (HGL) 19 Uc 8
Strood Green **GB** (WSX) 71 Zc 42
Stroove **IRL** (DON) 78 Ta 17
Stroud **GB** (GLS) 61 Xe 38
Stroud **GB** (HAS) 70 Za 42
Stroud Common **GB** (SUR) 71 Zc 41
Stroxton **GB** (LIN) 47 Zc 31
Struan **GB** (HGL) 13 Td 4
Strubby **GB** (LIN) 47 Ab 29
Struy **GB** (HGL) 14 Vc 4
Stryt-yr-hwch **GB** (CLW) 44 Xa 30
Stuartfield **GB** (GRP) 17 Xf 3
Stubbington **GB** (HAS) 70 Ye 44
Stubhampton **GB** (DOS) 69 Xf 43
Stubton **GB** (LIN) 46 Zb 30
Stuck **GB** (STC) 24 Uf 13
Stuckgowan **GB** (STC) 24 Vb 11
Stuckton **GB** (HAS) 69 Yb 43
Stud Green **GB** (BKS) 63 Zb 40
Studham **GB** (BFS) 63 Zc 38
Studland **GB** (DOS) 69 Ya 45
Studley **GB** (WIL) 61 Xf 40
Studley **GB** (WWH) 53 Ya 35
Studley Roger **GB** (NOY) 36 Yc 24
Stuntney **GB** (CBS) 56 Ab 34
Sturbridge **GB** (SFS) 45 Xe 31
Sturminster Marshall **GB** (DOS) 69 Xf 44
Sturminster Newton **GB** (DOS) 68 Xe 43
Sturry **GB** (KEN) 65 Ba 41
Sturton by Stow **GB** (LIN) 46 Zb 29
Sturton le Steeple **GB** (NTS) 46 Zb 28
Stuston **GB** (SUF) 57 Ba 34
Stutton **GB** (NOY) 40 Ye 25
Stutton **GB** (SUF) 57 Ba 37
Styal **GB** (CHS) 45 Xe 28
Styrrup **GB** (NTS) 40 Yf 28
Subulter **IRL** (COR) 98 Rb 35
Suckley **GB** (HWC) 53 Xd 36
Sudborough **GB** (NRH) 55 Zc 34
Sudbrook **GB** (GWE) 61 Xb 39
Sudbrook **GB** (LIN) 47 Zc 31
Sudbury **GB** (DSH) 45 Yb 31
Sudbury **GB** (SUF) 56 Ae 36
Sudgrove **GB** (GLS) 61 Xf 38
Suffield **GB** (NOR) 49 Bb 31
Suffield **GB** (NOY) 37 Zd 23
Sugarloaf Hill **IRL** (ROS) 93 Rf 29
Sugarlof **GB** (KEN) 72 Af 42
Sugnall **GB** (SFS) 45 Xe 31
Sulby **GBM** 29 Vd 23
Sulgrave **GB** (NRH) 54 Ye 36
Sulham **GB** (BKS) 63 Yf 40
Sulhamstead **GB** (BKS) 63 Yf 40
Sullington **GB** (WSX) 71 Zd 43
Sullom **GB** (SHL) 2 Yd 106
Sully **GB** (SGL) 60 We 40
Sumburgh **GB** (SHL) 3 Ye 109
Summerbridge **GB** (NOY) 39 Yb 24
Summercourt **GB** (CNW) 75 Va 46
Summer Cove **IRL** (COR) 104 Rc 38
Summerfield **GB** (NOR) 48 Ad 31
Summer Hill **GB** (CLW) 44 Wf 30
Summerhill **IRL** (KLK) 94 Sf 32
Summerhill **IRL** (MT) 90 Tb 25
Summerhill **IRL** (MT) 90 Tb 28
Summerhill House **IRL** (MAY) 81 Qe 23
Summerhill House **IRL** (MT) 90 Tb 28
Summerhill House **IRL** (OFF) 93 Sb 31
Summerleaze **GB** (GWE) 61 Xb 39
Summertown **GB** (OXS) 62 Ye 38
Summit **GB** (GRM) 39 Xf 26
Sunadale Cott **GB** (STC) 23 Ud 15
Sunbury **GB** (SUR) 63 Zd 40
Suncroft **IRL** (KIL) 94 Ta 30
Sunderland **GB** (CUB) 34 We 20
Sunderland **GB** (TAW) 33 Yd 19
Sunderland Bridge **GB** (DUR) 36 Yc 20
Sundon Park **GB** (BFS) 63 Zd 37
Sundridge **GB** (KEN) 64 Aa 41
Sunhill **GB** (GLS) 62 Yb 38
Sunk Island **GB** (HUS) 41 Zf 27
Sunninghill **GB** (BKS) 63 Zb 40
Sunningwell **GB** (OXS) 63 Ye 38
Sunniside **GB** (DUR) 36 Yb 20
Sunniside **GB** (TAW) 33 Yc 19
Sunnyhill House **IRL** (KIL) 95 Tb 30
Sunnylaw **GB** (CEN) 25 Wa 12
Surbiton **GB** (GRL) 64 Ze 40
Surfleet **GB** (LIN) 47 Zf 31
Surfleet Seas End **GB** (LIN) 47 Zf 31
Surlingham **GB** (NOR) 57 Bc 33
Sustead **GB** (NOR) 49 Bb 31
Susworth **GB** (LIN) 40 Zb 27
Sutcombe **GB** (DEV) 66 Vd 43
Sutterton **GB** (LIN) 47 Zf 31
Sutton **GB** (BFS) 55 Ze 36
Sutton **GB** (CBS) 55 Aa 34
Sutton **GB** (GRL) 64 Ze 40
Sutton **GB** (KEN) 73 Bb 41
Sutton **GB** (NTS) 46 Za 28
Sutton **GB** (NTS) 46 Za 31
Sutton **GB** (SFS) 45 Xd 32
Sutton **GB** (SHS) 44 Xc 31
Sutton **GB** (SHS) 52 Xb 34
Sutton **GB** (SUF) 57 Bc 36
Sutton **GB** (WSX) 70 Zc 43
Sutton Abinger **GB** (SUR) 71 Zd 41
Sutton Bassett **GB** (NRH) 54 Za 33
Sutton Benger **GB** (WIL) 61 Xf 39
Sutton Bonington **GB** (NTS) 54 Ye 32
Sutton Bridge **GB** (LIN) 48 Ab 32
Sutton Cheney **GB** (LEC) 54 Yd 33
Sutton Coldfield **GB** (WMD) 53 Yb 33
Sutton Courtenay **GB** (OXS) 62 Ye 39
Sutton Crosses **GB** (LIN) 47 Aa 32
Sutton Grange **GB** (NOY) 36 Yc 24
Sutton Green **GB** (SUR) 71 Zc 41
Sutton Hampton **GB** (SHS) 52 Xd 34
Sutton Holms **GB** (DOS) 69 Ya 43
Sutton Howgrave **GB** (NOY) 36 Yc 23
Sutton in Ashfield **GB** (NTS) 46 Ye 30
Sutton-in-Craven **GB** (NOY) 39 Ya 25
Sutton Lane Ends **GB** (CHS) 45 Xe 29
Sutton Leach **GB** (MES) 44 Xb 28
Sutton le Marsh **GB** (LIN) 48 Ab 29
Sutton Maddock **GB** (SHS) 52 Xd 34
Sutton Mallet **GB** (SOM) 68 Xa 42
Sutton Mandeville **GB** (WIL) 69 Xf 42
Sutton-on-Hull **GB** (HUS) 41 Ze 26
Sutton on Sea **GB** (LIN) 48 Ab 29
Sutton-on-the-Forest **GB** (NOY) 40 Yf 24
Sutton on the Hill **GB** (DSH) 45 Yc 31
Sutton on Trent **GB** (NTS) 46 Zb 29
Sutton Poyntz **GB** (DOS) 68 Xd 45
Sutton Saint Edmund **GB** (LIN) 47 Aa 32
Sutton Saint James **GB** (LIN) 47 Aa 32
Sutton Saint Nicholas **GB** (HWC) 52 Xb 36
Sutton-under-Brailes **GB** (WWH) 54 Yc 36
Sutton-under-Whitestonecliffe **GB** (NOY) 36 Ye 23
Sutton Veny **GB** (WIL) 69 Xf 41
Sutton Waldron **GB** (DOS) 69 Xe 43
Sutton Wick **GB** (OXS) 62 Ye 39
Suville **IRL** (COR) 104 Rf 37
Swaby **GB** (LIN) 47 Aa 29
Swadlincote **GB** (DSH) 45 Yc 32
Swaffham **GB** (NOR) 48 Ae 33
Swaffham Bulbeck **GB** (CBS) 56 Ab 35
Swaffham Prior **GB** (CBS) 56 Ab 35
Swafield **GB** (NOR) 49 Bc 31
Swainby **GB** (NOY) 36 Ye 22
Swainshill **GB** (HWC) 52 Xb 36
Swainsthorpe **GB** (NOR) 57 Bb 33
Swainswick **GB** (AVN) 61 Xd 40
Swalcliffe **GB** (OXS) 54 Yd 36
Swallow **GB** (LIN) 41 Ze 27
Swallowcliffe **GB** (WIL) 69 Xf 42
Swampton **GB** (HAS) 69 Yd 41
Swan **IRL** (LAO) 94 Sf 31
Swanage **GB** (DOS) 69 Ya 45
Swanbourne **GB** (BUS) 63 Zb 37
Swancote **GB** (SHS) 53 Xd 34
Swanland **GB** (HUS) 41 Zd 26
Swanley **GB** (KEN) 64 Ab 40
Swanlinbar **IRL** (CAV) 83 Sb 23
Swanmore **GB** (HAS) 70 Ye 43
Swannington **GB** (LEC) 46 Yd 32
Swannington **GB** (NOR) 49 Ba 32
Swanscombe **GB** (KEN) 64 Ab 40
Swansea **GB** (WGL) 59 Wa 39
Swanton Abbot **GB** (NOR) 49 Bc 32
Swanton Morley **GB** (NOR) 48 Af 32
Swanton Novers **GB** (NOR) 48 Ba 31
Swanwick **GB** (DSH) 46 Yd 30
Swanwick **GB** (HAS) 70 Ye 43
Swarby **GB** (LIN) 47 Zd 31
Swardeston **GB** (NOR) 57 Bb 33
Swarkestone **GB** (DSH) 46 Yd 31
Swarland **GB** (NHL) 33 Yb 17
Swaton **GB** (LIN) 47 Ze 31
Swatragh **GB** (LDR) 79 Tc 19
Swavesey **GB** (CBS) 55 Zf 35
Sway **GB** (HAS) 69 Yc 44
Swayfield **GB** (LIN) 47 Zc 32
Sweep, The **IRL** (KLK) 100 Sd 34
Swefling **GB** (SUF) 57 Bc 35
Swepstone **GB** (LEC) 54 Yd 32
Swerford **GB** (OXS) 62 Yd 37
Swettenham **GB** (CHS) 45 Xe 29
Swillington **GB** (WYO) 40 Yd 26
Swimbridge **GB** (DEV) 66 Wa 42
Swimbridge Newland **GB** (DEV) 66 Wa 42
Swinderby **GB** (LIN) 46 Zb 30
Swindon **GB** (GLS) 61 Xf 37
Swindon **GB** (SFS) 53 Xe 33
Swindon **GB** (WIL) 62 Yb 39
Swine **GB** (HUS) 41 Ze 26
Swinefleet **GB** (HUS) 40 Zb 26
Swineshead **GB** (BFS) 55 Zd 35
Swineshead **GB** (LIN) 47 Zf 31
Swineshead Bridge **GB** (LIN) 47 Ze 31
Swiney **GB** (HGL) 9 We 119
Swinford **GB** (LEC) 54 Yf 34
Swinford **GB** (OXS) 62 Yd 38
Swinford **IRL** (MAY) 87 Ra 25
Swingfield Minnis **GB** (KEN) 73 Ba 42
Swinhoe **GB** (NHL) 27 Yb 15
Swinhope **GB** (LIN) 41 Ze 28
Swining **GB** (SHL) 2 Ye 106
Swinithwaite **GB** (NOY) 36 Ya 23
Swinscoe **GB** (SFS) 45 Yb 30
Swinside Hall **GB** (BOR) 32 Xd 16
Swinstead **GB** (LIN) 47 Zd 32
Swinton **GB** (BOR) 27 Xe 14
Swinton **GB** (GRM) 39 Xd 27
Swinton **GB** (NOY) 36 Yb 23
Swinton **GB** (SOY) 40 Ye 28
Swintonmill **GB** (BOR) 27 Xe 14
Swithland **GB** (LEC) 46 Ye 32
Swordale **GB** (HGL) 15 Vd 3
Swyddffynnon **GB** (DYF) 51 Wa 35
Swyncombe **GB** (OXS) 63 Yf 39
Swynnerton **GB** (SFS) 45 Xe 31
Swyre **GB** (DOS) 68 Xb 44
Sychdyn=Soughton **GB** (CLW) 44 Wf 29
Syde **GB** (GLS) 61 Xf 38
Sydenham **GB** (OXS) 63 Za 38
Sydenham Damerel **GB** (DEV) 75 Ve 45
Syderstone **GB** (NOR) 48 Ae 31
Sydling Saint Nicholas **GB** (DOS) 68 Xc 44
Sydmonton **GB** (HAS) 62 Ye 41
Sykehouse **GB** (SOY) 40 Yf 27
Sykes **GB** (LCS) 38 Xc 25
Sylen **GB** (DYF) 59 Vf 38
Symbister **GB** (SHL) 2 Yf 106
Symington **GB** (STC) 25 Wc 15
Symington **GB** (STC) 30 Vc 15
Symondsbury **GB** (DOS) 68 Xb 44
Symonds Yat **GB** (HWC) 61 Xc 37
Syngefield **IRL** (OFF) 93 Sa 30
Synod Inn **GB** (DYF) 50 Ve 36
Syre **GB** (HGL) 8 Ve 118
Syresham **GB** (NRH) 54 Yf 36
Syston **GB** (LEC) 54 Yf 32
Sytchampton **GB** (HWC) 53 Xe 35
Sywell **GB** (NRH) 54 Zb 35

T

Tackley **GB** (OXS) 62 Ye 37
Tadcaster **GB** (NOY) 40 Ye 25
Tadden **GB** (DOS) 69 Xf 44
Taddingstone **GB** (SUF) 57 Ba 37
Taddington **GB** (DSH) 45 Yb 29
Tadley **GB** (HAS) 63 Yf 40
Tadlow **GB** (CBS) 55 Zf 36
Tadmarton **GB** (OXS) 54 Yd 36
Tadworth **GB** (SUR) 64 Ze 41
Tafarnaubach **GB** (GWE) 60 We 38
Tafarn-y-Gelyn **GB** (CLW) 44 We 30
Taghboy **IRL** (ROS) 88 Re 27
Taghmon **IRL** (WEX) 101 Tc 35
Taghshinny **IRL** (LGF) 89 Sb 27
Tagoat **IRL** (WEX) 101 Td 35
Tahilla **IRL** (KER) 102 Qa 38
Tai-bach **GB** (CLW) 43 We 31
Tain **GB** (HGL) 6 We 117
Tain **GB** (HGL) 8 Vf 2
Tai'n Lôn **GB** (GWY) 42 Ve 30
Takeley **GB** (ESS) 64 Ab 37
Talachddu **GB** (POW) 60 Wd 37
Talacre **GB** (CLW) 43 We 28
Talaton **GB** (DEV) 67 We 44
Talbenny **GB** (DYF) 58 Uf 38
Talbolton **GB** (STC) 30 Vd 15
Talcolneston **GB** (NOR) 57 Ba 33
Talerddig **GB** (POW) 51 Wc 33
Talgarreg **GB** (DYF) 50 Ve 36
Talgarth **GB** (POW) 60 We 37
Talisker **GB** (HGL) 13 Td 5
Talke **GB** (SFS) 45 Xe 30
Talkin **GB** (CUB) 32 Xb 19
Talladale **GB** (HGL) 7 Ud 2
Tallaght **IRL** (DUB) 95 Td 29
Talla Linnfoots **GB** (BOR) 31 Wd 16
Tallanstown **IRL** (LOT) 90 Tc 25
Tallarn Green **GB** (CLW) 44 Xa 31
Tallentire **GB** (CUB) 34 Wd 20
Talley **GB** (DYF) 59 Wa 37
Tallington **GB** (LIN) 55 Zd 33
Tallow **IRL** (WTF) 99 Rf 36
Tallowbridge **IRL** (WTF) 99 Rf 36
Tallyho **IRL** (WKL) 95 Td 32
Tallyho **IRL** (WMT) 89 Sd 28
Tallyho Lodge **IRL** (LIM) 98 Ra 33
Talmine **GB** (HGL) 5 Vd 117
Talog **GB** (DYF) 59 Vd 37
Tal-sarn **GB** (DYF) 50 Vf 35
Talskiddy **GB** (CNW) 75 Va 46
Talwrn **GB** (CLW) 44 Wf 30
Talwrn **GB** (GWY) 42 Ve 29
Tal-y-bont **GB** (DYF) 51 Wa 34
Tal-y-bont **GB** (GWY) 42 Vf 32
Tal-y-Bont **GB** (GWY) 43 Wa 29
Talybont-on-Usk **GB** (POW) 60 We 37
Tal-y-cae **GB** (GWY) 42 Vf 29
Tal-y-llyn **GB** (GWY) 51 Wa 33
Talyllyn **GB** (POW) 60 We 37
Talysarn **GB** (GWY) 42 Ve 30
Tal-y-Wern **GB** (POW) 51 Wb 33
Tamerton Foliot **GB** (DEV) 76 Vf 46
Tamlaght **GB** (FER) 83 Sc 23
Tamworth **GB** (SFS) 53 Yb 33
Tandragee **GB** (ARG) 84 Td 22
Tandridge **GB** (SUR) 71 Zf 41
Tanfield **GB** (DUR) 33 Yb 19
Tang **IRL** (WMT) 88 Sb 27
Tangaveane **IRL** (DON) 77 Rf 20
Tangley **GB** (HAS) 69 Yc 41
Tangmere **GB** (WSX) 70 Zb 43
Tankardstown House **IRL** (MT) 90 Tc 26
Tan-lan **GB** (GWY) 43 Vf 31
Tannach **GB** (HGL) 6 Wf 118

134 GB IRL Stanford on Avon – Tannach

Tannadice **GB** (TYS) 22 Xa 8
Tannersrath **IRL** (TIP) 99 Sb 34
Tannington **GB** (SUF) 57 Bb 35
Tansley **GB** (DSH) 45 Yc 30
Tansor **GB** (NRH) 55 Zd 34
Tantobie **GB** (DUR) 33 Yb 19
Tanton **GB** (NOY) 37 Ye 22
Tanworth-in-Arden **GB** (WWH) 53 Yb 34
Tan-y-fron **GB** (CLW) 43 Wc 30
Tan-y-Groes **GB** (DYF) 50 Vc 36
Taplow **GB** (BUS) 63 Zb 39
Tarbert **GB** (HGL) 11 Tb 1
Tarbert **GB** (STC) 23 Ub 13
Tarbert **GB** (STC) 23 Ub 14
Tarbert **GB** (STC) 23 Ud 13
Tarbert **IRL** (KER) 97 Qd 33
Tarbet **GB** (HGL) 4 Uf 118
Tarbet **GB** (STC) 24 Vb 11
Tarbock Green **GB** (MES) 44 Xb 28
Tarbrax **GB** (STC) 25 Wc 14
Tardy Gate **GB** (LCS) 38 Xb 26
Tarfside **GB** (TYS) 22 Xb 7
Tarland **GB** (GRP) 16 Xa 6
Tarleton **GB** (LCS) 38 Xb 26
Tarlton **GB** (GLS) 61 Xf 38
Tarmon **IRL** (KER) 97 Qd 33
Tarnbrook **GB** (LCS) 38 Xc 25
Tarnock **GB** (SOM) 68 Xa 41
Tarporley **GB** (CHS) 44 Xb 30
Tarr **GB** (SOM) 67 We 42
Tarrant Crawford **GB** (DOS) 69 Xf 44
Tarrant Gunville **GB** (DOS) 69 Xf 43
Tarrant Hinton **GB** (DOS) 69 Xf 43
Tarrant Keyneston **GB** (DOS) 69 Xf 43
Tarrant Launceston **GB** (DOS) 69 Xf 43
Tarrant Monkton **GB** (DOS) 69 Xf 43
Tarrant Rawston **GB** (DOS) 69 Xf 43
Tarrel **GB** (HGL) 9 Wa 2
Tarring Neville **GB** (ESX) 71 Aa 44
Tarrington **GB** (HWC) 52 Xc 36
Tarsappie **GB** (TYS) 21 Wd 10
Tarskavaig **GB** (HGL) 13 Ua 6
Tarves **GB** (GRP) 17 Xe 4
Tarvie **GB** (HGL) 14 Vc 3
Tarvin **GB** (CHS) 44 Xb 29
Tasburgh **GB** (NOR) 57 Bb 33
Tasley **GB** (SHS) 52 Xd 33
Tassagh **GB** (ARG) 84 Tc 23
Taston **GB** (OXS) 62 Yd 37
Tatenhill **GB** (SFS) 45 Yb 32
Tathwell **GB** (LIN) 47 Zf 29
Tatsfield **GB** (SUR) 64 Aa 41
Tattenhall **GB** (CHS) 44 Xb 30
Tatterford **GB** (NOR) 48 Ae 32
Tattersett **GB** (NOR) 48 Ae 32
Tattershall **GB** (LIN) 47 Ze 30
Tattershall Bridge **GB** (LIN) 47 Ze 30
Tattyboy **IRL** (MOG) 90 Tc 24
Tatworth **GB** (SOM) 68 Xa 43
Taunton **GB** (SOM) 67 Wf 42
Taur **IRL** (COR) 98 Qf 35
Taverham **GB** (NOR) 49 Bb 32
Tavernspite **GB** (DYF) 58 Vc 38
Tavistock **GB** (DEV) 76 Vf 45
Taw Bridge **GB** (DEV) 66 Wa 43
Taw Green **GB** (DEV) 66 Wa 44
Tawnaghbaun **IRL** (GAL) 86 Qa 28
Tawnaghbeg **IRL** (MAY) 88 Rc 25
Tawny **IRL** (DON) 77 Sb 17
Tawny **IRL** (DON) 82 Rc 21
Tawnyinah **IRL** (MAY) 87 Rb 25
Tawnyslinnaun **IRL** (MAY) 86 Qb 26
Tawstock **GB** (DEV) 66 Vf 42
Tayinloan **GB** (STC) 23 Uc 15
Taylors Cross **GB** (CNW) 66 Vd 43
Taynton **GB** (GLS) 61 Xd 37
Taynton **GB** (OXS) 62 Yc 38
Taynuilt **GB** (STC) 19 Ue 10
Tayport **GB** (FIF) 22 Xa 10
Tayvallich **GB** (STC) 23 Uc 12
Tealby **GB** (LIN) 41 Ze 28
Teanamachar **GB** (HGL) 10 Sd 3
Teangue **GB** (HGL) 13 Ua 6
Tebay **GB** (CUB) 35 Xc 22
Tebworth **GB** (BFS) 63 Zc 37
Tedavnet **IRL** (MOG) 84 Sf 23
Tedburn Saint Mary **GB** (DEV) 67 Wb 44
Teddington **GB** 61 Xf 37
Tedstone Delamere **GB** (HWC) 52 Xd 35
Tedstone Wafre **GB** (HWC) 52 Xd 35
Teedehan **IRL** (CAV) 89 Sd 25
Teelin **IRL** (DON) 82 Rc 21
Teer **IRL** (KER) 96 Pe 35
Teeranearagh **IRL** (KER) 102 Pe 37
Teerelton **IRL** (COR) 103 Ra 37
Teermaclane **IRL** (CRE) 92 Ra 32
Teernacloghane **IRL** (CRE) 91 Qd 32
Teeton **GB** (NRH) 54 Za 35
Teevurcher **IRL** (MT) 89 Ta 25
Teffont Evias **GB** (WIL) 69 Xf 42
Teffont Magna **GB** (WIL) 69 Xf 42
Tegryn **GB** (DYF) 58 Vc 37
Teigh **GB** (LEC) 46 Zb 32
Teigngrace **GB** (DEV) 76 Wc 45
Teignmouth **GB** (DEV) 76 Wd 45
Telford **GB** (SHS) 52 Xd 32
Telham **GB** (ESX) 72 Ad 43
Tellisford **GB** (SOM) 68 Xe 41
Telscombe **GB** (ESX) 71 Zf 44
Templand **GB** (DAG) 31 Wd 18
Temple **GB** (CNW) 75 Vc 45
Temple **GB** (LOT) 26 Wf 14
Temple, The **GB** (DOW) 85 Ua 22
Temple Bar **GB** (DYF) 50 Vf 36
Templeboy **IRL** (SLI) 81 Rb 23
Temple Cloud **GB** (AVN) 68 Xc 41
Templecombe **GB** (SOM) 68 Xd 43
Templederry **IRL** (TIP) 93 Rf 32
Temple Ewell **GB** (KEN) 73 Ba 42
Temple Grafton **GB** (WWH) 53 Yb 35
Temple Guiting **GB** (GLS) 62 Ya 37
Temple Hill **IRL** (COR) 104 Rc 37
Templeludigan **IRL** (WEX) 100 Ta 34
Templemartin **IRL** (COR) 104 Rb 38
Templemore **IRL** (TIP) 93 Sa 32
Templenoe **IRL** (KER) 102 Qb 37
Temple Normanton **GB** (DSH) 46 Yd 29
Templeoran **IRL** (WMT) 94 Sd 28
Templeshanbo **IRL** (WEX) 101 Tb 33
Temple Sowerby **GB** (CUB) 35 Xc 21
Templeton **GB** (DYF) 58 Vb 38
Templeton Bridge **GB** (DEV) 67 Wc 43
Templetouhy **IRL** (TIP) 93 Sb 32
Templetown **IRL** (WEX) 100 Ta 35
Templeusaue **IRL** (COR) 104 Rd 37
Tempo **GB** (FER) 83 Sd 22
Tempsford **GB** (BFS) 55 Ze 36
Ten Acres **IRL** (WMT) 89 Sd 27
Tenbury Wells **GB** (HWC) 52 Xc 35
Tenby **GB** (DYF) 58 Vb 38
Tendring **GB** (ESS) 65 Ba 37
Ten Mile Bank **GB** (NOR) 56 Ac 33
Tenterden **GB** (KEN) 72 Ae 42
Terally **GB** (DAG) 28 Va 20
Terenure **IRL** (DUB) 95 Te 29
Terling **GB** (ESS) 65 Ad 38
Termon **IRL** (CRE) 91 Qc 33
Termon **IRL** (DON) 77 Sb 18
Termonbarry **IRL** (ROS) 88 Sa 26
Termoncarragh **IRL** (MAY) 80 Pf 23
Termon Cross Roads **IRL** (CAV) 89 Sf 25
Termonfeckin **IRL** (LOT) 90 Te 26
Termon House **IRL** (GAL) 92 Ra 30
Terregles **GB** (DAG) 31 Wb 18
Terrington **GB** (NOY) 37 Za 24
Terrington Saint Clement **GB** (NOR) 48 Ab 32
Terrington Saint John **GB** (NOR) 48 Ab 32
Terryglass **IRL** (TIP) 93 Re 30
Tervoe House **IRL** (LIM) 98 Rb 33
Teston **GB** (KEN) 65 Ac 41
Tetbury **GB** (GLS) 61 Xf 39
Tetbury Upton **GB** (GLS) 61 Xe 39
Tetchill **GB** (SHS) 44 Xa 31
Tetford **GB** (LIN) 47 Zf 29
Tetney **GB** (LIN) 41 Zf 28
Tetney Lock **GB** (LIN) 41 Aa 27
Tetsworth **GB** (OXS) 63 Yf 38
Teversal **GB** (NTS) 46 Ye 30
Teversham **GB** (CBS) 56 Ab 35
Teviothead **GB** (BOR) 32 Xa 16
Tevrin **IRL** (WMT) 89 Se 27
Tewin **GB** (HTS) 64 Zf 38
Tewkesbury **GB** 61 Xf 37
Teynham **GB** (KEN) 65 Ae 41
Thainston **GB** (GRP) 22 Xc 7
Thakenham **GB** (WSX) 71 Zd 43
Thame **GB** (OXS) 63 Za 38
Thames Haven **GB** (ESS) 65 Ad 39
Thanington **GB** (KEN) 65 Ba 41
Thankerton **GB** (STC) 25 Wc 15
Tharston **GB** (NOR) 57 Bb 33
Thatchham **GB** (BKS) 62 Ye 40
Thatto Heath **GB** (MES) 38 Xb 28
Thaxted **GB** (ESS) 56 Ac 37
Theakston **GB** (NOY) 36 Yc 23
Thealby **GB** (HUS) 40 Zc 27
Theale **GB** (BKS) 63 Yf 40
Theale **GB** (SOM) 68 Xb 41
Theberton **GB** (SUF) 57 Bd 35
The Bloody Hollow **IRL** (GAL) 93 Re 29
The Burf **GB** (HWC) 53 Xe 35
The Butts **IRL** (CLW) 94 Tb 33
The Cedars **IRL** (WKL) 95 Tf 31
The Common **GB** (BUS) 63 Za 37
Thedden Grange **GB** (HAS) 70 Yf 42
Theddingworth **GB** (LEC) 54 Yf 34
Theddlethorpe All Saints **GB** (LIN) 47 Ab 28
Theddlethorpe Saint Helen **GB** (LIN) 48 Ab 28
The Derries **IRL** (OFF) 93 Sa 30
The Fourteen Roads **IRL** (TIP) 93 Sa 31
The Grande **IRL** (LIM) 98 Rc 33
The Grange **GB** (NOY) 37 Yf 22
The Grange **GB** (SUR) 71 Zf 41
The Green Door **IRL** (GAL) 93 Re 30
The Harrow **IRL** (WEX) 101 Td 33
The Hill **GB** (CUB) 34 We 23
The Howe **GB** (CUB) 35 Xa 23
The Howe **GBM** 29 Vb 24
The Laurels **GB** (NOR) 57 Bc 33
Thelbridge Barton **GB** (DEV) 67 Wb 43
The Leap **IRL** (WEX) 101 Tb 34
Thelnetham **GB** (SUF) 56 Af 34
Thelveton **GB** (NOR) 57 Bb 34
Thelwall **GB** (CHS) 44 Xc 28
Themelthorpe **GB** (NOR) 49 Ba 32
The Mythe **GB** (GLS) 61 Xf 36
The Node **GB** (HTS) 64 Ze 37
The Pike **IRL** (TIP) 93 Rf 30
The Pike **IRL** (WTF) 98 Sc 36
The Pike **IRL** (WTF) 99 Sa 36
The Point **IRL** (DON) 77 Sb 17
Therfield **GB** (HTS) 55 Zf 36
The Rodney **IRL** (COR) 98 Ra 35
The Rowe **GB** (SFS) 45 Xe 31
The Rower **IRL** (KLK) 100 Ta 34
The Sweep **IRL** (KLK) 100 Sd 34
Thetford **GB** (NOR) 56 Ae 34
The Wyke **GB** (SHS) 52 Xd 33
Theydon Bois **GB** (ESS) 64 Aa 38
Thickwood **GB** (WIL) 61 Xe 40
Thimbleby **GB** (LIN) 47 Zf 29
Thimbleby **GB** (NOY) 36 Ye 22
Thirkleby **GB** (NOY) 36 Ye 23
Thirlby **GB** (NOY) 36 Ye 23
Thirlestane **GB** (BOR) 26 Xb 14
Thirn **GB** (NOY) 36 Yb 23
Thirsk **GB** (NOY) 36 Yd 23
Thistleton **GB** (LEC) 47 Zc 32
Thistley Green **GB** (SUF) 56 Ac 34
Thixendale **GB** (NOY) 40 Va 24
Thockrington **GB** (NHL) 33 Xf 18
Tholomas Drove **GB** (CBS) 55 Aa 33
Tholthorpe **GB** (NOY) 40 Ye 24
Thomas Street **IRL** (ROS) 88 Re 28
Thomastown **GB** (GRP) 17 Xb 4
Thomastown **IRL** (KLK) 100 Sf 33
Thomastown **IRL** (LIM) 98 Rc 34
Thomastown **IRL** (MT) 90 Tb 26
Thomastown **IRL** (WMT) 89 Sf 28
Thomastownpark **IRL** (ROS) 93 Rf 28
Thompson **GB** (NOR) 56 Ae 33
Thomshill **GB** (GRP) 16 We 3
Thong **GB** (KEN) 64 Ac 40
Thoralby **GB** (NOY) 36 Ya 23
Thore Kirkby **GB** (CUB) 35 Xc 21
Thoresby **GB** (NTS) 46 Yf 29
Thoresway **GB** (LIN) 41 Ze 28
Thorganby **GB** (NOY) 40 Za 25
Thorgill **GB** (NOY) 37 Za 22
Thorington **GB** (SUF) 57 Bd 35
Thorington Street **GB** (SUF) 57 Af 37
Thormanby **GB** (NOY) 36 Ye 23
Thornaby-on-Tees **GB** (CLE) 36 Ye 21
Thornage **GB** (NOR) 49 Ba 31
Thornberry House **IRL** (CRE) 92 Qe 33
Thornborough **GB** (BUS) 54 Za 36
Thornborough **GB** (NOY) 36 Yc 23
Thornbury **GB** (AVN) 61 Xc 39
Thornbury **GB** (DEV) 66 Ve 43
Thornbury **GB** (HWC) 52 Xc 35
Thornby **GB** (NRH) 54 Yf 34
Thorncliffe **GB** (SFS) 45 Ya 30
Thorncombe **GB** (DOS) 68 Xa 44
Thorncombe Street **GB** (SUR) 70 Zc 41
Thorndon **GB** (SUF) 57 Ba 35
Thorne **GB** (SOY) 40 Za 27
Thorner **GB** (WYO) 40 Yd 25
Thornes **GB** (SFS) 53 Ya 33
Thorne Saint Margaret **GB** (SOM) 67 We 43
Thorney **GB** (BUS) 63 Zd 40
Thorney **GB** (CBS) 55 Zf 33
Thorney **GB** (NTS) 46 Zb 29
Thorney **GB** (SOM) 68 Xb 43
Thorney Hill **GB** (HAS) 69 Yb 44
Thornfalcon **GB** (SOM) 68 Wf 42
Thornford **GB** (DOS) 68 Xc 43
Thornford **IRL** (MOG) 90 Tb 24
Thorngumbald **GB** (HUS) 41 Ze 26
Thornham **GB** (NOR) 48 Ad 31
Thornham Magna **GB** (SUF) 57 Ba 35
Thornhaugh **GB** (CBS) 55 Zd 33
Thornhill **GB** (CEN) 25 Vf 11
Thornhill **GB** (DAG) 31 Wb 17
Thornhill **GB** (MGL) 60 We 39
Thornhill Edge **GB** (WYO) 39 Yc 27
Thornicombe **GB** (DOS) 69 Xe 44
Thornley **GB** (DUR) 36 Yb 20
Thornley **GB** (DUR) 36 Yd 20
Thornliebank **GB** (STC) 25 Ve 14
Thorns **GB** (SUF) 56 Ad 35
Thornthwaite **GB** (CUB) 34 We 21
Thornthwaite **GB** (NOY) 39 Yb 24
Thornton **GB** (BUS) 54 Za 36
Thornton **GB** (FIF) 26 Wf 12
Thornton **GB** (HUS) 40 Za 25
Thornton **GB** (LCS) 38 Xa 25
Thornton **GB** (LIN) 47 Zf 29
Thornton **GB** (NHL) 27 Xf 14
Thornton **GB** (TYS) 22 Xa 9
Thornton **GB** (WYO) 39 Ya 26
Thornton Curtis **GB** (HUS) 41 Zd 27
Thornton Hough **GB** (CHS) 44 Wf 29
Thornton-le-Beans **GB** (NOY) 36 Yd 23
Thornton-le-Clay **GB** (NOY) 40 Za 24
Thornton-le-Dale **GB** (NOY) 37 Zb 23
Thornton-le-Moor **GB** (NOY) 36 Yd 23
Thornton-le-Moors **GB** (CHS) 44 Xa 29
Thornton-le-Street **GB** (NOY) 36 Yd 23
Thorntonloch **GB** (LOT) 27 Xd 13
Thornton Lodge **IRL** (KIL) 95 Tb 30
Thornton Rust **GB** (NOY) 36 Xf 23
Thornton Steward **GB** (NOY) 36 Yb 23
Thornton Watlass **GB** (NOY) 36 Yc 23
Thornwood Common **GB** (ESS) 64 Aa 38
Thoroton **GB** (NTS) 46 Za 31
Thorp Arch **GB** (WYO) 40 Yd 25
Thorpe **GB** (DSH) 45 Yb 30
Thorpe **GB** (LIN) 48 Ab 29
Thorpe **GB** (NOR) 57 Bd 33
Thorpe **GB** (NOY) 39 Ya 24
Thorpe **GB** (SUR) 63 Zc 40
Thorpe Abbots **GB** (NOR) 57 Bb 34
Thorpe Acre **GB** (LEC) 46 Ye 32
Thorpe Arnold **GB** (LEC) 46 Za 32
Thorpe Audlin **GB** (WYO) 40 Ye 27
Thorpe Bassett **GB** (NOY) 37 Zb 24
Thorpe by Water **GB** (LEC) 55 Zb 33
Thorpe Constantine **GB** (SFS) 53 Yc 32
Thorpe End Garden Village **GB** (NOR) 49 Bc 33
Thorpe Hall **GB** (NOY) 37 Yf 23
Thorpe Hesley **GB** (SOY) 40 Yd 28
Thorpe in Balne **GB** (SOY) 40 Yf 27
Thorpe Langton **GB** (LEC) 54 Za 33
Thorpe Larches **GB** (CLE) 36 Yd 21
Thorpe-le-Soken **GB** (ESS) 65 Ba 37
Thorpe Malsor **GB** (NRH) 54 Zb 34
Thorpe Mandeville **GB** (NRH) 54 Ye 36
Thorpe Market **GB** (NOR) 49 Bb 31
Thorpe Morieux **GB** (SUF) 56 Ae 36
Thorpeness **GB** (SUF) 57 Bd 35
Thorpe on the Hill **GB** (LIN) 47 Zc 29
Thorpe Saint Andrew **GB** (NOR) 49 Bb 33
Thorpe Saint Peter **GB** (LIN) 48 Ab 30
Thorpe Salvin **GB** (SOY) 46 Ye 29
Thorpe Satchville **GB** (LEC) 54 Za 32
Thorpe Thewles **GB** (CLE) 36 Yd 21
Thorpe Tilney Dales **GB** (LIN) 47 Ze 30
Thorpe Underwood **GB** (NOY) 40 Ye 24
Thorpe Waterville **GB** (NRH) 55 Zd 34
Thorpe Willoughby **GB** (NOY) 40 Yf 26
Thorpland **GB** (NOR) 56 Ac 33
Thorrington **GB** (ESS) 65 Ba 37
Thorton-in-Craven **GB** (NOY) 39 Xf 25
Thorverton **GB** (DEV) 67 Wc 44
Thrandeston **GB** (SUF) 57 Ba 34
Thrapston **GB** (NRH) 55 Zc 34
Threapwood **GB** (CHS) 44 Xa 31
Three Bridges **GB** (WSX) 71 Ze 42
Three Chimneys **GB** (KEN) 72 Ad 42
Three Cocks **GB** (POW) 60 We 36
Three Crosses **GB** (WGL) 59 Vf 39
Three Cups Corner **GB** (ESX) 72 Ab 43
Three Holes **GB** (NOR) 56 Ab 33
Three Leg Cross **GB** (ESX) 72 Ac 42
Three Legged Cross **GB** (DOS) 69 Ya 43
Three Mile Cross **GB** (BKS) 63 Za 40
Three Mile House **IRL** (MOG) 83 Sf 23
Threemilestone **GB** (CNW) 74 Uf 47
Threlkeld **GB** (CUB) 34 Wf 21
Thringstone **GB** (LEC) 46 Yd 32
Thrintoft **GB** (NOY) 36 Yc 22
Thriplow **GB** (CBS) 56 Aa 36
Throckley **GB** (TAW) 33 Yb 19
Throckmorton **GB** (HWC) 53 Xf 36
Thropton **GB** (NHL) 33 Ya 17
Throwleigh **GB** (DEV) 66 Wa 44
Thrumster **GB** (HGL) 6 Wf 118
Thrunton **GB** (NHL) 33 Ya 16
Thrupp **GB** (GLS) 61 Xe 38
Thrushgill **GB** (LCS) 38 Xc 24
Thrussington **GB** (LEC) 46 Yf 32
Thruxton **GB** (HAS) 69 Yc 41
Thrybergh **GB** (SOY) 40 Ye 28
Thryxton **GB** (HWC) 61 Xb 37
Thulston **GB** (DSH) 46 Yd 31
Thundergay **GB** (STC) 23 Ud 14
Thundridge **GB** (HTS) 64 Zf 38
Thurcaston **GB** (LEC) 54 Yf 32
Thurcroft **GB** (SOY) 46 Ye 28
Thurgarton **GB** (NOR) 49 Bb 31
Thurgarton **GB** (NTS) 46 Za 30
Thurgoland **GB** (SOY) 39 Yc 27
Thurlaston **GB** (LEC) 54 Ye 33
Thurlbear **GB** (SOM) 67 Wf 43
Thurlby **GB** (LIN) 47 Zc 30
Thurlby **GB** (LIN) 47 Zd 32
Thurleigh **GB** (BFS) 55 Zd 35
Thurles **IRL** (TIP) 99 Sb 32
Thurlestone **GB** (DEV) 76 Wa 47
Thurloxton **GB** (SOM) 67 Wf 42
Thurlstone **GB** (SOY) 39 Yc 27
Thurlton **GB** (NOR) 57 Bd 33
Thurmaston **GB** (LEC) 54 Yf 32
Thurne **GB** (NOR) 49 Bd 32
Thurnham **GB** (KEN) 65 Ad 41
Thurnham **GB** (LCS) 38 Xb 25
Thurning **GB** (NOR) 49 Ba 32
Thurning **GB** (NRH) 55 Zd 34
Thursby **GB** (CUB) 32 Wf 19
Thursley **GB** (SUR) 70 Zb 42
Thurso **GB** (HGL) 6 Wd 117
Thurstaston **GB** (CHS) 44 Wf 28
Thurston **GB** (SUF) 56 Ae 35
Thurstonfield **GB** (CUB) 32 Wf 19
Thurstonland **GB** (WYO) 39 Yb 27
Thurton **GB** (NOR) 57 Bc 33
Thurvaston **GB** (DSH) 45 Yc 31
Thuxton **GB** (NOR) 57 Af 33
Thwaite **GB** (NOY) 35 Xf 22
Thwaite Saint Mary **GB** (NOR) 57 Bc 33
Tibbermore **GB** (TYS) 21 Wc 10
Tibberton **GB** (GLS) 61 Xd 37
Tibberton **GB** (HWC) 53 Xf 35
Tibberton **GB** (SHS) 44 Xd 32
Tibbie Shiels Inn **GB** (BOR) 31 We 16
Tibenham **GB** (NOR) 57 Ba 34
Tibertich **GB** (STC) 23 Ud 12
Tibohine **IRL** (ROS) 88 Rc 25
Tibshelf **GB** (DSH) 46 Yd 30
Tibthorpe **GB** (HUS) 41 Zc 25
Ticehurst **GB** (ESX) 72 Ac 42
Tichbery **GB** (DEV) 66 Vc 42
Tichborne **GB** (HAS) 70 Ye 42
Tickenham **GB** (AVN) 61 Xb 40
Tickhall **GB** (SOY) 40 Yf 28
Ticklerton **GB** (SHS) 52 Xb 33
Ticknall **GB** (DSH) 46 Yd 32
Tickton **GB** (HUS) 41 Zd 25
Ticroghan **IRL** (MT) 89 Sf 28
Tiddington **GB** (WWH) 53 Yb 35
Tidebrook **GB** (ESX) 72 Ab 42
Tideford **GB** (CNW) 75 Ve 46
Tidenham Chase **GB** (GLS) 61 Xc 38
Tideswell **GB** (DSH) 45 Yb 29
Tidmarsh **GB** (BKS) 63 Yf 40
Tidmington **GB** (WWH) 53 Yc 36
Tidpit **GB** (HAS) 69 Ya 43
Tierernane Lodge **IRL** (LAO) 94 Ta 31
Tiermore House **IRL** (LIM) 98 Qf 33
Tiers Cross **GB** (DYF) 58 Uf 38
Tiershanaghan **IRL** (KER) 97 Qa 34
Tieveborne **IRL** (DON) 78 Sd 18
Tievebrack **IRL** (DON) 83 Sc 20
Tievelough **IRL** (DON) 77 Rf 20
Tiffield **GB** (NRH) 54 Za 36
Tifty **GB** (GRP) 17 Xd 4
Tigerton **GB** (TYS) 22 Xb 8
Tigh-na-Blair **GB** (TYS) 20 Wa 11
Tighnabruaich **GB** (STC) 24 Ue 13
Tighnafiline **GB** (HGL) 7 Uc 1
Tigley **GB** (DEV) 76 Wb 46
Tilbrook **GB** (BFS) 55 Zd 35
Tilbury **GB** (ESS) 64 Ac 40
Tile Cross **GB** (WMD) 53 Yb 34
Tile Hill **GB** (WMD) 53 Yc 34
Tilford **GB** (SUR) 70 Zb 41
Tillathrowie **GB** (GRP) 16 Xa 4
Tillers Green **GB** (GLS) 61 Xd 37
Tillicoultry **GB** (CEN) 25 Wb 12
Tillingham **GB** (ESS) 65 Af 38
Tillington **GB** (HWC) 52 Xb 36
Tillington **GB** (WSX) 70 Zc 43
Tillington Common **GB** (HWC) 52 Xb 36
Tillycorthie **GB** (GRP) 17 Xf 5
Tillyfourie **GB** (GRP) 17 Xc 5
Tillygreig **GB** (GRP) 17 Xe 5
Tilmanstone **GB** (KEN) 65 Bb 41
Tilney All Saints **GB** (NOR) 48 Ab 32
Tilney High End **GB** (NOR) 48 Ab 32
Tilstock **GB** (SHS) 44 Xb 31
Tilston **GB** (CHS) 44 Xb 30
Tilstone Fearnall **GB** (CHS) 44 Xc 30
Tilsworth **GB** (BFS) 63 Zc 37
Tilton on the Hill **GB** (LEC) 54 Za 33
Tiltups End **GB** (GLS) 61 Xe 39
Timadooaun **IRL** (GAL) 87 Rc 27
Timahoe **IRL** (KIL) 94 Ta 28
Timahoe **IRL** (LAO) 94 Se 31
Timberland Dales **GB** (LIN) 47 Ze 30
Timbersbrook **GB** (CHS) 45 Xf 30
Timberscombe **GB** (SOM) 67 Wd 42
Timoleague **IRL** (COR) 104 Rb 39
Timolin **IRL** (KIL) 94 Tb 31
Timoney Park **IRL** (TIP) 93 Sb 31
Timsbury **GB** (AVN) 61 Xd 41
Timsbury **GB** (HAS) 69 Yd 42
Timsgarry **GB** (HGL) 11 Sf 119
Timullen **IRL** (LOT) 90 Td 26
Tincleton **GB** (DOS) 68 Xe 44
Tincoora **IRL** (COR) 98 Ra 36
Tindale **GB** (CUB) 32 Xc 19
Tingewick **GB** (BUS) 63 Yf 37
Tingley **GB** (WYO) 39 Yc 26
Tingrith **GB** (BFS) 55 Zc 37
Tinker's Cross Roads **IRL** (COR) 104 Rb 36
Tinkerstown Cross Roads **IRL** (WEX) 101 Tc 33
Tinmuck **IRL** (OFF) 93 Sb 28
Tinnacarrick **IRL** (WEX) 100 Ta 34
Tinnacree **IRL** (WEX) 101 Te 33
Tinnakilla **IRL** (WEX) 101 Tc 34
Tinny Park **IRL** (ROS) 88 Rd 26
Tinsley **GB** (SOY) 46 Yd 28
Tintagel **GB** (CNW) 75 Vb 45
Tintern Parva **GB** (GWE) 61 Xb 38
Tintinhull **GB** (SOM) 68 Xb 43
Tintwistle **GB** (DSH) 39 Ya 28
Tinure Cross **IRL** (LOT) 90 Td 26
Tinwald **GB** (DAG) 31 Wc 18
Tiobraid Árann = Tipperary **IRL** (TIP) 99 Re 34
Tipperary **IRL** (TIP) 99 Re 34
Tipperty **GB** (GRP) 17 Xf 4
Tiptoe **GB** (HAS) 69 Yc 44
Tipton **GB** (WMD) 53 Xf 33
Tipton Saint John **GB** (DEV) 67 We 44
Tiptree **GB** (ESS) 65 Ae 38
Tirabad **GB** (POW) 51 Wc 36
Tirley **GB** (GLS) 61 Xe 37
Tirmoghan Common **IRL** (KIL) 95 Tb 28
Tirril **GB** (CUB) 35 Xb 21
Tisbury **GB** (WIL) 69 Xf 42
Tissington **GB** (DSH) 45 Yb 30
Titchfield **GB** (HAS) 70 Ye 43
Titchmarsh **GB** (NRH) 55 Zd 34
Titchwell **GB** (NOR) 48 Ad 31
Tithby **GB** (NTS) 46 Za 31
Titley **GB** (HWC) 52 Xa 35
Titson **GB** (CNW) 66 Vd 44
Titsy **GB** (SUR) 64 Aa 41
Tittensor **GB** (SFS) 45 Xe 31
Tittleshall **GB** (NOR) 48 Ae 32
Tiverton **GB** (CHS) 44 Xb 30
Tiverton **GB** (DEV) 67 Wd 43
Tivetshall Saint Margaret **GB** (NOR) 57 Bb 34
Tixall **GB** (SFS) 45 Xf 32
Tixover **GB** (LEC) 55 Zc 33
Toab **GB** (ORK) 6 Xa 115
Toab **GB** (SHL) 3 Ye 109
Toames **IRL** (COR) 103 Ra 37
Tober **IRL** (CAV) 82 Rf 23
Tober **IRL** (OFF) 94 Sc 28
Toberadora **IRL** (TIP) 99 Sa 33
Toberaneague **IRL** (COR) 99 Re 36
Tober Cross Roads **IRL** (WKL) 95 Tb 30
Tobercurry **IRL** (SLI) 87 Rb 24
Toberdan **IRL** (ROS) 88 Rf 27
Tobergal **IRL** (WEX) 101 Td 33
Tobermacloughlin **IRL** (ROS) 88 Rf 28
Tobermore **GB** (LDR) 84 Tb 20
Tobermory **GB** (STC) 18 Tf 9
Tobernabrone **IRL** (KLK) 100 Se 34
Tobernaclougha Cross Roads **IRL** (COR) 98 Qf 35
Tobernamoodane **IRL** (KER) 96 Pe 36
Tobernaskeha **IRL** (ROS) 88 Sa 26
Toberneu **IRL** (LIM) 98 Rc 34
Toberonochy **GB** (STC) 23 Uc 11
Tobson **GB** (HGL) 11 Ta 119
Tocher **GB** (GRP) 17 Xc 4
Tockenham **GB** (WIL) 62 Ya 39
Tockenham Wick **GB** (WIL) 62 Ya 39
Tockholes **GB** (LCS) 38 Xc 26
Tockington **GB** (AVN) 61 Xc 39
Tockwith **GB** (NOY) 40 Ye 25
Toddington **GB** (BFS) 63 Zc 37
Toddington **GB** (GLS) 62 Ya 37
Todenham **GB** (GLS) 53 Yc 36
Todhills **GB** (CUB) 32 Xa 19
Todmorden **GB** (WYO) 39 Xf 26
Todwick **GB** (SOY) 46 Ye 28
Toft **GB** (CBS) 55 Zf 35
Toft **GB** (LIN) 47 Zd 32
Toft **GB** (SHL) 2 Ye 106
Toft Hill **GB** (DUR) 36 Yb 21
Toft next Newton **GB** (LIN) 47 Zd 28
Toftrees **GB** (NOR) 48 Ae 32
Togher **IRL** (COR) 103 Qf 38
Togher **IRL** (LOT) 90 Te 25
Togher **IRL** (MT) 89 Ta 28
Togher **IRL** (OFF) 94 Se 28
Togherstown **IRL** (MT) 90 Tb 26
Togston **GB** (NHL) 33 Yc 17
Tokavaig **GB** (HGL) 13 Ua 6
Tolkers Green **GB** (OXS) 63 Za 40
Tolland **GB** (SOM) 67 We 42
Tollard Royal **GB** (WIL) 69 Xf 43
Toller Down Gate **GB** (DOS) 68 Xb 44
Toller Porcorum **GB** (DOS) 68 Xc 44
Tollerton **GB** (NOY) 40 Ye 24
Tollerton **GB** (NTS) 46 Yf 31
Tollesbury **GB** (ESS) 65 Ae 38
Tolleshunt D'Arcy **GB** (ESS) 65 Ae 38
Tolleshunt Knights **GB** (ESS) 65 Ae 38
Tolleshunt Major **GB** (ESS) 65 Ae 38
Toll of Birness **GB** (GRP) 17 Ya 4
Tolpuddle **GB** (DOS) 68 Xe 44
Tolsta Chaolais **GB** (HGL) 11 Tb 119
Tomatin **GB** (HGL) 15 Wa 4
Tombreck **GB** (HGL) 15 Ve 4
Tombreen House **IRL** (WKL) 101 Tc 32
Tomfarney Upper **IRL** (WEX) 101 Tb 34
Tomhaggard **IRL** (WEX) 101 Tc 35
Tomintoul **GB** (GRP) 16 Wd 5
Tomintoul **GB** (GRP) 16 Wd 6
Tomnavoulin **GB** (GRP) 16 We 5
Tompsons Town **IRL** (DON) 78 Se 18
Tonabrocky **IRL** (GAL) 92 Qf 29
Tonacurra **IRL** (GAL) 88 Rd 28
Tonbaun Wood **IRL** (KER) 97 Qd 35
Tonbridge **GB** (KEN) 72 Ab 41
Tondu **GB** (MGL) 60 Wc 39
Toneen Lodge **IRL** (LGF) 89 Sd 26
Tonevane Cross Roads **IRL** (KER) 97 Qb 35
Tong **GB** (SHS) 53 Xe 34
Tonge **GB** (LEC) 46 Yd 32
Tongham **GB** (SUR) 70 Zb 41
Tongland **GB** (DAG) 30 Vf 19
Tong Norton **GB** (SHS) 53 Xe 32
Tong Street **GB** (WYO) 39 Yb 26
Tongue **GB** (HGL) 5 Vd 118
Tongwynlais **GB** (SGL) 60 We 39
Tonlegee **IRL** (WKL) 95 Tf 31
Tonmawr **GB** (WGL) 59 Wb 39
Tonna **GB** (WGL) 59 Wb 38
Tonwell **GB** (HTS) 64 Ab 38
Tonyduff **IRL** (CAV) 89 Sf 25
Tonyglassan **IRL** (MOG) 90 Ta 24
Tonypandy **GB** (MGL) 60 Wd 39
Tonyrefail **GB** (MGL) 60 Wd 39
Toom **IRL** (COR) 103 Qf 38
Toomaghera **IRL** (CRE) 92 Qe 30
Tooman **IRL** (LET) 88 Sa 25
Toomard **IRL** (GAL) 88 Rd 27
Toome **GB** (ANT) 84 Td 20
Toomyvara **IRL** (TIP) 93 Rf 31
Tooradoo **IRL** (WTF) 99 Rf 35
Tooraree **IRL** (LIM) 98 Qe 33
Tooravoola **IRL** (GAL) 92 Rc 30
Toorboney **IRL** (KER) 98 Qe 36
Tooreen **IRL** (MAY) 87 Qe 26
Tooreen **IRL** (MAY) 87 Rb 26
Tooreenavuscaun **IRL** (COR) 98 Qf 35
Tooreencahill **IRL** (KER) 97 Qe 36
Tooreenclassagh **IRL** (KER) 98 Qe 36
Tooreendermot **IRL** (COR) 98 Qf 35
Tooreenfineen **IRL** (COR) 98 Qe 35
Toorgarriff **IRL** (COR) 98 Rd 36
Toorlestraun **IRL** (SLI) 87 Ra 24
Toormakeady **IRL** (MAY) 87 Qd 27
Toormore **IRL** (COR) 102 Qc 39
Toornafulla **IRL** (LIM) 98 Qf 34
Tootagh **IRL** (MAY) 87 Ra 26
Toot Baldon **GB** (OXS) 63 Ye 38
Toot Hill **GB** (ESS) 64 Ab 38
Toothill **GB** (HAS) 69 Yd 43
Tooting **GB** (GRL) 64 Ze 40
Topcliffe **GB** (NOY) 36 Yd 23
Topcroft **GB** (NOR) 57 Bc 34
Top End **GB** (BFS) 55 Zd 35
Topings **GB** (GRM) 38 Xd 27
Toppesfield **GB** (ESS) 56 Ad 36
Topsham **GB** (DEV) 67 Wd 44
Topsham Bridge **GB** (DEV) 76 Wb 46
Torbay **GB** (DEV) 76 Wc 46
Torbeg **GB** (STC) 28 Ue 15
Torboll **GB** (HGL) 8 Vf 1
Torcross **GB** (DEV) 76 Wc 47
Tordarroch **GB** (HGL) 15 Ve 4
Tordstown **IRL** (MT) 89 Ta 27
Tore **GB** (HGL) 15 Ve 3
Toreen **IRL** (WTF) 99 Sc 35
Torksey **GB** (LIN) 46 Zb 29
Torlum **GB** (HGL) 12 Sd 4
Torlundy **GB** (HGL) 19 Uf 7
Tormarton **GB** (AVN) 61 Xd 39
Tormisdale **GB** (STC) 22 Td 14
Tormitchell **GB** (STC) 30 Vb 17
Tormons **IRL** (KER) 102 Pf 37
Tormore **GB** (STC) 28 Ud 15
Tornagrain **GB** (HGL) 15 Vf 3
Tornaveen **GB** (GRP) 17 Xc 6
Torrachrasky **GB** (HGL) 14 Va 5
Torness **GB** (HGL) 15 Vd 5
Tornhill House **IRL** (CLW) 95 Tb 32
Torpenhow **GB** (CUB) 34 We 20
Torphichen **GB** (LOT) 25 Wc 13
Torphins **GB** (GRP) 17 Xc 6
Torpoint **GB** (CNW) 75 Ve 46
Torpys Cross Roads **IRL** (COR) 98 Rc 35
Torquay **GB** (DEV) 76 Wc 46
Torquhan **GB** (BOR) 26 Xa 14
Torr **GB** (DEV) 76 Wa 46
Torran **GB** (STC) 23 Ud 11
Torrance **GB** (STC) 25 Ve 13
Torrans **GB** (STC) 18 Tf 10
Torridon **GB** (HGL) 14 Ud 3
Torrin **GB** (HGL) 13 Tf 5
Torrisdale **GB** (HGL) 5 Ve 117
Torrisholme Torris-Holme **GB** (LCS) 38 Xa 24
Torroble **GB** (HGL) 8 Vd 120
Torry **GB** (GRP) 16 Xa 4
Torryburn **GB** (FIF) 25 Wc 12
Torrylinn **GB** (STC) 28 Ue 16
Torterston **GB** (GRP) 17 Ya 3
Torthorwald **GB** (DAG) 31 Wc 18
Tortington **GB** (WSX) 71 Zc 44
Tortworth **GB** (AVN) 61 Xd 39
Torvaig **GB** (HGL) 13 Te 4
Torver **GB** (CUB) 34 Wf 22
Torwood **GB** (CEN) 25 Wa 12
Torworth **GB** (NTS) 46 Yf 28
Tory Hill **IRL** (LIM) 98 Rb 33
Tosberry **GB** (DEV) 66 Vd 43
Toscaig **GB** (HGL) 13 Ub 4
Toseland **GB** (CBS) 55 Ze 35
Tosside **GB** (LCS) 38 Xd 25
Tostock **GB** (SUF) 56 Af 35
Totaig **GB** (HGL) 12 Tc 4
Tote **GB** (HGL) 13 Tf 3
Totegan **GB** (HGL) 5 Vf 117
Totford **GB** (HAS) 70 Ye 42
Totland **GB** (HAS) 69 Yc 44
Totley **GB** (DSH) 45 Yc 29
Totnes **GB** (DEV) 76 Wb 46
Toton **GB** (NTS) 46 Ye 31
Totronald **GB** (STC) 18 Tc 9
Tottenham **GB** (GRL) 64 Zf 39
Tottenhill **GB** (NOR) 48 Ac 33
Totteridge **GB** (GRL) 64 Ze 39
Tottington **GB** (GRM) 39 Xd 27
Totton **GB** (HAS) 69 Yd 43
Touchen End **GB** (BKS) 63 Zb 40
Tournaig **GB** (HGL) 7 Uc 2
Toux **GB** (GRP) 16 Xb 3
Toux **GB** (GRP) 17 Xf 3
Tovil **GB** (KEN) 65 Ad 41
Toward **GB** (STC) 24 Va 13
Towcester **GB** (NRH) 54 Za 36
Towednack **GB** (CNW) 74 Uc 47
Tower **IRL** (LIM) 98 Ra 33
Tower Hamlets **GB** (GRL) 64 Zf 39
Towersey **GB** (OXS) 63 Za 38
Towie **GB** (GRP) 16 Xa 5
Towiemore **GB** (GRP) 16 Wf 3
Tow Law **GB** (DUR) 36 Yb 20
Townhead **GB** (DAG) 29 Vf 20
Townhead of Greenlaw **GB** (DAG) 31 Wa 19
Townhill **GB** (FIF) 25 Wd 12
Town Row **GB** (ESX) 72 Ab 42
Townshend **GB** (CNW) 74 Ud 48
Town Yetholm **GB** (BOR) 27 Xe 15
Towthorpe **GB** (NOY) 40 Yf 24
Towton **GB** (NOY) 40 Ye 25
Towyn **GB** (CLW) 43 Wc 29
Toynton **GB** (LIN) 47 Aa 30
Toy's Hill **GB** (KEN) 71 Aa 41
Trabboch **GB** (STC) 30 Vd 16
Traboe **GB** (CNW) 74 Uf 48
Tracking Station **IRL** (COR) 103 Qc 39
Tralee **IRL** (KER) 97 Qb 35
Trá Lí = Tralee **IRL** (KER) 97 Qb 35
Trallong **GB** (POW) 60 Wc 37
Trallwng = Welshpool **GB** (POW) 52 Wf 33
Tramore **IRL** (WTF) 100 Sf 36
Tranent **GB** (LOT) 26 Xa 13
Trantlemore **GB** (HGL) 5 Wa 118
Tranwell **GB** (NHL) 33 Yb 18
Trapp **GB** (DYF) 59 Wa 37
Traprain **GB** (LOT) 26 Xc 13
Traquair **GB** (BOR) 26 Wf 15
Travara Bridge **IRL** (COR) 102 Qa 38
Trawden **GB** (LCS) 39 Xf 25
Trawlebane **IRL** (COR) 103 Qd 38
Trawlebane **IRL** (COR) 103 Qd 39
Trawnbaun **IRL** (GAL) 91 Qc 29
Trawsfynydd **GB** (GWY) 43 Wa 31
Treales **GB** (LCS) 38 Xa 26
Trean **IRL** (MAY) 87 Qd 27
Treanlaur Lodge **IRL** (MAY) 86 Qc 25
Treantagh **IRL** (DON) 77 Sa 19
Treantagh **IRL** (DON) 78 Sd 19
Trearddur **GB** (GWY) 42 Vc 29
Treaslane **GB** (HGL) 13 Td 3
Trebarrow **GB** (CNW) 66 Vd 44
Trebartha **GB** (CNW) 75 Vd 45
Treborough **GB** (SOM) 67 Wd 42

Tannadice – Treborough (GB) (IRL) 135

Wareside **GB** (HTS) 64 Aa 38
Waresley **GB** (CBS) 55 Ze 35
Warfield **GB** (BKS) 63 Zb 40
Wargrave **GB** (BKS) 63 Za 40
Warham **GB** (NOR) 48 Af 31
Waringstown **GB** (DOW) 84 Te 22
Wark **GB** (NHL) 27 Xe 15
Wark **GB** (NHL) 32 Xe 18
Warkleigh **GB** (DEV) 66 Wa 43
Warkworth **GB** (NHL) 33 Yc 16
Warkworth **GB** (NRH) 54 Ye 36
Warlaby **GB** (NOY) 36 Yd 23
Warland **GB** (WYO) 39 Xf 26
Warleggan **GB** (CNW) 75 Vc 46
Warlingham **GB** (SUR) 64 Zf 41
Warmfield **GB** (WYO) 40 Yd 26
Warmingham **GB** (CHS) 44 Xd 30
Warmington **GB** (NRH) 55 Zd 33
Warmington **GB** (WWH) 54 Yd 36
Warminster **GB** (WIL) 69 Xe 41
Warmlake **GB** (KEN) 72 Ad 41
Warmley **GB** (AVN) 61 Xd 40
Warmsworth **GB** (SOY) 40 Yf 28
Warmwell **GB** (DOS) 68 Xd 44
Warnford **GB** (HAS) 70 Yf 42
Warnham **GB** (WSX) 71 Zd 42
Warningcamp **GB** (WSX) 71 Zc 43
Warninglid **GB** (WSX) 71 Ze 42
Warren **GB** (CHS) 45 Xf 29
Warren **GB** (DYF) 58 Va 39
Warrenpoint **GB** (DOW) 90 Te 24
Warren Row **GB** (BKS) 63 Zb 39
Warren Street **GB** (KEN) 65 Ae 41
Warrington **GB** (CHS) 44 Xc 28
Warsash **GB** (HAS) 70 Ye 43
Warslow **GB** (SFS) 45 Ya 30
Warsop **GB** (NTS) 46 Yf 29
Warter **GB** (HUS) 40 Zb 25
Warthill **GB** (NOY) 40 Za 25
Wartling **GB** (ESX) 72 Ac 43
Warton **GB** (LCS) 35 Xb 24
Warton **GB** (LCS) 38 Xa 26
Warton **GB** (NHL) 33 Ya 17
Warton **GB** (WWH) 53 Yc 33
Warwick **GB** (CUB) 32 Xa 19
Warwick **GB** (WWH) 53 Yc 35
Warwick Bridge **GB** (CUB) 32 Xb 19
Wasbister **GB** (ORK) 5 Wf 113
Wasdale Head **GB** (CUB) 34 We 22
Washbourne **GB** (DEV) 76 Wb 46
Washford **GB** (SOM) 67 Wd 42
Washingborough **GB** (LIN) 47 Zd 29
Washington **GB** (TAW) 33 Yc 19
Washington **GB** (WSX) 71 Zd 43
Waskerley **GB** (DUR) 36 Ya 20
Wass **GB** (NOY) 37 Yf 23
Watchet **GB** (SOM) 67 We 41
Watchfield **GB** (OXS) 62 Yc 39
Watchfield **GB** (SOM) 68 Xa 41
Watchgate **GB** (CUB) 35 Xb 22
Watch House Village **IRL** (WEX) 101 Tc 32
Water **GB** (LCS) 39 Xe 26
Waterbeach **GB** (CBS) 56 Ab 35
Waterbeck **GB** (DAG) 31 We 18
Water End **GB** (HTS) 63 Zd 38
Waterfall **GB** (SFS) 45 Ya 30
Waterfall **IRL** (COR) 104 Rc 37
Waterfoot **GB** (LCS) 39 Xe 26
Waterfoot **GB** (STC) 25 Ve 14
Waterford **GB** (HTS) 64 Zf 38
Waterford **IRL** (WTF) 100 Sf 35
Watergrasshill **IRL** (COR) 99 Rd 36
Waterhouses **GB** (SFS) 45 Ya 30
Wateringbury **GB** (KEN) 65 Ac 41
Waterloo **GB** (NOR) 49 Bb 32
Waterloo **GB** (STC) 25 Wa 14
Waterloo **GB** (TYS) 21 Wc 9
Waterloo **IRL** (CAV) 89 Sf 25
Waterloo Cross **GB** (DEV) 67 Wd 43
Waterlooville **GB** (HAS) 70 Yf 43
Watermeetings **GB** (STC) 31 Wc 16
Watermillock **GB** (CUB) 35 Xa 21
Water Orton **GB** (WWH) 53 Yb 33
Waterperry **GB** (OXS) 63 Yf 38
Waterrow **GB** (SOM) 67 Wd 42
Watersfield **GB** (WSX) 71 Zc 43
Waterside **GB** (STC) 24 Vd 15
Waterside **GB** (STC) 30 Vd 16
Waterston **GB** (DYF) 58 Va 38
Water Stratford **GB** (BUS) 54 Yf 36
Waters Upton **GB** (SHS) 44 Xc 32
Waterville **IRL** (KER) 102 Pe 38
Water Yeat **GB** (CUB) 34 Wf 23
Watford **GB** (HTS) 63 Zd 38
Watford **GB** (NRH) 54 Yf 35
Wath **GB** (NOY) 36 Yc 23
Wath **GB** (NOY) 39 Yb 24
Wath upon Dearne **GB** (SOY) 40 Yd 28
Watlington **GB** (NOR) 48 Ac 33
Watlington **GB** (OXS) 63 Yf 39
Watten **GB** (HGL) 9 We 118
Wattisfield **GB** (SUF) 56 Af 35
Wattisham **GB** (SUF) 57 Af 36
Watton **GB** (HUS) 41 Zd 25
Watton **GB** (NOR) 56 Ae 33
Watton at Stone **GB** (HTS) 64 Zf 37
Wattstown **GB** (MGL) 60 Wd 39
Wattsville **GB** (GWE) 60 Wf 39
Waunarlwydd **GB** (WGL) 59 Vf 39
Waun Fawr **GB** (DYF) 51 Vf 34
Waunfawr **GB** (GWY) 42 Ve 30
Waverton **GB** (CUB) 34 We 20
Wawne **GB** (HUS) 41 Zd 26
Waxham **GB** (NOR) 49 Bd 32
Waxholme **GB** (HUS) 41 Aa 26
Waytown **GB** (DOS) 68 Xb 44
Way Village **GB** (DEV) 67 Wc 43
Weachyburn **GB** (GRP) 17 Xc 3
Wealdstone **GB** (GRL) 64 Ze 39
Weare Giffard **GB** (DEV) 66 Vf 43
Wearhead **GB** (DUR) 35 Xe 20
Wearne **GB** (SOM) 68 Xb 42
Weasdale **GB** (CUB) 35 Xd 22
Weasenham All Saints **GB** (NOR) 48 Ae 32
Weasenham Saint Peter **GB** (NOR) 48 Ae 32
Weatheroak Hill **GB** (HWC) 53 Ya 34
Weatley **GB** (HAS) 70 Za 42
Weaverham **GB** (CHS) 44 Xc 29
Weaverthorpe **GB** (NOY) 37 Zc 24
Webheath **GB** (HWC) 53 Ya 35
Webton **GB** (HWC) 61 Xa 36
Wedderlairs **GB** (GRP) 17 Xe 4
Weddington **GB** (WWH) 54 Yd 33
Wedhampton **GB** (WIL) 62 Ya 41
Wedmore **GB** (SOM) 68 Xb 41
Wednesbury **GB** (WMD) 53 Xf 33
Wednesfield **GB** (WMD) 53 Xf 33
Weedon **GB** (BUS) 63 Zb 37
Weedon Bec **GB** (NRH) 54 Yf 35
Weedon Lois **GB** (NRH) 54 Yf 36
Weeford **GB** (SFS) 53 Yb 33
Week **GB** (DEV) 67 Wb 43
Weekly **GB** (NRH) 55 Zb 34
Week Saint Mary **GB** (CNW) 66 Vd 44
Weeley **GB** (ESS) 65 Ba 37
Weeley Heath **GB** (ESS) 65 Ba 37
Weem **GB** (TYS) 21 Wa 9
Weeping Cross **GB** (SFS) 45 Xf 32
Weethly **GB** (WWH) 53 Ya 35
Weeting **GB** (NOR) 56 Ad 34
Weeton **GB** (HUS) 41 Ab 27
Weeton **GB** (LCS) 38 Xa 26
Weeton **GB** (NOY) 39 Yc 25
Weir **GB** (LCS) 39 Xe 26
Welbourn **GB** (LIN) 47 Zc 30
Welbourne **GB** (NOR) 49 Ba 33
Welburn **GB** (NOY) 40 Za 24
Welbury **GB** (NOY) 36 Yd 22
Welches Dam **GB** (CBS) 56 Aa 34
Welchtown **IRL** (DON) 77 Sa 20
Welcombe **GB** (DEV) 66 Vc 43
Weldon **GB** (NRH) 55 Zc 34
Welford **GB** (BKS) 62 Yd 40
Welford **GB** (NRH) 54 Yf 34
Welford-on-Avon **GB** (WWH) 53 Yb 35
Welham **GB** (LEC) 54 Za 33
Welham Green **GB** (HTS) 64 Ze 38
Well **GB** (HAS) 70 Za 41
Well **GB** (LIN) 47 Aa 29
Well **GB** (NOY) 36 Yc 23
Welland **GB** (HWC) 53 Xe 36
Wellbank **GB** (TYS) 22 Xa 9
Wellesbourne Hastings **GB** (WWH) 53 Yc 35
Wellesbourne Mountford **GB** (WWH) 53 Yc 35
Well Hill **GB** (KEN) 64 Aa 40
Wellingborough **GB** (NRH) 55 Zb 35
Wellington **GB** (HWC) 52 Xb 36
Wellington **GB** (SHS) 52 Xc 32
Wellington **GB** (SOM) 67 We 43
Wellingtonbridge **IRL** (WEX) 101 Tb 35
Wellington Heath **GB** (HWC) 52 Xd 36
Wellington House **IRL** (TIP) 93 Re 31
Wellmount **IRL** (GAL) 93 Re 30
Wellow **GB** (AVN) 61 Xd 41
Wellow **GB** (NTS) 46 Za 29
Wells **GB** (SOM) 68 Xc 41
Wellsborough **GB** (LEC) 54 Yd 33
Wells-next-the-Sea **GB** (NOR) 48 Af 31
Welney **GB** (NOR) 56 Ab 33
Welshampton **GB** (SHS) 44 Xa 31
Welsh Bicknor **GB** (GLS) 61 Xc 37
Welsh End **GB** (SHS) 44 Xb 31
Welsh Hook **GB** (DYF) 58 Va 37
Welsh Newton **GB** (HWC) 61 Xb 37
Welshpool **GB** (POW) 52 Wf 33
Welton **GB** (AVN) 68 Xd 41
Welton **GB** (CUB) 34 Wf 20
Welton **GB** (HUS) 41 Zc 26
Welton **GB** (LIN) 47 Zf 29
Welton **GB** (NRH) 54 Yf 35
Welton le Marsch **GB** (LIN) 47 Zd 29
Welton le Wold **GB** (LIN) 47 Zf 28
Welwick **GB** (HUS) 41 Aa 26
Welwyn **GB** (HTS) 64 Ze 38
Welwyn Garden City **GB** (HTS) 64 Ze 38
Wem **GB** (SHS) 44 Xb 31
Wembley **GB** (GRL) 64 Ze 39
Wembury **GB** (DEV) 76 Vf 47
Wembworthy **GB** (DEV) 66 Wa 43
Wemyss Bay **GB** (STC) 24 Va 13
Wendens Ambo **GB** (ESS) 56 Ab 36
Wendlebury **GB** (OXS) 63 Ye 37
Wendling **GB** (NOR) 48 Af 32
Wendover **GB** (BUS) 63 Zb 38
Wendron **GB** (CNW) 74 Ue 48
Wendy **GB** (CBS) 55 Zf 36
Wenhaston **GB** (SUF) 57 Bd 35
Wenlli **GB** (CLW) 43 Wb 29
Wennington **GB** (GRL) 64 Ab 39
Wennington **GB** (LCS) 38 Xc 24
Wensley **GB** (DSH) 45 Yc 30
Wensley **GB** (NOY) 36 Ya 23
Wentbridge **GB** (WYO) 40 Ye 27
Wentnor **GB** (SHS) 52 Xa 33
Wentworth **GB** (SOY) 40 Yd 28
Wenvoe **GB** (SGL) 60 We 40
Weobley **GB** (HWC) 52 Xa 36
Weobley Marsh **GB** (HWC) 52 Xa 36
Wereham **GB** (NOR) 56 Ac 33
Wernrheolydd **GB** (POW) 60 Xa 38
Werrington **GB** (CBS) 55 Ze 33
Werrington **GB** (SFS) 45 Xf 30
Wervin **GB** (CHS) 44 Xa 29
Wesham **GB** (LCS) 38 Xa 26
Wessington **GB** (DSH) 46 Yd 30
West Acre **GB** (NOR) 48 Ad 32
West Allerdean **GB** (NHL) 27 Xf 14
West Alvington **GB** (DEV) 76 Wb 47
West Amesbury **GB** (WIL) 69 Yb 41
West Ashby **GB** (LIN) 47 Zf 29
West Ashling **GB** (WSX) 70 Za 43
West Ashton **GB** (WIL) 69 Xe 41
West Auckland **GB** (DUR) 36 Yb 21
West Bagborough **GB** (SOM) 67 We 42
West Barns **GB** (LOT) 26 Xc 13
West Bay **GB** (DOS) 68 Xb 44
West Beckham **GB** (NOR) 49 Bb 31
West Benhar **GB** (STC) 25 Wb 13
Westbere **GB** (KEN) 65 Ba 41
West Bergholt **GB** (ESS) 65 Af 37
West Bilney **GB** (NOR) 48 Ad 32
West Blatchington **GB** (ESX) 71 Ze 43
Westborough **GB** (LIN) 46 Zb 31
Westbourne **GB** (WSX) 70 Za 43
West Bretton **GB** (WYO) 39 Yc 27
West Bridgford **GB** (NTS) 46 Yf 31
West Bromwich **GB** (WMD) 53 Xf 33
West Buckland **GB** (DEV) 66 Wa 42
West Buckland **GB** (SOM) 67 We 43
West Burton **GB** (NOY) 36 Ya 23
West Burton **GB** (WSX) 71 Zc 43
Westbury **GB** (SHS) 52 Xa 32
Westbury **GB** (WIL) 69 Xe 41
Westbury Leigh **GB** (WIL) 69 Xe 41
Westbury-on-Severn **GB** (GLS) 61 Xd 38
Westbury-sub-Mendip **GB** (SOM) 68 Xb 41
West Caister **GB** (NOR) 49 Be 33
West Calder **GB** (LOT) 25 Wc 13
West Challow **GB** (OXS) 62 Yd 39
West Charleton **GB** (DEV) 76 Wb 47
West Chevington **GB** (NHL) 33 Yc 17
West Chiltington **GB** (WSX) 71 Zd 43
West Chinnock **GB** (SOM) 68 Xb 43
West Clandon **GB** (SUR) 71 Zc 41
Westcliff-on-Sea **GB** (ESS) 65 Ae 39
West Clyne **GB** (HGL) 9 Wa 120
West Coker **GB** (SOM) 68 Xb 43
Westcombe **GB** (SOM) 68 Xd 42
West Compton **GB** (DOS) 68 Xc 44
West Compton **GB** (SOM) 68 Xc 41
Westcote **GB** (GLS) 62 Yb 37
Westcott **GB** (BUS) 63 Za 37
Westcott **GB** (DEV) 67 Wd 44
Westcott **GB** (SUR) 71 Zd 41
West Cross **GB** (WGL) 59 Wa 39
West Curry **GB** (CNW) 66 Vd 44
West Curthwaite **GB** (CUB) 34 Wf 20
Westdean **GB** (ESX) 71 Aa 44
West Dean **GB** (WIL) 69 Yc 42
West Dean **GB** (WSX) 70 Zb 43
West Deeping **GB** (LIN) 55 Zd 32
West Derby **GB** (MES) 44 Xa 28
West Dereham **GB** (NOR) 56 Ac 33
West Ditchburn **GB** (NHL) 33 Yb 16
West Down **GB** (DEV) 66 Vf 42
West Drayton **GB** (NTS) 46 Za 29
West End **GB** (AVN) 61 Xb 40
West End **GB** (OXS) 62 Yd 38
West End **GB** (SUF) 57 Bd 34
West End **GB** (SUR) 63 Zc 41
Westerdale **GB** (HGL) 6 Wd 118
Westerdale **GB** (NOY) 37 Za 22
Westerfield **GB** (SUF) 57 Bb 36
Wester Fintray **GB** (GRP) 17 Xe 5
Wester Gruinards **GB** (HGL) 8 Vd 1
Westerham **GB** (KEN) 64 Aa 41
Westerleigh **GB** (AVN) 61 Xd 39
Wester Newburn **GB** (FIF) 26 Xa 11
Wester Skeld **GB** (SHL) 2 Yd 107
Westerton **GB** (TYS) 22 Xc 8
West Farleigh **GB** (KEN) 65 Ac 41
West Farndon **GB** (NRH) 54 Ye 35
West Felton **GB** (SHS) 44 Xa 32
Westfield **GB** (ESX) 72 Ad 43
Westfield **GB** (HGL) 5 Wc 117
Westfield **GB** (LOT) 25 Wb 13
West Firle **GB** (ESX) 71 Aa 43
West Fleetham **GB** (NHL) 27 Yb 15
Westgate **GB** (DUR) 35 Xf 20
Westgate **GB** (HUS) 40 Za 27
West Gerinish **GB** (HGL) 12 Sd 4
West Ginge **GB** (OXS) 62 Yd 39
West Grafton **GB** (WIL) 62 Yc 40
West Grimstead **GB** (WIL) 69 Yb 42
West Haddlesey **GB** (NOY) 40 Yf 26
West Haddon **GB** (NRH) 54 Yf 34
West Hagbourne **GB** (OXS) 62 Ye 39
West Hall **GB** (CUB) 32 Xb 18
Westhall **GB** (SUF) 57 Bd 34
West Hallam **GB** (DSH) 46 Yd 31
West Halton **GB** (HUS) 40 Zc 26
Westham **GB** (ESX) 72 Ab 44
Westham **GB** (SOM) 68 Xa 41
Westhampnett **GB** (WSX) 70 Zb 43
West Handley **GB** (DSH) 46 Yd 29
West Hanney **GB** (OXS) 62 Yd 39
West Hanningfield **GB** (ESS) 65 Ac 39
West Harptree **GB** (AVN) 68 Xc 41
West Harting **GB** (WSX) 70 Za 43
West Hatch **GB** (SOM) 68 Wf 43
Westhay **GB** (SOM) 68 Xb 41
Westhead **GB** (LCS) 38 Xa 27
West Helmsdale **GB** (HGL) 9 Wb 120
West Hendred **GB** (OXS) 62 Yd 39
West Heslerton **GB** (NOY) 37 Zc 23
Westhide **GB** (HWC) 52 Xc 36
West Hill **GB** (DEV) 67 We 44
Westhill **GB** (GRP) 17 Xe 6
West Hoathly **GB** (WSX) 71 Zf 42
West Holme **GB** (DOS) 69 Xf 44
Westhope **GB** (HWC) 52 Xb 36
Westhope **GB** (SHS) 52 Xb 34
West Horndon **GB** (ESS) 64 Ac 39
Westhorpe **GB** (LIN) 47 Ze 31
Westhorpe **GB** (SUF) 57 Af 35
West Horrington **GB** (SOM) 68 Xc 41
West Horsley **GB** (SUR) 71 Zd 41
West Hougham **GB** (KEN) 73 Ba 42
Westhoughton **GB** (GRM) 38 Xc 27
Westhouse **GB** (NOY) 35 Xc 24
Westhouses **GB** (DSH) 46 Yd 30
West Ilsley **GB** (BKS) 62 Ye 39
Westing **GB** (SHL) 2 Za 104
West Itchenor **GB** (WSX) 70 Za 44
West Keal **GB** (LIN) 47 Aa 30
West Kennett **GB** (WIL) 62 Ya 40
West Kilbride **GB** (STC) 24 Va 14
West Kingsdown **GB** (KEN) 64 Ab 40
West Kington **GB** (WIL) 61 Xe 40
West Kirby **GB** (CHS) 44 We 28
West Knighton **GB** (DOS) 68 Xd 44
West Knoyle **GB** (WIL) 69 Xe 42
Westlake **GB** (DEV) 76 Wa 46
West Langdon **GB** (KEN) 73 Bb 41
West Lavant **GB** (WSX) 70 Zb 43
West Lavington **GB** (WIL) 69 Ya 41
West Lavington **GB** (WSX) 70 Zb 43
West Layton **GB** (NOY) 36 Yb 22
West Leake **GB** (NTS) 54 Ye 32
Westleigh **GB** (DEV) 66 Ve 42
Westleton **GB** (SUF) 57 Bd 35
West Lexham **GB** (NOR) 48 Ae 32
Westley **GB** (SHS) 52 Xa 33
Westley **GB** (SUF) 56 Ad 35
Westley Waterless **GB** (CBS) 56 Ac 35
West Lilling **GB** (NOY) 40 Yf 24
Westlington **GB** (BUS) 63 Za 38
West Linton **GB** (BOR) 26 Wd 14
Westlinton **GB** (CUB) 32 Xa 19
West Littleton **GB** (AVN) 61 Xd 40
West Looe **GB** (CNW) 75 Vd 46
West Lulworth **GB** (DOS) 68 Xe 45
West Lutton **GB** (NOY) 37 Zc 24
West Lydford **GB** (SOM) 68 Xc 42
West Lyng **GB** (SOM) 68 Xa 42
West Lynn **GB** (NOR) 48 Ac 32
West Malling **GB** (KEN) 65 Ac 41
West Malvern **GB** (HWC) 53 Xd 36
West Marden **GB** (WSX) 70 Za 43
West Markham **GB** (NTS) 46 Za 29
West Marton **GB** (NOY) 39 Xf 25
West Meon **GB** (HAS) 70 Yf 42
West Mersea **GB** (ESS) 65 Af 38
Westmeston **GB** (ESX) 71 Zf 43
Westmill **GB** (HTS) 64 Zf 37
West Milton **GB** (DOS) 68 Xb 44
Westminster **GB** (GRL) 64 Zf 40
West Molesey **GB** (SUR) 64 Zd 40
West Monkton **GB** (SOM) 67 Wf 42
West Mors **GB** (DOS) 69 Ya 44
Westmuir **GB** (TYS) 22 Wf 9
West Muir **GB** (TYS) 22 Xb 8
Westness **GB** (ORK) 5 Wf 114
Westnewton **GB** (CUB) 34 Wd 20
West Newton **GB** (HUS) 41 Ze 26
West Newton **GB** (NOR) 48 Ad 32
West Ogwell **GB** (DEV) 76 Wb 45
Weston **GB** (CHS) 44 Xb 29
Weston **GB** (CHS) 44 Xd 30
Weston **GB** (DEV) 67 We 44
Weston **GB** (DOS) 68 Xd 45
Weston **GB** (HTS) 64 Zf 37
Weston **GB** (LIN) 47 Zf 32
Weston **GB** (NOY) 39 Yb 25
Weston **GB** (NRH) 54 Yf 36
Weston **GB** (NTS) 46 Za 29
Weston **GB** (SFS) 45 Xf 31
Weston **GB** (SHS) 44 Xc 31
Weston **GB** (SHS) 52 Xc 33
Westonbirt **GB** (GLS) 61 Xe 39
Weston by Welland **GB** (NRH) 54 Za 33
Weston Clinton **GB** (BUS) 63 Zb 38
Weston Colville **GB** (CBS) 56 Ac 36
Weston Green **GB** (NOR) 49 Ba 32
Weston Heath **GB** (SHS) 53 Xe 32
Weston Hills **GB** (LIN) 47 Zf 32
Westoning **GB** (BFS) 55 Zd 37
Weston-in-Gordano **GB** (AVN) 61 Xb 40
Weston Jones **GB** (SFS) 45 Xd 32
Weston Longville **GB** (NOR) 49 Ba 32
Weston Lullingfields **GB** (SHS) 44 Xa 32
Weston-on-the-Green **GB** (OXS) 62 Ye 37
Weston-on-Trent **GB** (DSH) 46 Yd 31
Weston Patrick **GB** (HAS) 70 Yf 41
Weston Rhyn **GB** (SHS) 44 Wf 31
Weston-Sub-Edge **GB** (GLS) 53 Yb 36
Weston-Super-Mare **GB** (AVN) 60 Xa 40
Weston-under-Lizard **GB** (SFS) 53 Xe 32
Weston under Penyard **GB** (HWC) 61 Xc 37
Weston under Wetherley **GB** (WWH) 54 Yd 35
Weston Underwood **GB** (BUS) 54 Zb 36
Westonzoyland **GB** (SOM) 68 Xa 42
West Overton **GB** (WIL) 62 Yb 40
Westow **GB** (NOY) 40 Za 24
West Pennard **GB** (SOM) 68 Xc 42
West Pentire **GB** (CNW) 74 Uf 46
West Porlock **GB** (SOM) 67 Wc 41
Westport **GB** (SOM) 68 Xa 43
Westport **IRL** (MAY) 86 Qc 26
Westport Quay **IRL** (MAY) 86 Qc 26
West Quantoxhead **GB** (SOM) 67 We 42
West Rainton **GB** (DUR) 36 Yc 20
West Rasen **GB** (LIN) 47 Zd 28
Westrigg **GB** (LOT) 25 Wb 13
West Rounton **GB** (NOY) 36 Yd 22
West Rudham **GB** (NOR) 48 Ae 32
West Runton **GB** (NOR) 49 Bb 31
Westruther **GB** (BOR) 26 Xc 14
Westry **GB** (CBS) 54 Aa 33
West Saltoun **GB** (LOT) 26 Xa 13
West Sandwick **GB** (SHL) 2 Ye 105
West Scrafton **GB** (NOY) 36 Ya 23
West Stafford **GB** (DOS) 68 Xd 44
West Stockwith **GB** (NTS) 40 Zb 28
West Stoke **GB** (WSX) 70 Zb 43
West Stonesdale **GB** (NOY) 35 Xe 22
West Stoughton **GB** (SOM) 68 Xa 41
West Stour **GB** (DOR) 68 Xe 42
West Stourmouth **GB** (KEN) 65 Bb 41
West Stow **GB** (SUF) 56 Ad 35
West Stowell **GB** (WIL) 62 Yb 40
West Stratton **GB** (HAS) 70 Ye 42
West Street **GB** (KEN) 65 Ae 41
West Tanfield **GB** (NOY) 36 Yc 23
West Taphouse **GB** (CNW) 75 Vc 46
West Tarbert **GB** (STC) 23 Ud 13
West Thorney **GB** (WSX) 70 Za 44
West Thurrock **GB** (ESS) 64 Ab 40
West Tilbury **GB** (ESS) 64 Ac 40
West Tisted **GB** (HAS) 70 Yf 42
West Tofts **GB** (TYS) 21 Wd 10
West Torrington **GB** (LIN) 47 Ze 29
Westtown **IRL** (WTF) 100 Se 36
West Tytherley **GB** (HAS) 69 Yc 42
West Tytherton **GB** (WIL) 61 Xf 40
West Village **IRL** (COR) 104 Rc 37
West Walton **GB** (NOR) 48 Ab 32
Westward **GB** (CUB) 34 Wf 20
Westward Ho! **GB** (DEV) 66 Ve 42
Westwell **GB** (GLS) 62 Yb 38
Westwell **GB** (KEN) 72 Af 41
Westwell Leacon **GB** (KEN) 72 Ae 41
West Wellow **GB** (HAS) 69 Yc 43
West Wemyss **GB** (FIF) 26 Wf 12
Westwick **GB** (CBS) 55 Aa 35
Westwick **GB** (DUR) 36 Ya 21
Westwick **GB** (NOR) 49 Bc 32
West Wickham **GB** (CBS) 56 Ac 36
West Williamston **GB** (DYF) 58 Va 38
West Winch **GB** (NOR) 48 Ac 32
West Winterslow **GB** (WIL) 69 Yc 42
West Wittering **GB** (WSX) 70 Za 44
West Witton **GB** (NOY) 36 Ya 23
Westwood **GB** (DEV) 67 Wd 44
Westwood **GB** (WIL) 61 Xe 41
West Woodburn **GB** (NHL) 33 Xe 17
West Woodhay **GB** (BKS) 62 Yd 40
West Woodlands **GB** (SOM) 68 Xe 41
Westwoodside **GB** (HUS) 40 Za 28
West Worldham **GB** (HAS) 70 Za 42
West Worlington **GB** (DEV) 67 Wb 43
West Wycombe **GB** (BUS) 63 Zb 39
West Yell **GB** (SHL) 2 Ye 105
Wetheral **GB** (CUB) 32 Xa 19
Wetherby **GB** (WYO) 40 Yd 25
Wethersfield **GB** (ESS) 56 Ac 37
Wethersta **GB** (SHL) 2 Yd 106
Wetherup Street **GB** (SUF) 57 Ba 35
Wetley Rocks **GB** (SFS) 45 Xf 30
Wettenhall **GB** (CHS) 44 Xc 30
Wetton **GB** (SFS) 45 Yb 30
Wetwang **GB** (HUS) 41 Zc 24
Wetwood **GB** (SFS) 45 Xd 31
Wexcombe **GB** (WIL) 62 Yc 41
Wexford **IRL** (WEX) 101 Td 34
Weybourne **GB** (NOR) 49 Ba 31
Weybread **GB** (SUF) 57 Bb 34
Weybridge **GB** (SUR) 63 Zd 40
Weydale **GB** (HGL) 6 Wd 117
Weyhill **GB** (HAS) 69 Yc 41
Weymouth **GB** (DOS) 68 Xd 45
Whaddon **GB** (BUS) 54 Zb 36
Whaddon **GB** (GLS) 61 Xe 38
Whaddon **GB** (WIL) 69 Yb 42
Whale **GB** (CUB) 35 Xb 21
Whaley **GB** (DSH) 46 Ye 29
Whaley Bridge **GB** (DSH) 45 Ya 29
Whalley **GB** (LCS) 38 Xd 26
Whalton **GB** (NHL) 33 Yb 18
Wham **GB** (NOY) 38 Xd 24
Whaplode **GB** (LIN) 47 Zf 32
Whaplode Saint Cathrine **GB** (LIN) 47 Zf 32
Wharfe **GB** (NOY) 38 Xd 24
Wharles **GB** (LCS) 38 Xa 26
Wharncliffe Side **GB** (SOY) 39 Yc 28
Wharram le Street **GB** (NOY) 40 Zb 24
Wharton **GB** (CHS) 44 Xc 29
Wharton **GB** (HWC) 52 Xb 35
Whashton **GB** (NOY) 36 Yb 22
Whatcombe **GB** (DOS) 68 Xe 44
Whatcote **GB** (WWH) 54 Yc 36
Whatfield **GB** (SUF) 57 Af 36
Whatton **GB** (NTS) 46 Za 31
Whauphill **GB** (DAG) 29 Vd 20
Wheatenhurst **GB** (GLS) 61 Xd 38
Wheathampstead **GB** (HTS) 64 Ze 38
Wheathill **GB** (FER) 83 Sb 23
Wheathley **GB** (OXS) 63 Yf 38
Wheatley Hill **GB** (DUR) 36 Yd 20
Wheaton Aston **GB** (SFS) 53 Xe 32
Wheddon Cross **GB** (SOM) 67 Wc 42
Wheedlemont **GB** (GRP) 16 Xa 5
Wheelerstreet **GB** (SUR) 70 Zc 42
Wheelock **GB** (CHS) 44 Xd 30
Wheelton **GB** (LCS) 38 Xc 26
Wheen **GB** (TYS) 21 Wf 8
Wheldrake **GB** (NOY) 40 Za 25
Whelford **GB** (GLS) 62 Yb 38
Whenby **GB** (NOY) 37 Yf 24
Whepstead **GB** (SUF) 56 Ae 35
Wherstead **GB** (SUF) 57 Ba 36
Wherwell **GB** (HAS) 69 Yd 41
Wheston **GB** (DSH) 45 Yb 29
Whetsted **GB** (KEN) 72 Ac 41
Whicham **GB** (CUB) 34 We 23
Whichford **GB** (WWH) 54 Yc 36
Whickham **GB** (TAW) 33 Yb 19
Whiddon Down **GB** (DEV) 66 Wa 44
Whigstreet **GB** (TYS) 22 Xa 9
Whilton **GB** (NRH) 54 Yf 35
Whimple **GB** (DEV) 67 Wd 44
Whimpwell Green **GB** (NOR) 49 Bd 32
Whinburgh **GB** (NOR) 48 Af 33
Whinnyfold **GB** (GRP) 17 Ya 4
Whipsnade **GB** (BFS) 63 Zc 37
Whipton **GB** (DEV) 67 Wd 44
Whisby **GB** (LIN) 47 Zc 29
Whissendine **GB** (LEC) 46 Zb 32
Whistley Green **GB** (BKS) 63 Za 40
Whiston **GB** (MES) 44 Xb 28
Whiston **GB** (NRH) 54 Zb 35
Whiston **GB** (SFS) 45 Ya 30
Whiston **GB** (SOY) 46 Ye 28
Whitbeck **GB** (CUB) 34 Wd 23
Whitbourne **GB** (HWC) 52 Xd 35
Whitburn **GB** (LOT) 25 Wb 13
Whitburn **GB** (TAW) 33 Yd 19
Whitby **GB** (CHS) 44 Xa 29
Whitby **GB** (NOY) 37 Zc 22
Whitchurch **GB** (AVN) 61 Xc 40
Whitchurch **GB** (BUS) 63 Zb 37
Whitchurch **GB** (CHS) 44 Xb 31
Whitchurch **GB** (DYF) 58 Ue 37
Whitchurch **GB** (HAS) 70 Ye 41
Whitchurch **GB** (SGL) 60 We 39
Whitchurch Canonicorum **GB** (DOS) 68 Xa 44
Whitcombe **GB** (DOS) 68 Xd 44
Whitcott Keysett **GB** (SHS) 52 Wf 34
White's Cross **IRL** (COR) 104 Rd 37
Whiteacen **GB** (GRP) 16 We 3
Whiteash Green **GB** (ESS) 56 Ad 37
Whitebridge **GB** (HGL) 15 Vd 5
Whitebrook **GB** (GWE) 61 Xb 38
Whitecairns **GB** (GRP) 17 Xf 5
White Castle **IRL** (DON) 78 Se 18
Whitechurch **IRL** (COR) 98 Rc 37
Whitechurch **IRL** (KIL) 95 Tc 29
Whitechurch **IRL** (TIP) 100 Sd 34
Whitechurch **IRL** (WEX) 100 Ta 35
Whitechurch **IRL** (WTF) 99 Sb 36
Whitechurch Hill **GB** (OXS) 63 Yf 39
White Coppice **GB** (LCS) 38 Xc 26
Whitecroft **GB** (GLS) 61 Xc 38
Whitecross **GB** (ARG) 84 Td 23
Whitecross **GB** (CEN) 25 Wc 13
White End **GB** (GLS) 61 Xe 37
Whiteface **GB** (HGL) 8 Ve 1
Whitefield **GB** (GRM) 39 Xe 27
Whitefield **GB** (TYS) 21 Wd 10
Whitefield **IRL** (DON) 78 Se 17
Whiteford **GB** (GRP) 17 Xd 5
Whiteford **IRL** (OFF) 93 Sa 30
Whitegate **GB** (CHS) 44 Xc 29
Whitegate **IRL** (COR) 104 Re 38
Whitegate **IRL** (CRE) 93 Rd 31
Whitegate **IRL** (WMT) 89 Se 26
White Gate Cross Roads **IRL** (KER) 97 Qb 35
Whitehall **GB** (ORK) 5 Xc 114
White Hall **IRL** (COR) 103 Qd 39
Whitehall **IRL** (ROS) 88 Sa 26
White Hall **IRL** (WKL) 95 Te 30
White Hall **IRL** (WMT) 89 Sb 28
Whitehaven **GB** (CUB) 34 Wc 21
Whitehead **GB** (ANT) 85 Ub 20
Whitehill **GB** (HAS) 70 Za 42
Whitehill **GB** (KEN) 65 Af 41
Whitehill **GB** (STC) 24 Vb 14
Whitehill **IRL** (DON) 78 Sd 19
White Hill **IRL** (DON) 82 Rd 20
Whitehills **GB** (GRP) 17 Xc 2
Whitehouse **GB** (ANT) 85 Ua 20
Whitehouse **GB** (GRP) 17 Xc 5
Whitehouse **GB** (STC) 23 Ud 14
Whitekirk **GB** (LOT) 26 Xc 12
White Lackington **GB** (DOS) 68 Xd 44
Whitelackington **GB** (SOM) 68 Xa 43
White Ladies Aston **GB** (HWC) 53 Xf 35
Whiteley Bank **GB** (IOW) 70 Ye 45
Whitemans Green **GB** (WSX) 71 Zf 42
Whitemire **GB** (GRP) 15 Wb 3
White Moor **GB** (DSH) 46 Yd 30
Whitemount **IRL** (KLK) 100 Sd 33
White Notley **GB** (ESS) 65 Ad 38
Whiteparish **GB** (WIL) 69 Yc 42
White Pit **GB** (LIN) 47 Aa 29
White Quarry **IRL** (MT) 90 Tb 26
Whiterashes **GB** (GRP) 17 Xe 5
Whiterath Cross Roads **IRL** (LOT) 90 Td 25
Whiterhurst **GB** (ESX) 72 Ac 43
White Roothing or White Roding **GB** (ESS) 64 Ab 38
Whiterow **GB** (HGL) 6 Wf 118
Whiteshill **GB** (GLS) 61 Xe 38
Whiteside **GB** (LOT) 25 Wc 13
Whitesmith **GB** (ESX) 71 Ab 43
Whitestone **GB** (DEV) 67 Wc 44
Whitestone **GB** (GRP) 17 Xc 6
Whites Town **IRL** (LOT) 90 Tf 25
Whitestown House **IRL** (WTF) 100 Sd 35
White Waltham **GB** (BKS) 63 Zb 40
Whiteway **GB** (GLS) 61 Xf 38
Whiteway House **GB** (DEV) 76 Wc 45
Whitewell **GB** (LCS) 38 Xc 25
Whitewreath **GB** (GRP) 16 We 3
Whitfield **GB** (AVN) 61 Xd 39
Whitfield **GB** (KEN) 73 Bb 41
Whitfield **GB** (NHL) 32 Xd 19
Whitfield **GB** (NRH) 54 Yf 36
Whitfield Court **IRL** (WTF) 100 Se 35
Whitford **GB** (CLW) 43 We 29
Whitford **GB** (DEV) 67 Wf 44
Whitgift **GB** (HUS) 40 Zb 26
Whitgreave **GB** (SFS) 45 Xf 31
Whithorn **GB** (DAG) 29 Vd 20
Whiting Bay **GB** (STC) 28 Uf 16
Whitland **GB** (DYF) 58 Vc 38
Whitletts **GB** (STC) 30 Vc 16
Whitley **GB** (BKS) 63 Za 40
Whitley **GB** (NOY) 40 Yf 26
Whitley Bay **GB** (TAW) 33 Yd 18
Whitley Chapel **GB** (NHL) 33 Xf 19
Whitley Lower **GB** (WYO) 39 Yc 27
Whitley Row **GB** (KEN) 71 Aa 41
Whitlock's End **GB** (WMD) 53 Ya 34
Whitminster **GB** (GLS) 61 Xe 38
Whitmore **GB** (SFS) 45 Xe 31
Whitnash **GB** (WWH) 54 Yc 35
Whitney-on-Wye **GB** (HWC) 52 Wf 36
Whitrigg **GB** (CUB) 31 We 19
Whitrigg **GB** (CUB) 34 We 20
Whitsbury **GB** (HAS) 69 Yb 43
Whitsome **GB** (BOR) 27 Xe 14
Whitson **GB** (GWE) 60 Xa 39
Whitstable **GB** (KEN) 65 Ba 40
Whitstone **GB** (CNW) 66 Vd 44
Whittingham **GB** (NHL) 33 Ya 16
Whittingslow **GB** (SHS) 52 Xa 34
Whittington **GB** (DSH) 46 Yd 29
Whittington **GB** (GLS) 62 Ya 37
Whittington **GB** (HWC) 53 Xe 35
Whittington **GB** (LCS) 35 Xc 23
Whittington **GB** (NOR) 56 Ad 33
Whittington **GB** (SFS) 53 Xe 34
Whittington **GB** (SFS) 53 Yb 32
Whittington **GB** (SHS) 44 Wf 31
Whittlebury **GB** (NRH) 54 Za 36
Whittle-le-Woods **GB** (LCS) 38 Xc 26
Whittlesey **GB** (CBS) 55 Zf 33
Whittlesford **GB** (CBS) 56 Aa 36
Whitton **GB** (BOR) 32 Xd 16
Whitton **GB** (CLE) 36 Yd 21
Whitton **GB** (HUS) 40 Zc 26
Whitton **GB** (POW) 52 Wf 35
Whitton **GB** (SHS) 52 Xc 34
Whitton **GB** (SUF) 57 Ba 36
Whittonditch **GB** (WIL) 62 Yc 40
Whittonstall **GB** (NHL) 33 Ya 19
Whitway **GB** (HAS) 62 Yd 41
Whitwell **GB** (DSH) 46 Ye 29
Whitwell **GB** (HTS) 64 Ze 37
Whitwell **GB** (IOW) 70 Ye 45
Whitwell **GB** (LEC) 55 Zc 32
Whitwell **GB** (NOY) 36 Yc 22
Whitwell-on-the-Hill **GB** (NOY) 40 Za 24
Whitwick **GB** (LEC) 46 Yd 32
Whitwood **GB** (WYO) 40 Yd 26
Whitworth **GB** (GRM) 39 Xf 27
Whixall **GB** (SHS) 44 Xb 31
Whixley **GB** (NOY) 40 Ye 24
Whorlton **GB** (DUR) 36 Ya 21
Whorlton **GB** (NOY) 36 Ye 22
Whygate **GB** (NHL) 32 Xd 18
Whyteleafe **GB** (SUR) 64 Zf 41
Wibdon **GB** (GLS) 61 Xc 38
Wichenford **GB** (HWC) 53 Xe 35
Wichling **GB** (KEN) 65 Ae 41
Wick **GB** (AVN) 61 Xd 40
Wick **GB** (HGL) 6 Wf 118
Wick **GB** (HWC) 53 Xf 36
Wick **GB** (MGL) 60 Wc 40
Wick **GB** (WIL) 69 Yb 43
Wick **GB** (WSX) 71 Zc 44
Wicken **GB** (CBS) 56 Ab 35
Wicken **GB** (NRH) 54 Za 36
Wicken Bonhunt **GB** (ESS) 56 Ab 37
Wickenby **GB** (LIN) 47 Zd 29
Wickersley **GB** (SOY) 40 Ye 28
Wickford **GB** (ESS) 65 Ad 39
Wickham **GB** (BKS) 62 Yd 40
Wickham **GB** (HAS) 70 Ye 43
Wickham Bishops **GB** (ESS) 65 Ad 38
Wickhambreaux **GB** (KEN) 65 Ba 41
Wickhambrock **GB** (SUF) 56 Ad 36
Wickhamford **GB** (HWC) 53 Ya 36
Wickham Heath **GB** (BKS) 62 Yd 40
Wickham Market **GB** (SUF) 57 Bc 36
Wickham Saint Paul **GB** (ESS) 56 Ad 37
Wickham Street **GB** (SUF) 57 Ba 35
Wick Hill **GB** (KEN) 72 Ad 42
Wicklow **IRL** (WKL) 95 Tf 31
Wick Saint Lawrence **GB** (AVN) 60 Xa 40
Wickwar **GB** (AVN) 61 Xd 39
Widcombe **GB** (SOM) 67 Wf 43
Widdington **GB** (ESS) 56 Ab 37
Widdrington **GB** (NHL) 33 Yc 17
Widecombe in the Moor **GB** (DEV) 76 Wb 45
Widegates **GB** (CNW) 75 Vd 46
Widemouth Bay **GB** (CNW) 66 Vc 44
Wide Open **GB** (TAW) 33 Yc 18
Widewall **GB** (ORK) 6 Xa 116
Widford **GB** (HTS) 64 Aa 38
Widmerpool **GB** (NTS) 46 Yf 31
Widnes **GB** (CHS) 44 Xb 28
Widworthy **GB** (DEV) 67 Wf 44
Wigan **GB** (GRM) 38 Xc 27
Wiggaton **GB** (DEV) 67 We 44
Wiggenhall Saint Germans **GB** (NOR) 48 Ac 32
Wiggenhall Saint Mary Magdalen **GB** (NOR) 48 Ac 32
Wiggenhall Saint Mary the Virgin **GB** (NOR) 48 Ac 32

Wareside – Wiggenhall Saint Mary the Virgin (GB) (IRL) **137**

Wigginton **GB** (HTS) 63 Zc 38
Wigginton **GB** (OXS) 62 Yd 37
Wigginton **GB** (SFS) 53 Yb 33
Wigglesworth **GB** (NOY) 39 Xe 24
Wiggonby **GB** (CUB) 32 Wf 19
Wiggonholt **GB** (WSX) 71 Zd 43
Wighill **GB** (NOY) 40 Ye 25
Wighton **GB** (NOR) 48 Af 31
Wigmore **GB** (HWC) 52 Xa 35
Wigmore **GB** (KEN) 65 Ad 40
Wigston **GB** (LEC) 54 Yf 33
Wigston Parva **GB** (LEC) 54 Ye 33
Wigtoft **GB** (LIN) 47 Zf 31
Wigton **GB** (CUB) 34 Wf 20
Wigtown **GB** (DAG) 30 Vd 19
Wilberfoss **GB** (HUS) 40 Za 25
Wilburton **GB** (CBS) 56 Ab 34
Wilby **GB** (NOR) 57 Af 34
Wilby **GB** (NRH) 55 Zb 35
Wilby **GB** (SUF) 57 Bb 35
Wilcot **GB** (WIL) 62 Yb 40
Wilcott **GB** (SHS) 44 Xa 32
Wilcrick **GB** (GWE) 61 Xa 39
Wildboarclough **GB** (CHS) 45 Xe 29
Wilden **GB** (BFS) 55 Zd 35
Wilden **GB** (HWC) 53 Xe 34
Wildhern **GB** (HAS) 69 Yd 41
Wildsworth **GB** (LIN) 40 Zb 28
Wilkesley **GB** (CHS) 44 Xc 31
Wilkhaven **GB** (HGL) 9 Wb 1
Wilkieston **GB** (LOT) 26 Wd 13
Wilkins Green **GB** (HTS) 64 Ze 38
Wilkinstown **IRL** (MT) 90 Tb 26
Willand **GB** (DEV) 67 Wd 43
Willaston **GB** (CHS) 44 Wf 29
Willaston **GB** (CHS) 44 Xd 30
Willen **GB** (BUS) 55 Zb 36
Willenhall **GB** (WMD) 53 Xf 33
Willenhall **GB** (WMD) 54 Yd 34
Willerby **GB** (HUS) 41 Zd 26
Willerby **GB** (NOY) 37 Zd 23
Willersey **GB** (HWC) 53 Ya 36
Willersley **GB** (HWC) 52 Wf 36
Willesborough **GB** (KEN) 72 Af 42
Willesden **GB** (GRL) 64 Ze 39
Willett **GB** (SOM) 67 We 42
Willey **GB** (SHS) 52 Xd 33
Willey **GB** (WWH) 54 Ye 34
William's Grove **IRL** (GAL) 88 Rc 28
Williamstown **IRL** (GAL) 88 Rc 26
Williamstown **IRL** (WMT) 88 Sa 28
Williamstown Castle **IRL** (LIM) 98 Rc 33
Williamstown Lodge **IRL** (WMT) 89 Sc 27
Willian **GB** (HTS) 64 Ze 37
Willifield House **IRL** (WMT) 89 Sc 27
Willingale **GB** (ESS) 64 Ab 38
Willingdon **GB** (ESX) 72 Ab 44
Willingham **GB** (CBS) 55 Aa 35
Willington **GB** (BFS) 55 Zd 36
Willington **GB** (DUR) 36 Yb 20
Willington **GB** (TAW) 33 Yc 18
Willington Corner **GB** (CHS) 44 Xb 29
Willitoft **GB** (HUS) 40 Za 26
Williton **GB** (SOM) 67 We 42
Willoughby **GB** (LIN) 47 Zf 29
Willoughby **GB** (WWH) 54 Ye 35
Willoughby Waterleys **GB** (LEC) 54 Yf 33
Willoughton **GB** (LIN) 41 Zc 28
Willowbrook **IRL** (LET) 88 Sa 25
Willsborough House **IRL** (TIP) 93 Re 31
Willsworthy **GB** (DEV) 76 Vf 45
Wilmcote **GB** (WWH) 53 Yb 35
Wilmington **GB** (DEV) 67 Wf 44
Wilmington **GB** (ESX) 71 Ab 44
Wilmington **GB** (KEN) 64 Ab 40
Wilmslow **GB** (CHS) 45 Xe 29
Wilnecote **GB** (SFS) 53 Yc 33
Wilpshire **GB** (LCS) 38 Xd 26
Wilsden **GB** (WYO) 39 Ya 26
Wilsford **GB** (LIN) 47 Zc 31
Wilsford **GB** (WIL) 69 Yb 42
Wilsill **GB** (NOY) 39 Yb 24
Wilsley Green **GB** (KEN) 72 Ad 42
Wilsontown **GB** (STC) 25 Wb 14
Wilstead **GB** (BFS) 55 Zd 36
Wilsthorpe **GB** (LIN) 47 Zd 32
Wilton **GB** (CLE) 37 Yf 21
Wilton **GB** (NOY) 37 Zb 23
Wilton **GB** (WIL) 62 Yc 40
Wilton **GB** (WIL) 69 Ya 42
Wilton Castle **IRL** (WEX) 101 Tc 34
Wilton Dean **GB** (BOR) 32 Xb 16
Wimbish **GB** (ESS) 56 Ab 36
Wimbledon **GB** (GRL) 64 Ze 40
Wimbletown Lodge **IRL** (DUB) 90 Te 27
Wimblington **GB** (CBS) 54 Aa 33
Wimborne Minster **GB** (DOS) 69 Ya 44
Wimborne Saint Giles **GB** (DOS) 69 Ya 43
Wimbotsham **GB** (NOR) 56 Ac 33
Wimpstone **GB** (WWH) 53 Yb 36
Wincanton **GB** (SOM) 68 Xd 42
Winchburgh **GB** (LOT) 25 Wd 13
Winchcombe **GB** (GLS) 62 Ya 37
Winchelsea **GB** (ESX) 72 Ae 43
Winchelsea Beach **GB** (ESX) 72 Ae 43
Winchester **GB** (HAS) 70 Yd 42
Winchet Hill **GB** (KEN) 72 Ac 42
Wincle **GB** (CHS) 45 Xf 29
Windermere **GB** (CUB) 35 Xa 22
Winderton **GB** (WWH) 54 Yc 36
Windgap **IRL** (KLK) 100 Sd 34
Windgate **IRL** (WKL) 95 Tf 29
Windlesham **GB** (SUR) 63 Zb 40
Windley **GB** (DSH) 45 Yc 30
Windley Meadows **GB** (DSH) 46 Yc 31
Windmill Cross Roads **IRL** (KIL) 94 Ta 28
Windmill Hill **GB** (ESX) 72 Ac 43
Windmill Hill **GB** (SOM) 68 Xa 43
Windrush **GB** (GLS) 62 Yb 38
Windsor **GB** (ANT) 85 Ua 21
Windsor **GB** (BKS) 63 Zc 40
Windsor House **IRL** (COR) 104 Re 37
Windy **IRL** (MT) 90 Tc 26
Wineham **GB** (WSX) 71 Ze 43
Wine Town **IRL** (WMT) 89 Sb 27
Winfarthing **GB** (NOR) 57 Ba 34
Winford **GB** (AVN) 61 Xb 40
Winforton **GB** (HWC) 52 Wf 36
Winfrith Newburgh **GB** (DOS) 68 Xe 45
Wing **GB** (BUS) 63 Zb 37
Wing **GB** (LEC) 55 Zb 33
Wingates **GB** (NHL) 33 Ya 17
Wingfield **GB** (SUF) 57 Bb 34
Wingfield House **IRL** (TIP) 93 Sa 30
Wingfield House **IRL** (WEX) 95 Td 32
Wingham **GB** (KEN) 65 Bb 41
Wingrave **GB** (BUS) 63 Zb 37
Winkburn **GB** (NTS) 46 Za 30
Winkfield **GB** (BKS) 63 Zb 40
Winkfield Row **GB** (BKS) 63 Zb 40
Winkhill **GB** (SFS) 45 Ya 30
Winkleigh **GB** (DEV) 66 Wa 43
Winksley **GB** (NOY) 36 Yc 24
Winkton **GB** (DOS) 69 Yb 44
Winless **GB** (HGL) 9 We 118
Winmarleigh **GB** (LCS) 38 Xb 25
Winnards Perch **GB** (CNW) 75 Va 46
Winsford **GB** (CHS) 44 Xc 29
Winsford **GB** (SOM) 67 Wc 42
Winsham **GB** (SOM) 68 Xa 43
Winshill **GB** (SFS) 45 Yc 32
Winskill **GB** (CUB) 35 Xc 20
Winslade **GB** (HAS) 70 Yf 41
Winsley **GB** (WIL) 61 Xe 40
Winslow **GB** (BUS) 63 Za 37
Winson **GB** (GLS) 62 Ya 38
Winster **GB** (CUB) 35 Xa 23
Winster **GB** (DSH) 45 Yc 30
Winston **GB** (DUR) 36 Yb 21
Winston **GB** (SUF) 57 Bb 35
Winstone **GB** (GLS) 61 Xf 38
Winswell **GB** (DEV) 66 Vf 43
Winterborne Houghton **GB** (DOS) 68 Xe 43
Winterborne Kingston **GB** (DOS) 69 Xe 44
Winterborne Monkton **GB** (DOS) 68 Xd 44
Winterborne Stickland **GB** (DOS) 68 Xe 43
Winterborne Whitechurch **GB** (DOS) 69 Xe 44
Winterborne Zelston **GB** (DOS) 69 Xf 44
Winterbourne **GB** (AVN) 61 Xc 39
Winterbourne **GB** (BKS) 62 Yd 40
Winterbourne Abbas **GB** (DOS) 68 Xc 44
Winterbourne Bassett **GB** (WIL) 62 Ya 40
Winterbourne Dauntsey **GB** (WIL) 69 Yb 42
Winterbourne Earls **GB** (WIL) 69 Yb 42
Winterbourne Monkton **GB** (WIL) 62 Ya 40
Winterbourne Steepleton **GB** (DOS) 68 Xc 44
Winterbourne Stoke **GB** (WIL) 69 Ya 41
Winterburn **GB** (NOY) 39 Xf 24
Winterhill **IRL** (DON) 82 Rf 20
Winteringham **GB** (HUS) 41 Zc 26
Winterley **GB** (CHS) 44 Xd 30
Winterslow **GB** (WIL) 69 Yb 42
Winthorpe **GB** (LIN) 48 Ab 30
Winthorpe **GB** (NTS) 46 Zb 30
Winton **GB** (CUB) 35 Xd 22
Wintringham **GB** (NOY) 37 Zc 24
Winwick **GB** (CBS) 55 Zd 34
Winwick **GB** (NRH) 54 Yf 34
Winyates **GB** (HWC) 53 Ya 35
Wippingham **GB** (IOW) 70 Ye 44
Wirksworth **GB** (DSH) 45 Yc 30
Wirswall **GB** (CHS) 44 Xb 31
Wisbech **GB** (NOR) 48 Ab 33
Wisbech Saint Mary **GB** (CBS) 55 Aa 33
Wisborough Green **GB** (WSX) 71 Zc 42
Wishaw **GB** (STC) 25 Wa 14
Wishaw **GB** (WWH) 53 Yb 33
Wisley **GB** (SUR) 63 Zd 41
Wispington **GB** (LIN) 47 Ze 29
Wissett **GB** (SUF) 57 Bc 34
Wistanstow **GB** (SHS) 52 Xa 34
Wistanswick **GB** (SHS) 44 Xd 31
Wistaston **GB** (CHS) 44 Xd 30
Wiston **GB** (DYF) 58 Va 38
Wiston **GB** (STC) 25 Wc 15
Wistow **GB** (CBS) 55 Zf 34
Wistow **GB** (NOY) 40 Yf 26
Wiswell **GB** (LCS) 38 Xd 25
Witcham **GB** (CBS) 56 Aa 34
Witchampton **GB** (DOS) 69 Xf 43
Witchford **GB** (CBS) 56 Ab 34
Witham **GB** (ESS) 65 Ad 38
Witham Friary **GB** (SOM) 68 Xd 41
Witham on the Hill **GB** (LIN) 47 Zd 32
Witherdale Street **GB** (SUF) 57 Bb 34
Witherenden Hill **GB** (ESX) 72 Ac 42
Witherfield **GB** (SUF) 56 Ac 36
Witheridge **GB** (DEV) 67 Wb 43
Witherley **GB** (LEC) 54 Yc 33
Withern **GB** (LIN) 47 Aa 29
Withernsea **GB** (HUS) 41 Ae 26
Withernwick **GB** (HUS) 41 Ze 25
Witherslack **GB** (CUB) 35 Xa 23
Withiel **GB** (CNW) 75 Vb 46
Withiel Florey **GB** (SOM) 67 Wd 42
Withington **GB** (CHS) 45 Xe 29
Withington **GB** (GLS) 62 Ya 37
Withington **GB** (HWC) 52 Xc 36
Withington **GB** (SFS) 45 Ya 31
Withington **GB** (SHS) 52 Xc 32
Withington Green **GB** (CHS) 45 Xe 29
Withleigh **GB** (DEV) 67 Wc 43
Withnell **GB** (LCS) 38 Xc 26
Withybrook **GB** (WWH) 54 Yd 34
Withyham **GB** (ESX) 71 Aa 42
Withypool **GB** (SOM) 67 Wc 42
Witley **GB** (SUR) 70 Zc 42
Witnesham **GB** (SUF) 57 Bb 36
Witney **GB** (OXS) 62 Yd 38
Wittering **GB** (CBS) 55 Zd 33
Wittersham **GB** (KEN) 72 Ae 42
Witton **GB** (DUR) 36 Yb 20
Witton Bridge **GB** (NOR) 49 Bc 32
Witton Gilbert **GB** (DUR) 36 Yc 20
Witton Park **GB** (DUR) 36 Yb 21
Wiveliscombe **GB** (SOM) 67 We 42
Wivelsfield **GB** (ESX) 71 Zf 43
Wivelsfield Green **GB** (ESX) 71 Zf 43
Wivenhoe **GB** (ESS) 65 Af 37
Wiveton **GB** (NOR) 49 Ba 31
Wix **GB** (ESS) 65 Ba 37
Wixford **GB** (WWH) 53 Ya 35
Woburn **GB** (BFS) 55 Zc 37
Woburn Sands **GB** (BFS) 55 Zc 36
Wogdland **GB** (DOS) 68 Xe 43
Wokefield Park **GB** (BKS) 63 Yf 40
Woking **GB** (SUR) 63 Zc 41
Wokingham **GB** (BKS) 63 Za 40
Wolborough **GB** (DEV) 76 Wc 45
Woldingham **GB** (SUR) 64 Zf 41
Wold Newton **GB** (HUS) 41 Zf 28
Wolferlow **GB** (HWC) 52 Xd 35
Wolferton **GB** (NOR) 48 Ac 32
Wolfhill **GB** (TYS) 21 Wd 10
Wolfhill **IRL** (LAO) 94 Sf 31
Wolf's Castle **GB** (DYF) 58 Va 37
Wolfsdale **GB** (DYF) 58 Uf 37
Woll **GB** (BOR) 32 Xa 16
Wollaston **GB** (NRH) 55 Zc 35
Wollaston **GB** (SHS) 52 Xa 32
Wollerton **GB** (SHS) 44 Xc 31
Wolley **GB** (AVN) 61 Xd 40
Wolmersley **GB** (NOY) 40 Ye 27
Wolsingham **GB** (DUR) 36 Ya 20
Wolsten **GB** (WWH) 54 Yd 34
Wolvercote **GB** (OXS) 62 Ye 38
Wolverhampton **GB** (WMD) 53 Xf 33
Wolverley **GB** (HWC) 53 Xe 34
Wolverley **GB** (SHS) 44 Xb 31
Wolverton **GB** (BUS) 54 Zb 36
Wolverton **GB** (HAS) 63 Ye 41
Wolverton **GB** (WWH) 53 Yb 35
Wolveshewton **GB** (GWE) 61 Xb 38
Wolvey **GB** (WWH) 54 Yd 34
Wolviston **GB** (CLE) 36 Ye 21
Wombleton **GB** (NOY) 37 Za 23
Wombourne **GB** (SFS) 53 Xe 34
Wombwell **GB** (SOY) 40 Yd 27
Womenswold **GB** (KEN) 65 Bb 41
Wonastow **GB** (GWE) 61 Xb 38
Wonersh **GB** (SUR) 71 Zc 41
Wonson **GB** (DEV) 66 Wa 44
Wonston **GB** (HAS) 70 Ye 42
Wooburn **GB** (BUS) 63 Zb 39
Wooburn Green **GB** (BUS) 63 Zb 39
Wood **IRL** (OFF) 94 Se 28
Woodale **GB** (NOY) 36 Ya 23
Woodbastwick **GB** (NOR) 49 Bc 32
Woodbeck **GB** (NTS) 46 Za 29
Woodborough **GB** (NTS) 46 Yf 30
Woodborough **GB** (WIL) 69 Ya 41
Woodbridge **GB** (SUF) 57 Bb 36
Woodbrook **IRL** (DUB) 95 Tf 29
Wood Burcote **GB** (NRH) 54 Za 36
Woodburn **GB** (ANT) 85 Ua 20
Woodbury **GB** (DEV) 67 Wd 44
Woodchester **GB** (GLS) 61 Xe 38
Woodchurch **GB** (KEN) 72 Ae 42
Woodcote **GB** (GRL) 64 Zf 40
Woodcote **GB** (OXS) 63 Yf 39
Woodcroft **GB** (GLS) 61 Xc 39
Woodcutts **GB** (DOS) 69 Xf 43
Wood Dalling **GB** (NOR) 49 Ba 32
Woodditton **GB** (CBS) 56 Ac 35
Woodenbridge **IRL** (WKL) 95 Te 31
Wood End **GB** (BFS) 55 Zc 36
Woodend **GB** (CUB) 34 We 22
Wood End **GB** (GRL) 64 Zd 39
Wood End **GB** (HTS) 64 Zf 37
Woodend **GB** (NRH) 54 Yf 36
Wood End **GB** (WWH) 53 Ya 34
Wood End **GB** (WWH) 53 Yc 33
Wood Enderby **GB** (LIN) 47 Zf 30
Woodfalls **GB** (WIL) 69 Yb 43
Woodfield **GB** (HTS) 64 Zf 38
Woodfield **IRL** (COR) 103 Ra 39
Woodfield **IRL** (LAO) 94 Sd 29
Woodford **GB** (CNW) 66 Vc 43
Woodford **GB** (GLS) 61 Xd 39
Woodford **GB** (GRL) 64 Zf 39
Woodford **GB** (GRM) 45 Xe 28
Woodford **IRL** (KER) 97 Qd 36
Woodford Halse **GB** (NRH) 54 Ye 35
Woodfort **IRL** (GAL) 93 Rd 30
Woodgate **GB** (HWC) 53 Xf 35
Woodgate **GB** (WMD) 53 Xf 34
Woodgreen **GB** (ANT) 84 Te 20
Woodgreen **GB** (HAS) 69 Yb 43
Woodhall **GB** (NOY) 36 Xf 23
Woodhall Spa **GB** (LIN) 47 Ze 30
Woodham **GB** (SUR) 63 Zc 40
Woodham Ferrers **GB** (ESS) 65 Ad 39
Woodham Mortimer **GB** (ESS) 65 Ad 38
Woodham Walter **GB** (ESS) 65 Ad 38
Woodhead **GB** (GRP) 17 Xd 4
Woodhill **GB** (SHS) 53 Xd 34
Woodhouse **GB** (LEC) 46 Ye 32
Wood House **IRL** (OFF) 93 Rf 31
Woodhouse Cross Roads **IRL** (WTF) 99 Sb 36
Woodhouse Eaves **GB** (LEC) 46 Ye 32
Woodhurst **GB** (CBS) 55 Zf 34
Woodingdean **GB** (ESX) 71 Zf 43
Woodlana **IRL** (DON) 77 Sb 19
Woodland **GB** (DEV) 76 Wb 45
Woodland **GB** (DUR) 36 Ya 21
Woodland House **IRL** (WTF) 100 Sf 35
Woodlands **GB** (DOS) 69 Ya 43
Woodlands **GB** (GRP) 17 Xd 6
Woodlands **GB** (HAS) 69 Yc 43
Woodlands **IRL** (DON) 77 Sb 20
Woodlawn **IRL** (GAL) 93 Rd 29
Woodleigh **GB** (DEV) 76 Wb 47
Woodlesford **GB** (WYO) 40 Yd 26
Woodley **GB** (BKS) 63 Za 40
Woodmancote **GB** (GLS) 62 Ya 38
Woodmancote **GB** (WSX) 70 Za 43
Woodmancote **GB** (WSX) 71 Ze 43
Woodmancott **GB** (HAS) 70 Ye 41
Woodmansey **GB** (HUS) 41 Zd 26
Woodmansterne **GB** (SUR) 64 Ze 41
Woodmount **IRL** (ROS) 93 Rf 28
Woodmount House **IRL** (WKL) 95 Te 32
Woodnewton **GB** (NRH) 55 Zd 33
Wood Norton **GB** (NOR) 49 Af 32
Woodpark House **IRL** (TIP) 92 Rd 32
Woodpark House **IRL** (TIP) 93 Re 31
Woodplumpton **GB** (LCS) 38 Xb 26
Woods Cross Roads **IRL** (CAV) 89 Sf 26
Woodseaves **GB** (SFS) 45 Xe 32
Woodseaves **GB** (SHS) 44 Xd 31
Woodsend **GB** (WIL) 62 Yb 40
Woodsetts **GB** (SOY) 46 Ye 28
Woodsford **GB** (DOS) 68 Xe 44
Woodside **GB** (BKS) 63 Zc 40
Woodside **GB** (FIF) 26 Wf 11
Woodside **GB** (GRL) 64 Zf 40
Woodside **GB** (HTS) 64 Ze 38
Woodside **GB** (SHS) 52 Wf 34
Woodstock **GB** (OXS) 62 Yd 37
Woodstown **IRL** (WTF) 100 Sf 35
Wood Street **GB** (SUR) 70 Zc 41
Woodthorpe **GB** (LEC) 46 Ye 32
Woodton **GB** (NOR) 57 Bc 34
Woodtown **GB** (DEV) 66 Vf 42
Woodtown **IRL** (MT) 90 Tc 26
Woodtown **IRL** (WEX) 101 Td 35
Woodville **GB** (DSH) 46 Yc 32
Woodville **IRL** (KER) 97 Qc 35
Woodville **IRL** (LGF) 89 Sc 25
Woodville **IRL** (OFF) 93 Sa 30
Woodwalton **GB** (CBS) 55 Ze 34
Woodyates **GB** (WIL) 69 Ya 43
Wookey **GB** (SOM) 68 Xb 41
Wookey Hole **GB** (SOM) 68 Xb 41
Wool **GB** (DOS) 69 Xe 44
Woolacombe **GB** (DEV) 66 Ve 41
Woolage Green **GB** (KEN) 73 Bb 41
Woolaston **GB** (GLS) 61 Xc 38
Woolavington **GB** (SOM) 68 Xa 42
Woolbeding **GB** (WSX) 70 Zb 43
Wooler **GB** (NHL) 27 Xf 15
Woolfardisworthy **GB** (DEV) 66 Vd 43
Woolfords Cottages **GB** (STC) 25 Wc 14
Woolhampton **GB** (BKS) 63 Ye 40
Woolhope **GB** (HWC) 61 Xc 36
Woolley **GB** (CBS) 55 Ze 34
Woolley **GB** (WYO) 39 Yc 27
Woolmere Green **GB** (HWC) 53 Xf 35
Woolmer Green **GB** (HTS) 64 Ze 37
Woolpit **GB** (SUF) 56 Af 35
Woolsington **GB** (TAW) 33 Yb 18
Woolstaston **GB** (SHS) 52 Xb 33
Woolsthorpe-by-Belvoir **GB** (LIN) 46 Zb 31
Woolston **GB** (CHS) 44 Xc 28
Woolston **GB** (SHS) 44 Wf 32
Woolston **GB** (SHS) 52 Xa 34
Woolstone **GB** (OXS) 62 Yc 39
Woolton **GB** (MES) 44 Xa 28
Woolton Hill **GB** (HAS) 62 Yd 40
Woolverstone **GB** (SUF) 57 Bb 36
Woolverton **GB** (SOM) 68 Xe 41
Woolwich **GB** (GRL) 64 Aa 40
Woonton **GB** (HWC) 52 Xa 35
Wooperton **GB** (NHL) 33 Ya 16
Woore **GB** (SHS) 45 Xd 31
Woorton **GB** (OXS) 62 Yd 37
Wootton **GB** (BFS) 55 Zc 36
Wootton **GB** (HAS) 69 Yc 44
Wootton **GB** (HUS) 41 Zd 27
Wootton **GB** (OXS) 63 Ye 38
Wootton **GB** (SFS) 45 Xe 31
Wootton **GB** (SFS) 45 Ya 31
Wootton Bassett **GB** (WIL) 62 Ya 39
Wootton Bridge **GB** (IOW) 70 Ye 44
Wootton Common **GB** (IOW) 70 Ye 44
Wootton Courtenay **GB** (SOM) 67 Wc 41
Wootton Fitzpaine **GB** (DOS) 68 Xa 44
Wootton Rivers **GB** (WIL) 62 Yb 40
Wootton Saint Lawrence **GB** (HAS) 70 Yf 41
Wootton Wawen **GB** (WWH) 53 Yb 35
Worcester **GB** (HWC) 53 Xe 35
Wordsley **GB** (WMD) 53 Xf 34
Wordwell **GB** (SUF) 56 Ae 35
Workington **GB** (CUB) 34 Wc 21
Worksop **GB** (NTS) 46 Yf 29
Worlaby **GB** (HUS) 41 Zd 27
World's End **GB** (BKS) 62 Ye 40
Worlds End **GB** (HAS) 70 Yf 43
Worle **GB** (AVN) 60 Xa 40
Worleston **GB** (CHS) 44 Xc 30
Worlingham **GB** (SUF) 57 Bd 34
Worlington **GB** (SUF) 56 Ac 34
Worlingworth **GB** (SUF) 57 Bb 35
Wormbridge **GB** (HWC) 61 Xa 37
Wormegay **GB** (NOR) 48 Ac 32
Wormhill **GB** (DSH) 45 Yb 29
Wormingford **GB** (ESS) 56 Ae 37
Worminghall **GB** (BUS) 63 Yf 38
Wormington **GB** (GLS) 53 Ya 36
Worminster **GB** (SOM) 68 Xc 41
Wormit **GB** (FIF) 22 Xa 10
Wormley **GB** (SUR) 70 Zc 42
Wormshill **GB** (KEN) 65 Ae 41
Wormsley **GB** (HWC) 52 Xa 36
Worplesdon **GB** (SUR) 70 Zc 41
Worrall **GB** (SOY) 39 Yc 28
Worstead **GB** (NOR) 49 Bc 32
Worsthorne **GB** (LCS) 39 Xe 26
Worth **GB** (KEN) 65 Bb 41
Worth **GB** (WSX) 71 Zf 42
Wortham **GB** (SUF) 57 Ba 34
Worthen **GB** (SHS) 52 Xa 33
Worthenbury **GB** (CLW) 44 Xa 30
Worthing **GB** (NOR) 49 Af 32
Worthing **GB** (WSX) 71 Zd 44
Worthington **GB** (LEC) 46 Yd 32
Worth Matravers **GB** (DOS) 69 Xf 45
Wortley **GB** (GLS) 61 Xd 39
Wortley **GB** (SOY) 39 Yc 28
Worton **GB** (WIL) 62 Xf 41
Wotherton **GB** (SHS) 52 Wf 33
Wotton **GB** (SUR) 71 Zd 41
Wotton-under-Edge **GB** (GLS) 61 Xd 39
Wouldham **GB** (KEN) 65 Ac 40
Wrabness **GB** (ESS) 57 Ba 37
Wrafton **GB** (DEV) 66 Vf 42
Wragby **GB** (LIN) 47 Ze 29
Wragholme **GB** (LIN) 41 Aa 28
Wramplingham **GB** (NOR) 57 Ba 33
Wrangham **GB** (GRP) 17 Xc 4
Wrangle **GB** (LIN) 47 Aa 30
Wrangle Bank **GB** (LIN) 47 Aa 30
Wrangle Lowgate **GB** (LIN) 47 Aa 30
Wrangway **GB** (SOM) 67 We 43
Wrantage **GB** (SOM) 68 Wf 43
Wrawby **GB** (HUS) 41 Zd 27
Wraxall **GB** (SOM) 68 Xc 42
Wraxall **GB** (WIL) 61 Xe 40
Wraxhall **GB** (AVN) 61 Xb 40
Wray **GB** (LCS) 38 Xc 24
Wray Castle **GB** (CUB) 35 Xa 22
Wraysbury **GB** (BKS) 63 Zc 40
Wrea Green **GB** (LCS) 38 Xa 26
Wreay **GB** (CUB) 35 Xa 20
Wreay **GB** (CUB) 35 Xa 21
Wrekenton **GB** (TAW) 33 Yc 19
Wrelton **GB** (NOY) 37 Zb 23
Wrenbury **GB** (CHS) 44 Xc 30
Wreningham **GB** (NOR) 57 Bb 33
Wrentham **GB** (SUF) 57 Bd 34
Wressle **GB** (HUS) 40 Za 26
Wrestlingworth **GB** (BFS) 55 Ze 36
Wrest Wratting **GB** (CBS) 56 Ab 36
Wretham **GB** (NOR) 56 Ae 34
Wretton **GB** (NOR) 56 Ac 33
Wrexham **GB** (CLW) 44 Xa 30
Wrexham Industrial Estate **GB** (CLW) 44 Xa 30
Wrightington Bar **GB** (LCS) 38 Xb 27
Wrinehill **GB** (SFS) 45 Xd 30
Wrington **GB** (AVN) 61 Xb 40
Writhlington **GB** (AVN) 68 Xd 41
Writtle **GB** (ESS) 64 Ac 38
Wrockwardine **GB** (SHS) 52 Xc 32
Wroot **GB** (HUS) 40 Za 27
Wrotham **GB** (KEN) 64 Ab 41
Wrotham Head **GB** (KEN) 64 Ac 41
Wroughton **GB** (WIL) 62 Yb 39
Wroxall **GB** (IOW) 70 Ye 45
Wroxall **GB** (WWH) 53 Yb 34
Wroxeter **GB** (SHS) 52 Xc 32
Wroxham **GB** (NOR) 49 Bc 32
Wroxton **GB** (OXS) 54 Yd 36
Wyaston **GB** (DSH) 45 Yb 31
Wyboston **GB** (BFS) 55 Ze 35
Wybunbury **GB** (CHS) 44 Xd 30
Wychbold **GB** (HWC) 53 Xf 35
Wych Cross **GB** (ESX) 71 Aa 42
Wyck **GB** (HAS) 70 Za 42
Wyck Rissington **GB** (GLS) 62 Yb 37
Wycomb **GB** (LEC) 46 Za 32
Wyddial **GB** (HTS) 55 Aa 37
Wye **GB** (KEN) 72 Af 41
Wyke **GB** (WYO) 39 Yb 26
Wykeham **GB** (NOY) 37 Zb 23
Wykeham **GB** (NOY) 37 Zc 23
Wyken **GB** (SHS) 53 Xd 34
Wyke Regis **GB** (DOS) 68 Xd 45
Wykey **GB** (SHS) 44 Xa 32
Wylam **GB** (NHL) 33 Yb 19
Wyle **GB** (WIL) 69 Ya 42
Wymeswold **GB** (LEC) 46 Yf 32
Wymington **GB** (BFS) 55 Zc 35
Wymondham **GB** (LEC) 46 Zb 32
Wymondham **GB** (NOR) 57 Ba 33
Wynford Eagle **GB** (DOS) 68 Xc 44
Wyre Piddle **GB** (HWC) 53 Xf 36
Wysall **GB** (NTS) 46 Yf 31
Wythall **GB** (HWC) 53 Ya 34
Wytham **GB** (OXS) 62 Ye 38
Wythburn **GB** (CUB) 34 Wf 21
Wyton **GB** (CBS) 55 Zf 35
Wyverstone **GB** (SUF) 57 Af 35
Wyville **GB** (LIN) 46 Zb 31

Y

Yafford **GB** (IOW) 70 Yd 45
Yafforth **GB** (NOY) 36 Yd 22
Yalding **GB** (KEN) 72 Ac 41
Yaleley **GB** (HAS) 63 Za 40
Yanworth **GB** (GLS) 62 Ya 38
Yapham **GB** (HUS) 40 Zb 25
Yapton **GB** (WSX) 70 Zc 44
Yarburgh **GB** (LIN) 41 Aa 28
Yarcombe **GB** (DEV) 67 Wf 43
Yardley **GB** (WMD) 53 Yb 34
Yardley Gobion **GB** (NRH) 54 Za 36
Yardley Hastings **GB** (NRH) 55 Zb 35
Yardro **GB** (POW) 52 Wf 35
Yarkhill **GB** (HWC) 52 Xc 36
Yarlet **GB** (SFS) 45 Xf 31
Yarley **GB** (SOM) 68 Xb 41
Yarmouth **GB** (IOW) 69 Yd 44
Yarnfield **GB** (SFS) 45 Xe 31
Yarnscombe **GB** (DEV) 66 Vf 43
Yarnton **GB** (OXS) 62 Ye 38
Yarpole **GB** (HWC) 52 Xb 35
Yarrow **GB** (BOR) 32 Wf 15
Yarrow Feus **GB** (BOR) 32 Wf 15
Yarsop **GB** (HWC) 52 Xa 36
Yarwell **GB** (NRH) 55 Zd 33
Yate **GB** (AVN) 61 Xd 39
Yatesbury **GB** (WIL) 62 Ya 40
Yattendon **GB** (BKS) 63 Ye 40
Yatton **GB** (AVN) 61 Xb 40
Yatton **GB** (HWC) 52 Xa 35
Yatton **GB** (HWC) 61 Xc 37
Yatton Keynell **GB** (WIL) 61 Xe 40
Yaverland **GB** (IOW) 70 Yf 45
Yaxham **GB** (NOR) 48 Af 33
Yaxley **GB** (CBS) 55 Ze 33
Yaxley **GB** (SUF) 57 Ba 35
Yazor **GB** (HWC) 52 Xa 36
Y Drenewydd = Newtown **GB** (POW) 51 We 33
Yeadon **GB** (WYO) 39 Yb 25
Yealand Conyers **GB** (LCS) 35 Xb 24
Yealand Redmayne **GB** (LCS) 35 Xb 23
Yealmpton **GB** (DEV) 76 Wa 46
Yearsley **GB** (NOY) 37 Yf 24
Yeaton **GB** (SHS) 44 Xa 32
Yeaveley **GB** (DSH) 45 Yb 31
Yedingham **GB** (NOY) 37 Zc 23
Yelford **GB** (OXS) 62 Yd 38
Yelland **GB** (DEV) 66 Vf 44
Yelling **GB** (CBS) 55 Zf 35
Yellow Furze **IRL** (MT) 90 Tc 26
Yellow Walls **IRL** (MT) 90 Tc 27
Yelvertoft **GB** (NRH) 54 Yf 34
Yelverton **GB** (DEV) 76 Vf 46
Yenston **GB** (SOM) 68 Xd 43
Yeoford **GB** (DEV) 67 Wb 44
Yeolmbridge **GB** (CNW) 66 Vd 45
Yeomadon **GB** (DEV) 66 Vd 44
Yeovil **GB** (SOM) 68 Xc 43
Yeovil Marsh **GB** (SOM) 68 Xc 43
Yerbeston **GB** (DYF) 58 Vb 38
Yesnaby **GB** (ORK) 6 Wd 114
Yetlington **GB** (NHL) 33 Ya 16
Yetminster **GB** (DOS) 68 Xc 43
Yettington **GB** (DEV) 67 Wd 45
Yetts o'Muckhart **GB** (CEN) 25 Wc 11
Y Fan **GB** (POW) 51 Wc 34
Y Felinheli **GB** (GWY) 42 Ve 29
Y-fenni = Abergavenny **GB** (GWE) 60 Wf 38
Y Ffôr **GB** (GWY) 42 Vd 31
Yieldshields **GB** (STC) 25 Wb 14
Ynysddu **GB** (MGL) 60 We 39
Ynyshir **GB** (MGL) 60 Wd 39
Ynyslas **GB** (DYF) 51 Vf 33
Ynystawe **GB** (WGL) 59 Wa 38
Ynysybwl **GB** (MGL) 60 Wd 39
Yockenthwaite **GB** (NOY) 35 Xf 23
Yockleton **GB** (SHS) 52 Xa 32
Yokefleet **GB** (HUS) 40 Zb 26
Yoker **GB** (STC) 24 Vd 13
Yoletown **IRL** (WEX) 100 Tb 35
Yonder Bognie **GB** (GRP) 17 Xc 3
York **GB** (NOY) 40 Yf 25
Yorkletts **GB** (KEN) 65 Af 40
Yorkley **GB** (GLS) 61 Xc 38
Yorton **GB** (SHS) 44 Xb 32
Youghal **IRL** (COR) 104 Sa 37
Youldonmoor Cross **GB** (DEV) 66 Vd 43
Youlgreave **GB** (DSH) 45 Yb 29
Youlstone **GB** (DEV) 66 Vd 43
Youlthorpe **GB** (HUS) 40 Zb 25
Youlton **GB** (NOY) 40 Ye 24
Young's End **GB** (ESS) 65 Ad 37
Yoxall **GB** (SFS) 45 Yb 32
Yoxford **GB** (SUF) 57 Bd 35
Ysbyty Ifan **GB** (GWY) 43 Wb 30
Ysbyty Ystwyth **GB** (DYF) 51 Wa 35
Ysceifiog **GB** (CLW) 43 We 29
Ystalyfera **GB** (WGL) 59 Wb 38
Ystrad **GB** (MGL) 60 Wd 39
Ystrad Aeron **GB** (DYF) 50 Vf 35
Ystradfellte **GB** (POW) 60 Wc 38
Ystradffin **GB** (DYF) 51 Wb 36
Ystradgynlais **GB** (POW) 59 Wb 38
Ystradmeurig **GB** (DYF) 51 Wa 35
Ystrad Mynach **GB** (MGL) 60 We 39
Ystradowen **GB** (SGL) 60 Wd 40
Ythanbank **GB** (GRP) 17 Xf 4
Ythanwells **GB** (GRP) 17 Xc 4
Ythsie **GB** (GRP) 17 Xe 4

Z

Zeal Monachorum **GB** (DEV) 67 Wb 44
Zeals **GB** (WIL) 68 Xe 42
Zelah **GB** (CNW) 74 Uf 47
Zennor **GB** (CNW) 74 Uc 47

⇛ Laufzeit 1998

© RV Reise- und Verkehrsverlag GmbH, München · Stuttgart
© Kartografie: GeoData

Printed in Germany by Neef + Stumme, Wittingen
ISBN 3.575.11877.9 (3.)

138 GB IRL **Wigginton – Zennor**

Stadtpläne · City maps · Plans de villes · Stadsplattegronden
Piante di città · Planos de ciudades · Byplaner · Stadskartor
Zeichenerklärung · Legend · Légende · Legenda · Segni convenzionali
Signos convencionales · Tegnforklaring · Teckenförklaring
1:20.000

(D)	(GB)		(F)	(NL)
Autobahn	Motorway		Autoroute	Autosnelweg
Vierspurige Straße	Road with four lanes		Route à quatre voies	Weg met vier rijstroken
Durchgangsstraße	Through road		Route de transit	Weg voor doorgaand verkeer
Hauptstraße	Main road		Route principale	Hoofdroute
Sonstige Straßen	Other roads		Autres routes	Overige wegen
Fußgängerzone	Pedestrian zone		Zone piétonne	Voetgangerzone
Parkplatz, Parkhaus	Parking	P	Parking	Parkeerplaats
Hauptbahn	Main railway		Chemin de fer principal	Belangrijke spoorweg
Nebenbahn	Other railways		Chemin de fer secondaire	Spoorweg
S-Bahn	Rapid city railway	S	Réseaux express régional	Stadsspoor
U-Bahn	Subway	M U	Métro	Ondergrondse spoorweg
Information	Information	i	Information	Informatie
Polizei	Police station		Poste de police	Politiebureau
Post	Post office		Bureau de poste	Postkantoor
Krankenhaus	Hospital	+	Hôpital	Ziekenhuis
Denkmal	Monument		Monument	Monument
Jugendherberge	Youth hostel	▲	Auberge de jeunesse	Jeugdherberg
Bebauung – Öffentliches Gebäude	Built-up area – Public building		Zone bâtie – Bâtiment public	Woongebied – Openbaar gebouw
Industriegebiet	Industrial area		Zone industrielle	Industrieterrein
Park, Wald	Park, forest		Parc, bois	Park, bos

(I)	(E)		(DK)	(S)
Autostrada	Autopista		Motorvej	Motorväg
Strada a quattro corsie	Carretera de cuatro carriles		Firesporet vej	Fyrfilig väg
Strada di attraversamento	Carretera de tránsito		Hovedvej	Genomfartsled
Strada principale	Carretera principal		Anden vigtig vej	Huvudled
Altre strade	Otras carreteras		Anden mindre vej	Annan väg
Zona pedonale	Zona peatonal		Gågade	Gågata
Parcheggio	Aparcamiento	P	Parkere	Parkering
Ferrovia principale	Ferrocarril principal		Hovedjernbane	Stambana
Ferrovia secondaria	Ferrocarril secundario		Sidebane	Annan järnväg
Ferrovia urbana	Metro	S	Bybane	Snabbtåg
Metropolitana	Subterráneo	M U	Underjordisk bane	Tunnelbana
Informazioni	Información	i	Information	Information
Posto di polizia	Comisaria de policia		Politi	Polisstation
Ufficio postale	Correos		Posthus	Postkontor
Ospedale	Hospital	+	Sygehus	Sjukhus
Monumento	Monumento		Mindesmærke	Monument
Ostello della gioventù	Albergue de juventud	▲	Vandrerhjem	Vandrarhem
Caseggiato – Edificio pubblico	Zona edificada – Edificio público		Bebyggelse – Offentlig bygning	Bebyggt område – Offentlig byggnad
Terreno industriale	Zona industrial		Industriområde	Industriområde
Parco, bosco	Zona verde		Park, skov	Park, skog

Aberdeen

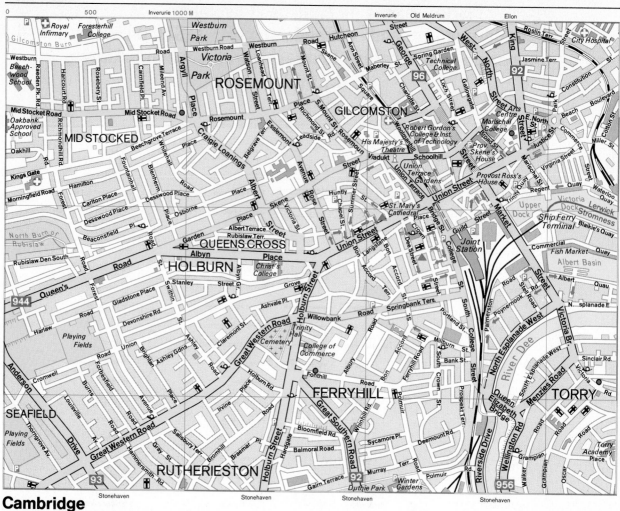

Cambridge

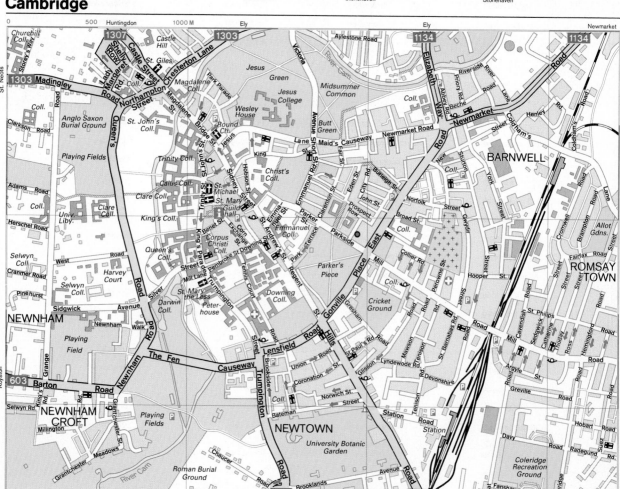

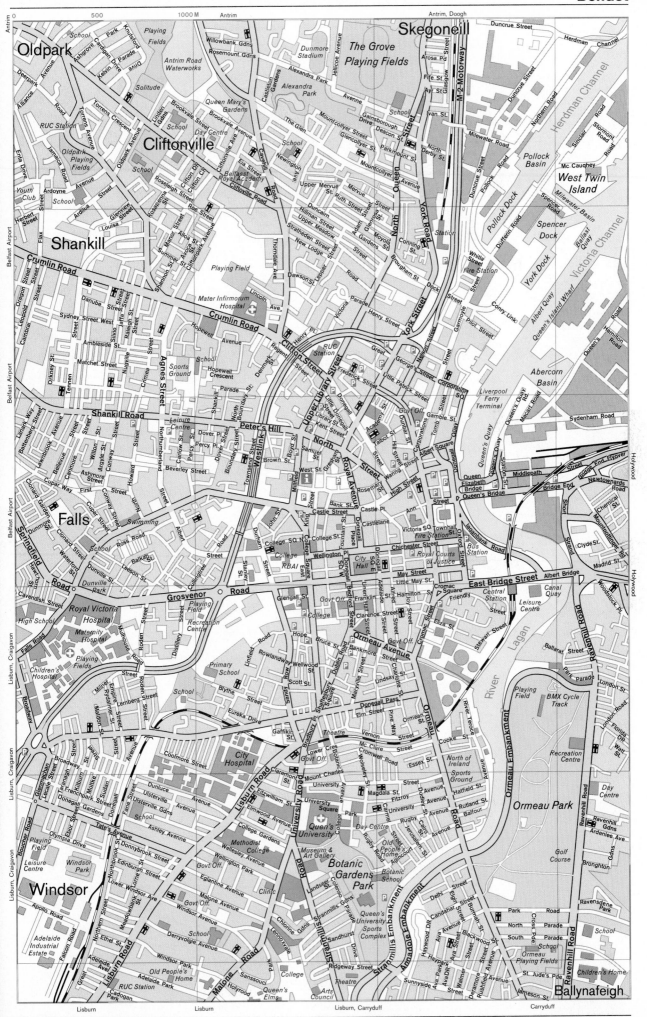

Antrim

Antrim, Doogh

Oldpark

Skegoneill

Cliftonville

The Grove
Playing Fields

Shankill

Crumlin Road

Crumlin Road

Shankill Road

Falls

Grosvenor Road

Royal Victoria
Hospital

Belfast Airport

Lisburn, Craigavon

Windsor

City Hall

City Hospital

Queen's
University

Botanic
Gardens
Park

Lisburn

West Twin
Island

Spencer
Dock

Victoria Channel

Abercorn
Basin

York Dock

Ormeau Park

Golf
Course

River Lagan

Ballynafeigh

Cardiff

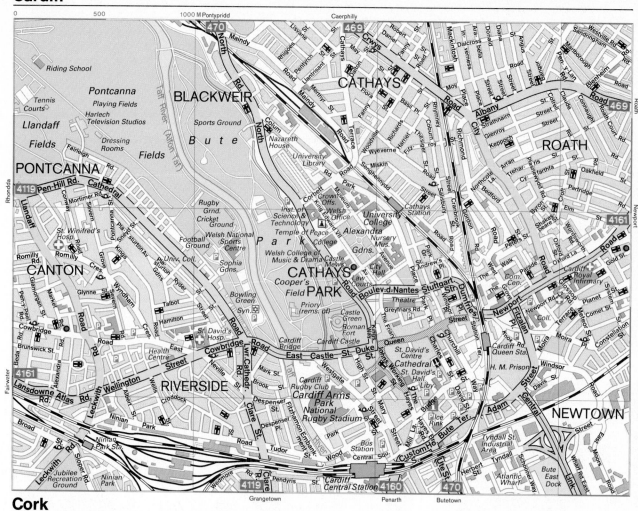

Cork

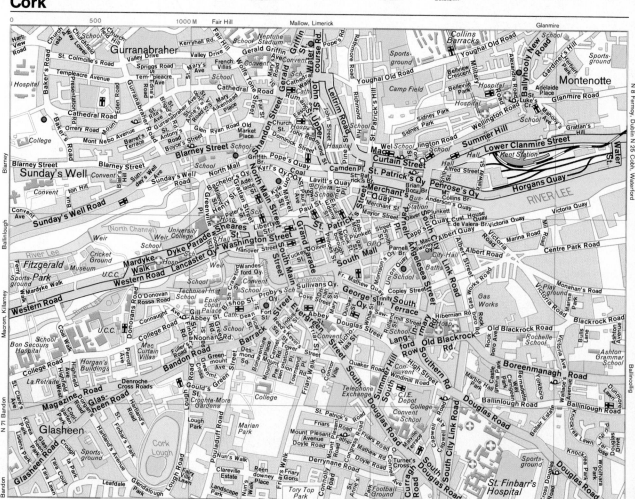

Edinburgh

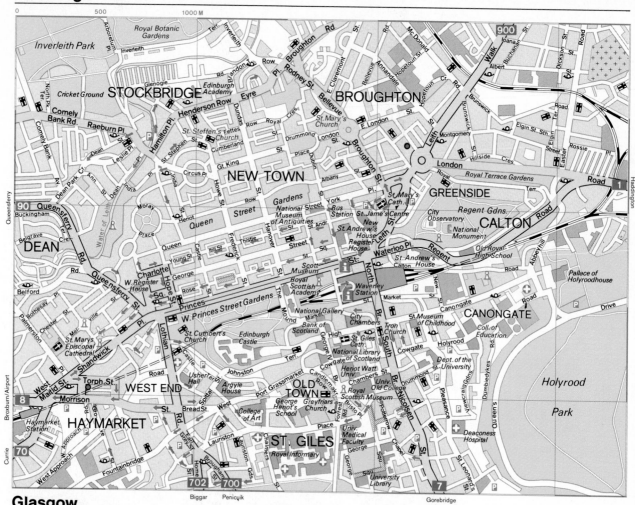

Glasgow

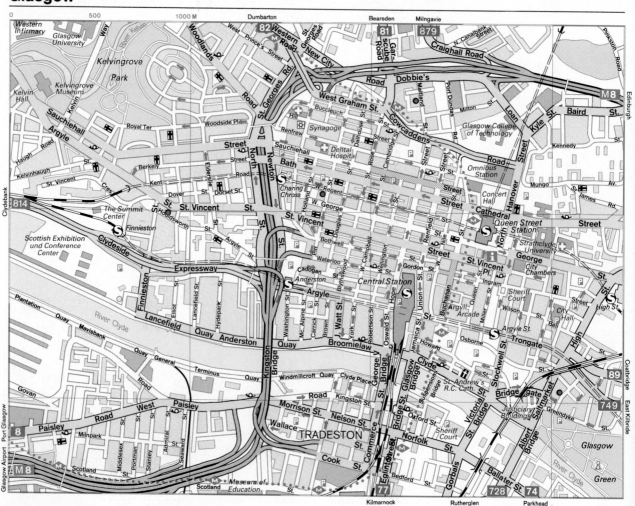

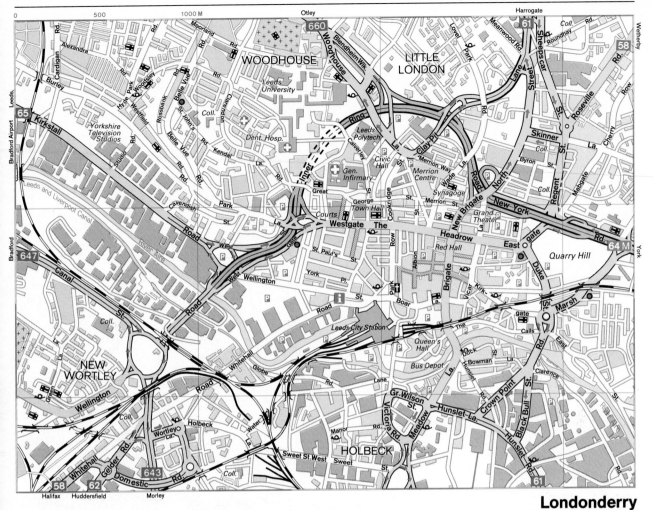

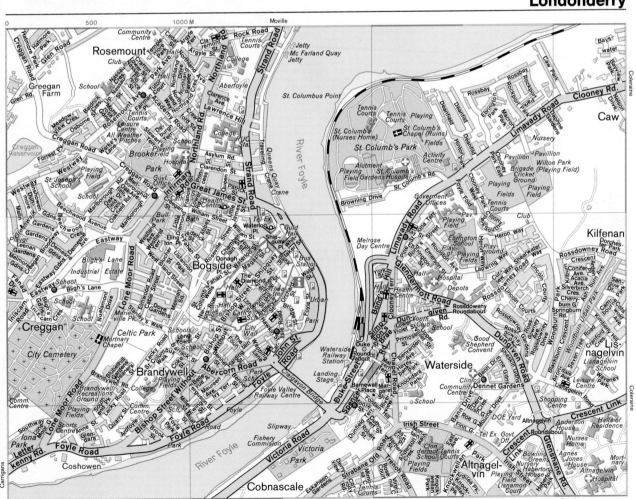

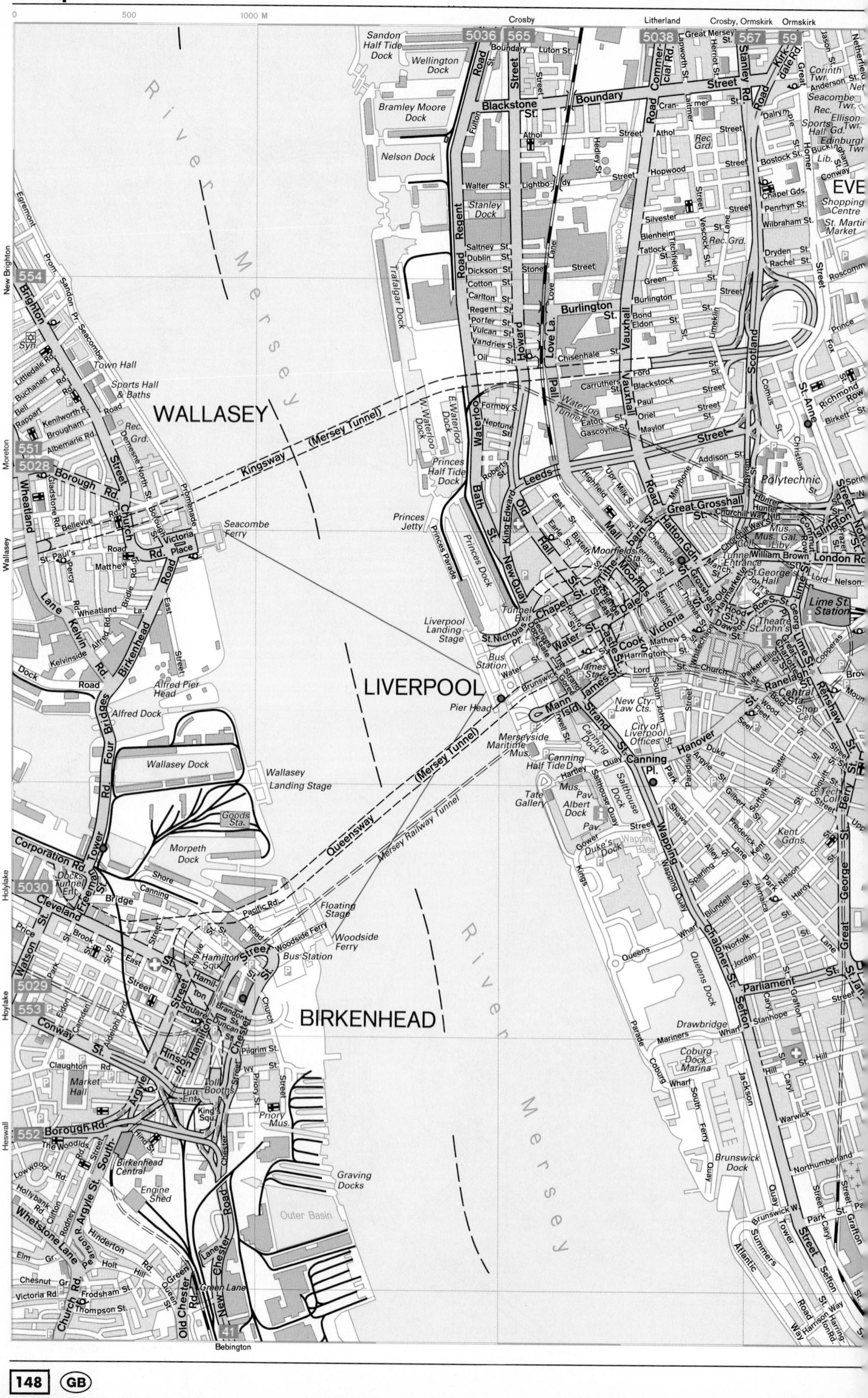

0   500   1000 M

Crosby   Litherland   Crosby, Ormskirk   Ormskirk

`5036` `565`   `5038` `567` `59`

WALLASEY

LIVERPOOL

BIRKENHEAD

EVE

River Mersey

(Mersey Tunnel)

Kingsway

Queensway

(Mersey Tunnel)

Mersey Railway Tunnel

`554`
`551`
`5028`
`5030`
`5029`
`553`
`552`

`41`

Bebington

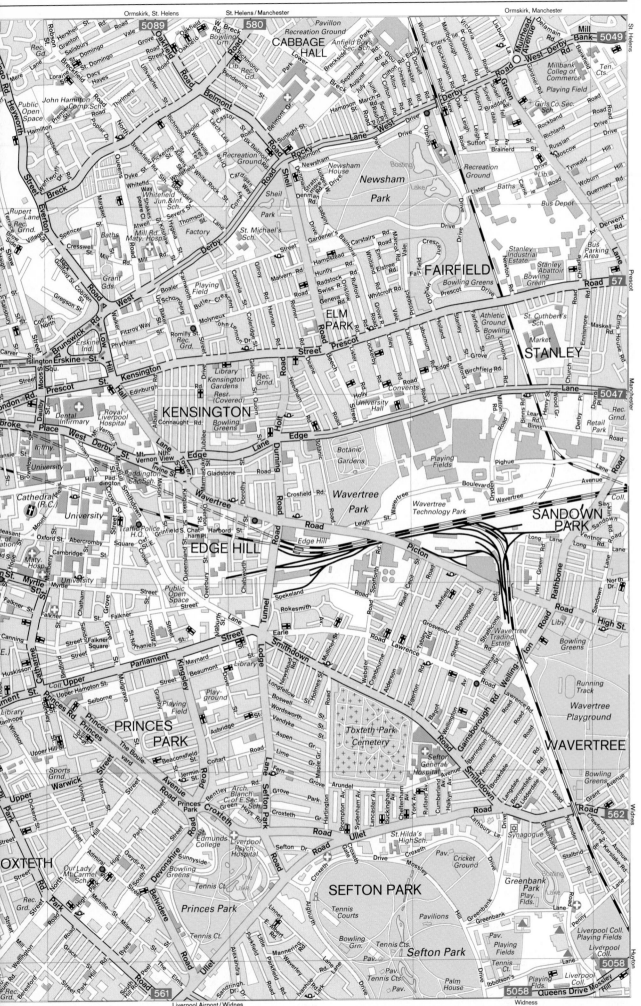

London

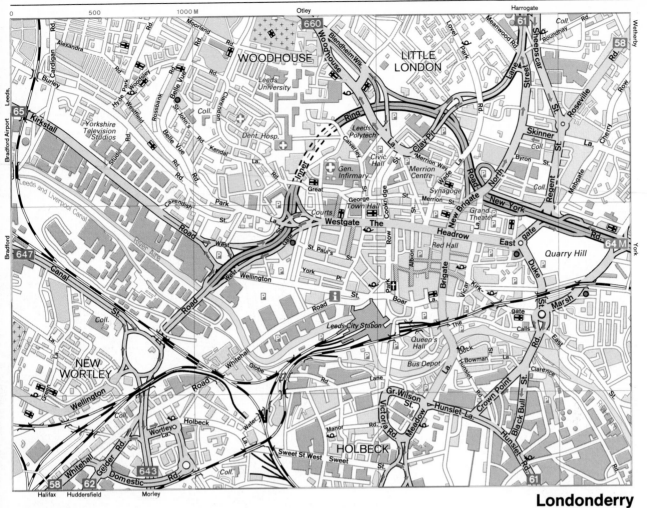

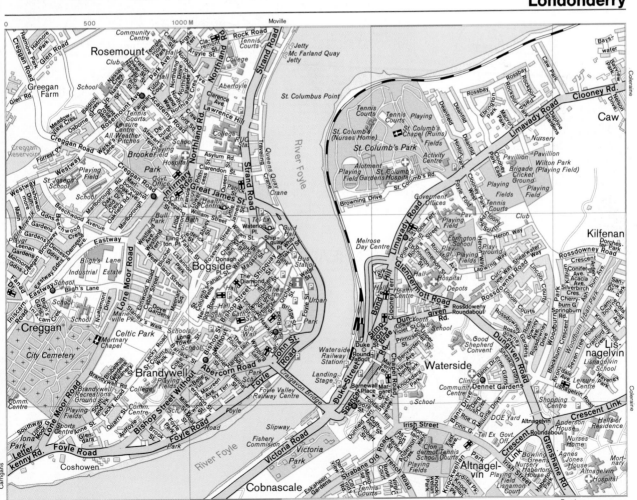

0   500   1000 M

Crosby   Litherland   Crosby, Ormskirk   Ormskirk

5036 565   5038   567 59

Great Mersey St.   Stanley Rd   Kirk-dale Rd   Great Homer St.

Sandon Half Tide Dock   Wellington Dock   Larworth St.   Commercial Rd.   Herriot St.

Corinth Twr.   Anderson   Netherfield

Boundary   Luton St.   Street   Seacombe Rec. Twr.   Ellison Twr.

Blackstone St.   Boundary   Cran-   Laimer   Dalrymple   Sports Hall Gd.   Edinburgh Twr.

Bramley Moore Dock   Athol   Athol   Hopwood   Bostock St.   Lib.   Conway

Nelson Dock   Hedley St.   Street   Homer   St. Anne

Walter   St.   Lightbo-dy   Street   Chapel Gds   Penrhyn St.   EVE

Stanley Dock   Dryden St.   Shopping Centre

Regent Road   Saltney St.   Stoney   Silvester   Wilbraham St.   Rachel St.   St. Martin Market

Dublin St.   Blenheim   Vescock St.   Roscomm

Dickson   Street   Rec. Grd.   Roscomm

Trafalgar Dock   Cotton   Street   Green   St.

Carlton   Burlington   St.   Bond   Dryden St.   Lincoln

Regent   Burlington   St.   Eldon   St.

WALLASEY   Porter   Vulcan   Chisenhale   St.   St. Anne

New Brighton   Vandries   Carruthers   Prince   Fox

Brighton   554   Oil   Vauxhall   Blackstock   St.   St. Anne   Richmond Row

Sandon Pt   Seacombe   E. Waterloo Dock   Ford   Paul   Birket   St.

Promenade   W. Waterloo Dock   Formby St   Eaton   Oriel   Maylor   Polytechnic   Christian

Town Hall   Neptune St.   Gascoyne St.   Addison   St.

Littledale Rd   Syn.   Kingsway (Mersey Tunnel)   Bath   Waterloo   Highfield   Hunter St.   Spir

Buchanan   Rec. Grd.   Roberts   Upr Milk St   Churchill Way   Mus.   Nor

Rapport   Kenilworth Rd   Princes Half Tide Dock   King Edward   Leeds   St.   Mus. Gal. Liby.

Albemarle Rd   Brougham   Road   Old   Mall   Cheapside   Tunnel   William Brown   London Rd

Moreton   551   Borough Rd   Princes Jetty   Great Grosshall   St.   Entrance   St. George's

5028   Bellevue   East   St. Paul's   Church   Victoria   Place   Seacombe Ferry   Princes Parade   Princes Dock   Moorfields   Byxteth   Vernon   St.   Churchill Way   St. John's   Lime St. Station

Wallasey   St. Percy   Matthew   Road   Moorfields Sta.   Dale   Theatre   Hall

Lane   Kelvin   Wheatland   La.   St. Nicholas   Water   St.   Castle   Cook   Victoria   Parker Elliot   i

Kelvinside   Liverpool Landing Stage   Pl.   Harrington   Church   Ranelagh   Central Sta.   Shop Cen

Dock   Road   Bus Station   Brunswick   James   Lord   Wood   Renshaw

Alfred Pier Head   Water   New City Law Cts.   New City   Seel   Mour

Alfred Dock   LIVERPOOL   Pier Head   Mann   City of Liverpool Offices   Hanover   Duke

Four Bridges   Wallasey Landing Stage   Merseyside Maritime Mus.   Canning   Pl.   Paradise   Kent

Wallasey Dock   Canning Half Tide D.   Quay   Canning   Shaw   Gilbert   Lane   Frederick   Gdns.

Goods Sta.   Tate Gallery   Hanley   Mus.   Salthouse Quay   Gower   Kent

Corporation Rd   Morpeth Dock   Queensway (Mersey Tunnel)   Pav.   Albert Dock   Pav.   Wapping   Blundell   Nelson   Hardy

5030   Docks Tunnel Ent.   Shore   Mersey Railway Tunnel   Duke's Dock   Wapping Basin   Starling   Norfolk   Jamaica

Cleveland   Bridge   Canning   Wapping Quay   Park

Price   Brook   St.   Pacific Rd   Road   Jordan

Watson   East   Floating Stage   Queens   Wharf   Parliament

5029   Hamilton Squ.   Woodside Ferry   Queens Dock   Caryl

553   Hamil-ton   Woodside   Bus Station   Sefton

Conway   Camden   Brandon   Duncan St   Drawbridge   Mariners   Stanhope

BIRKENHEAD   Church   St.   Coburg Dock Marina   Hill

Claughton Rd   Pilgrim St.   Coburg   Wharf   Jackson

Hinson St.   IVY   St.   South   Ferry   Warwick

Market Hall   King's Squ.   Priory Mus.   Brunswick Dock

Argyle   Lun Ent.   Toll Booths   Priory   St.   Brunswick W.

552   Borough Rd   The Woodlds.   King's   Quay

Heswall   Birkenhead Central   Caryl   Park

Lowwood   Clifton   Engine Shed   Atlantic

Hollybank Rd.   Grove   Graving Docks   Harrison Way

Whetstone Lane   Elm   Chesnut Gr   Holt   Rd   Green Lane

Victoria Rd   Frodsham   Old Chester Rd   Outer Basin   New Chester Road

Thompson St.   41   Bebington

River Mersey

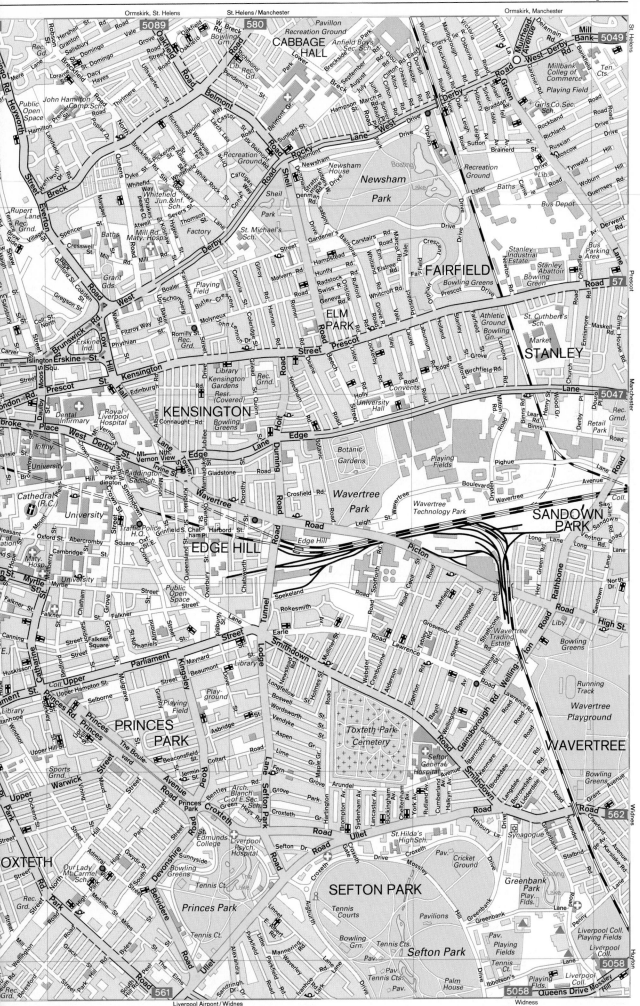

London

Manchester

Oxford

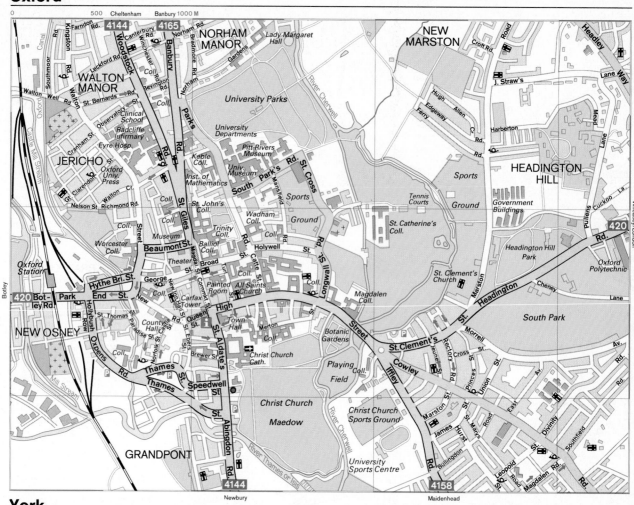

York

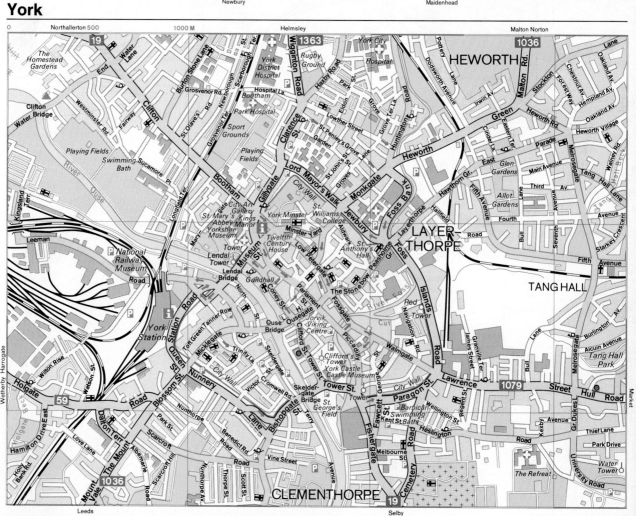

Europa · Europe
1 : 4.500.000

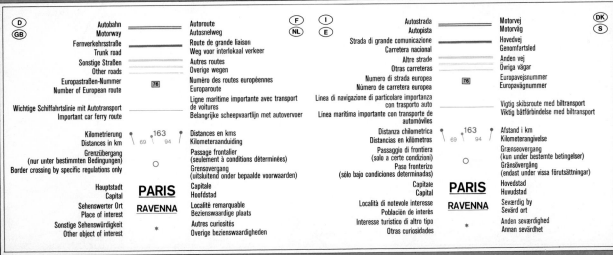

D GB	Autobahn Motorway	Autoroute Autosnelweg	F I NL E	Autostrada Autopista	Motorvej Motorväg	DK S
	Fernverkehrsstraße Trunk road	Route de grande liaison Weg voor interlokaal verkeer		Strada di grande comunicazione Carretera nacional	Hovedvej Genomfartsled	
	Sonstige Straßen Other roads	Autres routes Overige wegen		Altre strade Otras carreteras	Anden vej Övriga vägar	
	Europastraßen-Nummer Number of European route	Numéro des routes européennes Europaroute	76	Numero di strada europea Número de carretera europea	Europavejsnummer Europavägnummer	
	Wichtige Schiffahrtslinie mit Autotransport Important car ferry route	Ligne maritime importante avec transport de voitures Belangrijke scheepvaartlijn met autovervoer		Linea di navigazione di particolare importanza con trasporto auto Línea marítima importante con transporte de automóviles	Vigtig skibsroute med biltransport Viktig båtförbindelse med biltransport	
	Kilometrierung Distances in km	Distances en kms Kilometeraanduiding	163 69 94	Distanza chilometrica Distancias en kilómetros	Afstand i km Kilometerangivelse	
	Grenzübergang (nur unter bestimmten Bedingungen) Border crossing by specific regulations only	Passage frontalier (seulement à conditions déterminées) Grensovergang (uitsluitend onder bepaalde voorwaarden)	○	Passaggio di frontiera (solo a certe condizioni) Paso fronterizo (sólo bajo condiciones determinadas)	Grænseovergang (kun under bestemte betingelser) Gränsövergång (endast under vissa förutsättningar)	
	Hauptstadt Capital	Capitale Hoofdstad	PARIS	Capitale Capital	Hovedstad Huvudstad	
	Sehenswerter Ort Place of interest	Localité remarquable Bezienswaardige plaats	RAVENNA	Località di notevole interesse Población de interés	Seværdig by Sevärd ort	
	Sonstige Sehenswürdigkeit Other object of interest	Autres curiosités Overige bezienswaardigheden	*	Interesse turistico di altro tipo Otras curiosidades	Anden seværdighed Annan sevärdhet	

ÍSLAND

Horn
Dranga
925 jökull
Bolungarvík
Ísafjördhur
Thingeyri   141
Hólmavík
Vatneyri   62
Breidhafjördhur   558
Stykkishólmur
Sandur
Kolbeinsstadhir
Borgarnes
Faxaflói   162
Akranes
Reykjavík
Hafnarfjördhur
Keflavík   45
Grindavík
Thorlákshöfn

Arctic Circle

Raufarhöfn   Rifstangi   Fontur
Kópasker   Thistilfjördhur
Thórshöfn
43   132
Húsavík
Siglufjördhur   Vopnafjördhur
Dalvik   90   Grimsstadhir
Saudhárkrókur   141   303
Blönduós   150
Akureyri   Egilsstadhir   27
Hvammstangi   Seydhisfjördhur   Thórshavn
137   135   Neskaupstadhur
ÍSLAND   Eskifjördhur
449   1765
          Hofsjökull   233
          Langjökull
          1400   2000   Djúpivogur
          Vatnajökull
Laugarvatn   Höfn
Thing-   Flúdhir   Öræfajökull
valla-   2119
vatn   Selfoss   Hella   732   280
          Kirkjubæjarklaustur
Myrdals-
jökull
1450
Vík
Vestmannaeyjar   135

ÍSLAND
Lerwick

NORWEGIAN

SEA

Arctic Circle

Vesterålen
Lofoten   Andøy   Andsfjorden
Langøy   Sortland   Harstad
          191   Hinnøy
Vestvågøy   Stokmarknes   Lødingen   10
          Austvågøy   Bognes
Stamsund   Svolvær   Ulvsvåg
          Skutvik   230
Vestfjord   411
Sommarset
Bodø
Saltfj.   Fauske   69
Rognan   Sulitjelma
Glomfjord   1913
Svartisen
1600   112   6
R   Jäckvik
Mo i Rana
Sandnessjøen   Korgen   Ammarnäs
139   Rössvatn
Mosjøen   12   Västansjö
Vega   Hattfjelldal   245   Sorsele
Brønnøysund   Trofors   481
Vendesund   Dikanäs
Vikna   Foldereid   164   Majavatn
Gardstad   Limingen   Saxnäs
506   Tunnsjö   Risbäck
Folda   Grong   Nordli   Gäddede   Vilhelmi
Namsos   Formofoss   Sørli   N   o   R   r
76   Dorotea
Froya   Frohavet   Steinkjer
Frøya   Åfjord   O   Verdalsøra   Strömsund   Lövberga
Hitra   Stranda   Sandvika   Kall-   Lillholmsjö
Smøla   90   sjön
Kristiansund   Orkanger   Stjørdal   14   117   Duved   Hammerdal   Ramsele   A   Näså
          Kvisvik   Halsa   TRONDHEIM   Järpen   114   Östersund
Molde   Angvik   Duved   Stor-   sjön   Ragunda   Solle
Ålesund   Sunndalsøra   Støren   Jämtland   459   E
          Åndalsnes   163   6   120   Röros   Håtledalen   Bispfors   Krar
Romsdal   126   200   Oppdal   Glomma   Bräcke
Trollstigveien   234   2286   80   Tynset   Femund   Åsarna   Rätansbyn   191   14
Måløy   Volda   108   Dovre-   fjell   Alvdal   Vemdalen   Ostavall   Sun
Eid   Stryn   Dalsnibba   Dombås   Dreysjø   Idre   Sveg   Ljungan
Flöro   Nordfj.   2083   Lom   Otta   Åsheim   Särna   Los   Ljusdal
Jostedalsbreen   2470   Jotunheimen   Østerdalen   Nybergsund   Älvdalen   Voxna   219   Hud
Moskog   Skjolden   Ringebu   219   Dala   Norra   Siljan   Bollnäs   Söde
Leirvik   Dragsvik   Gudbrandsdal   353   Elverum   Ny   Mora   Rättvik   402
Sognefj.   567   Fagernes   Lillehammer   Höljes   Malung   Sandviken
Gudvangen   159   Z   Gjøvik   Vansbro   Falun
Borgund   Gol   Hamar   Flisa   Vansbro Ny   Borlänge   116
Knarvik   86   Stalheim   Rands-   Brandbu   99   S   Gysinge
BERGEN   16   fj.   Nes   Mjøsa   Kongsvinger   Ludvika   Gä
Kvanndal   Voringfoss   Geilo   132   Elverum   v   Avesta
130   Voringfoss   178   138   Rødberg   Hønefoss   Skotterud   Sä   S   Fagersta   133   Sala
Kinsarvik   Hardangervidda   Klofta   Sunne
58   1691   Löfallstrand   OSLO   Örebro   Stockholm
Skåre   Rjukan   Drammen   430   35
Sauda   120   Haukeligrend   Kristiansand   Göteborg   4
Haugesund   Sand

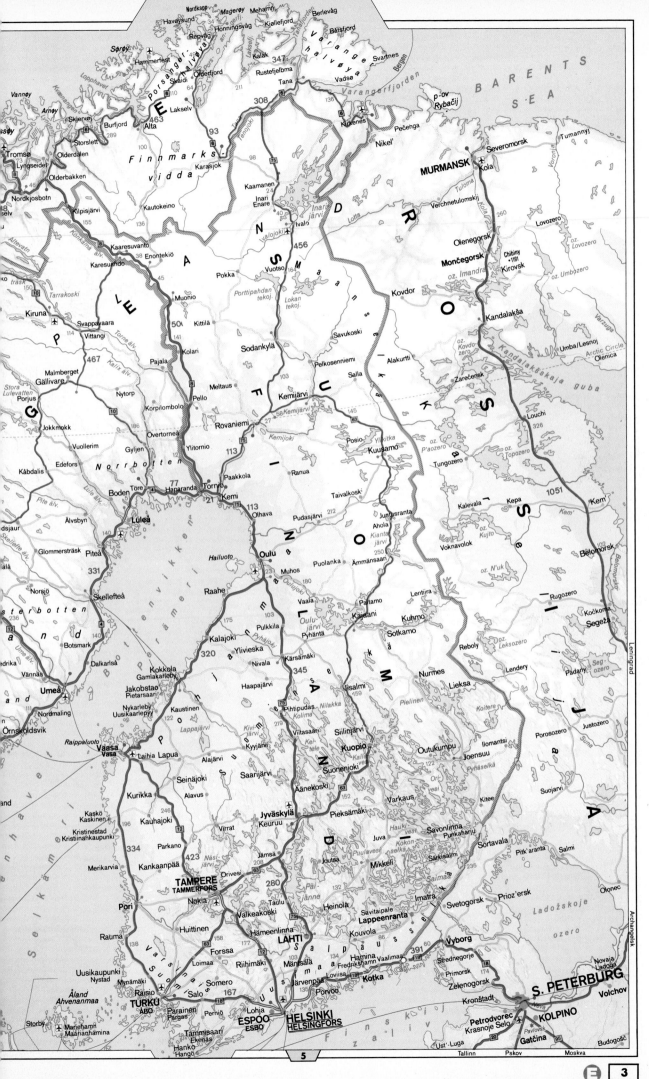

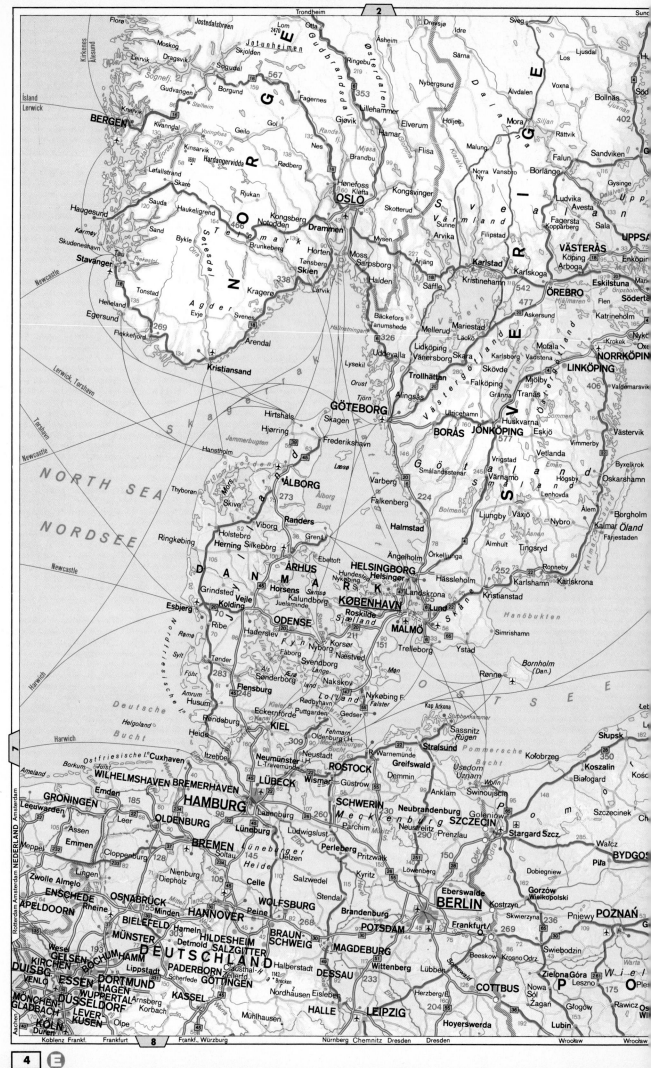

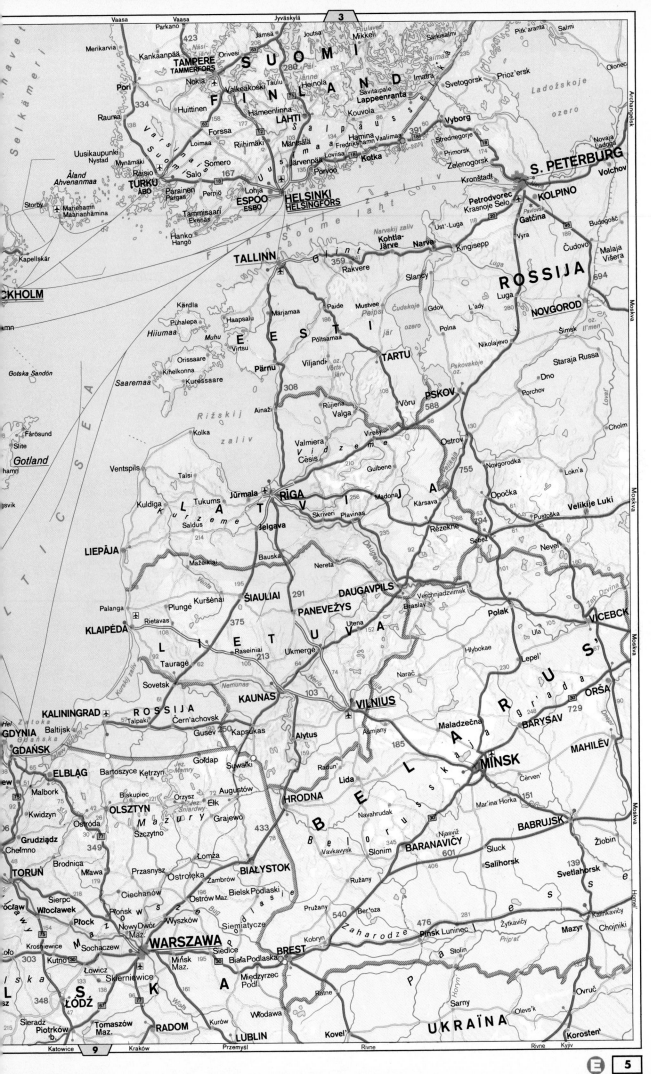

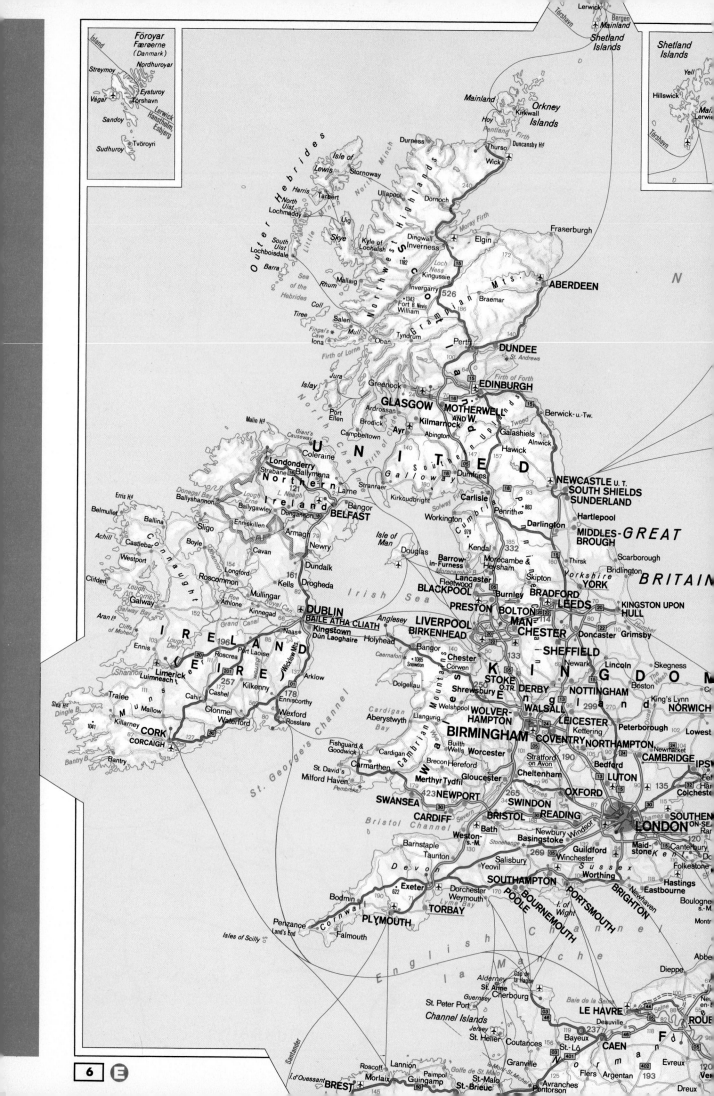

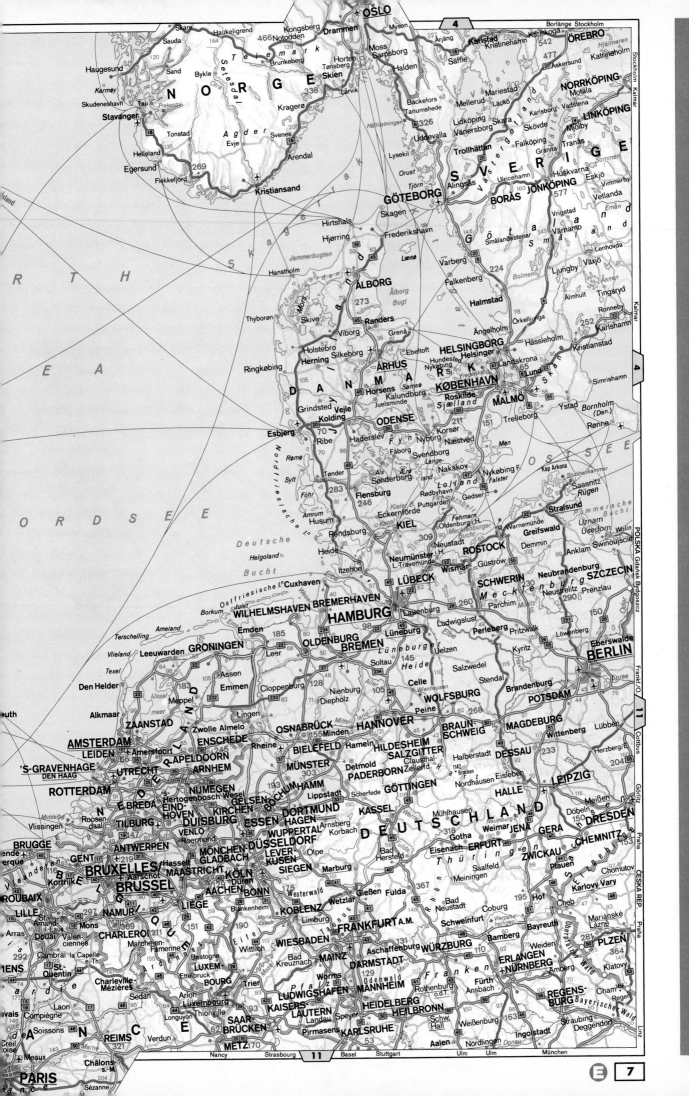

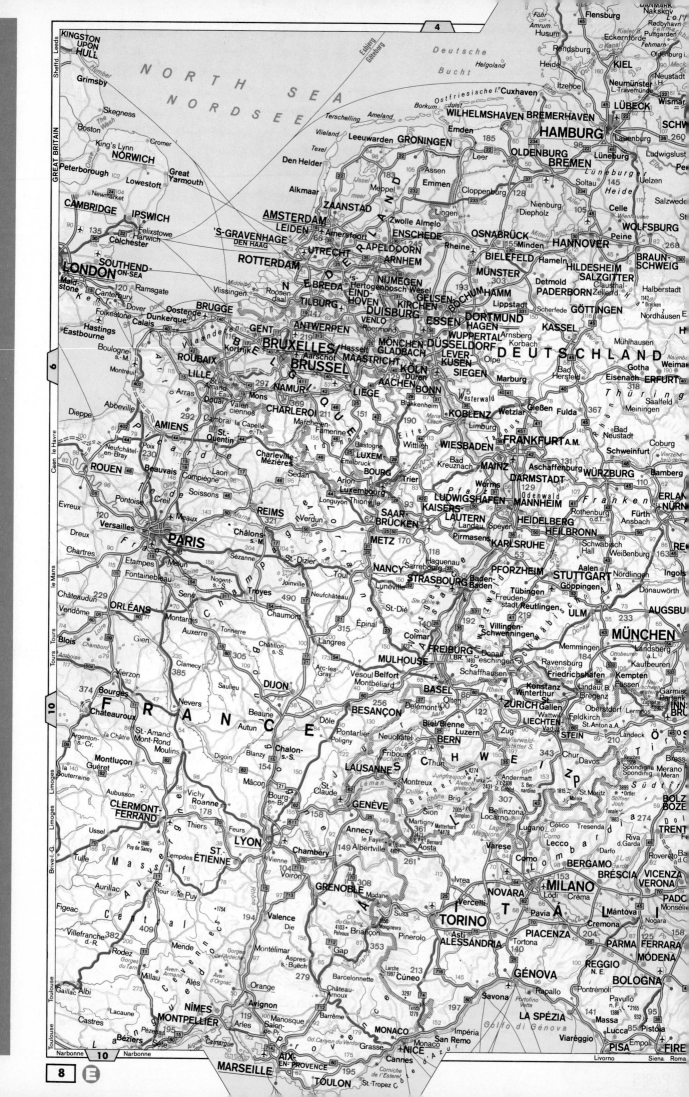

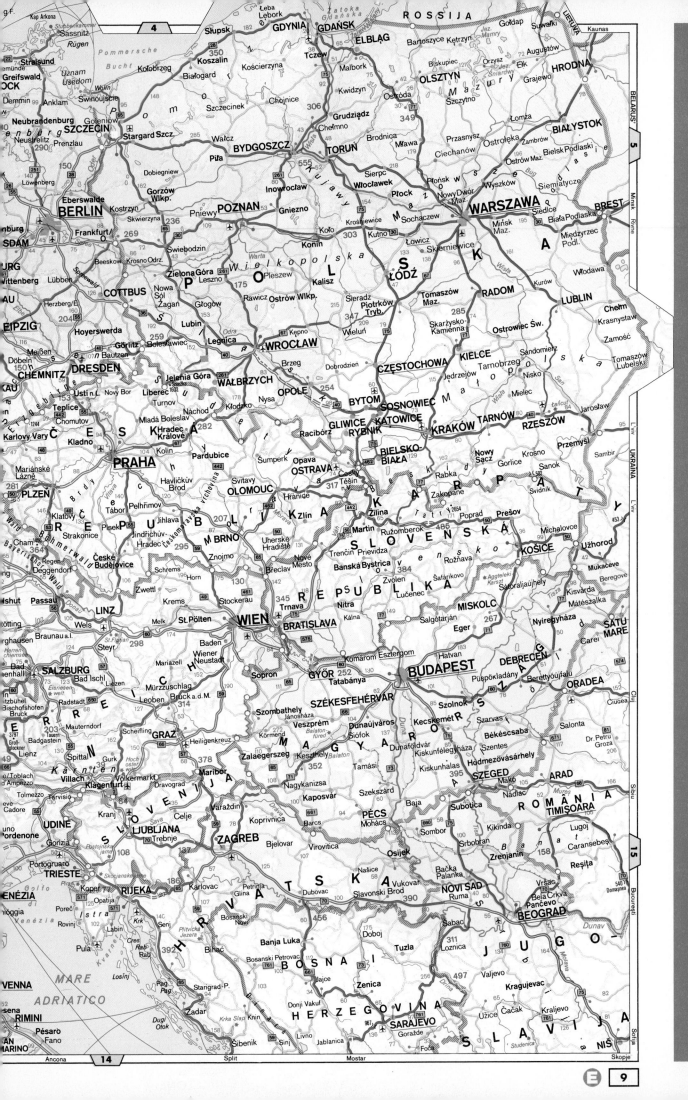

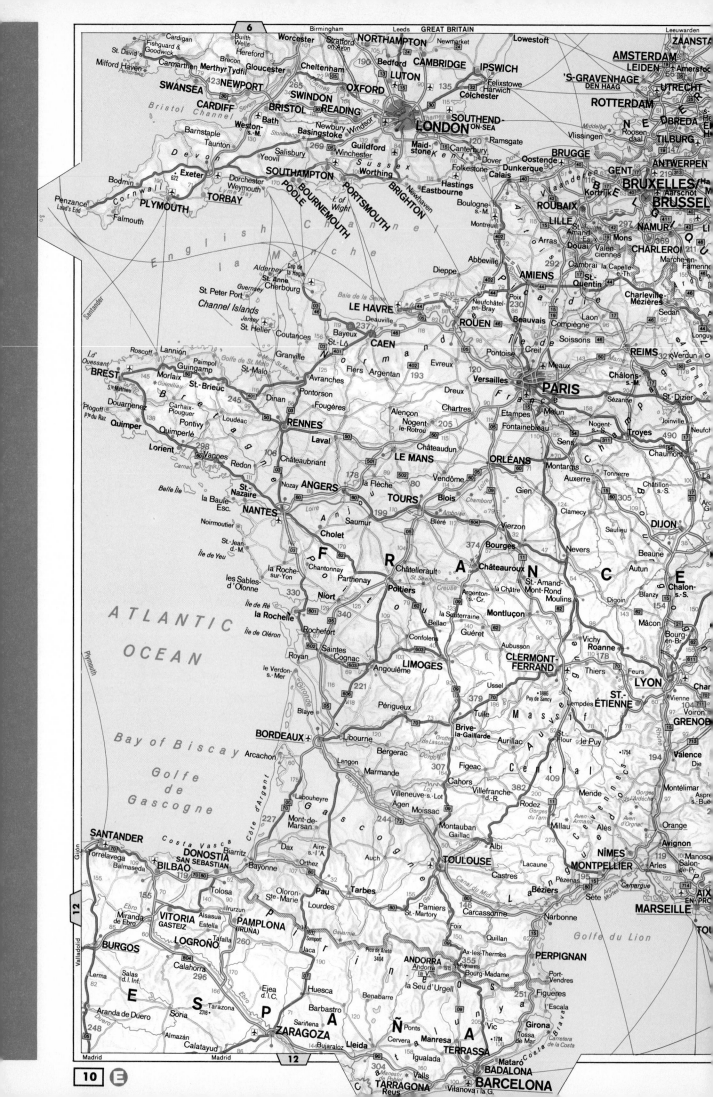

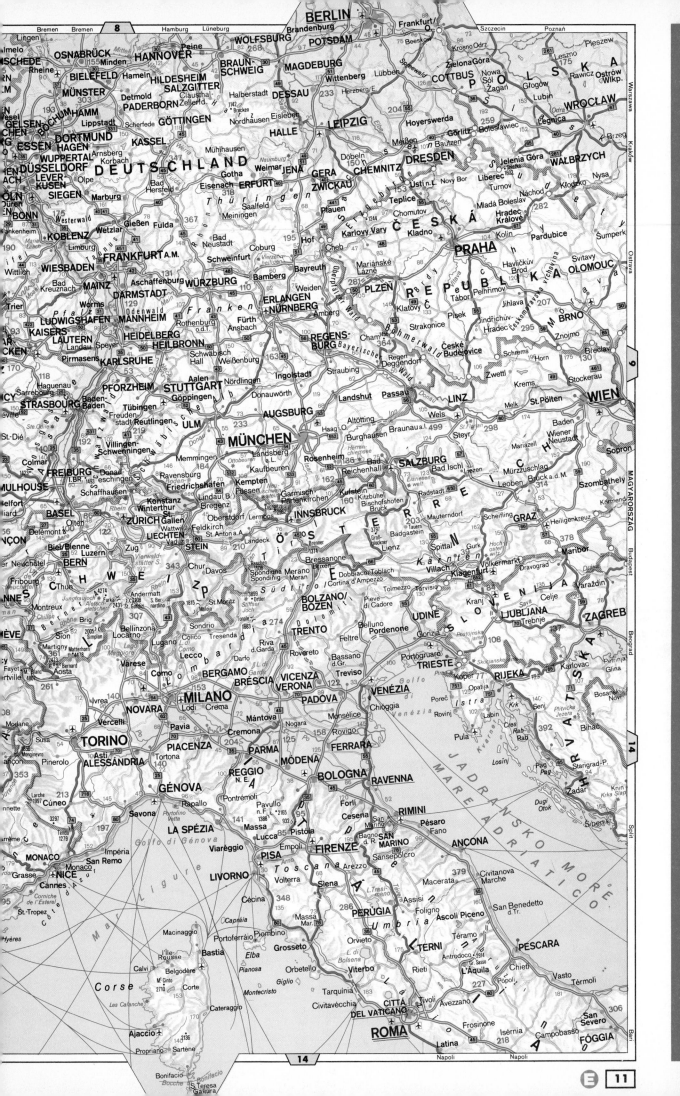

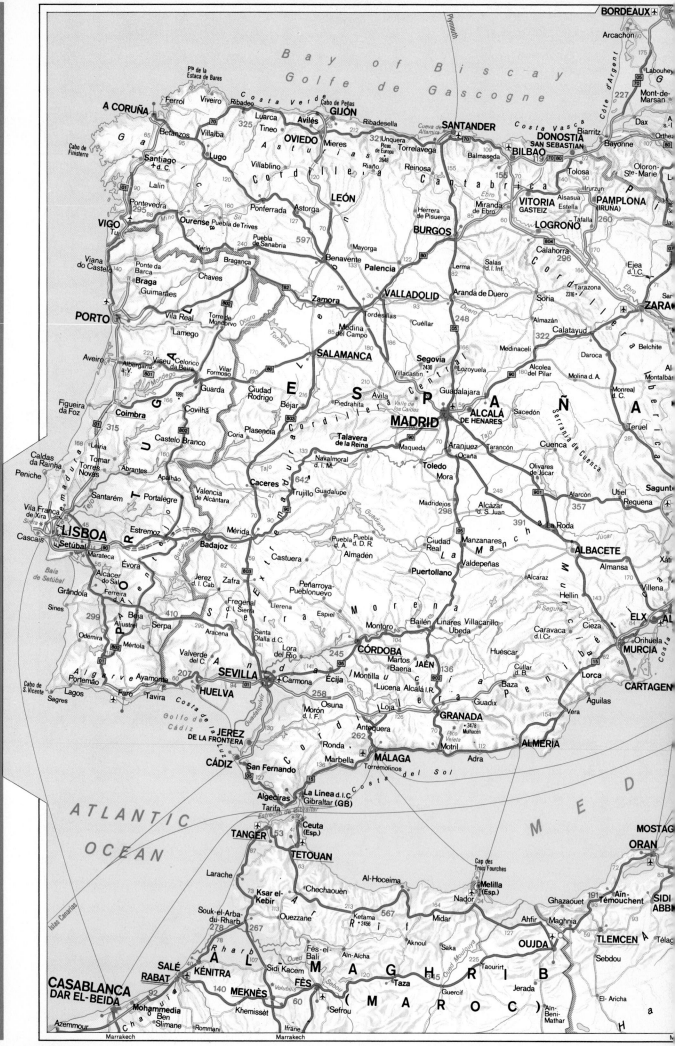